Phonology in Generative Grammar

or

A Plethora of Confusion

Blackwell Textbooks in Linguistics

Phonology in Generative Grammar

Michael Kenstowicz

BLACKWELL
Cambridge MA & Oxford UK

First published 1994

Blackwell Publishers
238 Main Street
Cambridge, Massachusetts 02142
USA

108 Cowley Road
Oxford OX4 1JF
UK

Library of Congress Cataloging-in-Publication Data

Kenstowicz, Michael J.
    Phonology in generative grammar / Michael Kenstowicz.
        p.   cm.
    Includes bibliographical references and index.
    ISBN 1-55786-425-X.—ISBN 1-55786-426-8
        1. Grammar, Comparative and general—Phonology.   2. Generative
grammar.   I. Title.
    P217.6.K46   1993   92-37749
    414—dc20   CIP

British Library Cataloguing in Publication Data

A CIP catalogue record for this book is available from the British Library.

Typeset in 10 on 12 pt Times Roman
by Maryland Composition Co., Inc.
Printed in the United States of America

This book is printed on acid-free paper

Contents

11 Prosodic Morphology   622

Preface

My aim in writing this book has been to provide a thorough introduction to generative phonology. By reading the text and working through the exercises, the student will develop a basic understanding of the fundamental concepts of phonology and the ability to apply them to the analysis of novel data. It is my hope that the reader will acquire the background and tools not only to read the current literature with critical understanding but also to become an active participant in phonological research.

I see the book as being useful to three sorts of readers. First, it can serve as the core text for a one- or two-semester course in phonology at the advanced undergraduate or beginning graduate level. Second, it can be used to provide an overview or to fill in the gaps for instructors who wish to develop a different approach to the subject or to treat a particular topic in depth. Finally, it is suitable for self-study, giving a sense of the kinds of questions phonologists ask and how they go about answering them.

The first three chapters introduce the basic descriptive concepts and analytic techniques of "classical" generative phonology, covering some of the same ground as Kenstowicz and Kisseberth 1979. In conjunction with chapter 4, they are suitable for an undergraduate phonology course. Remaining chapters survey the major lines of generative research that have opened up in the ensuing period. Each motivates the questions being explored, presents the basic results, and then surveys the contemporary scene. These chapters can be read more or less independently. All chapters in the book are accompanied by a list of suggested readings and a set of exercises ranging in difficulty and type. There are more exercises than could reasonably be worked through in a single course. Instructors are urged to pick and choose the ones that work best.

Acknowledgments

This book grew out of the lecture notes for a course on generative phonology I gave in 1987 at the Scuola Normale Superiore in Pisa. I wish to thank my hosts Pier-Marco Bertinetto and Pino Longobardi for their support and interest. Thanks also to Cinzia Avesani, Alessandra Giorgi, Jim Higginbotham, Michele Loporcaro, Giovanna Marotta, and Mario Vaira. Much of the data and many of the ideas for the book result from work over the years with students at the University of Illinois and later at MIT. I wish to thank in particular Mohammad Abasheikh, Kamal Abdul-Karim, Issam Abu-Salim, Mohammad Alghazo, Irja Alho, Yousef Bader, Christina Bethin, Rakesh Bhatt, Zoann Branstine, Maria Carreira, Farida Cassimjee, Raung-fu Chung, Abigail Cohn, Laura Downing, Donna Farina, Anne Garber, Ghassan Haddad, Abdel Halim Hamid, Omar Irshied, Omar Ka, Mairo Kidda, Scott Krause, Shlomo Lederman, Michal Livnat, Hassan Marchad, David Odden, Meterwa Ourso, Trudi Patterson, Elizabeth Pearce, Pilar Prieto, Teoh-Boon Seong, Hyang-Sook Sohn, Wafaa Wahba, Uthaiwan Wong-opasi; and Zhiming Bao, Eulàlia Bonet, Lisa Cheng, Chris Collins, Hamida Demirdache, San Duanmu, Alicja Gorecka, Tom Green, Mark Hewitt, Bill Idsardi, Peter Ihionu, Janis Melvold, Rolf Noyer, Brian Sietsema, Kelly Sloan, Tony Bures, Colin Phillips, and Vaijayanthi Sarma. Colleagues at Illinois, Venice, and MIT who provided input and support include C. C. Cheng, Guglielmo Cinque, Rodolfo Delmonte, Morris Halle, Jim Harris, Hans Hock, Jay Keyser, Charles Kisseberth, Philip Khoury, Pino Longobardi, Alec Marantz, Wayne O'Neil, Donca Steriade, and Ken Stevens.

For checking data and (dis)confirming various facts I thank Paola Benincà, José Hualde, Greg Iverson, Aditi Lahiri, Utpal Lahiri, Joan Mascaró, Carole Paradis, Jean-François Prunet, Jerzy Rubach, Miklós Törkenczy, Hubert Trockenbrodt, Laura Vanelli, and Draga Zec. Abigail Cohn, Nick Clements, John Harris, and Iggy Roca offered valuable comments and criticism on various chapters. Andrea Calabrese, Bruce Hayes, David Odden, Keren Rice, and Moira Yip read the entire manuscript and provided very penetrating comments that have markedly improved the presentation. I am especially grateful to Morris Halle for help with chapter 4. Also, I wish to thank Anne Mark and Ruth Myott for turning the manuscript into a book and to Philip Carpenter for his persistent interest in the project. Words cannot express the debt I owe to my wife Tamara for her enduring patience and indulgence over the course of this too long project.

Finally, I dedicate the book to the three individuals from whom I have learned the most about phonology: Theodore Lightner, who introduced me to the subject; Charles Kisseberth, fellow graduate student, faculty colleague, and research collaborator; and Morris Halle, colleague and mentor, the founder and leading proponent of phonology in generative grammar.

Introduction

Generative grammar is an approach to linguistics developed at MIT (Massachusetts Institute of Technology) by Noam Chomsky and Morris Halle in the 1950s. It has since become the received theory of phonology and syntax in the United States. Many generative linguists are also active in Canada, Western Europe, Japan, Korea, Australia, and elsewhere. The major goal of generative linguistics has been to solve what Chomsky (1986) has termed *Plato's problem:* any speaker knows many surprising things about the structure of his or her language, things whose internalization is difficult to understand if based solely on evidence from the linguistic environment. Chomsky illustrates this point with the paradigm in (1).

(1) a. I wonder who [the men expected to see them]
     b. [the men expected to see them]
     c. John ate an apple
     d. John ate
     e. John is too stubborn to talk to Bill
     f. John is too stubborn to talk to

In (1a) the pronoun *them* may take *the men* as antecedent; but this anaphoric relation is impossible in (1b), even though exactly the same sequence of words is involved. In (1b) *the men* and *them* must be understood to refer to different individuals. These judgments are quite sharp and immediate and will be readily assented to by any speaker of the language. How are they possible? No one has ever taught them to us; in fact, they were only recently discovered. Nevertheless, every mature speaker comes to share these intuitions. A traditional explanation of language learning is that it proceeds by analogy from the most frequent or salient patterns and structures. It is easy to show that analogy is incapable of explaining many such facts. For example, comparing (1c) and (1d), one might infer that if the object of the verb is dropped, the verb is interpreted as taking an arbitrary, unspecified object (John ate something). But this explanation immediately runs afoul of examples such as (1e) and (1f), where the object of the verb *talk to* is also missing. Here object deletion does not result in an unspecified noun phrase interpretation; the missing object in (1f) must refer to *John*.

Chomsky's point is that these judgments are immediate, intuitive, and natural. A child learning English would never generalize from (1c,d) to (1e,f). But "mistakes" of this kind are just what we should expect to find if language acquisition proceeds by analogy, stimulus generalization, and the other learning mechanisms proposed in classical empiricism.

Over 30 years' study of Plato's problem suggests a different picture. Rather than emphasizing how different from one another languages are, linguists are much more impressed with their basic similarity. For many deep-seated properties such as those illustrated in (1), languages seem to be identical or exhibit only a small range of variation. The knowledge of language revealed in speakers' judgments of coreference in (1) and in many other syntactic structures is quite rich and specific in character. Since this knowledge is so different and remote from overt speech behavior, the most promising and natural explanation for its existence and origin is that humans share a common core of Universal Grammar (UG) as part of their genetic endowment. It is in terms of this common core that language develops in the individual in response to the language of the environment, evolving into Korean, French, English, and so on, as depicted in (2). Languages are so similar or even identical in their underlying structure because they develop from this common core. What systematic differences do exist involve choosing among a constrained set of options (parameter fixing).

(2)   UG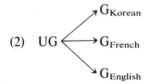

Phonology is the component of our linguistic knowledge that is concerned with the physical realization of language. Possession of this knowledge permits us to realize words and the sentences they compose as speech (or as gestures in the language of the deaf) and to recover them from the acoustic signal (or visual sign display). Phonology differs from syntax in that knowledge of the pronunciation of lexical items must be stored in memory; since the relation between sound and meaning is arbitrary, there is no way to predict that 'man's best friend' is *dog* in English, *Hund* in German, *chien* in French, and so on. This basic fact allows for more unpredictable differences among languages that must be learned in the development of an individual grammar from UG. Nevertheless, for a significant range of phenomena, the same general picture depicted in (2) appears accurate. There are many recurrent aspects of phonological structure of a highly specific and rich character whose acquisition cannot be explained on the basis of analogy or stimulus generalization in any useful sense of these terms. These properties are also most naturally explained as reflections of UG.

In this Introduction we discuss a few examples to motivate this general point of view. We then summarize the kinds of questions generative phonologists have been asking and preview the book's survey of the answers that have been offered. In his celebrated (1933) paper "The Psychological Reality of Phonemes," the American linguist Edward Sapir (1884–1939) pointed to the existence of several puzzles posed by the sound structure of language that are as striking as the syntactic ones illustrated in (1). In the course of his fieldwork on American Indian languages, Sapir was struck by the fact that his language consultants would hear sounds that were not objectively present in their speech. Let us consider one of Sapir's examples in some detail. While studying the Canadian Athabaskan language Sarcee, he was puzzled by his informant John Whitney's insistence that there was a difference between *dìní* 'this one' and *dìní* 'it makes a sound' even though the two were phonetically homophonous to Sapir's trained ears.

> When I asked him what the difference was, he found it difficult to say, and the more often he pronounced the words over to himself the more confused he became as to their phonetic difference. Yet all the time he seemed perfectly sure that there was a difference. At various moments I thought I could catch a slight phonetic difference, for instance, (1) that the *-ní* of "this one" was on a slightly lower tone than the *-ní* of "it makes a sound"; (2) that there was a slight stress on the *dì-* of "this one" . . . and a similarly slight stress on the *-ní* of "it makes a sound"; (3) that the *-ní* of "this one" ended in a pure vowel with little or no breath release, while the *-ní* of "it makes a sound" had a more audible breath release, [and] was properly *-ní'*. These suggestions were considered and halfheartedly accepted at various times by John, but it was easy to see that he was not intuitively convinced. The one tangible suggestion that he himself made was obviously incorrect, namely, that the *-ní* of "it makes a sound" ended in a "*t*". John claimed that he "felt a *t*" in the syllable, yet when he tested it over and over to himself, he had to admit that he could neither hear a "*t*" nor feel his tongue articulating one. We had to give up the problem, and I silently concluded that there simply was no phonetic difference between the words . . . (p. 26; all page references are to Makkai 1972)

Sapir's discussion concerns what he calls a *phonetic illusion*. Two objectively identical stimuli *dìní* are perceived as different when they are associated with different meanings. Furthermore, the difference is of a precise form; Whitney felt that the *-ní* of 'it makes a sound' ended in a [t] while *dìní* 'this one' did not. What could be the basis of this strange illusion? Clearly, unlike other well-known illusions in which identical stimuli are interpreted differently depending on context (e.g., the Müller-Lyer illusion in which a line looks longer between outward-pointing than between inward-pointing arrowheads: ↔ vs. ⟩—⟨), the *dìní* case depends on having very specialized knowledge – being a speaker of Sarcee.

Sapir goes on to say that as his understanding of the structure of Sarcee increased, the source of the "mysterious *t*" that his informant intuited became clear. The final syllables of *dìní* 'this one' and *dìní* 'it makes a sound' behave differently when suffixes such as the inferential *-la* and the relative *-i* are added, as shown in (3). *-la* is unchanged after 'this one' but devoices its initial lateral consonant to [ɬ] after 'it makes a sound'. Before the relative suffix, a [t] appears in 'it makes a sound' while *i + i* contract to a long [a] in 'this one'.

(3)

	inferential -la	relative -i
dìní 'this one'	dìníla	dìná:[a]
dìní 'it makes a sound'	dìníɬa	dìnít'í

Sapir explains,   *unconsciously, but not actively so.*

> There are phonologically distinct types of final vowels in Sarcee: smooth or
> simple vowels; and vowels with a consonantal latency, i.e., vowels originally
> followed by a consonant which disappears in the absolute form of the word
> but which reappears when the word has a suffix beginning with a vowel or
> which makes its former presence felt in other sandhi phenomena. (p. 26)

In other words, the postulated latent consonant intuited by John Whitney for *dìní*
'it makes a sound' actually emerges before the relative *-í* in *dìnít'-í.* Its presence
is also detectable in the devoicing of the inferential *-ła* suffix: *dìní-ła.*

In order to explain his informant's intuition, Sapir postulates that the final
claims
vowels of words like *dìní* 'it makes a sound' have a "latent" consonant. What
this means is that there is another, psychologically more accurate representation
of the word that records the presence of this intuited sound: [dinit]. Following
Sapir, let us refer to this representation as the *phonological representation.* Sapir
concludes,

> It is clear that, while John was phonetically amateurish, he was phonologically
> subtle and accurate. His response amounted to an index of the feeling that
> *dìní* "this one" = *dìní,* that *dìní* "it makes a sound" = *dìní',* and that this
> *-ní'* = *-nít'.* (p. 27)

Lest we conclude that such phonological illusions are only to be found in "exotic" languages, Sapir discusses an analogous case from English. He states that

> [his informant] John's certainty of difference in the face of objective identity
> is quite parallel to the feeling that the average Englishman would have that
> such words as *sawed* and *soared* are not phonetically identical. It is true that
> both *sawed* and *soared* can be phonetically represented as *sɔ·d,* but the *-ing*
> forms of the two verbs (*sawing, soaring*), phonetically *sɔ·-iŋ* and *sɔ·r-iŋ,* and
> such sentence sandhi forms as "Saw on, my boy!" and "Soar into the sky!"
> combine to produce the feeling that the *sɔ·d* of *sawed* = *sɔ·-d* but that the
> *sɔ·d* of *soared* = *sɔ·r-d.* In the one case zero = zero, in the other case zero = r.
> (p. 27)

Thus, in this particular *r*-less dialect of English, *saw* and *soar* are homophonous
as [sɔː]([ɔː] indicates a long back vowel). But the native speaker nevertheless
distinguishes them as [sɔ] vs. [sɔr], the [r] in *soar* being supplied in the same way
as the [t] that John Whitney heard in Sarcee *dìní* 'this one'.

Sapir concludes his discussion of the intuitions of native speakers with respect
to the pronunciation of their language with the remark that

> *= Spelling*
> Among educated but linguistically untrained people who discuss such matters
> differences of orthography are always held responsible for these differences
> of feeling. This is undoubtedly a fallacy, at least for the great mass of people,
> and puts the cart before the horse. Were English not a written language, the

configuratively determined phonologic difference between such doublets as *sawed* and *soared* would still be "heard," as a collective illusion, as a true phonetic difference. (p. 27)

In other words, phonetic illusions are found in languages that lack an orthography. Indeed, the phenomenon arose for Sapir in the context of the linguistic description practiced at that time in which large bodies of text (myths, riddles, stories, etc.) were gathered to serve as a data base for linguistic analysis. An efficient way to collect the data was to train the native informants to transcribe them; designing an orthography was thus a prerequisite to linguistic analysis. The phonetic illusions were manifested in the informants' tendency to spell sounds that were objectively absent in their pronunciation. Since the phenomenon happens in unwritten languages, the orthography cannot be responsible. Rather, the reverse is true: it is precisely because of the existence of such illusions that native speakers feel compelled to represent such latent sounds.

Granted the existence of the phenomenon, the important question then becomes how to explain it. Why are Sarcee speakers compelled to represent *dìní* 'this one' as [dìnít] and *r*-less English speakers [sɔː] 'soar' as [sɔr]? How does a child growing up in the Sarcee/English language environments where the relevant sounds are always absent in the pronunciation of these words discover them in the course of acquiring the language? A reasonable first guess is that the phantom [t] in Sarcee and the [r] in English derive from the fact that these sounds actually appear in the related suffixed words *dinit'-i* and [sɔriŋ] *soaring*. But what precisely do we mean by a related word? How is it possible for the pronunciation of one word to influence another? Why doesn't the influence run in the opposite direction: that is, why doesn't the absence of a final consonant in the isolation form induce deletion in the suffixed forms? Providing a serious scientific answer to these kinds of questions forms an essential part of the research program of generative phonology.

Let us consider some additional examples of phonetic illusions. English speakers tend to perceive the intersyllabic consonantal material in *camper* and *anchor* as analogous to *clamber* and *anger*. This is an illusion, however. In most dialects (Malécot 1960) the nasal consonant is phonetically absent before such sounds as [p,t,k,s], so that *camper* and *anchor* have the same gross phonetic shape (C)ṼCVC (Ṽ a nasal vowel) as (C)VCVC *wrapper* and *acre*. While ṼCVC *anchor* belongs with VCVC *acre* phonetically, English speakers have the strong intuition that psychologically it belongs with VCCVC *anger*. Somehow the nasality of the vowel in *anchor* signals the presence of a following latent nasal consonant. But why do we hear the nasal consonant after the vowel instead of before? Why is the sequence ṼCVC interpreted as VNCVC and not as NVCVC? Notice that in this case, unlike the examples from Sarcee and *r*-less English, there is no suffixed form of the word in which the latent nasal emerges. For these dialects, under normal circumstances *anchor* is always pronounced without a nasal consonant. Nevertheless, the child acquiring these English dialects comes to interpret [æ̃kər] as having the VNCVC shape of *anger* [æŋgər] and not the VCVC shape of *acre* [ekər]. On what basis is this perception acquired?

Lahiri and Marslen-Wilson (1991) report experimental evidence that corrobo-

rates the contention that English speakers interpret nasality in the vowel as reflecting a following nasal consonant. In a word completion task in which subjects
hear stimuli of the form CV and are asked to supply a continuation as rapidly as
possible, English-speaking subjects tend to complete CṼ with CṼN (N =
[m,n,ŋ]); their performance differs significantly from that of Bengali subjects, who
tend to complete the CṼ stimuli with an oral consonant: for instance, [p,t,k]. This
consistent difference between the Bengali- and English-speaking subjects reflects
the different phonological status of vowel nasality in the two languages: Ṽ implies
a following nasal in English but not in Bengali, where nasal vowels comprise an
important subset of the vocalic inventory. Interestingly, the difference is also
reflected in the orthography of the two languages. Bengali has a diacritic mark
for nasal vowels while English does not and, if our analysis is correct, could not
have an analogous device such as the nasal tilde. Another important difference
between the two languages is that in English a nasal vowel is always followed by
a nasal consonant unless a consonant from the voiceless [p,t,k,s] series follows.
In other words, while English has lexical items such as *camp* with the shape CṼX
(X = [p,t,k,s]), it lacks items with the shapes CṼ or CṼX (X = [b,l,r,v], etc.).
In Bengali no such restriction holds. We will see later why factors of this kind
could be relevant to the differing interpretations of the same phonetic stimuli in
the two phonological systems.

Phonetic illusions do not just involve the addition of "phantom" sounds. We
often misperceive sounds that are objectively present in the speech signal. Consider the well-known pairs *write* vs. *ride* and *writer* vs. *rider* in (4), taken from
many American English dialects.

(4)		write	ride	writer	rider
	phonological representation	raı̯t	raı̯d	raı̯t-er	raı̯d-er
	phonetic representation	raı̯t	ra:ı̯d	raı̯D-ər	ra:ı̯D-ər

Most speakers of this dialect hear a clear difference between *writer* and *rider* and
localize it in the medial dental consonant: *writer* has a medial [t] while *rider* has
a medial [d]. The pronunciations of *writer* and *rider* are indeed different. But
phonetic study reveals that the medial dental consonants are in fact pronounced
identically – as a rhotic, *r*-like consonant called a *flap* (found in Spanish *pero*
'but') and symbolized here as [D]. The difference instead resides in the vowel –
it is longer in *rider* than in *writer*. Unless one has had phonetic training, however,
this vowel length difference is ignored because it is below the threshold of consciousness.

The *writer-rider* pair thus presents us with another phonetic illusion. Our ears
must detect the vowel length difference: we do hear these words as different, and
this is where the objective difference lies. But somehow our consciousness interprets the contrast as located in the following consonant. Furthermore, it does
so in a very precise way – the medial flap of *writer* is perceived as [t] while that
of *rider* is perceived as [d]. Once again, how is this possible?

It appears that we must recognize at least two different conceptualizations or
representations for phonological information: a *phonetic* one indicating how the
lexical item is to be realized in speech and an additional *phonological* one that

helps to explicate the "illusions" we have been discussing. These contrasting representations play a significant role in the development of an orthography. Phonetic differences that are overlooked (such as the vowel length in [ra:ịd]) will typically fail to receive an orthographic registration. Phonetically accurate (but psychologically misleading) orthographies have frequently had to be abandoned as impracticable – precisely because they attempt to record distinctions that are below the level of consciousness of ordinary speakers. Clearly it would be absurd to require English spelling to indicate the vowel length difference in *writer-rider*. But just as clearly, rational orthographies will often require spelling differently what is phonetically the same sound. For example, orthographic reformers would correctly point to the irrational spelling distinction between the "wr" in *writer* and the "r" in *rider* for what is clearly the same sound. But no one would ever propose spelling the medial dental consonants the same in *writer* and *rider* – precisely because they are perceived as different by English speakers.

There is an interesting regularity that supports this interpretation. As just noted, the vowel of *rider* is longer than that of *writer*. This vowel length difference runs throughout English and is strictly correlated with the type of consonant that follows the vowel. Examination of the data in (5) shows that short vowels are associated with such consonants as [p,t,k,s] while long ones are associated with [b,d,g,z].

(5) tăp   ta:b
     bĕt   be:d
     bŭck   bu:g
     dŏse   do:ze

The former (voiceless) consonants are articulated with a stiff glottis position while the latter (voiced) consonants have the glottis in a slack (vibrating) position. If *writer* [raịDər] is represented as [raịter] and *rider* [ra:ịDər] is represented as [raịder], then the same regularity observed in (5) explains the vowel length difference in *writer-rider* as well: [t] belongs to the voiceless set and hence calls for a preceding short vowel while [d] belongs to the voiced set and hence calls for a long vowel.

These considerations suggest that English speakers conceptualize the phonological information comprising the lexical units of their language in two different ways. A phonetic representation such as that in (4) indicates how the word is actualized in speech – the instructions sent to the vocal apparatus to articulate the sounds and acoustic properties that are isolated in order to decode the speech signal. The phonological representation is more abstract. It is called into play when speakers have occasion to represent the word in spelling; it may be revealed in language games (e.g., "Say *writer* or *anchor* backward") and judgments of poetic rhyme. The phonological representation also allows us to explain regularities in the phonetic signal (e.g., the vowel length in *rider-writer*). Phonologists believe that it is essentially the form in which the lexical item is stored in memory. The two representations are systematically related by phonological rules that delete, insert, or change sounds in precise contexts. In the *rider-writer* case, the two rules are first a rule that introduces a vowel length distinction as a function of the nature of the following consonant ([p,t,k,s, . . .] vs. [b,d,g,z, . . .], followed by a process that transforms [t] and [d] to the flap [D] in an intervocalic context (V___V).

It is clear that these rules and representations are under the active control of the speakers and not simply a legacy of the historical development of General American English. This point is seen in the ability of many persons to shift from one dialect or accent to another in response to a change in geographic locale or social setting. For example, in his study of English accents, Wells (1982:31–2) says of one of his best Cockney informants,

> For telling a joke involving an upper class figure, he can put on quite a flawless U-RP accent. But his everyday speech is rather broad Cockney. Clearly he has within his competence not only the local working class accent but also the local upper class accent. . . . It seems likely that most speakers, perhaps all except younger children, have the ability to "raise" or "lower" the apparent social class characteristics of their speech in this way.

To develop this point further, consider a person who moves from a nonflapping dialect area to a flapping one. Although the process is acquired more or less effortlessly and unconsciously, flapping represents a computational feat of considerable complexity. One must be able to isolate the consonant [t] and then substitute for (better, modify) this speech segment another of a very precise character – the flap [D] – a sound that speakers of the flapping dialect find virtually impossible to pronounce in other contexts such as the beginning of a word. One is not taught to do this – and could not be if it is correct that speakers of the flapping dialect are not even conscious that they make this sound. Furthermore, the [t] is changed only in a particular context whose exact character involves not only the features of the surrounding sounds but also the stress contour: for instance, *átom* has a [D] but in *atómic* the flap is impossible. Finally, the change is extended quite naturally to [d] (as in *rider*) but not to [p] or [k]. For example, in learning the flapping accent, no one would generalize the rule so that *wiper* is changed to *wi*[D]*er*. Similarly, no child learning this dialect as his or her first language will ever make this false analogy. But why not?

The general answer that has emerged from over 30 years' study of the problem is that speech sounds are represented in memory as *distinctive features* – linguistic categorizations with precise phonetic correlates. Sound changes are defined over these feature structures. The [t] and [d] (as well as flap [D]) of *writer* and *rider* share the feature of being articulated with the tongue tip and thus form a natural class; the [p] of *wiper* is articulated with the lips. The change of [t] and [d] to the flap [D] proceeds along the same phonological dimension; [p] → [D] cuts across this dimension and thus is an unnatural change. In other words, what is a possible sound change is constrained by the feature structure inherent in the sound's linguistic representation. Because speech sounds are encoded in memory as feature bundles, the range of modification a sound may undergo in phonetic realization is considerably narrowed – so much so that [p] → [D] will not even be considered as a possible phonological rule.

The conceptualization of speech sounds as bundles of features is not something that children are taught. We do not show children where to put the tongue to articulate a [t] the way we must teach them how to hold a spoon or tie a shoe. Rather, the features are known in advance as part of UG. It is in virtue of this knowledge that the continuous speech signal can be segmented, the resultant pieces stored in memory as *dog, Hund, chien, write, ride,* and so on, and the proper adjustments made in response to differing morphological and syntactic contexts.

Let us consider a final example of phonological knowledge of a somewhat different character – the formation of hypocoristics (nicknames).

(6) a.   Jennifer   Jennie
          Abigail   Abbie
          Madeline   Maddie
          Penelope   Pennie
          Rebecca   Beckie

     b.   Margaret   Margie
          Amanda   Mandie
          Patricia   Pattie, Tricia
          Victoria   Vickie
          Jacqueline   Jackie

From the examples in (6a) – the majority – one might infer the rule that extracts a vowel plus a consonant on each side from a prominent position of the base (the stressed or initial vowel) and adds the diminutive suffix *-ie.* (The doubled consonant in *Pennie,* etc., is an orthographic device to indicate the quality of the preceding vowel; it does not denote two consonants.) But in other cases more than a single consonant is extracted: *Patricia* may shorten to *Tricia,* taking in the entire preceding cluster, and *Margaret* and *Amanda* may shorten to *Margie* and *Mandie,* taking two consonants after the vowel. But *Alberta* shortens to *Bertie,* not *Lbertie,* and two postvocalic consonants are impossible in cases such as *Patricia* → *Pattie* and *Victoria* → *Vickie: Patrie* and *Victie* (and *Jacquie*) are distinctly odd. These judgments are quite sharp. They carry over more or less productively to non-English names as well: *Helmut* → *Helmie,* but *Zygmunt* → *Zyggie,* not *Zygmie.* Once again, the question is why not? Why does *Helmie* sound perfectly natural and *Zygmie* so awful? If learning is simply a matter of habit formation and generalization of the strongest, most frequent pattern, such errors are expected. But this is just what we do not seem to find. Rather, children and adults home in on the correct solution very quickly. Why is this so?

In this case the answer runs roughly as follows. Hypocoristic formation is a prosodic operation defined over syllables. Specifically, a prominent vowel (initial or stressed) is located and as many surrounding consonants are packed into the nickname as can be accommodated by the language's syllable template. The result is suffixed by the diminutive *-ie:* [Jennifer] → [Jenn] → [Jenn + ie].

Like the notion of distinctive feature, *syllable* is a UG primitive that cannot be defined in physical terms; rather, it is an abstract linguistic category that the child brings to the language development process. Organization into syllables is fundamental; the rest of the language's prosodic structure and much of its segmental phonology takes its syllable structure into account. The syllable template is subject to limited parametric variation. All languages start with a CV core and most allow it to expand to include CVC sequences as well. Some, such as English (but not Japanese, Korean, or many languages of Africa), extend the syllable template to CCVCC; but there are severe limitations on just which particular consonants may combine. For example, while [tr] may cluster together in the prevocalic onset, the inverse cluster [rt] is impossible in this position (*trip, true, train* are common English words, but *rtip, rtue* are unpronounceable); also in *atrocity* the syllable boundary falls between the [a] and the [tr] cluster (a.tro.ci.ty) while in *articulate* it splits the cluster (ar.ti.cu.late). Conversely, while [rt] is a possible postvocalic coda (*mart*), [tr] is not (*metre* is pronounced as two syllables). Thus, the reason *Margaret* can truncate to *Margie* but *Patricia* can shorten only to *Pattie* and not to **Patrie* is that while [marg] is a possible UG syllable, [patr] is not. Finally, both principles combine to determine Bertrand Russell's nickname of *Bertie* (**Bertrie, *Betrie, *Betie, *Berie* are ungrammatical). In sum, we see that it is a deep-seated property of UG that underlies the judgments concerning the paradigm in (6) – one that resembles the syntactic judgments from (1) that started the discussion of Plato's problem.

[handwritten margin note: Shorten]

If we accept this general point of view, then the major research questions that arise are the following. For any given language, what are the phonological representations and rules that have developed from UG in individual speakers as a result of exposure to the language of their environment? How do these rules apply to compute the phonetic representation? At a more theoretical level, what is a possible rule and representation? What elements are representations composed of? What principles govern their combination? Precisely how does UG develop into G_{Korean}, G_{French}, and so on, in response to the language of the environment?

This book explores the answers that generative linguists have given to these questions. Chapter 1 surveys the UG phonetic alphabet to give a sense of the range of speech sounds and the features that underlie them. Chapter 2 considers how lexical items are stored in memory and how phonological rules compute the corresponding phonetic representation. Chapter 3 studies more complex systems with several interacting rules. Chapter 4 returns to the features, examining their phonetic foundations in order to arrive at a more accurate and adequate representation. Chapter 5 considers the effect of morphological context on phonological rules. Chapter 6 develops a formal representation of the syllable. The next three chapters concern the ways in which features depart from a simple one-to-one relation with positions in the linear sequence of phonological segments. Chapter 7 focuses on tone, chapter 8 looks at the interface between speech sounds and syllables, and chapter 9 surveys the remaining features from a nonlinear perspective. The final two chapters return to prosodic structure. Chapter 10 pursues the idea that stress reflects a chunking of speech sounds into metrical constituents. Chapter 11 examines processes such as reduplication and hypocoristic formation that manipulate prosodic structure.

Suggested Readings

Chomsky, Noam. 1986. Knowledge of language: Its nature, origin, and use. New York: Praeger. Chapters 1 and 2.

Sapir, Edward. 1933. The psychological reality of phonemes. Reprinted in Selected writings of Edward Sapir in language, culture, and personality, ed. by D. Mandelbaum, 46–60. Berkeley: University of California Press, 1949. Also in Phonological theory: Evolution and current practice, ed. by V. Makkai, 22–31. New York: Holt, Rinehart and Winston, 1972.

1 The Sounds of Speech

This chapter has several goals. First, it surveys the sounds of speech from a traditional phonetic point of view, introducing the customary categorizations for the most common sounds in the world's languages. Second, it illustrates the basic notion of phonological natural classes and motivates the distinctive feature notation to express such classes. It then systematically surveys the universal phonetic alphabet, introducing a set of features to serve as the notational foundation for the analytic concepts and techniques of chapters 2 and 3. Finally, it familiarizes the reader with the most common systems of phonetic transcription.

In its desire to give a reasonably complete first-pass survey of the phonetic alphabet, this chapter is necessarily lengthy. Readers wishing to get to the phonological action sooner may content themselves with reading the first five or six sections. Those desiring more background should consult a phonetics text such as Ladefoged 1993.

1.1 The Saussurean Sign

According to Miller and Gildea (1987), in the normal course of development a child learns a vocabulary of some 80,000 lexical items. Many adults have lexicons of much greater size. Lexical acquisition is the one most obvious aspect of language development that requires a large contribution of memorization and learning. At the level of discussion relevant here, we conceive of the lexical item as a Saussurean sign. Our discussion focuses on the *signifiant* (*phonological form* in generative parlance). To build a large vocabulary, the learning system must have the capacity to readily perceive the information constituting the *signifiant* in the linguistic environment, to store and recall it at will, and to articulate it through a channel that offers easy transmission. The natural mode of articulation for human language is speech (though when the auditory system is impaired, language is readily expressible in the visual modality of sign language). To understand some of its most basic properties, we can ask what design features it would be desirable to build into a language articulation system so that it may subserve vocabulary acquisition. Surely one requirement is that the system be able to assign different lexical items distinct articulations that are detectable by the human ear. Second, the faster the item can be articulated and the more quickly the information contained in the acoustic signal can be recovered, the better. Third, the system itself must be easy to learn and to operate.

While a groan and a giggle are readily distinguished from one another, no language encodes its vocabulary in such gross vocal wholes. Think of the cognitive hardware that would be required to perceive, learn, and put into operation 80,000 different gestures. A much more efficient system would stipulate a small number of basic atoms and some simple method for combining them to produce structured wholes. For example, two iterations of a concatenation operation on an inventory of 10 elements (say, the digits 0,1,2,3,4,5,6,7,8,9) will distinguish 10^3 items (e.g., 000, 001, 002, . . . , 999). As a first approximation, it can be said that every language organizes its lexicon in this basic fashion. A certain set of speech sounds is stipulated as raw material. Distinct lexical items are constructed by chaining these elements together like beads on a string. Two lexical items are *distinct* if they differ in length (e.g., *us, bus, bust, burst, bursts*) or have different elements at any given position in the string (e.g., *bus, sub, rub, urb*). The fact that all languages studied so far submit to an alphabetic representation and that such writing systems are learned with relative ease reflects this basic mode of linguistic organization. However, languages typically utilize more than ten basic elements. Also, while the digits {0,1,2, . . . , 9} can be combined in any order to produce a code, human languages impose severe constraints on possible sound sequencing. Phonology can be defined as the attempt to reach a deeper understanding of the nature of these constraints.

Some constraints clearly reflect exigencies of the articulatory hardware. For example, longish sequences of consonants are not preferred. Too many unreleased consonants shut off airflow and transmission ceases. As frequently observed, the human vocal apparatus did not evolve specifically in order to articulate language. The lungs, tongue, and lips were present in the species well before the advent of language, which has had to make do with these anatomical givens (though see Lieberman 1984 for arguments that certain evolutionary developments such as the lowering of the larynx have accommodated the language faculty). But while some features of phonological structure are explicable in mechanical terms, many others are not. There appear to be principles, laws, tendencies, and modes of organization that are more cognitively based. Their discovery, study, and formulation is what animates much of the interest in the subject.

1.2 Speech Sounds: An Internal Dimension

Lexical items (*dog, cat, man*) resolve themselves into strings of speech sounds ([dɔg], [kæt], [mæn]). In addition to this "horizontal" dimension, the individual speech sounds themselves submit to further analysis. They are not the atoms of linguistic organization but constellations of still more fundamental categories. Study of the sound systems of the many different languages described over the past two centuries strongly suggests that the sounds of speech are drawn from a tightly constrained, *universal phonetic alphabet* with a surprisingly rich internal structure. This structure in large part reflects categorizations imposed by the vocal apparatus.

1.2.1 The Vocal Apparatus and the Articulation of Consonants

We can get a sense of this inner dimension of linguistic organization by a brief review of the gross structure of the vocal apparatus (see chapter 4 and figures 4.1 and 4.5 for more extensive discussion). Human speech has often been described as "movements made audible by the vocal apparatus." Between the time that air is first expelled from the lungs and the time it finally exits the oral and nasal cavities, it is excited and modified by the organs of speech in specific ways to which the auditory system is sensitive. Recent research suggests that after air has been expelled from the lungs into the trachea or windpipe, six separate *articulators* may modify it in linguistically significant ways. These articulators are the *larynx,* the *tongue root,* the *velum,* the *tongue body,* the *tongue blade,* and the *lips.*

The larynx houses the vocal cords (folds) – two elastic lips that form a valve sitting across the glottis. The vocal folds can assume a number of configurations that are linguistically significant. Here we distinguish two. First, the folds may be brought together (*adducted*) along their entire length in such a way as to be set in vibration when air passes between them. Sounds produced with this laryngeal configuration are called *voiced.* They are opposed to *voiceless* sounds, which lack vibration due to an instruction to either separate the folds or increase their tension. For example, the initial [s] and [z] sounds of *sip* and *zip* are opposed as voiceless to voiced.

After the airstream leaves the larynx, it passes through as many as three cavities whose specific properties excite it in particular ways. These are the *pharyngeal, nasal,* and *oral cavities.* In the pharynx, the root of the tongue may be projected forward to create a greater pharyngeal opening or it may fail to be so advanced. This advancement of the tongue root is the basis of the distinction between the relatively tense-feeling, crisper vowels of *beat* and *bait* and the more lax vowels of *bit* and *bet.* Prolongation of the vowel in *beat* produces the sensation of a noticeable tensing of the tongue muscles; the tension reflects the advancement gesture. As we will see, *advancement* of the tongue root (ATR) is significant not only in English but also in many African languages, which have a principle of vowel harmony that prohibits the mixture of advanced and nonadvanced vowels within a word.

After the airstream reaches the upper portion of the pharyngeal cavity, it may be expelled entirely into the oral cavity or part of it may enter the nasal cavity by lowering of the velum (the back portion of the roof of the mouth, sometimes also called the *soft palate*), which acts as a valve shutting off the nasal passage. Sounds produced with a lowered velum are called *nasal;* those produced with the velum in a raised position are called *oral.* The distinction between the raised and lowered velum position is what distinguishes the English words *bat, dip* from *mat, nip.* Virtually all languages distinguish at least one nasal consonant from a corresponding oral one. Vowel sounds may also be either oral or nasal. In the speech of most English speakers, the vowel of *can't* is noticeably nasalized as compared to the vowel of *cat.* In some American dialects the [n] is deleted, so that the nasalization in the vowel is the only feature distinguishing *can't* from *cat.*

The three remaining articulators are housed in the oral cavity. From front to back, they are the lips, the front portion (blade) of the tongue, and the tongue body. The term *labial* designates sounds articulated by the lips. Sounds articulated with the muscles controlling the front portion of the tongue are known as *coronals*, and those articulated by the tongue body are termed *dorsal* or *velar*. Labial sounds include the initial consonants in *pit, bit,* and *mitt;* the final consonants in *fat, fad,* and *fan* are coronals; and *tack, tag,* and *tang* end in velar consonants.

So far, each of the phonetic dimensions we have looked at is localized in a particular articulator. For example, the voicing dimension is a function of the larynx, and nasality is a function of the velum. Degree of stricture is a phonetic category that cuts across several different articulators. *Occlusive* or *stop* consonants are formed by having the articulator produce a closure that temporarily interrupts the flow of air. They are opposed to *fricatives,* in which the articulator forms a stricture that is narrow enough to create air turbulence but not so narrow as to interrupt the airflow. For example, the stop [p] of *pile* is produced by making a closure at the lips; in the fricative [f] of *file,* the lower lip touches the upper teeth but the contact is not sufficient to block airflow past the teeth. Similarly, in the stop [t] of *tin,* the front of the tongue makes a closure sufficient to interrupt airflow, while in the [s] of *sin,* the tongue is positioned with respect to the teeth and gum ridge so as to create turbulence but not to interrupt airflow. The initial labials in *bile* and *vile* and the coronals in *dip* and *zip* exemplify the same stop versus fricative opposition – but combined with a voicing of the vocal folds. While not bound to a particular articulator and thus somewhat more abstract, the stop-fricative distinction is nevertheless an important one in many languages. For example, Hebrew has a rule that relates stops and fricatives in particular phonological contexts: compare the perfect and imperfect forms of the verbs [p]*agaš,* *yi*-[f]*goš* 'meet'; [b]*aḥar, yi*-[v]*ḥar* 'choose'; and [k]*atab, yi*-[x]*tob* 'write'. It is interesting that such stop-fricative pairs as *p-f, b-v, k-x* are spelled by the same letter in the Hebrew alphabet. Whether the letter stands for a stop or a fricative is indicated by context as well as by the presence versus absence of a diacritic (a dot known as the *daghesh*). Recourse to this diacritic reveals an intuitive facility for resolving speech sounds into their constituent features.

The consonants made available by the various articulatory categories surveyed above are tabulated in (1). They are designated by the customary phonetic symbols. The only ones not found in English are the velar fricatives [x] and [ɣ]. The former occurs as the final consonant in German *Bach* and the latter is the phonetic realization of the second consonant in Spanish *lago* 'lake'.

(1)	labial	coronal	velar
voiceless stops	p	t	k
voiced stops	b	d	g
voiceless fricatives	f	s	x
voiced fricatives	v	z	ɣ
nasals	m	n	ŋ

Several points are worth noting. The first is a combinatoric one. In terms of its articulation, every speech sound in (1) is the product of a specific choice for each of the phonetic gestures introduced above: Are the vocal folds brought together or separated? Is the velum raised or not? Does the stricture interrupt the airflow? Thus, [p] shares the stop property with [b] and [k]. It shares the labial property with [f] and [v] and the voiceless property with [x] and [s]. From this perspective, we see that the phonetic gestures (the distinctive features) are the ultimate units of speech. Any particular sound is a macrolevel constellation of such properties – a bundle of distinctive features.

One might wonder, however, whether this phonetic reductionism has any linguistic relevance. After all, tables and chairs are composed of atoms and molecules; but we experience these objects as tables and chairs – not as atoms. Note first of all that cross-classification of the set of speech sounds into such a densely packed network is an efficient way to catalogue a large inventory of items (such as the vocabulary of a language). Just as the appropriate shoes in a shoestore can be quickly located because they are shelved in terms of a relatively small number of categories (adult vs. child, sex, length, width, color, style, etc.), so a large vocabulary can be deployed in speech if individual lexical items can be located quickly. From the table in (1), we have seen how just four parameters (place of articulation, voicing, nasality, and continuancy) yield fifteen distinct sounds. Furthermore, it is obviously significant that while the various phonetic gestures composing a sound can be produced simultaneously, the auditory system is still able to resolve the resultant complex sound into its constituent parts. The payoff is the increased efficiency with which messages can be transmitted (coded and decoded). Thus, while with just four phonetic parameters 15 distinct messages can be transmitted in one unit of time, 15 * 15 distinct messages are possible in two units of time. This mode of articulation makes it possible to transmit a greater number of messages per unit of time. Finally, since the phonetic dimensions comprising the universal phonetic alphabet are the same for all languages, the basic system is already "wired in" and need not be learned. What must be learned are which particular dimensions and combinations are employed in the language of the environment.

A few important qualifications to the combinatorics are necessary here. First, certain features are more compatible than others. Note from (1) that while voicing and continuancy (the stop vs. fricative dimension) combine freely at all three points of articulation, nasality is more restricted. There is a marked preference for voiced nasals. Although voiceless nasals can be found (e.g., in Burmese), they are decidedly rare. Also, nasality combines with oral closure in [m], [n], and [ŋ]. Nasal fricatives do not make for a happy combination of features – perhaps because so much airflow is diverted to the nasal cavity that not enough remains to generate the turbulence required of a fricative. Which feature combinations are optimal and why is still a poorly understood problem. The table in (1) represents most of the frequently occurring consonants. Later we will see how the system can be augmented to describe the fuller range of consonants found in the world's languages.

In generative grammar the major source of evidence for the features has been their utility in providing the natural cuts of phonetic space needed to understand phonological patterning. For example, recall from our discussion of *writer-rider* in the Introduction that vowels in English are shorter before [p,t,k,s] than before [b,d,g,z]. We now see that the basis of this difference is not haphazard or arbitrary; it can be expressed as a function of the voicing of the following consonant: vowels are short before the voiceless consonants [p,t,k,s] and long before the voiced [b,d,g,z]. Similarly, the English dialect in which *limp, lint,* and *link* are realized as [lĭp], [lĭt], and [lĭk] has a rule that deletes nasal consonants before voiceless stops. Before developing a more precise notation to express such natural classes, we will briefly survey the articulation of vowels.

1.2.2   Vowels

Vowels are distinguished from consonants primarily by a less radical degree of constriction imposed by the lips and tongue on the flow of air through the mouth. Distinctions within the class of vowels are created by the specific shape of the lips and the precise positioning of the tongue body. It is traditional to describe these tongue positions by reference to a neutral point such as that corresponding roughly to the location the tongue body occupies in pronouncing the vowel in the English word *bed*. (Just before the onset of speech, the vocal apparatus shifts to a "get-ready" configuration in which the vocal folds are in the voiced position, the velum is raised, and the tongue is positioned in the mid front region where the vowel of *bed* is articulated.) The vowel of *bit* is articulated by raising the tongue body above the neutral position of *bet*. A similar raising distinguishes the ATR vowel of *beat* from that in *bait*. The vowel in *bat* is produced by lowering the tongue below the neutral position. Finally, comparison of the tongue positions for the vowels in pairs such as *bet* vs. *bought* or *bait* vs. *boat* reveals a retraction from the neutral position. Vowels produced with a raising, lowering, and retraction of the tongue body are called *high, low,* and *back* vowels, respectively. While the tongue cannot be simultaneously raised and lowered, the retraction gesture combines freely with the instructions to raise, lower, or retain the tongue in the neutral position. Various English words whose vowels differ in relative tongue positioning in just these ways are displayed in (2). (The [+ATR] vowels of *beat, bait, food,* and *boat* are also longer than their [−ATR] counterparts.) The corresponding symbols that customarily designate these vowel qualities are indicated in (3). The high lax [−ATR] vowels are represented here by small capitals [ɪ] and [ʊ]; the International Phonetic Association (IPA) utilizes the special symbols [ɩ] and [ɷ] instead.

(2)

	front		back	
	[+ATR]	[−ATR]	[−ATR]	[+ATR]
high	beat	bit	foot	food
mid	bait	bet	bought	boat
low		bat	Bach	

(3)

	i	ɪ	ʊ	u
	e	ɛ	ɔ	o
		æ	ɑ	

1.3 Natural Classes

After this brief phonetic review, we begin looking at some of the phonological properties of speech sounds. One of the basic insights of 20th-century linguistics is that an individual sound tends to pattern with certain other sounds in the overall fabric of any given language. Such sound groupings are termed *natural classes*. Our first illustration comes from Chamorro, an Austronesian language of Guam (Topping 1968). Chamorro distributes its vowels in front-back pairs over the three tongue heights (4). (In unstressed syllables the distinctions between [i] and [e], [u] and [o], [æ] and [a] are lost, a detail that we overlook here.) In Chamorro, the first vowel of certain words shows a systematic change when preceded by certain particles whose precise characterization is not important at this point (5).

(4)

	front	back
high	i	u
mid	e	o
low	æ	a

(5)

gumə	'house'	i gimə	'the house'
tomʊ	'knee'	i temʊ	'the knee'
lahɪ	'male'	i læhɪ	'the male'
gwihən	'fish'	i gwihən	'the fish'
pecʊ	'chest'	i pecʊ	'the chest'

In (5) we see that a noun such as *gumə* 'house' whose first syllable contains [u] replaces that vowel with [i] when preceded by the definite particle *i*. In a similar way, [o] alternates with [e] in *tomʊ* 'knee' and [a] with [æ] in *lahɪ* 'male'. The vowels [i,e,æ] fail to change in this environment; only [u,o,a] alternate. Given the six-element inventory of (4), twenty possible three-member subsets can be formed. But only a very small percentage ever figure in the grammar of a language in the systematic way in which [u,o,a] function in Chamorro. Other logically possible drawings such as [i,o,æ] or [u,e,a] seldom appear in any rule in any language. This is a remarkable and significant fact that any theory of phonology must explain.

To continue our discussion of natural classes, the definite particle *i* is not the only one that activates the Chamorro vowel alternation. The examples in (6) show that *en, sæn, mi,* and *gi* do as well.

(6)

tunʊʔ	'to know'	en tinʊʔ	'you know'
hulʊʔ	'up'	sæn hilʊʔ	'upward'
otdʊt	'ant'	mi etdʊt	'lots of ants'
oksʊʔ	'hill'	gi eksʊʔ	'at the hill'
lagʊ	'north'	sæn lægʊ	'toward north'

The vowels in these particles are restricted to [i,e,æ]. This set (the complement of [u,o,a]) is the only other three-member subset drawn from (4) that appears with any frequency in the world's languages. It too constitutes a natural class.

We have noted two ways in which natural classes figure in phonological alternations: in defining the set of segments participating in the alternation, and in defining a conditioning environment. The individual pairings that comprise an alternation constitute a third way in which sounds organize themselves into natural groupings. For example, given the six-vowel inventory [i,e,æ,u,o,a], there are many logically possible mappings of [u,o,a] onto some other subset that could in principle define an alternation. However, only a very small number are attested empirically. Pretheoretically, some notion of "phonological distance" constrains the possible pairings. Segments are not equidistant in "phonological space." For example, [o]≈[u] is a frequent alternation; but the chances of encountering [a]≈[s] are virtually nil. Each pairing displayed in the Chamorro alternation ([u]≈[i], [o]≈[e], and [a]≈[æ]) is widely attested. *phonological alternations must make sense.*

Finally, there is characteristically an internal coherence to the various pairings that comprise a phonological alternation. While [o]≈[u] is as natural a pairing as [o]≈[e] is, it is very unlikely that [o] will alternate with [u] in the same circumstances in which [a] alternates with [æ] and [u] with [i]. In a crucial sense, the pairing of [o] with [e] is of the same kind as the [u]≈[i] and [a]≈[æ] pairings.

To sum up, only certain restricted combinations of sounds are likely to constitute the various components of a phonological alternation: the *focus* or input (e.g., [u,o,a] in Chamorro), the *image* or output (Chamorro [i,e,æ]), and the *conditioning context* (Chamorro [i,e,æ] in a particle). "Natural phonological class" is not a recent discovery. Designations such as "voiceless stops" and "front vowels" appear in many of the sound laws discovered in the 19th century. The important question is, Why is human language organized in this fashion? Although "back vowel" is defined with respect to the neutral tongue position, the latter, so far as is known, has no independent motivation outside of language. The tongue does not naturally gravitate toward [ɛ], except in the articulation of human language. Consequently, the natural phonological classes must arise from and be explained by the particular way in which UG organizes the information that determines how human language is articulated and perceived. The real question then is the nature of this organization.

1.4 Distinctive Features

The Russian-born linguist Roman Jakobson (1896–1982) proposed an answer to this question that is generally regarded as one of the most important discoveries in the history of the discipline. Jakobson's proposal (based on collaboration with his compatriot Nikolai Trubetzkoy (1890–1938)) is that phonological segments can be analyzed into complexes of *distinctive features* that cross-classify the entire inventory of possible speech sounds into a densely packed network. In general, each feature comprehends two possible values, represented as plus or minus. Also, each feature has its own characteristic articulatory and acoustic correlate.

For example, the vowels of (2) receive the distinctive feature analysis in (7). (When the distinction between back [ɑ] and central [a] is not relevant, [ɑ] will be transcribed as [a].)

(7)
	i	ɪ	e	ɛ	æ	a	o	ɔ	u	ʊ
high	+	+	−	−	−	−	−	−	+	+
low	−	−	−	−	+	+	−	−	−	−
back	−	−	−	−	−	+	+	+	+	+
ATR	+	−	+	−	−	−	+	−	+	−

We may interpret [+high] as the instruction the brain sends to the vocal apparatus to raise the tongue body above the neutral point. Segments with the [−high] designation do not raise the tongue body. Sounds that are [+back] are articulated by retracting the tongue body from the reference point. [−back] defines a sound whose articulation lacks this tongue retraction. As a first approximation, each feature implies an independent phonetic dimension. Specification as plus or minus picks out a particular end point on the relevant dimension. The complete stock of features thus constitutes a hypothesis about the phonologically significant phonetic dimensions along which possible speech sounds can vary. An adequate system should be able to resolve any sound from any language into its constituent features. Jakobson's proposal thus encourages us to think of phonological segments such as [i] and [u] as the *feature matrices* in (8). Each such matrix indicates the linguistically significant configurations the vocal apparatus assumes in order to articulate the corresponding sound.

(8) [i] = $\begin{bmatrix} +\text{high} \\ -\text{low} \\ -\text{back} \\ +\text{ATR} \end{bmatrix}$ [u] = $\begin{bmatrix} +\text{high} \\ -\text{low} \\ +\text{back} \\ +\text{ATR} \end{bmatrix}$

The proposal to represent phonological segments as feature matrices has a number of positive consequences for the issue of natural classes. First, it now becomes possible to formalize the notion of phonological distance in terms of shared feature specifications. Given the feature system in (7), [a] is closer to [æ] than [o] is, because [a] and [æ] differ by just one feature while [o] and [æ] differ in three features. Second, we can begin to understand why certain collections of segments are more natural than others. For example, the set [u,o,a] can be extracted from the Chamorro inventory [u,i,o,e,a,æ] by the simple designation [+back]. Similarly, the vocalic segments [i,e,æ] that constitute the environment for the Chamorro alternation can be specified as all and only the vowels of the language with the feature [−back].

We also note that there is no way in which such unnatural sets as [u,e,a] or [i,o,æ] can be uniquely identified as a conjunction of features. In order to specify exactly the set [u,e,a] and leave out [i,o,æ], several disjunctive statements are required. For example, while [u,a] are back vowels, [+back] also includes [o] and excludes [e]. To let in [e] but leave out [o] necessitates a complicated statement such as "[−back] only if [−high, −low] and otherwise [+back, +high] or

[+back, +low]." But this is precisely the result we seek. If natural classes have simple analyses and unnatural ones do not, then the theory is drawing the empirically correct distinctions and offers a formal basis for explaining, as opposed to simply describing, why things are as we appear to find them.

Finally, we can reconstruct the notion of the internal coherence of an alternation by noting the extent to which the feature differences between the two terms [a]≈[b] in one alternating pair are matched by corresponding differences in the other alternating pairs [c]≈[d], and so on. Given the feature system in (7), we see that the Chamorro pairings [u]≈[i], [o]≈[e], and [a]≈[æ] reflect the same feature change of [+back] to [−back].

The payoff is that we can formalize the Chamorro sound change by the rule in (9). (We assume a feature [±consonantal] to distinguish [+consonantal] consonants from [−consonantal] vowels; see section 1.8.)

(9)
$$\begin{bmatrix} -\text{cons} \\ +\text{back} \end{bmatrix} \rightarrow [-\text{back}] \ / \ \begin{bmatrix} -\text{cons} \\ -\text{back} \end{bmatrix} C_0 \underline{\quad\quad}$$

The *rule* in (9) is interpreted as follows. The *focus* [−consonantal, +back] to the left of the arrow defines the input to the alternation as the back vowels. The matrix [−back] to the right of the arrow indicates the feature change introduced by the rule – the *structural change* (SC). The slant / is read "in the context." The accompanying *environment dash* ____ locates the focus relative to the conditioning context. Finally, C_0 denotes a string of zero or more consonants. The statement in (9) thus says that back vowels are changed to the corresponding front vowels when preceded by a front vowel with an intervening string of zero or more consonants. The expression formed by combining the rule's focus and conditioning context (if any) is known as the *structural description* (SD) of the rule. Thus, A → B / ____ C has the SD AC; the SD of A → B / C ____ is CA; and the context-free rule A → B has A as its SD.

The vowel fronting in (9) illustrates the most common type of sound change: a sound *assimilates* a feature of the local environment. Our feature system can characterize assimilation by the extent to which the feature specifications in the structural change match the specifications in the conditioning context. Chamorro exhibits assimilation for backness. Since assimilation is the most common type of sound change, we can begin to understand how the class of possible phonological changes [x] → [y] might be constrained. As a first approximation, we expect [x] to become [y] in those contexts [z] where [z] has one or more of the features mentioned in [y].

Finally, with features we can begin to give a plausible answer to the question posed in the Introduction about sound change. Recall that the problem is to explain how it is possible to systematically modify our speech in a very precise but largely unconscious way as we move from one dialect (regionally or socially defined) to another. We may now say that the information the brain sends to the vocal apparatus in order to articulate a given lexical item is represented in memory in the form of a string of speech sounds, where each sound is a distinctive feature matrix. For example, in many Southern dialects of American English, the vowel [ɛ] is raised to [ɪ] before a nasal consonant so that *pen* becomes homophonous with *pin* and *hem* with *him*. At the level of detail we are considering here, the word *pen* will have the representation in (10).

(10)
$$
\begin{bmatrix} +\text{cons} \\ -\text{continuant} \\ +\text{labial} \\ -\text{voiced} \end{bmatrix}
\qquad
\begin{bmatrix} -\text{cons} \\ -\text{high} \\ -\text{low} \\ -\text{back} \\ -\text{ATR} \end{bmatrix}
\qquad
\begin{bmatrix} +\text{cons} \\ +\text{nasal} \\ +\text{coronal} \end{bmatrix}
$$

[p]   [ε]   [n]

As a first approximation, we may say that this dialect has the rule stated in (11).

(11)
$$
\begin{bmatrix} -\text{cons} \\ -\text{low} \\ -\text{back} \\ -\text{ATR} \end{bmatrix} \rightarrow [+\text{high}] \, / \, \underline{\quad} \, [+\text{nasal}]
$$

Application of this rule thus alters the realization of every [ε] before a nasal – regardless of the lexical item in which it occurs. Speakers applying this rule in their speech thus compute a different pronunciation for *hem* and *pen,* one that matches *him* and *pin.*

Assuming that speech sounds are bundles of distinctive features, we conceive of sound change as an alteration of the plus/minus specifications of the entries in the feature matrix. Let us examine some additional vocalic alternations to begin learning the kinds of changes these segments are subject to. The Bizcayan dialect of Basque (de Rijk 1970) has the five-vowel system [i,e,a,o,u]. The indefinite morpheme *bat* 'one' and the definite suffix show an alternation between [a] and [e].

(12)

noun	indefinite	definite	
sagar	sagar bat	sagar-a	'apple'
gison	gisom bat	gison-a	'man'
buzten	buztem bat	buzten-a	'tail'
belaun	belaum bet	belaun-e	'knee'
cakur	cakur bet	cakur-e	'dog'
agin	agim bet	agin-e	'tooth'
mutil	mutil bet	mutil-e	'boy'

Examination of the data reveals that these morphemes are pronounced with an [e] when a high vowel [i,u] occurs in the immediately preceding syllable and with an [a] when the mid [e,o] or the low [a] precedes. Since the indefinite morpheme has the shape *bat* in isolation, the *bet* alternant appears to be the derivative one. We can characterize the relationship between the alternants by the rule in (13). It says that a low vowel changes its values for [low] and [back] to minus when preceded by a high vowel. (This rule may be interpreted as a restricted assimilation of [−low] from a subset of the nonlow vowels – those that are [+high]. The change to [−back] is best seen as a subsidiary adjustment.)

(13) $\begin{bmatrix} -\text{cons} \\ +\text{low} \end{bmatrix} \rightarrow \begin{bmatrix} -\text{low} \\ -\text{back} \end{bmatrix} / \begin{bmatrix} -\text{cons} \\ +\text{high} \\ -\text{low} \end{bmatrix} C_0 \underline{\hspace{1cm}}$

The rule thus explains why the definite and indefinite suffixes change their pronunciation after *cakur* 'dog', *belaun* 'knee', *agin* 'tooth', and *mutil* 'boy' but not after the other nouns in (12). We see that the high vowels [i] and [u] form a natural class in triggering this rule. Given our feature system, the simple designation [+high] can isolate this class of vowels. [+low] picks out the [a] vowel as the rule's focus – the only segment that alternates in this context in Basque. It shows that a single segment may constitute a natural class.

The high vowels figure in another rule of this Basque dialect that operates in the definite forms of the nouns in (14). These stems end in a high vowel. As predicted by rule (13), the low vowel of the suffixes has changed to [e].

(14)

noun	indefinite	definite	
erri	erri bet	erriye	'village'
ari	ari bet	ariye	'thread'
buru	buru bet	buruwe	'head'
iku	iku bet	ikuwe	'fig'

The *semivowels* or *glides* [y] and [w] are close kin to the corresponding high vowels [i] and [u]. If one articulates an [i] and then slowly constricts the tongue body, the pronunciation shades into the *jod* [y]. [u] shades into [w] under similar constriction. Intuitively, [y] and [w] are consonantal variants of the vowels [i] and [u]. The emergence of the semivowels in the definite forms of (14) can be explained in the following way. Vowel sequences (V + V) are phonologically unstable; affixation of the definite suffix [-a] creates such a *hiatus*. One response is to separate the vowels by a "dummy" or "generic" consonant: V + V → VCV. Basque realizes this dummy as the consonantal variant of the preceding high vowel. In an intuitive sense (which will be made more precise in chapter 4), the features of the preceding high vowel seep into this position, giving rise to [y] and [w]. This idea is sketched in (15).

(15)

$$\begin{matrix} \text{V} \quad\quad \text{C V} \\ \begin{bmatrix} +\text{high} \\ \pm\text{back} \end{bmatrix} \end{matrix}$$

1.5 Round and Central Vowels

We have characterized vowel quality in terms of tongue body position. The configuration of the lips may also play a distinctive role. Vowels with essentially the same tongue positioning may nevertheless contrast in quality. For example, the vowels in German *Tier* 'animal' and *Tür* 'door' are both articulated with the tongue in a relatively high front position. The difference lies in the fact that for the vowel of *Tür* the lips are rounded and/or protruded while the vowel of *Tier* is articulated with the lips in a neutral or spread position. To account for this additional phonetic dimension, we augment the feature system with [±round]. In German each of the nonround front vowels [i,e,ɛ] has a distinctive rounded counterpart. We follow German orthography and transcribe the front rounded vowels with the umlaut as [ü,ö,ɔ̈]. Other languages with one or more front rounded vowel include French, Swedish, and Finnish. In similar fashion, many languages (e.g., Russian, Mandarin, Korean) have one or more back unrounded vowel. As with the front rounded vowels, the symbolization of the back unrounded vowels is varied. (16) displays the two most common systems of vocalic transcription: the system of the International Phonetic Association (IPA) and a system more commonly employed in America. The IPA tends to utilize special symbols while the American system relies more on diacritics. In generative phonology, the American system has been more commonly employed. One reason is that it more closely reflects the idea that sounds are composed of features; it also has the advantage of having fewer basic symbols to learn and is easier to deploy typographically (at least until the advent of word-processing software, which brings the special IPA fonts within easy reach). In general, the American system will be employed here, except that IPA [ɯ] and [ɤ] will be used instead of [ï] and [ë].

(16)

	[−back]		[+back]	
	[−round]	[+round]	[−round]	[+round]
[+ATR]				
[+high]	i	y	ɯ	u
[−high]	e	ø	ɤ	o
[−ATR]				
[+high]	ɩ	Y		ɷ
[−high]	ɛ	œ	ʌ	ɔ

IPA transcription of front and back round and nonround vowels

	[−back]		[+back]	
	[−round]	[+round]	[−round]	[+round]
[+ATR]				
[+high]	i	ü	ï	u
[−high]	e	ö	ë	o
[−ATR]				
[+high]	ɪ	Ü	ï	U
[−high]	ɛ	ɔ̈	ʌ	ɔ

Alternative "American" transcription of front and back round and nonround vowels

Complicating the matter of transcription further is the fact that many philological and linguistic traditions specializing in particular language families have developed their own transcription systems (some of which take into account the graphic traditions of the individual languages). Thus, in Slavic linguistics the high back unrounded vowel is traditionally transcribed as [y] and the front palatal glide jod as [j]. In general, generative phonologists prefer to retain the transcription of their sources; and so the confusing plethora of symbols is a fact of life that readers of the literature must make the best of. To minimize confusion, IPA or "American" equivalents are normally indicated. Pullum and Ladusaw 1986 is a very useful guide to phonetic symbolization.

To show the independence of lip rounding and tongue position, some minimal pairs are cited from German (17a) and Korean (17b).

(17) a. Tier   [i] 'animal'   Tür   [ü] 'door'
          Sehne   [e] 'tendon'   Söhne [ö] 'sons'
      b. kul   [u] 'cave'   kɯl   [ɯ] 'script'
          sol   [o] 'brush'   sɤl   [ɤ] 'frost'

Turkish has the vowel system shown in (18a), with matched sets of round and nonround vowels in the high front and back regions. For many Turkish suffixes, the feature values for [back] and [round] are determined by the corresponding values of the root vowels and thus do not form lexical contrasts. The data in (18b) illustrate this *vowel harmony*. The plural suffix takes the back vowel alternant *-lar* when the root contains one of the back vowels [u,ɯ,o,a] and the front vowel alternant *-ler* when the root contains one of the front vowels [i,ü,e,ö]. Similarly, the [±back] value of the accusative suffix is determined by the root; it is [+back] when the root contains a back vowel and [−back] when the root contains a front vowel.

(18) a. i ü   ɯ u
          e ö   a o

	i	e	ü	ö	ɯ	u	o	a
high	+	−	+	−	+	+	−	−
back	−	−	−	−	+	+	+	+
round	−	−	+	+	−	+	+	−

b.

noun	pl.	acc.	
dal	dal-lar	dal-ɯ	'branch'
kol	kol-lar	kol-u	'arm'
kɯz	kɯz-lar	kɯz-ɯ	'daughter'
kul	kul-lar	kul-u	'slave'
yel	yel-ler	yel-i	'wind'
göl	göl-ler	göl-ü	'sea'
diš	diš-ler	diš-i	'tooth'
gül	gül-ler	gül-ü	'rose'

If we let the variable α range over plus and minus, then the backness harmony rule can be expressed as (19a). This rule says that for any given vowel V (= [−consonantal]), its value for [back] is the same as the [back] value of the preceding vowel; C_0 stands for zero or more consonants and is a notational device allowing the rule to apply regardless of the number of consonants intervening between the vowels.

(19) a. V → [αback] / V   C$_0$ ____
                        [αback]

      b.   V   → [αround] /   V   C$_0$ ____
          [+high]   [αround]

Suffixal high vowels, such as the accusative, also harmonize in rounding with the root vowel in Turkish. Thus, after the [+round] root vowels [u] and [o] we find suffixal [u] if the root vowel is also [+back] and suffixal [ü] if the root vowel is [−back] [ü] or [ö]. We express the rounding harmony with the help of rule (19b).

Within the class of low vowels, different dialects of English (as well as other languages) make various distinctions. Most dialects distinguish the [−back] [æ] of *cat* from the [+back] [ɑ] of *father*. A number of dialects have another vowel [a] intermediate in quality: for example, the Eastern Massachusetts [a] of *car*, *park*, *yard*, and so on, and the Chicago vowel of *pop* [a] distinct from the [ɑ] of *balm* and the [æ] of *cat*. Other dialects distinguish the vowel of *bomb* from the [−round] [ɑ] of *balm* and the [−low] [ɔ] of *bought*. This vowel is transcribed as [ɒ] and has the featural representation [+low, +back, +round].

Traditional phonetics recognizes a distinct class of central vowels in the mid and high range as well. Both round and nonround variants are allowed. In the high range they are transcribed as barred [ɨ] and [ʉ]. In the mid range the central vowels include schwa [ə] and the retroflexed (*r*-colored) vowel of *bird* [ɜ] (formed by curling the tip of the tongue back). Most generative phonologists have eschewed introducing a distinct central category in addition to front and back; they have attempted to accommodate these vowels in other ways. In many languages the central vowels arise as reduced variants of front and back vowels in unstressed position and so do not contrast with full vowels: in English, for example, compare the high reduced vowel [ɨ] in the initial syllable of *demonic* with the mid schwa [ə] of *atomic*. In other cases the feature [round] may be invoked. For example, the Togolese language Lama (Ourso 1989) exhibits a three-way contrast among the high vowels: [−back, −round] [i] (e.g., *litə* 'tease'), [+back, +round] [u] (e.g., *lutə* 'stir up'), and a distinct vowel intermediate in quality between these two (which Ourso transcribes as schwa but shows to be [+high] on both acoustic phonetic and phonological grounds): *lətə* 'skin an animal'. Since this vowel lacks lip rounding, it could be described as [+back, −round] [ɯ]. But it is unclear whether there is any motivation for grouping it with the [+back] [u] other than the desire to avoid central vowels. Finally, there are cases in which this maneuver is precluded: Clements (1991a) mentions a dialect of Swedish spoken in Finland that distinguishes among three high vowels all of which are [+round]: the front [ü] of *dyr* 'expensive', the central [ʉ] of *bur* 'cage', and the back [u] of *bor* 'lives'. This is a case where a third category must be introduced (see section 9.3). This discussion can be summarized with the table in (20), where the central vowels are distinguished by the lack of a specification for [back].

(20)   æ a ɑ ɒ ə ɨ ʉ
      high   − − − − − + +
      low   + + + + − − −
      back   −   + +
      round   − − − + − − +

1.6 Features for Consonants

$S+\!$

Table (1) of the most frequent consonants is repeated in (21).

(21)

	labial	coronal	velar
voiceless stops	p	t	k
voiced stops	b	d	g
voiceless fricatives	f	s	x
voiced fricatives	v	z	ɣ
nasals	m	n	ŋ

Corresponding to the phonetic dimensions discussed earlier, we introduce the features [±continuant], [±voiced], and [±nasal]. The stops (produced with a constriction blocking airflow) are [−continuant], while the fricatives (which permit turbulent airflow) are [+continuant]. Nasals (produced with lowered velum) are [+nasal], while oral segments are [−nasal]. [+voiced] denotes sounds produced with a vibration of the vocal folds; [−voiced] sounds lack this vibration. The table in (22) illustrates how these features differentiate the coronal consonants of (21). The labials and velars receive a corresponding analysis.

(22)

	t	d	s	z	n
continuant	−	−	+	+	−
voiced	−	+	−	+	+
nasal	−	−	−	−	+

The [continuant] value of the nasal consonants is not completely clear. Since airflow is not interrupted, nasals can be prolonged like fricatives (humming) and consequently might be considered [+continuant]. On the other hand, they are produced with an oral closure and hence might better be treated as [−continuant]. The latter decision is supported by the frequent shift of fricatives to stops after a nasal, a change that can be viewed as the assimilation of [−continuant] from the nasal (compare Spanish *la* [ɣ]*ata* 'the cat' fem. but *u*[ŋ] [g]*ato* 'a cat' masc.).

1.6.1 *Place of Articulation: The Articulator Theory*

Traditional phonetics recognizes some eleven distinct points of articulation dispersed along the vocal tract, as depicted in figure 1.1. Bilabials are produced by a constriction at the lips, while for labiodentals the constriction is formed by the lower lip and the upper teeth. The (inter)dentals, dental-alveolars, and alveo-palatals constrict the tongue blade respectively at the back of the upper teeth, the alveolar ridge, and the roof of the mouth at the point where it slants upward toward the soft palate. Velars and postvelars (uvulars) form constrictions with the tongue dorsum. In pharyngeals the tongue root approximates the back wall of the pharynx, while the laryngeals utilize the vocal folds as articulators.

Recent research amalgamates some of the traditional place-of-articulation cat-*Join into one; unite* egories according to the active articulator that forms the consonantal constriction: the lower lip [labial], the tongue blade [coronal], the tongue body [dorsal], the tongue root [radical], and the vocal folds [laryngeal]. The oral articulators [labial],

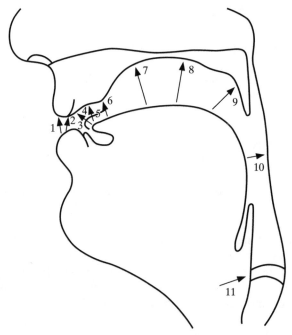

Figure 1.1 Places of articulation: 1 bilabial; 2 labiodental; 3 dental; 4 alveolar; 5 retroflex; 6 alveopalatal; 7 palatal; 8 velar; 9 uvular; 10 pharyngeal; 11 laryngeal. (Adapted from Ladefoged 1975:6.)

[coronal], and [dorsal] function as a group for one of the most widespread phonological processes: nasal assimilation to the place of articulation of a following consonant. This process is reflected in the varying realizations of the prefix in *co*[m]-*pact, co*[n]-*tact, co*[ŋ]-*gress*. It suggests that there is a phonological dimension "place" that has more than two values, including at least labial, coronal, and dorsal. In chapter 4 we will undertake a more precise characterization of the place features. For now, we content ourselves with [±labial], [±coronal], and [±dorsal].

This interpretation of place of articulation departs from earlier treatments in generative grammar where labial, dental-alveolar, palatal, and velar were differentiated by two binary cuts. The precise subgroupings varied somewhat from one researcher to another. As with so many other aspects of generative theory, the interpretation put forth in Chomsky and Halle's (1968) landmark study *The Sound Pattern of English* (henceforth *SPE*) served as the unofficial standard. In *SPE* the features [anterior] and [coronal] partitioned the oral place of articulation as in (23).

(23)

	anterior	coronal
labial	+	−
dental-alveolar	+	+
alveopalatal	−	+
velar	−	−

The feature [coronal] was defined essentially as here, while [anterior] split the oral cavity into two broad regions at the point where the alveolar ridge rises upward (roughly where the first consonant in *ship* is articulated). However, subsequent research has shown that [coronal] and [anterior] do not have the same status. While there are many sound changes that distinguish dentals and palatals from labials and velars, few convincing cases partition the four major places of the oral cavity as {labial, dental} vs. {palatal, velar}, as predicted by the [±anterior] distinction proposed in (23). Furthermore, while changes can be found that relate velars and labials on the one hand and dentals and palatals on the other, these changes never occur in the same context – a surprising empirical gap if [±anterior] is defined as claimed in (23).

1.6.2 Subsidiary Place Distinctions

Each of the articulators imposes further refinements that have traditionally been subsumed under the label "place of articulation." In this section we will briefly survey these subcategorizations.

Labial

Labial consonants can be distinguished as *bilabials* and *labiodentals*. In the former, the consonantal constriction is made by the two lips; the latter are articulated by an approximation of the lower lip and the upper teeth. The customary symbols are shown in (24).

(24)	bilabial	labiodental
stop	p b	
fricative	Φ β	f v
nasal	m	ɱ

The fricatives in [f]*ile* and [v]*ile* are labiodental; the fricative of Spanish *la* [β]*arca* 'the boat' is bilabial. The nasal [ɱ] appears in some pronunciations of *emphasis*. It invariably arises from a rule of place assimilation and is not an independently occurring segment. A few languages contrast the bilabial and labiodental fricatives. Ladefoged (1975) cites such minimal pairs as *èβè* 'Ewe' vs. *èvè* 'two' and *éΦá* 'he polished' vs. *éfá* 'he was cold' from the West African language Ewe. For the fricatives, languages more commonly select the labiodentals [f,v] than the bilabials [Φ,β]. This asymmetry is customarily explained on acoustic grounds. The labiodentals have a higher degree of turbulence and hence are more salient than the mellow-sounding bilabials. Some researchers have distinguished the two subclasses by invoking a feature [strident]: the harsher labiodentals are [+strident] in opposition to the [−strident] bilabials. But since stridency is a property of fricatives and not nasals, this feature cannot be the one that is assimilated in *emphasis*. If this type of assimilation is phonological and not merely phonetic *coarticulation* (overlap of articulatory gestures), then an additional feature must be introduced to group [ɱ] with [f] and [v]. We leave this question open, pending further evidence.

Coronal

The coronal articulator exhibits the largest number of refinements. *Dental-alveolar* versus *alveopalatal* is the most basic distinction. In the former class the front portion of the tongue creates a constriction either at the back of the upper teeth (pure dentals) or on the hard gum ridge immediately behind (alveolars). The alveopalatals (a term often abbreviated to palatals) are produced with a constriction farther back, at the point where the roof of the mouth begins to slant upward toward the soft palate. Many languages draw coronals from these two regions. Minimal pairs from English are cited in (25). They are distinguished with the help of the *SPE* feature [anterior] but its use is explicitly restricted to the coronals.

(25)   [+anterior]   [−anterior]
       s   š   (IPA ʃ)   sun   vs.   shun
       z   ž   (IPA ʒ)   miser   measure
       t   č   (IPA tʃ)   tin   chin
       d   ǰ   dump   jump
       n   ñ   money   onion

The palatal nasal is found in some pronunciations of *onion* (i.e., *o*[ñ]*on*) and occurs in Spanish.

The dental-alveolars are more common than the alveopalatals. Virtually every language selects at least one (and usually several) consonants from the [+anterior] column while many shun [−anterior] altogether. This asymmetry is also reflected in languages like Spanish where the [−anterior] [ñ] and [ʎ] are replaced by the corresponding [+anterior] [n] and [l] in the coda of a syllable: compare *Do*[ñ]*a* 'lady' but *Do*[n] and *Donce*[ʎ]*a* 'lass' but *Donce*[l] 'lad'. A neutralization of the opposition from [+anterior] to [−anterior] is much less common in this position.

The coronals are partitioned in two other ways as well. The traditional phonetic category of *interdentals* is comprised of the voiceless and voiced fricatives represented by the initial consonants of English *thin* [θɪn] and *then* [ðɛn]. They are produced by placing the tongue blade parallel to the roof of the mouth in such a way that the tip touches or projects slightly beyond the upper teeth. Air is expelled over the tongue, between the teeth. In English these fricatives are opposed to the [s] of *sin* and the [z] of *Zen* in which the tip of the tongue makes a constriction at the alveolar ridge. Many languages of Australia distinguish between dental and alveolar stops. Also, in the Irish English brogue the interdentals are replaced by dental stops, creating a dental-alveolar contrast (marked by the presence versus absence of the underbridge) between *thin* [t̪]/*though* [d̪] and *tin* [t]/*dough* [d] (Wells 1982:428). Most researchers have sought to distinguish the interdental, dental, and alveolar categories by differences in tongue shape rather than as differences in point of articulation, adding precision to the traditional phonetic distinction of *apical* (tongue-tip) versus *laminal* (tongue-blade) articulation. In *SPE* the apical-laminal distinction is implemented by a feature [distributed]: [+distributed] are sounds produced with a constriction that extends a considerable distance parallel to the direction of airflow; [−distributed] sounds are produced with a constriction that extends for just a short distance along the direction of airflow. On these grounds, the interdentals are [+distributed]. The [±distributed] feature can also be used to distinguish the retroflex consonants found in many languages of India; these consonants are produced by curling the tongue back to make a constriction with the tip or the underside of the tongue in the alveopalatal region. The [ṭ] in [ṭ]*rip* is retroflexed for many English speakers. Retroflexion is commonly denoted by underdotting. The IPA uses an undertail. The table in (26) summarizes the partitioning of the coronal articulator induced by the features [anterior] and [distributed].

(26)

		[anterior]	[distributed]
interdental	θ	+	+
dental-alveolar	s	+	−
alveopalatal	š	−	+
retroflex	ṣ, ṣ	−	−

Traditional phonetics distinguishes another point of articulation at the flat upper surface of the hard palate between alveopalatals and velars. It is usually referred to as (pure) *palatal;* it is articulated with the tongue blade and hence a species of coronal. Sounds in this category include the voiceless and voiced palatal stops of Hungarian *kutya* 'dog' and *Magyar* 'Hungarian' (transcribed [c] and [ɟ] by the IPA) and, according to Ladefoged (1975), the German ich-laut (a voiceless fricative) in words such as *ich* 'I' and *nicht* 'nothing', transcribed with the [ç]. Rather than adding another point-of-articulation distinction within the coronals, most phonologists have tried to accommodate these segments through appeal to the stricture features of [continuant] and [strident] (see section 1.7).

Affricates

Languages frequently distinguish one or more *affricates* among their coronal consonants. For example, Russian opposes its dental stop [t] and fricative [s] to the affricate [tˢ]: [t']*elo* 'body', [s']*elo* 'village', [tˢ]*eloe* 'entire' neut. sg. (the apostrophe in Russian [t'] and [s'] denotes palatalization; see section 1.10). In German the stop [t] of *Teller* 'plate' is opposed to the affricate [tˢ] that begins *Zelle* 'cell'. The affricate is produced with an initial closure; but unlike the closure of a stop, the closure of an affricate is released gradually, sounding very much like a fricative. The affricates cannot be treated as a stop-fricative sequence since they freely occur in so-called CV languages that otherwise do not allow consonant clusters. Also, some languages such as Polish distinguish affricates from the corresponding consonantal sequence; compare the cluster of *trzy* [tši] 'three' with the affricate in *czy* [tˢi] 'whether'. The interpretation of affricates is controversial. While most other sounds combine their features simultaneously, the affricate seems to require an internal sequencing of the feature [continuant].

(27)

```
        [+coron]                        [+coron]
           |                               |
        [+anter]                        [−anter]
         /    \                          /    \
 [−contin][+contin]              [−contin][+contin]
        [tˢ]                            [tˢ]
```

This representation is supported by phonological rules that treat the left face as a stop and the right as a fricative. In the alveopalatal-palatal region, the affricates [tˢ,dᶻ] are preferred over the stops [c,ɟ]. Thus, when [t] and [s] assimilate the palatality of a front glide [y], the stop [t] typically changes to the affricate [tˢ] while [s] remains a fricative and appears as [+continuant] [š]: *met you* → *me*[tˢ]*you* but *miss you* → *mi*[š]*ou*. The affricates are tabulated in (28) in voiceless-voiced pairs, along with the most common transcriptional alternatives.

(28)

	[+anterior]	[−anterior]
stop	t, d	c, ɟ
fricative	s, z	š, ʒ
		ʒ, dᶻ
affricate	tˢ, dᶻ	tˢ, ǰ
	ȼ	č, ǯ
		tʃ,

Dorsal Consonants

The tongue body is capable of producing constrictions over a broad spectrum of the vocal tract, as shown by points 8 and 9 in figure 1.1. *Prevelars* and *velars* require essentially the same tongue body positioning as the front and back vowels, respectively, and so can be distinguished by the feature [±back]. We can see this in the varying realizations of [k] in response to the front versus back vocalic environment: compare the relatively front prevelar of the initial stop in *keep* with the relatively back velar of *coop*.

   In *uvulars*, the tongue dorsum makes a constriction at the uvula. Arabic opposes voiceless stops at the velar and uvular points of articulation: velar *kalb* 'dog', uvular *qalb* 'heart'. The Parisian [ʁ] of *rouge* 'red' is a voiced uvular approximant. Aside from *k* (velar) and *q* (uvular), the transcription of the prevelar, velar, and uvular varieties of dorsal consonants is not standardized. Here a prime will be used for prevelars and underdotting for uvulars. IPA alternants for the uvulars are also shown.

(29)

	prevelar	velar	uvular	
voiceless stop	k′	k	q	
voiced stop	g′	g	g̣	[ɢ]
voiceless fricative	x′	x	x̣	[χ]
voiced fricative	ɣ′	ɣ	ɣ̣	[ʁ]
nasal	ŋ′	ŋ	ŋ̣	[ɴ]

Gutturals

Traditional grammar groups laryngeal, pharyngeal, and sometimes some uvular consonants under the category of *gutturals*. Contrasts among these three points of articulation are found in Classical Arabic. *Pharyngeals* are formed by a constriction at the back wall of the pharynx with the root of the tongue; [ħ,ʕ] and [ḥ,9] are transcriptional alternatives. *Laryngeals* have the vocal folds as articulators: the glottal stop [ʔ] constricts the folds to briefly shut off airflow while the [h] permits air to pass through the glottis. Some minimal pairs are cited in (30b).

(30) a.

	uvular	pharyngeal
voiceless	x̱	ḥ
voiced	ẏ	ʕ

laryngeal
h
ʔ

b. xaali   'my maternal uncle'
    ɣaali   'expensive'
    ḥaali   'my condition'
    ʕaali   'high'
    haal   'mirage'
    ʔaal   'family, kin'

McCarthy (1991) documents the phonological relevance of the gutturals. Let us look briefly at two types of sound change that single out these consonants. The gutturals frequently condition lowering in an adjacent vowel. For example, the root vowel in Classical Arabic verbs undergoes *ablaut* (phonetically unconditioned change of a root vowel) in forming the perfect (*CaCVC*) versus imperfect (*CCVC*) distinction. The high vowels [i] and [u] ablaut with [a]: *katab – ktub* 'write', *ḥamal – ḥmil* 'carry'. However, roots whose second or third consonant is a guttural show the low vowel in both the perfect and imperfect: *saʔal – sʔal* 'ask', *ðahab – ðhab* 'go', *fataḥ – ftaḥ* 'open', *baʕat – bʕat* 'send'. Many Bedouin Arabic dialects shun preconsonantal gutturals, metathesizing the preceding vowel (VGC → GVC) to avoid closing the syllable with a guttural. This process distorts the underlying morphological templates in the following paradigms from the Hijaazi dialect of Saudi Arabia.

(31)
template	plain root	guttural root
CaCC + a	sawda 'black'	bɣaθa 'grey'
		dḥama 'dark red'
ma + CCuuC	maktuub 'written'	mʕazuum 'invited'
		mḥazuum 'tied'
		mxaṣuur 'neglected'

Having surveyed the various points of articulation, we might ask what evidence justifies grouping the consonants in terms of the three major articulators: labial, coronal, dorsal? After all, in our survey we have examined some ten different categories dispersed along the vocal tract. Traditional phonetics sees these as ten separate points along the dimension of consonantal place. Hybrid labels like labiodental might suggest placing [f] between the bilabial and dental categories, sharing the lower lip of [p] and the upper teeth of [t] and [θ]. Yet we have assigned [f] and [v] the labial articulator, implying that they have more in common with [p] than with [t]. Several pieces of evidence support this interpretation. Many phonological systems select a stop and corresponding fricative from each of the oral place regions. For example, typically [k] is paired with [x], [t] with [s], and *spirantize – a consonantel sound, as (sh) or (v) produced by the passage of breath through the partially closed oral cavity; fricative.*

[p] with [f]. A system where [t] pairs with [f] (instead of [s] or [θ]) and [p] with [Φ] is unheard of. The claim that [f] and [v] are basically labial is also reflected in sound change. For example, many languages spirantize stops to fricatives (lenition), so that the velar [k] is replaced with [x]. In these languages we find [p] changing to [f] – not to [θ] or [s]. This process is often inverted (fortition); once again, [f] typically alternates with [p], not with [t]. This point is also explained if it is the feature [continuant] that changes while the [labial] articulator remains constant.

lenis – articulated w/ little muscle tension and little or no aspiration – (eg) [b] or [d]

1.7 Stricture

@ antonym (Fortis)

Fortis – articulated w/ much muscle tension & usu. w/ strong aspiration eg – (p) or (t) initial English

a limiting or stricting condition.

Traditional phonetics recognizes three categories of consonantal constriction: *stops* (also called *occlusives*) interrupt airflow, *fricatives* constrict airflow in such a way as to generate turbulence, and *approximants* have nonturbulent airflow. Common representatives of each category are depicted in (32).

(32) occlusives   p   t   č   k
      fricatives   f   s   š   x
      approximants   w   l,r   y

CONTINUENT

Stops / Fricatives difference

Occlusives are distinguished from fricatives by the feature [continuant]. [−continuant] sounds are produced with an oral stricture that interrupts airflow. On these grounds, [p,t,č,k] are [−continuant] while [f,s,š,x] are [+continuant]. Nasals [m,n,ñ,ŋ] fail to participate in a stop-fricative opposition the way [p] and [f] do, but they induce occlusion on following consonants and for this reason are usually classed as [−continuant]. Approximants include the liquids [l] and [r] and the glides [w] and [y]. These sounds form a natural class in virtue of their distribution in syllable structure rather than because of any property they impart to neighboring sounds via assimilation. For example, in English syllable onsets may include a stop plus liquid or glide (*clean* [kl], *cream* [kr], *queen* [kw], *cue* [ky]) but not a stop plus nasal such as [kn] (in *knee* the *k* is silent). While the approximants could be defined indirectly as nonnasal sonorants, some researchers have preferred the feature [±approximant] so that the shared distribution of the liquids and glides can be expressed directly.

Having surveyed the major stricture categories, we now consider each of them in turn. Most phonological systems select an occlusive for each oral articulator, the coronal often taking two – typically a [+anterior] such as [t] and a [−anterior] such as [č]. Affricates are more common than stops at the alveopalatal point of articulation; they can also be found at the lips and dorsum (e.g., standard German [pf] and dialectal [kx]). Because of the difficulty of interrupting airflow at certain points of articulation (e.g., interdental and pharyngeal), there are more continuants than stops. In some systems, the interdentals [θ,ð] are distinguished from the harsher [s,š], the latter termed *sibilants*. Some phonologists have proposed a feature [+strident] (greater turbulence) to distinguish the sibilants from the [−strident] interdentals. Among the approximants, the liquids [l,r] and the glides [w,y] form easily distinguished subsets. In Maddieson's (1984) survey of more than three hundred phonological inventories, over 95 percent of languages chose at least one liquid and most (77 percent) more than one, with the lateral being slightly more popular. Liquids are prone to dissimilate; in Latin [l] turned to [r] when the stem contained a lateral. This dissimilation is evident in the distribution of the *-al* and *-ar* alternants of the adjectival suffix in *pap-al, tot-al, coron-al, guttur-al* but *vel-ar, pol-ar, angul-ar*. A *lateral* is produced by making a constriction with the central portion of the tongue but lowering one or both margins so that air flows out the side of the mouth. Laterals may be aspirated or voiceless (transcribed as a barred [ɬ]); they can be affricated; and while typically coronal (with the dental-alveolar [+anterior] [l] favored over the alveopalatal [−anterior] [ʎ]), they can be articulated with the tongue body. Whether coronal versus velar lateral is a possible phonemic contrast is unclear. *Rhotics* come in several varieties as well. The trilled versus flap opposition of Spanish *perro* 'dog' vs. *pero* 'but' is well known. In a *trill,* the articulator is held loosely so that it can be set in vibration by the passing air. According to Ladefoged (1982:153), "a *flap* is caused by a single contraction of the muscles so that one articulator is thrown against another. It is often just a very rapid articulation of a stop closure," as produced by English speakers who flap the medial consonants in *latter, ladder, tanner.* Phoneticians have devised a panoply of special symbols to distinguish among the various rhotics. For example, the French uvular rhotic is indicated by a small capital, inverted to distinguish the Parisian fricative/approximant [ʁ]*ouge* 'red' from the Midi's trilled [R]*ouge*. The rhotic of English *red* is a weak approximant (IPA [ɹ]) with no contact between the tip of the tongue and the roof of the mouth. It patterns with the glides in allowing the flapping of a following dental stop, which itself is transcribed [ɾ]: *writer* [ayɾ], *outer* [awɾ], *Carter* [aɹɾ] but *welder* [ɛld]. We will distinguish the rhotics and laterals with the help of a feature [±lateral] whose articulatory correlate is the presence or absence of lowering at the tongue margin(s). Finally, the pharyngeals [ħ,ʕ] and laryngeals [h,ʔ] are sometimes treated as approximants instead of fricatives.

Sound changes from left to right on the stop-fricative-approximant dimension are known as *weakenings* (*lenition*) while changes from right to left are *strengthenings* (*fortition*). Postvocalic context is the most typical environment for the change from stop to fricative (a process also known as *spirantization*). This is the environment where Tiberian Hebrew changes its stops [p,t,k] and [b,d,g] to the fricatives [f,θ,x] and [v,ð,ɣ]. Many systems restrict weakening to contexts in which a vowel follows as well as precedes: for instance, intervocalic flapping of dental stops in many English dialects. It is unclear whether spirantization is properly viewed as assimilation of the open position of the neighboring vowel and hence whether vowels are properly viewed as [+continuant]. Fortitions from fricative to stop tend to occur in the complementary set of contexts: post-consonantal and initial. In some cases only certain consonants call for a following occlusive. For example, in Spanish the voiced stops [b,d,g] and the corresponding fricatives [β,ð,ɣ] are in complementary distribution. The fricatives occur after [r] (*cur*[β]*a* 'curve', *ver*[ð]*e* 'green', *lar*[ɣ]*o* 'long') and stops after a (homorganic; i.e., same point of articulation) nasal: *hom*[b]*re* 'man', *don*[d]*e* 'where', *an*[g]*osto* 'narrow') as well as initially ([b]*ola* 'ball', [d]*uro* 'hard', [g]*ato* 'cat'). After the lateral, [d] appears in place of [ð] (*cal*[d]*o* 'broth') while noncoronals are realized as [+continuant] (e.g., *cal*[β]*o* 'bald', *al*[ɣ]*o* 'something'). The fact that nasals favor a following occlusive justifies categorizing them as [−continuant] even though they themselves typically do not spirantize. The inconsistent behavior of the lateral leaves the [±continuant] status of [l] unresolved. *Gemination* (doubling) is a context that inhibits lenition and promotes fortition. Thus, in Tiberian Hebrew postvocalic stops systematically fail to spirantize when geminate. Conversely, geminated approximants often strengthen to homorganic obstruents: for instance, in Faroese (Anderson 1972) **yy > ggj* [ǰ] and **ww > gv*.

1.8 Major Class Features

The features [sonorant] and [consonantal] each partition the set of speech sounds into two broad classes, as depicted in (33). Like [continuant], these features are not bound to a particular articulator; instead, they specify phonologically critical degrees of constriction imposed by essentially any articulator.

(33) | | [sonorant] | [consonantal] | |
|---|---|---|---|
| vowels | + | − | a,i,u,o,e, . . . |
| glides | + | − | y,w |
| liquids | + | + | l,r |
| nasals | + | + | m,n,ñ,ŋ |
| obstruents | − | + | t,d,s |

[±sonorant] classifies sounds in terms of the effect their stricture has on the flow of air across the glottis and hence the capacity to induce vibration of the vocal folds. Vocal fold vibration is influenced by several factors; but the most important is airflow. The folds cannot vibrate if no air is passing through the glottis. In order for air to flow, the supralaryngeal pressure must be less than the sublaryngeal. The degree of stricture made during the articulation of a sound may increase the supralaryngeal pressure and hence tend to shut off voicing unless other adjustments are made. Stops and fricatives have a stricture that inhibits spontaneous voicing. The stricture associated with [+sonorant] segments does not disrupt airflow enough to inhibit voicing. Thus, the natural state for sonorants is [+voiced] and for nonsonorants (termed *obstruents*) is [−voiced].

Of all speech sounds, vowels and glides are produced with the least constriction and hence allow the freest flow of air. While nasals are articulated with an oral closure, the nasal cavity is open and hence airflow is not impeded. In the production of a lateral, a closure is made; but the lowering of the tongue margins allows sufficient airflow to maintain voicing. Finally, the various rhotics (retroflexed approximants, trills, flaps) either do not make a sufficiently narrow stricture, or if they do, it is not held long enough to inhibit spontaneous voicing.

From these remarks, it is clear that [+voiced] is the natural laryngeal state for a sonorant. A special laryngeal adjustment is required to inhibit voicing. Thus, while voiceless sonorants occur, they are distinctly dispreferred to voiced ones. In obstruents the opposite state of affairs obtains. The optimal stop or fricative is voiceless. A language typically augments its inventory with a voiced obstruent only after the corresponding voiceless one has been chosen. The special status of [+voiced] in obstruents is shown by the fact that in many languages (e.g., Slavic) obstruents induce voicing assimilation in adjacent obstruents while sonorants are inert, neither causing nor undergoing such changes: compare Russian *pro*[s']-*it* 'requests', *pro*[z']-*ba* 'a request' with *ne*[s]-*ut* 'carries' 3pl., *ne*[s]-*la* past fem. Two additional properties distinguish sonorants. First, in many languages a syllable can only terminate in a sonorant: for example, Lama has words ending in liquids or nasals but none ending in obstruents. Second, in a number of languages (e.g., Lithuanian) a sonorant consonant in the coda of a syllable may count as a tone-bearing unit; obstruents typically shun tones.

The feature [+consonantal] denotes sounds with a radical constriction in the supralaryngeal cavity. Vowels and the corresponding glides are [−consonantal]. Note that in the system being described here the high vowels [i] and [u] and the corresponding glides [y] and [w] have the same feature structure. They differ in terms of their location within the syllable. A vowel occupies the nuclear peak while a glide appears in the margins – the prevocalic onset or the postvocalic coda. The equivalence of [i] – [y] and [u] – [w] is seen in a number of processes. For example, many dialects of Arabic avoid words ending in consonant clusters. When the 2sg. suffix is removed from the stems in *dalw-ak* 'your pail' and *jady-ak* 'your kid', the glides are turned to the corresponding vowels: *dalu* 'pail', *jadi* 'kid'. Another reflection of the close relation between [i] and [y] and between [u] and [w] is seen in Basque. As noted in section 1.4, when the definite suffix -*a* is added to a stem ending in a high vowel, a corresponding glide fills the gap to provide the second syllable with an onset: *ari* 'thread' and *iku* 'fig', but [ari+a] and [iku+a] are realized as [ariya] and [ikuwa] or, depending on the dialect, as [ariye] and [ikuwe] by another rule. When glides occupy the syllable nucleus as part of a *diphthong* (a tautosyllabic sequence of [−consonantal] segments), they are sometimes called *semivowels* and transcribed with an inverted breve ([ai̯], [au̯]). In the early stages of generative phonology, the syllabicity of a sound was characterized by a feature [±syllabic]. This feature stood out from the others, however, in its lack of any precise phonetic correlate. A major theoretical development of the 1970s and 1980s was the articulation of the more traditional conception of the syllable as a prosodic constituent. In current generative thinking, the syllabicity of a sound is a function of its location in this constituent – not a matter of its feature structure. Syllabic consonants are transcribed by an under-ring or understroke: for example, Czech *vlk* 'wolf' is [vl̥k] or [vl̩k].

The table in (34) summarizes the manner-of-articulation features for a representative set of speech sounds.

(34)

	t	s	θ	n	l	r	y	i
consonantal	+	+	+	+	+	+	−	−
sonorant	−	−	−	+	+	+	+	+
approximant	−	−	−	−	+	+	+	+
continuant	−	+	+	−	+	+	+	+
lateral	−	−	−	−	+	−	−	−
nasal	−	−	−	+	−	−	−	−
strident	−	+	−	−	−	−	−	−

1.9 Laryngeal Features

The stops in *s*[p]*in*, *s*[t]*un*, *s*[k]*in* exhibit the optimal laryngeal state for occlusive consonants: voiceless, unaspirated, unglottalized. However, many systems augment their stock of phonemes through modifications of the sound wave introduced by the vocal folds in the larynx. French, Mandarin, and Nootka illustrate the most common options. In French voiceless stops are opposed to voiced, in Mandarin to aspirated, and in Nootka to glottalized (transcribed with a glottal superscript [p$^\gamma$] or apostrophe [p']).

(35)   <u>French</u>

[p]as	'not'	[t]u	'you'	[k]uand	'when'
[b]as	'low'	[d]u	'of'	[g]ant	'glove'

<u>Mandarin</u>

pei	'back'	tai	'to bring'	kan	'to do'
p^{h}ei	'to match'	t^{h}ai	'very'	k^{h}an	'to see'

<u>Nootka</u>

pa:-	'go'	ta:-	'long'	kaɬ-	'branch'
p$^\gamma$a-	'give away'	t$^\gamma$aq-	'just'	k$^\gamma$o:-	'a little way'

Many languages combine these options to make a three-way contrast among laryngeal features. For example, in Thai [t] is opposed to [d] as well as to [t^h], while in Amharic [t] is opposed to [d] and to [t$^\gamma$]. Finally, some systems such as Hindi make a four-way distinction among laryngeal features, combining both voicing and aspiration (examples from Ladefoged 1975).

(36)   <u>Thai</u>

bàa	'shoulder'	dam	'black'		
pàa	'forest'	tam	'to pound'	kàt	'to bite'
p^{h}àa	'to split'	t^{h}am	'to do'	k^{h}àt	'to interrupt'

<u>Amharic</u>

dɨl	'victory'	gərr	'innocent'
tɨl	'worm'	kɨrr	'thread'
t$^\gamma$ɨl	'quarrel'	k$^\gamma$ɨr	'stay away'

<u>Hindi</u>

pal	p^{h}al	bal	b^{h}al
'take care of'	'edge of knife'	'hair'	'forehead'
tan	t^{h}an	dan	d^{h}an
'mode of singing'	'roll of cloth'	'charity'	'paddy'
ʈal	ʈ^{h}al	ɖal	ɖ^{h}al
'postpone'	'place for buying wood'	'branch'	'shield'
kan	k^{h}an	gan	g^{h}an
'ear'	'mine'	'song'	'kind of bundle'

The interpretation of the laryngeal features adopted here is based in part on the model developed by Halle and Stevens (1971). Two phonetic dimensions are distinguished: the amount of space between the vocal folds (glottal width) and the amount of tension in the folds. Given that the voiceless unaspirated unglottalized series defines the optimal laryngeal state, we take it to be the neutral configuration of the glottis. Aspirated sounds are produced by spreading the vocal folds while glottalized sounds constrict the folds. The former are accordingly [+ spread gl, − constr gl] while the latter are [+ constr gl, − spread gl]. The neutral [p,t,k] are [− spread gl, − constr gl]. The absence of [+ constr gl, + spread gl] reflects the impossibility of realizing two opposing mechanical gestures simultaneously. The diagram in (37) depicts this tripartite division of glottal width.

(37)

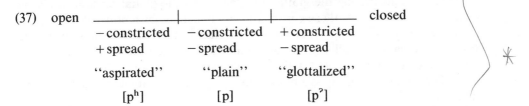

open ————————|—————————|———————— closed

− constricted	− constricted	+ constricted
+ spread	− spread	− spread
"aspirated"	"plain"	"glottalized"
[pʰ]	[p]	[pˀ]

With this background, let us briefly survey the three laryngeal categories. The *aspiration* of a stop as in English [pʰ]*in* has traditionally been described as a "puff of air" occurring after the release of the stop closure or as a delay in the onset of vocal cord vibration in the production of the following vowel. The Halle-Stevens model sees both of these phenomena as consequences of the instruction to spread the vocal folds. Accordingly, aspirated stops are [+ spread gl] and hence [− constr gl]. The voiced aspirates of Hindi are an embarrassment to the traditional "lag in onset of vibration" theory since the folds must be vibrating in the execution of the stop as well as the following vowel. We will follow Halle and Stevens in construing voicing as a function of glottal tension (noting, however, that this interpretation of vocal fold vibration awaits experimental phonetic confirmation). Even though the folds are separated, they may still vibrate if they are held loosely. Thus, [− voiced] will denote sounds produced with greater vocal fold tension, and [+ voiced] will denote sounds in which the folds are held more loosely. (Halle and Stevens suggest the features [stiff] and [slack], but this terminology has not been widely accepted. We will retain the traditional label [± voiced] but will follow Halle and Stevens in construing vocal fold vibration as a function of glottal tension.) The table in (38) shows how the stops of French, Thai, and Hindi are characterized in the proposed system.

(38)

	pʰ	bʰ	p	b
spread gl	+	+	−	−
constr gl	−	−	−	−
voiced	−	+	−	+

Glottalized consonants are produced by constricting the vocal folds. For example, the medial stop in English *button* is glottalized for many speakers: simultaneous with the oral closure, the vocal folds are constricted to yield a [tˀ].

In some casual pronunciations the oral closure may be suppressed, unveiling the laryngeal constriction in the form of a glottal stop: *bu*[ʔ]*on*. In many languages the glottal constriction in stop consonants is enhanced by raising the larynx in the throat. This gesture compresses the air behind the oral closure; when it is released, a sharp, crackling sound is produced. So far as is known, these *ejectives* do not contrast with plain glottalized consonants and so the laryngeal raising, while dramatic, might best be considered a matter of phonetic implementation rather than a distinct phonological category. Such ejectives are found in many American Indian languages, where they are customarily transcribed with an apostrophe [p',t',k'].

A similar phenomenon occurs with the voiced glottalized segments, which are produced by constricting the glottis but slackening the glottal tension to permit vibration. In many cases these consonants are enhanced by a noticeable lowering of the larynx in the throat. This action may decrease the air pressure in the supralaryngeal cavity, leading to an ingression of air when the oral closure is released. Sounds supplemented with this laryngeal lowering are known as *implosives*. They are customarily symbolized as [ɓ,ɗ,ɠ] and are found in many African languages.

Halle and Stevens (1971) suggest dividing the dimension of glottal tension into three categories instead of just two. For the [−spread gl, −constr gl] group, this move allows them to distinguish the voiced stops of Romance languages like French from the initial stops in English *bun, done, gun*. In the former, vocal fold vibration begins more or less simultaneously with the oral closure; in the latter, there is a considerable delay in the onset of voicing until well after the initial closure. Halle and Stevens see the English [b,d,g] as having an intermediate degree of tension between the totally voiceless (stiff) [p,t,k] of *spin, stun,* and *skin* and the fully voiced (slack) [b,d,g] of French. They also exploit the possibility of an intermediate degree of glottal tension to try to explain a puzzling contrast in Korean. As pointed out originally by Kim (1965), Korean stops display three contrasting laryngeal configurations, none of which involve vocal fold vibration: *tʰal* 'mistake', *t*al* 'daughter', *tal* 'moon'. Halle and Stevens suggest placing the [t*] in the aspirated [+spread gl] series but distinguish it from [tʰ] as well as from the voiced [dʰ] of Hindi by assigning it an intermediate degree of glottal tension. Subsequent research has shown that the "tense" [t*] is actually produced with a constricted glottis but lacks the ejection of the glottalized consonants of the American Indian languages. Iverson (1987) suggests the features [+constr gl, +stiff vf].

The table in (39) summarizes the laryngeal features. If the distinction between the fully voiced [b] of French and the partially voiced [b] of English is simply a matter of different phonetic implementation, we may replace [stiff vf] and [slack vf] with [voiced]. (Voiceless sonorants are transcribed by an underring (e.g., [m̥]) or by small capitals.)

(39)	spread gl	constr gl	stiff vf	slack vf	(voiced)
pʰ	+	−	+	−	−
bʰ (Hindi)	+	−	−	+	+

	spread gl	constr gl	stiff vf	slack vf	(voiced)
p	−	−	+	−	−
b (English)	−	−	−	−	+
b (French)	−	−	−	+	+
p^{ʔ}	−	+	−	−	−
p∗ (Korean)	−	+	+	−	−
ɓ	−	+	−	+	+

1.10 Secondary Articulations and Complex Segments

Many languages amplify their segmental inventories by superimposing the vowel quality features of lip rounding and tongue body palatality or velarity on their consonants. Imposition of [+round], [−back], and [+back] produce the *secondary articulations* of labialization, palatalization, and velarization, respectively; pharyngealization arises from retraction of the tongue body and/or tongue root toward the back wall of the pharynx.

Labialization is usually transcribed by a superscripted *w;* a labialized consonant simultaneously combines lip rounding with the primary articulation. Examples of (near) minimal pairs from the West African language Margi (Hoffman 1963) appear in (40).

(40) pá   'build'   sà   'drink'   gà   'and'
      p^{w}á   'pour in'   s^{w}á   'shut'   g^{w}à   'enter'

Even though rounding is produced by the lips, this gesture is still compatible with a labial constriction; Margi has a full suite of labialized labials: *b^{w}àŋ* 'hip', *ɓ^{w}à* 'cook', *f^{w}àŋ* 'hollow', *m^{w}àl* 'friend', *v^{w}ĭ* 'gourd-plant'. As we might expect, labialized consonants often arise through the assimilation of [+round] from adjacent rounded vowels. For example, in their description of Nootka, Sapir and Swadesh (1939) posit a stem [ki:ɬ] 'making'. When this stem is preceded by the prefix ʔo-, the velar is labialized: *ʔo-k^{w}i:ɬ* 'making it'.

In Russian essentially all consonants are accompanied by a raising of the tongue body as a secondary articulator. If it is [−back], the consonant is *palatalized;* if it is [+back], the consonant is *velarized*. This contrast is fundamental, appearing in prevocalic, preconsonantal, and word-final positions. (In Slavic linguistics, palatalization is usually denoted by the apostrophe; elsewhere, a superscripted *y* is more common. There is no standard notation for velarization; the plain letters are used here with the explicit understanding that the tongue is in a high back position.) The chain of minimal pairs in (41) illustrates this [±back] opposition on Russian consonants.

(41) m'at'   'to rumple'
      mat'   'mother'
      mat   'checkmate'
      m'at   'rumpled'

Palatalization and velarization freely combine with labials and most dentals in Russian. But in the [−anterior] alveopalatals they are distributed complementarily: [č] is palatalized ([−back]) while, at least in the standard dialect, [š,ž] are velarized ([+back]). This difference shows up in the effects these consonants have on the following vowel: the phoneme /i/ is realized as [−back] [i] after [č] but as [+back] [ɯ] after [š,ž]: *uč'-it* 'teaches', *duš*-[ɯ]*t* 'smothers', *druž*-[ɯ]*t* 'befriends'. Because we have viewed the feature [back] as a dependent of the dorsal articulator, when velar [k] assimilates [−back] it changes its point of articulation to prevelar [k']; but palatalization of [p] or [t] entails no necessary change in point of articulation. Compare the palatalizations induced by the dat.sg. suffix -*e*: *ruk-a, ruk'-e* 'hand'; *rabot-a, rabot'-e* 'work', *tolp-a, tolp'-e* 'crowd'. In many cases, however, dental, velar, and sometimes labial consonants change their primary place of articulation to alveopalatal when palatalized by a front vocalic segment, especially the high vowels [i,ü] and the corresponding glides [y,ẅ] ([ẅ] = IPA [ɥ]). Precisely how to express this change is a subject of continued debate in feature theory; see section 9.3 for discussion.

The tongue root or body may be retracted during the production of an oral consonant – a secondary articulation known as *pharyngealization*. This gesture underlies the "emphatic" consonants in Arabic (usually transcribed by underdotting or capitals), where we find such minimal pairs as *sayf* 'sword' vs. *ṣayf* 'summer' and *tiin* 'figs' vs. *ṭiin* 'mud'. According to Ghazeli (1977), the emphatics [ṣ,ṭ,ẓ,ð̣] are produced with a tongue body constriction in the upper pharynx.

The secondary articulations will be treated here as single segments rather than consonant-glide clusters. A number of considerations support this decision. First, many languages that otherwise lack consonant clusters freely permit C^w and C^y. Second, a secondarily articulated consonant may contrast with a consonant-glide cluster: compare Russian *s'est'* 'sit down' with *syest'* 'eat up'. Finally, when consonants with a secondary articulation simplify, the residue is typically a single segment. Two patterns of simplification will illustrate this. First, the primary articulation may be suppressed, leaving just the secondary articulation in the form of a glide. For example, in Polish the velarized [+back] lateral (orthographic *ł*) is now realized (in the standard dialect) as [w]: *Łódz* is [wuć]. Alternatively, the secondary place of articulation may be promoted to primary, displacing the original articulator. For example, the labialized velars k^w and g^w of Latin appear as bilabial stops in Romanian: Latin *aqua* 'water', *lingua* 'tongue' > Romanian *apă*, *limbă*. In this sound change, the [−continuant] feature is executed by the lips instead of by the tongue dorsum.

The most salient phonological property of the secondary articulations is their propensity to stretch over successive consonants or even syllables, mimicking the behavior of the corresponding features in vowel harmony. For example, in many Arabic dialects the pharyngealization of the emphatic phonemes spreads to other consonants of the root and beyond. In an analysis of the Lebanese dialect, Haddad (1983) shows that when the root [rxṣ] 'become cheap' maps to the C*i*C*i*C template, pharyngealization spreads from the final consonant to the remaining segments of the word, causing a nonfinal [i] to be realized as [u]: *ruẋiṣ* 'became cheap' vs. *rixis* 'became tender', built on the radical [rxs].

Consonants exist in which two articulators combine to form a single segment where the constriction of each is greater than a simple vowel or glide. The clearest examples of such *complex segments* are the *labiovelars* [kp] and [gb] found in many West African languages such as Ewe (Ladefoged 1975), with the minimal pairs shown in (42a).

(42) a. ekpā   'he faded'   egba   'he roofed'
          eka   'he chipped'   egã   'he became rich'
          epɔ   'he was wet'   eba   'he cheated'

      b. epla   'he hurt'
          eklɔ   'he washed'
          ekpla   'he girded'

      c. fo   'to beat'   fofo   'beating'
          ci   'to grow'   cicii   'grown up'
          fle   'to buy'   feflee 'bought'
          kplo   'to lead'   kpokplo 'leading'

These segments have the distribution of single consonants. The only clusters in Ewe consist of a consonant plus [l]; the labiovelar forms this cluster just like simple labial and velar stops (42b). Also, CV reduplication takes the first consonant and vowel of the stem (42c); once again, the labiovelar patterns as a single segment. When the labiovelars condition nasal assimilation, the result, at least in some languages, is a doubly articulated nasal [mŋ]. This suggests that the labial and velar components are unordered – at least phonologically. A controversial question in feature theory is whether one of the articulators must be singled out as primary. In the absence of such a distinction, we expect any rule mentioning labial or velar to be activated by the labiovelar complex. Not enough languages have been studied to know whether this expectation is justified.

Given that the labial and velar articulators may combine, it is natural to inquire about the behavior of the coronal. Sagey (1986) interprets the clicks of the Khoisan languages as dorsal consonants with coronal as a radically constricted secondary articulation. *Clicks* are formed by simultaneous constrictions of the tongue blade and dorsum, creating a temporary air chamber between the two closures. This chamber is rarified by sliding the tongue dorsum back along the soft palate, increasing the volume and consequently lowering the air pressure. When the coronal stricture is released, air flows into the mouth to create the distinctive click sound. These dramatic consonants are largely restricted to the languages of southern Africa, where they have been thoroughly integrated into the sound system. In Buru (Traill 1985) clicks combine with other manner-of-articulation features to produce some twenty distinct consonantal segments. While clicks are phonetically dramatic, their phonological behavior remains to be assessed.

Given that dorsal combines with both labial and coronal, we predict the existence of labiocoronals. Hoffman (1963) reports such consonants for Margi, citing *bdà* 'to sting (bee), to kick (donkey)', *bzə́r* 'child', *ptə́l* 'chief, king', *psár* 'grass'. He argues that these are single segments rather than clusters on the grounds that *ptə̀* 'to be insufficient' reduplicates as *ptə̀ptə̀* just as *sà* 'to drink' reduplicates as *sàsà*. As Maddieson (1987) points out, this argument is vitiated by examples such

as *tˢàgàlà*, which reduplicates as *tˢàgàlàtˢàgàlà*, suggesting that the Margi reduplication is at the level of the entire stem and not just the first CV. If so, then
the labiocoronals could be treated as consonant clusters instead of single segments. Sagey (1986) analyzes such clusters as *tkʷ*, reported for certain Shona
dialects by Doke (1931) as triply articulated single consonants. This interpretation
has, however, been called into question.

1.11   Prosodic Features

The properties of length, stress, and tone are traditionally isolated from the other
features into a special category of *prosodic* or *suprasegmental* features. Their
distribution and phonological behavior characteristically ignores the features defining a sound's inherent quality. The autonomy of the suprasegmentals (and indeed the term itself) is reflected in the fact that orthographic systems register
their presence (if at all) through diacritic marks or accents rather than with separate letters. The prosodic features have received intensive scrutiny during the
past two decades. The insights acquired in the study of these categories have
profoundly influenced phonologists' conception of the segmental features. We
will review this research in considerable detail in later chapters. At this point we
will content ourselves with a brief overview of the prosodic terrain.

Quantity

Many languages oppose long vowels and consonants to short. Phonetically, the
duration of the longer sound exceeds that of the shorter by a factor of one-half
to one-and-a-half or more. In consonants, length is usually indicated by *gemination* (doubling): Italian *nono* 'ninth' vs. *nonno* 'grandfather', Arabic *darasa*
'studied' vs. *darrasa* 'taught', Japanese *saka* 'slope' vs. *sakka* 'author'. Long
vowels are variously transcribed as geminates (*taa*), by a colon (*ta:*), or by the
macron (*tā*). Short vowels are unmarked (*ta*) or indicated by the breve (*tă*): Latin
mālus 'apple tree' vs. *malus* 'evil', Arabic *kataba* 'wrote' vs. *kaataba* 'corre-
sponded with', Japanese *tori* 'bird' vs. *toori* 'road'. Given the autonomy of suprasegmentals, quantity oppositions are usually distributed freely across a language's vowel or consonant inventory. There are, however, occasional gaps: for
example, in Tiberian Hebrew geminates are excluded from the class of gutturals;
in the Roman dialect of Italian palatals such as [č,š,ǰ,y] are phonologically geminate. In many systems length consists in the assignment of a phonological position
after the syllable's nuclear vowel. This "slot" is then filled by either the following
consonant or the preceding vowel. Such a conception of length affords a straightforward explanation for the behavior of the Hebrew definite prefix *ha*. When
added to most stems, it geminates the following consonant: *seefer* 'book', *has-
seefer* 'the book'; *melex* 'king', *hammelex* 'the king'. But when the noun begins
with a guttural (which resists gemination), the vowel of the prefix lengthens instead: *ʔiiš* 'man', *haaʔiiš* 'the man', *ʕaam* 'people', *haaʕaam* 'the people'. Intuitively, the prefix has the phonological form *haX*, where *X* is an empty position
that prefers to be occupied by the following consonant but when this is impossible

then by the preceding vowel. We will develop this conception of "phonological position" in chapter 8.

Long consonants typically span the syllable break and often shorten when such syllable sharing is not possible. In Tiberian Hebrew the geminate of the root [dall-] 'poor' is realized as such before a vowel-initial suffix such as the plural: *dall-i:m* (syllabified [dal.li:m]). In the masculine singular, where there is no suffix, the final consonant degeminates: *dal.* In vowels length is often incompatible with a following tautosyllabic consonant. For example, a CVVC stem may realize its ~redundancy~ long vowel before a suffixal vowel but shorten when no suffix follows and the consonant closes the syllable. Length is also intimately connected with the presence of stress in many systems. In Yupik Eskimo a stressed vowel is lengthened so long as the following consonant does not close the syllable (i.e., . . . CVCV is realized as CV́:CV). In Egyptian Arabic the long vowel of *báab* 'door' shortens when the stress shifts to the dual suffix: *bab-éen* 'two doors'.

The increment of length that distinguishes long vowels from short (often called *MORA - an arbitrary unit of syllabic length* a *mora*) is sometimes required to be [+high]. The result is a diphthong consisting of two successive vowels agreeing in backness and rounding but changing in tongue aperture. The high vocalic element is known as a glide. If it precedes the vocalic core, we speak of an *onglide* and a *rising diphthong*. If it follows, we speak of an *offglide* and a *falling diphthong*. (With respect to diphthongs, "rise" and "fall" refer not to the constriction of the tongue but rather to the degree of aperture.) Examples of rising and falling diphthongs are furnished by Slovak and certain Italian dialects, respectively. In Slovak the genitive plural of feminine nouns is formed by lengthening the final syllable of the stem. In this context the high vowels [i,u] and the low vowel [a] simply lengthen while the mid vowels diphthongize with onglides.

(43)

nom.sg.	gen.pl.	
lipa	li:p	'linden tree'
mucha	mu:ch	'fly'
lopata	lopa:t	'shovel'
kazeta	kaziet	'box'
sirota	siruot	'orphan'

In the southern Italian dialect of Altamura (prov. Bari, Loporcaro 1988), a word-final schwa deletes before pause. When the preceding syllable is stressed and not closed by a consonant, the vowel is diphthongized with an offglide. The stressed vowel is indicated with a vertical stroke: ['ɛ], ['o], and so on.

(44)

phrase-medial	phrase-final	
k'ɛnə	k'ɛi̯n	'dog'
v'ɛvə	v'ɛi̯f	'to drink'
k'ošə	k'ou̯š	'to cook'
kr'ɔšə	kr'ɔu̯š	'cross'
s'ɔrdə	s'ɔrt	'deaf'
p'ortə	p'ort	'door'
purt'ɔnə	purt'ɔu̯n	'gate'

The term "diphthong" is often used more broadly to denote any sequence of tautosyllabic vowels. They need not necessarily share any phonological features and the entire sequence may count as a single timing unit (mora). In Spanish vowel clusters arising across word boundaries contract into a unit. Both phonetic measurements as well as poetic meter suggest that the resultant combination is equivalent to a single mora. For the Chicano dialect, Clements and Keyser (1983) report contractions such as those in (45) (from Hutchinson 1974).

(45) i # i →   i
      i # u   i̯u
      i # e   i̯e
      e # i   i
      e # e   e
      e # o   i̯o
      e # a   i̯a

These data motivate a UG convention of automatic degemination when two identical segments occupy the same phonological position. This convention explains such equations as $i\#i = i$ and $e\#e = e$. When the vowels are not identical, the first turns to a [+high] onglide (if possible). If the result is a sequence of identical segments, they degeminate as well. Thus, $e\#i = i\#i = i$.

The distinction between tautosyllabic (diphthongal) and heterosyllabic vowel sequences helps us to understand the behavior of stress in Fijian (Dixon 1988). Stress normally appears on the second-last vowel of the word: for example, *líga* 'arm'. When a suffix is added to the stem, the stress shifts: *ligá-mu* 'his arm'. Vowel sequences contrast in their effect on stress. If the stem contains a [−high] [+high] sequence, then no stress shift occurs upon the addition of the suffix: *táu* 'touch down', *táu-ta* (transitive). Other vowel sequences show the normal shift of stress: *lúa* 'vomit', *luá-ca* (transitive). This difference is explained if the [−high] [+high] sequence forms a tautosyllabic diphthong while other sequences remain heterosyllabic. The penultimate stress rule (redefined to operate at the level of the syllable σ) then shifts the stress in one case (46b) but fails to do so in the other (46a).

(46) a. tau   tau-ca   b. lu a   lu a-ca
          ＼＼   ＼＼ ＼   ＼｜ ＼｜ ＼
          'σ   'σ   σ   'σ σ σ 'σ σ

Tone and Intonation

Pitch (rate of vibration of the vocal folds) is used contrastively in the realization of an intonation contour as well as to encode lexical contrasts. For example, in English a yes-no question typically has a pitch rise on the final accented syllable; in a statement the pitch descends at this point. In other situations more elaborate intonation contours are imposed. For example, Liberman (1975) describes a vocative used to call someone out of sight in terms of a Low-High-Mid (L-H-M) sequence that is mapped to the segmental string in such a way that the High is attracted to the final accented syllable while the Low and Mid fill out the remaining portions of the string. When the accent shifts, the intonation contour is modified, as we can see by comparing the vocatives in (47).

(47) a. oh 'Isadore   b. oh Isad'ora   c. oh Mary'ann

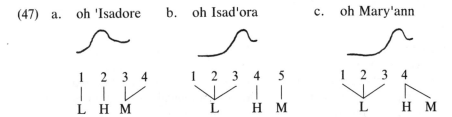

Many languages of Africa, Asia, and the Americas use pitch changes comparable to those found on the final two syllables of (47b) or the final syllable of (47c) to distinguish lexical items. Most common is a two-way tonal distinction of high versus low (typically analyzed as [+ hi tone] vs. [− hi tone]); three, four, and even five levels of pitch have been reported. In a two-tone system, the high tone is customarily transcribed with the acute (e.g., *tá*), while low tone is either unmarked (*ta*) or signaled by the grave (*tà*). In three-tone languages such as Yoruba, the mid is unmarked or transcribed with the macron (*tā*). For more complex systems the notation is not standardized. See chapter 7 for discussion of the tonal features underlying these more complex systems.

(48) <u>Margi</u> (Hoffman 1963)
      shú   tail   yíná   'to dye'   ámà   'husband's mother'
      shù   'to dry up'   yìnà   'to rinse'   àmá   'but'

    <u>Yoruba</u> (Pulleyblank (1986)
      high   kọ́   'build'
      mid   kọ̄   'sing'
      low   kọ̀   'refuse'

    <u>Grebo</u> (Newman (1986b)
      high   tó   'store'
      higher-mid   tu̍   'tree, stick'
      lower mid   mɔ̄   'you' sg.
      low   fã̄   'herring'

Contour (rising and falling) tones accompany level tones in many systems. A *rising tone* is customarily marked by the wedge (*tǎ*) and the *falling tone* by a circumflex (*tâ*). As this symbolization suggests, rising and falling tones often can be analyzed as low + high and high + low combinations on a single vowel or syllable. The circumstances under which this decomposition is appropriate continues to be a basic analytic and theoretical issue in tonology. The Thai examples in (49) illustrate the combination of plain and contour tones in the same system.

(49)   <u>Thai</u> (Ladefoged 1975)
    high   ná: 'aunt'
    mid   na: 'field'
    low   nà: a nickname
    rising   nǎ: 'thick'
    falling   nâ: 'face'

Stress

Unlike length and tone, stress has no uniform phonetic correlates. The perception of stress may be elicited by increased duration, heightened pitch, or sometimes more subtle aspects of vowel or consonant quality. In a sense that will be made precise in chapter 10, *stress* is an abstract phonological category of prominence whose presence is signaled through other (usually prosodic) features. Stress is a property of vowels or more generally of syllables. In many systems a vowel bears a stress not in virtue of any inherent property but simply due to its location in the word. Initial stress is found in Czech, Finnish, and Latvian, but final stress in French, Turkish, and Farsi. In many systems (e.g., Polish) the second-last, penultimate syllable is stressed. The distribution of stress often takes syllable weight into account. In Latin stress falls on the third-last, antepenultimate syllable so long as the penult is *light* (consists of a single short vowel and no closing consonant). *Heavy* penults (containing a long vowel and/or a closing consonant) prevent stress from receding to the antepenult: *r'eficit, ref'ectus, ref'ēcit*. Many systems distinguish several degrees of prominence. For example, in *Tènnessée* English speakers perceive the final syllable to be stronger than the first (thus contrasting with *Hénnessy*). But in *Ténnessèe State* the prominence reverses: here the initial [Ténn] is stronger than the final [sèe]. Notationally, a stressed syllable is distinguished from an unstressed one by the acute accent or by a vertical stroke (usually before the vowel). Secondary stresses are indicated by a grave accent or by assigning a single stroke to the secondary and a double stroke to the primary: *Tènnessée* or *T'enness''ee*.

The location of stress is a crucial determinant for many sound changes. Vowel contrasts are often reduced in unstressed positions: compare the alternations with schwa as the stress is moved in [t'ɛləgr'æ]*ph*, [təl'ɛgrə]*phy*. Unstressed syllables (especially in the middle of the word) often delete entirely (*syncope*): trisyllabic *memory* may reduce to disyllabic *mem*[ ]*ry*. The location of the stress also affects consonants. For example, in English [h] deletes in an unstressed noninitial syllable: compare the absence and presence of [h] in *v'e*[ ]*icle, v'e*[h]*'icular* as the stress slides from one syllable to the next. As we will see, in English a sequence of a stressed plus following unstressed syllable forms a metrical constituent called a *foot*. The [h]≈∅ alternation can be defined in terms of a rule that deletes [h] when not initial in the metrical foot.

Suggested Readings

Jakobson, Roman. 1949. On the identification of phonemic entities. Travaux du Cercle Linguistique de Copenhague 5.205–13. Reprinted in Selected writings, vol. 1, 418–25.

The Hague: Mouton, 1962; and in Phonological theory: Evolution and current practice, ed. by V. Makkai, 318–22. New York: Holt, Rinehart and Winston, 1972.

Ladefoged, Peter. 1993. A course in phonetics. 3d ed. New York: Harcourt Brace Jovanovich.

Pullum, Geoffrey, and William Ladusaw. 1986. Phonetic symbol guide. Chicago: University of Chicago Press. Introduction.

Exercises

1.1   Features and Symbols

These exercises test the reader's understanding of the features and phonetic symbols.

A. Provide the phonetic symbols for the following sounds.

(1) a. velar nasal   ŋ
     b. low front vowel   æ
     c. voiceless aspirated bilabial stop   pʰ
     d. voiced velar fricative   ɣ
     e. voiceless alveopalatal affricate   č
     f. glottal stop   ʔ
     g. long high front tense vowel   iː

B. Characterize the following phonetic symbols in terms of the traditional phonetic categories of place and manner of articulation.

(2) a. [f] = voiceless labiodental fricative
     b. [x]
     c. [ü]
     d. [š]
     e. [ɑ]
     f. [ħ]
     g. [ð]

C. Label the feature matrices with the correct symbol.

(3)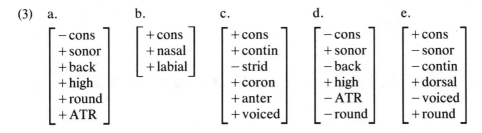

a.	b.	c.	d.	e.
− cons	+ cons	+ cons	− cons	+ cons
+ sonor	+ nasal	+ contin	+ sonor	− sonor
+ back	+ labial	− strid	− back	− contin
+ high		+ coron	+ high	+ dorsal
+ round		+ anter	− ATR	− voiced
+ ATR		+ voiced	− round	+ round

D. Supply the feature matrices for the following sounds.

(4) a. [ñ]
     b. [ɛ]
     c. [θ]
     d. [l]
     e. [ɯ]
     f. [ɟ]

1.2 Transcription Exercises

A. Phonetically transcribe the following English words; check your answers in a dictionary.

(1) a. sun   f. sheep
     b. moon   g. wrong
     c. cough   h. right
     d. shampoo   i. Hughes
     e. garage   j. moth

B. Give the orthographic representation of the following English phrase.

(2) ðə kʰæw ɟʌmpt ovə ðə muːn

C. The following phrases are from three English dialects: American, Southern British, and Scottish. Can you match each with the appropriate dialect? (Adapted from the IPA 1949.)

(3) a. ðə nɔrθ wɪnd ənd ðə sʌn wər dɪspjutɪŋ hwɪtʃ wəz ðə strɔŋgər
     b. ðə nɔɹθ wɪnd n̩ ðə sən wɪ aɹgjuɪŋ hwɪtʃ wəz strɔŋgɹ
     c. ðə nɔːθ wɪnd ənd ðə sʌn wə dɪspjuːtɪŋ wɪtʃ wəz ðə strɒŋgə

D. Find a fellow student or colleague who speaks a language you do not know. Elicit five words (e.g., *dog, sun, eat, two,* etc.). Transcribe them phonetically, noting any sounds that do not occur in English.

1.3 Natural Classes

A. Eliminate one segment to form a natural class; supply the features that define that class.

(1) a. [p,t,s,k]
     b. [m,n,l,r]
     c. [ɯ,ə,ʌ,ɑ]
     d. [β,ð,z,ɣ]

B. Indicate which features must be changed in order to implement the sound change.

(2) a. [p] → [b]
     b. [ε] → [ɪ]
     c. [s] → [š]
     d. [u] → [ü]
     e. [k] → [x]

C. Tell the results of applying the rules underlying the respective sound changes
    in (2) to the following sounds.

(3) a. [x]
     b. [o]
     c. [t]
     d. [ɑ]
     e. [p]

D. In order to define some natural classes, we must indicate sounds that agree
    in their plus/minus specifications for two features. For example, with the
    understanding that alpha is uniformly replaced by either plus or minus, the
    expression in (4a) includes [u,i] but excludes [ü,ɯ]. Which class of sounds
    is characterized by the expression in (4b)? Use the device of the Greek letter
    variables to form the classes in (4c) and (4d).

(4) a. $\begin{bmatrix} -\,\text{cons} \\ +\,\text{high} \\ \alpha\text{back} \\ \alpha\text{round} \end{bmatrix}$

     b. $\begin{bmatrix} +\,\text{cons} \\ +\,\text{labial} \\ \alpha\text{sonor} \\ \alpha\text{voiced} \end{bmatrix}$

     c. [t,d,s,z] but not [θ,ð]

     d. [iː,uː,ε,ɔ] but not [ɪ,ʊː,e,o]

1.4 English Pre-rhotic Vowels

The following table (based on Wells 1982:434) shows the phonetic realization of
vowels before [r] in two English dialects: Irish English and General American.
Which dialect reflects an earlier stage of the language and why? What sound
changes have occurred in the other? Try to subsume these changes under one
rule.

(1)   <u>I</u>   <u>GA</u>
     weary   i: ɪ
     spirit   ɪ   ɪ
     fairy   e: ɛ
     ferry   ɛ   ɛ
     marry   æ   ɛ
     war   ɔ: ɔ
     story   o: ɔ
     hurry   ʌ   ʌ
     jury   u: ʊ

1.5 Arabic Sun and Moon Letters

Traditional Arab grammarians divide the consonants of their language into two groups on the basis of their effect on the definite prefix *ʔal:*- the "sun" letters induce a complete assimilation of the lateral consonant in the prefix while the "moon" letters have no effect. Study the following examples to determine the basis for the distinction.

(1) ʔal-qamr   'the moon'   ʔaš-šams   'the sun'
     ʔal-faras   'the mare'   ʔad-daar   'the house'
     ʔal-kitaab 'the book'   ʔaz-zayt   'the oil'
     ʔal-ḥarb   'the war'   ʔan-nahr   'the river'
     ʔal-ʔab   'the father'   ʔaθ-θawb   'the garment'

Given your answer, predict the definite form of the following nouns.

(2) ražul   'man'   ðalq   'tip of tongue'
     xaatam   'ring'   walad   'boy'
     baab   'gate'   tižaara   'commerce'
     sana   'year'   laban   'milk'
     mawt   'death'   ɣada   'lunch'
     harab   'escape'

1.6 Tamil Vowel Sequences

Tamil has the vocoid (glide and vowel) inventory shown in (1). According to Christdas (1988), certain glide + vowel sequences are possible within roots while others are not. Relying on the Greek letter notation for variables, formalize a constraint that will distinguish the valid from the invalid combinations. (Hint: It is simpler to characterize the glide + vowel sequences that are excluded.)

(1) i   u   *yi, *ye, ya, yo, yu
     e   o   wi, we, wa, *wo, *wu
        a
     y   w

1.7 English Diphthongs

The following table (from Wells 1982, transcription altered) shows the diphthong evolution from three socially stratified accents of British English: Received Pronunciation (RP), PL (Popular London), C (Cockney). Describe the various sound changes in terms of features.

(1)

	face	goat	price	mouth
RP	ɛɪ	ʌU	aɪ	ɑU
PL	əɪ	əU	ɑɪ	æU
C	aɪ	aU	ɒɪ	æː

As shown by the diagram in (2) (from Wells 1982:310), the vowel nuclei in *price* and *mouth* appear to "cross over" as we move from RP to PL. If speech sounds are simply specifications for a particular acoustic-articulatory target, is this type of change expected (or even possible)?

(2) RP   aɪ   ɑU

     PL   æU   ɑɪ

1.8 Moore Vowels

Moore is a Gur language of Burkina Faso with the seven-vowel system indicated below. Characterize the alternation in suffixal vowels in terms of natural phonological classes. The source of the data (Kenstowicz, Nikiema, and Ourso 1988) has been followed here in transcribing the high [−ATR] vowels as [i̧] and [u̧].

(1)

	i	i̧	u	u̧	e	o	a
high	+	+	+	+	−	−	−
back	−	−	+	+	−	+	+
ATR	+	−	+	−	+	+	−

(2)

kor-go	'sack'	kug-ri	'stone'
laŋ-go	'hole'	tu̧b-re	'ear'
bi̧d-go	'sorrel'	gob-re	'left hand'
zu-gu	'head'	la-re	'hatchet'
pil-gu	'granary'	rakil-li	'fagot of wood'
ru̧g-go	'pot'	gel-le	'egg'
sen-go	'rainy season'		

1.9 Biblical Hebrew Imperfects

In Biblical Hebrew roots of the shape CVCVC appear as CCVC after the imperfect prefix yi-. Characterize the alternations in consonants in terms of distinctive features.

(1)

perfect	imperfect	
bāḥar	yi-vḥar	'choose'
gānav	yi-ɣnov	'steal'
dāraš	yi-ðroš	'inquire'
pāɣaš	yi-fgoš	'meet'
kāθav	yi-xtov	'write'

1.10   Lithuanian Prefixal Alternation

In Lithuanian the prefix cognate with English/Latin *con-* shows various shapes depending on the following consonant. Characterize the distribution of the prefixal variants in terms of distinctive features. Stems are cited in the native orthography; *j* = the palatal glide jod, *y* = [i:], *ė* = [e:]

(1)

sam-būris	'assembly'	būrys	'crowd'
sam-pilas	'stock'	pilnas	'full'
san-dora	'covenant'	dora	'virtue'
san-taka	'confluence'	tekėti	'to flow'
saŋ-kaba	'connection'	kabė	'hook'
sa:-voka	'idea'	vokti	'to understand'
sa:-skambis	'harmony'	skambėti	'to ring'
sa:-šlavos	'sweepings'	šluoti	'to sweep'
sa:-žine	'conscience'	žinoti	'to know'
sa:-rašas	'list, register'	rašyti	'to write'

1.11   English [yu]

One feature that distinguishes the American and British dialects of English is the distribution of the [yu] sequence. Examine the following data to determine the difference.

(1)

American	British
am[yu]se	am[yu]se
b[yu]ty (beauty)	b[yu]ty
c[yu]be	c[yu]be
d[u]pe	d[yu]pe
f[yu]me	f[yu]me
l[u]rid	l[yu]rid
n[u]ws (news)	n[yu]ws
p[yu]ny (puny)	p[yu]ny
pre[zu]me (presume)	pre[zyu]me
st[u]pid	st[yu]pid
s[u]t (suit)	s[yu]t

1.12   Sudanese Arabic Consonant Assimilation

In Sudanese Arabic (Hamid 1984) a stop assimilates to a following fricative. Examine the following "Noun *of* Noun" paradigms to determine when this process applies. Briefly discuss the relevance of this phenomenon to the notion "consonantal point of articulation."

(1)   kitáab 'book'   bít 'daughter'   sámak 'fish'

kitáa[f] Fáthi	bí[t] Fáthi	sáma[k] Fáthi
kitáa[p] Samíir	bí[s] Samíir	sáma[k] Samíir
kitáa[p] Šaríif	bí[š] Šaríif	sáma[k] Šaríif
kitáa[p] Xáalid	bí[t] Xáalid	sáma[x] Xáalid
kitáa[p] Hásan	bí[t] Hásan	sáma[k] Hásan

1.13 *Lama Paragoge*

The list in (2) is a sample of completive (basic underived) verbs in Lama, a Gur language of Togo (Ourso 1989). Assume that these verbs are phonologically mono-syllabic. When is the final schwa added? How is the tone and ATR value of the schwa determined? Lama is a two-tone language in which high tones are transcribed by the acute and low-toned syllables are unmarked. The vowels have the feature interpretation indicated in (1).

(1)

	i	i̧	e	ȩ	ə	ə̧	a	ʌ	u	u̧	o	o̧
high	+	+	−	−	+	+	−	−	+	+	−	−
back	−	−	−	−	+	+	+	+	+	+	+	+
round	−	−	−	−	−	−	−	−	+	+	+	+
ATR	+	−	+	−	+	−	−	+	+	−	+	−

(2)

sé	'run'	kár	'lock'	rǫn	'repair'
kpá	'catch'	sál	'crunch'	waal	'gather'
rí̧	'put'	sáal	'wander'	tǫm	'mix'
lu	'forge'	tə̧l	'open'	maw	'beat'
lu̧	'wrestle'	cín	'exhort'	sén	'moan'
le	'weave'	lɔ́m	'dive'	hȩm	'change'
ñǫ	'burn'	kǫ́r	'pick up'	mə̧l	'twist'

wéetə̧	'sell'
hátə̧	'pound'
fȩsə̧	'deny'
takə	'touch'
hǫpə	'squat'
kútə́	'fold'
cuutə	'shake'
rȩ́kə̧	'visit'
fítə́	'hurry'
fetə	'fall down'
lətə	'skin an animal'

1.14 *Klamath Diminutives*

In this American Indian language of Oregon (Barker 1964), the addition of the diminutive suffix leads to a glottalization of the final consonant of the stem plus a reduplication of the initial syllable. The resultant structure is then subject to a general rule of syncope deleting a short medial vowel: [weloč] → [we + weloč + ʔak] → [wewloč'ak]. Characterize the changes in laryngeal features that follow in the wake of the syncope rule.

(1)

weloč	wewloč'āk	'pup'
pʰeč	pʰepč'ak	'foot'
kʰow'e	kʰokw'eʔāk	'frog'
dot	dott'āk	'tooth'
bok	bopk'āk	'book'
n'ep	n'enp'āk	'hand'
w'an	w'awn'āk	'red fox'

1.15   Fijian Stress

Recalling the discussion of Fijian in section 1.11, explain why the stress lodges on the prefix in *tá + uru* 'become slack' and *tá + isi* 'be torn', but remains on the stem in *ta + músu* 'be broken'.

2 Phonological Rules and Representations

When generative linguists study the phonology of a language, they try to discover three kinds of generalizations. They look for regularities that help to define the language's inventory of phonological elements: its vowels, consonants, syllables, tones. They determine patterns in the distribution of these elements in the language's representations: may they appear or are they banned from initial, medial, final positions in the word, from stressed/unstressed syllables?; may an element of type *a* immediately precede/follow an element of type *b*?; and so on. Finally, they investigate alternations in the shapes of morphemes composed of these elements within the word and variant pronunciations of words within the sentence. The regularities that emerge from such study are assumed to be the joint product of the principles and parameters of Universal Grammar and the rules and representations that develop through the course of language acquisition. Although other more "experimental" approaches have been proposed from time to time (see Ohala 1986), the study of the "corpus-internal" generalizations just enumerated continues to be the major avenue of research into the speaker's internalized grammar.

The goal of this chapter and the next is to examine some of the basic questions that arise in the study of such generalizations, and the answers that generative phonology has given to these questions. These chapters also introduce the most important analytic techniques used to discover these regularities as well as the concepts and notation required to express them in the grammar.

2.1 Distinctive versus Redundant Features

Let us consider regularities of distribution first, beginning with a simple example from English. Study of English quickly reveals that the articulator feature in stops is in general unpredictable. Labial, coronal, and velar stops occur freely in initial, medial, and final positions. There are numerous examples of morphemes whose pronunciation differs solely in virtue of the point of articulation of the stop: for example, *pin, tin, kin, bun, dun, gun*. Specifications for the features [labial], [coronal], and [dorsal] thus are irreducible, arbitrary features of these particular lexical items. If one knew the rest of English grammar and did not happen to know the pronunciation of a word such as *ketch*, there would be no way to predict that the initial consonant has the value [dorsal]. It could have been [coronal] and pronounced *tetch*. Information of this kind is used to encode the vocabulary of the language and must be memorized in the course of language development.

that which cannot be reduced

Consequently, as in most other languages, the point-of-articulation features are *distinctive* for the stop consonants of English.

Now consider the laryngeal features that characterize the English stop system.

(1) [−voiced, −spread gl]   p t k
     [−voiced, +spread gl]   pʰ tʰ kʰ
     [+voiced, −spread gl]   b d g

(2)   initial   medial   final
     [pʰ]in [b]in   ra[p]id   ra[b]id   la[p]   la[b]
     [tʰ]ot [d]ot   a[t]om   A[d]am   ma[t]   ma[d]
     [kʰ]ap [g]ap   jac[k]et jag[g]ed   pic[k] pi[g]

Examination of the data in (2) reveals an important difference in the status of the voicing and aspiration features. Ignoring for the moment contexts adjacent to a consonant, we see that the feature specifications for voicing (i.e., [+voiced] and [−voiced]) have essentially free distribution: each appears initially, medially, and finally. There are many minimal pairs for this feature. The same is not true for aspiration ([+spread gl]), however. Careful study of English shows that the distribution of this feature is severely limited. First, [+spread gl] appears only on voiceless stops. All other consonants (as well as vowels) are [−spread gl]. In addition, [pʰ,tʰ,kʰ] occur only at the beginning of a syllable. At any other position in the syllable voiceless stops are unaspirated. For example, the voiceless stops in *s*[p]*in, s*[t]*em, s*[k]*in* as well as *la*[p], *ma*[t], and *pic*[k] are not aspirated. Finally, another key distributional regularity is that unaspirated voiceless stops are not found in syllable-initial position (the case of *ra*[p]*id* is discussed below). The sound sets [pʰ,tʰ,kʰ] and [p,t,k] thus have *complementary distributions:* they never appear in exactly the same phonological context.

These distributional regularities are summarized in (3).

(3) a. All segments except for voiceless stops are [−spread gl].
     b. [pʰ,tʰ,kʰ] only appear syllable-initially.
     c. [p,t,k] do not appear syllable-initially, but freely occur in other positions in the syllable.

These results suggest that, unlike the features for place of articulation and for voicing, aspiration is entirely *redundant*. For any given English sound, we may predict its [±spread gl] value by determining whether it is a voiceless stop (if not, then automatically [−spread gl]); and if it is a voiceless stop, then its location in the syllable. Consequently, in learning English vocabulary, the developing grammar need not list the [±spread gl] value individually for each lexical item. If the generalizations in (3) are known, then in learning a new word such as *ketch,* the grammar can deduce that the initial consonant is aspirated, once having determined that it is a voiceless stop.

It is quite clear that these distributional generalizations follow from the English speaker's internalized grammar. For example, consider what typically happens when English speakers acquire a second language such as French, which lacks aspirated stops. In general, they have little difficulty in pronouncing and distinguishing such idiosyncratic features as [voiced] or point of articulation: they can differentiate *pas* [pa] from *bas* [ba] and *tas* [ta] from *pas* [pa]. However, English speakers typically pronounce French *pas* and *tas* as [pʰa] and [tʰa] instead of [pa] and [ta]. When this error is pointed out, they often have difficulty hearing the difference between their [tʰ]*a* and the French [t]*as*. This pronunciation error cannot be explained simply by saying that unaspirated [p] and [t] are foreign sounds – English speakers have no trouble producing them in s[p]*in* and s[t]*em*. It's just that they have great difficulty pronouncing unaspirated [p] and [t] at the beginning of a French word. This difficulty can be explained by assuming that the generalization "syllable-initial voiceless stops are aspirated" is part of the grammar of English and that this rule is superimposed on the English speaker's pronunciation of French. In order to pronounce a foreign language accurately, one must often suppress the phonological rules of one's own language.

Slips of the tongue also argue that the principle governing the distribution of aspiration is part of the speaker's internalized grammar. When *tail spin* is transposed to *pail stin*, the aspiration on the voiceless stops is automatically adjusted to accommodate the new location of the shifted sounds so that [tʰ]*ail* s[p]*in* → [pʰ]*ail* s[t]*in*. If the distribution of aspiration is controlled by the rule that voiceless stops are aspirated syllable-initially, then the otherwise mysterious transformations of [p] to [pʰ] and of [tʰ] to [t] are explained.

Before asking how to express formally the rule governing the distribution of aspiration, let us consider another example of distinctive versus redundant features. At the level of detail we are considering here, the features defining the tongue body position for the vowel in *tab* [tʰæ:b] are idiosyncratic ones that must be memorized. The fact that the vowel of *tab* is [+low] is unpredictable. The word could have been pronounced with a [−low] vowel as [tʰe:b] or with a [+high] vowel as [tʰi:b]. No rule of English phonology predicts the [+low] and [−back] features in *tab*. On the other hand, the fact that the vowel of *tab* is pronounced long is principled. In stressed syllables, English vowels systematically lengthen before voiced obstruents and shorten before voiceless ones – as shown by minimal pairs such as *tab* [tʰæ:b] vs. *tap* [tʰæp], *hid* [hɪ:d] vs. *hit* [hɪt], *dug* [dʌ:g] vs. *duck* [dʌk]. If the English speaker knows the rule that vowels lengthen before voiced obstruents and shorten before voiceless ones, then the length of the vowels in these words need not be memorized because it is predictable information.

2.2 Two Levels of Representation

Conclusion/result

The upshot of the above discussion is that, for English, aspiration in consonants and length in vowels have a different status from such features as consonantal point of articulation or vocalic tongue position. The latter are essentially unpredictable while the former instantiate systematic regularities in the sound pattern of the language. Data from second language acquisition and from speech errors support the contention that speakers of English tacitly know these rules. Granting this, the question now becomes, How is the distinction between the predictable

to represent by a concrete example

not expressed or declared openly, but implied or understood.

(redundant, nondistinctive) and the unpredictable (contrastive, distinctive) features to be expressed? Generative grammar's answer to this question is based on the hypothesis that the human capacity for language is designed in such a way as to minimize the amount of information that must be stored in the speaker's mental lexicon. If storage space is at a premium, then the more information that can be predicted by simple and general rules, the more space will be available to store additional lexical items. In this way, the acquisition and seemingly effortless deployment of a large vocabulary becomes comprehensible.

2 Levels of Representation

1. underlying

If we accept this line of reasoning, then a particular approach toward drawing the distinction between the idiosyncratic and systematic features of pronunciation rather naturally emerges. Let us suppose that the grammar contains two levels of representation for phonological structure. An *underlying* or *phonological representation* will contain all and only the unpredictable (distinctive) information for each lexical item. Predictable features of pronunciation are added to the underlying phonological representation by grammatical rules and principles. These rules operate on the basis of the information in the lexical item's phonological representation and the context in which it is located. For each possible word constructed by the morphology and for each possible sentence constructed by *2. Surface* the syntax, the phonological rules will thus "compute" or "derive" a (*surface*) *phonetic representation*. For example, the word *tab* will, at the level of discussion relevant here, have the underlying representation shown in (4).

(4)

	t	æ	b
consonantal	+	−	+
sonorant	−	+	−
continuant	−	0	−
coronal	+	0	−
labial	−	0	+
voiced	−	0	+
nasal	−	0	−
spread gl	0	0	0
low	0	+	0
high	0	−	0
back	0	−	0
long	0	0	0

The pluses and minuses represent unpredictable information that must be memorized when learning *tab*. It is in virtue of this information that one lexical item is distinguished from another. For example, the [−voiced] of the initial consonant distinguishes *tab* from *dab*. Changing the final consonant from [+voiced] to [−voiced] gives the phonological representation of *tap*. And changing the vowel from [+low] to [−low] gives *teb* – a possible but at present unoccupied slot in the English lexicon. The zeros represent information that is predictable and hence are not counted in calculating the complexity of a representation. Instead of being filled with zeros, the predictable values are often left blank to express more graphically the idea that this information entails no storage cost. The zeros (or blanks) will be filled in by rules and principles of the grammar. The discussion in section 2.1 mentioned two of these rules, which are stated in (5).

(5) a. $\begin{bmatrix} -\text{contin} \\ -\text{voiced} \end{bmatrix} \rightarrow [+\text{spread gl}] /$ syllable-initial

  b. $V \rightarrow [+\text{long}] / \underline{\hspace{1cm}} \begin{bmatrix} +\text{cons} \\ +\text{voiced} \end{bmatrix}$

  c. $V \rightarrow [-\text{long}] / \underline{\hspace{1cm}} \begin{bmatrix} +\text{cons} \\ -\text{voiced} \end{bmatrix}$

(5a) anticipates later discussion by stating the context for aspirated consonants as the beginning of a syllable. Since the first sound in any word normally begins the first syllable of the word, the context in (5a) will correctly assign aspiration in [tʰ]*ab* and will do much additional work later. This rule does not apply in *s*[t]*ab* since here the voiceless stop does not initiate the syllable. (5b) lengthens vowels before voiced consonants and thus applies in the derivation of *tab,* while (5c) assigns a shortened vowel in [tæp]. Application of the rules in (5) thus changes the [0spread gl] feature of [t] to [+spread gl] and the [0long] of [æ] to [+long]. (In actuality, length is not a feature but an extra position (see section 6.9); we will overlook this fact here, however, since it does not materially affect the point that length is predictable from the voicing of the following consonant.)

Note that our discussion of *tab* is incomplete in several respects. We have not specified the final [b] with respect to aspiration. In addition, we have not specified the consonants [t] and [b] for the tongue body features [high], [low], and [back]; nor have we specified the vowel [æ] for voicing and nasality as well as the features [coronal] and [labial]. These features are predictable by a combination of UG and English rules. But unlike aspiration in voiceless stops and length in vowels, they are not assigned on the basis of the context in which the segment is located. Rather, they are implemented by a series of context-free rules assigning "default" values.

2.3 Default Rules and Unmarked Feature Values

Given that any phonological segment is defined by the UG set of features, we can view the construction of a phonological inventory as the grammar's utilizing a subset of these features to encode the language's lexical representations. Certain features are always selected (e.g., all grammars distinguish high from nonhigh vowels and coronal from noncoronal consonants); other features are language-particular choices that must be learned. For example, consider the laryngeal features of [voiced] and [spread gl]. French encodes its lexicon with the help of the [voiced] feature and thus opposes [t] to [d], while Mandarin Chinese employs [spread gl] to oppose [t] to [tʰ]. Thai utilizes both the [voiced] and the [spread gl] dimensions to make a three-way distinction among [t], [tʰ], and [d]. Hindi utilizes both dimensions fully in its four-way contrast of [p], [pʰ], [b], and [bʰ]. Some languages (e.g., Finnish) choose neither of these features to encode their lexical representations. An important insight due to the Prague School linguists Trubetzkoy and Jakobson is that the two poles of the [voiced], [spread gl], and [constr gl] features are not of equal status. In an important sense [−voiced], [−spread gl], and [−constr gl] are more basic values and denote more stable states. Linguists refer to the fundamental value of a feature as the *unmarked value*. For obstruents, the unmarked value for voicing is [−voiced]. For aspiration, it is [−spread gl]; [+voiced] and [+spread gl] are the *marked* values.

The marked-unmarked distinction for these features is reflected in a number of asymmetries. First, the unmarked values appear in all grammars. According to Maddieson (1984), all languages have at least some voiceless stops. While many languages supplement their stock of obstruents by adding further laryngeal distinctions of aspiration and glottalization, many others do not. For the latter, the unmarked [−voiced], [−constr gl], and [−spread gl] are the values chosen. Thus, Finnish stops are [p,t,k], not [b,d,g]. Second, according to Jakobson (1941), the unmarked values are the first to emerge in language acquisition and the last to disappear in language deficits. Finally, many languages neutralize underlying contrasts among the laryngeal features in particular positions such as the coda of the syllable or the end of the word. In general, it is the unmarked value that emerges in these positions. For example, while Thai contrasts [p,pʰ,b] in the syllable onset, only [p] appears in the syllable coda.

Generative phonologists encode the marked-unmarked distinction by supposing that for each feature exhibiting such a distinction, there is a UG rule assigning the unmarked value. This implies the rules shown in (6).

(6) a. [−sonor] → [−voiced]
      b. [−sonor] → [−spread gl]
      c. [+sonor] → [+voiced]
      d. [   ]   → [−constr gl]

A number of consequences ensue from assuming the existence of such *default rules*. First, if a particular language does not utilize one of these features to encode its lexical representations, then the relevant default rule will automatically assign the unmarked value for that feature. (This conclusion is based on the assumption that the default rules are present in UG, and that every language develops from UG.) On the face of it, this is somewhat surprising. Since glottalization is essentially irrelevant in English, one might expect the articulators to randomly glottalize or not glottalize any given segment and that the system would simply overlook this feature. But this is not what is found. If a grammar fails to utilize a given phonological dimension to encode its lexical representations, the articulators still assume a definite state with respect to that dimension – in general, the unmarked one predicted by the rules in (6). In other words, in the absence of language-particular information, UG assigns a default value for each articulatory state. (Recent research suggests that this position may be too strong; see section 9.10 for discussion.)

To illustrate this point further, consider that the English plural suffix agrees in voicing with a preceding segment: *lip*[s], *cat*[s], *duck*[s], but *tub*[z], *bed*[z], *rug*[z].

Unlike obstruents, sonorant consonants in English have no underlying voicing opposition. Consequently, rule (6c) assigns these segments their [+ voiced] value by default. Note that the plural suffix does not vacillate when added to *gun* or *bell*. It is uniformly pronounced with the same value that emerges after a voiced stop such as [b] or [g]: just as English speakers say *lab*[z] and *bug*[z], they say *gun*[z] and *bell*[z] – never *gun*[s] or *bell*[s]. Consequently, both underlyingly distinctive as well as default values can define the context for phonological rules.

Another consequence of assuming the rules in (6) is that if a particular feature encodes lexical items, then the corresponding default rule must be suppressed. Given that *bit* is lexically distinguished from *pit* by designation of [+ voiced], the default rule (6a) must be prevented from applying. This is ensured by stipulating that default rules are restricted to filling in information that is lacking (so-called *feature filling*); they cannot change a feature that has been specified as plus or minus. Finally, even though a given laryngeal feature is not contrastive, that feature may nevertheless be assigned by a language-particular rule in the course of the phonological derivation. In general, we expect such rules to assign the marked value, because the unmarked value will emerge in any case by the UG default rule. For example, aspiration is not contrastive in English. Nevertheless, the grammar has a rule assigning [+ spread gl] in syllable-initial position. The [− spread gl] feature is assigned in the complementary contexts by the default rule (6b).

Most of the other zero specifications for *tab* in (4) are assigned plus and minus values by UG default rules that supply the unmarked value for the relevant feature. For example, English does not employ the secondary articulations of palatalization, labialization, or velarization to distinguish lexical items. Consequently, the unmarked, minus values for the tongue body features [high], [low], and [back] are assigned to consonants regardless of context. Similarly, [− nasal] is the unmarked value for nasality in vowels and [+ voiced] is the unmarked value for voicing in sonorants. UG default rules assigning these features determine the states of the glottis and the velum in the articulation of the vowel in *tab*. The result is the surface phonetic representation in (7) in which each of the three segments in the string is specified plus or minus for each of the features defined by UG.

(7)	t^{h}	æ:	b
consonantal	+	−	+
sonorant	−	+	−
continuant	−	+	−
coronal	+	−	−
labial	−	−	+
voiced	−	+	+
nasal	−	−	−
spread gl	+	−	−
low	−	+	−
high	−	−	−
back	−	−	−
long	−	+	−

To briefly summarize the discussion to this point, we see that the surface phonetic representation is the product of three sorts of information: the unpredictable
lexical specifications used to encode the vocabulary, language-particular rules
supplying predictable feature specifications on the basis of context, and UG default rules assigning the unmarked value for nondistinctive features.

Excursus – a lengthy digression, as in a literary work,
a detailed discussion of some point in a work, added as an appendix

2.4 Excursus on Unmarked Values

The unmarked values and attendant default rules for the major phonological features are listed in (8). Note first that not all features seem to display the unmarked-
marked asymmetry. In general, the major class features [consonantal], [sonorant]
show no preference for one value over the other. Every language contrasts vowels
and consonants and within the latter, sonorants and obstruents.

unmarked   marked

(8) a. stricture features
   i. $[-\text{sonor}] \rightarrow [-\text{contin}]$

   ii. $\begin{bmatrix} +\text{sonor} \\ +\text{nasal} \end{bmatrix} \rightarrow [-\text{contin}]$

   iii. $[+\text{sonor}] \rightarrow [+\text{contin}]$

   iv. $\begin{bmatrix} -\text{sonor} \\ +\text{contin} \end{bmatrix} \rightarrow [+\text{strid}]$

   v. $[\quad] \rightarrow [-\text{strid}]$

   b. laryngeal features
   i. $[-\text{sonor}] \rightarrow [-\text{voiced}]$
   ii. $[+\text{sonor}] \rightarrow [+\text{voiced}]$
   iii. $[\quad] \rightarrow [-\text{spread gl}]$
   iv. $[\quad] \rightarrow [-\text{constr gl}]$

   c. nasality
   i. $[\quad] \rightarrow [-\text{nasal}]$

   d. consonantal place features
   i. $[+\text{cons}] \rightarrow [+\text{coron}]$
   ii. $[+\text{coron}] \rightarrow [+\text{anter}]$
   iii. $[+\text{cons}] \rightarrow [-\text{high}]$
        $\rightarrow [-\text{low}]$
        $\rightarrow [-\text{back}]$
        $\rightarrow [-\text{round}]$

   e. vowel quality
   i. $[-\text{cons}] \rightarrow [+\text{high}]$

   ii. $\begin{bmatrix} -\text{cons} \\ -\text{low} \\ \alpha\text{back} \end{bmatrix} \rightarrow [\alpha\text{round}]$

(8a) records the default rules for continuancy and stridency. At the points of articulation where a stop-fricative contrast is phonetically possible, [−continuant] is unmarked: segmental inventories generally choose a stop before including a fricative; some languages of Australia lack fricatives entirely; and when a [±continuant] contrast is neutralized nonassimilatorily, it is typically in favor of [−continuant] (e.g., consonants closing the syllable in Korean must be [−continuant] (Kim 1972)). Rule (8ai) encodes the unmarked status of stops over fricatives. If postvocalic spirantization of stops (e.g., Spanish *Ma[ð]ri[ð]*) is an assimilatory phenomenon, then [+continuant] is redundant in vowels and may be assigned by (8aiii). The spirantization of [b,d,g] in Spanish also argues that nasals are [−continuant] while liquids are [+continuant]: *hom*[b]*re* 'man' vs. *cal*[β]*o* 'bald', *ver*[ð]*e* 'green'. Since default rules are feature-filling operations, applying (8aii) before (8aiii) preempts application of the latter to a nasal. For stridency, (8aiv) records the observation that the optimal fricative is [+strident]: languages prefer [s] to [θ]. Besides enhancing fricatives, this feature seems to play no role; all other segments are thus [−strident].

For the laryngeal features, we have observed that [+voiced] is unmarked for sonorants while [−voiced] is the optimal value for obstruents. Aspiration and glottalization are marked in both sonorants and obstruents. These observations imply the default rules in (8b). (8c) states that vowels and consonants are optimally oral; [+nasal] is always a marked feature.

For consonantal place of articulation, there is debate as to whether a particular value should be singled out as unmarked, and if so which one (see the discussion in section 9.11). The most popular choice is [+coronal]; (8di) reflects this point. Within the class of coronals, the [+anterior] dental-alveolar category is clearly unmarked in comparison to the [−anterior] alveopalatals. Phonological inventories select [t,s,n] before [č,š,ñ]. The battery of rules in (8diii) indicate that secondary articulations of labialization, palatalization, velarization, and so on, are marked. More generally, phonological segments with complex, multiple articulations are marked in comparison to singly articulated ones.

For vocoids (8e), mid [e] and [o] are marked in comparison to the high vowels [i] and [u]. Glides are typically [+high], and many languages either reject mid vowels entirely in favor of high or limit their appearance to "strong" positions such as stressed or initial syllables. It is difficult to determine an unmarked value for the [±back] feature. Finally, in nonlow vowels, rounding enhances backness: for back vowels [+round] [u,o] are chosen over [−round] [ɯ,ɣ], and [−round] [i,e] are chosen over [+round] [ü,ö]. In section 4.4 we will see the phonetic rationale for this enhancement relation between [round] and [back].

2.5 The Phoneme

One of the factors that initiated the development of phonology as a branch of linguistics distinct from phonetics was the discovery that native speakers often judge sounds to be identical that are clearly distinct phonetically – sometimes quite radically so. For example, in many dialects of American English the coronal stop [t] has as many as eight distinct pronunciations.

(9) [t]   "plain"   stem
     [tʰ]   aspirated   ten
     [ṭ]   retroflexed   strip
     [D]   flapped   atom
     [N]   nasal flap   panty
     [tˀ]   glottalized   hit
     [ˀ]   glottal stop   bottle
     [ ]   zero   pants

def. of allophone

Such variants (*allophones*) of the same underlying sound (*phoneme*) are the product of systematic rules that modify the segment depending on the context in which it finds itself. (In structural and early generative phonology, phonemes were distinguished notationally from allophones by enclosing them in slanted brackets. One spoke of the phoneme /t/ with its allophones [t], [tʰ], and so on. This notational distinction is no longer systematically enforced; it will be employed here on occasion, when the distinction between an underlying and a derived representation is crucial to the point under discussion.) We are in general unconscious of these rules. But if we come into contact with a speaker who fails to follow them, we may feel that he or she is not "one of us" and speaks with an accent or somehow sounds "funny." In some cases these variant pronunciations are quite puzzling. For example, although we perceive *tents* as having five sounds, phonetic instrumentation reveals that in fact no consonant appears between the [n] and the [s]. The same gap is found in *tends,* yet we feel that the two words are somehow still different. As we saw in the Introduction, Edward Sapir referred to these phenomena as "collective phonetic illusions" – we hear things that objectively are not there, we fail to notice elements that are present, and we judge sounds to be identical that are demonstrably quite different. Thus, in order to speak English, we must learn the rule that omits the [t] and [d] in *tents* and *tends*. Furthermore, it is by virtue of having internalized this rule that we can recognize the defective stimuli [tʰɛns] as the plural of *tent* and [tʰɛ:nz] as *tends*. The mysterious thing is how we learn these rules. No one has taught them to us. We are unable to discover them through introspection. Yet we all tacitly know them if we are native speakers of English. As stated in the Introduction, generative phonologists have set themselves the task of giving a serious, scientific answer to this question.

In this section we augment our sketch of English phonology by examining the rules that account for the varying realizations of the [t] phoneme. The retroflex stops – essentially equivalent to the [ṭ] and [ḍ] of Hindi – have a very limited distribution in English: they appear only before [r]. Compare the plain [t] and [d] of *s[t]ay* and *[d]ip* with the retroflex variants in *s[ṭ]ray* and *[ḍ]rip*. Since the rhotic [r] of *rip* is produced by curling back the tip of the tongue, it is natural to interpret this sound change as one in which the coronal stops assimilate the [−anterior, −distributed] features of the following [r] (IPA [ɹ]). The rule in (10) expresses this assimilation.

(10) $\begin{bmatrix} -\text{contin} \\ +\text{coron} \end{bmatrix} \rightarrow \begin{bmatrix} -\text{anter} \\ -\text{distrib} \end{bmatrix} / \underline{\hspace{1cm}} \begin{bmatrix} +\text{sonor} \\ -\text{anter} \\ -\text{distrib} \end{bmatrix}$

Another "exotic" segment hidden inside English phonetics is a voiceless lateral, similar to the one found in Welsh. Careful listening to the following paradigms reveals that the liquids are voiceless [r̥] and [l̥] after voiceless stops.

(11) [r̥]im   [r̥]ip   [l̥]ean
      b[r]im   d[r]ip   g[l]ean
      p[r̥]im   t[r̥]ip   c[l̥]ean
      f[r]om   sh[r]imp   s[l]ip

While we can easily write a rule to devoice liquids after voiceless stops, we may ask why the voiceless fricatives in *f[r]om, sh[r]imp,* and *s[l]ip* fail to trigger the change. An attractive answer is suggested by the observation that the voiceless stops in *p[r̥]im, t[r̥]ip,* and *c[l̥]ean* are aspirated. This observation in turn suggests that the real process underlying the liquid devoicing is one in which the liquids assimilate the [+ spread gl] feature, which will naturally tend to suppress vocal fold vibration in a sonorant. We can test this alternative hypothesis because we know a context in which the voiceless stops are unaspirated: when they are preceded by [s]. The fact that *st[r]ip* rhymes with *d[r]ip* rather than with *t[r̥]ip* confirms this analysis. We express the rule generating the voiceless liquids as (12). It will also aspirate the [w] in *t[w̥]elve* and the [y] in *c[y̥]ue (cue),* whose glides are essentially equivalent to the aspirated ones in [wʰ]*ich* and [yʰ]*uge (huge).*

(12)   [+ sonor] → [+ spread gl] / [+ spread gl] ____

Besides the aspirated and the retroflexed variants, the phoneme [t] has two additional realizations in many American dialects: a glottalized version (13a) and a flap (13c).

(13) a. hi[tʔ], ho[tʔ], ou[tʔ]
      b. bel[t], raf[t], ap[t]
      c. hitter (hi[D]er), hottest (ho[D]est), outing (ou[D]ing)

The glottalized [tʔ] is articulated by making simultaneous closures at the glottis and at the alveolar ridge. The flap [D] (IPA [ɾ]) is a variety of [r] quite similar to the tap in Spanish *pero.* Comparison of the forms in (13a) and (13b) suggests that the glottalized allophone arises after a vocalic segment. When the items in (13a) are followed by a vowel, the [t] emerges as a flap (13c) in the dialect in question. Since the flap is a rhotic, and since in many languages [r] arises from an intervocalic dental obstruent (a form of lenition), we will posit a similar analysis for English. Note that the voiced stop [d] of *ride, mad,* and *bed* also flaps in the same context.

(14)   ride, ri[D]er; mad, ma[D]est; bed, be[D]ing

There is a curious restriction on this lenition process in English. Comparison of the forms *átŏm* [D] vs. *prótòn* [tʰ] and *Ádăm* [D] vs. *rádàr* [d] shows that flapping cannot take place when the vowel following the coronal stop is stressed. We know that in *atomic* the [t] is aspirated; and so it might be argued that the aspiration rule applies first to generate a [t^h]. Flapping could then be defined over the [−spread gl] [t] in the intervocalic environment. However, the fact that the unaspirated [d] of *rádàr* is not flapped either suggests that stress is involved directly in the flapping rule. As we will see in chapter 10, the combination of a stressed plus unstressed syllable forms a metrical constituent in English known as a *foot*. A number of other rules of English phonology are sensitive to this environment: *cónsti*[t^h]*ùte,* but *constí*[č]*uent.* We therefore express the flapping rule as (15), requiring the flanking vowels to belong to the same metrical foot.

(15) $\begin{bmatrix} -\text{contin} \\ +\text{coron} \end{bmatrix} \rightarrow [+\text{sonor}] / V_1 \underline{\quad} V_2$

(where V_1 and V_2 belong to the same foot)

The rule will now apply to the intervocalic stops in *átom* and *Ádam* but not in *prótòn* and *rádàr* because the flanking stressed vowels of the latter pair belong to separate metrical feet.

Let us now turn to a problem posed by *rá*[p]*id, rác*[k]*et* (and *á*[t]*om* in the dialects without flapping). The lack of aspiration in these cases has traditionally been explained by restricting the aspiration rule to the onset of stressed syllables. However, two facts noted by Kahn (1976) call this analysis into question. First, the initial consonants in *Pacífic, terrífic,* and *collápse* are generally perceived as aspirated even though the following vowel is unstressed. A rule assigning aspiration to the onset of stressed syllables would incorrectly overlook these cases. Second, the data in (16) suggest that liquids devoice after a voiceless stop even when they occupy the unstressed syllable of a metrical foot. If the earlier hypothesis that voiceless liquids reflect aspiration of the preceding stop is correct, then aspiration must be assigned to the medial voiceless stops in (16) even though they initiate a stressless syllable.

(16) áp[r̥]on
   mát[r̥]on, mát[r̥]ess
   ác[r̥]id, ácc[l̥]imate

These arguments indicate that the original generalization − aspirate a syllable-initial voiceless stop − is correct. To explain the lack of aspiration in *rá*[p]*id, á*[t]*om,* and *rác*[k]*et,* we can suggest that they reflect another "branch" of the intervocalic lenition process that operates in the flapping dialects. Let us therefore posit the rule in (17).

(17) $[-\text{contin}] \rightarrow [-\text{spread gl}] / V_1 \underline{\quad} V_2$

(where V_1 and V_2 belong to the same metrical foot)

Note that if we accept this analysis, then two rules are competing for the same input. Being syllable-initial, the aspiration rule would assign the [p] of *rapid* the feature [+spread gl]. But since the [p] of *rapid* also finds itself in the context of (17) that assigns [−spread gl], a contradiction arises. In the case of such competing rules, a principle (due originally to the Sanskrit grammarians) generally obtains according to which the rule applying in the more specific context "wins out." In this case, the general aspiration rule is preempted by the more specific lenition rule (17).

To complete the discussion of [t] realizations, note that the glottalization observed in (13a) is also found for many speakers on the [p] of *captain* and the [k] of *buxom*. We account for this fact by invoking the rule in (18), which assigns the feature of glottal closure to a voiceless stop when it belongs to the same syllable as the preceding vowel.

(18) $\begin{bmatrix} -\text{contin} \\ -\text{voiced} \end{bmatrix} \rightarrow [+\text{constr gl}] \ / \ V \underline{\hspace{1cm}}$

(where V is tautosyllabic)

Our discussion of flapping abstracts away from certain complications. In many dialects the [t] of *capácity* is flapped (though less uniformly than the [t] of *atom*). In this case each of the flanking vowels is unstressed. If rule (15) is correct, then we might infer that the stressed antepenult heads a metrical foot that takes in both of the following unstressed syllables. Also, many speakers can extend the flapping process to intervocalic stops that arise in sentential contexts: for example, the final [t] of *hit* and *merit* can flap in *hit Ann* and *merit action*. In these cases the requirement that the flanking vowels belong to the same foot is dropped. But since the rule never extends to the [t] of *my tie*, we see that aspiration and flapping are still incompatible. For further discussion, see Kahn 1976, Selkirk 1982b, Harris 1990, Harris and Kaye 1990.

2.6   One or Two Levels of Representation?

The rules of English phonology examined so far (aspiration, flapping, retroflexion, and glottalization) define generalizations that are true of the surface phonetic level. For example, when we examine intervocalic position in the flapping dialect, we consistently encounter a [D] in place of [t] or [d]. We have characterized this state of affairs in terms of abstract representations of [t] that are then assigned the features [+spread gl], [+sonorant], [−distributed], [+constr gl] in the appropriate contexts to produce the allophones [tʰ], [D], [t̪], and [tˀ]. However, it is not obvious that another representation distinct from the phonetic level must be invoked to explain these generalizations of English phonology. We could interpret a rule like (18) as simply an if-then declarative statement of the form "If a voiceless dental stop immediately follows a tautosyllabic vowel, then it is glottalized." Under such an interpretation, no generalization is missed or fact left out. To use a crude analogy, we may state the law that "All swans are white" without appealing to a colorless swan that is "assigned" the property white. As we have seen, generative phonologists have postulated abstract, redundancy-free representations on the assumption that the grammar is designed (through evolution) to minimize the amount of information that must be stored, allowing the development of a large lexicon (Bromberger and Halle 1989). However, with the advent of neural science and more accurate estimates of the capacity of the human brain, this "economy of storage" argument is not compelling in and of itself. Phonologists have proposed two additional types of argument in order to motivate the distinction between phonological and phonetic representations.

First, expressing the difference between distinctive and redundant information as the presence versus absence of material in the phonological representation provides a natural formal basis for understanding why redundant features are often inert. To take a well-known example, in Russian consonants the voicing feature is contrastive among obstruents but redundant in sonorants. The [+ voiced] feature of liquids and nasals can thus be supplied by the UG default rule of (8bii). As the paradigms in (19) demonstrate, Russian consonants are devoiced at the end of a word (*vez-u* but *ve*[s]), and in consonant clusters the voicing of the final member is assimilated by nonfinal members (*vez-u* but *ve*[s]-*ti*). Sonorant consonants neither trigger nor undergo the rule (*nes-la, sn-a, son, rt-a*).

(19)
1sg.	vez-u	nes-u	
masc. past	ve[s]	nes	
infin.	ve[s]-ti	nes-ti	
fem. past	vez-la	nes-la	
	'transport'	'carry'	
nom.sg.	voš	rot	son
inflected	[f]š-i	rt-a	sn-a
	'louse'	'mouth'	'sleep'

Furthermore, as shown by the preposition *iz-* 'from' in the phrases *iz Moskvi* 'from Moscow' vs. *i*[s] *Mcenska* 'from Mcensk', sonorants fail to interrupt the assimilation of voicing. This set of facts is naturally explained if the final devoicing and voicing assimilation rules operate over representations in which sonorants lack any specification for the feature [voiced]. But if these rules must be defined over the phonetic representations that contain the redundant [+ voiced] on the nasals in *Mcensk*, it is unclear why this [+ voiced] feature fails to interrupt the propagation of the voicing change through the cluster in *i*[s] *Mcenska* as well as why it neither initiates nor undergoes voicing assimilation itself.

A second reason to posit more than a single level of representation is simply that there are many empirical generalizations that cannot be stated over just a single level. The length of vowels before voiced versus voiceless consonants in English provides a well-known example. Recall that rule (2b) accounts for the difference between *cab* [kʰæ:b] and *cap* [kʰæp]. As shown in (20), many additional pairs of words distinguished solely by the voicing of the final consonant exhibit this vowel length difference: *r*[ɪː]*b* vs. *r*[ɪ]*p*; *b*[æː]*g* vs. *b*[æ̆]*ck*; *b*[ʌː]*zz* vs. *b*[ʌ̆]*s*. The feature worthy of note is that most dialects preserve the length distinction when the flapping rule merges the underlying contrast between [t] and [d]. This point is illustrated by the paradigms in (20). For speakers of this dialect, *writer* and *rider* are not homophonous. While the distinction is heard in the consonants, this is an illusion, since the words are pronounced the same in this position. Instead, they differ phonetically in the length of the preceding vocalic nucleus.

(20) wet   [wĕt]   wetting   [wĕDɪŋ]
      wed   [wɛ:d]   wedding   [wɛ:Dɪŋ]

      seat   [sĭt]   seated   [sĭDəd]
      seed   [si:d]   seeded   [si:Dəd]

      write [răi̯t]   writer   [răi̯Dər]
      ride   [ra:i̯d]   rider   [ra:i̯Dər]

If phonological rules are restricted to stating generalizations defined on and holding over the information contained in the phonetic transcriptions alone, then the vowel length in *rider* cannot be predicted. The phonetic representation of this word is identical to that of *writer* – save for the vowel length. To assign a long vowel in *rider* but not *writer,* the rule must "know" that the flap [D] in *rider* derives from a [d]. In other words, the grammar must define another representation in which the neutralized [t] vs. [d] contrast is restored. But this other representation is automatically supplied – if we agree to characterize the predictable features such as aspiration and glottalization in terms of redundancy-free underlying representations (UR). All we need assume is that the rule assigning vowel length applies before the sonorization rule neutralizing the voicing distinction. Under such an analysis, the following derivations (ordered sequence of rule applications) emerge for *write-writer* versus *ride-rider.*

(21) /rai̯t/   /rai̯t-ər/   /rai̯d/   /rai̯d-ər/   UR
     răi̯t   răi̯tər   ra:i̯d   ra:i̯dər   length (5b,c)
     ——   răi̯Dər   ——   ra:i̯Dər   sonorization (15)

If the theory of grammar does not permit a second level of representation, then an important generalization of English phonology is missed. For the labial and velar stops in *r*[ɪ:]*b-r*[ɪ:]*bbing* vs. *r*[ĭ]*p-r*[ĭ]*pping* or *b*[æ:]*g-b*[æ:]*gging* vs. *b*[æ]*ck-b*[æ]*cking,* the presence versus absence of vowel length uniformly correlates with the voicing of the following consonant. Furthermore, this correlation holds for the coronals in *w*[ɛ:]*d* vs. *w*[ɛ]*t.* The one situation in which it appears to break down is before the flap. But this is precisely the context in which another rule neutralizes the contrast between voiced [d] and voiceless [t]. There is, moreover, a regular connection among the words in a paradigm built from the same stem. If a stem ending in [d] has a long vowel (e.g., *w*[ɛ:]*d*), then vowel length emerges in words formed by suffixation (e.g., *w*[ɛ:D]*ing, w*[ɛ:D]*ed*). This correlation is also explained if the vowel length generalization is stated before the voicing contrast is neutralized. But if the phonological model is required to define its rules over the phonetic level alone, then the generalization will be lost. Vowel length becomes unpredictable – but only in preflap contexts. Furthermore, it turns out to be a complete accident that the dialect has a rule neutralizing the [t]-[d] contrast in this very context.

In the face of this argument, one might try to salvage the single-level model as follows. We grant that the vowel length contrast in *writer-rider* depends on a prior voicing distinction in the following consonant and thus that the grammar must "compute" representations with a [t] for *writer* and a [d] for *rider*. But we observe that the latter exist in the related words *write* and *ride*. Furthermore, *writer* and *rider* are obviously constructed morphologically from the bases *write* and *ride*. We might thus revamp the single-level model to allow phonological rules to state generalizations over the phonological representations that appear at each layer in the morphological construction of a word. The vowel length rule states a generalization that holds over the information contained in the base forms *write* [răit] and *ride* [ra:ịd]. The morphology then suffixes the agentive -*ər*, setting up the context for the sonorization rule predicting a flap. The flap rule likewise states a generalization that holds of the surface forms [răịDər] and [ra:ịDər]. Thus, while a complex word may have several representations, they are products of the morphology – not the phonology. Only a single phonological representation exists at any given point in the construction of the paradigm. Phonological rules state systematic relations holding within the information structures contained in these representations.

While there may be some merit in the view that vowel length is assigned to the stems in (20) before the suffixes are added, there are many other phonological alternations that cannot be explained in this way. For example, the words *tent* and *tend* contrast in the voicing of their final consonants; this contrast is responsible for the concomitant vowel length difference *t*[ε:]*nd* vs. *t*[ἔ]*nt*. Consider now the effect of suffixing plural and 3sg. affixes. For many speakers, the dental stops terminating the stem are deleted: they say [tʰἔns] for *tents* and [tʰε:nz] for *tends*. We may account for this alternation by the rule shown in (22).

$$(22) \quad \begin{bmatrix} +\text{coron} \\ -\text{contin} \end{bmatrix} \rightarrow \emptyset \: / \: [+\text{nasal}] \underline{\quad\quad} \begin{bmatrix} +\text{coron} \\ +\text{contin} \end{bmatrix}$$

Let us grant that this rule defines a generalization over the surface phonetic representations. We may also assume that, as in the case of *writer* vs. *rider*, the vowel length contrast is defined in [tʰἔns] vs. [tʰε:nz] before the suffix is added. The problem is to explain the voicing difference in the inflectional suffix itself. In the dual-level model, this difference is derived by the general rule that assimilates the voicing of a suffixal obstruent to the preceding segment – the rule that operates in *cup*[s], *hut*[s], *duck*[s] vs. *tub*[z], *bud*[z], *bug*[z]. We need merely stipulate that the voicing assimilation rule is defined on the underlying representation of these words – not on the surface form, where the opposition between [t] and [d] has been neutralized.

(23)	/tɛnt-z/	/tɛnd-z/	UR
	tɛnt-s	——	voicing assimilation
	tĕnt-s	tε:nd-z	length
	tĕn-s	tε:n-z	deletion (22)

The crucial point is that, unlike in the case of the vowel length, we cannot assign the voicing contrast in the suffix on an earlier morphological stratum. The suffix only appears on the second stratum. It is only by the morphological act of combining stem and suffix that we bring the affixal consonant into phonological proximity with the preceding consonant. But it is precisely at this stratum that the determinant voicing difference in the dental stop is missing from the surface representations: [tʰɛ̆n-s] vs. [tʰɛ:n-z]. It thus looks as if the single-level model must abandon all hope of stating the obviously systematic correlation that exists between the voicing of the suffixal consonant and the voicing of the stem-final consonant.

Another example making the same point is to be found in Mohanan's (1992b) discussion of some rules in the Singapore dialect of English. Like many other varieties of English, the Singapore dialect simplifies consonant clusters composed of a fricative plus stop at the end of the word through deletion of the stop (perhaps reflecting more rigid constraints on syllabification). As a result, words such as *lift*, *ask*, and *list* are pronounced [lɪf], [ɑ:s], [lɪs]. For many speakers, the underlying stop appears before suffixes beginning with a vowel: *lif*[t]-*ing*, *as*[k]-*ing*, *lis*[t]-*ing*, and so on. As in other dialects, the plural suffix -*es* in Singapore takes a reduced schwa-like vowel when the stem ends in a sibilant: *raise*-[ə]*s*, *hiss*-[ə]*s*, *watch*-[ə]*s*. After nonsibilants the suffix consists of just the consonant, appearing as [-s] or [-z] as a function of the voicing of the final segment of the stem: *set*-*s*, *laugh*-*s* with [-s] and *bag*-*s*, *see*-*s* with [-z]. The relevant fact here is that the plurals of *list* [lɪs] and *task* [tɑ:s] are not *liss*-*es* and *tass*-*es* with a schwa parallel to *hiss*-*es* but rather simply *list*-*s* [lɪs] and *task*-*s* [tɑ:s]. This contrast follows straightforwardly if the rule determining whether or not the plural suffix takes a schwa is controlled by the underlying phonological representation of the stem: /hɪs/ vs. /lɪst/. The former forces the schwa-initial variant of the plural while the latter with its final [t] chooses [-s]. The resultant [lɪst + s] then simplifies to [lɪs] by the cluster reduction process mentioned above. Once again we cannot escape the force of this example by appeal to an earlier morphological cycle. The presence or absence of the schwa is a function of adding the plural suffix. But the proper choice crucially depends on a sound that is not pronounced in the plural.

To summarize the results of this section: We have seen how a variety of different English sounds ([t], [tʰ], etc.) manifest the same phonological category: the phoneme [t]. The phonological rules that realize the [t] operate in a very general and largely unconscious manner. It takes phonetic training for English speakers to realize that the [t]'s of *take* and *stake* are different sounds. They are typically unaware of the flap in *writer*, and no orthographic reformer would propose introducing a special letter to spell this consonant. Such a policy would be impracticable – precisely because most speakers are not aware of this sound. The phonological rules define a given language's sound pattern. In general, speakers of a different language (i.e., one with a different set of rules) will categorize the same sounds differently. For example, while English speakers interpret the intervocalic flap as a dental stop [t] or [d], Spanish speakers assign their flap to a rhotic phoneme. Given these differences among languages, the important question is, How are these assignments made?

When this question was first posed in the early part of the 20th century (in structural linguistics), it was suggested that each phoneme was defined by an invariant set of phonetic features common to all its allophones. For example, the [pʰ] of *pin* and the [p] of *spin* share the features [+labial, −voiced, −continuant]. It was this common core of distinctive features that was thought to define the phoneme [p] for English. But it soon became clear that this answer runs into serious problems. We have seen that the English [t] phoneme has the allophones [t], [tʰ], [ɾ] (flap), [tˀ], [ʔ], and [ ]. Clearly, there is no invariant core here. Furthermore, this set of realizations overlaps the [d] phoneme, which also appears as [ɾ] and [ ]. A procedure that groups allophones on the basis of an invariant core will never arrive at the psychologically correct categorizations. Various solutions to these problems were proposed in the American structuralism of the 1930s and 1940s, but each was found to be seriously defective. In the 1950s Noam Chomsky and Morris Halle concluded that these defects arose from the basic methodological premise of American structuralism that the phonemic structure could only be induced from information present in the (overt) speech act – a strong form of empiricism known as *behaviorism*. Chomsky and Halle rejected this point of view and advocated a mentalist approach to phonology similar to that envisioned by Edward Sapir, for whom a language's phonemic inventory is a conceptual system of "ideal sounds" in terms of which the phonetic segments of speech are perceived and articulated. The phonological representations and rules are thus hypotheses about the information structures of the individual speaker – what he or she has stored in the mind/brain after learning to speak a given language.

If we accept this general point of view, then a number of questions arise. These questions constitute the research program of generative phonology. Descriptively, we ask, For any given language X, what features has it selected from the UG phonetic alphabet to construct its lexicon? What are the phonological representations of language X and its corresponding rules? How do the rules apply to derive (compute) the phonetic representations? At the theoretical level, we ask, What is a possible representation and rule? Since the language faculty has developed for millennia, the number and variety of phonological systems is large. But many aspects seem to be variations on a limited number of themes. The range of possible rules and representations seems to be sharply constrained. If these constraints are wired into the system (if the child "knows" them at birth as part of genetic endowment), they may circumscribe and direct the learning process and make more plausible how such an intricate system as language is acquired in the first place.

2.7 Dual-Level Model: Additional Evidence

2.7.1 Polish

In this section we examine two additional cases in which the grammar must postulate an abstract phonological representation in order to state the proper generalizations. The first example comes from the West Slavic language Polish. Inspection of the singular and plural forms of the masculine nouns in (24) reveals two note-worthy alternations.

(24)

sg.	pl.	
klup	klubi	'club'
trup	trupi	'corpse'
dom	domi	'house'
šum	šumi	'noise'
snop	snopi	'sheaf'
žwup	žwobi	'crib'
trut	trudi	'labor'
dzvon	dzvoni	'bell'
kot	koti	'cat'
lut	lodi	'ice'
grus	gruzi	'rubble'
nos	nosi	'nose'
vus	vozi	'cart'
koš	koše	'basket'
nuš	nože	'knife'
wuk	wugi	'lye'
wuk	wuki	'bow'
sok	soki	'juice'
ruk	rogi	'horn'
bur	bori	'forest'
žur	žuri	'soup'
vuw	vowi	'ox'
ul	ule	'beehive'
sul	sole	'salt'
buy	boye	'fight'

In some stems the final obstruent consonant alternates in voicing, appearing as voiced before the plural suffix and as voiceless in word-final position. For example, there is a [p]≈[b] alternation in 'club', a [t]≈[d] alternation in 'labor', an [s]≈[z] alternation in 'rubble', a [š]≈[ž] alternation in 'knife', and a [k]≈[g] alternation in 'lye'. There are two possible descriptions of this alternation, depending on whether the voiced or voiceless obstruent is posited as underlying. If voiced obstruents are underlying, a rule is needed to devoice them at the end of the word (25a). This rule is found in many languages (e.g., German, Russian, Catalan). However, perhaps equally as widespread is the process that voices obstruents intervocalically (25b). (As a notational convenience, we assume that the word boundary symbol # appears at the beginning and end of each phonological word. We can then refer to the final phoneme of the word as the one that stands before #; the initial phoneme immediately follows #.)

(25) a. [−sonor] → [−voiced] / _____ #
b. [−sonor] → [+voiced] / V _____ V

Thus, on grounds of phonological plausibility, either (25a) or (25b) is a reasonable first guess concerning the rule that underlies the voicing alternation. However, two additional facts motivate the devoicing analysis (25a). The first is that Polish has an equally large number of stems with a final voiceless consonant that never changes to voiced before the plural suffix. The morphemes meaning 'corpse', 'cat', 'nose', and so on, belong to this class. In a grammar with rule (25b), the underlying representations of such lexical items could not be simply [trup], [kot], [nos]. Some additional information indicating that they exceptionally fail to undergo the voicing rule would have to be added. But if (25a) is selected, then the underlying representations do not require this additional information. A learning procedure striving for maximally simple grammars will thus choose (25a) over (25b).

Another reason for selecting this analysis is that Polish has no stems with a final voiced obstruent that remains voiced at the end of the word. Although there are stems such as [trup] with a constant voiceless final consonant, and there are stems such as [klub] where the final obstruent alternates, there are no stems in which the final obstruent is always voiced. The final devoicing rule of (25a) states a generalization of Polish phonetics that is without exception and thus may be said to explain this gap in the distribution of voiced obstruents. If (25b) were the rule, then it would turn out to be a complete accident that Polish has no word-final voiced obstruents. In other words, the grammar incorporating (25b) would fail to relate the distributional gap (no final voiced obstruents) with the alternation exhibited by 'club', 'crib', 'labor', and so on. A separate rule would be required to state the distributional gap. In the alternative analysis, one rule (25a) accounts for the alternation and simultaneously explains the distributional gap. Once again, it is a simpler grammar.

The final devoicing rule (25a) is a *neutralization* rule. Polish utilizes [±voiced] to encode its lexicon. The voicing contrast surfaces before vocalic suffixes such as the plural. But when no suffix follows, the final devoicing rule neutralizes the underlying contrast by changing the specification of an obstruent from [+voiced] to [−voiced]. By virtue of this rule, underlying [b,d,g,z,ž] become identical with underlying [p,t,k,s,š]. Where the [±voiced] specification in the final consonant is the only difference between a pair of morphemes, the two pronunciations merge (e.g., in 'lye' and 'bow'). The following is a good descriptive heuristic. If a morpheme exhibits an alternation between [x] and [y] and one of the two terms of the alternation (say, [x]) is also found in a class of morphemes that fail to alternate in the same way, then try positing the other term of the alternation [y] as underlying.

Let us apply this heuristic to the analysis of the vocalic alternation in (24) between [o] and [u] found in such stems as 'crib', 'ice', 'cart', 'horn'. Since [o] and [u] differ just by the feature [high], the structural change of the rule will be easy to state. However, whether it is [o] or [u] that underlies the alternation is rather more difficult to determine. We may reason as follows. If [u] were underlying, it is unclear why the vowel lowers in *bur, bori* 'forest' and *sul, sole* 'salt' but fails to do so in *žur, žuri* 'soup' and *ul, ule* 'beehive', where we find a stable, nonalternating vowel. [b] and [s] together, excluding [ž], do not form a natural class. If phonological rules are defined over natural classes, we must seek another analysis for the alternation. Our descriptive heuristic suggests that [o] is basic to the alternation and thus that the underlying representations for the alternating morphemes are [žwob], [lod], [voz], [noz], [rog] – essentially, the stem shapes that appear in the plural. To maintain this analysis, a rule is needed to raise [o] to [u] in the singular. But we must formulate the rule so that it does not change the nonalternating [o] in such stems as [snop], [kot], [nos], [koš], and [sok]. The generalization is now obvious. [o] raises before a voiced consonant – but only when that consonant is word-final, since no change occurs in the plural. Furthermore, nasal consonants systematically fail to condition the rule. We may incorporate these observations into the rule stated in (26), which correctly delimits the contexts in which [o] changes to [u] in Polish.

(26) $$\begin{bmatrix} -\text{cons} \\ +\text{back} \\ -\text{low} \end{bmatrix} \rightarrow [+\text{high}] \ / \ \underline{\hspace{1cm}} \begin{bmatrix} +\text{cons} \\ +\text{voiced} \\ -\text{nasal} \end{bmatrix} \#$$

Clearly this rule must apply before devoicing since the [o] → [u] change depends on the voicing contrast that the devoicing rule neutralizes. An ordering restriction "raising precedes final devoicing" guarantees this result. A word such as *vus* 'cart' thus receives the derivation in (27a). If final devoicing had applied first, /voz/ would appear as [vos]. The raising rule would then be unable to apply and we would derive the incorrect *[vos] (27b).

(27) a. /#voz#/   UR   b. /#voz#/   UR
          vuz   raising   vos   devoicing
          vus   devoicing   inappl.   raising

The Polish raising rule has a status similar to that of the English vowel-lengthening rule operative in the *writer-rider* contrast. Both rules crucially refer to a voicing distinction in the following consonant that is neutralized by a subsequent rule. But in the case of Polish *vus*, the triggering voiced consonant does not appear on a earlier stratum in the morphological structure of the word. Unlike English *rid-er*, Polish *vus* is a root. It is not derived from any simpler form. Furthermore, unlike in the case of English *tents* (*tĕn*[s]) vs. *tends* (*tɛ:n*[z]), where the vowel length might be considered an enhancement of the obstruent voicing, the [o]≈[u] alternation cannot be construed as incorporating a distinctive feature from the following consonant. The Polish data thus furnish additional evidence for phonological versus phonetic representations. To account for the systematic raising of [o] to [u] in nom. sg. forms of 'cart', 'knife', 'horn', and so on, the grammar must contain representations with a final voiced obstruent ([voz], [nož], [rog]) even though that voiced obstruent is uniformly pronounced voiceless. Such "abstract" representations will be formed by a grammar that seeks to maximize the simplicity of its rules and representations.

Two additional observations are in order. First, we defined the context for both Polish rules in essentially phonological terms instead of referring to the grammatical context in which the stem finds itself (e.g., devoice the final consonant of the stem in the nominative singular). For final devoicing, this decision is motivated by the fact that no word in the language ends in a voiced obstruent, regardless of grammatical category. In addition, there are several other morphological contexts that have no overt suffix and thus place the stem in word-final position. In each case the final devoicing and raising rules apply – as predicted by the formulations in (25a) and (26). One of these is the genitive plural of feminine and neuter nouns; the other is the imperative singular of the verb.

(28)

nom.sg.	gen.pl.		1sg.	imper.	
swov-o	swuf	'word'	rob'e	rup	'do'
brod-a	brut	'beard'	vodze	vuć	'lead'
proz'b-a	prus'p	'request'	odvože	odvuš	'open'
drog-a	druk	'road'	zwov'e	zwuf	'catch'
bžoz-a	bžus	'birch'	stoye	stuy	'stand'
komor-a	komur	'closet'	ogole	ogul	'shave'
pol-e	pul	'field'			

In general, when rules are formulated in terms of phonological contexts, they make predictions that go beyond the data at hand. In our descriptive work, we may discover additional data that require modification of our initial formulations. Experienced phonologists have strong intuitions about what rules are likely to underlie a given alternation and readily use this "expert system" to develop hypotheses about the rules and representations that constitute the grammar. Our descriptive work constantly seeks to test these hunches and extend the empirical coverage of the proposed rules. Needless to say, one often guesses wrong and the system turns out to be quite different from what was initially expected. Sometimes this is because a crucial piece of information is missing and, once discovered, radically alters the interpretation of the data. At other times the language may be truly odd and not behave the way the theory predicts. This should not be too surprising because any phonological system is also the product of historical evolution whose preceding sound changes may leave arbitrary gaps and create missing links. Finally, descriptive failure may indicate that the underlying theory is simply incorrect and must be revised.

A second point worthy of note is that unlike most of our previous rules, the Polish raising rule cannot readily be assigned to a natural phonological category. It is not a rule of assimilation, weakening, strengthening, enhancement, and so on. Polish raising typifies what Jan Baudouin de Courtenay (1845–1929) called a *sinnlos* ("irrational") alternation. It is unlikely that any other language has a rule of exactly this form. While the environment for the rule forms a natural class and the structural change is very simple, there is no good reason why this particular vowel change ([o] → [u]) should take place in this particular context (before voiced oral consonants). (The answer to this puzzle lies in the history of the language. See Kenstowicz and Kisseberth 1977:64 for discussion.) But even though the [o]≈[u] alternation is phonologically arbitrary, it is clear that it is still a genuine rule of Polish phonology. For example, Bethin (1978) notes that it regularly extends to loanwords in the genitive plural (e.g., *doz-a, dus* 'dose'; *pagod-a, pagut* 'pagoda'), but interestingly not in the nominative singular, where many exceptions have developed (*snop, snob-a* 'snob'; *epizot, epizod-a* 'episode'; *gol* 'goal').

2.7.2 Icelandic

In this section we will examine one more example to motivate the dual-level model of phonological representation. Our discussion focuses on the *u*-epenthesis rule of Modern Icelandic. Orešnik (1972) discusses several independent lines of evidence that converge on the conclusion that the [u] in *dag-ur* and *hest-ur* (29a) is inserted by the rule shown in (29b) and thus that the underlying representation of the nom.sg. suffix in this declension class is [-r].

(29) a.
nom.sg.	dag-ur	hest-ur	bæ-r
acc.sg.	dag	hest	bæ
	'day'	'horse'	'farmhouse'

b. $\emptyset \rightarrow u \; / \; C \underline{\hspace{1cm}} r \; \#$

A rule breaking up final C*r* clusters is a natural process termed *epenthesis* in traditional grammar. But deletion of one vowel after another is also very common. Thus, considerations of rule naturalness do not resolve the analysis of the [-r]≈ [-ur] alternation. We must consider the effects the insertion analysis has on other rules of the grammar. Orešnik's first argument runs as follows. If [u] underlies the [u]≈∅ alternation, a rule is needed to delete it after vowel-final stems such as [bæ]. But Icelandic already has a rule of truncation eliminating a V-V cluster for data not considered here. This rule deletes the first vowel in the cluster, however, not the second. Orešnik concludes that epenthesis underlies the alternation since, if the language already has a means to eliminate vowel clusters, why is it not utilized here? This argument is based on the premise that underlying V-V sequences should be eliminated in the same way, regardless of the particular vowels filling the first and second positions. While true in general, this is not very strong justification for an underlying [-r] rather than [-ur] because an additional rule is required in any case. The analysis of the [u]≈∅ alternation as epenthesis receives much stronger support from its interaction with two other phonological alternations.

The first of these is evident in the paradigms of (30a), where stems such as [lyfj] lose their final [j] (a front glide) before a consonant or word boundary. [v] (underlying [w]) has a parallel distribution. As we will see when we develop the theory of syllabification, this is a common alternation. A consonant-glide sequence is difficult to incorporate into the syllable coda. Many languages follow Icelandic in simplifying such clusters through deletion of the second member. This rule can be stated informally as in (30b).

(30) a.
nom.sg.	lyf-ur	byl-ur	beð-ur	söng-ur
acc.sg.	lyf	byl	beð	söng
gen.sg.	lyf-s	byl-s	beð-s	söng-s
dat.pl.	lyfj-um	bylj-um	beðj-um	söngv-um
gen.pl.	lyfj-a	bylj-a	beðj-a	söngv-a
	'medicine'	'storm'	'bed'	'song'

b. $[j,v] \rightarrow \emptyset \; / \; C \underline{\hspace{1cm}} \left\{ \begin{matrix} \# \\ C \end{matrix} \right\}$

Returning to the [u]≈∅ alternation, if the underlying representation of the nom.sg. ending is [-ur], then we expect the glides to surface before the vowel – as they do in the dative and genitive plural: *lyfj-um, lyfj-a*. But this is not what we find. Instead, the glide deletion rule uniformly applies: the nominative singular is *lyf-ur*, not *lyfj-ur*. As Orešnik observes, the loss of the glide is explained if zero underlies the [u]≈∅ alternation. Then the nom.sg. suffix will have the same monoconsonantal shape as the gen.sg. [-s] and thus will activate rule (29b). Of course, the glide deletion rule must be ordered before epenthesis so that derivations such as those in (31) obtain.

(31)   /#bylj-um#/   /#bylj-s#/   /#bylj#/   /#bylj-r#/   UR
       ―――――   byl-s   byl   byl-r   glide deletion (30b)
       ―――――   ―――   ―   byl-ur   epenthesis (29b)

If the rules had applied in the opposite order, then [bylj-r] would become [bylj-ur] by epenthesis and the stem-final glide could not delete by (30b).

The general point to emerge from this discussion is that application of the glide deletion rule in the derivation of *byl-ur* crucially depends on positing that the underlying representation of the nom.sg. suffix begins with a consonant [-r]. Yet in every pronunciation of this word (and all stems ending in C-glide), the suffix has the shape [-ur].

The *u*-umlaut rule in Icelandic independently supports this analysis. As illustrated in (32a), many suffixes containing a [u] such as the dative plural, the diminutive, and the first person plural of the verbal inflection mutate the [a] of a preceding syllable to [ö]. This rule is stated informally in (32b).

(32)   a.   barn   nom.sg.   baggi   kalla   1sg.
            börn-um   dat.pl.   bögg-ull   köll-um   1pl.
            'child'   'bundle', 'parcel'   'call'

       b.   [a] → [ö] / ____ C₀ [u]

There is one systematic exception to umlaut: the nom.sg. [-ur]. As the data in (33) demonstrate, [-ur] does not umlaut the preceding stem.

(33)   nom.sg.   hatt-ur   dal-ur   stað-ur
       acc.sg.   hatt   dal   stað
       dat.pl.   hött-um   döl-um   stöð-um
                 'hat'   'valley' 'place'

The lack of umlaut has nothing to do with the roots, since they regularly submit to the rule in the dative plural. The assumption that the underlying representation of the nom.sg. suffix is [-r] helps us to understand why this suffix fails to umlaut a preceding root. If the umlaut rule is defined to operate at a point that precedes the epenthesis rule, the suffix will lack a vowel to trigger the umlaut. Under this analysis, *hatt-ur* and *hött-um* receive the following derivations.

(34) /#hatt + r#/   /#hatt + um#/   UR
                          hött-um   *u*-umlaut (32b)
      ————
      hatt-ur   ————   epenthesis (29b)

Thus, two separate aspects of the *-ur* suffix's behavior are explained if its underlying representation lacks a vowel. If the theory of grammar posits just a single level of phonological representation, we would be unable to explain the systematic behavior of the suffix – and the hundreds of words in which it is attached – in this way. To ensure that the umlaut and glide deletion rules operate on this more abstract representation, we stipulate that each precedes application of epenthesis.

To summarize the results of this section, we have examined several cases indicating that the phonological structure of a given lexical item may require the application of rules that crucially refer to information that is not present in the item's phonetic representation. But in each case the missing information is present in the underlying phonological representation – that is, in the representation that arises from consistent elimination of predictable information and assignment of this information by general phonological rules.

Suggested Readings

Anderson, Stephen. 1985. Phonology in the twentieth century. Chicago: University of Chicago Press. Chapters 11 and 12.

Bromberger, Sylvain, and Morris Halle. 1989. Why phonology is different. Linguistic Inquiry 20.51–70.

Halle, Morris. 1962. Phonology in generative grammar. Word 18.54–72. Reprinted in Phonological theory: Evolution and current practice, ed. by V. Makkai, 393–400. New York: Holt, Rinehart and Winston, 1972.

Kenstowicz, Michael. 1992. American structuralist phonology. International encyclopedia of linguistics, vol. 3, ed. by W. Bright, 215–17. Oxford: Oxford University Press.

Sapir, Edward. 1925. Sound patterns in language. Language 1.37–51. Reprinted in Selected writings of Edward Sapir in language, culture, and personality, ed. by D. Mandelbaum, 33–45. Berkeley: University of California Press, 1949; in Readings in linguistics I, ed. by M. Joos, 19–25. Chicago: University of Chicago Press, 1957; in Phonological theory: Evolution and current practice, ed. by V. Makkai, 13–21. New York: Holt, Rinehart and Winston, 1972.

Exercises

2.1 *English Allophones*

Review the analysis of (American) English developed in the text. Tell what allophone it assigns to the boldfaced segments in the following words. If the result is different from your dialect, tell what the difference is.

(1) pin   hug   laugh   rat
     stupid   true   Santa Cruz   atlas
     martyr   mástodòn   actress   chowder
     antler

2.2 English Minimal Pairs

The system of stops and nasals to be found in English is tabulated in (1). These segments are built from combining [±voiced] and [+nasal] with the three articulators [labial], [coronal], and [dorsal].

(1)

	labial	coronal	dorsal
voiceless stops	p	t	k
voiced stops	b	d	g
nasals	m	n	ŋ

   Listed in (2) are minimal triples constructed over the three classes of consonants in (1). In these examples the consonants appear in both initial and final position. (2a,b) indicate that the articulator features [labial], [coronal], and [dorsal] are contrastive. (2c,d) suggest that the features [voiced] and [nasal] are also utilized to encode the lexicon. There is of course one major distributional gap: the velar nasal does not appear word-initially (see the discussion in section 3.4).

(2) a. pin, tin, kin; bun, dun, gun; mutt, nut
     b. lip, lit, lick; robe, road, rogue; dim, din, ding
     c. pat, bat, mat; tip, dip, nip; cut, gut
     d. rope, robe, roam; mate, made, main; pick, pig, ping

   Try to construct minimal *n*-tuples (pairs, triples, quadruples) over the set of English fricatives listed in (3) for both initial and final position. Which of these segments appear to have restricted distributions?

(3) f θ s š
     v ð z ž

2.3 English sC Clusters

Although voiced and voiceless stops freely contrast initially, medially, and finally in English, there is one position where the opposition is suspended: after morpheme-initial [s] (e.g., s[p]*in*, s[t]*em*, s[k]*in*). What significance is to be attached to the fact that neither voiced nor aspirated stops are found here instead?

2.4 Korean

The liquids [l] and [r] are in complementary distribution in Korean (data from Demers and Farmer 1991). State the context where each is found. What difficulty is a name such as *Lori Roland* likely to present to the Korean learner of English?

(1) mul ᵈ/ᵉ 'water'   mal ᵈᵗ/ᵉ 'horse'
     mulkama 'place for water'   malkama 'place for horse'
     mure   'at the water'   mare   'at the horse'

     pal   'foot'   səul   'Seoul'   rupi   'ruby'
     pari 'of the foot'   ilkop 'barber'   ratio 'radio'

2.5 Singapore English

In his discussion of Singapore English, Mohanan (1992b) notes a process whereby
[sp] in the coda of the syllable metathesizes to [ps]; [st] and [sk] clusters reduce
by the process mentioned in section 2.6.

(1) lisp   [lips]   list   [lis]   risk   [ris]
     crisp [krips]   mist   [mis]   whisk   [wis]
     grasp [grɑ:ps]   past   [pɑ:s]   mask   [mɑ:s]

Before vocalic suffixes speakers break into the two groups illustrated in (2).

(2)   group 1   group 2
     lisping   [lisp-iŋ]   [lips-iŋ]
     crispy   [krisp-i]   [krips-i]
     grasping   [grɑ:sp-iŋ]   [grɑ:ps-iŋ]

Mohanan reports that both groups of speakers treat plurals and 3sg. present verb
forms the same, as indicated in (3).

(3) sg.   pl.
     hiss   [his]   hisses   [hisəs]
     eclipse [eklips]   eclipses   [eklipsəs]
     lapse   [læps]   lapses   [læpsəs]
     lisp   [lips]   lisps   [lips]
     grasp   [grɑ:ps]   grasps   [grɑ:ps]

Discuss the implications of these data for the issue of single- vs. dual-level models
of phonological representation.

2.6 Friulian

A. In the Friulian dialect of Italian (Vanelli 1979, 1986), there is an alternation
    between voiced and voiceless obstruents. Suggest a rule to account for the
    following voicing alternations.

(1) wárp   'blind'   kwárp   'body'
     warb-ít 'sty'   kwarp-út   dimin.

     piérd-i 'to lose'   dínt   'tooth'
     piért   3sg.   dint-isín dimin.

B. Accented vowels seem to contrast in length: for example, *lá:t* 'went' vs. *lát* 'milk', *pá:s* 'peace' vs. *pás* 'step'. But in many cases the length is predictable. Suggest a rule to account for the length in the following data. How must your rules be ordered? How does your analysis bear on the issue of one level of representation versus two?

(2) lá:t   'went'   brút   'ugly'
     lád-e   fem.   brút-e   fem.

     nervó:s   'nervous'   rós   'red'
     nervóz-e   fem.   rós-e   fem.

     tróp   'flock'   ló:f   'wolf'
     trop-út   dimin.   lov-út   dimin.

     sék   'dry'   fí:k   'fig'
     séc-e   fem.   fig-ón   'big fig'

     vjód-i   'to see'
     vjó:t   3sg.

C. Friulian has recently borrowed many words from Standard Italian. What bearing do these loanwords have on the analysis?

(3) Friulian   Italian
     impjegá:t   impiegato   'clerk'
     impjegád-e   impiegata   fem.
     istitú:t   istituto   'institute'
     istitud-út   dimin.
     steká:t   steccato   'fenced'
     stekad-út   dimin.
     afít   affitto   'rent'
     afit-út   dimin.

2.7 *Northern Salentino*

As in Standard Italian, the Northern Salentino dialect distinguishes seven vowels in stressed position (Calabrese 1984).

(1)   i   e   ɛ   a   ɔ   o   u
     high   +   −   −   −   −   −   +
     low   −   −   −   +   −   −   −
     back   −   −   −   +   +   +   +
     ATR   +   +   −   −   −   +   +

A. In the following paradigms, the root vowels change in response to the shift of accent – generally on the penultimate syllable. Postulate a rule to account for the alternations in vowel quality that result from the shift of stress. What is the underlying representation? Justify your choice. State the rule, utilizing

distinctive features. Show how the analysis works by giving the derivations
for *kanósku* and *kanuššímu*.

(2) 1sg.   kréu   séntu   kanósku   trɔ́u
     3sg.   kréti   sénti   kanóšši   trɔ́a
     1pl.   kritiámu   sintímu   kanuššímu   truámu
            'believe'   'feel'   'recognize' 'find'

B. Some suffixes cause a mutation of the root vowel (known as *metaphony* in
    Romance linguistics). Examine the following paradigms and suggest a rule
    to account for the metaphony.

(3) masc.sg.   karúsu   rússu   frísku   fríddu   krútu   vívu   sánu
     fem.sg.   karósa   róssa   fréska   frédda   krúta   víva   sána
     masc.pl.   karúsi   rússi   fríski   fríddi   krúti   vívi   sáni
                'young' 'red'   'cool'   'cold'   'raw'   'alive' 'healthy'

C. In contrast to the suffixes in (3), other suffixes do not cause metaphony.
    While they may be treated simply as exceptions, a phonological explanation
    is also possible. Suggest an analysis along the latter lines. Must the rules be
    ordered? Show how the analysis works by deriving the words *karósi* and
    karúsi.

(4) a. fem.pl.   karósi   róssi   fréski   fréddi
         masc.pl.   karúsi   rússi   fríski   fríddi
                    'young'   'red'   'slow'   'cold'

     b. sg.   mési   pésši   nóči   krɔ́či
         pl.   mísi   písši   núči   krúči
                    'month'   'fish'   'nut'   'cross'

     c. 3sg.   véti   kréti   kanóšši
         2sg.   víti   kríti   kanúšši
         1sg.   vétu   kréu   kanósku
                    'see'   'believe' 'recognize'

2.8 Yakut

Yakut is an Altaic language spoken in Siberia (Kruger 1962). The data for this
exercise, shown in (1), consist of nouns in various case forms. Asterisked items
have been constructed from attested models to fill out the paradigms.

(1)

gloss	absolute	plural	dative	accusative	partitive	our N	your N
'father'	aɣa	aɣalar	aɣaɣa	aɣanɯ	aɣata	aɣabɯt	aɣaɣɯt
'child'	oɣo	oɣolor	oɣoɣo	oɣonu	oɣoto	oɣobut	oɣoɣut
'lake'	küöl	küöller	küölge	küölü	küölle	küölbüt	küölgüt*
'horse'	at	attar	akka	atɯ*	atta*	apput	akkɯt
'duck'	kus	kustar	kuska*	kuhu*	kusta*	kusput	kuskut
'bull'	oɣus	oɣustar	oɣuska*	oɣuhu*	oɣusta	oɣusput	oɣuskut

gloss	absolute	plural	dative	accusative	partitive	our N	your N
'tool'	sep	septer	sepke	sebi	septe	seppit	sepkit
'meat'	et	etter	ekke	eti	ette	eppit	ekkit
'arrow'	ox	oxtor	oxxo	oɣu	oxto	oxput	oxxut
'knee'	tobuk	tobuktar	tobukka	tobugu	tobukta	tobukput	tobukkut
'elder brother'	ubay	ubaydar	ubayga*	ubayɯ*	ubayda	ubaybɯt	ubaygɯt
'stallion'	atɯɯr	atɯɯrdar	atɯɯrga*	atɯɯrɯ*	atɯɯrda	atɯɯrbɯt	atɯɯrgɯt
'squirrel'	tiiŋ	tiiŋner	tiiŋŋe*	tiiŋi	tiiŋne	tiiŋmit	tiiŋŋit
'door'	aan	aannar	aaŋŋa	aanɯ	aanna	aammɯt	aaŋŋɯt
'ford'	olom	olomnor	olomŋo	olomu	olomno	olommut	olomŋut

Segment the words into root plus suffix. Note the many alternations. Tabulate the sounds that comprise the phonetic inventory. Only a subset of these appear in underlying representations. Following Kruger, you may postulate the following phonemic inventory.

(2)　high vowels　　　 i　　ü　　　　　ɯ　　u
　　　nonhigh vowels　　 e　　　　　　　 a　　o

　　　voiceless stops　　　　　p　　t　　k
　　　voiceless fricatives　　　　　 s　　x
　　　nasals　　　　　　　　　 m　　n　　ŋ
　　　approximants　　　　　　　l r
　　　　　　　　　　　　　　　 y

The point of this exercise is to discover the rules realizing this system of phonemes in the various nominal paradigms. You may orient your analysis around the following questions.

A.　Yakut contrasts seven root vowels, distinguished by appropriate choices among [±high], [±back], [±round]. Only one of these three features is contrastive in suffixes. Which one? How are the other features determined?

B.　[±voiced] is not underlyingly contrastive. Assuming the appropriate default rules of section 2.4, account for the appearance of [±voiced] in the phonetic representations. You may assume a special rule that deletes the initial -n of the accusative suffix after a stem ending in a consonant.

C.　Postulate additional rules to account for the remaining alternations. Must they apply in a particular order?

2.9　Kire Nasalization and Orthography

Pryor and Clifton (1987) explain how difficulties with the orthographic registration of vowel nasality in the Papua New Guinean language Kire encouraged a reinterpretation of the phonological structure of the language, which in turn led to a more efficient orthography. Primarily on the basis of such contrasts as *pi* 'to eat' vs. *pī:* 'breadfruit tree', Pryor's original analysis of Kire concluded that vowel nasality was phonemic in the language. Accordingly, he proposed the use of the dieresis for the native orthography. The above words were thus originally spelled as *pi* and *pïï* (gemination used to indicate long vowels). The authors state (p. 34),

> Though this symbolisation was accepted by the Kire people, problems arose in deciding which vowels should be marked with the dieresis. Literate Kires began putting the dieresis on vowels that had previously been declared oral and omitting them on obviously nasal vowels following or preceding nasal consonants. In addition analysis of the morphophonemics of Kire indicated that at least some nasalisation was predictable.

The authors cite the data in (1a) to illustrate the point that vowel nasality is predictable from a tautosyllabic nasal consonant. This interpretation is also supported by the alternations in vowel nasality in (1b), which respond to changes in syllabification due to the addition of affixes.

(1) a.

vap	'fire'
pʰɨkta	'shoulder'
bẽm	'tree species'
dõmdori	'roll over'
mõmūk	'tree species'
mõnūm	'fish species'
faramē	'thumb'

b.

sg.	dual	pl.	
gumã	gumãnɨ	gūmgi	'man'
kɨn	kɨnãnɨ	kɨnɨ	'banana'

Finally, Pryor and Clifton note that while Kire contrasts [m], [n], and [ŋ] in the onset of the syllable, [ŋ] is phonetically absent at the end of a syllable. They propose to analyze such words as those in (2a) with the underlying phonological representations in (2b) and posit the rule (2c) that deletes the velar nasal from the syllable coda.

(2) a.

	b.		
pī:		/pi:ŋ/	'breadfruit tree'
bī		/biŋ/	'bird species'
tʰā:		/tʰa:ŋ/	'bamboo'

  c. [ŋ] → ∅ at the end of the syllable

The authors state (p. 41),

> Long before the reanalysis outlined in [(2)] was completed, it had become clear that at least the majority of nasalised vowels were predictable. At the same time the dieresis was proving increasingly problematic. The major problem was the difficulty writers had in using it consistently. . . . Because of these difficulties, the possibility of eliminating the dieresis from the orthography was discussed with those Kires who had been trying to use the dieresis.

During these discussions they indicated their feelings that nasalised vowels were generally conditioned by neighboring nasal consonants, and not "basic" as the use of the dieresis would indicate. After explaining the possibility of using "silent" ŋ as a spelling device to signal nasalised vowels not flanked by a nasal consonant, they were enthusiastic about eliminating the dieresis.

Discuss the relevance of these comments from Pryor and Clifton to the issues of phonetic versus phonological accuracy in orthography. Why did the Kires have so much trouble with the dieresis? Why was the use of the ŋ more readily accepted?

3 Phonological Alternations and Derivations

The discussion in this chapter proceeds on both the descriptive and theoretical levels. Given that phonological rules state generalizations about the sound structure of a language, the immediate descriptive question confronting any generative phonologist is, What are the phonological rules and underlying representations of the language under analysis? This question is usually answered through the study of alternations in a paradigm. We construct paradigms of words to look for regular alternations in the phonetic shape of the stem as different affixes are added, as well as for systematic differences in the realization of the affix as a function of the stem. We may also study variations in the pronunciation of a word as the phrasal context changes. If the alternations are regular, we assume that the morpheme has a unique underlying representation, such that the various phonetic shapes arise from sound changes introduced by context-sensitive phonological rules. This chapter illustrates this descriptive methodology. Although the examples are carefully chosen pedagogically, and hence are not representative of real-life phonological description, they do illustrate the kinds of questions asked in order to discover the rules of a given language as well as a standard format in which to present the results.

Through analysis of the paradigms, we will isolate *alternations* in which sound (or sound sequence) [x] alternates with [y] in a given context ([x] or [y] may be zero). There are always at least two possible analyses for the [x]≈[y] alternation that must be considered. Either [x] is underlying, and a given rule applies to change [x] to [y] in some context Z; or [y] is underlying, and some rule changes [y] to [x] in the complementary set of contexts Z'. We will identify the kinds of criteria phonologists appeal to in order to resolve this analytic choice.

On the theoretical front, we will return to the dual representation model developed in chapter 2. We will raise the question whether the two representations are on a par or whether the phonetic representation is derivative and computed from the underlying representation. We will look at arguments in favor of the latter view and discuss how the rules apply to derive the phonetic representation from the underlying one. We will then look at more complex cases of multiple alternation in which a given lexical item participates in several alternations simultaneously. Multiple alternation increases the number of possible underlying representations. We will ask whether the choice of the underlying representation can be constrained, given the set of surface alternants. Finally, we will see that the methods devised for the analysis of alternations can be used to reconstruct earlier stages in a language's historical development.

3.1   Ordered Rules

Our first example of the analysis of alternations comes from the South Slavic language Serbo-Croatian. Consider the phonological alternations that occur in the adjectival paradigms of (1).

(1)

masc.	fem.	neut.	pl.	
mlád	mladá	mladó	mladí	'young'
púst	pustá	pustó	pustí	'empty'
zelén	zelená	zelenó	z>elení	'green'
čést	čestá	čestó	čestí	'frequent'
bogat	bogata	bogato	bogati	'rich'
sunčan	sunčana	sunčano	sunčani	'sunny'
rapav	rapava	rapavo	rapavi	'rough'

It is apparent that these words consist of a root to which are suffixed the morphemes [-a], [-o], and [-i] to represent gender and number. As in many other languages, the masculine is not marked by an affix. Words transcribed with an accent such as [mlad] and [pust] are representative of a class of Serbo-Croatian stems (traditionally called "oxytones") for which the location of accent is predictable: the accent falls on the suffix, and in the absence of a suffix, on the preceding stem vowel. (In the standard dialect another rule retracts the accent one syllable to the left, where it is heard as a rising tone. Our discussion abstracts away from this retraction.) For these words, the accent may be assigned by the rule in (2).

(2) $V \rightarrow \acute{V} / \underline{\hspace{1cm}} C_0 \#$ or Stem $V \rightarrow \acute{V} / \underline{\hspace{1cm}} (C) \#$

(2) accents a vowel that is separated from the right edge of the word by zero or more consonants and thus isolates the last vocalic segment in the word. Stems such as [bogat] and [sunčan] belong to a different class in which the location of accent is unpredictable. Since their accent is not relevant to the following discussion, it will not be transcribed.

The stems in (3) show an alternation between the liquid [l] and the back vowel [o].

(3)

masc.	fem.	neut.	pl.	
debéo	debelá	debeló	debelí	'fat'
posustao	posustala	posustalo	posustali	'tired'
béo	belá	beló	belí	'white'
mío	milá	miló	milí	'dear'
céo	celá	celó	celí	'whole'

There are two possible analyses for this [l]≈[o] alternation. Either [o] is underlying and a rule converting [o] to [l] is required, or [l] is underlying and is changed to [o] in some context. Since the [o] is found word-finally and the [l] between vowels, we might postulate (4a) if the [o] underlies the alternation or (4b) if [l] is underlying.

(4) a.   [o] → [l] / V ____ V
     b.   [l] → [o] / ____ #

There are two reasons to believe that (4b) is the correct analysis. First, the change of [l] to a back vocalic segment such as [o] in word-final (or syllable-coda) position is a natural process found in many languages. For example, English velarizes [l] in syllable codas. Many speakers of the Cockney dialect delateralize such segments as well, so that *field* is pronounced [fiod]. Also, children frequently substitute glides for liquids. The conversion of [l] to [o] thus constitutes one additional step (to [−high]) beyond this very common feature change. By contrast, the transformation of a vowel into an [l] is a nearly unprecedented phonological change. Considerations of phonological plausibility thus strongly favor the analysis that posits rule (4b).

Considerations internal to the grammar of Serbo-Croatian also motivate this analysis. As the forms *béo* and *mío* indicate, the [o] that alternates with [l] is systematically skipped by the accent rule (2). In this respect, it differs from the [o] of the neuter suffix, which readily accepts the accent when preceded by a stem belonging to the predictable accent class: *bel-ó, mlad-ó,* and so on. If *béo* is derived from [bel], and if the accent is assigned in terms of the underlying representation, then we can explain why [o]'s that alternate with [l] are skipped by the accent rule: at the point where accent is assigned, these segments are consonants. Like all other Serbo-Croatian consonants, they are not stress-bearing segments. We may ensure that the accent rule skips the vocalized [l] by ordering this rule prior to *l*-vocalization. The derivation in (5) illustrates the suggested analysis.

(5) /#bel#/   UR
     bél   accent (2)
     béo   *l*-vocalization (4b)

Next consider the alternation displayed in (6).

(6) | masc. | fem. | neut. | pl. | |
     | --- | --- | --- | --- | --- |
     | ledan | ledna | ledno | ledni | 'frozen' |
     | dóbar | dobrá | dobró | dobrí | 'good' |
     | jásan | jasná | jasnó | jasní | 'clear' |
     | sítan | sitná | sitnó | sitní | 'tiny' |
     | óštar | oštrá | oštró | oštrí | 'sharp' |
     | mókar | mokrá | mokró | mokrí | 'wet' |

These stems have an [a] in the masculine that is missing in the suffixed forms: *dóbar, dobr-á, dobr-ó,* and so on. Deletion of vowels (especially when unaccented) in a context such as VC____CV is quite common (cf. English *general* and *gen'ral*) and so the hypothesis that Serbo-Croatian syncopates [a] in this position cannot be faulted on grounds of phonological plausibility. However, there are reasons to doubt the validity of this deletion analysis for the [a]≈∅ alternation. First, the language has numerous stems of the shape CVC*a*C whose [a] does not alternate with ∅. Morphemes from (1) such as [bogat] and [rapav] would be lexical exceptions to the proposed analysis. By the heuristic mentioned in the discussion of Polish in section 2.7, we must entertain the hypothesis that ∅ underlies the alternation and thus that the underlying forms for 'good' and 'clear' are [dobr] and [jasn]. To generate the CVCaC alternants from these representations, a rule is needed to insert [a]. In many languages word-final consonant clusters terminating in a sonorant are dispreferred and subject to epenthesis – the insertion of a vowel. For example, English *cycle* rhymes with *angel* ([sáykəl], [éynǰəl]). But these items contrast before -*ic,* a suffix that uniformly accents the preceding vowel: *angél-ic* vs. *cýcl-ic.* The latter observation suggests that *cycle* is underlyingly monosyllabic and hence that its schwa is epenthetic. This reasoning implies the formulation in (7) for the Serbo-Croatian [a]≈∅ alternation.

(7)　∅ → [a] / C ＿＿＿　　C　　#
　　　　　　　　　　　　　[+sonor]

Rule (7) breaks up the clusters in [ledn] and [dobr] but correctly allows the fricative-stop cluster of *púst* to emerge unchanged since the final [t] is [–sonorant].

　　Independent confirmation of this analysis is furnished by the forms *dóbar* and *jásan.* They illustrate the important point that the [a] that alternates with ∅ is systematically ignored by the accent rule. (The discussion here abstracts away from other [a]≈∅ alternations in Serbo-Croatian in which [a] is underlying. For these, the [a] is counted by the accent rule.) If ∅ underlies the [a]≈∅ alternation, then this generalization is explained. As in the case of *l*-vocalization, all we need to say is that accent is assigned in terms of the information present in the underlying representations [dobr] and [jasn]. Since the epenthetic [a] is not present, the accent is assigned to the initial (and only) syllable of these words. Subsequent epenthesis yields [dóbar] and [jásan]. The stipulation that rule (2) precedes epenthesis produces the proper interplay between the rules. The derivation in (8) illustrates the proposed analysis.

(8)　/#dobr#/　　UR
　　　dóbr　　　　accent (2)
　　　dóbar　　　epenthesis (7)

　　We have not yet determined any ordering between the vocalization rule and epenthesis; yet potentially they interact. Since epenthesis breaks up final consonant clusters, and since vocalization changes the consonantal [l] to a vocalic segment [o], an early or late vocalization of [l] can materially affect the insertion of [a]. Words such as *okrúgao* in (9) furnish evidence bearing on the ordering of *l*-vocalization and epenthesis.

(9)　| masc. | fem. | neut. | pl. | |
| --- | --- | --- | --- | --- |
| okrúgao | okruglá | okrugló | okruglí | 'round' |
| óbao | oblá | obló | oblí | 'plump' |
| nágao | naglá | nagló | naglí | 'abrupt' |
| pódao | podlá | podló | podlí | 'base' |

These stems manifest both the [l]≈[o] and the [a]≈∅ alternations. If our analysis of these alternations is correct, we are committed to the underlying representation [okrugl]. We may obtain the correct phonetic representation with the rules at our disposal by simply ordering epenthesis before *l*-vocalization. The derivation in (10) then ensues.

(10) /#okrugl#/   UR
      okrúgl   accent (2)
      okrúgal   epenthesis (7)
      okrúgao   *l*-vocalization (4b)

The form *okrúgao* is significant in several respects besides fixing the order of the rules. First, it confirms the implicit prediction that is made when rules are formulated in terms of natural classes. Recall from our discussion of the data in (6) that the simplest way to include [r] and [n] together to the exclusion of [t] requires reference to the class of consonantal sonorants. The fact that [l] also triggers epenthesis corroborates this decision. Second, the insertion of [a] takes place at a certain level of abstraction. In order to know that [a] is to be inserted in *okrúgao* but not in (for example) *mlad-ó*, we must know that the [o] in *okrúgao* derives from a consonant. But this is only possible if the insertion of [a] is defined in terms of the more abstract underlying representation. In other words, just as in the case of the [o] → [u] rule in Polish, the Serbo-Croatian *a*-epenthesis rule does not state a generalization that can be defined over the surface phonetic representations. This point is even more forcefully made by the accent in *okrúgao*. For most words of the predictable accent class, the accent falls on the final vowel. But *okrúgao* is doubly exceptional. The accent has been assigned to the third-last vowel. If the grammar provides an underlying representation along the lines sketched in the above discussion, then this antepenultimate accent – bizarre as it may seem on the surface – is exactly what we expect. Given that the [o] of *okrúgao* derives from [l] and the [a] from ∅, and given that the accent rule applies before the epenthesis and vocalization rules, third-last accent is precisely what the description implies.

(11a,b) summarize the results of the analysis.

(11) a.   rules
           $\overline{V → Ṽ / \_\_\_\ C_0\ \#}$ accent (2)
           ∅ → [a] / C ____   C   #   epenthesis (7)
                               [+ sonor]
           [l] → [o] / ___ #   *l*-vocalization (4b)

      b.   ordering restrictions
           Accent precedes epenthesis.
           Accent precedes *l*-vocalization.
           Epenthesis precedes *l*-vocalization.

In the discussion of the Serbo-Croatian data, we have brought three considerations to bear on the choice of the underlying representation of a phonological alternation: the avoidance of lexical exceptions in rules of neutralization, the naturalness and plausibility of the rules, and the implications that the analysis of one alternation has on the analysis of other alternations. The last point figured in our treatment of both the [l]≈[o] and the [a]≈∅ alternations, when we argued for a particular solution on the basis of its effect on the accent rule.

Both a theoretical and an analytic remark are in order here. Theoretically, each of these three factors is a variation on one general theme: the overall *simplicity* of the rules and representations of the grammar. Lexical exceptions obviously complicate the grammar, because one must record not only the distinctive segments that make up the underlying representation but also the information that the item fails to undergo a rule for which its phonological representation qualifies it. With respect to natural rules, generative phonologists have assumed that an adequate feature system should provide simple characterizations of natural phonological classes and recurrent phonological processes. If we have adopted the correct feature system, then choosing the simpler rule should also choose the more natural rule. Finally, if, in our analysis of alternation A, we refer to alternation B, we are concerned with the simplifying effects of B on A (e.g., by positing that [l] underlies the Serbo-Croatian [l]≈[o] alternation, we can maintain a simple statement of the accent rule). Given that simplicity is the driving force behind the analysis of alternations, one can begin to understand how the rules and representations that underlie the generative approach to alternations could develop in the course of language acquisition – by a learning procedure that is preprogrammed to entertain simple grammars before complex ones.

The descriptive point is that with three separate factors that can potentially be brought to bear on the analysis of a given alternation, we have the possibility of independent confirmation. This is fortunate since our confidence in the analysis is increased to the extent that it successfully passes the test posed by the other factors. If our general descriptive and theoretical framework achieves this result in a significant number of cases, then we may legitimately place some confidence in the analyses that ensue when only one such factor can be applied.

3.2 Feeding and Bleeding

In generative phonology it has become customary to describe the ordering relation between rules in terms of the potential effect (positive or negative) that the application of one rule has on the application of another. To describe this effect, Kiparsky (1968a) introduced the terms *feeding* and *bleeding*.

(12) a. Two rules A and B stand in a potentially feeding relation if the application of A creates new input to B. If B applies, then A is said to *feed* B; if B does not apply, then A and B stand in a *counterfeeding* relation.

  b. Two rules A and B stand in a potentially bleeding relation if the application of A removes inputs to B. If B does not apply, then A is said to *bleed* B; if B does apply, then A and B stand in a *counterbleeding* relation.

$$\begin{bmatrix} -cor \\ -cnt \\ -vc \end{bmatrix} \rightarrow [+s.g.] / \_\_ \#$$

$$\begin{bmatrix} -cor \\ -cnt \\ +vc \end{bmatrix} \rightarrow [+c.g.] / \_\_ \#$$

Pl   Sg.

kæt|s   kæt

bʌg|z   bʌg

bʌsəz   bʌs

bʊšəz

næt+bə   næb

A   [næb]   (næpilsa

B   V → ∅ / __ #

A   [-son] → [-vc] / __ #   næt+mar

      S   Pl   næp

  næp   næbisa

Linguistics Club Colloquium
English Linguistics Forum

THE FORM & FUNCTION
OF SUBJECT-VERB INVERSION
IN ENGLISH

Professor Doo-Shick Kim

English

Gyeongsang National University

Chinju City, Korea

FRIDAY, JANUARY 28, 1994

3:35 P.M.

50 FOLWELL HALL

Feeding relations can be illustrated with an example from Tangale, a Chadic language of Nigeria (Kidda 1985). In the following nominal paradigms, suffixes mark the definite and pronominal possession.

(13)

'N'	loo	bugat	tugat	aduk	kúluk
'the N'	loo-í	bugat-í	tugad-í	aduk-í	kúlug-í
'my N'	loo-nó	bugad-nó	tugad-nó	adug-nó	kúlug-nó
'your N'	loo-gó	bugat-kó	tugad-gó	aduk-kó	kúlug-gó
'her N'	loo-dó	bugat-tó	tugad-dó	aduk-tó	kúlug-dó
	'meat'	'window'	'berry'	'load'	'harp'

-í marks the definite and *-nó* the 1sg. possessive. The 2sg. and 3sg. fem. possessive suffixes show parallel voicing alternations: *-kó*≈*-gó* and *-tó*≈*-dó*. The final obstruent of the noun stem also alternates: *bugat*≈*bugad, tugat*≈*tugad,* and so on. Careful examination of the data reveals no contrast between voiced and voiceless obstruents in the prepausal form, yet the stems do display a voicing contrast before the definite suffix *-í*. The noun stems also contrast before the obstruent-initial 2sg. and 3sg. fem. pronominal suffixes: *bugat-kó* vs. *tugad-gó*. Since *bugat-í* and *tugad-í* are virtual minimal pairs, we must posit an underlying voicing contrast in the final obstruent. The contrast is neutralized to voiceless before pause (the isolation form) and to voiced before the 1sg. suffix *-nó*. While final devoicing is ubiquitous, many languages (e.g., Catalan, Cracow Polish) also voice obstruents before sonorant consonants. We might therefore expect the voicing before *-nó* in Tangale to be an example of this more general phenomenon. This suspicion is confirmed by the fact that the 1pl. pronominal suffix *-mú* and the 3pl. *-wú* also voice a preceding obstruent: *bugat-í, bugad-mú, bugad-wú.* However, Tangale has a large number of words such as *pítlá* 'ant', *basre* 'work' in which a voiceless consonant precedes a sonorant. The voicing rule must be prevented from affecting these forms. An obvious difference between the two cases is that in the former the obstruent and the triggering sonorant belong to different morphemes while in the latter the two consonants are tautomorphemic. We appeal to this difference in the statement of the rule, requiring the focus and the triggering sonorant to span a morpheme boundary (indicated by the bracket "]").

$$(14) \quad [-\text{sonor}] \rightarrow [+\text{voiced}] \: / \: \underline{\quad} \:] \begin{bmatrix} +\text{cons} \\ +\text{sonor} \end{bmatrix}$$

The rule will thus apply to the representation [[bugat] nó] but fail to apply to *pítlá,* since no bracket separates the [t] and [l]. Similar juncture conditions hold in Catalan and Cracow Polish.

Let us turn to the alternation in the suffixal obstruents. It is easy to see that the variation between *-kó* and *-gó* and between *-tó* and *-dó* is determined by the voicing of the stem-final segment: voiceless after a voiceless obstruent and voiced after a voiced segment (consonant or vowel). This alternation differs in one respect: while stem-final consonants underlyingly contrast in voicing, suffixal obstruents never do. Such a stem versus affixal asymmetry in the contrastive use of a distinctive feature is actually quite common (recall Turkish vowel harmony from section 1.5). The suffixal alternations are accounted for with the rule in (15).

(15)   [−sonor] → [αvoiced] / [αvoiced] ⎯⎯ (feature filling)

With the voicing alternations as background, let us consider the noun paradigms in (16).

(16)   wudó   lútu   taga   duka
       wud-í   lút-í   tag-í   duk-í
       wud-nó   lút-nó   tag-nó   duk-nó
       wud-gó   lút-kó   tag-gó   duk-kó
       wud-dó   lút-tó   tag-dó   duk-tó
       'tooth'   'bag'   'shoe'   'salt'

       tuužé   kagá   yáará   ŋúlí
       tuuž-í   kag-í   yáar-í   ŋúl-í
       tuuž-nó   kag-nó   yáar-nó   ŋúl-nó
       tuuž-gó   kag-gó   yáar-gó   ŋúl-gó
       tuuž-dó   kag-dó   yáar-dó   ŋúl-dó
       'horse'   'spoon'   'arm'   'truth'

These nouns are composed of two syllables in the isolation form but lack their final vowel in the presuffixal contexts. The vowel≈∅ alternation must be characterized as deletion instead of insertion. While there are languages (e.g., the Dravidian languages of India) that insert vowels at the end of words that would otherwise end in a consonant, such an analysis is not viable for Tangale, where many words end in a consonant. Furthermore, it is not possible to predict the quality of the vowel that alternates with ∅ in (16); this is memorized information that must be included in the lexical representation of the noun stem. Thus, a rule is needed to elide the stem-final vowel when some phonological material follows. This rule is expressed in (17).

(17)   V → ∅ / ⎯⎯] X

Elision is another rule that applies at a boundary; vowels that are not the final segment of a stem are stable in Tangale.

Vowel elision pervades Tangale phonological structure and activates a number of other alternations. Comparison of forms such as *wud-gó* and *lút-kó* shows that the rule of progressive voice assimilation (15) will account for the suffixal alternations displayed by the data in (16). However, we must ensure that the voicing assimilation rule applies to the representation that results from application of elision. It is only by deletion of the stem-final vowels of *wudó* and *lútu* that the suffixal consonants come to stand immediately after the root consonants. In this case elision creates an input to the progressive assimilation rule. The two rules thus stand in a feeding relation. But as shown by *lút-nó* from [lútu-nó], elision stands in the inverse, counterfeeding relation with respect to regressive assimilation (14). Here application of elision creates a potential input to sonorant voicing, but the latter rule systematically fails to apply in these cases. In other words, "counterfeed" means "fails to feed." The derivations in (18) illustrate the proper sequencing of the rules; G denotes a consonant that is [0 voiced].

(18) | [wudó]Gó | [lútu]Gó | [lútu]nó | UR |
|---|---|---|---|
| ——— | ——— | ——— | regressive voicing (14) |
| wud Gó | lút Gó | lút nó | elision (17) |
| wud gó | lút kó | ——— | progressive voicing (15) |

The bleeding relation between a pair of rules is well illustrated using data from Bright's (1957) description of the American Indian language Karok. The alternation between [s] and [š] evident in (19a) may be accounted for by the rule (19b).

(19)   a.

imperative	1sg.	3sg.	
pasip	ni-pasip	ʔu-pasip	'shoot'
kifnuk	ni-kifnuk	ʔu-kifnuk	'stoop'
si:tva	ni-ši:tva	ʔu-si:tva	'steal'
suprih	ni-šuprih	ʔu-suprih	'measure'
ʔaktuv	ni-ʔaktuv	ʔu-ʔaktuv	'pluck at'

   b.   [s] → [š] / [i] ——

   c.

ʔaxyar	ni-xyar	ʔu-xyar	'fill'
ʔiškak	ni-škak	ʔu-skak	'jump'
ʔuksup	ni-kšup	ʔu-ksup	'point'
ʔikšah	ni-kšah	ʔu-ksah	'laugh'

The data in (19c) show two additional rules: one truncates the second of two successive vowels, while the other helps to maintain the Karok requirement that every word begin with a consonant by supplying vowel-initial stems with a glottal stop. Finally, forms such as *ni-kšup* and *ni-kšah* show that palatalization may cross a consonant. The required rules are stated in (20).

(20)   a.   V → ∅ / V ——
   b.   ∅ → ʔ / # —— V
   c.   [s] → [š] / [i] (C) ——

The derivation in (21) of *ʔu-skak* reveals a bleeding relation between truncation and palatalization. The initial representation satisfies the palatalization rule since it contains an [is] substring. Application of truncation removes the [i] and thus deprives the palatalization rule of a potential input. Truncation thus bleeds palatalization.

(21) | /# ʔu-iskak #/ | /#ni-uksup#/ | UR |
|---|---|---|
| ʔu-skak | ni-ksup | truncation (20a) |
| ——— | ni-kšup | palatalization (20b) |

But in the derivation of *ni-kšup* (21) truncation feeds palatalization. The underlying representation does not satisfy the palatalization rule, because the vowel preceding the [s] is [u], not [i]. By truncating the [u], we bring the [i] into the local environment of the [s] and thus create an input to palatalization. The derivations in (21) reveal the important point that feeding and bleeding are derivative notions that depend on the ordering relation between the rules. Given one representation, ordering A before B may result in feeding; but given another, the side effect is bleeding.

Finally, to illustrate counterbleeding, let us return to the Icelandic rules of glide deletion and epenthesis discussed in section 2.7.

(22) a. nom.sg.   lyf-ur
       acc.sg.   lyf
       gen.sg.   lyf-s
       dat.pl.   lyfj-um
       gen.pl.   lyfj-a
                 'medicine'

    b. /#lyfj-r#/   UR
       lyf-r   glide deletion
       lyf-ur   epenthesis

Recall from the paradigm in (22a) that a C*j* cluster loses its glide before a consonant or word boundary but preserves it before a vowel. The only exception is the nom.sg. suffix -*ur*. But we argued that this suffix is underlyingly [-r] and that its vowel arises from epenthesis in the derivation (22b). By supplying the suffix with a vowel, we potentially remove an input to the glide deletion process. Icelandic does not in fact exercise this option, a point we explained by ordering epenthesis after glide deletion. In this case the rules of epenthesis and glide deletion stand in a counterbleeding relation; that is, one rule fails to bleed the other.

The concepts of feeding and bleeding were introduced by Paul Kiparsky (1968a) in his early work on language change. Kiparsky had corroborated with additional examples the important discovery of Halle (1962) that two dialects or two stages in the historical development of a language could have the same underlying representations and the same rules, but differ simply in virtue of the ordering of the rules – a new category of linguistic change. On the basis of the small number of cases known at the time, the diachronic change in the ordering relation seemed to proceed from a counterfeeding to feeding relation or from a bleeding to counterbleeding one. Since feeding and counterbleeding are derivations where both rules A and B apply, Kiparsky conjectured that maximal utilization of the rules was a natural state toward which grammars would gravitate in historical evolution.

Subsequent discovery of additional rule order changes as well as the increasing number of phonologies described in terms of ordered rules led Kiparsky (1971) to modify the definition of the unmarked ordering relation to include feeding and bleeding but exclude counterbleeding. In the feeding and bleeding ordering relations, rule B is *transparent* in the sense that it states a generalization that holds over the phonetic representation. This point is most easily seen in the Karok example. At the phonetic level, we never find [s] after [i]; and where we might expect such a string to result from morpheme concatenation, we find [š] instead.

By ordering palatalization after truncation (feeding), this transparent generalization (i.e., [š] after [i]) is maintained. An [i] that comes to stand before [s] via truncation results in palatalization: underlying [ni-uksup] emerges as *ni-kšup*. Had palatalization been ordered before truncation (i.e., had it been defined on the underlying representation), then an [i] that came to stand next to [s] by virtue of truncation would not induce palatalization. In this case the phonetic level would contain [i(C)s] substrings that would appear to violate the palatalization rule. Under such a counterfeeding relation, the palatalization rule would be *opaque*.

Bleeding and counterbleeding induce the same transparent versus opaque distinction. The [i] that triggers Karok palatalization is always present in the phonetic representation. An [i] that is adjacent to [s] in the underlying representation but then deleted by the truncation rule does not induce palatalization. Underlying [ʔu-iskak] is realized as *ʔu-skak* (bleeding), not as *ʔu-škak* (counterbleeding). Had *ʔu-škak* been the correct surface form, the palatalization rule would be rendered opaque in the sense that the triggering [i] is not present in the surface phonetic representation.

This line of thought led to the *thesis of rule transparency:* the ordering of rules will tend toward a relation that maximizes the transparency of the rules involved. The transparency thesis had an obvious learnability implication. Transparent rules were considered easier to learn since all of the information needed for the formulation of the rule is present in the phonetic representation. Kisseberth (1973a) raised significant objections to the transparency thesis. If opaque rules are marked, why are they so often found in phonological structure? He argued that opaque relations can also play a functional role in helping to preserve underlying phonological contrasts. For example, in the case of the *writer-rider* contrast, the flapping rule neutralizes the underlying voicing contrast. Although opaque from the phonetic surface, application of lengthening in *rider* helps to signal that a voiced stop follows in the underlying representation. Perhaps such *clues* aid in the recovery of the underlying representation during language acquisition and language processing.

Some support for this point of view is provided by the rule of Canadian Raising. In many Canadian English dialects, the low vowel nucleus in the [ay] and [aw] diphthongs raises before voiceless consonants. Chambers (1973) cites the data in (23). This rule is also responsible for such alternations as *kn*[ʌy]*f*≈*kn*[ay]*ves* and *h*[ʌw]*s*≈*h*[aw]*ses,* where the root vowel alternates in response to the rule that voices the final root consonant in the plural.

(23)   [ʌy]   [ʌw]
    type
    tight   tout
    tyke   south
    rife   mouse
    rice   couch

Many of these Canadian dialects also have a rule neutralizing the intervocalic [t]-[d] contrast (apparently in favor of [d] instead of a flap). In these dialects *metal* and *medal* are homophonous. In the 1940s Joos (1942) reported two dialects with respect to the interaction between the raising and voicing neutralization processes. Dialect A distinguishes *writer* and *rider,* while in dialect B they are homophonous. In dialect B the rules apply in the transparent, bleeding order; in dialect A they apply in the opaque, counterbleeding fashion.

(24) <u>dialect A</u>

/#rayt#/	/#rayd#/	/#rayt-ər#/	/#rayd-ər#/	UR
rʌyt	——	rʌytər	————	Canadian Raising
——	——	rʌydər	————	voicing neutralization

<u>dialect B</u>

/#rayt#/	/#rayd#/	/#rayt-ər#/	/#rayd-ər#/	UR
——	——	raydər	————	voicing neutralization
rʌyt	——	————	————	Canadian Raising

According to Chambers (1973), dialect B has disappeared from contemporary speech, while "dialect A is ubiquitous throughout heartland Canada." In this case the rule interaction that gives rise to phonetic transparency has been eliminated in favor of grammatical opacity. The Canadian data thus suggest that there is nothing particularly unnatural or unstable in the opaque rule interaction. (It should be noted that the very existence of dialect B has been called into question by Kaye (1990c).)

3.3   Intermediate Representations

The dialect difference detected by Joos suggests that grammars can differ solely in the ordering of their rules. This has naturally led to the view that the phonetic representation is computed from the phonological representation by an ordered sequence of rules with various intermediate stages. However, the examples that we have seen so far would be compatible with an alternative view that eliminates the notion of derivation by granting equal status to the phonological and the phonetic representations. Given an ordering restriction "A precedes B," rule A could be interpreted as stating a generalization that holds over information in the underlying phonological representation and rule B could be viewed as stating a generalization that holds over the phonetic representation. An unordered rule holds of both representations. These two views of rule ordering differ with respect to whether or not intermediate stages need to be invoked in the phonological derivation. On the first view, we would not be surprised to discover situations in which rule A precedes rule B while rule B must precede another rule C – indeed, under this view we would be surprised if these cases did not arise. The alternative claims that such cases are impossible.

Canadian Raising furnishes crucial data bearing on this point. Like other varieties of English, the Canadian dialect has the rule that voices stem-final fricatives before the plural suffix in a lexically defined set of cases: *wolf-wolves, wreath-wrea*[ð]*es.* Chambers (1973) reports that the root vowel in the forms in (25) alternates in tandem with the voicing of the consonant.

(25) house   [hʌws]   mouth   [mʌwθ]
      houses   [hawzəz]   mouths   [mawð̃z]
      wife   [wʌyf]   knife   [nʌyf]
      wives   [wayvz]   knives   [nayvz]

In these cases the rule voicing the stem-final consonant must precede the rule raising the diphthongal nucleus. Thus, Canadian Raising cannot be formulated to apply solely to the underlying representations of the language, lest an unacceptable plural such as *w[ʌy]ves* be generated. But the *writer-rider* distinction discussed earlier shows that the rule cannot be defined exclusively on the phonetic representation either. Instead, it must operate at a point in the grammar that lies between these two different voicing rules.

Another example requiring reference to intermediate stages of representation comes from Kiamu (Marshad 1982), a Bantu language of Kenya. The verbal paradigms in (26a) show that the high vowels of the infinitive prefix *ku-*, the object prefix *i-*, and the agentive *mu-* devocalize by the process in (26b). Additional rules convert the agentive [mu-] to syllabic [m̩-] through syncope of [u] before a consonant and syllabification of the resultant consonant cluster: [mu+tunda] → [m+tunda] → [m̩+tunda]. Finally, [wo] simplifies to [o] via absorption of the glide: [ku+oweka] → [kw+oweka] → [k+oweka].

(26) a.	infinitive	infinitive-'it'	agentive
kutunda	kuitunda	m̩tunda	'pick'
kubana	kuibana	m̩bana	'squeeze'
kuzaña	kuizaña	m̩zaña	'spell'
kufunua	kuifunua	m̩funua	'open'
kuvaa	kuivaa	m̩vaa	'wear'
kwandika	kuyandika	mwandika	'write'
kweneza	kuyeneza	mweneza	'spread'
kuunda	kuiunda	muunda	'model'
kuiza	kuiiza	muiza	'refuse'
koweka	kuyoweka	moweka	'soak'

      b. [i,u] → [y,w] / _____ V
                            [−high]

With the devocalization rule as background, consider the nominal paradigms in (27).

(27) | class 3 (sg.) | class 4 (pl.) | |
      | --- | --- | --- |
      | m̩gomba | migomba | 'banana plant' |
      | m̩rašo | mirašo | 'small goat' |
      | m̩biringani | mibiringani | 'eggplant' |
      | mwavuli | ñavuli | 'umbrella' |
      | mwezi | ñezi | 'month' |
      | moši | ñoši | 'smoke' |
      | muuwa | miuwa | 'flowering plant' |
      | mui | mii | 'town' |

class 7 (sg.)	class 8 (pl.)	
kiti	ziti	'chair'
kibuzi	zibuzi	'small goat'
kisu	zisu	'knife'
čango	zango	'cloth hanger'
čembe	zembe	'arrow'
čowa	zowa	'ringworm'
kiuno	ziuno	'waist'
kiini	ziini	'egg yolk'

We see that the prefixes [mi-] and [ki-] alternate with [ñ-] and [č-], respectively. The palatal alternants occur when the stem begins with a nonhigh vowel. Since this is precisely the context in which devocalization turns [i] to [y], and since [y] is the premier palatalizer, it is natural to postulate that Kiamu has the rules shown in (28a) ordered after devocalization. A final rule (28b) deleting postconsonantal jod completes the derivations of such forms as *č-ango* and *ñ-avuli* (28c).

(28) a. [m] → [ñ] / ___ [y]
     [k] → [č] / ___ [y]

   b. [y] → ∅ / C ___

   c. /#ki-ango#/   /#mi-avuli#/   UR
      ky-ango   my-avuli   devocalization (26b)
      čy-ango   ñy-avuli   palatalization (28a)
      č-ango   ñ-avuli   jod deletion (28b)

If palatalization is not activated by the output of devocalization and we are instead required to define the environments for the rules in (28a,b) on the underlying representation, then we will have to recompute inside the palatalization rules themselves precisely the contexts in which [y] appears. For the [m]≈[ñ] alternation, the rule in (29) will do the job.

(29) [m] → [ñ] / ___ i   V
                    [−high]

However, it should be clear that a grammar incorporating (29) is inadequate on both descriptive and theoretical grounds. Descriptively, it is a pastiche that repeats the environment of devocalization. When one phonological rule repeats the information contained in another rule – especially if the information is complex – one immediately suspects that a descriptive generalization is being missed. Theoretically, it is unlikely that a rule such as (29) will be found in another language unless like Kiamu that language has an additional rule generating a palatalizing element (such as [y]) in the same context. To state the point differently, while palatalization before a high front vocalic element such as [y] or [i] is natural, a palatalization rule such as (29) that looks beyond the immediately adjacent segment to the following vocalic context is not natural. A theory that strives for natural rules would not consider (29) a potential member of the grammar.

Thus, the palatalization rules must be defined on the output of devocalization. But note that the triggering glide does not appear on the phonetic surface. It is deleted by a rule such as (28b) – a rule that clearly must follow palatalization. Jointly, the ordering restrictions "palatalization precedes glide deletion" and "devocalization precedes palatalization" furnish the two premises of the syllogism that implies an intermediate level of representation. The Kiamu palatalization rules crucially refer to information (the $[k+y]$ and $[m+y]$ strings) that appears neither in the underlying nor in the surface representation. An intermediate stage must be computed.

Before concluding this discussion, we should note that the arguments from Canadian Raising and Kiamu palatalization for intermediate representations are not as strong as they might at first appear. For the latter, we might view Kiamu *ñavuli* as arising from [my-avuli] through a merger of the palatal point of articulation of the [y] with the preceding nasal. If so, then in a sense still to be made precise (see section 4.3), the palatal glide is still present in the surface representation – it is inside the nasal [ñ]. Thus, appeal to an intermediate stage may not be required in this case. As for the Canadian English example, the voicing rule operative in the plural *w[ʌy]ves* differs in two important respects from the one involved in *writer*. First, it applies to a lexically restricted class of stems; second, it is triggered by a limited set of suffixes (e.g., *roof, rooves,* but *roofing*). The voicing of intervocalic [t] takes place regardless of the lexical and the grammatical context. When we consider the theory of Lexical Phonology in chapter 5, we will see that the sequencing of the plural voicing rule and Canadian Raising can be predicted from the architecture of the grammar as a whole and thus may not have to be stipulated separately for this pair of rules. In general, more enriched representations and a more articulated conception of the grammar's internal architecture have taken over much of the explanatory burden that was borne by the rules in earlier generative analyses. For example, Goldsmith (1990) sketches a phonological model with just three levels of representation, corresponding very roughly to the morphophonemic, phonemic, and phonetic levels of American Structuralism. It remains to be seen whether the more complex cases of ordered rules can be naturally expressed in these more restrictive models without loss of descriptive generalization. See Bromberger and Halle 1989 and Goldsmith 1993 for further discussion.

3.4 Multiple Alternation

The preceding sections have illustrated the analysis of alternations – a primary source of evidence for phonological rules. Given that [x] alternates with [y], the decision whether [x] or [y] underlies the alternation is in general resolved by appeal to the criteria of *predictability* and the *naturalness* of the corresponding rules – reflections of a more general criterion of simplicity. We have seen that it is not uncommon for a given morpheme to participate in several alternations simultaneously. In most of the examples of such multiple alternation examined so far, the morpheme alternant containing the underlying segment for one alternation has also contained the underlying segment for the other alternations. For example, the Polish stem for 'cart' *vus* (sg.), *vozi* (pl.) manifests both the [o]≈[u] alternation and the final devoicing alternation. Earlier discussion (section 2.7) indicated that [o] underlies the first alternation and voiced [z] the second. The result of these two analytic steps is the underlying representation [voz]. And in fact it is precisely this representation that surfaces in the plural. Similarly, the Serbo-Croatian stem *okrúgao* participates in the [a]≈∅ and the [l]≈[o] alternations; we have seen that the [a] is best treated as inserted and the [o] as derived from [l], and thus that the underlying form is [okrugl]. But this representation is identical to the form of the stem that surfaces in the feminine *okrugl-á*. These examples rather naturally lead to the following conjecture.

(30)   The segments underlying a lexical item with multiple alternants will emerge simultaneously in at least one of the item's phonetic realizations – the *basic alternant*.

If true, this conjecture simplifies the task of arriving at the underlying representation – an obviously welcome result. For example, given that *okrugao* exhibits two alternations, there are four possible choices among the [a]≈∅ and [l]≈[o] terms with respect to the appropriate underlying form. But the stem has only two paradigmatic alternants: [okrugao] and [okrugl]. Given (30), only two analytic options need to be considered. In more complex cases, the doctrine of the basic alternant would do more work for us.

However, if we accept the general approach to phonological structure developed so far, we should be suspicious of a condition such as (30). On this approach, the underlying representation depends solely on the simplicity and the naturalness of the corresponding rules. It would be quite surprising if application of the phonological rules were suspended to respect such a condition. To see this point, consider the reduction of unstressed vowels in English. Disyllabic stems such as *atom* ([ǽ]t[ə]m), *atomic* ([ə]t[á]mic) or *metal* (m[έ]t[ə]l), *metallic* (m[ə]t[ǽ]lic) show an unstressed vowel in each of their alternants and hence always contain an ambiguous schwa. In order to respect the basic alternant thesis, vowel reduction would have to be suspended in one of the alternants. No such suspension is found in English – nor is it typically found in other languages that reduce vowels. It would complicate the simple, general rule "reduce unstressed vowels." But what about cases in which the multiple alternation is the product of two (or more) distinct rules? In this case, might one rule be held off in order to satisfy (30)? In this section we will examine a few cases bearing on this question.

3.4.1   The Basic Alternant: A Counterexample

Our first example comes from Chukchee, a language of Eastern Siberia (Krause 1979, Kenstowicz 1979, 1986a). The data in (31) show nouns in the absolute singular and plural as well as the ergative case. The noun stems in (31a) end in a coronal consonant; those in (31b) end underlyingly in a vowel.

(31)   abs.sg.   abs.pl.   erg.
   a.   eŋer   eŋer-ti   eŋer-e   'star'
         tintin   tintin-ti   tintin-e   'ice'
         uul   uul-ti   uul-e   'chisel'
         ococ   ococ-te   ococ-a   'leader'
         qʔawal   qʔawal-te   qʔawal-a   'corner'

   b.   ŋileq   ŋileqe-t   ŋileqe-te   'match'
         milut   milute-t   milute-te   'rabbit'
         ajkol   ajkola-t   ajkola-ta   'bed'
         uqqem   uqqeme-t   uqqeme-te   'dish'
         uwequc   uwequci-t   uwequci-te   'husband'

The contrast between consonant-final and vowel-final stems is crucial for the allomorphy exhibited by the ergative suffix, which loses its initial consonant after a stem ending in a consonant. (*Allomorphy* is an alternation exhibited by a lexically restricted class of elements. While the class of items undergoing a rule of allomorphy is lexically restricted, the context can often be defined in general phonological terms. For example, the indefinite *an* has the allomorph *a* before a consonant: *an apple* vs. *a pear*.) This rule is stated informally in (32).

(32)   [te] → [e] / C ____

The final vowel of the stem is systematically missing in the absolute singular, suggesting the apocope rule (33). (*Apocope* refers to the deletion of word-final vowels.)

(33)   V → Ø / ____ #

The apocope rule also appears to delete the vowel of the plural suffix in (31b); but it must be prevented from applying to plurals from (31a) such as *eŋer-ti*. Since no Chukchee word may end in a consonant cluster, we might propose that application of the rule is blocked if it would create an illicit word-final consonant cluster. While attractive, this hypothesis runs afoul of the data in (34), where the vowel of the plural suffix does delete. However, the language still satisfies the ban on final consonant clusters by inserting schwa.

(34)   abs.sg.   abs.pl.   erg.
       rʔew   rʔew-ət   rʔew-e   'whale'
       wejem   wejem-ət   wejem-e   'river'
       watap   watap-ət   watap-a   'moss'
       tig   tig-ət   tig-e   'ski'
       rileq   rileq-ət   rileq-e   'spine'

Notice that the stems in (31a) all end in a coronal consonant while those in (34) end in noncoronals. We thus assume that the apocope process is blocked when the final vowel is preceded by a cluster of coronal consonants. Otherwise, it applies generally. (The vowel of the ergative suffix must be exempted from apocope. In fact, all inflectional case suffixes systematically fail to apocopate; see Krause 1979 for discussion.) The ban on final clusters is enforced by the epenthesis rule stated in (35).

(35) $\emptyset \rightarrow [\partial]$ / C ___ C#

The word *wejem-ət* 'rivers' thus receives the derivation in (36).

(36)   /#wejem-ti#/   UR
            wejem-t   apocope (33)
            wejem-ət   epenthesis (35)

In sum, we assume the rules in (32), (33), and (35) with the restrictions that (33) does not affect case suffixes and that it fails to apply after a cluster of coronal consonants.

With this analysis as background, consider the nouns in (37).

(37) | abs.sg. | abs.pl. | erg. | |
| --- | --- | --- | --- |
| imət | imti-t | imti-te | 'load' |
| ekək | ekke-t | ekke-te | 'son' |
| ceŋəl | cenle-t | cenle-te | 'box' |
| loŋəl | lonla-t | lonla-ta | 'walrus fat' |
| wiŋər | winri-t | winri-te | 'hoe' |

These stems end in an underlying VCCV sequence. Being vowel-final, they allow the consonant of the ergative suffix [-te] to escape deletion and permit the vowel of the plural suffix [-ti] to apocopate without creating a cluster. However, in the absolute singular, deletion of the final vowel of the stem does lead to a consonant cluster, which is broken by schwa. The point we are building up to is the proper underlying representation for the forms in (37) that show the [ŋ]≈[n] alternation. There are three reasons to suppose that [ŋ] underlies this alternation. First, with this underlying representation, the change to [n] can be characterized as the very natural process of nasal assimilation of the coronal point of articulation of the following consonant. Second, a rule assimilating [ŋ] to the point of articulation of a following consonant is needed anyway in Chukchee for other alternations not discussed here. Finally, on grounds internal to the description of Chukchee, if [n] were to underlie the alternation, then we would fail to explain why apocope applies to [cenle], since the deleting vowel would be preceded by a cluster of coronal consonants, which otherwise inhibit the loss of final vowels.

There is thus good reason to believe that the underlying representations are [ceŋle], [wiŋri], and [loŋla]. But notice that these representations never surface directly in Chukchee. If the final vowel fails to apocopate, then the velar nasal obligatorily assimilates to the following coronal. And if the final vowel does delete, then an inorganic schwa breaks up the final cluster, allowing the underlying [ŋ] to surface. The derivations in (38) illustrate this point.

(38)	/#ceŋle#/	/#ceŋle-ti#/	/#ceŋle-te#/	UR
	inappl.	inappl.	inappl.	allomorphy (32)
	ceŋl	ceŋle-t	inappl.	apocope (33)
	ceŋəl	inappl.	inappl.	epenthesis (35)
	inappl.	cenle-t	cenle-te	ŋ-assimilation

A theory that analyzes alternations in terms of phonological naturalness and plausibility thus treats [ŋ] as underlying and the schwa as inserted in the [ceŋəl]≈[cenle] multiple alternation. These analyses are reached independently of each other. The result is that sometimes an underlying representation takes shape that never surfaces directly. This leads to complexity and abstractness and thus is undesirable if one believes that the phonological structure is induced from the phonetic surface by general analytic procedures. From such a viewpoint, a requirement that the underlying representation be identical with one of its alternants makes sense as a way of limiting the hypothesis space. But if underlying representations are selected in order to simplify the individual rules and representations of the grammar, then the fact that this representation never surfaces directly should come as no particular surprise.

3.4.2 Abstract Underlying Representations

In this section we examine data from the Yawelmani dialect of Yokuts, an American Indian language of California, that bear directly on the thesis of the basic alternant. These data have played a prominent role in generative phonology, where they were discussed first by Kuroda (1967), later by Kisseberth (1969) and Kenstowicz and Kisseberth (1977, 1979), and then by Archangeli (1984, 1991). All these writers have relied on the original description of the language by Stanley Newman (1944).

As shown in (39), five short vowels and three long vowels are found in Yawelmani phonetic representations. (Our discussion abstracts away from a general rule that contracts the diphthongs [iy] and [uw] to [i:] and [u:] in closed syllables; see Kenstowicz and Kisseberth 1979 for details.)

(39)	short vowels		long vowels	
	i	u		
	(e)	o	e:	o:
	a			a:

The short nonhigh front vowel is shown in parentheses because it is a predictable variant of the underlying long [e:] and arises from a vowel-shortening process to be discussed momentarily.

Yawelmani: Some Basic Rules

Three vocalic alternations pervade Yawelmani phonological structure: vowel harmony, vowel shortening, and epenthesis. We will look at each in turn. The paradigms in (40) illustrate the fact that virtually all suffixes exhibit two variants as a function of the rounding of the root vowel. Suffixes such as the nonfuture [hin] and gerundive [mi] have the alternants [hun] and [mu] when the preceding root contains [u], while the dubitative and participative suffixes [al] and [xa] have the variants [ol] and [xo] when an [o] precedes.

(40)　　xat-hin　　xat-mi　　xat-al　　xat-xa
　　　　bok-hin　　bok-mi　　dub-al　　giy-xa
　　　　xil-hin　　xil-mi　　xil-al　　dub-xa
　　　　dub-hun　　dub-mu　　koʔ-ol　　bok-xo

　　　　[xat] 'eat', [bok] 'find', [xil] 'tangle', [dub] 'lead by hand', [giy] 'touch', [koʔ] 'throw'

The most natural analysis posits a rule of vowel harmony that extends [+round] from one vowel to the next, but only when the two vowels have the same value for the feature [high].

(41)　　　　V　　　　　　　　V　　C$_0$ ____
　　　[αhigh] → [+round] / $\begin{bmatrix} αhigh \\ +round \end{bmatrix}$

The paradigm in (42a) shows two suffixes (the indirect [sit] and nonfuture [hin]) harmonizing to the root vowel in *tul-sut-hun* 'burns for'.

(42)　a.　max-sit-hin　　b.　bok-ko
　　　　　koʔ-sit-hin　　　　bok-sit-ka
　　　　　tul-sut-hun

　　　　[max] 'procure', [koʔ] 'throw', [tul] 'burn', [bok] 'find'

There are two possible interpretations of this multiple harmony. Either each suffix harmonizes directly with the root vowel or the harmony is broken down into a series of steps such that the root first changes the suffix [sit] to [sut], which then in turn passes on the rounding to the next suffix [hin]. The paradigm in (42b) supports the second interpretation. Here the imperative suffix [ka] harmonizes to [ko] when immediately preceded by the root [bok]. But when [sit] intervenes, the imperative suffix may not change to [ko]. This point is explained if harmony is determined by the immediately preceding vowel. Since [sit] has a high vowel, the "same-height" requirement on harmony is not satisfied in [bok-sit-ka]. But if all vowels harmonize directly with the root vowel, then we incorrectly predict *bok-sit-ko*, since the nature of the intervening vowels should not matter.

　　A vowel-shortening rule underlies the alternation in length exhibited by the stems in (43a).

(43)　a.　future　　　　dubitative　　imperative　　nonfuture
　　　　　wo:n-en　　　wo:n-ol　　　won-ko　　　won-hin　　　'hide'
　　　　　do:s-en　　　do:s-ol　　　dos-ko　　　dos-hin　　　'report'
　　　　　la:n-en　　　la:n-al　　　lan-ka　　　lan-hin　　　'hear'
　　　　　me:k-en　　　me:k-al　　　mek-ka　　　mek-hin　　　'swallow'

　　　b.　V: → V / ____ CC

The root vowel is long when the suffix begins with a vowel, but is systematically shortened when the suffix begins with a consonant. These roots contrast with those in (40), which have a constant CVC shape. By the logic of avoiding lexical exceptions, we must posit the CV:C shape as basic for (43) and invoke a rule to shorten a long vowel when two consonants follow. Choice of the short-vowel alternant CVC as underlying would fail to distinguish this class of roots from the nonalternating roots of (40) and thus would require a division of the roots into two arbitrary lexical classes. No such division is necessary if the CV:C alternant is underlying. The required shortening rule is stated in (43b). Shortening vowels before two consonants is a very common process. Indeed, as we will see later, it is what ultimately underlies the vowel quality alternation in English *deep* vs. *dep-th*.

Finally, epenthesis underlies the [i]≈∅ alternation found in the verbs of (44).

(44)

future	dubitative	gerundive	nonfuture	
paʔt-en	paʔt-al	paʔit-mi	paʔit-hin	'fight'
lihm-en	lihm-al	lihim-mi	lihim-hin	'run'
logw-en	logw-ol	logiw-mi	logiw-hin	'pulverize'
ʔugn-on	ʔugn-al	ʔugun-mu	ʔugun-hun	'drink'

These stems show the shape CVCC before vowel-initial suffixes but CVC*i*C before consonant-initial ones. While we could posit a rule of syncope that converts CVCVC-V to CVCC-V, we will treat the vowel as inserted instead. The reasoning behind this move is as follows. We have seen that suffixes contrast for vowel height. If CVCVC were the underlying shape, we would, other things being equal, expect to find stems whose second vowel is nonhigh ([o] or [a] depending on the rounding of the first vowel). However, such disyllabic stems are systematically missing. This gap is explained if we say that underlyingly Yawelmani stems are essentially monosyllabic and thus allow just one vowel phoneme. The CVCVC shape arises from a rule of epenthesis inserting an [i] in the context C _____ CC in order to break up clusters of three consonants. In this respect, Yawelmani resembles many other languages that avoid clusters of three successive consonants. If we accept this interpretation of the [i]≈∅ alternation, then the epenthesis rule must be ordered before harmony, because the epenthetic vowel harmonizes when preceded by a [u]. *ʔugun-hun* thus receives the derivation in (45a).

(45) a. /#ʔugn-hin#/   b. /#logw-xa#/   UR
         ʔugin-hin   logiw-xa   epenthesis
         ʔugun-hun   ————   harmony (41)

By ordering epenthesis before harmony, we make an interesting prediction about the pronunciation of a C*o*CC stem plus a consonant-initial suffix containing a nonhigh vowel. If epenthesis precedes harmony, and if harmony is dependent on the immediately preceding vowel, then [Ca] suffixes should fail to harmonize when added to [CoCC] roots, because the intervening epenthetic vowel will have the opposite value for the feature [high]. This prediction is confirmed by a form such as *logiw-xa* 'let's pulverize'. It receives the derivation in (45b) in which epenthesis bleeds harmony.

We have not yet determined the ordering relation between epenthesis and vowel shortening. The data in (46) furnish the needed evidence.

(46)

	dubitative	gerundive/ nonfuture	
	sonl-ol	so:nil-mi	'put on the back'
	?aml-al	?a:mil-hin	'help'
	moyn-ol	mo:yin-mi	'get tired'
	salk-al	sa:lik-hin	'wake up'

These stems participate in each of the three Yawelmani alternations we have discussed. When they contain a round vowel, they initiate harmony. They also show the alternation between long and short vowels: a long vowel appears when just a single consonant follows, while the corresponding short vowel occurs before two consonants. Finally, these stems participate in the [i]≈∅ alternation: the CVCC shape appears when the suffix begins with a vowel, while the CV:CiC alternant arises when the suffix begins with a consonant. We argued earlier that the long vowel underlies the long-short alternation, and that ∅ must underlie the [i]≈∅ alternation. Consequently, the most natural underlying representations have the canonical shape [CV:CC]. We obtain the correct derivations with the rules already at our disposal by simply ordering epenthesis prior to shortening. (47) shows how *sonl-ol* and *so:nil-hin* are derived.

(47)

/#so:nl-al#/	/#so:nl-hin #/	UR
————	so:nil-hin	epenthesis
so:nl-ol	————	harmony (41)
sonl-ol	————	shortening (43b)

Epenthesis bleeds the shortening rule by breaking up the [V:CCC] string into [V:CiCC].

This analysis is precluded by a theory requiring that the underlying representation be identical with one of its surface alternants. The postulated [CV:CC] shape never emerges directly. When followed by a vowel-initial suffix, the long vowel shortens to yield CVCC. But when a consonant-initial suffix follows, the epenthetic vowel is inserted. In order to satisfy the thesis of the basic alternant (30), either CVCC or CV:CiC would have to be postulated as underlying. But either of these representations is a serious compromise that leads to a loss of generalization. If we start with CVCC, then the rule generating the long vowel will have many lexical exceptions: all the stems like those in (40) with a constant short vowel. If CV:CiC is basic, then a rule of syncope is needed to delete [i] in the set of contexts that exactly complement the range of environments where another rule inserts [i]. A grammar that seeks simple rules and simple representations must postulate [CV:CC] – in direct violation of the basic alternant requirement.

The Yawelmani data and the parallel example from Chukchee suggest that the "basic alternant" conjecture is too strong. We must allow the underlying representation to be pieced together on the basis of an independent analysis of each of the alternations it participates in.

Absolute Neutralization

A weaker constraint – but one that is compatible with all of the data discussed so far – is stated in (48). It simply requires that each segment in the underlying representation emerge in some phonetic alternant.

(48)   Each segment in the underlying representation must appear in some phonetic realization of the morpheme.

(48) is a corollary to the procedure that resolves any alternation [x]≈[y] with an underlying [x] or an underlying [y]. It prohibits positing some [z] that is phonologically distinct from both [x] and [y] as underlying the alternation. However, a convincing case can be made for precisely this state of affairs in Yawelmani. Recall that under our interpretation of the vowel harmony, the [o] of a stem rounds nonhigh suffixal vowels but leaves high suffixal vowels unchanged. While a large number of roots behave this way, an equally large number do not. Examples of each type appear in (49).

(49)   do:s-ol   sonl-ol   co:m-al   wo?y-al
       dos-hin   so:nil-hin   com-hun   wo:?uy-hun

     [do:s] 'report', [so:nl] 'pack on the back', [co:m] 'destroy', [wo:?y] 'fall asleep'

The "irregular" roots [co:m] and [wo:?y] are not simply exceptions to harmony. They do trigger the rule. But perversely so: only when the suffix contains a high vowel. A key to understanding this perplexing behavior lies in the observation that such irregular roots are drawn exclusively from the CV:C and CV:CC root shapes. They do not populate the CVC or CVCC classes. Recall the Yawelmani vowel inventory, which is repeated in slightly altered form in (50). There are four phonologically distinct short vowels and four phonologically distinct long vowels: [e:], [a:], and the two kinds of [o:].

(50) | short vowels | | long vowels | |
|---|---|---|---|
| i | u | | |
| o | | e: | o:, o:* |
| a | | | a: |

Suppose that the irregular [o:*] derives from [u:]. Two immediate consequences ensue. First, we are able to explain why this vowel harmonizes high suffixal vowels and fails to harmonize nonhigh ones. At the point where harmony applies, it bears the feature [+high]. Second, the inventory of vowels becomes more symmetric. It now contains long and short vowels for each of the three back vowel qualities. In fact, we can make the system completely symmetric if we also derive [e:] from [i:], as depicted in (51a).

(51)   a.   i   u   i: u:
                   ↓   ↓
          o   e: o:*, o:
          a   a:

     b.   V: → [−high]

A corollary of this analysis is a rule that lowers the long high vowels, which is stated in (51b). This is a rule of *absolute neutralization*. It merges the contrast between underlying [u:] and [o:] in all environments and is thus to be distinguished from the more familiar *contextual neutralization* rules that merge phonological contrasts in particular environments (e.g., the Yawelmani contrast in vowel length is neutralized before a consonant cluster). Rules of absolute neutralization are descriptively controversial and are typically not postulated unless a good deal of language-internal motivation can be mustered. It turns out that in addition to explaining the peculiar double exceptions to vowel harmony, the postulated long high vowels elucidate a number of other peculiarities in Yawelmani phonological structure. Let us look at two additional pieces of supporting evidence.

First, the language has a class of underlying disyllabic roots of the shape CVCV:C. Given that there are four distinct vowel qualities, we expect, other things being equal, sixteen possible patterns. Of course, other things are not equal, since the language has rounding harmony. But even when the harmony factor is removed, we will expect initial-syllable [i] to combine with [a:] or initial [a] to combine with [i:]. In fact, as the data in (52) show, only four root patterns are found: $CaCa:C$, $CiCe:C$, $CoCo:C$, and $CuCo:C$. Furthermore, note that $CuCo:C$ behaves "irregularly" with respect to vowel harmony.

(52) paxa:t-al   paxat-hin   yawa:l-al   yawal-hin
      hiwe:t-al   hiwet-hin   hibe:y-al   hibey-hin
      ?opo:t-ol   ?opot-hin   yolo:w-ol   yolow-hin
      sudo:k-al   sudok-hun   tuno:y-al   tunoy-hun

[paxa:t] 'mourn', [hiwe:t] 'walk', [?opo:t] 'arise from bed', [sudo:k] 're-move', [yawa:l] 'follow', [hibe:y] 'bring water', [yolo:w] 'assemble', [tuno:y] 'scorch'

Given that [e:] and "irregular" [o:] derive from underlying high vowels, we see that $CiCe:C$ and $CuCo:C$ roots parallel $CaCa:C$ and $CoCo:C$ in repeating the same vowel quality in both syllables. (Newman (1944) calls these "echo" verbs.) Vowel lowering transforms the postulated $CiCi:C$ and $CuCu:C$ roots into the surface $CiCe:C$ and $CuCo:C$ shapes. This rule is essential to capture the "echoing" pattern that underlies these roots.

The vowel-lowering rule must be ordered after vowel harmony, because the harmonic behavior of the two kinds of [o:] is our primary reason for postulating the difference. The lowering rule must apply before shortening, however, because it is the [– high] quality that shows up before a consonant cluster. Vowel lowering is thus another rule that must be defined on an intermediate level of representation. The derivations in (53) illustrate this analysis.

(53) /#hiwi:t-hin#/   /#sudu:k-hin#/   /#yowo:l-al#/   UR
          inappl.   sudu:k-hun   yowo:l-ol   harmony (41)
          hiwe:t-hin   sudo:k-hun   inappl.   lowering (51b)
          hiwet-hin   sudok-hun   inappl.   shortening (43)

The other evidence that supports the long high vowels comes from various rules of Yawelmani morphology that assign different canonical shapes to the stem. If a root with a basic long high vowel is assigned to a canon calling for a short vowel, then the postulated [+high] feature emerges. As a brief illustration of one such case, consider the deverbal nouns in (54).

(54) underlying root   verbal noun
      [bo:k]   bok   'find'
      [logw]   logiw   'pulverize'
      [mo:yn]   moyin   'get tired'
      [ʔi:dl]   ʔidil   'gets hungry'
      [wu:ʔy]   wuʔuy   'falls asleep'

Deverbal nouns are formed by shortening the verb's root vowel (if long). For example, [bo:k] 'find' has the nominal *bok*. Underlying [logw] 'pulverize' nominalizes as *logiw* by virtue of epenthesis breaking up a final consonant cluster. The neutralization of length is illustrated by the root [mo:yn] 'get tired'. Its nominal form is *moyin*. This morphological shortening applies before vowel lowering and thus allows the underlying [+high] postulated for the roots in *ʔe:dil-hin* 'gets hungry' and *wo:ʔuy-hun* 'falls asleep' to emerge phonetically. The fact that the [o:] of *wo:ʔuy-hun* 'falls asleep' alternates with nominal [u] while the [o:] of *mo:yin-hin* 'gets tired' does not is automatically explained by deriving the former from an underlying [u:].

Given the vowel-lowering rule, the distinctive features composing the [u:] never emerge as a phonetic ensemble. The lowering rule changes the [+high] specification to [−high] in the context of length. As we have just seen, sometimes the morphology may shorten the vowel, allowing [+high] to surface – but, crucially, only in the absence of [+long]. Thus, for at least some roots, we can see both facets of the postulated long high vowels. But because of the vowel-lowering rule, they can never be seen simultaneously.

A similar state of affairs exists in other languages. For example, English has many alternations between the diphthong [ay] and the high lax vowel [ɪ]: for example, *five*, *divine* [ay] vs. *fif-th*, *divin-ity* [ɪ]. As we will see later (section 5.1), these vowels derive from an underlying long [i:]. Shortening rules, some completely analogous to the Yawelmani shortening before two consonants, produce [ɪ]. When [i:] is not shortened, it undergoes the so-called Vowel Shift rule, which transforms it into the diphthong [ay]. Thus, just as in Yawelmani, the underlying vowel quality of [fi:v] 'five' is revealed in the short vowel alternant *f*[ɪ]*fth*, while the underlying quantity is realized (obliquely) in the diphthong *f*[ay]*ve*. But because of the Vowel Shift rule, the length and quality features never surface together. Since well-motivated examples of this kind are found in several languages, we must abandon conjecture (48) and allow ourselves the freedom to postulate that a distinct [z] underlies an [x]≈[y] alternation when the evidence warrants.

In view of these examples we might weaken (48) to (55).

(55) Each distinctive feature in the underlying representation must emerge in at least one phonetic realization of the morpheme.

While this constraint permits the long high vowels to be posited for the Yawelmani material considered so far, there are other data for which it would deprive us of an internally well motivated explanation. For example, consider the alternation exhibited by the future suffix in (56).

(56) bok-en   'find'
      dub-on   'lead by hand'
      xat-en   'eat'
      giy-en   'touch'

This alternation follows automatically from the rules discussed so far, provided the suffix is assigned the underlying shape [i:n]. Given that the vowel is high, it will round to [u:n] after a root containing [u] such as [dub]. Subsequent lowering and shortening transform [i:n] and [u:n] to the [en] and [on] found in (56). (In Yawelmani vowels systematically shorten before two consonants as well as before a single-word final consonant.) The problem here is that being an affix, the future suffix does not participate in the morphological processes that would shorten its vowel and thus allow the postulated [+high] to emerge. Furthermore, the morphology of the language is such that this suffix always appears at the end of a word. Its postulated length thus never emerges phonetically either. In this case a majority of the distinctive features composing this segment are never pronounced. Nonetheless, the harmonic behavior is precisely that of a high vowel. A theory that seeks the most economical grammar – one with the simplest rules and representations compatible with the data – would almost inevitably be led to postulate just such a vowel.

There is only one situation that could be argued to be more abstract: one in which none of the distinctive features constituting a segment surface directly because the segment is always deleted. The phonological literature – both generative and nongenerative – is replete with analyses that posit such "phantom" segments. Such analyses are generally viewed with some skepticism and are only postulated when strong internal evidence is available. One well-known example is found in English. Three nasal consonants contrast in final position: *su*[m], *su*[n], and *su*[ŋ] (*sung*). However, the velar nasal has a defective distribution. It does not appear morpheme-initially (*map, nap* but not **ŋap*) or morpheme-internally before a vowel (*smack, snack, *sŋack*). Furthermore, [n] and [ŋ] have largely complementary distributions. [ŋ] occurs to the exclusion of [n] before the velars [k,g] (e.g., *tha*[ŋ]*k, a*[ŋ]*gry*), the latter part of a larger generalization in which nasals assimilate the point of articulation of a following consonant. Finally, while we find final homorganic nasal plus voiceless stop clusters (*da*[mp], *wa*[nt], *tha*[ŋk]), final [ŋg] clusters are systematically missing (as are final [mb] clusters). This gap can be accounted for by postulating a rule that deletes [g] in the context [+nasal] ____ #. Putting all these facts together, we may postulate the underlying representation of [sɪŋ] 'sing' as [sɪŋg] and derive it as shown in (57).

(57) /#sɪŋg#/   UR
      sɪŋg   nasal assimilation
      sɪŋ   *g*-deletion

3.5 Linguistic Reconstruction

The regularity of sound change makes it possible to reconstruct the earlier stages of a language and lies at the basis of the Comparative Method developed in 19th-century linguistics. Phonological reconstruction starts from the observation of systematic *sound correspondences* between words of the same or similar meaning in two or more languages that cannot reasonably be attributed to borrowing or chance. The hypothesis is that the related words descend from a common ancestor and that the differences arise from sound changes that the individual languages have experienced in the course of historical development. Words so related are called *cognates;* languages so related are known as *sister languages* with respect to one another and *daughter languages* of the ancestor or parent tongue. Application of the Comparative Method involves discovering the sound correspondences between presumed cognate words and trying to assign a unique protoform such that the individual daughter languages can be derived by plausible sound changes. The reconstructed form is marked with an asterisk to distinguish it from actually attested words, indicating its hypothetical (as opposed to attested) nature. The entire procedure is similar in certain ways to the discovery of a word's synchronic underlying representation on the basis of its phonetic alternants. This is not surprising since, as argued in the Introduction, systematic sound changes typically arise from the addition of phonological rules to the grammar of a given language or dialect. The underlying representations of the synchronic grammar thus often reflect earlier surface pronunciations. However, this is sometimes an oversimplification because the synchronic system is developed anew by each generation of language learners on the basis of data in the linguistic environment. This can lead to a reinterpretation or *restructuring* of the earlier historical state of affairs or indeed to creation of underlying representations that correspond to no earlier historical source (e.g., in the adaptation of loanwords). Finally, the synchronic order of the rules often reflects the actual diachronic sequencing of the sound changes. But again this is not always the case, as the discussion of Canadian Raising in section 3.3 made clear. Of course, the rules and representations of the grammar are justified solely on the basis of data in the synchronic linguistic environment since children do not have access to comparative evidence.

In this section we will see how the Comparative Method applies to two particular cases. We will begin by considering and amplifying Jeffers and Lehiste's (1979) discussion of data such as those in (58) from three closely related Balto-Finnic languages. Finnish and Estonian words are cited in the native orthography, where long vowels are geminates; *ä* is the low front vowel [æ]; *d* and g represent voiceless lenis (unaspirated) stops in Estonian.

(58)

	Livonian	Finnish	Estonian	
a.	säv	savi	savi	'clay'
b.	tämm	tammi	tamm	'oak'
c.	säpp	sappi	sapp	'bile'
d.	lüm	lumi	lumi	'snow'
e.	sül	süli	süli	'womb'
f.	töb	topi	tobi	'sickness'
g.	ä:rga	härkä	härg	'ox'

Examination of the data in (58) reveals that the consonants are unchanged while the vowels differ. Initial-syllable [ä] and [ü] in Livonian correspond to back vowels [a] and [u] in Finnish and Estonian (58a–e). Given Livonian *ä:rga* 'ox', where initial [ä] corresponds to Finnish and Estonian [ä], it is reasonable to suppose that Livonian [ä] and [ü] in (58a–e) derive from earlier back vowels via a process of vowel fronting (*umlaut*) caused by a no longer pronounced front vowel. The fact that these nouns end in [i] in Finnish suggests that the Livonian forms ended in an [i] that deleted at some earlier stage of the language. Note that if it were not for the clue provided by the Finnish cognates, there would be no particular reason to suppose that the Livonian [ä]'s of 'clay' and of 'ox' have different origins. We thus reconstruct *savi, *tammi, *sappi,* and *lumi* for the ancestor language. The present-day Livonian forms descend from the sound changes sketched informally in (59). These rules must have applied in the order indicated at some earlier stage of the language and perhaps reflect a corresponding chronology.

(59)   umlaut $V \rightarrow [-\text{back}] / \underline{\quad} C_0 \text{ [i]}$

        apocope $\text{[i]} \rightarrow \emptyset / \underline{\quad} \#$

The Estonian forms in (58) show the loss of final [i] in 'oak' and 'bile'. This reflects a more general apocope process that has deleted final vowels in the forms in (60). It is regularly suspended in words of the shape CVCV. In section 11.3 we will see that vowel deletion is often blocked if it would bring a word below a certain minimal size. Livonian apocope, while restricted to [i], is evidently not subject to this word-size limitation.

(60)

	Livonian	Finnish	Estonian	
a.	ko:r	kaari	kaar	'rib'
b.	mo:	maa	maa	'land'
c.	o:da	hauta	haud	'grave'
d.	so:na	sauna	saun	'sauna'
e.	ja:lga	jalka	jalg	'foot'
f.	suormǝd	sormet	sormed	'finger'
g.	vierda	verta	verd	'blood'
h.	o:r'a	harja	hari	'sandbank'

The forms (60a–d) reveal that Livonian [o:] corresponds to either [a:] or [au] in Finnish and Estonian. The simplest hypothesis is that Livonian has two separate sound changes: *a: > o: and *au > o:. Next we note that the [h] of Finnish and Estonian 'ox', 'grave', and 'sandbank' corresponds to ∅ in Livonian. The most plausible analysis postulates a rule deleting *h in Livonian. The alternative would be a prothesis rule inserting [h] in the historical development of Finnish and Estonian. The first analysis would be supported by vowel-initial cognates in Finnish and Estonian as well as cases of *h-deletion word-medially in Livonian. The remaining Livonian forms (60e–h) reveal long vowels cognate to Finnish and Estonian short vowels in syllables closed by a liquid. We therefore postulate the Livonian rule in (61).

(61)   V → V: / _____ [liquid]

   Condition: V and liquid are tautosyllabic.

The fact that the vowel of Livonian *sül* 'womb' is short suggests that (61) preceded the loss of final vowels; at the point where apocope applies, the form is **süli* and hence lacks a closed syllable. We note that the long mid vowels of 'blood' and 'finger' are realized with the ongliding diphthongs [ie] and [uo]. The Livonian diphthongization of mid vowels is reflected in such cognates as Livonian *suo* 'marsh', *miez* 'man' vs. Finnish *soo, mees*. Finally, the palatalized consonant of Livonian *o:r'a* reflects an original palatal glide (preserved in Finnish) that has merged with the liquid, presumably after vowel lengthening. In Estonian the glide [j] has vocalized to [i] after apocope: **harja → harj → hari*.

   This analysis is summarized in (62), where the reconstructions for the cognates are listed along with the postulated sound changes. Note that most of the sound changes have occurred in Livonian. It is interesting that several similar sound changes (apocope, diphthongization) are found in the genetically unrelated but geographically proximate Baltic language Latvian. Language contact and the accompanying bilingualism are frequent sources of sound change.

(62)   a.   *savi, *tammi, *sappi, *lumi, *süli, *topi, *härka, *ka:ri, *ma:, *hauta, *sauna, *jalka, *sormet, *verta, *harja

   b.   Livonian
      V → [−back] / _____ C$_0$ [i]
      [i] → ∅ / _____ #
      [h] → ∅, [a:] → [o:], [au] → [o:]
      V → V: / _____ [l,r]
      [o:] → [uo], [e:] → [ie]

      umlaut precedes apocope
      liquid lengthening precedes
         diphthongization and apocope
      diphthongization precedes [a:] → [o:]

      Estonian
      V → ∅ / _____ #
      [j] → [i] / C _____ #

      apocope precedes glide
      vocalization

3.6   Algonquian

The Comparative Method grew out of work in the 19th century on the Indo-European as well as Semitic and Finnic languages, where reconstructions could be checked against the testimony of written records of some antiquity. The resultant reconstructions reached back several millennia and, as the appellation "Proto-Indo-European" (PIE) suggests, established genetic relations among widely dispersed languages. The discovery of the attendant sound laws and precise cognates over such a large body of material was the crowning achievement of 19th-century linguistics and justly established the discipline as the "queen" of the social-cultural sciences. The 19th and early 20th centuries also saw considerable descriptive work on the languages of the New World and Africa, often carried out under the aegis of the European colonial powers as well as missionaries. As far as is known, these languages lack written records from all but the past few centuries. The question was raised whether linguistic reconstruction was possible under these circumstances. For example, in the 1924 edition of *Les langues du monde,* the eminent Indo-Europeanist Antoine Meillet (1866–1936) wondered "if the American languages . . . will ever lend themselves to the establishment of precise and complete comparative grammars" (Meillet 1926–1936, 2:61). Meillet's challenge was taken up by Leonard Bloomfield (1887–1949). Building on the earlier studies of Michelson and others plus his own fieldwork on Menomini, Bloomfield (1925, 1928, 1946) worked out the sound correspondences among four Central Algonquian languages in his influential reconstruction of Proto-Algonquian. His analysis is commonly regarded as a classic example of the application of the Comparative Method in the absence of written records (Hockett 1948); it vindicated the Neogrammarian idea of regular sound change in all languages; and it laid a firm foundation for further reconstruction that has established genetic connections among languages of considerable geographic and historical separation that rivals the 19th-century work on the better-known European languages. In the remainder of this chapter we will survey selected aspects of this Algonquian reconstruction.

(63) lists cognates from the four Central Algonquian languages that form the original core of Bloomfield's work: Fox, Cree, Menomini, Ojibwa. (The data are taken from Cowan 1972; the transcriptions have been normalized, following Cowan.)

			Fox	Cree	Menomini	Ojibwa
(63)	1.	'above'	ahpemeki	ispimihk	espēm-	išpimik
	2.	'big'	kehči	kisči	kēʔč	kičči
	3.	'belch'	šekiwa	sikiw	sekēw	šiki
	4.	'he comes'	očīwa	ohčīw	ohčēw	ončī
	5.	'crow'	-ahō-	ahā-	aʔa-	aʔā-
	6.	'my eye'	neškīšek-	niskīsik	neskēhse-	niškīnšik
	7.	'he embarks'	pōsiwa	pōsiw	pōsew	pōsi
	8.	'he fears'	sēkesiwa	sēkisiw	sēkesew	sēkisi
	9.	'fire'	aškotēwi	iskotēw	eskōtēw	iškotē
	10.	'grandfather'	omešōmesani	omosōma	omēhsomēhsan	omiššōmissan
	11.	'grandmother'	nōhkomesa	nōhkom	nōhkomɛh	nōkkomis
	12.	'his head'	–	ostikwān	–	oštikwān
	13.	'he hunts'	māčīwa	māčīw	māčīw	māčī
	14.	'he kicks'	takeškawēwa	tahkiskawēw	tahkēskawɛw	tankiškawa-
	15.	'knock down'	kaweni	kawin	kawēn-	kawin
	16.	'louse'	ihkwa	ihkwa	ehkuah	ikkwa
	17.	'make'	išihčikēwa	isīhčikew	esēhčekɛw	išiččikē
	18.	'make so'	išihtōwa	isīhtāw	esēhtaw	išittōt
	19.	'mistakes'	pehtena-	pistinam	pɛʔtɛnam	pittina-
	20.	'he pursues'	–	nōspinatam	nōčpen-	nōppinata-
	21.	'palate'	–	nayakašk	nenākačk-	ninakašk
		'old'	kehkyēwa	–	kečkīw	–
	22.	'is red'	meškosiwa	mihkosiw	mehk-	miskosi
			Swampy Cree	mihtkosiw		
	23.	'he ruins'	–	kōhpačihēw	kōhpačehēw	kōppačihā-
	24.	'he sees'	osāpamēwa	osāpamēw	ohsāpamɛw	onsāpamā-
	25.	'sister'	nemis-	nimis	nemēhs-	nimiss-

		Fox	Cree	Menomini	Ojibwa
26.	'he sits'	-nāhapiwa	nahapiw	-nāhapεw	nahapi
27.	'sleepy'	kawekwašiwa	kawihkwasiw	-kūhkwaʔsew	kakwinkwašši
28.	'my son'	nekwisa	nikosis	nekīʔs	ninkwiss-
29.	'he takes'	otenam-	ohtinam	ohtēnam	ontina-
30.	'up'	op-	ohp-	ohp-	omp-
31.	'brings inside'	pi:tikewa	pi:htukew	pi:htikew	pi:ntike

Simplifying slightly, we may set up the following table of correspondences among the vowels in the initial syllable. Bloomfield (1925) remarks that in initial syllables there appears to have been no Proto-Algonquian (PA) contrast between *e and *i; the high vowel appears initially and the mid vowel after a consonant.

(64)

PA	F	C	M	O	
*a	a	a	a	a	14,15
*a:	a:	a:	a:	a:	13
*e	e	i	e	i	3,6
*e:	e:	e:	ε:	e:	8
*o	o	o	o	o	4
*o:	o:	o:	o:	o:	7
*i	i	i	e	i	16,17,18
*i:	i:	i:	i:	i:	31

Examination of such cognates as 3, 6, 16, 17 reveals two correspondence sets: [e,i,e,i] and [i,i,e,i]. We see that Cree and Ojibwa [i] has two possible cognates in Fox: [i] or [e]. By the logic of predictability employed in the analysis of alternations (section 2.7), we are led to reconstruct an *i vs. *e contrast for the protolanguage that has been neutralized in Cree and Ojibwa through raising of *e to [i] and in Menomini through lowering of *i to [e].

Similar reasoning applies in the interpretation of the consonant correspondences in (65). We momentarily set aside the initial element of clusters since it presents certain complications. These excluded, the table in (65) may be set up.

(65)

PA	F	C	M	O	
*p	p	p	p	p	1,5,19
*t	t	t	t	t	14,29
*č	č	č	č	č	4,13
*k	k	k	k	k	2,3,15
*s	s	s	s	s	8,24,25
*š	š	s	s	š	3,9,17
*m	m	m	m	m	13,10,25
*n	n	n	n	n	6,25,15
*w	w	w	w	w	3,4,15
*h	h	h	h	h	26
*ʔ	h	h	ʔ	ʔ	5

Cree and Menomini [s] corresponds to either an [s] or a [š] in Fox and Ojibwa: [s,s,s,s] vs. [š,s,s,š]. Furthermore, the correspondences are exact; where Cree has [s] and Fox [š], the cognate Menomini and Ojibwa words match [s] with [š], respectively. Such systematic sound correspondences replicate the kind of results established in Indo-European reconstruction; they constitute solid evidence for a genetic relation among the languages and more generally the assumption of regular sound change upon which the Comparative Method rests. We postulate that Cree and Menomini have merged the PA *s* vs. *š* contrast by a regular sound change *š > s*. A similar point can be made by the [h] and [ʔ] correspondences in the last two lines of (65). Where we find [h] across the board, we reconstruct PA *h;* cases such as 5 in (63) suggest a merger of *ʔ > h* in Menomini and Ojibwa.

Turning to the vowels in noninitial position, we note three sound changes that account for many of the divergences. First, Fox has preserved the PA word-final vowels that the other languages have dropped. Ojibwa takes the reduction a step further, deleting final glides as well: *po:siwa > po:siw > po:si*. Menomini has undergone two special developments. First, when the first syllable contains a short vowel, the vowel of the second syllable lengthens (1,3,9, etc.). Second, *i* has lowered to a mid vowel (3,4,6,7) while original *e* has lowered to open [ɛ] (1,8).

So far the sound correspondences and their interpretation have been fairly straightforward. Let us now consider some more complex cases. The forms in (66) illustrate the general problem of *overlapping correspondences* (data from Gleason 1961).

(66)

	Fox	Cree	Menomini	Ojibwa	
a.	pema:tesiwa	pima:tisiw	pema:tesew	pima:tisi	'he lives'
b.	ni:yawi	ni:yaw	ne:yaw	ni:yaw	'my body'
	kenosiwa	kinosiw	keno:sew	kinosi	'he is long'
c.	anemwa	atim	anɛm	anim	'dog'
	ni:nemwa	ni:tim	ne:nem	ni:nim	'my sister-in-law'
d.	ineniwa	iyiniw	ene:niw	inini	'man'
	ne:se:wa	ye:hye:w	nɛ:hnew	ne:sse:	'he breathes'

The forms in (66a) and (66b) illustrate across-the-board correspondences of [t] and [n]. But (66c) displays cases where Cree [t] corresponds to [n] in the remaining languages; and in (66d) Cree [y] is matched by an [n] in the remaining languages. In view of the [t,t,t,t] and [n,n,n,n] correspondences (66a,b), (66c) can be derived from neither PA *t* nor PA *n*. Furthermore, there are too many such correspondences to dismiss the problem as accidental. Rather, as in the case of the Yawelmani long [o:] (section 3.4), we must assume that Proto-Algonquian had an additional pair of phonemes – one of which merged with *t* in Cree and *n* in the remaining languages (66c), the other of which appears as Cree *y* and merges with *n* in Fox, Menomini, and Ojibwa (66d). Faced with such a situation, phonologists must fall back on their general conception of natural sound changes and plausible phonemic inventories in order to narrow down the choices. In both the [n,t,n,n] and the [n,y,n,n] cases, the reflexes are coronal; consequently, the PA sources are likely to be coronals as well. Bloomfield in fact reconstructed the [n,y,n,n] correspondence as PA *l, knowing that this sound appeared as [l] in other Eastern Algonquian languages (e.g., compare Penobscot *wálakesk*ʷ with Fox *anake:hkwa*, Cree *wayake:sk*, Menomini *wana:kɛ:h*, Ojibwa *wanake:kk* reconstructed as PA *walake:θkwa* 'bark' by Siebert (1941)). Moreover, Bloomfield (1925) observes that the word *Illinois* derives from PA *ileniwa* 'man' from Peoria (via French); compare (66d).

Bloomfield reconstructed the [n,t,n,n] set with the symbol *θ. According to Goddard (1979), it is unclear whether this was just a lucky guess or whether he in fact knew that the sound appears as [θ] in Arapaho: PA *aθenwa* 'dog' > Arapaho-Atsina *oθem* > Arapaho *éθ*. The implied sound changes of *l > y and *l > θ > n are not unusual, and *θ and *l are therefore reasonable reconstructions. Historical linguistics is filled with examples where researchers have postulated "abstract" segments to account for overlapping correspondences only to have their conjectures confirmed by subsequent discovery of additional languages or documents. The PIE *coefficients sonantiques* (laryngeals) postulated by Saussure constitute the most celebrated example.

Let us now turn to the Central Algonquian consonant clusters. There has obviously been a partial neutralization in preconsonantal position. Two questions arise: what the correct correspondences are, and how they are to be interpreted phonetically and phonologically. As far as the first question is concerned, Bloomfield demonstrates that the languages are remarkably consistent in their development. (67) reproduces the major table of correspondences that Bloomfield established; numerals in the right-hand column refer back to (63).

(67)   nasal clusters

PA	F	C	M	O	
*mp	p	hp	hp	mp	30
*nt	t	ht	ht	nt	29
*nč	č	hč	hč	nč	4
*nk	k	hk	hk	nk	14,27
*ns	s	s	hs	ns	24
*nš	š	s	hs	nš	6

h-clusters

PA	F	C	M	O	
*hp		hp	hp	pp	23
*ht	ht	ht	ht	tt	18
*hč	hč	hč	hč	čč	17
*hk	hk	hk	hk	kk	11,16
*hs	s	s	hs	ss	10,25
*hš	š	s	hs	šš	10

ʔ-clusters

PA	F	C	M	O	
*ʔt	ht	st	ʔt	tt	19
*ʔč	hč	sč	ʔč	čč	2
*ʔs	s	s	ʔs	ss	28
*ʔš	š	s	ʔs	šš	27

č-clusters

*čp		sp	čp	pp	20
*čk	hk	šk	čk	šk	21

š-clusters

*šp	hp	sp	sp	šp	1
*št		st		št	12
*šk	šk	sk	sk	šk	6,9,14

The interpretation of the nasal clusters is fairly straightforward. They are attested only in Ojibwa where there is neutralization of place and are lost entirely in Fox. Cree and Menomini have replaced the nasal by [h], with the complication that Cree deletes the [h] before the fricative reflexes of *s and *š. The laryngeal clusters are based on a contrast of *h vs. *ʔ that shows up in Menomini (and Cheyenne). These segments completely assimilate the following consonant in Ojibwa to create a geminate. The Cree [st] and [sč] reflexes of *ʔt and *ʔč are anomalous; they suggest that the preconsonantal glottal stop reflects some underlying oral consonant – but which one is difficult to tell in the absence of evidence from alternations. š-clusters reflect the *š > s sound change in Cree and Menomini. The [šk] reflex in Fox is idiosyncratic; elsewhere, Fox has neutralized the initial consonant in a cluster to [h].

In sum, while certain developments are unclear, the overall pattern is remarkably systematic, a fact that impressed linguists at the time and vindicated application of the Comparative Method in the Americas and, in Bloomfield's (1925: 130) words, helped to "dispose of the notion that the usual processes of linguistic change are suspended on the American continent."

In his original (1925) reconstruction, Bloomfield noted that the [šk,hk,hk,šk] correspondence for the cluster in the stem meaning 'is red' did not match any of the others and so he was forced to postulate a unique source symbolized by [çk].

(68)

PA	F	C	M	O	
*meçkw-	meškusiwa	mihkusiw	mehk-	miškusi	'(he is) red'

Sometime after the publication of this reconstruction, Bloomfield had the opportunity to do fieldwork on the Swampy Cree dialect, where he discovered that the cluster in the stem 'red' appeared as [htk]: *mihtkusiw* 'he is red'. In a (1928) note publishing this observation, he saw this as a vindication for the general assumption underlying phonological reconstruction: namely, that sound change is regular. Without this assumption, it would have been possible to simply dismiss the [šk,hk,hk,šk] correspondence in (68) as a case of "sporadic sound change." This point drew further commentary in the later literature. Bloomfield (1946) notes that "the fuss and trouble behind my note in *Language* . . . would have been avoided if I had listened to O, which plainly distinguishes sk (<PA çk) from šk (<PA šk); instead, I depended on printed records which failed to show the distinction." Subsequent work on other Algonquian languages found additional reflexes of the postulated [çk] cluster, justifying the original distinction (Geary 1941).

Of course, the true phonetic nature of the postulated [ç] remains unclear; see Goddard 1979 for discussion.

Sapir (1931) also called attention to the importance of Bloomfield's adherence to the principle of regular sound change, drawing certain methodological parallels from his own work on Athabaskan reconstruction. His example is interesting in its own right; it is briefly summarized here. Like Algonquian, the Athabaskan languages are dispersed over a wide geographic expanse, including a Northern group in western Canada (comprising Sarcee and Chipewyan among others), a Southern group in Arizona and New Mexico (Navaho), and a small Pacific group in Oregon and northern California (Hupa). Sapir reconstructed the following correspondences among the obstruent consonants in these languages.

(69)

Athabaskan	Hupa	Chipewyan	Navaho	Sarcee
*s	s	θ	s	s
*z	s	ð	z	z
*dz	dz	dð	dz	dz
*ts	ts	tθ	ts	ts
*ts'	ts'	tθ'	ts'	ts'
*š	W	s	š	s
*ž	W	z	ž	z
*dž	dž	dz	dž	dz
*č	čʷ	ts	č	ts
*č'	č'	ts'	č'	ts'
*x'	W	š	s	š
*y	y	y	y	y
*g'	g'	dž	dz	dž
*k'	k'	č	ts	č
*k''	k''	č'	ts'	č'

Looking first at Navaho and Sarcee, we find a puzzling case of overlapping correspondences. Taking the voiceless affricate series as representative, Navaho matches its [ts,č,ts] to Sarcee's [ts,ts,č]. While the corresponding [ts]'s in the first series suggest Proto-Athabaskan *ts, it is unclear whether to reconstruct *č or *ts for the second or the third series; and in any case, another consonant will still be required to distinguish among them. If one did not believe in the regularity of sound change, one might simply conclude that there is no systematic correspondence in these consonants between Navaho and Sarcee (other than a negative one that [č] never matches). The Chipewyan [tθ,ts,č] correspondence corroborates the decision to isolate the Sarcee and Navaho matching [ts]'s as a distinct series; and its point-by-point correspondence with Sarcee in the second and third series reconfirms our faith in regular sound change. However, the Chipewyan data still leave the phonetic nature of the Proto-Athabaskan sources for the second and third series unresolved. It is the Hupa [ts,čʷ,k'] series that answers this question: the alveolar representatives for the first series match Navaho and Sarcee; the alveopalatal second series matches Navaho (with fricative rounding as a separate

Hupa development). Most important are the prevelar representatives of the third series, which provide a plausible story for the puzzling developments in the remaining languages: the prevelars *k' have shifted to alveopalatals č in Sarcee and Chipewyan and to alveolars *ts* in Navaho, where they merge with the original alveolar series. Sarcee and Chipewyan have shifted the original alveopalatal series *č to alveolar, neutralizing it in Sarcee but keeping it distinct in Chipewyan, where the original alveolars have turned to interdentals.

These data provide an impressive demonstration of the regularity of sound change and the resultant systematic sound correspondences that permit the ancestor Proto-Athabaskan to be reconstructed and the historical development of the various daughter languages to be precisely described. They also demonstrate that sound change operates over natural classes of sounds, as is evident from the way in which Sapir has grouped the segments. Both properties follow from the basic premise of generative phonology that a language's vocabulary is stored in the memory of individual speakers as phonological representations composed of strings of feature matrices that can be modified in very precise ways by the ordered application of context-sensitive phonological rules.

Sapir gives a practical illustration of the predictive power of the assumption of regular sound change. His original reconstruction included the cognates for 'rain' from Chipewyan (*čą*), Navaho (*tsą*), and Sarcee (*čą*). The Hupa word for 'rain' was missing from the available descriptive materials, however. The Chipewyan-Navaho-Sarcee [č,ts,č] correspondence fixes the Proto-Athabaskan consonant as [k']. Sapir states that he was later able to confirm this prediction, collecting the Hupa word *k'aŋ-k'oh* 'hailstorm' (lit. 'rain-big').

To close the discussion, let us consider a few examples from Goddard's (1974) reconstruction of Arapaho, an Algonquian language of the Great Plains. Unlike the Central Algonquian languages, the connection of Arapaho to the other languages is considerably less obvious to the casual observer. Nevertheless, Goddard convincingly shows how many Arapaho words can be derived from the common PA sources by a regular (if lengthy) series of sound changes. Some of the major changes are listed in (70a), with a few illustrations in (70b).

(70) a. V → Ø / ___ #
 Gl → Ø / C ___ #
 [we] → [o]
 [o] → [i]
 [e] → [i] / # ___
 [m,n] → Ø / ___ #
 V → Ø / ___ #
 [m] → [b]
 [s] → [h]
 [h] → Ø / ___ #

   b. *meto:ni 'mouth'   *eleniwa 'man'
 meto:n   eneniw
 meti:n   eneni
 meti: ineni
 beti: inen

*aθemwa	'dog'	*mo:swa	'moose'
aθemw		mo:sw	
aθem		mo:s	
eθem		mi:s	
eθe		mi:h	
eθ		bii	

*maxkeseni 'moccasin'
maxkesen
maʔkesen
maʔesen
moʔesen
moʔoson
moʔohon
woʔohon
woʔoho
woʔoh   (cf. F mahkes-ehi, C maskisin, M mahkɛsin,
          O mahkisin)

Suggested Readings

Bloomfield, Leonard. 1939. Menomini morphophonemics. Travaux du Cercle Linguistique de Prague 8.105–15. Reprinted in Phonological theory: Evolution and current practice, ed. by V. Makkai, 58–70. New York: Holt, Rinehart and Winston, 1972; and in A Leonard Bloomfield anthology, ed. by C. Hockett, 351–62. Bloomington: Indiana University Press, 1970.

Hock, Hans. 1986. Principles of historical linguistics. Berlin: Mouton. Chapters 18 and 19.

Kenstowicz, Michael, and Charles Kisseberth. 1979. Generative phonology: Description and theory. New York: Academic Press. Chapters 3 and 4.

Kiparsky, Paul. 1968. Linguistic universals and language change. Universals in linguistic theory, ed. by E. Bach and R. Harms, 191–212. New York: Holt, Rinehart and Winston. Reprinted in Explanation in phonology, 13–43. Dordrecht: Foris, 1982.

Lakoff, George. 1992. Cognitive phonology. To appear in The last phonological rule, ed. by J. Goldsmith. Chicago: University of Chicago Press.

Payne, David. 1981. The phonology and morphology of Axininca Campa. Summer Institute of Linguistics, Publication in Linguistics no. 66. Arlington, Tex.: University of Texas. Chapters 4, 5, 6, 9.

Exercises

3.1   Serbo-Croatian

The verbs in (1) provide additional data bearing on the analysis of Serbo-Croatian given in section 3.1. Segment these words into their constituent morphemes and list the underlying representations for each root and each affix. At least two additional rules are required. State them in distinctive feature format. How must these rules be ordered with respect to those already developed? Illustrate your analysis by deriving *povéo* and *povelá*. [ṛ] denotes a syllabic liquid.

(1)

1sg. pres.	masc. past	fem. past	neut. past	
cṛpém	cṛpao	cṛplá	cṛpló	'drain'
grebém	grébao	greblá	grebló	'scratch'
tresém	trésao	treslá	tresló	'shake'
pasém	pásao	paslá	pasló	'graze'
muzém	múzao	muzlá	muzló	'milk'
vezém	vézao	vezlá	vezló	'convey'
pletém	pléo	plelá	pleló	'plait'
ubodém	ubóo	ubolá	uboló	'prickle'
metém	méo	melá	meló	'sweep'
povedém	povéo	povelá	poveló	'lead'
pečém	pékao	peklá	pekló	'bake'
obučém	obúkao	obuklá	obukló	'dress'
žežém	žégao	žeglá	žegló	'burn'
vodim	vodio	vodila	vodilo	'lead'
tepam	tepao	tepala	tepalo	'babble'

3.2 *Basque*

A. Recall from section 1.4 the rules accounting for the glide≈∅, [a]≈[e], and mid vowel≈high vowel alternation in the Biscayan dialect of Basque. The relevant data are repeated in (1). Characterize the ordering relations among these rules in terms of the notions "feeding" and "bleeding."

(1)

noun	definite	
sagar	sagar-a	'apple'
gison	gison-a	'man'
buzten	buzten-a	'tail'
čakur	čakur-e	'dog'
mutil	mutil-e	'boy'
buru	buru-we	'head'
mendi	mendi-ye	'mountain'
ate	ati-e	'door'
asto	astu-e	'donkey'

B. Nouns in the bare and definite forms from the Baztan dialect (Hualde 1991) are listed in (2). In what ways does this dialect differ from Biscayan?

(2)

noun	definite	
gison	gison-a	'man'
egun	egun-e	'day'
mendi	mendi-e	'mountain'
buru	buru-e	'head'
eče	eči-a	'house'
ašto	aštu-a	'donkey'

C. The Baztan data in (3) require another rule. Give the derivations for 'limit'. Can you explain the contrasting behavior of *eče* and *muge* in the definite? How do these forms bear on the question of intermediate representations? (The form *fabrik-e* is inferred from the data source by analogy to *mug-e*.)

(3)

noun	definite	
alaba	alab-a	'daughter'
neska	nesk-a	'girl'
muge	mug-e	'limit'
fabrike	fabrik-e	'factory'

D. The paradigms in (4) come from the Arbizu dialect. In what ways does it differ from the Baztan and Biscayan dialects?

(4)

stem	ergative	
gison	gisonak	'man'
čakur	čakurek	'dog'
ašto	aštuek	'donkey'
berde	berdiek	'green ones'
ešku	eškubek	'hand'
mendi	mendijek	'mountain'
alaba	alabak	'daughter'

3.3 *Chukchee*

Incorporate the following Chukchee data into the text analysis of section 3.4. State your rules. How must they be ordered with respect to each other and to those already postulated? What would be the consequences for your analysis if the requirement that the underlying representation be identical with one of its surface alternants were accepted? The paradigms in (1) include an additional case form, the comitative. A few examples discussed in the text are repeated here.

(1)

abs.sg.	abs.pl.	erg.	comit.	
eŋer	eŋerti	eŋere	aŋarma	'star'
ococ	ococte	ococa	ococma	'leader'
milut	milutet	milutete	melotama	'rabbit'
ajkol	ajkolat	ajkolata	ajkolama	'bed'
rileq	rileqət	rileqe	relaʔma	'spine'
watap	watapət	watapa	watamma	'moss'
wiŋər	winrit	winrite	wenrema	'hoe'
qepəl	qeplət	qeple	qapləma	'ball'
miməl	mimlət	mimle	memləma	'water'
lewət	lewtət	lewte	lawtəma	'head'
titəl	titlət	title	tetləma	'door'
jaʔjaq	jaʔjaqət	jaʔjaqa	jaʔjaʔma	'seagull'
meqəm	meʔmit	meʔmite	maʔmema	'arrow'
aqən	aʔnət	aʔna	aʔnəma	'fishing pole'
weqən	weʔnət	weʔne	waʔnəma	'fish species'

abs.sg.	abs.pl.	erg.	comit.	
rəpən	rəmnət	rəmne	rəmnəma	'flesh side of hide'
rətən	rənnət	rənne	rənnəma	'tooth'

3.4 Yawelmani and English

Review the Yawelmani analysis of section 3.4. Must any of the rules be defined on an intermediate level of representation distinct from the underlying and the phonetic? Review the analysis of the English velar nasal in section 3.4. Discuss the relevance of the following observation for the analysis of [ŋ]: while it is possible to find stem morphemes ending in a labial or dental nasal consonant preceded by the diphthong [ay] (e.g., *dime, dine, lime, line*), cases of a velar nasal in the same position are impossible.

3.5 Somali

A. Parse the singular, singular definite, and plural nouns in (1) into root plus suffix and isolate the alternations. For each alternation, justify your choice of an underlying representation. Formulate rules to account for the alternations. Must the rules be ordered? Provide derivations for the forms of 'sea'. You may assume a phonetically arbitrary rule that replaces [lt] with [š]. Transcription notes: [β,ð,ɣ] are voiced fricatives, [ḍ] is a retroflex stop, and [ṛ] is a retroflex fricative.

(1)

sg.	sg. def.	pl.	
daar	daarta	daaro	'house'
gees	geesta	geeso	'side'
lug	lugta	luɣo	'leg'
naag	naagta	naaɣo	'woman'
tib	tibta	tiβo	'pestle'
sab	sabta	saβo	'outcast'
bad	bada	baðo	'sea'
ʕid	ʕida	ʕiðo	'person'
feeḍ	feeḍa	feeṛo	'rib'
ul	uša	ulo	'stick'
bil	biša	bilo	'month'
meel	meeša	meelo	'place'
kaliil	kaliiša	kaliilo	'summer'

B. The data in (2) require an additional rule. State it in features. Justify your choice of an underlying representation.

(2)

sg.	sg. def.	pl.	
sun	sunta	sumo	'poison'
laan	laanta	laamo	'branch'
sin	sinta	simo	'hip'
dan	danta	dano	'affair'
daan	daanta	daano	'riverbank'
saan	saanta	saano	'hide'

C. The data in (3) show a vowel-zero alternation. Justify your choice of an underlying representation and formulate the rule to account for the alternation. Must the rule be ordered with any other rules? If yes, tell why for each ordering. Give derivations for the forms of 'mule' and 'hole'.

(3)

sg.	sg. def.	pl.	
nirig	nirigta	nirgo	'baby female camel'
gaβaḍ	gaβaḍa	gabḍo	'girl'
gaʕan	gaʕanta	gaʕmo	'arm'
hoɣol	hoɣoša	hoglo	'downpour'
baɣal	baɣaša	baglo	'mule'
waḥar	waḥarta	waḥaro	'female kid'
kefed	kefeda	kefeðo	'pan'
ʕilin	ʕilinta	ʕilino	'female dwarf'
bohol	bohoša	boholo	'hole'

D. The verbs in (4) provide additional examples of the alternations already encountered. What underlying representations does your analysis assign to the verb roots and affixes? Illustrate how your analysis works by giving derivations for the forms of 'talk'.

(4)

3sg.masc.	3sg.fem.	1pl.	
suɣay	sugtay	sugnay	'wait'
kaβay	kabtay	kabnay	'fix'
siðay	siday	sidnay	'carry'
dilay	dišay	dillay	'kill'
ganay	gantay	gannay	'aim'
tumay	tuntay	tunnay	'hammer'
argay	aragtay	aragnay	'see'
gudbay	guðubtay	guðubnay	'cross river'
qoslay	qosošay	qosollay	'laugh'
hadlay	haðašay	haðallay	'talk'

E. Does your analysis contain any rules that must be defined on intermediate levels of representation? Illustrate and discuss their theoretical significance.

3.6 *Sudanese Arabic (Hamid 1984)*

A. The data in (1) illustrate the Sudanese Arabic stress rule that accents the rightmost heavy syllable and otherwise the initial. A heavy syllable contains a long (geminate) vowel or a short vowel followed by two consonants. Stress is transcribed on the first half of the geminate; [j] denotes an alveopalatal affricate.

(1)

bána	'he built'	jamaléen	'two camels'
ʔákal	'he ate'	masaakíin	'poor' pl.
ʔagúul	'I say'	hammalíin	'porters'
ʔáakul	'I eat'	máktab	'office'
baabéen	'two doors'	maktabéen	'library'
ʔakálna	'we ate'	tárjam	'he translated'
kátabu	'they wrote'	tárjamu	'they translated'
kátabat	'she wrote'	tarjámna	'we translated'

B. Develop an analysis for the data in (2), indicating the underlying representations for all of the roots and affixes; state your rules and any ordering restrictions required. Show how your analysis works by deriving *jámalu, jamála, šúɣlu, šuɣúla, dáwa, dawáak, dawáaha, sít, síttaha.*

(2)	'N'	jámal	sádur	šúɣul	ḥímil	dárib
	'your N'	jámalak	sádrak	šúɣlak	ḥímlak	dárbak
	'his N'	jámalu	sádru	šúɣlu	ḥímlu	dárbu
	'our N'	jamálna	sadúrna	šuɣúlna	ḥimílna	daríbna
	'your pl. N'	jamálkum	sadúrkum	šuɣúlkum	ḥimílkum	daríbkum
	'her N'	jamála	sadúra	šuɣúla	ḥimíla	daríba
	'their N'	jamálum	sadúrum	šuɣúlum	ḥimílum	daríbum
		'camel'	'chest'	'work'	'burden' (cf. ḥumúula 'load')	'path'

	'N'	dáwa	dálu	jádi	ʔúm	sít
	'your N'	dawáak	dalúuk	jadíik	ʔúmmak	síttak
	'his N'	dawáa	dalúu	jadíi	ʔúmmu	síttu
	'our N'	dawáana	dalúuna	jadíina	ʔúmmana	síttana
	'your pl. N'	dawáakum	dalúukum	jadíikum	ʔúmmakum	síttakum
	'her N'	dawáaha	dalúuha	jadíiha	ʔúmmaha	síttaha
	'their N'	dawáahum	dalúuhum	jadíihum	ʔúmmahum	síttahum
		'medicine'	'pail'	'kid'	'mother' (cf. ʔumúuma 'motherhood')	'lady'

C. Verbs exhibit the same alternations as nouns; your analysis should generalize to these data with perhaps only minimal changes. Pronominal direct objects are marked by essentially the same series of suffixes that mark pronominal possession on nouns. Indicate your underlying representations for the roots and suffixes in (3) and give derivations for *ḥamála, ḥamaltíi.*

(3)	šírib	'he drank'	ḥámal	'he carried'
	šírbat	'she drank'	ḥámalat	'she carried'
	siríbti	'you fem. drank'	ḥamálti	'you fem. carried'
	siríbta	'I drank'	ḥamálta	'I carried'
	šírbu	'they drank'	ḥámalu	'they carried'
	siríbtu	'you pl. drank'	ḥamáltu	'you pl. carried'
	síribna	'we drank'	ḥamálna	'we carried'

ḥámal	'he carried'	
ḥámalak	'he carried you'	
ḥámalu	'he carried him'	
ḥamálna	'he carried us'	
ḥamála	'he carried her'	
ḥamálum	'he carried them'	

ḥamálna	'we carried'
ḥamalnáak	'we carried you masc.'
ḥamalnáa	'we carried him'
ḥamalnáaha	'we carried her'
ḥamalnáahum	'we carried them'

ḥámalu	'they carried'	
ḥamalúuk	'they carried you masc.'	
ḥamalúuna	'they carried us'	
ḥamalúuha	'they carried her'	
ḥamalúuhum	'they carried them'	

ḥamálti	'you fem. carried'
ḥamaltíi	'you fem. carried him'
ḥamaltíina	'you fem. carried us'
ḥamaltíiha	'you fem. carried her'
ḥamaltíihum	'you fem. carried them'

D. How might the verb+object paradigm in (4) be explained in terms of the analysis you have developed?

(4) ḥamálta   'I carried'
     ḥamáltak   'I carried you masc.'
     ḥamáltu   'I carried him'
     ḥamáltakum   'I carried you pl.'
     ḥamáltaha   'I carried her'
     ḥamáltahum   'I carried them'

E. In what way does the paradigm in (5) bear on the analysis in question D, especially when the paradigm for *sit* in question B is recalled? Carefully formulate your rules to account for these data.

(5) ḥárat   'he plowed'
     ḥarátta   'I plowed'
     ḥaráttu   'I plowed it masc.'
     ḥaráttaha   'I plowed it fem.'
     ḥaráttahum   'I plowed them'

F. The 2sg. fem. suffix exhibits an idiosyncratic alternation that can be observed in the data in (6). State the principle underlying this idiosyncratic alternation and discuss how it bears on the question of what the underlying representation for the 1sg. perfect (subject) suffix is.

(6) ḥámal   'he carried'   ḥámalik   'he carried you fem.'
     ḥamálna 'we carried'   hamalnáaki   'we carried you fem.'
     jámal   'camel'   jámalik   'your fem. camel'
     dáwa   'medicine'   dawáaki   'your fem. medicine'
     ʔúm   'mother'   ʔúmmik   'your fem. mother'

     ḥamálta 'I carried'   ḥamáltik   'I carried you fem.'

3.7 *Trukese (Quackenbush 1970)*

Trukese is a Micronesian language spoken on the Caroline Islands in the South Pacific. The following data are from four of the many island dialects. Sonsoral is the westernmost island. Satawal, Pullap, and Moen are about 800, 900, and 1,000 miles, respectively, to the east. Reconstruct the vowel system for Proto-Trukese. What sound changes must be assumed to have taken place in the individual dialects? Quackenbush's (1970) transcription is followed here: long vowels are geminate, [r] is a dental trill, [ṛ] is retroflex, [c] is an alveolar affricate, [j] a palatal glide, [g] a velar fricative, [ḷ] a velarized lateral, and [θ] an interdental.

(1) vowels   i   y   u
                   e   ə   o
                   ä   a   ǫ

(2)

	i	e	ä	y	ə	a	u	o	ọ
high	+	−	−	+	−	−	+	−	−
low	−	−	+	−	−	+	−	−	+
back	−	−	−	+	+	+	+	+	+
round	−	−	−	−	−	−	+	+	+

(3)

Sonsoral	Satawal	Pullap	Moen	
ŋii	ŋii	ŋii	ŋii	'tooth'
jee	jee	jee	jee	'he'
ryy	lyy	nyy	nyy	'coconut tree'
waa	waa	waa	waa	'canoe'
soo	ṛoo	ṛoo	coo	'copra'
jita	jit	jit	jit	'name'
tyty	tyt	tyt	tyt	'breast'
fasa	faṛ	faṛ	fac	'pandanus'
wuŋa	wuŋ	wuŋ	wuŋ	'pole'
loŋo	roŋ	roŋ	roŋ	'to hear'
mawuri	mawul	mawun	mawun	'war'
gasii	gäri	järi	jäci	'toddy'
meta	met	met	met	'what'
tati	sät	hät	sät	'the sea'
ḷari	rän	rän	rän	'day'
gapi	jäp	jäp	jep	'buttock'
ppare	ppäl	ppäl	ppäl	'light'
jaθo	jọs	jọh	jọs	'roof'
raŋo	lọŋ	lọŋ	nọŋ	'fly'
nnaty	nnat	nnat	nnət	'scaevola'
faty	fat	fat	fət	'eyebrow'
mʷare	mʷäl	mʷäl	mʷän	'man'
maθe	mää	mää	mää	'to die'
jawo	jọọ	jọọ	jọọ	'fishline'
rago	lọọ	lọọ	nọọ	'to go'
rawo	lọọ	nọọ	nọọ	'wave'
tawy	təə	təə	təə	'to climb'
sawy	ṛəə	ṛəə	cəə	'leaf'

3.8 Polynesian Reconstruction

A. (1) lists cognates from four Polynesian languages (Walsh and Biggs 1966). Determine the second correspondences among the consonants and reconstruct the consonant system of the protolanguage, arranging the consonants in a phoneme chart. Reconstruct each cognate set. Determine the sound changes that characterize the development of the individual daughter languages. Can the relative chronology of certain sound changes be determined? Do shared changes allow you to make any subgroupings among the languages?

(1)

	Hawaiian	Maori	Tongan	Samoan	
1.	ʔele	kere	kele	ʔele	'black'
2.	ʔula	kura	kula	ʔula	'red'
3.	halo	whare	fale	fale	'house'
4.	heʔe	wheke	feke	feʔe	'octopus'
5.	kalo	taro	talo	talo	'taro'
6.	kahu	tahu	tafu	tafu	'cook'
7.	kai	tai	tahi	tai	'sea'
8.	haʔa	haka	haka	saʔa	'dance'
9.	liʔi	riki	iiki	liʔi	'small'
10.	luʔu	ruku	uku		'dive'
11.	lama	rama	ama	lama	'torch'
12.	puna	puŋa	puŋa	puŋa	'coral'
13.	piko	pito	pito	pito	'navel'
14.	nuku	ŋutu	ŋutu	ŋutu	'beak'
15.	nalu	ŋaru	ŋalu	ŋalu	'wave'
16.	niho	niho	nifo	nifo	'tooth'
17.	moko	moto	moto	moto	'strike with fist'
18.	moe	moe	mohe	moe	'sleep'
19.		aŋa	haŋa	aŋa	'to face'
20.	iho	iho	hifo	ifo	'downwards'
21.	aʔe	ake	hake	aʔe	'upwards'
22.	honu	honu	fonu		'turtle'
23.	ihi	ihi	hihi	isi	'to strip, peel'
24.	aka	ata	ata	ata	'dawn'
25.	awa	awa	ava	ava	'channel'
26.	wahine	wahine	fefine	fafine	'woman'
27.	pee	pee	peʔe	pee	'overripe'
28.	ao	ao	ʔaho	ao	'day'
29.	au	au	ʔahu	au	'gall'
30.	aloha	aroha	ʔaloʔofa	alofa	'love, pity'
31.	wai	wai	vai	vai	'water'
32.	waʔa	waka	vaka	vaʔa	'canoe'
33.	wae	wae	vaʔe	vae	'leg'
34.	hau	hau	hau	sau	'dew'
35.	hiʔu	hiku	hiku	siʔu	'tail'
36.	iwa	iwa	hiva	iva	'nine'
37.	ihu	ihu	ihu	isu	'nose'
38.	noho	noho	nofo	nofo	'sit, dwell'
39.	leo	reo	leʔo	leo	'voice'
40.	lele	rere	lele	lele	'fly, run'
41.	lemo	remo	lemo	lemo	'drown'
42.	lehu	rehu	efu	lefu	'ashes'
43.	mimi	mimi	mimi	mimi	'urinate'
44.	mana	maŋa	maŋa	maŋa	'branch'
45.	hala	whara	faa	fala	'pandanus'
46.	hana	whaŋa	faŋa	faŋa	'bay'
47.	ʔapo	kapo		ʔapo	'grasp'

B. Fijian is a more distantly related language. What is the significance of the forms in (2)?

(2) kele   'black'   cf. 1
     kula   'red'   2
     vale   'house'   3
     dalo   'taro'   5
     lomo   'drown'   41
     ravu   'ashes'   42
     vara   'pandanus'   45

3.9 Algonquian

Relying on the discussion in section 3.6, reconstruct the Proto-Algonquian forms of the following words.

(1)

Fox	Cree	Menomini	Ojibwa	
ana:kani	uya:kan	una:kan	unakan	'dish'
ana:kwa	ata:hk	ana:hku-k pl.	ana:nk	'star'
ihkwewa	iskwew		ikwe:	'woman'

3.10 Muskogean Consonants

A. (1) lists cognates from four major Muskogean languages (Haas 1941, 1945, 1947): Choctaw, Hitchiti, Koasati, and Creek. Set up the sound correspondences among the consonants and try to reconstruct the consonant system for Proto-Muskogean. What sound changes have occurred in the development of the individual daughter languages? In certain cases the transcription has been normalized. All Hitchiti nouns end in the suffix -*i*.

(1)

Choctaw	Hitchiti	Koasati	Creek	
ahi	a:h-i	aha	aha	'potatoes'
opa	o:p-a:k-i	opa	opa	'hoot owl'
koni	ko:n-i	kono	kono	'skunk'
tana		taθa	taθ-ita	'to weave'
nani	θa:θ-i	θaθo	θaθo	'fish'
haši	ha:s-i	hasi	hasi	'sun'
šawi	sa:w-i	sawa		'raccoon'
nusi	nu:č-i	nuči	nuč-ita	'sleep'
losa	lo:č-i	loča		'black'
	θa:f-i	θafi	θafo	'winter'
lakna	lakn-i	la:na	la:n-i	'yellow'
sakli		ča:lo	ča:lo	'trout'
okla	okl-i	o:la		'town, people'
homma		homma		'red'
minko	mik-i	mi:kko	mi:kko	'chief'
	hayohk-i	hayo:ki		'deep'
ayokpa		ayokpa		'happy'

B. The forms in (2) present a puzzling correspondence between [b] and [k]. In what ways is this correspondence problematic for your analysis? A new phoneme *X must be posited as the source for this correspondence. What properties must *X have? Suggest some likely candidates.

	Choctaw	Hitchiti	Koasati	Creek	
(2)	bihi	bih-hasi	bihi-čuba	ki:	'mulberry'
	bayyi		baya	kala	'white oak'
		bakč-i	bakču	kaču:	'brier, black-berry'
	umbi			uθku	'pawpaw'
	biyaŋkak		biyakka	kiya:kka	'chicken hawk'

4 The Phonetic Foundations of Phonology

We have a number of goals in this chapter. First, we will return to a more complete description of the vocal apparatus and its role in the production of speech. Second, we will sketch a particular conception of the organization of the features based on the Articulator Model. We will then look at the acoustics of speech in a nontechnical way. Finally, we will survey some of the issues that arise in speech perception, concentrating on evidence that speech is perceived by a special module.

4.1 Introduction

A range of opinion has arisen on the role of phonological versus phonetic considerations in the development of a feature system to represent the articulation of the Saussurean sign (''phonological form'' in generative parlance). One extreme, represented by Hjelmslev's glossematics (see Anderson 1985), claims that phonological behavior involves patterns and categories that are unconstrained by phonetics (the physical realization of language as speech). On the other side, much work in phonetics concerns itself with discovering and quantifying systematic articulatory and acoustic differences in the realization of members of the same phonological category. Most generative theorists have taken the position that both phonological and phonetic considerations are important. On the one hand, the gestures of speech reflect abstract linguistic categories and can be expected to differ from possibly identical physical movements that do not realize linguistic categories. On the other hand, the phonological categories we do find empirically attested are constrained by the vocal tract and the human auditory system – anatomical apparatus not specifically evolved for the articulation and perception of language. Phonological distinctions and categorizations display gaps that appear arbitrary from a purely abstract, classificatory point of view but seem to reflect contingencies of the articulatory and acoustic systems that realize language in speech. Finding the proper balance between these phonological and phonetic considerations in an explicit representational scheme for the sounds of language continues to be a central question of linguistic theory.

We may distinguish two general approaches to phonological features: those that see features as realizing a certain action or movement and those that see features as static targets or regions of the vocal tract. The latter represents a more traditional point of view that is embodied in the International Phonetic Alphabet (IPA). For example, on the basis of their own extensive language sample as well as a survey of the phonetics literature, Ladefoged and Maddieson (1988) isolate some seventeen distinct consonantal constrictions that would be categorized as "places of articulation" in traditional phonetic terms.

(1)   1.   bilabial
      2.   labiodental
      3.   linguolabial
      4.   interdental
      5.   apical dental
      6.   (laminal) dentialveolar
      7.   apical alveolar
      8.   laminal alveolar
      9.   apical retroflex
     10.   (laminal) palatoalveolar
     11.   sublaminal (retroflex)
     12.   palatal
     13.   velar
     14.   uvular
     15.   pharyngeal
     16.   epiglottal
     17.   glottal

Although minimal pairs are not available in all cases because of the rarity of certain types (e.g., epiglottals), we assume that these categories are capable of distinguishing one sound from another on a systematic basis. But if we accept the thesis that phonetics represents the physical realization of abstract linguistic categories, the important question is how these various sound types behave phonologically. As we will see, there is good reason to believe that a much simpler system underlies the notion "place of articulation." By concentrating on articulatory accuracy, we are in danger of losing sight of the phonological forest among the phonetic trees.

For example, we observed in section 1.6 that although the labiodental [v] shares properties with both the bilabial [β] and interdental [ð] and thus might be said to stand between them (and is so listed in the IPA), [v] consistently patterns phonologically with the bilabials rather than with the dentals in sound changes and constraints: for example, [p] → [f], [f] → [p], not [f] → [t]. A related point is that the various places of articulation in (1) are not phonologically equidistant. For example, only a few languages contrast consonants from the first and second categories (e.g., Ewe bilabial [Φ] vs. labiodental [f]), while many more contrast consonants from the second and third categories (e.g., English, Arabic [f] vs. [θ]). Finally, complex segments simultaneously combine certain points of articulation in one sound: for example, the labiovelar stop [kp] found in many West African languages is articulated with closure at the lips and dorsum and thus combines bilabial and velar. But there are no sounds that can be described as simultaneously combining bilabial and labiodental (though they may be sequenced, as in the affricate [pf]). This difference makes sense if such multiply articulated consonants are generated according to the articulator active in the production of the two sounds: the tongue dorsum for [k] and the lower lip for [p]. Since [p] and [f] have the same articulator (labial), they could not combine to form a multiply articulated segment.

The IPA system describes vowels with a system of articulatory targets that differs radically from the one employed for consonants: the highest point of the tongue arch. There are major problems with this system; we will look at two. First, it is simply not accurate as a description of the actual location of the tongue. For example, in a critique of this model, Wood (1982) finds that the highest point of the tongue arch for the lax high front vowel [ɪ] is actually lower than for the mid vowel [e]. If we were solely interested in achieving phonetic accuracy, we could simply rearrange the relative positions of these two vowels. However, because sounds represent phonological categories, this move is not open to us. We must be able to group [i] and [ɪ] together as a natural class to the exclusion of [e]. For example, Canadian French affricates [t] before [i] and [ɪ] but not before [e]. The proper conclusion to draw is that the articulatory definition of vowels in terms of the highest tongue arch is incorrect. Some other articulatory correlate must be found. Another major flaw of the traditional IPA system is its failure to provide a uniform set of categories to describe both consonants and vowels. After all, speakers do not have two mouths (one for consonants and the other for vowels), and it is clear that many phonological processes (e.g., palatalization) cut across the consonant-vowel division.

These problems prompted Halle (1983) to develop an alternative model in which features are viewed as neural commands to activate certain articulators with specific muscular gestures.

> The process of speech production consists in moving an articulator from one position to another, where by an articulator is meant a recognized anatomical entity such as the lower lip, the body of the tongue, or the vocal cords, but not an entity defined purely ad hoc such as the highest point of the tongue arch which varies constantly in the course of an utterance. (p. 97)

For Halle, features are abstract neural categories with specific articulatory and acoustic correlates. To justify this more abstract conception of the features, he points to a number of cases showing the lack of a one-to-one relation between a given feature's acoustic and articulatory correlates. For example, place of articulation in a stop such as [k] is associated with two acoustic cues: the frequency pattern of the spectral burst produced by release of the stop closure and the formant transitions to and from the adjacent vowels. The latter cue is missing in interconsonantal contexts; only the former differentiates strings such as *asks* and *asps*. An inverse case in which a given acoustic state has different articulatory correlates is represented by voicelessness, which can be achieved either by stiffening the vocal folds or by spreading the vocal folds. The important point is that phonological rules never distinguish a sound depending on its associated phonetic correlate. They always equate the two and hence must operate at a more abstract level. The specific connections between the articulation and the acoustics are mediated by the features. These connections are not learned. Rather, they are "wired-in" as part of the genetic endowment the child brings to language acquisition, allowing the system to get off to a running start. Without these connections, acquisition would be stymied by another lack of invariance in the speech signal. More generally, this state of affairs recalls the point made by Sapir (1925) in his celebrated discussion comparing the sounds made in blowing out a candle with the [wh] in words such as *when* and *whether*. From a purely physical point of view, the two sounds have essentially identical muscular movements and spectral properties. But they have a totally different psychological or cognitive status. The [wh] of *when* is part of a system of phonological categories that cross-classifies all speech sounds; candle blowing is a single isolated act that, so far as is known, is unconnected with others like sighing, whistling, and clucking. The general point is that the same physical hardware can be operated by distinct neural (software) systems in producing and interpreting the sounds involved in sighing, whistling, and so forth, on the one hand, and the sounds of natural language on the other. Linguists are interested in the neural systems that activate the vocal apparatus to produce speech. As Halle puts it, "On this view the distinctive features correspond to controls in the central nervous system which are connected in specific ways to the human motor and articulatory systems" (1983:95).

In Halle 1983 and much subsequent work, generative phonologists have developed a model for the representation of speech sounds that is premised on a close relation between phonetics and phonology in which the articulators involved in the production of speech play a central role. This *Articulator Model* postulates a set of six articulators with special formal properties. Certain features reflect general properties of the strictures made by the various articulators; other features are bound to particular articulators, implying a certain hierarchical organization. Finally, a given sound may be the product of several different articulators working in concert. In order to better appreciate the Articulator Model, let us first review the anatomy of the vocal apparatus, identifying the various pieces of articulatory hardware and the features they implement.

4.2   The Articulators

While it is possible to speak for a brief duration on inhalation, speech is normally realized under exhalation. The lungs are a pair of elastic cavities that expand and contract to take in and expel air during breathing. They are connected to the trachea through the bronchi (figure 4.1). Since breathing and feeding share some of the same anatomical passageways, evolution has designed several valves to ensure that food and other solid matter do not enter the lungs. One occurs at the top of the trachea; it is known as the *larynx,* a complex structure composed of several cartilages and ligaments (figure 4.2). At the top front of the larynx is a large flange-shaped protective cartilage (the thyroid cartilage), which protrudes sharply in the throat of adult males – the so-called Adam's apple. Behind this cartilage at the top of the trachea lies the crycoid cartilage, which forms the base supporting the entire laryngeal assembly. For our purposes, the most important part of the assembly is the *arytenoid* cartilages, which connect to the thyroid by two pairs of ligaments – the upper one known as the "false" vocal folds and the lower the "true" vocal folds. They seal off the trachea, preventing the intrusion

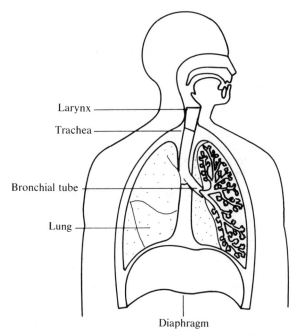

Figure 4.1   Lungs, bronchial tubes, and trachea: general arrangement. (From Clark and Yallop 1990:23; adapted by Clark and Yallop from Minifie, Hixon, and Williams 1973:78.)

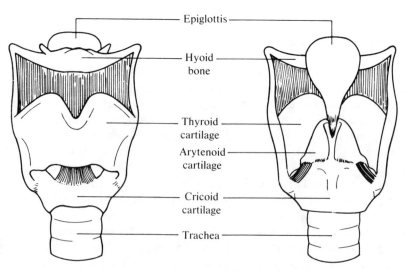

Figure 4.2   The larynx: anterior and posterior views. (From Clark and Yallop 1990:30.)

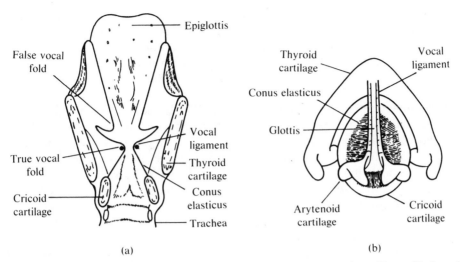

Figure 4.3 Vocal fold structure. (a) Anterior view. (b) Coronal section. (From Clark and Yallop 1990:32; adapted by Clark and Yallop from (a) Zemlin 1968:131 and (b) Minifie, Hixon, and Williams 1973:137.)

of foreign matter that could cause suffocation. They also permit air to be trapped in the lungs to form a fulcrum for lifting with the arms. The arytenoid cartilages and vocal folds jointly form the long slit-like valve known as the *glottis* (figure 4.3). For speech only the lower, "true" vocal folds are relevant. They are controlled by the arytenoid cartilage and some 23 accompanying muscles. One manner of control determines the amount of opening between the folds. This glottal opening ranges from a relatively wide position for normal breathing, to a narrowing of the folds found in the sound [h], to a tight closure for the glottal stop [ʔ]. Opening the vocal folds is known as *abduction*, closing the folds as *adduction*. Halle and Stevens (1971) postulate that these muscles realize the features [±spread gl] and [±constr gl]. (Recall that [+spread gl] characterizes aspirated consonants and [+constr gl] ejective – "glottalized" – consonants.) The arytenoids may also rock back and forth, thereby changing the tension of the folds. This gesture realizes the features [±stiff vf] and [±slack vf] (figure 4.4).

Figure 4.4 Posterior cricoarytenoid muscle: superior view showing action. (From Clark and Yallop 1990:33; adapted by Clark and Yallop from Schneiderman 1984:70.)

According to Halle and Stevens (1991), these features provide another example of the absence of a simple one-to-one relation between the articulatory and acoustic correlates of a feature. Recall that periodic vibration in the acoustic signal – vibration of the vocal folds – is a function of (i) a pressure drop across the glottis required to generate the airflow necessary to set the folds in vibration as well as (ii) the stiffness of the folds themselves. Halle and Stevens observe that in sounds with relatively minimal supralaryngeal constriction such as vowels, an increase in glottal stiffness increases the rate of vibration and thus serves to implement the phonological category of tone. But in sounds with greater supralaryngeal constriction (obstruents), increased stiffness shuts off vibration and thus implements a voiceless consonant. Hence, the same articulatory gesture [+ stiff vf] can lead to fundamentally different acoustic effects, depending on the nature of the supralaryngeal constriction. The fact that the upper register tones of Tianjin (section 7.8) are associated with voiceless obstruents and the lower register tones with voiced obstruents now finds a natural interpretation: the glottal stiffness of the preceding onset consonant has a direct effect on the vocal fold stiffness of the accompanying vowel's tone.

The supralaryngeal articulations involve three cavities: pharyngeal, oral, and nasal (figure 4.5). The tongue constitutes the lower margin of the first two and the palate (roof of the mouth) the lower margin of the third. It is these lower elements that are movable; the upper ones are essentially fixed. Halle's hypothesis is that speech is articulated through the action of the lower articulators – the

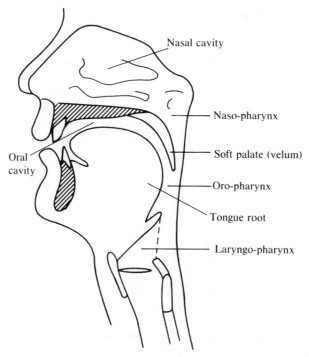

Figure 4.5   Supralaryngeal cavities. (Adapted from Clark and Yallop 1990:43.)

"dramatis personae" of articulation. The Tongue Root is the principal actor in the lower pharynx. It may project forward, creating greater pharyngeal volume. This gesture realizes the [ATR] feature ("advanced tongue root") that underlies the tense vowels of English and the harmony systems of many West African languages such as Lama. The tongue root may also be retracted toward the back wall of the pharyngeal cavity to produce the pharyngeal consonants [ħ,ʕ] found in Arabic, perhaps reflecting a consonantal feature [RTR] ("retracted tongue root") comparable to the vocalic [ATR]. Lowering the velum to produce [+nasal] sounds is the joint responsibility of the palatopharyngeal and palatoglossus muscles. The palatal tensor muscle and the levator palatine muscle raise the velum and thus implement [−nasal] (figure 4.6). Instead of the term "velum," Halle employs Soft Palate to designate the articulator that implements nasality.

The tongue is a large and elongated mass of muscles capable of a variety of movements and is proprioceptively the most active element in speech. It is thus no accident that the morpheme for "language" derives etymologically from 'tongue'. At the opposite end from the root, the blade of the tongue articulates coronal sounds such as [θ,s,š]. Coronals are produced by contracting the superior longitudinal muscles of the tongue and relaxing the inferior longitudinal muscles

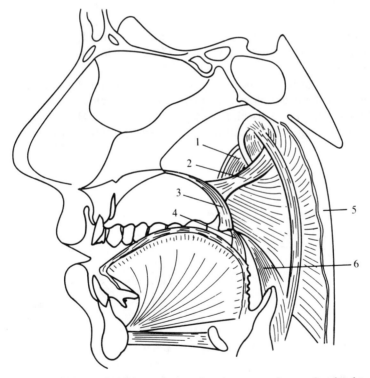

Figure 4.6 Supraglottal vocal tract showing soft palate musculature: 1 palatal tensor muscle; 2 levator palatine muscle; 3 uvular muscle; 4 palatoglossus muscle; 5 palatopharyngeal sphincter; 6 palatopharyngeal muscle. (From Clark and Yallop 1990:45; adapted by Clark and Yallop from Zemlin 1968:299.)

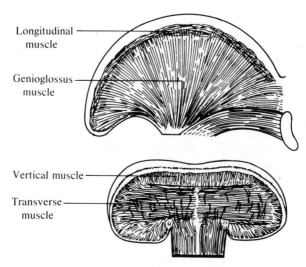

Figure 4.7   Intrinsic muscles of the tongue. (From Clark and Yallop 1990:50; adapted by Clark and Yallop from Sonesson 1968:68.)

(figure 4.7). The extrinsic muscles of the tongue control the movement of the tongue body; they connect the tongue to fixed bone masses in the skull (figure 4.8). The genioglossus connects the tongue body with the lower jaw and pulls the tongue forward to produce front vowels. The styloglossus connects the tongue to two processes at the base of the skull; it retracts the tongue body and is active in the production of back vowels. Raising and lowering the tongue body is the responsibility of the palatoglossus and hyoglossus muscles, respectively. The former implements high vowels and the latter low vowels. Halle cites EMG (electromyographic) recordings by Alfonso et al. (1982) to support these connections

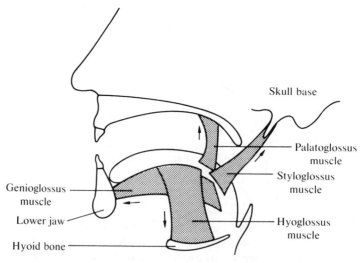

Figure 4.8   Extrinsic muscles of the tongue. (From Clark and Yallop 1990:49; adapted by Clark and Yallop from Sonesson 1968:67.)

between particular features and articulators. Finally, the lower lip is the active articulator in the production of labial consonants. It also helps to execute the feature [round].

The articulators and the features they execute are listed in (2)

(2) [round] ———— Labial

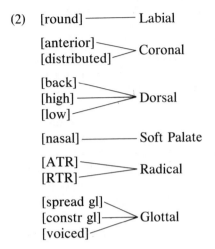

Conceiving of features in this way begins to answer some of the criticisms raised earlier against the traditional point-of-articulation scheme. First, both consonants and vowels are described with the same set of articulators and so the model promises to capture consonant-vowel homologies (though exactly how remains a hotly debated question; see sections 9.2, 9.3 for discussion). Second, both [p] and [f] are implemented with the Labial articulator, in contrast to [ð] and [d], which share the Coronal articulator. This explains their affinities even though the precise point of stricture may vary. As we will see, it is at the level of the articulator that many phonological rules and constraints operate.

To sum up, under the Articulator Model, the features are claimed to control specific muscular activations. This view contrasts with the more traditional one, which sees place of articulation as a division of the vocal tract into an ordered series of regions or zones without paying special attention to the articulators that are activated in each zone. While the Articulator Model claims that the six articulators are the basic actors in the production of speech, specific points along the vocal tract may establish proprioceptive feedback relations (Perkell 1980) that guide the act of articulation. An active role for feedback is supported by the observation of readjustments that the articulators make in producing speech after the loss of teeth or certain surgical interventions that radically alter the production mechanism.

4.3   The Feature Tree

Until this point in our exposition of the generative model, the features composing a sound have been represented as an unorganized bundle. This gives the misleading impression that the features may freely combine in the construction of a phonemic inventory as well as in defining natural classes of segments in phonological rules and constraints. But this is clearly false – for at least two reasons.

First, some features are best thought of as introducing a subdistinction within the category defined by another feature. For example, [distributed] and [anterior] only seem relevant for Coronal consonants. Although we may specify [g] or [h] as [−distributed] by default, this move opens up the possibility that some language could contrast [±distributed] velars and laryngeals, parallel to [θ] vs. [s]. It also leads us to expect rules or constraints that depend on grouping [−distributed] [t] with [h]. No evidence exists to support either of these predictions. To take another case, certain stricture features are only appropriate for consonants. Thus, it makes no sense to mark a vowel such as [a] for the features [lateral] and [strident]. In sum, we need to encode these limitations on the ability of the features to combine and thereby create contrasting phonological categories.

Second, as stressed by Clements (1985a), certain features form recurrent groupings in phonological rules and constraints. For example, one vowel may assimilate the place features [high], [low], and [back] from an adjacent vowel but ignore the latter's specification for [hi tone] and [nasal]. Assimilation of [hi tone], [nasal], and [back] (but not [high] and [low]) would be very unusual if not impossible. If we take seriously the idea that features are executed by articulators, then [high], [low], and [back] have a special affinity – they are all bound to the Dorsal articulator. The fact that they function together in rules and constraints is no longer mysterious.

In order to capture formally such natural feature groupings and restrictions on feature combination, generative phonologists have pursued the hypothesis that the features are organized in a hierarchical tree structure. There are various competing proposals about the nature of the organization and many details remain to be worked out. We will survey some of these issues in chapter 9. The model in (3), based on proposals by Halle (1992), serves as our point of departure.

(3)

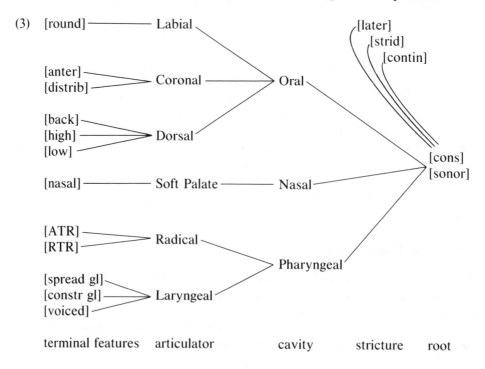

terminal features   articulator   cavity   stricture   root

In this model, several hierarchical distinctions are introduced among the features. The terminal features ([round], etc.) are related to the *SPE* major class features [consonantal] and [sonorant], which form the root of the tree, through two intermediate levels of structure: the six articulators and the three cavity nodes to which they are assigned. Off to the side are a set of features characterizing the degree and type of stricture made by the articulator in its cavity. The feature tree can be thought of as a segment generator. The claim is that any member of the UG phonetic alphabet can be generated by choosing the appropriate articulator and dependent feature(s), the cavity in which the articulator forms a stricture, and general characteristics of the degree and type of stricture, which lead to the segment's identity as an obstruent, sonorant consonant, or vowel.

Organizing the features in a hierarchical tree provides a natural formalism to express the fact that certain features refine distinctions in other features. For example, we observed earlier that [+distributed] only seems relevant for coronal consonants. The tree graph formally expresses this point by making [distributed] a daughter of Coronal. [distributed] can only be accessed through the Coronal articulator and is thus incompatible with any other articulator. The hierarchical tree also provides a natural formalism to express recurrent feature groupings. Mention of a particular node in the tree will be interpreted to imply all of the information dominated by that node. Two features can thus be expected to cooccur in rules or constraints only if they share a common node in the tree. For example, [high], [low], and [back] group together since they are daughters of the node Dorsal. Conversely, [high] and [nasal] should not join up since there is no single node that dominates just these features. We will return to this point in greater detail momentarily.

Depending from the root in (3) are two types of features: those that can be localized to a particular articulator (*articulator-bound* features) and the *stricture* features [continuant], [strident] (and perhaps [lateral]), which combine more freely and are thus not bound to a particular articulator as the terminal features are. Because the stricture features are much less well understood, our discussion here concentrates primarily on the remaining features; see section 9.5 for further discussion of stricture.

Certain restrictions hold on the combination of the root features with each other and with the articulators. Vowels are [−consonantal, +sonorant], sonorant consonants are [+consonantal, +sonorant], and obstruents are [+consonantal, −sonorant]. The fourth combination, [−consonantal, −sonorant] is precluded because a [−consonantal] segment's lack of constriction in the oral cavity implies the spontaneous voicing indicative of a [+sonorant] segment. Also, Halle (1992) proposes a constraint that requires [+consonantal] to dominate the Oral cavity and thus restricts its implementation to the Labial, Coronal, or Dorsal articulator. This proposal implies that pharyngeals such as [ḥ,ʕ] and laryngeals such as [h,ʔ] will pattern as [−consonantal] glides – a prediction that seems to be borne out in many cases where it can be tested.

There are still certain gaps in our knowledge of how the stricture features combine. [continuant] combines freely with the oral articulators: many languages have stop-fricative oppositions implemented by the Labial, Coronal, and Dorsal articulators. Conclusive evidence for [continuant] in the Pharyngeal cavity is lacking, however. Consequently, this feature might be regarded as a dependent of the Oral

cavity instead of the root node; or perhaps it joins [+ consonantal] in being restricted to the oral articulators. [strident] most clearly characterizes coronals; its
appearance under Labial depends on whether the bilabial [β] vs. labiodental [v]
distinction is best treated as one of stridency. There is little evidence one way or
the other on this question. Finally, [lateral] is almost always a coronal; but rules
assimilating the Coronal articulator often fail to spread [lateral]. This is a case
where evidence from contrast and from assimilation (see section 4.3.1) fail to
converge.

Feature trees generated from (3) for a few selected segments are shown in (4).

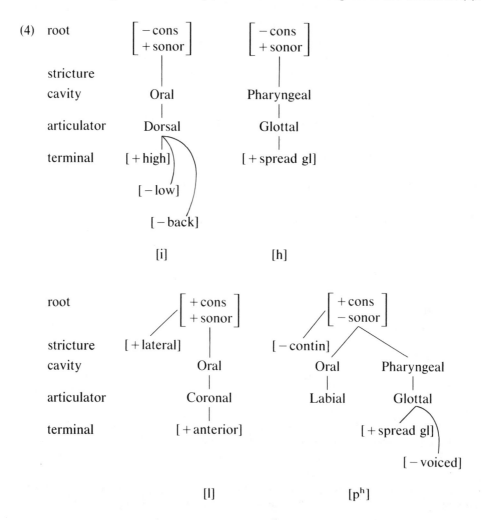

In the representation of sounds in terms of the feature tree in (3), any given
terminal feature implies the presence of the corresponding articulator and all
higher nodes. Thus, [round] implies Labial; [+ spread gl] implies Glottal; and so
on. Furthermore, each articulator can be reached from the root of the tree only
through a cavity. An interpretive convention is also required to indicate which

articulator executes the root features (as well as other stricture features not dedicated to a particular articulator). Sagey (1986) employs an arrow pointing from the root to the relevant articulator. To reduce notational clutter, the major articulator is indicated here with an asterisk. Segments such as [m], [æ], and [kʷ] thus receive the representations in (5). The asterisk ensures that in the implementation of the labiovelar [kʷ], the [+consonantal, −sonorant] root features and the [−continuant] stricture feature are jointly executed by the Dorsal articulator.

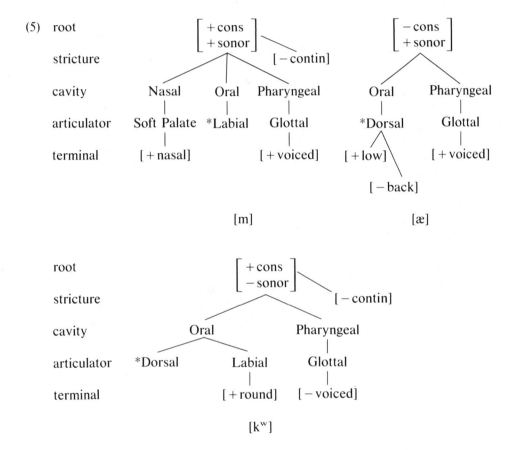

An essential property of the tree graph is the relation of *dependency* and/or *dominance*. We can single out a group of features by mentioning the corresponding node in the graph that dominates all and only those features. Stated differently, any nonterminal node in the graph forms the root of a subtree composed of all the nodes that it dominates. Thus, Coronal groups [anterior] and [distributed]; Oral groups Labial, Coronal, and Dorsal and therefore also groups the Coronal dependents [anterior] and [distributed]. As we will see, this dominance/dependency property is crucial to the formal expression of numerous phonological processes and constraints. On the other hand, no significance is to be attached to the order of the branches (e.g., to whether Oral precedes or follows Pharyngeal at the cavity level, or whether Labial precedes or follows Dorsal at the articulator level). In the diagrams shown here, the order of the branches depending from the same node will be shifted freely in order to overcome the limitations of the two-dimensional page. In sum, within the segment it is the presence or the absence of features and their hierarchical arrangement that is important.

The next three subsections illustrate the utility of the feature tree in formulating three broad categories of sound change: assimilation, reduction, and dissimilation.

4.3.1 Assimilation

Conceiving the features as distributed in a tree provides a natural representation of assimilation as establishing a new connection or *association* between two nodes in the graph. Assimilation is represented by a dotted line connecting the features of the *source* to the *target* or *focus* of the rule. Three kinds of assimilation are distinguished: *single-feature assimilation,* corresponding to the extension of a terminal feature or "leaf" in the tree; *complete assimilation,* which joins segments at the root; and *partial assimilation,* in which the information at some intermediate node in the graph spreads to an adjacent position.

To take the simplest case, assimilation of an individual feature will consist in associating a feature to the corresponding mother node in an adjacent segment. If the assimilating segment is unspecified for the relevant feature, then it simply acquires the specification of the source segment (a so-called *feature-filling* or *structure-building* operation). An example is provided by the voicing assimilation of the regular verbal and nominal inflections in English, such as the plural *cat* + [s] vs. *dog* + [z] and the past tense *reap* + [t] (*reaped*) vs. *rub* + [d] (*rubbed*). These suffixes do not contrast underlyingly in voicing and assimilate the voicing of the final segment of the stem. The rule in (6a) says that the [±voiced] specification "spreads" to the bare Glottal articulator of the following consonant of the inflectional suffix. The application of the rule is shown in (6b,c), where [S] stands for a dental fricative unspecified for voicing. The result is that two successive segments terminate at the same leaf node: the [±voiced] specification that underlyingly characterizes the final segment of the stem (6b,c).

(6)   a.   Glottal$_i$ Glottal$_j$ (where Glottal$_j$ is unspecified)

          [±voiced]

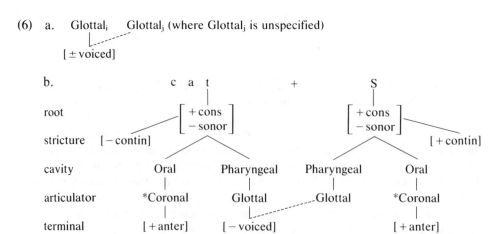

c.

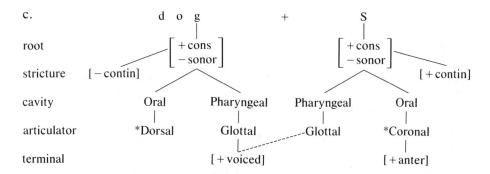

In the regressive assimilation of *fi*[v]*e* vs. *fi*[f]-*th,* the [−voiced] of the suffix [-θ] spreads leftward to the consonant, displacing the underlying [+voiced] specification of the [v] (a *structure-changing* operation). The delinking of the original feature is represented by "z" in the rule (7a). The application of this rule to the underlying [v]+[θ] substring of [fiv+θ] is depicted in (7b,c). Once again, it results in a representation where two successive consonants share the same [−voiced] feature specification.

(7) a.

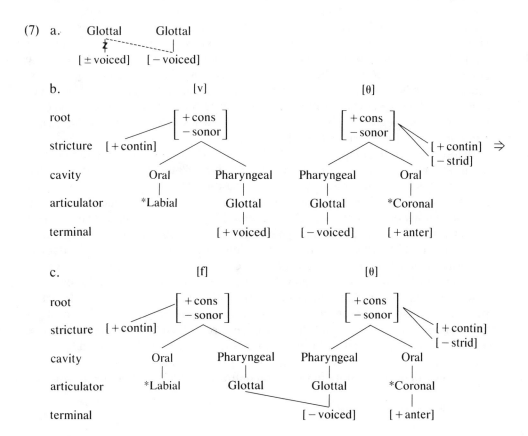

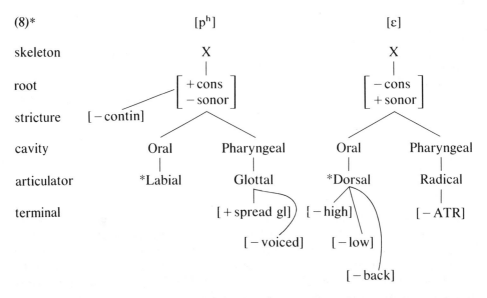

(8)*

In the general case, then, assimilation takes the form of associating a node in the graph with the appropriate mother node of the adjacent segment. If the segment undergoing assimilation bears a specification for the spreading feature, it is typically delinked from the tree, giving the appearance of a change in feature values. However, it is crucial to realize that under this view of assimilation, the plus or minus feature values of one segment are not changed to agree with those of the adjacent segment. Rather, the feature specification of the conditioning context literally spreads to the focus of the rule, displacing any information that occupies that site in the graph. The result is a single feature specification that extends over two successive segments. In later chapters we will explore in detail the formal consequences of this conception of assimilation.

Before we turn to complete assimilation, let us anticipate a result from chapter 8 and assume a *three-dimensional* representation of phonological structure that distinguishes between a phoneme and the position that it occupies in the linear string of segments. Segments are ordered in virtue of a linear sequence of "skeletal" positions or "timing slots," represented by Xs and reflecting the fact that speech is realized over time. The segments flesh out the empty timing slots forming the skeleton. The ordering of the timing slots in the skeleton of course depicts an abstract or virtual time; in physical articulation the various gestures overlap considerably. A word such as *penny* receives the schematic representation in (8) under the conception that features are organized in hierarchical trees. In interpreting this diagram, in order to overcome the limitations imposed by the two-dimensional page, imagine that the root nodes are rotated 90°. If *penny* comprises a four-segment "pipe" [pʰ][ɛ][n][i] that we rotate in order to look down the front end, then the root nodes for [ɛ], [n], and [i] will be hidden behind that of [pʰ]. We assume that each feature in the graph defines a special type of linear sequence

* This diagram reads across pages 152 and 153.

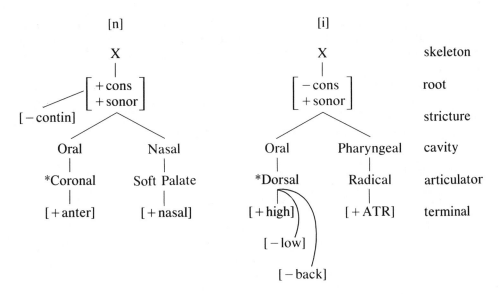

known as a *tier*. Like the levels of seating in a stadium, we can talk about feature specifications across the string of segments as being located on the same tier relative to one another. Thus, at the root *penny* is comprised of the sequence [+cons] [−cons] [+cons] [−cons] on the [consonantal] tier. For the feature [ATR], *penny* defines the tier [−ATR] [+ATR]. Note in particular that a consonant such as [n] is inherently unspecified for [ATR]; as a result, the surrounding vowels are adjacent on the ATR tier. This *underspecification* will be of considerable importance in maintaining the hypothesis that rules and constraints apply in local contexts – a desirable hypothesis because of the constraints it places on the grammar's learnability. In order to visualize the tiers more clearly, it helps to imagine that the feature trees are mobiles. When we rotate the root nodes, the [ATR] specifications of the [ɛ] and [i] will align and not be interrupted by any terminal features of the intervening [n], which fails to receive a registration for [ATR].

Biblical Hebrew provides examples of complete assimilation that receive a natural interpretation under the tree graph notation for features. The dental nasal [n] assimilates completely to a following consonant, as we can see from the paradigms in (9), where the CV̄CVC root of the perfect shrinks to CCVC, bringing the first and second radical (root) consonants next to one another; initial [n] of 'fall', 'give', and 'approach' then completely assimilates to the second radical.

(9) perfect   kātab   nāpal   nātan   nāgaš
     imperfect yi-ktob   yi-ppol   yi-tten   yi-ggaš
                'write'   'fall'   'give'   'approach'

In this case all the features characterizing [n] must assimilate: consonantality, voicing, articulator, nasality, and so on. This is easy to express if the features form a tree structure. We simply say that given an [n]C string (where C is any

consonant), the root node comprising the C is associated to the timing slot that
dominates the preceding [n], simultaneously delinking all the features of the original [n] by detaching it from its timing slot. The result is a sequence of two skeletal
positions associated with the same root node – a geminate. This rule is formulated
in (10a); just enough information is specified to isolate the [n]C string that undergoes the rule. (10b) sketches the effects of the rule on the underlying [np] string
in [yi-npol] → *yi-ppol;* (10bi) shows the input [np] and (10bii) the output [pp],
where the root node of the original [n] has been cut away.

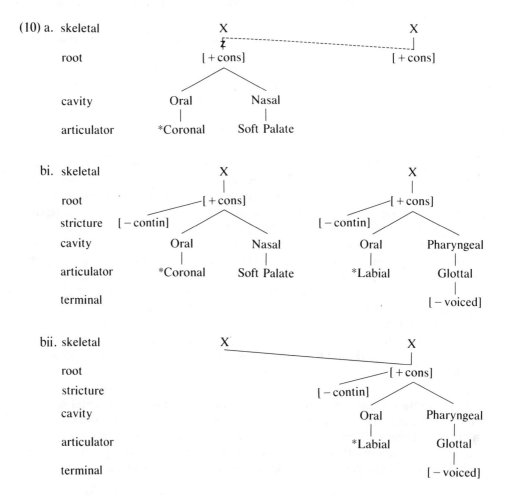

The formalism in (10) expresses the essence of complete assimilation: no trace
of the original segment is left – just its position, which is filled by the spreading
segment. Under the earlier generative conception of the features as an unstruc-
tured bundle, complete assimilation is rather mysterious. Simply listing all features
as changing simultaneously makes for a complex rule. Furthermore, if all features
can assimilate, then why not all but one or all but two? But such cases are rare
or nonexistent. The general point is that the earlier formalism fails to isolate
complete assimilation as a natural and recurrent process. Unhappiness with this

state of affairs is reflected in the fact that previous generative descriptions typically invoked some ad hoc convention such as [n] → [αFs] / ⎯⎯ [αFs], where [Fs] abbreviated all the features of a segment. But a variable such as [Fs] has no natural standing in the theory in comparison to the root node of the feature tree that serves as the anchoring point for the view of complete assimilation developed here.

To take another case from Biblical Hebrew, recall from section 1.11 that the definite prefix geminates a following consonant, unless it is a guttural, in which case the preceding vowel is lengthened (reflecting a restriction against long gutturals): *ham-melek* 'the king' but *haa-ʕiir* 'the city'. Given the notions of the skeleton and features as rooted tree graphs, we may represent the prefix as composed of three positions, the third of which is not associated to a root node. This empty position then links to any following nonguttural consonant, producing gemination. Otherwise, it is filled by the preceding vowel.

(11) skeleton   X X X   X X X X X X X X   X X X X X X X
                  │ │   │ │ ╲ │ │ │ │   │ ╱ │ ╱ │
      root   h a   h a m e l e k   h a   ʕ i   r

In this case complete assimilation at the root node has no preexisting features to displace; it is a structure-building rather than a structure-changing operation.

Multiple feature assimilation has played a critical role in the development of feature theory. In a very influential study, Clements (1985a) observes that only a small number of the logically possible combinations of features spread together in rules of assimilation. For example, given the features {a,b,c,d,e}, we may find that {a,b} and {c,d} form recurrent groupings while {b,c} and {d,e} do not. As Clements points out, organizing the features in a rooted tree graph provides a natural formalism to express this fact. Two or more features will figure in a rule or constraint only if they share a common dominating node in the tree. Stated differently, if phonological rules are defined over nodes in the tree graph, then certain feature grouping are simple to express while others become more complex. In our abstract example, suppose that {a,b,c,d,e} are organized as in (12). Then we can isolate {a,b} by mentioning {f} and {c,d} by mentioning {g}. But we cannot group {d,e} without also including {c}. Finally {b,c} should function together only if {a,d,e} are also included – that is, only in complete assimilation.

(12)

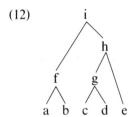

Some of the simplest and clearest cases of multiple feature assimilation strongly support the articulator groupings depicted in the feature tree of (3). In the rest of this subsection we will survey a few examples.

Consider first one of Clements's examples from English (13). In informal speech, the [−continuant] coronals [t,d,n] appear as interdental before [θ], as postalveolar before [š,ž], and as retroflex before [r].

(13)   [t]   [d]   [n]
      ____ θ   eighth   hundredth   tenth   [+distrib, +anter]
      ____ š   eight shoes   eight gems   insure   [+distrib, −anter]
      ____ r   tree   dream   enroll   [−distrib, −anter]
      ____ s   hats   reads   ensue   [−distrib, +anter]

This collection of sound changes can be described as assimilation of the features [distributed] and [anterior]. Why [distributed] and [anterior] (rather than, say, [distributed] and any other randomly selected feature such as [nasal] or [spread gl])? Given the feature tree (3), [distributed] and [anterior] share a special relation: they are dependents of the same mother node, the Coronal articulator. This sister relation allows the process to be expressed as in (14): a dental-alveolar [−continuant] (i.e., [t,d,n]) assimilates the subsidiary place features of the following coronal consonant, simultaneously delinking its original specifications. In other words, the precise point of articulation of the second coronal is transmitted to a preceding coronal occlusive.

(14) stricture/root   [−contin]   [+cons]

      cavity   Oral   Oral

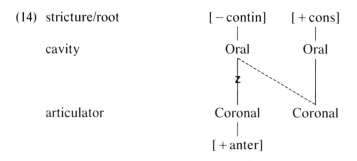

      articulator   Coronal   Coronal

                              [+anter]

This example also indicates that the feature [lateral] is not a dependent of Coronal even though it is typically associated with coronals. If it were, then we should expect [d] to turn to [l] in *badly*.

Ancient Greek provides an example in which the dependents of the Glottal articulator spread as a group. This language contrasts voiceless, aspirated, and voiced stops, as depicted in (15a). The paradigms in (15b) from Buck 1933 indicate that the underlying [voiced] and [spread gl] values of a stem-final consonant are replaced by the following suffix-initial obstruent's specifications for these features.

(15) a. p,t,k   = [−voiced, −spread gl]
          pʰ,tʰ,kʰ   = [−voiced, +spread gl]
          b,d,g   = [+voiced, −spread gl]

b. tríb-ō   tetrīp-tai   'rub'
    grapʰ-ō   gegrap-tai   'write'
    pɛmp-ō   ɛpɛmpʰ-tʰēn   'send'
    tríb-ō   etrīpʰ-tʰēn   'rub'
    klɛpt-ō   klɛb-dēn   'steal'
    grapʰ-ō   grab-dēn   'write'

Given the feature tree of (3) in which [voiced] and [spread gl] are dependents of the Glottal articulator, the regressive assimilation seen in (15b) may be expressed by the rule in (16): it simply extends the Glottal node of the second obstruent to the preceding one, delinking the latter's underlying Glottal specification. The result is a representation in which a single laryngeal specification characterizes the entire consonant cluster.

(16) root   [−sonor]   [−sonor]

      cavity   Pharyngeal   Pharyngeal

      articulator   Glottal   Glottal

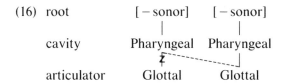

It is instructive to compare this formulation with the one in (17) implicated by a theory in which the features are not organized into a tree but form an unordered bundle.

(17) $[-\text{sonor}] \rightarrow \begin{bmatrix} \alpha\text{voiced} \\ \beta\text{spread gl} \end{bmatrix} / \underline{\hspace{1cm}} \begin{bmatrix} \alpha\text{voiced} \\ \beta\text{spread gl} \end{bmatrix}$

This notation employs the Greek letters α and β as variables ranging over plus and minus and is designed to say that the feature in the structural change has the same value as the feature of the conditioning context. It is subject to a number of serious criticisms. First, it fails to explain why [voiced] pairs with [spread gl] rather than any other randomly chosen feature. Under the feature tree analysis this is no accident – both features are dependents of the Glottal articulator and thus close kin. Second, the theory that allows (17) fails to explain why we do not find rules in which the value for the feature in the structural change is determined by the specification of a different feature in the rule's context: for example, [αvoiced] by [αlateral]. If the features are not organized into tiers, then assimilation as a spreading operation has no natural or privileged status. But if features define tiers in the feature tree, then rules like [X] → [αvoiced] / ⎯⎯ [αlateral] can be formally distinguished from the more natural ones that spread a node in the tree. The latter merely rearrange the geometry of the representation by extending the domain of a feature or feature group. The former change feature coefficients without any formal connection between the focus and the triggering context. Finally, formulating rules in terms of higher-level nodes leads us to expect that other dependents of the same node will exhibit similar behavior. For example, we expect languages with glottalized consonants to spread [constr gl] along with features of aspiration and voicing – a prediction that is well supported on cross-linguistic grounds. Once again, no such prediction is made by a theory that does not impose an internal organization on the features.

The presence of the cavity nodes in the feature tree of (3) is motivated at present more on phonetic than on phonological grounds. However, it is clear that many phonological processes single out the Labial, Coronal, and Dorsal articulators. For example, in Sudanese Arabic (Hamid 1984) the coronal nasal [n] assimilates the point of articulation of the following consonant, becoming the labial [m] before [b], the coronal [n] before [z], and the velar [ŋ] before [k].

(18)   <u>perfect</u>   <u>imperfect</u>

nabaḥ	ya-mbaḥ	'bark'
nafad	ya-ɱfid	'save'
nazal	ya-nzil	'descend'
nasaf	ya-nsif	'demolish'
našar	ya-ñšur	'spread'
naǰaḥ	ya-ñǰaḥ	'succeed'
nakar	ya-ŋkur	'deny'
naxar	ya-ŋxar	'puncture'
nagal	ya-ŋgul	'transfer'
naḥar	ya-nḥar	'slaughter'
niʕis	ya-nʕas	'fall asleep'
nahab	ya-nhab	'rob'

The [n] remains unchanged before the pharyngeal [ḥ] and the laryngeal [h]. We take this as phonological evidence for a division of the vocal tract into oral and pharyngeal cavities. The assimilation can then be expressed as spreading of the Oral cavity node of the following consonant leftward to a preceding coronal nasal, delinking the original Oral cavity node.

(19)   root

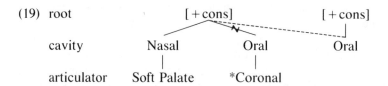

cavity	Nasal	Oral	Oral
articulator	Soft Palate	*Coronal	

More evidence for the Pharyngeal cavity is discussed in section 9.2. The Sudanese Arabic example recalls the observation of Halle (1992) that the tree structure the phonological evidence leads us to impose on the feature bundle by and large matches the structure motivated on phonetic grounds – in particular, the organization into articulators and cavities. This remarkable convergence is presumably no accident but rather indicates a deep connection between the phonology and the phonetics – in other words, that the sounds of language reflect a special linguistic organization and are thus different from the sounds produced when blowing out a candle, yawning, and so forth. We will return to this point in section 4.5.

4.3.2 Reduction

The feature tree of (3) allows a formalization of the traditional intuition that sound changes falling under the rubric of reduction in "weak" position involve the loss of information. To take a simple example, consider vowel reduction to schwa in unstressed position: for example, [æ] → [ə] in *átom, atómic*. Given the feature tree, this process can be described as simply delinking the Dorsal articulator, leaving a bare [−consonantal] root node without any terminal articulator features.

(20) root

articulator

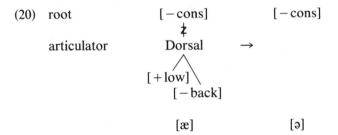

This is a natural representation for the colorless schwa. Previous frameworks required finding some combination of feature values among [high, low, back] to distinguish schwa. But this is problematic in languages such as English that have independent front and back unrounded mid vowels [ɛ] and [ʌ]. Furthermore, even if a vacant feature combination can be found, it still fails to single out the schwa from the other vowels the same way the reductive account does. Finally, the claim that schwa lacks an articulator node explains its propensity to assimilate vowel quality features from the local consonantal and vocalic environment.

Following an insight first expressed by Lass (1976), many researchers have viewed such sound changes as the Spanish dialectal "aspiration" of [s] to [h] (e.g., *me*[h], *mes-e*[h] 'month' sg., pl.) and British English "glottalling" of [t'] to [ʔ] (e.g., *a*[t']*om* → *a*[ʔ]*om*) as a suppression of the supraglottal articulation. Given that [t'] is [+constr gl], [ʔ] is what remains once the supralaryngeal features have been excised (21).

(21) root

stricture
cavity

articulator

terminal

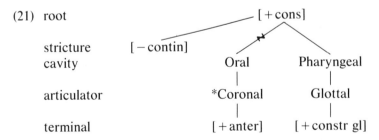

To bring the [s] → [h] change under this rubric, we must establish a link between the [+spread gl] feature marking [h] and the voiceless fricative [s] that is not completely understood. Also, the status of [continuant] in these changes is controversial. Some researchers see [h] as preserving the [+continuant] of [s] and [ʔ] as preserving the [−continuant] of a stop (not necessarily glottalized), accounting for the generalization that fricatives debuccalize as [h] and stops (both glottalized and plain) as [ʔ]. However, there is little independent evidence that [ʔ] and [h] are opposed as [±continuant]. In many languages these sounds pattern with the glides [y,w]. We will return to this issue in section 9.5.

Another common form of reduction is the suppression of laryngeal distinctions in the coda of the syllable. For example, many languages oppose plain, aspirated, and voiced stops [p,b,pʰ] in syllable onsets but limit their coda to just [p]. Given the feature tree, this sound change can be described as the delinking of the Glottal articulator and replacement with a default [−spread gl, −voiced] specification. Evidence that such neutralizations are to be described as delinking rather than as simply a plus-to-minus change in the laryngeal features is the fact that the delinked material can sometimes show up at another position in the string. As we will see in chapter 7, this is a general trait of tonal features. Other laryngeal features sometimes display similar behavior. A possible example is Bartholomae's Law in the development of Sanskrit where an Indo-European [bh+t] cluster is realized as [b+dh], with the apparent transfer of voicing and aspiration from the coda [bh] to the following onset [t] (followed by the regular regressive voicing assimilation). Under the earlier theory in which features form an unorganized bundle, this sound change requires a simultaneous modification of the coefficients of both [spread gl] and [voiced] at two successive positions in the cluster (22a).

(22) a.
$$\begin{bmatrix} +\text{spread gl} \\ +\text{voiced} \end{bmatrix} \begin{bmatrix} -\text{spread gl} \\ -\text{voiced} \end{bmatrix} \rightarrow \begin{bmatrix} -\text{spread gl} \\ +\text{voiced} \end{bmatrix} \begin{bmatrix} +\text{spread gl} \\ +\text{voiced} \end{bmatrix}$$

$\qquad\qquad$ [bʰ] $\qquad\qquad\quad$ [t] $\qquad\qquad\qquad$ [b] $\qquad\qquad$ [dʰ]

b.

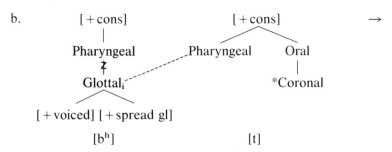

But given the Articulator Model, it can be described as the delinking and subsequent relinking of the Glottal$_i$ articulator. The [p] resulting from delinking the Glottal$_i$ articulator from [b^h] then turns to [b] by the regular rule of regressive voicing assimilation spreading [voiced] from right to left. We assume that when the spreading feature lacks the proper sponsoring articulator node, one is interpolated by convention. This is the source of the new Glottal$_j$ specification supporting the [+voiced] spread from the [d^h] in (22b).

Complex segments with a primary and secondary articulation often reduce by loss of one of the two articulators. Two examples are found in Ukrainian and Romanian. In Ukrainian palatalized labial consonants depalatalize at the end of the word (more generally in the coda of the syllable) – a process evident by comparison with the Russian cognates in (23a). The depalatalization is expressed in (23b) as a delinking of the secondary place features (indicated by the absence of the asterisk designating the primary articulator). The depalatalization of [m'] is sketched in (23c).

(23) a.

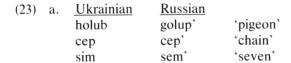

	Ukrainian	Russian	
	holub	golup'	'pigeon'
	cep	cep'	'chain'
	sim	sem'	'seven'

b.

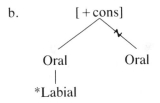

c.

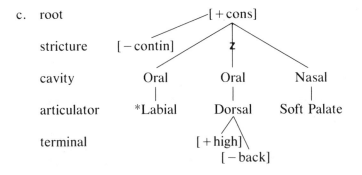

The evolution of Romance *k^w to [p] in Romanian (cf. Latin *aqua* 'water' and Romanian *apă*) can be expressed as the delinking of the primary Dorsal articulator. The secondary Labial articulator is then promoted to primary, realizing the [+consonantal] and [−continuant] stricture features.

(24)

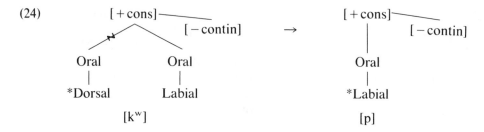

4.3.3 Dissimilation

In many languages root morphemes exhibit gaps in the otherwise expected free
distribution of features to encode the lexicon. These gaps often reflect dissimilatory constraints: avoidance of successive elements drawn from the same category. What counts as the same category should receive a simple formal expression. The study of such constraints is thus another source of evidence bearing on
feature organization. We will review two cases here.

In Japanese the combination of voiced obstruents within a root is avoided in
the native Yamato vocabulary (Itô and Mester 1986). Thus, while voiceless obstruents and voiced and voiceless obstruents combine freely (*futa* 'lid', *fuda*
'sign', *buta* 'pig'), voiced ones do not (**buda*). The constraint is actively enforced
by blocking or undoing an otherwise general rule voicing the initial obstruent in
the second member of a compound (Lyman's Law). Thus, while *iro* 'color' + *kami*
'paper' give *iro* + *gami* 'colored paper', [kami + kaze] 'divine wind' surfaces as
kami + *kaze,* not **kami* + *gaze.* Itô and Mester (1986) express the contrast between
iro + *gami* and *kami* + *kaze* as a dissimilation process that deletes the voicing specification inserted in compounds when another one follows in the same morpheme.
So long as this process is ordered before the default insertion of voicing on sonorants, it can be expressed as a rule that deletes one [+ voiced] specification
when followed by another on the [voiced] tier (25a). The derivation of *kami* + *kaze*
is shown in (25b).

(25) a. [+ voiced] → ∅ / ___ [+ voiced]

    b. kami + k a z e → kami + g a z e → kami + k a z e
              | | | |
        [+ vd]   [+ vd] [+ vd]   [+ vd]

It is worth observing that if the intervening vowels are not underspecified for
voicing and the input to dissimilation is thus (26a), the rule becomes much more
complex. First, we must allow a potentially unbounded number of [+ voiced]
specifications to intervene between the obstruents; second, the rule will have to
look down to the root node where the [± sonorant] contrast is registered. (26b)
states the rule under these assumptions. One job of underspecification is to place
gaps in phonological representations so that rules can be expressed more simply
and insightfully, as comparison of (25a) and (26b) shows. We will return to this
issue in section 9.11.

(26) a.

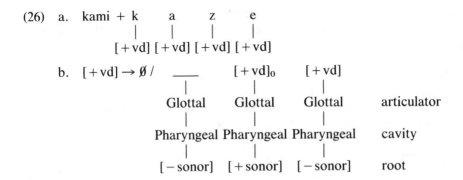

    b. $[+vd] \rightarrow \emptyset /$ ____

Another frequent type of root constraint avoids segments chosen from the same place of articulation. When examined in detail, "place" typically is found to be more general than the precise location of a consonantal stricture in the sense of (1) and tends to support the Articulator Model. We will review one of the best-documented cases of this form here, the root cooccurrence constraints in Arabic studied by McCarthy (1991).

As we will see in section 8.1, Arabic root morphemes are composed typically of three (and sometimes two or four) consonants: for example, [md] 'stretch', [ḥb] 'love', [ktb] 'write', [rsm] 'draw', [sfr] 'travel', [trgm] 'translate'. Developing an observation of Greenberg (1950), McCarthy demonstrates a statistically significant tendency to avoid adjacent consonants produced by the same articulator. The consonants of Arabic are listed in (27). (28) tabulates how these consonants distribute themselves through a sample of 2,703 triradical roots taken from the first half of Wehr's (1976) Standard Arabic dictionary. Capitals (T,D,S,Z) denote pharyngealized consonants ("emphatics"). In the case of the coronals, the pattern breaks down into several subparts depending on the features [sonorant] and [continuant].

(27) a. labials   [f,b,m]
     b. coronal sonorants [l,r,n]
     c. coronal stops   [t,d,T,D]
     d. coronal fricatives [θ,ð,s,z,S,Z,š]
     e. dorsals   [g,k,q]
     f. gutturals   [x̣,ɣ,ḥ,ʕ,h,ʔ]

(28) adjacent consonants ($C_1 C_2$ and $C_2 C_3$) in triliteral $C_1 C_2 C_3$ roots

	a	b	c	d	e	f
a	0	210	125	138	82	151
b	196	15	122	161	165	208
c	118	153	7	26	29	105
d	196	211	58	5	89	168
e	118	167	66	105	1	79
f	211	252	148	182	81	11

In the matrix of (28) the vertical axis represents the first of two adjacent root consonants while the horizontal axis represents the second. Thus, at C_1-C_2 [ktb] 'write' is one of the 66 roots in the survey that combine a dorsal with a following coronal stop; and at C_2-C_3 [ktb] is one of the 118 roots that combine a coronal stop with a following labial.

Examination of the table (28) reveals that the smallest numbers run along the diagonal, evidencing a strong dispreference for adjacent consonants drawn from the groupings in (27). Putting the gutturals aside (see discussion in section 9.2), it is clear that the dissimilatory classes are defined by the articulators Labial, Dorsal, Coronal (the latter refined into three disjoint subsets by the features [sonorant] and [continuant]). In no case does a dissimilatory class combine consonants produced by different articulators. Note also that the fricatives range across several of the traditional IPA points of articulation: labiodental [f], interdental [θ], alveolar [s], and alveopalatal [š]. Given that the constraint is defined in terms of the articulators, it is no accident that this set is partitioned {f} vs. {θ,s,š} rather than {f,θ} vs. {s,š}, or {f,θ,s} vs. {š}: [f] is produced by the Labial articulator while [θ,s,š] are produced by the Coronal articulator.

Again sidestepping the issue of the gutturals, we may express the Arabic root constraint as in (29). It marks as ill formed two successive entries on the articulator tier that choose identical values from among the options listed.

(29)   articulator   *[x] [x]

        (where x = Labial, Dorsal, Coronal, Coronal)
                                    | | ⁀[αcontin]
                           [+sonor] [−sonor]

4.3.4   Tiers and Adjacency

Another perhaps more surprising result is that a similar (albeit somewhat weaker) avoidance constraint also holds between the first and third consonants of the Arabic triliteral root [$C_1C_2C_3$]. As shown by the table in (30), except for the [b,b] cell, the small numbers once again run along the diagonal, indicating a tendency to disprefer consonants with the same articulator. Thus, [ktb] 'write' is one of 74 roots in the survey that combine an initial dorsal and a final labial.

(30)   nonadjacent consonants (C_1 C_3)

	a	b	c	d	e	f
a	20	88	53	37	41	79
b	97	76	52	83	47	85
c	36	53	9	29	28	45
d	93	127	61	14	46	88
e	74	72	44	53	3	54
f	126	162	66	85	64	37

As McCarthy (1991) points out, if we are to explain this phenomenon by positing that constraint (29) rules out adjacent identical articulators, then we must conclude that Labial, Coronal, Dorsal each define their own separate tier. To see this, consider a hypothetical ill-formed root such as [ftb], where the first and third radicals have a Labial articulator. In order to be ruled out by (29), the [f] and the [b] must be able to "see" each other through the [t]. If Labial and Coronal occupied the same tier (31a), then the two instances of Labial would be separated by the intervening Coronal; hence, they would not fall under (29), which rules out identical articulators only when they are adjacent. But if each articulator defines its own tier, then the two Labial specifications of [ftb] are adjacent because the medial radical [t] has no registration on the Labial tier (31b). If this interpretation is correct, it implies that the articulators have a different status from terminal features such as [±back] in which both values of the feature occupy the same tier.

(31)   a.

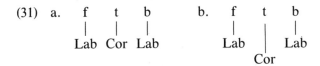

The *n*-retroflexion rule of Sanskrit (Steriade 1986, Schein and Steriade 1986) provides another case in which the same conclusion has been drawn. In Sanskrit the features [anterior] and [distributed] define a three-way contrast among alveolar, palatal, and retroflex, as indicated in (32).

(32)   alveolar   palatal   retroflex

       t   č   ṭ
       s   ś   ṣ
       n   ñ   ṇ
                             r

$$\begin{bmatrix} +\text{anter} \\ -\text{distrib} \end{bmatrix} \qquad \begin{bmatrix} -\text{anter} \\ +\text{distrib} \end{bmatrix} \qquad \begin{bmatrix} -\text{anter} \\ -\text{distrib} \end{bmatrix}$$

The rule of *n*-retroflexion states that suffixes with an [n] take a retroflex alternant with [ṇ] when the stem contains a retroflex continuant [ṣ] or [r].

(33)   a.   *-na:* present
           mrd-na: 'be gracious'   iṣ-ṇa: 'seek'
     b.   *-na* passive participle
           bhug-na- 'bend'   pu:r-ṇa 'fill'
                                  vrk-ṇa- 'cut up'
     c.   *-a:na* middle participle
           marj-a:na- 'wipe'   pur-a:ṇa 'fill'
           kṣved-a:na- 'hum'   kṣubh-a:ṇa 'quake'
     d.   *-ma:na* middle participle
           krt-a-ma:na 'cut'   krp-a-ma:ṇa 'lament'

As the examples in (33) make clear, the source and the focus of the assimilation may but need not be adjacent: for example, in [kṣubh-a:ṇa] and [krp-a-ma:ṇa], the focus [n] is separated from the source [ṣ] or [r] by one and even two intervening labial consonants. Significantly, the rule is blocked by intervening coronals such as the [t] in *krt-a-ma:na* (cf. *krp-a-ma:ṇa*). The challenge is to make sense of this contrast.

Schein and Steriade propose the rule shown in (34); it spreads the Coronal articulator dominating a [−anterior, −distributed] continuant to a following coronal nasal, delinking the latter's original coronal specification. (Pl is equivalent to the Oral node.)

(34)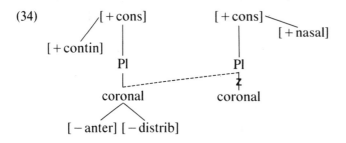

Implicit in the statement of the rule is the assumption that the source and the focus are adjacent on the Coronal tier. On this assumption, the rule will apply in (35b) since nothing intervenes on the Coronal tier between the [r] of the root and the [n] of the suffix. And for exactly the same reason, the rule blocks in (35a) because the [t] intervenes. Furthermore, the [t] itself cannot undergo the rule since (34) is restricted to nasals. As in the Arabic case of (31), this explanation crucially depends on the premise that each articulator defines its own tier – a point expressed in (35b) by placing Labial, Coronal, Dorsal at different levels in order to overcome the limitations of the two-dimensional page.

(35)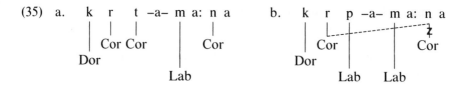

Let us close the discussion with another long-distance assimilation that is similar to but not exactly the same as the one found in Sanskrit. In the California American Indian language Chumash (Poser 1982), the coronal fricatives and affricates contrast for the feature [anterior].

(36)

	stop		
stop	t		
affricate	c	č	
fricative	s	š	
sonorant	n,l		

[+anter] [−anter]

There is a sibilant harmony process whereby a coronal affricate or fricative assimilates the anteriority of a following coronal affricate or fricative. The source of the spreading [±anterior] may be found in a suffix or a root, and the recipient can be in a root or a prefix. The process clearly operates from right to left.

(37) a.

k-sunon-us	'I obey him'	/k + sunon + us/
k-šunon-š	'I am obedient'	/k + sunon + š/
saxtun	'to pay'	/saxtun/
šaxtun-ič	'to be paid'	/saxtun + ič/

3sg. prefix *s-*

s-ixut	'it burns'	/s + ixut/
s-aqunimak	'he hides'	/s + aqunimak/
š-ilakš	'it is soft'	/s + ilakš/
š-am-moč	'they paint it'	/s + am + moč/
š-kuti-waš	'he saw'	/s + kuti + waš/

b. dual subject *iš-*

p-iš-anan'	'don't you two go'	/p + iš + al + nan'/
s-is-tisi-yep-us	'they two show him'	/s + iš + tiši + yep + us/

We observe that sibilants contrast for anteriority and that both values assimilate: in (37a) [s] assimilates [−anterior] from [š] and [č]; in (37b) [š] assimilates [+anterior] from [s]. Consequently, the harmony rule spreads both values of [±anterior] and must delink both values of [±anterior] from the underlying focus of the rule. It is thus a structure-changing operation. We may formulate the rule as in (38).

(38) Coronal   Coronal

    ≠--------------⏌

[±anter]   [±anter]

As the forms in (39) show (from Shaw 1991a), the nonsibilant coronals [t,n,l] neither trigger (39a), nor undergo (39b), nor block (39c) the assimilation of [anterior].

(39) a.

š-api-čo-it	'I have good luck'
s-api-co-us	'he has good luck'

b.

k-šunon-š	'I am obedient'
k-sunos-us	'I obey him'

c.

ha-s-xintila	'his Indian name'
ha-š-xintila-waš	'his former Indian name'

To explain the first two properties, we might add a restriction on rule (38) that the source and the focus of the harmony bear the stricture feature [+strident], indicating a sibilant. However, this would still not explain why such segments fail to block the propagation of harmony across them. This is particularly puzzling when we compare the Sanskrit *n*-retroflexion rule. Recall that the spread of retroflexion to a following [n] was blocked by an intervening coronal [t] (35a). Thus, in both Sanskrit and Chumash [t] fails to undergo or to trigger the relevant rule; but the languages still behave differently when a [t] intervenes between the source and the recipient of assimilation. Finding a formal explanation for this kind of contrast has emerged as a central question in feature theory. One approach to the problem is premised on the observation that Chumash [t] lacks a [−anterior] counterpart in the language's phonemic inventory and hence can be underspecified for [anterior] at the point where the harmony rule applies. On the other hand, Sanskrit opposes [+anterior] [t] to [−anterior] [ṭ] in its phonemic inventory and hence must specify the Coronal articulator to support the underlying [t] vs. [ṭ] opposition. We will return to a fuller discussion of this issue in section 9.9.

To summarize this section, we see that imposing a hierarchical organization on the features promises to sharply constrain the range of natural phonological rules and constraints. The fact that the preliminary phonological evidence implicates a feature organization that in large part mirrors the organization motivated on phonetic grounds is a significant convergence that strengthens the idea that conceiving of speech sounds as feature trees is a basic property of the human language faculty.

4.4   Acoustic Phonetics

When we speak, the air at our mouth and nostrils is alternately compressed and rarefied. Air is an elastic medium and will transmit these patterns of compression and rarefaction to our listeners by setting their eardrums in motion. The resultant motion is converted into electrical impulses in the inner ear that are transmitted to the brain. This section introduces some basic concepts of acoustic phonetics in order to provide a preliminary understanding of this aspect of speech.

4.4.1   Vibratory Motion

The compression and rarefaction of the air can be understood as a type of vibratory phenomenon. To gain an understanding of how sound is transmitted through the air, it is useful to think of the air as being composed of little cubes. Since air is elastic, when one of the cubes is squeezed it will bounce back when the squeeze is released. If the elasticity is great, this bouncing back and forth will be repeated several times before the cube returns to its original state of rest. The alternating compression and rarefaction of the elastic cube illustrates a phenomenon that occurs widely in nature. More familiar examples include the swing of a pendulum and the behavior of a spring fixed at the top and supplied with a weight at the bottom (figure 4.9). If we gently tug at the end of the spring, we set up a repetitive up-and-down motion. We see a record of this motion in the graph in figure 4.10. This curve, known technically as a *sine wave*, is defined by two properties: the *period*, T (the time required for the spring to execute a complete up-and-down movement), and the *amplitude*, A (the maximal displacement of the free end of the spring from its rest position). It is a fact of elementary physics that the period and amplitude are independent of one another. More surprising perhaps is the fact that once a spring is set in motion, its period never changes: the period is

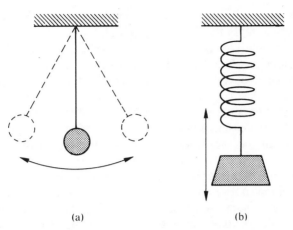

(a)   (b)

Figure 4.9 Simple vibrating systems. (a) Pendulum. (b) Spring-mass. (From Clark and Yallop 1990:187.)

determined by the material of which the spring is made. The vibration ceases not because the spring bobs more slowly but because its amplitude decreases over time; that is, the displacement from the rest position becomes smaller and smaller until ultimately the bobbing stops altogether. It is often useful to think in terms of the reciprocal of the period, a quantity termed the *frequency* (f): rather than speaking of the time taken by one vibration, we speak of the number of vibrations (cycles) per unit of time, standardly the second. The relation between period and frequency is expressed by the formula in (40).

(40)   frequency $= \dfrac{1}{\text{period}}$

If the period is 2 seconds, the frequency is ½ vibration (bob) per second. It is

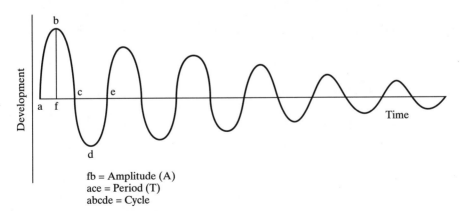

fb = Amplitude (A)
ace = Period (T)
abcde = Cycle

Figure 4.10 Simple waveform.

standard in physics to refer to cycles per second with the term *hertz* (abbreviated Hz). Thus, in our example the frequency is $\frac{1}{2}$ Hz.

Let us now ask how sound propagates across space. A useful analogy is to think of what happens when a pebble is dropped in a pool of water. When the pebble hits the surface of the water, some water will be pushed down. However, water (like air) is an elastic medium and so, like the spring bob, it will eventually push upward and even surpass the level of the undisturbed surface. The water thus bobs up and down essentially like the spring in figure 4.10; this up-and-down motion is evident in the movements of a leaf or twig on the water's surface. However, water is a viscous medium and will consequently transmit the motion generated at the point of the stone's impact to the surrounding water. In a uniform medium, the bobbing motion is transmitted at a constant speed – in our hypothetical example, let us suppose 10 feet per second. This implies that after 1 second the water at a distance of 10 feet from the source will begin to bob; after 2 seconds the water 20 feet away will begin to move up and down; and so on. Figure 4.11

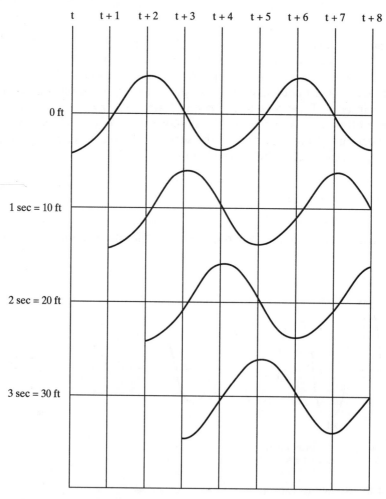

Figure 4.11   Propagation of waveform.

depicts the state of the water at various points from the source as a function of time. The important point is that at each 10-foot interval the water exhibits the same bobbing motion. Of course, at any given point in time the water's displacement above or below the pool's original surface level at each 10-foot interval will vary as a function of the amount of time required for the original bobbing motion to be transmitted from the pebble's point of impact. In our example the period is 4 seconds – the time required for water at the point of impact to move up and return to the same position.

Imagine now that we are able to take a photograph of the surface of the pool of water at $t+6$ seconds, where t is the point in time when the pebble impacts the water's surface. This snapshot of the water's surface would show the sinusoidal shape depicted in figure 4.12. This wave has a length – the distance from one peak to the next – which in our case is 40 feet. The relation between the length (λ) of the wave and the frequency of the bobbing motion of the water at any point along the wave is determined by the formula in (41a). It expresses the fact that the length of the wave is inversely proportional to the frequency; and since the frequency = 1/period, the length is directly proportional to the period. For our particular example, the wavelength is calculated in (41b).

(41) a. $\text{wavelength} = \dfrac{\text{speed of propagation}}{\text{frequency}}$

  b. $40 \text{ ft} = \dfrac{10 \text{ ft per sec}}{\frac{1}{4} \text{ cycle per sec}}$

Because the speed of propagation in water is constant, the length of the wave can be decreased by increasing the frequency. For example, if the surface of the water is struck by a pebble every 2 seconds instead of every 4, then the frequency would be $\frac{1}{2}$ cycle per second; that is, one-half of the periodic motion would be completed in a second. When this shorter time span is translated into the related

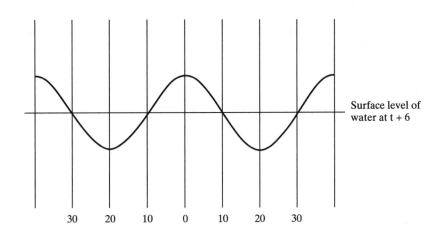

Surface level of water at t + 6

| 30 | 20 | 10 | 0 | 10 | 20 | 30 |

Distance from point of impact

Figure 4.12 Waveform.

spatial dimension, the length of the corresponding wave will traverse half of the original distance – that is, 20 feet. Similarly, we can increase the wavelength by increasing the amount of time required to complete a cycle.

Like water, air is an elastic medium. When we strike a tuning fork, the prongs are set in vibration. They create a series of alternating compressions and rarefactions in the surrounding air that are transmitted to the neighboring air molecules and expand outward in all directions, eventually reaching the eardrum where the movement is perceived as sound by our brains. Of course, the air particles themselves are not transferred from the vicinity of the tuning fork to our ears – rather, it is the alternating pattern of compression and rarefaction that is propagated through the air. As an analogy, think of a row of bowling balls touching one another on the return rack. When the ball at the near end of the row is struck by a returning ball, the ball at the far end flies away while the ones in the middle remain stationary. The striking force is simply passed from one ball to the next. The obvious conclusion is that sound cannot be transmitted in the absence of a medium. This is dramatically illustrated by the experiment (going back to Robert Boyle in the 17th century) in which a ringing bell is enclosed in a glass jar. When the air is pumped out of the jar, the sound of the ringing dies away even though we can see the bell clappers vibrating vigorously.

There is one important difference between the waves on the surface of the pool and sound waves (produced for example by a tuning fork). In the former case the up-and-down vibratory movement created by the falling pebble takes place in a plane that is perpendicular to the direction of propagation; in the case of the tuning fork the alternating compressions and rarefactions of the air occur in the same plane as the propagation of the motion. The former waves are known as *transverse* waves and the latter as *longitudinal* waves. In the case of sound, then, the disturbance radiates outward in all three dimensions from the source of vibration. The intensity varies inversely with the square of the distance from the source. Thus, the sound will be four times weaker at a distance of 2 meters than at a distance of 1 meter and nine times weaker at a distance of 3 meters from the source. We can enhance a sound's intensity by enclosing the medium (air) in a tube or pipe. The ticking of an otherwise inaudible watch is heard quite distinctly across a room when listened to through a tube. Tyndall (1896:43) remarks that "The celebrated French philosopher, Biot, observed the transmission of sound through the empty water-pipes of Paris, and found that he could hold a conversation in a low voice through an iron tube 3,120 feet in length." This observation is important because speech can, to a first approximation, be thought of as the transmission of sound through a column of air enclosed by the vocal tract.

4.4.2 Wave Analysis

As figure 4.13 illustrates, the waves of speech sounds may be of great complexity. Significant insight into their nature is obtained from a notable mathematical theorem proven in 1822 by the French mathematician Fourier. The *Fourier theorem* states that a large class of curves may be analyzed as sums of a series of sinusoidal waves, differing in frequency, amplitude, and phase; the frequency of each sinusoid is an integral multiple (not a fraction) of the sinusoid of lowest frequency.

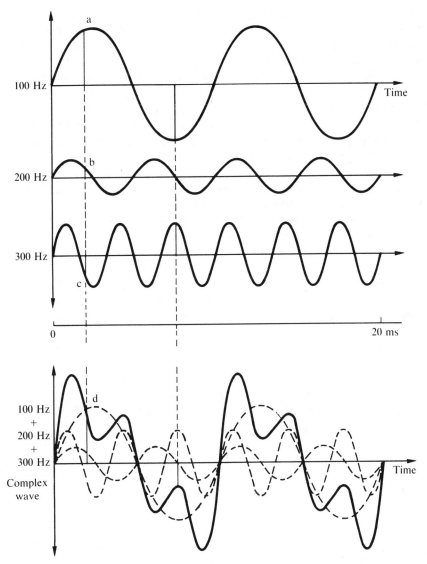

Figure 4.13 Complex wave with three sinusoidal components (100 Hz, 200 Hz, 300 Hz). (From Clark and Yallop 1990:193; adapted by Clark and Yallop from Ladefoged 1962:35.)

The sinusoidal components of a wave are traditionally called *harmonics;* the sinusoid with the lowest frequency is known as the *fundamental* (f_0). The term *phase* refers to the correspondence (or lack of correspondence) of different parts of the period in two (or more) waves. If two sinusoids reach their maximum at the same time, we say they are *in phase;* otherwise, they are *out of phase.* Although phase relations play an important role in sound perception, they will be disregarded here because, unlike amplitude and frequency, phase effects are quite indirect in speech production.

Figure 4.13 illustrates the Fourier analysis of the complex wave shown in (d) by means of adding the three simple sinusoids (a,b,c). In this example the sinusoids are all in phase. Because our discussion disregards phase, the different harmonics of the wave can be represented simply by a *spectrum,* where the vertical axis represents the amplitude and the horizontal the frequency of the different harmonics. The complex wave of figure 4.13 has the spectrum shown in figure 4.14.

A pure tone, such as the one emitted by a tuning fork, has only a single harmonic. (The tuning forks used in musical performances are tuned to 440 Hz, the middle A.) We know from experience that the amplitude of the vibrations emitted by a tuning fork decays very slowly; the tone the fork emits may last for many seconds. Such a sound has very *low damping.* It contrasts with clicks or snaps that decay rapidly and are therefore said to be *highly damped.* There is an inverse relationship between the damping of a sound and the number of harmonics: sounds with few or no harmonics have low damping; highly damped sounds are composed of a large number of harmonics.

When we strike an object such as a glass or a box, the object gives off a characteristic sound. We call this sound the *natural mode(s) of vibration* of the object or its *resonances.* The resonances of an object are determined primarily by the geometric shape of the object and of its apertures. Because in speaking we constantly change the geometry of the vocal tract and its apertures, we expect that the acoustic speech signal that we produce in this manner will reflect variations in the resonances of the vocal tract. As we will see directly, this expectation is fully borne out. We must therefore look at the nature of resonance in greater detail.

As noted, different cavities have different resonances. For tubes of uniform cross section, the height of the tube is the only determinant of resonance. Experimentally minded readers might wish to perform the following simple exper-

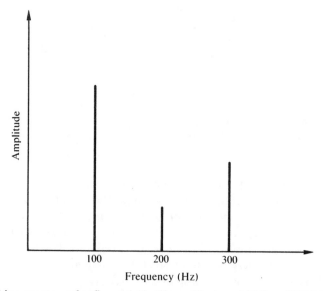

Figure 4.14   Line spectrum for figure 4.13. (From Clark and Yallop 1990:203.)

iment. Take a glass cylinder at least 18 inches tall, a tuning fork tuned to 256 Hz, and a container filled with water (figure 4.15). When you strike the tuning fork and hold it over the cylinder, you will observe that hardly any sound is emitted. Next, gradually pour water into the cylinder. You will observe that the cylinder begins to "resonate" to the tuning fork as the water level rises; it reaches a maximum at about 5 inches water (or 13 inches cylinder height), after which the sound intensity progressively lessens. If you substitute forks tuned to different frequencies, you will observe the same general behavior, but the maximum will occur at different water levels in the cylinder.

The explanation for this phenomenon runs as follows. When the air is excited (made to bob) at the top end of the column of air in the cylinder, the excitation is transmitted down to the other end of the column. When it reaches the bottom end, the transmission of the excitation (bobbing) reverses direction and now travels in the opposite direction, back toward the top end of the column. As a result, at some points in the air column an "up-bob" (compression) of the air traveling downward meets an "up-bob" traveling upward; the two reinforce one another, resulting in a more radical upward movement or compression of the air. At some other point, however, an "up-bob" will meet a "down-bob" (rarefaction) traveling in the opposite direction, and the two will cancel each other out. In general, such reinforcements and cancellations appear at different points along the column at different times, and nothing special can be said about them. It is, however, possible to arrange matters so that the reinforcements and cancellations appear at fixed points in the column. In this case there will be certain points in the column where the air is stationary and other points where the air movement is maximal.

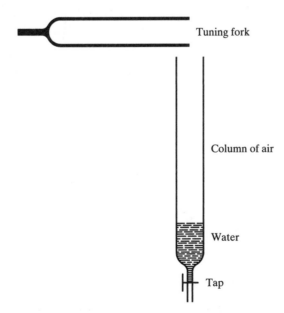

Tuning fork

Column of air

Water

Tap

Figure 4.15 A typical laboratory arrangement for producing a vibrating column of air. (From Ladefoged 1962:69.)

The sound wave associated with such a state of affairs is known as a *stationary* or a *standing wave*.

A more easily visualized example of a standing wave (adapted from Tyndall 1896) can be produced by shaking a rope that is fastened at one end to a wall or a ceiling. If we give the rope a sudden jerk, we produce a "hump" that runs along the rope to the fixed point and is then reflected back to our hand (figure 4.16a). Let the time required for the pulse to reach the fixed end be 1 second. Suppose now that a succession of jerks is given, sending a series of pulses along the rope. In $\frac{1}{2}$ second the pulse will reach point *b* of figure 4.16bi, and in 1 second it will reach point *c* (figure 4.16bii). Now at the moment when reflection begins, we deliver another jerk that initiates a second pulse; the configuration of figure 4.16biii results. Point *b* is now subject to two competing motions. The reflected hump *cb* wants to travel down the rope and displace *b* to the left; but the new hump *ab* wants to travel up the rope and displace *b* to the right. The result is that *b* is impelled by two equal forces in opposite directions and so does not move at all. Under these circumstances the two halves of the rope *ab*, *bc* will oscillate as if they were independent of each other (figure 4.16biv). Thus, by two accurately

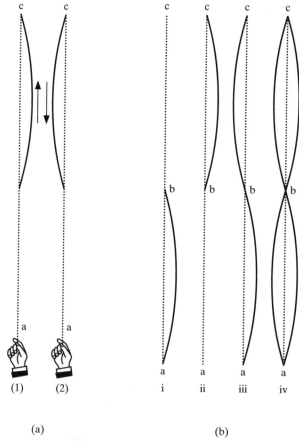

Figure 4.16 Standing waves in rope. (Adapted from Tyndall 1896:121–2.)

timed jerks of the rope, we produce two stationary pulses. The result is a standing wave.

A similar standing wave pattern can be generated in the air column in our cylinder, except that the air moves up and down the cylinder, whereas in the rope the movements are perpendicular to the rope. Recall that the rope produces a given standing wave pattern only when shaken at a particular rate; when it is shaken at a different rate, either a different standing wave pattern will be produced or no pattern whatever will emerge. We have seen in our "experiment" that the cylinder resonates at a given frequency. In fact, the different standing wave patterns in the rope and in the column of air are a function of the resonating properties respectively of the air column and of the rope. In the case of an air column closed at one end and open at the other, it turns out that there are an infinite number of standing wave patterns whose lengths are related to the height of the column L according to the series in (42) – that is, odd-numbered fractions of four times the height of the column.

(42) $4 \times L, \frac{4}{3} \times L, \frac{4}{5} \times L, \frac{4}{7} \times L, \ldots$

In other words, we find standing wave patterns such as those illustrated in figure 4.17. The longest is four times the length of the cylinder, the next is $\frac{4}{3}$ the length of the cylinder, then $\frac{4}{5}$, and so on.

We are especially interested in cylinders closed at one end because, as a first approximation, the vocal tract can be thought of as such a cylinder (figure 4.18). It is closed at the glottis and open at the lips; under very special circumstances (such as when we pronounce the vowel [æ] or [ʌ]) the cross-sectional area of the vocal tract approaches that of a tube of uniform cross section. Of course, the cross section of the vocal tract is not uniform for the vast majority of speech

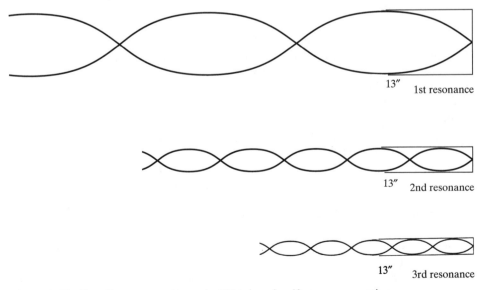

13″   1st resonance

13″   2nd resonance

13″   3rd resonance

Figure 4.17 Standing wave patterns in 13″ tube of uniform cross section.

Lips

Glottis

Figure 4.18 Schematic representation of vocal tract.

sounds; but the uniform cross section provides a useful starting point for dealing with the rest.

With the help of formula (43), we can calculate the frequencies of the different standing waves in figure 4.17.

(43) $F_k = \dfrac{\text{speed of propagation}}{\text{length of tube}} \times \dfrac{2k - 1}{4}$

In the case of interest to us, the speed of sound in air at a room temperature of 60° F is 340 m ($= 34{,}000$ cm) per sec. We have seen that a cylinder of 13 in. will resonate at 256 Hz. Converting 13 in. to centimeters (2.54 cm = 1 in.), we obtain 33.02 cm. Substituting these values into the formula (43) yields the standing wave frequencies shown in (44a).

(44) a. $F_1 = \dfrac{34 \times 1000}{33.02 \times 4} = 257$ cps   b. $F_1 = \dfrac{34 \times 1000}{17 \times 4} = 500$ cps

$F_2 = \dfrac{34 \times 1000}{33.02 \times \frac{3}{4}} = 771$ cps $F_2 = \dfrac{34 \times 1000}{17 \times \frac{3}{4}} = 1500$ cps

$F_3 = \dfrac{34 \times 1000}{33.02 \times \frac{5}{4}} = 1285$ cps $F_3 = \dfrac{34 \times 1000}{17 \times \frac{5}{4}} = 2500$ cps

In the case of speech sounds, the height of the cylinder is not 33.02 cm but about 17 cm. (According to Clark and Yallop (1990:219), the average vocal tract length for an adult male is 17.6 cm from the glottis to the lips; for a woman it is about 80%–90% of a man's; and for a child, depending on age, it may be around 50% of a man's.) As a consequence, the resonances are about double the frequencies of the cylinder in our earlier example – that is, 500, 1500, 2500 (44b). In speech science, the harmonics are known as *formants;* for vowels, the first three formants are the basic determinants of the sound's quality. Figure 4.19 sketches the stationary waves associated with these frequencies. These waves represent the velocity of air movement at different points in the cylinder or tube. It is obvious that there is no movement at the closed end of the cylinder, but there will always be maximum movement at the open end. The locations with no movement are called *nodes* and those with maximal movement *loops.*

The Japanese researchers Chiba and Kajiyama (1941) discovered an important rule of thumb to estimate the resonant frequencies for vowels articulated with vocal tract configurations that depart from a tube with a uniform cross section. Their rule is stated in (43).

(43) When the cross-sectional area of the tube is reduced at or near a loop, the frequency of the corresponding resonance is lowered; when the cross-sectional area of the tube is reduced at or near a node, the frequency of the corresponding resonance is raised.

We can appreciate the utility of this rule by first considering a vowel articulated with lip rounding, such as [u]. It is of course produced by a constriction at the lips. As we have just seen, for each of the first three resonances in figure 4.19, the lips at the open end of the tube correspond to a loop; hence, Chiba and Kajiyama's rule predicts that the corresponding resonances will be lower for the [u] in comparison with the values for the uniform tube. The representative vowel formants for adult male speakers of American English (from Peterson and Barney 1952) confirm this prediction (44). Both formant values for [u] are lower than those for [ʌ] or [æ] – the vowels whose vocal tract configuration approximates the uniform tube in figure 4.18. Now consider the high front vowel [i]; it is articulated with a fairly radical constriction in the vocal tract at a point that is roughly one-third in from the lips. This corresponds to a node for the second resonance in figure 4.19; Chiba and Kajiyama's rule consequently predicts a higher value for this resonance when compared with the values of [æ] and [ʌ]. Once again, the data in (44) confirm this prediction.

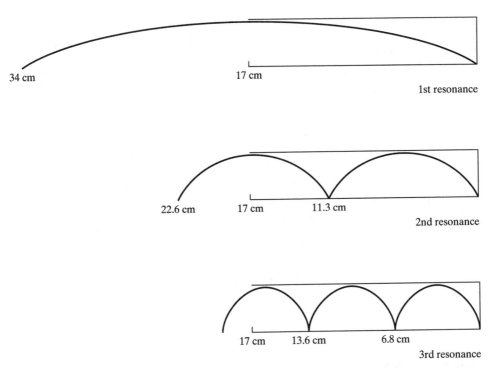

34 cm   17 cm
1st resonance

22.6 cm   17 cm   11.3 cm
2nd resonance

17 cm   13.6 cm   6.8 cm
3rd resonance

Figure 4.19   Standing wave patterns in 17-cm tube of uniform cross section approximating vocal tract.

(44) F$_1$ 270   660   640   300
      F$_2$ 2290 1720 1190 870
           [i]   [æ]   [ʌ]   [u]

The resonance properties of consonants are more complex. As a first approximation, they are produced with a constriction that divides the vocal tract into
two cavities: one before and one after the stricture. The cavity between the glottis
and the stricture is more or less closed at both ends and hence requires that its
resonances be calculated in a different way – by the rule in (45a).

(45) a. $$\text{frequency} = \frac{\text{speed of propagation}}{\text{length of tract}} \times \frac{n-1}{2}$$

  b. F$_1$ = 0
      F$_2$ = 1000
      F$_3$ = 2000

          [b]

In this formula when $n = 1$, a value of 0 is obtained. This means that the first
resonance is 0 in consonants – a fact that is dramatically clear from spectrograms
(visual displays of the formant and other structures; see below). When we consider
a labial consonant, the cavity closed at both ends comprises essentially the entire
vocal tract. Taking the 17 cm standard, we obtain the values in (45b). If we track
the formants of a vowel such as [æ], which approximate the 500, 1500, 2500 of a
uniform tube, we see that all three go down adjacent to a [b]. This formant transition is an essential acoustic cue for the bilabial point of articulation. (See figure
4.21 and discussion in section 4.4.3.)

When the consonantal constriction is made farther back in the vocal tract, the
size of the back cavity is reduced and that of the front cavity is increased. Re-
membering their respective formulas ((45a), (43)), we see that the resonances in
the back cavity will increase in value while those in the front cavity will decrease.
This point is shown by the graph in figure 4.20, which plots the resonances of the
two cavities as a function of the length of the back cavity. (The lowest resonance
of the combined cavities is at a very low frequency and is not shown here.) We
also note that there are certain points where the lines cross, indicating places
where the resonances of the two cavities reinforce one another, producing peaks
in the spectra of the stop bursts and fricative turbulences corresponding to consonantal constrictions made at these points. It turns out that these tend to be just
the points along the vocal tract where languages prefer to implement their consonantal constrictions. For example, the lowest resonances of the two cavities
cross at 8–9 cm – a position corresponding to the velar point of articulation. The
lowest resonance of the front cavity crosses the second resonance of the back
cavity at about 10–11 cm, a region that corresponds roughly to where dental-
alveolar and alveopalatal consonants are produced.

4.4.3 The Sound Spectrograph

A graphic display of the sound wave's components is made by a *sound spectro-
graph,* a mechanical device equipped with a series of filters that monitor the

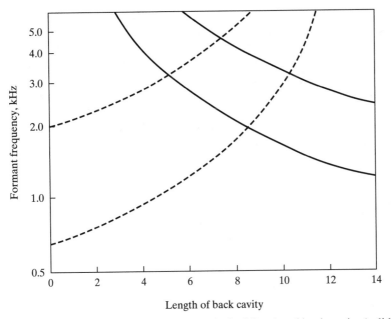

Figure 4.20 Lowest resonances of front cavity (dashed lines) and back cavity (solid lines). (Based on Stevens 1972:61.)

frequency range between 0 and 8 kHz. Each filter is connected to an amplifier and averaging device that convert energy picked up from the acoustic signal into electrical energy that controls the illumination of a light bulb. A photographic film is exposed to the light to produce a visual display of the energy present at the frequencies sampled by the filters. The example in figure 4.21 shows the spec-

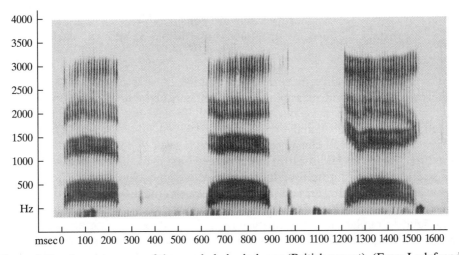

Figure 4.21 A spectrogram of the words *bab, dad, gag* (British accent). (From Ladefoged 1975:177.)

trogram for *bab, dad, gag*. The horizontal axis displays time (typically up to 2 seconds) and the vertical axis the frequencies. The darker the bar, the stronger the energy at the corresponding frequency in the acoustic signal. The first three formants of this speaker's [æ] appear at roughly 500, 1400, and 2300 Hz. The formants adjacent to the consonants reflect the changing shapes of the vocal tract as the articulators implement their neural commands. Both the second and the third formants descend for the labial in *bab;* the second and the third formants converge in *gag*. The first formant descends in all three cases, reflecting the special property of a cavity closed at both ends (45a).

The list in (46) (from Ladefoged 1975) describes some of the clues that phoneticians use to interpret spectrograms.

(46)   <u>Acoustic correlates of consonantal features</u>

Note: These descriptions should be regarded only as rough guides. The actual acoustic correlates depend to a great extent on the particular combination of articulatory features in a sound.

Voiced	Vertical striations corresponding to the vibrations of the vocal cords.
Bilabial	Locus of both second and third formants comparatively low.
Alveolar	Locus of second formant about 1700–1800 Hz.
Velar	Usually high locus of the second formant. Common origin of second and third formant transitions.
Retroflex	General lowering of the third and fourth formants.
Stop	Gap in pattern, followed by burst of noise for voiceless stops or sharp beginning of formant structure for voiced stops.
Fricative	Random noise pattern, especially in higher-frequency regions, but dependent on the place of articulation.
Nasal	Formant structure similar to that of vowels but with nasal formants at about 250, 2500, and 3250 Hz.
Lateral	Formant structure similar to that of vowels but with formants in the neighborhood of 250, 1200, and 2400 Hz. The higher formants are considerably reduced in intensity.
Approximant	Formant structure similar to that in vowels, usually changing.

It is important to realize that the interpretation of spectrograms is an art that requires experience and guesswork. In spite of considerable research on the problem, speech scientists have not yet succeeded in devising a mechanical method to decode the acoustic signal.

In section 4.5 we will consider why this has proved to be such a difficult problem. First, however, let us return to the observation made in section 2.1 that there is a strong tendency for lip rounding to correlate with backness in nonlow vowels: languages prefer [u] to [ɯ] and [i] to [ü]. Since the tongue body and the lips are independent articulators, this coupling of rounding with tongue body retraction is difficult to explain in articulatory terms. But it does have an acoustic explanation. As the table in (47) shows, there is an inverse relation between vowel height and the first formant: the lower the vowel, the higher the first formant.

The data also reveal that retracting the tongue tends to lower the second formant: compare the F_2 values for such front-back pairs as [æ] vs. [a], [ɛ] vs. [ɔ], and [i] vs. [u]. Retracting the tongue increases the length of the front cavity between the lips and the constriction; as suggested by figure 4.20, a lowering of F_2 and F_3 is the expected acoustic correlate. Lip rounding and protrusion also increase the length of this cavity and hence tend to lower F_2 as well. Thus, lip rounding tends to reinforce the acoustic difference between front and back vowels. Stevens and Keyser (1989) suggest that several other phonological features serve to *enhance* more basic acoustic parameters in this way.

(47) formant frequencies for eight American English vowels (from Ladefoged 1982:176)

F_3	2890	2560	2490	2490
F_2	2250	1920	1770	1660
F_1	280	400	550	690
	[i]	[ɪ]	[ɛ]	[æ]
F_3	2540	2540	2380	2250
F_2	1100	880	1030	870
F_1	710	590	450	310
	[a]	[ɔ]	[o]	[u]

Finally, it should be observed that when linguists and phoneticians describe vocalic series such as [i,e,æ] and [u,o,ɑ] as front high, mid, low versus back high, mid, low, they are referring to relative auditory quality rather than to actually observed points of tongue body constriction. X-ray studies reveal that the positioning of the tongue is considerably more complex, with no point-by-point correlation between the locus of constriction and formant structure or auditory impression. Ladefoged (1975) observes that in certain cases a fairly good match can be obtained between points in the traditional vowel chart and acoustic parameters, however, showing that the vowels of American English align themselves as indicated in figure 4.22 if F_1 is plotted along the vertical axis and the difference between F_1 and F_2 is plotted along the horizontal axis.

4.5   Speech Perception

Speech scientists have developed devices that convert sound spectrograms into acoustic signals. Such *synthetic speech* has become a basic research tool that has been the object of intensive study at Haskins Laboratories (New Haven); it has led to several significant discoveries that indicate that human beings possess from birth special devices for the perception of speech that differ from the neural and cognitive equipment used to perceive other sounds. In this section we will review a few highlights of this "speech is special" theme.

The original motivation for the Haskins Laboratories research was to develop a reading machine for the blind that could convert letters to speech sounds (via a phonetic transcription) so that blind people could "read" printed texts. The

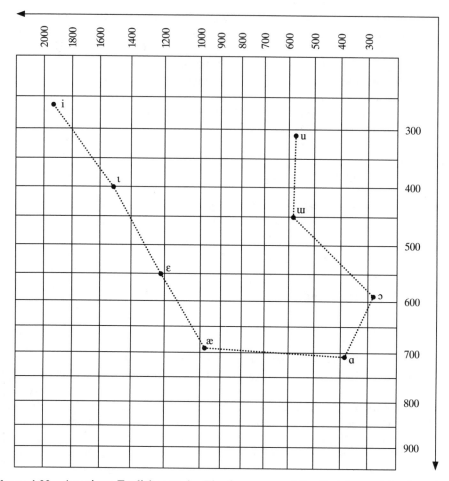

Figure 4.22   American English vowels. The frequency of the first formant is plotted on the ordinate (the vertical axis), and the difference between the frequencies of the second and first formant is plotted on the abscissa (the horizontal axis). (From Ladefoged 1975: 190.)

project was a failure but one that led to important discoveries about the nature of speech perception. According to Lieberman (1984), the naive starting assumption was that speech is structured as a string of sounds. Accordingly, one should be able to segment an utterance such as *cat* into its constituent allophones [kʰ], [æ], and [t] and connect up the resultant segments as the acoustic output of a typing machine. With due allowance for the vagaries of English spelling, one should thus in theory be able to design a "talking machine." Two immediate problems arose. First, it proved impossible to segment normal speech into the constituent allophones. Because of coarticulation, the successive sounds radically overlap one another. We simply cannot splice out a [kʰ] from *cat* without including some of the adjacent vowel. Second, one might try to get around this problem by synthesizing prototypes of the [kʰ], [æ], and [t] allophones. The problem with this approach was that the transmission time was much too slow. In normal speech some 20–30 segments are articulated per second. Utterances composed of the synthesized [kʰ], [æ], and [t] could only be processed at rates of 7–9 segments per second – too slow to be useful (Miller 1956). On the other hand, if one tried to speed up the synthesized utterances, they turned into an acoustic blur. The result was to pose a significant puzzle. Linguistically (phonologically), utterances are structured as a sequence of features/segments/syllables. When speech is articulated, the gestures overlap one another considerably (coarticulation). The payoff is rapid transmission. But the apparent downside is an acoustic signal with no sharp boundaries. Somehow human beings are able to overcome this blur and restore the original structure. Charles Hockett (1955:210) posed the problem with the following striking analogy.

> Imagine a row of Easter eggs carried along a moving belt; the eggs are of various sizes, and variously colored, but not boiled. At a certain point, the belt carries the row of eggs between the two rollers of a wringer, which quite effectively smash them and rub them more or less into each other. The flow of eggs before the wringer represents the series of impulses from the phoneme source; the mess that emerges from the wringer represents the output of the speech transmitter. At a subsequent point, we have an inspector whose task it is to examine the passing mess and decide, on the basis of the broken and unbroken yolks, the variously spread out albumen and the variously colored bits of shell, the nature of the flow of eggs which previously arrived at the wringer.

An influential theory designed to explain the speed with which speech is processed has been the *Motor Theory* (Liberman et al. 1967, Liberman and Mattingly 1985). It claims that the interpretation of the acoustic signal is guided by articulatory gestures that produce the overlap that is responsible for the segmentation problem. There are a variety of acoustic "cues" for a given feature. None is essential. What is essential is the articulatory gesture they point to. One early finding that supports this point of view comes from Delattre, Liberman, and Cooper (1955). These researchers synthesized stimuli composed of first and second vowel formants of a constant fundamental. By systematically varying the initial transitions, they were able to elicit from listeners the perception of a voiced stop [b,d,g]. As shown in figure 4.23, there is no consonant sound preceding the vowel formants – just silence. Rather, the differing stops are somehow supplied in virtue of the following onset formant – a kind of "illusion." Note also that the type of formant transition that give rises to the perception of a particular stop varies radically with the nature of the following vowel. For example, in [di] the F_2 transition points down, while in [du] it points up. According to the Motor Theory, what allows the listener to equate the differing formant transitions as [d] is their rigid connection with articulation: in effect, the system "knows" it coarticulates and so can use this fact to equate all the transitions in figure 4.23.

In another set of experiments, Liberman (1970) showed that the perception of speech sounds is *categorial* in nature. These studies tested the ability of listeners to discriminate and identify synthetically prepared stimuli. In one experiment, a

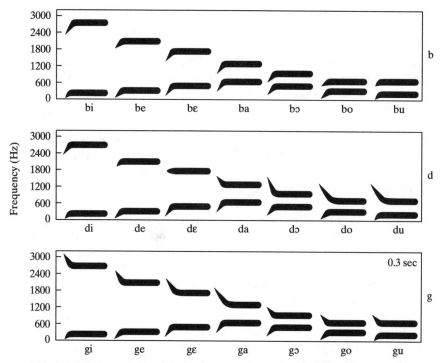

Figure 4.23 Synthetic spectrograms using only F_1 and F_2 information that produce the voiced stops before various vowels. (From Lieberman and Blumstein 1988:144; adapted by Lieberman and Blumstein from Delattre, Liberman, and Cooper 1955.)

range of equally spaced F_2 transitions to a following [æ] were prepared (figure 4.24). Listeners' responses divide the scale into three ranges with very little overlap as [bæ], [dæ], and [gæ]. There is thus a sharp perceptual boundary at certain points along the scale. Furthermore, subjects are unable to distinguish elements within a given category: for example, stimuli −6 . . . −2 may all be perceived as [bæ]. This shows that speech sounds are interpreted as exemplars of a given category much as the figures in (48) are seen as instances of the letter *s*. It contrasts with responses to nonspeech sounds such as the notes on a piano; even the musically untrained can normally discriminate one note from another, but assigning them to specific categories presents great difficulty (even for those with musical training).

(48) ∽ ∫ ৎ

Furthermore, when the transitions of figure 4.24 are presented in isolation from the following vowel, listeners can easily discriminate among them. But under this condition they are no longer perceived as speech but as "chirps." This result suggests that the transition to the following vowel formant is automatically interpreted as a particular point of articulation. We cannot help hearing it in these linguistic terms. Such categorial perception has an obvious processing advantage.

Even though the [b]'s in [tab] and [taba] may differ acoustically, they are perceived as instances of the same phonetic category and so allow a given lexical item to be equated across varying acoustic contexts.

Eimas et al. (1971) showed that such categorial perception of speech is also present in infants. In these experiments infants are trained to suck on a pacifier in response to the presentation of visual and auditory stimuli. Repeated presentation of the same stimulus leads to a drop in sucking rate, indicating boredom. When a new stimulus is introduced, the sucking rate increases. This "high-amplitude sucking technique" allows investigators to get at what counts as the same versus different stimuli for infants (who obviously cannot be asked whether they can hear a difference). Only those stimuli that can be distinguished will lead to a change in the sucking response. The major finding is that 1- to 4-month-old infants have a pattern of responses similar to that of adults: they can discriminate between phonetic categories but not within them. In a review of the literature,

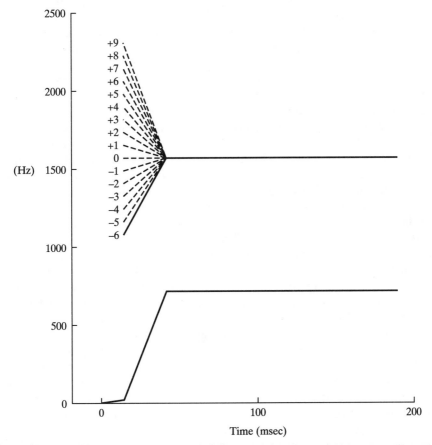

Figure 4.24 Schematic representation of two formant frequency patterns that will produce the sounds [bæ], [dæ], and [gæ]. The numbers −6 through +9 reference the different signals. (From Lieberman and Blumstein 1988:157; adapted by Lieberman and Blumstein from Liberman 1970.)

Werker (1989:45) states, "Experiments in the 17 years since Eimas's original study have shown that infants can discriminate nearly every phonetic contrast on which they are tested but are generally unable to discriminate differences within a single phonemic category."

Werker has studied infants' sensitivity to phonetic contrasts not present in the language of the environment. In her experimental setup, infants are induced to turn their head in response to the presentation of a novel stimulus. Werker found that English-speaking adults had considerable difficulty in distinguishing such Hindi contrasts as [pa] vs. [pʰa] and [ba] vs. [bʰa] as well as dental-alveolar [t] vs. retroflex [ṭ]. However, young infants from monolingual English environments did not; they were able to discriminate these contrasts. In other experiments Werker asked how long this ability is maintained and found that it begins to decline between 6 and 12 months. Subsequent studies have shown infant sensitivity to other contrasts not found in English such as the velar-uvular [k] vs. [q] of many languages of the Pacific Northwest. These results indicate that the ability to distinguish different members of the UG phonetic alphabet (and to ignore differences within these categories) is present at birth and is not learned.

Although systematic study of all phonetic contrasts has not yet been carried out, the results to date suggest that young infants can discriminate any phonetic contrast. Assuming that this reflects the ability to encode sounds in memory, it would imply that young children's inability to articulate certain contrasts (e.g., [l] vs. [y]) is a production difficulty, perhaps requiring some maturation or learning in articulation. This would be consistent with the repeated observation that children readily perceive phonetic contrasts that they are incapable of producing.

Stevens (1972, 1989) has argued that of the many possible articulatory-acoustic couplings that can be produced in the vocal tract, UG seeks out relations that are nonlinear in nature. The basic idea can be illustrated with the following simple experiment. Position the tongue tip at the upper teeth to form an [s]. Hold the shape of the tongue constant and slowly draw the constriction backward toward the palate. One should observe a relatively long region that produces essentially no change in quality followed by an abrupt change to [š]. There is thus a nonlinear (*quantal*) relation between the articulatory and the acoustic/auditory dimensions that can be depicted in the diagram in figure 4.25. The plateau I designates a region in which a change in the articulatory parameter correlates with a stable acoustic/auditory state; the steep rise II defines a boundary region where small changes in articulation coincide with abrupt changes in the acoustic correlate; it is followed by another plateau, III, producing a stable acoustic output across a range of articulatory targets. The acoustic steady state generated by the articulatory plateau identifies the corresponding feature's acoustic correlate. Stevens sees a major functional advantage for such quantal relations between articulation and acoustics. The articulator does not have to hit a precise target but has a considerable margin of error in which to produce the desired acoustic effect. This presumably allows for faster articulation. In a number of cases the "lazy" S shape in figure 4.25 is created by two features acting in concert, one enhancing the acoustic dimension created by the other; see Stevens and Keyser 1989 for discussion.

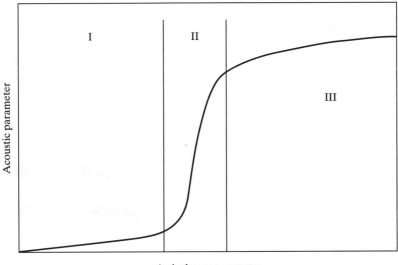

I

II

III

Acoustic parameter

Articulatory parameter

Figure 4.25   (After Stevens 1989:4.)

Another basic claim of Liberman and Mattingly's (1985; Mattingly and Liberman 1990) Motor Theory is that speech perception is the product of a special
module that operates independently from the analysis for pitch and timbre employed in the perception of other nonspeech sounds. In one series of experiments
they synthesized brief resonances with a changing center frequency (figure 4.26).
When presented in isolation, these "glides" are heard as nonspeech "chirp"- like
sounds and are readily distinguished from one another (figure 4.26a). But when
they are combined as F_3 transitions with a base as in figure 4.26b, listeners perceive a [da] or [ga]. Listeners are unable to perceive the chirp inside the Ca
syllable. Furthermore, they perform at no better than chance levels when asked
to match the rising or falling chirps of figure 4.26a with [da] or [ga] from figure
4.26b. Liberman and Mattingly conclude that a special phonetic module automatically integrates the information in figure 4.26 into a single percept. This module has priority over the more general-purpose, nonspeech module; it uses up the
"glide" and thus prevents the chirp from being isolated in the [da] or [ga].

A similar conclusion is drawn from phenomenon of *duplex perception*. In these
experiments the stimuli are synthesized from the components shown in figure
4.27. If (a) is presented in isolation, listeners report a buzz; if (b) is presented in
isolation, subjects hear a CV syllable that is ambiguous between [da] and [ga]
since it lacks the distinguishing F_3 transition. When the two stimuli are combined
– either diotically (both parts to both ears) or dichotically (one part to one ear
and one part to the other) – listeners naturally integrate them and hear [da] or
[ga]. To produce the phenomenon of duplex perception, the two stimuli are modified by assigning them different fundamental frequencies. In such cases another
auditory module of "scene analysis" might be expected to be called into play.
Scene analysis segregates the acoustic signal into different streams on the basis

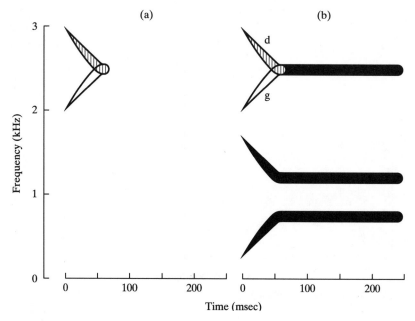

Figure 4.26   Patterns that illustrate the "domain specificity" of speech perception. (a) Isolated resonances. (b) The same resonances producing [d] and [g] in a speechlike context. (From Mattingly and Liberman 1990:503.)

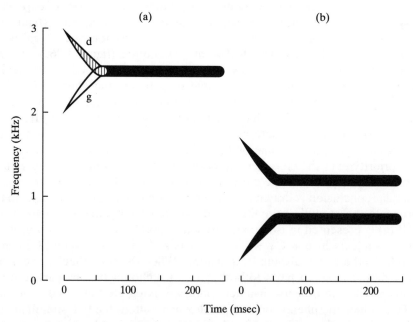

Figure 4.27   One way of partitioning the stimulus pattern so as to produce duplex perception. (a) The third formant with its variable [d]-producing and [g]-producing resonances. (b) The fixed remainder of the pattern. (From Mattingly and Liberman 1990:506.)

of differences in pitch, loudness, and timbre. It analyzes the sound impinging on the ears as originating from different sources in the environment – different voices, the vacuum cleaner versus the lawn mower, and so on. If scene analysis operates on the combination of figure 4.27a,b first, we might expect two different percepts: the buzz and a syllable that would be ambiguous between [da] and [ga]. The surprising result is that listeners report two percepts: the buzz and an *un*ambiguous [da] or [ga], depending on the nature of the brief resonance onset. Evidently, F_3 is being used simultaneously to form two different percepts: the buzz and the [da] or [ga]. Once again, Liberman and Mattingly conclude that the phonetic module takes priority, integrating the two stimuli despite their different fundamentals. Only after this module has operated does scene analysis step in to assign the stimuli to separate sources on the basis of the differing fundamentals.

Finally, let us note two experiments that demonstrate a relation between the auditory and visual modalities that makes sense under the tight bond between particular articulatory and acoustic states implied by a phonological feature. In the so-called *McGurk effect,* subjects see a video display of a head saying [ba] repeatedly: [ba], [ba], [ba]. The video is synchronized with a recording of [ga], [ga], [ga]. If speech was perceived by a set of general cognitive categories unconnected to language, listeners should have no difficulty hearing [ga], [ga], [ga]. But if speech is processed as a linguistic category that implies a particular articulatory-acoustic connection, then the sound [ga] is directly tied to a velar articulation and thus will be incompatible with the bilabial visual cue. In fact, subjects hear neither [ga], [ga], [ga] nor [ba], [ba], [ba], but [da], [da], [da] – an illusion whose effect is quite stunning. (See Summerfield 1991 for recent discussion.) Such bimodal visual-aural equivalences have also been detected in infants. In one experiment (Kuhl and Meltzoff 1982), 4-month-old infants were shown two faces side by side with a loudspeaker in between. One facial image articulated [a] and the other [i]. When the loudspeaker presented matched [a] and [i] stimuli, infants chose to look at the face that matched the aural cue some 73% of the time. Once again, these results suggest a hard-wired connection between articulation and acoustics that is implied by the theory of distinctive features.

Suggested Readings

Clark, John, and Colin Yallop. 1990. An introduction to phonetics and phonology. Oxford: Blackwell Publishers. Chapters 2 and 7.

Clements, George N. 1985. The geometry of phonological features. Phonology Yearbook 2.225–52.

Halle, Morris. 1983. On distinctive features and their articulatory implementation. Natural Language & Linguistic Theory 1.91–105.

Lieberman, Philip. 1984. The biology and evolution of language. Cambridge, Mass.: Harvard University Press. Chapters 7 and 8.

McCarthy, John. 1988. Feature geometry and dependency: A review. Phonetica 43.84–108.

Exercises

4.1 *Articulators*

A.   What are the primary effects of contracting the hyoglossus?

B.   What muscles control the positioning of the tongue body?

C.   Where is the styloglossus located?

D.   Identify the muscles involved in the production of [i] and [m].

4.2 *Feature Trees*

A.   Label the following feature trees with the appropriate phonetic symbol.

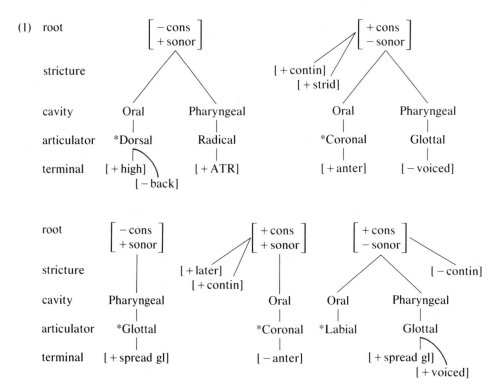

B.   Draw feature trees for the following sounds.

(2)   [æ]   [ɣ]   [ʔ]   [ṇ] (retroflex)   [ö]

4.3 *Polynesian*

Express the sound changes postulated in exercise 3.8 (Polynesian) in terms of the
feature tree developed in section 4.3.

4.4 Arabic Sun and Moon Letters

Review the discussion of complete assimilation in section 4.3.1 and then return
to exercise 1.5 to formalize the rule underlying the variation in the Arabic definite
prefix.

4.5 Irish-English

Wells (1982:434) states that the substitution of bilabial for labiodental fricatives
is a feature characteristic of the Irish-English brogue, so that *loaf* and *leave* are
pronounced (lo:Φ] and [le:β]. He mentions that "A trace of this [sound change]
remains in the fact that the Irish surname *ó Faoláin* has two competing anglici-
zations, *Phelan* and *Whelan:* in the first Irish [Φ] becomes English /f/, in the second
English /hw/." Express the [Φ] > [f] and [Φ] > [hw] sound changes in terms of
the feature tree.

4.6 Bengali

Organizing features in a hierarchical tree allows a distinction to be drawn between
single-feature and multiple-feature assimilation and delinking. With this distinction in mind, express the processes underlying the laryngeal neutralizations
evident in the following Bengali data. Like Hindi, Bengali makes an underlying
four-way distinction among voicing and aspiration in its occlusives: for example,
[p] vs. [pʰ] vs. [b] vs. [bʰ].

(1) prepausal

dialect I	dialect II	
ḍab	ḍab	'unripe coconut'
labʰ	lab	'profit'
bap	bap	'father'
lapʰ	lap	'jump'
kādʰ	kād	'shoulder'
pɔtʰ	pɔt	'street'
mɔt	mɔt	'opinion'
bagʰ	bag	'tiger'
bag	bag	personal name
ākʰ	ak	'sugarcane'
ḍak	ḍak	'call'

(2) preconsonantal (no dialect difference)

pɔtʰ	+	dækʰa	→	pɔddækʰa
'road'		'seeing'		
mačʰ	+	dʰɔra	→	majdʰɔra
'fish'		'catching'		
pāč	+	gun	→	pajgun
'five'		'times'		

labʰ	+	kɔra	→	lapkɔra
'profit'		'making'		

šat	+	bʰali	→	šadbʰali
'seven'		'brothers'		

lobʰ	+	tʰaka	→	loptʰaka
'greed'		'remaining'		

mɔd	+	kʰaoa	→	mɔtkʰaoa
'alcohol'		'drinking'		

4.7 Lyman's Law in Japanese

Review the analysis of Lyman's Law in Japanese compounds in section 4.3.3. Provide derivations for the following two compounds, explaining the difference in voicing. Briefly discuss the role that the notion of tier plays in accounting for this difference.

(1) ko   +   tanuki   →   kodanuki
     'child'   'raccoon'   'baby raccoon'

(2) taikutsu   +   šinogi   →   taikutsušinogi
     'boredom'   'avoiding'   'time-killer'

4.8 Acoustic Phonetics

A. Calculate the first three resonance frequencies of a tube closed at one end that is 10 cm long. What is the wavelength of the lowest resonance?

B. The speed of sound in water is 1,520 meters per second. Calculate the first three frequencies at which a tube closed at one end whose length is 17 cm will resonate in water.

C. Using the Chiba-Kajiyama rule, label the cells in the following table as higher or lower with respect to the values for the neutral vowel schwa. Hint: Rely on the diagrams in figure 4.19 and assume that [u] is produced with a constriction at the lips, [i] with a constriction about 5 cm in from the lips, and [a] with a constriction about 11 cm in from the lips. Verify your results by referring to figure (47).

(1) F_1 500 Hz   ____ ____ ____
     F_2 1500 Hz ____ ____ ____
           [ə]   [u]   [i]   [a]

5   Lexical Phonology

In this chapter we will look at generative research into the relation between phonology and morphology. We will begin with evidence that phonological rules fall
into two broad classes: one sensitive to the morphological and lexical environment
and the other not. We will then note another criterion of lexical rules – sensitivity
to derived contexts – and examine attempts to subsume this property under the
notion of strict cyclicity. After a review of early work in generative morphology,
we will see how phonology and morphology are integrated in Kiparsky's (1982a)
Lexical Phonology model – the received generative interpretation of the relation
between phonology and morphology. We will examine the model's basic concepts
and claims and in the final sections turn to current issues and problems that
confront the model.

5.1   Introduction

Since the inception of the scientific study of phonology, linguists have noted that
phonological alternations and the rules that underlie them tend to fall into two
broad classes. These classes are distinguished by several properties, which are
listed in (1).

(1)   a.   relevance of lexical information
      b.   distinctive nature of alternating sounds
      c.   phonetic motivation for alternation

As illustration, let us compare two rules of English phonology: the flapping rule
that converts intervocalic dental stops to a sonorant [D] (IPA [ɾ]) and the so-
called trisyllabic laxing rule (TSL) that shortens a vowel when followed by two
syllables. These rules differ with respect to each of the features listed in (1). First,
the context in which the flapping rule applies can be stated in purely phonological
terms as V́___V. The rule converts an intervocalic dental stop to a sonorant
essentially without exception. It applies both morpheme-internally (2a) and when
the V́___V context is interrupted by a morpheme boundary (2b). Flapping also
applies at the phrasal level, where the following vowel is contributed by another
word (2c).

(2)   a.   a[D]om   cf. atom-ic
      b.   mee[D]-ing   cf. meet
      c.   wha[D] is wrong? cf. what

The flapping rule exhibits the two other features of (1) that often accompany such purely phonologically conditioned rules. The [D] that is the output of the rule is not a member of the underlying inventory of contrasting phonological segments in English. This sound arises only as a product of the flapping rule. For this reason English speakers are typically unaware of the sound substitution introduced by this rule. It takes phonetic training to realize that the [t]'s in *atom* and *atomic* are in fact different sounds. Finally, the sonorization of an intervocalic stop is a natural phonological process that is widely distributed through the languages of the world and can be viewed as an assimilation of the sonority of the adjacent vowels.

The TSL rule differs in each of these respects. Before developing this point, we need to assemble some background on this rule, which has played a prominent role in generative phonology. TSL is responsible for many of the vocalic alternations running through the phonology of English. Its precise statement is still a matter of some controversy. For purposes of discussion here, we will accept the formulation given by Kiparsky (1982a), listed in (3a); see section 10.9 for further discussion. This rule shortens a long vowel when followed by two syllables, the first of which is unaccented. (The latter restriction prevents application of the rule in *títán-ic, Hĕbrá-ic, Plãtón-ic,* etc.) After TSL has applied, another rule known as Vowel Shift transforms the vowels that have escaped shortening in the manner indicated in (3b).

(3) a. $\bar{V} \rightarrow \breve{V}/ \underline{\quad\quad} C\ V_1\ C\ V_2$
          (where V_1 is not stressed)

     b.   ī → aj
          ē → ij
          ǣ → ej

The rules in (3a,b) jointly account for the vowel alternations exemplified in (4a). (In dialects where long vowels are not diphthongized, the alternations take the form [ē] → [ī] and [ǣ] → [ē]; also, short [i] and [e] are realized as [−ATR] lax vowels [ɪ] and [ɛ].)

(4) a.   divīne   [aj]   divĭn-ity   [i]
          serēne   [ij]   serĕn-ity   [e]
          profǣne   [ej]   profǎn-ity   [æ]

     b.   div[ī]ne   div[ī]n + ity   UR
          inappl.   [i]   TSL
             [aj]   inappl.   Vowel Shift

We will follow the analysis of these alternations developed in *SPE*, which assumes the underlying long vowels reflected in the orthography. The pair *divine-divinity* receives the derivations in (4b).

Additional suffixes whose attachment to a stem invokes TSL are listed in (5).

(5) [-ify]   vīle   vĭl-ify
                 clēar   clăr-ify
     [-ual]   rīte   rĭt-ual
                 grāde   grăd-ual
     [-ize]   tȳrant   tȳrann-ize
                 pēnal   pĕnal-ize
     [-ous]   tȳrant   tȳrann-ous
                 fāble   făbul-ous

With this background, let us now consider the ways in which the TSL rule differs from the flapping rule. First, specification of the context in purely pho-nological terms as ____CVCV is not sufficient to characterize the precise range of application of the rule. There are a significant number of stems with a long tense vowel followed by two syllables. These V̄CVCV strings show no tendency to shorten the initial vowel (6a). Consequently, the rule is only conditioned by the addition of a suffix. Second, not all suffixes activate the rule. While [-ity] and [-ify] regularly initiate shortening, the suffixes in (6b) systematically fail to do so.

(6) a.   nīghtingale, stēvedore, īvory
     b.   brăv-ery, mīght-ily, pīrat-ing

Finally, within the class of suffixes that trigger TSL, there are still idiosyncratic lexical exceptions: *obēsity* fails to undergo the rule and be pronounced as *obĕsity*. Consequently, precise delimitation of the extension of TSL requires information about the lexical and morphological environment in which the V̄CVCV string is located. By contrast, the domain of the flapping rule can be specified in purely phonological terms.

In addition, TSL differs from flapping in that it relates segments that occur as independent phonemes in English. The [ij]≈[ɛ] alternation of *serēne-serenity* re-lates phonological segments that contrast in such minimal pairs as *beat* vs. *bet*. English speakers have no difficulty in perceiving the sound substitutions effected by TSL in such pairs as *serene-serenity* even if they are not reflected in the orthography. This [ij] vs. [ɛ] difference is one to which proponents of orthographic reform are likely to appeal in order to justify a change in English spelling. It is noteworthy that the *t*'s in *atom-atomic* differ by just as many features as the *e*'s in *serene-serenity*. But few would argue that *atom* and *atomic* should be distin-guished orthographically – precisely because this sound difference is below the threshold of consciousness for most speakers. Finally, given the formulation of TSL as in (3a), the environment of the rule is not a particularly natural one for vowel shortening (closed syllable, unstressed syllable, etc.).

The flapping and TSL rules thus contrast with respect to each of the properties of (1). Other rules often fail to display all three features. But this does not in-validate the classification. Rather, the features of (1) should be thought of as relations that constrain the range of properties any given phonological rule is likely to display. If a rule introduces allophones, then it typically lacks lexical condi-tioning and tends to be phonetically motivated. If a rule substitutes sounds in a phonetically irrational way, then the terms of the alternation are usually elements of the underlying phonemic inventory, and the rule will quite likely display or develop lexical restrictions.

Let us consider another example in which the distinction between these two kinds of phonological rules is evident. Recall from section 2.7 the rule of Polish that raises [o] to [u] when followed by a word-final voiced nonnasal consonant (7b). This rule accounts for the alternations in (7a).

(7) a. bup   bob-u   'bean'
         xut   xod-u   'pace'
         kot   kot-a   'cat'
         vus   voz-u   'cart'
         dzvon   dzvon-u   'bell'

     b. [o] → [+high] / ____ [+cons, −nasal, +voiced] #

Polish raising displays many of the characteristics of English TSL. First, it has lexical exceptions: for example, *skrop* 'scratch' imper. from underlying [skrob] (cf. 1sg. *skrob'-e*). It also has some morphological conditioning. According to Bethin (1978), the rule applies much more often in feminine and neuter nouns than in masculines. The latter point is shown also by extension of the rule to loanwords: the feminines *doz-a* 'dose', *pagod-a* 'pagoda', *mod-a* 'fashion' show raising in the suffixless genitive plural: [dus], [pagut], [mut]. Bethin reports that there is no tendency to extend the rule to such masculines as [mop] 'mob', [snop] 'snob'. In contrast, the final devoicing rule is completely regular. Its context and extent of application do not require access to any lexical or morphological information. Second, Polish speakers are aware of the sound substitution effected by the raising rule since [o] and [u] are contrastive segments. In fact, this sound change is reflected in the orthography: the [u] derived from raising is spelled *ó*. The voicing change is essentially below the level of consciousness; it is not reflected in the orthography. It happens to be the case that each voiced obstruent phoneme in Polish is matched by a corresponding voiceless one. Consequently, the final devoicing rule has no opportunity to introduce allophones. It should be noted that the discussion here abstracts away from the effects of the phrasal context. When the following word begins with a voiced obstruent, the final obstruent of the preceding word will assimilate in voicing. This process may introduce allophones. For example, the voiceless fricative [x] lacks a voiced counterpart as an independent phoneme. But this gap fails to constrain the change of [x] to [ɣ]: for example, *Lech Wałęsa* is phonetically [. . .ɣ # v. . .]. Thus, when the proper conditions obtain, the rule(s) responsible for the voicing of word-final obstruents in Polish display the range of features predicted by the classification in (1). Finally, while final devoicing is one of the most common kinds of phonological rule, the raising of [o] to [u] before a voiced nonnasal consonant is an arbitrary and phonetically unmotivated sound substitution.

Thus, the Polish raising and devoicing rules classify with respect to the properties in (1) in essentially the same way as the English TSL and flapping rules do. However, the Polish data bring out an additional point. Recall that the raising rule must precede the devoicing rule. This ordering reflects the generalization that lexically restricted rules typically precede rules of the second type. This is another important difference between the two rule classes that must be explained. Anticipating later discussion, we will refer to rules whose application is sensitive to the morphological or lexical context of the phonological string as *lexical* rules. The second class of rules is termed *postlexical*.

Let us continue developing the distinction between lexical and postlexical rules by looking at another example from Polish. Here we will rely on the discussion of Rubach (1984). Polish has a general rule palatalizing dental consonants such as [t,d,s,n,] to [ć,ǯ,ś,ń] before suffixes beginning with front vowels, such as the loc.sg. [-e]. The data in (8a) illustrate.

(8) a.   nom.sg.   loc.sg.
          ------   ------
          brat   bra[ć]e   'brother'
          cud   cu[ǯ]e   'miracle'
          pas   pa[ś]e   'belt'
          dzwon   dzwo[ń]e   'bell'

     b.   wtedy 'then', deptać 'tread', sejm 'parliament'

     c.   [ć]eń 'shade', [ǯ]eń 'day', [ś]eń 'hallway', [ń]e 'no'

Polish also has a significant number of root morphemes containing substrings composed of a dental plus front vowel (8b). Rubach reports that there is no tendency to generalize the palatalization rule to these morpheme-internal strings. However, Polish also has a significantly larger number of stems containing a palatal plus front vowel sequence (8c).

The data in (8) pose a significant theoretical problem. Two analyses are possible. The morphemes in (8c) can be assigned underlying representations composed of a dental plus front vowel: [ten], [sen], and so on. If the palatalization rule is permitted to apply morpheme-internally as well as across a morpheme boundary, then these morphemes will be assigned surface representations with a palatal. On this analysis, the items in (8b) are treated as idiosyncratic exceptions to the palatalization rule. Alternatively, an analysis might be proposed in which the palatalization rule is restricted to *heteromorphemic* contexts: the focus of the rule (the dental consonants) is contributed by one morpheme, while the triggering context (front vowel) is contributed by a different morpheme. On this alternative analysis, the items in (8b) are not idiosyncratic exceptions. They are systematically excluded by virtue of the fact that their dental + front vowel substrings do not span a morpheme boundary. An important corollary of this alternative analysis is that the palatal consonants in (8c) must be part of the underlying representations. They cannot be derived by the palatalization rule, which is restricted to apply at the morpheme boundary.

The table in (9) summarizes the opposing analyses.

(9)   analysis A
      ----
      a.   domain of palatalization rule is unrestricted
      b.   [ć]*eń* derives from underlying [t]*eń*
      c.   *wtedy* is an idiosyncratic exception to the palatalization rule

analysis B
a.   domain of palatalization is restricted to heteromorphemic contexts
b.   [ć]*eń* derives from underlying [ć]*eń*
c.   *wtedy* is not an idiosyncratic exception to the palatalization rule

English TSL poses a similar analytic indeterminancy. If the rule is allowed to apply morpheme-internally, then words such as *elephant* and *pyramid* could be derived from underlying representations with a long vowel: [ēlephant], [pȳramid]. Forms such as *ivory* and *stēvedore* would have to be marked as lexical exceptions. But if TSL is restricted to heteromorphemic environments, then *elephant* must be derived from an underlying short vowel and *ivory* is not a lexical exception. In general, any lexical phonological rule allows these alternative analyses. An adequate theory of phonology will resolve the indeterminacy by imposing a consistent choice between the alternatives.

Rubach (1984) shows that the adaptation of loanwords in Polish strongly supports the second analysis, which restricts the rule to heteromorphemic contexts. In etymologically foreign words, a stem-final dental consonant regularly palatalizes before a front vowel suffix. The data in (10) are representative.

(10)   Fiat   'Fiat'   Fia[ć]-ik   dimin.
       Ford   'Ford'   For[ž]-e   loc.sg.
       ras-a   'race'   ra[ś]-ista   'racist'
       dżentelmen   'gentleman'   dżentelme[ń]-i pl.
       serwis   'auto service' serwi[ś]-e   loc.sg.
       tez-a   'thesis'   te[ź]-e   loc.sg.

The important point is that the palatalization rule just as systematically fails to affect morpheme-internal dental + front vowel sequences. Note the unpalatalized dentals in *dżentelmen, serwis, teza*. This is a striking contrast. Why should the initial [s] in *serwis* fail to palatalize while the final one undergoes the rule? The contrast is exactly what we expect under analysis B of (9), which restricts palatalization to heteromorphemic dental + front vowel strings. It remains unexplained under analysis A, in which the rule applies in unrestricted, across-the-board fashion.

The Polish data suggest that the class of lexical rules is systematically restricted from applying to morpheme-internal strings. This is an additional criterion to distinguish lexical from postlexical rules: the latter apply without regard to the morphemic constituency of the phonological string. In the next section we will see that delimiting the domain of application of the lexical rules is actually a more complex matter than the tautomorphemic/heteromorphemic distinction found in Polish.

5.2   Derived Environment Rules

Kiparsky (1973a) discovered a class of lexical phonological rules whose application is sometimes extended to tautomorphemic strings and sometimes not. Let us begin with an example from Finnish, which has a rule converting [t] to [s] before suffixal [i] (11a). This rule accounts for the alternation in (11b) but must be prevented from affecting the morpheme-internal [ti] strings in such lexical items as those in (11c).

(11) a. [t] → [s] / ____ [i]
      b. halut-a 'to want', halus-i 'wanted'
      c. tila 'room', äiti 'mother'

So far this is exactly the behavior we expect of lexical rules. What makes the Finnish example noteworthy is the existence of a class of morpheme-internal [ti] strings that, unlike those in (11c), do undergo the rule – and systematically so. These [ti] strings derive from underlying [te] sequences through another rule of Finnish that raises word-final [e]. This raising rule, which is stated in (12a), accounts for the alternations in (12b). (12c) cites stems that end in [te]. Observe that in the latter case both rules apply.

(12) a. [e] → [i] / ____ #

      b. joki   'river'   joke-na   essive sg.
          äiti   'mother'   äiti-nä   essive sg.

      c. vesi   'water'   vete-nä   essive sg.
          käsi   'hand'   käte-nä   essive sg.

Vesi must therefore be derived as shown in (13a).

(13) a. [vete]   b. [äiti]   UR
          veti   inappl.   raising
          vesi   block   *t → s*

But now there is a serious problem – namely, how to permit the *t → s* rule to apply to the [ti] sequence in (12c) but at the same time prevent it from affecting the morpheme-internal [ti] strings of the items in (11c). There is of course a systematic difference in the two classes of tautomorphemic [ti] strings: the ones in *tila* and *äiti* are present in the underlying representation, while the one in [veti] arises from the application of the raising rule to [vete]. The *t → s* rule blocks on underlying [ti] sequences but applies to derived ones.

In earlier chapters we have seen that rule ordering may sometimes be used to distinguish between underlying and derived strings. More specifically, ordering of rules is relevant to situations in which a given rule A applies to an underlying string [x] but fails to apply to an identical string [x] derived from another rule B. We simply order A before B. But in the present case rule ordering is of no avail. The *t → s* rule must apply to the output of raising and therefore is ordered later. Yet somehow the grammar must be constructed so that this rule applies to derived [ti] strings but blocks on underlying [ti] strings.

After the publication of Kiparsky 1973a, phonologists discovered a number of other cases of rules whose application is restricted to such "derived contexts."

The *ruki* rule of Sanskrit furnishes an additional example. This rule turns [s] to the retroflex [ṣ] after [r], velars, and high vowels. Following Kiparsky's discussion of the phenomenon, we will assume that the feature [+high] adequately characterizes the environment for this rule. The retroflexion rule applies quite regularly across morpheme boundaries. Suffixes beginning with [s] appear with an [ṣ] in the [r,u,k,i] environment.

(14) [-si] 2sg.   [-sya] future
      da-dā-si   'you give'   kram-sya-ti   'he will go'
      bi-bhar-ṣi   'you carry'   vak-ṣya-ti   'he will say'

      [-s] aorist   [-su] loc.pl.
      a-yā-s-am   'I wanted'   senā-su   'armies'
      a-bhār-ṣ-am   'I carried'   agni-ṣu   'fires'

There are a substantial number of lexical items with unretroflexed [s] appearing tautomorphemically in the ruki environment: *bisa* 'lotus', *busa* 'mist', *barsa* 'tip'. However, the retroflexion rule cannot be restricted to apply just across morpheme boundaries. When rules of ablaut modify the root vowel so as to create a ruki context morpheme-internally, the rule regularly applies. For example, the root *sās* 'instruct' ablauts to [i] in the participle, triggering retroflexion: *śiṣ-ṭa* 'taught'. Also, *ghas* 'eat' loses its vowel in the reduplicated [ga + ghas + anti], resulting in a [velar + s] cluster that undergoes retroflexion: *ja-kṣ-ati* 3pl. Thus, just as in Finnish, underlying [s] in a tautomorphemic ruki environment must be prevented from undergoing the rule, while derived tautomorphemic strings do undergo it.

Rules that block on underlying tautomorphemic strings but apply either (i) to strings that span a morpheme boundary or (ii) to tautomorphemic strings derived by a previous rule have become known as *derived environment rules*. They pose a serious theoretical problem. Somehow, the underlying [ti] string in Finnish *tila* 'room' and underlying [is] in Sanskrit *bisa* must be prevented from being inputs to the *t → s* and retroflexion rules. But at the same time, the [ti] string derived from Finnish raising and the [is] string derived from Sanskrit ablaut must be inputs to these same rules.

One possible solution to the problem is to allow the application of individual rules to be determined not only by the immediately preceding step in the derivation, but also by information contained in the underlying representation. For example, the Finnish *t → s* rule might be formulated so as to apply to a representation just in case it contains a [ti] string that does not derive from an underlying [ti] string. This *global* condition will block application to *äiti* 'mother' in (13b), since its [ti] string is underlying. But the rule will apply in the derivation of *vesi* 'water' in (13a), because the [ti] string that is input to the rule does not derive from an underlying [ti] string. While this proposal generates the correct outputs, it is theoretically undesirable. If the theory grants any individual rule the power to look back to the underlying representation, then the class of possible grammars is increased significantly. It would be preferable to impose a general condition that predicts when any given rule will block on tautomorphemic underlying strings (i.e., in nonderived contexts). If such a condition can be formulated, then the class of grammars is not increased at all. In fact, it becomes internally more articulated.

At the time of Kiparsky's discovery and formulation of the problem (1973), many linguists were skeptical about whether such a general condition could be found (see discussion in Kenstowicz and Kisseberth 1977). For there are a significant number of situations in which phonological rules quite clearly do apply in nonderived contexts. Four types are listed in (15).

(15) a. allophonic rules (e.g., English aspiration [tʰ]*eam*)
      b. cyclic stress (e.g., English *América*)
      c. context-free "absolute" neutralization (e.g., Yokuts lowering)
      d. contextual neutralization (e.g., Chukchee [ŋ] assimilation)

In view of the fact that the rule types in (15) freely apply in nonderived contexts, the problem reduces to the following two questions. How do the Finnish $t \rightarrow s$ and the Sanskrit retroflexion rules differ from the rules in (15)? Does the purported difference provide a natural explanation for why the former rules block in nonderived contexts, while the latter do not (rather than the other way around, for example)?

Answering these two questions has turned out to be a very difficult problem. An early answer, given by Kiparsky (1973a), noted that the Finnish and Sanskrit rules are neutralization rules. Both [t] and [s] contrast before [i] as well as in many other contexts in Finnish; and both [s] and [ş] contrast after [i] as well as in other contexts in Sanskrit. Application of Finnish $t \rightarrow s$ to [tila] would produce **sila*. But since the [ti] string is morpheme-internal, no alternation will be produced and *sila* would naturally tend to be reanalyzed as [sila]. Thus, one might plausibly argue that the $t \rightarrow s$ rule blocks on underlying tautomorphemic [ti] strings, so that a greater range of underlying lexical contrasts surface phonetically. However, while this may be true, the rules in (15c,d) also neutralize underlying contrasts. Why isn't their application blocked morpheme-internally as well? Kiparsky noted that the rules in (15c,d) tend to be automatic rules with no lexical exceptions. Apparently, the Finnish $t \rightarrow s$ and Sanskrit retroflexion rules have exceptions. Thus, the existence of lexical exceptions might permit the two classes of neutralization rules to be distinguished. However, it is hard to see how this purported difference explains why neutralization rules with exceptions block in nonderived contexts while automatic rules do not. Why couldn't the two classes be reversed, so that it is the automatic rules that are restricted to nonderived contexts? As we will see, an answer to this question only emerged much later.

5.3 Strict Cyclicity

The next significant advance on the problem of derived environment rules was made by Mascaró (1976), who discovered reasons to believe that the restriction to derived contexts is a property of *cyclic* rules. Cyclic application refers to a situation in which the derivation proceeds in stages, through the repeated application of the same set of ordered rules to successively larger, more inclusive strings. The derivation of a big string VWXYZ thus works in successive cycles, from the inside out, rather than in one single run through the rules. Given a string VWXYZ, first an inner substring X is submitted to the cyclic rules. They apply to derive VWX'YZ. The derivation then moves out to a more inclusive substring WX'Y. This substring WX'Y is submitted to the same set of cyclic rules. Their application yields a string X". The resultant VX"Z is then cycled through the rules again until the outermost cycle comprehending the entire string has been processed. Of course, one assumes that the delimitation of the cyclic domains has some motivation independent of the phonology. A natural proposal is that the cyclic domains mirror the morphological structure of the word, such that each successive level of affixation defines a separate cycle. For example, for the word [origin + al + ity], the stem [origin] would constitute the first cyclic domain, [[origin]al] the second, and the entire word [[[origin]al]ity] the third.

Before considering how cyclic application is connected to the derived environment problem, we might ask if it makes any material difference whether or not phonological rules are applied cyclically. Often the result is the same as under noncyclic application. But there are situations in which the cyclic mode has empirical consequences. Sometimes application of a rule on an earlier cycle supplies information that is crucial to the proper application of another rule on a later cycle. The *SPE* analysis of English provides a classic example. According to *SPE*, some English dialects assign different stress contours to the words *compensation* and *condensation*. The second syllable of *comp*[ə]*nsation* bears no stress and so its vowel is reduced to schwa. But in these dialects, for some reason, vowel reduction blocks on the second syllable of *cond*[ɛ]*nsation*. The pronunciation **cond*[ə]*nsation* with a schwa is unacceptable. If the derivations start with [compensat + ion] and [condens + ation], it will be impossible to explain the contrast in the second syllables, since the words are virtually equivalent. However, the contrast finds a natural explanation in the observation that *cond*[ɛ]*nsation* derives from *condénse* while *comp*[ə]*nsation* derives from *cómpensàte*. If the stress rule is applied cyclically, as in (16), then *condensation* has a stress placed on its second syllable in an earlier cycle. This stress will then block vowel reduction. Since *compensate* assigns no stress to the medial syllable, vowel reduction may apply in this word. Later rules of stress neutralization may leave the medial vowel distinction as the only contrastive feature.

(16)   [condens]ation   [compensat]ion

		first cycle
[condense]	[compensate]	
condénse	cómpensàte	stress
		second cycle
[condéns]ation	[cómpensàt]ion	
condènsátion	còmpensátion	stress
		later rules
———————	còmpənsátion	vowel reduction
còndɛnsátion	———————	stress neutralization

In sum, cyclic application of stress provides a natural basis for distinguishing the otherwise equivalent *compensation* and *condensation*.

Cyclic application also solves certain ordering paradoxes in which application of a given rule A must both precede and follow application of another rule B. Such a situation can arise when the rules apply in the order [A,B] on one cycle and then rule A applies over again on a subsequent cycle. To take a simple example, the paradigm for [bɛn] in (17) illustrates two rules of Catalan phonology.

(17)   a.   mol   bɛn   3sg.
            mol-s   bɛn-s   2sg.
            mol-k   bɛŋ   1sg.
            mul-íə   bən-íə   3sg. past
            'grind'   'sell'

       b.   bint-έ   'twentieth'
            bin   'twenty'
            bim pans   'twenty breads'
            biŋ kaps   'twenty heads'

The first rule assimilates the point of articulation of the dental nasal to that of a following consonant. The second deletes a word-final stop after a nasal. In the derivation of [bɛŋ] from [bɛn + k], nasal assimilation clearly must precede cluster simplification. But the phrases *bim pans* and *biŋ kaps* show that nasal assimilation follows cluster simplification as well; for it is only by deletion of the final stop in [bint] 'twenty' that the dental nasal comes to immediately precede the initial stops of the following words.

Thus, nasal assimilation both precedes and follows cluster simplification. Such a state of affairs poses a significant problem for a theory in which the underlying representation is passed through the rules just once. But the paradox is solved if the nasal assimilation process applies on two separation cycles in Catalan: once on the word level and a second time on the phrasal level. The derivations in (18) illustrate the proposed solution.

(18)   [bɛn + k]   [bint] [kap + s]
                                          first cycle
        bɛŋ + k   bint ———   nasal assimilation
        bɛŋ   bin   ———   cluster simplification

                    [bin] [kaps]
                                          second cycle
                    biŋ kaps   nasal assimilation

Having seen that cyclic application can sometimes be empirically detected, let us now return to the derived environment problem. Mascaró (1976) demonstrated that certain rules of Catalan are subject to an opacity constraint that can be explained if it is assumed (i) that the rules apply in a cycle and (ii) that they display the property of *strict cyclicity* (Chomsky 1973). He then showed that the derived environment restriction could be subsumed under the independently needed strict cycle constraint. The rest of this section recapitulates his important result.

Three rules of Catalan phonology are relevant to the discussion. First, although stress falls on one of the last three syllables of the word in Catalan, which particular syllable bears the accent is, in general, unpredictable. Mascaró assumes that the stress is located in the underlying representation. Given this assumption, then a rule destressing a vowel before another stressed vowel is required, since any stem loses its stress whenever it is followed by a stressed affix. In general, only the rightmost underlying accent surfaces phonetically. A rule that removes a stress when followed by another stress accounts for this accentual limitation: $\acute{V} \rightarrow V / \underline{\hspace{1cm}} \ldots \acute{V}$. Second, Catalan contrasts the seven vowels [i,u,e,o,ɛ,ɔ,a] in stressed syllables. However, in unstressed syllables [e,ɛ,a] reduce to schwa and [o,ɔ] reduce to [u]. As the forms in (19) show, the stress deletion rule feeds the reduction process. An underlying representation such as [nɔ́bl + ɛ́z + ə] first loses its initial stress to become [nɔbl + ɛ́z + ə], and then reduces to [nubl + ɛ́z + ə].

(19) nɔ́bl-ə   'noble'
      nubl-ɛ́z-ə   'nobility'

The final rule relevant to the discussion devocalizes unstressed high vowels after a vowel. This rule is stated informally in (20a). Its application is illustrated in (20b), where the conjunction [i] 'and', the inflectional suffix [-u], and the adjectival suffix [-ik] devocalize postvocalically.

(20) a. [i,u] → [y,w] / V __ (in unstressed syllable)

      b. sál i pá   'salt and bread'   pá y sál   'bread and salt'
          féɾ-u   'iron'   dé-w   'God'
          fér-ik   'ferrous'   əlžəbrá-yk   'algebraic'

Devocalization must precede destressing, because a postvocalic high vowel does not turn to a glide when it loses its stress. This is clear from the examples *rəim-ét* and *ruin-ós* in (21a).

(21) a. rəím   'grape'   rəim-ét   dimin.
          ruín-ə   'ruin'   ruin-ós   'ruinous'

      b. [[ruín] ós]
                              second cycle
          inappl.   devocalization
          ruin ós   destressing
          inappl.   vowel reduction

The derivation of *ruin-ós* must be as shown in (21b). On the first cycle [ruín], no rules are applicable and so we pick up the derivation on the second cycle. If devocalization is ordered first, it (correctly) fails to apply since the postvocalic [i] is stressed. Subsequently, the stress on the stem is deleted by the destressing rule. Vowel reduction is inapplicable, and *ruinós* is derived. If devocalization applied to the output of destressing, then [ruin]*ós* would incorrectly become disyllabic **ruynós*. We prevent this derivation by ordering devocalization first.

There are, however, some additional cases in Catalan where devocalization does apply to a vowel that has been destressed. The paradigms in (22a) illustrate this situation.

(22)   a.   óbr-ə   'opens'
           ínst-ə   'instates'

      b.   ubr-ír   'to open'
           inst-ár   'to instate'

      c.   à wbrír   'in order to open'
           nò ystár   'not to instate'

The roots, shown in (22a), are [óbr] and [ínst]. In (22b) the stressed infinitival suffixes trigger loss of stem stress and vowel reduction. In (22c) the infinitives are preceded by *a* 'in order to' and the negative *no*, which devocalize the following vowel. (The vowels in these particles apparently retain some degree of prominence and thus fail to reduce. This is informally recorded with a grave accent: *à, nò*.) The derivations appear in (23).

(23)   [[óbr] ír]   [[ínst] ár]

                            second cycle
      inappl.   inappl.   devocalization
      obr ír   inst ár   destressing
      ubr ír   inappl.   reduction

      à [ubrír]   nò [instár]
                            third cycle
      à wbrír   nò ystár   devocalization
      inappl.   inappl.   destressing
      inappl.   inappl.   reduction

The important point that emerges from the discussion so far is that devocalization applies to the output of destressing in (23). But this rule interaction fails to obtain in the derivation of *ruinós* in (21b). Here the [i] does not turn to [y] in spite of the fact that it has been destressed and is preceded by a vowel. Mascaró observed that this mysterious contrast finds a natural explanation if the rules are applied cyclically. In *nò* [ynstár], *nò* devocalizes a vowel [i] that has been destressed on a previous cycle. The third cycle thus starts with an unstressed [i]. But in *ruinós* of (21b), the [i] is still stressed at the point when the devocalization rule is reached on the next cycle. Consequently, devocalization cannot apply.

In order to maintain this attractive explanation, however, we must ask what happens to *ruinós* when another affix is added, forcing the [ui] string to go through the rules again. Will devocalization apply to the unstressed [i] at the start of the next cycle? The answer is evident from the superlative form *ruinuz-ízim* 'very ruinous'. Devocalization does not apply. The disyllabic [ui] string established on the earlier cycle by ordering devocalization before destressing is carried through the subsequent cycles. Thus, devocalization must somehow be prohibited from returning to affect the material of an earlier cycle. Note, however, that the superlative suffix does trigger destressing and vowel reduction on the preceding stem. The derivation consequently must be as shown in (24).

(24)   [ruinós] ísim
       block   devocalization
       ruinosísim   destressing
       ruinusísim   reduction
       ruinuzízim   other rules

The problem then is that we must block devocalization in (24) but still permit it to apply in derivation (23) of *nò ystár* from *nò* [instár]. Mascaró pinpointed the relevant difference between the two cases. In the former, the [ui] string is completely contained within the bounds of an earlier cycle. But in the latter, the [òi] string straddles a cyclic boundary. The Catalan data indicate that information drawn exclusively from an earlier cycle constitutes an opaque domain to which rules applying on a later cycle are blind. This, in essence, is the strict cyclicity requirement that Chomsky (1973) argued to hold of the transformational cycle in syntax. The phonological version of the constraint can be formulated as shown in (25). (This formulation departs slightly from that of Mascaró 1976 and follows more closely the statement of the condition in Halle 1978.)

(25)   <u>Strict Cycle Condition (SCC)</u>
       A cyclic rule may apply to a string *x* just in case either of the following holds:

       a.   The rule makes crucial reference to information in the representation that spans the boundary between the current cycle and the preceding one.

       b.   The rule applies solely within the domain of the previous cycle but crucially refers to information supplied by a rule operating on the current cycle.

In essence, the SCC requires a cyclic rule to refer to a mixture of information – one portion drawn from the earlier cycle and the other contributed by the current cycle.

The SCC succeeds in explaining the intricate pattern of application and blocking of the Catalan devocalization and stress reduction rules. Some important theoretical consequences follow from the assumption that cyclic rules are subject to this condition. To begin with, the first rule to apply on any cycle must apply by case (a), since a rule can apply by case (b) only if some preceding rule has applied on the current cycle. But if the first application on any cycle goes by case (a), then it also follows that no cyclic rule may apply on the innermost cycle of a derivation – for lack of a cyclic boundary. This in turn implies that the underlying representation of the root morpheme is an opaque domain. No cyclic rule may enter this domain directly, without the assistance of an affix.

It should now be apparent how the SCC draws precisely the same distinction between derived and nonderived contexts that is needed to block improper application of the Finnish $t \rightarrow s$ rule. If we suppose that $t \rightarrow s$ (and thus by implication the raising rule) is cyclic, then just the right patterns of application take place for *halus-i, vesi,* and *tila.* This point is illustrated in (26).

(26) [halut] i   [vete]   [tila]

			first cycle
——	——	—	raising
——	——	—	$t \rightarrow s$
			second cycle
——	veti	—	raising
halus i	vesi	—	$t \rightarrow s$

By the SCC, no cyclic rules may apply on the innermost root-level cycle. On the second cycle raising applies to [vete] since, we assume, the triggering word boundary lies outside the root [# [vete] #] and thus becomes visible only on the final word-level cycle. This application takes place in virtue of condition (a). The [+high] introduced by raising will trigger application of $t \rightarrow s$ by condition (b). *halus-i* is derived by condition (a) since it combines information that spans the boundary between the stem and the suffix. But the rule blocks on [tila], which satisfies neither condition of the SCC.

To summarize, Mascaró 1976 is an important contribution – for several reasons. The first is theoretical economy. The derived context restriction can be reduced to a condition on rule application (the SCC) that is independently needed for cyclic rules. The theory now admits two classes of rules: cyclic and noncyclic. On the conceptual level, it is natural to try to identify the cyclic-noncyclic classification with the lexical-postlexical distinction developed earlier. In this way, cyclicity becomes another trait of the lexical class of rules. Construing the derived context limitation in terms of strict cyclicity also endows the theory with sharper empirical consequences. We have seen that the cyclicity of a rule is sometimes independently detectable. The implication is that if a rule must be restricted to derived contexts, then it should also display cyclic characteristics; similarly, any cyclic rule will have to apply in derived contexts. In addition, if cyclicity is a function of the lexical-postlexical distinction, then a further prediction is made. The lexical-postlexical distinction traces a line through a language's set of phonological rules. Consequently, any rule A ordered before another rule B that is restricted to derived contexts must also be cyclic. And any rule ordered after a rule that does not respect strict cyclicity will have to be a postcyclic rule.

Tying the derived context problem to strict cyclicity in this way should thus make the validity of the overall theory easier to assess. However, some nagging problems still remain. Most striking is the fact that the English stress rule does not fall into place properly. *SPE* – and later Kiparsky (1979) – showed it to be a paradigm example of a cyclic rule; yet it apparently applies on the root cycle in *América.*

5.4 Morphological Preliminaries

Besides work on the derived environment problem, the other important line of
research of the 1970s leading to the development of the Lexical Phonology model
took place in morphology. In this section we will review some of the highlights
of this research. In its initial stages, generative grammar did not develop a distinct
theory of morphology and instead tended to adopt, essentially by default, the
assumptions underlying the morphological theory and analysis of the earlier structuralist period – in particular, the conception of the morpheme as a minimal
meaningful element.

Aronoff 1976 represents the first serious generative attempt to deal with morphology on its own terms. Two of Aronoff's most significant results relate to the
nature of morphemes and to constraints on morpheme concatenation. First, he
shows that while the *morpheme* is the minimal unit in word structure, it need not
have any constant meaning or indeed any meaning at all. For example, morphological analysis of paradigms such as [permit, remit, commit], [perceive, receive,
conceive] isolates the prefixes [per-, re-, con-] and the roots [mit] and [ceive].
Even though no constant semantic value can be assigned to these elements, the
grammar nevertheless analyzes them as distinct units. This is evident from various
allomorphy rules. For example, the morpheme [mit] has the alternant [mis] before
the suffix [-ive]: *permissive, remissive,* and so on. This rule does not apply to just
any [mit] string – in fact, it applies only to those that comprise the root [mit] (cf.
vomit, *vomissive). Consequently, [mit] must be a linguistic unit even if it has no
consistent semantic value independent of the particular word in which it occurs.

Aronoff also discusses the notion of *morphological blocking*. In general, lexical
items can be located in an abstract morphological space or grid. The same sector
is often occupied by items that are the product of distinct *word formation rules*
(WFRs). The term "blocking" refers to the fact that the output of a more idiosyncratic, less productive WFR often preempts or blocks application of a more
general and productive rule. For example, the regular rule for forming the English
past tense suffixes [-ed]: *compute, computed.* The past tense is also formed by
less productive rules of ablaut (*sing, sang*) or by suppletion (*be, was*). These less
productive formations block the creation of **sing-ed* and **be-ed.* To cite one more
example, the productive rule for constructing agentive nouns suffixes [-er]: *compute, computer.* Less productive are the WFRs that add [-ant] (*inhabit, inhabitant*)
or that form the agentive directly from the verb by so-called zero derivation (*to
guide, a guide*). The less productive rules occupy the lexical building site first,
blocking the construction of **inhabiter, *a guider.* (*Guider* is a possible word;
but like *cooker,* it is restricted to inanimate denotees.)

Another finding of the early generative morphologists was that the *SPE* distinction between primary and secondary affixes crucial for the proper operation
of several phonological rules in English is also crucial to the morphology. English
affixes fall into two classes with respect to their effect on stress placement and
vowel length. The syllables comprising such primary affixes as [-al] and [-ous]
are counted in the computation of antepenultimate position (27a). But secondary
affixes such as [-ship, -less] have no effect on the location of the accent (27b).
The same distinction also applies to the rule of trisyllabic laxing. Affixes drawn

from the former class may trigger a shortening of the root vowel, but those from the latter class never do (27c,d).

(27) a. pýramid   [pyrámid]al
          hómonym   [homónym]ous

      b. pártisan   [pártisan]ship
                        *[partísan]ship

      c. nātion   [nătion]al
          ōmen   [ŏmin]ous

      d. sēaman   [sēaman]ship
                        *[sĕaman]ship

      e. in[potent]   im[potent]
          un[popular]   *um[popular]
          in[legal]   il[legal]
          un[lawful]   *ul[lawful]

A similar distinction shows up among prefixes (27e). The negative [in-] may, at least sometimes, count for stress while the negative [un-] never does. Correlated with this contrast is the fact that the nasal of [in-] assimilates to a following consonant while that of [un-] does not.

Three generalizations emerging from the study of English word structure also distinguish between primary and secondary affixes. First, primary affixes may be added to bound morphs such as [ept], [ert], [leg]: *in*[ept], *in*[ert], [leg]*al*, [curi]*ous*. But secondary ones may not: **un*[ept], **[leg]ness*, **[curi]less*. (There are a few isolated exceptions such as *unkempt*.) Second, as the terms primary and secondary suggest, there appears to be an ordering among the affixes. A secondary affix such as [-ness] can, in general, be added to a base with a primary affix such as [-al]. From [parent]*al* we may form [parental]*ness*. But a primary affix may not be attached to a base that contains a secondary affix. This explains why **[[happy]ness]al* sounds much worse than [parental]*ness*. Similarly, the secondary prefix [un-] may be added to *ir*[regular] (from *in*[regular]) to form *un*[ir[regular]]. But addition of primary [in-] to a base with a secondary affix yields ungrammatical results – the word *in*[un[regular]] is impossible. Finally, secondary affixes tend to have more coherent semantics. The meaning of *un*[credible] is more or less adequately described as "not capable of being believed." But *in*[credible] means much more, having an added, unpredictable dimension of "amazement."

One more result is due to Siegel (1978), who observes that WFRs exhibit an *opacity* property similar to the subjacency property of syntactic transformational rules. Aronoff (1976) had noted that some WFRs are sensitive to lexical properties of the base such as whether or not it is drawn from the Latinate sector of the vocabulary. To take a simple example, [-ity] attaches to Latinate bases. This explains why **[weird]ity* is odd while [equal]*ity* is not. The word [drink]able is composed of a Latinate affix and a non-Latinate root. Since [-ity] successfully attaches to this base ([drinkabil]*ity*), it appears that when the base contains conflicting [±Latinate] specifications, it is the one added on the preceding cycle that determines the outcome. In other words, the [−Latinate] feature of the base [drink] is no longer visible when the [-ity] affixation rule applies. To take another example, the prefix [un-] does not in general attach to bases containing the prefix [dis-]; this restriction must be built into the *un*-prefixation rule.

(28)   *un[dis[sonant]]   *un[dis[tinct]]
       *un[dis[loyal]]   *un[dis[honest]]

However, it then is mysterious why such words as *undismayed* and *undiscoverable* are completely well formed. As Siegel points out, the mystery vanishes once the internal structure of the bases [dismayed] and [discoverable] is taken into account. They derive from [dismay]*ed* and [discover]*able*. The [dis-] prefix is added on a cycle prior to the one that immediately precedes attachment of [un-].

(29)   un[dis may ed]   un [dis cover able]

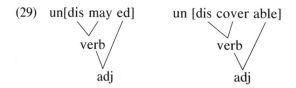

The information that the bases [dis[may]]*ed* and [dis[cover]]*able* contain the prefix [dis-] thus appears to be inaccessible to the *un*-prefixation rule. This result follows if information only from the immediately preceding cycle is available to the WFRs. Then, when the *un*-prefixation rule becomes applicable, it will be able to analyze the adjectives *dismayed* and *discoverable* into just the two immediate constituents [dismay]*ed* and [discover]*able*.

One mechanical way to implement the opacity restriction is to suppress the internal bracketing at the end of a given cycle. To illustrate, *undiscovered* and *undisloyal* would be derived as in (30).

(30)   cover → dis[cover]   loyal → dis[loyal]
       dis[cover] → [dis[cover]]ed   dis[loyal] → *un[dis[loyal]]
       [discover]ed → un[[discover]ed]

In the transition from the second to the third step, the internal bracketing showing that *discovered* is composed of a complex stem containing a prefix [dis-] and a root [cover] is erased. Consequently, at the point where *un*-prefixation applies, the string [dis] of *discovered* has the same status as the three-phoneme sequence beginning *discotheque*. By contrast, the information that *disloyal* is composed of the prefix [dis-] and the root [loyal] is still accessible to the *un*-prefixation rule because these two morphemes have been concatenated on the immediately preceding cycle.

Pesetsky (1979) noted a serious problem with this *bracket erasure* proposal. The WFRs apply in the lexicon. Nevertheless, a record of the internal bracketing is crucial for the phonology, because it delimits the domains for the cyclic application of the phonological rules. Pesetsky proposed the following bold solution to the problem: assume that the cyclic phonological rules apply inside the lexicon, after the application of each WFR, as depicted in (31).

(31) | WFRs | ⇌ | cyclic phonology |

Several noteworthy consequences ensue from this proposal. First, the cyclicity of the phonological rules no longer has to be stipulated. It now follows from the decision to organize the grammar as depicted in (31). More importantly, we now have a partitioning of the phonological rules into two classes that follows from their location in the overall model of grammar. Kiparsky (1982a) showed that many of the differences between the two classes of rules begin to make sense when the grammar is organized in this fashion. In the next section we turn to this influential work.

5.5 Lexical Phonology

The research on the derived environment problem and the role of morphology in phonology was synthesized by Paul Kiparsky into the theory of Lexical Phonology. In two highly influential papers, Kiparsky (1982a, 1985) developed and articulated Pesetsky's proposal that phonological rules appear at two distinct points in the grammar: in the lexicon and in the postsyntactic, phonological component. Given these two locations, many of the long-noted differences between the two classes of phonological rules begin to make sense. If the lexical phonological rules apply after each WFR, then this class of rules is inherently cyclic. Their cyclic application does not have to be stipulated; it follows from the organization of the grammar. From the work of Mascaró (1976), we know that limitation to derived contexts follows, in turn, from strict cyclicity. Finally, since the lexical rules are interleaved with the WFRs, it is natural for them to have access to the lexical properties of a given word's immediate constituent morphemes. Postlexical rules, on the other hand, apply outside the lexicon to the output of the syntactic component. By virtue of their different location, they can be expected to display different properties. First, since they are postsyntactic, their application may take a word's phrasal environment into account. Lexical rules of course may never do so, since they appear in the presyntactic component. Second, the postlexical rules have no direct access to the lexical properties of the constituent morphemes composing a word. This information is closed off by the bracket erasure convention. This explains why the paradigm postlexical rules – phrasal and allophonic rules – typically are automatic and have no lexical exceptions. Finally, if cyclicity is a function of interleaving with the WFRs, then there is no reason to suppose that the postlexical rules are cyclic. They are consequently free to apply in across-the-board (ATB) fashion and hence are not restricted to derived contexts by strict cyclicity.

Kiparsky's proposal to draw the lexical-postlexical distinction in this way is theoretically very attractive – for several reasons. First, it comes to terms with the intuition, dating back to the beginning of the study of phonological structure, that there are two different kinds of phonological rules – a distinction that was essentially denied by the earlier generative models. Second, it makes this distinction not by stipulation but rather by a specific proposal about the internal architecture of the grammar; furthermore, this proposal explains, at least in gross terms, why the two classes of rules display the specific properties they do. Third, the lexical-postlexical distinction helps to articulate and individuate the grammar; it thus accords with the modularity thesis that has become a methodological cornerstone of generative grammar. Finally, the Lexical Phonology model makes concrete predictions about how individual languages will have to look under this conception of the grammar. For these reasons, this model has become the focus for most generative research, both of a descriptive and of a theoretical nature, concerned with the relation of phonology to word structure.

In the following sections we will examine the basic concepts and principles of Lexical Phonology. We will also try to distinguish areas where there is basic agreement from those that are more unsettled.

5.5.1   The Model

Lexical Phonology develops the distinction between primary and secondary affixes noted by the early generative morphologists into a level-ordered morphology. The basic proposal is that the word formation rules (WFRs) and the lexical phonological rules can be partitioned into a series of *levels* or *strata*. Figure 5.1 illustrates Kiparsky's (1982a) conception of how the English lexicon is organized. Primary inflection includes the umlaut of *tooth-teeth*, the ablaut of *sing-sang*, and the past tense [-t] of *sleep*-[slep]*t* in addition to the primary derivational affixes in such items as [pyrámid]*al,* [ómen]*ous,* [dĕp]*th, im*[potent]. Secondary derivation is illustrated by the affixes in *un*[happy], [loneli]*ness,* [labor]*er.* The remaining inflection includes the regular plural in [cat]*s* and [brush]*es* and the past tense of [leap]*ed* and [pleat]*ed.* In this model, each level has the lexical phonological rules distinctive of that level. The morphological structure of a word is characterized by tracing its development through the paths indicated by the arrows. For example, the structure of *codifiers* is analyzed as follows. The word is composed of the base [côde], which has been submitted to the lexical phonological rules of level 1 (stress being the only relevant rule to apply). Then the verbalizing WFR affixing *-ify* applies to yield the representation [côd]*ify.* This representation is submitted to the phonological rules of level 1, where TSL applies to derive [cŏd]*ify.* The latter representation then enters level 2. No phonological rules are applicable, and the agentive suffix is added to give [cŏdifi]*er.* Finally, at level 3 the plural suffix is added to yield [codifier]*s.* It is apparent that this model defines a set of lexical items by a hierarchy of WFRs.

Two additional points should be noted about figure 5.1. First, any derivation proceeds through all the levels even if no relevant morphology applies at that level. Thus, the word *cat* is derived by submitting it to the lexical phonological rules of each of the three levels. Second, the output of each level is a *lexical item.* This is a technical term for Kiparsky; and as we will see, it plays a central role in the theory.

It should be clear that the model straightforwardly accounts for several generalizations about English word structure noted earlier. For example, the contrast

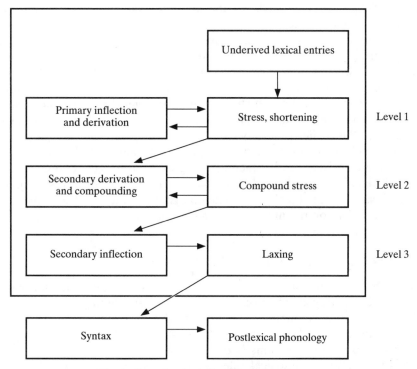

Figure 5.1 Lexical phonology in English.

between the relative well-formedness of *parentalness* and the marked deviance of **inunregular* can now be explained as follows. In the Lexical Phonology model, words are formed by the successive application of the WFRs. Prefixation and suffixation rules thus create successive layers of affixation. *Parentalness* arises from suffixation of *-al* to the base [parent] at level 1, followed by suffixation of *-ness* at level 2. **Inunregular* would have to arise from prefixation of *in-* to the base [unregular]. But the WFR prefixing *in-* applies at level 1, while the base [unregular] only arises at level 2. Since there is no provision to return to an earlier level in the model of figure 5.1, once [unregular] has been formed, the prefix *in-* cannot be attached. In this way, the generalization that primary affixes may not appear outside secondary affixes is captured.

Kiparsky also assumes that the output of each level is a full-fledged lexical item. If this assumption is granted, then we can explain why bound roots such as [ept] only appear with level 1 affixes: compare *in*[ept] with **un*[ept]. The latter can only be constructed by prefixing *un-* at level 2. Because the morphological levels are ordered, the bound morph [ept] must traverse level 1. But this will be impossible if the output of each level must be a full-fledged lexical item.

Another noteworthy feature of the model is that an underived base is passed through the level 1 phonological rules before any WFRs are applied. In many cases this step will be vacuous if application is blocked by the SCC. But recall that at least some rules such as stress assignment must be permitted to operate on the initial cycle. Since, in general, phonological rules may precede the application of WFRs, it is possible for the latter to take into account information supplied by a phonological rule. A possible example is furnished by deverbal nominalizations in *-al*. This suffix attaches only to bases whose final syllable is accented: [acquít]*al,* [rebút]*al,* *[devélop]*al*. The requirement that the final syllable of the base be accented forms a clause in the [-al] WFR, thus blocking the construction of deviant items such as *develop-al*. This example is an important one for several reasons. First, it shows that phonological rules (in this case stress assignment) can apply prior to a WFR (*-al* suffixation). Such a state of affairs is impossible in the earlier generative models where all morphology takes place in the lexicon and all phonology in the postsyntactic component. Second, it is crucial that an underived base such as [acquit] be passed through the phonological rules of level 1 before any WFR applies so that it may pick up the stress required by the *-al* affixation rule. Finally, this example shows that the stress rule must be permitted to apply on the initial cycle and so must not be blocked by the SCC.

5.5.2   *Conjunctive versus Disjunctive Ordering*

Kiparsky has an interesting answer to the question of why stress assignment applies on the root cycle while rules such as trisyllabic laxing (TSL) are blocked by the SCC. Before examining his solution to this problem, we must consider an additional concept: the *Elsewhere Condition* (Kiparsky 1973b). It is a proposal to account for *disjunctive* relations between phonological rules. To this point, we have assumed that phonological rules apply *conjunctively.* If rule A applies to derive a representation [x], a subsequently ordered rule B must apply to [x] if [x] satisfies the structural description of rule B. The final output is thus the conjunction of the application of rules A and B. A disjunctive relation holds when either rule A or rule B, but not both, may apply. It typically arises when rule A applies to a certain subset of strings and rule B applies to the remainder as the "elsewhere" case. Let us look at a simplified example adapted from Kiparsky 1973b. In Sanskrit, word-final [s] assimilates the precise point of articulation of a following coronal consonant, becoming retroflex before a retroflex and palatal before a palatal (32a). Elsewhere, it turns to [h] (32b).

(32)   a.   s#t → st
            s#ṣ → ṣṣ
            s#ć → ść

       b.   s#m → hm
            s#a → ha
            s#pause → h pause

(33)   a. $s \rightarrow [\alpha Fs] /$ ____ $\begin{bmatrix} +\text{coron} \\ \alpha Fs \end{bmatrix}$

       b. $s \rightarrow h /$ ____ $\{$ C,   V, pause$\}$
            $[-\text{coron}]$

       c. $s \rightarrow h /$ ____ #

(33a) expresses the assimilation rule (where F is an ad hoc designation of the features for the retroflex and palatal points of articulation). One could express the $s \rightarrow h$ rule by enumerating the precise set of contexts that form the complement of the assimilation rule, as in (33b). However, this is a complex and unnatural rule. It should only be found in a language that also has a rule such as (33a) operating in the complementary set of contexts. There is thus a descriptive generalization about the relation between the rules that (33b) fails to express. The most natural statement of the $s \rightarrow h$ rule appears in (33c). Intuitively, the relation between the assimilation and aspiration rules is that [s] assimilates to a coronal and *elsewhere* turns to [h]. This relation can be expressed if it is the natural rules of (33a) and (33c) that appear in the grammar of Sanskrit. There is one problem with this description, however. The aspiration rule must be prevented from affecting a string that has undergone the assimilation rule – for example, the string $s\#t$. In other words, the relation between assimilation and aspiration is disjunctive. Conjunctive application must be prevented, since otherwise underlying [s#t] will be incorrectly converted to [h#t].

The theoretical problem the Sanskrit data raise is to find a general way to predict when a disjunctive relation will be imposed between a pair of rules instead of the normal conjunctive relation under which both rules may apply. Kiparsky's (1982a) proposal is stated as (34), the *Elsewhere Condition*.

(34)   Rules A and B in the same component apply disjunctively to a form θ if and only if

    a.   The structural description of A (the special rule) properly includes the structural description of B (the general rule).

    b.   The result of applying A to θ is distinct from the result of applying B to θ.

In that case A is applied first, and if it takes effect, then B is not applied.

A number of technicalities arise in applying this constraint to any given case. We will content ourselves here with understanding its basic intent. In essence, (34) claims that application of rule B will be suspended when the information defining the inputs to rule A subsumes all of the information defining inputs to B. This condition holds in the Sanskrit case. The assimilation rule applies to the class of strings denoted by its structural description [s#coronal consonant]. This expression clearly subsumes the information content of [s#] – the set of strings forming the elsewhere case. In general, the structural description of the elsewhere rule can be derived by cancelling out material from the structural description of the special rule (in our case, [+coronal, αFs]). The requirement that the structural changes of the rules be distinct means that the disjunctive relation will only be imposed when the feature changes of the two rules are contradictory or otherwise incompatible. For example, we would not want to impose disjunctive ordering on rules palatalizing obstruents after [i] and spirantizing obstruents after all vowels. The incompatibility requirement is also satisfied in the Sanskrit case because the aspiration rule defines a point of articulation that is distinct from the one assigned by the assimilation rule. Thus, with the Elsewhere Condition available, the Sanskrit treatment of final [s] can be analyzed by the natural rules (33a,c).

Note that the Sanskrit data provide a compelling argument for disjunctive ordering only if assimilation is treated as feature changing. If assimilation arises from the spread of a feature (as argued in section 4.3), then an underlying [s#t] string will come to share the same [coronal] specification.

(35)   s   #   t   s # t
            | | →   \ /
          [coron] [coron]   [coron]

The aspiration rule can then be made sensitive to this formal property, applying to singly linked coronals and passing over multiply linked ones. Indeed, the failure of aspiration to apply to multiply linked structures may reflect a general constraint on rule application (as argued in section 8.4) and thus have nothing to do with a disjunctive relation between assimilation and aspiration.

Another possible example motivating disjunctive ordering is furnished by the TSL rule of English: *serēne, serĕn-ity; crīme, crĭm-inal*. As argued in section 10.9, we will assume that the rule is restricted to the stressed member of a disyllabic (trochaic) foot (36a).

(36)   a. $\bar{V} \rightarrow \check{V} /$ ____ C_0 V
                                    | |
                                  ('σ   σ)

        b.   Jordan   Jordān-ian
             colony   colōn-ial
             melody   melōd-ious

        c. $\check{V} \rightarrow \bar{V} /$ ____ C i V
                                    | |
                                  ('σ   σ)

A number of rules lengthen vowels in the same metrical context but under more restricted segmental conditions. One accounts for the alternations of (36b), lengthening nonhigh vowels when followed by an [i + V] string. The rule governing this alternation can be formulated as (36c) with the same stressed plus unstressed metrical conditioning. The shortening rule of (36a) represents the elsewhere case, while lengthening is a special rule applying to only a subset of the cases that meet the general metrical condition. A disjunctive relation must obviously be imposed on the rules since the lengthened vowels in (36b) escape shortening by (36a).

Having seen the motivation for the Elsewhere Condition, let us now turn to its role in the Lexical Phonology model. Kiparsky argues that the phenomenon of morphological blocking can be construed as a reflex of the Elsewhere Condition. For example, consider the two rules in (37) marking the English plural.

(37)   a.   pl → en / [X ____] (where X = ox, child, . . .)
        b.   pl → es / [X ____]

The structural description of (37a) clearly subsumes that of (37b). The former rule lists a particular set of lexical items. But in (37b) X is a variable standing for any noun and thus designates the elsewhere case. If the Elsewhere Condition applies in this case, then we explain why words with double marking of the plural such as *childrens* and *oxens* are ill formed. Application of the lexically restricted -*en* rule preempts the regular plural rule and thus blocks the construction of such doubly marked words. Kiparsky then observes that inherent plurals such as *people* and *cattle* work the same way as *children* and *oxen* do. These words are peculiar in a couple of respects. First, they are grammatically plural since they impose plural verbal agreement: *The people/cattle *is/are coming*. But they lack any overt morphology (i.e., an affix or an ablaut) and hence are not derived by any WFR from a singular base. They are thus underived lexical items that, unlike most nouns, happen to be plural instead of singular. Since these items are plural, it is now necessary to explain why the regular plural rule (37b) fails to apply and produce *peoples, *cattles. These items are ill formed and the grammar must prevent their generation. But now there is a problem. We cannot evidently invoke the Elsewhere Condition since *people* and *cattle* are not the product of any WFR. Yet because they are inherent plurals, it seems entirely natural that the rule suffixing [-es] is suspended.

Kiparsky proposes to solve this puzzle by construing each lexical representation as an identity rule mapping the string into itself. To make this proposal more intuitive, one might suppose that a derivation is launched by making a copy of the lexical representation. This cloning thus maps every lexical item into itself.

(38)   cattle pl → cattle pl

The "rule" in (38) will now invoke the Elsewhere Condition with respect to the regular plural rule in essentially the same way that the rule forming *ox-en* does. (In the context of this discussion, "rule" is understood as any licensed transition from one representation to the next in the derivation.) The information contained in *cattle* is clearly much richer and subsumes the information content of the plural rule (37b).

5.5.3   Strict Cyclicity and the Elsewhere Condition

Armed with the Elsewhere Condition and the construal of each lexical item as an identity rule, we can now return to the strict cyclicity problem. Kiparsky (1982a) notes that the two clauses defining a derived context (across cyclic boundaries and information derived on the same cycle) do not form a natural class conceptually. Rather, they appear to designate the complement of a more basic notion: the material contained in the underlying representation at the start of each cycle. Somehow, this material prevents the application of rules that would have the effect of altering its information content. But, Kiparsky reasons, this is analogous to the relation between (38) and the plural rule (37b). If each lexical item initiating a cycle is the product of an identity rule such as (38), then the Elsewhere Condition will suspend application of any rule that would change the information content of the lexical item. In this way, the underlying representation itself prevents application of rules that will alter its content.

Let us see how this works by returning to the Finnish $t \rightarrow s$ rule. The rules are formulated in (39).

(39)   a. $\begin{bmatrix} -\text{cons} \\ -\text{back} \end{bmatrix} \rightarrow [+\text{high}] / \underline{\hspace{1em}} \#$

    b. $\begin{bmatrix} -\text{contin} \\ +\text{coron} \end{bmatrix} \rightarrow [+\text{contin}] / \underline{\hspace{1em}} \begin{bmatrix} -\text{cons} \\ +\text{high} \\ -\text{back} \end{bmatrix}$

    c.   [tila] $\rightarrow$ [tila]

First consider [tila]. It defines the identity rule in (39c). The structural description of this rule is much richer and subsumes the partial specification of the [ti] string that forms the structural description of the $t \rightarrow s$ rule (39b). Furthermore, and crucially, the structural changes of the two rules are inconsistent. The latter assigns [+continuant] and the identity rule assigns [−continuant]. Consequently, (39c) and (39b) fall under the Elsewhere Condition. The more specific rule (39c) thus preempts application of the more general $t \rightarrow s$ rule.

Now consider the two cases of derived contexts. Recall that [halut]*i* becomes [halus]*i*. The Elsewhere Condition will not apply in this case because the relevant identity rule [halut] $\rightarrow$ [halut] does not subsume the [ti] string in [halut]*i*. The suffixal [i] is left out. In general, any combination of information taken from separate cyclic domains will suffice to turn off the Elsewhere Condition, because the relevant identity rule will be unable to cover the material introduced on the current cycle.

Next consider the case of new information derived on the same cycle. Recall that Finnish #[vete]# becomes #[veti]# and then #[vesi]#. The first step involves material spanning the cyclic brackets (assuming that the word boundary # marks a separate domain) and so proceeds essentially just like [halut]*i*. This step assigns the feature [+high] to the final vowel. But this operation suffices to remove the stem from the control of the [vete] $\rightarrow$ [vete] identity rule. The [−high] feature on the final vowel of [vete] now fails to cover the [+high] assigned by the raising rule. The Elsewhere Condition is thus not invoked and the $t \rightarrow s$ rule may now enter inside the root. In general, any information change introduced by transboundary application drives a wedge into the root through which subsequent phonological rules may enter.

Finally, recall the remark that the output of any phonological cycle is a lexical item. As such, it may serve as the base for a subsequent WFR. Furthermore, being a lexical item, it defines an identity rule. This is crucial for a proper account of the strict cyclicity of Catalan [ruin]*ós,* derived from [ruín]*ós.* Given that [ruin]*ós* is a lexical item, the identity rule [ruin]*ós* $\rightarrow$ [ruin]*ós* is induced. This rule then blocks application of devocalization to the [ui] substring in [ruinus]*ísim* on the next cycle.

To summarize the discussion, we see that the Strict Cycle Condition is derivable from the Elsewhere Condition – a constraint that is needed anyway to characterize disjunctive rule application. Finally, Kiparsky argues that if strict cyclicity is viewed as a function of the Elsewhere Condition, then we can make sense of the fact that stress rules may apply on the root cycle in apparent disregard of the Strict Cycle Condition. The stress rule operating in *América* does not alter the feature content of the underlying representation but rather supplements it by erecting a metrical structure. Stress is by and large predictable in English. Since stress is not utilized to encode the English lexicon, it will not trigger the Elsewhere Condition. This in turn permits the stress rule to apply on the initial cycle. But in a language such as Russian, where the accent unpredictably falls on any syllable of the morpheme, stress information must be present in the underlying representation. This in turn activates the Elsewhere Condition and blocks stress rules from applying on the initial cycle (Halle and Vergnaud 1987).

5.6   Structure Preservation

Another basic concept of Lexical Phonology is Structure Preservation. The idea runs as follows. Each grammar stipulates a set of underlying contrastive segments (the phonemic inventory). According to Structure Preservation, representations within the lexicon may only be composed of elements drawn from the phonemic inventory. The phonemic inventory thus constrains the kinds of phonological rules that may apply in the lexicon. If a rule introduces or refers to a noncontrastive segment, then, by Structure Preservation, that rule can only apply postlexically. To take a simple example, we know from chapter 2 that the flap in English is a predictable segment and thus not a phoneme. Structure Preservation requires the flapping rule to be postlexical. In a well-articulated model such as Lexical Phonology, this claim has consequences. For example, it allows us to explain why, although stress is assigned cyclically, we do not find [atóm]*ic* realized as *a*[D]*ómic*. The latter representation could arise if the flapping rule applied on the first cycle, giving *a*[D]*om*. The principle of Structure Preservation prohibits such a derivation because the flapping rule must be postlexical and hence cannot apply at level 1. Structure Preservation can also be argued to confer learnability advantages on the theory of Lexical Phonology. If one assumes that the phonemic inventory can be determined independently of the phonological rules, then it automatically follows that a rule will be postlexical if it either introduces or refers to an element not belonging to the set of contrastive segments. More generally, the Lexical Phonology model curtails (but does not completely eliminate) the need for extrinsic ordering statements; if the various criteria we have outlined distinguish a pair of rules as lexical versus postlexical, then their ordering need not be stipulated but rather follows from the overall architecture of the grammar.

Let us illustrate these points further by some material from Spanish (Harris 1983, Wong-opasi 1986). Within the vowel system of Spanish, there is a contrast between the mid vowels [e,o] and the diphthongs [ie,ue]. There is also a well-known alternation between diphthongs in accented syllables and corresponding mid vowels in unaccented syllables. We will follow Harris (1985b) in assuming that the diphthongs underlie this alternation and that they simplify by the rule in

(40b). (For the point to be made here, we could also derive the diphthongs from stressed mid vowels.)

(40) a. inf.   bebér   perdér   contár   cosér
          1sg.   bébo   piérdo   cuénto   cóso
                   'drink'   'lose'   'count'   'sew'

      b. [ie,ue] → [e,o] / in unaccented syllables

Spanish has compound nouns such as *hierbabuéna* and *cuentagótas* in (41) whose stress contour is the same as that of monomorphemic *Venezuéla* in containing just a single word accent on the penultimate syllable.

(41) hiérba   'grass'   contár   'to count'
      herbóso   'grass' adj.   cuénto   'I count'
      hierbabuéna   'mint'   cuentagótas   'eyedropper'

The unaccented diphthongs in the initial member of the compounds can be explained if monophthongization (40b) applies at level 1 and the compounds are formed at a later stratum of the lexicon, where there is a rule suppressing the accent of the initial member of the compound. We thus postulate the derivation of (42) for *hierbabuéna*.

(42) level 1   [hierb-a] [buen-a]
                 hiérb-a   buén-a   penultimate accent
                 inappl.   inappl.   monophthongization

      level 3   [[hiérba] + [buéna]]   compounding
                 hierba buéna   deaccenting

The point of this discussion is the following. Since compounding is a lexical process, and since the [e]≈[ie] alternation in *hiérba* must be implemented before the compounding in *hierbabuéna,* it follows that the phonological rule responsible for the [e]≈[ie] alternation must be a lexical rule. This analysis is permitted by Structure Preservation, because as evidenced by such minimal pairs as *neto* 'net' and *nieto* 'grandson', both [e] and [ie] belong to the phonemic inventory of Spanish.

  Another example of the role of Structure Preservation in Spanish is furnished by a rule depalatalizing the nasal [ñ] and the lateral [lʸ]. (43a) contains paradigms built on the stems [desdeñ] and [doncelʸ]. The final consonant of these bases is depalatalized when the stem is unaffixed by the general rule (43b) of Spanish that bars [ñ] and [lʸ] from syllable codas (Harris 1983). Interestingly, the vowel-initial plural suffix [-es] fails to "restore" the palatals, in contrast to stem-forming suffixes such as the feminine [-a], the infinitival [-ar], or the derivational [-os].

(43) a. desdeñ-ar   'to disdain'   doncelʸ-a   'lass'
          desdeñ-os-o   'disdainful'   doncelʸ-a-s   'lasses'
          desden   'disdain' noun   doncel   'lad'
          desden-es   noun pl.   doncel-es   'lads'

      b. [ñ,lʸ] → [n,l] / in coda

These data are explained if the plural suffix [-es] is added at a later lexical stratum (level 2) and the depalatalization rule applies at this level. The [desdeñ] paradigm then receives the derivation in (44).

(44)

[desdeñ]	[desdeñ]	[desdeñ]	level 1
des.deñ	des.deñ	des.deñ	syllabification
[des.deñ]ar	———	———	WFR
des.de.ñar	———	———	resyllabification
[des.de.ñar]	[des.deñ]	[des.deñ]	level 2
inappl.	des.den	des.den	depalatalization
		[des.den]es	WFR
———	———	des.de.nes	syllabification

On the root cycle at level 1, syllabification puts [ñ] in the coda. But this segment will not change to [n] because the depalatalization rule only operates at level 2. Addition of a suffix such as [-ar] at level 1 prompts resyllabification of the [ñ] to syllable onset in [des.de.ñar]. Both this representation and [des.deñ] then enter level 2, at which point the depalatalization rule becomes applicable. It applies to [des.deñ] but fails to apply to [des.de.ñar] since the latter's nasal has been shifted to onset position by resyllabification at level 1. The representation [des.den] now serves as the base for the plural suffix, yielding [des.den.]*es*. Resyllabification produces [des.de.nes]. No further lexical rules of relevance are applicable and the representations [des.de.ñar], [des.den], and [des.de.nes] result.

The upshot of the above analysis (due to Harris (1983)) is that the depalatalization rule must apply at level 2 and hence must be a lexical rule. Structure Preservation requires that both the inputs [ñ,lʸ] and the outputs [n,l] of depalatalization belong to the phonemic inventory. This requirement is met, as suggested by such minimal pairs as *cana* 'grey hair' vs. *caña* 'cane' and *polo* 'pole vs. *pollo* 'chicken'.

Let us now look at two cases where Structure Preservation blocks a rule from applying in the lexicon. Two of the best-known processes operating in Spanish dialects are an aspiration rule turning [s] to [h] and a velarization rule turning [n] to [ŋ] (Harris 1983). Both operate in syllable codas.

(45)

standard	dialectal		
cantan	ca[ŋ]ta[ŋ]		'sing' 3pl.
desden	de[h]den *or* de[h]de[ŋ]		'disdain'

The aspiration and velarization processes differ from monophthongization and depalatalization in that the [h] and [ŋ] segments introduced by these rules are not contrastive elements in most dialects. Rather, they arise only from these rules. Consequently, the principle of Structure Preservation bars these segments from the lexicon and predicts that they will only develop postlexically. One immediate consequence is that [h] and [ŋ] will not be introduced before the plural suffix [-es]. This prediction is confirmed by the paradigms in (46). When [-es] is suffixed at level 2, the final consonants of [mes] and [pan] resyllabify to onset position and thus escape postlexical aspiration and velarization.

(46)   standard   dialectical
       mes   me[h]   'month'
       mes-es   mes-e[h]   'months'

       pan   pa[ŋ]   'bread'
       pan-es   pan-e[h]   'breads'

Since compounding is also a lexical process, we predict that stem-final [s] and [n] will be preserved by lexical resyllabification before a vowel-initial second member of the compound. Wong-opasi (1986) cites the paradigms in (47) that confirm this prediction.

(47)   mu[h]   'mouse'   pa[ŋ]   'bread'
       mus-e[h]   'mice'   panikeso   'name of a dish'
       mus-araña   'shrewmouse'   pa[ŋ][i] queso   'bread and cheese'

In *panikeso* the three morphemes are compounded lexically. Resyllabification applies to place the nasal in onset position, [pa.ni.ke.so], preempting postlexical velarization. Velarization does apply to the phrasal combination [paŋ] [i] [keso] and must precede application of resyllabification at the phrasal level.

5.7   Multistratal Rules

In Kiparsky's original exposition of the Lexical Phonology model (1982a), it was assumed that the rules applying at the various lexical levels form disjoint blocks. In a study of Malayalam, Mohanan (1982) posited a number of distinct lexical strata but found that a given phonological rule appears to apply in more than one lexical stratum. If the lexical rules form disjoint blocks, then it would be an accident that the same phonological process applies in several different strata of the same grammar. This rule overlap prompted Mohanan to propose that the phonological rules of the grammar constitute a single system, individual members of which may be assigned to a particular lexical stratum or to the postlexical component of the grammar. From the Lexical Phonology perspective, we may compare the lexical and postlexical applications of what appear to be the same rule. Since lexical applications are constrained by Structure Preservation while postlexical applications are not, the same phonological process may display different properties depending upon which module of the grammar (the lexicon or the syntax) the rule applies in.

As illustration, let us look at a Catalan example drawn from Kiparsky's (1985) discussion of this modularity. According to Kiparsky, Catalan has nasal phonemes at four distinct points of articulation: [m,n,ñ,ŋ]. A number of additional nasals are produced by a postlexical rule that assimilates [n] to the precise point of articulation of the following consonant.

(48) unassimilated alveolar   so[n] amics   'they are friends'
      bilabial   so[m] pocs   'they are few'
      labiodental   so[m̩] felicos   'they are happy'
      dental   so[n̪] dos   'they are two'
      alveolar   so[n] sincers   'they are sincere'
      postalveolar   so[n̪]rics   'they are rich'
      palatal   so[ñ] [lʸ]iures 'they are free'
      velar   so[ŋ] grans   'they are big'

The feature [distributed] that differentiates between the bilabial and labiodental
and between the dental and alveolar points of articulation is predictable in Catalan
and hence is barred from the lexicon by Structure Preservation. The [+contin-
uant] labiodental [f] is [+distributed], while the [−continuant] nasal [m] and stops
[p,b] are bilabial [−distributed]; similarly, the [+coronal, +anterior] stops [t,d]
are [+distributed], while the nasal [n] is alveolar [−distributed]. The fact that
the nasal assimilation in (48) takes place between words means that the rule is
applying postlexically. Hence, it may take the [distributed] feature into account.
Catalan also has a lexical rule simplifying clusters composed of a homorganic
sonorant plus stop through the deletion of the stop. The rule applies when the
cluster is in the syllable coda. The stems [kamp] and [bint] illustrate this rule.

(49) kamp-et dimin.   bi[n̪t̪]-e   'twentieth'
      kam-s   pl.   bi[n]   'twenty'
      kam   'field'   bi[m] pans 'twenty breads'
      kam es   'field is' bi[ŋ] kaps 'twenty heads'

As in many other languages, in Catalan the point of articulation of a nasal in a
tautomorphemic nasal-consonant sequence is (barring a few isolated exceptions
such as *prems*[ə] 'press') predictable from the following consonant by nasal assimilation. Thus, in [kamp] the labial feature of the nasal arises from assimilation
to the [p] and the dental in [bint] from assimilation to the [t]. It is clear that this
nasal assimilation must precede the cluster simplification rule; otherwise, the
homorganic requirement of the latter process will not be satisfied. The paradigm
for [bint] also shows that if an alveolar nasal comes to stand at the end of a word
through cluster simplification, it assimilates the point of articulation of the following consonant. Thus, nasal assimilation must apply both before and after cluster simplification. From the standpoint of a theory in which the phonetic representation arises from one pass through the phonological rules, this is a paradoxical
state of affairs. But since the Lexical Phonology model distinguishes the lexical
and postlexical components, it is possible for the same rule to apply in both
components. However, if this is so, then the rule should display different properties, depending on whether the application takes place in the lexicon (where
Structure Preservation holds) or in the postlexical component (where it does not).
In this respect the difference between the [+distributed] dental nasal in [bin̪t̪-e]
and the [−distributed] alveolar in [bin] is particularly significant. If it really is
the same rule of nasal assimilation applying in both cases, then why do the prod-

ucts of the rule differ? The Structure Preservation principle answers this question. Because it is not contrastive, the [+distributed] feature of the dental stop [t] only enters the representation postlexically. Since this feature is barred from the lexicon, the lexical application of nasal assimilation will not assign [+distributed]. Consequently, when the [t] of [bint] is deleted lexically, the nasal will be unable to receive the [+distributed] feature. It instead takes the default value [−distributed] that is assigned to unassimilated [+coronal, +anterior] nasals postlexically. But in [bint̪-e], the [t] is assigned [+distributed] postlexically. Postlexical nasal assimilation then transmits this property to the nasal consonant. The nasal in [bin̪t̪-e] thus undergoes two rounds of nasal assimilation. Lexically, it is assigned the distinctive [+coronal, +anterior] features of the [t]; postlexically, it assimilates the [+distributed] feature of the [t].

If more cases like the Catalan one just reviewed are uncovered in which the different properties displayed by the lexical and postlexical applications of a phonological process are predictable on general grounds, then we are justified in claiming that indeed it is the same phonological rule applying at two separate points in the grammar. Suppose that this turns out to be true. Then Mohanan's conception of the phonological rules as forming a single system separate from the lexical and postlexical positions in the grammar at which they apply would be validated (50). The question then arises whether any principles constrain the assignment of a given phonological rule to the various levels of the grammar.

(50)   level 1   rule 1
       level 2   rule 2
         .   .
         .   .
         .   .
       level *n*   rule *n*
       postlexical

One principle we are familiar with is Structure Preservation, which bars rules assigning or referring to nondistinctive features from the lexicon. An additional principle suggested by Mohanan's study of Malayalam is that if a phonological rule is assigned to more than one level, then the levels must form a continuum. Kiparsky (1985) suggests a still stronger constraint (the *Strong Domain Hypothesis*), according to which all rules are free to apply at the earliest lexical level. (Structure Preservation will of course bar lexical application for many rules whose domain assignment is thereby restricted to the postlexical level.) For any given rule, one must simply stipulate when the rule ceases to apply. Thus, for example, TSL in English would have to be marked as holding of just the initial level, while nasal assimilation in Catalan is unrestricted and free to apply at all levels. Much further study of individual grammars from the Lexical Phonology standpoint is needed before it can be determined which of these hypotheses is closest to the truth.

5.8 Outstanding Problems

In this section we will review some of the unresolved problems that confront the Lexical Phonology model. One problem is presented by rules triggered by the word boundary. The Dutch rule devoicing syllable-final obstruents furnishes a simple example (Booij and Rubach 1987). In virtue of this rule, underlying [hɛld] 'hero' is realized as [hɛlt]. Addition of vowel-initial suffixes prompts resyllabification of the stem-final consonant to onset with the following vowel. This process bleeds the devoicing rule. Thus, the underlying voiced consonant of [hɛld] emerges in [hɛl.d-in] 'heroine'. Assuming that syllabification is assigned cyclically, the devoicing rule cannot itself be cyclic. It must wait until all suffixes have been added that prompt resyllabification and thus bleed the rule. But there is evidence that syllable-final devoicing cannot be postlexical either. In casual speech, Dutch also resyllabifies a consonant across word boundaries. But this process does not bleed syllable-final devoicing. According to Booij and Rubach (1987), *een hoed opzetten* 'to put on a hat' is realized [ən. hu.t ɔp.sɛ.tən]. Here the underlying voiced consonant of /hud/ 'hat' is devoiced even though it is in onset position.

5.8.1 *The Word Level*

The Dutch data suggest that there is a stage – after all of the affixation takes place but before the word is inserted into the phrase – at which the syllable-final devoicing process is defined to operate. To accommodate such cases, Booij and Rubach (1987), Kiparsky (1985), and others have postulated a special component of *postcyclic lexical rules*. This block of rules (often called the *word level*) intervenes between the cyclic lexical rules and the postlexical, phrasal rules. Any representation is passed through the phonological rules of this component just once. Being noncyclic, it is a natural location for the rules of absolute neutralization such as Yawelmani vowel lowering (section 3.4) or the English Vowel Shift (section 5.1), which apply morpheme-internally and thus violate the SCC. Although such rules are generally automatic, they typically do not apply at the phrasal level – a fact that would follow from their being lexical.

We can flesh out the role of this postcyclic lexical component by recapitulating some of the rules of Polish phonology discussed by Booij and Rubach (1987). The Polish rule raising [o] to [u] before a word-final voiced nonnasal consonant is a natural candidate for the postcyclic lexical rule block. Recall from section 2.7 that this rule (plus final devoicing) accounts for the realization of the root [rob] 'do' as *rup* in the imperative. Since raising is triggered by the word boundary, it cannot be a cyclic rule. Any suffixation automatically displaces the triggering word boundary: for example, *rob'-e* 1sg. We must wait until all suffixation has taken place in order to apply the rule. But the fact that the rule has exceptions (e.g., [skrob] 'scratch' is realized as *skrop,* cf. *skrob'-e* 1sg.) suggests that it is a lexical rule.

Another argument that raising is a postcyclic lexical rule derives from the fact that it is ordered after a rule that applies in nonderived contexts; hence, raising must be postcyclic by the rule-ordering thesis. Like other Slavic languages, Polish has a pair of abstract vowels – known as *yers* – that are phonologically distinct in that they delete in contexts where other vowels do not. For example, *lew* and *sweter* participate in the alternation while the nearly identical *zlew* and *krater* do not (51a). It is not possible to analyze all yers as epenthetic vowels, since there are consonant clusters that remain unseparated by a yer (51b).

(51) a. lew   'lion'   zlew   'sink'
          lw-em   instr.sg.   zlew-em   instr.sg.

          sweter   'sweater'   krater   'crater'
          swetr-y   pl.   krater-y   pl.

      b. mask-a   'mask' nom.sg.   trosk-a   'concern' nom.sg.
          masek   gen.pl.   trosk   gen.pl.

          dekl-a   'cap' gen.sg.   cykl-u   'cycle' gen.sg.
          dek'el   nom.sg.   cykl   nom.sg.

When a derivational suffix follows a yer, sometimes the root yer emerges and sometimes it does not. It turns out that those suffixes that allow a preceding yer to surface themselves contain a yer; furthermore, their yer emerges when they in turn are followed by another yer suffix. The yers thus "vocalize" when followed by a yer or by the "zero" nom.sg. and gen.pl. suffixes. Elsewhere they appear as $\emptyset$. The vocalization rule can be simplified if we say that these "zero" suffixes are also yers. Since they are never themselves followed by a suffix, this point cannot be verified directly. But it is a natural analytic step, given the overall framework. The basic generalization thus is that the yers delete everywhere, except when the following syllable contains a yer. In the latter case they surface as [e] – a process traditionally known as "vocalization" of the yers. We can account for the Polish yer phenomenon by the rules in (52a,b), which yield the derivations of (52c). (*Y* is used here as a cover symbol for a yer.)

(52) a. yer → [e] / ____ C_0 yer

      b. yer → $\emptyset$

      c. [lYw-Y]   [lYw-em]   [zlew-Y]   [zlew-em]
          lew-Y   inappl.   inappl.   inappl.   yer vocalization
          lew   lw-em   zlew   inappl.   yer deletion

For our purposes, the most important point about the yers is that the rule deleting the yer applies in a nonderived context. Like Yawelmani vowel lowering and English Vowel Shift, it neutralizes an underlying phonemic contrast in a context-free fashion and thus must be postcyclic. By the ordering thesis, any rule ordered after yer deletion must be postcyclic. In particular, the raising rule must be postcyclic, for it is only in virtue of the loss of the final yer in underlying [voz-Y] that the triggering voiced consonant comes to stand at the edge of the word, so that [voz] gives [vuz] (and eventually [vus]).

The diagram in (53) depicts the Lexical Phonology model of Polish. By their ordering with respect to the yer deletion process, Booij and Rubach (1987) pinpoint the location of several other rules of Polish phonology.

(53) lexical rules
         cyclic
             palatalization
             yer vocalization
         postcyclic
             yer deletion
             raising
      postlexical rules
             final devoicing

One of these rules devoices the fricatives [v] and [ž] after a voiceless consonant. The [ž] itself derives from a palatalized [r'] by a special rule [r'] → [ž]. Thus, in the contexts where other consonants simply palatalize (54a), [r] is replaced by [ž].

(54) a.   vus   'cart'   voz'-e   loc.sg.   [voz] root
           kar-a   'penalty'   kaž-e   dat.sg.   [kar]
      b.   Piotr   'Peter'   Piot[š-e]   voc.sg.   [Piotr]
      c.   kufer   'trunk'   kuf[š-e]   loc.sg.   [kufYr]
           list[f-a] 'board'   liste[v]-ek dimin.gen.pl. [listYv]

In *Piot*[š-e] we see voicing assimilation applying within a morpheme. This application is consistent with the Lexical Phonology model if the rule belongs to the noncyclic component. Assignment to this component is confirmed by the fact that the rule must be ordered after yer deletion – a rule that we know to be postcyclic on independent grounds. This point is shown by the forms in (54c); *kuf*[še] has the derivation in (55).

(55) [kufYr-e]   cyclic
      kufYr'-e   palatalization

                    postcyclic
      kufYž-e   r' → ž
      kufž-e   yer deletion
      kufš-e   progressive assimilation

   To briefly summarize the discussion, we have located three rules in the postcyclic lexical component of Polish: yer deletion, raising, and progressive voicing assimilation. We have strong grounds for the first assignment because yer deletion applies in a nonderived context. The other two cannot be cyclic because they are ordered after yer deletion. But what about the postlexical component? Can any of these rules be assigned there? Raising cannot, since it has lexical exceptions. Yer deletion is not likely to be, because it is a rule of absolute neutralization. But what about progressive assimilation and final devoicing?

Evidence from the phrasal phonology helps us to answer some of these questions. The key is provided by another voicing assimilation rule, the more pervasive regressive assimilation of all remaining obstruent clusters. This process has both voicing and devoicing components; furthermore, it operates between words as well as within the word (56).

(56) a. Warsza[v-a]   'Warsaw'   Warsza[f]-ski   adj.
          pros'-ic'   'to request'   pro[z']-ba   'a request'

      b. zakaz-y   'prohibitions'   zaka[s] postoj-u   'no parking'
          kryzys-y   'crises'   kryzy[z] gospodarczy 'economic crisis'

In this respect it differs from progressive assimilation, which may not apply between words. This point is illustrated by the fact that *but* [V]*ojtk-a* 'Wojtek's shoe' is pronounced *bu*[d V]*ojtka* and not *bu*[t F]*ojtka*. This difference is automatically explained if progressive assimilation is a lexical rule while regressive assimilation is postlexical and thus may apply at the phrasal level.

Regressive voicing assimilation also establishes a difference between the raising rule and final devoicing – both rules triggered by the word boundary. Regressive assimilation may undo the effects of final devoicing. This is shown by the derivations of *sad wiśniowy* 'cherry tree orchard' and *sad owocowy* 'fruit tree orchard' in (57).

(57) sad viśnovɨ   sad ovocovɨ
      sat viśnovɨ   sat ovocovɨ   final devoicing
      sad viśnovɨ   inappl.   regressive voicing
                                      assimilation

But the raising rule is never undone when the word is placed in the phrase. [voz] undergoes raising even if the triggering voiced consonant is devoiced by assimilation: *v*[us K]*atarzyny* 'Katherine's cart'. This difference is explained if raising is assigned to the lexical phonology while final devoicing is a postlexical rule.

To summarize the discussion, we have looked at several pieces of evidence, some stronger than others, for the rule assignment depicted in (58).

(58)   lexical rules
           cyclic
               palatalization
               yer vocalization
           postcyclic
               yer deletion
               raising
               progressive voicing assimilation
       postlexical rules
           final devoicing
           regressive voicing assimilation

For the Polish data, suffixation always suppresses the application of a rule triggered by the word boundary (e.g., the raising rule). Such suppression does not always obtain under affixation. The rule of English phonology that simplifies final [mn] clusters through deletion of the [n] furnishes a simple example. This rule, stated in (59a), accounts for the "silent" [n] of *damn, hymn,* and so on (59b). The data in (59c) show that the rule cannot be cyclic; otherwise, the [n] would never emerge to the surface.

(59) a. [n] → ∅ / [+nasal] ____]
      b. dam[ ]; hym[ ]
      c. damn-ation, damn-atory; hymn-al, hymn-ology
      d. dam[ ]-ing, dam[ ]-s, dam[ ]-ed; hym[ ]-s, hym[ ]-less

We thus assign the rule to the postcyclic lexical component. But unlike Polish raising, the English cluster simplification rule is not suspended when level 2 suffixes are added (59d). We can account for these forms by assuming that the affixes of (59d) are added in the postcyclic lexical component. This effectively identifies level 2 with the word level. Since this component is not cyclic, only one run through the rules will take place. Hence, the triggering bracket will still be present. However, the internal brackets will crucially have been erased from the level 1, cyclic suffixes of (59c) by the bracket erasure convention. Under these assumptions, the following derivations obtain for *damn, damnation,* and *damning.*

(60) [damn]   [damn]   [damn]   cyclic
                  [[damn]ation]   affixation
                                                no phonological
                                                  rules apply
                  [damnation]   bracket erasure

      [damn]   [damnation]   [damn]   postcyclic
                                   [[damn]ing] affixation
      [dam]   inappl.   [[dam]ing]   cluster simplification (59a)

Since [n] does not delete after a liquid in words such as *kiln* and *corn,* it is natural to pursue a slightly different analysis that treats the deletion in [damn] as the elimination of a syllabically "stray" consonant (see section 6.5): {dam}*n* → {dam}, where braces indicate the syllabification. The rules of English syllabification (section 6.3) will group a vowel-liquid-nasal sequence into a syllable but will fail to group a vowel plus two successive nasals, taking in just the vowel plus the first nasal to give {dam}*n.* However, certain problems arise with this approach. The lexical items in (59b) are the morphological bases for the words in (59c). But the nasal may not delete before the level 1 affixes are added. The deletion of the unsyllabified nasal must wait so that the addition of the level 1 suffixes prompts syllabification of the nasal to onset position, saving it from deletion: [{dam}*n*]*ation* → {dam}{na}{tion}. If we assume that the distinction between syllabically incorporated and syllabically stray material introduced by the syllabification rules does not constitute a derived context, then the lack of deletion follows from the SCC.

The identity rule *damn* → *damn* subsumes and hence blocks the rule deleting the stray nasal by the Elsewhere Condition. On this account, the problem then becomes one of explaining how deletion is possible in the first place, since it is not triggered by another morpheme and hence may not go by case (a) of the SCC. This problem arises more generally with any rule that is triggered by the word boundary (e.g., the Finnish rule that raises word-final [e] to [i]). We know that postlexical rules are not subject to the SCC. But the nasal deletion rule cannot be postlexical: the bracket erasure operation obliterates the distinction between the stem + level 1 form *damn-ation,* where no deletion occurs, and the stem + level 2 form *damn-ing,* where deletion does apply. Consequently, *damn-ation* and *damn-ing* would be equivalent at the postlexical level. The deletion process would be unable to distinguish the two cases. Thus, the deletion rule must be lexical even though it violates the SCC. These data appear to require relaxation of the SCC in certain cases.

One solution suggested by Kiparsky (1985) simply stipulates that the final stratum of the grammar – the word level – is not subject to the SCC. We can then locate the deletion rule at this stratum. The derivations in (61) illustrate how this solution is supposed to work.

(61)　[damn]　　　　　[damn]　　　[damn]　　level 1
　　　{dam}n　　　　 {dam}n　　　{dam}n　　syllabification
　　　[{dam}n]ation　　　　　　　　　　　　WFR
　　　{dam}{na}{tion}　　　　　　　　　　　syllabification

　　　[{dam}{na}{tion}]　 [{dam}n]　　[{dam}n]　level 2
　　　inappl.　　　　　 {dam}　　　{dam}　　stray nasal deletion
　　　　　　　　　　　 {dam}ing　　　　　　WFR
　　　　　　　　　　　 {da}{ming}　　　　　(re)syllabification

On the first cycle at level 1, syllable structure is assigned and the [n] is defined as stray. The WFR affixing *-ation* applies and resyllabification places the [n] in onset position. The derivation then enters level 2, where the rule eliminating syllabically stray nasals is housed. It will apply to [{dam}n] since the SCC is stipulated to be inapplicable at this level.

There are a couple of unsettling features of this analysis. Deletion of the syllabically stray nasal must apply before the rule suffixing *-ing.* If the suffix is added first, then rules of syllabification would be expected to intervene and to parse the stray nasal as onset to the vowel of the suffix and thus to block deletion of the nasal. While the derivation in (61) avoids this outcome by ordering stray nasal deletion before affixation, one should expect the rules of affixation to apply first before any phonological rules, given that level 2 is noncyclic and the representation is passed through the rules just one time. Furthermore, this solution fails to generalize to the Finnish raising rule. On the strength of [vete-nä], the raising rule cannot apply on the root cycle [vete] and in fact will be barred from applying there by the SCC. Just as in the case of the English *n*-deletion rule, we might pursue a solution that suspends the SCC at the final lexical level in order to permit the raising of the final [e] of [vete] to [veti]. But if we do so, we then lose the explanation for why the $t \to s$ rule applies on [veti] but blocks on [äiti]. Consequently, the SCC must still hold for the $t \to s$ rule even though the derived context is created by a word-level rule.

Evidently we need to (re)introduce the word boundary symbol from the earlier generative model and stipulate that it may count as defining a derived environment for phonological rules. This is not a very attractive solution, however, because the elimination of boundary symbols was one of the early signs that the Lexical Phonology model was on the right track. Clearly, rules applying at the word boundary constitute a problem that requires further study. See sections 5.8.4 and 11.4.4 for further discussion.

Borowsky (1986, 1992) undertakes a more systematic study of level 2 in English. The next few paragraphs summarize her results. In addition to the cluster simplification found in *dam[n]≈damnation,* several other rules operate at the word level. They share two peculiarities. First, they introduce allophones and hence violate Structure Preservation (in contrast to the aspiration and velarization rules of Spanish discussed in section 5.6).

(62) a. $[b,g] \to \emptyset / [+\text{nasal}]$ ___]

lon[g̶]	lon[g̶]-ing	elong-ate
stron[g̶]	stron[g̶]-ly	strong-est
bom[b̶]	bom[b̶]-ing	bomb-ard

   b. $[l,r] \to [\mathring{l},\mathring{r}] / C$ ___]

cyc[l̩]e	cyc[l̩]-ing	cycl-ic
cente[r̩]	cente[r̩]-ing	centr-al
mete[r̩]	mete[r̩]-ing	metr-ic

   c. $[t,d,n] \to [+\text{distrib}] /$ ___ (ə)r ...]

dental	alveolar
spi[d̪]er	wi[d]er
pi[l̪]ar	fi[ll]er
ma[t̪t̪]er	fa[tt]er

One rule deletes noncoronal voiced stops after a tautosyllabic nasal (62a) while another converts stray sonorant consonants to syllabic nuclei (62b). They cannot apply at level 1 because they must wait until all level 1 affixes have been added, allowing the stem-final consonant to onset the following vowel and hence escape the rule. Both rules violate Structure Preservation: sonorant syllabification introduces syllabic liquids while deletion of the [g] in *long* generates a free-standing velar nasal [lɔŋ]. Borowsky points to a number of dialectal processes applying at level 2 that also introduce allophones. For example, in Belfast English (Harris 1989) the alveolar noncontinuants [t,d,n,l] are dentalized before tautosyllabic [r]: [t,d] are dental ([+distributed]) in [t̪]*rain*, [d̪]*rain, sani[t̪]ary* but remain alveolar in *bedroom* and *hard rain,* where a strong juncture separates the following rhotic. The rule cannot be postlexical because it fails to apply before the level 2 comparative and agentive suffixes (62c). Given bracket erasure, a postlexical application would be unable to distinguish the dental [d̪] of *spider* from the alveolar [d] of *wider*. This example illustrates a second peculiarity of level 2 in English: the rules applying at this level treat the stem and affix independently from each other and never have to refer to both. That is to say, there are no level 2 rules of assimilation or dissimilation that require simultaneous reference to both the stem and the affix. As a result, the stem is treated as if it ended the word. In the Lexical Phonology model, boundaries are not elements present in the string but simply reflect different morphological domains. Consequently, Borowsky proposes to account for the isolation of the stem and affix in English by a parameter that allows the stem and the affixes to enter the level 2 rule block before they are concatenated by the morphology. They are only joined together after the level 2 phonological rules have applied. Given this architecture, the stem and suffix are phonologically invisible to one another at level 2. Any interaction between them (as in the flapping in *eat* vs. *ea[D]ing*) must take place postlexically.

The representations that arise at the two different levels have distinct formal properties as well. Since Structure Preservation holds at level 1, the output of a level 1 rule has the same phonotactic structure as words lacking any internal morphology. Representations arising from level 2 rules are quite different: they contain allophones as well as clusters not found morpheme-internally (e.g., the [rldl] substring in *world-ly*). Borowsky proposes to explain this difference by restricting Kiparsky's notion of "lexical item" to the product of level 1 rules. These items are independently listed in the lexicon; the level 1 rules can be thought of as relating items in this list. Allophones (elements not belonging to the phonemic inventory and hence not listed) thus cannot be introduced by the level 1 rules. Kaye and Vergnaud (1990) hypothesize that words constructed at level 2 are processed differently from level 1 items in speech recognition. Items listed in the lexicon will be derived by simple lookup. Words containing level 2 morphology are not stored; hence, in order for them to be recognized, the parser must recover the stem and affixal components. The introduction of allophones and complex consonant clusters in close proximity to the stem-affix juncture thus has a functional advantage in marking the position where the parser must make a cut in order to recognize the string. Other things being equal, we expect a stem + level 2 suffix to take longer to recognize than a stem + level 1 structure. This implication has yet to be tested experimentally.

5.8.2   *Affixal Ordering and Bracketing Paradoxes*

Another well-known problem is presented by cases in which a level 1 affix appears outside a level 2 affix. Aronoff (1976:85) noted the data in (63) as potential counterexamples to Siegel's affixal ordering generalization.

(63)   a.   ánalyze   b.   ánalyzable   c.   analyzabílity
            stándard   stándardize   standardizátion
            góvern   góvernment   governméntal

The problem is the following. The affixes [-able, -ize, -ment] do not trigger the reapplication of stress to a preceding heavy syllable. They thus contrast in behavior with an affix like [-al]: *párent, parént-al;* but *góvern-ment,* not *govérn-ment.* This difference could be explained if these morphemes were treated as level 2 affixes like [-less] (e.g., *párent-less*). But then the forms in (63c) become problematic. They are completed by the addition of a level 1 suffix that does count for stress, attracting the accent to the preceding heavy syllables. Consequently, if there is no provision to return from level 2 back to level 1, then the Lexical Phonology model cannot derive a word such as *governmental.* The alternative is to treat [-ment], [-ize], and [-able] as level 1 affixes that exceptionally fail to count for stress.

A similar problem is presented by so-called *bracketing paradoxes.* These are cases in which the morphology demands a certain constituent structure while the phonology appears to require a different one. A much-discussed example is the word *ungrammaticality.* The [un-] prefix attaches to adjectival bases (e.g., *un*[lucky], *un*[American]), not to nominal bases (**un*[luck], **un*[America]). Consequently, [un-] must take as its sister constituent the adjectival base [grammatical] and not the nominal [grammaticality]. Since *un*[grammatical] is still an adjective, it may serve as the base for the WFR that suffixes the nominalizing [-ity]. Hence, the morphological structure of *ungrammaticality* must be that in (64a).

(64) a. [[un[grammatical]] ity]
      b. [un [[grammatical] ity]]

However, as observed earlier, there are phonological reasons for distinguishing [un-] from [in-] in terms of levels. The latter prefix may at least sometimes count for stress. It also undergoes nasal assimilation while the former does not: *ím-potent.* This phonological contrast might be explained by assuming that [in-] attaches at level 1 and [un-] at level 2. But if this is so, then *ungrammaticality* must have the constituent structure of (64b) in which the level 2 [un-] appears outside the base [grammaticality] containing the level 1 suffix [-ity]. However, as we have just seen, this structure is inconsistent with the constituent analysis required by the morphology: [un-] may not attach to a nominal base.

The literature is replete with attempted solutions to these bracketing paradoxes. Some major references are Selkirk 1982a, Mohanan 1982, Kiparsky 1983, Booij and Rubach 1984, Pesetsky 1985, Halle and Vergnaud 1987, Inkelas 1989. Halle and Vergnaud (1987) propose that individual affixes must be lexically marked for activating the cyclic phonological rules of a given lexical level. On this view, the constituent structure of *ungrammaticality* is that required by the morphology – namely, (64a). The [un-] prefix is lexically marked as [−cyclic]. Consequently, the morphological constituent *un*[grammatical] is simply not submitted to the cyclic phonological rules. But [-ity] is [+cyclic] and so stress and TSL will be applicable to the representation [ungrammatical]*ity* that arises from affixation of [-ity]. The SCC prevents the cyclic rules from affecting the [un-] prefix on subsequent cycles. If we have the option of marking any given affix as [±cyclic] independent of its ordering with respect to other affixes, then we can also account for *government* and *standardize.* The [-ment] and [-ize] affixes will be [−cyclic] and thus stress is not reassigned upon affixation of these suffixes to the bases in [góvern]*ment* and [stándard]*ize.* It should be noted that this solution is not equivalent to simply marking these morphemes as exceptions to stress. They do count for stress upon subsequent affixation of the [+cyclic] [-al], as in [governmént]*al*. An additional strong claim is made. Since they are [−cyclic], we predict that these affixes will fail to trigger other cyclic rules such as TSL. Forms such as [lēgal]*ize*, [blāzon]*ment*, [īron]*able* corroborate this analysis.

Halle and Vergnaud (1987) adopt Mohanan's (1982) idea that phonological rules may occupy more than one lexical stratum. This assumption is crucial to their solution to another well-known bracketing paradox noticed for Russian originally by Lightner (1972) and later by Pesetsky (1979). Like Polish, Russian has the yer≈∅ alternation. Yers "vocalize" when the following syllable contains a yer and delete otherwise. These rules are repeated in (65a). Vocalization is cyclic; but yer deletion is necessarily postcyclic, since it applies in a nonderived context. The paradox concerns the behavior of prefixal yers (65b).

(65) a.   yer → V / ___ C_0 yer
           yer → ∅

      b.   <u>verb</u>   <u>UR</u>
           pod-žok   [podY + žYg + Y]   'he burned up'
           podo-žg-la   [podY + žYg + la]   'she burned up'

Vocalization of the prefixal yer in [podY] is contingent on whether or not the yer in the root [žYg] is vocalized. But the latter is determined by whether or not the inflectional affix is a yer. Given that yer vocalization is cyclic, it appears that the root must group with the inflectional suffix before it groups with the prefix: *podY*[[žYg]Y]. But this bracketing contradicts the one required by the morphology and the semantics. The prefix is a derivational affix more closely bound to the root than the inflection is.

Halle and Vergnaud's solution is based on two key assumptions. First, they mark the prefix [−cyclic]; consequently, it fails to initiate a pass through the cyclic rules. No rules apply to the [prefix[root]] assembly and the derivation moves out to the inflectional affixes, which are [+cyclic]. The representation is now submitted to the cyclic phonological rules. In [podYžYg]*Y*, vocalization does not apply to the substring comprising the first two yers because they are contained within the domain of a preceding cycle. But the rule may vocalize the root yer, because it is followed by the suffixal yer that spans a cyclic boundary. No rules apply in [podYžYg]*la*.

(66) [podY[žYg]]   [podY[žYg]]
      no rules apply   no rules apply   cycle II

      [[podYžYg]Y]   [[podYžYg]la]   cycle III
      podYžog Y   inappl.   yer vocalization

      [podYžogY]   [podYžYgla]   postcyclic
      inappl.   podožYgla   yer vocalization
      podžog   podožgla   yer deletion

These representations are now submitted to the postcyclic component. Suppose crucially that yer vocalization is also assigned to this stratum. The Elsewhere Condition orders vocalization before deletion. It now vocalizes the prefixal yer in [podYžYgla], since the SCC is suspended in the postcyclic stratum. Subsequent yer deletion yields [podožgla]. For the masculine form [podYžogY], only yer deletion is applicable, resulting in [podžog].

This intricate rule application follows from the network of assumptions underlying the model. While the intermingling of cyclic and noncyclic affixes weakens the original Lexical Phonology model, this move appears to be required empirically. Fabb (1988) shows that the original affixal ordering generalization was too hastily formulated and not based on a thorough survey of English word structure.

5.8.3 P1 versus P2 Rules

Analogous to the lexical versus word-level distinction in the lexical phonological rules, there is evidence that the postlexical, phrasal rules subdivide into two broad classes, termed *postlexical 1* (P1) and *postlexical 2* (P2) rules by Kaisse (1985). In the original Lexical Phonology model, the paradigm postlexical rules are those like Polish regressive voicing assimilation which are totally automatic (no exceptions), may introduce allophones, and hence are typically below the threshold of consciousness and consequently not reflected orthographically. On the other hand, there are phrasal rules whose application requires relatively rich information on grammatical context (e.g., to distinguish noun from verb, or head from complement), and which may apply cyclically instead of across-the-board, may be restricted to applying at the juncture between words and hence show strict cyclic effects, and may have lexical exceptions. Let us look at a few examples of these P1 rules.

Kaisse (1987) argues that the English "rhythm rule" that retracts the prominence from the end of the word to an earlier stressed syllable under stress clash with a following word is a P1 rule. This rule accounts for the stress shift in such cases as *Mìssissíppi*, but *Míssissìppi délta*. It displays a number of lexical-like features. First, its input and output are independently contrastive stress contours (*álligàtor* vs. *màcaróni*), and thus it is structure-preserving. Second, the rule has many lexical exceptions in disyllabic cases: while *àbstráct* and *còmpléx* retract their stress, *àbsúrd* does not (*an àbstràct nótion* vs. *an àbsúrd nótion*). Also, as Kiparsky (1982a:144) observes, the stress-shifted output may be lexicalized: *ábstràct art* has the meaning 'art that is not representational'. Finally, cyclic application of the rhythm rule accounts for the contrasting stress contours in such four-word phrases as **one-thirteen Jay Street** vs. *Bill's **thirteen clothes** pins*.

Another much-discussed phrasal rule with lexical characteristics is Kimatuumbi vowel shortening (Odden 1987). In this Bantu language, a long vowel located in a noun or verb shortens when followed by a phrasal complement. Following Odden, we will express the rule as (67a), deleting the second half of a tautosyllabic (essentially geminate) vowel when located in the head of a phrase X and followed by some phonological material Y in the same phrase. The "same phrase" requirement distinguishes (67b) from (67c,d). In the former, the two words share the same maximal projection (NP); in the latter, *kįkóloombe* occupies a different projection than the following word does. The lack of shortening on *kįkeéle* in (67e) shows that the rule isolates the phrasal head.

(67) a.   σ
             /\
          $V_1 \, V_2 \rightarrow V_1 \, / \, [[\underline{\quad\quad}]_X Y]_{X'}$

   b.   kįkóloombe 'cleaning shell'
        kįkólombe chaángu 'my cleaning shell'
   c.   kįkóloombe chaapúwaanįįke 'the shell broke'
   d.   naampéį kikóloombe Mambóondo 'I gave Mamboondo the shell'
   e.   kįkólombe kįkeéle chaángu 'my red shell'

The Kimatuumbi shortening interacts with long vowels that are the by-products of a glide formation process. The glide formation in turn is intricately tied to the constituent structure of the verbal and nominal word phrase. Odden distinguishes three levels: 1 root + derivation suffixes, 2 inflectional prefixes + stem, and 3 locative (prepositional) prefixes. Glide formation devocalizes a prevocalic high vowel, lengthening the conditioning vowel if short: $i,u + V \rightarrow yVV, wVV$. For example, the class 4 nominal prefix *mį-* (e.g., *mį-kaáte* 'loaves') illustrates glide formation at level 2 when added to the root [otó] that appears in *ma-otó* 'large fires': *my-oótó* 'fires' (from [mį + oto]). The locative prefix *kų-* (e.g., *kų-sųúle* 'to school') devocalizes before the class 8 prefix in *kw-įįsįwá* 'to the islands', which in turn derives from *į-sįwa* 'the islands'. A form such as *kųyaáį* 'to the cooking pots' from [kų[į[aaį]]] shows that glide formation applies cyclically: the class 8 prefix in *į[aaį]* must devocalize before the locative prefix *kų-* does. A similar inside-out application of glide formation is required by *mųyuúlá* 'in the frogs' from [mų[į-úlá]].

Let us now consider the interaction between the two rules. A long vowel derived from glide formation at level 2 or 3 does not undergo phrasal shortening, while one derived on the stem at level 1 does. These points are revealed in the following paradigms.

(68) a.   ák-a   'to net-hunt'
           ák-**an**-a   'to net-hunt each other'
           ák-y-**aan**-a   'to net-hunt for each other' [ak-į-an-a]

      b.   twaakyana įtúmbili   'we net-hunt monkeys for each other'
             < [tų-ak-į-an-a]
           twaamámandwįle ñųýmba   'we plastered a house'
             < [tų-a-mámaandųįle]

The last form in (68a) illustrates glide formation and lengthening at level 1 [stem + suffix]: *ák-y-aan-a*. When embedded in a phrase, this vowel shortens: note *twaakyana* in (68b). But a lengthened prefixal vowel does not: *twaakyana*.

To account for this difference, Odden (1990) assigns the shortening rule to level 1 of the lexical phonology. However, the rule is granted the power to look outside the word into the phrasal context, in a derivation such as (69). Shortening does not affect the lengthened prefix vowels because they are derived at level 2 while shortening is assigned to the level 1.

(69) ak-į-an-a įtúmbili   level 1
      akyaana įtúmbili   glide formation
      akyana įtúmbili   shortening

      tų-akyana įtúmbili   level 2
      twaakyana įtúmbili   glide formation

This analysis abandons the assumption that the lexical phonology precedes the syntax. Like Halle and Vergnaud's analysis of the Slavic yers, it rejects Lexical Phonology's interleaving of the word formation and lexical phonological rules and returns to the earlier generative model in which morphology is separated from phonology but still defines the cyclic domains required for the phonology. It also permits the earliest phonological stratum to access the syntactic phrase and thus effectively denies any correlation between the power to refer to the syntax and the depth of the lexical stratum.

Another possible interpretation of these data more in keeping with the tenets of the Lexical Phonology model is that vowel shortening is a P1 phrasal rule, but one whose application ignores the inflectional prefixes. In some Bantu languages, the stem is prosodically separated from its inflectional prefixes (as revealed in the tonology). It is possible that this prosodic constituency defines the domain for the Kimatuumbi shortening rule rather than the purely grammatical domain. The juncture between a prefix and a following stem often has a different phonology from the stem + suffix juncture. This asymmetry may reflect a parsing advantage for signaling the onset of the stem – the semantically heaviest and most valuable information in the decoding of the speech signal. See Hayes 1990 for another interpretation of these controversial Kimatuumbi data.

5.8.4 P-Structure Rules

Building on the work of Clements (1978) and Chen (1985, 1987), Selkirk (1986) singles out for special treatment rules that display traits intermediate between those of Kaisse's P1 and P2 rules. Unlike P1 rules, these "prosodic" rules are generally automatic (no lexical exceptions) and typically fail to distinguish noun from verb, or head from complement; rather, they treat all phrases of a given complexity of branching the same. But unlike the typical P2 rule (e.g., Catalan nasal assimilation), the prosodic rules do not apply between any arbitrary pair of words but instead are sensitive to the phrasing. However, while based on the surface syntax, the phrasing does not coincide exactly with syntactic constituent structure. Rather, the prosodic grouping reflects an impoverishment of the surface syntax arising from the elimination of all but a designated set of syntactic constituent boundaries. The boundaries that survive impoverishment are then interpreted as divisions within the string of phonological segments. Phonological rules applying at this point or later thus do not see surface syntax directly but only obliquely through the bracketing that survives impoverishment. Such rules are thus predicted to be sensitive to only a limited amount of syntactic information.

The syntactic constituent boundaries that are passed on to define the phonological phrasing are defined by two parameters in Selkirk's model: (i) the level of syntactic projection: X^{lex} (where X = a Noun, Verb, Adjective) or X^{max} (Noun Phrase, Verb Phrase, Adjective Phrase); and (ii) the left or right edge of the projected constituent. Since only one edge (right or left) is projected, the resultant phonological phrasing will not necessarily delimit a syntactic constituent. In a number of well-documented cases, this failure of the syntax and the prosodic grouping to coincide gives exactly the correct phonological delimitations. To close this chapter, we will look at examples from two languages. For further discussion and exemplification, see Selkirk 1986, Nespor and Vogel 1986, Kaisse and Zwicky 1987, and Inkelas and Zec 1990.

One of Selkirk's best examples concerns the realization of vowel length in the Bantu language Chi Mwi:ni (based on data from Goodman 1967 and from Kisseberth and Abasheikh 1974). In Chi Mwi:ni long vowels come from several sources: from underlying lexical contrasts (e.g., *x-so:ma* 'to read' vs. *x-tufa* 'to spit'); from rules lengthening vowels before certain suffixes such as the locative *-ni* (e.g., *madrasa* 'school', *madrasa:-ni* 'at school') and in word-final phrase-medial position (e.g., *na* 'by', *na: noka* 'by a snake'; *hujo* 'one who eats', *hujo: mbele* 'the one who eats first'). Vowel length is realized phonetically only within a maximal three-syllable window at the end of the phonological phrase: long vowels falling outside this window are shortened: *x-so:m-a* 'to read', *x-so:m-esh-a* 'to teach', but *x-som-esh-añ-a* 'to teach each other'. Furthermore, the window shrinks to two syllables when the penult of the phrase is heavy: *su:xu* 'market', *suxu:-ni* 'at the market'; *xsoma: chuwo* 'to read a book'; *xfungula xalbi* 'to open one's heart'.

Building on an earlier proposal of Hayes (1981), Selkirk develops a metrical interpretation of the Chi Mwi:ni window that is equivalent to the structure underlying the Latin stress rule: it may reach to the antepenultimate syllable, but only when the penultimate syllable is light; if it is heavy, then the window stops at the penult. The derivations in (70) illustrate the intended analysis.

(70)

[xso:mesha]	[su:xu-ni]	[xso:ma chuwo]	UR
————	su:xu:-ni	xso:ma: chuwo	lengthening
{xso:mesha}	su:{xu:-ni}	xso:{ma: chuwo}	metrical window
————	su{xu:-ni}	xso{ma: chuwo}	shortening

We now turn to certain properties of the vowel-shortening phenomenon and its bearing on the phonological phrasing. First, certain pairs of words in Chi Mwi:ni join together to form a phrase for the realization of the metrical window while others do not.

(71) a. nthi: nkhavu   'dry land'
      b. nthi ni: nkhavu   'land is dry'
      c. mayi malada   'fresh water'
      d. ma:yi ni malada   'water is fresh'

For example, when *nthi* 'land' and *nkhavu* 'dry' are combined into a Noun Phrase (71a), they form a single prosodic phrase. This phrasing is relevant for two rules: medial lengthening and pre-antepenult shortening. Since the final vowel of *nthi* 'land' falls inside the metrical window, it emerges lengthened at the phonetic surface. But when *nthi* and *nkhavu* form a subject + predicate construction (71b), they belong to separate prosodic phrases. Consequently, no vowel length is assigned to the final syllable of *nthi* 'land'; rather, the copula *ni* and the following adjective *nkhavu* form a phonological phrase. Being phrase-medial and word-final, the vowel of the copula *ni* is lengthened; and once again this length may surface because it falls within the phrase-final three-syllable window. In (71c) the underlying vowel length in *ma:yi* is shortened since it groups with *malada* and hence lies outside the three-syllable window. For exactly the same reason, vowel length does not surface on the final syllable of the noun *ma:yi*. But in the copular construction (71d), the subject phrases separately from the following predicate. The underlying length in *ma:yi* now surfaces. But the length assigned to the final vowel of the copula *ni* does not because it lies outside the window, given that the predicate adjective *malada* 'fresh' is trisyllabic.

From these examples as well as others such as (72), it is evident that the proper phrasing can be determined by projecting the right edges of maximal phrasal categories.

(72) verb + object NP
      xfungula xalbi 'to open one's heart' (cf. xfu:ngula 'to open')

      preposition + NP
      na: noka 'by a snake' (cf. na 'by')

      NP + VP
      mwa:rabu vete chile:mbe 'an Arab has put on a turban' (cf. ve:te 'has put on')

In other words, the phonological phrasing in Chi Mwi:ni is determined by the following parameter settings for the impoverishment operation: X^{max}, right. The three-syllable window is then measured right to left from the resultant boundaries. The derivations in (73) show how this analysis works. The syntactic brackets that survive impoverishment and thus translate into prosodic boundaries are notated by parentheses.

(73) [mwa:rabu]$_{NP}$ [ve:te [chile:mbe]$_{NP}$]$_{VP}$ UR
      mwa:rabu)   ve:te chile:mbe)   impoverishment
      inappl.   ve:te: chile:mbe)   medial lengthening
      {mwa:rabu}   ve:te: chi{le:mbe}   metrical window
      inappl.   vete chi{le:mbe}   shortening
      mwa:rabu   vete chile:mbe   surface

Since just the right edges of phrasal constituents define prosodic phrasing in Chi Mwi:ni, the material lying between any two such boundaries need not form a syntactic constituent by itself. Two examples will illustrate this point. In (74)

the NP subject of the complement clause projects its right edge and so groups
with the preceding complementizer and head noun *munthu* into a prosodic phrase.
But *munthu wa Ja:ma* 'the man who Jama' clearly is not a syntactic constituent.

(74)

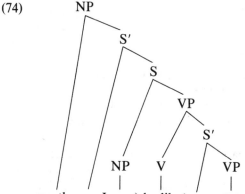

munthu wa Ja:ma) hadilo kuwa ile)   '(the) man who Ja:ma said that came'

In (75) the PP takes an NP complement that itself consists of an NP with a PP
complement. Once again, the syntactic and phonological groupings do not coincide.

(75)

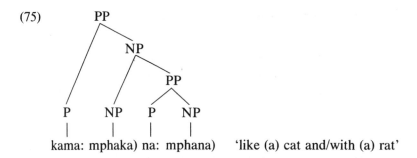

kama: mphaka) na: mphana)   'like (a) cat and/with (a) rat'

   An example in which the left edge of a maximal phrase defines prosodic boundaries is provided by the tonal phonology of the Anlo dialect of Ewe (Clements
1978). Anlo Ewe distinguishes three tonal levels in isolation: high, mid, and low
(marked by the acute, macron, and grave, respectively): *ètó* 'mountain', *ētō* 'mor-
tar', and *ètò* 'buffalo'. As shown by the alternation of *àkplò* 'spear' but *ākplō dyí*
'on a spear', certain low tones neutralize to mid when not phrase-final. The rule
of interest here is one that raises a mid tone (basic or derived) to superhigh (marked
by the double acute) between high tones. This rule is stated informally in (76).

(76) $\bar{V} \rightarrow \ddot{V} / \acute{V} \underline{\quad} \acute{V}$

It accounts for a number of the alternations observed in the phrases in (77) such
as the superhigh on the postposition *mĕgbé* 'behind' in *èkpĕ mĕgbé* 'behind a
stone' or the superhigh in *àtyíkĕ dyí* 'on medicine', where the final low tone on

àtyíkè has shifted to mid in phrase-medial position and then raised to superhigh between the high tones of [tyí] and [dyí]. An underlying high tone may optionally assimilate to a following superhigh: [èkpé mēgbé] → [èkpé mḗgbé] → [èkpé mḗgbé].

(77)

àkplò	èkpé	àtyíkè	N
ākplō ó	èkpé ó	àtyíkḗ ó	N pl.
ākplō dyí	ékpé dyí	àtyíkḗ dyí	'on N'
ākplō mēgbé	èkpḗ mēgbé	àtyíkē mēgbé	'behind N'
m' ākplō dzrá-gé	mè kpé dzrá-gé	m' àtyíkḗ dzrá-gé	'I'll sell N'
m' ākplō flē-gé	mè kpé flé-gé	m' àtyíkē flē-gé	'I'll buy N'
'spear'	'stone'	'medicine'	

Anlo Ewe has a number of constructions in which the verb precedes its complement NP. In these cases the verb and the NP belong to different prosodic phrases because the mid tones do not shift to superhigh even though they are located between high tones. A few examples are cited in (78). We may account for the difference in terms of Selkirk's phrasing parameter by saying that Anlo Ewe projects {X^{max}, left}. An NP is thus separated from the preceding verb even though they evidently form a syntactic constituent. Once again, a parenthesis marks the constituent boundary that survives impoverishment.

(78)

àblá kplé kōfí 'Abla and Kofi'	NP and (NP
kpɔ́ ānyí 'saw (a) bee'	V (NP
mē ná àtyí kōfí 'I gave (a) stick (to) Kofi'	V (NP (NP
mē xé fē né kòdzó 'I paid (a) debt to Kwadzo'	V (NP (PP
mē yī dé tɔ̄ tó 'I went to the riverside'	V V (NP
wő nɔ̃ví 'their brother' (cf. nɔ̃ví 'brother')	(NP N
kófí yī dé kḗtá 'Kofi went to Keta'	V (PP
mí ā-dzó 'we will leave'	NP Infl (VP
wó má-ā dzó ò 'they will not leave'	neg-tense (VP

Suggested Readings

Booij, Geert, and Jerzy Rubach. 1987. Postcyclic versus postlexical rules in lexical phonology. Linguistic Inquiry 18.1–44.

Borowsky, Toni. 1992. On the word-level. To appear in Studies in lexical phonology, ed. by S. Hargus and E. Kaisse. San Diego, Calif.: Academic Press.

Kiparsky, Paul. 1982. Lexical phonology and morphology. Linguistics in the morning calm, ed. by I. S. Yang, 3–91. Seoul: Hanshin. Abridged version published as "From cyclic to lexical phonology" in The structure of phonological representations (part I), ed. by H. van der Hulst and N. Smith, 131–75. Dordrecht: Foris.

Kiparsky, Paul. 1985. Some consequences of lexical phonology. Phonology Yearbook 2.83–138.

Selkirk, Elisabeth. 1986. On derived domains in sentence phonology. Phonology Yearbook 3.371–405.

Exercises

5.1 Icelandic (Anderson 1974)

A. Recall the *u*-umlaut rule (1a) from section 2.7 that accounts for alternations
such as those in (1b).

(1) a.   [a] → [ö] / ____ C_0 [u]

    b.   barn   'child'   börn-um   dat.pl.
           svangt   'hungry'   svöng-u   dat.sg.
           kall-a   'I call'   köll-um   'we call'

Formulate a syncope rule that accounts for the V≈∅ alternation in the data of
(2a) and use the data in (2b) to order syncope and *u*-umlaut. (The nom.sg. suffix
-r assimilates to a preceding sonorant, and stress is on the initial syllable.)

(2) a.   hamar   'hammer'   hamr-i   dat.sg.
           fífil-l   'dandelion'   fifl-i   dat.sg.
           morgun-n   'morning'   morgn-i   dat.sg.

    b.   ketil-l   'kettle'   regin   'gods'
           katl-i   dat.sg.   ragn-a   gen.pl.
           kötl-um   dat.pl.   rögn-um   dat.pl.

What problem do the data in (3) pose for the analysis? Suggest a solution.

(3) bagg-i   'pack'   jak-i   'piece of ice'
    bögg-ul-l   'parcel'   jök-ul-l   'glacier'
    bögg-l-i   'parcel' dat.sg.   jök-l-i   'glacier' dat.sg.

    þagg-a   'to silence'
    þög-ul-l   'taciturn'
    þög-l-an   'taciturn' acc.sg.masc.

B. Recall from section 2.7 the paradigms in (4a) that motivate [-r] as the underlying representation for the nom.sg. suffix in the *r*-stem nouns. Following
Kiparsky (1984), the epenthesis rule may be expressed as (4b) to insert a [u]
before an unsyllabifiable [r] (indicated by the tick), assuming that the syllable-
building rules fail to syllabify an [r] in the context C____# (unless followed
by a vowel). Treating epenthesis as supporting an unsyllabified consonant
implies the derivation in (4c).

(4) a.   hom.sg.   dag-ur   hest-ur   bæ-r
           acc.sg.   dag   hest   bæ
                      'day'   'horse'   'farmhouse'

    b.   ∅ → u / ____ r'

c. [#dag+r#]   [#bæ+r#]
    {dag}+r   {bæ+r}   syllabification
    {dag}+ur   ———   epenthesis
    {da}{g+ur}   ———   resyllabification

Relying on the concept of strict cyclicity as a reflex of the Elsewhere Condition, develop an analysis for the paradigms in (5). *#inn* is the definite clitic, added in the syntax as a separate word. Hint: Consider assigning epenthesis to both the lexical and the postlexical modules.

(5) nom.sg.   lifur   dag-ur   akur   hamar
     dat.sg.   lifr-i   dag-i   akr-i   hamr-i
     dat.pl.   lifr-um   dög-um   ökr-um
     nom.sg.def. lifr#inn   dag-ur-#inn akur#inn   hamar#inn
                  'liver'   'day'   'acre'   'hammer'

5.2 Polish

This exercise (based on Rubach 1984) introduces several additional rules of Polish phonology. Building on the text analysis developed in section 5.8.1, determine the grammatical component (cyclic, postcyclic lexical, postlexical) of each rule. What reasons can be given for each assignment?

A. Formulate a rule to account for the alternations between [t',d',n'] and [t,d,n]. Determine its ordering with respect to other rules of Polish developed in the text.

(1) a. <u>noun</u>   <u>adjectival</u>
         sekret   sekret-n-i   'secret'
         brut   brud-n-i   'dirt'
         s'an-o   s'en-n-i   'hay'

         vilgot'   vilgot-n-i   'humidity'
         čelad'   čelad-n-i   'household'
         kon'   kon-n-i   'horse'

     b. vin-a   'fault'   podob-n-i   'similar'
         vin'-en 'guilty' masc.sg.   podob'-en-stv-o 'similarity'
         vin-n-a fem.sg.
         vin-n-i attributive

     c. d'en'   'day'   star-i   'old'
         dn'-a   gen.sg.   staž-ec   'old man'
         d'en-n-i 'daily'   star-c-a   gen.sg.

     d. dobrot'   'goodness'   jes'en'   'autumn'
         dobrot-liw-i   'good-hearted'   jes'en-n-i   adj.
         dobrot' ludzka   'human   jes'en' našego   'autumn of
                          goodness'   žyt'a   our life'

B. The front vowel [i] is assigned the feature [+back] after nonpalatalized
    [+back] coronal consonants, where it is realized as [ɨ] (orthographic *y*). This
    rule is responsible for the alternations displayed by the *-it'* and *-ist* deriva-
    tional suffixes. You may assume a rule [r'] → [ž].

(2) a.   <u>noun</u>   <u>derived verb</u>
          kapris   kapris'-it'   'whim'
          vus   voz'-it'   'cart'
          brut   brud'-it'   'dirt'
          tentn-o   tentn'-it'   'pulse'
          tovažiš   tovažiš-it'   'companion'
          partač   partač-it'   'bungle'
          kuš   kuž-it'   'dust'
          xmur-a   xmuž-it'   'cloud'

     b.   zwot-o   'gold'   zwot'-ist-ɨ   'golden'
          srebr-o   'silver'   srebž-ist-ɨ   'silvery'

C. Consider the realization of "i" in loanword adaptation. What bearing does
    it have on the nature of the backing rule?

(3) a.   kretin   'idiot'   crétin   French
          krip-a   'boat'   Krippe   German
          cipel   'cape'   Zipfel   German
          šifr   'code'   chiffre   French
          pilot   'pilot'   pilote   French
          vitraš   'stained-glass   vitrage   French
                     window'
          kitel   'frock'   Kittel   German

     b.   <u>U.S. Polish</u>
          sink   'sink'
          strita   'street'
          grinhorn   'greenhorn'
          ofis   'office'
          spikovat'   'to speak'

5.3 Chumash

Review the discussion of Chumash sibilant harmony in section 4.3.4. Recall that
coronal affricates and fricatives assimilate the [±anterior] value of a following
sibilant. As a result, the 3sg. subject prefix [s-] of *ha-s-xintila* 'his Indian name'
appears as [−anterior] [š] in *ha-š-xintila-waš* 'his former Indian name', where the
suffix [-waš] has been added. The data in (1b) motivate another rule (1a) that
assigns [−anterior] to [s] when it appears before the nonstrident coronals [t,l,n].

(1) a.   [s] → [š] / ____ [Coronal, −strid]
     b.   š-nanʔ   'he goes'   /s+nanʔ/
          š-tepuʔ   'he gambles'   /s+tepuʔ/
          š-loxitʔ   'he surpasses me'   /s+loxitʔ/

The [š] that arises from (1a) has the following two special properties: (i) it fails to harmonize with a following sibilant, and (ii) it starts a new harmonic domain, causing all sibilants to its left to harmonize to it. The first property is evident in (2a), where the [š-] prefix derived by (1a) fails to harmonize to the [+anterior] [s] of the suffix; and the second is evident in (2b), where the [š] of the dual prefix /-iš/ starts a new harmonic domain.

(2) a. š-ti-yep-us   'he tells him'   /s+ti+yep+us/
      b. š-iš-lu-sisin 'they two are gone awry' /s+iš+lu+sisin/

Poser (1982) accounts for this range of data by breaking the sibilant harmony process of (38) in section 4.3.4 into two parts: the first delinks all but the rightmost specification on the [±anterior] tier when the anchoring root is [+strident]; the second is a feature-filling process that spreads [±anterior] leftward to [+strident] segments that lack an anterior specification.

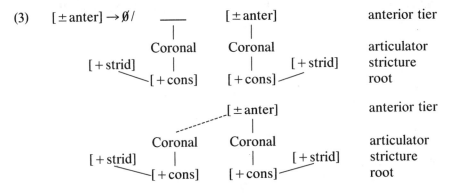

(3)   [±anter] → Ø/

The rule of (1a) is ordered in between the delinking and spreading parts of the harmony. To see how this solution works, examine the derivation in (4), where [S] stands for a sibilant unspecified for [±anterior].

(4) ha+s+xintila+waš   s+   iš+ lu+sisin   UR

      [+ant]   [−ant]   [+ant][−ant] [+ant]

    ha+S+xintila+waš   S+iS+lulu+sisin   delinking

          [−ant]   [+ant]

    inappl.   S+iš+lu+sisin   (1a)

                    [−ant] [+ant]

    ha+š+xintila+waš   š+iš+lu+sisin   spread

            [−ant]   [−ant] [+ant]

(5a) lists tautomorphemic [s] + nonstrident coronal clusters. How can they be exempted from the rule in (1a)? (5b) exemplifies the stem /wašti/ 'of a flow, liquid in motion'. Assuming the analysis developed above, show the derivation of *swastilokʔinus* (5c) and compare it with the derivations in (4). What role does the SCC play in your analysis?

(5)　a.　stumukun　　　'mistletoe'
　　　　　slowʔ　　　　　'eagle'
　　　　　wastuʔ　　　　'pleat'

　　　b.　wašti-nanʔ　　'to spill'　　/wašti + nanʔ/

　　　c.　s-wasti-lokʔin-us　'the flow stops on him'　/s + wašti + lokʔin + us/

5.4　Sundanese

In Sundanese (Robins 1953, 1957) vowels assimilate the nasality of a preceding nasal consonant (1). Nasality propagates through a string of vowels (2) and is interrupted by a supralaryngeal consonant (1). There is one systematic exception to this statement: nasality crosses a liquid, but only when it comprises the infix-*ar/al-* marking plurality in verbs (3).

(1)　mãke　　　'to use'
　　　ŋũsap　　　'to stroke'
　　　mãrios　　'to examine'
　　　ŋũliat　　'to stretch'

(2)　mĩãk　　　'to stand aside'
　　　ñãũr　　　'to say'
　　　ñãĩãn　　'to wet'
　　　nĩʔĩr　　'to pierce'
　　　mãhãl　　'to be expensive'

(3)　ñ-ãr-ãhõ　　cf.　ñãhõ　　'to know'
　　　n-ãr-ĩʔĩs　　　　　nĩʔĩs　　'to cool oneself'
　　　m-ãr-ãhãl　　　　mãhãl　　'to be expensive'
　　　ñ-ãl-ãũr　　　　　ñãũr　　'to say'

Develop an analysis for these data that will account for the behavior of the infix and thus explain the contrast between *mãrios/ŋũliat* and *mãrãhãl/ŋãlãũr*. Briefly discuss the relevance of these data to the issue of whether morphology precedes phonology or is interleaved with it. Are the data susceptible to an analysis along the lines suggested by Halle and Vergnaud (1987) for Russian (section 5.8.2) in which morphemes can be marked [±cyclic]? (For the data in (3), Robins transcribes the vowel that immediately follows the liquid of the infix as oral. In her phonetic study, Cohn (1990) found such denasalization only in certain contexts and with certain speakers. The transcriptions given here abstract away from this complication.)

5.5　Chi Mwi:ni

The following sentences are taken from a Chi Mwi:ni folktale (Kisseberth 1986). Assuming Selkirk's (1986) analysis discussed in section 5.8.4 in which the phonemic string is metrically parsed according to the Latin stress rule and vowels are shortened in nonprominent position, examine the following sentences to determine what their prosodic phrasing must be. Mark the constituent boundaries that survive impoverishment by a parenthesis. Indicate which cases are consistent with the parameter settings of Selkirk's analysis and which ones (if any) are not; comment on cases where there is a disparity between the syntactic and the prosodic constituency. (Hints: Recall the rule lengthening a word-final vowel that is not phrase-final; long vowels shorten in closed syllables; homorganic nasal-stop clusters count as syllable onsets.)

(1) sku mo:yi jira:ni   wa?ale numba:-ni   wamwambile mamaye
    one day   neighbors came house-loc [and] they-tell   mother-of

    Hasi:bu kuwa: wo   wanakenda maduri:-ni xtinda skuñi   na
    Hasib   that   they were-going forest-loc to-cut firewood and

    wataxpenda Hasi:bu kenda na: wo.
    they-wanted Hasib   to-go with them

    (cf. nu:mba 'house', ma:ma 'mother')

(2) ma:ma shxi:ra   chiwa?ambila kuwa: ye tamulila   mphu:nda
    mother agreed [and] told-them   that she would-buy a-donkey

    (cf. x-wa:mbila 'to tell')

(3) sku ya pi:li wachenda te:na   wachiruda na   skuñi   zi:ŋgi.
    day of p.   they-went again [and] returned with firewood much
    'The next day they went again and returned with much firewood.'

(4) ichanza kuña: nvula.
    it-began to-rain rain
    'It began to rain.'

(5) Hasi:bu chimuza ma:maye zi:kopi   ziwo za wa:waye.
    Hasib   asked   mother-his where-be books of father-his
    'Hasib asked his mother where the books of his father were.'

(6) ma:ma chimji:ba ya kuwa ziwo za wa:waye zimo nthini ya mivu:ŋgu.
    mother answered him that books of father-his are under of bed
    'Mother answered him that the books of his father are under the bed.'

6   The Syllable and Syllabification

The role of the syllable in phonological theory has been controversial. Like the notions "word" and "sentence," it is part of the conceptual baggage left from traditional grammar. At various points in the history of linguistics, the syllable has been jettisoned in favor of a sparser theoretical vocabulary. Generative grammar is no different in this respect. During the *SPE* period, the notion had no official recognition. However, through subsequent research, generative phonologists have come to appreciate that the syllable is an essential concept for understanding phonological structure. One reason the syllable has proved so elusive is that it lacks any uniform or direct phonetic correlates: it is not a sound, but an abstract unit of prosodic organization through which a language expresses much of its phonology. Furthermore, the exact shape of the syllable varies from one language to another. Finally, the organization of sounds into syllables can take place at a certain level of abstraction; more superficial features often obscure the underlying organization. Phonologists have only begun to grasp the factors determining syllabification. Much work still remains to be done. But there can be no doubt that the syllable is an essential unit of phonological organization and hence a principal research objective.

In this chapter we will survey the major results of generative research on the syllable. We will look first at motivations for the syllable in phonological theory, and then at the concept of core syllable and the Sonority Sequencing Principle. In the ensuing sections we will survey some known determinants of syllabification and the kinds of questions that remain to be answered.

6.1   Motivations for the Syllable

Three kinds of justification have been offered for the syllable. First, the syllable is a natural domain for the statement of many phonotactic constraints. Second, phonological rules are often more simply and insightfully expressed if they explicitly refer to the syllable. Finally, several phonological processes are best interpreted as methods to ensure that the string of phonological segments is parsable into syllables. Let us illustrate these points with a few examples from English (Kahn 1976).

Phonotactic constraint refers to limitations on the distribution of sounds and sound sequences at various points (initial, medial, final) in the phonological word or phrase. Typically, these limitations are not the result of a phonological rule changing one sound into another. Yet it is quite clear that they must follow from the speaker's internalized grammar. For example, all English speakers tacitly know that while lexical items may begin with the strings #*tr* and #*str*, sequences such as #*tl* and #*nt* are not possible initial clusters in their language. If we say that every word must be parsed into syllables, and that [tr] is a well-formed syllable onset while [tl] is not, then this aspect of the speaker's knowledge of English is accounted for. One might respond that there is little apparent difference between saying that no word may begin with [tl] and that no syllable may begin with [tl]. However, reference to the syllable also helps us to explain why the first [t] in a word such as *A*[tˀ]*lantic* is glottalized while the [t] in *a*[tʰ]*rocious* is aspirated. If every word must be parsed into syllables, and if we stipulate that [tl] is not a possible syllable onset while [tr] is, then *Atlantic* will have a syllable break within the [tl] cluster and *atrocious* will not: [At.lan.tic] vs. [a.tro.cious]. Rules aspirating syllable-initial [t] and glottalizing syllable-final [t] can then produce the appropriate allophones. But if the absence of initial [tl] clusters is viewed simply as a constraint on word shapes, then it is mysterious why what is a possible word-initial cluster should have any bearing on the behavior of word-medial [tl] and [tr] sequences.

Certain aspects of English stress also make this point. The string of syllables that precedes the primary accent is assigned a subsidiary alternating stressed-unstressed contour that starts with the first syllable: *Àpalàchicóla, Àlabáma*. As the examples in (1) demonstrate, when the initial syllable abuts the primary stress, it is sometimes stressed and sometimes not. The key determinant is the consonant cluster that separates the first vowel from the second.

(1)   a.   América   b.   Mòntána
            Nebráska   àrcáde
            atrócious   Àtlántic
            astrónomy   àrthrític

The consonant strings [m,br,tr,str] that follow the initial vowel in (1a) are possible word-initial sequences (e.g., [m]*ilk,* [br]*ain,* [tr]*ip,* [str]*eet*). But those in (1b) are not: no English words begin with [nt,rk,tl,rθ]. Again it is puzzling why what is a possible word-initial consonant sequence should be relevant when the cluster is buried inside the word. But if we accept the view that the phonological string is parsed into syllables, then the following explanation is possible. Assume that as many consonants as possible syllabify with the following vowel; those that remain are then parsed with the preceding vowel. This procedure distinguishes the initial vowels in (1a) and (1b) in the appropriate way. Since the clusters in (1a) are possible syllable onsets, the preceding vowels terminate their own syllable (an open syllable): [A.mérica], [Ne.bráska], [a.trócious], [a.strónomy]. But the consonant that escapes the following vowel in (1b) closes the preceding syllable: [Mòn.tána], [àr.cáde], [Àt.lántic], [àr.thrític]. Cross-linguistically, open syllables are more susceptible to reduction; the fact that the initial syllables in (1a) appear unaccented now has a natural explanation. (In more casual speech, the initial vowels in *Atlantic, athletic,* and so on, may also reduce to schwa; nevertheless, while it is perfectly natural to pronounce these words with a nonreduced initial vowel, it is quite unnatural for the words in (1a).)

To briefly summarize, we have seen three different rules (aspiration, glottalization, destressing and reduction) that apply word-medially but are sensitive to what is a possible word-initial cluster. Crucially, each rule consistently distinguishes the [tl] and [tr] clusters in *Atlantic* and *atrocious*. The grammar would be significantly more complex if the formal statement of each rule had to refer to what is a possible word-initial cluster. An important generalization would be lost. But if the segmental string is parsed into syllables, and we stipulate that [tr] is a possible onset while [tl] is not, then not only do we explain why [tl] and [tr] differ as possible word beginnings; we also simplify the statement of several rules with the help of such natural categories as "syllable-initial" and "syllable-final."

Let us now discuss the third motivation for developing an explicit theory of the syllable. Consider the following phonotactic constraints from English phonology. While words may terminate in the sequences [rt], [lt], and [mθ] (e.g., *cart, belt, warmth*), the inverse strings [tr], [tl], [θm] are not possible final clusters. In fact, the underlying cluster in *rhythm* /rɪθm/ ends up sounding very much like the disyllabic word *atom* (cf. [æDəm] vs. [rɪðəm]) through epenthesis of a schwa. (The schwa must be inserted rather than underlying, given the contrast between trisyllabic *atom-ic* and disyllabic *rhythm-ic*.) The alternation of [rɪðəm] and [rɪðm]*ic* can be explained as follows. In [rɪðm]*ic,* each segment can be assigned to a syllable: *rið.mic*. But since the string [ðm] is not a possible coda, the [m] in underlying [rɪðm] will be left "stranded." There are two common strategies to deal with such *stray* consonants: one assigns them to a "dummy" syllable (*anaptyxis*), the other suppresses them. The former strategy is adopted in the case of disyllabic *rhythm,* while the latter is employed for *dam(n)* (cf. *damn-ation*). Without the notion of the syllable, it is difficult to understand why languages should have rules to insert vowels out of nowhere into quite specific points in the phonological string. With the syllable, the mystery is explained: the vowels are inserted to syllabify unparsed consonants.

Finally, organization into syllables serves as the base over which the rules and principles of prosody are defined: for example, the alternating stress pattern of *Àpalàchicóla* is assigned in terms of the number and character (light or heavy) of syllables.

To summarize, we have ample justification to develop a theoretical account of the syllable. A number of questions now ensue. What is the structure of the syllable? Is this structure predictable? If so, how is syllabification assigned? Where is it assigned? Although detailed answers still remain to be found, we will look at a promising approach to these questions developed originally by Kiparsky (1981), Steriade (1982), and Levin (1985).

6.2   Syllable Structure and Syllabification: Basic Concepts

As far as its internal structure is concerned, the syllable has traditionally been seen as containing an obligatory *nucleus* preceded by an optional consonantal *onset* and followed by an optional consonantal *coda*. The nucleus plus coda form a tighter bond than the onset plus nucleus. Consequently, traditional grammar recognizes an additional subconstituent called the *rhyme* (or *rime*) that includes the nucleus and the coda. The constituents of the traditional syllable are depicted in (2a).

(2) a.

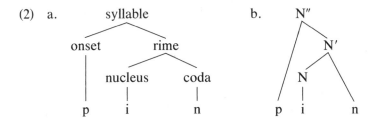

There is reason to believe that the nucleus has a special status as the only oblig-atory constituent. For example, {CV, VC, V, CVC} represents one of the most primitive syllable inventories. A significant number of the world's languages draw their syllables from this limited stock. More complex systems invariably arise from augmenting this basic inventory. The nuclear vowel V is the only constant factor among these four primitive syllables. The special status of the nucleus also shows up in its role as the optimal tone- or stress-bearing element. Deletion of the syllable's vocalic nucleus typically relocates the tone or stress. But loss of a consonantal onset or coda does not disturb the syllable count, and thus the location of accent or tone.

The evidence thus suggests that the nucleus is the syllable's essential core. This idea is formally reflected in the theory of syllabic representation developed by Levin (1985) in which the syllable is a projection of the single primitive category "nucleus," represented by N in (2b). We can then define the coda as the "com-plement" (right sister) of the nucleus, dominated by the first projection N'. The onset may be defined as the "specifier" of the syllable (left sister of N'), dominated by the second-level projection N". On this view, the syllabic constituent "rime" is then nothing but the first projection N'. (Just as a noun may constitute an NP in the absence of a complement or specifier, so a nuclear vowel may function as a syllable in the absence of an onset or coda. The first syllable of *atom* has an N' and N" projection just like the second. However, for notational convenience these may be suppressed.)

In most languages the syllabification assigned to a string of phonemes is pre-dictable from other aspects of the representation, in particular whether the seg-ment is a consonant or a vowel. Since the consonantal or vocalic status of a segment is generally assumed to be given independent of syllable structure by the feature [±consonantal] (or its equivalent), this information can be used to for-mulate rules to syllabify the segmental string. These syllable-building rules are very similar from one language to another and so can be viewed as the contribution of UG. Since the nucleus is the basis of the syllable, it is not surprising that the syllable is constructed outward from this core. In most languages, syllabic nuclei are coextensive with the set of vocalic segments. We thus have the rule (3a), which assigns a vowel to the nucleus. The second rule, (3b), assigns a prevocalic consonant to onset position.

(3) a.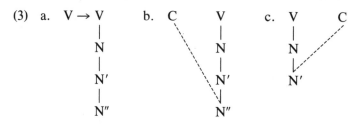

All grammars possess these two rules. In a few languages (e.g., Senufo, Hawaiian) these are the only rules of syllabification. As a result, their syllable inventory is limited to {V, CV}. However, most languages augment their stock of syllables to {V, CV, VC, CVC} with the help of (3c), which adds a single unincorporated consonant into the coda. The rules of (3) apply in the order indicated. One consequence is that a VCV string syllabifies to [V.CV], with the single intervocalic consonant onsetting the second syllable rather than closing the first. [VC.V] syllabifications are unusual and arise from language-particular rules. This is one aspect of a general tendency to avoid onsetless syllables. We will return to this point later.

A significant number of languages (e.g., Somali (exercise 3.5), Tangale (section 3.2), Yawelmani (section 3.4.2)) exploit just the rules in (3), so that their syllable inventories are restricted to {V, CV, VC, CVC}. Important consequences of this limitation are that no word can begin or end in a cluster of consonants and no word-medial consonant cluster can contain more than two elements. In these languages, #CC, CCC, and CC# strings typically evoke rules of epenthesis or cluster simplification. For example, recall from section 3.2 that Tangale (Kidda 1985) elides the final vowel of a stem when an affix is added: *duka* 'salt', *duk-nó* 'my salt'. When a suffix is added to CVCCV stems, elision creates a triconsonantal cluster that is broken by epenthesis of [u] between the first and second consonants unless they take the form of a homorganic nasal plus consonant, in which case the cluster is simplified by deletion of the medial stray consonant: *líprá* 'needle', *lípúr-nó* < /lípr-nó/ 'my needle' vs. *landa* 'dress', *lan-nó* < /land-nó/ 'my dress' (see Nikiema 1989 for a different interpretation).

The more complex syllable inventories found in languages such as English, Polish, and Sanskrit arise from selecting the option to incorporate additional consonantal material into the onset or coda. Typically, the creation of such complex onsets and codas is severely constrained. It has been known for over a century that the construction of complex onsets and codas is guided by a *Sonority Sequencing Principle* (SSP) that requires onsets to rise in sonority toward the nucleus and codas to fall in sonority from the nucleus. Although a simple phonetic correlate to the phonological property of sonority has yet to be discovered, phonologists agree that the entire class of speech sounds can be scaled as in (4a), with the vowels as most sonorous and the obstruents as least.

(4) a. vowels
        glides
        liquids
        nasals
        obstruents

b.

G	L	N	O	
+	−	−	−	vocoid
+	+	−	−	approximant
+	+	+	−	sonorant
3	2	1	0	

We adopt Clements's (1990:293) feature [approximant] ("any sound produced with an oral tract stricture open enough so that airflow through it is turbulent only if it is voiceless") to group together liquids and glides as in (4b). The hierarchy among nonnuclear segments can then be defined in terms of the rankings shown (G = glide, L = liquid, N = nasal, O = obstruent).

Given the syllable-building rules of (3), our initial statement of the Sonority Sequencing Principle claims that if a $C_wC_xVC_yC_z$ string has been syllabified by incorporating C_x into the onset and C_y into the coda, then C_w may be added to the onset only if it is less sonorous than C_x and C_z may be added to the coda only if it is less sonorous than C_y. These rules are stated in (5). Following Steriade (1982), (5a) will be referred to as *onset augmentation* and (5b) as *coda augmentation*. Syllables constructed with rules (3a,b,c) and (5a,b) are known as *core syllables*.

(5) a. N″

  C_w C_x (where C_w is less
    sonorous than C_x)

  b. N′

  C_y C_z (where C_z is less
    sonorous than C_y)

c.
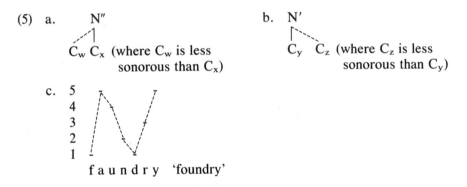

f a u n d r y 'foundry'

Given these rules, the sonority of the syllable thus peaks at the nucleus and descends toward the margins (reflected in the sonority graph of the word *foundry* in (5c)).

Two qualifications to this statement are in order here. First, while vowels are certainly the optimal syllabic nuclei, many systems allow sonorant and some even obstruent consonants to fill the nuclear slot. When this happens, such segments need not always bear greater sonority than adjacent nonnuclear segments. Clements (1990) cites English *yearn* [yr̩n], German *wollen* [voln̩], Berber *t-wn̩-tas* 'you climbed on him', Bella Coola *mn̩mn̩ts* 'children'. In many of these cases the syllabicity of a consonant is predictable from its position in the word. Second, adjacent vowels often combine to form a single syllable. For example, recall from section 1.11 that in Fijian (Dixon 1988) a nonhigh vowel combines with a following high vowel to form a diphthong (a tautosyllabic sequence of vocoids); the inverse sequences of high vowel plus nonhigh vowel form separate syllables, as evidenced by the fact that the rule stressing the penultimate syllable shifts the stress when the transitive suffix is added to *lú.a* 'vomit' but no shift of stress occurs when *táu̯* 'touch down' is transitivized: *lu.á-ca* vs. *táu̯.-ca*. This has led most phonologists to believe that glides [y,i̯] and [w,u̯] and the cognate vowels [i] and [u] have the same feature structure and differ simply in terms of their nuclear, nonnuclear position. However, there are other cases in which high vowels and glides contrast. It is unclear whether the appropriate move in such cases is to postulate a lexical syllabification or to distinguish the glides in terms of their feature structure.

6.3   The Syllables of English: A Sketch

Let us examine the role of the SSP in the construction of English onsets. The table in (6a) lists all possible two-consonant C_1C_2 onsets, with C_1 depicted along the vertical axis and C_2 along the horizontal; examples follow in (6b).

(6)   a.   <u>English onsets: two consonants</u>

```
        w  y  r  l  m  n  p  t  k
    p   −  +  +  +  −  −  −  −  −
    t   +  +  +  −  −  −  −  −  −
    k   +  +  +  +  −  −  −  −  −
    b   −  +  +  +  −  −  −  −  −
    d   +  +  +  −  −  −  −  −  −
    g   +  +  +  +  −  −  −  −  −
    f   −  +  +  +  −  −  −  −  −
    θ   +  +  +  −  −  −  −  −  −
    š   −  −  +  −  −  −  −  −  −
    s   +  +  −  +  +  +  +  +  +
```

  b.

	p[y]uke	priest	plate
twin	t[y]une*	trap	
quit	c[y]ute	crawl	clean
	beauty [byu]	brick	black
dwell	d[y]une*	drip	
Gwen	ambig[y]uity	grip	glad
	f[y]ume	free	flow
thwart	enth[y]use*	three	
		shrill	
sweet	s[y]uit*		slip smell snow spa stem skip

(*for dialects such as British Received Pronunciation (RP), see exercise 1.11)

If we set [s] aside for the moment, it is clear that all occurring onsets conform to the SSP. The pluses appear under columns headed by the more sonorous glides and liquids and in rows headed by the less sonorous obstruents. The two consonants occupying the onset tend to be chosen from opposite regions of the sonority scale. English systematically excludes clusters of a stop plus a nasal, for example, even though they would satisfy the SSP (cf. the "silent" [p] and [g] in *pneumatic* and *gnostic* with *ap.nea* and *ag.nostic,* where these consonants emerge phonetically in the coda of the preceding syllable). We might capture this aspect of the syllabification routine by requiring that adjacent consonants in the onset differ by a certain increment of sonority, with a preference to maximize this value. An obstruent-nasal cluster such as [pn] would consequently be dispreferred to an obstruent-liquid cluster like [pl], explaining why the former is generally chosen only if the latter has been too (e.g., in Ancient Greek).

While the SSP does a good deal of work in explaining the permitted clusters, there are still clusters with rising sonority that are systematically excluded. A number of these can be construed as reflecting a tendency to avoid successive consonants drawn from the same point of articulation. For example, this tendency explains why the labials [p,b,f] do not combine with [w] and why the coronals [t,d,θ] do not cluster with [l] in the onset. However, coronal [r] violates this tendency by freely combining with [t,d,θ]. It is unclear whether or not the tendency to avoid concatenating consonants with the same point of articulation should be raised to the level of a general principle. If so, then [t,d,θ] + [r] clusters must be generated by a language-specific stipulation; if not, then [t,d,θ] + [l] clusters must be excluded by a filter. For purposes of exposition, we will follow Clements and Keyser (1983) and stipulate the filters in (7).

(7)

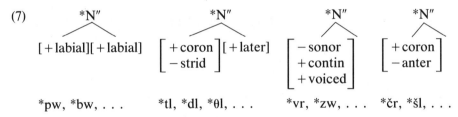

*pw, *bw, . . .   *tl, *dl, *θl, . . .   *vr, *zw, . . .   *čr, *šl, . . .

We have now developed apparatus sufficient to explain the contrast between *A[tˀ]lantic* and *a[tʰ]rocious* noted at the outset of this chapter. Application of the nuclear placement and the onset rules yields the representations in (8a).

(8)

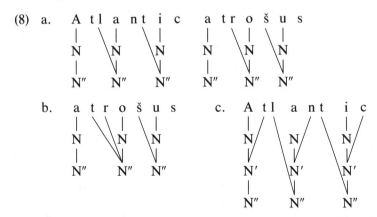

For *a.tro.cious,* we must incorporate the [t] into the following onset. Like many Indo-European languages, English maximizes its onsets: given a VC$_x$C$_y$V string, if C_x may form a legitimate onset with C_y, then the string will syllabify $V.C_xC_yV$. To obtain this result (8b), we order the onset augmentation rule (4a) before the coda rule (3c). Onset augmentation will block on the first [t] of [At.lan.tic] given the second filter in (7). This segment is then assigned to the coda of the preceding syllable (8c) by the coda rule (3c). We now have the appropriate representations to serve as input to the rules aspirating syllable-initial [t] and glottalizing syllable-final [t].

We now return to consider the special status of [s] in English. First, a minor point. The palatal consonants [č,š,ž] systematically fail to share the onset with any other consonant and must be excluded by the special stipulation in (7). The only exception to this generalization is the cluster [šr]. But the unexpected existence of [šr] is matched by the surprising absence of [sr]. The natural decision is to derive [šr] from [sr] by a special rule palatalizing [s] before [r] in the onset. As for the remaining [sC] clusters, the reduction of the first vowel in *asparagus* as well as the absence of aspiration on the [p] suggest that the [s] is in onset position. But the [s] of such [sC] clusters systematically violates each of the three principles we have claimed to govern the structure of English onsets. It violates the ban on shared point of articulation by combining with [l] (e.g., *slow*, in contrast to [θ], for example). [s] also violates the sonority increment requirement by freely combining with a following nasal (e.g., *smell, snow*). Finally, [s] combines with a following voiceless stop to yield a sequence of two obstruents. We can account for the exceptional behavior of [s] if we postulate a special rule adding [s] to the onset.

(9)   N″

Strong support for this rule derives from the fact that it automatically generates the attested three-member onsets depicted in (10a) and exemplified in (10b).

(10) a. <u>English onsets: three consonants</u>

	w	y	r	l	m	n
sp	−	+	+	+	−	−
st	−	+	+	−	−	−
sk	+	+	+	+	−	−

b.

	spume	spray	spleen
	st[y]lupid	strip	
squeeze	skew	scream	sclerosis

Each of these clusters begins with [s]. Furthermore, each can be segmented into [s] plus a possible two-consonant onset. Given the existence of rule (9) adding [s] to an onset, the three-member clusters in (10) are automatically generated. We do not need any additional machinery to account for them. However, we must assume that the ban against palatals in complex onsets constrains (9). Rule (9) also generates [stw] clusters; their absence is predicted to be an accidental gap.

To briefly summarize, we have seen that the syllable onsets in English are defined by a combination of universal and language-particular information. The contribution of the UG SSP plays the major role. The language-particular adjunction rule (9) is a complication that must be learned. The special status of the [sC] clusters is evident in their unique metrical properties in the Indo-European languages (Anderson 1969) and their tendency to emerge later in language acquisition.

Let us now briefly consider the structure of the English coda. Kiparsky (1981) observes that while both tense [+ATR] (diphthongized) and lax vowels combine freely with single consonants (11a,b), and while a lax vowel may freely combine with two consonants (11c), a tense vowel may in general not do so (11d). A syllable of the form [eylm] does not occur and is judged odd by native speakers.

(11)   [ɛ]   [ē]   [ɛ]   *[ē]

     a.   bell   b.   bale   c.   helm   d.   [eylm]
         hem   aim   elf   [eylf]
         pep   tape   hemp   [eymp]

     e.   N'   f.   N'

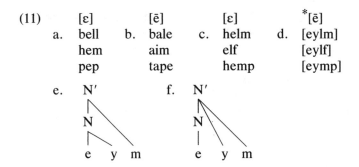

We assume that diphthongs such as [ey] derive from underlying long [+ATR] vowels such as [e:]. It is unclear whether the diphthongal offglide is best treated as part of a branching nucleus or as directly dominated by N' in the coda so that *aim* thus has the alternative representations in (11e) and (11f). On the latter interpretation, (11d) can be excluded by restricting N' to a maximum of three branches: at most one for the nucleus and at most two for the coda. However, in many languages (e.g., Yawelmani; section 3.4) long vowels are barred from combining with a coda consonant; if the second half of a long vowel is immediately dominated by the nucleus, then restrictions such as that observed in (11d) cannot be stated directly at the level of N' but must take into account the number of terminal positions that the syllable rime N' may dominate independently of how these positions are parceled out between the nucleus and the coda. The proper way to express this limitation is an unsolved problem.

Just as in the syllable onset, the SSP is the major determinant of consonant clustering in the coda. The table in (12) shows that the string VC_yC_z may constitute a coda just in case C_z is less sonorous than C_y. If the diphthongal offglides in *file* [ay], *coin* [oy], *louse* [aw], and so on, occupy the coda, then they also conform to the SSP. (We assume that the [r] in *curl, girl,* and so on, is a syllabic vocoid rather than a liquid.)

(12) helm
      elf   triumph
      help   hemp

Thus, the liquid [l] freely combines with a following nasal (*helm, kiln*), fricative (*elf, health*), or stop (*help, belt, belch, milk*). A nasal combines with a following fricative (*triumph, tenth*) or stop (*hemp, hint, bench, thank*). But a nasal may not be followed by a more sonorous liquid or an equivalently sonorous additional nasal (e.g., *dam*[ ], but *dam*[n]*ation*); also, while *pa*[lm] is monosyllabic, English speakers find it difficult to articulate the inverse cluster in *pa*[ml] without vocalizing the [l]. Finally, the principle that operates in the onset, favoring consonants chosen from opposite regions of the sonority scale, is not invoked in the English coda.

To briefly summarize the discussion so far, the grammar of English stipulates an upper bound of three positions on its syllable rime. The SSP does the major share of the work in defining the well-formed sequences of phonological segments that occupy these three positions.

There is, however, one glaring class of exceptions to the analysis: the coronal obstruents [t,d,θ,s,z]. They violate the SSP by combining with a preceding stop or fricative: *depth, apse, adze, fifth, act, apt*. They also violate the length restriction: *wild* [ayld], *paint* [eynt], *fifths* [ɪfθs], *sixths* [ɪksθs]. To accommodate these exceptions, we may postulate a special rule that adds an anterior coronal obstruent to a core syllable that is otherwise well formed with respect to the more universally based principles developed above. This rule is expressed in (13).

(13)   N′
$$
\begin{array}{cc}
\overset{\displaystyle\Gamma^{\cdots\cdots}}{C\quad x} & \text{(where } x = \begin{bmatrix} -\,\text{sonor} \\ +\,\text{coron} \\ +\,\text{anter} \end{bmatrix})
\end{array}
$$

The presence of this rule might be attributed to the fact that the inflectional suffixes in English are composed of segments drawn from the set of coronal obstruents. In the absence of this rule, many English stems would have defective paradigms. On the other hand, dental-alveolar appears to be the unmarked point of articulation for consonants. One might thus reverse the argument: if the syllable canons are to be augmented, then it is reasonable that the least marked elements will be the first to emerge.

The treatment of the final clusters in cases such as *depth, wild, sixths* remains an outstanding problem. The following major alternatives have been proposed. The rule in (13) simply adds the coronals to the coda at a later stage in the derivation (level 2 or postlexical). Once incorporated, the resultant syllable is no different from a syllable such as *help* (14a). Alternatively, the special status of the coronal clusters has been indicated structurally by housing them in an *appendix* that is adjoined either to the preceding syllable ((14b); see Halle and Vergnaud 1980) or to a higher-order (prosodic) constituent such as the phonological word ((14c); see Booij and Rubach 1984). Still another approach does not relate the coronals to the preceding syllable in any special way. Two varieties of this approach can be distinguished. One simply licenses such segments at the edge of the word (or other relevant domain) by a special rule or stipulation ((14d); see Itô 1986). The other houses the coronals as onsets to syllables that contain an empty nucleus (Kaye 1990b) or null vowel (Burzio 1988). This option produces the analysis in (14e).

(14) a.

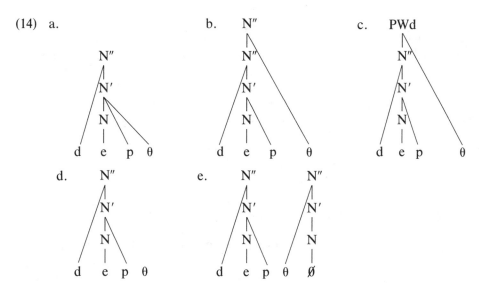

Instead of Kiparsky's (1981) three-slot rime, Borowsky (1986, 1989) interprets the shortening contrasts between *drēam, drĕam-t* vs. *drēam-ed* and *fīve, fĭf-th* vs. *fīve-s* as reflecting a level 1 restriction of English that limits syllable rimes to two slots VX plus a final "extrasyllabic" consonant (see section 6.7). *Dream* thus has the analysis {dree}⟨m⟩, with angled brackets marking the extrasyllabic consonant. When the level 1 suffix [-t] is added, the [m] is no longer at the edge of the domain and hence loses its extrasyllabicity; it syllabifies and the root vowel then shortens to maintain the restriction on two-slot syllable rimes: {drĕm}⟨t⟩. Since Structure Preservation does not hold at level 2 (recall section 5.8.1), addition of the regular past tense inflection occasions no shortening; rather, the syllable is allowed to expand to take in the [m], creating a three-position rime: {dreem}⟨d⟩ (with the final [d] in the syllable appendix). Since the rime is limited to two slots at level 1, it is predicted that nonfinal syllable rimes will be composed of just a long vowel or a short vowel plus a single consonant. In fact, both VVC and VCC rimes occur, but they are largely restricted to consonants that agree in point of articulation with a following consonant: *chāmber, council, maintain; antler, symptom, texture.* Only a few exceptions to this generalization exist: for example, *deictic, arctic, sculptor.* If this analysis is correct, it suggests that restrictions on the size of syllabic constituents are not merely a function of the number of segmental slots but must take account of the segments filling the slots in such a way that sharing a place of articulation with a following consonant reduces the overall phonotactic burden of the cluster in ways that remain to be understood.

6.4 Medial versus Marginal Clusters

As we have just seen, strict restrictions on consonant clustering are often relaxed at the margins of the word. This point is further illustrated by Rubach and Booij's (1990) findings on Polish syllabification. Polish is notorious for its consonant clustering, making syllabification appear chaotic. For instance, *pstry* [pstri] 'mottled' starts with four consonants and *przestępstw* [pšestempstf] 'crime' gen.pl. ends in five consonants. Furthermore, many Polish clusters violate the SSP. Some examples are listed in (15), where N = nasal, L = liquid, V = vowel, S = sonorant, O = obstruent, and the letter *y* stands for the vowel [ɨ]. Cases such as *rtęć* 'mercury' are monosyllabic rather than disyllabic with a syllabic liquid. Polish speakers perceive just a single sonority peak in such words; more importantly, the language's penultimate stress rule fails to place a stress on the [r].

(15) #NN,NN#   **mn**ożyć 'multiply', hy**mn** 'anthem'
      #LNV   **ln**u 'linen' gen.sg.
      VNL#   Kre**ml** 'Kremlin'
      #SOV   **rt**ęć 'mercury', **lw**y [lvɨ] 'lions'
      VOS#   my**śl** 'idea', ry**tm** 'rhythm', tea**tr** 'theater'

A closer look, however, reveals that the SSP is involved in Polish too, just as in English. First of all, the sonority violations occur almost exclusively at the margins of the word; while the initial or final consonant may violate the SSP, internal clusters are more severely constrained. Two sorts of evidence support this contention. First, while consonant triples freely combine obstruents, sonorants are out of sequence only at the edge of the word. For instance, in *lśnić* 'shine' the initial liquid is misaligned; but the [śn] substring conforms to the SSP. Rubach and Booij state that an initial liquid-nasal-obstruent string that reverses the sonority curve in the second and third positions is impossible. Similarly, while *sióstr* 'sister' gen.pl. terminates in a postconsonantal liquid, a final C-liquid-C sequence is impossible. (A few initial triples with an internal liquid are found, however (e.g., *krtań* 'larynx'); see Gussmann 1992 for discussion and alternative analysis.) We may account for these phonotactics by having the SSP erect core syllables and then incorporate the violations at the word margins.

This analysis is supported by the syllabification of word-internal clusters. Testing the intuitions of Polish university students, Rubach and Booij report variation in the parsing of obstruent + consonant strings, with a clear preference for maximal onsets. The favored syllabifications of *dobry* 'good' and *pat*[š]*eć* 'look' are thus *do.bry* and *pa.t*[š]*eć*, though *dob.ry* and *pat.*[š]*eć* are possible as well. These results contrast sharply with judgments concerning sonorant + obstruent clusters. For these the only syllabification possible is the one that splits the cluster: [kor.mo.ran], never [ko.rmo.ran] 'cormorant'; [kon.takt] and [par.tia], never [ko.ntakt], [pa.rtia] – even though [rt] is a possible initial cluster (*rtęć* 'mercury'). If the SSP controls word-internal syllabifications, then sonorant + obstruent strings will never be incorporated into the onset. They can only arise at the left edge of the word by a language-particular rule. We will see several other manifestations of this medial-marginal asymmetry in this chapter.

Clements (1990) conjectures that the stricter requirements on medial clusters reflect an avoidance of ambiguous parsing. If the SSP bars the medial C_i of a VCC_iCV string from the preceding coda and the following onset, then language-particular rules would be required to syllabify such a segment. If the language has heavy clustering at both the right and left word margins anyway, such that $\#C_iC$ and $CC_i\#$ are attested, then the assignment of the medial consonant in a

VCC$_i$CV string will be ambiguous. Both VCC$_i$.CV and VC.C$_i$CV divisions would be consistent with the syllabifications found at the word margins. Precisely this issue arises in Polish in medial clusters composed of a sonorant trapped between two obstruents, as in *piosnka* 'song'. Rubach and Booij report considerable variation in the intuitions of Polish speakers concerning the syllabification of the [snk] string – in marked contrast to the virtual unanimity of intuitions in cases like [kon.takt].

Unlike in English, there are not many phonological rules in Polish that directly refer to syllable structure and hence can corroborate the above analysis. In the absence of such information, one might then question the motivation for introducing the syllable into the analysis. What good does it do and what evidence could the language learner rely on to construct the proper syllabifications? From the perspective of current generative grammar, this is an erroneous view of syllabification. The core syllable-building rules and the SSP are assumed to be part of UG and hence are necessarily present in any particular language that develops from UG. On this view, organizing the phonemic string into syllables is an activity that comes naturally to the child and hence does not have to be learned. What must be shaped by language development are certain options such as whether onsets may be augmented, whether the rime is restricted to three positions, and so on.

It turns out that there is evidence crucially relying on the syllable at a few small corners in the phonology of Polish. One such piece of evidence concerns the comparative suffix, which is normally *sz* [š] but takes the allomorph [ejš] when the preceding stem ends in a C-sonorant string. Several examples are given in (16), where *y* = [ɨ], *ł* = [w], *cz* = [č], *rz* = ž < [r'], and *j* is the palatal glide.

(16)	grub-y	grub-sz-y	'fat'
	młod-y	młod-sz-y	'young'
	star-y	star-sz-y	'old'
	prost-y	prost-sz-y	'simple'
	tę[m]p-y	tę[m]p-sz-y	'blunt'
	podł-y	podl-ejsz-y	'mean'
	szczodr-y	szczodrz-ejsz-y	'generous'
	czarn-y	czar[ń]-ejsz-y	'black'
	fajn-y	faj[ń]-ejsz-y	'nice'

If the SSP guides the construction of core syllables, then the comparatives of *te*[m]*p-y* and *podł-y* contrast in a natural way: the latter terminates in an unparsed consonant, while the former has syllabified all of its consonants (17a).

(17) a.   temp-š   podl-š

b. [š] → [ejš] / C' _____

We can now express the allomorphy as (17b), a rule that transforms the com-

parative suffix [š] to [ejš] after an extrasyllabic consonant (abbreviated as C').
(Forms such as *czarńejszy* and *fajńejszy* suggest that Polish does not incorporate
more than a single sonorant into its core coda – perhaps reflecting a sonority
distance requirement.) If the decision to organize phonemes into syllables had to
be motivated on language-particular grounds, then it is very unlikely that the
concept could play a role in the phonology of Polish because the evidence forcing
its postulation is so diffuse. But if syllabification is a product of UG, then the
organization is present in all languages and available to any particular rule.

6.5   Core Syllables in Ancient Greek and Sanskrit

In this section we will extend our theory of syllabification with material from
Greek and Sanskrit. Our discussion focuses on the major results of Steriade's
(1982) influential study of these languages. For Ancient Greek, in addition to the
rules and phonotactic constraints of the grammar, certain metrical conventions
provide evidence concerning the syllabification operative in the language. The
opposition between light and heavy syllables lies at the base of the metrics. Normally the first vowel in a VCCV sequence scans as heavy. But an optional metrical
rule (correptio Attica) counts this vowel as light when the following consonant
cluster is composed of a stop plus sonorant. Since these clusters have rising
sonority, it is natural to conclude that they syllabify as onsets (V.CCV) while all
other clusters span the syllable break (VC.CV). In the latter case the consonantal
coda counts as the increment of quantity making the syllable heavy.

   The contrast between these two types of clusters shows up elsewhere in Greek.
One noteworthy place is in the perfect of the verb. Greek perfects are marked
by a CV prefix whose vowel is [e] and whose consonant position sometimes
reduplicates the initial consonant of the following root. Examples are cited in (18).
(The root vowel is often altered ("ablauted") in the perfect.)

(18)		root	perfect	
	a.	lū	le-luka	'untie'
		sēman	se-sēmēna	'signify'
	b.	angel	āngelka	'announce'
		opʰel	ǭpʰēlēka	'owe'
	c.	klepʰ	ke-klopʰa	'steal'
		tlā	te-tlamen	'endure'
		knai	ke-knēsmai	'scrape'
		pneu	pe-pneuka	'breathe'
		grapʰ	ge-grapʰa	'write'
	d.	sper	e-sparmai	'sow'
		zdeug	e-zdeugmai	'yoke'
		kten	e-ktona	'kill'
		psau	e-psauka	'touch'
		smukʰ	e-smugmai	'smolder'

When the root begins with a single consonant, there is reduplication (18a). When the root begins with a vowel, there is no reduplication; the prefix and root vowels contract: [e] + V → V: (18b). When the root begins with a cluster, sometimes the first consonant reduplicates (18c) and other times it does not (18d). Careful examination of the reduplicating clusters reveals that they are composed of a stop plus sonorant – exactly the clusters that the metrical evidence suggests are onsets word-medially. Most of the clusters in (18d) violate the SSP. There are some (e.g., [sm]) that have a rising sonority profile yet still fail to reduplicate. We put these aside for the moment.

The important question is how to distinguish between the reduplicating and nonreduplicating clusters in a natural way. Steriade shows that if the SSP controls the construction of core onsets, then exactly the correct distinctions are drawn. Since the clusters in (18c) have rising sonority, they will parse as core onsets. But the initial consonants in (18d) will fail to enter the onset; we assume they are incorporated by a language-particular adjunction rule. If the rule spelling out the perfect prefix, stated informally in (19a), applies between the construction of the core syllable and the adjunction rule, then the contrast between (18c,d) is accounted for. Derivations for the pair *ke-klop^{h}a* 'steal' and *e-ktona* 'kill' are shown in (19b); tautosyllabic segments are enclosed in curly brackets.

(19)   a.   [e] → [C$_i$e] / ——— $_{stem}$[C$_i$
                                                    |
                                                   N″

b. | klop^{h}a | ktona | klep^{h}a | ktena | UR |
|---|---|---|---|---|
| {klo}{p^{h}a} | k{to}{na} | {kle}{p^{h}a} | k{te}{na} | SSP |
| {e}{klo}{p^{h}a} | {e}k{to}{na} | | | prefixation |
| inappl. | {ek}{to}{na} | inappl. | inappl. | coda rule |
| {ke}{klo}{p^{h}a} | inappl. | inappl. | inappl. | reduplication |

In the first step, the SSP constructs core syllables. We assume that Ancient Greek maximizes onsets; the entire [kl] cluster in [klop^{h}a] thus enters the onset while only the second element of the [kt] cluster in [ktona] does. On the next cycle, the prefix is added and its vowel is assigned to a nucleus. The initial [k] in the root for 'kill' is free and thus may enter the coda with the preceding vowel. But the initial consonant of [klop^{h}a] may not, since it was parsed on the preceding cycle. Given the different syllabifications, we now have a natural representational difference to which the reduplication rule may refer: whether or not the initial consonant of the stem belongs to a core onset (is immediately dominated by N″). The prefix thus reduplicates the initial consonant in [klop^{h}a] but not that in [ktona].

Turning now to the unprefixed roots, we have two options. The [k] in [ktena] 'kills' might be adjoined to the initial syllable by a special rule. Alternatively, it might remain unsyllabified. As we will see momentarily, there are reasons to maintain the former position. Anticipating this result, we state the rule in (20) that adjoins a single stray consonant to the syllable in word-initial position.

(20) [C   C   [C   C
      | →   \\ |
      N″   \\   N″
                           \\ |
                              N″

Given this rule, the initial clusters in (18d) are now fully syllabified. Following the terminology introduced earlier, we will refer to the onsets in (18c) as *core onsets* and those in (18d) as *marginal onsets*.

Let us now turn to syllable codas in Ancient Greek. (21) shows the kinds of medial clusters found on the surface (focusing on the most salient features of the Greek coda; see Steriade 1982 for discussion of additional complexities). They are parsed into C_1 + core onset strings.

(21) a.   V-sonorant: ar.nos 'lamb', ar.tʰron 'joint', an.tʰrōpos 'man'
      b.   V-s: ʰes.pe.ra 'evening', as.tron 'star', as.tʰma 'panting'
      c.   V-stop: ok.tō 'eight', skēp.tron 'scepter', tit.tʰos 'breast'
      d.   V-sonorant-stop: ark.tos 'bear', tʰelk.tron 'charm', pʰtʰenk.tos 'ut-
            tered', pemp.tos 'sent'

As we see, the C_1 string may be represented by a single consonant selected from any position on the sonority scale (21a,b,c) or by two consonants chosen from opposite regions of the scale (21d) – in the order of falling sonority, of course. The syllabification of the [elktro] substring in a form such as *tʰelk.tron* proceeds straightforwardly from the UG SSP. The universal onset rule assigns [r] to the onset, which is then augmented with [t] [{e}lk{tro}n]. The onset does not expand further since [k] is not less sonorous than [t]. The [lk] substring now remains to be picked up by the coda rules. After incorporation of the [l] [{el}k{tron}], the less sonorous stop [k] may be added [{elk}{tron}].

This analysis of Greek syllabification is independently supported by the existence of underlying consonant clusters that do not reach the phonetic surface intact. They suppress one of their components. Our syllabification procedure precisely isolates the suppressed consonants. A survey of the relevant types appears in (22).

(22) a.   stop-*s*-stop: /ge-grapʰ-stʰai/ 'to have been written' → ge-grapʰ-[ ]tʰai
      b.   stop-*s*-nasal: /ploksmos/ 'locks' → plok[ ]mos
      c.   nasal-*s*-stop: /pepʰan-stʰe/ 'you have been revealed' → pepʰan-[ ]tʰe

First consider (22a). The [s] cannot be assigned to a core onset; it does not have a lower sonority value than the following stop. For the same reason, it cannot be assigned to the preceding coda. It thus remains a "stray" consonant. Letting the tick stand for an unsyllabified segment, we may account for the cluster simplification by the simple rule of *stray erasure* in (23). This rule deletes the unsyllabified [s] in (22a): {ge}{grapʰ}s{tʰai} → {ge}{grapʰ}{tʰai}.

(23) C′ → ∅

In order to maintain (23), the initial consonant of a form such as *kten-a* from (18d) must be exempted. As in the case of the dentals in English *si*[ksθs], this can be done by invoking a later adjunction rule. The Greek metrics treat various #CCV strings differently when embedded in the phrase. The initial vowel of a V#CCV string scans as light when the consonant cluster forms a core onset, but as heavy otherwise. Steriade (1982) shows that stray erasure in Greek operates in the lexical phonology. Consequently, the first consonant in *kten-a* must be syllabified or otherwise licensed to escape deletion. But when the words are embedded in a phrase, the postlexical phonology must be able to discriminate between the two types of #CCV clusters to explain the metrical contrast. This distinction is drawn rather naturally if it is the adjunction rule in (20) (or one of the other alternatives mentioned in (14)) that saves the initial consonant from stray erasure. Simple onset augmentation would merge the contrast between the two types of cluster that is crucial for the subsequent phrasal phonology.

Let us now consider the remaining cases of cluster simplification in (22). The simplest hypothesis is that they also follow from stray erasure (23). This hypothesis is supported by the fact that the types of cluster involved are exactly those that the reduplication evidence suggests are not core syllables. For example, just as the lack of reduplication in the perfect *e-smugmai* (root [smukʰ] 'smolder') suggests that [sm] is not a core onset, so does the cluster simplification in (22b) *plok*[ ]*mos*. Since stop + nasal clusters are core onsets, [s] + nasal must be treated differently. One way to derive this result is to introduce finer distinctions in the sonority scale on a language-particular basis. Steriade (1982) pursues this hypothesis and partitions obstruents into stops and fricatives, assigning the latter a greater degree of sonority. Fricatives and nasals then occupy adjacent positions in the sonority scale. As with the English onset, we might now require a certain increment of sonority to separate elements of the core onset. The fricative [s] can then be prevented from combining with the following nasal. The same minimal sonority distance requirement seems to operate in the codas as well. Recall that the Ancient Greek codas that surface consist of a sonorant plus voiceless stop (21d). Evidently the elements comprising the [ns] string in (22c) are too close in sonority to form a legitimate coda. Given the sonority scale "stop-fricative-nasal-liquid," the reduplication and cluster simplification facts now follow if we require an interval of two positions between members of core onsets and core codas. Also, if the elements in the onset and coda must be separated by a two-step interval on the four-position sonority scale, it then follows that no core onset or coda can contain more than two members. This correctly predicts an upper bound of four for word-medial intervocalic clusters in Greek. It also leads to the conjecture (not so far well supported) that the number of positions available in a core onset or coda does not in general have to be stipulated but instead follows from setting the sonority distance parameter properly.

For other data not considered here, Steriade shows that not only the stop versus fricative contrast but also the voicing and point of articulation of the consonants must be taken into account in the precise definition of the core syllable for Greek. She proposes to adjust the definition of sonority on a language-particular basis in order to capture these finer distinctions. Most other researchers have preferred to retain the more traditional and general definition of the sonority scale given in

(4); they try to explain the role of voicing and place of articulation (especially coronal versus noncoronal) in other terms (see section 9.11 for brief discussion; see also Goldsmith and Larson 1990 for proposals to allow sonority settings to vary from one language to another as well as to take on nonintegral values as a function of the local context).

The perfect reduplication and cluster simplification found in the Sanskrit aorist displays variations on the same general syllabification themes observed in Greek. On the surface, Sanskrit reduplication looks rather different.

(24)	a.	C	tud	tu-tud	'push'
			rud^h	ru-rud^h	'obstruct'
	b.	stop + sonorant	jña:	ja-jña:	'know'
			dru	du-druv	'run'
	c.	s + sonorant	smi	si-ṣmi	'smile'
			śrat^h	śa-śrat^h	'slacken'
	d.	stop + s	kṣam	ca-kṣam	'endure'
			psa:	pa-psa:	'devour'
	e.	s + stop	stu	tu-ṣtu	'praise'
			ścut	cu-ścut	'drip'
	f.	stop + s + sonorant	kṣṇu	cu-kṣṇu	'whet'

First of all, the phonology of the CV prefix is slightly different in that the vowel also reduplicates. Second, the prefixal consonant reduplicates not only the initial member of clusters whose elements come from opposite poles of the sonority spectrum (24b) but, unlike in Greek, also those occupying adjacent regions (24c). Furthermore, as evidenced by the forms in (24d), obstruent clusters whose second element is a coronal fricative also reduplicate the initial consonant; ([k] becomes [c] by another rule). This follows if we accept the proposal to partition the obstruents into stop versus fricative subclasses: the resultant stop-fricative sequence has rising sonority and thus qualifies as a core onset. Further support for this move appears in (24e), where the [s] of an s + stop cluster is not copied. If [s] is truly more sonorous, then onset augmentation fails to incorporate it next to a stop. Sanskrit's larger inventory of reduplicating clusters is matched by a correspondingly smaller number of clusters showing stray erasure. Unlike Greek, Sanskrit preserves an interconsonantal [s] adjacent to a nasal (25a).

(25)	a.	a-ta:r-ṣ-ma	'we passed'
		yut-s-mahi	'we fought'
		a-tan-s-ta	'you stretched'
		a-ka:r-ṣ-tam	'you did'
	b.	/a-rud^h-s-ta/ → /a-rud^h-[ ]-ta/	'you obstructed'
		→ surface *a-rud-d^{h}a* by Bartholomae's Law	
		/śap-s-ta/ → śap-[ ]-ta	'you cursed'
		/a-prk-s-t^{h}a:s/ → a-prk-[ ]-t^{h}a:s	'you mixed'

In fact, the only deletions occur when the [s] is trapped between stops (25b). But this is exactly where the UG SSP does not incorporate the [s] into a core syllable! Finally, note that since Sanskrit builds onsets and codas from adjacent regions of the sonority spectrum, longer onsets and codas are possible. This prediction finds some confirmation in the existence of a few core onsets containing three elements (24f).

The Sanskrit data thus motivate essentially the same syllable-building routine that we saw operating in Ancient Greek. A small distinction in just one parameter (distance apart on the sonority scale) accounts for the observed differences in (i) reduplication, (ii) cluster simplification, and (iii) onset length. More generally, the reduplication and cluster simplification patterns crucially depend on the distinction between core and marginal syllables. It is hard to see how a distinction of this nature could be learned. But if a sonority-based syllabification of the phonemic string is contributed by UG, then the core-marginal distinction will automatically be imposed, elucidating not only the inner nature of the reduplication and cluster simplification alternations but more importantly how they might plausibly develop in the course of language acquisition. Steriade's (1982) study was a major advance; it demonstrated that the syllable is not just relevant for the assignment of allophones but essential to understanding processes operating at deeper levels of the grammar.

6.6   Continuous Syllabification and Syllable Templates

In the earliest works introducing the syllable into generative phonology, syllabification is performed by a battery of rules applied at a single point in the derivation (Kahn 1976) or cyclically (Steriade 1982). An alternative view has emerged according to which at least a rudimentary organization into syllables holds at all levels of phonological representation (McCarthy 1979a). There is no point where syllabification originates or ceases. Proponents of this view point to allomorphy rules such as the Polish comparative (section 6.4) that apply at the earliest stage of the derivation and still require a syllabification of the base.

Another argument for continuous syllabification comes from successive steps in the derivation, each of which requires a reparsing of the phonemic string. The syllabically defined rules of syncope and epenthesis in many Modern Arabic dialects illustrate this point. For example, in the Bedouin dialect of the Bani-Hassan (Irshied 1984) word-final consonants syllabify as onset to a following vowel: *ðarab alwalad* 'he hit the boy' is parsed [ða.ra.b al.wa.lad]. When resyllabification opens a syllable whose nucleus is an unstressed high vowel, syncope occurs: *širib almáyyah* 'he drank the water' is realized as [šír.b almáyyah]. (That the [i] of *širib* cannot be inserted is clear from such CVRC nominals as *šírb* 'a drink'.) The syncope can be expressed as deletion of a high vowel when it is the final phoneme in the syllable (N″) and medial in the phrase.

(25)   V $\rightarrow \emptyset /$ _____]$_{N''}$ W   (where W is some phonological material and V
         [+high]   is unstressed)

As in other Arabic dialects, clustering of consonants is avoided through epenthesis. While many words begin with a cluster of two consonants in isolation (e.g., *ktáab, lsáan, wtáan*), the first syllabifies as the coda of the preceding syllable as soon as these words are embedded in a phrase. The nucleus may be contributed by the final vowel of the preceding word: for example, *ištara ktáab* 'he bought a book' is parsed [iš.ta.ra k.taab]. If the preceding word ends in a consonant, as in *ištarat* 'she bought', epenthesis occurs: [ištara.t ik.taab]. The epenthesis rule can be expressed as (26), where C′ is an unsyllabified consonant.

(26) $\emptyset \rightarrow$ [i] / ____ C′

We can now ask what happens when *ktáab* is placed after a verb such as *fíhim* 'he understood', which contains an unstressed high vowel. The answer is that epenthesis feeds syncope: [fíh.m ik.táab] 'he understood a book'. In the derivation of this phrase, syllabification is relevant at each step. First, a stray consonant must be defined in order to initiate epenthesis: [k′.táab] → [ik.táab]. The word-final consonant then resyllabifies to onset the anaptyctic syllable: [fí.hi.mik.táab]. This in turn opens the final syllable of *fíhim*, leading to its syncope: [fíh.mik.táab]. Consonant clusters that result from syncope are also reparsed into syllables. This point is made by a form such as *yíhrig* 'he burns', which syncopates before a vowel, creating a triconsonantal cluster /yih.r.gal.wa.lad/ that is broken by epenthesis: [yíhirg ál walad] 'he burns the boy'. Finally, in [yíhirg iktáab] 'he burns a book', we see two rounds of resyllabification. First, syllabification of [yíh.rig. k.táab] defines the stray consonant [k′], triggering epenthesis and resyllabification [yíh.ri.g ik.táab]. The resultant open syllable then syncopates, creating a new stray consonant, [yíh.r.g ik.táab], which is housed in an anaptyctic syllable via epenthesis: [yí.hir.gik.táab]. In this case the requirement that the phonemic string parse into syllables guides each step of the derivation.

   Itô (1986, 1989) has used epenthesis sites like those found in Bani-Hassan to argue for *templatic syllabification*. On this view, the grammar defines a template that characterizes the gross prosodic shape of the maximal core syllable (e.g., for Arabic CV(V)C). Syllabification consists in a directional mapping of the phonemic string to appropriate positions in the template, matching vowels with V-positions and consonants with C-positions. Itô shows that templatic syllabification allows a simpler analysis of epenthesis than the syllabification-by-rule model. As we have just seen, on the latter view anaptyxis consists in first defining a stray consonant C′, then inserting an epenthetic vowel before or after the C′, and finally submitting the result to the syllable-building rules, with possible resyllabification. But if syllabification consists in mapping to a preexisting template, then the location of the epenthetic vowel relative to the stray consonant is fixed by the template. What must be specified is its phonetic value. The templatic model restricts the range of epenthesis options in ways that the alternative relying on rules such as (26) does not. The following paragraphs will examine two of these restrictions.

   First, if the language has several epenthesis rules, syllabification-by-rule gives us no reason to expect any correlation in the location of the epenthetic vowel relative to the stray consonant because this must be stipulated in each epenthesis rule. But if epenthesis consists in matching to the syllable template, then the left-to-right/right-to-left direction of template mapping should be fixed for a given language and mirror its direction of syllabification. In support of this idea, Itô points to Spanish, where Harris (1983) postulates three separate epenthesis rules inserting [e] in the contexts #___*s'*C, C___*s'*#, and C___*r'*C (the tick marks the stray consonant): the first accounts for the alternation in *yugo-slavo* 'Yugo-slav' but *eslavo* 'Slavic'; the second for the *-es* plural of *mes* 'month', *mes-es* 'months'; and the third for the alternation in *abr-ir* 'to open' but *aber-tura* 'open-ing'. In each case the inserted [e] lies before the stray consonant: *s*{la}{vo}, {mes}*s*, {ab}*r*{tu}{ra}. This consistent location follows necessarily if Spanish maps its pho-nemic string to a CCVC syllable template in a right-to-left direction: a single stray consonant will enter the syllable coda, because the right edge of the template is the first available consonantal position under right-to-left mapping. Since no vowel is present in the segmental string before the stray [s] in a #___*s*C sequence, the nuclear V-slot of the template is realized as [e]. The adapted loanword *esplín* 'spleen' receives the analysis sketched in (27).

(27)   [C C V C]   [C C V   C]
                        : : : : |
     # s p l i n → s p l i n →   s p l i n →
                                               \\|/
                                                σ

     s p l i n → e s p l i n
     |/ \\|/ | \\|/
     σ   σ   σ   σ

If right-to-left syllabification can be independently motivated for Spanish, then we have evidence for the templatic view.

Another of Itô's arguments for template matching comes from systematic dif-ferences in the location of the epenthetic vowel among various Arabic dialects. Broselow (1982) noted that both the Cairene and Iraqi dialects avoid triconsonantal clusters through epenthesis: in Cairene an [i] is inserted between the second and third consonants, while Iraqi places the vowel between the first and second.

(28)   Cairene: Ø → i / CC ___ C
          ʔul-t   'I said'
          ʔul-t-ilu   'I said to him' from /ʔul+t+lu/

       Iraqi: Ø → i / C ___ CC
          gil-t≈gil-it   'I said'
          gil-it-la   'I said to him' from /gil+t+la/

Under rule-driven syllabification, we stipulate the insertion of the epenthetic vowel after the stray consonant for Cairene and before it for Iraqi (29a). Sub-sequent application of the syllable-building rules organizes the inserted vowel plus stray consonant into a syllable (with possible resyllabification to avoid an onsetless syllable), as in (29b).

(29)   a.   Cairene: ∅ → i / C' _____   Iraqi: ∅ → i / _____ C'

      b.   {ʔul}t{lu}   {gil}t{la}
             {ʔul}ti{lu}   {gil}it{la   epenthesis
             {ʔul}{ti}{lu}   {gi}{lit}{la}   (re)syllabificatic

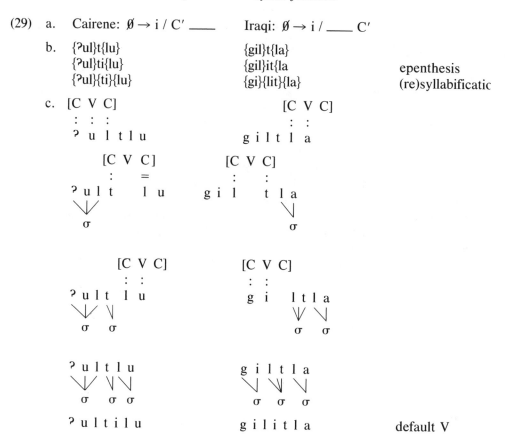

In templatic syllabification, the dialects differ in the direction of mapping to Arabic's CVC template (29c): left to right for Cairene and right to left for Iraqi. (The mapping procedure implicitly assumes a one-segment look-ahead so that VCV parses as V.CV in order to avoid onsetless syllables – a detail marked by the = in (29c) that we overlook here.) Thus, the medial consonant C_i in a VCC_iCV string enters the prevocalic onset in left-to-right Cairene but the postvocalic coda in right-to-left Iraqi (29c). After the mapping is completed, a later default rule supplies the appropriate vowel to the phonemic string, spelling out the nucleus of the epenthetic syllable as [i] in Arabic, [e] in Spanish, and so on.

So far the two models appear equivalent. They predict different outcomes for a VCCCCV string, however. With four intervocalic consonants, the two medial ones are stray: VC.C'C'.CV. Since the CVC syllable template has two consonantal positions, only one epenthetic vowel is required for this case under templatic syllabification. We can guarantee this outcome by requiring syllabification to map as many phonemes as possible to the template – a natural condition to impose on template matching. Furthermore, left-to-right and right-to-left mapping converge on the same output in this case. Consequently, we predict an identical location for the epenthetic vowel in the two Arabic dialects – a true prediction, as shown by the forms in (30a) and their derivations in (30b).

(30) a. <u>Cairene</u>   <u>Iraqi</u>
          ʔultilha 'I said to her'   giltilha 'I said to her'
          from /ʔul+t+l+ha/   from /gil+t+l+ha/

      b.

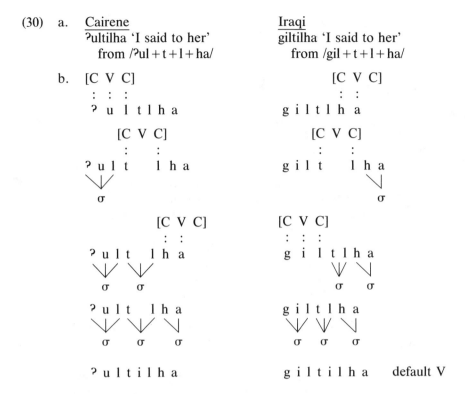

On the other hand, rule-driven epenthesis predicts that an epenthetic vowel should lie adjacent to each stray consonant – to the left in Iraqi and to the right in Cairene, as in (31). But this is incorrect.

(31) <u>Cairene</u>   <u>Iraqi</u>
      {ʔul}tl{ha}   {gil}tl{ha}
      {ʔul}tili{ha}   {gil}itil{ha}   epenthesis
      {ʔul}{ti}{li}{ha}   {gi}{li}{til}{ha}   (re)syllabification

At this point, two observations are in order. First, rule-driven syllabification can simulate the effect of templatic syllabification by applying the epenthesis rules of (29a) in an iterative fashion: left to right in Cairene and right to left in Iraqi. For this to produce the correct results, however, the syllable-building rules must follow each iteration, ensuring that the vowel inserted after [t] in Cairene {ʔul}*til*{ha} takes the following {l} as a coda, bleeding epenthesis to the stray {l}: {ʔul}{til}{ha}. But this grants the template model's basic point that the rules of epenthesis and syllabification are the same basic phenomenon: mapping to the syllable template. Second, the argument from Arabic is complicated by the fact that like Bani-Hassan, the Egyptian and Iraqi dialects have high vowel syncope. So long as the missing vowel predicted by the epenthesis rules in (29a) cannot be excluded by syncope, the argument goes through. More generally, while templatic syllabification simplifies considerably the statement of epenthesis in languages with an elementary syllable inventory such as Arabic, it remains to be tested on languages with more complex onsets and codas.

6.7   Continuous versus Staged Syllabification

If syllabification is reduced to template matching, then epenthesis will, other things being equal, arise on the initial right-to-left/left-to-right scan of syllabification across the string. There are, however, well-known cases in which epenthetic vowels contrast with underlying ones in a fashion that is naturally explained by delaying epenthesis until a later stage in the derivation. For example, in Levantine Arabic dialects such as Palestinian, vowel-initial suffixes allow stress to appear on the initial syllable of a CVCVC verbal root while consonant-initial ones close the root's final syllable, creating a heavy syllable that attracts stress: compare *kátab-u* 'they wrote' and *katáb-na* 'we wrote'. Underlying /katab + t/ 'wrote' 1sg. surfaces with epenthesis in the final cluster but still takes penultimate stress: *katáb-it*. This suggests that the final syllable of the root counts as closed at the point where stress is assigned and thus attracts stress in the same fashion as *katáb-na*. But such a contrast is unavailable if epenthesis occurs on the initial scan of syllabification that feeds stress assignment. Templatic syllabification might accommodate this case by invoking the device of *extrasyllabicity* for final consonants (32a). This diacritic feature allows segments to be made invisible to the syllabification rules or algorithm. Phonologists have attempted to limit access to this powerful device by requiring that only segments at the periphery of a domain can be shielded from the syllabic parse (the so-called *Peripherality Condition*). Once affixation places a segment in medial position, its extrasyllabicity is lost and it becomes subject to syllabification. The [extrasyllabic] diacritic can also be revoked at some later point in the derivation – for example, postlexically. Appeal to extrasyllabicity allows the derivation of (32b) for *katáb-it;* the extrasyllabic consonant is enclosed in angled brackets.

(32)   a. $[+\text{cons}] \rightarrow [+\text{extrasyllabic}] /$ ____ #

   b.   /katab-t/   lexical
        katab-⟨t⟩   (32a)
        {ka}{tab}⟨t⟩   syllabification
        {ka}{táb}⟨t⟩   stress

                           postlexical
        {ka}{táb}t   revocation of extrasyllabicity
        {ka}{tá}{bit}   syllabification (epenthesis)

Although it seems very ad hoc, final extrasyllabicity accounts for other asymmetries of distribution in Arabic (all synchronic reflexes of final vowels that have been lost in the development of the modern dialects from the Classical language). Let us look at two. First, while medial closed syllables count as heavy and hence attract the stress, final ones do not: *katáb-na, kátab-u,* but *kátab* 'he wrote'. If final consonants are extrasyllabic, then [katab] scans as two light syllables and hence is metrically equivalent to *bána* 'he built'. Second, as shown by the paradigm in (33a), long vowels shorten before two consonants. If final consonants are extrasyllabic, then the shortening rule can be expressed as closed-syllable shortening – a widely attested and natural rule (32b).

(33)   a.   stašaar-u   3pl.
             stašar-na   1pl.
             stašaar   3sg.
             'consult'

       b.   /stašaar-u/   /stašaar-na/   /stašaar/
             ─────────   ─────────   stašaa⟨r⟩   (32a)
             s{ta}{šaa}{ru}   s{ta}{šaar}{na} s{ta}{šaa}⟨r⟩   syllabification
             ─────────   s{ta}{šar}{na}   ─────────   closed-syllable
                                                                shortening

In her comparison of templatic and rule-driven syllabification, Itô argues that templatic syllabification can dispense entirely with rules that could utilize the syllabified versus stray nature of a segment as a contextual diacritic for some sound change (for Itô, stray erasure itself is elevated to the status of a UG convention rather than a rule; see section 6.9). However, this conclusion has been challenged by Dell and Tangi (1991a), who formulate two rules for the Ath-Sidhar dialect of Rifian Berber that apply before an unparsed consonant. The first inserts [a] before any [r] that is not followed by a full vowel [i,u,a]. The second deletes nongeminate [r]'s that do not immediately precede a full vowel. The verbal paradigms in (34) show how these processes operate; following Dell and Tangi, schwa is transcribed here as [e] and pharyngealized consonants are transcribed as !C.

(34)

		perfect	imperfect	negative	
a.	UR	CCa	CCi	CC:a	
	/fna/	fna	fni	fenna	'adore'
	/šra/	šra	šri	šarra	'rent'
b.	UR	CCC	CCiC	CC:C	
	/nqs/	nqes	nqis	neqqes	'decrease'
	/frn/	fan	frin	farren	'sort'
c.	UR	CuCC	CuCuC		
	/nudm/	nudem	tt-nudum	'doze'	
	/!surf/	!soaf	!ssuruf	'stride'	

Dell and Tangi's analysis assumes two stages of syllabification. First an underlying vowel plus single preceding consonant combine into a CV syllable. Then remaining strings of unsyllabified consonants are grouped from right to left into CVC syllables whose nucleus is the epenthetic schwa, as indicated by the derivations sketched in (35).

(35) [nqs]   [nqis]   [nqqs]   [nudm]
      ——   n{qi}s   ——   {nu}dm   CV syllabification
      n{qes}   n{qis}   {neq}{qes} {nu}{dem}   coda and epenthesis

If *a*-insertion and *r*-deletion are ordered between these two points of syllabification, then these rules can be defined over a stray (unsyllabified) [r]′, as in (36a). The derivations in (36b) ensue.

(36) a. $\emptyset \rightarrow$ [a] / _____ [r]′
         [r]′ $\rightarrow \emptyset$ (where [r] is not geminate)

      b. /frin/   /frn/   /tt-!suruf/
          f{ri}n   ——   tt-{!su}{ru}f   CV syllabification
          ——   farn   —————————   *a*-insertion
          ——   fan   —————————   *r*-deletion
          ——   {fa}n   —————————   CV syllabification
          f{rin}   {fan}   tt{!su}{ruf}   right-to-left
                                                  coda formation

The *a*-insertion rule must precede epenthesis of schwa; otherwise, /nudm/ and /!surf/ become [nudem] and [!suref] and another otherwise unnecessary rule is needed to delete schwa later to derive the surface forms *nudem* vs. *!soaf*. In this case, unlike in Palestinian Arabic, final extrasyllabicity cannot delay epenthesis because the relevant consonants are not restricted to the right edge of the word. Rather, two rounds of syllabification are required: one triggered by a full vowel and a later one parsing the long strings of consonants for which Berber is justly famous. To accommodate these data, the templatic model must invoke two different templates: CV for the initial stage and CVC for the second, postlexical stage – a move that undermines the theory's basic intuition that syllable structure is the function of a fixed, static set of constraints encapsulated in the template and that takes it a step in the direction of the rule-driven model, which develops the syllable piece by piece through the course of the derivation.

On the other hand, there is evidence that the postlexical syllabification process in Berber requires some appeal to a CVC template. Two such arguments are based on the Ath-Sidhar paradigms in (37), taken from Dell and Tangi 1991b.

(37)

root	= imperative	[θ + root] = 3sg.fem.	[θ + root + m] = 2pl.masc.	
[xzn]	xzen	θexzen	θxeznem	'keep'
[wzn]	wzen	θewzen	θweznem	'weigh'
[uðf]	uðef	θuðef	θuðfem	'enter'

First, as the root [xzn] 'keep' suggests, the location of the epenthetic schwa is a function of the odd/even position of the surrounding consonants with respect to the right edge of the domain (basically the clitic group in this Berber dialect). This follows straightforwardly if the epenthetic vowel emerges from the right-to-left assignment of the consonantal string to onset and coda positions in a CVC template. The derivation in (38) indicates the intended analysis: we might imagine a conveyer belt shunting the phonemes past the syllable template, which assembles them into CVC packages.

(38)

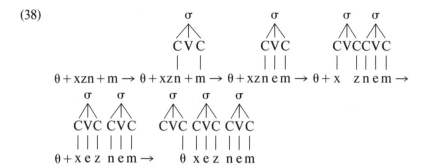

On the rule-driven model, syllabification is initiated by the projection of a nuclear position from some vocalic or otherwise locally sonorous segment. But this is precisely what is missing in Berber underlying representations such as [θ+xzn+m]. We might try to sidestep this stumbling block by somehow contriving to have odd-numbered consonants from the right edge of the word project a nucleus and invoke some later "diphthongization" process to emit a schwa (39).

(39)

$$\begin{array}{cccc} N'' & N'' & N'' & N'' \\ | & | & | & | \\ N & N & N & N \\ | & | & \backslash & \backslash \end{array}$$
θ+xzn → θ+ x z n → θ e xz e n

However, Dell and Tangi (1991b) thwart this move with the second and third members of the paradigms in (37). They illustrate a systematic contrast between high vowels and glides in Berber. If we accept the standard assumption that the high vowel [u] and the glide [w] have the same feature structure and differ in terms of their nuclear/nonnuclear position, then projection of an N category from an odd-positioned glide merges the contrast with vocalic [u]; we fail to capture the distinction between θuðen and θewzen.

(40)

Dell and Tangi account for this contrast by projecting a nucleus from the high vowels in the lexical representation (an idea of Guerssel (1986)) and then allowing the [−consonantal] [w] to enter the coda and onset slots in the template like a consonant. Templatic syllabification then identifies the lexically marked nucleus with the nuclear V-slot of the template (41).

(41)

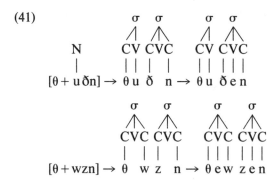

We conclude that some mechanism is required to parse the string of consonants. A CVC template is one option. But the *r*-replacement data from Berber indicate that the template can be altered in the transition from the lexical to the postlexical phonology. Presumably the alterations can be narrowly circumscribed. One reasonable constraint would be that the templates grow to accommodate more material rather than shrink to take in less; (however, see Wiltshire 1992 for apparent counterexamples). While templatic syllabification is a natural method to parse the consonantal strings of Berber, others are conceivable. As we will see in chapter 10, binary grouping is a basic mechanism to impose a metrical stress pattern on a string of syllables. The grouping of consonants (and more generally of phonemes) into syllables is a problem that raises many of the same issues as stress metrification.

To close this section, let us look at a more complex case of staged syllabification from Dell and Elmedlaoui's (1985) work on the Imdlawn Tashlhiyt dialect of Berber (ITB). In most languages segments can be divided into three categories: sounds that always form the syllable nucleus, sounds that never occupy the nucleus, and sounds that alternate between nuclear and nonnuclear positions depending on the context. For example, in French the first class is composed of the nonhigh vowels, the second of all consonants, and the third of high vocoids that alternate between vowels and glides: *loue* [lu] 'rents', *louer* [lwe] 'to rent'. For languages in which the third class is not empty, members are typically drawn from the high vocoids and the sonorant consonants. ITB is remarkable in that the third class spans the entire phonemic inventory. As shown by the examples in (42), any segment including stops may form the nucleus of a syllable. ((42) departs from Dell and Elmedlaoui's transcription, by representing nuclear consonants with an under ring.)

(42)   yattuy   'it is high'
       ikr̥zawn   'he ploughed for you'
       tṛgl̥t   'you locked'
       txzn̥t   'you stored'
       tm̥sx̥t   'you transformed'
       tf̥tk̥t   'you sprained'

Furthermore, unlike in the Ath-Sidhar dialect, in ITB the onset versus rimal (more accurately, nuclear) status of the variable segments is not entirely dependent on their odd-even position in the string. For example, the forms *ratlult* 'you will be born' from [ra-t-lUl-t] and *ratṛglt* 'you will lock' from [ra-t-rgl-t] each contain a string of five variable segments after the initial [ra]. But they nevertheless contrast as disyllabic versus trisyllabic.

In spite of these complexities, Dell and Elmedlaoui show that ITB syllabification follows strict rules governed by the sonority hierarchy. But instead of one directional sweep across the word, syllabification in ITB proceeds in a cascade, one for each level of the sonority scale. Dell and Elmedlaoui formulate the multistaged syllabification algorithm of (43).

(43)   Associate a core (onset-nucleus) syllable with any sequence (Y)Z, where Z
        is a low vowel, a high vocoid, a liquid, a nasal, a fricative, a stop.

According to (43), if the phonemic string contains a free element with the requisite sonority, it forms the nucleus Z of a core onset-nucleus sequence (Y)Z. (44) shows how Dell and Elmedlaoui's algorithm syllabifies underlying [t-IzrUal-In] 'those fem. from Tazrwalt' as *tizṛwalin*. (The transcriptions in (44) abstract away from pharyngealization.)

(44)   [t-IzrUal-In]
     low vowel   t-Izr(wa)l-In
     high vowel   (t-i)zr(wa)(l-i)n
     liquid   (t-i)(zṛ)(wa)(l-i)n

We derive the final form by assuming that onsetless syllables are avoided in non-initial position. The final consonant thus escapes the nasal portion of the syllabification routine (which would otherwise generate [. . . li.ṇ]) and is left to be assigned to a coda by a late adjunction rule. By balking on onsetless syllables, the algorithm avoids creating a sequence of syllabic nuclei. It resembles metrification processes, which frequently avoid the creation of adjacent (clashing) stressed syllables.

We see the importance of avoiding onsetless syllables in the derivation of underlying [I-ḥaUl-tn] 'he made them masc. plentiful' in (45), where the high-sonority [U] forms an onset with the following lower-sonority liquid. If the avoidance of onsetless syllables is not granted priority over the sonority-based syllabification algorithm, we incorrectly form a syllable nucleus on the (U) and derive *iḥaultṇ instead of *iḥawltṇ*.

(45)   [IḥaUltn]
     low vowel   I(ḥa)Ultn
     high vowel   (i)(ḥa)Ultn
     liquid   (i)(ḥa)(wḷ)tn
     nasal   (i)(ḥa)(wḷ)(tṇ)

In cases where a sequence of segments belong to the same sonority rank, Dell and Elmedlaoui report groupings that reflect a left-to-right iteration of the syllabification algorithm. For example, [sUI] with two successive high vocoids appears as *suy* 'let pass' rather than *syu; baynn* 'they masc. appear' from [baIn-n] and *tftkt* 'you sprained' from [t-ftk-t] make the same point, as shown by the derivations in (46). Right-to-left parsing generates the ill-formed **baynn* and **tftkt*.

(46)   [baIn-n]   [t-ftk-t]
    low vowel   (ba)In-n   ———
    high vowel   ———   ———
    liquid   ———   ———
    nasal   (ba)(yn̥)n   ———
    fricative   ———   (tf)tkt
    stop   ———   (tf)(tk̥)t
    coda   (ba)(yn̥n)   (tf)(tk̥t)

To conclude, syllabification in ITB proceeds in a series of steps down the sonority scale. Two observations are in order. First, this stepwise syllabification arguably reflects the unmarked UG option. In most languages the process cuts off at the high vocoids. ITB is unusual in extending it to all segments. Second, while Berber presents good evidence for a stage of core syllabification parsing CV before the incorporation of a coda, there is no comparable evidence for a stage in which syllabic nuclei are parsed without also incorporating a preceding available onset – that is, a stage where CVCV is parsed as C{V}C{V} and then later as {CV}{CV}. (However, see Carreira 1988 for a possible counterexample.)

6.8   Resyllabification

Prevocalic consonants prefer to occupy the syllable onset (part of a more general tendency to avoid onsetless syllables, at least word-medially). In many languages the onsetting of prevocalic consonants takes place even if a grammatical or word boundary intervenes. The result is a misalignment of the morphological and the prosodic structure: a word such as *condensation* divides grammatically as [condens + ation] but syllabifies as [con.den.sa.tion]. In some languages onsetting of prevocalic consonants crosses the word boundary. For example, French and Spanish are well known for syllabifying VC#V as V.C#V; Harris (1983) cites Spanish *Los otros estaban en el avión* 'The others were on the airplane', which syllabifies in casual speech as *Lo.s otro.s es.ta.ba.n e.n e.l a.vion*. In such cases it is natural to ask whether the onsetting consonant occupies the coda of the preceding syllable at an earlier stage of the derivation. When the relevant juncture is the word boundary, one can often detect the earlier coda position. For example, in Canadian French vowels are laxed in closed syllables and diphthongized in open syllables. The masculine form of *petit* 'small' is pronounced [ptˢij] while the feminine *petite* is [ptˢɪt]. When a vowel-initial word follows, the final consonant of the feminine adjective appears in the onset, but the lax vowel is retained: *ta petite amie* 'your girlfriend' is [pt^{s}ɪ.ta.mij]. Consequently, the final consonant must resyllabify from the coda [.pt^{s}ɪt.] (where it laxes the vowel) to the onset with the following word [pt^{s}ɪ.ta.mij]. Since we have assumed that the syllable-building rules operate exclusively on free (unparsed) elements, the resyllabification in French must be the result of a rule that alters the syllabic structure. The rule is stated informally in (47).

(47)   resyllabification: C.V → .CV

In general, such resyllabification only applies before a vowel. In languages where *tr*V is a legitimate onset, a V*t*#*r*V sequence does not (usually) resyllabify to V.*tr*V. (47) is thus best viewed as a device to avoid onsetless syllables.

We might pause to ask for positive evidence that a VC#V sequence has in fact resyllabified to V.C#V so that the consonant is treated as an onset by some rule of the postlexical, phrasal phonology. It turns out that there are few cases of this form on record. One is discussed by Harris (1983) for Spanish, where in emphatic speech [r] is trilled when it occupies the coda. Thus, *ma*[r]*tes* 'Tuesday' and *ma*[r] 'sea' may appear as *ma*[r̄]*tes* and *ma*[r̄] in "highly emphatic" speech. Harris states that when the final rhotic of *ma*[r] is followed by a consonant-initial word, alternation between plain and trilled [r] is possible: *ma*[r≈r̄] *verde* 'green sea'. But no alternation is possible in *ma*[r] *azul* 'blue sea', where the next word begins with a vowel. Harris explains this contrast with the premise that the final consonant has resyllabified to onset position and hence is no longer subject to trilling in the coda. This state of affairs is unusual. Spanish has a number of other rules affecting coda consonants (such as *s*-aspiration and [n]-velarization; see section 5.7) that are not bled by phrasal resyllabification: *tiene*.[h] *e*[h].*pacio* (*tienes espacio* 'do you have room?'), *Ramó*.[ŋ] *en.tró* (*Ramón entró* 'Ramon entered'). An attractive explanation for this asymmetry is that the application of coda-sensitive rules to a VC#V sequence serves as a parsing cue indicating a word division.

If phonological rules apply cyclically, then we might expect consonants to resyllabify in response to a vocalic affix as the derivation proceeds from one cycle to the next. Such resyllabification to avoid onsetless syllables is the key to an intricate pattern of devoicing in German (Rubach 1990). As the alternations in (48a) show, obstruents devoice in word-final position.

(48)   a.   kind-isch   [d]   'childish'   Kind   [t]   'child'
            Tag-e   [g]   'days'   Tag   [k]   'day'
            Häus-er   [z]   'houses'   Haus   [s]   'house'

       b.   jag-en   [g]   'to hunt'
            Jag-**d**-en   [kd] 'hunting' pl.
            Jag-**d**   [kt] 'hunting' sg.

       c.   [−sonor] → [−voiced] / ___
                                    |
                                    N′

However, the paradigm for the stem [jag] in (48b) reveals that obstruents also devoice word-medially: for example, *Ja*[k]*den*. Thus, we cannot simply say that obstruents devoice at the end of a stem. Although this formulation accounts for the devoicing of the [g] in *Jag-d-en* and *Jag-d,* it incorrectly predicts devoicing before the vowel in *jag-en*. In this case, however, the obstruent is a syllable onset. So if devoicing is defined on codas (48c), then all the data are handled correctly. The rule applies in [jag.den] and [tag.] and is inapplicable in [ja.gen]. A purely syllabic context for devoicing is also supported by loanword adaptation: the stem-internal [d] devoices in such words as *Admiral* [t], *Edna* [t], and *Edgar* [t], suggesting the syllabifications [Ad.mi.ral], [Ed.na], and [Ed.gar].

But other data seem to indicate that the location of grammatical boundaries *is* relevant and thus that devoicing cannot be defined in purely syllabic terms. For example, devoicing occurs in *glaub-lich* and *Wag-nis* even though [bl] and [gn] are legitimate onsets (as suggested by forms such as *Blatt* 'leaf' and *Gnade* 'grace').

(49) a.   glaub-en   [b]   'to believe'
           glaub-lich   [p]   'believable'

           wag-en   [g]   'to dare'
           Wag-nis   [k]   'risk'

           Hand   [t]   'hand'
           Händ-e   [d]   pl.
           hand-lich   [t]   'handy'

      b.   Handl-ung   [d]   'act'
           handel-n   [dl̥]   'to act'

           nebl-ig   [b]   'foggy'
           Nebel   [bl̥]   'fog'

More puzzling still is the fact that while there is devoicing in *hand-lich* and *glaub-lich,* the same [dl] and [bl] strings fail to devoice in *Handl-ung* and *nebl-ig* (49b). The difference systematically correlates with the location of the stem boundary: the consonants are tautomorphemic in *Handl-ung* and *nebl-ig,* while a morpheme boundary separates the clusters in *hand-lich* and *glaub-lich*. It thus appears that the devoicing rule must take account of the grammatical boundaries after all.

The key to this puzzling set of data lies in the observation that the [l] is syllabic in the related words *handel-n* (*han*[dl̩n]) and *Nebel* (*Ne*[bl̩]). More generally, the sonorant consonants of German are syllabic in the contexts C ____ # and C ____ C – that is, when they cannot be assigned to an onset or coda by the SSP. This can be treated as a variety of anaptyxis in which the stray sonorant forms the nucleus of the emergent syllable, obviating the need for an epenthetic vowel. Following Rubach, let us suppose that syllabification is cyclic. The contrasting *glaub-lich* and *nebl-ig* are then derived as follows. On the root cycle, [b] is assigned to the coda in [glaub-lich]; but in [nebl-ig] it occupies an onset to the syllabic sonorant, assuming that anaptyxis of a stray consonant is a cyclic rule. Alternatively, German may simply extend the SSP to sonorant consonants in a manner that partially mimics the syllabification observed in Imdlawn Tashlhiyt Berber in section 6.7.

(50)　a.　[glaub] → [glaub]
　　　　　　　　　　　 N″

　　c.　[glaub] lich → [glaub] lich
　　　　　　　　　　　　 N″　　　N″ N″

　　b.　[nebl] → [ne bl'] → [ne bḷ]
　　　　　　　　 N″　　　N″ N″

When -*lich* is affixed to [glaub], the [l] will be onset to the [i]. But the [b] remains in the coda of the preceding syllable: [glaub.lich]. It is not free, and onset augmentation (5a) applies only to free, unparsed elements. The [b] thus remains in the coda (50c), where it devoices by (48c). To explain why there is no devoicing in *glaub-en,* the [b] must resyllabify to onset the following syllable, by (47): [glaub.ən] → [glau.bən]. Postcyclic devoicing now correctly fails to apply. Finally, in *nebl-ig* we derive a sequence of two successive nuclei: the consonantal sonorant and the suffixal vowel, [ne.bḷ.iç]. Here Rubach reports a fair amount of idiosyncrasy as to whether the two syllables merge, depending on the particular consonants involved and other factors.

For our purposes, the most important point is that we may retain the purely syllabic formulation of coda devoicing (48c). But this requires a cyclic assignment of syllabification and a structure-changing rule to resyllabify a coda consonant to onset a suffixal vowel – a reflex of the more general tendency to avoid onsetless syllables that we see operating across word boundaries in many languages.

Clements (1990) interprets VC.V → V.CV resyllabification as reflecting a more general *Sonority Dispersion Principle* (SDP) that prefers to maximize the sonority slope in the "demisyllable" formed by the onset + nucleus and to minimize this value in the nucleus + coda demisyllable. He formulates an equation that generates the following rankings for initial and final two- and three-position demisyllables (V = vowel, G = glide, L = liquid, N = nasal, O = obstruent).

(51)　a.　CV: OV > NV > LV > GV
　　　b.　VC: VG > VL > VN > VO
　　　c.　CCV: OLV > ONV; OGV > NLV; NGV > LGV
　　　d.　VCC: VGL > VLN; VGN > VGO; VNO > VLO

This scale ranks OLV as the most optimal three-member initial cluster and VGL as the optimal final cluster. OLV spans the sonority gamut from O to V and places its second element squarely in the middle of the five-position (O-N-L-G-V) scale. ONV and OGV also run the sonority gamut but combine two adjacent positions and hence are less optimal. NLV and NGV are worse still since they fail to span the scale; LGV is worst of all because it comprises three successive positions at the high end of the scale. The inverse VGL, on the other hand, is the best syllable rime, since it minimizes the sonority drop from the peak.

Clements's SDP ties together a number of generalizations that have emerged in the study of syllabification. First, it is supported by implicational universals derived from Greenberg's (1978) survey of phonotactic patterns in the descriptive literature – for example, that ONV implies the presence of OLV (e.g., Ancient Greek). The SDP accounts for languages such as Lama whose rimes are restricted to vowel-glide or vowel-sonorant (exercise 1.13): such high-sonority codas minimize the sonority drop in the syllable rime. Second, the SDP successfully isolates CV as the optimal syllable: the presence of an onset ranks it ahead of an onsetless syllable and the absence of a coda ranks it before (C)VC syllables. Consequently, we derive the generalization that every language has the CV syllable. Another corollary is the tendency for vowel-initial words to acquire an onset (prothesis) and consonant-final words to lose their consonant. In addition, single-onset consonants can be expected to move down the sonority scale and single-coda consonants to move up the scale. This accounts for the tendency of onset glides to harden to obstruents (Basque) and obstruent codas to sonorize (Japanese).

Finally, the SDP explains some characteristic syllabifications of intervocalic consonant clusters noted by Murray and Vennemann (1983). Three of these bear mentioning. First, [ap.a] is the worst "syllable contact" since the preceding syllable has a sharp sonority fall in its rime and no sonority rise in the following demisyllable. [a.pa] optimizes the syllable contact by terminating the first syllable with high sonority and starting the next with low sonority. The first demisyllable thus minimizes the sonority curve while the second maximizes it. Given these sharply different evaluations of VC.V and V.CV strings, the strong tendency to resyllabify VC.V to V.CV begins to make sense. Second, the SDP explains the tendency to parse the stop-liquid sequence of [atra] as [a.tra] instead of [at.ra] but to split the inverse cluster in [ar.ta] (52). The latter combines a relatively gently sloping rime with a sharply sloping initial demisyllable; [a.tra] increases the sonority break between the syllables even more with its nonsloping rime and sloping initial demisyllable; and [at.ra] is dispreferred since the falling slope in the rime is steeper than the following rise. Thus, the trough in the sonority wave is optimally an onset. Finally, the SDP explains the second link in the diachronic chain *venirá > venrá > vendrá* found in the evolution of the Spanish future as one that increases the sonority slope of the onset through the insertion of the stop.

(52)
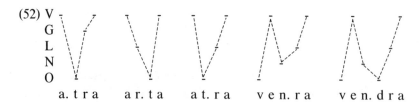

In each of these syllable contacts, the sonority distance between the close of the first syllable and the initiation of the second is increased. Perhaps this difference helps to perceptually highlight the syllable break, aiding in speech perception; see Mehler et al. 1981 for preliminary evidence that the syllable plays a role in speech perception.

We observed earlier that consonantal accretions to the core onsets and codas constructed by the SSP must be the product of language-particular stipulations.

It is a striking fact that in many systems these accretions are restricted to the class of anterior coronals. In other words, dental/alveolars concatenate more freely than other points of articulation. To briefly illustrate, the well-known example *sixths* [ksθs] terminates in a sequence of three alveolars. Other fricatives are impossible in this position. English codas may combine a fricative with a following stop, but the fricative must be [s]: *asp, fast, ask,* but **a*[fk]. [f] can occur before a stop but only if that stop is [t]: for example, *raft.* The same asymmetry appears in Ancient Greek. Recall that core onsets consist not only of a stop plus liquid but also of a stop plus nasal. However, the nasal must be [n]. While [pn] and [kn] reduplicate as core onsets, there are no cases where stop plus [m] does. In other words, in stop plus consonantal sonorant (nonglide) core onsets, the sonorant is a dental [l,r,n]. We might understand this asymmetry by saying that if a language is going to augment its onset or coda, then the unmarked element is chosen first. (See Paradis and Prunet 1991 for discussion of coronals as the unmarked consonantal place of articulation and dentals as the optimal coronal.) Goldsmith (1990) sees the impossibility of English **a*[fk] as part of a more general tendency to allow just one contrastive feature in the onset or coda. This explains the strong tendency for onset and coda clusters to agree in voicing and more generally in laryngeal and secondary articulation features such as palatalization and labialization. On this view as well, dental functions as a wild card that can be added to any hand. Thus, in Ancient Greek the consonantal sonorant in the core onset can be [l,r,n] but not [m] because dental may not contrast with any other point of articulation in this position.

6.9 Prosodic Licensing and Exhaustive Syllabification

We have seen that many phonotactic restrictions can be understood as constraints on syllabification. In an influential study, Itô (1986) develops a general theory of prosodic licensing to account for syllable-based phonotactics. She interprets syllabification as template matching. Building on McCarthy's (1979a) idea that phonemic material that fails to map to the template is suppressed, she extends stray erasure to a general constraint on phonological representation: all phonological segments must be prosodically licensed. There are two ways to achieve prosodic licensing: association to the syllable template or declaration as extrasyllabic at the edge of the relevant prosodic domain (for marginal consonant clusters). Material that is not prosodically licensed is deleted by Stray Erasure, now raised to the level of a general condition on phonological representation. Stray Erasure functions as a "last resort"; rules of epenthesis or resyllabification across a juncture may rescue a segment from deletion.

One of the most impressive cases supporting this theory is Itô's treatment of certain consonantal truncations in the Australian language Lardil (also see Wilkinson 1988). Examination of Lardil stems such as those in (53a) reveals that the language has a CVC syllable template with a restriction barring labials and velars from the coda unless they are homorganic with a following onset consonant. Coronals enter the coda freely.

(53) a. pir.ŋen   'woman'   wa.ŋal   'boomerang'
         rel.ka   'head'   wu.lun   'fruit species'
         kar.mu   'bone'   ma.yar   'rainbow'
         kan.tu   'blood'   yaR.put   'snake, bird'
         kuŋ.ka   'groin'   ŋam.pit   'humpy'

    b. *[−coron]   (unless homorganic with following consonant)
            |
            N′

The filter in (53b) expresses this constraint; it blocks association of a noncoronal
to the syllable coda unless it is homorganic with a following onset consonant. In
Itô's terms, the onset consonant "licenses" the preceding labial or velar.
   Lardil has stems such as those in (54) in which a final noncoronal alternates
with ∅.

(54) <u>absolute</u>   <u>inflected</u>
      ŋalu   ŋaluk-in   'story'
      thurara   thuraraŋ-in   'shark'

While we could posit a rule to delete final noncoronals, such an analysis fails to
connect the alternation with the fact that such segments are barred from the
syllable coda. If underlying [ŋaluk] is parsed according to the Lardil syllable
template, the final [k] will be stray. The process of stray erasure in (55) makes
the connection to syllable structure explicit.

(55) C′ → ∅

There is further evidence that syllable structure underlies phonological alternations in Lardil. As the data in (56b) show, a final vowel apocopates in stems
containing three or more syllables. This rule is stated in (56a).

(56) a. V → ∅ / VCVC ____ #

      b. <u>absolute</u>   <u>inflected</u>
          yalul   yalulu-n   'flame'
          mayar   mayara-n   'rainbow'
          yiliyil   yiliyili-n   'oyster species'

      c. yukar   yukarpa-n   'husband'
          kantukan   kantukantu-n   'red'

When (56a) is applied to a word such as [kantukantu] 'red', the output [kantukant]
might be expected. But in fact *kantukan* surfaces. We could postulate a rule to
simplify a final CC cluster. But recalling that the Lardil syllable template allows
no clustering of consonants in the onset or the coda, the loss of the final [t] in
[kantukant] can also be subsumed under stray erasure (55) – on the natural assumption that apocope of the nuclear vowel deforms the syllable and that sylla-

bification extends beyond the initial level to govern the output of apocope. The derivation runs as follows.

(57) {kan}{tu}{kan}{tu}   initial syllabification
      {kan}{tu}{kan}t   apocope
      {kan}{tu}{kan}   stray erasure

Striking independent support for this analysis is the fact that the ban on coda labials and velars also constrains the output of apocope. While the stems in (56b) merely apocopate, those in (58a) lose their final consonant as well. If the output of apocope must resyllabify (via template matching), and if the same templatic constraints hold (in particular, (53b)), then coronal-final *yalul* is correctly distinguished from noncoronal-final *putu*, as shown by the derivations sketched in (58b).

(58) a. <u>absolute</u>   <u>inflected</u>
          putu   putuka-n   'short'
          murkuni   murkunima-n   'nullah'
          tipiti   tipitipi-n   'rock-cod species'

      b. {ya}{lu}{lu}   {pu}{tu}{ka}   initial syllabification
          {ya}{lu}l   {pu}{tu}k   apocope
          {ya}{lul}   inappl.   resyllabification
          inappl.   {pu}{tu}   stray erasure

Lardil clearly lends further support to the thesis of continuous syllabification – that the output of a phonological rule is subject to syllabification constraints holding at an earlier point in the derivation. In prosodic licensing theory, syllabification is viewed as a representational constraint that holds at essentially all points in the derivation. This idea is brought out more forcefully by the Lardil stem appearing in [muŋkumuŋku-n] 'wooden axe'. When [muŋkumuŋku] apocopates, the final [k] is desyllabified and hence is subject to stray erasure: {muŋ}{ku}{muŋ}k. But syllable-final [ŋ] is licensed by the following [k] in Lardil. If the latter is removed, then the [ŋ] becomes unlicensed. The fact that the surface form is [muŋkumu] encourages Itô to see the loss of [ŋ] as following from the loss of [k]. More generally, prosodic licensing sees syllabification as a static constraint on representations in which the presence of one element may be contingent on the satisfaction of some condition. Disruption of the latter may lead to unlicensing of the former – remedied by the Stray Erasure principle operating as a last resort. If syllabification is a simple structure-building mechanism operating at a certain point or points in the derivation, then we have no particular reason to expect the second [ŋ] in [muŋkumuŋku] to change its status once it has been assigned to the coda (unless some rule deforms its dominating N″ through elimination of the nucleus). The loss of the [ŋ] in [muŋkumuŋ] is thus surprising under rule-driven syllabification.

This analysis is impressive; it minimizes the language-particular stipulations that must be stated and learned for Lardil to essentially just the apocope rule and the coda constraint. All the remaining alternations follow from the proposed conception of UG – in particular, the idea that stray erasure can be promoted from a language-specific rule to a UG condition on phonological representation. This upgrading of stray erasure is, however, controversial. Let us look at three kinds of problems the proposal faces.

The first concerns pinpointing where the condition is enforced. The prima facie evidence indicates that this point varies from one language to another. Recall from section 5.8 that simplification of the final cluster in English *da*[mn] must preempt the resyllabification that would occur from the addition of the inflectional suffix in *damn-ing:* [dam-iŋ]. But in Canadian French, simplification of final consonant-liquid clusters must wait until phrasal resyllabification has the chance to bleed the process: *théât*[r] *anglais* vs. *théât*[ ] *français*. These cluster simplifications should follow from stray erasure, yet they occur at quite different points in the two languages: on the postcyclic word-level stratum in English but in the phrasal phonology of French. Such a difference is easy to understand if stray erasure is a rule that can be assigned to different sectors of the grammar and ordered with other rules. It is more problematic if stray erasure is regarded as a general condition on phonological representation.

Another possible challenge to generalized stray erasure are the many cases in which constraints on initial syllabification fail to govern the output of phonological rules and thus work differently from Lardil. To take a simple but representative example, in native Hindi stems nasals are homorganic with a following consonant: *lamba* 'tall', *tund* 'sharp', *paṇḍit* 'learned man', *gañǰ* 'marketplace', *uŋgli* 'finger'. The absence of heterorganic clusters can be attributed to a coda constraint barring assignment of a place feature unless it is homorganic with the following consonant. Hindi also has a general syncope rule creating consonant clusters in its wake. But in these clusters there is no requirement that the nasal agree in place features with the following consonant: *sanak* 'craze', *sank-ō:* pl.; *ki:mat* 'price', *ki:mt-i:* adj. The apparent failure to extend the initial syllabification constraints is a frequent phenomenon; it raises doubts about the generality of the Lardil state of affairs. More importantly, it provokes the question, What is the precise syllabic structure of the heterorganic clusters in *sank-ō:* and *ki:m-ti:?* Three different responses have been given to this question.

The most widespread view presumes that the nasal has resyllabified to the coda (to respect continuous syllabification) but the homorganic constraint on nasal codas has been suspended: hence [san.kō:], [ki:m.ti:]. Some researchers propose extending the Lexical Phonology notion of structure preservation to syllabic structures (Borowsky 1986). The failure to extend the coda constraint in Hindi might thus reflect a lexical versus postlexical difference in the inventory of syllable templates. However, it is unclear how many cases of failure to extend the initial syllabification constraints can be explained in these terms. Depending on how widespread the phenomenon is, it potentially jeopardizes the claim that syllabification is a continuous constraint on phonological representation rather than a rule applying at a particular point in the phonological derivation.

Another response denies the premise that *sank-ō:* has changed its initial syllabification and thus that the coda constraint has been violated at all. On this view, the nasal remains in the onset of a syllable with a phonetically null nucleus: [sa.nV.kō:]. The problem then becomes to explain why Lardil does not maintain its apocopated syllables with a null vowel, allowing [putuka] to surface as [pu.tu.kV] (= phonetic *[putuk]). More generally, this view must substantiate the claim that [sa.nV.kō:] is phonologically trisyllabic even though it lacks a medial phonetic vowel. (See Kaye 1990a,b, Kaye, Lowenstamm, and Vergnaud 1990, and Charette 1991 for development of this line of thought.)

A third analysis of *sankō:* also claims that the coda constraint is still in force – not because of a phonetically null nucleus but rather simply because the nasal remains unsyllabified after syncope has removed the nuclear vowel: {sa}*n*{kō:}. But in order to maintain this interpretation, we must drop one of the twin assumptions of prosodic licensing theory: that syllabification is continuous and exhaustive. More generally, this response challenges the upgrading of stray erasure to a UG constraint on phonological representation from its original more modest status as a rule encoding one of a range of possible responses to extrasyllabic material: anaptyxis, resyllabification, deletion, no change.

A final challenge to generalized stray erasure comes from languages with words and phrases containing long strings of consonants lacking any phonemic vowel: for example, Tashlhiyt Berber (Dell and Elmedlaoui 1985) *tftktst, tfktstt* 'you sprained it fem., and then you gave it fem.' or Bella Coola (Bagemihl 1991) *c'ktskᵂc'* 'he arrived'. These languages are usually described as inserting short transitional or excrescent vowels at various points to aid in articulation. The controversial question is whether these vowels reflect a syllabic organization in any phonologically useful sense of the term. Bagemihl (1991) uncovers evidence from Bella Coola reduplication that bears on this question. Let us briefly review his results.

Two of the major Bella Coola reduplication patterns are illustrated in (59a) for vowels and (59b) for sonorants. (In the transcriptions of Bella Coola [ɬ] denotes a lateral obstruent.)

(59) a. | reduplication type | base | reduplication |
|---|---|---|
| CV- | qayt 'hat' | qaqayt-i 'toadstool' dimin. |
| CVC- | yaɬk 'do too much' | yaɬyaɬk contin. |

   b. | | | |
|---|---|---|
| CV- | tlk'ᵂ 'swallow' | tl̩tlk'ᵂ contin. |
| CVC- | mn̥ɬkᵂa 'bear berry' | mn̥ɬmn̥ɬkᵂ-ip dimin. |

The reduplication type (CV or CVC) is lexically determined and often accompanied by subsidiary changes that lengthen, shorten, delete, or insert material: for example, *X'ap* 'go' has the reduplicated form *X'anX'ap*. The fact that interconsonantal sonorants readily reduplicate in both types suggests that they form syllabic nuclei. They also parallel vowels by lengthening the penult in the formation of the habituative: compare *sk'ak'a-c* 'split', *sk'aak'a-c* hab. with *k'nk'nca-c* 'chop', *k'nk'nnca-c* hab. Since we assume that there is no feature [+syllabic], the parallel behavior of the [a] in [qayt] and the [l̩] in [tlk'ᵂ] can only be explained in virtue of their equivalent prosodic status as syllabic nuclei.

The crucial question now becomes the treatment of obstruent stems under reduplication. If their excrescent vowels reflect a rudimentary phonological syllabification, then they should also reduplicate. Bagemihl reports that the majority of such stems do not participate in reduplication at all. Those that do require preliminary modification such as the insertion of a vowel or sonorant to serve as a nucleus.

(60) base   ɬq'   kɬ   sx̣
      insertion   ɬnq'   knɬ   six̣
      reduplication   ɬnɬnq'   knɬknɬ   six̣six̣ → six̣sx̣ (syncope)
      CV/CVC   'slap'   'fall'   'peel'

These data suggest (i) that reduplication is defined in syllabic terms and (ii) that the excrescent vowels found in obstruent stems do not reflect a phonological syllabification. At the point where reduplication is defined, obstruent strings are unsyllabified. In order to reduplicate, a sonorant phoneme must be inserted to project the N″ required for reduplication.

Equally telling is the treatment of the prevocalic strings in (61). (61a) reveals that just a single obstruent reduplicates with the following vowel; recall that [ɬ] is a lateral obstruent. This follows straightforwardly if the SSP constructs the Bella Coola syllable and bars clustering of obstruents in (core) onsets. Syllabic sonorants again parallel vowels (61b).

(61)   base   reduplication
      a.   p'ɬa   p'ɬaɬa   'wink' → contin.
           tq'ɬa   tq'ɬaaɬa-y   'knife' → dim. (vowel
                                          lengthening)
           qpsta   qpstata   'taste' → iterative

      b.   tqn̥k   tqn̥qn̥k   'be under' → 'underwear'
           t'ksn̥   t'ksn̥sn̥   'shoot with bow' → contin.
           pɬtkn̥   pɬtkn̥kn̥-ɬp   'bark of bitter cherry tree' → 'tree'

      c.   p'ɬa   tq'ɬa   qpsta   tqn̥k   t'ksn̥   pɬtkn̥
            \/   \/   \/   \/   \/   \/
            N″   N″   N″   N″   N″   N″

The null hypothesis that the UG SSP syllabifies the phonemic string automatically defines the appropriate inputs to reduplication (61c) (given that Bella Coola allows sonorants as syllabic nuclei). This point is further supported by the forms in (62): here two prevocalic consonants reduplicate instead of just one. These consonant clusters differ from those in (61) in being composed of an obstruent plus sonorant rather than two obstruents.

(62)   xʷnaɬ   'spring of water'   xʷnxʷnaaɬ-i   dimin. (vowel length)
       skma   'moose'   skmkma-y   dimin.
       st'qʷlus   'black bear snare'   st'qʷlqʷlus-i dimin.

To generate these cases, all we need say is that Bella Coola (like English) permits two positions in the core onset. In Bagemihl's analysis, reduplication is performed by left-to-right mapping to a CV (light-syllable) or CVC (heavy-syllable) template that has been prefixed to the root syllable. Since Bella Coola allows sonorants to occupy the syllable nucleus, the [m] fills the V-slot of the template, preempting the appearance of the [a]. The derivation sketched in (63) indicates the intended analysis.

(63) skma →   skma → skma kma
     ╲╲   ╲╲ | | ╲╲
     N″   CV + N″   CV + N″

For our purposes, the most important point is that only the rightmost obstruent of a prevocalic cluster reduplicates. Since Bella Coola defines reduplication in terms of the syllable, we can conclude that the remaining prevocalic obstruents in *qpsta* and *st'q*ʷ*lus* are not syllabified. The question then becomes how they can be spared from stray erasure if the latter is a general constraint on representation rather than a rule that a given language may or may not select. Bagemihl shows that the two most apparent escapes from this dilemma are blocked. We cannot simply extend licensed extrasyllabicity from a single marginal consonant to an entire cluster. While this move could protect the cluster in *qpsta,* there are many word-medial obstruent strings that are unreachable in this way, to say nothing of the all-obstruent words such as *c'ktsk*ʷ*c'* 'he arrived' in which the entire string would have to be extrasyllabic. The other possible response is to say that the obstruents remain extrasyllabic until the postlexical phonology. Bagemihl argues against this hypothesis on the basis of allophonic rules whose proper application depends on essentially the same syllabification as the one required by the (lexical) reduplication rules. In an effort to preserve the prosodic licensing theory in the face of these data, Bagemihl suggests that the Bella Coola obstruents are dominated by a mora and that the language is special in allowing this more primitive prosodic unit to license a segment instead of the syllable. To become compelling, this hypothesis will have to pass a test that discriminates moraic from nonmoraic material analogous to the way that the Bella Coola reduplication discriminates syllabic from nonsyllabic material.

6.10   Syllable Quantity and Weight

Traditional grammar distinguishes between light and heavy syllables for a variety of processes and constraints. In this section we survey these phenomena and develop a particular formalization of phonological weight, employing the notion ''mora.''

6.10.1   Light and Heavy Syllables

Phonological quantity often determines the distribution of stress. For example, consider the paradigm of trisyllabic words in (64) from Egyptian Arabic (long vowels and consonants transcribed as geminates).

(64)   a.   garíida   'newspaper'
            fukáaha   'humor'
            kiníisa   'church'

       b.   bisílla   'green peas'
            žakítta   'jacket'

       c.   fasúlya   'green beans'
            gawánti   'gloves'
            ṭaráblus   'Tripoli'

       d.   ʕínaba   'a grape'
            ʕárabi   'Arabic'
            ẓáḷaṭa   'stone'

When the word ends in a short vowel (CV), stress lodges on the penult if it contains a long vowel (CVV) (64a), a short vowel followed by a geminate consonant (64b), or the first consonant of a cluster (64c). If the penult contains a single short vowel, stress falls on the initial CV syllable (64d). This kind of stress distribution depends solely on the gross prosodic structure of the syllables – the quality of the particular consonants and vowels rarely matters. Following traditional nomenclature, we will refer to syllables in the first class as *heavy* and to those in the second as *light*.

The stress pattern of many other languages depends on a similar division of syllables into these two classes. For example, Latin accents a heavy penult: *ref'ēcit, ref'ectus* 'set over' 3sg. perf., past part. Stress may recede to the antepenult, but only if the penult is light: *ex'istimō* 'esteem' 1sg. Latin illustrates an additional point: onset consonants do not count in the determination of weight. According to Allen (1973), a short penultimate vowel followed by a stop-liquid cluster gives antepenultimate stress: *vólucres* 'winged' pl. But when the cluster is reversed, the penult is closed, hence heavy, hence stressed: *pepércī* 'spare' 1sg. perf.

The same opposition between light and heavy syllables is relevant to other Cairene Arabic stress patterns. Consider the paradigm of trisyllabic words in (65).

(65)   kátabu   'they wrote'
       mára?a   'broth'
       wálad-i   'my boy'

       qaahíra   'Cairo'
       ʕaalámu   'his world'
       ṭaalíba   'student' fem.

       falsáfa   'philosophy'
       maktába   'library'
       busṭági   'mailman'

       faṣṣáru   'they explained'
       ṣalláḥit   'she repaired'

When the first syllable is light (L), stress lodges on the initial syllable – this is the LLL pattern seen in (64d). But when the initial syllable is heavy (H), stress appears on the penult (65). Once again, CVV, CVG (G = geminate), and CVC behave as a group.

The question now is to find a formal invariant that underlies the three types of heavy syllable and distinguishes them from the light one in a natural way. One of the most popular generative treatments of this question recruits the notion of mora from traditional grammar to express the idea that a light syllable consists of a single unit of quantity while heavy syllables contain two units. In the model of McCarthy and Prince (1986) and Hayes (1989), the canonical light syllable [ta] is represented as in (66a) while the three species of heavy syllable receive the bimoraic representations in (66b,c,d): [taa], [tapta], [tappa].

(66)

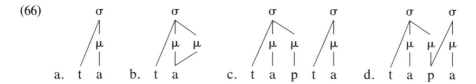

a. t a   b. t a   c. t a p t a   d. t a p a

Various properties of these representations need to be explicated. First, the key idea is that the mora is not a species of sound but rather an elementary prosodic unit that, like the syllable, organizes the phonemes in a particular way. Second, the mora is a constituent of the syllable intervening between the [σ] and the phonemic string. Third, what unifies the various heavy syllables is their bimoraic structure; they differ in how the second mora relates to the phonemic string. In a CVV long-voweled syllable (66b), a single vowel [a] spans two moras. In a CVC closed syllable (66c), the vowel occupies the first mora while the second is filled by the coda consonant. In the case of a geminate (66d), a single consonant simultaneously occupies the second mora and the onset of the following syllable. The geminate consonant thus arches across two syllables. Fourth, prenuclear, onset consonants do not pass through a mora and hence are weightless. This formalizes the generalization that stress rules sensitive to weight do not take account of onset consonants.

Another significant point is that on this interpretation of quantity, long vowels and consonants are single phonemic segments associated with two successive positions in syllable structure – so-called true geminates. This representation helps us to understand the observation of Kenstowicz (1970) that rules and constraints referring to or changing the feature structure of a sound in response to the segmental context typically treat long and short segments alike; it is rules that refer to syllable structure that normally differentiate long from short. For example, when a coronal consonant palatalizes before a front vowel, we expect the rule to be triggered equivalently by long and short [i], just as we expect it to apply indiscriminately to single and geminate consonants. Thus, in Japanese underlying [s] is realized as [š] in *suši* 'sushi', *hišši* 'desperate', *hošii* 'want', *raššii* 'Lassie'. Under the two-level representation for length, long and short [i] and [s] have the same representation at the phonemic level – as single segments. Rules applying at that level can thus be expected to treat them alike. This is not to say that segmental rules could not distinguish long from short; if necessary, they can do so by referring to the number of associated moras.

Prince (1984) makes the same point with regard to several phonotactic constraints in Finnish whose expression is considerably simplified by the two-level interpretation of geminates. For example, Finnish freely concatenates the obstruents [p,t,k,s], with one systematic gap: in a C_1C_2 cluster, C_2 cannot be [p]. This calls for a phonotactic constraint: *[−sonorant] [p]. However, geminate VppV sequences are abundant: *kippis* 'cheers'. They slip past the constraint. To cite another example, the middle C in a CCC sequence must be [s], demanding a filter barring a string *[+cons][−contin][+cons]. Once again, geminates elude the constraint: *helppo* 'easy', *poltta* 'burn'. The two-level representation of length explains why geminates systematically escape these phonotactic constraints. The constraints hold at the phonemic level; but at this level geminates are represented as single segments.

(67)

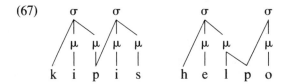

It is as syllable terminals that geminates count as two elements. Thus, rules that refer to syllable structure are where we expect long vowels and consonants to parallel sequences. To take an example from Japanese, long foreign words often truncate to disyllabic, in which case the second syllable must be light (Itô 1990). Thus, *herikoputaa* 'helicopter' shortens to *heri*. But *demoNsutareešon* 'demonstration' and *rokeešoN* 'location' shorten to *demo* and *roke*. This is easily described in moraic terms: we impose the prosodic requirement [σσ_μ] (σ_μ a monomoraic syllable) on the truncated words. The final mora in [demoN] and [rokee] is eliminated. The consequence is that the [ee] of disyllabic [rokee] shortens while the [N] of [demoN] undergoes stray erasure.

(68)

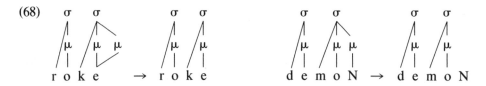

Finally, since moras are constituents of syllables, the determination of weight will be a function of syllable structure. Because the latter varies from one language to another, moraic structure will as well. For example, syllable onsets in Arabic are not complex; a stop-liquid cluster must consequently be heterosyllabic. The result is that the stop-liquid and liquid-stop sequences in Egyptian *madrása* 'school' and *martába* 'mattress' are not distinguished syllabically and consequently the words have equivalent HLL prosodic profiles.

6.10.2 Additional Weight Reflections

Before we ask how moraic structure is assigned, let us examine additional phenomena that motivate these representations. Compensatory lengthening (CL) receives a simple interpretation under the representations in (69). The most prevalent form of CL involves the loss of a coda consonant with concomitant lengthening of the adjacent nuclear vowel. The following paradigm from Komi illustrates this type (Harms 1968).

(69) | stem | 1sg. past | infinitive | |
|------|-----------|------------|---|
| lïy | lïy-i | lïy-nï | 'to shoot' |
| mun | mun-i | mun-nï | 'to go' |
| kïl | kïl-i | kï:-nï | 'to hear' |
| sulal | sulal-i | sulo:-nï | 'to stand' |

On the moraic theory of length, [kïlnï] has the underlying representation in (70a).

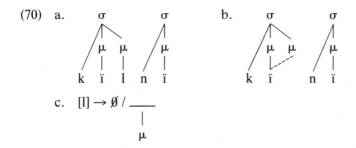

CL is now easy to express. We simply say that the [l] deletes from the coda (redefined as "dominated by a mora") but that its mora remains (70c). This vacated prosodic position is then reassigned to the preceding vowel, creating a geminate (70b). In other words, the basic quantitative structure of the syllable remains even though the phonemic expression is changed. If we lacked the notion of "prosodic position" provided by the mora, the change would have to be expressed as deletion plus inducement of [+long] on the preceding vowel – a clumsy statement to say the least (see Kisseberth 1973b for discussion).

In a survey of the CL literature, McCarthy and Prince (1986) and Hayes (1989) report that the loss of an onset consonant characteristically remains uncompensated by the lengthening of a following (or preceding) vowel. This point is seen most clearly in languages where consonants delete from both onset and coda positions. For example, according to Sezer (1986), [v] optionally deletes before labial segments in Turkish. Only coda [v] induces CL; onset [v] does not. *savmak* 'to get rid of' may surface as [sa:mak], but *davul* 'drum' is realized as [daul], not *[da:ul]. To the extent that this generalization holds up, it indicates that CL also diagnoses syllable weight – the same representation that calculates light versus heavy for stress. The correlation follows if weight is expressed as moras, if onsets do not project moras, and if CL is conservation of moras under segmental deletion or reshuffling.

Language games and speech disguises sometimes demonstrate the independence of the phonemic level from the gross prosodic shape of the syllable. A striking example is provided by the secret language called *Kinshingelo* played by speakers of the Bantu language Sanga (Coupez 1969). As shown by the examples in (71), the disguise consists in interchanging the final two syllables of the word. However, the weight of the syllable remains unaltered. Thus, the Light-Heavy-Light profile of Sanga *múkwèètù* is preserved in Kinshingelo *mútùùkwè*.

(71)   Sanga   óbé múkwèètù twáàyáá kú múkólá
       Kinshingelo   béó mútùùkwè yáàtwáá kú múlákó
       gloss   'You, my companion, come with me to the river!'

The constancy of weight is easy to express under the model in (66); *múkwèètù* has the representation in (72a).

(72)   a.   b.

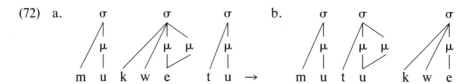

Interchanging the phonemic content of the last two syllables (the segments dominated by σ) while preserving the syllabic and moraic structure yields the correct result (72b). We also observe that monosegmental [t] and disegmental [kw] interchange with no side effects. If onset consonants are weightless, then according to the moraic model such elements cannot in principle leave a prosodic trace.

In a number of languages, word formation processes are reflected in a modification of syllable structure rather than by the more familiar affixation. The root-and-pattern morphology found in such Semitic languages as Arabic and Hebrew is a prime example of this "templatic" morphology. For example, in Arabic the causative of the verb is marked by geminating the middle radical.

(73)   šarib   'drink'   šarrab   'make drink'
       daras   'study'   darras   'teach'
       ḥamal   'carry'   ḥammal   'load'

In terms of the system in (66), we can express this process as adjunction of a mora to the initial syllable of the verb, realized by gemination of the consonant.

(74)

A similar phenomenon occurs in Biblical Hebrew (Lowenstamm and Kaye 1986). But unlike in Arabic, where every consonant has a geminate counterpart, in Biblical Hebrew the gutturals only occur as single consonants. When we examine morphological categories such as the *hitpaʕel* conjugation of the verb that call for gemination of the middle radical (e.g., *hit-gaddeel* from [gdl]), we find that the first vowel of verbs whose middle radical is a guttural is lengthened here – and only here: for example, *hit-paaʔeer* from [pʔr]. Once again, this is easy to explain under the moraic theory: a constraint against geminate gutturals blocks linking a mora to the guttural. The free mora is then linked to the nuclear vowel as a default option. This demonstrates that in Biblical Hebrew the second mora in a heavy syllable is a pure prosodic position that under the appropriate circumstances can be filled by the preceding vowel, a coda consonant, or the first half of a geminate.

Several widespread phonological processes receive a simple and enlightening interpretation under the moraic representation of quantity. Closed-syllable shortening can be understood as a coda consonant crowding out a vowel from the second mora in order to escape stray erasure. For example, in Egyptian Arabic *baab* 'door' shortens the root vowel before two consonants: *baab-i* 'my door' vs. *bab-na* 'our door'. In the moraic theory we may understand this in the following terms. Final consonants are extraprosodic. When the suffix *-na* is added, the final [b] is no longer licensed and so maps to the second mora. Assuming that Egyptian Arabic bars two phonemes from sharing the same mora, the link between the vowel and the second mora is thus suppressed, entailing a shortening of the vowel.

(75)

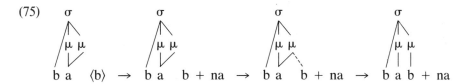

To take another case, in many systems a stressed syllable is required to be bimoraic. Underlying monomoraic syllables increment a mora, expressed as vowel lengthening or gemination. For example, in Italian underlying *nono* 'ninth' is realized as [n'o:no] by lengthening the vowel. No vowel lengthening occurs in *nonno* 'grandfather' or *monte* 'mountain' since the initial stressed syllables are already bimoraic. When the accent shifts, unstressed vowels shorten; but consonants do not degeminate in unstressed syllables, arguing that vowel length is assigned under stress rather than underlying. In word-final position, however, stressed vowels are not lengthened. Rather, the second mora is filled by gemination across the word boundary in the process called *radoppiamento sintattico: parlerò* 'I will speak', *parlerò bbene* 'I will speak well'.

Let us close this survey by looking at two additional phenomena that are often claimed to reflect phonological weight: minimality and tone-bearing units. Minimality refers to the requirement that a freestanding, stressable (nonclitic) word have a certain minimal weight (typically disyllabic or bimoraic). Lexical items below the minimum are either avoided or augmented to satisfy the requirement. McCarthy and Prince (1990) discuss in detail a bimoraic minimality requirement in Arabic. Given that final consonants are extrasyllabic, words of the shape CV and CVC are consequently subminimal. In fact, only a handful of such forms occur; they are restricted to particular sectors of the lexicon (principally body-part and kin terms: e.g., *dam* 'blood', *ʔab* 'father'); and they tend to be augmented in productive morphology (e.g., *ʔabaw-aan* 'two fathers', *ʔabaw-iy* 'paternal'). Loanwords of illicit shape are modified to conform to the requirement: 'bar', 'gas', 'shawl' are Arabized as *baar, gaaz, šaal* in the Standard dialect. In Saudi

Bedouin dialects we find *natt* 'nut, *rigg* 'rig'. This example demonstrates once again that the second mora is pure position, realized as gemination or vowel lengthening depending on the dialect. More importantly, the fact that final consonants are scrupulously excluded in the minimality calculation recapitulates the same exclusion observed in stress and closed-syllable shortening. This supports the idea that weight is a function of syllable structure and that these various phenomena converge on the same representation.

Similar convergence is often found in the realization of tonal patterns. To take a simple example, consider the paradigm in (76) from the Bantu language Luganda (Hyman and Katamba 1992). When combined with the morpheme *kyàngè*, the infinitival verb stem takes on a tonal pattern that depends on the weight of its first two syllables: if the first syllable contains a short vowel, then the second syllable appears with a simple high tone if it is short and with a falling tone if it is long (transcribed as the circumflex on the first half of the geminate vowel). On the other hand, if the first syllable of the stem contains a long vowel, then it takes a rising tone when combined with *kyàngè* (later simplified to high by a general rule).

(76) ku-lagira   'to command'   ku-lagírà kyàngè   'my commanding'
      ku-tamiir-a   'to get drunk'   ku-tamîirà kyàngè   'my getting drunk'
      ku-saaba   'to smear'   ku-sǎabà kyàngè   'my smearing'
                                         (> *kusáabà kyàngè* by later rule)

If long vowels are represented as two moras and short vowels as just a single mora, then the tonal pattern induced by *kyàngè* has a very simple analysis: a high tone [+hi] is assigned to the second mora of the stem (77). If this mora forms the first half of a long vowel, a falling tone is heard; if it forms the second half of a long vowel, a rising tone results. We will turn to an explicit consideration of tone in the next chapter. For now it should be clear that analyzing long vowels into two moras is the key to a simple statement of the *kyàngè* tonal pattern.

(77)
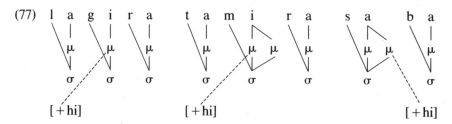

Suggested Readings

Clements, George N. 1990. The role of the sonority cycle in core syllabification. Papers in laboratory phonology 1: Between the grammar and physics of speech, ed. by J. Kingston and M. Beckman, 283–333. Cambridge: Cambridge University Press.

Dell, François, and Mohamed Elmedlaoui. 1985. Syllabic consonants and syllabification in Imdlawn Tashlhiyt Berber. Journal of African Languages and Linguistics 7.105–30.

Itô, Junko. 1986. Syllable theory in prosodic phonology. Amherst: University of Massachusetts Ph.D. dissertation. Published by Garland Press, New York, 1988. Chapters 1 and 3.

Kaye, Jonathan, Jean Lowenstamm, and Jean-Roger Vergnaud. 1990. Constituent structure and government in phonology. Phonology 7.193–231.

Selkirk, Elisabeth. 1982. The syllable. The structure of phonological representations (part II), ed. by H. van der Hulst and N. Smith, 337–83. Dordrecht: Foris.

Exercises

6.1 *Lebanese Arabic (Haddad 1984)*

In this dialect of Arabic syllables take the shapes CV, CVC, CVV, CVVC, and CVCC. This exercise concerns the construction of CVCC syllables. CVCC underlies a well-populated nominal template. In some cases the stem surfaces directly; in others an epenthetic vowel is inserted in a prepausal or preconsonantal context. The result is paradigms like the following.

(1) underlying shape /dars/   /ʔakl/
     Noun   dars   ʔakil
     'your masc. N'   dars-ak   ʔakl-ak
     'our N'   dars-na   ʔakil-na
                       'lesson' 'food'

The precise phonetic realization of the epenthetic vowel varies with context; here, abstracting away from this variation, it is transcribed uniformly as /i/. (3) presents underlying representations for numerous Lebanese Arabic words. If no additional form is cited, then the phonetic representation is the same as the underlying one. In the other cases epenthesis has applied. Develop an analysis to account for the epenthetic vowel. Which aspects of your analysis are the product of UG; which are language-particular? No examples of the following underlying sequences could be found: /CVyw/, /CVln/, /CVlr/, /CVnm/, /CVrl/, /CVfb/. What pronunciation does your analysis assign to these unattested cases? The Lebanese Arabic consonant inventory is given in (2); [ṭ,ḍ,ṣ,ẓ] are pharyngealized; [ḥ,ʕ] are pharyngeals.

(2) stops   t,ṭ   k   ʔ
                    b   d,ḍ
     fricatives   f   s,ṣ   š   x   ḥ   h
                        z,ẓ   ž   ɣ   ʕ
     nasals   m   n
     liquids   l,r
     glides   w   y

(3) /ʕawy/ → ʕawi   'barking'   /žaly/ → žali   'washing'
     /dalw/ → dalu   'pail'   /bary/ → bari   'sharpening'
     /žarw/ → žaru   'puppy'   /bany/ → bani   'building'
     /ħamw/ → ħamu   'cold sores'   /ramy/ → rami   'throwing'
     /ʕafw/ → ʕafu   'pardon'   /ħašy/ → ħaši   'stuffing'
     /ʔabw/ → ʔabu   'basement'   /ʔazy/ → ʔazi   'hurting'
     /nafy/ → nafi   'denying'   /raty/ → rati   'seaming'
     /ħaky/ → ħaki   'talking'

     /ħawl/   'around'   /xayl/   'horses'   /dawr/   'turn'
     /ɣayr/   'other than'   /ʕayn/   'eye'   /lawm/   'blame'
     /xawf/   'fear'   /mawz/   'bananas'   /žayš/   'army'
     /bayt/   'home'   /ʕayb/   'shame'   /ʔawd/   'leading'
     /layk/   'look'

     /hafar-l-na/ → hafarilna   'he dug for us'
     /kan-l-na/ → kanilna   'he was for us'

     /ħiml/ → ħimil   'load'   /ʔifl/ → ʔifil   'lock'
     /nasl/ → nasil   'progeny'   /ʔakl/ → ʔakil   'food'
     /šikl/ → šikil   'shape'   /nisr/ → nisir   'eagle'
     /ħafr/ → ħafir   'digging'   /ħibr/ → ħibir   'ink'
     /zikr/ → zikir   'souvenir'   /nimr/   'tiger'
     /farm/ → farim   'chopping'   /ʔism/ → ʔisim   'name'
     /ʕatm/ → ʕatim   'darkness'   /ħikm/ → ħikim   'ruling'
     /firn/ → firin   'oven'   /ʔamn/ → ʔamin   'peace'
     /dafn/ → dafin   'burial'   /ħuṣn/ → ħuṣin   'fortress'
     /ʔibn/ → ʔibin   'son'   /rikn/ → rikin   'nook'
     /ħilm/   'dream'

     /nasf/ → nasif   'detonation'   /ražf/ → ražif   'trembling'
     /natf/ → natif   'plucking'   /ʕakf/ → ʕakif   'leaning to'
     /balf/   'bluffing'   /ħarf/   'letter'

     /nasž/ → nasiž   'weaving'   /ʔas-š/ → ʔasiš   'he didn't
                                                          measure'

     /ħažz/ → ħažiz   'booking'   /fils/   'small coin'
     /talž/   'snow'   /ʕirs/   'wedding'   /marž/   'meadow'
     /ramz/   'symbol'   /ʔins/   'humans'   /ɣinž/   'wantonness'
     /nafs/   'self'   /ʕafs/   'furniture'   /ħabs/   'prison'
     /l-ʔids/ 'Jerusalem'   /nakz/   'poking'   /ʔaṭš/   'cutting off'

     /kalb/   'dog'   /žild/   'weather'   /darb/   'road'
     /fark/   'rubbing'   /ħamd/   'praise'   /bint/   'girl'
     /ħank/   'jaw'   /kizb/   'lying'   /wizk/   'win'
     /ʔusṭ/   'fee'   /mušṭ/   'comb'   /mažd/   'glory'
     /xaṣb/   'fertile'   /lift/   'turnip'   /safk/   'bloodletting'

     /sakt/   'silence'   /rakd/   'running'   /ʕabd/   'slave'
     /labṭ/   'kicking'
     /ħabk/ → ħabik   'weaving'   /fatk/ → fatik   'eradicating'
     /nadb/ → nadib   'wailing'   /rikb/ → rikib   'riding'

6.2 Ancient Greek (Steriade 1982)

A. Both Attic (4th century BC) Greek and Sanskrit are Indo-European languages. A natural question to ask is whether the richer stock of core syllables found in Sanskrit or the more restricted Attic inventory reflects the Proto-Indo-European (PIE) system. The following data from Mycenean (2d millennium BC) Greek, excerpted from Steriade 1982, shed light on this question. Mycenean Greek had a syllabic writing system (Linear B), where each graph marks a particular vowel or consonant + vowel combination. In an alphabetic writing system the number of graphs typically equals the sum of the consonants and vowels. But in a syllabic system the number of graphs is much larger, approaching the arithmetic product of the vowels and consonants. In a string of alternating consonants and vowels CVCVCV . . . , each segment finds a representation. But some supplemental decision is required to represent consonant clusters in a syllabic system. Some examples of Mycenean spelling are cited in (1). The words in the first column are reconstructions of the pronunciation of selected Mycenean words. The second column indicates the spelling these words received in the Mycenean syllabic system. First, determine what decision the system makes to deal with the problem posed by consonant clusters. Second, does this result shed any light on the syllabic structure operative in this dialect of Greek? Third, assuming that the Attic dialect discussed in section 6.5 is a later descendent of Mycenean, can you say anything about whether Sanskrit or Attic syllabification more closely reflects the system that must have operated in PIE?

(1)
Aleksandra	personal name	a-re-ka-sa-da-ra
Knossos	place name	ko-no-so
dosmiya	'gifts'	do-si-mi-ja
deksiwos	'right'	de-ki-si-wo
ksenwos	'foreigner'	ke-se-nu-wo
pʰasgana	'swords'	pa-ka-na
pʰulakpʰi	'to the guardians'	pu-ra-pi
aiksma	'sword'	a-ka-sa-ma

B. In the development of Greek from Indo-European, PIE *[s] turned to [h] in certain contexts but not in others. On the basis of the following data, formulate a simple rule that predicts exactly where the sound change takes place. Also, can you say anything about what relative point (early, middle, or late) in the development of Ancient Greek this sound change must have occurred? (The forms in parentheses are later Attic developments.)

(2) PIE *[s] → [h]
#___V	*sekwomai	hepomai	'I follow'
#___sonor	*swekuros	hekuros	'father-in-law'
V___V	*nesomai	nehomai (neomai)	'I return'
sonor___V	*ansiā	anhiā (hāniā)	'rein'
sonor___sonor	*arsma	arhma (harma)	'wheel, chariot'
V___sonor	*naswos	nahwos (nāos)	'temple'

(3)   PIE *[s] is retained

#____obstruent	spḗrǭ	'I sow'
obstruent____V	akʰsios	'worth'
V____obstruent	astḗr	'star'
____#	nomos	'law'

6.3   Italian Onsets

A.   The possible word-initial consonants and consonantal clusters for Italian are listed in (1) and (2). Both divide into two remarkably consistent groups with respect to a number of phonological rules and constraints outlined in questions B–E. Try to explain the basis for the groupings.

(1)

group A			group B		
[p]	ponte	'bridge'	[š]	sciopero	'strike'
[t]	topo	'mouse'	[tˢ]	zio	'uncle'
[k]	corpo	'body'	[dᶻ]	zaino	'knapsack'
[b]	bagno	'bath'	[ñ]	gnocco	'dumpling'
[d]	dente	'tooth'			
[g]	gatto	'cat'			
[č]	cielo	'sky'			
[ǰ]	giorno	'day'			
[f]	forno	'oven'			
[v]	volo	'flight'			
[s]	segno	'mark'			
[m]	mondo	'world'			
[n]	nome	'name'			
[l]	ladro	'thief'			
[r]	regalo	'gift'			

(2)

group A			group B		
[pr]	proposito	'purpose'	[sp]	specchio	'mirror'
[pl]	plastico	'plastic'	[st]	studio	'office'
[tr]	treno	'train'	[sk]	scudo	'shield'
[dr]	drappo	'cloth'	[zb]	sbaglio	'mistake'
[kr]	croce	'cross'			
[fr]	fratello	'brother'	[sf]	sfogo	'outlet'
[fl]	flagello	'whip'	[ps]	psicologo	'psychologist'
[py]	piatto	'dish'	[spr]	sprone	'spur'
[fy]	fiore	'flower'	[zbr]	sbrano	'tear'
[ky]	chiaro	'bright'			

B.   Many prenominal modifiers (specifiers) lose their final [o] when the following word begins with a vowel or with a single consonant or a consonant cluster belonging to group A. Single consonants or consonant clusters from group B never permit the preceding -o to be dropped. How can this difference be accounted for?

(3) definite article
    l anno   'the year'
    il ponte   'the bridge'
    il proposito   'the purpose'
    lo sciopero   'the strike'
    lo specchio   'the mirror'

    indefinite article
    un amico   'a friend'
    un topo   'a mouse'
    un treno   'a train'
    uno zio   'an uncle'
    uno sbaglio   'a mistake'

    demonstrative
    quell amico   'that friend'
    quel volo   'that flight'
    quel drappo   'that cloth'
    quello zaino   'that knapsack'
    quello sfogo   'that outlet'

    negative
    nessun altro   'no other'
    nessun gatto   'no cat'
    nessun fratello   'no brother'
    nessuno gnocco 'no dumpling'
    nessuno psicologo 'no psychologist'

C. When the preceding word ends in a stressed vowel, we find gemination of the following consonant in words belonging to group A and to single consonants belonging to group B. But an [sC] cluster does not geminate the [s]. How can this asymmetry be explained? (After Chierchia 1986.)

(4) | | | | |
|---|---|---|---|
| pulita | 'clean' | città [pp]ulita | 'a clean city' |
| triste | 'sad' | città [tt]riste | 'a sad city' |
| freddo | 'cold' | caffè [ff]reddo | 'cold coffee' |
| sciupato | 'ruined' | città [šš]upata | 'a ruined city' |
| sporco | 'filthy' | città [s]porca | 'a filthy city' |
| | | *città [ss]porca | |
| spesso | 'thick' | caffè [s]pesso | 'thick coffee' |
| | | *caffè [ss]pesso | |
| santa | 'holy' | città [ss]anta | 'holy city' |
| serale | 'evening' | caffè [ss]erale | 'evening coffee' |

D. In the standard Roman or Tuscan dialects of Italian, the affricates [tˢ] and [dᶻ] and the palatals [ñ] and [š] are always long intervocalically within a word: for example, *pozzo* [pottˢo] 'well', *legno* [leñño] 'wood', *fascia* [fašša] 'bandage'. What relevance does this fact have to the distribution in questions B and C?

E. In standard Italian most words end in a vowel. However, in the Piedmontese
    dialects nonlow final vowels have been lost. According to Clivio (1971), words
    beginning in [sC] clusters have developed a schwa, but generally only when
    the preceding word ends in a consonant.

(5) steịla   'star'   speč   'mirror'
     la steịla   'the star'   n əspeč   'a mirror'
     sɛt əstɛịle   'seven stars'   sɛt əspeč   'seven mirrors'

     zǰaf   'slap'
     n əzǰaf   'a slap'
     dez əzǰaf   'ten slaps'

In addition, certain other initial clusters have arisen through the loss of an unstressed vowel. Some of these also develop a schwa.

(6) pnas   'tail'   dez əpnas   'ten tails'
     mluŋ   'melon'   dez əmluŋ   'ten melons'
     vziŋ   'neighbor'   dez əvziŋ   'ten neighbors'

Clivio states that appearance of the schwa is optional after words ending in [r,ị,ụ,l].
How might this be explained?

(7) ən fɛr əspɔrk ≈ ən fɛr spɔrk   'a dirty iron'
     n anel əspɔrk ≈ n anel spɔrk   'a dirty ring'

6.4 English

A. In one of the first generative publications, Halle (1962) called attention to
    the remarkable ability of English speakers to divide the phonemic strings
    brick [brɪk], *blick* [blɪk], and *bnick* [bnɪk] into three categories: actual word
    of English, possible but nonoccurring word of English, impossible or dis-
    tinctly un-English-sounding word. How do English speakers develop this
    ability? What are the relative contributions of UG and the language of the
    environment in the process?

B. Recall from exercise 1.11 that the palatal glide [y] associated with the letter
    u occurs freely after all coronal consonants except [r] in the RP dialect of
    British English: *t*[yu]*ne*, *d*[yu]*ne*, *n*[y]*ew*, *s*[y]*uit*, *l*[y]*ute*, *l*[y]*urid*. According
    to Kaye (1992), the glide must be dropped in such cases as *fl*[ ]*uid* (*fl*[y]*uid*),
    pl[ ]*umage* (*pl*[y]*umage*), *gl*[ ]*ue* (*gl*[y]*ue*), *bl*[ ]*ew* (*bl*[y]*ew*). How might
    this fact be accounted for? How do the forms *st*[y]*upid*, *sp*[y]*ew*, *sk*[y]*ewer*,
    sl[y]*ew*, *sl*[y]*euth* bear on the analysis of *s*C clusters?

6.5 Arabic Dialects

Review the text discussion in section 6.6. Broselow (1982) mentions that Egyptian
Arabic speakers tend to pronounce English *Fred* as *F*[i]*red* while Iraqi speakers
say [i]*Fred*. How can this difference be explained?

6.6 Imdlawn Tashlhiyt Berber (Dell and Elmedlaoui 1985, 1988)

A. Recall from the text discussion (section 6.7) that ITB *ratlult* 'you will be born' from [ra-t-lUl-t] and *ratṛglt* 'you will lock' from [ra-t-rgl-t] contrast as disyllabic versus trisyllabic. They differ (sonority-wise) in just the fifth segment. Use Dell and Elmedlaoui's syllabification algorithm to explain this difference. (Note: Final suffixal [t] may be treated as extrasyllabic.)

B. Many triradical verbs form their imperfective stem by geminating either the first or the second consonant. Explore Dell and Elmedlaoui's algorithm to find a formal basis for determining which consonant geminates to form the imperfect.

(1) | perfect | imperfect | |
     |---------|-----------|---|
     | zlf | zzlf | 'singe' |
     | xng | xxng | 'choke' |
     | mrz | mmrz | 'wound in head' |
     | knd | kknd | 'dupe' |
     | | | |
     | zdm | zddm | 'gather firewood' |
     | xtl | xttl | 'feint' |
     | mgr | mggr | 'harvest' |
     | ršq | rššq | 'be happy' |

6.7 American English Schwa Syncope (Hooper 1978)

In American English schwa deletes in medial posttonic syllables (the weak position in a metrical foot). The syncope is constrained by the surrounding consonantal context. Examine the following data and develop an analysis that accounts for when syncope occurs and when it is blocked. In these transcriptions the syncopated vowel is bracketed.

(1) syncope permitted

sep[a]rate	choc[o]late	pers[o]nal
temp[e]rature	ped[a]ling	ars[e]nal
elab[o]rate	awf[u]lly	op[e]ner
fact[o]ry	des[o]late	def[i]nite
adult[e]ry	jav[e]lin	pris[o]ner
bound[a]ry	especi[a]lly	nati[o]nal
lic[o]rice	fin[a]lly	marg[i]nal
myst[e]ry	fam[i]ly	
mis[e]ry		
inj[u]ry		
cent[u]ry		
fish[e]ry		
gen[e]ral		
Laz[a]rus		
cam[e]ra		
cel[e]ry		
brew[e]ry		

(2) syncope blocked
      monog[a]my   quarr[e]ling
      ult[i]mate   fel[o]ny
      rock[e]ting   ir[o]ny
      ball[o]ting   col[o]ny
      mon[i]tor
      opac[i]ty
      goss[i]ping

The following cases have an intermediate status; syncope is possible but seems less natural than in the cases in (1). Can you explain this intermediate status?

(3) fem[i]nine
      prom[i]nent
      nom[i]nal
      dom[i]nant

When [t] is flapped, it seems to inhibit syncope. Why should this be?

(4) syncope possible   syncope inhibited
      fact[o]ry   wat[e]ry
      adult[e]ry   flatt[e]ry
      myst[e]ry   art[e]ry

6.8 Egyptian Arabic

Egyptian Arabic is traditionally described as having three types of syllable: light (CV), heavy (CVV, CVC), and extraheavy (CVVC, CVCC). The extraheavy syllables are restricted to word-final position. Syncope of unstressed short high vowels in open syllables pervades the language. The rule is formulated in (1). The paradigms in (2a) illustrate application of the rule at the word level and those in (2b) at the phrasal level. The syncopating vowel is marked in bold.

(1)   V   → Ø / X [____]$_\sigma$ Y (where σ has a nonbranching rime and V is
        [+high]   not stressed)

(2) a. fíhim   'he understood'   bi-tí-ktib   'she is writing'
         fíhm-u   'they understood'   bi-t-šúuf   'she is seeing'
                                          bi-ti-ktíb-ha 'she is writing it'

          bi-y-áakul 'he is eating'
          bi-y-ákl-u 'they are eating'

     b. kitaab   'book'   kútub   'books'
         báaʕ kitáab   'he sold a book'   kutúb-ha   'her books'
         báaʕu ktáab   'they sold a book' báaʕu ktúb-ha 'they sold her
                                                           books'

With the syncope rule as background, develop an analysis for the vowel length alternations in the following paradigms. What role does syllable structure play in the analysis? What principles and assumptions of syllable theory are crucial to your analysis? Show how your analysis works by giving derivations for *kitáab, kitáab-u, kitáb-ha, ṣáḥb-u*.

(3) kitáab   'book'   ṣáaḥib   'friend'
     kitáab-u   'his book'   ṣáḥb-u   'his friend'
     kitáab-ak   'your book'   ṣáḥb-ak   'your friend'
     kitáb-ha   'her book'   ṣaaḥíb-ha   'her friend'
     kitáb-na   'our book'   ṣaaḥíb-na   'our friend'

6.9 German

A. As in English, German [ŋ] derives from an underlying [ng] sequence. Sometimes the [g] surfaces and other times it deletes. Examine the data in (2) (simplified from Moltmann 1990) to determine the context for the *g*-deletion rule. (It is not stray erasure!) For this alternation as well as several others, the German affixes fall into two classes: the first (composed mostly of words of foreign origin but thoroughly integrated into the grammar) blocks deletion, while the second (composed of native derivational and inflectional suffixes) permits it. However, both classes take the preceding consonant as onset.

(1) Diphth[oŋg-i:]   Diphth[oŋ-ə]

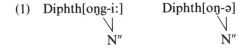

Recalling the Lexical Phonology model, how might this be explained? Be sure to clarify your assumptions concerning the ordering of the rules and the number and character of strata. How are the rules of *g*-deletion and [x]≈[ç] ordered with respect to the devoicing and resyllabification rules discussed in section 6.8? If syllabification is relevant, explain how. Show how your analysis works by deriving *Diphthong-ie* and *Diphthong-e*.

(2) [g] → ∅   [g]
     Tang   (Ta[ŋ])   Tango   (Ta[ŋg]o)
       'seaweed'   'tango'
     Ring   (Ri[ŋ])   Linguistik   (Li[ŋg]uistik)
       'ring'   'linguistics'
     Angst   (A[ŋ]st)   Linguine   (Li[ŋg]uine)
       'fear'   'linguini'
     Hengst   (He[ŋ]st)   Ingolf   (I[ŋg]olf)
       'stallion'   name
     längs   (lä[ŋ]s)   Mangan   (Ma[ŋg]an)
       'along'   'manganese'

     Thüring-isch   (Thüri[ŋ]-isch) Angl-ist   (A[ŋg]l-ist)
       'Thuringian'   'English philologist'
     Häng-ung   (Hä[ŋ]-ung)   Angl-ikaner   (A[ŋg]l-ikaner)
       'hanging'   'Anglican'

Diphthong-e 'diphthong'	(Diphtho[ŋ]-e)	Laryng-al 'laryngeal'	(Lary[ŋg]-al)
Ring-er 'wrestler'	(Ri[ŋ]-er)	Diphthong-ie 'diphthonging'	(Diphtho[ŋg]-ie)
Ring-e 'rings'	(Ri[ŋ]-e)	Schelling-ianer 'disciple of Schelling'	(Schelli[ŋg]-ianer)
		Möhring-esk 'like Möhring'	(Möhri[ŋg]-esk)

B. The dorsal fricative (orthographic *ch*) has two allophones: [ç] [−back] and [x] [+back]. Determine their distribution from the following data and state the relevant rule.

(3)
Chile [ç] 'Chile'	Lurch [urç] 'batrachian'	Schacht [axt] 'shaft'
Charisma [ç] 'charisma'	Kelch [elç] 'chalice'	Loch [ox] 'hole'
Cholesterol [ç] 'cholesterol'	manch [anç] 'many a'	Fluch [ux] 'curse'
Hypochonder [ç] 'hypochondriac'	Licht [içt] 'light'	Lauch [awx] 'leek'
Kolchose [ç] 'kolkhoz'	Recht [eçt] 'right'	
	keucht [oyçt] 'gasps'	
	leicht [ayçt] 'light, easy'	

Masoch [o:x] name	Masoch-ismus [o:ç] 'masochism'
Eunuch [u:x] 'eunuch'	Eunuch-ismus [u:ç] 'eunuchism'
Buch [x] 'book' nom.sg.	Buch-es [ux] 'book' gen.sg.
Bach [ax] 'brook' nom.sg.	Bach-e [ax] 'brook' gen.sg.

C. Leonard Bloomfield called attention to near minimal pairs (4) in which the [ch] phoneme is implemented differently depending on the location of the grammatical boundaries (Bloomfield 1930). This observation provoked considerable discussion in later American Structuralism about whether statements of the distribution of allophones could properly refer to grammatical information or had to be defined solely in terms of phonetic information (cf. discussions of the relation between morphology and syntax today). How does your analysis account for the difference?

(4)
Kuch-en [x] 'cake'	Kuh-chen [ç] 'little cow'
Fauch-en [x] 'spitting' (of cats)	Pfau-chen [ç] 'little peacock'

D. In the light of the data in this exercise, review the text discussion in section
    6.8 arguing that the rules of core syllabification in German are cyclic. Can
    the core syllabification rules be noncyclic and still account for the contrast
    between *glauben* [b] and *glaublich* [p]?

6.10   Somali Accent (Hyman 1981)

In Somali many pairs of masculine and feminine nouns are distinguished solely
by accent. Some singular – plural forms are differentiated in the same way, plural
being treated as a subtype of feminine. Three accent types are transcribed here:
falling accent [â], rising accent [ā], and plain high-pitched accent [á]. The rising
and falling accents are restricted to syllables containing a long vowel or diphthong;
the high-pitched accent is restricted to syllables containing a short vowel. Three
subtypes of accent shift are distinguished below. Relying on the notion "mora,"
develop an analysis that reduces the accent representation and shift to a single
factor.

(1)   shift in accent location

ínan	'boy'	inán	'girl'
nácas	'stupid man'	nacás	'stupid woman'
kálax	'ladle'	kaláx	'ladles'
bálli	'water reservoir'	ballí	'water reservoirs'

(2)   shift in accent type

damê:r	'young donkey' masc.	demē:r	'young donkey' fem.
darmâ:n	'colt'	darmā:n	'filly'
tû:g	'thief'	tū:g	'thieves'
êi	'dog'	ēi	'dogs'

(3)   shift in both location and type

qā:lin	'young camel' masc.	qa:lín	'young camel' fem.
So:mā:li	'Somali man'	So:ma:lí	'Somali people'

6.11   Finnish

As shown by the paradigm in (1) (Keyser and Kiparsky 1984), Finnish has a
process of gradation, one branch of which involves degemination. Develop an
analysis to state the precise context where the [kk] of *mykkä* 'mute' degeminates.
What role does the notion "mora" play in your analysis?

(1)

nominative sg.	talo	mykkä
essive sg.	talo-na	mykkä-nä
genitive sg.	talo-n	mykä-n
ablative sg.	talo-lta	mykä-ltä
inessive sg.	talo-ssa	mykä-ssä
	'house'	'mute'

7 Autosegmental Phonology

In this chapter we return to the feature tree introduced in section 4.3 and its conception of assimilation as the extension of a feature to adjacent positions in the linear string of segments. This view is depicted abstractly in (1), where F is some node in the feature tree (a terminal feature, an articulator, a cavity, or the root) and X is the appropriate mother node in an adjacent segment (order irrelevant).

(1) anchor   X   X

            feature   F

This conception of assimilation introduces an inherently *nonlinear* character to phonological representation: there is no longer a one-to-one relation between segments of the string and feature specifications. One piece of information [F] is distributed over more than a single position. As a result, this conception crucially departs from generative phonology's earlier linear representations (inherited from structuralism). On the *linear* view, any lexical item is a sequence of speech sounds, each sound characterized in turn as a feature matrix. For example, *stamp* has the representation sketched in (2).

(2)
$$
\begin{bmatrix} +\text{cons} \\ -\text{sonor} \\ +\text{contin} \\ +\text{coron} \\ +\text{anter} \\ -\text{voiced} \end{bmatrix}
\begin{bmatrix} +\text{cons} \\ -\text{sonor} \\ -\text{contin} \\ +\text{coron} \\ +\text{anter} \\ -\text{voiced} \end{bmatrix}
\begin{bmatrix} -\text{cons} \\ +\text{sonor} \\ +\text{contin} \\ +\text{low} \\ -\text{back} \\ +\text{voiced} \end{bmatrix}
\begin{bmatrix} +\text{cons} \\ +\text{sonor} \\ -\text{contin} \\ +\text{labial} \\ +\text{nasal} \\ +\text{voiced} \end{bmatrix}
\begin{bmatrix} +\text{cons} \\ -\text{sonor} \\ -\text{contin} \\ +\text{labial} \\ -\text{nasal} \\ -\text{voiced} \end{bmatrix}
$$

What sort of information does (2) provide? First it tells us that *stamp* consists of five sequential positions. Second, it implicates another dimension that assigns each position in the sequence a value in the phonetic alphabet. More precisely, (2) assumes a function mapping each position to a plus or minus value for each distinctive feature provided by UG. The result is a fully specified phonetic representation. Phonological rules change sounds by altering their feature coefficients. To describe the assimilation of the nasal with the following stop evident in *stamp*, a rule is needed to ensure that the [+nasal] segment has a [+labial] specification that mimics the following [p]. Thus, the linear view of assimilation posits two [+labial] specifications: one for the [m] and another for the [p]. The nonlinear representation of *stamp* is quite different: a single [labial] specification spans two positions. Similarly, a single [−voiced] marks the [sp] cluster as a whole. (The diagram of *stamp* in (3) is incomplete, highlighting only the nonlinear character of [labial] and [−voiced].)

(3)

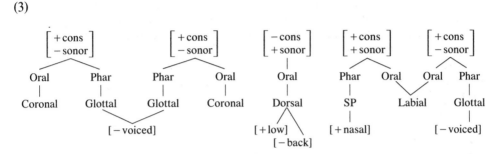

Phar = Pharyngeal
SP = Soft Palate

Recapitulating in part some of the insights of the Firthian School, generative phonology has found solid evidence for such multiply linked representations.

Once the requirement of a one-to-one relation between features and positions is dropped, we are free to entertain other nonlinear relations in phonological representation. Substantial evidence has emerged for the relations depicted in (4), where F denotes some feature on its tier and X is the relevant mother node in the tree graph.

(4)

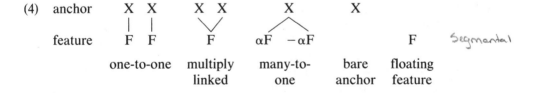

Our goal in this chapter and the next two will be to review the evidence that such nonlinear relations pervade phonological representation. The discussion in chapter 7 concentrates on tone – the first feature for which substantial nonlinearity was detected. In chapter 8 we will see that nonlinear relations obtain at the intersection of segmental and prosodic structure as well. Chapter 9 surveys the evidence for the nonlinear character of other features and returns to the question of how the features are organized in the hierarchical feature tree.

Our discussion of nonlinear phonology begins with tone. There are several reasons for this choice. First, tonology provided the first substantial evidence for representations of the type depicted in (4). Second, tone behaves independently from other features and so can be discussed in relative isolation. Finally, there is a substantial descriptive and theoretical literature to draw on. We will begin in section 7.1 with Margi, a typical tonal language with each of the nonlinear relations depicted in (4). We will then proceed in sections 7.2 and 7.3 to the Bantu languages Shona and Venda, where there is evidence for a representational distinction between singly and multiply linked structures. Section 7.4 reviews early generative work on vowel harmony demonstrating that vocalic features – especially [ATR] – also take part in nonlinear relations. The discussion in the next two sections focuses on anchoring elements and the parameters that establish their nonlinear relation with tone. Section 7.8 reviews some of the generative work on the tonology of Asian languages.

7.1   Margi

7.1.1   *Margi Contour Tones*

The Chadic language Margi (Hoffman 1963) spoken in Nigeria illustrates well some of the conceptual problems that arise when tone is treated as a feature of vocalic segments in the linear model. Margi contrasts three tones on single syllables: high *kʸí* 'compound', low *tì* 'mourning', and rising *fí* 'to swell'. However, on descriptive grounds the Margi rising tone must be analyzed as the combination of a low + high tone. At least three distinct lines of evidence support this interpretation.

First, a rising tone automatically results as the tonal by-product of a rule reducing a pair of adjacent vowels through devocalization or truncation. For example, the definite suffix has the underlying shape [-árì] (5a). It devocalizes a preceding high vowel (5b).

(5)   a.   sál   sál-árì   'man'
           kùm   kùm-árì   'meat'
      b.   ʔímí   ʔímy-árì   'water'
           kú   kw-árì   'goat'
           tágú   tágw-árì   'horse'
      c.   tì   ty-ǎrì   'morning'
           hù   hw-ǎrì   'grave'
           úʔù   úʔw-ǎrì   'fire'

If the high vowel has an underlying low tone, the contracted syllable containing the glide + *á* has a rising tone (5c). It is entirely natural to see the rising tone in *tyǎrì* as a combination of the low of [tì] plus the high of [-árì].

A second respect in which the Margi rising tone parallels a low + high tone combination appears in the verb. As in many other African languages, Margi verbs display the phenomenon known as *tonal melodies*. Given that the language has three contrasting tones, one might expect the number of tonal patterns a word displays to increase in geometric proportion to the number of syllables. Disyllabic verbs should then have $3 \times 3 = 9$ possible tonal patterns. In a language with tonal melodies, the number of tonal patterns remains constant, regardless of the number of syllables. Like a melody, the tonal pattern shrinks or expands in response to the length of the syllabic "text." Margi disyllabic verbs have not nine tonal patterns but only three: high on both syllables, low on both, or low on the first and high on the second. Monosyllabic verbs also have just three shapes: high, low, and rising. Examples appear in (6).

(6) a. tsá   'beat'   ndábyá   'touch'
         sá   'go astray'   tɔ́dú   'fall down'
     b. dlà   'fall'   gɔ̀rhù   'fear'
         ghà   'reach'   dzàʔù   'pound'
     c. hǔ   'grow up'   pɔ̀zú   'lay eggs'
         vǎl   'fly'   ŋgùrsú   'bend'

Clearly, the monosyllabic *tsá* and the disyllabic *ndábyá* belong to the same tonal pattern, as do *ghà* and *dzàʔù*. If rising tone is treated as the combination of a low tone plus a high tone, then monosyllabic *vǎl* can be assigned to the same tonal class as disyllabic *pɔ̀zú*.

In sum, the rising tone in Margi has a limited and predictable distribution. It arises as either a by-product of the contraction of V + V sequences or the monosyllabic realization of the LH melody. Hence, it is not a member of the inventory of basic tones, which is limited to high and low. The low-high nature of the rising tone is also brought out by a number of Margi clitic morphemes that exhibit *tonal polarity*. Tonal polarity is a common state of affairs in two-tone systems. It means simply that a given affix has a tonal specification that is the opposite of that of the base. Among the Margi polarity morphemes are the present tense element [a], which precedes the verbal base, and certain pronominal elements that follow the base. Examples are cited in (7).

(7) a. à sá gù   'you go astray'
         à tsú gù   'you beat'
     b. á wì gú   'you run'
         á dlà gú   'you fall'
     c. á vǎl gù   'you fly'

In (7a) the high-toned verbs induce a low on the tense morpheme [a] and the pronominal [gu], while the low-toned bases of (7b) induce a high. Now consider the behavior of a rising-toned base such as [vǎl] in these circumstances. If the rising tone is really the combination of a low followed by a high, as claimed, then we predict that the tense morpheme [a] will polarize with respect to the following low component and thus should appear with a high tone. On the other hand, the pronominal [gu] will polarize with respect to the preceding high component of the rising tone in [vǎl]. It should thus appear with a polar low tone. The form *á vǎl gù* of (7c) dramatically confirms this prediction of the analysis.

Thus, on internal descriptive grounds, there is good reason to believe that the grammar of Margi analyzes rising tones as the concatenation of a low followed by a high tone. Now consider the dilemma the linear model of representation faces in coming to terms with this aspect of Margi phonology. If tone is treated as a feature of vocalic segments analogous for example to [±back], then the rising tone on the vowel of [vǎl] must be represented with a feature such as [+rising]. It cannot be represented as a [−hi] [+hi] sequence since this violates the basic premise of the linear model that each feature specification marks a segment [+F] or [−F] for each feature. To mark the same segment both [+F] and [−F] is thus a contradiction. This [+rising] feature can be given a precise phonetic definition and would consequently distinguish rising tones from simple highs and lows. Further, all of the Margi tonological alternations could be accurately described with such a feature. For example, the rule in (8) would correctly generate the low-toned alternant for the present tense morpheme in (7b,c).

$$(8) \quad [a] \rightarrow [á] / \underline{\hspace{1cm}} \left\{ \begin{array}{c} [-\text{hi}] \\ [+\text{rising}] \end{array} \right\}$$

The problem of course is that under this theory, although the fact that the behavior of the rising tone parallels that of a low-high sequence can be described, it is not explained. In other words, the parallel in no way follows from the theory; rather, it must be built into each rule and principle in the grammar that refers to it.

To develop this point further, recall that when the rising tone of *vǎl* is analyzed as a LH sequence, we not only explain why the past tense particle appears with a high tone before *dlà* and *vǎl*; we also predict that the suffix [gù] will appear with a low tone after *sá* and *vǎl*. Confirmation of such predictions is diagnostic of a successful theory: one that helps us to gain a deeper understanding of why things are the way they are rather than some other way. In contrast, the analysis of *vǎl* as [+rising] only succeeds in describing the facts. It does not explain them. While we may write a rule such as (8), there is no reason why [+rising] should combine with [−hi] (rather than [+hi]) in requiring a low tone on the preceding tense morpheme. In fact, [+rising] combines with [+hi] in another rule of Margi – the one requiring a low tone on the following [gù]. But why should [+rising] parallel [+hi] with respect to tonal change on a following element (rather than, say, on a preceding element)? Why couldn't the facts have been the opposite?

The parallel of rising tones to a LH sequence is not a peculiarity of Margi. Rising tones parallel LH sequences and falling ones parallel HL sequences in many languages. To cite one more example, Lama, a Togolese Gur language (Kenstowicz, Nikiema, and Ourso 1988), contrasts high and low tone; but a low tone changes to falling after a high tone.

(9) a. yó   'child'
         rì   'mother'
         yó rî   'child's mother'

b.   L → [+falling] / H ____

c.   L → [+rising] / H ____

We could write a rule such as (9b) to describe this situation. But since the linear model forces us to treat contour tones as unanalyzed [+rising] and [+falling] wholes, it implicitly claims that we are just as likely to find that a low tone changes to rising after a high (9c). However, while a change of [áCà] to [áCâ] is one of the most common tonal rules, a change of [áCà] to [áCǎ] is very unusual. An adequate theory of phonology should help us to understand why the former is widespread and the latter is not.

7.1.2   *Autosegmental Representation*

Contour tones, as well as many other aspects of tonology, thus pose a serious challenge to any theory of grammar. In his Ph.D. dissertation "Autosegmental Phonology" (1976), John Goldsmith proposed a brilliant solution to this tonal challenge. He diagnosed the problem as lying with the method of phonological representation assumed at the time in generative phonology. As noted earlier, the representation of *cat* as [kʰat] contains two kinds of information: first, that the lexical item is composed of three sequential positions and second, that each position is assigned to a feature matrix containing a ± specification for each feature made available by UG. No overlap among features is permitted in the representations of the linear model. Goldsmith saw that many of the puzzling properties of tone can be explained if this ban on feature overlap is relaxed. In particular, he proposed that the information representing a HL word such as Margi *ú?ù* 'fire' (10a) be displayed on two separate levels or *tiers*: a tonal tier consisting of the linear sequence of tones and a segmental tier consisting of the sequence of phonemes (10b). Both the tonal tier and the segmental tier consist of a series of feature sets (10c).

(10)   a.   ú ? ù
             high   +   +
             low   −   −
             back   +   +
             hi   +   −

b.   u ? u   segmental tier

       H   L   tonal tier

c. $\begin{bmatrix} -\text{cons} \\ +\text{high} \\ -\text{low} \\ +\text{back} \end{bmatrix}$ $\begin{bmatrix} -\text{cons} \\ +\text{constr gl} \end{bmatrix}$ $\begin{bmatrix} -\text{cons} \\ +\text{high} \\ -\text{low} \\ +\text{back} \end{bmatrix}$ segmental tier

       [+hi]   [−hi]   tonal tier

Each tier is autonomous; neither one is subordinate to the other. They are just different locations for the display of the information in *ú?ù*. (10b,c) thus inform us that *ú?ù* contains two tones concatenated in the order high – low. There is, however, one respect in which the representations are incomplete. We must indicate how the information in the two tiers is synchronized. This is accomplished by *association lines* linking tones and selected units of the segmental tier called *tone-bearing units* (TBUs). In most languages the syllabic nucleus constitutes the TBU. And since many languages do not contrast short versus long (geminate) vowels, the number of syllables and the number of vowels are equivalent. In this case we speak of the association as holding between vowels and tones. Margi *ú?ù* can thus be represented as in (11).

(11)   u ? u   segmental tier
       | |
       H   L   tonal tier

From the simple decision to partition the features composing a representation into distinct levels, a number of important consequences follow. Indeed, much of the research conducted in generative phonology after the appearance of Goldsmith's thesis focused on a rigorous pursuit of the implications of his proposal. Let us return to some of the problems noted earlier and see how they can be addressed from an autosegmental perspective. First consider the Lama data of (9), which provoked the observation that an [áCà] sequence is much more likely to change to [áCâ] than to [áCǎ]. Given that the tonal features occupy a distinct level of representation, 'child's mother' will have the underlying representation of (12a).

(12) a.   yo ri   b.   yo ri
           | | ⋉
           H L   H L

To derive the phonetic representation, all we need say is that the duration of the high tone extends to the position associated with the vowel of *rì* (12b). The vowel of *rì* thus becomes associated with two tones: the high of *yó* and its own lexical low. We will assume that a HL sequence associated with the same TBU is interpreted phonetically as a falling pitch contour. Thus, from the autosegmental perspective, the change of [áCà] to [áCâ] can be treated as a form of assimilation: the vowel of *rì* assimilates the high tone of the immediately preceding *yó*.

We can now also explain why the change of [áCà] to [áCǎ] is very uncommon. We assume of course that a rising tone is represented as a LH sequence associated to the same position. In order to derive such a structure from [áCà], we would have to make a copy of the high tone and place it after the low (13a). Spreading of the high tone past the low, as in (13b), will be prevented because it yields an ill-formed representation in which the high tone originally associated with *yó* both precedes and follows the low associated with *rì*.

(13) a. V V   V V   b. V V
          | | | ⌐\ |⟋⟍
          H L → H L H   H L

The tonal tier, like all other tiers, is strictly ordered. A representation such as (13b) is thus ill formed since the high both precedes and follows the low. This constraint is usually expressed in the autosegmental literature by saying that "association lines may not cross." As we will see, it is critical in constraining the range of tonal operations. Thus, the only way to implement an [áCà] → [áCǎ] change is by the copying plus relocation operation seen in (13a). Such a rule requires transformational power and is more complex formally. Autosegmental representations thus distinguish some common tonal changes from some more unusual ones – the hallmark of a good theory. (Representation (13b) is excluded under the intended interpretation of our autosegmental diagrams, in particular that the various tiers are parallel to one another and that the association lines are straight and not curved.)

The autosegmental representation of Lama *yó rî* 'child's mother' in (12b) violates the ban on feature overlap of the linear model in two ways. Not only are two tones linked to the same vowel; the high tone is linked to two successive syllables. We will see the consequences of this momentarily.

To briefly summarize the discussion so far, the autosegmental analysis hinges on the possibility of representing a contour tone as two tones (H or L) linked to a single tone-bearing unit. This in turn is made possible by the decision to represent the tonal features and the segmental features on separate levels. The linear model cannot avail itself of such an explanation and is doomed to failure.

7.1.3 *Margi: An Autosegmental Perspective*

We now reexamine the various aspects of Margi tonology discussed earlier from our new, autosegmental perspective, developing the necessary notational apparatus as we proceed. First consider the phenomenon of tonal melodies. Recall that the problem is to represent the tonal patterns at a level abstract enough so that they can shrink or expand in response to the number of syllables in the segmental tier. The decision to represent tonal features on a separate tier should produce this effect. However, we need an explicit procedure to synchronize the tones with the tone-bearing units of the phonemic tier. We will assume that Margi verbs lexically select one of just three tonal patterns (H, L, or LH) regardless of their segmental length. We will also assume a two-stage procedure to associate the tonal melodies to the segmental tier. The first step is stated in (14) and is known as the *Universal Association Convention* (UAC) (Goldsmith 1976, Pulleyblank 1986).

(14) Match the tones and tone-bearing units (TBUs) one to one, left to right.

For monosyllabic verbs this procedure yields the surface representation directly for items belonging to the high and low classes, such as *tsá* 'beat' and *dlà* 'fall'

(15a). But for verbs in the LH pattern such as *fĭ* 'swell', the high tone is left dangling or "floating" (15b). We can derive the correct surface representation by simply linking the floating tone to the only available TBU, thereby creating the rising tone (15c). (Recall from section 4.3 that a dashed or broken line indicates the linking process in operation; a solid line denotes a link already established in the representation.)

(15) a.   tsa dla   b.   fi   c.   fi

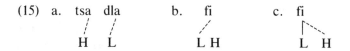

The question naturally arises whether the association of the floating tone in (15c) results from a convention of UG or must be stipulated as a rule of individual grammars. Goldsmith (1976) originally assumed the former; but subsequent research has shown that floating tones must, at least in some cases, remain unlinked (Pulleyblank 1986). Consequently, the operation in (15c) must arise from a rule of Margi, stated in (16). Following the notation introduced by Pulleyblank (1986), unlinked elements are indicated with a circle.

(16) V

    ⌐╲╲

    t Ⓣ

This rule says to associate an unlinked tone to the TBU associated with the immediately preceding tone.

    Margi disyllabic verbs present the opposite state of affairs. The UAC yields a perfect matching for the LH pattern in *mbìdú* 'blow'. But verbs in the high and the low classes such as *ndábyá* 'touch' and *ùlṳ* 'see' will lack a tonal association on their final syllables (17b).

(17) a.   mbidu   b.   ndabya   ulu

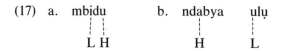

We can derive the correct surface form by postulating that the tone associated with the initial syllables spreads to all of the following toneless syllables by the process stated in (18).

(18) V   Ⓥ

    L----╱

    t

Goldsmith (1976) assumed that such tonal extension to unlinked syllables followed automatically from UG and enforced a requirement that all TBUs be matched with some tone. Pulleyblank (1986) and others have argued that this position is too strong. Some grammars select another option whereby vowels remain unlinked to the tonal tier until a relatively late point in the derivation, where they are assigned a *default tone*. (In two-tone systems the default tone is low, while in three-tone systems it is generally mid.)

We have now explained the limited distribution of the rising tone in Margi and its parallel to the LH sequence. Verbs such as *fǐ* belong to the same melodic class as *mbìdú* and thus both have LH on their tonal tiers in the lexicon. The rising tone is restricted to monosyllabic stems, because this is the only occasion in which the mapping procedure fails to assign the individual elements of the LH melody to separate syllables. The rule in (16) associates the dangling high to the same syllable the low is linked to, thereby deriving a contour tone.

This is an appropriate point to consider the tonology of Margi verbal suffixes. According to Hoffman (1963), there are just two types: suffixes like -*bá* with a fixed high tone and another class whose tone alternates between high and low, such as -*na*.

(19) a.   cú   'speak'   cí-bá   'tell'

            ghà   'reach'   ghà-bá   'reach'

            fǐ   'swell'   fì-bá   'make swell'

      b.   sá   'go astray'   sá-ná   'lead astray'

            dlà   'fall'   dlà-nà   'overthrow'

            bdlǔ   'forge'   bdlə̀-ná 'forge'

      c.   sa+na   bdlə+na   UR

            H   LH

            sa+na   bdlə+na   UAC

             | | |

            H   L H

            sa+na   inappl.   tone spread (18)

             ⌶

            H

Clearly [ba] has a high tone in the lexicon. Given the framework developed so far, the behavior of [na] follows if we assume that it has no underlying tone. It will acquire a tone from the root – either the second element of the LH melody by the UAC or via the spreading rule in (18). Sample derivations for *sá-ná* and *bdlə́-ná* are given in (19c). In the first step the UAC applies. In the second step the spreading rule supplies the suffix [-na] with a tone.

So far we have examined three tonal patterns for the Margi verb: H, L, and LH. There is in fact a fourth stem class, which Hoffman calls the "changing" verbs. These verbs are low when unaffixed but appear with high tone when combined with a high-toned suffix such as [-bá] or [-ŋgə́rí].

(20) high   cú   cí-bá   cí-ŋgə́rí   'speak'

      low   ghà   ghà-bá   ghà-ŋgə́rí 'reach'

      changing hù   hə́-bá   'take'

                  fà   fá-ŋgə́rí   'take many'

Since the changing roots differ systematically from high and low roots, they must
be assigned a different underlying representation. Following a suggestion of Pulleyblank (1986), suppose that they are underlyingly toneless. If the tone of the
affixes is not lexically linked, then we will have the underlying representation in
(21a) for *fá-ŋgárí*.

(21)   a.   [fa] ŋgəri   b.   [fa] ŋgəri

       H   H

The UAC, matching free tones and free TBUs left to right, links the high to the
initial syllable of the root, whence it spreads by (18) to the remaining toneless
syllables of the word (21b). This analysis obviates another rule spreading tone
from the suffix to the preceding stem and utilizes machinery already developed
in the analysis. It illustrates the phenomenon of *tonal displacement*. Even though
the high tone of (21a) is a lexical property of the suffix, it makes its initial association to the segmental tier on the root. If Margi had selected the option of
assigning toneless syllables a default tone instead of invoking spreading, the result
would have been *fá-ŋgàrì*.

     Returning to the Margi "changing" verbs, when these toneless stems appear
in isolation or in combination with a toneless affix, their phonetic interpretation
is not variable. In fact, it is systematically identical to basic low-toned items. To
explain this neutralization, we will follow Pulleyblank (1986) and assume that at
a certain point in the derivation, a TBU not linked to the tonal tier is assigned a
default low tone by the rule in (22a). In virtue of this rule, the changing verb
hù receives the derivations in (22b).

(22)   a.   (V) → V

            |

            L

       b.   hu   'take'   hə + na   'take away'

            hu   hə + na   default-L insertion

            | | |

            L   L   L

     We have so far seen three of the four possible mismatches violating the one-
to-one relation among features imposed by the linear model: two tones mapped
to a single vowel (e.g., a contour tone such as the Margi rising tone of *fǐ* 'swell'),
one tone spread over two vowels (e.g., a bisyllabic verb in the high melody class
such as *ndábyá* 'touch'), and finally a vowel with no (underlying) tonal specification (e.g., a "changing" verb such as *hù* 'take'). The fourth logically possible
mismatch is an element of the tonal tier that is not associated to any member of
the segmental tier. But recall that this is precisely what we found in the Margi
reduction of underlying vowel sequences: the tone associated with one vowel
persists after the reduction of the other, creating a contour tone in the process.

Let us examine this vowel reduction process more closely. Margi has six vowel phonemes: [i,u,e,o,a,ə]. When the definite suffix [-árì] is added to a stem to create a V + á cluster, the V turns to a glide if it is high, the [a] of the definite suffix truncates when V is mid, and the V deletes when it is [ə]. When both vowels are [a], it is unclear which one deletes. Arbitrarily assuming that it is the first, the ordered rules in (23b) can be formulated to account for these segmental alternations.

(23)   a.

ʔímí	ʔímyárì	'water'
kú	kwárì	'goat'
šèré	šèrérì	'court'
tóró	tórórì	'threepence'
ə́ncàlá	ə́ncàlárì	'calabash'
tì	tyǎrì	'mourning'
hù	hwǎri	'grave'
cédè	céděrì	'money'
fà	fǎrì	'farm'

     b. $[i,u] \rightarrow [y,w]$ / ____ V

             $V \rightarrow \emptyset$ / [e,o] ____

             $V \rightarrow \emptyset$ / ____ V

The tonal modifications arising from the reduction of the V + V sequences pose insuperable difficulties for the linear model. We will consider this point only briefly, as it will become obvious. Since the tonal and segmental features are represented as an unordered set much like the coins in one's pocket, in the linear model it is not possible to delete the vowel without deleting the tone. But whether the tone on the deleting vowel is high or low is obviously crucial for the proper tonal modification. Consequently, the tonal modifications will have to precede the deletion rules of (23b). What rules will be required to implement these modifications? A rule must change the first vowel of [árì] to rising after a low tone (e.g., *hwǎrì*). But this only happens when the [a] vowel is retained. When the stem ends in a mid vowel, for example, it is the mid vowel that survives. Consequently, another rule will be needed to change its tone from low to rising (e.g., *céděrì*). Thus, not only are two additional tone rules needed; but with their reference to whether the stem ends in a high or a mid vowel, these rules repeat portions of the contexts of the segmental reduction rules. Clearly, these ad hoc rules are nothing but a roundabout procedure to identify the tone of the deleted or devocalized vowel. In an autosegmental representation, the tone of the deleted vowel can be identified directly. It is the unassociated tone that is left *floating* on the tonal tier after the deletion or devocalization of the associated vocalic phoneme has removed a TBU, a phenomenon Goldsmith (1976) dubs *tonal stability*.

We must now stipulate a rule or principle to associate this floating tone to the timing tier. Clements and Ford (1979) suggest that a derived unassociated tone typically associates to the TBU that provokes the loss of the original TBU. This

Stranded Tone Principle correctly predicts that in (24a) the low tone set afloat by devocalization of the glide will associate to the vowel of the definite suffix, while in (24b) the high tone of the definite associates to the preceding mid vowel.

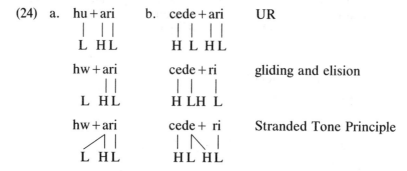

(24) a. hu + ari   b. cede + ari   UR
         | | | | | | | |
         L H L   H L H L

         hw + ari   cede + ri   gliding and elision
          | | | | | |
         L H L   H LH L

         hw + ari   cede + ri   Stranded Tone Principle
          /| | | \ |
         L H L   H L H L

7.1.4 Multiple Linking and the Obligatory Contour Principle

Let us now step back from what we have done. If the autosegmental perspective is adopted, then two major analytic questions arise in tonology.

(25) a.   How many tones does each lexical item have?
      b.   How are these tones associated to the TBUs?

In regard to the first question, the linear model had a simple answer. Margi ʔímí 'water' has two syllables and thus must have two occurrences of [+hi]. Hence, it has two tones. But in the autosegmental model, nouns such as ʔímí or làgù 'road' could have a representation with two tones, each linked to a single vowel, or one with a single tone, multiply linked to both syllables.

(26) a.   ʔimi   lagu
            | | | |
            H H   L L

      b.   ʔimi   lagu
            \/   \/
            H   L

This representational difference between (26a,b) can have empirical consequences. Consider the way in which disyllabic low-toned nouns behave in the definite.

(27) làgù   làgwárì   'road'
      màlà   màlárì   'woman'

If *làgù* has the singly linked representation of (26a), then in the course of the derivation of (28a) devocalization creates a floating low. By the Stranded Tone Principle, this floating tone links to the suffixal vowel, creating a rising tone. To derive the correct form *làgwárì*, we must postulate an additional rule to delete a floating low after a low tone.

(28) a. lagu   lagw + ari   lagw + ari = *làgwărì

      | | → | | | → | /| |

      L L   L L   HL   L   L HL

   b. lagu   lagw + ari

      |/ → | | |

      L   L   HL

But if *làgù* is assigned the multiply linked representation of (26b), then upon devocalization no floating tone is created, because the L remains anchored to the first syllable. No rising tone develops and the correct *làgwárì* is derived directly (28b). We thus reach the perhaps surprising conclusion that *làgù* is best regarded as having just one tone, not two.

The possibility of single versus multiple linking thus introduces a certain indeterminacy in the theory. A CV̀CV̀ string has two possible representations. Trisyllabic CV̀CV̀CV̀ could have many more depending on whether it is assigned one, two, or three tones, and how these tones are linked to the segmental tier. But tonological systems seldom, if ever, make use of this potential in encoding their lexical representations. For example, as far as is known all Margi disyllabic nouns behave like *làgù* in consistently requiring the multiply linked representation. This indeterminacy problem was recognized in the earliest stages of autosegmental tonology. A principle known as the *Obligatory Contour Principle* (OCP), originally due to Leben (1973), has been proposed to resolve the problem.

(29) Obligatory Contour Principle
      Adjacent identical tones are banned from the lexical representation of a morpheme.

According to the OCP, successive occurrences of the same tonal specification ([+ hi] or [− hi]) cannot appear in the lexical representation of a morpheme. If two tones succeed one another, then they must differ by at least one tonal feature. One consequence of the OCP is that all low-toned disyllabic (and trisyllabic or longer) noun stems must have lexical representations with just a single low tone. The OCP thus, correctly in this case, enforces the multiply linked representation (26b) for Margi.

Let us now briefly address the second question of (25), the direction of mapping. This question arises if we assume a condition such as the OCP that constrains the inventory of tonal sequences. For Margi disyllabic nouns there are four possible patterns. As we have seen, the OCP requires the representations in (30).

(30) ʔímí   làgù   šèré   cédè

     H   L   L H   H L

The surface forms can be derived with left-to-right association and then rightward spreading to toneless vowels. But they can just as easily be derived through right-to-left association and leftward spreading. To resolve the directionality question, we must turn to longer words. If the association were from left to right, then we would expect a spreading of tones on the right portion of the word (31a). Spreading in the left-hand portion of the word would be indicative of right-to-left association (31b).

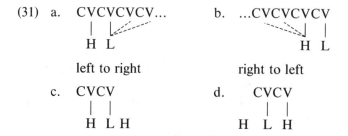

(31)   a.   CVCVCVCV...   b.   ...CVCVCVCV
            | | | |
            H   L   H   L

            left to right   right to left

       c.   CVCV   d.   CVCV
            | | | |
            H L H   H L H

Another directional diagnostic is the location of dangling tones or contour tones. This test is applicable when the number of tones exceeds the number of TBUs – for example, in the association of a three-tone melody to a two-tone text. Under left-to-right mapping the final high of a HLH melody dangles on the right (31c), while under right-to-left mapping the first tone of the melody dangles at the beginning of the word (31d). When the floating tone docks, a contour tone is created. If the language restricts its contour tones to the initial or the final positions of a domain, this can be a clue to the directionality of tonal assignment.

To briefly summarize the discussion, there are three ways in which a TBU may acquire its initial tonal association: (i) through unpredictable linking in the lexical representation (e.g., Shona; section 7.2), (ii) through application of the UAC either via direct matching with an underlying tone or via the tonal spreading parameter (e.g., Margi), and (iii) via a default rule (e.g., Margi changing verbs).

7.2   Shona and the Obligatory Contour Principle

In this section we will examine additional evidence bearing on autosegmental representations – in particular, multiple linking and the OCP. The discussion will focus on Shona, a Southern Bantu language spoken in Zimbabwe, and builds on the results of Odden (1980) and Myers (1987a).

Shona contrasts high and low tones. High-toned syllables are transcribed by the acute, while low tones are unmarked. Shona fully utilizes this two-way tonal opposition to encode its noun stems. The data in (32) show that whether a given syllable of the stem is high or low is unpredictable.

(32)   mbwá   'dog'   bwe   'stone'
       hóvé   'fish'   badzá   'hoe'
       sadza   'porridge'   gárwe   'crocodile'
       mbúndúdzí   'army worms'   hákáta   'diviner's bones'
       shámwarí   'friend'   chapúpu   'witness'
       dikitá   'perspiration'   dhuvhání   'tin cup'
       dandadzi   'cobweb'   séndere   'place forbidden
       bénzíbvunzá   'inquisitive fool'   for farming'

The existence of such contrasting tonal shapes as *hákáta* vs. *séndere* presents an analytical problem. We cannot simply posit a HL melody for each, since the method of association is not predictable: in *hákáta* the first two syllables are high, while in *séndere* only the first one is. The UAC mapping a HL tonal sequence from left to right would incorrectly assign these nouns the same tonal shape. The same problem arises under right-to-left association. One solution is to expand the inventory of melodies to include HHL in addition to HL. An alternative posits a single tonal shape HL for both stems but lexically records (at least some of) the associations between the tonal and segmental tiers. The representations in (33) illustrate these two different analyses.

(33) a.   hakata   b.   hakata

     H H L   H   L

Odden (1980) discovered evidence that favors the second solution. Many Bantu languages have a dissimilation rule changing one of two adjacent high tones (typically the second) to low. This process is known as *Meeussen's Rule* (after the Belgian linguist who first detected its existence). In the Shona dialect studied by Odden, Meeussen's Rule operates at the juncture (marked by a #) between a cliticized element (e.g., a preposition such as *né* 'with' or *sé* 'like') and its host. Its effect on some of the stems of (32) is seen in (34).

(34) a.   mbwá   'dog'   né#mbwa   'with a dog'
          hóvé   'fish'   né#hove   'with a fish'
          mbúndúdzí   'army worms'   sé#mbundudzi   'like army worms'
          hákáta   'diviner's bones'   sé#hakata   'like diviner's bones'
          badzá   'hoe'   né#badzá   'with a hoe'
          chapúpu   'witness'   sé#chapúpu   'like a witness'
          bénzíbvunzá   'inquisitive fool'   sé#benzibvunzá   'like an inquisitive fool'

     b.   Fárái   personal name   na#Fárái   'with Farai'

     c.   mbwá   'dog'   sá-mbwá   'owner of dog'

We see that a string of one or more successive high-toned syllables shifts to low. Forms such as *bénzíbvunzá* show that not all high-toned syllables of the stem change to low – just those that are not separated from the high tone of the clitic by a low. The forms in (34b,c) reveal certain important details: *na#Fárái* shows that only high-toned clitics induce the change, and *sá-mbwá* shows that only clitics trigger the rule – not just any high-toned prefix such as the honorific *sá-*.

If *hákáta* and *hóvé* have single, multiply linked high tones, then Meeussen's Rule can be expressed quite simply as (35a). On the tonal tier, the first high of the stem changes to low when it immediately follows a high belonging to a cliticized element.

(35) a.   H → L / H # _____

     b.   ne#hove   ne#hakata   ne#mbundudzi   ne#chapupu

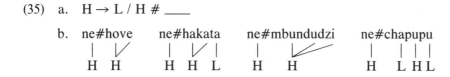

Given the multiply linked representations of (35b), all the high-toned syllables of *hákáta, hóvé,* and *mbúndúdzí* simultaneously change to low because the syllables all share the same high tone. The rule also correctly fails to dissimilate the medial high tone of *chapúpu* and the final high of *bénzíbvunzá* since a low tone intervenes between them and the clitic high that initiates the dissimilation. Meeussen's Rule applies to a H#H string but not to H#LH.

Contrast the situation with singly linked representations. Odden points out that if *hákáta, hóvé,* and so on, have singly linked high tones, then it becomes quite difficult to state the tonal change formally. To appreciate this point, consider the derivation of *né#hove* under single linking (36a).

(36) a. ne#hove   b. ne#hove
          | | | | | |
          H H H   H L H

If the rule iterates from left to right, the first application (shown in (36b)) changes a HH stem to LH. But now the contrast with underlying LH nouns such as *badzá* will have been merged; we will be unable to explain why the rule applies to *hóvé* but not to *badzá*. Right-to-left iteration is of no help either. The rule will not apply until the scansion reaches the first high of the stem, since that is the one that precedes the triggering clitic high. *hóvé* then changes to *hové*. But now the rule will be unable to return to the final syllable in order to change its high to low (without again introducing an unwanted change in *badzá*). Thus, with the singly linked representation of (36a) the only way the rule can be made to work is to reformulate it to change an entire string of high tones simultaneously. The introduction of essential variables such as H^1 (a string of one or more successive highs) permits Meeussen's Rule to be expressed as (37).

(37) $H^1 \rightarrow L \, / \, H \, \# \, \underline{\hspace{1.5em}}$

But this move increases the expressive power of the rule formalism and thus undesirably broadens the class of possible grammars. Furthermore, even this solution will not work without additional stipulation. In Shona it is possible to stack clitics: *sé#ne#hóvé* 'like with a fish'. Since (37) changes a string of successive highs after a high-toned clitic, it should transform [sé#né#hóvé] into the ungrammatical *sé#ne#hove*. A string of high tones follows the *sé* across a clitic boundary. Why doesn't Meeussen's Rule transform all of them into low? This is the result we expect from a rule defined on an unbounded string.

The solution sketched earlier that relies on multiple linking does not face a similar problem with *sé#ne#hóvé*. If multiple linking is a function of the OCP, and if the OCP governs just the underlying representation of the morpheme, a heteromorphemic high-toned sequence will not necessarily collapse into a single high tone. On these assumptions, the representation of (38) ensues.

(38) se#ne#hove
      | | |/
      H H H

So long as Meeussen's Rule iterates from left to right (or applies anticyclically), it will change the high of *né* to low before the high tone of *hóvé* is scanned. By the time the rule reaches the high tone of *hóvé*, the preceding tone will have changed to low and so the rule will correctly fail to apply.

Several conclusions emerge from this discussion. First, the across-the-board (ATB) tonal change we see in *né#hove* follows automatically from the representation with multiple linking by a paradigm phonological rule – one that changes one feature in strict adjacency to another (albeit in a special morphological configuration). Second, such ATB tonal changes as Meeussen's Rule furnish another diagnostic of multiple linking besides the multiple anchoring effect detected in Margi *làgù* (26b). Third, the multiple linking of both Margi *làgù* and Shona *hóvé* follows automatically if the OCP governs the underlying, lexical representation of morphemes. Finally, since Shona *hákáta* exhibits the ATB lowering, it must have the multiply linked high of (33b). An important corollary of this line of reasoning is that at least some associations between the tonal and segmental tier must be recorded in the underlying representations of morphemes. Not all associations can be produced by the left-to-right UAC. Stated differently, two morphemes such as *hákáta* and *séndere* can have identical representations on the tonal tier and contrast solely in terms of the associations between those tones and the TBUs of the segmental tier.

In addition to excluding the empirically unsupported lexical representations of (33b), the OCP also helps to solve the indeterminacy problem inherent in unconstrained autosegmental representations. In this regard an additional point is perhaps worth making. It has sometimes been argued that the OCP does not have to be stated independently but follows directly from a procedure that always seeks the simplest representation. After all, if Shona *hóvé* can be represented with just one high tone, isn't that simpler than a representation with two?

(39) a.   hove   b.   hove

          $\bigvee$

          H   H H

However, this reasoning seems fallacious. While (39a) has fewer tones than (39b), it has more association lines. Thus, unless tones and association lines are to be weighted differently, neither representation in (39) seems materially simpler than the other. This suggests that the OCP has the character of other constraints uncovered in generative grammar: a condition on representations of a rather specific character that is not obviously subsumed under more general cognitive considerations such as economy of information structure.

7.2.1 An Ordering Paradox

The contrasting behavior of two classes of enclitics in Shona furnishes an additional argument for autosegmental representations. One class includes *wó* 'also' and *sá* 'too'.

(40) bwe   'stone'   bwe#wó   'stone also'
      shámwarí   'friend'   shámwarí#wo   'friend also'

      pfúpi   'short'   pfúpi#sá   'too short'
      ndefú   'long'   ndefú#sa   'too long'

They appear as high-toned after a base whose final syllable is low and low-toned after a preceding high tone. Since the clitic boundary is the juncture across which Meeussen's Rule applies in Shona, we can easily account for the alternation by assigning these clitics an underlying high tone. Meeussen's Rule will transform underlying [ndefú#sá] into *ndefú#sa*.

The other clitic set is represented by *po* 'there'; it is high-toned after a word ending in a high, and low-toned after a word ending in a low.

(41) ákáénda   'he went'   ákáénda#po   'he went there'
      ákaóná   'he saw'   ákaóná#pó   'he saw there'

We may account for its behavior by stipulating a rule of assimilation that spreads a high tone to the right. Whether *po* has an underlying low tone or is toneless does not matter for the point to be made here. For concreteness we will assume it is toneless and stipulate the rule in (42a); *ákaóná#pó* receives the derivation shown in (42b).

(42) a. V (V)
           |---´
           H

      b. a ka o na#po   →   a ka o na#po
          | | ⌄ | | ↙
          H LH   H LH

Recall that assimilation in the autosegmental formalism is conceived as the extension of a feature from one TBU to an adjacent one. The result is a multiply linked tone – a representation that contrasts with the two successive high tones of [ndefú#sá] found in the underlying forms of (40). In other words, even though the H-spread rule (42a) makes the *po* clitic high, it does not merge the contrast with the successive high tones in [ndefú#sá]. This is the key to understanding an otherwise puzzling state of affairs. One rule of the language removes successive high-toned syllables in the V́#V́ context, while another turns right around and creates this very sequence in exactly the same context. From the autosegmental perspective, there is no mystery here. Meeussen's Rule dissimilates one high tone when adjacent to another: H#H. But, by hypothesis, the product of (42a) is just a single high tone. The representations are thus distinct.

This is of course a distinction that the linear model cannot make. In this model, assimilation is understood as a process that assigns a given segment (in this case the vowel of *po*) a feature specification that is identical with the triggering context (in this case [+hi]). But then the contrast with V́#*sá* is neutralized, and Meeussen's Rule will fail to distinguish the two cases (43a).

(43) a. V́#sá   V́#po

      —————   V́#pó   assimilation

      V́#sa   V́#po   Meeussen's Rule

   b. V́#sá   V́#po

      V́#sa   —————   Meeussen's Rule

      V́#sá   V́#pó   assimilation

Furthermore, applying the rules in the opposite order is of no avail (43b). Meeussen's Rule will change the [+hi] of *sá* to [−hi], effectively merging the contrast with *po*. Subsequent assimilation then incorrectly reassigns a high tone to *sá*. Thus, no matter in which order the rules are applied, an irrecoverable contrast is lost.

Some important conclusions can be drawn from this discussion. First, we have additional evidence for the distinction between singly and multiply linked high tones. Even though the representations in (44a) and (44b) have the same phonetic implementation as two successive high-pitched syllables, they are crucially distinguished by the phonological rules.

(44) a. V V   b. V V

     | | \\/

    H H   H

(44a) arises from morpheme concatenation while (44b) can have two sources: the lexical representation of two successive V́-toned syllables (an OCP requirement) or the product of an assimilation rule. Finally, the evidence suggests that assimilation rules such as the one affecting the clitic *#po* are autosegmental operations extending the domain of a feature from one TBU to the adjacent one.

7.2.2 Stevick's Rule

Having established the necessity for multiply linked representations in Shona, let us now look at an additional alternation in the language that, at first blush, seems to call such representations into question. The data in (45a) show that when words ending in two successive high-toned syllables such as *hóvé* or *murúmé* are followed by a word that begins with a high, the final high of the first word changes to low. (45b) shows that a single word-final high does not change. (45c) shows that the tonal change does not occur when the following word begins with a low tone. This tonal change, which may be dubbed *Stevick's Rule* after Stevick (1965), is informally expressed as HH##H → HL##H.

(45) a. hóvé   'fish'   murúmé   'man'

      húrú   'big'   ákafá   'he died'

      hóve húrú 'big fish'   murúme ákafá 'the man died'

   b. shámwarí   'friend'   mbwá   'dog'

      shámwarí ákafá 'the friend died'   mbwá yákafá 'the dog died'

   c. akáfá   '(the one) who died'

      murúmé akáfá   'the man who died'

In virtue of the ATB effect of Meeussen's Rule on *hóvé* in *né#hove,* we know that *hóvé* has a multiply linked high tone. The input to *hóvé húrú* must thus be (46).

(46)   hove   huru
        ⋁   ⋁
        H   H

But if *hóvé* has just a single high tone, how can the change to the two-tone sequence HL be expressed? It looks as if the multiply linked high must be split in two and then the second high in the resultant HH##H string changed to low. But such tonal dissection is a complication that seriously compromises the entire thrust of the analysis.

   We may avoid this undesirable outcome by appealing to the notion of "default rule." Recall from the discussion of Margi that in two-tone systems the default tone is generally low. Following Myers (1987a), we will assume that Stevick's Rule is expressed as the delinking of the word-final syllable from a multiply linked high when followed by a high (47a). The result is a bare TBU unassociated to the tonal tier. The UG default rule (47b) then supplies this vowel with a low tone.

(47)   a.

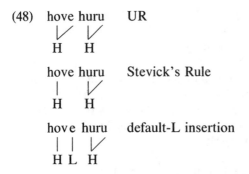

On this view, *hóvé húrú* receives the derivation in (48).

(48)   hove huru   UR
        ⋁   ⋁
        H   H

       hove huru   Stevick's Rule
        | ⋁
        H   H

       hove huru   default-L insertion
        | | ⋁
        H L H

   The forms in (49) show that Stevick's Rule must precede Meeussen's Rule. Otherwise, the high-toned clitics would incorrectly change to low.

(49)   mukúrú   'large'   mukúru#sá   'too large'
       hóvé   'fish'   hóve#wó   'fish also'

Now consider the data in (50), which bear on the ordering of Stevick's Rule with respect to H-spread (42a). We assume that the verb [tora] has a single high linked by the UAC to the initial syllable [to]. H-spread (42a) then extends the high to the toneless [ra] and #*po* (see later discussion of verbal tone): [ákatóra#po] → [ákatórá#pó].

(50) a. ákatórá#pó   'he took there'
       b. ndakátórá#pó badzá   'I took there a hoe'
       c. ndakátórá#po hárí   'I took there a pot'

The clitic *po* assimilates the preceding high tone from the verb 'took' in (50b). But when the following word begins with a high tone, this process is blocked (50c). Since Stevick's Rule delinks a high tone in precisely this context, we may account for the absence of a high tone on *po* in (50c) by letting Stevick's Rule trim off the final high tone produced by H-spread, as in (51).

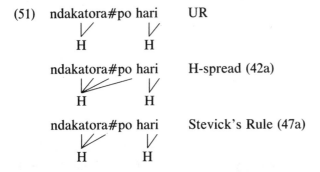

(51) ndakatora#po hari   UR

      ndakatora#po hari   H-spread (42a)

      ndakatora#po hari   Stevick's Rule (47a)

The significance of this derivation is that the multiply linked high that results from H-spread onto the toneless clitic *po* also undergoes Stevick's Rule – just like the underlying multiply linked high of *hóvé*. This is further evidence that H-spread creates a multiply linked structure, and more generally that assimilation is autosegmental spreading.

7.2.3 Shona Verbs

Compared to noun stems, where any syllable can be unpredictably high or low, verb stems in Shona have a much simpler underlying tonal structure. The Shona verb stem comprises a root followed optionally by a set of extensional suffixes and completed by a final-vowel suffix. The extensions mark changes in the verb's argument structure (e.g., causatives, benefactives, reciprocals). The tone of the extensional suffixes and the final vowel is predictable from the root tone. Roots fall into two classes. In verb stems built from a root in the high-toned class such as [teng], all the syllables of the root as well as the extensions and the final vowel bear a high tone (for the dialects under consideration here). The high tone of the root is thus distributed throughout the verb stem. In stems built from roots in the low-toned class such as [ereng], all syllables are pronounced low.

(52) ku-téng-á   'to buy'
      ku-téng-és-á   'to sell'
      ku-téng-és-ér-á   'to sell to'
      ku-téng-és-ér-án-á   'to sell to each other'

      ku-ereng-a   'to read'
      ku-ereng-es-a   'to make read'
      ku-ereng-es-er-a   'to make read to'

The most natural analysis assigns roots such as [teng] a single high on the tonal tier and treats the extensional and final-vowel suffixes as underlying toneless. After the UAC associates the high to the initial vowel, H-spread (repeated in (53a)) extends the high tone to the right, making all vowels in the stem high (53b).

(53) a.   V Ⓥ
           |--⁻⁻⁻
           H

      b.   teng-es-er-a   c.   ereng-es-a   d.   ereng-es-a
              ↙↙↙↙ |
              H   L

      e.   Ⓥ → V
               |
               L

    Now what about the roots in the low-toned class? Prima facie two hypotheses are plausible. We might assign these roots an underlying low tone and then generalize (53a) to also spread the low. On this analysis *ku-ereng-es-a* has the representation shown in (53c). Alternatively, we could postulate that the roots are toneless (53d) and assigned a low tone by the UG default rule (53e).

    Myers (1987a) uncovered evidence in the Southeastern dialects of Shona that supports the second interpretation. Object prefixes such as [rí] and [mú] have a lexical high tone; they have no material effect on a following stem whose root is high-toned (54a). But when appended to a verb whose root belongs to the low-toned class, the high of the object prefix spreads through the stem, encompassing all but the final vowel (54b).

(54) a.   ku-téng-és-á   'to sell'
           ku-rí-téng-és-á   'to sell it'

      b.   ku-ereng-er-a   'to read to'
           ku-mú-éréng-ér-a   'to read to him'

Descriptively, we clearly want to say that the rightward extension of the object high tone is produced by the same rule that extends the high of the root in (53a). (Otherwise, it would be an accident that two separate rightward extensions exist in the same grammar.) But if the low-toned verbs have the analysis shown in (53c), it is not clear why H-spread is not blocked by the association line linking the low tone and the root-initial syllable. If, on the other hand, the low-toned roots are underlyingly toneless, then the same rule (53a) extending the high rightward from a verb root [téng] will also extend the high of the object prefix. Still unexplained, however, is the puzzling behavior of the final syllable: *ku-téng-és-á* vs. *ku-mú-éréng-ér-a*. Why should the tonal character of a syllable at the far right edge of the word be affected by whether the spreading high originates from an object prefix or from the root? Isn't this a violation of locality?

An attractive answer to this question appeals to the grammatical structure of these words. Myers assembles evidence that the verb stem constitutes a domain in the lexical phonology of Shona separate from the word. For instance, this is the domain over which reduplication is defined: *ku-téng-és-á* reduplicates as *ku-téng-és-á-teng-es-a*. Extensional suffixes and the final vowel must be reduplicated (**ku-téng-és-á-teng-a*), but an object prefix may not be (*ndi-nó-mu-kúmbírá-kumbira* 1sg.-habitual-3sg.-ask for-ask for 'I keep asking him'). Following Myers, let us postulate a special rule marking the final syllable *extratonal*, in effect shielding it from the tonal rules in rather the same way that licensed extrasyllabic consonants are ignored by the syllabification rules. We assign this rule to the word level. We also assign H-spread to both the stem level and the word level. The final syllable will consequently be shielded from the effects of H-spread – but only in the word level. Spreading from the root takes place on the stem level and thus encompasses the final syllable. The distribution of rules in the two lexical strata is depicted in (55).

(55) verb stem stratum   UAC
                            H-spread

      word level   UAC
                            final syllable extratonality
                            H-spread
                            default-L insertion

To illustrate this solution, let us derive *ku-rí-téng-és-ér-á, ku-ereng-es-a,* and *ku-rí-éréng-és-a*. To simplify the displays, we will let V stand for a given TBU.

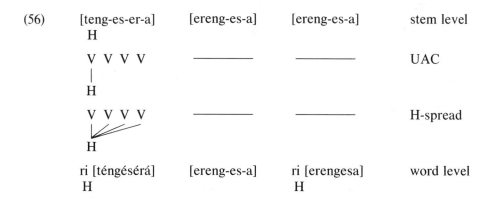

(56) [teng-es-er-a]   [ereng-es-a]   [ereng-es-a]   stem level
        H

       V V V V   ————————   ————————   UAC
         |
         H

       V V V V   ————————   ————————   H-spread
         ⟍⟍
         H

       ri [téngésérá]   [ereng-es-a]   ri [erengesa]   word level
          H   H

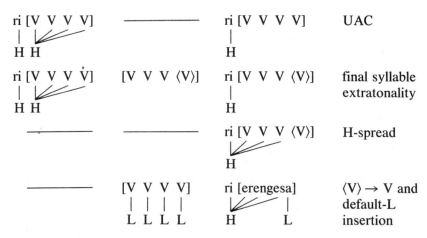

ri [V V V V]	———————	ri [V V V V]	UAC
H H		H	
ri [V V V V̇]	[V V V ⟨V⟩]	ri [V V V ⟨V⟩]	final syllable
H H		H	extratonality
———————	———————	ri [V V V ⟨V⟩]	H-spread
		H	
———————	[V V V V]	ri [erengesa]	⟨V⟩ → V and
	L L L L	H L	default-L
			insertion

In the first step the high of [teng] is associated to the TBU at the left edge. H-spread then extends this H to all remaining vowels of the verb stem, completing this stratum. Since the root [ereng], by hypothesis, lacks any tones, no tonal rules are applicable. We then enter the word-level stratum, where the object prefix becomes visible. The UAC attaches it to the leftmost position – the *ri*. But now the special rule of extratonality applies to shield the final syllable from application of H-spread (marked by the angled brackets). Consequently, all syllables of the following stem are linked to the object high save the last. The derivation is completed by the revocation of extratonality and the default rule assigning the erstwhile extratonal syllable as well as all syllables of [ereng-es-a] a low tone.

This analysis crucially depends on the low-toned roots being toneless at the point where the object prefix is encountered. If a low tone had already been assigned (as in (53c)), then the H-spread rule would be unable to extend the object high past the initial syllable (by the line-crossing ban). As a matter of fact, there is another dialect of Shona where precisely this state of affairs obtains. In Southern Karanga the tonal assignment inside the verb stem is identical to that of the Southeastern dialect. But an object prefix in Southern Karanga alters only the tone on the immediately following syllable. Subsequent syllables in the stem remain unchanged.

(57) <u>Southern Karanga</u>   Southeastern
      ku-vereng-er-a   ku-vereng-er-a
      ku-mú-véreng-er-a   ku-mú-véréng-ér-a

We can account for this dialect difference quite simply with the assumption that in Southern Karanga the default-L insertion rule has moved up into the first lexical stratum. Consequently, when a stem enters the word-level stratum, all of its syllables will have been assigned a tone. The input to H-spread on the word level is thus (58a).

(58) a.   mu [verengera]   b.   mu [verengera]

          H LL LL   H LL LL

If H-spread (53a) is reinterpreted as spreading a high rightward until an association line is encountered, the rule will only be able to extend the domain of the prefixal high to the first vowel of the stem (58b). The result is a doubly linked vowel. Since Shona has no contour tones, a ban on more than one association per TBU will lead to a delinking of the original low tone, deriving [mú-vérengera]. We have seen in earlier chapters that one of the ways in which dialects can differ is in the ordering of the phonological rules. Appealing to this device thus seems reasonable in this case.

If we accept the implication of Myers's analysis that the underlying tonal opposition in Shona is not H vs. L but rather H vs. Ø, then two remarks are in order. First, Meeussen's Rule can now be expressed as the deletion of a high rather than as a change from high to low. We might then entertain generalizing the rule inside the verb. A form such as *ku-rí-téng-és-á* 'to sell it' (54a) could be derived as follows. At the word level, the object high on [rí] dissimilates the following multiply linked high of the stem to derive a toneless stem [ku-rí-teng-es-a]. The H-spread rule then fills in the gap with the high of the object prefix to yield [ku-rí-téng-és-á]. So long as the extratonality rule is ordered before Meeussen's Rule, the final vowel will not be marked extratonal and hence will be able to accept the object marker's spreading. While this analysis works, it fails to generalize to the phrasal level. Recall that [né#hóvé] becomes *né#hove*. To obtain this result, H-spread must be ordered before Meeussen's Rule. There appears to be no advantage to generalizing Meeussen's Rule to the word level at the expense of inconsistent ordering restrictions. To conclude, Meeussen's Rule may still be expressed as a deletion process; but it must be restricted to the clitic context in Shona.

Second, if the underlying tonal opposition is (linked) H vs. Ø, the OCP must be reinterpreted in order to allow for such cases as *shámwarí* 'friend'.

(59)   shamwari
       | |
       H   H

In (59) there is no longer any element intervening between the two high tones. In order to permit this representation but still maintain the OCP's ban on adjacent identical tones, Myers refines the notion of adjacency so that the TBUs must be taken into account. Two tones are *adjacent* iff the following restrictions hold: (i) no distinct tone appears between them and (ii) if they are associated to the segmental tier, then no distinct TBU may intervene between their TBUs. The high tones in (59) thus satisfy the first clause of the definition but not the second. They now count as nonadjacent and hence do not violate the OCP.

7.2.4 OCP Extensions

In our discussion of Shona we have argued that the OCP plays a fundamental role in controlling the distribution of multiple linking for the underlying representation. It is this principle that forces a single high tone in *hóvé*, *hákáta*, and so on. In addition, we have examined two rules (Meeussen's Rule and Stevick's Rule) that eliminate adjacent high tones that arise from morpheme and word concatenation:

the former deletes one of the abutting highs, while the latter delinks. This suggests that the OCP holds for later levels of representation beyond the underlying level. Myers (1987a) explores this question for Shona. In addition to motivating the existence of rules eliminating adjacent high tones that arise from morpheme and word concatenation, Myers sees the OCP as monitoring the H-spread rule – blocking its application just when it would give rise to adjacent high tones. We may appreciate this point in the following paradigms, where H-spread extends across the word boundary. The high cannot spread beyond the initial syllable since, by this time, all default low tones will have been inserted.

(60) zvirongó   'water pots'
      zvina   'four'
      zvirongó zvína   'four water pots'

      akabika   'and then he cooked'
      Chipó   personal name
      Chipó ákabika   'and then Chipo cooked'

      mukómana   'boy'
      ndakáóná   'I saw'
      ndakáóná mukómana   'I saw the boy'

      badzá   'hoe'
      ndakáténgá   'I bought'
      ndakáténgá badzá   'I bought a hoe'

Note that while [LL. . . words are transformed to [HL. . . , [LH. . . words such as *badzá* remain unchanged. Myers sees this as an effect of the OCP blocking the spread of the high just in case it creates two adjacent high-toned syllables. Unfortunately, it is not clear that this conclusion can be drawn with certainty. Recall that Stevick's Rule applies in exactly this context. The lack of a surface high tone on the initial syllable of *badzá* might reflect Stevick's Rule trimming the final syllable from the domain of the spreading high. Whether the OCP may inhibit the application of a phonological rule remains a hotly debated question in autosegmental phonology; see Odden 1986, 1988 for discussion.

If the OCP governs later stages of the derivation, then we might wonder whether two adjacent identical tones that straddle a constituent boundary (i.e., H [H or H] H) and have failed to be eliminated by a phonological rule, merge into a single tone. Rules applying on later lexical or phrasal domains could detect such a merger. Myers appears to have identified a case of this form in the subjunctive of Shona. The subjunctive consists of a high-toned subject prefix plus a verb stem whose final vowel is [e]. Examples for the verbs *ku-téng-és-á* 'to buy' and *ku-tar-is-a* 'to look' appear in (61a).

(61) a. tí-téng-és-é   tí-tár-ís-e
            'that we might sell'   'that we might look'

      b. ti-teng-es-e   ti-tar-is-⟨e⟩

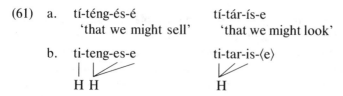

c.   há#ti-teng-es-e   há#ti-tar-is-e
     'let us sell'   'let us look'

In *tí-tár-ís-e* the high of the prefix *tí* spreads through the stem built on the toneless root [tar] (with extratonality of the final vowel). *tí-téng-és-é* has the representation shown in (61b). Neither Meeussen's nor Stevick's Rule is applicable. The former does not apply because the subject prefix is not clitic to the verb, and the latter because the first high is not multiply linked. The hortatives in (61c) are formed from the subjunctive by the prefix *há-*. If *há* is clitic to the verb, then Meeussen's Rule will lower the multiply linked high originating in the [tí] prefix in *há#ti-tar-is-e*. The problem is to explain why the high tone of the prefix [tí] and the multiply linked high originating in the root [téng] both lower in *há#ti-teng-es-e*. If the two highs of (61b) have merged at the end of the preceding cycle/stratum, then this result follows automatically. We might thus posit a UG principle of last resort that merges adjacent identical elements at the end of each cycle. This convention ensures that the input to the next cycle (and presumably to the phonetics) contains no OCP violations.

Once again, while this proposal is attractive, the evidence from Shona is not conclusive. We know that the language spreads its high tones to the right. In some cases, the high spreads to a toneless vowel. But in other cases it spreads to a TBU linked to a low tone. It thus appears that the rule does not care about the tonal structure to the right: it simply extends the high until an association line is encountered. On this view, a high tone should also spread to a following TBU that is linked to a high (62a).

(62)   a.   V V   b.   V   c.   V   d.   V V

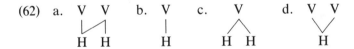

There are few if any cases on record in which a language must distinguish between one and two identical tones mapped to the same TBU (as in (62b) vs. (62c)). This has led to the convention merging two identical tones into one when they lodge on the same TBU (presumably a subcase of the OCP). Such a convention automatically transforms (62a) into (62d). The effect we see in the Shona subjunctive thus might reflect this convention rather than a last resort merger. To differentiate the two proposals, we need to find a system isomorphic to Shona but lacking the H-spread rule. If the OCP holds for later levels of representation, then two adjacent highs resulting from morpheme concatenation or the application of a phonological rule should always merge and be treated as a single tone by rules applying on later cycles. Finding evidence to confirm or disconfirm such a prediction is one of the outstanding questions of autosegmental phonology.

To briefly summarize, we have seen that the OCP plays a major role in the tonology of Shona. First, it enforces the multiple linking in lexical representations that is crucial to explaining the ATB effects displayed by Meeussen's Rule. Second, it may function as an output condition blocking the application of H-spread just in case the latter creates two adjacent high-toned syllables. Third, it can be seen as the driving force behind Meeussen's Rule and Stevick's Rule – both of which eliminate successive high-toned syllables that arise from the concatenation of morphemes and words. Finally, it may function as a last resort process, merging any remaining adjacent high tones at the end of a cycle.

The discussion of Shona illustrates a more general point. As we saw in our study of syllabification in chapter 6, much of the phonology of a language can be seen as operations designed to advance structures to a more optimal state or configuration (Goldsmith 1990). In line with recent speculations in syntax, we might conjecture that these states and configurations are interface conditions mediating between the grammar and other cognitive systems – in this case phonetics. The OCP requirement that [XX] be avoided in favor of [XY] or in the limit [X] makes sense on perceptual grounds and may have articulatory motivation as well in minimizing muscular and/or neural fatigue.

7.3   Venda

In this section we will explore the autosegmental view of tone further with material from Venda, a Bantu language of South Africa. The discussion is based on the analysis by Cassimjee (1983, 1987). The syllables of Venda have three surface tones: high (marked by the acute), low (unmarked), and falling (circumflex). The predictable falling tone is restricted to the penultimate syllable of the phrase. Venda nominals have radically different tonal shapes depending on their location in the phrase. In particular, they have one shape in isolation or when the preceding word ends in a low tone and a quite different shape when the preceding word ends in a high tone, such as when object of *ndivhóná* 'I see'. (63) illustrates these alternations for disyllabic roots.

(63)	post-L and isolation	post-H	
	mu-tuka	mú-tûka	'youth'
	mu-rathú	mú-râthú	'brother'
	mu-sélwa	mú-sêlwa	'bride'
	mu-sádzí	mú-sâdzi	'woman'

The nominals in (63) contain a low-toned prefix *mu-*. They show all four possible combinations of high and low tone on the root syllables in the post-L/isolation context. These tonal contrasts are sharply reduced in the post-H forms, where the prefix has become high and the root-initial syllable falling. The post-L forms are underlying and the post-H arise from extension of the high tone of the preceding word. But how?

The low-initial roots *mu-tuka* and *mu-rathú* take a falling tone on the initial syllable of the root in the post-H forms *mú-tûka* and *mú-râthú*. Since a falling tone is equivalent to a HL combination on a single syllable, the best hypothesis is that the high of the preceding word has spread to the root-initial syllable to create a contour falling tone. But we also know that spreading rules cannot cross association lines (64a). Consequently, the prefix *mu-* must lack an association to the tonal tier at the point where the high spreads past it to the root. Cassimjee postulates the special rule of (64b) to delete word-initial lows. Since there is quite a bit of evidence for this rule, we will accept this analysis here. The H-spread rule is stated in (64c). It is formulated simply to spread a high tone to a following syllable. We will assume that the rule iterates until it is blocked by an association line. The form *mú-râthú* is derived in (64d).

(64)　a.　[mu-rathu]

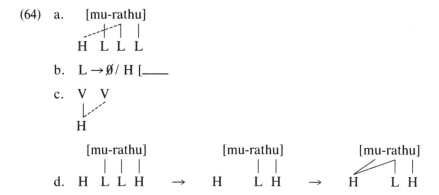

　　b.　$L \rightarrow \emptyset / H [\underline{}$

　　c.　V　V

　　　　　H

　　　　[mu-rathu]　　　　　[mu-rathu]　　　　　[mu-rathu]

　　d.　H　L　L　H　　→　　H　　L　H　　→　　H　　L　H

Now consider a root with an initial high tone such as *mu-sélwa*. Its post-H form *mú-sêlwa* also starts with a falling tone. After L-deletion, the representation in (65a) results.

(65)　a.　[mu-selwa]　　b.　[mu-selwa]　　c.　[mu-selwa]

　　　　H　　H　L　　　　　H　　L　L　　　　　H　　L　L

Cassimjee shrewdly observes that the low required for the second half of the falling tone can be produced by calling on the dissimilation rule in (66) that changes a high to low after a high, a reflex of Meeussen's Rule that we saw operating in Shona.

(66)　$H \rightarrow L / H \underline{}$

Like the H-spread rule, (66) also applies after L-deletion. Its application in (65a) produces representation (65b), to which the H-spread rule may apply to derive the falling tone in *mú-sêlwa* (65c).

With Meeussen's Rule added to the analysis, we can now deal with the change of *mu-sádzí* to *mú-sâdzí*. The two possible underlying representations for the root are given in (67).

(67)　a.　[mu-sadzi]　　　　b.　[mu-sadzi]

　　　　L　H　H　　　　　　　L　H

It should be clear that (67b) is the one we want. Meeussen's Rule will change the multiply linked high to a low. Spreading of the high from the preceding word then yields the required falling tone on the root-initial syllable. Besides being required on descriptive grounds, (67b) is the only permissible representation if we accept the OCP, which bars successive identical tones within a morpheme. The derivations in (68) summarize the analysis to this point.

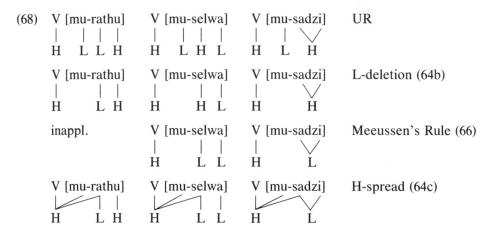

(68)

	V [mu-rathu]	V [mu-selwa]	V [mu-sadzi]	UR
	H LLH	H LHL	H L H	
	V [mu-rathu]	V [mu-selwa]	V [mu-sadzi]	L-deletion (64b)
	H L H	H H L	H H	
	inappl.	V [mu-selwa]	V [mu-sadzi]	Meeussen's Rule (66)
		H L L	H L	
	V [mu-rathu]	V [mu-selwa]	V [mu-sadzi]	H-spread (64c)
	H L H	H L L	H L	

Now let us consider some additional root types. Monosyllabic roots have just two contrasting tonal shapes – as we might expect if the inventory of basic tones is just high and low. (69) illustrates the alternations that befall these nouns in the two phrasal contexts.

(69)

post-L	post-H	
mu-thu	mú-thu	'person'
mu-rí	mú-ri	'tree'

Clearly 'person' has a lexical low and 'tree' a lexical high tone. But our rules do not derive the correct results in the post-H context, as (70) shows.

(70) a.

    [mu-ri]   [mu-ri]   [mu-ri]   [mu-ri]

H   L H → H   H → H   L → H   L

b.   V   V

      H L → H L   (where V is posttonic)

c.   V   V

      H L → H L   (where V is pretonic)

The rules predict *mú-rî* with a final fall. There is actually a rather simple explanation available here. The penultimate syllable of the phrase in Venda carries an accent (manifested phonetically by increased vowel duration). Complex structures often simplify in unaccented positions. Tone appears to be no different. We thus complete the derivation in (70a) with the rule in (70b) that delinks the spreading high tone from an unaccented syllable. Anticipating later discussion, we express simplification of rising tones in prepenultimate syllables as delinking of the low tone (70c).

The paradigm in (71) illustrates the behavior of trisyllabic roots in the two phrasal contexts.

(71)

	post-L	post-H	
LLL	mu-kalaha	mú-kálaha	'old man'
LLH	mu-tukaná	mú-túkaná	'boy'
LHL	mu-lambóni	mú-lámb'óni	'at the river'
LHH	mu-tańgá	mú-tá'ńngá	'young man'
HLL	ma-díngwâre	má-díngware	personal name
HLH	tshi-vhávhâlá	tshí-vhávhalá	'wild beast'
HHL	mu-dúhúlu	mú-dúhulu	'grandchild'
HHH	mu-kégúlú	mú-kégulu	'old woman'

The alternations in (71) are quite complex. First of all, the post-L forms *ma-díngwâre* and *tshi-vhávhâlá* have a fall on their penults. If these roots take the underlying HLL and HLH shapes, respectively, then they complete the inventory of $2 \times 2 \times 2 = 8$ possible tonal patterns available in a two-tone system. The fall derives from spreading of the root-initial high to the following syllable. Presumably there is also H-spread to the final syllable in the LHL *mu-lambóni*. But the resultant falling tone simplifies because it is located in an unaccented syllable.

Before discussing the post-H forms, we take note of two new concepts: downdrift and downstep. In many African tonal languages the pitch register drops in absolute value as the phrase is articulated. This declination takes a number of forms, and the precise details are not well understood. A prevalent form of *downdrift* realizes a string of high-toned syllables after a low at a slightly lower pitch value than the preceding high. In other words, each successive high in a HLHLHLH sequence is thus articulated at a slightly lower value. In some languages the low tones also drop but in others they do not. The schematic phrase of (72a) receives the implementation in (72b).

(72) a. CÝCVCÝCVCÝ   b. –
  –
  –
  – –

Venda has downdrift; the high tone on the final syllable of *mú-túkaná*, the post-H form of 'boy', is spoken at a lower level than the high tone spread over the first two syllables.

Downstep indicates a situation in which a high tone has a downdrifted phonetic value but there is, at least on the surface, no preceding low tone to mark the division from the preceding high, which is articulated at the "normal" value. Downstep is usually marked by the *!* sign placed between one high and the following downstepped high. Thus, in Venda *mú-lámb'óni* the high tone on the syllable [bó] is pitched slightly lower than the preceding high tone spread over the first two syllables (73a). A sequence of downstepped highs thus looks quite literally like the steps in a staircase (73b).

(73) a. mú-lámbʼóni   b. CV́CʼV́CʼV́CʼV́

    ‾ ‾   ‾

        ‾   ‾

                                  ‾

        ‾   ‾

The analysis of downstep and downdrift is controversial. Here we will adopt the interpretation of downdrift as a left-to-right parsing of the tonal tier into L_1H_1 "tonal feet" (Clements 1979, Huang 1985). Each foot is assigned a pitch value lower than the preceding one. For example, a V́V́V́VV́VV́VV́V́ sequence is parsed [V́][VV́][VVV́V́][VV́]. The feet constitute miniregisters in which a low is articulated toward the bottom of the register and a high toward the top. In phonetic implementation each foot as a whole is pitched at a lower level than the preceding one and so the absolute values drift downward across the utterance.

With this background we can now return to the Venda post-H forms in (71). Consider first the low-initial *mú-túkaná*. Deletion of the low tone from the prefix and spreading of the high yields the representation in (74a) with high and low linked to the root-initial syllable.

(74) a.   [mu + tukana]   b.   [mu + tukana]   c.   [mu + tukana]
              ╱│ │ │   ╱   │ │   ╱   │ │
            H   L L H   H   L H   H   L L H

Since this syllable is unaccented, the correct surface form can be derived through simplification of the contour tone (70c). We have two options: either the root-initial low deletes to give (74b) or it delinks to give (74c). In either case we derive a HL_1H sequence that yields downdrifting of the second high by the phonetic interpretation procedure mentioned earlier. At this point the choice between (74b) and (74c) may seem of slight importance. However, turning to a form such as *mú-lámbʼóni*, we see that there are good reasons to prefer the delinking formulation of tonal simplification. After L-deletion and H-spread, *mú-lámbʼóni* has the representation in (75a).

(75) a.   [mu + lamboni]   b.   [mu + lamboni]   c.   [mu + lamboni]
              ╱│ │ │   ╱   │ │   ╱   │ │
            H   L HL   H   L HL   (H)   (L H)(L)

Delinking of the low portion of the contour tone yields (75b). But now the procedure parsing the tonal tier to implement downdrift will group the floating low and the following high into a foot (75c). Like any other foot, this one will be pitched at a slightly lower level than the preceding foot. As a result, the overt high is automatically dropped to yield the downstep. No special rule is required, and downstep can be assimilated to the downdrift phenomenon. This explanation hinges crucially on the tonal tier containing information – the floating low – that is not directly realized phonetically. It thus constitutes another strong reason to adopt the autosegmental approach to tone.

Recall from the discussion of *mu-sádzí≈mú-sâdzi* in (67) that it was crucial that the OCP banning successive highs on the tonal tier be respected in Venda underlying representations. We thus predict that HHL and HHH stems will lower each high. This prediction is dramatically confirmed by *mu-dúhúlu≈mú-dúhulu* and *mu-kégúlú≈mú-kégulu*. The latter is derived in (76).

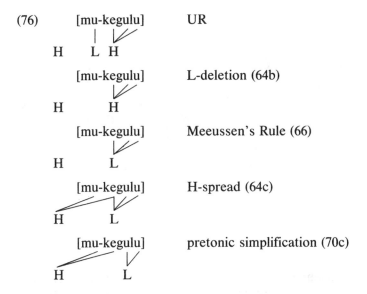

(76)   [mu-kegulu]   UR

    H   L   H

        [mu-kegulu]   L-deletion (64b)

    H   H

        [mu-kegulu]   Meeussen's Rule (66)

    H   L

        [mu-kegulu]   H-spread (64c)

    H   L

        [mu-kegulu]   pretonic simplification (70c)

    H   L

This derivation appeals to locality – a fundamental notion in generative grammar. Phonological rules typically relate (near) adjacent elements. Strong locality confers a learnability advantage on the theory. If the element activating a rule is consistently found in the local environment, then the learner's hypothesis space is restricted – narrowing the class of grammars. But the alternation of *mu-kégúlú* with *mú-kégulu* is prima facie inconsistent with a strong version of the locality thesis. The final syllable *-lu* systematically alters its tone as a function of the final tone of the preceding word. This change operates across three intervening syllables. But not all final syllables in trisyllabic stems behave this way. The high of *mu-thakaná* 'boy' never changes. It appears that we must consider the nature of the intervening syllables in order to explain the difference between *mu-kégúlú* and *mu-thakaná*. But an autosegmental representation of tone and the OCP (proposed to solve the indeterminacy problem) motivates a representation with just one high tone spanning the three stem syllables in *mu-kégúlú*. Consequently, a rule changing a high tone to low immediately after a high has the surprising effect of changing the final syllable of *mu-kégúlú* (as well as the two preceding syllables) in response to the preceding word. The Venda data thus turn out to support the locality thesis.

The final set of Venda nominals we will consider appears in (77). They lack a prefix and provide independent evidence for the rule of L-deletion.

(77) | post-L and isolation | post-H | |
|---|---|---|
| bofu | bófu | 'blind person' |
| thukú | thúku | 'scoundrel' |
| ndémwa | ndêmwa | 'naughty child' |
| ṭhólí | ṭhôli | 'spy' |

The post-H forms *ndêmwa* and *ṭhôli* are straightforward. The latter is derived in (78).

(78)   [ṭholi] →   [ṭholi] →   [ṭholi]

      H H   H L   H L

Since there is no prefix, L-deletion is inapplicable. In the first step the multiply linked high dissimilates to low by Meeussen's Rule. The high of the preceding word then spreads onto the initial syllable to create the falling tone. Since this syllable is the penult, it is accented and so no tonal simplification occurs.

Consider now the *thukú≈thúku* alternation. The underlying representation is given in (79a).

(79) a. [thuku]   b.   [thuku]

      L H   H L H

If Venda lacked the rule deleting an initial low, then spreading of the preceding high should yield *thûkú,* with a falling tone in the post-H context (79b). But the correct pronunciation is *thúku* – with a simple high on the first syllable. Post-H *thúku* (and *bófu*) are the only forms encountered so far with a plain high instead of a fall on an accented, root-initial syllable. But if Venda deletes initial lows, then the lexical low of *thukú* will be preempted from forming the second portion of the contour falling tone. Thus, the otherwise mysterious absence of a falling tone in post-H *thúku* is predicted. The derivation is given in (80).

(80)   [thuku] →   [thuku] →   [thuku] →   [thuku] →   [thuku]

    H L H   H H   H L   H L   H L

In the first step L-deletion applies; then the high on the final syllable turns to low by Meeussen's Rule. The high spreads from the preceding word, and the intermediate falling tone on the unaccented final syllable simplifies.

Finally, consider the *bofu≈bófu* alternation. The two possible underlying representations are given in (81a) and (81c).

(81) a. [bofu]   b.   [bofu] →   [bofu] →   [bofu]

      L   H L   H   H

c. [bofu]   d.   [bofu] → [bofu] → [bofu] → [bofu]

    | | | | | ⟋⟋| ⟋ |

    L L   H L L   H   L   H   L   H   L

If (81a) is chosen, then the result is the derivation in (81b) in which the single low is deleted, yielding two bare syllables. We have assumed that H-spread is unbounded and blocked only by an association line. Consequently, the rule should spread the high onto both syllables of the root, deriving the incorrect *bófú*. On the other hand, if the root has two low tones, as in (81c), then L-deletion eliminates only the first (81d). H-spread and simplification then yield the correct post-H form *bófu*.

Thus, on descriptive grounds the representation in (81c) with two separate low tones, each linked to a different syllable, is the correct one. Yet Venda has also shown that in roots with high tones the highs must be multiply linked. This assumption was crucial to our account of the across-the-board change of high to low tone affected by Meeussen's Rule. There is thus a puzzling asymmetry in the representation of the high and low tones in Venda. A possible explanation for this difference is that low is the default tone in Venda and thus is inserted by the rule in (82) that assigns any toneless vowel a low on the tonal tier. The result is a single linking of low tones.

(82) Ⓥ → V

         |

         L

This interpretation implies that Venda underlying representations in general contain only linked high tones that respect the OCP. On this account, the stems in (77) have the lexical representations in (83a).

(83) a. [bofu]   [thuku]   [ndemwa]   [ṭholi]

                 | | &nbsV

                 H   H   H   H

    b. [bofu]   [thuku]   [ndemwa]   [ṭholi]

          | | | | | | V

          L L   L H   H L   H

At some point in the derivation prior to the operation of the phrasal rules discussed in this section, rule (82) will insert low tones to yield the representations in (83b). These representations are then input to the phrasal rules.

Bruce Hayes (personal communication) suggests an alternative analysis that permits underlying multiply linked low tones and thus removes the high-low asymmetry. First, Cassimjee's L-deletion (64b) is replaced by a delinking rule (84a). Second, Meeussen's Rule is reordered after H-spread and reformulated to change high to low after a tautosyllabic high, eliminating a syllable-internal downstep (84b). Under this analysis, the post-H forms of *bofu* and *mu-sélwa* receive the derivations in (84c).

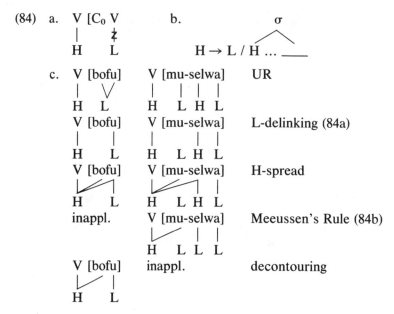

(84) a. V [C₀ V   b.   σ
          | ⌇   ╱‾‾╲
          H   L   H → L / H ... ___

      c. V [bofu]   V [mu-selwa]   UR

          V [bofu]   V [mu-selwa]   L-delinking (84a)

          V [bofu]   V [mu-selwa]   H-spread

          inappl.   V [mu-selwa]   Meeussen's Rule (84b)

          V [bofu]   inappl.   decontouring

Under this alternative Myers's conception of adjacency (section 7.2.3) is not violated as it is in the derivation of post-H *mú-sêlwa* in (68).

Let us close the discussion with two observations. First, it should be clear that if we invoke the notion of default low tone, then the high tones must be linked in the underlying representation. Otherwise, there is no nonarbitrary way to associate a high tone by the UG UAC and at the same time distinguish a CV́CV vs. CVCV́ contrast. Second, if low tones are not inserted by the default rule, then a system with four contrasting disyllabic stems could be assigned the representations in (85).

(85) CV́CV́   CV́CV   CVCV́   CVCV
      CVCV   CVCV   CVCV   CVCV

      H   H L   L H   L

The UAC plus spreading of high and low tones to unlinked syllables would yield the correct surface forms. But a system such as Venda with an eight-way contrast on trisyllabic stems requires prelinking if the OCP is respected. Otherwise, it will be impossible to generate a HHL vs. HLL contrast, as shown in (86).

(86) CV́CV́CV   CV́CVCV
        ╲╱╱   │╱╱
        HL   HL

7.4 Vowel Harmony

In this section we will survey some of the early generative research on vowel harmony, setting the stage for further discussion of vocalic features in chapter 9.

(See Clements 1980, 1985b and Ringen 1975 for valuable discussion.) Vowel harmony is a phonological state in which the vowels in a given domain share or harmonize for a particular feature. It differs from other processes affecting adjacent vowels (e.g., umlaut) in that typically all of the vowels of the language participate in the harmonic constraint. In addition, the harmony applies in an essentially unbounded fashion, affecting all the relevant vowels within the domain (typically the word). Virtually any of the common features used to distinguish among vowels have been discovered to seat a harmonic system, including vowel height, backness, rounding, nasality, and pharyngeal opening or [ATR]. Vowel harmony exhibits many of the "action-at-a-distance" properties displayed by tone. It is not surprising, then, that the analysis of this phenomenon has been a major focus of generative research. In this section we will see that many of the puzzling properties of tones that motivate the autosegmental approach are also found in vowel harmony; the discussion recapitulates a number of points made in Clements 1980.

7.4.1 Wolof: A Linear Analysis

The ATR-based system found in the West Atlantic language Wolof (Ka 1988) illustrates a number of the typical properties of vowel harmony. The vowels fall into the two groups shown in (87). Long vowels are transcribed as geminates. The high vowels as well as the long low vowel [aa] have special harmonic properties and so we momentarily put them aside.

(87) [+ATR] i   u   [−ATR]
               é   ó   e   o
                  ë   a

Restricting the discussion to the remaining nonhigh vowels, we find that Wolof exhibits the two chief traits of harmonic systems. First, the vowels that appear in root morphemes are drawn from two disjoint sets: the [+ATR] vowels {é,ó,ë} and the [−ATR] vowels {e,o,a}.

(88) [+ATR]   [−ATR]
       béréb   'place'   doole   'strength'
       gétën   'to bother'   cere   'couscous'
       jéégó   'to step'   lempo   'tax'
       géléém   'camel'   xandoor   'to snore'
       xóóyël   'to dilute'   nelaw   'to sleep'

Combining vowels from the two sets is systematically prohibited. Roots of the shape *CéCe, *CoCó, *CëCa, and so on, are impossible in Wolof. The data in (89) illustrate a second trait of harmonic systems: affixes regularly alternate for the feature [ATR] in agreement with the root.

(89) instrumental/locative -é≈-e
       dóór-é   'to hit with'   xool-e   'to look with'
       réér-é   'to be lost in'   dem-e   'to go with'
       gë-né   'to be better in'   xam-e   'to know in'

participant *-lé≈-le*

dóór-lé	'to help hit'	jox-le	'to help give'
réér-lé	'to lose one's property'	dee-le	'to lose a relative'
yëg-lé	'to announce'	takk-le	'to help tie'

past tense *-óón≈-oon*

réér-óón	'was lost'	reer-oon	'had dinner'
ñów-óón	'came'	jox-oon	'gave'
bëgg-óón	'wanted'	takk-oon	'tied'

benefactive *-ël≈-al*

lééb-ël	'to tell stories for'	bey-al	'to cultivate for'
fóót-ël	'to launder for'	woor-al	'to fast for'
jënd-ël	'to buy for'	wax-al	'to speak for'

possessive *-ëm≈-am*

sófóór-ëm	'his driver'	nelaw-am	'his sleep'

comitative *-ëndóó≈-andoo*

génn-ëndóó	'to go out together'	dend-andoo	'to be neighbors'
tóx-ëndóó	'to smoke together'	topp-andoo	'to imitate'
dëkk-ëndóó	'to live together'	wax-andoo	'to say together'

Monosyllabic suffixes such as the participant and past tense as well as polysyllabic ones such as the comitative systematically vary the quality of their vowels in accord with the root. If the word contains more than one suffix, then the harmonic effect propagates from the root through the suffixes to the end of the word.

(90) jubbëntééndóó 'to rectify together'
      from [jubb-anti-andoo]
   muñëndééndóó 'to be a little patient together'
      from [muñ-andi-andoo]

An "action-at-a-distance" effect is thus produced: variation in the first root vowel systematically alters the quality of the final vowel across a potentially unbounded distance.

Now let us consider the challenges a harmony system poses for the linear model. Recall that in this model each feature is the property of a position in the phonemic string and every segment of the string is exhaustively specified plus or minus for each feature. This "linearity" requirement poses significant problems for the assignment of an underlying representation to a polysyllabic root morpheme in Wolof. Consider for example the root *nelaw*. Since the vowels of the root harmonize for [ATR], the [−ATR] feature of the first vowel is predictable from that of the second. But the value of the second is equally predictable from that of the first. A similar indeterminacy is posed by the suffixes. We could postulate an underlying [+ATR] and change it to [−ATR] to agree with [−ATR] roots. But it appears just as valid to set up the affixes as [−ATR] and change them to [+ATR] when the root is [+ATR]. Second, we must postulate a rule of assimilation changing the suffixal vowel so as to agree with the [ATR] feature of the root. But which root vowel should serve as the trigger? Since each vowel of the root is [−ATR], it would seem arbitrary to single out the first or second as the origin. The problem is compounded in an ATR harmonic system such as that of Akan (Clements 1985b) in which both prefixes and suffixes harmonize to the root. (Nonlow [−ATR] vowels are marked by under dots in Akan (91).)

(91) o-fiti-i   'he pierced it'
      ọ-cirẹ-ị   'he showed it'

Does the prefixal vowel harmonize with the first or the second root vowel? Which of the two root vowels initiates harmony in the suffix?

7.4.2 The Root-Marker Theory

It seems that the vowel harmony in a Wolof form such as *nelaw-am* 'his sleep' is not the function of a particular vowel of the root or word but rather a property of the root as a whole. *nelaw* belongs to the [−ATR] class of roots; this phonological property is distributed throughout the word. This intuition underlies the first generative analysis of vowel harmony: the so-called *root-marker* theory of Lightner (1965). On this approach the analysis of vowel harmony is broken down into two steps. First, the roots are divided into two arbitrary lexical classes, say, [+Z] roots and [−Z] roots. A UG convention distributing such lexical features as gender and number through the word also marks every phonological segment [±Z]. Second, a phonological rule translates the [±Z] classification into a phonological distinction by assigning each [+Z] vowel one value for the harmonic feature (say, [+ATR]) and each [−Z] vowel the other value (say, [−ATR]). On this view, *nelaw-am* 'his sleep' is derived as in (92).

(92)   [−Z]   [−Z]

[n E l A w] + A m → [n E l A w] + A m → n e l a w + a m
                                         + − + − +   − + [cons]
                                         −   −   −   [ATR]

For the root-marker theory, harmony is not the product of a phonological rule but a UG convention that distributes lexical and grammatical features to every position in the word. Lightner explicitly draws an analogy between such a [±Z] classification and a [±masculine] classification of the nouns in a language such as Spanish or Italian. Just as it makes no sense to locate the [+masculine] of Italian *problem-a* in one of the root phonemes (it is a property of the root as a whole), so, Lightner reasons, the harmonic property of a root such as Wolof *nelaw* is not a feature of one of the vocalic phonemes but rather a property of the whole morpheme.

The root-marker theory obviates an arbitrary choice among the root vowels in order to seat the harmonic feature. But it does so at considerable cost. This theory is fundamentally misleading because it denies the obvious fact that the classification of the Wolof roots is in reality phonologically based. The only justification for assigning a given root to the [+Z] or [−Z] class is its [+ATR] or [−ATR] harmonic behavior. But translating this phonetic distinction into an arbitrary lexical one violates Jakobson's basic insight that the vocabulary of a language is encoded in terms of natural phonological features that are grounded in overt phonetic distinctions, reflecting the (presumed) fact that it is much easier to store and search a large set of items if they are catalogued in terms of such natural properties as [±voice], [±round], rather than an arbitrary coding (sec. 1.4). Root-marker theory, with its arbitrary [±Z], denies that the Wolof opposition [réér] 'to be lost' vs. [reer] 'to dine' is of the same sort as English [pit] vs. [bit].

But if we refuse to accept this bizarre conclusion and return to the representation of the distinction between [réér] and [reer] as one between [+ATR] and [−ATR], then, in the linear model, we are also inevitably returned to the indeterminacy problem. A Wolof [CéCé] root differs from a [CeCe] root in that the former has a [+ATR] specification on the first and second root vowels while the latter has a [−ATR] specification in both these positions. But these representations are redundant − one specification for [ATR] is predictable from the other. We are trapped in this dilemma by the basic representational assumption of the linear theory that any feature is a property of individual matrices and consequently cannot span more than one position in the phonological string.

Disharmonic roots pose an additional problem for the root-marker theory. Harmonic systems often have roots that violate the harmonic law by combining vowels from the two harmonic classes. For example, in Akan we find the examples of (93a).

(93)   a.   bisa   'ask'   b.   o-bisa-i   'he asked it'
            kari   'weigh'   ọ-kari-i   'he weighed it'
            ñinsẹn   'be pregnant'   o-ñinsẹn-i   'she became pregnant'
            pịrako   'pig'   fuñanị   'to search'

While these roots deviate (in a regular fashion, as we will see) from the harmonic principle, their effect on affixes is not haphazard: prefixal vowels harmonize to the first root vowel while suffixal vowels harmonize to the last (93b). Finnish loanwords such as *afääri* 'affair' and *Camüs* in which a [+back] vowel is followed by a [−back] one furnish another example of this phenomenon. These words take front vowel suffixes: *afääri-ä* part.sg., *Camüs-tä* part.sg. Lightner's theory in which affixal harmony arises from distribution of the arbitrary root marker is in principle incapable of describing this situation. The roots of (93) can be assigned neither to the [+Z] nor to the [−Z] lexical class since they contain vowels drawn from each harmonic group. There is thus no root marker to distribute through the word. Consequently, their systematic harmonizing effect on affixes is completely mysterious.

7.4.3 *Harmony as a Morpheme Structure Constraint*

These problems prompted Kiparsky (1968b) to abandon the root-marker approach. Kiparsky proposed an alternative theory in which harmony is broken down into two separate statements. To handle the harmony of roots, a so-called *morpheme structure condition* was proposed. Such MSCs were essentially descriptive generalizations over the lexical representations of the grammar. Although their precise form was a matter of some debate at the time, we will ignore this point here and simply formulate the Wolof and Akan root constraints as in (94a). It states that the vowels in a morpheme share the same value ($\alpha = [\pm]$) for the feature [ATR].

(94) a. C_0 V ... C_0 V C_0
      $[\alpha ATR]$ $[\alpha ATR]$

   b. V → $[\alpha ATR]$ / ___ C_0 V
                              $[\alpha ATR]$

      / V C_0 ___
       $[\alpha ATR]$

Disharmonic roots are then treated as exceptions to the descriptive statement. In the case of both the regular harmonic roots such as [fiti] and the irregular disharmonic ones such as [ñinsẹñ], each vowel of the root is specified for its [ATR] value in the lexical representation. These specifications are not assigned by any rule. The affixal alternations arise from an assimilation rule (94b) that assigns the affixal vowel a plus or minus value for the harmonic feature that agrees with the closest root vowel – the first vowel in the case of a prefix and the last in the case of a suffix. The harmony rule is thus no different in form from a local rule of assimilation such as umlaut. However, unlike the latter, the harmony rule is given the power to iterate (apply to its own output). Given that the rule can iterate, the harmonic feature is spread throughout the harmonic domain (the word) by successive local changes.

   Although this alternative approach achieved greater descriptive success than the root-marker theory, a number of serious problems nevertheless arose. For one thing, many harmonic systems display what have come to be called *opaque* vowels. For example, the Wolof agentive suffix [-kat] exceptionally fails to alternate, appearing as $[-ATR]$ regardless of the root vocalism.

(95) tëgg-kat   'drummer'   tëgg-kat-am   'his drummer'
      fóót-kat   'launderer'   fóót-kat-am   'his launderer'
      ligééy-kat 'worker'   ligééy-kat-am 'his worker'
      togg-kat   'cook'   togg-kat-am   'his cook'
      jangale-kat 'teacher'   jangale-kat-am 'his teacher'

Although this suffix fails to harmonize, its effect on following vowels is not haphazard: they systematically surface as $[-ATR]$. The agentive suffix thus appears to harmonize following elements to itself while being itself an exception to the

rule. This halfway exceptionality is difficult to understand in a system that implements harmony as a feature-changing process. If a vowel exceptionally fails
to assimilate to a preceding vowel, why should it nevertheless provoke the same
harmonic change in a following element? At the very least, it leads one to expect
the opposite state of affairs in which an affix undergoes the rule but fails to transmit
the harmonic change to a following element. While the former type of exceptions
are quite prevalent in harmonic systems, the latter are not. The linear approach
has no explanation for this asymmetry.

The feature-changing view of harmony also runs into certain ordering paradoxes. The phenomenon of palatal umlaut found in certain Istanbul dialects of
Turkish is a notorious example (Kumbaraci 1966). This rule raises and unrounds
vowels before palatal consonants such as the jod that begins the imperative suffix
(96a).

(96) a.   infinitive   imperative
           ye-mek   yi-yin   'eat'
           üšü-mek   üši-yin   'be cold'
           oku-mak   okɯ-yɯn   'read'

   b. $V \rightarrow \begin{bmatrix} +\text{high} \\ -\text{round} \end{bmatrix} / \underline{\hspace{1cm}} \begin{bmatrix} +\text{cons} \\ +\text{high} \\ -\text{back} \end{bmatrix}$

   c. $V \rightarrow [\alpha\text{round}] / \quad V \quad C_0 \underline{\hspace{1cm}}$
        $[+\text{high}]$ $[\alpha\text{round}]$

The problem is the ordering of palatal umlaut (96b) with respect to the Turkish
labial harmony rule (96c) that rounds a high vowel after a round vowel. If labial
harmony applies first, it will iterate through the word, rounding all the vowels to
convert underlying [üšü-yIn] to [üšü-yün]. Palatal umlaut then derives the incorrect *üši-yün*. To avoid this effect, we must order palatal umlaut before labial
harmony. If root harmony is the product of a MSC and suffixal harmony arises
from a local feature-changing rule triggered by the preceding vowel, then *üši-yin*
is successfully derived. Underlying [üšü-yIn] is umlauted to [üši-yIn]; labial harmony then assimilates the suffixal vowel to the final stem vowel, giving [üši-yin].
Since labial harmony (96c) does not apply within the root, the final root vowel
will not harmonize to the first vowel and thereby undo the effect of rule (96b).
The problem with this analysis, noted by Clements (1980), is that it does not
generalize to cases in which the vowel undergoing palatal umlaut belongs to a
suffix. For example, underlying [dur-IyIm] 'let me stop' is realized as *dur-ɯyɯm*.
Application of umlaut first gives [dur-ɯyIm]. But if labial harmony is an iterative
feature-changing process, labialization will incorrectly spread from the root
through the word to produce *dur-uyum*.

Intuitively, it seems that the palatal umlaut phenomenon erects a barrier past
which the labial harmony cannot spread, just as in Wolof the [-kat] suffix defines
a barrier blocking the spread of harmony from the root. But if harmony is viewed
as a rule that changes the features of one vowel to agree with those of the preceding
one, this notion of "barrier" is difficult to reconstruct.

In addition to these problems, there is good reason to doubt the basic assumption of the alternative theory that the harmony found in roots and affixes is the product of two separate grammatical mechanisms: a morpheme structure condition and a feature-changing rule. The agreement in the feature [ATR] between the first and second syllables of the Wolof root *jéégó* 'to step' seems to be essentially the same phenomenon as the suffixal harmony in *réér-óón* 'was lost'. The linear model claims that there is no connection between the two. It implies the existence of languages in which all the suffixes systematically harmonize to the root but the roots show no restrictions on vowel combinations or in which the opposite state of affairs holds (i.e., the root vowels harmonize but affixes fail to alternate). Study of dozens of harmony systems reveals a very strong tendency for these phenomena to cooccur.

7.4.4 *Harmony: An Autosegmental Perspective*

Suppose that we drop the linearity assumption on phonological representation and instead adopt the autosegmental perspective. We may then capture the basic insight of the root-marker theory that harmony is typically the property of the entire root morpheme rather than any particular vowel. Since autosegmental representation permits a one-to-many relation between features and positions in the string, we may represent the harmonic contrast in phonological terms. Appeal to an abstract and ad hoc root marker is unnecessary. A Wolof root belonging to the [+ATR] class such as [béréb] 'place' will be represented as in (97).

(97)   bErEb

        [+ATR]

Like the tonal melodies of Margi (section 7.1), each root will lexically select a [+ATR] or a [−ATR] specification. This feature appears on an autosegmental tier separate from the other features. The UAC associates the autosegment to the leftmost or rightmost relevant segment (in this case a vowel). An additional rule then extends the autosegment to unlinked vowels until another association line is encountered, blocking the spread of the harmonic feature.

The autosegmental approach has a number of advantages. It captures the intuition of the root-marker theory that the harmonic feature is a property of the entire root morpheme rather than any one of its individual vowels. But it maintains Jakobson's insight that phonological contrasts are represented in phonetically grounded distinctive features. In addition, the fact that root harmony and affixal alternations naturally accompany one another will follow from the assumption that underlying representations minimize redundancy. If the specification of a given feature in affixes is always predictable from the root, then elimination of redundancy will posit underlying representations with no specification for that feature. And if roots show no contrast in the location of the feature, then a system striving for the most economical underlying representations will simply classify roots into the two contrasting harmonic classes. Harmony systems thus reflect a phonological state in which the encoding potential of a given feature is only partially utilized. From this perspective, the "root control" property of harmony makes sense as well. If a phonological system introduces a feature for lexical encoding, more vocabulary can be distinguished if the feature is applied to the open lexical class of roots than if it is applied to the closed affixal class.

The autosegmental perspective also helps us to understand the behavior of such opaque elements as the Wolof suffix [-kat]. We need merely assume that in its lexical representation this suffix is supplied with a [−ATR] specification as in (98a) (where for typographical reasons *ATR* is shortened to *A*).

(98) a. fOOt-kat-Am   b. fóót-kat-Am   c. fóót-kat-am
          | L---+--- | |/
       [+A][−A]   [+A][−A]   [+A][−A]

Since it has its own [ATR] specification, it will block spreading past it from a [+ATR] root (98b) by the ban on crossing association lines. In addition, if we assume that (at least for Wolof) there is no vowel harmony analogue of contour tones in which two autosegments associate to the same vowel, then the unbounded spreading rule will not extend the harmonic feature of the root to the vowel of [-kat]. This explains why [-kat] fails to alternate. Finally, given that [-kat] has its own lexically supplied autosegment, it will initiate a harmonic span of its own, explaining why suffixes that follow are consistently [−ATR] (98c).

Many ATR systems have no underlying contrast between plus and minus [ATR] low vowels. In such systems the low vowel invariably displays [−ATR] harmony. This property holds of the Wolof long vowels, for example. While long mid vowels contrast for ATR (e.g., [réér] 'be lost' vs. [reer] 'dine', [fóót] 'launder' vs. [woor] 'fast'), this opposition is suspended in the long low vowels: [aa] occurs but [ëë] is missing from the Wolof segment repertoire both underlyingly and at the phonetic surface. Furthermore, morphemes that contain [aa] may not also draw a vowel from the [+ATR] set {é,ó,ë}; [aa] finds its confreres only among the [−ATR] set (e.g., [kontaan] 'be satisfied', [perkaal] 'percale', [paase] 'to iron', [jaaro] 'ring'). Finally, as we might expect, when [aa] appears in a suffix, all following vowels are [−ATR]: for example, *dóór-aat-e* 'to hit usually', *génn-aale* 'to go out also'.

A similar state of affairs exists in Akan – but with an interesting twist. In Akan there is no underlying contrast of [ATR] in the low vowels (vowel length is not relevant). But unlike in Wolof, in Akan [a] freely combines with both [+ATR] and [−ATR] vowels inside root morphemes (99a).

(99) a. kari   'to weigh'
          yarị   'to be sick'
          bisa   'to ask'
          pịra   'to sweep'
          pịrako   'pig'
          fuñanị   'to search'

      b. piñcẹ   'to come close'
          ñinsẹñ   'to be pregnant'

c.   k A r I   b I s A
     | |
     [−A][+A]   [+A][−A]

We might construe the difference between the two systems as reflecting a Wolof ban against more than a single autosegment per morpheme. Akan relaxes this constraint to permit two autosegments. This interpretation is corroborated by the existence of at least a few disharmonic Akan roots in (99b) that combine vowels from the two harmonic classes. Ka (1988) reports no such comparable structures in Wolof. On this analysis, Akan *kari* and *bisa* have the underlying representations shown in (99c). From these representations it is easy to see how the inflected forms *ọ-kari-i* 'he weighed' and *o-bisa-ị* 'he asked' are derived.

The possibility of combining more than a single autosegment also helps us to understand the phonology of the Akan roots in (100).

(100) jʷanị   'to flee'   o-jʷanị-ị   'he fled'
       sʸanị   'to come down'   o-sʸanị-ị   'he came down'

Etymologically, these roots derive from [juanị] and [sianị]. Clements (1985b) suggests they have been restructured to [jʷanị] and [sʸanị]. If so, then linear analyses face a serious problem. Although the first vocalic segment in the root is the [−ATR] low vowel, these roots consistently induce [+ATR] in prefixes. If we adopt the autosegmental representation in which the harmony autosegments appear on a separate tier, the diachronic restructuring is easy to understand. The former trisyllabic roots of (101a) have been reinterpreted as disyllabic (101b) by a restructuring of the segmental tier. But the harmonic tier has remained unchanged.

(101)   a.   [jUAnI]   [sIAnI]   b.   [jʷAnI]   [sʸAnI]
                | | | |
                [+A][−A]   [+A][−A]   [+A][−A]   [+A][−A]

The result is a representation with a "floating" harmonic autosegment. When a prefix is affixed, the floating [+ATR] autosegment – being the leftmost autosegment in the root – will induce [+ATR] harmony in the prefixal vowel. Once again this analysis is only possible if Akan permits more than a single [ATR] autosegment per morpheme. If correct, this analysis provides very strong support for the autosegmental treatment of vowel harmony. In the linear model, the notion of a floating autosegment is incoherent.

7.4.5   *Neutral Vowels*

We now turn to the harmonic behavior of the high vowels in Wolof. These vowels do not contrast for the feature [ATR] at either the underlying or the phonetic level. According to Ka (1988), they are phonetically realized as [+ATR] in all positions. When the high vowels occupy the first syllable of the root (and hence the first syllable of the word), they have the harmonic properties we expect: as shown in (102a), all following vowels in the stem are [+ATR] (save the long low vowel [aa]). In addition, suffixes show their [+ATR] variants (102b).

(102) a. dibéér   'Sunday'
           gumbë   'be blind'
           guró   'cola nut'
           guné   'infant'

       b. tiit-óón   'was afraid'
           gis-léén   'look!'
           njur-éél   'posterity'
           sumb-lé   'help start'
           dugub-ëm   'his millet'
           suul-ël   'bury for'
           ligéé-ël   'work for'

But when they occupy a noninitial syllable, the high vowels display a suite of properties that is puzzling. First, they fail to alternate, remaining constantly [+ATR] (103a). Second, they freely combine with both preceding and following [−ATR] vowels (as well as [+ATR] ones) (103b). Finally, and most puzzling of all, the harmony of following vowels systematically correlates with the harmonic value of the preceding vowel. For example, the imperative suffix in (103c) agrees with the [ATR] specification of the initial vowel, in seeming disregard for the [ATR] value of the intervening high vowel.

(103) a. *-si* motion toward
           dëkk-si   'come and live'
           wax-si   'come and say'

           -it residual
           ñóóx-it   'residue'
           dog-it   'bit'

           -i reversive
           wédd-i   'take out of leaning position'
           lemm-i   'unfold'

           -u reflexive, passive
           sëlm-u   'wash face'
           wat-u   'have haircut'
           létt-u   'braid hair'
           seet-u   'look in mirror'

       b. barigo   'barrel'
           kabine   'toilet'
           ʔaddina   'world'

c. tekki-leen   'untie'
    moytu-leen   'avoid'
    watu-leen   'have haircut'

    léttu-léén   'braid hair'
    sóóbu-léén   'plunge'
    gëstu-léén   'research'
    ʔubbi-léén   'open'
    gimmi-léén   'open eyes'

In the vowel harmony literature, elements behaving like the Wolof high vowels are called *neutral* vowels. They have been identified in a number of harmony systems (e.g., Finnish, Mongolian, Hungarian). Many able phonologists have tried to understand their properties. Here we will look at three solutions to the problem of neutral vowels.

The first proposes that when a neutral vowel is preceded by a [−ATR] vowel, the harmony rule spreads this feature to each vowel in the word, including the high vowels. The resultant [−ATR] high vowels are then readjusted to [+ATR] by a later rule. On this analysis, the forms *léttu-léén* and *tekki-leen* receive the derivations in (104).

(104)   a.   lEtt-U-lEEn → létt- U-lEEn → létt-u-téén
                      | | ⟋
                   [+A]   [+A]   [+A]

        b.   tEkk-I-lEEn → tekk-I-lEEn → tekk-i̧-leen → tekk-i-leen
                      | | ⟋ | | ＼
                   [−A]   [−A]   [−A]   [−A][+A][−A]

The roots [létt] and [tekk] belong to the [+ATR] and [−ATR] classes, respectively. In the first step the harmonic autosegment is associated to the first syllable. In the second step this feature is extended to the remaining vowels in the word. In the case of (104b), a [−ATR] high vowel [i̧] is derived. A subsequent rule changes the high vowel to [+ATR].

While this solution "works," it has a couple of unsettling properties. First, it crucially relies on an "abstract" intermediate stage of the derivation. There are no [−ATR] high vowels in the underlying representation and none on the phonetic surface either. Yet this analysis posits their existence at an intermediate level. But phonologists have not discovered any independent evidence that would corroborate this hypothetical intermediate stage for neutral vowels. We cannot invoke the [−ATR] feature on the following vowels as support since this is exactly what the hypothetical intermediate stage is posited to explain. Another weakness is that the last step of the derivation in (104b), which switches the [−ATR] high vowel to [+ATR], is quite complex in autosegmental terms. Since a single autosegment spans several positions, in order to assign the opposite feature specification to an internal position, the original [−ATR] autosegment must be split into two pieces to make room for the [+ATR] specification on the high vowel.

Our notation suggests that positions internal to such an autosegmental span should be inaccessible to this kind of feature change.

The second proposal renders the high vowels inaccessible to the vowel harmony rule by not representing their [ATR] specification on the same tier as the harmony-producing autosegment. Under one version of this approach, an autosegmental representation arises from the decision to "project" a given feature on a separate tier. The Wolof high vowels would be special in failing to license this projection, retaining their [+ATR] in a segmental "core." On this approach the Wolof word *tekk-i-leen* has the following underlying representation.

(105) [t] $\begin{bmatrix} -\text{high} \\ -\text{back} \end{bmatrix}$ [kk] $\begin{bmatrix} +\text{high} \\ -\text{back} \\ +\text{ATR} \end{bmatrix}$ [l] $\begin{bmatrix} -\text{high} \\ -\text{back} \end{bmatrix}$ [n]

$\qquad\qquad$ [−ATR]

Since the high vowel has its [ATR] specification in the "segmental core," it will not be able to receive a second, contradictory specification from the harmonic autosegment. The vowel harmony rule extending the autosegment in *tekk-i-leen* thus skips over or bypasses the intervening high vowel.

This proposal has not received much favor since it opens up the organization of the features to considerable language-particular manipulation. Not only does it permit individual grammars to project or not to project a given feature, it also makes this decision dependent on other properties (e.g., whether the vowel is high or not). Nor can we say that all predictable [ATR] specifications remain in the core. The long low vowel [aa] is predictably [−ATR]. But it must project to the autosegmental tier to block extension of a [+ATR] autosegment past it.

A third view sees the [−ATR] specification on the suffix [-leen] in *tekk-i-leen* not as connected to the root specification but rather as the product of a later default rule. Recall from section 7.2.4 that we found it useful to treat low tones in Shona verbs as arising from a default rule. This proposal extends the notion to harmony systems. Under one version of this approach, the [±ATR] root contrast is construed as an opposition between [+ATR] roots and unspecified roots. The UAC associates the [+ATR] autosegment to the first vowel of the word, from which it spreads by the rule shown in (106a). On this analysis, *létt-u-léén* receives the derivation in (106b).

(106) a. $\quad$ V$\quad$V

$\qquad\qquad$ [ATR]

b. lEtt-U-lEEn → létt-U-lEEn → létt-u-léén

$\qquad\qquad$ [+A] $\qquad\quad$ [+A] $\qquad\qquad$ [+A]

c. tEkk-I-lEEn → tekk-i-lEEn → $\quad$ tekk-i-leen

$\qquad\qquad\qquad\qquad$ [+A] $\qquad$ [−A][+A][−A]

tekkileen has the derivation shown in (106c). By assumption, the root lacks an autosegment. The high vowel receives the predictable [+ ATR] specification by the rule in (107a). Finally, the remaining vowels receive a [− ATR] specification by the default rule (107b) that assigns [− ATR] to all vowels that have failed to receive an [ATR] specification. For this approach to work, it is crucial that the insertion of the [+ ATR] autosegment on high vowels take place after the harmonic spread rule (106a) because we do not want this autosegment to start a new harmonic domain.

(107)   a.   V   →   V
              [+ high] |
                            [+ ATR]

        b.   Ⓥ   →   V
                             |
                          [− ATR]

This analysis faces problems as well. First, it does not capture the generalization that when the initial root vowel is high, the remaining vowels of the word are [+ ATR]: for example, *ligéé-ël*. The [+ ATR] specification on the following vowels cannot arise from spreading the product of (107a) because, as we have just seen, high vowels do not initiate harmonic domains when medial in the word. Another problem is caused by the opaque low vowel in a case like *fóót-kat-am*. If it is assigned a lexical [− ATR], it correctly blocks the spread of [+ ATR] from the preceding root. But what prevents [-kat] from incorrectly passing on its [− ATR] to a following high vowel, creating the impossible [i̧,u̧]? To solve this problem, we might contemplate restricting the spread rule (106a) to just [+ ATR]. But this move undermines the original motivation for interpreting the [± ATR] opposition in Wolof as [+ ATR] vs. ∅. Somehow, the existence of the [+ ATR] [i,u] entails the absence of their [− ATR] counterparts. Precisely how to express this relation remains an outstanding problem. (See Archangeli and Pulleyblank 1993 for discussion.)

7.5   Makua

In this section we will examine aspects of the tonology of Makua, a Bantu language of Mozambique and Tanzania. The discussion is based on the extensive description of Cheng and Kisseberth (1979, 1980, 1981). In Makua the tone interacts with the syllable structure in an intricate fashion, motivating the mora as the tone-bearing unit.

Makua high tones almost always span two successive syllables on the phonetic surface (108a). In certain cases this high-tone doubling occurs between the final vowel of a verb and the initial syllable of the following word (108b).

(108)   a.   ki-no-thúmíh-a meele   'I'm selling millet'
        b.   ki-na-á-váhac-á méele   'I'm giving them millet'

The rule of (109) spreading a high tone to the following vowel accounts for both of these features of the language.

(109)   V V
        ⌐⟋
        H

Since all the published data on Makua tonology deal with the verb, we will focus on this category. The verb *ki-no-á-túm-ih-a* 'I'm selling them' has the structure shown in (110): subject-marking prefixes precede the tense-aspect elements, which in turn precede the object prefix. The root may be augmented by verbal extensions marking causative, passive, and applicative elements. The whole assembly is finished off by a final vowel suffix of unclear exponence.

(110)   subj-tense-obj-root-extensions-final vowel

        ki   no   a   tum   ih   a

The root plus extensions is generally referred to as the "stem" in Bantu linguistics. The stem forms a unit for the assignment of the verb's basic tonal pattern. Unlike the verbal roots of some other Bantu languages (e.g., Shona), those of Makua do not distribute themselves into tonal classes. Rather, all roots behave alike with respect to the surface tonal pattern: a string of highs starts on the first syllable of the root and continues until the fourth syllable is reached. After this point, the tonal pattern mysteriously drops to low. The infinitives, marked by the prefix [u-], illustrate.

(111)   medial   prepausal
        u-lím-á   u-lím-a   'cultivate'
        u-váh-á   u-váh-a   'give'
        u-lówól-a   u-lówól-a   'transport'
        u-lókóth-a   u-lókóth-a   'pick up'
        u-rámúcél-á   u-rámúcél-a   'greet'
        u-lókóthél-á   u-lókóthél-a   'pick up for'
        u-lókótáníh-a   u-lókótáníh-a   'pick up' pl.
        u-kákámálíher-a   u-kákámálíher-a   'use something to
                                                   strengthen'
        u-kákámáláherac-a   u-kákámáláherac-a   'use something to
                                                   strengthen' pl.

In certain cases the tone of the final vowel is altered before pause. We momentarily put these prepausal forms to the side.

   Given the high-tone spreading rule (109), we may account for the upper bound of four successive high-toned syllables by assigning a HLH tonal melody to the stem from left to right (112a). At some point later in the derivation, the remaining vowels of the word are assigned a default low tone to give the representation in (112b). High-tone spreading (109) then extends the high tones to the following syllables. Since Makua does not allow more than one tone per TBU, the spreading high tone displaces the low. The result is a string of four high-toned syllables (112c).

(112) a. [kakamalaherac]   b. [kakamalaherac]a   c. [kakamalaherac]a

In a disyllabic stem such as [lowol] the last high of the HLH melody remains unassigned (113a); and in the monosyllabic [lim] the last two tones are unassigned (113b).

(113) a. [lowol]   b. [lim]
          | | |
         H L H   H L H

Under certain circumstances the dangling high surfaces on the final vowel (e.g., (108b)). Since this aspect of Makua is not well understood (see Cheng and Kisseberth 1981 for discussion), we will ignore this detail of the analysis. For purposes of discussion, we will assume that the dangling tones are pruned after the assignment of the tonal melody to the stem.

Now let us consider the prepausal forms of (111). The final vowel alternates between a phrase-medial high and a prepausal low when the stem is monosyllabic or trisyllabic. With disyllabic stems the final vowel is low in both positions. We can account for this tonal alternation on the final vowel as follows. First, we assume that H-spread (109) and default-L insertion are late rules in Makua, operating after words have been situated into the syntax. Second, we posit a special phrase-level rule (114a) that marks the final vowel extratonal before pause. As in the case of Shona discussed in section 7.2, extratonality shields the TBU from the tonal tier. Any existing tonal association on the final vowel blocks the rule.

(114) a. V → ⟨V⟩ / ___ pause

    b. u [ramucel] ⟨a⟩
              | | |
             H L H

    c. u [lowol] a   u [lowol] a   u [lowol] a
            | | | | ⌐
          H L H→   H L →   H L

(114a) shields the final vowel of prepausal *u-rámúcél-a* from H-spread (114b). The first high spreads to displace the low, yielding three successive highs. In phrase-medial position the final vowel is not protected by (114a); consequently, both highs spread and four successive high-toned syllables ensue. In a disyllabic stem (114c) the final high of the HLH melody is pruned, leaving just a single high followed by low. H-spread extends the high only one syllable in both the phrase-medial and the pausal form.

For our purposes, the most important feature of Makua is the behavior of its long vowels. Consider the forms in (115).

(115)

	medial	prepausal	
a.	u-máál-a	u-máal-a	'to be quiet'
	u-thééš-a	u-théeš-a	'lift'
b.	u-máálíh-á	u-máálíh-a	'to quieten'
	u-váráán-á	u-váráán-a	'be stuck together'
c.	u-kúmááníh-a	u-kúmááníh-a	'join together'
d.	u-kóróméélih-a	u-kóróméélih-a	'cause to be suspended'

In (115c,d) the stems have three and four syllables, respectively. But the assignment of the HLH tonal sequence is quite different from the assignment in trisyllabic *u-rámúcél-á* and quadrisyllabic *u-lókótáníh-a*, where four successive syllables receive a surface high. If the syllable were the TBU of Makua, we would expect **u-kúmááníh-á*, parallel to trisyllabic *u-rámúcél-á*. This discrepancy is explained if the second mora of a long vowel also counts as a TBU in Makua. The forms in (116) show the assignment of the HLH melody under this assumption.

(116)   [koromeelih]   [kumaanih]   [maalih]   [varaan]   [maal]
         | | | | || ||| | || ||
         H L H   H LH   HLH   HLH   HL

H-spread yields the correct surface tonal pattern for all the phrase-medial forms. Prepausal *u-máal-a,* where a falling tone surprisingly appears on the long root vowel, presents a slight complication. Evidently, the H-spread rule is suspended in certain cases. Since the penultimate syllable of the phrase is the locus of an accent in many Bantu languages, it is possible that H-spread is, for some reason, barred from applying within an accented syllable in Makua. Alternatively, there may be a special rule that spreads the final low tone leftward to the penultimate mora.

Now consider the behavior of vowel-initial stems in the infinitive.

(117)

medial	prepausal	
w-aáp-á	w-aáp-a	'whisper'
w-iíhán-a	w-iíhán-a	'call'
w-iíhánél-á	w-iíhánél-a	'call for'

In these forms the infinitive prefix [u] has devocalized to [w]. It is followed by a long vowel with a rising tone. Viewed from the phonetic surface, it appears as if the initial mora of the root has been skipped in the assignment of the HLH melody. We may account for these data by postulating that Makua has the rule shown in (118a) that spreads the vowel of the root leftward to the mora of the infinitive prefix, creating [waa] and [wii] long vowel diphthongs. (118b) illustrates this proposal.

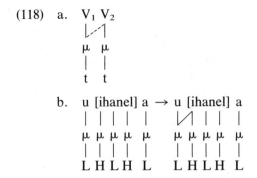

(118) a. V₁ V₂

b. u [ihanel] a → u [ihanel] a

Now consider the effect that high-toned object prefixes such as [kí-] 'me', [á] 'them', and [ú-] 'you' have on the verb. Phrase-medial forms are cited in (119).

(119) u-léél-a   u-máálíh-á   infin.
       u-kí-léel-a   u-kí-máalíh-á   'to V me'
       w-aá-léel-a   w-aá-máalíh-á   'to V them'
       w-uú-léel-a   w-uú-máalíh-á   'to V you'
       'tell'   'make quiet'

Comparison of *u-léél-a* 'to tell' and *u-kí-léel-a* 'to tell me' makes it appear as if the addition of the object prefix triggers the loss, not of the immediately following high tone, but of the second one down the line. However, when we remember that Makua surface tones come in pairs and originate from H-spread (109), the alternation between *u-léél-a* and *u-kí-léel-a* may be viewed as a reflex of Meeussen's Rule turning the first of two successive high tones to low. The derivation of *u-kí-léel-a* appears in (120a).

(120) a. ki [leel] a   ki [leel] a   ki [leel] a

           H HL → H LL → H L L

       b. ki [maalih] a   ki [maalih] a   ki [maalih] a

           H HLH → H LLH → H L LH L

Also, if we are correct in positing HLH as the underlying tonal melody for the root, then when a prefixal high dissimilates a following high to low, it should affect only the first high of the HLH melody. We thus predict that the second high will not dissimilate to low. This prediction is confirmed by *u-kí-máalíh-á* (120b).

7.6 Latent Tones in Ga'anda

In this section we will examine another case in which the mora functions as the tone-bearing unit. We will also extend the notion of "floating tone." The discussion is based on Ma Newman's (1971) analysis of the Chadic language Ga'anda.

Ga'anda is a three-tone language. Both mid and low tones cause the downdrift of a following high. For instance, the high on the plural suffix [-cá] is implemented at a lower pitch than the high of the initial syllable in *dúkwè-cá* 'buttocks'. In addition, the language has extensive downstepping of high tones. For example, while the high tone of the definite suffix [-án] is realized at the same level as the final high of the stem in *sáfàtá-án* 'the cold season', it is downstepped when appended to a stem such as *ɓə́ndú* 'granary': *ɓə́ndú-w'án* 'the granary'. In order to explain this differential downstepping potential of the two classes of stems, Ma Newman posits a "latent" low tone at the end of the latter. The latent tone actually emerges to the phonetic surface when the final syllable of this class of stems takes a certain segmental shape. Specifically, if this syllable contains a long vowel (121a) or a short vowel plus sonorant consonant (121b,c), then a falling tone is heard. Assuming that a fall reflects a HL combination, the latent low provides the second half of the falling tone. Apparently, the emergence of these falling tones on syllables closed by a sonorant consonant is optional before a suffix such as the plural [-cá]. If it fails to occur, then the latent low triggers a downstep on the suffix.

(121) a. cə̀cî: 'porcupine'   cə̀cî:-cá   pl.

       b. sàlâr   'lizard'   sàlâr-cá   pl.
                                         sàlár-ˈcá

       c. wássân   'squirrel'   wássân-cá   pl.
                                         wássán-ˈcá
                                         wássán-ˈán   def.

       d. ɓə́ndú   'granary'   ɓə́ndú-ˈwán   def.

We may account for these data by postulating a rule that associates the latent low to the second mora of a heavy syllable (122a,b). The rule is optional when that mora is contributed by a consonant, at least before the plural suffix. If it does not apply, then the floating low produces a downstep on the plural suffix (122c).

(122) a. cəci i   b. sala r ca   c. salar ca
           | | ┊ | | ┊ | | | |
           L HL   L H L H   L H L H

The latent tone thus only docks when the final syllable of the stem is bimoraic. This explains why the definite suffix [-án] permits just the downstepping option. In *wássán'án* (121c) the final consonant of the stem is a syllable onset [wás.sá.nˈán]. The stem-final syllable thus contains just a single mora and so the floating low tone has no position to which it can associate (123a). The lack of a second mora explains why the latent low never emerges in the case of stems ending in a short vowel such as *ɓə́ndú*. Its only manifestation is an indirect phonological one – initiating a downstep on a following high tone (123b).

(123)   a.   was.sa.n-an   b.   ɓəndu

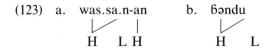

The sensitivity of the tonology to syllable weight underlies some additional tonal alternations in Ga'anda. According to Ma Newman, the monosyllabic roots in (124a) are lexically assigned a LHL tonal sequence. But the realization of this pattern varies with the syllabification of the stems. (It should be noted that Ma Newman cites *cùkû:* (124b) as *cùkû* with a final short vowel; we will assume this to be a misprint in view of the fact that otherwise falling tones are said to occur on heavy syllables.)

(124)   a.   [cuk]   'pound'
              [piš]   'spray'
              [kərs]   'be patient'
              [cams]   'chicken'

        b.   cù.kû: 'pound!'
              pì.šá.mà   'let's spray'

        c.   ˈcúk.tà   'pounding'
              ˈpíš.tà   'spraying'

        d.   ŋgɔ́ ŋgɔ́t ˈpíštà wà   'I will not spray'

Let us consider first roots with the shape CVC. Before a vowel-initial suffix, the initial low appears on the root while the high and following low of the LHL sequence appear on the suffix (124b). But when the suffix begins with a consonant, the high of the LHL tonal sequence appears on the root (124c), displacing the initial low. This displaced low manifests itself phonologically, however; when these forms are embedded in a phrase, the high tone of the root is downstepped (124d) in relation to the high of a preceding word. Clearly, this downstep reflects the initial low of the LHL sequence. If the mora counts as the TBU in Ga'anda, then we may propose an analysis in which the initial syllable of the CVC roots houses the first two of the three tones composing the LHL sequence (125a). But, as in the case of *wássân*, addition of a vowel-initial suffix opens the syllable, leading to a loss of the second mora. The high tone becomes floating and may associate to the suffix (125b).

(125)   a.   p i š   b.   p i š - a m a   c.   p i š - t a   d.   σ

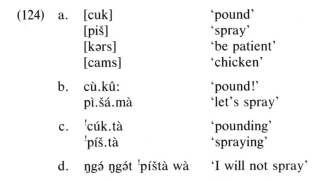

In order to account for (124c), we will assume that Ga'anda has the rule (125d) found in many other languages (e.g. Luganda section 6.10.2) that spreads a H to

a tautosyllabic mora; this rule reflects the fact that Ga'anda has no surface rising tones.

Now consider the behavior of the CVCC stems [kərs] and [cams] in these two syllabic contexts.

(126) a. ꞌkə́rs-ìncɔ́   'I am patient'
           ꞌcáms-àn   'the chicken'

       b. kə̀rɔ́s-tà   'to be patient'
           càmɔ́s-cà   'chickens'

In contrast to the CVC roots of (124), the CVCC roots do not open their syllable when a vowel-initial suffix is added. This syllable remains closed. It thus contains two moras and consequently may host the first two tones in the LHL sequence (127b). Rule (125d) delinks the initial low to create a downstep.

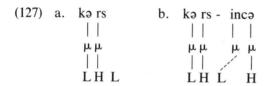

(127) a. kə rs   b. kə rs - incə

But when a consonant-initial suffix is appended to a CVCC root, a syllabically illicit three-consonant cluster is created. Epenthesis occurs, inserting a dummy syllable whose nucleus is schwa and whose onset is the medial consonant of the CVCC root. The root-initial syllable is thus opened and in the process loses its second mora. The result is a floating high tone that, we assume, associates to the epenthetic vowel. The derivation sketched in (128) illustrates the proposed analysis. (The forms ꞌcámsàn and càmɔ́scà indicate that the final low in the LHL sequence can displace the suffixal high tone of the [-an] and [-ca] suffixes.)

(128)   kə rs - ta   kərəs - ta   kərəs - ta

        μ μ   μ   μ   μ   μ μ   μ

        L H   L →   L H   L →   L H   L

We have so far seen two different situations to which the term *floating tone* is applicable. The most common is when an already associated tone becomes disassociated from its TBU through deletion or devocalization of the syllabic nucleus (e.g., Margi), or through loss of a mora via resyllabification (Ga'anda). A second sense in which linguists use the term "floating tone" is illustrated by Ma Newman's "latent tone." Stems such as cɔ̄má 'husband' and ɓə́ndú 'granary' differ from ɓə̄rtá 'stream' and ɓɔ́rtá 'ditch' by inducing the downstep of a following high tone. Since downstep is regularly triggered by a floating low in Ga'anda, the natural analysis assigns these stems a final low on the tonal tier that is not associated to any TBU. As we have seen, under certain syllabic circumstances this floating low actually appears in the guise of the second half of a fall.

(129)   6ərta   cəma   6ərta   6əndu
        | | | | \/   \/
        M H   M H L   H   H L

In these cases the floating tone is postulated as an unpredictable feature of the lexical representation that distinguishes one class of stem from another.

Ga'anda furnishes an example of a third sense of "floating tone." Recall that the autosegmental system permits underlying representations that lack a tonal specification. This was crucial in explaining the distinctive behavior of the Margi changing verbs (section 7.1.3). The absence of a tonal specification creates an open position that enables these verbs to acquire the tonal specification of the suffix and thus to alternate in tonal value – in contrast to stems with an underlying high or low tone, which remain constant regardless of the tone of the suffix. Since the tonal and segmental tiers are autonomous, we should also be prepared for the opposite state of affairs – that is, a morpheme that contains a tonal specification but lacks a segmental one. This expectation is firmly supported. The tonal literature is replete with "tonal particles" – grammatical morphemes whose phonological substance is purely tonal.

Associative (Noun *of* Noun) phrases are one of the most common constructions in which such tonal particles appear. Ga'anda associative constructions exhibit a systematic but puzzling tonal change. The initial mid- or low-toned syllable of the second noun appears with a high tone. For example, *cùnèwà* 'elephant' appears as *cúnèwà* in 'bone of elephant'. This tonal change cannot be attributed to any special property of the first noun. It takes place regardless of the tonal shape of the first noun.

(130)   āl   'bone'   6ár   'bark'
        cùnèwà   'elephant'   pūnó   'maize'
        āl cúnèwà   'bone of elephant' 6ár pú'nó   'husk of maize'

        pérrá   'bride'   cōmá   'husband'
        Músá   name   pérrá   'bride'
        pérrá Músá   'bride of Musa'   cōmá 'pérrá   'husband of bride'

        shìkècá   'friend'   cōmá   'husband'
        mbēɗétá   'grasshopper'   mbēɗétá   'grasshopper'
        shìkècá mbé'ɗétá 'friend of   cōmá 'mbé'ɗétá   'husband of
                           grasshopper'   grasshoper'

Although the shift of [cùnèwà] to [cúnèwà] might be described as a change from low tone to high, this interpretation would not explain the downstep that results in a case such as *6ár pú'nó*. Rather than a tonal change, we must treat this alternation as the product of a rule that associates a high tone to the initial syllable of the second noun. If the initial syllable is light, the linking of the high leads to a floating tone, which downsteps a following high. The derivations in (131) illustrate.

(131) ɓar   puno   ɓar   puno   ɓar puno
       | | | | ╱| | | ╱ |
       H H M H →   H H M H →   H H MH

The high tone that initiates these displacements is not part of the lexical representation of either the first or the second noun. Rather, it only occurs when the nouns participate in the associative construction. The distribution of this tone is thus grammatical in nature. If our theory of representation posits an autonomy between the segmental and tonal tiers, then there is nothing anomalous in postulating a morpheme whose only phonological substance is a tonal specification. In fact, we should be surprised if this possibility did not occur. Of course, such particles or their effect must ultimately be projected on the segmental tier in order to be detected. Consequently, they are limited in number and drawn from the grammatical rather than the lexical sector of the vocabulary.

Let us conclude the discussion of latent tones and downstep with a phenomenon found in a number of African tonal systems, such as the Nigerian language Yala (Armstrong 1968). Yala contrasts tones at three levels, as shown by the minimal triple *à kú* 'you bit', *à kū* 'you defecated', *à kù* 'you ran'. There is also downdrift of high tones after mid and low and of mid tones after low. Finally, a low tone is realized as a fall after a high: *útù* 'maternal kindred' is pronounced [útû]. Mid tone is unchanged after high, motivating the rule in (132).

(132)   V   V
        └--┐
        H   L

Consider now the paradigm in (133). The rule in (132) derives the falling tone in *ǫ́ kwęnyà*. In order to account for the systematic correlation between the presence of a downstep and the absence of high tone spread in *kó'sósí* and *kǫ́ kwęnyà*, Armstrong postulates a latent tone between [kó] and the verb (133b).

(133) a.   à sósí   'you cut the tree'   à kwęnyà   'you ran'
            ó sósí   'he cut the tree'   ǫ́ kwęnyà   'he ran'
            kó 'sósí   'let him cut the tree'   kǫ́ kwęnyà   'let him run'

       b.   ko   sosi   kǫ   kwęnya
            | V | V
            H M H   H M   L

The latent tone serves two functions in Armstrong's analysis: first, it downsteps a following high; second, it prevents the high of *kó* from spreading to the low of *kwęnyà*. We do not capture the latter aspect of Armstrong's solution with the line-crossing convention. Since the floating tone is not attached to the segmental tier, no association line bars the spreading of the high. In order to incorporate Armstrong's insight into our theoretical framework, we need to add two clarifications. First, recall from (59) that Myers (1987a) defines adjacency so that the tones in Shona (134a) count as nonadjacent and hence escape the OCP. We will extend the definition to (134c) so that the TBUs in Yala (134b) also count as nonadjacent.

(134)   a.   Shona   V   V   V   b.   Yala   V   V
                      | | | |
                      H   H   H   M   L

   c. x_i and y_i are adjacent on $tier_i$ iff the following restrictions hold: (i) no distinct element z_i occurs between them, and (ii) if x_i and y_i are linked to x_k and y_k on $tier_k$, then no distinct z_k occurs between x_k and y_k.

Second, we will make the general assumption that rules operate in local environments unless stated otherwise. Given these assumptions, the rule in (132) spreading a high to the right-adjacent TBU linked to a low will now correctly block in (134b).

7.7   Parameters of Association

Although left-to-right matching of tones and TBUs is the most prevalent form of autosegmental association, other types exist. For example, Newman (1986a) presents a good case for right-to-left mapping in Hausa. Hausa has a number of suffixes that suppress the tones of the base, distributing their own melody over the entire word. Such formations have tonal plateaus at their left edge, arguing for right-to-left association. A few examples are reproduced in (135), preserving Newman's transcription. A general rule truncates the final vowel of the stem before a suffix. The tone of long vowels is marked on the first half of the geminate.

(135)   plurals
        taatsuuniyaa LHLH + ooCii HH   →   táatsúuníyóoyíi HH   'folktales'
        riigaa LH + unaa HL   →   ríigúnàa HL   'gowns'
        raanaa HH + aikuu LH   →   ràanàikúu LH   'days'
        hankaakaa LHL + ii LH   →   hànkàakíi LH   'crows'

        derivational suffixes
        shuugabaa LLH + ancii HL   →   shúugábáncìi HL   'leadership'
        yaaroo HL + antakaa LHL   →   yàaràntákàa LHL   'childishness'
        tagangana LHL + ee LH   →   tàgàngànée LH   'sitting with
                                                                legs apart'

   Another form of association anchors tones to the edges of the word. The middle is then filled in by spreading from one or the other edge or by default. We will look at two examples where this *edge-in association* has been used effectively (see Yip 1988b for discussion). The first comes from Rialland and Badjimé's (1989) analysis of certain Bambara constructions in which a high *ton de liaison* is inserted between the head noun and a following particle such as the presentationals *dòn* 'it is' and *té* 'it is not'.

(136)   indef.   bá dôn   bá té   'river'
        def.   bá dòn   bá 'té

        indef.   bà dôn   bà té   'goat'
        def.   bǎ dòn   bǎ 'té

        indef.   bálá dôn   bálá té   'balafon'
        def.   bálá dòn   bálá 'té

        indef.   mùsò dôn   mùsò té   'woman'
        def.   mùsó dòn   mùsó 'té

The liaison high is realized on the particle, manifested as a change of the low of *dòn* to falling. In the case of high-toned *té,* no overt change occurs. We assume that the floating high is mapped to the particle and then "absorbed" by the UG convention merging two identical tones associated to the same TBU. The rule associating the liaison tone is stated in (137).

(137)   V

In the definite forms, the *ton de liaison* fails to associate to the particle. Rialland and Badjimé posit a floating low between the liaison high and the particle to mark the definite. This tone blocks association of the liaison high and triggers a downstep on *té.* Just in case the liaison high fails to associate to the particle, it is realized on the preceding noun stem, as a rising tone on *bà* 'goat' and as a plain high on the final syllable of *mùsò* 'woman'. The intended analysis is illustrated in (138) with the various forms of 'woman'.

(138)   muso   don   muso   tɛ   indef.

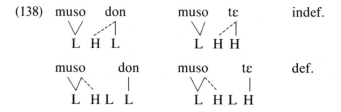

With this analysis as background, consider the paradigms of the longer trisyllabic and quadrisyllabic stems in (139).

(139)   indef.   gàlàmà dôn   gàlàmà té   'louche'
        def.   gàlàmá dòn   gàlàmá 'té

        indef.   súngúrún dôn súngúrún té   'girl'
        def.   súngúrún dòn súngúrún 'té

        indef.   mángòrò dôn   mángòrò té   'mango'
                 mángórò dôn   mángórò té
        def.   mángòró dòn   mángòró 'té

indef.	bànfúlá dôn	bànfúlá té	'hat'
	bànfùlá dôn	bànfùlá té	
def.	bànfúlá dòn	bànfúlá 'té	

The point of interest is the variation in the indefinite of 'mango' and 'hat'. Specifically, the former shows a HLL≈HHL alternation and the latter LHH≈LLH variants. No variation is reported for 'louche' and 'girl'. While one might argue that the right-to-left/left-to-right direction of association is in free variation, the alternation makes more sense if Bambara tones associate to the stem from the edge inward. Given a trisyllabic stem and a two-tone melody, edge-in association fills the first and third positions, leaving a gap in the middle. The variation then consists precisely in whether the vacant syllable associates to the preceding or to the following tone.

(140)

No comparable variation occurs in the definite forms, where the liaison high has been assigned to the final syllable. In this case the final tone of the stem has been displaced from the right edge and so naturally seeks out the vacant position in the middle of the stem.

Finally, consider four-syllable stems (141). For HL 'bowl' and LH 'chance', we find neither free variation nor the trisyllabic plateau that would be expecte* if the association proceeded from one edge or the other.

(141)	indef.	bùgùnìnkà dôn	bùgùnìnkà té	'whip'
	def.	bùgùnìnká dòn	bùgùnìnká 'té	
	indef.	jánkárúbú dôn	jánkárúbú té	'cheat'
	def.	jánkárúbú dòn	jákárúbú 'té	
	indef.	kúlúkùtù dôn	kúlúkùtù té	'bowl'
	def.	kúlúkùtú dòn	kúlúkùtú 'té	
	indef.	gàrìjégé dôn	gàrìjégé té	'chance'
	def.	gàrìjégé dòn	gàrìjégé 'té	

Edge-in association derives the representations in (142).

(142)

The vacant TBUs appear to associate to the "cl*ading to fill in the
or from side to side. Rialland and Badjimé cite*ddle syllable.
LH melody. If the two edge tones are sim*
middle, we predict variation comparable to*

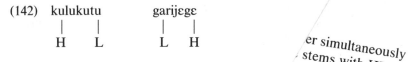

Hewitt and Prince (1989) rely on edge-in association to explain a complex paradigm from Shona that Odden (1984, 1986) argued to require a tonal melody that violates the OCP. Specifically, Odden reports the data in (143) for the Northern Karanga dialect. (The "nonassertive" is the form the verb takes in certain subordinate clauses.)

(143)   a.   high-toned roots

assertive	nonassertive
ku-téngá	handáka tóra
ku-téngésá	handáka tóresá
ku-téngéséra	handáka tóréserá
ku-téngésérana	handáka tóréséraná
ku-tóréséserana	handáka tóréséresaná

HH	HL
HHH	HLH
HHHL	HHLH
HHHLL	HHHLH
HHHLLL	HHHLLH

   b.   low-toned/toneless roots

ku-bika	handáká biká
ku-bikisa	handáká bikísa
ku-bikisira	handáká bikísíra
ku-bikisirana	handáká bikísísira
	handáká bikísísirana

LL	LH
LLL	LHL
LLLL	LHHL
LLLLL	LHHLL
	LHHLLL

In

m... analysis, the nonassertive schema arises from a [BHHL^{1}B] tonal suc...re B equals the "basic" tone of the root (high or low). With its also...h tones, this melody violates the OCP; and with its variable B, it latio... the claim that phonological structure traffics in purely local re- sourc...and Prince (1989) show how employing the full descriptive re- permit...mental phonology, reliance on the OCP and edge-in association in fact ...e interpretation that respects locality – one in which locality Let us r...force behind this seemingly complex descriptive statement. The fir... mally, ph...eir analysis. counting a...ncerns the tone tripling found in high-toned verbs. Nor- string of ex...do not count past two (which can be construed as not maintain the...examining one item in strict adjacency to another). A ...s thus challenges this basic generalization. In order to ...g, Hewitt and Prince break the tone tripling down into two local spreading operations, the first triggered by the left stem bracket, the second being Myers's (1987a) general H-spread rule.

(144) a. [V   V   b. V   H
           └--⟋   └--⟋
           H   H

Given that (144a) is triggered by the stem bracket, it can only apply once and thus does not iterate across the string. Although the restriction appears ad hoc, it explains the behavior of these stems in the nonassertive, as we will see momentarily. Downing (1988) proposes a similarly restricted rule of "local" H-spread for the related Southern Bantu languages of Xhosa and Zulu.

Granted the rules in (144), a four-syllable stem receives the derivation sketched in (145). In the first step the root high spreads one to the right. Default lows are then inserted at the word level, followed by the general rule of H-spread and finally tonal delinking, suppressing contour tones.

(145) [V V V V → [V V V V → [V V V V → [V V V V
        | ⟋   ⟋ | | ⟋ |
        H   H   H L L   H   L

Given this analysis of the triple high, let us now consider the nonassertive forms. They clearly involve the addition of a high suffix to the stem. In toneless roots this suffixal high appears on the second syllable of the stem (146a). Under left-to-right association, we expect the suffixal high to emerge on the first syllable of the stem. The attraction to second position suggests either that the first syllable is extratonal or that it is occupied by a lexical low (and hence that the opposition between the two classes of verb roots is H vs. L rather than H vs. Ø). Hewitt and Prince pursue the extratonality option. Since the high is associated to the second syllable of the stem, it cannot spread to the right by (144a) because this rule requires the source of the spreading high to be the first vowel of the stem. The general, postlexical H-spread rule then doubles the H on the following syllable to give the LHHL pattern of the toneless stems.

(146) a. V V V V V   b. V V V V V
              ⟍--------⟍ |
                       H   H   H

Now consider the analysis of the high-toned class. Since the nonassertive marks an inflectional category, it arguably appears at a later lexical level, after the stem (root plus derivational suffixes) has been processed. If we grant this point, then high-toned roots will have already associated their lexical tone with the initial position. The input to the second lexical stratum is thus (146b). Left-to-right association would now land the suffixal high adjacent to the root high – an OCP violation. Hewitt and Prince assert that the OCP blocks this association, leaving the high unmapped. Shona then places the free tone at the opposite edge of the word under the option of edge-in association. When the stem is trisyllabic or longer, this association can be made. But in disyllabic stems the left edge is unavailable since an OCP violation would occur here as well. In this case the suffixal high fails to associate and is suppressed. Finally, in HLH and HHLH stems the OCP constrains the two spreading rules from bumping up against the right-edge high.

Like Myers (1987a), Hewitt and Prince (1989) get a good deal of mileage out of the OCP. This suggests that, contrary to the doubts of Odden (1986), the OCP is a fundamental principle of Shona tonology that not only constrains the initial lexical representations but also drives much of the later tonology that must smooth out the rough edges arising from affixation and syntactic combination.

At this point it would be useful to consider the parameters that underlie autosegmental rules, reviewing some of the many examples discussed in this chapter. Given that features are organized into hierarchical trees, phonological rules are defined over graphs consisting of nodes and connecting branches ("links" or "paths" are common terminological alternatives). In general, they add or delete nodes and branches. Some of these operations may follow from general UG conventions while others must be stipulated and learned as rules of individual languages. Determining the balance between rules and conventions continues to be a primary research objective.

First let us consider deletion. We start with the convention that deletion of a node automatically eliminates the branches connecting it to other nodes. If the deleted element is an anchoring vowel, the result will be a floating tone – provided the tone is not associated with some other TBU (147a). We recall from section 7.1 that this distinction is crucial to explaining the alternation between a high and a rising tone on the Margi definite suffix *-ári*. Deletion of a tone has comparable effects (147b). If the associated vowel is linked to another tone, then in general nothing else happens. But if it is not, then a toneless vowel results, which may in turn receive a default tone or be subject to spreading from an adjacent tone on the left or the right. The Venda rule of section 7.3 deleting an initial low tone illustrates this state of affairs: in the post-H context the toneless vowel of the prefix *mu-* assimilates a preceding high; elsewhere it takes a default low (147b). Finally, the association line connecting the tone and the TBU may be eliminated. If the tone is not associated with any other TBU, the result is a floating tone. We appealed to this property in the simplification of unaccented falling tones in Venda, postulating a rule to remove the second link in a pretonic syllable; the resultant floating low triggers downstep (147c).

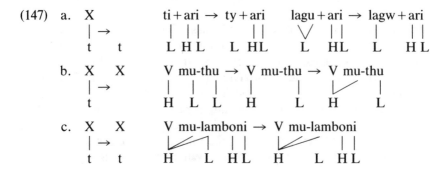

Comparable to deletion is the insertion of a TBU, tone, or connecting path. For path insertion, two subcases can be distinguished: spread and initial association. The former characterizes the addition of an association line to the tone in the graph of (148a).

(148)   a.

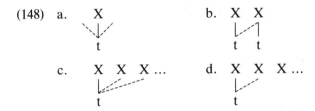

We must distinguish the direction of extension (leftward or rightward spread) as well as whether or not the target is already linked to the tonal tier. In the former case the ban on crossing association lines blocks further spread (148b), resulting in a contour tone that may or may not simplify. Rightward H-spread in Makua (109) and Yala (132) illustrates these options. If the target is toneless and the rule is thus "feature-filling," it may be necessary to parameterize further for whether the rule iterates or applies just once. The [±iterative] option allows an alternative analysis for the two Shona dialects of (57). Instead of trading on a difference in the ordering of the H-spread and default-L insertion rules, we may order H-spread first in both dialects and treat the difference as a [+iterative] setting for the Southeastern dialect (148c) versus a [−iterative] setting for Southern Karanga (148d). Finding the evidence to distinguish between these alternatives is an unresolved issue of autosegmental phonology.

A related question is whether or not it is possible to reinterpret feature-changing dissimilation processes such as Meeussen's Rule as the composite of the more elementary operations of deletion and default insertion, as depicted in (149a).

(149)

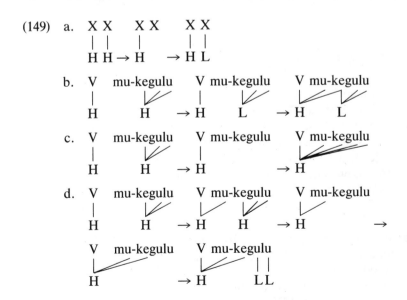

The Venda alternation of *mu-kégúlú* and *mú-kégulu* is relevant here. Following Cassimjee (1983), we treated the process as a feature change from [+high tone] to [−high tone] (149b). The two-step deletion+insertion alternative encounters problems with this case. If H-deletion precedes H-spread, we are unable to prevent the high from spreading too far (149c). The two-step version of Meeussen's Rule requires (i) marking H-spread as [−iterative] and (ii) allowing it to both precede and follow H-deletion. It is unclear whether this alternative (depicted in (149d)) is descriptively feasible.

Finally, let us consider insertion of nodes and links into the feature graph. Insertion of a TBU arises from rules of epenthesis and vocalic lengthening (in systems that take the mora as a TBU). In Ga'anda we saw that the epenthetic syllable may host a floating tone (128). In cases where there is no floating tone in the vicinity of the epenthetic vowel, we can ask whether it acquires its tonal specification from the left, from the right, or by default. If the language has rules of spread or directional association, we can ask whether they are pressed into service to associate the epenthetic syllable to the tonal tier. Not enough cases are known to be able to tell whether the tonology of epenthetic syllables is predictable, given the nature of the rest of the system. Similar questions arise for the association of tones inserted in particular morphological contexts: recall Bambara's *ton de liaison* (137) and the floating high in Ga'anda associative constructions (131). Finally, as we saw from Hausa (135) and Bambara (141), initial tonal association can be parameterized for direction and mode: left to right, right to left, and edge-in. A significant question is whether these options are best viewed as parameters for the entire phonological system or as more humble rules that are ordered to apply at particular points in the derivation. The former, stronger hypothesis predicts that epenthetic syllables and floating tones should associate according to the parameters for initial association. Not enough cases are on record to know whether this prediction is valid. See Archangeli and Pulleyblank 1993 for a full-scale decomposition of autosegmental rules into more elementary operations.

7.8   Tone in Asian Languages

The tonal systems of many East Asian languages are superficially rather different from the typical African system. The inventory of tone levels and shapes is often larger and the distribution of the complex tones is freer. This led to the intuition that the Asian systems are organized in a fundamentally different way from the African, which typically have a smaller inventory of basic tones (Wang 1967). However, Yip (1980) showed that many of the autosegmental concepts developed in the analysis of African languages can be fruitfully applied to the Asian systems as well. However, certain problems remain. Recent innovations in feature geometry have furnished new ways of looking at the issues; but many questions are still unresolved. In this section we will briefly survey some of the results to get a sense of these tonal systems and how they differ from the more widely studied and better understood African systems. See also Chen 1991.

In the Asian tradition, tones are represented as points along a five-step scale, a notation based on that of Chao (1930) and followed as a transcriptional practice in subsequent studies, even if the official representation is quite different. For example, the four tones of Mandarin are represented in the familiar paradigm of (150).

(150) ma 55   'mother'
       ma 35   'hemp'
       ma 214 'horse'
       ma 51   'scold'

The numbers are misleading since it is unclear whether they are intended as phonetic or phonological categories. If the latter, it is much more plausible that they denote relative rather than absolute values. While humans are good at discriminating pitches as higher or lower and at judging up or down changes in pitch value over time, they have difficulty estimating absolute values. This accounts for the fact that the same tone is often transcribed differently (e.g., the Mandarin third tone is variously represented as 214, 213, 312). However, all descriptors agree that the third tone is concave in shape and contrasts with the other tones. Despite its shortcomings, we will follow traditional practice and also employ the Chao numbering system in transcriptions.

7.8.1 Register

In a number of Asian systems the pitch range splits into an upper and lower register (Yip 1980). In some cases this doubles the number of tones by in effect adding a new dimension, much in the way that lip rounding doubles the front-back opposition to transform an [i,u] system to [i,ü,ï,i]. This suggests that articulatorily register reflects a separate feature whose effects on the pitch range are secondary. Indeed, register distinctions often arise from the effects of laryngeal features in the consonantal onset. A particularly clear example is furnished by the Songjiang dialect of suburban Shanghai (Bao 1990). The tonal inventory comprises the eight elements of (151) transcribed in the Chao numbering system.

(151) 53 44 35 5   yin register
       31 22 13 3   yang register

The tones can be matched for shape: two falling tones (53, 31), two rising tones (35, 13), and two pairs of level tones (44, 22) and (5, 3). The latter are restricted to short syllables closed by a glottal and hence may be seen as variants of the former. When displayed on the 5-to-1 pitch range, the pairings become particularly clear.

(152)
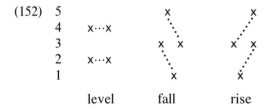

level   fall   rise

The motivation for these pairings is strengthened by the fact that the tones are largely in complementary distribution. Specifically, the 22, 31, 13 tones are never found after a voiceless onset, while 44, 53, 35 are absent after voiced obstruents. The tones partially contrast after sonorants. We might describe this system by saying that there are three basic tones – a level, a rise, and a fall {h, lh, hl} – and that the [±stiff] feature characterizing the vocal cords in the onset spreads onto the following vowel, where it modifies the pitch of the nucleus and hence the realization of the tone in much the way that lip rounding lowers the second formant of a vowel.

This way of looking at the phenomenon implies that the tonal effect of the onset is largely a phonetic matter. However, in many systems the correlation of register with laryngeal voicing has been broken, leading to an independent phonological dimension, along which tones may continue to alternate. A particularly clear example is furnished by Tibetan. In the dialect studied by Meredith (1990) we find the inventory shown in (153).

(153)

long syllables	short syllables	
55, 52	5, 53	upper register
24, 31	23	lower register

Once again, the short level 5 and falling 53 can be treated as variants of the basic 55 and 52 tones found on long syllables. The falling 31 of the lower register pairs with upper register 52. As we will see, the 24 rise alternates with 55; Meredith suggests that 24 derives from a basic level tone by a rule adding a high on the right. This analysis reduces the system to four basic tones, with a level and a falling tone in each register. In Meredith's notation, adopted from Bao 1990, these tones receive the representations shown in (154). Each tone consists of an obligatory register designation r, which may be either [+stiff] H or [−stiff] L. The tone may also be supplemented with a "contour" node, which subdivides each register. Meredith speculates that this tonal feature is a reflex of [+slack] l or [−slack] h. In this way, four possible tone heights are distinguished.

(154)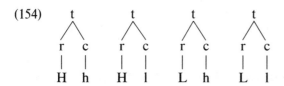

As its name implies, the contour node's [±slack] h and l dependents are allowed to sequence, generating a rise or a fall. With this notation, the four basic tones of Tibetan can be represented as in (155).

(155)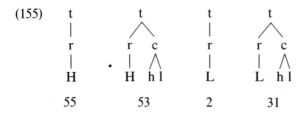

The independence of the register and contour features in Tibetan is revealed in the tonal modifications that accompany compounding. When two monosyllabic morphemes combine to form a compound, the second syllable is more prominent than the first. In response to the weak-strong stress contour, the sixteen possible tonal combinations reduce to just four, as shown in (156).

(156)

input			compound	
first syllable	second syllable	⇒	first syllable	second syllable
H-level	H-level		H-level	H-level
H-fall	H-level		H-level	H-level
L-level	H-level		L-level	H-level
L-fall	H-level		L-level	H-level
H-level	H-fall		H-level	H-fall
H-fall	H-fall		H-level	H-fall
L-level	H-fall		L-level	H-fall
L-fall	H-fall		L-level	H-fall
H-level	L-level		H-level	H-level
H-fall	L-level		H-level	H-level
L-level	L-level		L-level	H-level
L-fall	L-level		L-level	H-level
H-level	L-fall		H-level	H-fall
H-fall	L-fall		H-level	H-fall
L-level	L-fall		L-level	H-fall
L-fall	L-fall		L-level	H-fall

Some examples illustrating this pattern of reduction appear in (157). The last two are from Chang and Chang 1968 (transcription altered); the others are from Meredith 1990.

(157) phöö 2 'Tibet'
mi 2 'person'
phöö-mi 2-5 'Tibetan'

thuu 52 'banner'
caa 52 'iron'
thuu-caa 5-52 'iron banner fixture'

ree 31 'cotton'
see 2 'robe'
ree-see 2-5 'cotton robe'

yum 2 'mother'
chēē 5 'great'
yum - chēē 2-5 'mother' (honorific)

see 52 'knowledge'
yöö 2 'possessor'
see yöö 5-5 'intellectual'

> cu 55 'ten'
> kɛɛ 31 'eight'
> copkɛɛ 5-52 'eighteen'
>
> cee 31 'track, print'
> qopcee, qupcii 5-52 'impression left by buttocks (on e.g. sand)'

The reduction may be succinctly characterized as the elimination of tonal contour in the first position and as a change from the lower to the upper register in the second position. We can see both of these modifications in 'cotton robe', where $31 + 2$ is transformed into $2 + 5$.

(158)
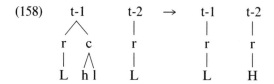

Without the concept of register as a separate tonal dimension, the changes become more complex to express. Since the 4 of 24 is derivative and since levels 1 and 2 do not contrast, we might try to reduce the tones to a three-way high, mid, low system.

(159)   55 = H   52 = HM   31 = ML   24 = LH or MH

There are at least two problems with this analysis. First, to describe the change in the second element of the compound, where 31 becomes 52 and 2 becomes 5, we must distribute the pitch rise across both tones of the ML contour so that the mid 3 raises to high 5 and the low 1 raises to mid 2. This change on two successive tones is difficult to state and violates the thesis that phonological changes are basically local in nature. Second, in the elimination of the contour on the first syllable, the HM 52 appears as high and thus appears to lose its second element; but when the ML appears as 2, it is unclear whether this should be seen as loss of the first tone or the second. Autosegmentally, we want to eliminate the second element so that the two changes can be collapsed. But some kind of adjustment of the output is still needed. Given the notion of register, no such adjustment is needed. Elimination of the contour node collapses the four-way distinction into a two-way distinction.

7.8.2   Contour Tones as Units

Another striking difference between the Asian and African tonal systems concerns the distribution of contour tones. As the discussion of Margi revealed, contour tones typically arise from the association of floating or dangling tones to a singly linked TBU. In the Asian systems the contour tones enjoy a much freer distribution. A typical example is provided by many Wu dialects, where noninitial syllables in the phrase become toneless and hence susceptible to spreading from the initial syllable. For example, Wang (1983) reports the data in (160) for the Suzhou dialect. In sandhi phrases, the tone of noninitial morphemes is suppressed and the first element spreads its final tone to fill in the gap.

(160) le 13   pae 52   za? 3   13 44 22
       'blue' 'precious' 'stone'   → 'sapphire'

       hiã 13 mae 13 hy 13   tcin 44 → 13 33 33 31
       'lamb' 'wool' 'wrap' 'scarf'   'wool scarf'

       pe 44 ts'o 52 si 412 ka 412   → 44 44 44 31
       'sad'   'world'   'Les misérables'

In contrast to Margi, where the combination of rising *bdlŭ* with the toneless suffix -*na* yields low + high *bdlɜ̀* + *ná,* in Suzhou the initial syllable retains the contour. However, the rising tone still reveals its low + high nature by spreading its high portion to the following toneless syllables. The derivation is completed with the addition of a low "boundary" tone to the final syllable.

(161) CV CV CV CV   →   CV CV CV CV
         ∧   ∧
        1 3   1 3   1

Two explanations have been suggested for the contrasting behavior of the contour tones in Margi and Suzhou. One, represented in the work of Woo (1969) and later Duanmu (1990), sees the difference as a function of the number of TBUs deployed by the two systems. In particular, for Suzhou the isolation form of a morpheme and the initial syllable of the phrase are claimed to contain two TBUs while noninitial syllables contribute just a single TBU (perhaps reflecting the absence of stress). Given that there are two TBUs to house the two tones composing the 13-rise, the initial syllable remains unaltered. The remaining TBUs assimilate the final element of the initial syllable contour (162).

(162) CVV CV CV CV   →   CVV CV CV CV
        | | | |
        1 3   1 3   1

An alternative interpretation, championed by Yip (1989) and Bao (1990), sees the contour tones of Chinese acting as a unit grouped under a single tonal node, much the way an affricate such as [tˢ] sequences [−continuant] [+continuant] under a basic coronal point of articulation. Given that the 13 contour of Suzhou links to the TBU as a unit via the tonal root node, it remains associated to the initial syllable. However, its final component is allowed to spread as a single element, analogous to the way that segmental rules treat the right face of a [tˢ] affricate as an [s].

(163) CV CV CV CV → CV CV CV CV

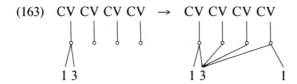

1 3   1 3   1

Yip (1989) reports that the more complex convex and concave tones of Suzhou split apart in the sandhi phrases in a way that parallels the Margi breakup of the contour tones. This suggests that the Asian systems allow at most two elements to combine in a single tonal unit, again much like an affricate. For example, the fall + rise 523 and the inverse rising-falling 242 lose their final upglide or dip in sandhi and realize it as a high or a low on the following toneless syllable (164) (no glosses given).

(164) a. kau 523 i 523   →   52 44
       b. mo 242 ko 523   →   23 11

Yip analyzes the convex and concave tones of Suzhou into an initial HL fall or LH rise – followed by a separate high or low level tone. So long as the autosegmental associations are conducted via the tonal root nodes, the alternations in (164) parallel the breakup of the contour tone in Margi. For example, (164b) receives the analysis in (165).

(165) mo   mo ko

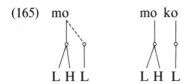

       L H L   L H L

The alternative view of Duanmu (1990) sees the concave and convex tones as reflecting the addition of a mora before pause, creating a trimoraic syllable that has the capacity to encompass the entire HLH or LHL sequence.

Proponents of the aggregate view of contour tones have interpreted dissimilation processes defined over these elements as support for their position. For example, the Tianjin dialect (Chen 1985) has four tones: H, L, HL, LH. Of the sixteen possible combinations arising from the juxtaposition of two syllables in the phrase, only four change. These sandhi modifications are listed in (166) (examples from Bao 1990).

(166) xi LH lian LH   →   HH LH   'wash face'
       song HL xin HL   →   LL HL   'send letter'
       kan HL shu LL   →   HH LL   'read book'
       chou LL yan LL   →   LH LL   'smoke cigarette'

If the rise and fall form units, then the tonal change can be expressed rather simply as follows.

(167)

$$x_1\ y_1\ \ x_2\ y_2 \qquad \text{(when } x_1 = x_2 \text{ and } y_1 = y_2, \text{ delete } x_1)$$

Opponents of the aggregate theory have challenged the assumption that the dissimilation is a true generalization in Tianjin. They point to the two additional tonal changes that occur in (166) and propose a different grouping of the data. However, the alternative grouping does not appear to be motivated by anything other than the refusal to see the first two changes in (166) as true dissimilations. Nevertheless, it is true that so far no one has succeeded in isolating a dissimilation based on shape from all other changes the same way Grassmann's Law in Indo-European ($*C^h. . .C^h \rightarrow C. . .C^h$) isolates the feature of aspiration. If contour tones reflect a separate phonological category, such cases should exist.

If the contour tones of the Asian systems really do function as units, then we also expect them to associate and spread as a bundle. Proponents of the aggregate theory claim to have identified cases of this sort, but the interpretations of the data are open to challenge as well. For example, in the Wuxi dialect Yip (1989) reports such paradigms as (168).

(168) a.

gʌ	'to do'	131
gʌ tshin	'to do completely'	24 21
gʌ tshin tshʌw	'to make clear'	24 44 21
gʌ və? tshin tshʌw	'unable to make clear'	24 4 44 21

b.

di	'to address'	213
di tchi	'to bring up'	12 41
di tchi le	'to bring up'	12 44 41
di və? tchi le	'unable to bring up'	12 4 44 41

Paradigm (168a) is composed of an initial rise that continues as high and then falls to low, while (168b) seems to have a final fall and initial low, with the interval assimilating the high portion of the final fall. Yip sees these two cases as each spreading a LHL tonal sequence but differing in the parsing of the tonal string as (LH)L or L(HL). The two tonal nodes are then associated to the edges of the phrase and the toneless syllables in between receive their pitch values via phonetic interpolation. For our purposes the important points are (i) that each paradigm involves the same LHL sequence but differs in the grouping and (ii) that the groups associate as a unit to the edges of the domains. For example, (168a) receives the derivation sketched in (169).

(169) CV CV CV CV   →   CV CVCV CV   →   CV CV CV CV

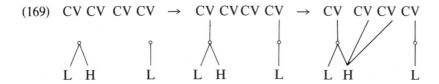

     L H   L   L H   L   L H   L

The spreading of a contour tone has been proposed for the Wu dialect of Dan-yang. Six basic tones appear in isolation: a high, mid, and low, plus a rise.

(170)   11   lan   'rotten'   3   yiʔ   'one'
        33   wang   'net'   4   fuʔ   'coat'
        55   tu   'earth'
        24   fang   'house'

When morphemes are combined in certain grammatical configurations, the iso-lation tones are replaced by a tonal melody that is unrelated to the synchronic underlying tone – presumably the isolation form. The inventory of melodies over two-, three-, and four-syllable domains are schematized in (171).

(171)   a.   11-11   11-11-11   11-11-11-11   L
        b.   33-33   33-33-33   33-33-33-33   M
        c.   55-55   55-55-55   55-55-55-55   H
        d.   24-55   24-55-55   24-55-55-55   LH
        e.   42-11   42-11-11   42-11-11-11   HL
        f.   42-24   42-42-24   42-42-42-24

These cases could be described as left-to-right association of the tonal melodies listed in the right column, with spreading of the rightmost tone. The controversial cases appear in (171f). Yip interprets this as a falling plus rising melody that maps to the edges of the sandhi domain, followed by a left-to-right spreading of the contour tonal node.

(172)   CV CV CV CV   →   CV CV CV CV

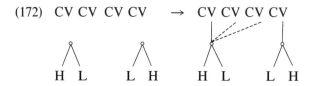

              H L   L H   H L   L H

Bao notes that the falling 42 is not a member of the basic (isolation) inventory of tones and proposes a rule, suggested by the original descriptor of Danyang (Lü 1980), that dissimilates the first of two rising tones to a fall (24-24 → 42-24), which then spreads as a unit.

Duanmu (1990) challenges this interpretation of the data. He notes that the pattern in (171f) has a different phrasal distribution from the others. More im-portantly, while the tonal melodies of the other patterns are unconnected with the isolation forms, for (171f) "most or all of the component syllables have the citation tone [24]" (Duanmu 1990:145). He concludes that the 42-42. . .24 arises from an underlying string of 24-24. . .24 by iterative application of the dissimi-lation rule. If correct, this interpretation seriously undermines one of the strongest arguments for the aggregate theory of contour tones.

Suggested Readings

Archangeli, Diana, and Douglas Pulleyblank. 1993. Grounded phonology. Cambridge, Mass.: MIT Press. Chapter 4.

Cassimjee, Farida. 1990. An autosegmental analysis of Venda tonology. New York: Garland Press. Chapter 1.

Chen, Matthew. 1991. An overview of tone sandhi phenomena across Chinese dialects. Languages and dialects of China, ed. by W. Wang, 113–58. Journal of Chinese Linguistics, monograph series no. 3.

Clements, George N. 1985. Akan vowel harmony: A nonlinear analysis. African linguistics: Essays in memory of M. W. K. Semikenke, ed. by D. Goyvaerts, 55–98. Amsterdam: Benjamins.

Odden, David. 1986. On the role of the Obligatory Contour Principle in phonological theory. Language 62.353–83.

Exercises

7.1 *Siane*

Siane is a tonal language spoken in the Highlands of Papua New Guinea (James 1981). In the transcriptions given here, ´ and ` denote high and low tones, respectively, while ˇ is rising and ˆ is falling. A syllable's tone is marked on its vocalic nucleus. For each noun, indicate the information that must be included on its tonal tier in order to predict the tonal shape of the words in its paradigm. Which tonal patterns are problematic for the Universal Association Convention? Show how your analysis works by deriving a few words. Briefly state in what way these data depart from a one-to-one relation between tones and tone-bearing units. (Note: There appear to be no monosyllabic nouns with a falling tone. Treat this as an arbitrary gap.)

(1)	noun	'our' N	'the' N	'by' N	
	nó	nóté	nómá	nókáfó	'food'
	kò	kòtè	kòmà	kòkàfò	'rain'
	yǒ	yòté	yòmá	yòkáfó	'fire'
	nǒ	nòté	nòmá	nòkáfó	'water'
	nǒi	nòité	nòimá	nòikáfó	'tree species'
	kúlá	kúláté	kúlámá	kúlákáfó	'dog'
	mèinà	mèinàtè	mèinàmà	mèinàkàfò	'payment'
	màfó	màfóté	màfómá	màfókáfó	'taro'
	àumá	àumáté	àumámá	àumákáfó	'bone'
	lónò	lónòtè	lónòmà	lónókàfò	'work'
	móità	móitàtè	móitàmà	móitákàfò	'rubbish'
	kétúfú	kétúfúté	kétúfúmá	kétúfúkáfó	'saliva'
	kòsìnà	kòsìnàtè	kòsìnàmà	kòsìnàkàfò	'sky'
	kìlífú	kìlífúté	kìlífúmá	kìlífúkáfó	'trap'
	máfùnà	máfúnàtè	máfúnàmà	máfúnàkàfò	'owl'
	kólìpá	kólìpáté	kólìpámá	kólìpákáfó	'pine'
	kêfá	kéfàté	kéfàmá	kéfàkáfó	'meat'

7.2   Mende (Leben 1973, Rialland and Badjimé 1989)

The data in (1) illustrate the possible tonal patterns for one-, two-, and three-syllable noun stems in Mende. Develop an analysis that derives the surface tonal patterns from an underlying tonal specification. List the inventory of tonal patterns. What descriptive generalizations can be made? What justification can be given for fixing the direction of tonal association? What role does the OCP play in the analysis? How are the data in (2) relevant? (The form glossed 'companion' has a rising-falling pitch contour.)

(1)

monosyllables		disyllables		trisyllables	
kɔ́	'war'	pɛ́lɛ́	'house'	háwámá	'waist'
kpà	'debt'	bɛ̀lɛ̀	'pants'	kpàkàlì	'three-legged chair'
mbû	'owl'	ngílà	'dog'	félàmà	'junction'
mbǎ	'rice'	fàndé	'cotton'	ndàvúlá	'sling'
mb'â	'companion'	nyàhâ	'woman'	nìkílì	'peanut'

(2)

noun	noun + ma 'on'
kɔ́	kɔ́-má
mbû	mbú-mà
mbǎ	mbà-má
pɛ́lɛ́	pɛ́lɛ́-má
bɛ̀lɛ̀	bɛ̀lɛ̀-mà
ngílà	ngílà-mà
nyàhâ	nyàhá-mà

7.3   Kanakuru (Newman 1974)

Develop an analysis for the tonal patterns of the verbs in this Chadic language. For each verb, list its underlying tonal specification. What rules and principles are required to derive the observed surface forms? Briefly compare this system with that of Mende in exercise 7.2. Assume that [ai], [ui], and [ua] are diphthongs.

(1)

gâi	'to enter'	bûi	'to shoot'
`túa	'to eat'*	`wái	'to get'
gɔ́rè	'to leave'	lákè	'to untie'
tùké	'to hide'	wùpé	'to sell'
tàkàlé	'to trick'	ˌlùkùré	'to disperse'
bómbɔ́lè	'to scrape'	lápɔ́rè	'to hold down'

*cf. mɔ́n ꞌtúa   'we ate it'

7.4   Proto-Bantu

The following data are taken primarily from Greenberg 1948 and van Spaandonck 1971. Cognate nominal stems from a number of Bantu languages are listed in (1). In most cases the stem was amplified with a CV prefix, many of which have lost their vowel in the course of history. The prefixes were uniformly low in tone. On the basis of these data, reconstruct the Proto-Bantu tonal shapes of the noun stems. How many different tonal patterns are there? What tonal changes must be assumed to have operated in the evolution of the individual languages? The transcriptions have been normalized: acute marks high tone; a low-toned syllable is unmarked. For the Tonga forms, *i#* is a so-called pre-prefix, akin to a definite determiner. The available data do not allow a totally satisfactory explanation for the development of the rising tone in Holoholo. For Tonga, it may be useful to appeal to lexical strata.

(1)

Lomongo	nyama	Lomongo	botá
Shambala	nyama	Shambala	utá
Holoholo	nyama	Holoholo	butǎ
Tonga	i#nyama	Tonga	í#búta
Chiluba	nyámá	Chiluba	búta
	'meat, animal'		'bow (and arrow)'

Lomongo	li-lɔ́tɔ́	Lomongo	li-élɛ
Shambala	n-dótó*	Shambala	u-vyélé
Tonga	í#cí-loto	Holoholo	i-beelé
Chiluba	cí-loota	Tonga	í#b-beele
	'dream'	Chiluba	dí-beelá
			'breast'

Lomongo	m-búla	Lomongo	lo-kónyi
Shambala	fúlá	Holoholo	lu-kuní
Holoholo	m-bilá	Tonga	í#lú-kunyi
Tonga	í#m-vula	Chiluba	lú-kunyí
Chiluba	m-vulá		'firewood'
	'rain'		

Lomongo	n-kíngó	Lomongo	n-jala
Shambala	šíngó	Shambala	sala
Holoholo	n-kingó	Holoholo	n-jala
Tonga	í#n-singo	Tonga	i#n-zala
Chiluba	n-si:ŋu	Chiluba	n-zálá
	'neck'		'hunger'

Lomongo	u-kɔ́kɔ́	Lomongo	i-longó
Shambala	n-gúkú	Shambala	n-yungú
Holoholo	n-kokó	Holoholo	mu-ungú
Tonga	í#n-kuku	Tonga	í#bú-lóngo
Chiluba	mú-kuuku		'cooking pot'
	'fowl'		

Lomongo	lɔ-kɛndo	Lomongo	fafá
Shambala	lu-ɣendo	Shambala	taté
Holoholo	lw-endo	Holoholo	taatǎ
Tonga	i#lw-eendo	Tonga	táata
Chiluba	lu-éndú	Chiluba	táatu
	'voyage'		'father'

*Van Spaandonck (1971) cites *n-dóto;* this appears to be a misprint.

Goldsmith (1990) has proposed that individual grammars may set lower and upper bounds on the number of autosegmental links their tones and TBUs may display. Rules that overload a given node automatically activate a delinking repair strategy in order to restore the system's equilibrium. On this view, Shona's TBU (section 7.2) has a (0,1) setting: toneless (unlinked) vowels are allowed (at least until the default rule is applied) while contour (rising and falling) tones are banned. The delinking of a low tone that occurs under high-tone spread (2) would thus not have to be stipulated.

(2)

As far as its tone is concerned, Shona would have the setting (1,n). There is no upper bound, so high-tone spread is free to extend a high until an association line blocks the rule; but delinked low tones are deleted – there is no downstep – and so the lower limit is not zero. In what ways is Goldsmith's proposal useful in analyzing the data in this exercise?

7.5 Venda

Listed in (1) are some prefixless Venda nominals. Assuming the analysis developed in section 7.3, determine the appropriate underlying representation for each and then the predicted post-H form.

(1)   thamaha   'male beast with certain markings'
       mádzhîe   personal name
       danána   'fool'
       khókhôlá   'ankle-bone'
       phapháná   'type of calabash'
       dukaná   'monstrous boy'
       dákálo   'joy'
       góŋóŋó   'bee'
       ḍabaḍaba   'fool'
       buvhikhomú   'species of spider'
       bubuséla   'woolen blanket'
       dziŋgándêvhé   'deaf person'
       bwerepwéré   'coward'
       bókól'íko   'species of bird'
       bólóŋgóndó   'heavy, thick pole'
       bélétshédzo   'reparation'
       pfúmélelo   'intercession'
       súdzúŋgw'áné   'species of shrub'

7.6 Finnish Vowel Harmony (Välimaa-Blum 1986, Alho 1987)

Examine the data in (1) and (2) to determine the various parameters of harmony in Finnish: the harmonic feature, root control, direction of spread, disharmonic roots, opaque and neutral elements. What aspects of autosegmental representation are crucial to your analysis? (Transcription note: [y] is a high front vowel; long vowels are geminates.)

(1)

	i	e	ä	y	ö	o	a	u
high	+	−	−	+	−	−	−	+
low	−	−	+	−	−	−	+	−
back	−	−	−	−	−	+	+	+
round	−	−	−	+	+	+	−	+

(2)

infinitive		infinitive		partitive	
tie-tää	'know'	tava-ta	'meet'	syndän-tä	'heart'
piir-tää	'draw'	halu-ta	'want'	katu-a	'street'
len-tää	'fly'	koka-ta	'cook'	rivi-ä	'row'
kään-tää	'turn'	tykä-tä	'like'	neiti-ä	'miss'
pyy-tää	'ask for'	kado-ta	'disappear'	äiti-ä	'mother'
löy-tää	'find'	filma-ta	'film'	ikkuna-a	'window'
mur-taa	'break'	ruve-ta	'start'	kyynel-tä	'tear'
sor-taa	'oppress'	menettä-ä	'lose'	tuoli-a	'chair'

infinitive	present passive	participle	
tul-la	tul-la-an	tul-nut	'come'
juo-da	juo-da-an	juo-nut	'drink'
syö-dä	syö-dä-än	syö-nyt	'eat'
men-nä	men-nä-än	men-nyt	'go'
luke-a	lue-ta-an	luke-nut	'read'

arka	'timid'	ark-uus	'timidity'
tyyni	'calm'	tyyne-ys	'calmness'
syvä	'deep'	syv-yys	'depth'
kaunis	'beautiful'	kaune-us	'beauty'
naivi	'naive'	naivi-us	'naiveness'
seniili	'senile'	seniili-ys	'senility'

väri	'color'	väri-käs	'colorful'
koti	'home'	kodi-kas	'cozy'
tyyli	'style'	tyyli-käs	'stylish'
ilme	'expression'	ilme-käs	'expressive'

question particle	
syön#kö	'do I eat?'
menet#kö	'do you go?'
olette#ko	'are you pl.?'

-kko	
mysti-kko	'mystic'
kehi-kko-j-a	'frames'

recent borrowings

afääri-ä	'affair' partitive
vulgääri-ä	'vulgar' partitive'
kamyy-tä	'Camus' partitive
tornado-a	'tornado' partitive

7.7 Makua

Review the discussion of section 7.5 to develop an analysis for the following verb forms from Makua. Is a cyclic application of the rules helpful?

(1) diminutive [ší]

u-ší-lówol-a	'to transport small things'
u-ší-lókotáníh-a	'to pick up small things'
u-ší-páparúlél-a	'to detach small things'
u-ší-kí-paparúlél-a	'to detach small things for me'

tense [-ahó]

k-a-hó-lókotáníh-a	'I picked up pl.'
y-a-hó-kí-hukulél-á	'he sieved for me'
y-a-hó-ší-ki-lokotáníherac-a	'he picked up small things for me'

7.8 Ga'anda

Review the discussion in section 7.6 and then determine the underlying representations and derivations for the following associative constructions from Ga'anda.

(1)

āl	'bone'	ɓár	'bark'
cùnèwà	'elephant'	pūnó	'maize'
āl cúnèwà	'bone of elephant'	ɓár pú'nó	'husk of maize'
pérrá	'bride'	cāmá	'husband'
Músá	name	pérrá	'bride'
pérrá Músá	'bride of Musa'	cāmá 'pérrá	'husband of bride'
shìkècá	'friend'	cāmá	'husband'
mbēɗétá	'grasshopper'	mbēɗétá	'grasshopper'
shìkècá mbé'ɗétá	'friend of grasshopper'	cāmá 'mbé'ɗétá	'husband of grasshopper'

7.9 Moore

A. Moore is a two-tone Gur language spoken in Burkina Faso (Kenstowicz, Nikiema, and Ourso 1988). In the transcriptions below, high-toned syllables are marked by the acute; low-toned syllables are unmarked. The language has a system of noun class suffixes marking singular and plural. Examples from the most productive classes are listed in (1). What principle underlies the alternation in suffixal tone?

(1)

sg.	pl.	
kor-gó	kor-dó	'sack'
ro:-gó	ro-tó	'house'
wób-go	wób-do	'elephant'
láŋ-go	lán-do	'hole'
tị̀:-gá	tị̀:-sé	'tree'
ke:-gá	ke:-sé	'green'
sá:-ga	sá:-se	'broom'
wáŋ-ga	wám-se	'hollow'
gob-ré	gwab-á	'left hand'
tụb-ré	tụb-á	'ear'
kúg-ri	kúg-a	'stone'
bẹ́d-re	bẹ́d-a	'big'

B. Moore has downdrift of high tones; the high tone on the final syllable of *zá
léŋgə-ré* 'bring the bowl' is implemented at a lower pitch value than the high
tones of the first two syllables. Develop an analysis to account for the appearance of the downstep in the data of (2). In the first paradigm the nouns
sá:-ga 'broom' and *kor-gó* 'sack' appear as complements to the verbs *zá*
'bring' and *ko* 'give'. The second paradigm consists of noun + adjective constructions. This construction has the peculiarity that the morphology does
not generate a number suffix on the noun in Moore.

(2)

ko sá:ga	'give a broom'
ko korgó	'give a sack'
zá sá:ga	'bring a broom'
zá kór'gó	'bring a sack'
kor bẹ́da	'big sacks'
kor ke:gá	'green sack'
sá bẹ́da	'big brooms'
sá ké:'gá	'green broom'

C. In Moore a suffixal vowel is deleted when a word appears in medial position
of the phrase. Examine the associative constructions in (3) and discuss the
tonal effects produced by the deletion rule. Derive each of the phrases, explaining the steps involved.

(3)

nẹ́d-a	'man'	na:-bá	'chief'
nẹ́d korgó	'man's sack'	na:b kór'gó	'chief's sack'
nẹ́d 'sá:ga	'man's broom'	na:b sá:ga	'chief's broom'

D. So far we have seen two tonal patterns for Moore nominals: low on the root
and high on the suffix (e.g., *kor-gó*) and high on the root and low on the
suffix (e.g., *sá:-ga*). There is in fact an additional tonal pattern: a high appears

on both the root and the suffix (4). But nominals with a low tone on both the root
and the suffix are absent in Moore.

(4) bíd-gó   bí-tó   'sorrel'
     mó:-gó   mó:-dó   'straw'
     bá:-gá   bá:-sé   'dog'
     bṳ́:-gá   bṳ́:-sé   'goat'
     wám-dé   wám-á   'calabash'
     rá:-ré   ré-yá   'day'

These nominals appear with a low tone when combined with a following adjective
(5).

(5) mo saŋgó   'good straw'
     bṳ saŋgó   'good goat'
     ba bɛ́da   'big dogs'
     wam ke:gá   'green calabash'

Develop an analysis to explain this alternation as well as the absence of nominals
with a low on both the root and the suffix. You should also be able to assign a
nonarbitrary underlying tone to the number suffixes and state a natural rule that
accounts for the alternation between high and low tone. (Note that the root vowel
alternates in length in many of these examples, appearing as long before the
number suffix. You may ignore this alternation; it has no bearing on the tone.)

7.10 Lama (Ourso 1989)

Lama is a two-tone language of the Gur family (related to Moore) spoken in Togo.
Three contrasting surface tones occur before pause: high (e.g., *ná* 'see!'), low
(e.g., *na* 'with'), and falling (e.g., *nâ:* 'cow'). Phrase-medially only high and low
tones occur phonetically; falling tone is systematically barred except before pause.
Monosyllabic nouns fall into four distinct classes in terms of their tonological
behavior. However, before pause the four classes merge into three distinct phonetic types and phrase-medially into only two. Examples of the four distinct
classes appear in (1).

(1) a.   ci   'father'
          ri   'mother'
          ra   'friend'

     b.   wá:l   'husband'
          yír   'person'
          lé:l   'widow'

     c.   nâ: 'cow'
          sî: 'sheep'
          tî: 'elephant'

     d.   yal   'wife'
          ra:l   'brother'
          nun   'aunt'

A. Develop an analysis to account for the tonal effects of class (1a) and class (1b) nouns on the words *tẹ* 'under' and *ra* 'friend'.

(2) ci   'father'   ri   'mother'
     ci tẹ   'under father'   ri tẹ   'under mother'
     ci ra   'father's friend'   ri ra   'mother's friend'

     wá:l   'husband'   yír   'person'
     wá:l tệ   'under husband'   yír tệ   'under person'
     wá:l râ   'husband's friend'   yír râ   'person's friend'

B. Now consider class (1c) words in the same contexts; formulate a rule to account for the alternation between fall and high. Must this rule be ordered with respect to the one developed for (2)? If yes, why? If no, why not?

(3) nâ: 'cow'   tî: 'elephant'
     ná: tẹ   'under cow'   tí: tẹ   'under elephant'
     ná: ra   'cow's friend'   tí: ra   'elephant's friend'

C. The postposition *tẹ́* means 'chez', 'at the house of'. Can you explain the downsteps in the following paradigms?

(4) ci tẹ́   'chez father'   ri tẹ́   'chez mother'
     wá:l tẹ́   'chez husband'   yír tẹ́   'chez person'
     ná: t'ẹ́   'chez cow'   tí: t'ẹ́   'chez elephant'

     wá:l râ   'husband's friend'
     wá:l rá tẹ   'under husband's friend'
     wá:l rá t'ẹ́   'chez husband's friend'

D. The verb *sewá* 'ran' systematically varies its tone depending on the tone type of the preceding noun. Your analysis should be able to explain each example in (5).

(5) ci sewá   'father ran'
     wá:l séw'á   'husband ran'
     ná: sewá   'cow ran'
     wá:l rá sewá   'husband's friend ran'

E. Now consider nouns from class (1d). In what ways are they similar to and different from the other types? Develop an analysis to explain these differences.

(6) yal   'wife'   ra:l   'brother'
     yal tệ   'under wife'   ra:l tệ   'under brother'
     yal râ   'wife's friend'   ra:l râ   'brother's friend'
     yal tẹ́   'chez wife'   ra:l tẹ́   'chez brother'
     yal séw'á   'wife ran'   ra:l séw'á 'brother ran'

7.11 Suzhou (Bao 1990)

Review the analysis of Suzhou in section 7.8.2. In (1) are listed the tonal shapes for one-, two-, three-, and four-syllable phrases. Instead of the Chao numbering, develop an analysis using high and low tones. Which cases are consistent with the text analysis? Which are not? Is the notion of extratonality useful? ʔ55 and ʔ23 are tones found on syllables whose coda is a glottal stop. Must they be considered separate tones as the Chao numbering implies?

(1) | monosyllabic | disyllabic | trisyllabic | quadrisyllabic |
|---|---|---|---|
| 44 | 55 21 | 55 55 21 | 55 55 33 21 |
| 52 | 52 21 | 52 22 21 | 52 22 22 21 |
| 13 | 22 44 | 22 55 21 | 22 55 44 21 |
| ʔ55 | ʔ55 34 | ʔ55 34 21 | ʔ55 34 44 21 |
| ʔ23 | ʔ23 55 | ʔ23 55 21 | ʔ23 55 44 21 |

7.12 Pinyao (Bao 1991)

The Chinese dialect Pinyao (data from Hou 1980) has three isolation tones: *ti* 13 'animal's foot', *ti* 35 'field', and *ti* 53 'top'. The 31 tone apparently occurs only in sandhi. Use Bao's (1990) conception of the tonal node as dominating sister register and contour nodes to characterize the sandhi changes. (Hint: Postulate a special rule to reduce case (1e) to case (1b).) Bao's analysis involves a rule for dissimilation of shape (1b,e,i) followed by an assimilation of register (1c,d). How strongly do these data support the distinction between the register and contour components of the tonal node?

(1) a. $13 + 13 > 13\ 13$ t'aŋ u 'embezzle'; ts'əu tç'iɛ 'draw lottery'
      b. $13 + 35$ 31 35   tsəu ti 'rent land'; pu taŋ 'hatch egg'
      c. $13 + 53$ 35 53   ts'uŋ mi 'grind rice'; tçi ma 'ride horse'
      d. $35 + 13$ 13 13   t'uæ paŋ 'quit class'; xa kuei 'start cooking'
      e. $35 + 35$ 31 35   pæ çiŋ 'upset'; ts'ɿ ts'æ 'cut vegetables'
      f. $35 + 53$ 35 53   xa y 'rain'; tuŋ xuei 'get angry'
      g. $53 + 13$ 53 13   tsaŋ iɔ 'stretch waist'; tsəu sei 'meteorite'
      h. $53 + 35$ 53 35   suaŋ tç'i 'breathe heavily'; ti sɿ 'useful'
      i. $53 + 53$ 35 53   ta tiŋ 'take a nap'; mæ çi 'curry favor'

8 The Phonological Skeleton

In the preceding chapter we saw that the fundamental insight of Goldsmith's (1976) autosegmental model is that tone occupies a separate tier from the associated segmental phonemes, allowing for multiple linking, underlying toneless vowels, and latent tones. Shortly after the appearance of Goldsmith's dissertation, phonologists started to consider extending autosegmental thinking to other phonological problems. A significant breakthrough came in John McCarthy's (1979a, 1981) work on Semitic. He showed that the notorious problem of the root-and-pattern morphology in these languages could be solved if an Arabic word such as *katab* 'he wrote' is analyzed in terms of a [ktb] root morpheme that associates to a CVCVC template in essentially the same way that a LH tonal melody maps to *ŋgùrsú* 'bend' in Margi (section 7.1). Clements and Keyser (1983) extended this multilinear conception of phonological representation, pointing to segmental analogues of toneless vowels and latent tones as well as one-to-many relations in more familiar and well-studied languages such as English, Spanish, and French. They developed a three-dimensional model of phonological representation that is based on a fundamental distinction between a phoneme and the position it occupies in phonological structures. Clements and Keyser refer to the sequence of positions as the *CV* or *skeletal tier*, assigning a word such as *dog* the representation sketched in (1).

(1)   σ   syllable tier

      C V C   CV, skeletal tier

      d ɔ g   segmental tier

In the ensuing years two models of the skeleton have emerged: an X-slot model that continues the original conception of McCarthy and of Clements and Keyser in essential respects and a moraic model in which phonological positions are viewed as terminal points in prosodic structure.

In this chapter we will survey the research that has developed around the phonological skeleton. We will begin with a brief sketch of the root-and-pattern morphology of Arabic in order to appreciate the kind of problem that McCarthy confronted. We will then survey some of the major evidence and implications of adopting the autosegmental approach to Semitic – again focusing on Arabic. In the final sections we will examine the ways in which phonologists have employed the distinction between a segment and its position in phonological structure, comparing the X-slot and the moraic conceptions of the skeleton.

8.1 Arabic Root-and-Pattern Morphology

One of the most striking features of Arabic word structure is that the constituent morphemes seem to be sprinkled through the word rather than to occupy some continuous subsegment. This property is evident in the following paradigms.

(2) a. daras-a   ḥamal-a   rasam-a   šarib-a
         'he studied'   'he carried'   'he drew'   'he drank'

     b. darras-a   ḥammal-a   rassam-a   šarrab-a
         'he taught'   'he loaded'   'he made   'he made
                                             draw'   drink'

     c. dars-un   ḥiml-un   rasm-un   šurb-ah
         'a lesson'   'cargo, load'   'a drawing'   'a drink'

     d. darraas-un   ḥammaal-un   rassaam-un   šarraab-un
         'student'   'porter'   'draftsman'   'drunkard'

     e. diraas-ah   ḥimaal-ah   risaam-ah
         'studies'   'trade of   'ordination'
                            porter'

     f. madras-ah   marsam-un   mašrab-un
         'Koranic   'studio'   'tavern'
         school'

     g. daaris   ḥaamil   raasim   šaarib
         'studying'   'carrying'   'drawing'   'drinking'

The suffixes -*a*, -*un*, and -*ah* are inflectional affixes. In these families of semantically related words, the only constant formal property is that each stem has located within it three consonants in a fixed order: [drs], [ḥml], [rsm], [šrb]. These "radicals" are interspersed with the vowels in seemingly chaotic fashion. However, comparison of the paradigms reveals deeper regularities. All words in the (a) form have the canonical structure CVCVC in which the C-positions are occupied by the radical consonants, the first V is [a], and the second is [a] or [i] (lexically determined). The gerundives (g) have the shape CVVCVC, where the first long vowel is [a] and the second vowel is [i]. The resultative nominals of (c) take a CVCC stem shape with the V-slot unpredictably filled by one of the language's three vocalic phonemes. Thus, minimally we can say that words belonging to the same morphological category (resultative nominal, agentive nominal, etc.) have the same template characterizing the relative position of the radical consonants to the vowels. This feature of the Semitic languages differs strikingly from the more prevalent affixational morphology in which suffixes and prefixes are concatenated to the stem to build up (sometimes quite lengthy) chains of morphemes. Arabic also employs affixational processes, but the nonconcatenative morphology evident in (2) pervades most of the derivational system and a good portion of the inflection as well. It is clearly the language's basic mode of morphological organization and has always posed a challenge to methods of analysis based on the notion of affixation to a stem such as the structuralist item-and-arrangement approach in which words are segmented into parts whose distribution must then be stated. The problem here is that the relevant units [ktb], [drs], and so on, cannot be isolated in any simple, mechanical fashion.

With the advent of autosegmental phonology, the idea that elements may occupy distinct tiers suggested a fresh approach to the problem. As we have seen, the only invariant running through the slots of the paradigms in (2) is the gross prosodic shape: the causative has the form CVCCVC with gemination of the middle radical, the agentive CVCCVVC has medial gemination plus a long second vowel, and the participle CVVCVC has a long first vowel. It does not matter which particular phonemes occupy the template slots; their individual character is irrelevant in marking these morphological categories. What matters is the canonical shape of the words. McCarthy's idea was that just as a tone language selects the option to encode its vocabulary in terms of the features [±hi tone], [±upper reg], and so on, so the Semitic languages recruit the feature [±consonantal] as an autosegmental tier to encode their morphological categories. At the most basic level, then, the verbs *daras* and *rasam* and their derivative causatives and agentives have the representations in (3).

(3)

```
      d r s              d r s              d r s
     / | \              / ∧ \              / ∧ \
     CVCVC              CVCCVC             CVCCVVC
       V                  V                  V
       a                  a                  a

      r s m              r s m              r s m
     / | \              / ∧ \              / ∧ \
     CVCVC              CVCCVC             CVCCVVC
       V                  V                  V
       a                  a                  a
```

Stated differently, the distribution of consonants versus vowels in Arabic is not lexically contrastive the way it can be in English (cf. VCC *art,* CVC *rat;* CVCC *tort,* CCVC *trot*); instead, it is determined by the CV template that characterizes the morphological category a given word belongs to.

Another noteworthy feature of Arabic morphology is that the vowel phonemes mark inflectional categories such as tense in verbs and number on nominals. This point is reflected in the paradigms in (4), where the [ui] melody distinguishes the passive from the [a] that fills the vowel slots in the active form of the verb. CVVCVC is another measure of the verb known as the "participative" (involving the object as a participant). The important point is that the active and passive forms in each measure (derivational category) preserve the same prosodic shape: the difference in voice is signaled by the vowels.

(4)   active   passive
      I   katab-a   'he wrote'   kutib-a   'it was written'
      II   kattab-a 'he made write'   kuttib-a   'he was made to write'
      III   kaatab-a 'he corresponded   kuutib-a   'he was corresponded
                       with'   with'

      I   šarib-a   'he drank'   šurib-a   'it was drunk'
      II   šarrab-a 'he made drink'   šurrib-a   'he was made to drink'
      III   šaarab-a 'he had a drink   šuurib-a   'he was had a drink
                       with'   with'

In other cases individual templates determine the vowel pattern: for instance, the
CVVCVC participles have [ai] vocalism. Vowels contrast lexically in only a small
number of cases (e.g., CVCC nominals). Finally and most importantly, vowels
never function as radicals. Root morphemes in Arabic are encoded solely by
consonantal phonemes (including the glides). This means that consonants and
vowels occupy distinct morphological and autosegmental tiers, and it gives rise
to the language's characteristic interweaving of the radical consonants and the
morphologically determined vowels. The word *kuutib* thus receives the autosegmental analysis in (5).

(5)   k   t   b   'write'
      | | |
      CVVCVC   'participative'
       \/ |
       u   i   'passive'

Projecting vowels and consonants on different autosegmental tiers (so-called
V/C segregation) is a frequent but by no means necessary property of templating
languages, whose basic feature is that the distribution of consonants and vowels
with respect to one another is determined by the template rather than being lexically contrastive (see McCarthy 1989 for discussion).

   To briefly sum up, consonants and vowels in Arabic are autosegmentally related
to positions in the template. Consequently, we expect that essentially the same
properties that characterize the relation between a tone and a TBU should arise:
multiple linking, bare template slots, unassociated phonemes, directions of association, and so on. Much of McCarthy's research involved a rigorous pursuit
of the implications of his original proposal. In the following sections we will look
at some of the evidence that has emerged to support the autosegmental view of
Arabic.

8.2   Some Modern Arabic Dialects

In this section we will discuss a number of Arabic dialects, including Classical
(or Modern Standard) Arabic as well as such modern colloquial dialects as Levantine (Palestinian, Lebanese, Jordanian), Sudanese, and Bedouin (Kenstowicz

1986b). Since our discussion focuses on the syllable, a few general remarks are in order. The language has the core syllable inventory [CV, CVV, CVC]. Extra-heavy CVVC and CVCC syllables arise word-finally or before a vowel deletion site. We will focus on the pandialectal processes of vowel syncope and epenthesis. Both crucially interact with stress, whose placement follows the Latin stress rule in essential respects. The antepenultimate syllable bears the word stress if the penult is a light CV syllable; otherwise, stress is assigned to the penult unless the final syllable is extraheavy, in which case it takes the stress (6).

(6)   wálad-i   'my boy'   walád-na   'our boy'   sakán-t   'I settled'
      báarak-at   'she blessed'   makáatib   'offices'   makatíib   'letters'
      máktab-a   'library'

The first dialect we will examine is that of the Ajloun Mountains spoken in northern Jordan. The discussion will follow closely the analysis developed by Alghazo (1987). In the Ajloun dialect the creation of extraheavy CVCC syllables is severely constrained. They arise only when the two consonants in the coda form a geminate. In all other cases the stray consonant of CC# and CCC clusters is assigned to the coda of an anaptyctic syllable whose vowel is [i]. The epenthesis process inserting this dummy [i] vowel must follow the stress rule. This ordering is justified by paradigms such as those in (7).

(7)   a.   ḍaráb-it   b.   ḥímil   ḥúbb
         ḍárab-ič   ḥíml-u   ḥúbb-u
         'strike'   ḥímil-ha   ḥúbb-ha
                       'load'   'love'

The stress in *ḍaráb-it* 'I struck' is superficially anomalous since a light penult has been accented instead of the antepenult, which is where the stress usually falls in words whose second last syllable has the CV shape (cf. *ḍárab-ič* 'he struck you'). Since a VCC# sequence always attracts the stress in Arabic, the aberrant stress in *ḍaráb-it* is explained if it derives from the underlying representation [ḍarab + t]. This analysis is supported by a number of stem allomorphy rules that are sensitive to whether the suffix is consonant- or vowel-initial. Each one treats the 1sg. suffix as if it begins with a consonant. The paradigms in (7b) are deverbal nominals with a CVCC canonical shape. The [-u] and [-ha] suffixes mark 3sg. masc. and fem. pronominal possession. In the Ajloun dialect the underlying CVCC shape emerges to the phonetic surface only when the final cluster is a geminate; otherwise, the stray consonant is assigned to an anaptyctic syllable. Notice that in *ḥímil-ha* from [ḥiml + ha] epenthesis has created another superficial exception to the stress rule. This time it appears that a heavy penult has been skipped in favor of a light antepenult. Ordering stress assignment before epenthesis explains this anomaly as well: [ḥiml + ha] → [ḥíml + ha] → [ḥímil + ha].

Having motivated the epenthesis rule, let us now turn to its formulation. In the linear model the rule can be stated to simply insert the epenthetic vowel before a stray consonant, as in (8a). But in a model with a distinct timing tier, a two-step approach to epenthesis is possible. First, a nuclear skeletal slot is inserted; second, that slot is assigned the value [i] on the phonemic tier (8b).

(8)   a. $\emptyset \rightarrow i / \underline{\hspace{1cm}} C'$

    b. $C' \rightarrow \textcircled{V}C'$ $\textcircled{V} \rightarrow V$
                | |
                N   [i]

We will argue that there is descriptive as well as theoretical motivation for this two-step approach to epenthesis in Arabic. But first let us look at another process relevant to the discussion: a syncope rule deleting unstressed high vowels from word-medial short open syllables. This rule permeates the entire morphological system of Arabic. The paradigms in (9) illustrate the syllabic gaps this rule creates. The suffixes [-ha] and [-u] mark pronominal possession on nouns and objects on verbs; the prefix [ʔa-] marks a 1sg. subject in the imperfect. Vowel-initial suffixes open the final syllable of the stem, leading to the deletion of the [i].

(9)   makáatib   ʔa-ʕállim   ʔa-báarik
      makaatíb-ha   ʔa-ʕallím-ha   ʔa-baarík-ha
      makáatb-u   ʔa-ʕállm-u   ʔa-báark-u
      'offices'   'I teach'   'I bless'

Although the distribution of the [i] appearing in these paradigms parallels that of the vowel of (7), it cannot be the epenthetic vowel since it counts for stress. But the epenthetic vowel arises after the word stress has been assigned. Consequently, the [i] that alternates with $\emptyset$ in (9) must be an underlying [i]. To sum up, we have developed a partially ordered set of three rules: stress precedes syncope and epenthesis.

    Now consider the paradigms for imperfect verb roots of the shape CCVC.

(10)   ʔá-fham   ʔá-ḥrig   ʔá-ḥrus   'I verb'
       ʔa-fhám-ha   ʔa-ḥríg-ha   ʔa-ḥrús-ha   'I verb her'
       ʔá-fham-u   ʔá-ḥirg-u   ʔá-ḥurs-u   'I verb him'
       'I understand' 'I guard'   'I burn'

Roots with a high vowel such as [ḥrig] and [ḥrus] have CVCC alternants when the following suffix begins with a vowel. Roots with a low vowel such as [fham] do not alternate. The most natural analysis assumes that syncope deletes the root vowel, creating a CCC cluster whose stray consonant activates epenthesis. The derivations of (11) illustrate this proposal.

(11)   a.   ʔa-ḥrig-u   b.   ʔa-ḥrus-u
         ʔá-ḥrig-u   ʔá-ḥrus-u   stress
         ʔá-ḥrg-u   ʔá-ḥrs-u   syncope
         ʔá-ḥirg-u   ʔá-ḥurs-u   epenthesis

While this analysis is attractive, it faces a serious problem: in (11a) the epenthetic vowel is [i] but in (11b) it is [u]. From a study of hundreds of roots, Alghazo

(1987) reports that CC*i*C roots consistently have a C*i*CC alternant while CC*u*C roots always take C*u*CC. In other words, the vowel in the CVCC alternant systematically matches the vowel in the CCVC alternant. But in the derivations in (11) the root vowel is deleted by the syncope rule. In order to capture Alghazo's generalization, the epenthesis rule must restore a vowel identical to the underlying vowel.

We have assumed that the application of a phonological rule is determined by two factors: the immediately preceding representation in the derivation, and UG and language-particular constraints on rule application. But in (11) the information that determines the proper epenthetic vowel is absent from the preceding step of the derivation. Nor can this information be supplied by a general constraint because the [i] vs. [u] contrast is unpredictable information comprising the lexical representation of each root. Consequently, to maintain the analysis embodied in (11), the epenthesis rule would have to be granted the power to look back to the underlying representation in order to insert the proper epenthetic vowel. While descriptively attractive in this case, such "global" rules are theoretically undesirable because they significantly increase the class of potential grammars.

A descriptive alternative is to derive the CVCC alternant directly from the CCVC shape before syncope eliminates the root vowel. However, as Alghazo shows, this analysis is not very appealing either. The metathesis rule must be stated as in (12).

(12)   C C V C + V $\Rightarrow$ 1 3 2 4 5
$$\begin{array}{c} | \\ [+\text{high}] \\ 1\ 2\ 3\ 4\quad 5 \end{array}$$

This rule repeats information contained in the independently needed syncope and epenthesis rules. Like syncope, it must be ordered after the stress rule to avoid accent on the metathesized vowel. Its restriction to [+high] vowels in an open syllable repeats the structural description of the syncope rule. Finally, the metathesized vowel is placed in the context C____CC – exactly the site of the epenthetic vowel. Clearly, descriptive generalizations are missed by the metathesis rule.

Representing Arabic words as three-dimensional objects provides an escape from this dilemma. As Alghazo observes, all we need say is that the syncope rule deletes a nuclear V-slot of the skeletal tier when it is associated with a high vowel in a nonfinal syllable (13a). The phoneme associated with this skeletal slot remains on the vocalic tier (13b). If, as suggested, epenthesis inserts a bare nuclear V-slot, then a representation with an unlinked V-slot and an unlinked vocalic phoneme is derived (13c). A plausible UG association principle will link these elements (13d), preempting the default rule that assigns [i] to a bare V-slot.

(13)   a.   ḥ r s   b.   ḥ r s   c.   ḥ r s   d.   ḥ r s   root tier
            | | | | | | | | | | | |
            CCVC   →   CCC   →   CVCC   →   CVCC   skeletal tier
            | |
            u   u   u   u   inflection

The analysis in (13) strongly resembles the phenomenon of tonal stability (section 7.1), a major motivation for the autosegmental representation of tone. However, the vowel stability evident in (13) seems less prevalent than tonal stability. This apparent disparity could reflect the special status of the Semitic root vowels as occupants of a distinct autosegmental tier. Alternatively, it might lie in the fact that the derivations in (13) involve the contingency of vowel deletion and then insertion in the same vicinity, giving the floating vowel the opportunity to re-emerge.

Another crucial assumption of the analysis in (13) is that epenthesis is a two-stage affair – insertion of a bare V-slot followed by a separate rule that phonetically interprets the slot as [i]. Some support for this approach derives from the observation, originally made by Harris (1983) for Spanish, that when a language has several distinct epenthesis rules, each rule usually inserts the same vowel. This holds for Ajloun Arabic. Alghazo (1987) motivates two additional vowel insertion rules. In both cases the inserted vowel is [i]. The imperatives in (14) illustrate one such case.

(14) šuuf   íḥmal   'verb!'
      šuuf-ha   ḥmál-ha   'verb her!'
      'see'   'carry'

In Arabic, as in many other languages, the imperative consists of just the root of the verb. The analytic question is the status of the initial vowel in *íḥmal*. If it were an underlying prefix, we could not explain its deletion in *ḥmál-ha* by syncope since this rule applies only in an open syllable. On the other hand, the vowel cannot be the epenthetic support of stray consonants because the Ajloun dialect permits words to begin with two consonants (e.g., *ktáab* 'book'). Furthermore, the [i] in *íḥmal* is stressed, but epenthesis applies after stress. Consequently, this vowel cannot be the epenthetic vowel. Rather, it reflects a minimality constraint (see section 11.2 for discussion) found in other Levantine dialects, which adds a mora to bare CCVC roots to ensure that each word has at least two moras – the minimal stress unit. The important point is that the dummy syllable realizing the extra mora takes [i] as its vocalic nucleus – the same vowel that fills the anaptyctic syllable. Why should these vowels be the same?

In both cases the vowels are dummy placeholders that fill in a bare prosodic position rather than serving any contrastive function. Recall that in Shona (section 7.2) there is motivation for deriving the surface {H,L} tonal inventory from underlying representations with vowels linked to a high tone or vowels linked to no tone. The toneless vowels then acquire a "default" low tone at some point in the derivation. It has been argued, most forcefully by Archangeli (1984, 1988), that vocalic systems are organized in a similar fashion with one element singled out as the default element. On this view, an *n*-vowel system in general has $n-1$ underlying vowel phonemes. The vowel subtracted from the inventory is assigned by default to bare V-slots. Arabic would be analyzed with [i] as the default and the underlying inventory reduced to {a,u}. If we accept the view that every grammar designates a particular vowel as default to fill bare V-slots, then it is natural that the same default rule will fill the V-slots inserted by epenthesis rules. In this way, vowel epenthesis rules appear to always insert the same vowel. The important point is that a default rule only makes sense in a model that distinguishes between the segmental and skeletal tiers. The linear model equates a segment's phonemic substance and its position relative to other segments and thus has no provision for such a notion.

The solution in (13) crucially hinges on the distinction between the segmental and skeletal tiers of the nonlinear model. By deletion of the nuclear skeletal slot, the syncope rule creates a floating vowel that reanchors to the nucleus of the anaptyctic syllable. Pursuing the tonal analogy, one wonders whether floating phonemic segments can be posited for underlying representations. An example is furnished by the phenomenon of *wasla* "joining" in Arabic. We will follow the analysis developed by Hamid (1984) for the Sudanese dialect. (Essentially the same phenomenon occurs in Classical Arabic.) Sudanese Arabic displays certain prefixes such as the passive of *in-kátal* 'was killed' whose vowel escapes the stress normally assigned to the antepenult (cf. *tárjamat* 'translated' 3sg.fem., *yáktub-u* 'they write'). The aberrant stress is explained if the underlying form is [n-katal]. The [n] fails to parse into a core syllable and is later assigned to a dummy syllable by the epenthesis process described earlier. In the Sudanese dialect epenthesis must occur in the phrasal phonology because it is suspended when the preceding word ends in a vowel. In such postvocalic contexts *wasla* "joining" occurs: the stray consonant joins the coda of the preceding syllable (cf. (15b), (15c)). The rule is formulated in (15d). It applies before epenthesis and thus preempts emergence of the anaptyctic syllable.

(15) a. inkátal   'was killed'
      b. alwála.d in.kátal   'the boy was killed'
      c. wála.du n.kátal   'his boy was killed'
      d. V   [C'
          |------
          N'

Now consider the phonology of the definite prefix [al-]. It also shuns the accent (16a) and is missing its vowel after a word ending in a vowel, such as *kátal-u* 'they killed' (16c).

(16) a. al-wálad   'the boy'
      b. káta.l al.wálad   'he killed the boy'
      c. káta.lu l.walad   'they killed the boy'

The [a] of the definite prefix thus has the distribution of the epenthetic vowel in (15). As Hamid points out, this point is explained if the definite prefix has the underlying form shown in (17a). In this representation the phoneme [a] is not associated with a skeletal position of its own. In order to escape stray erasure, it must acquire a link to the skeletal tier through the epenthesis rule.

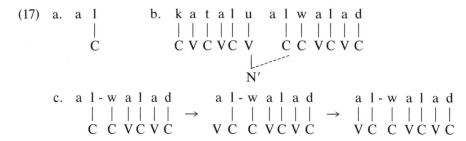

Since all Arabic roots begin with a consonant, the [l] of the definite prefix will never be assigned to a core syllable. But it may join the coda of the preceding word ending in a vowel (17b) by (15d). Because the [a] is not linked to the skeletal tier in (17b), it undergoes stray erasure to give [katalu l-walad]. If the stray [l] is preceded by a consonant or pause, then no "joining" occurs. Instead, the same epenthesis process operative in (15) inserts a bare V-slot: the unlinked [a] can now associate to the bare V-slot, preempting insertion of the default [i] vowel and deriving [al-walad] (17c). The parallel between the distribution of the [a] vowel of the definite prefix and that of the epenthetic vowel thus follows entirely from the representation in (17a). No special rules or conditions of application are required.

Consider the dilemma the linear model faces in attempting to come to terms with the same data. To explain why the definite prefix escapes stress, it can be assigned the underlying representation [l]. Stress will then be assigned correctly to the first root vowel in [l+walad]. As in the three-dimensional analysis, the [l] remains a stray consonant and thus triggers insertion of the epenthetic vowel [i]. (In Sudanese Arabic [i] is the epenthetic vowel used in loanword adaptation: for example, *bálif* 'valve'.) But now a special rule is required to change the epenthetic vowel from [i] to [a]. This rule cannot be a general one, however; it must be triggered solely by the definite prefix. This analysis is suspect because phrasal rules are typically blind to the internal morphological structure of words. Furthermore, the rule must be limited to the epenthetic vowel. Other [i] vowels do not change to [a] in this context (e.g., *katal-ti l-walad* 'you fem.sg. killed the boy'). Clearly, the "rule" changing the epenthetic vowel to [a] merely disguises the fact that the [a] is an idiosyncratic feature of the definite prefix and thus should properly form part of its lexical representation. But if the underlying representation of the prefix is [al], then its vowel should receive the word stress in *al-wálad* and we are returned to the initial problem.

This dilemma does not arise in the nonlinear model, where exactly the right distinctions are drawn. The [a] is part of the lexical representation (17a) of the definite prefix. Yet it lacks a skeletal slot of its own and hence can never take the stress because the prosodic rules of syllabification and stress operate off of the skeletal tier. It only manages to reach the phonetic surface through the epenthesis process. Consequently, its distribution is entirely parallel to that of the epenthetic vowel. The presence or absence of the [a] thus follows from general principles and not from an arbitrary and suspect rule.

The underlying representation of the definite prefix for Sudanese Arabic and for Classical Arabic, where essentially the same facts hold, violates the one-to-one relation between the segmental and skeletal tiers. Therefore, it might be argued to constitute a more complex phonological state. Support for this view derives from the tendency to reanalyze this morpheme in the individual modern Arabic dialects in such a way as to bring its representation in line with a one-to-one relation. For example, in the Levantine area the floating [a] has been lost so that the prefix is simply [l]. (18) represents the situation in the Ajloun dialect.

(18) a. gátal il-wálad   'he killed the boy'
      b. gáta.lu l.wálad   'they killed the boy'
      c. l-wálad   'the boy'
      d. n-gátal   'was killed'

When the definite prefix is preceded by a consonant, epenthetic [i] appears (18a); when it is preceded by a vowel, joining occurs (18b). However, unlike in the Sudanese dialect, a special adjunction rule or licensing statement operates post-pausally in the Ajloun dialect to preempt epenthesis (18c). This accounts for the existence of the many words that begin with consonant clusters in the Levantine dialects (e.g., *ktáab* 'book'). As we would expect, it also applies to the passive prefix (18d). Given this syllabification, the floating *a* of the definite prefix never surfaces and so the prefix is naturally restructured to [l-].

We now turn to another Arabic dialect that ties together a number of strands in the preceding discussion: the dialect of the Bani-Hassan, a Bedouin clan of the Jordanian desert (Irshied 1984). In this dialect the definite prefix has been simplified in a different way. Its vowel counts for stress (*ál-walad*), suggesting that the one-to-one principle has restored a skeletal slot to the [a] vowel so that the prefix has the underlying representation shown in (19a). The vowel of the definite prefix truncates the vowel of a preceding word (19b). This rule is formulated in (19c).

(19) a. a l
          | |
          V C

      b. ál-walad   'the boy'
          gtál-u   'they killed'
          gtál ál-walad   'they killed the boy'

      c. $V \rightarrow \emptyset / \underline{\quad} V$

Now consider the paradigm in (20), illustrating the behavior of the passive prefix in the Bani-Hassan dialect.

(20) a. ín-gital   'was killed'
      b. wlíd-u   'his boy'
      c. wlí.dún.gital   'his boy was killed'

Since its vowel counts for stress, the prefix must have an underlying V-slot. In (20c) the [u] and [i] appear to have merged into an accented [ú]: [wlíd-u íngital]

→ [wlí.dún.gi.tal]. In the linear model this contraction requires another rule to delete the [i] and shift its stress to the preceding [u]. Contraction must be a rule separate from the truncation operating in (19c) because the latter deletes the first vowel in the sequence. A rather different analysis is available in the nonlinear model that distinguishes the skeletal and phonemic tiers. Recall the proposal to extend default rules to vowel systems. Clearly, [i] is the default vowel in Arabic since it is the one that is assigned to a bare V-slot under epenthesis. Consequently, at the word juncture in (20c) the relevant representation is (21a).

(21) a. V] [V   b.   ] [V
          | ⁄⁄⁄
          u   u

If truncation (19c) is interpreted as an operation on the skeletal tier deleting one V-slot before another, then a floating vowel is created. By now-familiar principles, the floating vowel reattaches to the bare V-slot of the passive prefix (21b). No complex vowel merger and stress movement processes are required. The independently motivated truncation rule (19c) derives the correct results. Thus, by assuming that [i] vowels really constitute bare V-slots, they may serve as landing sites for vowels set adrift by truncation.

This analysis claims that the apparent deletion of the [i] and the accompanying shift of stress in the paradigms of (20) are in reality entirely a function of the truncation rule (19c). Independent support for this interpretation derives from the fact that the Bani-Hassan truncation rule does not apply to long vowels. Since no vocalic phoneme will be set adrift from a long vowel, we predict that the bare V-slot in the passive prefix will undergo the default rule when the preceding word ends in a long vowel because the default will not be preempted by the attachment of the floating vowel. The paradigm in (22) dramatically confirms this prediction. (22a,b) parallel the data in (20).

(22) a. áxu   'brother'
      b. ála.xún.gital   'the brother was killed'
      c. axúu   'his brother'
      d. axúu íngital   'his brother was killed'

Suffixation of [-u] 'his' to [axu] creates a long vowel (22c). This long vowel does not truncate in (22d). Consequently, the prefixal vowel of the following verb does not "shift" its stress and instead is assigned the value [i] by the default rule.

To summarize, we have postulated bare skeletal V-slots unassociated to any phoneme. They acquire a vowel by attachment of a floating segment or via the default rule. We have also postulated floating vowels – both in the underlying representation and as the by-product of rules deleting skeletal positions. Neither a bare V-slot nor a floating phoneme is a notion that is available (or even coherent) in the linear model of representation that imposes a strict one-to-one relation between phonemes and the positions they occupy. The Arabic data indicate that this condition must be relaxed in order to reach the level of descriptive adequacy.

In the next section we will examine evidence in Semitic for the other logically possible violation of the one-to-one relation: multiply linked structures.

8.3   Semitic Biradicals and Multiple Linking

In section 8.1 we saw that the key to understanding the root-and-pattern system of Semitic morphology was to recognize a distinct skeletal tier upon which word formation rules may stipulate a particular patterning of CV elements. A second result was that Semitic root morphemes are composed entirely of consonants; the vowels in a stem are markers of inflectional categories or otherwise the product of the word formation rule responsible for the individual lexical item. We accounted for this second feature of the system by assuming that consonants and vowels are projected on distinct autosegmental tiers. A word such as *duuris* 'study' (passive, measure III) thus consists of three distinct morphemes, each displayed as a separate autosegmental tier.

(23)   d   r s   'study'
         | | |
       CVVCVC   measure III
         V |
          u   i   passive perfect

In this section we will examine a distinct class of roots that we will claim to have just two radical consonants, even though on the surface they are always realized with at least three consonants. These *biconsonantal* roots have several intriguing properties. For example, Greenberg (1950) discovered a number of generalizations about the structure of the Semitic root. One of the most striking of Greenberg's findings is that while there are numerous roots of the form $C_iC_jC_j$, where the last two consonants are identical, and a significant number of the form $C_iC_jC_i$, where the first and last are the same, there are virtually no roots of the form $C_iC_iC_j$, where the first two consonants are identical and distinct from the third. This constraint has been carried down into Arabic, where it remains in force today. It must be stated at the level of the root rather than at the level of the word, because Arabic has no hesitancy in attaching a prefix whose consonant is identical to the initial radical: for example, *ma-mluka* 'kingdom' [mlk], *ta-truku* 'leaves' 3sg.fem. [trk]. In a brilliant theoretical deduction, McCarthy (1979a, 1981) showed how the ban on $C_iC_iC_j$ roots can be explained within the nonlinear model. Three assumptions are required in McCarthy's explanation: first, that the root consonants are represented on a separate autosegmental tier; second, that these consonants associate to C-slots of the skeletal tier one to one, left to right; third, that the Obligatory Contour Principle (OCP) holds of the root tier. Let us see how these assumptions derive the forms *madad-na* 'we stretched' and *katab-na* 'we wrote'.

(24) a. k t b   k   t   b
                                   | | |
          CVCVC   →   CVCVC

      b. m d   m   d   m   d
                                   | | | /\
          CVCVC   →   CVCVC   →   CVCVC

In the first step, one-to-one left-to-right (L-R) matching of radicals with C-positions yields *katab-na* directly. For *madad-na* this procedure fills only the first two C-slots; another step is necessary to spread the final radical to the third C-slot. As with tone, it is unclear whether this second step arises from automatic spreading of the final autosegment or from a language-particular rule. For the point we wish to develop, it does not matter which alternative is correct. It is apparent that, given two distinct radical consonants, L-R mapping fills the first two slots of a CVCVC template. Consequently, a $C_iC_iC_j$ root can never be generated.

Both the L-R and the OCP assumptions are necessary to derive this result. If the biradical [md] were associated to the template from right to left, the [d] would map to the final C-slot and the [m] to the medial one. But then we must explain why the [m] could not spread to the initial C-slot to derive the ill-formed *[mmd]. Thus, L-R mapping is crucial. Now assume that the OCP banning successive occurrences of the same element on the root tier does not hold. If so, then *madad-na* could be derived from [mdd] by simple one-to-one matching. But if the radicals can be repeated, then we should expect to find [mmd] as well; specific stipulation would be required to exclude roots of this form.

Thus, it is only by maintaining both the L-R assumption and the OCP that we derive the ban on $C_iC_iC_j$ roots. But these are entirely natural assumptions. L-R association is found in many tonal languages; also, the OCP was crucial in Shona and Venda (see sections 7.2 and 7.3). The Semitic data thus suggest that the relation between the segmental and the skeletal tiers is governed by essentially the same principles as those holding between the tonal and the skeletal tiers. McCarthy's landmark study convinced most phonologists that a radical extension of autosegmental representations beyond tonology and vowel harmony was required.

Several consequences ensue from this analysis. First, it is imperative that the root [ktb] be a distinct unit at some level of analysis even though in *katab-na* the radical consonants are scattered through the word. Second, although a root such as 'stretch' is always pronounced with at least three consonantal segments, it must be a biradical underlyingly. Third, if the final radical in *madad-na* spreads to the third C-slot, then a multiply linked structure is derived (24b). We know from the study of tone that such one-to-many associations are sometimes detectable. The discovery of evidence bearing on this implied multiple association thus becomes a significant research topic in Semitic. In the remainder of this section we will survey the most important results discovered to date.

First, a number of Arabic dialects have a speech disguise that permutes the radical consonants in a word. For the Hijaazi of Saudi Arabia, Al-Mozainy (1982) reports that a word such as *difaʕ-na* 'we paid' has the range of disguises shown in (25a). (This dialect has the rule raising the vowel of a short open syllable not bounded by guttural consonants such as [ʕ]. The word thus has the CaCaC underlying shape.) Note first that the consonant of the [-na] suffix does not participate in the scrambling operation. Only radical consonants do. This point is more sharply illustrated by the infixed [t] in (25b), whose position remains constant under the permutation of the radicals [ḥrm] (cf. *ḥarim-a* 'be forbidden').

(25) a. difaʕ-na   b. iḥtaram   c. darras-na   d. madad-na
          daʕaf-na   iḥtimar   dassar-na   damam-na
          fidaʕ-na   irtaḥam   raddas-na   *mamad-na
          faʕad-na   irtimaḥ   rassad-na   *dadam-na
          ʕafad-na   imtaraḥ   saddar-na   *damad-na
          ʕadaf-na   imtaḥar   sarrad-na   *madam-na
          'pay'   'respect'   'teach'   'stretch'

  e. maddad-na
      dammam-na

  f.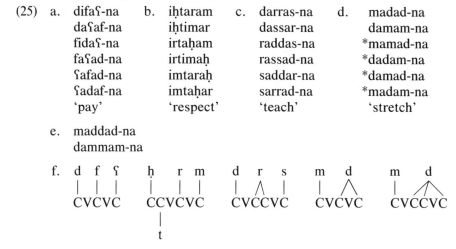

Given that the permutation rule operates at the level of the root, we predict that a form such as *darras-na* will have only six possible permutations instead of the $(4 \times 3 \times 2) \times \frac{1}{2}$ that would otherwise be expected if the disguise were defined on [drrs]. Further, for biradicals we predict just one possible disguised form, since a two-element string has just two permutations. In fact, just *damam-na* is accepted as a valid disguise for *madad-na*. Forms such as *damad-na* and *dadam-na*, which might otherwise be expected from a {m,d,d} set of generators, are rejected. Finally, just *dammam-na* is acceptable as a disguise for *maddad-na*. Clearly, the speech disguise respects the structural organization depicted in the autosegmental displays of (25f).

   Although the Arabic biradical and triradical roots have parallel morphological distribution in every respect, they have a slightly different surface phonology. The paradigms in (26) illustrate this point.

(26) katab-na   madad-na   1pl. perfect
      katab-a   madd-a   3sg.masc.perfect
      ya-ktub-na   ya-mdud-na   1pl. imperfect
      ya-ktub-u   ya-mudd-u   3sg.masc. imperfect
      'write'   'stretch'

Arabic roots drawn from measure I have a CVCVC canonical form in the perfect and a CCVC form in the imperfect. In roots whose final two consonants are identical, these stem shapes are altered when the stem is followed by a vowel-initial suffix. In the first generative analysis of Arabic, Brame (1970) formulated a rule of "identical consonant metathesis" that transformed strings of the shape C_1VC_2V into VC_1C_2V just in case $C_1 = C_2$. By this rule, underlying [ya + mdud + u] is converted to *ya-mudd-u*. The rule also transforms [madad + a] into [maadd + a]. Brame assumed another rule shortening a long vowel before two consonants, deriving *madd-a*. The important point for our purposes is that the metathesis must refer to consonants that belong to the root. No metathesis occurs in a measure VIII form such as *ktatab-a* 'he copied' even though the substring [tata] satisfies the rule. Given that the radical and affixal consonants are projected on distinct tiers, a form such as [madad + a] can be formally distinguished from one such as [ktatab + a].

(27) a. m   d   b. k   t   b
         | ∧ | | |
       CVCVC   CCVCVC
                            |
                            t

    c. [α]   [α]
        ∧   ∧
     CV$_i$CV →   V$_i$CCV

And given that *madd-a* is derived from a representation with just two radical consonants, it is possible to formulate metathesis as a relatively simple rule that transposes to the left an open syllable V-slot that is trapped between two C-slots associated to the same phoneme. The identical consonant metathesis of (27c) is thus a rule whose very formulation crucially depends on the biradical, multiply linked representation implicated by our general framework of assumptions.

8.4 The Integrity of Geminates

Our final arguments for multiple linking in the Arabic biradical roots require a digression into the phonology of geminates. These elements display curious properties that have been remarked upon since the inception of generative phonology. Kenstowicz and Pyle (1973) observed that in many languages geminates form a tight bond that resists disruption by phonological rules. There are two aspects to this "integrity" of geminates. First, geminates characteristically repel insertion of an intervening segment. Second, geminates often escape rules whose application would modify one half of the geminate while leaving the other unchanged. In the literature these aspects of geminate behavior have been called *inseparability* and *inalterability,* respectively. First, let us briefly consider the history of the problem.

In the linear framework two representations are available for a long consonant or vowel: it may be represented either by the feature [±long] or by a sequence of two identical feature matrices. In some situations the feature notation seems appropriate, while in others the sequence representation is required. For example, Sampson (1973) argued that the long consonants of Biblical Hebrew (BH) demand the feature notation. Such a representation simplifies the rule spirantizing post-vocalic stops. Recall from exercise 1.9 that [katab] becomes [kaθav] (eventually *kāθva*) while [yi-ktob] is realized *yixtōv*. As in many other languages, geminates in BH resist spirantization: [gibbōr] 'hero' is realized as *gibbōr*, not **givbōr*. If the geminate in [gibbōr] is represented as [+long], then the spirantization rule can be defined on postvocalic [−long] stops. But if the geminates are represented as a sequence, then spirantization is more complex to state. Even though triggered by a preceding vowel, the rule would have to look forward to check whether the stop is followed by an identical segment. This complicated procedure allows spirantization to apply to the labial stop in [yi-pgōš] to derive *yi-fgōš* (cf. *pāγaš* 'meet') but to block on the geminate in *sappir* 'sapphire'. We conclude that for the BH spirantization rule, the feature representation of length is appropriate.

But there are other respects in which it is the sequence notation that makes for a simpler grammar. Barkaï (1974) observes that geminates parallel consonant clusters for many other rules of BH phonology. For example, vowels regularly reduce to schwa in the context ＿CVCV́ in plural nouns: *malk-í* 'my king' but *məlax-ím* 'kings' from [malak+ím]. Reduction is blocked by a following cluster (*galgal-ím* 'wheels') as well as by a geminate (*sappir-ím* 'sapphires'). If geminates are represented as sequences of consonants, then the parallel behavior of *galgal-ím* and *sappir-ím* in inhibiting reduction is explained by the assumption that the [lg] and [pp] clusters close the preceding syllable. But if the geminate is represented as [+long], then the nasty disjunction "consonant cluster or single [+long] consonant" is required for vowel reduction (as well as several other rules of the language).

The paradoxical conclusion is that some rules are simplified if geminates are represented as sequences while other rules require the feature notation. But a given geminate cannot have both of these inconsistent representations. Geminates thus constitute another representational dilemma for the linear model.

Leben (1980) demonstrates that the nonlinear framework of autosegmental phonology offers an escape. In this system a long segment can be represented as a single phonemic element associated to two adjacent skeletal positions (28a).

(28) a. [α]
          ∧
         X X

b. m a l a k + i m   g a l g a l + i m   s a p i r + i m
    | | | | | | | | | | | | | | | | | ∧ | | | |
    C V C V C   V C   C V C C V C   V C   C V C C V C   V C
     ∨ ∨   ∨   ∨ ∨   ∨   ∨ ∨   ∨
     σ σ   σ   σ   σ   σ   σ   σ   σ

Autosegmental representations for relevant BH words appear in (28b). If we assume that syllable structure is erected on the skeletal tier, then the reduction rule operating in the ＿CVCV́ context will apply in [malak+ím] but block in [sappir+ím], because the skeletal C-slot forming the first half of the geminate closes the syllable in exactly the same way as the C-slot associated with the first consonant of the [lg] cluster in [galgal + ím] does. Leben also observes that the status of a phoneme as [±long] is determined by whether or not it is linked to two successive skeletal slots. We can thus formulate the spirantization rule to apply to [−continuant] segments that are singly linked. The rule will apply to derive *yi-fgōš* from [yi-pgōš] but block on the multiply linked [p] in *sappir*. In this way, the feature [±long] can be dispensed with. More generally, the representational paradox posed by the BH geminates is resolved.

While the nonlinear representation can distinguish long segments from short ones by the degree of linkage, the BH data raise an important question that remains to be answered. Many languages spirantize postvocalic or intervocalic stops. In virtually every case, a geminate consonant resists spirantization. An explanation is still needed for this generalization. Nothing said so far excludes a rule spirantizing postvocalic stops that are multiply instead of singly linked. But such a rule is never found. It illustrates the inalterability property of geminates mentioned earlier.

Before attempting a solution to this problem, let us look at another illustration of the phenomenon. We will borrow an example from Hayes (1986a), to whom the term "inalterability" is due. In Persian [v] is realized as [w] in the coda of a syllable. A subsequent rule shifts [æ] to [o] before this [w]. For example, the root [ræv] 'go' is realized as such in *mi:-ræv-æm* 'I am going', but is modified in the imperative *bo-row* 'go!'. Similarly, the [v] of [nov] emerges in a syllable onset in *nov-i:n* 'new', but appears as [w] in the coda of *now-ru:z* 'New Year'. The [v] → [w] rule blocks on the first half of a geminate even though it occupies the syllable coda: *ævvæl* 'first', *morovvæt* 'generosity', *qolovv* 'exaggeration', not *owvæl, *morowvæt, *qolowv.

A hint toward a resolution of the problem lies in the observation that only tautomorphemic [vv] sequences escape the rule. There are several Persian suffixes that begin with the [v] phoneme, such as the adjectival [-va:r] meaning 'like, having the qualities of'. When one of these suffixes is added to a stem ending in an underlying [v], a [v + v] sequence is created.

(29)   pi:š-row-va:r 'leader-like'
          (cf. pi:š-row 'leader' = [pi:š] 'ahead' + [ræv] 'go')
       pa:-dow-va:r 'runner-like'
          (cf. pa:-dow 'runner' = [pa:] 'foot' + [dov] 'run')

Just as in *ævvæl,* the underlying stem-final [v] in [pi:š + ræv + va:r] occupies the syllable coda. But this time it systematically undergoes the rule, turning to [w] in *pi:š-row-v:ar*. Thus, heteromorphemic [vv] sequences may be inputs to the [v] → [w] rule. But tautomorphemic ones resist this process.

This contrast is actually rather common: tautomorphemic geminates exhibit the integrity phenomenon while heteromorphemic ones do not. The distinction is reminiscent of Meeussen's Rule in Shona (section 7.2), where a string of tautomorphemic high-toned syllables dissimilate but a transmorphemic sequence does not. The proposed explanation appealed to the OCP and limited its scope of application to the morpheme. The result was that a tautomorphemic sequence of high-toned syllables is represented by one multiply linked high tone while heteromorphemic sequences have single linking (possibly transformed to multiple linking at the end of a cycle as a last resort). If Persian also restricts the scope of the OCP to the morpheme, then the theory draws a representational distinction between tautomorphemic and heteromorphemic geminates. The former are multiply linked (30a) and the latter singly linked (30b).

(30) a. æ v æ l   b. r o v + v a r
          | ∧ | | | | | | ∧ |
          V C C V C   C V C   C V V C

The Persian data thus suggest that inalterability is a property of multiply linked representations. This is a good result since now the phenomenon begins to make sense. The [v] segment in (30a) is subject to two contradictory instructions. Since it occupies the coda, the [v] → [w] rule requires it to change to [w]. But since it also occupies the onset of the following syllable, it cannot be [w], because [w] is otherwise barred from onset position. Given this contradictory set of instructions, two outcomes are possible a priori. We might expect the rule to "overapply" even though just one of the legs of the geminate satisfies it. Alternatively, the rule might be suspended even though one portion of the multiply linked representation does satisfy it. The latter strategy seems to be the one that UG imposes and is precisely the inalterability phenomenon. This line of reasoning suggests the following general constraint on rule application (adapted from Hayes 1986a, Schein and Steriade 1986).

(31) In order to change the feature content of a segment [A], every skeletal slot linked to [A] must satisfy the rule.

This constraint imposes a *Uniformity Condition* on rule application. It will block postvocalic spirantization of the BH geminate stop in *sappir* since the right leg is not postvocalic on the skeletal tier. Change of [v] to [w] in the syllable coda is prevented in Persian *ævvæl* (32) because the right leg is dominated by N″.

(32) a. [v] → [w] / ____   b. æ v æ l
                    | | ∧ | |
                    C   V CC V C
                    | ↙   ↘↓
                    N′   N′   N″

However, the rule will apply to the coda [v] of (30b) since this segment is linked to just a single skeletal slot and hence satisfies the constraint imposed by (31).

It should be noted that in general, the Uniformity Condition (31) blocks change in the feature content of a multiply linked segment only when the relevant rule crucially refers to the skeletal tier (e.g., in defining a position in the syllable). To appreciate this point, recall Meeussen's Rule in Venda, which changes a high ([+hi tone]) to low ([−hi tone]) when preceded by a high tone. This rule applies regardless of whether either high tone is singly or multiply linked and was used to illustrate the autonomy of the tonal tier. The rule has the simple formulation in (33a), in which only information from the tonal tier is mentioned. The Uniformity Condition (31) will not block application of the rule to *mu-sádzá* 'woman' in (33b), since each leg of the multiply linked high tone of the stem satisfies the rule: that is, each skeletal slot is linked to a [+hi] segment that immediately follows another [+hi] segment.

(33) a.   [+hi] → [−hi] / [+hi] ____
      b.   óná mu-sádzá
      c.   ona mu-sadza

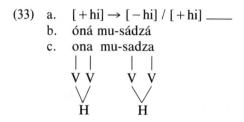

Application of the rule produces [mu-sadza], which is then subject to further modification (see section 7.3 for details).

Subsequent research on the inalterability phenomenon (e.g., Selkirk 1991) suggests that the failure of spirantization in BH *sappir* and of [v] → [w] in Persian *ævvæl* does not reflect a general constraint on rule application but rather some as yet poorly understood property of the stricture features [continuant], [consonantal], and [sonorant]. First, there is no evidence for the phenomenon in vowels: both context-free and context-sensitive vowel quality change and assimilation may be freely restricted to short or long vowels or apply indiscriminately to both. Second, within a geminate consonant nonstricture features can be modified on one-half of the geminate. For example, in Icelandic (Thráinsson 1978) voiceless stops are aspirated: /gata/ 'street' is realized as [ga:tʰa]. When a voiceless stop is combined with a preceding consonant in a cluster, the aspiration shifts to the first member: /telpa/ 'girl' is realized as [teḷpa] ([ḷ] marks an aspirated liquid). Geminates also undergo the rule, followed by a debuccalization process, so that /kappi/ 'hero' is realized as [kahpi]. While a variety of formalizations of the process can be given, the relevant point is that the shift of aspiration found in [lpʰ] → [ḷp] is not blocked in geminates. Finally, the rules involved in the inalterability syndrome have the one-way character of "weakening" the consonant, typically in virtue of the context on the left. For our purposes here the important point is that whatever the ultimate explanation for the phenomenon, it is clear that geminate inalterability depends on and thus may serve as a diagnostic for multiple linking.

We now turn to the inseparability aspect of geminate integrity. In many languages a geminate consonant resists separation by an epenthetic vowel that might otherwise be expected. As illustration, let us take an example from Guerssel's (1977, 1978) discussion of the phenomenon in the Ait Segrouchen dialect of Berber spoken in the Middle Atlas Mountains of Morocco. Guerssel motivates a rule to insert schwa obligatorily in the context C____CC and optionally in #____CC. The first context is illustrated by the prepositions [s] 'with' and [am] 'like' (34a), which trigger schwa insertion when the following stem begins with a cluster of consonants or a geminate. The free variation in (34b) exemplifies the second context.

(34)   a.   s wudi   'with butter'   am langliz   'like an Englishman'
           sə-tmaziġt   'in Berber'   amə-tfunast   'like a cow'
           sə-zzit   'with oil'   amə-ṭṭalyan   'like an Italian'

     b.   xdəm≈əxdəm   'to work'
           sdid≈əsdid   'to be thin'
           ffəġ≈əffəġ   'to go out'

In terms of the theory of syllabification developed in chapter 6, the data in (34) suggest that core syllables in this Berber dialect do not permit the clustering of consonants in the onset or coda. Stray consonants are assigned to the coda of a dummy syllable whose nucleus is schwa. Adjunction rules or licensing statements operating at the margins of the word allow more complex clusters, preempting epenthesis. The variation in (34b) suggests that the process is optional.

The important point for our purposes is that medial epenthesis blocks systematically on C_i___C_iC clusters. Guerssel cites forms such as *tazzla* 'running' and *sslil* 'to rinse'. **tazəzla* and **səslil* are sharply ungrammatical. To take just one more example, addition of the 3pl. obj. suffix triggers insertion of schwa in the root [ams]:*aməs-tən* 'rub them'. But epenthesis is blocked by the geminate in *ass-tən* 'tie them'.

The paradigm in (35) suggests that the inseparability phenomenon is also a function of multiply linking. Nominal complements to prepositions and nouns appear in a special form called the construct state in Berber. One morphological reflex of the construct state is loss of the prefixal vowel [a]. This process creates consonant clusters that are subject to the regular syllabification process.

(35)   t-a-məllal-t   'egg'   tməllalt   (construct state)
       t-a-šišaw-t   'chick'   tšišawt
       t-a-tərras-t   'adolescent' fem.   ttərrast
       t-a-tbirt   'pigeon'   tətbirt

Deletion of the prefixal vowel in [t+a+tbirt] creates a sequence of identical consonants. Yet in this case epenthesis is successful. There is thus a tautomorphemic≈heteromorphemic parameter at work in this aspect of geminate integrity as well. The natural conclusion to draw is that multiply linked segments resist separation while singly linked ones do not. The forms *ass-tən* and *tətbirt* will thus have the representations shown in (36a,b).

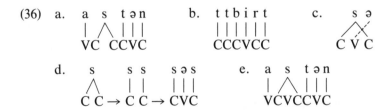

The schwa is freely inserted in (36b) since this representation has the same structure as a nongeminate cluster. The problem is to explain why insertion blocks on the multiply linked structure of (36a). Actually, the representation itself provides the basis for an attractive explanation. The schwa cannot be positioned after the geminate since an association line would be crossed (36c). This explains why [ass + tən] is not realized as *assətən. Nor can the schwa be inserted between the two halves of the geminate. Such insertion would necessitate an additional process to dissect the [s] into two pieces, in order to make room for the schwa on the segmental tier (36d). This explains why *asəs-tən is not produced. The multiply linked representation that results from assuming that the OCP holds in Berber provides an attractive explanation for the inseparability clause of the geminate integrity phenomenon.

This explanation faces a problem, however. Recall from section 8.2 that there is reason to break epenthesis into a two-stage process: insertion of a bare skeletal slot followed by later default spell-out of the slot on the segmental tier. By the logic of our account, the second step will be blocked in (36a) but the first should, other things being equal, take place to give (36e). However, this is dubious; given continuous syllabification, it would imply that the first half of the geminate is a syllable onset. We conclude that the precise formal explanation for geminate integrity remains to be discovered.

8.5   Tier Conflation

Given these insights on geminates, let us return to Semitic to examine additional evidence bearing on the multiply linked representation for biradical roots such as Arabic [md] 'stretch'. Recall that a representation such as (37) is required to explain the generalizations on root structure discovered by Greenberg, the Hijaazi speech disguise, and the identical consonant metathesis rule.

(37)   m   d
       │   /\
       CVCVC

In this section we will see that the representation in (37), although well motivated, poses significant problems with respect to the geminate integrity phenomenon. We will review these problems and then examine a solution. The discussion relies on McCarthy 1986a.

Consider first geminate separability. Recall that in the Jordanian Ajloun dialect, the ban on CC# and CCC clusters is universal except when the first two consonants are identical. (38) illustrates some relevant cases. (38a) exemplifies epenthesis.

(38)   surface   UR
      a.   ʔákil-na   [ʔakl + na]   'our food'
            ʔíbin-na   [ʔibn + na]   'our son'

      b.   sitt-na   [sitt + na]   'our grandmother'
            ḥúbb-na   [ḥubb + na]   'our love'

c. ḍaráb-it   [ḍarab + t]   'I hit'
   sakát-it   [sakat + t]   'I became silent'

In (38b) we see that geminates resist separation. *sakát-it* 'I became silent' in (38c) shows that a heteromorphemic [t + t] cluster is separable. The data in (38) thus strictly parallel the Berber material discussed earlier and should be susceptible to the same explanation. The problem is that the assumption that Semitic consonants and vowels are represented on separate tiers deprives us of the formal explanation we have appealed to in order to block epenthesis. A form such as *ḥúbb* will have the representation in (39a).

(39) a.   ḥ   b   b.   ḥ   b

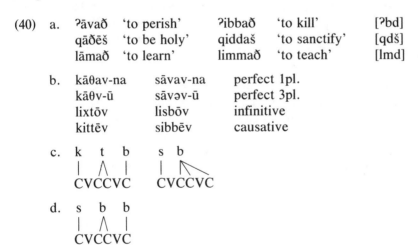

But if vowels appear on a separate tier, it becomes unclear why epenthesis cannot insert an [i] within the geminate cluster. In particular, no crossing of association lines takes place in (39b). Thus, the assumption that consonants and vowels occupy different tiers – crucial to the explanation of a variety of features of Semitic phonology and morphology – entails a serious formal problem.

Another problem arises with respect to inalterability. Recall the Biblical Hebrew rule of postvocalic spirantization. Being a Semitic language, BH also projects consonants and vowels on separate tiers. The paradigms in (40a) give a sense of the phenomenon.

(40) a.   ʔāvað   'to perish'   ʔibbað   'to kill'   [ʔbd]
            qāðēš   'to be holy'   qiddaš   'to sanctify'   [qdš]
            lāmað   'to learn'   limmað   'to teach'   [lmd]

    b.   kāθav-na   sāvav-na   perfect 1pl.
          kāθv-ū   sāvəv-ū   perfect 3pl.
          lixtōv   lisbōv   infinitive
          kittēv   sibbēv   causative

    c.   k t b   s b

          CVCCVC   CVCCVC

    d.   s b b

          CVCCVC

(40b) compares forms for the triradical [ktb] 'write' and the biradical [sb] 'to go around'. The medial radical is geminated in *kittēv* and thus escapes spirantization because its second leg in (40c) does not follow the triggering V-slot. The problem is to explain the pattern of spirantization in *sibbēv*. Given the multiply linked representation of (40c), the Uniformity Condition should block application to the final leg of the tripartite geminate since all three legs do not satisfy the rule. In particular, the middle leg does not follow a skeletal V-slot and so should prevent application of the rule to both the preceding and the following leg. While the former result is correct, the latter is not. The patterns of spirantization found in (40b) suggest that (40d) is the correct representation for *sibbēv*. But this representation is inconsistent with the other evidence, which tells us that [sb] is a biradical and not a triradical morpheme.

A final source of evidence bearing on the representation of the Semitic biradicals comes from the phenomenon of *antigemination* studied by McCarthy (1986a). McCarthy notes that in a significant number of languages general vowel deletion rules are suspended when they create a sequence of identical consonants. Let us look at an example from McCarthy's discussion of the phenomenon in the Cushitic language Afar. In Afar a general rule syncopates an unstressed vowel in the context #CVC___CV.

(41) wager-n-é   'we reconciled'   wagr-é   'he reconciled'
      digib-t-é   'she married'   digb-é   'I married'

A form such as *gonan-á* 'search for' suppresses the rule under the threat of deriving a geminate. Significantly, the rule applies, systematically, between identical consonants so long as they belong to separate morphemes: underlying [sas + is + étto] 'you will cause to spend the day' is realized as *sas-s-étto*. McCarthy attributes the tautomorphemic-heteromorphemic distinction to the OCP banning successive occurrences of identical segments within the morpheme. If the OCP also functions as a well-formedness condition on the output of rules, then it will block syncope in *gonan-á* lest **gonn-a* be derived. But the rule may apply in [sas + is + étto] since the [s]'s belong to different morphemes. While doubts have been expressed about the generality of the antigemination phenomenon (see Odden 1988), it seems to occur with sufficient frequency to motivate a UG explanation along the lines McCarthy proposes.

The antigemination phenomenon is also observed in Semitic. Recall the BH forms *kāθv-ū* and *sāvəv-ū* from (40b). There is evidence that the vowel deletion deriving *kāθv-ū* from [kātab-ū] takes place in two steps: first reduction to schwa [kāθəv-ū], and then syncope [kāθv-ū]. Biradical [sābab-ū] takes the first step to *sāvəv-ū*. But the second step is blocked – presumably a reflex of the same antigemination phenomenon observed in Afar. The problem is that we cannot appeal to the OCP to block schwa syncope if the biradical has the multiply linked representation of (42a).

(42) a.   s   b   b.   s   b   b
           | /\ | | |
          CVCVC   CVCVC

Since the [b] is multiply linked, deletion of the intervening vowel will not create an OCP violation consisting of two successive identical consonants. Rather, the representation shown in (42b) is required in order to appeal to antigemination.

But this representation is inconsistent with the biradical structure motivated by the evidence discussed earlier.

We have reached an impasse. A significant range of phenomena are explained by the multiply linked representation (42a) while another, equally significant range of properties requires the singly linked representation (42b). In order to bridge this gap, McCarthy (1986a) makes use of a suggestion due to Younes (1983). The proposal is that at a certain stage in the derivation, a principle of UG merges the consonant and vowel tiers. Folding the consonant and vowel tiers together transforms Semitic representations into the kind of structures found in most other languages where the vowels and consonants are not segregated into different morphemes. It is assumed that in the course of this *tier conflation,* a consonant whose multiple linking arches over a vowel is dissected into two identical parts by convention.

(43)   a.   s   b   b.   s i   b ē b
         │   ↖   │ │ ∧ │ │
       CVCCVC   CVCCVC
       │   │
       i   ē

Thus, when the consonant and vowel tiers of (43a) are folded together, the second and third legs of the multiply linked radical [b] are dissected, yielding (43b). But this is precisely the representation required to generate the correct pattern of spirantization! The first and second legs are still linked to the same phoneme and so the Uniformity Condition blocks spirantization. Spirantization then applies to the final leg, which has been cut free in the course of tier conflation.

Tier conflation also solves the antigemination and separability problems noted earlier. For example, BH *sāvəv-ū* has the derivation sketched in (44).

(44)   s   b   s a b a b   s a b ə b
      │   ∧   │ │ │ │ │   │ │ │ │ │
    CVCVC   →   CVCVC   →   CVCVC
     ∨
     a

In the first step the tiers are conflated. In the next, the second [a] is reduced to schwa. We now have a representation that blocks syncope: deletion of the schwa would bring together two identical tautomorphemic consonants. (Actually, there is evidence that schwa is the default vowel in BH. The vowel reduction rule thus might better be expressed as delinking or deletion of the [a] phoneme. The proper expression of the antigemination phenomenon then becomes more complex, requiring adjacency on the skeletal tier as well as the segmental one.)

Now, suppose Arabic epenthesis applies after tier conflation. Epenthesis then operates on the multiply linked representation in (45). Consequently, we may appeal to the explanation given earlier for Berber to block insertion within a geminate.

(45)
```
    ḥ  b          ḥ u b
    |  ∧          | | ∧
    CVCC    →    CVCC
    |
    u
```

Finally, note that this analysis depends on precisely locating conflation with respect to the various rules of the system. See McCarthy 1986a for discussion. We conclude that tier conflation provides an attractive solution to the geminate integrity phenomenon in Semitic.

8.6 Assimilation as Spreading

Preceding sections of this chapter uncovered several reflexes of multiply linked structures: geminate inseparability, inalterability, and across-the-board effects. In many languages multiple linking coincides with the morpheme, suggesting that it is the domain of the OCP. (In some languages such as Biblical Hebrew, the domain is extended across morpheme boundaries; see McCarthy 1986a for discussion.) Given that the properties of single versus multiple linking are relatively well understood, they can be used as diagnostics to probe the kinds of representations that phonological rules must produce – in particular, rules of assimilation.

Let us begin with a simple example from the South Semitic language Tigrinya (Schein 1981, Kenstowicz 1982). In Tigrinya velar stops spirantize after a vowel by the rule informally stated in (46a). It accounts for the alternations between [k] and [x] in (46b). Predictably, underlying geminates fail to spirantize (46c) – an inalterability effect. Heteromorphemic geminates arising from suffixation do exhibit spirantization (46d). (In some cases the combination of prefixal [k] plus root-initial [k] forms a geminate that resists spirantization; see Lowenstamm and Prunet 1986 for discussion.)

(46) a. [k] → [x] / ⎯⎯⎯
```
                |
            V   C
```

  b. kälbi   'dog'
      ʔaxaləb   'dogs'
      räxäb-ä   'he found'
      mə-rkab   'to find'

  c. fäkkär-ä   'he boasted'
      yə-räkkəb   'he finds'

  d. mərax-ka   'your calf'
      from [mərak + ka]
      bätäx-kum   'he cut you pl.'
      from [bätäk + kum]

The array of data in (46) is just what we are led to expect from the theory of the skeletal tier developed in the preceding sections. It provides some measure of assurance that the overall approach is on the right track and warrants extending the theory.

Consider the Tigrinya paradigms in (47), showing the behavior of the passive morpheme [tä].

(47)   active perfective   räxäb-ä   baräx-ä
       active jussive   yə-rkäb
       passive perfective   tä-räxb-ä   tä-baräx-ä
       passive jussive   yə-rräxäb   yə-bbaräx
                         'find'   'bless'

It is reasonable to analyze the root-initial gemination of the passive jussives *yə-rräxäb* and *yə-bbaräx* as arising from complete assimilation of the consonant of the passive prefix *tä-*, after the syncope of its vowel. On this analysis, underlying [yə-tä-räkäb] becomes [yə-t-räkäb] and then [yə-r-räkäb]. Assimilation of the passive [t] can be expressed as a rule of feature change (48a) or, given the skeletal tier, as an association of the root node of the root-initial consonant with the C-slot of the passive prefix, delinking the underlying [t]. This rule is stated informally as (48b).

(48)   a.   [t] → [αFs] / ____   C
                            [αFs]

     b.   [t] [α]   [t] [α]
          | | ⫽
          C C → C C

Which is correct? The distinction between single and multiple linking developed earlier makes a prediction here. Since the output of reassociation in (48b) is a multiply linked representation, it should display the properties we expect of such structures: inalterability and inseparability. We thus predict that when velar-initial roots are passivized, the geminate derived in the jussive should fail to spirantize. The paradigms in (49) show that this is a correct prediction.

(49)   active perfective   käfät-ä   kähas-ä
       active jussive   yə-xfät   yə-xhas
       passive perfective   tä-xäft-ä   tä-xähs-ä
       passive jussive   yə-kkäfät   yə-kkähas
                         'open'   'pay retribution'

This is a significant result, since it confirms the basic assumption that assimilation is autosegmental spreading. An important corollary is that we must either entirely ban or severely restrict recourse to such feature-changing operations as those in rule (48a). See Poser 1982 for discussion.

Now let us consider another prediction of the autosegmental approach to complete assimilation: inseparability. Recall the Berber data of section 8.4, where an epenthetic schwa supports a stray consonant in the context C___CC. Epenthesis blocks on tautomorphemic geminates such as *tazzla* – a reflex of inseparability.

Guerssel (1977) observes that Berber has a special rule that completely assimilates the genitive morpheme [n] to a following sonorant consonant (50a). Once again two possible statements of this rule exist (50b,c).

(50) a.   n-taddart   'house' gen.
           n-fəbrayr   'February' gen.
           l-litub   'book' gen.
           ṛ-ṛəbbi   'my God' gen.
           m-məmmi   'my son' gen.
           w-wadu   'wind' gen.
           y-yizi   'fly' gen.

     b.   [n] [+sonor]   [n] [+sonor]
           | | ↕-----|
           C   C   →   C   C

     c.   [n] → [αFs] / ____ $\begin{bmatrix} +\text{sonor} \\ \alpha Fs \end{bmatrix}$

If (50b) precedes epenthesis, then a multiply linked structure equivalent to an underlying geminate is created, which, like underlying geminates, should resist epenthesis (inseparability). The data in (51a) confirm this prediction.

(51) a.   nə-tračča   'net' gen.
           nə-bnadəm   'human being' gen.
           l-lwiski   'whisky' gen.
           m-mšərḍul   'grief' gen.
           w-wtəm   'male' gen.
           y-ysan   'horses' gen.

     b.   n+w t ə m   n+w t ə m
           | |||| ⟋||||
           C CCVC   →   C   CCVC

Guerssel explicitly states that pronunciations such as *ləlwiski,, *mə-m̃sərḍul are impossible. If the complete assimilation rule is ordered before epenthesis and is formulated as the autosegmental reassociation operation of (50b), then exactly the right predictions are made. A form such as *w-wtəm* has the derivation in (51b); its multiply linked [w] blocks insertion of schwa on the segmental tier.

Although more cases need to be studied, the integrity of geminates derived from rules of complete assimilation is a robust result (see Abu-Salim 1980 for another example). No cases are on record where such a derived geminate fails to show integrity. This suggests that the autosegmental analysis of complete assimilation is the correct one and provides further support for the nonlinear model that distinguishes the phonemic and skeletal tiers.

A natural question to ask at this point is, What are the properties of rules of partial assimilation with respect to the line of thought we have been developing? Will the products of partial assimilation also show inseparability and inalterability effects? Preliminary results suggest an affirmative answer to this question. The Dravidian language Kolami has a rule that transforms bases ending in the sequence V$_i$CC] into V$_i$CV$_i$C] before a consonant or word boundary. This rule is operative in (52b) and helps to explain the difference between these alternating verbs and ones like those in (52a) with a constant root shape.

(52)

		1sg.pres.	1sg.past	imper.	
	a.	suk-atun	suk-tan	suk	'whither'
		dakap-atun	dakap-tan	dakap	'push'
	b.	katk-atun	katak-tan	katak	'strike'
		melg-atun	melek-tan	meleg	'shake'
		kink-atun	kinik-tan	kinik	'break'
	c.	iḍḍ-atun	iṭ-tan	iḍ	'tell'
		aḍḍ-atum	aṭ-tan	aḍ	'thirst for'
	d.	mind-atun	min-tan	mind	'bury'
		poŋg-atun	poŋk-tan	poŋ	'bowl over'

The forms in (52c) show that the vowel insertion process may not split a geminate. But in (52d) we see that a nasal + consonant sequence sharing the same point of articulation also blocks copying of the vowel. (The loss of the medial dental stop in [iṭṭ + tan] and [mind + tan] presumably reflects stray erasure. Kolami also has a rule simplifying word-final [ŋg] clusters.) As in many other languages, root-internal NC clusters in Kolami share the same point of articulation. There are a few exceptions to this generalization such as [kink]; all involve a dental nasal that fails to assimilate to a following velar. These exceptional forms consistently exhibit vowel copy. They show that sharing the same point of articulation is the crucial factor explaining why the vowel copy process is suspended in (52d). If we postulate a rule of nasal assimilation, then we may pursue an explanation that attributes the integrity of NC clusters to the bond established by the assimilation rule. This requires autosegmentalization of the place features so that the same feature cluster may be extended over two successive segments, as in (53).

(53)

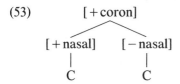

The fact that Kolami homorganic NC clusters exhibit the same effect as geminates in blocking epenthesis gives formal backing to the idea that the features are organized in a tree-like structure – a connection made originally by Steriade (1982).

A final example shows that rules of partial assimilation establish structures that also exhibit inalterability effects. The example is borrowed from Harris's (1985a) discussion of the phenomenon in Spanish (also see Hayes 1986b). In all Spanish dialects the voiced stops [b,d,g] spirantize after vowels. Some dialects extend the process after certain consonantal continuants such as glides, liquids, and even fricatives. For example, in the Havana dialect the forms *curva* and *purga* show spirantization in careful speech: *cur*[ß]*a, pur*[ɣ]*a*. In less monitored speech another rule takes over whereby the liquids assimilate in nasality and point of articulation to a following obstruent.

(54)

pulga	pu[gg]a	'flea'	purga	pu[gg]a	'purge'
el pobre	e[bp]o[ß]re	'the poor'	ser pobre	se[bp]o[ß]re	'be poor'
el tres	e[dt]res	'the three'	ser mata	se[mm]ata	'be crazy'
palco	pa[gk]o	'theater box'	parco	pa[gk]o	'park'
el fino	e[ff]ino	'the slender'	ser fino	se[ff]ino	'be slender'

This assimilation is not complete: the liquids retain their original voicing (except for [lf] → [ff] and [rf] → [ff], which, following Harris, we attribute to the fact that Spanish lacks a [v]). The assimilation then includes the supralaryngeal features of nasality, continuancy, and point of articulation – Clements's (1985a) supralaryngeal node. Autosegmental extension of this node onto a preceding liquid with delinking of the original supralaryngeal node produces a multiply linked structure such as (55) for the [bp] cluster of *el pobre*.

(55)

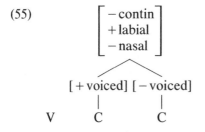

The problem now is to explain why the spirantization rule does not convert the [bp] cluster to *[ßp]. Harris notes that we cannot simply order spirantization before liquid assimilation. The reason is that in the Havana dialect stops spirantize after liquid continuants such as [r]. If spirantization applies first, [purga] should become *pur*[ɣ]*a* and then **pu*[ɣɣ]*a* by liquid assimilation. But if liquid assimilation is ordered first, then we can appeal to the Uniformity Condition to explain why spirantization fails to convert [bp] to [ßp]. The [−continuant] feature in (55) is multiply linked. However, only the first leg is adjacent to the triggering V-element. The second is not and so the rule is blocked.

In conclusion, geminate integrity and other diagnostics of multiple linking corroborate the autosegmental interpretation of assimilation as spreading a node in the feature tree.

8.7 Two Views of the Skeleton

In the ten years since the research by McCarthy and by Clements and Keyser established the skeleton, two competing theories have emerged: the X-slot model and the moraic model. Key references for the former include, besides McCarthy 1979a, 1981 and Clements and Keyser 1983, Kaye and Lowenstamm 1984, Halle and Vergnaud 1980, and Levin 1985. The moraic model is defended in Hyman 1985, McCarthy and Prince 1986, and Hayes 1989. In this section and the next we will compare these two views of the skeleton and try to clarify the differences between them.

(56) summarizes the phenomena whose elucidation has invoked the notion of phonological position. After illustrating each type, we will examine how the X-slot and moraic theories deal with them.

(56) a. phonological weight: light versus heavy syllable
　　　 b. phonological quantity: long (geminate) versus short vowels and consonants
　　　 c. compensatory lengthening
　　　 d. complete assimilation
　　　 e. underspecified (articulator-free) segments
　　　 f. latent segments

The prototypical light syllable [ta] has a single short vowel, while a heavy syllable may close with a long vowel [taa], a diphthong [tai], the first half of a geminate [tan.na], or a simple consonant [tan.ta]. The only common denominator running through the second class is the extra position that the light syllable lacks. Phonological weight is an essential ingredient in the stress patterns and prosodic templates of many languages. (See section 6.10 for exemplification.) The distinction between true and "fake" geminates (e.g., in Tigrinya; see section 8.6) crucially depends on one phonological segment spanning two (normally successive) positions. Compensatory lengthening consists in the spread of one phoneme to the position vacated by another. For example, in the development of Latin, [s] deleted before a sonorant, lengthening a preceding vowel if present: *kasnus > ka:nus* 'grey' vs. *snurus > nurus* 'daughter-in-law'. In complete assimilation one phoneme spreads to the position occupied by another, delinking the latter in the process. For example, the lateral of the Arabic definite prefix ʔal- completely assimilates to a following coronal consonant, producing a geminate: ʔal-qamr 'the moon' vs. ʔaš-šams 'the sun'. Finally, deletion alternations are often reanalyzed in terms of the presence or the absence of the corresponding position. For instance, Italian *tre* 'three' < Latin *trēs* geminates a following consonant, in contrast to *quattro* 'four', which does not, a phenomenon known as "raddoppiamento": *tre* [c]*cani* 'three dogs' vs. *quattro cani* 'four dogs'. The geminating *tre* reflects the etymological [s] that is no longer recoverable synchronically. All that remains is an empty position that is filled by the following consonant: [tre__]. The converse case is represented by the Sudanese Arabic definite prefix [al-], whose vowel lacks a skeletal position of its own; this segment emerges phonetically only when it is supplied a position by the epenthesis process (recall the discussion in section 8.2).

8.7.1 X-Slot Theory

The *X-slot* model of the skeleton evolved quite naturally from the CV theory originally proposed by McCarthy (1979a, 1981) and Halle and Vergnaud (1980).

Instead of defining the skeleton in terms of [±consonantal], Kaye and Lowenstamm (1984) and Levin (1985) propose a sequence of empty positions or slots labeled as simple points or Xs. A prime motivation for this refinement is the observation that, under appropriate circumstances, a skeletal position may associate with either a consonant or a vowel. This is hard to reconcile if [±consonantal] defines the skeleton – a point also made by Clements and Keyser (1983). The Tiberian Hebrew definite prefix provides a typical example. It geminates a following consonant unless guttural, in which case the preceding vowel lengthens: *ham-melek* 'the king' but *haa-ʕiir* 'the city'. If the prefix ends in an empty slot, then it is free to link to any segment regardless of its feature content. Another factor purging the skeleton of any phonetic content was the development of the feature tree. McCarthy (1988) combines [±consonantal] with the other major class features [±sonorant] and [±approximant] in the root of the tree, depriving [±consonantal] of its unique status as the only consistently "projectable" feature. Finally, for cases such as the Arabic CVCCVC and CVVCVC templates where the distinction between consonantal and vocalic slots is crucial, Levin reinterprets the V-slots as X-slots linked to a preassigned nucleus. Vocalic phonemes then associate to these X-slots; the consonantal radicals seek out nonnuclear slots.

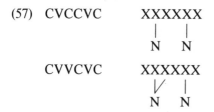

(57) CVCCVC   XXXXXX
                    | |
                    N   N

      CVVCVC   XXXXXX
                    V |
                    N   N

In the X-slot model, each phonological segment normally projects a single skeletal position. Rules of syllabification and metrification are defined over the skeletal X-slots, which constitute the points of intersection between the segmental phonemes (feature trees) and prosodic structures. The syllabification rules refer principally to the major class features ([consonantal, sonorant, approximant]) that drive the Sonority Sequencing and Dispersion Principles. As a result, we have additional motivation to place these features in the root of the tree: they are the features that are most readily accessible from or closest to the prosodic structure.

Let us see how the X-slot theory treats each of the phenomena in (56). In the case of Sudanese Arabic the definite prefix has the representation shown in (58a). Since the stress rules are defined in terms of (vocalic) X-slots, the vowel [a] is invisible to stress. It emerges only when the phrasal epenthesis rule provides a nuclear X-slot to the anaptyctic syllable that supports the stray consonant. If no epenthesis applies, the [a] fails to syllabify and thus deletes by stray erasure.

(58) a. a l   b. t r e   c a n i   c. ʔ a l [+cons]
          | | | | | | | | | | ɫ----˥
          X   XXXX   XXXX   XXX   X

Italian *tre* has the representation in (58b). A rule associating an empty X-slot to a following consonant produces the gemination of *tre* [c]*cani*. If no consonant follows, the slot remains empty and thus receives no phonetic interpretation. Complete assimilation of the Arabic definite prefix is expressed by the rule in (58c) that spreads a consonantal root node with a coronal articulator to the X-slot of the [l], delinking the latter; underlying [ʔal + šams] thus surfaces as *ʔaššams*. In compensatory lengthening, a segment deletes and the vacated skeletal slot is filled by a designated adjacent element. For example, in the development of Latin [s] deletes before a sonorant, compensatorily lengthening an immediately pre-ceding vowel. The rules in (59) characterize this two-step process. In principle, the two steps are separate and other rules might intervene. The circle will be used to designate an unassociated element. In practice, it is difficult to distinguish a complete assimilation process from the two-step deletion-plus-filling operation of compensatory lengthening.

(59)   a.   [s] → ∅ ____ [+sonor]

      b.   [−cons]
            ┌┄┄┄┄┄┄┐
            X   ⊗

Under the X-slot model, long vowels and consonants are distinguished from short by association to two successive skeletal positions. They may derive from rules of assimilation or appear as underlying contrastive elements. This multiple linking distinguishes the true geminates from successive consonants that arise from mor-pheme concatenation or deletion of intervening material (given the OCP).

    Finally, in the X-slot theory phonological weight is defined in terms of the presence or absence of two skeletal positions at certain levels of projection in the syllable. The range of variation is depicted in (60).

(60)

	light	heavy	branching location
English, Arabic	V	VV, VC	N, N'
Lardil, Cahuilla	V, VC	VV	N
Aklan	V	*VV, VC	N'

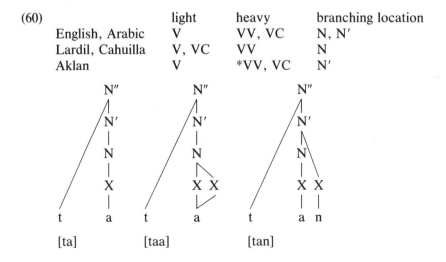

The most prevalent expression of weight counts long vowels and closed syllables as heavy and short open syllables as light. This is defined by the presence of a branching node dominating two skeletal slots at either the N or N' level, assuming that both slots of a vowel occur under the nucleus. Some languages such as Lardil count just long-voweled syllables as heavy and group closed syllables with short-voweled open syllables as light. In these systems the search for two skeletal positions is restricted to the nucleus node. Finally, languages such as Aklan lack long vowels but still distinguish open and closed syllables as light versus heavy. No cases are on record where closed syllables are treated as heavy and long vowels as light. This makes sense if the search for two positions proceeds from the lowest syllable projection, N, to the next higher, N'. Quite generally, onset consonants do not count for weight and so the rime N' of the syllable acts as a ceiling on the search for bipositionality.

8.7.2 Moraic Theory

While the X-slot model views the skeleton from the perspective of the segments, the *moraic* model develops a prosodic conception of the skeleton: phonological positions are certain terminal points where prosody intersects with segments or "melodies" (rooted feature trees). As seen in (61), prosodic rules and constraints categorize syllables as light monopositional versus heavy bipositional. These prosodic positions or *moras* are claimed to be the "genuine" or "authentic" units of prosody. All theorists agree that long vowels are distinguished from short as two versus one mora, as in (61a).

(61) a. μ   μ μ   b. μ   μ μ   skeletal tier
          | \/ | \/
          a   a   t   t   segmental tier

          [a] vs. [a:]   [t] vs. [tt]

There is also general agreement that moras dominating high-sonority, vocalic segments project a syllable. Some researchers posit an analogous monomoraic-bimoraic contrast for consonants, as in (61b). On this view, a consonant must lose a mora when it onsets the syllable, and so the moraic analogue of the X-slot theorist's onset rule deletes or merges it with the mora associated with the following vowel (Hyman 1985). Finally, an analogue to the coda rule allows [σ] to encompass an additional mora. But the syllable is normally constrained by an upper limit of two moras. Consequently, additional consonants incorporated into the syllable merge their moras with those already present. The schematic strings *ataa* and *atta* and *antta* receive the derivations sketched in (62).

(62)   a t a   a t a   a t a
       | | \ | | \ | \\
       μ μ μ μ   →   μ μ μ μ   →   μ μ μ
                          | \/ | \/
                          σ σ   σ σ

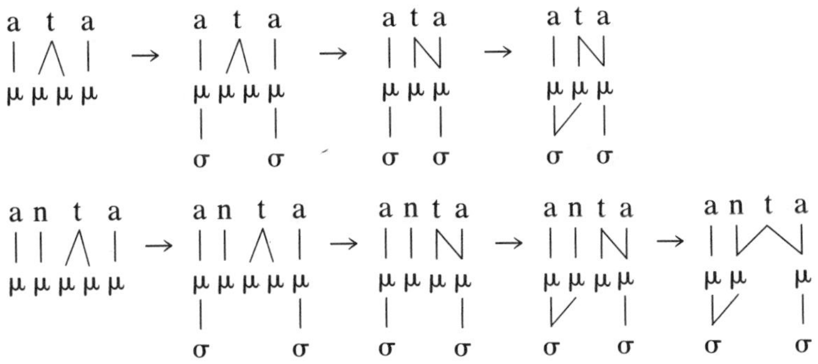

a t a → a t a → a t a → a t a

an t a → an t a → an t a → an t a → an t a

Hayes (1989) represents long versus short consonants as underlyingly moraic versus nonmoraic, respectively. Merging or deletion of consonantal moras is thus unnecessary. The onset rule is formulated to link a consonantal phoneme directly to [σ]. A coda rule then picks up the mora of the geminate consonant. The hypothetical strings [ataa] and [atta] receive the derivations shown in (63).

(63)   a t a → a t a → a t a

a t a → a t a → a t a → a t a

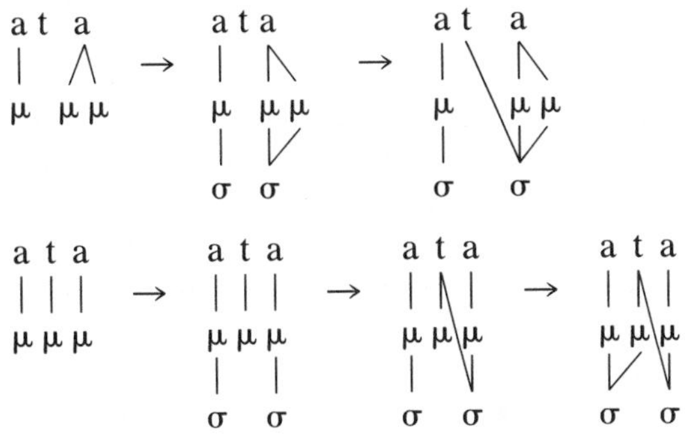

Since under Hayes' analysis single consonants start as weightless, they must be assigned a mora when they occupy the coda of a heavy syllable. This is accomplished through a *weight-by-position* rule. The WBP rule is not allowed to iterate; this stipulation ensures that syllables in general will respect a bimoraic limit.

(64)   σ → σ
        | /\
        μ   μ μ
        | | |
        α β   α β

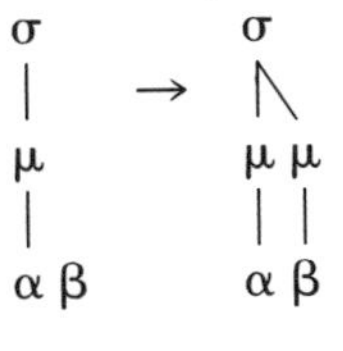

Subsequently, consonants adjoin to the left and right edges of the syllable already built, subject to sonority sequencing constraints. With this rule ordering, a geminate may be added to a syllable that has undergone the WBP rule, generating a trimoraic syllable.

(65)   a n t a   a n t a   a n t a   a n t a
       | | → | | → | \ | → | | \ |
       μ   μ   μ   μ   μ   μ   μ μ   μ
                      | | | | \ |
                      σ   σ   σ   σ   σ   σ

       a n t a   a n t a   a n t a   a n t a
       | | | → | \ | → | | \ | → | | \ |
       μ   μ μ   μ   μ μ   μ μ μ μ   μ μ μ μ
                       | | \ | \ |
                       σ   σ   σ   σ   σ   σ

Some noteworthy differences between the two models include the following.
First, Hyman's representations are strictly layered: all phonemes are dominated
by moras, which in turn are dominated by σ. For Hayes, onset consonants report
directly to the syllable node [σ] while coda consonants are sheltered under a mora.
The latter model allows the distinction between an onset and a rimal consonant
to be more simply expressed in terms of the absence or presence of a dominating
mora. Rules of English phonology such as the velarization of rimal [l] are thus
easy to formulate: [l]*eaf* vs. *fee*[ɫ], *f*[l]*eet* vs. *fie*[ɫ]*d*. Second, in Hyman's model
segments normally start out with a mora; onset consonants lose their mora in the
process of combining with a following vowel to form an onset. However, this
mora is in general undetected by processes such as compensatory lengthening
and thus has a rather dubious status. Third, languages such as Lardil that count
long vowels as heavy and closed syllables as light simply lack the WBP rule. For
Hyman, these consonants either lack any mora to begin with (if the language has
no geminates) or must lose or merge their mora as they syllabify. Finally, the
statement of constraints on particular classes of geminating consonants can be
more problematic in Hayes's model. For example, recall that in Biblical Hebrew
the guttural consonants never geminate. The simplest way to express this gap in
the phonemic inventory is with a constraint against underlying geminate gutturals
– expressed either as (66a) or as (66b).

(66)   a.   *μ μ   b.   *μ
              \/ |
          pharyngeal   pharyngeal

This constraint blocks association of gutturals to the empty mora of the definite
prefix and thus explains the contrast between *ham-melek* 'the king' and *haa-ʕiir*
'the city'. But if the guttural constraint is expressed as (66b), then it incorrectly
blocks the WBP rule from closing a syllable on a guttural. We then cannot explain
verbs such as *šaamáʕ* 'hear' whose final syllable must be heavy and thus bimoraic
in order to attract the stress. A bipositional representation for geminates does not
face this problem.

  Another issue is apparent trimoraic syllables. Hayes allows these as a marked
option, citing evidence such as the following. In Komi, where coda [l] deletes
with compensatory lengthening of the preceding vowel, no lengthening occurs in

[sultni] → *sutni*. This follows if Komi allows just two moras per syllable. The members of the [lt] cluster then share the same mora; when [l] deletes, no mora is freed up and so compensatory lengthening does not ensue. Hayes contrasts this case with Old English *θaŋx.ta → θa:x.ta 'thought'. Here compensatory lengthening appears to arise under analogous circumstances, suggesting that [θaŋx.ta] has a trimoraic initial syllable. A basic question this raises is whether there is independent evidence to establish the putative difference between Komi and Old English and how the child could discover it. Other evidence for trimoraic syllables includes languages such as Hindi whose stress distinguishes light (CV), heavy (CVV, CVC), and extraheavy (CVVC, CVCC) syllables, in such a way that the last acts as a heavy-light sequence, and languages such as Estonian with three superficial degrees of vowel length.

8.8 A Comparison

Now let us briefly compare the X-slot and moraic views of the skeleton. Moraic theorists have argued for their model on the grounds that the weightlessness of onset consonants does not have to be stipulated but is built into the theory as a fundamental property of the notation – either by virtue of the onset creation rule merging the C and V moras or because consonants acquire a mora only through the WBP rule, which is formulated so as to add a mora only on the right (coda) side of the syllable. Considered in isolation, this argument is hard to accept. Both the moraic and the X-slot models exclude onset positions from counting for weight essentially by stipulation – either by preventing onsets from projecting a mora and defining weight in terms of moras or by defining weight with respect to rimal (N and N′) slots. Another version of this argument runs as follows. Metrical stress constituents and prosodic templates "count" or group moras. For example, a common stress pattern equates a single heavy (H) syllable and two successive light (L) syllables: (H) and (LL) constituents can thus be analyzed as arising from a procedure that groups two successive moras. But we never find prosodic processes that group two successive X-slots: *(at), (aa)ta, (pa)ta, (tr)apa* are prosodically incoherent. Therefore, the X-slot skeleton does not constitute a valid level of representation. While it is certainly true that prosodic groupings such as *(at), (aa)ta,* and so on, are never found, the X-slot theorist will respond that this is expected because prosody traffics in light and heavy syllables and these are defined with respect to N and N′ constituents. Furthermore, in most cases a bimoraic stress grouping does not split a syllable and thus will not parse the first two moras of a light-heavy sequence such as *(tata)nta*. Consequently, the moraic model must also refer to a higher-level syllabic constituent in order to circumscribe the relevant skeletal positions.

Granted that both models must stipulate reference to the rime in the definition of weight, there is still a difference. The moraic model sets an upper limit of two skeletal positions and thus allows for two classes of syllables: monomoraic and bimoraic. Assuming that the Sonority Sequencing Principle allows for core syllable rimes of three, four, or more segments, the "counting" issue comes down

to whether prosodic rules ever use these additional slots to subcategorize syllables
– for example, to distinguish tripositional (trimoraic) rimes from mono- and bipositional ones. We saw that trimoraic syllables are an apparent option in Old
English and Estonian. In any case, it is safe to say that such putative trimoraic
syllables require much further scrutiny in order to bear one way or the other on
the "counting" issue.

The moraic argument against X-slots is stronger to the extent that other phenomena also ignore onsets. We can then conclude that the X-slot theory is too
rich and thus should be abandoned in favor of the more restrictive moraic model.
In a study of the compensatory lengthening (CL) literature, Hayes (1989) develops
the generalization noted by Hyman (1985) and McCarthy and Prince (1986) that
deletion of onset consonants fails to trigger CL of a tautosyllabic vowel – in
marked contrast to the deletion of coda consonants, which represents the paradigm case. If CL is the filling of a vacated skeletal position, then this onset-coda
asymmetry makes sense under the moraic model. For example, in Turkish (Sezer
1986) coda [h] optionally deletes before a nasal or fricative – with CL: *meh-
met≈me:met* 'Mehmet', *kahve≈ka:ve* 'coffee'. Onset [h] optionally deletes after
a vowel or voiceless consonant – but without CL: *mühendis≈müendis* 'engineer',
šüphe≈šüpe 'suspicion'. Assuming that coda consonants count for weight and
thus are moraic in Turkish, this onset-coda asymmetry follows straightforwardly
(67a).

(67) a.

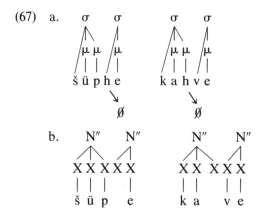

b.

In order to defend the representations in (67b), the X-slot theorist must try to
explain the CL asymmetry on other grounds. One line of argument appeals to
Clements's Sonority Dispersion Principle (section 6.8), which favors sonority
slopes in the onset and disfavors them in the coda. This principle would penalize
spreading a high-sonority vocalic element to a vacant onset slot (and thus derive
šüpe) but tolerate spreading to the coda (to derive *ka:ve*). Another conceivable
factor is the number of syllable projections intervening between the nucleus and
adjacent onset versus coda X-slots: a path between onset and nuclear slots must
traverse three syllable nodes N″, N′, N while a coda slot can be reached through
just two positions. A following tautosyllabic slot is thus "closer" to the nucleus,
and this might help to explain the difference.

While it is certainly true that the loss of coda consonants is the most prevalent source of CL, the moraic argument against the X-slot theory becomes compelling if CL can be used to confirm the postulated moraic status of coda consonants in languages where either WBP is limited to some subset of the consonant inventory (e.g., the sonorants) or the language lacks WBP but has geminates that count as heavy. In such a case only a subset of the coda consonants will bear a mora and only their deletion should induce CL. The X-slot theory makes no such connection, and CL should therefore be compatible with the deletion of any coda consonant regardless of its weight-bearing status for prosodic rules. Rubach (1992b) mounts an attack against the moraic model along these lines on the basis of yer vocalization in Slovak. His argument can be summarized as follows. Recall from section 5.8.1 that yers are the vocalic segments of Slavic languages that appear as Ø unless followed by another yer. Rubach's argument is premised on the idea (from Kenstowicz and Rubach 1987) that yers are "floating" vowels that lack a skeletal position and hence delete by stray erasure unless assigned one. Accordingly, he stipulates a rule supplying the first yer in a [yer-C-yer] sequence with a skeletal position. In Slovak there is another context of yer vocalization, however. A lexical rule of the verb phonology deletes a preconsonantal nasal across a morpheme boundary. In exactly this context a preceding yer vowel of the root vocalizes even when the following syllable fails to contain another yer and thus should otherwise define a context for stray erasure. The inflection of the verb [pän] 'bind', built from a yer root vowel, illustrates. In (68a) the yer [ä] undergoes stray erasure since the following vowel is not a yer. In (68b) the nasal deletes before the consonantal desinence; in precisely these cases the root vowel is "vocalized."

(68) a. za + pn + em   1sg.pres.
         za + pn + úc   gerund

      b. za + pä + l + a   past part. fem.
         za + pä + t + ý   passive part.

      c. p ä n t ý   p ä t ý
          | | | | | ＼ | |
          X X X X   →   X   X X X

As sketched in (68c), Rubach treats the vocalization as a compensatory phenomenon: the nasal deletes but its skeletal position remains, supporting the preceding yer and thus saving it from stray erasure.

So far, the facts seem compatible with either the X-slot or the moraic view of the skeleton. The difference is that Slovak has several rules that alter the weight of a syllable. The best known is the Rhythmic Law that shortens a long syllable after a long syllable. These rules never count coda consonants as contributing to weight: compare *lamp-a*, *lamp-ám* 'lamp', where the long vowel of the dat.pl. suffix [-a:m] fails to shorten, and *vín-o*, *vín-am* 'wine', where the long vowel of [vi:n-] triggers the Rhythmic Law (vowel length marked by the acute). The upshot is that the compensatory vocalization requires that nasal codas project a skeletal position, yet this position is systematically ignored by the quantity rules of the language. While the moraic theorist might postulate a special rule to supply the nasal verb roots with a mora or try to order WBP with respect to the rules sensitive to quantity, at the very least the differential behavior of the coda nasal in Slovak is surprising under this theory. If more cases of this character emerge in future research, they will challenge the assumption that quantity-sensitive rules and compensatory processes necessarily diagnose the same units and thus undermine the moraic model's claim to greater restrictiveness.

Finally, Hayes points to another CL asymmetry: cases in which deletion of a vowel lengthens the vowel of the preceding (but never the following) syllable. For example, Old English *tala* becomes Middle English *tāl* 'tale' through loss of schwa. Assuming that deletion of the nuclear vowel phoneme deforms the syllable, the autosegmental link between the onset consonant and the syllable node is lost to create both a stray mora and a stray consonant. Granting that the mora is filled by the vowel rather than the stray [l], a long vowel is produced. Final adjunction completes the derivation.

(69)

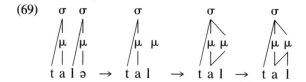

In the X-slot model, the skeletal position vacated by the schwa cannot directly link up with the preceding vowel across the intervening consonant without crossing an association line. This model thus cannot generate this type of nonlocal CL directly and must resort to other means. One alternative is to advance the stray consonant in crablike fashion to the vacated slot and then to degeminate, freeing up the slot adjacent to the vowel (70a).

(70)

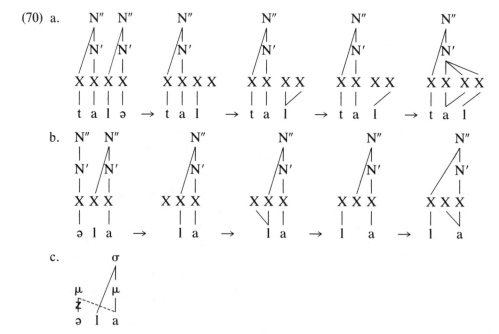

However, as Hayes shows with the derivation in (70b), this approach would be consistent with a CL triggered by the deletion of a preceding vowel: #əla → #laa. But this CL type is unattested. According to Hayes, it is excluded by the moraic model because the onset [l] remains attached to its syllable node and thus blocks rightward attachment of the mora vacated by the deletion of the schwa (70c).

While this argument is impressive, cases are on record in which it is concluded that a vacated onset must leave a trace of its skeletal slot. If valid, these cases are important because they provide positive evidence for onset skeletal slots, not just rationalizations for why they are not detected by weight-sensitive and CL processes. Rialland (1991) defends the X-slot model on this basis with the Kasem paradigms in (71).

(71)   sg.   pl.
       tu-gu   tu-ru   'stable'
       pur-u   pur-ru   'garbage heap'
       nagil-ʉ   nagil-lʉ   'anklet'
       kun-u   kun-nu   'fog'
       cəl-u   cəə-lu   'slag'
       can-u   caan-ʉ   'fish'

She sees the suffixal [r] as deleting after a (sonorant) consonant and leaving a skeletal slot that is filled by gemination of the preceding consonant. The geminate then degeminates after a nonhigh vowel, which spreads to the vacated coda slot (72a). In the singular the suffixal [g] is stipulated to delete along with its X-slot, creating a VC.V structure that resyllabifies to V.CV (72b).

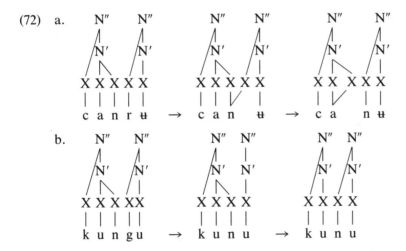

Rialland argues that under the moraic model there is no natural way to distinguish the behavior of the *-gu* and *-ru* suffixes. Since onset consonants are equivalent in lacking a skeletal slot, [kun + gu] and [kun + ru] should end up the same way (73). The only viable escape is to treat g-deletion as an allomorphy rule or otherwise order it before WBP, in contrast to r-deletion, which applies after WBP has assigned a mora to the preceding root syllable.

(73)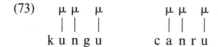

A parallel example is the deletion of [w] before a rounded vowel in the East Ionic dialect of Ancient Greek that lengthened the preceding vowel across an intervening consonant: **woikos > oikos* 'house', **newos > neos* 'new', but **odwos > o:dos* 'threshold'. Hayes posits a derivation like that in (74) in which deletion of the [w] creates a marked VC.V syllable juncture that is repaired by resyllabification of the [d] to onset the following syllable.

(74)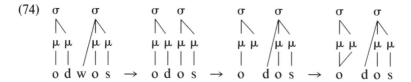

However, as Rialland (1991) observes, cyclic resyllabification does not typically leave a mora behind to produce a geminate. Once again the problem is to explain why cyclic resyllabification before a vowel produces no gemination (VC.V → V.CV) while resyllabification in the wake of the deleted onset [w] in **odwos* does. If the deleted [w] leaves a skeletal slot behind, the [d] may spread to this position to fill the onset and then later degeminate, freeing up a rimal slot to attract the preceding vowel (75).

(75)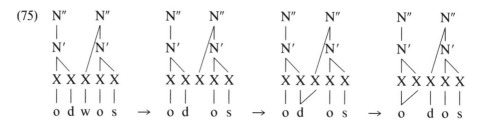

We conclude that while the bulk of the evidence from compensatory lengthening supports the moraic model, certain troublesome gaps remain.

8.9   Subsyllabic Constituency

In this section we will compare the two competing theories of the skeleton with respect to the internal structure they impose under the [σ] node. The X-slot theory posits three levels of projection of the nucleus and has an intermediate constituent N' or rime that is lacking in the moraic model. This makes for slight differences in the way in which several phenomena are treated. We will look at three.

Consider first closed-syllable shortening. In many languages long vowels may not combine with a following tautosyllabic consonant. When a CVVCCV sequence arises in which the medial cluster cannot form a complex onset, the first consonant of the cluster joins the initial syllable, triggering a shortening of the long vowel. This phenomenon is found in English, Arabic, and Yawelmani, to mention just a few cases (but see Kaye 1990b for a different interpretation). On the moraic theory, closed-syllable shortening can be seen as a repair strategy to maintain a restriction against mora sharing. For example, Cairene Arabic syncopates [kaa.ti.b + ah] to [kaa.t.b + ah]. In order to avoid stray erasure, the extrasyllabic [t] parses with the preceding syllable, creating a branching mora. If there is a constraint against mora sharing, the delinking of the preceding vowel can be seen as an adjustment to bring the representation in line with the constraint (rather than an arbitrary, unrelated change).

(76)

In order to implement this line of reasoning in the X-slot model, the constraint against VVC syllables would have to be expressed as barring the N' rimal node from dominating more than two skeletal positions. Kaye, Lowenstamm, and Vergnaud (1990) interpret the phenomenon as the reflection of a requirement of government under strict adjacency between the initial X-slot of the rime (the head) and any following sister element.

Another case where the two theories lead to slightly different treatments is found in the Uto-Aztecan language Cahuilla (Seiler 1977), where long vowels count as heavy while syllables closed by a consonant (except glottal stop) are light. This weight difference is reflected in the stress rule, which accents heavy syllables (H) and alternating light syllables (L) from left to right: *tákaličem* 'one-eyed ones' ('LL'LL), *táxmuʔàt* 'song' ('LL'L), *gá:nkìčem* 'palo verde' pl. ('H'LL). The X-slot analysis must restrict Cahuilla heavy syllables to those with two skeletal positions under the nucleus N node, while the moraic account treats Cahuilla as lacking the WBP rule so that only long vowels generate bimoraic syllables. The language has a morphological process of intensification in which CVCV or CVCCV stems "strengthen" or geminate their second consonant. As shown by the stress shifts in (77), this process turns the first syllable from light to heavy.

(77) čéxiwen   'it is clear'   čéxxìwen 'it is very clear'
      wélnet   'mean one'   wéllnèt   'very mean one'

Hayes (1991), following Seiler (1977), describes the intensification as incrementing a mora on the first syllable that is linked to a following consonant. The resultant syllables are now bimoraic and, like underlying long vowels, they require a stress on the immediately following syllable. The forms *wélnet* (78a) and *wéllnèt* (78b) thus differ in whether or not the [l] shares its mora with the preceding vowel.

(78) a.

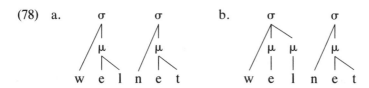

Long-voweled stems do not undergo the intensification process, presumably because their initial syllable is already bimoraic and thus cannot accommodate an
additional weight unit. It is worth observing that the contrast between (78a) and
(78b) is essentially structural in nature. The way in which it is manifested phonologically and phonetically could vary considerably. A similar issue arises with
stress (see section 10.1).

The X-slot theory cannot express the intensification as simply the addition of
a skeletal position linked to the following consonant. This would fail to distinguish
čéxxìwen from *wélnet* in the appropriate way unless the definition of weight refers
directly to multiply linked phonemes. Since heavy syllables in Cahuilla are defined
with respect to the N node, the contrast between *wélnet* and *wéllnèt* could be
expressed geometrically in terms of the location of the following consonant under
the nucleus node (79): in the former (79a) the X-slot of the [l] lodges under the
rimal N′, and in the latter (79b) it lodges under the nucleus N. This produces a
different stress pattern and arguably a difference in the "stronger" articulation
of the consonant, perceived as "gemination."

(79) a.

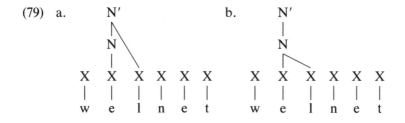

While this difference between domination by the N node and domination by
the N′ node may seem artificial, it allows certain distinctions to be made that
elude the moraic model without additional complications. Steriade (1990) discusses material from two dialects (or diachronic stages) of Classical Greek that
illustrate this point. In both dialects coda consonants define a heavy syllable for
purposes of the recessive accent rule and a minimality constraint. As the paradigm
in (80) demonstrates, final VVC, VV, and VCC syllables require penultimate
accent (marked in boldface), while V and VC finals allow accent on the antepenult.
If we invoke final-consonant extrasyllabicity, the VC reduces to V, while VVC,
VV, and VCC reduce to VV and VC. The recessive accent rule can now work
in terms of this derived light-heavy distinction in the final syllable. The important
point here is that all coda consonants (obstruents and sonorants) count in this
calculation for weight.

(80) **anthro:pos**   'man' nom.sg.
  anthro:pe   voc.
  anthro:po:n   gen.pl.
  anthro:po: dual
  lipotriks   'balding'

The same point holds for a minimality constraint inherited from Indo-European that requires monosyllabic nominal roots to be heavy: $C_0V:C_0$ or C_0VCC_0 (Golston 1990). Cluster simplifications taking roots below the minimum activate vowel lengthening: [pod-s] 'foot', [kher-s] 'hand' → [pos], [kher] → *pous* (= [poos]), *kheir* (= [kheer]). No lengthening occurs in *thriks* 'hair', indicating that [k] counts for weight. Assuming that both halves of a long vowel are under the nucleus, we have the representations in (81).

(81) a. lipotri k(s)   b. anthroopoo

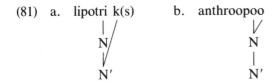

Thus, the calculation of weight must allow branching at two different structural levels in the X-slot model: under N for (81b) and under N' for (81a). The question is whether there are weight-sensitive processes that would need to distinguish the two locations.

Steriade recapitulates an argument to this effect due to Allen (1973), based on enclitic accent and the distribution of long vowels at two historical stages of Greek. In the Attic dialect [a'ngelo's tis] 'some messenger' and [phi'los tis] 'some friend' suggest that enclitic accent (= floating high tone) may dock on the final TBU of the stem so long as a representation with high tones on adjacent TBUs does not ensue (82a). The enclitic accent of [o'iko's tis] 'some house' (82b) indicates that the second element of a diphthong counts as a TBU, blocking adjacency between the [o] of the root [oik] and the [o] of the desinence [-os] and thus allowing the enclitic high to associate. Finally, cases like [a'llos tis] 'some other', [e'ntha te] 'thither and', [a'stu ti] 'some town' argue that coda sonorants do not count as TBUs; the emergence of the enclitic high thus is blocked (82c).

(82) a. angelos tis   philos tis (association blocked)

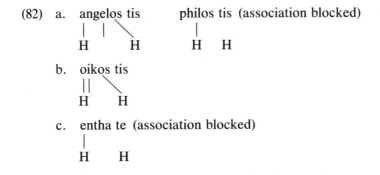

  b. oikos tis

  c. entha te (association blocked)

In contrast, Homeric [a'llo's tis] and [e'ntha' te] suggest that sonorants count as TBUs at an earlier stage of the language. Since tonal contrasts are typically realized on vocoids, and since vocoids seek out the nucleus, we might infer that TBUs are a property of the nucleus.

An additional parallel between vocoids and TBUs supports this line of reasoning. In general, phonological systems seem to allow just two vocoids per syllable. In supporting this proposition, Steriade points to Tryon's (1970a) statement that in Tahitian three-vowel sequences, the first two are tautosyllabic unless the first is long, in which case the syllable break falls between the first and second vowels. Thus, *oia* 'he, she' is syllabified as [oi.a], *fara:oa* 'bread' as [fa.ra:.oa], and *a?ahia: ta* 'dawn' as [a.?a.hi.a:.ta]. These divisions follow if the vocalic nucleus is restricted to two slots and a given vowel is barred from spanning two successive syllables.

Returning to Greek, on the basis of the Homeric [a'llo's tis] vs. Attic [a'llos tis] contrast, Allen infers that the former differs from the latter by assigning coda sonorants to the nucleus.

(83)

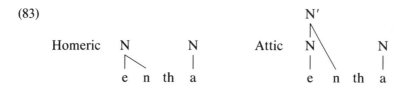

An additional fact supports this analysis. In Homeric Greek a long vowel shortens before a tautosyllabic sonorant (Osthoff's Law). Allen cites the data in (84) in support of this rule.

(84)   gra:u-s → graus 'old woman' vs. gra:u-os > gra:wos > gra:os
       gno:-nt-es → gnontes 'knowing' nom.pl. (cf. gi-gno:-sko:)

If there are just two skeletal slots in the nucleus and if sonorants are assigned to the nucleus N instead of to the coda under N', then shortening follows on the reasonable assumption that a consonant and a vowel cannot share the same skeletal slot. Once again the Attic dialect differs, freely allowing long vowel plus tautosyllabic sonorant: *ti:mo:ntos* 'value' past part. gen.sg., *ta:lla* 'the other' pl. To summarize, phonological weight for the recessive accent rule and minimality is defined by branching at either N or N' while the TBU and the domain of Osthoff's Law shortening are defined more narrowly as N in the Homeric dialect.

Steriade argues that these data do not conclusively support the X-slot model's nucleus-coda (N vs. N') distinction over the moraic theory. The latter can be enriched to encode the special status of the sonorants in the Homeric dialect through a rule or constraint, ordered after (or overridden by) the onset rule, requiring these consonants to associate with or project a mora. This special rule precedes the WBP rule, which is restricted to augmenting a monomoraic syllable to bimoraic. The effect is that syllables closed by a sonorant count as heavy for Osthoff's Law as well as the minimality and recessive accent rules. Nonsonorants (and all consonants in Attic) acquire a mora through WBP and thus will not trigger

Osthoff's shortening since WBP only applies when the syllable has just a single mora. So long as moras arising from WBP are excluded from the class of TBUs, the same pattern of data can be generated. The derivation of Homeric *e'ntha' te* and *gnontes* from [gno:-nt-es] sketched in (85) summarizes the proposed moraic analysis.

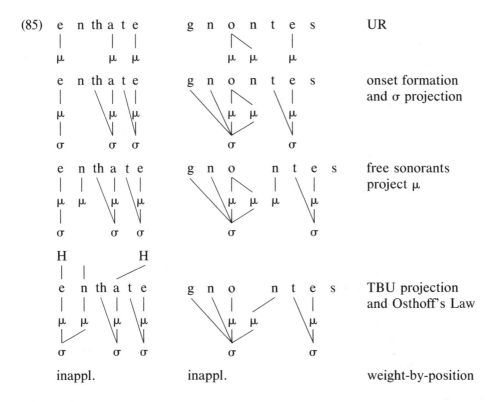

(85)   UR

onset formation and σ projection

free sonorants project μ

TBU projection and Osthoff's Law

inappl.   inappl.   weight-by-position

The Attic dialect differs in lacking the step that projects a mora over the sonorant consonants. They thus fail to count as TBUs and consequently block enclitic accent assignment in *e'ntha te;* they also fail to undergo WBP after a long vowel and hence will fail to trigger Osthoff's Law in *ti:mo:ntos*. The upshot is that in this case the moraic theory appears to encode the different status of the sonorants by stipulating a rule that must apply at a precise point in the derivation of the syllable. The stipulative nature of the solution might be mitigated by trying to construe Homeric Greek as similar to Imdlawn Tashlhiyt Berber (section 6.6) in allowing the projection of syllabic nuclei/moras to travel farther down the sonority scale than the vocoid cutoff point imposed by most systems.

     This discussion should reinforce the general impression that it is very difficult to tease apart the differences between the X-slot and moraic models and assess their empirical implications. Given the amount of maneuvering each model allows to protect itself from outright empirical disconfirmation, the differences seem at this juncture to lie more at the level of intuition than of hard evidence. Since the moraic model professes fewer skeletal distinctions, it has attracted greater alle-

giance on grounds of being the more restrictive theory. However, compelling
evidence one way or the other remains to be discovered.

Suggested Readings

Clements, George N., and Samuel Jay Keyser. 1983. CV phonology: A generative theory
    of the syllable. Cambridge, Mass.: MIT Press. Chapter 3.
Hayes, Bruce. 1989. Compensatory lengthening in moraic phonology. Linguistic Inquiry
    20.253–306.
Hyman, Larry. 1985. A theory of phonological weight. Dordrecht: Foris.
McCarthy, John. 1981. A prosodic theory of nonconcatenative morphology. Linguistic
    Inquiry 12.373–418.
Odden, David, 1986. Review of Larry Hyman, A theory of phonological weight. Language
    62.669–73.

Exercises

8.1 Chaha

This exercise concerns the principles controlling the assignment of the features
of palatalization and labialization that mark certain morphological categories of
the verb in Chaha, a South Semitic language (McCarthy 1983, 1986b). If the correct
representations have been established, then the realization of these features in
the designated morphological categories can be stated by two simple rules. Hence,
most of the work consists in establishing the correct representations. The rules
assigning palatalization and labialization are structure-preserving: their application is suspended if it would give rise to a segment that does not occur in the
inventory of underlying phonemes. The phonemes are listed in three groups. In
the first group [t] and [q] are ejectives (1a). The second group comprises the
palatalized consonants (1b). A low-level rule realizes palatalized coronals as alveopalatals (i.e., d^y = [ǰ], t^y = [č], etc.). Palatalization may not combine with
labial consonants or with coronal sonorants. The third group consists of labialized
consonants (1c). Coronals may not combine with labialization.

(1) a.   b,p   d,t,ṭ   g,k,q
          m   n,r
          f   z,s   x
          w   y

     b. d^y,t^y,$ṭ^y$ g^y,k^y
                        z^y,s^y x^y
                                       q^y

     c. b^w,p^w g^w,k^w
          f^w x^w
          m^w q^w

A. In the imperative the feminine is marked by palatalization.

(2)   imperative

2sg.masc.	2sg.fem.	
gʸækʸət	gʸækʸətʸ	'accompany'
nəmæd	nəmædʸ	'love'
nəqəṭ	nəqəṭʸ	'kick'
nəkəs	nəkəsʸ	'bite'
gəræz	gəræzʸ	'be old'
wəṭæq	wəṭæqʸ	'fall'
fəræx	fəræxʸ	'be patient'
nəkəb	nəkəb	'find'
bəkər	bəkər	'lack'

In the perfective a 3sg.masc. object is marked by labialization.

(3)

'he Verb-ed'	'he Verb-ed him'	
dænæg	dænægʷ	'hit'
nædæf	nædæfʷ	'sting'
qænæf	qænæfʷ	'knock down'
nækæb	nækæbʷ	'find'
sʸæfær	sʸæfʷær	'cover'
nækæs	nækʷæs	'bite'
kæfæt	kæfʷæt	'open'
bækær	bækʷær	'lack'
qæṭær	qʷæṭær	'kill'
mæsær	mʷæsær	'seem'
mækʸær	mʷækʸær	'burn'
sædæd	sædæd	'chase'

The impersonal of the verb is marked by both palatalization and labialization.

(4)

personal	impersonal	
kæfæt	kæfʷætʸ	'open'
nækæs	nækʷæsʸ	'bite'
ṭæbæs	ṭæbʷæsʸ	'fry'
dæmæd	dæmʷædʸ	'join'
bænær	bʷænær	'demolish'
qæṭær	qʷæṭær	'kill'
sʸægær	sʸægʷær	'change'
nækæb	nækæbʷ	'find'
sænæb	sænæbʷ	'spin'
ṭʸæfʷær	ṭʸæfʷær	'scratch and mark'
gʸækʸær	gʸækʸær	'straighten out'
bætæx	bætæxʷ	'dig out'
dænæg	dænægʷ	'hit'

Examine the data in (2)–(4) and briefly discuss the motivations for imposing a templatic representation. State the rules realizing the features of palatalization and labialization. Must the rules be ordered? Show how your analysis works by deriving the following items: *nəkəsʸ* 'bite!' fem.imper., *nəkəb* 'find!' fem.imper., *nækæbʷ* 'he found him', *nækʷæs* 'he bit him', *qʷæṭær* 'he killed him', *nækʷæsʸ* 'was bitten', *dænægʷ* 'was hit'.

B. The verbs in this section depart from the simple triconsonantal CVCVC shape of the previous data. In some cases this departure is predictable while in others it is lexically idiosyncratic. Propose representations for these verbs. What bearing do they have on the question of how the features of palatalization and labialization are realized?

(5)   imperative
        masculine   feminine
        bætət   bætʸətʸ   'be wide'
        fætət   fætʸətʸ   'be partial'
        nəzæz   nəzʸæzʸ   'dream'
        nəqəq   nəqʸəqʸ   'take apart'
        səkək   səkʸəkʸ   'plant in ground'

        personal   impersonal
        sækæk   sækʷækʷ   'plant in ground'
        gæmæm   gæmʷæmʷ   'chip the rim'

(6)   gərædæd   gʷərædʸædʸ   'cut in big pieces'
        məræqæq   məræqʷæqʷ   'scratch in a straight line'
        bərægæg   bərægʷægʷ   'be startled'
        nəsænæs   nəsʸænæsʸ   'sprinkle powder'
        gəzægæz   gʷəzʸægʷæzʸ   'cut a living being
                                       with a blunt knife'
        qətæqæt   qʷətʸæqʷætʸ   'hammer'
        fətæfæt   fʷətʸæfʷætʸ   'crumble bread'
        færæfær   fʷəræfʷær   'produce worms'
        bətæbæt   bʷətʸæbʷætʸ   'dissolve powder'
        təmætæm   təmʷætæmʷ   'wind down'
        səbæsæb   səbʷæsæbʷ   'gather'
        dəfædæf   dəfʷædæfʷ   'press lightly'
        nəqænæq   nəqʷænæqʷ   'shake'
        səxæsæx   səxʷæsæxʷ   'shell by grinding'

(7)   tætæ   tʸætʸæ   'twist a rope'
        qæqæ   qʷæqʷæ   'tie tightly'

Show how your analysis works by deriving the following items: *bætʸətʸ* 'be wide!' fem.imper., *bərægʷægʷ* 'was startled', *gʷəzʸægʷæzʸ* 'was cut a living being with a blunt knife', *qʷæqʷæ* 'was tied tightly'.

C. This question concerns the historical development of the system. It is known from comparison with closely related languages that Chaha underwent two sound changes reflected in (8a): devoicing of geminates followed by degemination. These rules are stated in (8b).

(8) a.

dæpær	'race'	*dæbbær
gætær	'put to sleep'	*gæddær
mækær	'suppurate'	*mæggær
gæt^{y}æ	'rope an animal'	*gæd^{y}d^{y}æ
gæs^{y}æ	'raid'	*gæz^{y}z^{y}æ

  b. $[-\text{sonor}] \rightarrow [-\text{voiced}]$ / ___

$$\underset{C \quad C}{\bigwedge}$$

$$\underset{C \quad C \rightarrow C}{\overset{\alpha \qquad \alpha}{\wedge \quad |}}$$

The devoicing and degemination have given rise to a voicing alternation in the middle radical of the verbal inflection. Where the earlier system opposed *sæbbær* 'he broke' to *yə-sæbər* 'he breaks', the present system opposes *sæpær* 'he broke' to *yə-sæbər* 'he breaks'. Also compare *gætær* with *yə-gædər* 'put to sleep' and *gæt^{y}æ* with *yə-gæd^y* 'rope an animal'. The forms in (9) are known by comparison with related languages to have also had an internal geminate. But unlike in the verbs in (8), no devoicing occurred, though degemination did. Can you explain the systematic difference between the verbs in (8) and (9)? In your discussion, make explicit all assumptions and principles that you appeal to.

(9)

gædæd	'tear'	*gæddæd
nædæd	'burn'	*næddæd
fægæg	'die (cattle)'	*fæggæg
næzæz	'dream'	*næzzæz
fæzæz	'be better'	*fæzzæz

An additional factor bearing on this question is that loanwords from Amharic show degemination but no devoicing.

(10)

nædæf	'sting'	Amharic *næddæf*
nægæs	'reign'	Amharic *næggæs*
næzæb	'be flexible'	Amharic *læzzæb*

8.2 *Levantine Arabic*

Review exercise 1.5. Formulate the rule for the complete assimilation of the lateral of the definite prefix seen in (1). Develop an analysis to explain the distribution of the epenthetic vowel in (2) versus (3). Discuss the bearing of these data on the representation of geminates and the nature of assimilation. Data for this exercise are based on Abu-Salim 1980.

	noun	definite	
(1)	walad	l-walad	'boy'
	mooz	l-mooz	'banana'
	kuusa	l-kuusa	'squash'
	hawa	l-hawa	'air'
	sana	s-sana	'year'
	nuur	n-nuur	'light'
(2)	blaad	li-blaad	'country'
	ktaab	li-ktaab	'book'
	ḥṣaan	li-ḥṣaan	'horse'
(3)	zbuun	z-zbuun	'customer'
	druus	d-druus	'lessons'
	treen	t-treen	'train'
	lḥaaf	l-lḥaaf	'blanket'

8.3 Hausa

These data from Kidda 1982 illustrate the formation of deverbal adjectives in Hausa. In what way do the concepts and principles of autosegmental phonology developed in this chapter help to elucidate the phonological structure displayed in these paradigms? Note that [y] is frequently employed in Hausa to break up vowel clusters. In these transcriptions the acute and grave accents mark high and low tone, respectively. Long vowels are transcribed as geminates.

	verb	masc.adj.	fem.adj.	pl.adj.	
(1)	dáf-à	dàfáfféé	dàfàffíyá	dàfàffúú	'cooked'
	kón-è	kònánnéé	kònánníyá	kònànnúú	'burnt'
	bùg-ú	bùgággéé	bùgággíyá	bùgàggúú	'drunk'
	sán-ì	sànánnéé	sànánníyá	sànànnúú	'known'
	túhùm-á	tùhùmámméé	tùhùmámmíyá	tùhùmàmmúú	'suspected'
	šàhár-à	šàhàrárréé	šàhàrárríyá	šàhàràrrúú	'well-known'
	bát-à	bàtáččéé	bàtáččíyá	bàtàttúú	'lost'
	búš-è	bùsáššéé	bùsáššíyá	bùsàssúú	'dried'
	máč-è	màtáččéé	màtáččíyá	màtàttúú	'died'
	húd-à	hùdájjéé	hùdájjíyá	hùdàddúú	'pierced'
	táfàs-á	tàfàsáššéé	tàfàsáššíyá	tàfàsàssúú	'boiled'
	só	sòyáyyéé	sòyáyyíyá	sòyàyyúú	'loved'
	sà	sàyáyyéé	sàyáyyíyá	sàyàyyúú	'worn'
	čí	čiyáyyéé	čìyáyyíyá	čìyàyyúú	'eaten'
	bà	bàyáyyéé	bàyáyyíyá	bàyàyyúú	'given'

8.4 Kàll

Kàll is a speech disguise employed by speakers of Wolof. According to Ka (1989), "it was used in precolonial times by the king to communicate with his people without strangers or foes understanding; during the colonial period to prevent representatives of the colonial power from knowing the intentions of the colonized; still today to treat appropriately a guest without his prior knowledge.'' Wolof surface syllables have the shapes CV, CVC, CVV, CVCC, CVVC, with vowel and consonant clusters restricted to geminates. What is the rule for the speech disguise? What does it reveal about the internal structure of the syllable and skeletal tier in Wolof? (Transcription note: [ë] is schwa.)

(1)

Wolof	Kàll	
sama	masa	'my'
jabar	barja	'wife'
yobbu ko	buko yoo	'bring it'
toggu ko	guko too	'cook it'
doom	mëdoo	'child'
kër	rëkë	'home'
yapp	pëyaa	'meat'

8.5 *Kwakala*

Adopting the moraic framework of Hayes (1989), state the distribution of stress in the following data from Kwakala, formally characterizing the required syllable distinctions. The data are from Zec 1988, based on Boas 1947.

(1)

qá:sa	'to walk'
c'é:kʷa	'bird'
xʷá:k'ʷəna	'canoe'
t'əlí:dᶻu	'large board on which fish are cut'
bəxá	'to cut'
w'ədá	'it is cold'
m'əkʷəlá	'moon'
gətəx̣ʷá	'to tickle'
səxʷc'á	'to be willing'
gasxá	'to carry on fingers'
maxʷc'á	'to be ashamed'
c'ətxá	'to squirt'
ánqa	'to squeeze'
m'ə́nsa	'to measure'
də́lxa	'damp'
dᶻə́mbətəls	'to bury in hole in ground'
məxə́nx̣ənd	'to strike edge'
an'qá	'to put fire among'
məl'qá	'to repair canoe'
kʷən'x̣á	'clams are spoiled'
gəm'x̣á	'to use the left hand'

8.6 *Low Norman French*

In the Northern Cotentin dialects of Low Norman French (Montreuil 1988), [r] completely assimilates to an adjacent consonant, but "only through schwa" (i.e., when an underlying schwa separates the [r] from the consonant). Develop an analysis for this phenomenon, comparing the X-slot and moraic theories. Is one more successful in explaining where [r] assimilation does and does not take place?

(1) | Low Norman | | French |
| --- | --- | --- |
| cop'pais | | couperais |
| bat'ties | | batteries |
| attend'dais | | attenderais |
| gaf'fais | | gafferais |
| s'sa | | sera |
| dor'rais | | dorerais |
| aim'mais | | aimerais |
| | | |
| mer'chin | [meššẽ] | médecin |
| ver'to | [vetto] | vérité |
| | | |
| patrie | *[pattie] | |
| effrayer | *[effayer] | |

8.7 *Altamura*

Recall from section 1.11 the paradigm in (1) from this Apulian Italian dialect (Loporcaro 1988). Two examples have been added involving geminate consonants. Develop an analysis for the compensatory lengthening in the X-slot and moraic theories. Do the geminate examples support one model over the other?

(1) | phrase-medial | phrase-final | |
| --- | --- | --- |
| k'ɛnə | k'ɛin | 'dog' |
| v'ɛvə | v'ɛif | 'to drink' |
| k'ošə | k'ou̯š | 'to cook' |
| kr'ɔšə | kr'ɔu̯š | 'cross' |
| s'ɔrdə | s'ɔrt | 'deaf' |
| p'ortə | p'ort | 'door' |
| m'elə | m'ei̯l | 'honey' |
| t'errə | t'err | 'earth' |
| s'ettə | s'ett | 'seven' |

8.8 *Bakwiri*

Speakers of Bakwiri (Hombert 1986) play a linguistic game to disguise their speech. Examine the following data to determine the rule for playing the game. Show how your analysis works to transform *lùùŋgá* into *ŋgàǎlú*. What aspects of the nonlinear conception of the skeleton are relevant to your analysis? (Transcription note: Long vowels are transcribed as geminates.)

(1) <u>normal</u> <u>disguised</u>
  mɔ̀kɔ̀ kɔ̀mɔ̀ 'plantain'
  lówá   wáló 'excrement'
  kwélí líkwé 'death'
  kóndì ndíkò 'rice'
  lìyé   yèlí 'stone'
  mɔ̀kɔ́ kɔ̀mɔ́ 'one person'
  kómbà mbákò 'take care of'
  záŋgò ŋgózà 'father'
  lùùŋgá ŋgàálú 'stomach'
  zééyá yáázé 'burn'

8.9 *Hausa Reduplication (Newman 1986c)*

In Hausa many nouns have reduplication as part of their inherent structure (as opposed to marking plurality). The problem concerns establishing the underlying representation of the reduplication base and the nature of the reduplication process itself. In addition, a number of phonological alternations are manifested in the reduplicated nouns. For the most part, these alternations are the product of general rules operative elsewhere in the language. Hausa syllables are of the form CV, CVV, CVC. There are three contrasting tones: high [á], low [à], and falling [â]. There are no rising tones. Long vowels are transcribed by geminates. The tone of the syllable is marked on the first vowel letter of a long vowel. You may assume a general rule lengthening word-final vowels in major lexical category words (i.e., nouns, verbs). In addition, the language has a rule of syncope deleting a stem-final vowel when it is not in final position in the word. The latter is illustrated by *rìigáa* 'robe' + *únàa* pl. suffix → [ríig]*únàa* 'robes' and *kútúrúu* 'leper' + *tàa* abstract marker → [kútúr]*tàa* 'leprosy'. (Transcription notes: [ɍ] is a trill, [kw] and [ky] denote labialized and palatalized velars, [k'] and [ɓ] are glottalized, [ts] is an affricate.)

A. Consider the following data.

(1) wárwáróo 'thin metal bracelet' kyáɍkèecíi 'wild hunting dog'
  bílbílóo   'butterfly'   gáɍgádáa 'mange of goat'
  zánzánáa 'small pock marks' kúɍkútúu 'small drum'
  túntúmíi 'sacred white ibis' gáɍgázáa 'cichlid perch'
  kúŋkúmíi 'type of drum'   kûɍkúdùu 'sandhopper'
  gwáŋgwáníi 'small metal basin' kwâɍkwátàa 'lice'
  tántáaníi 'membrane'   kwâɍkwáasàa 'driver ant'
  tántáamíi 'raised platform' díddígíi 'investigation'
  kûkkúukìi 'gum tree'   gággáafáa 'eagle'
  bâlbéelàa 'cattle egret'   dûddúfàa 'sacred white ibis'
  dándòonáa 'millet blight'   kúkkúɓáa 'cracked cooking pot'
  k'yâk'k'éegàa 'lame excuses' šíššígíi   'meddlesomeness'
  k'wáŋk'óoníi 'dark residual   bîbbígàa   'parakeet'
        groundnut oil' dâddóokàa 'western waterbuck'
  gúɍgúɍíi 'short person'

State the rules that account for the alternations in (1) along with any ordering restrictions. Show how your analysis works by deriving *bílbílóo* 'butterfly', *tántáamíi* 'raised platform', *bâlbéelàa* 'cattle egret', *kyár̥kèecíi* 'wild hunting dog', *bîbbígàa* 'parakeet'.

B. The direction of reduplication is unclear from the data in (1). How do the following data help to resolve this question? In the light of these data, informally state the reduplication rule.

(2) kàatúntúnáa   'amber necklace stone'
     cílíllígáa   'earring'
     káfáffágóo   'fig tree'
     k'àr̥fámfànáa   'lint at bottom of pocket'
     gàazúnzùmíi   'bedbugs'

C. Three sorts of tonal patterns have been observed so far, represented by *zánzánáa* 'pock marks', *k'âŋk'ánàa* 'measles', and *jánjàníi* 'refractory person'. The following data illustrate a tonal alternation that arises under an optional contraction process operating in the language. Formulate a rule to account for the tonal alternation. Does this analysis help in the analysis of the tonal patterns found in the reduplicated nouns?

(3) yáa káamàa ší → yáa káamás   'he seized him'
     sún kášèe tá → sún kášát   'they killed her'
     án zàaɓée nì → án zàaɓân   'I was chosen'

9 Feature Geometry, Underspecification, and Constraints

In this chapter we will first survey research developing the idea introduced in section 4.3 that features are organized hierarchically in a tree graph. This is one of the most active and unsettled areas of current phonological theory, with many competing proposals. The discussion reflects this lack of consensus. The goal will be to gain a sense of the types of questions being asked and the kinds of arguments and evidence that are employed in trying to answer them. The discussion is not intended to be a complete survey of the current scene, much less an endorsement of one view over others. It should be observed at the outset that this research is premised on the Jakobsonian idea that phonological segments are (internally structured) bundles of distinctive features whose behavior can be understood from the elucidation of this internal feature structure. A competing view should be mentioned here as well, namely, a conception of phonological segments as chemical elements with an internal molecular structure. On this view, just as water is composed of hydrogen and oxygen, so certain sounds are quite literally built out of others (e.g., [e] and [o] are composed of [i] + [a] and [u] + [a], respectively). Explanation of the behavior of phonological segments is to be sought in the nature and conditions under which elements combine and decompose. This idea is developed in various ways in Government and Charm Phonology (see Kaye, Lowenstamm, and Vergnaud 1985, Harris 1990), Dependency Phonology (Anderson and Ewen 1987, Durand 1990), as well as in work by Schane (1984) and van der Hulst (1989).

Next we will turn to underspecification. Given the idea that not all features can be combined to create phonological contrasts, certain segments will be unspecified for particular features. An especially fruitful line of attack on underspecification has been the study of processes and constraints that relate two positions across a third. The leading idea is that the intervening position is unspecified for the relevant feature and so the process or constraint is local in the relevant sense. We will survey some of the research that has grown up around this idea.

Finally, we will briefly consider the issue of rules versus constraints. The basic intuition is that phonological rules relate representations composed of segments and associated prosodic structures that can be characterized by a set of static well-formedness constraints (structural descriptions). What is the nature of these constraints? How are they deployed with respect to the more dynamic rules changing one representation into another? Is this a valid distinction?

9.1 Feature Geometry: A Review

In this section we will recapitulate the essentials of the Halle-Sagey Articulator Model of feature geometry introduced in section 4.3. Since much of the subsequent research in this area has extended, modified, or rejected various aspects of this model, it will serve as a good point of departure. The model's leading idea is that features are organized around the articulators – the movable parts of the vocal tract. This dynamic conception of the features contrasts with an earlier, more static view that emphasized the classificatory function of features as attributes of a sound without paying particular attention to how those attributes are generated by the vocal apparatus. The model recognizes six articulators. Some features are the sole responsibility of a particular articulator, while others combine more freely and are not dedicated to a particular articulator. (1) lists the articulators of the Halle-Sagey model, the features that depend on them, and the higher-order structure of the feature tree (based on Halle 1992).

(1)

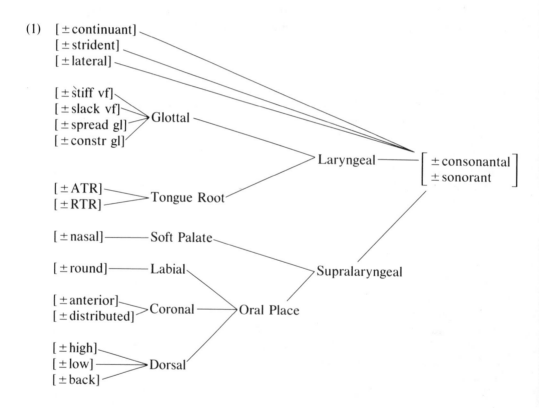

As discussed in section 4.3, grouping the features in terms of the articulators that execute them brings out a wealth of hidden connections that help to restrict the range of feature groupings in phonological rules and constraints. For example, the root cooccurrence restrictions in Arabic (section 4.3.3) hold over equivalence classes defined in terms of the articulators; also, the Sudanese Arabic rule (exercise 1.12) assimilating a stop to a following fricative only applies if the two consonants share the same articulator.

Other features are not bound to a particular articulator. Such articulator-free features fall into two groups: the major class features [consonantal] and [sonorant] and the stricture features [continuant], [strident], and [lateral]. Halle (1992) accepts McCarthy's (1988) proposal that [±consonantal] and [±sonorant] form the root of the feature tree. This move has a number of conceptual advantages. First, [±consonantal] and [±sonorant] seldom seem to spread outside of complete assimilation. Placing these features in the root of the tree explains this point. Second, every language distinguishes consonants from vowels and sonorants from obstruents. But while most also distinguish between at least one stop and fricative or nasal, these contrasts are not universal: some Australian languages lack fricatives and some Salish languages lack nasals. Placing [±consonantal] and [±sonorant] at the root of the feature tree expresses the intuition that higher-level features are more basic categories of contrast; terminal features such as [anterior] operate at the level of "micromanagement" and can be eliminated without affecting the gross character of the segmental inventory. Finally, [±consonantal] and [±sonorant] are major determinants of the sonority-driven syllabification routine that imposes the initial and most basic prosodic structure over the string of phonemes. Locating these features at the root highlights their special status in this regard also.

The root features define three major segment classes: obstruents are [+consonantal, −sonorant], sonorant consonants (liquids and nasals) are [+consonantal, +sonorant], and [−consonantal, +sonorant] defines the class of vocoids: vowels and glides. Halle (1992) follows many other researchers in assuming that the difference between a vowel and a glide is a function of whether or not the segment is dominated by the nucleus of the syllable. The vocal tract constriction demanded by an obstruent is incompatible with the absence of constriction required of a vocoid and so the [−consonantal, −sonorant] combination is excluded by definition.

Halle (1992) notes certain restrictions on the combination of root features with particular articulators. First, [+consonantal] segments must choose their articulator from among Labial, Coronal, and Dorsal. This restriction is written into the definition of [+consonantal] as "constriction in the central passage through the oral cavity." It is premised on the idea that the essential property of consonants is that they approximate a tube closed at both ends; recall from section 4.3 that this has the acoustic consequence that the lowest vowel resonance on the spectrogram descends to zero when next to a consonant. Only a constriction in the oral cavity is capable of achieving this approximation to a tube closed at both ends. The special status of the Labial, Coronal, and Dorsal articulators is signaled in (1) by grouping them into a special class called "(Oral) Place." This organization implies that pharyngeal and laryngeal segments will pattern as [−consonantal] glides. Another restriction requires a vowel ([−consonantal] segments dominated by the syllable nucleus) to choose the Dorsal articulator. This follows from the assumption that the vowel quality features [high], [low], and [back] are dependents of Dorsal. By contrast, [−consonantal] segments that are not syllable heads are unrestricted with respect to articulator (2).

(2)   Glottal   [h,ʔ]   Dorsal   [w,y]
      Tongue Root   [ḥ,ʕ]   Coronal   [j]
      Soft Palate   [N]   Labial   [w]

The nasal glide (N) is found in Japanese as the so-called mora nasal; it lacks an oral articulator of its own and may assimilate one from a following stop. The nasal glide is often found as the output of debuccalization processes that delink the Place node, as in many Spanish dialects (Trigo 1988). (2) predicts the existence of dorsal glides as distinct from labial and coronal ones. Halle points to Anderson's (1976b) analysis of Fula in which the glides [w,y] alternate sometimes with labials and coronals [b,ɟ] and at other times with the velars [k,g]. Careful phonetic study is required to determine whether the glides participating in these two different alternations are phonetically identical, as the traditional transcription implies. (Also see Paradis 1988a.)

If this view of the articulators in [−consonantal] segments is correct, it implies that the choice of articulator can only be determined once the syllabic nucleus is established. If the articulator choice is represented lexically, then a nuclear-non-nuclear distinction is implied and consequently a rudimentary syllabification is imposed on lexical representations. Also, rules vocalizing glides and devocalizing vowels may require a change of articulator in order to respect these constraints. Such implications of the constraint on articulator coupling with particular major class features remain unexplored.

In the Halle-Sagey model, the manner features [continuant], [strident], and [lateral] depend directly from the root and are thus articulator-free. [±continuant] freely combines with Labial, Coronal, and Dorsal to generate stops and fricatives at each of the three major oral places of articulation. But [±lateral] is almost always restricted to coronal consonants and so might be treated as a dependent of the Coronal articulator (Levin 1988a). Halle points to the velar laterals discovered in certain New Guinea languages, showing that coronality is not universal. Also problematic for the view of [lateral] as a Coronal dependent is the fact that assimilation for Place does not necessarily entail assimilation of laterality (e.g., Chukchee ŋ-assimilation, section 3.4). Finally, we lack evidence for whether the [±strident] distinction between [θ] and [s] is properly extended beyond the coronals. If no evidence is forthcoming, then it might be treated as a Coronal dependent.

Since the features for voicing and nasality are bound to the Glottal and Soft Palate (SP) articulators, respectively, the bilabial nasal [m] activates three articulators (3a).

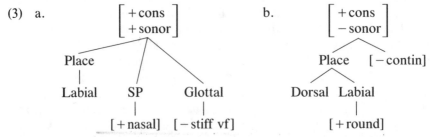

The oral articulators may also combine to form complex segments. For example, the labial-velar [kʷ] combines a dorsal closure with lip rounding and so activates both the Dorsal and Labial articulators. However, a representation such as (3b) is incomplete because it fails to indicate that the [−continuant] manner feature (as well as the root features) are executed by the Dorsal rather than the Labial articulator. This information is necessary for the proper phonetic interpretation of the segment as well as for the phonology: for example, to ensure that nasal assimilation to [gʷ] generates a velar nasal [ŋ] in *anguish* instead of the labial [m]. The integration of the manner/stricture features with place features has emerged as a major issue in phonological theory, generating a number of different accounts. The Halle-Sagey proposal distinguishes between a "major" and a "minor" articulator. In segments with multiple articulators, at least one is singled out as the major articulator; it executes the root and manner features. The major articulator is designated by an arrow pointing from the root of the tree. By convention, all of the stricture and root features are implemented by the articulator so designated. [kʷ] thus receives the representation in (4).

(4)

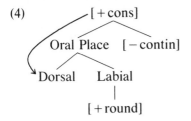

The Halle-Sagey model thus recognizes two different mechanisms to establish feature groupings: dependency and the arrow (in addition to certain restrictions on particular root-articulator combinations). Numerous researchers have attempted to eliminate the arrow by placing the stricture features (particularly [continuant]) at different locations. We will review some of these proposals in section 9.5. The stricture features of secondary articulations have also been studied by Sagey (1988), who claims that they are never contrastive in a given language although they may vary in their phonetic interpretation from one language to another: for example, [kʷ], [kᶠ], and [kp] have been identified as realizations of a labial-velar stop. These systematic differences are viewed as matters of phonetic implementation, conceived as copying the segment's stricture features under the major articulator and then adding the appropriate stricture specifications for the secondary articulator. The result is a phonetic representation with separate stricture specifications for each articulator, the vocoid [w] being the default value. On this view, (4) may be converted to any of the representations in (5) in the course of phonetic implementation.

(5)

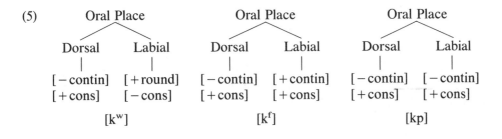

9.2   Gutturals

In a thorough study of the Semitic gutturals, McCarthy (1991) discusses the implications these consonants hold for feature theory – in particular the conception of Place. We will review his major results here. First and most importantly, the gutturals are implemented by three distinct articulators: the laryngeals [ʔ,h] by the "glottal" articulator, the pharyngeals [ḥ,ʕ] by retraction of tongue root constricting the lower pharynx, and the uvulars [x,ɣ] by a tongue-dorsum constriction at the posterior wall of the oropharynx. Nevertheless, the gutturals form a demonstrable phonological and phonetic class. McCarthy documents numerous sound changes and constraints that isolate [ʔ,h,ḥ,ʕ,x,ɣ]. First and most significantly, the gutturals participate fully in the Arabic root cooccurrence restrictions; there is a statistically significant avoidance of roots built from two distinct members from the guttural class (see section 4.3.4). Second, vowels lower in the environment of gutturals in several Semitic languages. For example, Classical Arabic distinguishes the perfect and imperfect of its basic (measure I) verbs by the quality of the vowel separating the second and third radicals. The chart in (6a) shows the relevant ablaut classes.

(6)	a.	a/u	katab/yaktub	'write'
		a/i	Darab/yaDrib	'beat'
		i/a	šarib/yašrab	'drink'
		a/a	faʕal/yafʕal	'do'
	b.		saʔal/yasʔal	'ask'
			nahab/yanhab	'rob'
			manaʕ/yamnaʕ	'prohibit'
			fataḥ/yaftaḥ	'open'
			maraɣ/yamraɣ	'loiter'
			ṣarax/yaṣrax	'scream'

The first three classes involve a change in the height of the vowel: imperfect [i,u] correspond to perfect [a] while imperfect [a] corresponds to perfect [i]. Members of the deviant [a]/[a] class almost all have a guttural in the second or third position and can be understood as reflecting a rule spreading a [low] tongue body feature to the vowel, which either preempts or reverses the change in height (see below for details). Other samples of this class are listed in (6b). Additional phenomena that single out the gutturals include a tendency to avoid closing the syllable on a guttural (e.g., Tiberian Hebrew and Bedouin Arabic, where underlying [V_iGC] is realized as V_iGV_iC) and guttural degemination (e.g., Tiberian Hebrew and Tigre, where $G_iG_i \rightarrow G_i$). These rules and constraints demonstrate that [ʔ,h,ʕ,ḥ,x,ɣ] form a natural phonological class. The gutturals also share clear phonetic correlates: acoustically, they are distinguished by their high first formant values; articulatorily, they are all produced in the posterior region of the vocal tract.

   McCarthy proposes the feature [pharyngeal] to define these segments. The next question is where to locate this feature in the hierarchical tree. Since they include the laryngeals [ʔ,h], one might see the gutturals as a ramification of the Glottal node. Two facts show this conclusion to be erroneous. First, the gutturals' participation in the root cooccurrence restriction argues for placing [pharyngeal] under the Place node. All the other equivalence classes in the constraint are defined by a Place category: [labial], [coronal] (with refinements), [dorsal]. Second, assimilation rules that neutralize voicing distinctions in the Semitic languages fail to alter the pharyngeal character of a guttural. If gutturals really were a subspecies of Glottal, we might expect them to delink in contexts where voice assimilates. Since such a phenomenon is never encountered, we have additional reason to locate [pharyngeal] under Place, as in (7).

(7)   Place

[labial] [coronal] [dorsal] [pharyngeal]

The fact that the [pharyngeal] class comprises three distinct articulators is surprising from the articulator-based conception of Place. McCarthy concludes that this fact supports Perkell's (1980) view of features as "orosensory goals" whose implementation requires feedback between the articulator and the constriction site. The geometry in (7) betrays an anatomical asymmetry that reinforces this interpretation. The single [pharyngeal] category spans a region that is equivalent to that subtended by the three separate [labial], [coronal], and [dorsal] articulators taken together. McCarthy speculates that feedback receptors are more diffused in the pharyngeal cavity in comparison to the densely packed oral cavity. This could also explain why the [labial], [coronal], and [dorsal] expansions of Place are always chosen before [pharyngeal], which, laryngeals aside, is lacking in most languages. A staunch supporter of the articulator model might speculate that the Glottal and Tongue Root articulators run along the same neural pathway and branch more superficially: the relevant sense of "articulator" would be defined at this more abstract level.

Whatever the eventual outcome of these speculations, the model in (7) overlooks a significant asymmetry noted first by Steriade (1987a), who observed a tendency for vowels to completely assimilate across [h] and [ʔ] in many languages. She explained this "laryngeal transparency" with the hypothesis that, in contrast to oral consonants such as [p], [h,ʔ] lack a Place node that could serve as a barrier to the spread of a vowel's Place node (8).

(8)   V   C   V   V   C   V

     Place   Place   Place Place Place

        [VhV]   [VpV]

McCarthy points out that in Semitic the entire class of gutturals is transparent – not just the laryngeals. For example, in Tiberian Hebrew the schwa of such prefixes as *lə* 'to' and *wə* 'and' assimilates the quality of a following reduced vowel – but only when a guttural intervenes. Other consonants block this vowel echo.

(9)   waʔᵃnī   'and I'
      leʔᵉkōl   'to eat'
      laʕᵃbōd   'to serve'
      loḥᵒlī   'for sickness'

There is thus a dilemma. The root cooccurrence restrictions argue that [pharyngeal] is Place category, while paradigms such as (9) indicate that the gutturals are permeable to spread of the vocalic Place node – a phenomenon that can be explained if they lack a Place specification. McCarthy's solution is to break the Place node into two branches: Oral and Pharyngeal.

(10)

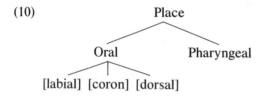

Just as the individual articulators define separate autosegmental tiers and hence can spread past one another (section 4.3.4), so do the Oral and Pharyngeal expansions. The consequence is that an oral consonant will block spreading a vowel's Place node but Pharyngeal will not; the asymmetry noted by Steriade is thereby addressed. The proper interpretation of the OCP-driven root restriction depends on a slight equivocation in the status of "pharyngeal." In the more densely populated oral cavity the cooccurrence constraint reaches down to the individual articulators; but in the pharyngeal cavity it remains at the category level, ignoring the individual articulators. As we saw in section 4.3.4, the statement of other cooccurrence constraints requires relativizing the OCP to particular tiers or combinations of tiers in the feature geometry and so this move appears justified.

(11a) shows McCarthy's conception of the internal structure of the Place node; (11b) illustrates various subtypes of [pharyngeal] consonants.

(11)   a.

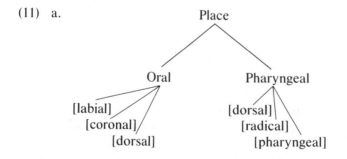

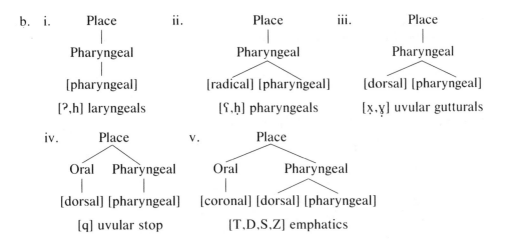

The following observations are in order. First, there are a couple of equivocations in the geometry. The term "pharyngeal" appears at two different levels in the tree. It denotes a category label standing for the whole class of gutturals and also appears as a terminal feature. Since no articulator is designated for the laryngeals, McCarthy apparently assumes that the "Glottal articulator" is pressed into service as a matter of phonetic implementation rather than in the phonology – a move whose validity remains to be assessed. Second, the [dorsal] articulator is reachable through either the Oral or the Pharyngeal branch. This makes sense since it lies at the boundary between the two cavities and can enter either. We will see additional examples of such "double domination" later in this chapter. Third, recall that in Semitic only the [x̱,ɣ̱] subset of the uvulars count as gutturals: the stop [q] does not. Instead of referring directly to a stricture feature, McCarthy draws the distinction between [x̱,ɣ̱] and [q] more subtly by trading on the ambiguous status of the [dorsal] articulator as a dependent of either the Oral or the Pharyngeal category node. The uvular stop [q] (11biv) has an Oral expansion lacking in the gutturals [x̱,ɣ̱] (11biii). Since both subtypes have identical terminal features, the guttural-nonguttural difference here is a purely formal one. It is designed to explain why uvular [x̱,ɣ̱] are transparent to rules that spread a vowel's Oral Place node while uvular [q] is opaque. Fourth, the emphatic consonants (11bv) have a secondary constriction in the upper oropharynx and thus take the [dorsal] and [pharyngeal] features as a secondary articulation. Finally, in all cases where an oral expansion of the Place node combines with a pharyngeal one, Oral is the primary Place category and Pharyngeal is subordinate. This primary-nonprimary distinction is critical to the statement of several constraints.

Let us now see how these representations permit various rules and constraints to be economically expressed. First, the root cooccurrence restriction on the gutturals is expressed in (12a) as an OCP restriction over the class [ʔ,h,ḥ,ʕ,x̱,ɣ̱] – that is, those consonants that lack an Oral expansion and hence for which Pharyngeal is the primary Place category. The remaining constraints over the oral articulators are expressed in (12b), with further refinements of the coronal class, a point we overlook here.

(12)   a.   <u>OCP</u>
            domain: primary [pharyngeal]

    b.   <u>OCP</u>
            domain: primary [labial], primary [coronal], primary [dorsal]

McCarthy cites the tables in (13) to show that the uvular gutturals [x̣,ɣ̣] actually overlap both the {g,k,q} and the guttural equivalence classes, discombining with both.

(13)   a.   <u>adjacent (C_1C_2,C_2C_3)</u>   <u>nonadjacent (C_1C_3)</u>

	A	B	C
A	1	0	79
B	3	0	2
C	78	3	6

	A	B	C
A	3	2	52
B	14	0	13
C	50	1	23

A = {g,k,q}
B = {x̣,ɣ̣}

C = {ʕ,ḥ,ʔ,h}

    b.   <u>OCP</u>
            domain: primary [dorsal]

This overlap follows straightforwardly if consonants taking the tongue dorsum as a primary articulator define an equivalence class. It groups {x̣,ɣ̣} with {g,k,q}.

The analysis of the emphatic consonants (11bv) as having a secondary uvular articulation and hence dominating a combination of [dorsal] and [pharyngeal] is the least well supported aspect of the proposed system. An alternative interprets "emphasis" as velarization and thus a secondary articulation of [+back]. The [k] vs. [q] opposition could then be expressed as [−back] vs. [+back] dorsals. There is minimal evidence for a [pharyngeal] component to the emphatics. Since these consonants freely combine with gutturals, the postulated [pharyngeal] component at best does no work and at worst must be overlooked. McCarthy mentions a couple of rules and constraints that index emphatics and uvulars: for example, Arabic [ẓ] corresponds to Ugaritic [ɣ]; also, while Classical Arabic [q] freely combines with emphatics, [k] does not. The [ẓ] > [ɣ] change is treated as loss of the coronal articulator accompanied by promotion of the secondary uvular articulation to primary. But if [back] is a dorsal dependent, the change could just as easily be described as the loss of the coronal articulator and promotion of the dorsal to primary. Similarly, the incompatibility of emphatics and [k] could be expressed in terms of [back] instead of [pharyngeal]. One phenomenon, however (noted originally in this connection by Herzallah (1990)), diagnoses the postulated [pharyngeal] component of the emphatics. In a number of Levantine dialects the feminine nominal suffix takes an [a] variant after laryngeals and pharyngeals, after uvulars, and after emphatics. Elsewhere it is [e] or [i] depending on the dialect. McCarthy cites the data in (14) from the Syrian dialect.

(14) mniiḥ-a   'good'
      Sanʕ-a   'handwork'
      waažh-a   'display'
      xərʔ-a   'rag'

      Tabx̣-a   'cooking'
      daggaaɣ-a   'tanning'

      ʔəSS-a   'story'
      ʕariiD-a   'broad'
      xayyaaT-a   'seamstress'
      baayZ-a   'foul'

      daraž-e   'step'
      kbiir-e   'large'
      madras-e   'school'
      šərk-e   'society'
      x̣afiif-e   'light'

Following Herzallah, McCarthy sees this distribution as arising from a special rule that spreads the [pharyngeal] component of a stem-final consonant to a postulated empty vowel for the suffix. An equivalence [pharyngeal] ↔ [+low] then realizes the suffixal vowel as low. The [e] and [i] variants arise by default rules filling in the empty vowel. An example from each subtype is sketched in (15).

(15)

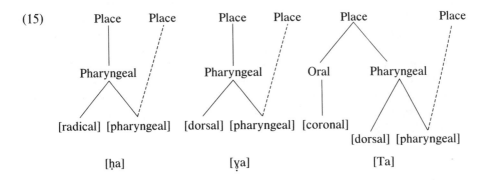

One point on which McCarthy is silent is how the laryngeal features of voicing, aspiration, and glottalization are to be represented in his model. In the Halle-Sagey articulator model of (1), these features are dependents of the Glottal articulator. In Semitic these features fail to classify a segment as a guttural – but why not? More broadly, this raises the question whether [ʔ,h] are properly viewed as gutturals in general or whether this is a special property of Semitic analogous perhaps to the different status of the oral glides [w] and [y] in Fula as labial/coronal versus dorsal. This is a topic that clearly requires further study.

9.3   Vocalic Place

In the Halle-Sagey model, consonantal Place is determined by the Labial, Coronal, and Dorsal articulators while vocalic Place is a function of the *SPE* tongue body features [high], [low], [back] as well as [round]. The former are dependents of the Dorsal articulator while [round] lies under the Labial node.

(16)

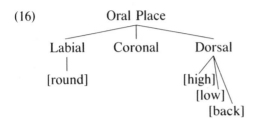

The only explicitly acknowledged formal connection between consonantal and vocalic Place relates Labial and [round]. Several lines of evidence support the idea that [round] is the vocalic expression of labiality in consonants. First, labial consonants induce lip rounding in vowels. For example, in the Dravidian language Tulu (Bright 1972) the accusative suffix is back unrounded [-ï] unless preceded by a labial consonant or a round vowel: *kaṭṭï* 'bond' but *kappu* 'blackness', *uccu* 'snake'. In this example [p] and [u] are equivalent in labializing the suffixal vowel – a process that may be characterized as a spread of the Labial articulator to the vowel, where it is realized as rounding. Similarly, a round vowel may induce a Labial articulator on a consonant. Clements (1991a) observes that Proto-Bantu **tʉ* is realized as [fu] in many daughter languages. The change can be understood as spread of the vowel's labial articulation to the preceding consonant, displacing the original Coronal articulator. In addition to assimilations that cross the consonant/vowel frontier, fortition and lenition processes also demonstrate the equivalence of rounded vowels and labials consonants: recall the hardening of the hiatus-breaking glide [w] to [v] or [b] in Basque (exercise 3.2) and Klingenheben's Law in Hausa where labial consonants weaken to [w] in the syllable's coda: compare *hawsii* 'barking of dog' and dialectal *hapsii*.

9.3.1   V-Place and C-Place: A Synthesis

Clements (1991a) argues for similar systematic relations between other consonantal and vocalic place features and concludes that Place is defined by a unified set of articulators for both vowels and consonants. He consolidates and simplifies the original Halle-Sagey articulator model. Let us review his major results and proposals.

As in the case of labial constriction and rounding, the place features have different phonetic expression because of the differing stricture properties of consonants and vowels, but they are fundamentally the same set of categories. Clements's Place features and their C and V expression are listed in (17).

(17) place   consonantal expression   vocalic expression
     labial   lip constriction   rounding
     coronal   constriction of tip/blade/front of   front and retroflex
                  tongue
     dorsal   constriction at back of tongue   back vowels
                  (palatine dorsum)
     radical   constriction in lower pharynx   low and pharyngealized

In this model the height features are segregated from the place features on a
separate branch labeled *Aperture,* as in (18a).

(18)   a. 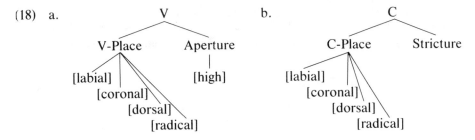   b.

In depending from both V and C, the place features are understood to occupy
different planes – a kind of double domination similar to that of the [dorsal]
articulator in McCarthy 1991, which is accessible from either the Oral or the
Pharyngeal cavity node. To visualize this point better, imagine looking at an el-
liptical-shaped object such as an American football or a watermelon from one
end. From the top seam (root) the features on the bottom can be accessed by
paths that run along either side of the ellipse. These paths correspond to different
planes that relate the root to the individual features (19).

(19)   root

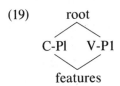

    Clements argues for this feature organization on both phonetic and phonological
grounds. It induces the following feature analysis of the familiar vowel triangle.
(Parentheses indicates cases where conclusive evidence for a binary versus monovalent opposition is lacking.)

(20)

	i	e	a	o	u
coronal	+	+	–	–	–
labial	(–)	(–)	(–)	+	+
dorsal	–	–	–	+	+
radical	(–)	(–)	+	(–)	(–)

Let us review the major points of difference with the Halle-Sagey model.

First, Clements's model eliminates the *SPE* feature [round]. Lip rounding is the vocalic expression of the labial articulator. Any more radical closure at the lips would be incompatible with a vocalic stricture. The same point holds for labialization in consonants such as [kʷ] and [pʷ], given that such labialization is a secondary articulation and hence a V-Pl feature (see below). Second, in the Halle-Sagey model [high], [low], and [back] are all dorsal features; they are defined with respect to a rest position that approximates the vowel [ɛ] (*SPE*). It is the job of the tongue dorsum to place the tongue in this rest position and this gives it a special status. Clements takes the presence of a constriction as positive evidence for the active involvement of an articulator in the production of a vowel. Since a number of phonetic studies have observed a pharyngeal constriction in low vowels (e.g., Delattre 1971), [æ,a,ɑ] are claimed to activate the radical articulator. Aside from the guttural-lowering phenomenon in Semitic, the implications of a pharyngeal articulator in the low vowels remain to be explored.

9.3.2   Front Vowels as Coronal

The major innovation of the Clements model is the hostile takeover of [back] by the coronal and dorsal articulators. Specifically, the back vowels are implemented by the dorsal articulator and front vowels by the coronal articulator. The claim that front vowels are coronal is supported on both phonetic and phonological grounds. Phonetic evidence is provided by Hume (1992), who cites X-ray tracings from the phonetic literature on a number of languages (German, Canadian French, Russian, Hungarian) indicating that front vowels (when compared with the corresponding back vowels) are articulated with a raising of the front of the tongue toward the hard palate. The major question is whether this raising reflects the coronal articulator or dorsal [– back]. For German and Hungarian, the front vowel constrictions appear comparable to those involved in the production of palatal consonants in these languages ([ç] in German and the palatal stops [c] and [ɟ] in Hungarian). And for Hungarian, Hume cites phonological evidence that groups [c] and [ɟ] with other coronal consonants and thus strengthens the hypothesis that front vowels such as [i] and [ö] are implemented by the same articulator as [t] and [c]. Phonologically, of course, there is a strong connection between front vowels (especially [i]) and alveopalatal consonants: for example, Slavic palatalization of velars [k,g,x] to [č,ž,š] before front vowels and glides [i,e,y], Russian ikan'e (raising and fronting of unstressed nonhigh vowels after [č,ž,š]), and Porteño Spanish fortition of onset [y] to [ž]. But whether this connection should be broadened to take in the lower vowels [e] and [æ] and the anterior coronals [t,s,n] is less clear. To support this point, Pulleyblank (1989) and Hume (1992) offer several cases of vowel fronting in the context of coronals, including dentals. For example, in the development of Cantonese from Late Middle Chinese, nonlow round vowels are fronted after coronals: *ty:n* ([y] = [ü]) 'end, tip' < LMC **tuan* (cf. Mandarin *duan*) vs. *ku:n* 'official' < LMC **kuan* (cf. Mandarin *guan*) and *pu:n* 'half' < LMC **puan* (cf. Mandarin *ban*). According to Cheng (1989), if the syllable onset and coda are both coronal in present-day Cantonese, a nonlow nuclear vowel must be front. And in Lhasa Tibetan, [u,o,a] fronted before coronal consonants but not before labials or velars (Michailovsky 1975). Final consonants have deleted in colloquial speech but are reflected in the written language: thus, written Tibetan *bdud* 'demon', *bod* 'Tibet', and *sman* appear as [tüü], [phöö], and [mɛ̃ɛ̃]; compare *nub* 'west', *goŋ* 'price', and *gyag* 'yak', which appear as [nuu], [qhŏŏ], and [yaa] and show no change in vowel quality.

The proposal to let the coronal and dorsal articulators do the work of [back] also provides a natural account of central vowels. In a system with just [back], a central vowel must be defined with the help of [round]. But Clements points to problematic cases such as the dialect of Swedish spoken in Finland, which contrasts three high round vowels: front [ü] *dyr* 'expensive', central [ʉ] *bur* 'cage', and back [u] *bor* 'lives'. Here appeal to [round] is of no avail. In the proposed new system, central vowels are distinguished from front and back by their [−coronal] and [−dorsal] specifications.

(21)   ü   ʉ   u
   labial   +   +   +
   coronal   +   −   −
   dorsal   −   −   +

We can also express processes such as the centralization of diphthongal nuclei found in many English dialects (see exercise 1.7) as delinking the V-Place node, leaving the nucleus to be defined in terms of just an aperture feature.

However, trading [back] for [coronal] and [dorsal] also introduces certain complications. First, we lose the insight that front and back vowels are opposites and thus cannot give a natural account of such dissimilations as the diphthong crossover in Australian English (Wells 1982) where the centralized nuclei of *price* and *mouth* have polarized with respect to the backness of the offglide: [ʌy] [ʌw] → [ɑy] and [æw]. Second, in the vowel harmony of such languages as Turkish, specification for [αback] blocks the spread of [−αback]. In order to preserve this effect in his system, Clements must stipulate that vocalic versions of the articulator features have binary values such that [+coronal] implies [−dorsal] and vice versa. However, [−labial] and [−radical] never seem to be needed in the way that [−coronal] is. When defining place of articulation in consonants, [coronal] and [dorsal] must be monovalent. Recall from section 4.3.3 that this point is crucial in order to state the Arabic root cooccurrence constraints: to rule out *[tkd], [t] must look past [k] to see [d]. If [k] were [−coronal], then it would block the line of sight between [t] and [d]. These facts indicate that the replacement of [±back] with [coronal] and [dorsal] is not entirely successful. A final point worth mentioning is that in the Halle-Sagey model Coronal is implemented by the intrinsic longitudinal muscles of the tongue while front vowels are produced by contraction of the genioglossus, an external muscle that connects the tongue body to the jaw. On this view, there is thus anatomical motivation for not identifying coronal consonants and front vowels.

9.3.3 *Secondary V-Place*

Another argument Clements offers for identifying the consonantal and vocalic place features is that this unification automatically circumscribes the range of secondary articulations: labialization, palatalization, velarization, and pharyngealization (as opposed to, for example, aperture features and [ATR]). Standing the traditional notation on its head, Clements represents [tʷ], [tʸ], and so on, as the subjunction of a V-Place subtree to a consonant's C-Place node, as in (22).

(22)

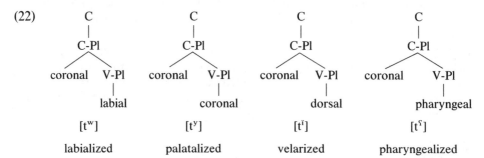

This notation has a number of noteworthy properties. First, since secondary articulation features are placed under the V-Pl node, we can distinguish between plain [p] and labialized [pʷ] without having to introduce the feature [round]: [labial] under the V-Pl node is interpreted as lip rounding, and under the C-Pl node as the constriction demanded by the consonant's stricture features. [p] is thus [labial] while [pʷ] is [labial [labial]]. The interpretation of [coronal [coronal]] and [dorsal [dorsal]] structures is less obvious; we will return to this point momentarily.

Second, a secondary place feature may supplant the primary one, a process Clements terms *promotion*. For example, Indo-European *[kʷ] appears as [p] in Greek. This change is sketched in (23) as loss of the dorsal articulator. Given that every consonant requires a primary articulator to execute its stricture features, the second step might follow by an interpretive convention.

(23)

```
      C                C             C
      |                |             |
    C-Pl       →     C-Pl     →    C-Pl
    ╱   ╲              |             |
 dorsal  V-Pl         V-Pl        labial
         |             |
       labial        labial
```

A vowel typically affects an adjacent consonant through spread of a place feature, interpolating a V-Pl node. The result is a secondarily articulated consonant: labialized [tʷ], palatalized [tʸ], and so on. What is less clear is how a vowel's V-Pl feature affects the primary point of articulation of an adjacent consonant, as in velar palatalization. This question is addressed by Hume (1992), who develops the idea that front vowels are coronal within the general framework of Clements's model. Hume's proposals can be summarized as follows. First, coronal is more articulated as a C-Pl feature, taking [anterior], [distributed], and [strident] as dependents. As a V-Pl feature, coronal lacks any contrastive dependents: [strident] is incompatible with a vocalic stricture, and there seems to be no [±anterior] contrast in front vowels comparable to that found in coronal consonants (see however Gorecka 1992). Hume assigns front vowels [−anterior] by a redundancy rule. This feature shows up when front vocoids are hardened and appear as [−anterior] palatals. One of Hume's major arguments for extending the coronal articulator to the front vowels is that this hypothesis provides a natural explanation for the ubiquity of palatalization, improving the account available with the Halle-Sagey model, which treats palatal consonants as coronals but front vowels as [−back] dorsals. The latter model can analyze velar fronting of [k] to [k'] in the context of front vowels as assimilation of [−back] but fails to give any privileged status to the change of dorsal [k'] to coronal [c]. The [k'] → [c] step must be stipulated as an arbitrary articulator change from dorsal to coronal; it remains mysterious why [k'] is not instead replaced with a labial or pharyngeal articulator. Hume's proposal is that both [k] → [k'] and [k] → [c] in the context of front vowels arise from spreading of V-Pl coronal. In the former, it appears as a secondary V-Pl articulator and is thus comparable to spread of [−back] (24a); but in the latter, it spreads to the velar's C-Pl node, delinking the original dorsal articulator. A dental-alveolar versus alveopalatal outcome might reflect the relative ordering of (24b) with respect to assignment of a redundant [−anterior] to the front vowel.

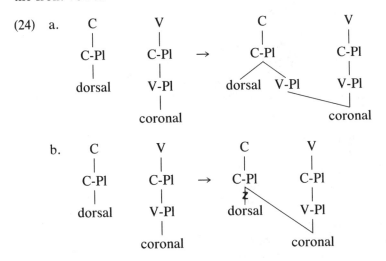

This analysis is an improvement over the Halle-Sagey account and constitutes a significant argument in favor of extending coronal to the front vowels. However, certain questions remain unanswered, of which we will consider two. First, while [k] → [c] is typically triggered by nonhigh front vowels, softening of dental [t] and labial [p] to coronal [c] is usually restricted to high front vocoids, often to just the glide [y]. This height asymmetry is not explained under the analysis in (24b). One might instead pursue an analysis in which [k] → [c] derives from intermediate [k'], where the palatality is an offglide, release feature (Calabrese 1992). From that point on, palatalization of [p], [t], and [k] would be comparable. In Clements's model, this idea might be pursued by exploring a connection between the Aperture node in (18a) and promotion of a V-Pl feature to C-Pl. Another asymmetry is that while [ke] → [ce] is quite common, [to] → [ko] with assimilation of dorsality is much less so. It is clear that there are still some major gaps in our understanding of the ways in which the V-Pl features do and do not influence C-Pl. See Gorecka 1989, Broselow and Niyondagara 1989, and Calabrese 1992 for further discussion of palatalization and feature geometry.

Rules spreading a place feature from a consonant to a vowel may distinguish the source feature as primary versus secondary. Two examples are furnished by Herzallah's (1990) study of emphatic consonants in Palestinian Arabic. Herzallah treats emphasis as secondary [dorsal] (and [pharyngeal]). The low vowel takes a back allophone after an emphatic (transcribed here with underdotting): [taab] 'repented' vs. [ṭɑɑb] 'got well'. Primary dorsal consonants [q,x,ɣ] fail to retract the vowel: [ṭɑxxat] 'she fired', [ṭaqam] 'he furnished'. Consequently, retraction must be expressed as spreading the [dorsal] feature that is dominated by the V-Pl node.

(25)

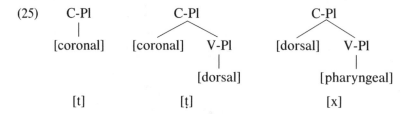

Another process spreads [dorsal] from both the C-Pl and the V-Pl nodes. In the Palestinian reflex of the [a]/[i] ablaut class for measure I verbs, the imperfect vowel is normally default [i] (26a); however, it appears as [u] when the root contains an emphatic consonant (26b) or a [q,x,ɣ] (26c).

(26) a.

perfect	imperfect	
katab	yi-ktib	'write'
fasad	yi-fsid	'decay'
tall	y-till	'snatch'
nass	y-niss	'sneak'

b.

perfect	imperfect	
naðam	yi-nðum	'compose'
šaṭab	yi-šṭub	'cross out'
ṭall	y-ṭull	'appear'
naṣṣ	y-nuṣṣ	'preach'

c.

perfect	imperfect	
saxan	yi-sxun	'get hot'
balaɣ	yi-bluɣ	'reach'
baxx	y-buxx	'spray'

Herzallah treats this process as spreading [dorsal] to a high vowel; a later rule enhances the resultant back vowel by adding a labial articulator. The source of the spreading [dorsal] is either a primary C-Pl [x,ɣ] (26c) or a secondary V-Pl [ṭ,ṣ, . . .] (26b). One might speculate that spreading a C-Pl feature implies spreading of the same feature from under V-Pl (if it occurs). More study is needed to confirm this conjecture.

9.3.4 Secondary V-Place Barriers

Attaching the V-Pl node as a subtree under C-Pl predicts that rules spreading a V-Pl feature from one vowel to another across an intervening consonant will block when the consonant is specified for the relevant feature as a secondary but not as a primary articulation. Although this prediction remains to be systematically investigated, there are cases on record that point in the right direction. Let us briefly look at two. Clements (1991a) points to Cook's (1987) analysis of a velarization prosody in the Athapaskan language Chilcotin. Like Arabic, this language opposes plain versus velarized/pharyngealized coronals and front versus back (velar versus uvular) dorsals. As in the case of Arabic, the precise articulatory correlates of the contrast are not clear. We will follow Cook in referring to the relevant feature as *flatting*. The flat consonants (both coronal and dorsal) retract and lower adjacent vowels, reflecting the spread of [+back] or [+dorsal]: for example, /ṣid/ 'kingfisher' is realized as [ṣˤit] but /sid/ 'I' is realized as [sit]. The strength of this process varies depending on whether the source is a primary coronal or dorsal and whether it applies from right to left or from left to right. For our purposes the interesting case is left-to-right spread from a coronal source. In [ṣVCV] strings, retraction can spread up to the second vowel: /ṣelin/ 'it's gotten bloody' is realized as [ṣəlˤin]. But front dorsals block the process: underlying /ṣegen/ 'it's dry' is realized as [ṣegɛn], not as [ṣəgən]. Following Cook, Clements treats these opaque elements as bearing an autosegmental specification on the secondary V-Pl tier. In particular, front (velar) and back (uvular) dorsals are distinguished as [±dorsal] under the V-Pl node (27).

(27)

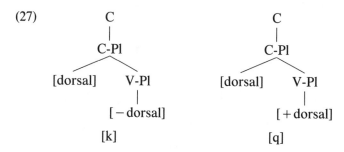

The blocking effect of the front dorsals on the spread of flatting now follows, as shown by the VCV substring of [ṣegɛn] in (28).

(28)

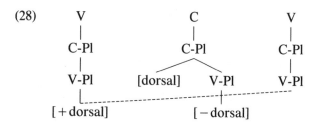

Cook states that velars do not block the right-to-left spread of flatting from a coronal source, citing underlying /tænink'æz/ 'water is getting cold', with a glottalized velar stop, realized as [taneŋk'az̧]. This suggests that the right-to-left flatting applies first and that plain velars lack an underlying V-Pl [−dorsal] specification, picking it up by a default rule ordered between the two spreading rules. On this analysis, the underlying velar-uvular contrast is represented as [dorsal] vs. [dorsal [+dorsal]]. It is worth observing that this recursion of the V-Pl [dorsal] under primary C-Pl [dorsal] encodes what is considered a contrast between two primary places of articulation (velar versus uvular) in more traditional theories.

To close this discussion, let us look at another example in which this recursion is used effectively to explain a blocking effect. Hume (1990) discusses an umlauting process in the Kyungsung dialect of Korean in these terms. The relevant underlying inventory (based on Sohn 1987) appears in (29); in the transcriptions used here, [p'] marks a tense consonant.

(29) p   t   c   k   i   u
      pʰ   tʰ   cʰ   kʰ   e   ə   o
      p'   t'   c'   k'   æ   a
           s   h
           s'
      m   n   ŋ
           l

[i] fronts central and back vowels in the preceding syllable. The rule applies across noncoronal consonants as well as across the anterior coronal [t] but is barred from crossing the palatal [c].

(30)   underlying   phonetic
       [koki]   [kegi]   'meat'
       [mək + hi + ta]   [mekʰida]   'to be eaten'
       [api]   [æbi]   'father'
       [sum + ki + ta]   [šimgida]   'to hide'

       [salpʰ + i + ta]   [sælpʰida]   'to inspect closely'
       [puti]   [pidi]   'by all means'
       [canti]   [cændi]   'lawn'

       [kacʰi]   [kacʰi]   'value'
       [huci + ta]   [hujida]   'to be old-fashioned'
       [toci + ta]   [tojida]   'worsening of an illness'

Hume treats umlaut as spreading V-Pl [coronal]. The fact that palatal [c] is a systematic barrier indicates that it has a V-Pl [coronal] specification (31a). By the same token, the permeable [t] must lack a V-Pl specification – at least at the time when the umlaut rule applies (31b).

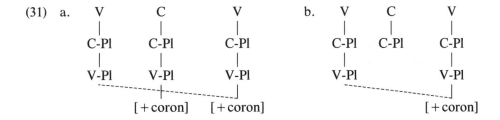

Here once again we see recursion of a place feature encoding as a primary-secondary opposition what for other theories is a contrast between two places of articulation: dental-alveolar [t] vs. alveopalatal [c]. But unlike in Chilcotin [k] vs. [q], the unmarked member [t] is not a barrier. Again this can be handled by judicious ordering of default rules (or it might indicate that the relevant feature is *SPE* [back] – Korean [c] being a [−back] coronal and Chilcotin [k] being a [−back] dorsal). The Korean example may be usefully compared with two other cases of transconsonantal assimilation of vocalic backness. In Hungarian (Hume 1992) palatals such as [c,ñ,ʎ] fail to block backness vowel harmony and so must lack a V-Pl specification for coronal: *szegé*[ʎ]*-es* 'having an edge' vs. *sú*[ʎ]*-os* 'heavy'; *la*[ñ]*-uŋk* 'our girl' vs. *me*[ñ]*-üŋk* 'our daughter-in-law'. On the other hand, Turkish palatal [ʎ] blocks the spread of backness from the preceding vowel and initiates its own harmonic domain: *ro*[ʎ]*-ü* 'role' acc.sg. (Clements and Sezer 1982). They are thus best analyzed as having a V-Pl [coronal] specification. The Korean example represents an intermediate case: [c] blocks harmony and thus has a V-Pl specification but fails to initiate its own domain. Consequently, in order to identify the source of the spreading V-Pl [coronal], the rule must look across the intervening V-Pl and C-Pl nodes to the root, where the [±consonantal] feature resides. This is a more complex statement and thus should represent a more marked situation. More generally, it raises the important question whether the assignment of a secondary V-Pl specification to a [−anterior] coronal can be made on purely phonetic grounds or requires reference to the phonology. The former position is clearly preferable on learnability grounds. Careful phonetic and phonological study of crucial examples will be required to resolve the matter.

9.3.5 Vowel Echo

A final observation on the V-Pl and C-Pl features. In the Halle-Sagey model, where vowel quality features are dependents of the Dorsal articulator, complete assimilation of a vowel across a consonant should be blocked by an intervening velar but not by a labial or a coronal. The data from Klamath (Odden 1991) in (32a) exhibit no such asymmetry: the *sn*V causative prefix copies the features of the following vowel regardless of the intervening consonant. If both vowels and velar consonants share the Dorsal articulator, then complete assimilation across a velar should be blocked, on the assumption that spread of the features [high], [low], and [back] implies extension of the dominating category in the feature tree (32b).

(32)   a.   sna-batgal   'gets someone up from bed'
            sne-l'e:ml'ema   'makes someone dizzy'
            sne-ge:ǰiga   'makes tired'
            sno-bo:stgi   'causes something to turn black'
            sni-nklilk'a   'makes dusty'

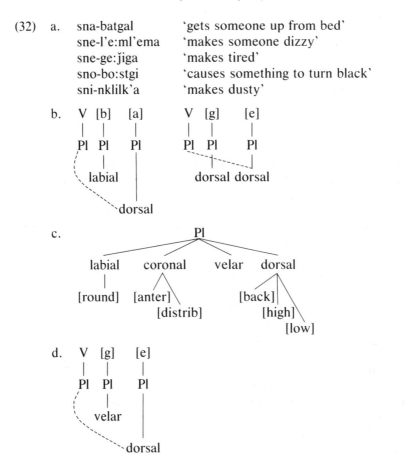

Steriade (1987b) eludes this problem with the hypothesis that the tongue body is the site of two different articulators depending on whether it implements a consonantal or a vocalic feature. The velar consonants [k,g,x] are produced by a Velar articulator and the vowels [a,e,i,o,u] by the Dorsal articulator. On this view, the Place features are arranged as in (32c). Since Velar and Dorsal are different articulators, they can spread past one another just like Labial and Coronal (32d). The introduction of the Velar versus Dorsal distinction is defensible if we accept Perkell's (1980) view of features as feedback patterns, given that the different stricture properties of velar consonants and vowels are sufficient to count as distinct proprioceptive patterns (Calabrese 1992). A proponent of the Halle-Sagey model might deny the premise of Steriade's argument that spreading to saturate the epenthetic vowel necessarily involves assimilating the entire articulator node in one fell swoop. It is conceivable that the empty vowel assimilates the features of the following vowel one by one. If so, we expect an intervening consonant to block assimilation only when it is specified for the relevant feature. Others should slip past. In the Steriade model, no such blockage is predicted. Since [high, back] are accessible from the Dorsal articulator, a vowel should be able to pass its [backness] across an intervening velar consonant. Of course, the saturation alternative requires some convention to ensure that the epenthetic vowel will draw all of its features from the same source – the vowel on the left or the right.

Clements (1991a) gets around the vowel echo problem in a different way. In his model the V-Pl features are subjoined to C-Pl features. This is even true when the C-Pl node is otherwise empty. That is to say, any vowel has a C-Pl specification intervening between the Root node and the V-Pl node. This aspect of the notation is designed to explain an asymmetry in the spreading behavior of consonants and vowels. There are many cases in which an (epenthetic) vowel copies the features of an adjacent vowel, as in the Klamath paradigm in (32a). Clements sees this process as spreading the Vocalic node that dominates V-Pl and Aperture features. He observes that there are few if any cases where the C-Pl feature bundle of a consonant spreads across a vowel. Assimilation for C-Pl features, as in nasal assimilation, always occurs under strict adjacency. If the vowel quality features are dependent on C-Pl, then this asymmetry finds a formal explanation.

(33)

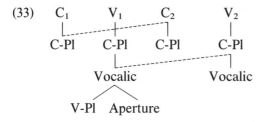

C-Pl for a consonant cannot cross a vowel without violating the autosegmental ban on line crossing: see, for example, the path between C_1 and C_2 in (33). On the other hand, the Vocalic node under V_1 may cross C_2 without violating the autosegmental line-crossing ban (so long as C_2 lacks secondary articulations for V-Pl). While this explanation is attractive, it remains to be seen whether the vowel's postulated C-Pl node does any additional work. Can it serve as an attachment site for a place feature? How can we tell whether a C-Pl feature from a consonant has attached to the C-Pl or the V-Pl node?

In the Clements model, the Vocalic node branches into V-Pl and Aperture. This groups vocalic rounding and backness together and isolates height – a natural acoustic parsing since height is primarily reflected in the first formant and backness and rounding in the second formant. On the other hand, the articulator-based Halle-Sagey model groups backness and height as Dorsal dependents and isolates rounding as a Labial dependent. Odden (1991) discusses a number of cases that appear to support the former partitioning. The strongest comes from Eastern Cheremis (Mari), which contrasts the vowels in (34).

(34)   i   ü   u
          e   ö   ə   o
                    a

	i	ü	e	ö	a	ə	o	u
high	+	+	−	−	−	−	−	+
low	−	−	−	−	+	−	−	−
back	−	−	−	−	+	+	+	+
round	−	+	−	+	−	−	+	+

The mid vowel of certain suffixes such as the 3sg. possessive -*že* alternates between [e], [o], and [ö] when word-final. We find [ö] after [ü] and [ö] (35a); [o] after [u] and [o] (35b); and [e] elsewhere (after [i], [a], [e], and [ə]; (35c)).

(35) a. üp-šö   'his hair'
          šör-žö   'its milk'
      b. surt-šo   'his house'
          boz-šo   'his wagon'
      c. kit-še   'his hand'
          šužar-že   'his sister'
          bokten-že   'beside it'

In Clements's model, [üp-še] → [üp-šö] can be described as spread of the labial and coronal features under the V-Pl node of [ü]; and [surt-še] → [surt-šo] as spread of V-Pl dominating labial and dorsal. The height feature is not spread and so the mid vowel retains its original height specification. The [surt-še] → [surt-šo] sound change is depicted in (36).

(36)

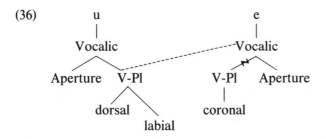

Odden shows on the basis of lexical exceptions and other idiosyncrasies that the transfer of labiality and backness cannot be divided into two separate rules, as in Turkish. Furthermore, given the [i] vs. [ü] and [e] vs. [ö] oppositions, rounding cannot be underspecified. A proponent of the Halle-Sagey model would have to treat the process as either complete assimilation or unrestricted spread of each individual vowel feature and then explain the failure of height to transfer on other grounds. It is unclear how descriptively feasible this alternative is since Odden cites no examples of final high vowels; the process must be defined over [−low] vowels, because suffixal [a] fails to alternate. If it can also be shown that high vowels fail to alternate, then the Eastern Cheremis data look like pretty strong evidence for the V-Pl node as distinct from Aperture. Odden presses the argument against the Halle-Sagey theory on another front as well. The Articulator Model predicts processes spreading the Dorsal-dependent height and backness features independently of rounding – an apparently unattested process. Once again, since the prediction can only be tested in the restricted set of languages that contrast both rounding and backness, it is unclear how much weight can be placed on this gap.

9.4 Vowel Height

In the Halle-Sagey model, vowel height is characterized by the features [high] and [low] (which group with [back] but not [round] under the Dorsal articulator). Like the other dorsal features, [high] and [low] are defined phonetically as tongue body displacements from a neutral position. Clements (1991b) challenges this interpretation of height on both phonetic and phonological grounds. In his view, vowel height is a uniform phonetic dimension that, like pitch, can be repeatedly subdivided into registers. Formally, each division is implemented by a feature [$open_i$]. The entire ensemble of [$open_1$] . . . [$open_n$] forms a hierarchical family of features housed under the Aperture node. Like other features, each [$open_i$] defines its own autosegmental tier and takes a binary value. The cardinal three- and five-vowel systems receive the interpretations in (37a,b). For comparison, the familiar analysis in terms of [high] and [low] is cited in (37c).

(37) a.

	i,u	a
$open_1$	−	+

b.

	i,u	e,o	a
$open_1$	−	−	+
$open_2$	−	+	+

c.

	i,u	e,o	a
high	+	−	−
low	−	−	+

Both models define essentially the same natural classes: high, mid, and low vowels as well as nonhigh [e,o,a] and nonlow [i,u,e,o]. And just like (37c), (37b) does not easily permit high and low vowels to be grouped together to the exclusion of mid. It is true that in the traditional model employing [high] and [low], [i,u] and [a] can be singled out with just one feature specification while mid [e,o] requires two. In the hierarchical model based on [$open_i$], two feature specifications are needed to distinguish both the high and the mid vowels. However, the relative markedness of the mid vowels in comparison to high and low is properly stated at the level of the inventory rather than individual rules. At this level, the Clements model singles out the three-vowel [i,u,a] system as the simplest because it is the starting point from which all the other height inventories are generated.

More substantive differences between the models arise in the interpretation of languages with four degrees of height such as many Bantu languages or Romance (Italian and French). Following the customary Bantu practice, the "superhigh" vowels are transcribed with a cedilla.

(38)

Bantu		Romance	
i̧	y̧	i	u
i	u	e	o
e	o	ɛ	ɔ
	a		a

In the *SPE* system, where [+low] and [+high] cannot be combined, another feature must be recruited in order to distinguish the fourth level. The most popular choice has been [ATR]. This feature was originally introduced by Stewart (1967) to describe the cross-height harmony systems found in many languages of West Africa where [ATR] can combine with all three heights to produce a ten-vowel system such as (39).

(39) [+ATR]   i   u   [−ATR]   i̜   u̜
                e   o   e̜   o̜
                   ʌ   a

Articulatory correlates of the [ATR] feature include an open pharynx and breathy voice. Researchers starting with Halle and Stevens (1969) have sought to equate the West African [i,u] vs. [i̜,u̜] and [e,o] vs. [e̜,o̜] with Bantu [i̜,u̜] vs. [i,u] and Romance [e,o] vs. [ɛ,ɔ]. However, it is unclear how well motivated this move is. There is no clear evidence for a pharyngeal expansion comparable to the West African case that would justify the putative activation of the tongue root in the production of these vowels. Another problem is that [ATR] is a dependent of the Tongue Root while [low] and [high] are Dorsal features. Yet there are cases in which these features spread as a group. For example, Odden (1991) points to the Kimatuumbi paradigm in (40) to make this point; the vowel transcription has been normalized to accord with the Bantu system in (38). Stem-initial vowels comprise a set of seven elements contrasting for four degrees of height. Noninitial vowels in the stem contrast for front versus back; but their height is predictable from the initial vowel as a copy of the height specification of nonlow vowels and otherwise [i̜,u̜]. These data imply a rule spreading the height features of at least [ATR] and [high]. The varying [-i̜y], [-iy], [-ey] realizations of the causative suffix *-Iy* illustrate.

(40)   u̜t-i̜y-a   'make pull'
       yi̜b-i̜y-a   'make steal'
       yuyuut-iy-a   'make whisper'
       biik-iy-a   'make put'
       goonj-ey-a   'make sleep'
       cheeng-ey-a   'make build'
       kaat-i̜y-a   'make cut'

Odden argues from these data that we must group [ATR] and height features under a single node if we are to maintain the leading idea that only nodes in the feature tree may spread. However, as Clements (1991b) observes, this conclusion is problematic if [ATR] is really a dependent of the Tongue Root while height features are Dorsal dependents: there is no node that uniquely dominates just these features. Clements takes this as evidence that the Bantu four-height contrast is based not on [ATR] but rather on the intercalation of another value for open, as shown in (41a). The Kimatuumbi rule can then be expressed as spreading the Aperture node from a [−open₁] nonlow vowel to a nowlow vowel within the stem (41b).

(41) a.

	i̧,u̧	i,u	e,o	a
open₁	−	−	−	+
open₂	−	−	+	+
open₃	−	+	+	+

b.

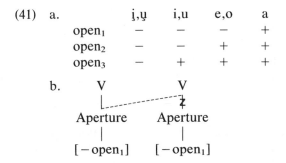

Another phenomenon that Clements claims to support the hierarchical model is scalar assimilations that shift vowels up or down one step. Let us look at a couple of his simpler Bantu examples (Clements 1991b). In the following discussion the vowel transcriptions are normalized according to the Bantu system of (38), departing from the original sources. In Kinande (Zaire) the rank 4 vowels [i̧,u̧] raise preceding vowels. This process neutralizes the contrast between [i̧,u̧] and [i,u] and introduces raised allophones [ẹ,ọ] for the mid vowels [e,o] and [ʌ] for the low vowel [a]. We see it operating in the paradigm (42a) where the [i̧,u̧] of the verbal roots [li̧m] and [hu̧k] raise the vowels of the infinitival prefix complex. In the paradigm (42b) the agentive suffix [-i̧] raises each of the preceding vowels (except that low vowels apparently raise only when long: ọ-mu̧-sat-i̧ 'dancer' but ọ-mu̧-kʌ:l-i̧ 'woman' from [o-mu-ka:li]).

(42) a. ẹ-ri̧-li̧m-a 'to exterminate' b. ọ-mu̧-li̧m-i̧ 'the exterminator'
      ẹ-ri̧-hu̧k-a 'to cook'   ọ-mu̧-hu̧k-i̧ 'the cook'
      e-ri-rim-a 'to cultivate'   ọ-mu̧-ri̧m-i̧ 'the farmer'
      e-ri-hum-a 'to beat'   ọ-mu̧-hu̧m-i̧ 'the beater'
      e-ri-hek-a 'to carry'   ọ-mu̧-hẹk-i̧ 'the porter'
      e-ri-boh-a 'to tie'   ọ-mu̧-bọh-i̧ 'the tier'

In the [ATR] model the alternation can be expressed as the spread of [+ATR] from a [+high] vowel and in the Clements model as the spread of [−open₃] (43).

(43)

	i̧,u̧	i,u	[ẹ,ọ]	e,o	[ʌ]	a
open₁	−	−	−	−	+	+
open₂	−	−	+	+	+	+
open₃	−	+	−	+	−	+

Clements argues that the latter analysis is preferable because it parallels other cases that cannot be described with [ATR]. One example is from Nzɛbi (Gabon), which has essentially the same underlying seven-vowel inventory of (43). Suffixal [-i̧] marking certain tenses shifts root vowels up one step rather than introducing novel segments, as in Kinande.

(44)

basic	shifted	stem	suffixed	
i	i̧	bit	bi̧t(-i̧)	'to carry'
u	y̧	kulən	ky̧li̧n(-i̧)	'to go down'
e	i	sy̧em	sy̧im(-i̧)	'to hide self'
o	u	tood	tuud(-i̧)	'to arrive'
a	e	sal	sel(-i̧)	'to work'

Clements treats the process as spreading a minus value for the feature [open] to the preceding root vowel (with a separate change of schwa to [i̧], which we ignore).

(45) Aperture   Aperture

        ┌- - - - - - - - - -┐
     [+open]   [−open]

The rule is interpreted as applying to any of the three ranks of [open] and trades on the special status of this feature as abbreviating a family of features cutting up a single phonetic dimension. Unlike in Kinande, application of this rule in Nzɛbi is controlled by Structure Preservation (section 5.6), which requires the output to be an independent phoneme of the system. This requirement ensures that the raised low vowel [a] appears as [e] rather than [ʌ] and [e,o] as high [i,u] rather than as the raised mid vowels [ȩ,o̧]. To see why, let us examine (46).

(46)

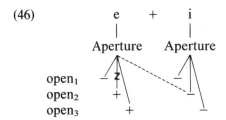

If [−open₃] were to spread to [e], we would derive [ȩ]. But [ȩ] is not an underlying phoneme of the system, and so Structure Preservation blocks extension of this feature. Similarly, in the low vowel [a] Structure Preservation blocks spread of both [−open₂] and [−open₃] (though it is unclear whether this is a meaningful distinction for the low vowels). Structure Preservation is understood as checking the compatibility of each feature change with the original feature specifications of the input; thus, spread of [−open₃] is blocked in virtue of its incompatibility with the original [+open₂].

Clements concludes that this analysis is superior to one invoking [ATR] because the latter would have to treat the Nzɛbi shifts as three separate rules: [a] → [e] as a change from [+low] to [−low], [e] → [i] as a change from [−high] to [+high], and [i] → [i̧] as a change from [−ATR] to [+ATR]. However, this argument only goes through if we do not allow repair rules as an alternative mechanism to instantiate Structure Preservation. An analysis couched in the traditional [ATR] model could spread [ATR] to produce intermediate [ʌ] and [ẹ,ọ] vowels and then say that Nzɛbi differs from Kinande in not licensing the appearance of these novel segments (perhaps because the rules appear in different strata of the respective grammars). Calabrese (1988) develops an analysis along these lines for metaphony (raising) processes in Italian dialects that parallels the Bantu cases discussed by Clements in essential respects. Repairs are implemented by UG processes of delinking or feature reversal, respecting a scale of complexity among phonological segments (see section 9.14). In Calabrese's model, the [a] → [ʌ] → [e] change could be treated as spread of [ATR] followed by delinking of [low]; the [e] → [ẹ] → [i] transformation would involve reversing the [+ATR, −high] of intermediate [ẹ] to [−ATR, +high]. We conclude that since scalar shifts can also be reasonably analyzed within the [ATR] framework, this argument for the hierarchical model of vowel height is not compelling. However, the problem of grouping the Dorsal features [high] and [low] with the Tongue Root dependent [ATR] still remains as an important consideration in favor of the Clements model.

Let us close this section by looking at a spectacular example from the Bantu language Esimbi (Cameroons) demonstrating the independence of the vocalic height and place features. The discussion is based on Clements 1991b and Hyman 1988, which rely on Stallcup's (1980) original analysis. Esimbi inverts the historical and synchronically underlying four-level height contrast in roots and the more restricted two-level contrast in prefixes: on the surface, prefixes exhibit four degrees of height, while the root vowel inventory is restricted to the high [i,ɨ,u]. For example, the class 9 nominal prefix vowel shows [i,e,ɛ] variants while class 3 alternates among [u,o,ɔ] and class 6 among [o,ɔ,a].

(47) underlying

root vowel	class 9		class 3 (sg.)	class 6 (pl.)	
[i]	i-bi	'goat'	u-tili	o-tili	'end'
[u]	i-su	'fish'	u-ku	o-ku	'death'
[e]	e-gbi	'bushfowl'	o-ki	ɛ-ki	'tail'
[o]	e-su	'hoe'	o-tu	ɔ-tu	'ear'
[ə]	e-bɨ	'canerat'	o-tɨ	ɔ-tɨ	'spear'
[ɛ]	ɛ-yisi	'hole'	ɔ-simi	a-simi	'grain'
[ɔ]	ɛ-zu	'snake'	ɔ-bu	a-bu	'hand'
[a]	ɛ-tlɨ	'place'	ɔ-bɨ	a-bɨ	'broom'

All analysts agree that the underlying contrast is registered on the root, whose height features are then transferred to the prefix by spreading and delinking, leaving the root vowel with just a V-Pl specification. It surfaces as high by a separate (default) rule. Esimbi thus replicates the phenomenon from Kimatuumbi in that three contrasting height levels must be spread, supporting the Aperture node. In Clements's model the rule is expressed as (48a). A form such as *ɛ-zu* 'snake' receives the derivation sketched in (48b).

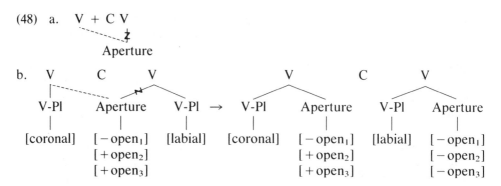

(48) a.   V + C V

b.

In the first step the Aperture node of the root vowel in [zɔ] spreads to the underspecified front vowel prefix, where it combines with the underlying [coronal] V-Pl feature to yield an [ɛ]. The Aperture node is delinked from the source and a separate default rule then assigns a maximal high vowel to the root, yielding a [u]. In each case, then, the V-Pl features of the root and the prefix remain in situ; just the height specification is replaced – a surgical operation that is possible only if the height features lodge under the Aperture node.

In the case of the underlying low vowel prefix of class 6 in (47), the surface value is one step lower than the underlying root vowel. Following the lead of the Nzɛbi analysis, Clements postulates a rule ordered before (48a) that spreads [+open] from a prefix to the following root. This rule is stipulated to preserve structure and hence, as in Nzɛbi, only certain values of the [+open$_i$] feature are accepted by the root vowel. The result is that the Aperture node of the root vowel shifts one step down: [i,u] → [e,o] → [ɛ,ɔ]. This derived root vowel height is then spread back to the prefix by the general rule of (48a). The derivation of *ɔ-tu* 'ear' pl. from [a-to] is sketched in (49).

(49)

V	C	V		V	C	V		V	C	V
	Aperture	Aperture	→	Aperture		Aperture	→	Aperture		Aperture
	[+open$_1$]	[−open$_1$]		[+open$_1$]		[−open$_1$]				[−open$_1$]
	[+open$_2$]	[+open$_2$]		[+open$_2$]						[+open$_2$]
	[+open$_3$]	[−open$_3$]		[+open$_3$]						[+open$_3$]
		[a+to]				[a+tɔ]				[ɔ+tu]

This elegant analysis fully utilizes the descriptive resources of the hierarchical model of vocalic height to account for a complex set of data in a maximally simple fashion.

9.5 Stricture Features

The features [consonantal], [sonorant] (and [approximant]), as well as [continuant] characterize the type of stricture involved in articulating a sound. Most researchers have accepted McCarthy's (1988) proposal that [consonantal] and [sonorant] occupy the root of the feature tree and hence are not freely manipulable outside of complete assimilation. These features thus behave rather differently from the others; they also stand out in lacking precise phonetic correlates and in general are not very well understood. There is considerably less consensus on the locus of [continuant] in the tree, and various proposals have been made concerning its relation to the Oral Place features. To appreciate this point, compare the relation between Place and features such as voicing or nasality. It is clear that [voiced] and [nasal] spread and dissimilate independent of Place. The typical voicing assimilation rule spreads [voiced] from an obstruent (or sonorant) to another obstruent regardless of the Place specification of the source and the target (e.g., Russian *pros'-it'* 'to ask', *proz'-ba* 'request'; *korob-a* 'bastbox' gen.sg., *korop-ka* dimin.). Similarly, Lyman's Law in Japanese (section 9.9) dissimilates [voice], again independent of Place. Although not nearly as ubiquitous as voicing assimilation, nasality seems to show a similar independence from Place. For example, Chukchee (Kenstowicz 1986a) contrasts nasals and voiceless stops at the labial, dental, and velar points of articulation. In a stop-nasal cluster, [nasal] spreads to the preceding stop, deriving the corresponding nasal regardless of the Place specifications of the source or the target (50a).

(50)	a.	pəne-k	'to grind'	ge-mne-lin	past
		rəpən	'flesh side of hide'	rəmn-ət	pl.
		pəŋəl	'news'	ga-mŋət-len	'having news'
		təm-ək	'to kill'	ga-nmə-len	past
		rətən	'tooth'	rənn-ət	pl.
		təŋe-k	'to grow'	ge-nŋe-lin	past
		plek-ət	'footwear'	te-pleŋ-ŋ-ək	'to make footwear'
	b.	taraŋ-ək	'to build a dwelling'	nə-taraɣ-more	'we built a dwelling'
		enawrəŋ	'to give as a gift'	enawrəɣ-nen	'he gave it'
		taaroŋ-ək	'to request'	ra-taaroɣ-ŋ-ətək	'you pl. will request'

Chukchee shows a limited form of nasal dissimilation as well (50b): [ŋ] denasalizes to [ɣ] when followed by a nasal. Again, the point of articulation of the trigger does not matter. Finally both [nasal] and laryngeal features may delink and be realized elsewhere in the string: recall the shift of voicing and aspiration under Bartolomae's Law in Sanskrit; also, VN(C) strings are often realized as V̂(C) with a shift of nasality (e.g., in French).

The relation between [continuant] and the Place features is much tighter. Whether one can spread or dissimilate independently from the other is considerably less clear. We will begin by reviewing the Halle-Sagey model's position on [continuant] and then examine several alternatives. Recall from section 9.1 that [continuant] stands out in the Halle-Sagey model as a feature that is not bound to any particular Oral articulator. It depends directly from the root of the tree. Nevertheless, in the process of phonetic implementation [continuant] (as well as the root features [consonantal] and [sonorant]) must be integrated with an articulator, which can be understood to execute the stricture features. The relevant articulator is dubbed the major articulator and is indicated by an arrow pointing from the root of the tree. Thus, in the Halle-Sagey representation of [m] in (51), Labial is the major articulator and hence the seat of the consonantal stricture.

(51)

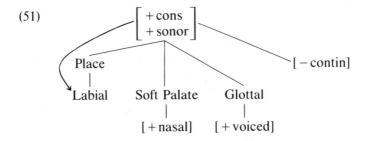

In complex segments with multiple articulators, at least one is singled out as a major articulator. The stricture of minor articulators is claimed to never be contrastive. In the process of phonetic implementation, the integration of the place and stricture features can be represented mechanically as copying or transferring the stricture features to a position under the articulator. Since [continuant] and Place are located at different points in the feature tree, the Halle-Sagey model predicts that they should assimilate independently. Sagey (1986) cites the nasal assimilation paradigm in (52) from Kpelle (based on Welmers 1973) to support this point; here the underlyingly placeless nasal prefix [N-] assimilates the point of articulation of the following consonant and appears as [m] before both the stop [p] and the labiodental fricative [f]. We will return to these data below for another interpretation.

(52) /N-polu/   [mbolu]   'my back'
      /N-tia/   [ndia]   'my taboo'
      /N-kɔɔ/   [ŋgɔɔ]   'my foot'
      /N-fela/   [mvela]   'my wages'
      /N-sua/   [nǰua]   'my nose'

Clements (1987) uses intrusive stop formation in English to argue for a special connection between [continuant] and the Oral Place specification: *prin*[t]*ce, ham*[p]*ster, heal*[t]*th.* In Clements's view, these data show the spreading of the oral closure of a [−continuant] segment onto a following consonant, creating a contour segment (analogous to a contour tone). The intrusive stop has the place and stricture specification of the preceding [−continuant] but the voicing of the following consonant (cf. also *lens* as *len*[d]*z,* for at least some speakers). Given his basic premise that spreading of two features implies a common node, Clements groups [continuant] and Place together under a node dubbed *oral cavity.*

(53)

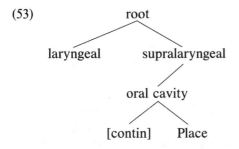

root

laryngeal   supralaryngeal

oral cavity

[contin]   Place

Like the Halle-Sagey model, (53) predicts that [continuant] and Place may spread independently. Evidence for this point is another of Clements's English examples, where the stops [t,d,n] assimilate the precise point of articulation of a following coronal consonant, appearing as interdental before [θ], postalveolar before [š,ž], and retroflex before [r] (Clements 1985a).

(54)

	[t]	[d]	[n]	
___ θ	eighth	hundredth	tenth	[+anter, +distrib]
___ š,ž	each	edge	inch	[−anter, +distrib]
___ r	tree	dream	enrol	[−anter, −distrib]

Clements treats this process as the leftward spread of the coronal articulator and its attendant dependents [distributed] and [anterior], with delinking of the alveolar occlusive's original place of articulation.

(55)

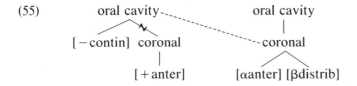

oral cavity ----   oral cavity

[−contin] coronal   ---- coronal

[+anter]   [αanter] [βdistrib]

Padgett (1991) argues for a still tighter connection between [continuant] and Place, with [continuant] as a dependent of Place (56).

(56)

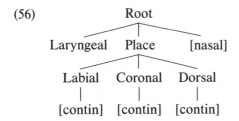

Root

Laryngeal   Place   [nasal]

Labial   Coronal   Dorsal

[contin]   [contin]   [contin]

In contrast to the Halle-Sagey model, (56) integrates [continuant] with the articulator at the outset. It also entails a strong form of double domination in which the same feature, [continuant], is accessible from three different tiers (given that the Labial, Coronal, and Dorsal articulators constitute separate tiers). Most other paths in the feature tree branch; the result is that any given feature can be uniquely placed with respect to the others in the tree. The model in (56) appears to abandon this formal property and thus endows [continuant] with a special status that recapitulates (albeit in a different fashion) the Halle-Sagey arrow. The most novel aspect of (56) is that [continuant] is a dependent of Place. This implies that there cannot be any assimilation of Place without dragging along the continuant specification as well. Like the Halle-Sagey and Clements models, it would be consistent with spreading of [continuant] independent of Place as a terminal feature.

Before we review Padgett's major arguments for this geometry, let us examine his reanalysis of the English and Kpelle paradigms cited by Clements and Sagey to support the independence of Place and [continuant]. With respect to the paradigm in (54), Padgett accepts the critique of Browman and Goldstein (1989) that these cases arguably involve a phonetic process of accommodation rather than a true autosegmental spreading. The basic idea is that speaking requires the precise timing of a variety of phonetic gestures; in connected speech the gestures overlap considerably, leading to two basic outcomes depending on whether the gestures are executed by the same or different articulators. The latter case is represented by the casual speech pronunciation of the phrase *seve*[m]*plus;* here the labial gesture of the [p] does not oust the coronal articulation of the underlying [n]. In fact, the tip of the tongue is raised to articulate an [n] – it is just masked by the overlapping labial gesture arising from the [p]. In case the two gestures are implemented by the same articulator (e.g., the coronals in *ten themes*), the Browman and Goldstein model predicts that alveolar and interdental gestures will blend to some intermediate value through mutual accommodation. As these researchers observe, gesture overlap is empirically distinct from autosegmental spreading in its prediction that the output should be some value intermediate between the two separate segments [n] and [θ]; autosegmental spreading plus delinking implies that the assimilating element takes on the same value as the source. The issue appears to come down to whether in the realization of the [n-θ] sequence of *ten-th* or *ten themes,* the nasal [n] is interdental and hence has the same place as the [θ] or whether the [n] and [θ] mutually assimilate to an intermediate value. But even if the latter is true, one might argue that it merely reflects a case of autosegmental spreading in which there is no delinking of the original Place feature, creating a kind of diphthong that is then "blended" in phonetic implementation.

In sum, the English rule cited by Clements for the oral cavity node might be reinterpreted as a phonetic implementation process; the fact that it applies at the phrasal level, may be affected by rate of speech, and is possibly gradient rather than categorical in nature is consistent with this point. If the distinction between autosegmental spreading (and delinking) and phonetic accommodation can be made more precise, then the data in (54) are not counterexamples to the claim that [continuant] is a dependent of Place. As far as the Kpelle paradigm in (52) is concerned, Padgett points to another discussion of the data by Welmers (1962), the language's original descriptor, in which the nasal assimilated to [v] is transcribed as a labiodental [ɱ]. Like its fricative counterpart [v], the nasal [ɱ] is legitimately characterized as [+continuant] since a labiodental constriction is not sufficient to block oral airflow (and in the production of the nasal most of the air is expelled through the nose in any case).

Padgett's major argument for [continuant] as a Place dependent is its role in explaining the following asymmetry: nasals readily assimilate to a stop but avoid assimilation to a fricative. In the nasal assimilation context a prefricative nasal either (i) fails to assimilate and acquires a default Place specification, (ii) deletes, or (iii) assimilates but induces a hardening of the fricative to a stop or affricate as a repair. Given that [continuant] is a Place dependent, the nasal-fricative sequence has the structure in (57).

(57) a.

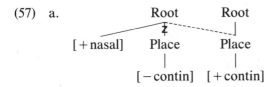

$$[+\text{nasal}]$$

Root   Root

Place   Place

$$[-\text{contin}] \quad [+\text{contin}]$$

Assimilation of Place creates a heavily marked [+nasal, +continuant] nasal fricative. Padgett presumes that nasal fricatives are never phonemic in any language and consequently must be blocked by a strong form of Structure Preservation barring their creation in the lexical phonology; languages may extend this ban into the postlexical phonology as well. Thus, the claim is that so long as the assimilation is lexical, it must be blocked or repaired. Assuming the stop-fricative asymmetry to be true, the implication is that the asymmetry is surprising under feature geometries that do not locate [continuant] under Place; but it follows if [continuant] is a Place dependent, activating the ban on nasal fricatives.

Let us look at a few of Padgett's examples supporting this asymmetry. The nasal of the English negative prefix *iN-* assimilates to the labial stops [p,b] but not to the fricatives [f,v]: *im-possible, im-bue, in-finite, in-valid*. This level 1 assimilation is clearly lexical; assuming Place-dependent [continuant], spread of the Labial articulator is permitted in the case of [p,b]. But assimilating the Place node of [f,v] creates a nasal fricative that will be blocked by the UG ban on such segments. In the prefricative context the nasal acquires the default coronal Place specification it has in such prevocalic cases as *in-articulate* and *in-active*.

Lithuanian contrasts [m] and [n] prevocalically; preconsonantal [n] assimilates the place of a following stop (58a); before fricatives [n] deletes, compensatorily lengthening the preceding vowel, as shown by the allomorphs of the prefix *saN-* (exercise 1.10).

(58) a.   sen-as   ʻold'   pin-a   ʻplaits'
         se[m]-bernis   ʻold fellow'   pin-ti   infin.
                                          pi[ŋ]-kite   imper.

      b.   sa[m]-buris   ʻassembly'
         sa[n]-taka   ʻconfluence'
         sa[ŋ]-kaba   ʻconnection'
         sa:-skambis   ʻharmony'
         sa:-šlavos   ʻsweepings'
         sa:-žine   ʻconscience'

c. tem-o   'darken' past
    tem-ti   infin.
    tem-kite   imper.

d. krims-ti   'to chew'   br[e:]s-ti   'to rot'
    kremt-o   past   brent-o   past

The paradigms in (58c,d) suggest that nasal deletion in the prefricative context
and nasal assimilation are tied to one another. Lithuanian [m] freely stands before
a consonant with no place assimilation and hence no linkage for Place. It contrasts
with [n], which does assimilate for Place. In (58d) [t] assibilates to [s] before the
infinitive suffix; the labial nasal is allowed to stand ([krims-ti]), while the dental
one is not ([brens-ti] → [bre:s-ti]). On Padgett's analysis, place assimilation to
the following fricative is blocked by the ban on nasal fricatives. Lithuanian differs
from English in lacking a rule assigning a default place specification to the nasal
segment. It consequently fails to surface for lack of an articulator, and its skeletal
position assimilates to the Root node of the preceding vowel to create a long
vowel.

Faced with these examples, a defender of the more traditional view of [con-
tinuant] as a Root dependent might pursue an analysis in which the nasal of the
iN- prefix in English and the *saN-* of Lithuanian is a bare nasal segment lacking
any place or stricture features. It would then acquire them from the following
segment by spreading of the Root node or through saturation (one-by-one spreading) as a feature-filling operation. The same UG filter against [+ nasal, + contin-
uant] would then block spread of [continuant] before a fricative but permit it before
a stop. As in Padgett's analysis, Lithuanian would differ from English in lacking
the default assignment of Place to the bare nasal, leading to its ultimate elimination.

While an alternative analysis along these lines is possible for Lithuanian, it will
not extend to Polish, where the stop-fricative asymmetry is displayed by several
nasals in differing contexts, precluding a bare nasal analysis. Nasal assimilation
in Polish arises from three distinct sources: nasal diphthongs, [n], and [m].

(59) a. ząb   [zomp]   'tooth'
          zęby   [zembɨ]   'teeth'
          ręce   [rence]   'hand' dat.
          węgiel   [veŋ'el]   'coal'
          mąż   [mow̃š]   'husband'
          węch   [vew̃x]   'smell'
          rzęsa   [žew̃sa]   'eyelash'

      b. kunszt   [kuw̃št]   'art'
          konflikt   [kow̃flikt]   'conflict'
          on śę ce ńi [ow̃ śew̃ ce ńi] 'he values himself'

      c. klamka   [klamka]   'doorknob'
          tramwaj   [traw̃vay]   'tram'
          tam vala   [taw̃ valow̃]   'they are hanging'
          chamski   [xamski]   'boorish'

The nasal diphthongs (represented by orthographic *ą* and *ę*) surface as mid vowels plus homorganic nasal before a stop and as vowel plus nasalized glide before a fricative (and word-finally). [n] shows a similar distribution but undergoes optional alternation across word boundaries (in fast speech). The labial [m] appears as a glide only when followed by [f] or [v] – an OCP effect of Place merger. The fact that [m] fails to assimilate to a following nonlabial stop [klamka] and fails to turn to a glide before a nonlabial fricative [xamski] supports the idea that nasalization arises only under Place assimilation. In the absence of such assimilation, a pre-fricative nasal is free to stand. In each case, the stop-fricative asymmetry follows if [continuant] is a Place dependent and assimilated along with Place assimilation. While the bare nasal alternative might be reasonably proposed for the nasal diph-thongs, the contrasting [n] and [m] must contain an underlying Place specification that is delinked in the process of nasal Place assimilation. The fact that the stop-fricative asymmetry arises under this Place delinking remains surprising if [continuant] is a Root dependent.

Padgett appeals to Place-dependent [continuant] to explain a curious asymmetry in the well-known Spanish paradigm in (60) that exemplifies another place-stricture coupling.

(60)

	[+contin]				[−contin]	
a.	ca[β]ello	'hair'		d.	[b]ueno	'good'
	la[ð]o	'side'			[d]edo	'finger'
	la[ɣ]o	'lake'			[g]ato	'cat'
b.	cur[β]a	'curve'		e.	ho[mb]ro	'shoulder'
	cal[β]o	'bald'			cua[nd]o	'when'
	pur[ɣ]a	'purge'			e[ŋg]año	'cheat'
	al[ɣ]o	'something'				
	car[ð]o	'plant species'				
	cal[d]o	'broth'				
c.	dis[ɣ]usto	'trouble'				
	a[βð]ika	'he abdicates'				
	a[ðβ]erso	'adverse'				

The fricative series [β,ð,ɣ] occurs after vowels, liquids, and both underlying fricatives such as [s] and the derived [β,ð,ɣ]. The stop series [b,d,g] occurs after pause as well as after a homorganic nasal. The relevant rule applies at the phrasal level and hence is postlexical in nature. There is some question whether the post-vocalic context should be viewed as assimilating [+continuant] from a vowel. For the point to be made here, this will not be crucial. The fact that the stop variant occurs in two distinct contexts (postpausal and after homorganic nasal) suggests that [−continuant] is a default value not determined by context and hence that the process is one of spirantization. The spirantization rule is feature-changing if the trigger is indeed [+continuant] from a preceding vowel because the voiced obstruent series will also have received the default [−continuant] value (given that default values for vowels and consonants are assigned at the same point in the derivation). The interesting problem is the fact that the rule applies after liquids except in one case: when the liquid is the lateral [l] and the stop is the coronal [d]: *cal*[d]*o,* not **cal*[ð]*o.* This fact suggests that homorganicity blocks the spread of continuancy – an inalterability effect (section 8.4). This suspicion is strengthened when we realize that [l] has assimilated the dependent coronal features of the following [d]: according to Harris (1985a), while [l] is normally alveolar and [d] dental, [l] is dental in *cal*[d]*o.* We accordingly assume the rule in (61).

(61)

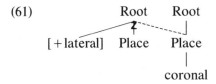

If [continuant] is a dependent of Place, then the [+continuant] [l] must assimilate the [−continuant] of [d] and delink its own [+continuant]. This is not blocked by any marking convention. The crucial point is that since [continuant] is a dependent of Place, the spirantization rule spreading [+continuant] must mention Place as the docking node (62a). We may now activate the condition on linked structures (section 8.4) to block the spread of [continuant] to *ca*[ld]*o* (62b), because the lateral lacks a [voiced] specification.

(62) a.   b.

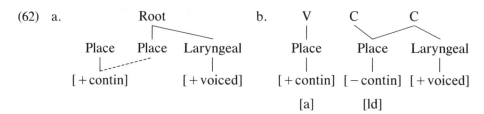

Since [l] only assimilates to [d], no inalterability is invoked in *cal*[β]*o* and so [+continuant] is free to spread from [l] to [b]. Since the rule of Place assimilation (61) does not apply to [r], it remains [+continuant] and hence can trigger spirantization of the following stop. In a model where [continuant] is not a Place dependent, [continuant] docks at a higher node: the Root node (Halle-Sagey) or the oral cavity node (Clements). In either case, whether the segment is Place-linked should not matter for the spread of [continuant] and the *cal*[d]*o* vs. *car*[ð]*o* asymmetry remains mysterious. Padgett's argument is quite intricate and depends on a variety of other assumptions, some controversial. It demonstrates the range of evidence and the delicate considerations that must be brought to bear on the more difficult problems facing feature theory.

  Let us close with several more observations on the stricture features. First, examples such as *a*[βð]*ika* in (60c) suggest that continuancy may spread independently of the place of articulation of the consonant, passing from the labial [β] to the dental [ð]. This follows straightforwardly in the Halle-Sagey and Clements models, where [continuant] and Place are not in a dominance relation. It is also permitted by Padgett's model, where [continuant] is a terminal feature below Place. This conclusion depends on the premise that [−continuant] underlies the

Spanish voiced obstruent series – a point that not all analysts have agreed on. It is therefore significant that in Spanish dialects that neutralize coda nasals to the velar [ŋ], a following obstruent is still realized as a stop: *cua*[ŋd]*o* 'when'. If the stop derives from an underlying spirant through assimilation of [−continuant] from the preceding nasal, then the conclusion that [continuant] spreads independent of Place still holds. Nevertheless, it must be acknowledged that the alleged independence of [continuant] from Place requires further documentation.

Second, in one of the first explicit discussions of feature geometry, Lass (1976) noted the frequency and naturalness of processes replacing oral stops and fricatives such as [t] and [s] with the laryngeal glides [ʔ] and [h], respectively. He saw these reduction processes as elimination of the Oral Place features with retention of the laryngeal specification and expression of the [±continuant] manner features at the larynx. While the original insight that such debuccalization processes involve elimination of the Oral Place specification is generally accepted, most subsequent researchers have rejected the idea that the [±continuant] distinguishing the oral stops versus fricatives is retained and expressed as a [ʔ] vs. [h] opposition. (See Durand 1987 and Iverson 1989 for defense of this view, however.) First, there is little independent evidence that other processes group [ʔ] with the oral stops and [h] with the oral fricatives. Second, while it seems true that fricatives reduce to [h] (instead of to [ʔ]), both Clements (1985a) and McCarthy (1988) suggest that this generalization reflects the phonetic fact that (voiceless) fricatives are produced with an open glottis (allowing the greater airflow required to generate the turbulence of an oral fricative). Rather, the received opinion is that the outcome of a reduced stop as [ʔ] vs. [h] reflects the laryngeal features of the original oral stop as glottalized versus aspirated. In many languages (e.g., English), a stop reducing to [ʔ] goes through the intermediate stage of glottalization: [t] → [tʼ] → [ʔ]. It remains to be seen, however, whether this missing link is always justified.

Third, while most researchers have accepted McCarthy's (1988) idea that [consonantal] forms the root of the feature tree and hence is incapable of spreading outside of complete assimilation, Kaisse (1992) points to some conflicting evidence from glide-hardening processes that operate only when adjacent to a consonantal segment. For example, in Cypriot Greek [y] turns to prevelar [kʼ] after most consonants: [aðerfi+a] → [aðerfya] → *aðerfkʼa* 'brothers', [traɣuðya] → *traɣuθkʼa* 'singing'. This rule cannot be explained away as hardening in the syllable onset in view of forms such as *yerakos* 'falcon' and *ayazin* 'chill wind'. Rather, Kaisse treats the process as autosegmental spreading of the [+consonantal] feature of the preceding consonant. If this is the correct interpretation, it dramatically illustrates spread of a stricture feature independent of Place and contradicts the proposition that [consonantal] forms the root of the feature tree. Unfortunately, the data assembled by Kaisse lack examples of two underlyingly adjacent glides. If the hardening process really pushes the glide across the vocalic-consonantal divide, we predict that a [−consonantal] glide will not trigger the process.

Finally, several researchers have observed that the most convincing cases of inalterability (section 8.4) in which a multiply linked structure blocks application of a rule typically involve changes in stricture features – particularly [continuant].

Selkirk (1991) notes that nasality and laryngeal features are often ignored in cal-culating identity for geminate integrity and inalterability: homorganic nasal+consonant clusters such as [mp] consistently parallel geminate [pp] in blocking the insertion of an epenthetic vowel; Havana liquid assimilation (section 8.6) creates [bp] geminates that differ in voicing; Icelandic preaspiration converts [pp] to [hp], again showing the independence of the laryngeal features from the rest of the geminate. Selkirk develops a "two-root" theory of geminates in which the multiple linking relevant for inalterability occurs lower in the feature tree at the level where [continuant] combines with Place. Geminates such as [pp] and [mm] receive the representations shown in (63). On this view, no inalterability effects are observed with laryngeal or nasal features since they are not multiply linked. Like Padgett's, this model also postulates a strong coupling of stricture with place features. However, in putting [continuant] above Place, it cannot spread the former without dragging along the latter and so must tell a different story for Spanish *a*[βð]*ika*. See Selkirk 1991 for details.

(63)

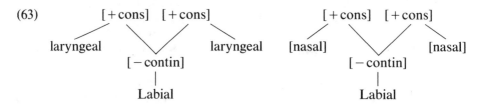

9.6 Nasal

Piggott (1992) discerns two cross-linguistic forms of nasal harmony. In the more prevalent type A, found in such languages as Warao, Malay, and Sundanese, the targets include vowels and normally the laryngeal and oral glides as well as some-times liquids and even fricatives; stops (and normally fricatives and liquids) are opaque. In type B harmony all sonorants are targets and obstruents are trans-parent. This harmony is found in Southern Barasano and Guarani, among others.

(64) type A

Warao | | Malay |
--- | --- | --- | ---
ināw̃āh̃ā | 'summer' | māỹãn | 'stalk'
mēh̃ōkohi | 'shadow' | mãʔãp | 'pardon'
mõãũpu | 'give them | mākan | 'eat'
 | to him' | məlaran | 'forbid'

type B
Southern Barasano

nasal words | | oral words |
--- | --- | --- | ---
māhãɲĩ | 'comer' | ⁿdiro | 'fly'
māsã | 'people' | waᵐba/waba | 'come'
w̃ātĩ | 'demon' | wati | 'going?'

Guarani

tũpã | 'god' | tupa | 'bed'
pĩr̃ĩ | 'to shiver' | piri | 'rush'

Instead of stipulating this difference directly in the [nasal] spread rules, Piggott sees a parametric distinction in the geometry of the feature [nasal]. In the unmarked type A, [nasal] is a dependent of the Soft Palate articulator, while in type B it is a dependent of the SV (Spontaneous Voicing) node. The latter takes up a suggestion of Avery and Rice (1989a,b) to characterize the voicing of sonorants with a special feature distinct from the obstruents' laryngeal-dependent [voiced]. Let us briefly review Piggott's results.

The basic intuition underlying the analysis of type A harmony is that nasality is a dependent feature of the Soft Palate (SP) articulator node. On phonetic grounds it makes sense to identify SP as an articulator because it is one of the independently movable elements of the vocal tract. It differs from other articulators such as Coronal and Dorsal in implementing just a single feature (i.e., [nasal]). Just as the representation of the labial [b] does not require a negative specification for the Coronal articulator, so nonnasal segments need not be specified [−nasal]. Hence, vowels are in general unspecified for SP; they may acquire a SP specification by contextual spreading just as a consonant may acquire a secondary place specification. This implies that in phonetic implementation, the velum is raised unless the segment is marked [+nasal]. Piggott treats [nasal] as a monovalent feature; this makes sense in that [−nasal] seldom seems to spread (see below). However, we encounter a problem in the type A nasal harmony systems in representing an opaque consonant such as [p] in Warao *mõãũpu:* the [p] interrupts the spread of nasality. Piggott proposes the representation in (65) where the opaque segment has a SP specification but no terminal feature.

(65)

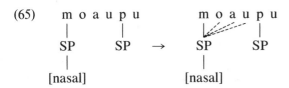

Nasal harmony is then formalized as spreading of the SP node. The undeveloped SP on the [p] blocks nasal harmony by the line-crossing constraint. This solution depends on the spreading taking place at the SP level rather than for the terminal feature [nasal]; to ensure this outcome, Piggott proposes a "maximal application" convention that requires a spreading rule to target the highest node in the feature tree consistent with the desired output. It is unclear whether this convention will induce spread of the bare SP node of the [p] to the following vowel in (65). Obstruents carry an SP specification universally while sonorants may or may not, depending on whether they arrest nasal harmony. The glottal stop in Malay *mãʔãp* has a SP [nasal] specification that spreads to the following vowel, indicating a lowered velum. But since the glottis is closed, it cannot deliver the nasal airflow normally found in [nasal] segments. This segment is thus intensionally [nasal] but extensionally oral.

In type B nasal harmony, obstruent consonants are not barriers to the spread of [nasal]. In many of these languages [nasal] is an autosegment that marks morphemes as a whole. Sonorant consonants as well as vowels are nasal in morphemes containing a [nasal] autosegment and oral in morphemes that lack the autosegment. Typically affixes harmonize as well, creating oral and nasal alternants. The Southern Barasano forms in (66) illustrate these points.

(66) māhāŋī   'comer'   ⁿdiro   'fly'
       māsā   'people'   waᵐba/waba   'come'
       w̄ātī   'demon'   wati   'going?'
       kāmōkā   'rattle'   wesika   'above'
       māhā-mā   'go up'   wa-ᵐba   'come!'
       ĩã-mī   'I saw'   wa-ᵐbi   'I went'
       hūnī-nē   'to hurt'   yi-re   'to say'
       mīnō-ñā   'leaf stream'   ⁿgahe-ya   'another stream'

The glides [w,y] appear as [w̄,ñ] in a nasal span while the liquid [r] alternates with [n]. A similar relation holds between the prenasalized [ᵐb,ⁿd,ᵑg] and the nasals [m,n,ŋ]. Previous researchers have analyzed the latter alternation with the [m,n,ŋ] nasal series as underlying. They derive the prenasalized [ᵐb,ⁿd,ᵑg] segments by a spread of [−nasal] from the following oral vowel to produce a contour segment with an internal [+nasal][−nasal] phase. Piggott rejects this approach. Developing an idea of Anderson (1976a), Piggott sees the nasal consonants in type B systems as arising from underlying [−continuant] sonorants that lack a specification for [nasal]. These sonorant stops appear as the [m,n,ŋ] nasals when associated with the [nasal] autosegment in a nasal span and as the prenasalized [ᵐb,ⁿd,ᵑg] series in an oral span. On this analysis, the nasal portion of the prenasalized consonants is a phonetic epiphenomenon that reflects the attempt of the vocal apparatus to realize spontaneous voicing in the presence of an oral closure: the nasal port opens to maintain the airflow needed to keep the vocal folds vibrating. Thus, the claim is that in the type B languages the [ᵐb,ⁿd,ᵑg]≈[m,n,ŋ] series are underlying nonnasal sonorants that are [−continuant]. They acquire a [nasal] specification from the context; otherwise, they are phonologically oral. The nasal phase of the [ᵐb,ⁿd,ᵑg] series is a matter of phonetic implementation. This treatment has the advantage of nullifying the major argument that [−nasal] can spread and takes feature theory a step closer to general monovalency.

In order to characterize the fact that nasal harmony targets all sonorants and skips over (voiceless) obstruents, Piggott treats [nasal] as a Spontaneous Voicing (SV) dependent in the type B systems. By definition, sonorants have a SV specification while (voiceless) obstruents lack one. The [nasal] autosegment thus targets SV nodes and consequently steps over obstruents that lack a SV specification. The intended analysis of Southern Barasano *w̄ātī* is sketched in (67).

(67)

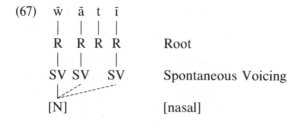

This analysis thus introduces a certain indeterminancy into the feature geometry: [nasal] can be a dependent of either the Soft Palate or the Spontaneous Voicing node. To maximize the proposal's learnability, Piggott posits SP as the default location. Positive evidence in the form of a noncontrastive complementary distribution between a [^{m}b,^{n}d,$^\eta$g] and a [m,n,ŋ] series is required to shift [nasal] to a SV dependency.

9.7 Laryngeal Features

The laryngeal features include aspiration, glottalization, and various types of voicing. Recall that Halle and Stevens (1971) define these features in terms of two phonetic parameters: glottal width and glottal tension. Aspirated segments are [+ spread gl], glottalized ones are [+ constricted gl]. These gestures are physically incompatible, and we thus correctly predict the absence of phonological segments that combine aspiration and glottalization (on the assumption that phonological features must be phonetically grounded). Phonologically there is a significant asymmetry between the two poles of the [constr gl] and [spread gl] features, however. Few if any rules and constraints single out [− constr gl] and [− spread gl] segments. Rather, phonological generalizations are almost always defined over the positive values of these features. This asymmetry has prompted many phonologists to treat [constr gl] and [spread gl] as monovalent features. A brief summary of the evidence follows.

Rules of neutralization typically replace [p^h] and [p'] with [p] rather than the inverse (e.g., Klamath, exercise 1.14). Languages may impose restrictions such as one aspirated (Sanskrit) or one glottalized (Yucatec Mayan) segment per stem. The inverse (i.e., one plain segment per stem) is not found. [+ spread gl] and [+ constr gl] may delink from one position and surface elsewhere (e.g. Grassmann's Law in Sanskrit). Once again, [− spread gl] and [− constr gl] fail to work in the same way. These asymmetries are explained if aspiration and glottalization are monovalent; the negative values do not exist and hence cannot figure in phonological rules and constraints. On this view, processes of neutralization are formulated to delink the monovalent [spread gl] or [constr gl] feature (or its dominating Laryngeal node). Segments without a laryngeal specification are phonetically implemented with an intermediate degree of glottal width.

A number of researchers have proposed generalizing laryngeal monovalency to voicing as well. This is prima facie plausible because [+ voiced] in obstruents parallels [+ constr gl] and [+ spread gl] in several respects. Just as phonemic inventories select [p] before they select [p^h] or [p'], so they also prefer [p] to [b]. In positions of neutralization (e.g., syllable-final, word-final), obstruents devoice. Final voicing is rarely found. Although not as prevalent, autosegmentalization of [voiced] is also possible. For example, Lyman's Law in Japanese (Itô and Mester 1986, Mester and Itô 1989) bars more than one voiced obstruent per stem (e.g., *kita* 'north', but **gida*); the constraint is also actively enforced by suppressing a process (*rendaku*) that voices the initial obstruent in the second member of a compound structure (e.g., [ori 'fold' + kami 'paper'] → *origami* 'origami paper', but [kita 'north' + kaze 'wind'] → *kitakaze* 'north wind', not **kitagaze*). Despite these parallels, however, monovalent [voiced] is a more controversial proposal simply because of the many rules and constraints in the phonological literature that have been defined over [– voiced]. They must be reinterpreted if this proposal is correct. Let us survey a few cases and the reanalyses that have been offered.

Consider first cases of voicing assimilation such as the one found in the English inflectional affixes. On the strength of the [-ɨz] alternant in *bush-es*, the derivation of the voiceless alternant in *cat*-[s] appears to involve spread of [– voiced] after deletion of the vowel. Mester and Itô (1989) propose to reinterpret this process as the by-product of a UG phonotactic constraint on syllabification – specifically, a requirement that tautosyllabic obstruent clusters agree in voicing. Thus, in order to syllabify the cluster in *ca*[t + z], the [z] deletes its [voiced]. This idea might be expressed in terms of a more general theory of prosodic licensing (see Goldsmith 1990) in which syllabic constituents such as the onset or coda are annotated with one occurrence of [voiced], which is interpreted as dominating all dependents. Sonorants (e.g., *tray, play*) would then have to pick up their voicing specification by default rules (assuming that the voicing of a sonorant such as [r] and that of an obstruent such as [d] are the same feature). If correct, this interpretation implies that the devoiced plural affix in *cat*-[s] is tautosyllabic with the preceding consonant.

Of course, in many languages voicing assimilation crosses syllable junctures. Where earlier analyses see a spread of [αvoiced], the monovalent model can only treat [+ voiced] in this fashion. Apparent assimilation of [– voiced] must be reanalyzed as simple delinking of the underlying [voiced] specification. Building on earlier work by Mascaró (1987), Lombardi (1991) develops a monovalent analysis that attempts to account for some subtle differences in the behavior of voicing in clusters. Her results can be summarized as follows. The German paradigm in (68) is significant in that it shows that there can be neutralization in a cluster without spread of [voiced]. Given monovalent [voiced], we predict the absence of languages that would voice obstruents in exactly the contexts where German devoices them (e.g., a paradigm such as *la*[s]-*en, la*[z], *la*[z]-*lich*).

(68)   lö[z]en   'loosen'
       lo[s]   'loose'
       lö[sb]ar   'solvable'
       lö[sl]ich   'soluble'
       lö[st]   'dissolves'

This alternation has generally been treated as delinking of [voiced] from the coda. Lombardi argues, however, that this formulation fails to extend to cases such as *Fein*[t] from *Feind* 'enemy'. There is some reason to believe that the underlying final [d] occupies the syllable appendix. A rule delinking [voiced] from the coda would bypass this case. In view of this point as well as some doubts about the legitimacy of the notion "coda," Lombardi turns the alternation on its head. Instead of saying where [voiced] is barred, the grammar states where it is permitted. In all other cases [voiced] is delinked from an obstruent. This "positive" condition can be expressed as (69); it licenses [voiced] when followed by a tautosyllabic sonorant.

(69)

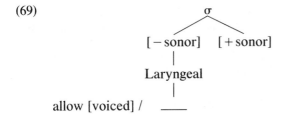

allow [voiced] / _____

Unless the language permits reversed sonority clusters in the coda, (69) amounts to saying that a voiced obstruent is allowed to stand in the syllable onset before a sonorant but not elsewhere. It thus devoices the relevant obstruents in (68) as well as in the appendix in *Fein*[t]. On the other hand, the [b]'s in *Baum* 'tree' and *Blatt* 'leaf' are allowed to stand.

Lombardi thus expresses the devoicing as a constraint rather than a rule. One motivation for doing so appears to be that it functions as a "soft" universal – a configuration of data that is found in many languages. The intuition is that such recurrent but not universal phonotactics have a different status from more arbitrary rules that must be learned. One might propose that (69) functions as a UG parameter that a given language may or may not choose to impose. German selects this option while English does not (at least at the word level). In other respects, however, (69) behaves much like a rule. In particular, it must be imposed at a specific point in the derivation, and there are options that must be selected regarding the fate of the unlicensed laryngeal feature: it may delete or relink at some adjacent position (e.g., the aspiration throwback of Grassmann's Law). On the other hand, if we interpret (69) as an active process, then it is a special kind of rule in which the structural change operates over the complement of the contexts defined in the rule itself.

The Dutch data in (70) differ minimally from the German data in combining neutralization in the coda with voicing assimilation. Under binary voicing, the alternation can be treated as a single process spreading [±voiced] leftward in obstruent clusters with delinking of the original [±voiced] specification. The privative theory breaks the process down into two steps: delinking of [voiced] from the coda consonant (perhaps reflecting the imposition of constraint (69)) and spread of [voiced] from a following obstruent to the laryngeally unspecified first consonant in the cluster (70b).

(70) a. hiu[z]en   'houses'   a[s]en   'ashes'
          hiu[s]   'house'   a[s]   'ash'
          hui[sk]ammer   'living room'   a[z]bak   'ashtray'
          hui[zb]aas   'landlord'

  b. [−sonor]   [−sonor]
      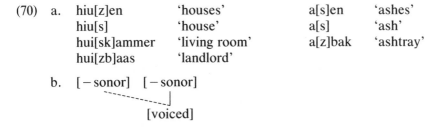
              [voiced]

For the underlying [zb] cluster of *huiz + baas* 'landlord', two derivations are possible: one delinks [voiced] from [z] followed by the spread of [voiced] from the

following onset [b]. An alternative analysis first merges the two [voiced] specifications and then requires the resultant multiply linked [voiced] to escape the
constraint in (69) by appeal to inalterability or perhaps by saying that [voiced] is
licensed via the following onset. Lombardi develops an argument for the latter
position on the basis of the past tense inflection in Dutch. In either case, two
rules/constraints are required that mimic the spread-plus-delinking operations that
are combined in the traditional analysis that assimilates [±voiced].

Ukrainian differs minimally from Dutch and German. Like Dutch, it spreads
[voiced] from a following obstruent (71a). However, it differs in not suppressing
[voiced] from the syllable coda: word-final (71b) as well as preconsonantal (71c)
voiced obstruents remain. In Lombardi's terms, Ukrainian follows English in
failing to impose constraint (69).

(71)   a.   pros'ity   'to request'
            proz'-ba   'a request'
            molot'   'to mill'
            molod'-ba   'milling'

       b.   bereg   'shore'
            viz   'cart'
            golub   'pigeon'

       c.   rid-ko   'rare'
            xobty   'trunk' gen.sg.
            vez-ty   'to drive'

Once again, the monovalent model predicts the absence of languages that would
reverse the Ukrainian situation by spreading [−voiced] but not [+voiced] and
thus realize [rid+ko] as *rit-ko* but [pros'-ba] as *pros'-ba*. The fact that such cases
are unattested makes monovalent [voiced] an attractive hypothesis.

Finally, there are languages such as Yiddish that follow Dutch in showing assimilation of voicing in obstruent clusters (72a) but follow Ukrainian in failing to
neutralize voicing word-finally (72b). Under the licensing model where voicing
assimilation reflects (69), we must say that Yiddish follows German in imposing
this constraint. However, word-final [voiced] in obstruents must then be licensed
by another statement. This situation is reminiscent of syllable phonotactics, where
word-final clusters are often more complex than word-medial ones. How to state
this connection precisely requires further research.

(72)   a.   bak   'cheek'   zis   'sweet'
            bagbeyn   'cheekbone'   zizvarg   'candy'

       b.   red   'I speak'   shrayb   'write'
            ret-st   'you speak'   shrayp-st   'you write'

The table in (73) summarizes the typology of [voiced] in clusters that emerges
from this discussion.

(73) Constraint (69) spreading (70b) final exception

+	−	−	German
+	+	−	Dutch, Polish, Catalan
+	+	+	Yiddish, Hungarian, Romanian
−	+	−	Ukrainian
−	−	−	English

Let us close with a few additional observations on the privative voicing theory. First, sonorant consonants are typically voiced. However, voicing in sonorants tends to pattern differently from voicing in obstruents. As we have seen, the latter triggers and undergoes assimilation and neutralization while the former typically does not. This asymmetry might suggest that voicing in sonorants and obstruents reflects two different phonological features. Alternatively, it may reflect a difference between the presence and the absence of [voiced] as a function of underspecification: obstruents are underlyingly specified as [voiced] but sonorants are unspecified until a relatively late point in the derivation. The Polish [o] → [u] rule (section 2.7) is problematic for either view. Recall that this rule raises [o] before word-final voiced obstruents as well as nonnasal sonorants: underlying [voz], [nos], [dzvon], and [bor] are realized as *vus* 'cart', *nos* 'nose', *dzvon* 'bell', and *bur* 'forest'. The specification [+ voiced, − nasal] subsumes exactly the class of conditioning consonants – but only if voicing in obstruents and sonorants is expressed by the same feature. Furthermore, this process must follow default [voiced] assignment to sonorants and precede final devoicing; but the latter fails to affect sonorants, a difference that must evidently be built into the rule.

Second, when sonorants change to obstruents, they typically appear as voiced rather than voiceless (e.g., hardening of glides). This also argues for identifying the [voiced] feature across both classes. Third, a number of languages are traditionally described as contrasting voiced and voiceless sonorants. Defenders of monovalent [voiced] have argued that when these cases are examined more closely, there is evidence that voiceless sonorants are really underlying aspirates and hence can be represented with [+ spread gl] rather than [− voiced].

Fourth, recall that Halle and Stevens (1971) establish a formal connection between voicing and tonal register features in order to capture the generalization that voiced consonants typically induce a lowering of pitch while voiceless ones are associated with a raised pitch. Specifically, [stiff vf] realizes voicelessness in obstruents and raised pitch in vowels while [slack vf] leads to lowering of pitch and voicing of obstruents. The tonogenesis found in many Asian languages receives a natural explanation in these terms (e.g., Songjiang, section 7.8). A voicing contrast in the syllable onset is associated with a tonal register difference in the following syllabic nucleus: voiceless (i.e., [+ stiff vf]) consonants with high-toned (i.e., [+ stiff vf]) vowels and voiced (i.e., [+ slack vf]) consonants with low-toned (i.e., [+ slack vf]) vowels. When the voicing contrast in the onset is neutralized, the associated tonal difference becomes phonemic.

If this idea is correct, we expect the influence to go in the opposite direction as well: a tonal difference affecting consonant voicing. Noyer (1991) interprets Verner's Law in these terms. Verner's Law explains apparent "exceptions" to Grimm's First Law whereby PIE voiceless stops **p, *t, *k* are reflected as Germanic voiceless fricatives $*f$, $*\theta$, $*x > h$. Verner noted that the latter relation holds initially as well as after a vowel that was stressed in PIE (74a). But after an unstressed PIE vowel (74b), the PIE voiceless stops appear as voiced fricatives in Germanic – a process that also affected PIE $*s$.

(74)

	PIE	Germanic	Gothic	Old Saxon	Greek	
a.	bhrá:ter	bró:θar	broθar	bro:θer	phrá:ter	'brother'
	dékm	téxun	taihun	tehan	déka	'ten'
	mú:s-	mu:s(i)-			mû:s	'mouse'
b.	pǝtér	faðár	faðar	fader	paté:r	'father'
	septṃ́	seβúm	siβun	sibun	hɛptá	'seven'
	ous-én	auzán		oora　Lith. ausìs		'ear'

c.

$$V \qquad C$$
$$\underset{\text{[slack vf]}}{\lfloor} \text{- - - - - - - - -} \underset{\text{[+contin]}}{\rceil}$$

Developing a suggestion of Morris Halle, Noyer (1991) sees the influence of stress in terms of the feature [stiff vf]. Specifically, suppose that PIE accented vowels were associated with [+stiff vf] and unaccented vowels with [+slack vf]. The voicing of Verner's Law can be formalized as a spread of [+slack vf] to a following continuant (74c) – a feature-filling operation given Noyer's analysis of the Germanic obstruent system. If the two-way connection between tone and consonantal voicing implied by Halle and Stevens's [stiff vf] and [slack vf] continues to hold up, then a serious challenge is posed for the monovalent theory of voicing. Finally, there are isolated cases such as Canadian Raising (section 3.2) that must be dealt with as well.

9.8 Contour Segments

We saw in chapter 7 that a major impetus to the development of autosegmental phonology was the decomposition of rising and falling tones into ordered sequences of [±hi] associated to a single vocalic segment. Such contour tones often arise from the combination of underlying simple tones. For example, Margi's rising tone in monosyllabic verbs realizes the LH melody. They also behave like LH and HL sequences as far as their effects on adjacent tones are concerned. Prenasalized stops and affricates are the two most common types of segments from traditional phonology for which a similar segment-internal sequencing of features has been proposed (Ewen 1982). The motivations for this decomposition are much the same as in the tonal case. In many Bantu languages a prenasalized [ⁿd] is easily demonstrated to arise from the combination of a nasal prefix plus a following coronal stop: [n] + [d] → [ⁿd]. Similarly, languages with [tˢ] and [č] affricates typically have [t], [s], and [š] as independent phonemes, justifying the decomposition: [t] + [s] → [tˢ] and [t] + [š] → [č]. However, just as contour tones may be associated with a single tone-bearing unit, so there is good reason to treat the prenasalized stops and affricates as single segments. As the Bantu languages demonstrate, homorganic NC sequences as well as affricates may arise in systems that otherwise lack any consonant clustering. Also, some languages contrast affricates and the corresponding stop-fricative sequences: for example, Polish *czy* 'whether' [č] vs. *trzy* 'three' [tš]. Given these parallels, it seems natural to extend the contour tone analogy and thus represent the prenasalized stop [ⁿd] and the affricate [tˢ] as a sequence of features associated with a single Root node.

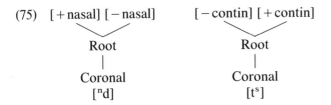

(75)   [+ nasal] [− nasal]   [− contin] [+ contin]

       Root   Root

     Coronal   Coronal

      [ⁿd]   [tˢ]

Further research has uncovered a number of problems with this line of thought; it suggests that the original analogy to contour tones was probably drawn too hastily. Let us survey some of the literature that has developed around these contour segments.

Sagey (1986) introduced a terminological distinction between *complex* segments such as the labiovelar [kp] of many West African languages and the *contour* segments (affricates and prenasalized stops). The labial and velar components of the former are unordered phonologically, while the [±continuant] and [±nasal] components of the latter are claimed to appear in a particular sequence. This difference is supposed to reflect a distinction in the formal status of the two types of features. The articulators can be combined in producing a single sound because they involve separate pieces of articulatory hardware. But the velum cannot be simultaneously raised and lowered and so the [+nasal] [−nasal] phases of a prenasalized stop must be sequenced. Also, if we accept the Halle-Sagey constraint that the major articulator of a segment must execute all its stricture features, then the affricate's [−continuant] and [+continuant] components cannot be implemented simultaneously – they involve the physically incompatible actions of narrowing and widening of the vocal tract.

Given the model's predilection to see a deep connection between the feature geometry and phonetic articulation, it was natural to carry the distinction between complex and contour segments over into the phonology. As phonological support for this move, Sagey pointed to rules of nasal assimilation that realize a nasal as the doubly articulated [mŋ] in front of [kp]; this process indicates that the Labial and Dorsal articulators can spread equally and independently from inside the same segment. On the other hand, the internal sequencing of the affricates and prenasalized stops was reflected in rules that see only one face of the contour segment. A rule whose structural description involves material to the left of a [tˢ] affricate would see the [−continuant] side and hence should group [tˢ] with stops such as [t]; a rule looking at the right face of an affricate would see [+continuant] and thus should group [tˢ] with [s]. To support this implication, Sagey drew attention to a rule of Zoque that voices postnasal stops and affricates but not fricatives (76a).

(76) a. [min-pa]   →   minba   'he comes'
            [pʌn-čʌki] →   pʌnȷ̌ʌki 'figure of a man'
            [winsaʔu]   →   winsaʔu 'he received'

b.

[nasal] [voiced] [−contin]

c.

     [−contin] [+contin] [−contin] [+contin]

       stop   fricative   affricate

The rule can be expressed as spreading [voiced] from a nasal to a following [−continuant] (76b). Given that an affricate starts with a [−continuant] specification, the rule will apply to a stop and an affricate but not to a fricative (76c). The distribution of the English plural allomorphs represents a rule sensitive to the right side of an affricate: [-ɨz] becomes [-z] (and then [-s] by voicing assimilation) unless deletion would create successive [+continuant] segments sharing the Coronal articulator. Deletion is thus possible in *cab*-[z], *cuff*-[s], and *cat*-[s] but not in *buss*-[ɨz] and *brush*-[ɨz]. The fact that deletion is blocked after the coronal affricates [č] and [ǰ] now makes sense: they terminate in [+continuant] and hence would give rise to successive [+continuant] specifications: *judg*-[ɨz], *church*-[ɨz].

Hualde (1987) discovered rules in Basque that appear to refer to the opposite edge of the affricate and thus call Sagey's interpretation into question. For example, one deletes a stop before another stop (77a).

(77) a. /bat paratu/   → ba paratu   'put one'
           /bat+naka/   → banaka   'one by one'
           /guk+piztu/ → gu-piztu   'we light'

      b. /hari[tˢ]-ki/ → hari[s]-ki   'oak wood'
           /ho[tˢ] bat/ → ho[s] bat   'a cold'

          /hi[tˢ] + tegi/ → hi[s]tegi   'dictionary'

If formulated as the deletion of the first of two successive [−continuant] segments, the [−continuant] [+continuant] components of the [tˢ] affricate should remain unaffected: the dissimilating [−continuant] specifications in a [tˢk] cluster are separated by the [+continuant] forming the release of the affricate. In fact, this prediction is wrong: the [tˢ] affricate also reduces by a loss of its plosive component (77b). Hualde concludes that the occlusive portion of the affricate and of the following stop must be able to see each other across the [+continuant] in order to dissimilate. He proposes a parameter to determine whether an affricate groups with a stop or a fricative in the interpretation of a given rule. The Basque paradigm in (77) thus seriously challenges the analogy of affricates with contour tones.

Lombardi (1990) tries to reconcile the Basque data with the edge facts discussed by Sagey. She notes that affricates differ from contour tones in that the order of the [−continuant] and [+continuant] components is fixed: the [−continuant] closure always precedes the [+continuant] release. Her hypothesis is that the affricate's pieces are unordered phonologically; the stop-fricative sequencing is imposed at the level of phonetic implementation (78).

(78)
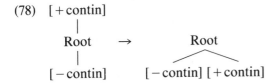

Thus, as far as the phonology is concerned, an affricate should behave like Sagey's multiply articulated [kp] segments. Both the [+continuant] and [−continuant] pieces are accessible from either side. This requires putting [−continuant] and [+continuant] on different tiers so that they can see past one another just like the articulators comprising the labiovelar [kp]. In effect, Lombardi denies Sagey's distinction between contour and complex segments, except possibly at the level of phonetics.

Since the [+continuant] and [−continuant] components are unordered in Lombardi's conception of the affricate, "anti-edge" rules such as the Basque occlusive simplification are no longer a problem. The rule is simply formulated to delete a [−continuant] specification when the following segment also is [−continuant]. It is understood to remove the stricture feature of a single stop, leading to its eventual demise; when it is applied to the affricate [tˢ], the [−continuant] occlusion is also removed but the [+continuant] portion remains and appears as the fricative [s] (79).

(79)

[+contin]			[+contin]	
|			|	
Root	Root	→	Root	Root
|	|			|
[−contin]	[−contin]		[−contin]	
[tˢ]	[k]		[s]	[k]

Zoque's same-side postnasal voicing can be defined over [−continuant] and will thus apply to both the stop and the affricate. Similarly, the basic [-ɨz] allomorph of the English plural converts to [-z] so long as successive [+continuant] specifications are not created on adjacent Root nodes. Since the affricate [č] contains a [+continuant] component, it blocks generation of the [-z] allomorph in *church*-[ɨz].

Lombardi's unordered representation predicts that phonological processes sensitive to one value for [continuant] will always pick out the affricate as well. Stated differently, it is incompatible with rules that single out stops to the exclusion of affricates and fricatives or with rules that single out fricatives to the exclusion of affricates and stops. Since it contains both a [+continuant] and a [−continuant] component, an affricate should elicit or undergo any rule that refers to either value of [continuant]. Lombardi (1990) disposes of several potential counterexamples by arguing that they are phonetic processes applying after the [−continuant] [+continuant] pieces have been sequenced.

Subsequent research has uncovered other possible counterexamples jeopardizing the basic premise of Lombardi's theory. For example, Rubach (1992a) points to several rules of Polish that are activated by fricatives but not by affricates or stops. One spreads [+anterior] from the fricative [s] to preceding obstruents, converting [š] to [s] and the affricates [č] and [tˢ] (= [ć] in Rubach's transcriptions) to [tˢ] (= Rubach's [c]). But the corresponding [+anterior] affricate [tˢ] does not share its [+anterior] feature with a preceding consonant.

(80) [š+s] → [s+s]   towarzysz [tovažiš]   towarzys+k+i [tovažiš-s-k-i]
                         'companion'   adj.
      [č+s] → [c+s]   partacz [partač]   partac-ki [partatˢ-s-k-i]
                         'bungler'
      [ć+s] → [c+s]   Noteć [noteć]   notec-k-i [notetˢ-s-k-i]
                         name   adj.
      [š+c] → [š+c]   głuszec [gwušec]   głuszc-a [gwušc-a]
                         'wood grouse'   gen.sg.
      [ć+c] → [ć+c]   sztuciec [štućuc]   sztućc-a [štućc-a]
                         'cutlery'   gen.sg.

Steriade (1989) also mentions several cases that single out fricatives from affricates and stops. For example, in Piro fricative clusters truncate their first element: [xs] → [s]. But affricate-fricative and fricative-affricate sequences remain unaltered: [xtˢ] and [tˢx]. In Lombardi's model, the Piro rule would have to be expressed as the deletion of the first of two [+continuant] obstruents so long as the second is not also associated with a Root node linked to [−continuant] – an awkward condition. A similar complication arises in delimiting the context of the Polish rule operative in (80). Both Rubach and Steriade conclude that the traditional intuition seeing affricates as the combination of a stop plus a fricative is incorrect.

Each researcher proposes that affricates are really a species of stops. Basing himself primarily on their behavior in Polish, Rubach treats affricates as [strident] stops, resuscitating the earlier interpretation of *SPE* and of Jakobson, Fant, and Halle (1951). The affricate develops a [+continuant] release as a matter of phonetic implementation. On this view, fricatives are distinguished from stops and affricates simply by being [+continuant]. The Polish paradigm (80) is no longer problematic. Rubach's model implies that rules will group affricates and fricatives together only to the extent that both are strident. This correctly encompasses many cases of sibilant harmony (e.g., Tahltan, section 9.11) and also plugs a hole in the English plural example: the [-ɨz] allomorph truncates to [-z] after the interdental fricative [θ]: *bath-s*. Given that [θ] lacks the [strident] feature found in [s], [š], and the affricates [č] and [ǰ], the rule can be expressed as truncating [-ɨz] to [-z] so long as successive strident segments are not created. But while the strident stop interpretation can deal successfully with most of the cases in the affricate literature, it still runs afoul of the Basque paradigm in (77) where [t] drops before a stop while [tˢ] simplifies to [s]. These two processes would have to be treated as separate rules.

Steriade (1989, 1991a,b) attempts to reconcile the conflicting data surrounding the affricate in a different way. Like Lombardi and Rubach, she rejects the contour tone analogy. Like Rubach, she treats the affricate as an underlying stop. However, she agrees with Lombardi that it has a [+continuant] component as well. The major innovation is the idea that stops and affricates are subtypes of a general category "plosive" that normally comprehends two positions: a closure followed by a release. These positions are characterized in terms of three degrees of consonantal stricture or aperture (81a): an occlusion A_0, a fricative A_f, and an approximant A_{max}.

(81) a. A_0 $= [-\text{contin}]$
A_f $= [+\text{contin}, -\text{sonor}]$
$A_{max} = [+\text{contin}, +\text{sonor}]$

b.

$A_0 A_{max}$	$A_0 A_f$	A_f	A_{max}	A_0
stop	affricate	fricative	approximant	unreleased stop
[t]	[tˢ]	[s]	[l]	[t⁰]

A released stop consists of a closure A_0 followed by a maximally open release A_{max} – the stricture that marks an approximant. The affricate also starts with an A_0 closure phase but has the A_f release properties that characterize a fricative. On this view, affricates parallel stops in two respects: they each have two phases, and they each have a closure component. They differ in their release properties – and it is precisely here that affricates can be expected to parallel fricatives.

Let us briefly consider how some of the preceding data sets would be formalized under Steriade's proposal. Zoque postnasal voicing spreads a nasal's [voiced] to a following consonant possessing an A_0 position. The English plural [-ɨz] simplifies to [-z] unless it results in adjacent A_f positions with an equivalent degree of turbulence. Piro only deletes the A_0 of an affricate if its release A_f is homorganic with a following A_f. The resultant [ss] then simplifies to [s]. The Basque case is more subtle. The A_0 closures of two successive plosives must be visible to one another across the release. Although this is not spelled out in detail, we presume that the premise that affricates are a species of stop entails that the affricate's A_0 closure phase is singled out as fundamental, a stricture analogue of the Halle-Sagey major versus minor articulator distinction.

Steriade sees the plosive's closure and release positions as seating different features. The release position is a natural docking site for aspiration and glottalization and perhaps secondary place specifications such as labialization and palatalization. The ubiquitous processes of deglottalization and deaspiration in preconsonantal position now begin to make sense. This is also the position in which stops are typically unreleased. The processes can be formalized as the elimination of the A_{max} release phase, unseating the laryngeal features. Latin's delabialization of coda [kʷ] might also be described in these terms.

Since fricatives and approximants have only a single aperture position, the model predicts various plosive-continuant asymmetries. Steriade (1991a,b) explores several. The laryngeal features [spread gl] and [constr gl] may be realized on either the closure or the release position as preaspiration/glottalization versus postaspiration/glottalization. Continuants offer just one attachment site and so should lack this positional contrast. In support of this distinction, Steriade (1991a) cites Hockett's (1955) inventory of Mazateco onset clusters: fricatives, as well as nasals, stops, and affricates, can be postaspirated; but only stops, affricates, and nasals can be preaspirated.

(82) <u>postaspirated</u>

bh	th	ch	čh	çh	kh
mh	nh				
		sh	šh		

<u>preaspirated</u>

hb	ht	hc	hč	hç	hk
hm	hn		hñ		

Docking of [nasal] offers another rich source of plosive-continuant disparities bearing on the model. In her survey of the descriptive literature, Steriade derives the generalization that while stops readily support pre- and postnasalization, fricatives and approximants in general do not (recalling Padgett's constraint against nasal fricatives, section 9.5). This asymmetry follows if (i) plosives allow two association sites for nasality while fricatives allow just one and (ii) we exclude the representations in (83) – either by a formal ban on multi-attachment of the same feature within a single segment or by postulating that [nasal] is a monovalent feature.

(83) [+nasal] [−nasal]   [+nasal] [−nasal]

A_f A_{max}

We are then left with the attachment options in (84).

(84)

A_0 A_{max}	A_0 A_{max}	A_0 A_{max}	A_0 A_{max}
N	N	N	
[^{n}d]	[d^n]	[n]	[d]
A_f	A_f		
N			
[z̃]	[z]		

Steriade (1991b) finds the stop-continuant asymmetry in rules spreading nasality from a consonant as well as from a vowel. We will examine one of each type.

The Sudanic language Zande illustrates the first. What Tucker and Hackett (1959) phonemicize as [nz] is realized as a nasalization of the fricative that spills over into the following vowel: underlying /binza/ 'doctor' surfaces as [bĩžã]. But with prenasalized stops as in *mbeda* 'to approach', the following [e] vowel remains oral. The stop-continuant contrast is also reflected in the operation of the so-called Ganda Law, a process that realizes NC clusters as N when followed by a nasal. For example, the prenasalized [mb] in *mbeda* 'to approach' is replaced by [m] in the reduplicated *membedi* 'close'; the underlying [mb] surfaces in the fully reduplicated alternant *mbedimbedi*. Steriade formulates the Ganda Law as (85).

(85) A_0 A_{max} V   A

       |

   [+nasal]   [+nasal]

Spreading [nasal] to the A_{max} release phase of the [mb] derives the fully nasal plosive [m]. The rule is also activated by [nz]: underlying [N-genze] 'snail' surfaces as [ŋenze]. But Tucker and Hackett state that the prenasalized fricatives [nz] and [nv] fail to undergo the rule: there is no Ganda Law effect in *nzunzu* 'correctly' and *nvunvu* 'dusk'. As Steriade explains, if what Tucker and Hackett transcribe as [nz] is realized as [ž], then it can be expected to show no effect of the Ganda Law since it is already nasalized.

In other languages prenasalized fricatives such as [nz] have a demonstrably oral section and so another analysis is required. Steriade suggests a nasal affricate: the closure A_0 seats the [nasal] while the underlying fricative surfaces as a release feature.

(86) A_0 A_f

      |

   [+nasal]

This analysis is supported by fact that languages that contrast stops and affricates typically neutralize the distinction under prenasalization: for example, in Venda [N+bv] → [mbv] and [N+v] → [mbv]. The [b] of these transcriptions is assumed to be a phonetic transitional element reflecting imprecision in the synchronization of the velum with the change in aperture internal to the plosive. Given the premises of her model, Steriade must treat this as a matter of phonetic implementation: these underlying clusters are realized on a single Root node; consequently, no more than two aperture positions are available; [nasal] is phonologically monovalent.

Processes spreading nasality from a vowel to adjacent consonants also treat plosives and continuants differently. For example, in Auca (Saint and Pike 1962) voiced stops are prenasalized after a nasal vowel while the approximant [w] and the flap [r] (optionally derived from an underlying [d]) are completely nasalized as [w̃] and what Saint and Pike transcribe as [ñ], respectively. Prenasalized voiceless stops are also optionally voiced.

(87) a. /õõgae/   → õõ^{n}gae   'I am going to hunt'
          /wī bika/   → wī^{m}bika   'he does not drink'
          /ītapa/   → ī^{n}tapa, ī^{n}dapa   'it was'
          /kõw̃i/   → kõw̃i   'always'
          /biwī-dia/ → biwī-^{n}dia, biwī-ñia 'younger brother'

  b.

    μ
    |
    A   A
    $\lfloor$-----
    [nasal]

Steriade suggests the rule in (87b) spreading nasality from a vowel (indicated by the mora) to the following A position. Since a continuant by assumption has just one aperture position, it will be fully nasalized; the stop realizes [nasal] on its closure phase, creating the prenasalized consonant. Saint and Pike also note that the contrast between [n] and [d] is preserved under prenasalization as the nasal flap [ñ] vs. [n]. Since nasals are plosives, the distinction can be represented as one versus two aperture positions.

(88) A_{max} A_0 A_{max}
        | $\diagdown\diagup$
      [nasal]   [nasal]

       [ñ]   [n]

This example suggests that weakening processes such as postvocalic spirantization can be treated as deletion of a stop's closure phase, with the nonstrident A_{max} release then surfacing as the spirant. This predicts that spirantized stops versus affricates may contrast in the output of spirantization as mellow versus strident fricatives – that is, [t] → [θ] vs. [t^{s}] → [s] – another possible implication of Steriade's model that remains to be explored.

9.9 Underspecification

Viewing the phoneme as a bundle of distinctive features has consequences for how the fundamental notion of contrast is represented. Let us first review the conception outlined in the initial chapters of this book, reflecting the consensus that developed on this issue in early generative grammar. On this view, languages differ in which features are recruited to encode the lexicon. To take a simple example, English distinguishes its stops in terms of [±voiced] (e.g., [p]*at* vs. [b]*at*) while Mandarin employs aspiration; English does possess [p] and [p^{h}] ([p^{h}]*in* and *s*[p]*in*), which are identical to the sounds in Mandarin at the phonetic level. It is at the phonological level that the two languages differ: aspiration is distinctive in Mandarin but not in English. Conversely, voicing is distinctive in English but not in Mandarin. We reflect this difference by saying that the stops in [p^{h}]*in* and *s*[p]*in* are unspecified for aspiration ([0spread gl]) at the lexical level. A context-

sensitive rule assigns [+spread gl] at the beginning of a (stressed) syllable while
a UG default rule assigns [−spread gl] in the remaining contexts. In Mandarin a
default rule assigns all obstruents the feature [−voiced]. Furthermore, both languages have rules assigning sonorants the feature [+voiced].

(89) a. [−sonor] → [−spread gl]
      b. [−sonor] → [−voiced]
      c. [+sonor] → [+voiced]

Application of these default rules produces fully specified phonetic representations in which each segment is plus or minus for every phonological feature regardless of whether or not it is contrastive in the system. The rules such as those
in (89) that assign redundant feature specifications on a context-free basis tend
to single out the same feature values: the unmarked ones. It is thus natural to
suppose that for every feature for which the marked-unmarked distinction can
legitimately be drawn, its special status will be reflected in a UG rule to assign
this feature. The child would not have to learn these rules; what must be learned
are the distinctive features used to encode the lexicon (plus the context-sensitive
rules assigning the marked values such as the English aspiration rule).

Subsequent research in the generative framework has both restricted and expanded the role of the default rules and the underspecification that they support.
First, a better comprehension of feature geometry has either curtailed the scope
of or entirely eliminated some of these rules. Two developments will be noted
here. If certain features are dependent on others, then the former no longer freely
cross-classify all segments and so the scope of the relevant default rule is curtailed.
For example, if [lateral] is a dependent of Coronal, then there is no point to
assigning [−lateral] to a labial stop such as [p], let alone to a vowel. These segments lack laterality in virtue of the feature organization itself rather than reflecting a rejection of the option to encode the lexicon with [−lateral]. Stated
differently, no language could choose to contrast labials or vowels for [±lateral].
Second, if a feature is monovalent, then its presence in a given context does not
automatically entail a default rule assigning the opposite value in complementary
contexts. Thus, if the major articulator features [labial], [coronal], [dorsal], and
so on, are unary, then there can be no default rule assigning [−coronal] (at least
in consonants). (If Lombardi (1991) is correct that laryngeal features for voicing,
aspiration, and glottalization are monovalent, then the rules in (89) may become
obsolete as well.)

A countervailing proposal of Kiparsky (1982a) and Archangeli (1984, 1988) has
expanded the role of default rules and underspecification. To appreciate this point,
let us consider the feature [voiced] in the Russian consonant system given in (90).

(90) stops   p,b   t,d   k,g
      affricates   tˢ   č
      fricatives   f,v   s,z   š,ž   x
      nasals   m   n
      liquids   l,r

Stops contrast in voicing while affricates do not; fricatives contrast as well, except at the velar point of articulation. Finally, sonorants do not contrast in voicing, being uniformly [+voiced]. Two views of how to characterize the distribution of [voiced] in a consonant system like (90) have emerged. Both agree that voicing is redundant in sonorants and assigned by the default rule in (91a).

(91)   a.   [+sonor] → [+voiced]
       b.   [−sonor] → [−voiced]

Both would also allow the affricates and velar fricative to be underspecified for voicing ([0voiced]) in the lexicon and receive their phonetic [−voiced] specification through the default rule (91b). Opinions diverge on the treatment of contrasting pairs such as [t] vs. [d] and [k] vs. [g]. *Radical Underspecification*, championed by Kiparsky (1982a) and, with certain additional assumptions, by Archangeli (1984, 1988) and Pulleyblank (1988), sees the underlying contrast as [+voiced] vs. [0voiced]. In other words, the UG default rule is claimed to assign all occurrences of [−voiced] regardless of whether or not it minimally contrasts one segment with another. In general, only marked features appear in the lexicon. An opposing school of thought known variously as *Contrastive* or *Restricted Underspecification* records the [t] vs. [d] opposition as [−voiced] vs. [+voiced] in the lexicon. The default rules assign only the redundant, predictable features in a given system – features that never distinguish a pair of otherwise identical segments (e.g., in the system of (90) [+voiced] in sonorants and [−voiced] in affricates).

Finding solid evidence bearing on this issue has proved to be very difficult. In cases where evidence has been found, the results are conflicting and consequently no consensus has emerged. Let us survey a few of the highlights. Steriade (1986, 1987a,b) has tried to get at this question through study of long-distance assimilation or dissimilation, asking whether or not particular intervening segments erect barriers to a given rule. Depending on the answer to this question, we may infer the feature structure of these segments at the point where the rule applies. To take a simple case, recall the Sanskrit *nati* rule discussed in section 4.3.4 in connection with the articulator nodes. As shown by the paradigms in (92a), [n] assimilates the retroflexion of a preceding continuant [ṣ] or [r].

(92)   a.   kṣubh-aṇa   'quake'   krp-aṇa   'hum'
            kṣved-ana   'lament'   krt-ana   'cut'

       b.

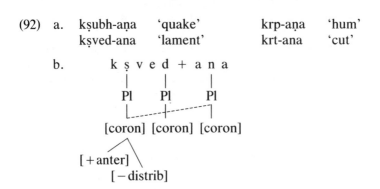

However, the process is systematically suspended when a plain dental consonant intervenes. This suggests that these consonants have some property that blocks the assimilation rule. On the assumption that the retroflex [ṇ] differs from plain [n] by two features ([−anterior, −distributed] vs. [+anterior, +distributed]), the rule must spread the dominating Coronal articulator. This simultaneously explains why dental consonants block the rule. As (92b) shows, extension of [coronal] would cross an association line. A significant implication of this analysis is that the articulator features (at least for consonants) cannot be binary. If labials were [−coronal], then they should block the rule as well. Since the dental articulator is not involved in the action of bilabial closure, it makes sense from the dynamic, articulator-based theory of feature geometry that a labial is not specified for coronality. This represents a case of obligatory or (in Steriade's terms) "trivial" underspecification: there is no freedom to choose [−coronal] on [b] and so it does not help to resolve the issue of Radical versus Restricted Underspecification.

Steriade (1987b) applies similar reasoning to cases where the relevant feature of the intervening segment is arguably binary. Under Restricted Underspecification, we expect the intervening segment to screen out the focus from the triggering context on the relevant autosegmental tier. Radical Underspecification will permit the rule to apply. To take a simple case, the Latin adjectival suffix *-alis* dissimilates to *-aris* when preceded by another lateral: *nav-alis* 'naval' but *sol-aris* 'solar'. The dissimilating laterals may be separated by intervening consonants: *milit-aris* 'military', *lun-aris* 'lunar'. The only consonant that blocks the rule is the other liquid [r]: *flor-alis* 'floral', *litor-alis* 'of the shore', *sepulchr-alis* 'funereal'. Steriade expresses the rule as dissimilation for [+lateral] (93a) and explains the special behavior of [r] as opposed to [n] and [t] with [−lateral] (93b).

(93)   a.   [+later] → [−later] / [+later] _____

      b. f l   o   r +   a l i s
            | | |
      [+lat] [−lat] [+lat]

By parity of reasoning, the [n] of *lun-aris* must be unspecified for [lateral], at least at the point where dissimilation applies. If [n] really is [−lateral] at some later point in the derivation, then we have an argument for Restricted Underspecification. A Radical Underspecification analysis must split the default rule assigning [−lateral] into two parts – application to [r] before dissimilation and to [n], [t], and so on, after dissimilation – an unnatural and arbitrary bifurcation of the same process. For Restricted Underspecification only [t], [n], and so on, undergo the default rule. By assumption, [r] does not receive its [−lateral] specification from the default rule; rather, it is [−lateral] in the lexical representation because the underlying [l] vs. [r] contrast is an opposition of [+lateral] vs. [−lateral].

When presented with this argument, the proponent of Radical Underspecification can offer two responses. First, the [−lateral] specification of [n] and [t] may be illusory; perhaps in the UG feature system [−lateral] only functions to distinguish [r] from [l]. Failure to detect it on Latin [n] and [t] would then show nothing. The scope of the default rule assigning [−lateral] could then be narrowed to just [r]; and for Latin, this rule can be ordered before dissimilation. Alternatively, the special behavior of [r] might be attributed to a dissimilatory output condition on the dissimilation rule itself, blocking application just in case two successive [r]'s are created.

Of course, in order for Radical Underspecification to play an explanatory role, there should be some cases in which a rule or constraint crosses one member of a binary opposition and blocks on the other. Mester and Itô (1989) discuss two processes from Japanese that bear on these questions. One involves the docking of a palatal autosegment in the so-called mimetic (onomatopoetic and ideophonic) vocabulary. These lexical items are normally bimoraic and reduplicated. The palatal prosody adds a meaning of "uncontrolledness." It seeks out the rightmost coronal consonant (except [r]) and otherwise docks on the initial consonant.

(94) hun^{y}a-hun^{y}a   'limp'
      kas^{y}a-kas^{y}a   'rustling'
      t^{y}oko-t^{y}oko   'childish small steps'
      z^{y}abu-z^{y}abu   'dabble in liquid'
      dos^{y}a-dos^{y}a   'in large amounts'
      net^{y}a-net^{y}a   'sticky'
      n^{y}oro-n^{y}oro   'slow, lazy' (*nor^{y}o-nor^{y}o)
      p^{y}oko-p^{y}oko   'jumping around imprudently'
      g^{y}obo-g^{y}obo   'gurgling'
      h^{y}oro-h^{y}oro   'looking thin and weak'

The refusal of [r] to seat the palatal prosody does not reflect a general ban on palatalized [r]. This sound is found outside the mimetic vocabulary: *r^{y}okoo* 'travel', *k^{y}oor^{y}uu* 'dinosaur'. Mester and Itô attribute the exceptional behavior of [r] to its special status in the underlying phonemic inventory of Japanese: it is the only consonant that does not contrast with another for oral place in its manner-of-articulation row.

(95) voiceless stops   p   t   k
      voiced stops   b   d   g
      voiceless fricatives   s   h
      voiced fricative   z
      nasals   m   n   N
      liquid   r
      glides   w   y

Accordingly, Japanese [r] is unspecified for [coronal] and receives this specification by default: [+consonantal] → [coronal]. So long as the rule realizing the palatal prosody on a coronal applies first, it will fail to sight an [r] and so the fact that [r] is skipped is accounted for. The other coronal consonants bear an underlying [coronal] specification that distinguishes them from the remaining points of articulation: [t,d] from [p,b], [k,g] and [s,z] from the "placeless" [h] ([h] derives from [f] and patterns as a fricative in Japanese phonology). Mester and Itô conclude that, as with the Latin *-alis* dissimilation, the mapping of the Japanese palatal prosody depends on underspecification and draws a crucial distinction between a noncontrastive segment and the unmarked element in a network of binary (or in this case ternary [labial], [coronal], [dorsal]) oppositions. Only the former are underspecified. Once again this supports the Restricted Underspecification position.

However, Mester and Itô report a second process from Japanese that appears to point in favor of Radical Underspecification. The initial obstruent of the second member of a compound is voiced ((96a), so-called *rendaku* voicing) unless followed in the same stem by another voiced obstruent (96b) (Lyman's Law).

(96) a. eda   + ke   → edage
          'branch'   'hair'   'split hair'
          unari   + koe   → unarigoe
          'moan'   'voice'   'groan'
          mizu   + seme   → mizuzeme
          'water'   'torture'   'water torture'
          ori   + kami   → origami
          'fold'   'paper'   'origami paper'
          neko   + šita   → nekoǰita
          'cat'   'tongue'   'aversion to hot food'

     b. kita   + kaze   → kitakaze (*kitagaze)
          'north'   'wind'   'freezing north wind'
          širo   + tabi   → širotabi (*širodabi)
          'white'   'tabi'   'white tabi'

Mester and Itô treat rendaku as the docking of a [+voiced] autosegment at the compound juncture and Lyman's Law as dissimilation of successive tautomorphemic [+voiced] specifications; *kitakaze* thus has the derivation in (97).

(97) k i t a + k a z e → k i t a + g a z e → k i t a + k a z e
                    | | | |
                 [+v]   [+v][+v]   [+v]

The fact that voiced sonorants do not initiate Lyman's Law could be explained by underspecifying them for voicing and assigning their [+voiced] by default after dissimilation. And the fact that dissimilation occurs across a sonorant consonant [n] as in (98) actually forces this underspecification. Otherwise, we should expect it to screen out the obstruent, permitting the ill-formed *taikutsuǰinogi*.

(98) taikutsu + šinogi → taikutsušinogi (*taikutsuǰinogi)
      'boredom' 'avoiding' 'time-killer'

          š   i   n   o   g   i
          | |
        [+v]   [+v]

We now have the tools to test the two models. Japanese contrasts voiced and voiceless stops and fricatives. If a voiceless obstruent intervenes and if the voiced-voiceless contrast is expressed as an underlying [+voiced] vs. [−voiced] opposition, then we expect dissimilation between voiced obstruents to be suspended. In fact, Lyman's Law regularly applies across voiceless obstruents (99a).

(99) a. onna   +   kotoba   →   onnakotoba (*onnagotoba)
          'woman'   'words'   'feminine speech'
          doku   +   tokage   →   dokutokage (*dokudokage)
          'poison'   'lizard'   'Gila monster'

      b.   g   o   t   o   b   a
             | | |
           [+v]   [−v]   [+v]

This is problematic under the Restricted Underspecification thesis; after rendaku voicing, *onnakotoba* has the representation of (99b) with an intervening [−voiced] that should block dissimilation. In order for Lyman's Law to operate correctly, [t] must not be specified for [−voiced]. It will not be under the Radical Underspecification thesis, which assigns all occurrences of [−voiced] by the default rule, regardless of its contrastive status.

The evidence from the behavior of barriers is thus not conclusive. Mester and Itô try to reconcile the contradictory results from Japanese with the hypothesis that [voiced] is in fact a UG monovalent feature marking just voiced obstruents. Voiceless obstruents are thus inherently unspecified for [voiced] and so Lyman's Law will automatically pass through a voiceless obstruent. The full implications of this proposal remain to be tested; privative laryngeal features are defended by Lombardi (1991) (see discussion in section 9.7). If monovalency for [voiced] is the appropriate solution, then we would appear to be justified in expecting the same for [lateral]. There is no convincing evidence for treating [−lateral] as a spreading autosegment. Yet the Latin dissimilation of *-alis* suggests that [r] bears some feature that screens out two [+lateral] segments when it stands between them. Ultimate resolution of these questions will require a much better understanding of the feature system and the apparently competing demands that it is being asked to satisfy: specification of natural classes in rules and constraints on the one hand, and representation of phonological contrasts on the other.

In addition to barriers, another source of evidence bearing on Radical versus Restricted Underspecification has been phonotactic constraints defined over the earliest (essentially underlying) lexical level. If a default rule functions like other phonological rules by being ordered to apply at a particular point in the derivation, then constraints defined at the earliest level should not refer to features assigned by the default rule. Christdas (1988) assembles cases where such constraints in fact involve redundant features. For example, Tamil has a five-vowel [i,u,e,o,a] system. The front and back glides freely combine with a following low vowel [a]; but [y] may not be followed by front vowels [i,e] and the back glide [w] does not combine with following [u,o] (recall exercise 1.6). We may make sense of this distribution in terms of a constraint barring a glide-vowel sequence whose members have the same value for [back].

(100) * Gl   V
          | |
       [αback] [αback]

The low back vowel [a] escapes this constraint if it is underlyingly represented as [+low] and its [+back] is assigned by a redundancy rule: [+low] → [+back]. If this analysis is correct, it implies that at the underlying level both values for [back] must be specified, since alpha in (100) ranges over both plus and minus. Radical Underspecification could be weakened to say that only some features are underspecified, in particular not [±back]. Alternatively, we might accept the postulate of Clements's model that front and back vowels are the products of the [coronal] and [dorsal] articulators and reinterpret the Tamil data as implying that neither one is necessarily a default.

Christdas points to other cases where features are strictly speaking predictable but still needed at the earliest lexical level for the expression of phonotactic constraints governed by sonority features. Perhaps if [±sonorant] is a Root feature, then it cannot be underspecified lest the remaining features have no node to which they may attach. It is to be hoped that as our understanding of the feature geometry improves, the proper constraints on just which features may be underspecified will become clearer.

9.10 Underspecification and Blocking in Nonderived Contexts

Recall from section 5.5 that a central result of Kiparsky's (1982a) Lexical Phonology model was the explanation of the blockage of rules in morpheme-internal, nonderived contexts as a reflex of strict cyclicity (derived in turn from the Elsewhere Condition). Kiparsky (1992) challenges the empirical adequacy of this result with convincing arguments that cyclicity is neither a necessary nor a sufficient condition to delimit the blocking contexts. He develops an alternative solution to the problem that crucially relies on Radical Underspecification. We will review his argument here, based on examples from Finnish.

Kiparsky first shows that cyclicity does not always entail blockage in nonderived contexts by exhibiting a cyclic rule that does apply in such contexts. A key feature of this counterexample is that the rule is optional. It simplifies a low-vowel diphthong by spreading the nonhigh onglide (101a); as a result, [a,ä] optionally assimilate to a preceding [e,o,ö]. The rule is cyclic in virtue of applying both before and after another rule (101b) that deletes intervocalic [t] after a short vowel not bearing primary (initial syllable) stress.

(101) a. [a,ä] → V_1 / V_1 _____ (where V_1 = [e,o,ö])

pimeä≈*pimee* 'dark' nom.sg.

b. [t] → Ø / $\check{V}_1$ _____ V_2 (where $\check{V}_1$ does not bear main stress)

-*tA* partitive sg.
jo+*ta* 'what', *veesee*+*tä* 'toilet', *hattu*+*a* 'hat' from /hattu+ta/

Contraction applies to the output of *t*-deletion so that underlying /nime + tä/ 'name' part.sg. appears as *nime-ä* or *nimee*. But contraction must also precede *t*-deletion because a long vowel arising from contraction suffices to block *t*-deletion. For example, when the partitive suffix is added to /pimeä/, the [t] deletes after the uncontracted stem alternant but blocks when the stem has undergone contraction: underlying /pimeä + tä/ surfaces as *pimeää* or *pimee-tä* but not **pimee-ä*. As the derivations in (102) show, this alternation is accounted for if *t*-deletion is ordered before contraction on the cycle.

(102)   1st cycle

/pimeä/		/nime/	
inappl.		inappl.	*t*-deletion
pimee	≈ pimeä	inappl.	contraction

2nd cycle

/pimee + tä/	/pimeä + tä/	/nime + tä/	
inappl.	pimeä + ä	nime + ä	*t*-deletion
inappl.	pimeä:*	nimee ≈ nimeä	contraction

(* We assume contraction of [ä + ä] to [ä:] takes precedence, perhaps reflecting the OCP.)

The contraction rule is thus cyclic but clearly applies in a nonderived, root-internal context. Stated in terms of Kiparsky's (1982a) Lexical Phonology model, the identity rule mapping /pimeä/ to itself must be prevented from activating the Elsewhere Condition that blocks application of contraction. This state of affairs is possible because the contraction rule is optional; failure to apply the rule allows the uncontracted (underlying) representation to be recovered. But, Kiparsky argues, we do not want the imposition of the Strict Cycle Condition or the Elsewhere Condition to depend on the obligatory versus optional status of the rules – if for no other reason than that no other grammatical principle refers to the optionality of a rule.

Kiparsky (1992) also assembles several cases of blocking in nonderived contexts where the rule is noncyclic. Recall *äiti* versus *vesi* from section 5.8.1. The Finnish *t* → *s* rule is fed by the rule raising word-final [e], so that /#vete#/ becomes /#veti#/ and then softens to /#vesi#/. Since raising is a word-level rule, *t* → *s* must apply at this level. But the word level is noncyclic (Booij and Rubach 1987). Another Finnish example making the same point is the gradation rule that degeminates a consonant at the onset of a closed syllable. This rule is responsible for the [hatu-] variant of the stem [hattu-] 'hat' in the paradigm of (103).

(103)

hattu	nominative	hatu-n	genitive
hattu-a	partitive	hatu-sta	elative
hattu-na	essive		

Degemination blocks in morpheme-internal position: *kippis* 'cheers', *attentatti* 'assassination'. This rule is also assigned to the word level because it applies to the output of another process deleting word-final [e] in polysyllables: /vaatteCe/ →

/vaatteC/ → *vaateC* (where C is an empty skeletal slot filled by the consonant beginning the following word). Kiparsky constructs an argument that degemination cannot be cyclic: it is not triggered by the genitive morpheme *-n,* which deletes before consonants by another rule of the phonology: /hattu + n + si/ 'your hat's' surfaces as *hattu-si.* If degemination were cyclic, then (other things being equal) /hattu + n/ should degeminate to /hatu + n/ before the addition of *-si,* resulting in the incorrect **hatu-si.* A final fact is that geminates derived by filling the empty C-slot from a clitic do not degeminate: /meneC#pas/ 'go!' surfaces as *meneppas.* This range of facts is explained if the degemination is restricted to the word level and thus counts as a postcyclic lexical rule like *t* → *s.* Yet as the *kippis* and *attentatti* examples make clear, the rule must be blocked from applying in nonderived contexts.

Thus, Kiparsky (1992) concludes that cyclicity is neither a necessary nor a sufficient condition for restriction to derived contexts. His alternative explanation is couched in the framework of Radical Underspecification and depends on the premises in (104).

(104) a. Features are binary.
      b. One value is underspecified.
      c. Underspecification may be context-sensitive.
      d. Underlying representations are redundancy-free.

The basic idea is that where possible, phonological rules are structure-building, feature-filling operations converting [0F] to [±F]. The distinction between default rules and rules describing alternations is thus merged. In effect, the latter rules also fill in redundant information (zeros) but in particular contexts. Hence, given a rule [X] → [αY] /___ Z, (where α = plus or minus), we are to assume that [αY] is redundant in the context ___ Z and that [−αY] is the context-free (default) value for the feature [Y]. To see how this is supposed to work, let us return to the familiar Finnish paradigm in (105).

(105) a. i. [e] → [i] / ___ #   b. i. [t] → [s] / ___ i
        ii. [E] → [+high] / ___ #   ii. [T] → [+contin] / ___ i
       iii. [E] → [−high]   iii. [T] → [−contin]

     c. vesi   'water'
         vete + nä   essive
         äiti   'mother'

Descriptively, the rules involve feature changes of [−high] to [+high] and of [−continuant] to [+continuant]. Hence, for dental obstruents as members of the /t/ vs. /s/ opposition, [+continuant] is redundant before [i]; furthermore, [−continuant] must be the default, context-free specification because this is the value that [t] assumes outside of the context ___ [i]. The upshot of this reasoning is that the dental consonant in /vete/ is underlyingly unspecified for [continuant] – that is, it is [0continuant]. (105bii) assigns [+continuant] before [i] and (105biii) assigns [−continuant] elsewhere. Similarly, given (105ai), [+high] is redundant in final position (for front vowels). The final vowel in /vete/ is thus underlyingly

[0high]. It is assigned [+high] by (105aii) in final position and [−high] by (105aiii) elsewhere. The derivations of (106) thus ensue.

(106) /#veTE#/   /#veTE-nä#/   /#äiti#/
     veTi   ———   —   (105aii)
    ———   veTe-nä   —   (105aiii)
    vesi   ———   —   (105bii)
    ———   vete-nä   —   (105biii)

Turning to *äiti* 'mother' and the blocking problem, the [−continuant] specification of the [t] is unpredictable and hence must be listed in the lexicon; *äiti* is thus in essence an exception to (105bii). Since (105bii) is a feature-filling rule converting underspecified [0continuant] to [+continuant], it will not apply to the specified [t] of *äiti*.

Kiparsky's proposed alternative to the Strict Cycle Condition has a number of implications whose validity remains to be assessed. First, since the raising and *t* → *s* rules apply at the word level, the underspecified values of the *t*≈*s* and *e*≈*i* segments for the features [continuant] and [high] are not filled in until this point, entailing that these features are unavailable at earlier strata in the grammar. Consequently, no cyclic lexical rule can depend on them. It is unclear whether this strong claim can be maintained. For example, the rule of *t*-deletion (101b) was demonstrated to be cyclic. Can we be assured that its scope of application can be delimited in the underspecification approach to the blocking problem? More generally, Kiparsky's solution implies that rules are in general feature-filling. It remains to be seen whether a consistent grammar can be constructed that also maintains strict adherence to such underspecification. In addition, it is unclear how the approach is to be extended to rules that manipulate the geometry of phonological representations in order to capture, for example, the contrast between /kippis/ (where degemination must block) and /hattu + n/ → *hatun* where the rule applies. See Kiparsky 1992 for some discussion of this question.

9.11   The Coronal Syndrome

Paradis and Prunet (1991) and their contributors document the generalization that [coronal] is the unmarked, default choice for the (Oral) Place node. This section summarizes the evidence and then some of the problems that arise in trying to express this idea. First, coronals are the most frequent articulator choice on a number of counts. In the UG phonetic alphabet, the Coronal articulator supports a larger number of dependent (consonantal) features than Labial, Dorsal, and Pharyngeal. In the phonemic systems of individual languages, coronals typically outnumber the other Place categories as well. Finally, they have been documented as among the most frequent consonants in speech corpora of English and Spanish. Second, coronal is the normal outcome of rules and constraints that neutralize Place contrasts: in Lardil and Carrier coda consonants are restricted to coronals; the syllable appendix in English is occupied exclusively by coronals (recall the [ksθs] cluster in *sixths*). Third, although no statistical evidence is available, phonologists have the impression that coronal is the most commonly chosen epenthetic or otherwise dummy oral consonant, as in French liaison: *il va* 'he goes', but *va-t-il* 'is he going'; *glouglou* 'noise in pipe', but *glouglouter* 'to make such noise'; *blabla* 'meaningless talk', but *blablater* 'to talk blabla' (Borowsky 1985). Fourth, coronals more freely combine with each other as well as with other consonants, eluding phonotactic restrictions that are enforced on labials and velars. For example, English morpheme-final clusters composed of stop and fricative must have one coronal: *ask, axe; asp, apse;* but **afk, *akf*. Fifth, coronals are more susceptible to Place assimilation than noncoronals: many languages (e.g., Lithuanian, Catalan) restrict nasal assimilation to [n], excluding [m] and [ŋ]; in Yakut (exercise 2.8) coda [t] assimilates to a following labial or velar while [p] and [k] do not. Finally, coronals are more likely to be transparent to transconsonantal vowel-echo rules than labials or velars. For example, Paradis and Prunet (1989) point to a constraint on disyllabic roots in the Ivory Coast Kru language Guere that bars the combination of two nonhigh vowels. Thus, while *nIme* 'bird', *zegU* 'chameleon', *kUla* 'hand' are well formed, structures such as **CeCa, *CeCe* are not. The only exceptions are roots of the form CV_iCV_i, where the two vowels are identical; in all these cases the medial consonant is a coronal [ɗ,n,l]: *wɔɗɔ* 'to wash', *beɗe* 'to hang', *pɔɗɔ* 'mud'.

Phonologists have sought to explain the suite of properties comprising the coronal syndrome by underspecification of the Place node and appeal to the corresponding default rule in (107) that assigns to a bare Place node the Coronal articulator.

(107)   Place   →   Place
                     |
                  Coronal

Let us consider how the explanation is supposed to work. Given the default rule (107), Coronal becomes a natural choice for an epenthetic consonant. A consonant is normally inserted to break a hiatus or fill some obligatory consonantal position in a prosodic template. The phonetic features of the epenthetic consonant play no distinctive lexical role and so it is natural for the UG rule (107) to step in to assign a generic place specification, as in (108a).

(108)   a.   V V   →   V C V   →   V   C   V
             | | | | | | | |
             Pl Pl   Pl Pl Pl   Pl Pl Pl
                                       |
                                    Coronal

        b.   C   C   c.   C   C   C
             | | | | |
             Pl Pl   Pl   →   Pl   →   Pl
             ↯---⌡ | | |
             artic artic   artic   Coronal

This "least effort" rationale also explains why coronals are more prone to Place assimilation. Assimilation of a labial or a velar requires two operations: spread of the adjacent articulator as well as delinking of the original articulator (108b). If coronals start out with a bare Place node, then only the first operation is required. Similar reasoning explains why Coronal is the typical outcome of neutralization for Place (108c): the original articulator is removed while the coronal substitute comes for free by the UG rule (107).

The transparency phenomenon demands a slightly different representation. Vowel echo (complete assimilation) across a coronal requires spreading the vocalic Place node that dominates the vowel quality and aperture features. A Guere form such as *bede* thus has a multiply linked geminate and so does not violate the constraint against two nonhigh vowels. This explanation seems to call for a representation such as (109) where the Coronal lacks any Place specification.

(109)

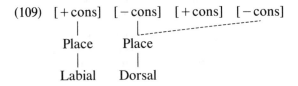

A similar representation seems to be necessary to explain the ease with which coronals cluster with other consonants. Yip (1991) notes that many languages impose a condition on consonant clustering that allows just one Place specification for the entire cluster. We might express this idea as (110), barring separate Place nodes for adjacent consonants.

(110)   *C   C
          | |
        Place Place

The West African language Diola Fogny (Sapir 1965) rigidly enforces this constraint, limiting its clusters to homorganic NC, nasal geminates, and coda liquids but only when followed by a coronal [t] (111). These clusters escape the constraint of (110) if they are represented with a single multiply linked Place node.

(111)   a.   mba   'or'
             ndaw   man's name
             ekumbay   'the pig'
             jensu   'undershirt'
             famb   'annoy'
             bunt   'lie'
        b.   nimammaŋ   'I want'
             niɲaŋŋan   'I cried'
        c.   salte   'be dirty'
             arti̱   'negative'

Yip shrewdly observes that English monomorphemic roots can be argued to impose essentially the same species of restriction on consonantal clustering if coronals are underspecified for Place. The table in (112) illustrates the range of clusters that are found. All are homorganic and thus share a single Place specification or else contain a coronal.

(112) a. stop-stop $C_2 = t,d$ chapter, factor, abdomen
       b. stop-fricative $C_2 = s,z$ capsule, axle, adze
       c. fricative-stop $C_1 = s$,   clasp, brisk, lift
                              or $C_2 = t,d$
       d. nasal-stop   homorganic   whimper, winter, wrinkle
       e. stop-nasal $C_2 = n$ signify (Greek sigma)
       f. liquid-stop   all OK   alder, garden, help, elk, lurk, harp
       g. stop-liquid   all OK   atlas, poplar, topple, wicker
       h. fricative-fricative $C_1 = s$ asphalt, aesthetic (rare)
       i. nasal-fricative $C_1 = n$ answer, panther, anvil, plinth
       j. fricative-nasal   very rare   prism
       k. liquid-fricative   all OK   elf, scarf, wealth, hearth, harsh
       l. fricative-liquid   all OK   Teflon, whiffle, usher

If coronals lack a Place node at the point where the constraint (110) is checked, then the clusters in which they participate pass the test, as shown by the representation for the [ps] of *capsule* in (113).

(113)
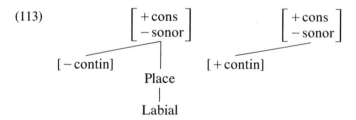

Yip notes a curious asymmetry in the location of the place features: Place associates with the leftmost [−continuant]; otherwise, with the rightmost position. Only the [ft] clusters fail to conform to the principle, a type of edge-in association with default to the opposite side similar to that found by Hewitt and Prince (1989) in the Shona verb (section 7.7).

To summarize, there is a slight inconsistency in the underspecification approach to the coronal syndrome: some properties require a bare Place node (underspecification of the articulator) while others seem to call for no Place specification at all. Future research must reconcile these two senses of underspecification.

A more serious problem arises in the expression of dependent features. Generally, it is the unmarked dental-alveolars [t,d,s,z,l,r] that manifest the suite of properties associated with the coronal syndrome. For example, in (112) fricative is filled by [s,z], not [š] or [θ]. As McCarthy and Taub (1992) point out, this follows from the logic of feature dependency. Given that [s] vs. [š] is expressed as two poles of the binary feature [±anterior], at least one value must be specified in underlying lexical representation (generally the [−anterior] of [š]). But we can only specify [−anterior] if we also specify the parent Coronal articulator. If underspecification is really the correct way to express the coronal syndrome, then it should only be exhibited by segments with unmarked dependent features. While this prediction holds for Yip's cluster condition, there are other phonotactic constraints applying at the earliest levels of English phonology that specifically single out coronals and yet fail to distinguish the marked [θ,š,č], etc., from the unmarked [t,d,s], etc. For example, syllable-onset [l] is incompatible not only with the marked [θ] but also with the unmarked [t]; the syllable appendix is composed of both types of coronals (*sixths* [k + sθs]); the diphthong [aw] may only be followed by coronals, again marked [θ], [č], [ǰ] (*mouth, couch, gouge*) as well as unmarked [t,d,n,r,l] (*out, crowd, ounce, hour, owl*). These constraints require Coronal to be specified at the point where they are checked and do not isolate just the marked [θ,š] but apply equally to the unmarked [s,t,n], etc. They seem to call the underspecification approach to the coronal syndrome into serious question.

Let us close the discussion by reviewing Shaw's (1991a) analysis of coronal harmony in the Athapaskan language Tahltan and the crucial role that underspecification and feature dependency play in the analysis. Tahltan has a complex set of place distinctions including five classes of coronals.

(114) b d   dl   dð   dz   dž   g   gʷ   G
          t   tɬ   tθ   ts   tš   k   kʷ   q
          t' tɬ' tθ' ts' tš' k' kʷ' q'
              ɬ   θ   s   š   x   xʷ   X   h
              l   ð   z   ž   ɣ   ɣʷ   R
       m n   y
          n'

The harmony process is exhibited by consonants from the [+ distributed] *dð*, the [+ strident] *dz*, and the [− anterior] *dž* series. These three segment classes also form the harmonic sources and count as barriers. The various realizations of the 1sg. subject affix [s] in (115a) illustrate this coronal harmony: in *dɛ[θ]kʷʊθ* from [deskʷʊθ], [s] harmonizes to [θ] across [kʷ].

(115) a. [s]   dɛ[θ]kʷʊθ   'I cough'
           [s]   ɛ[θ]du:θ   'I whipped him'
           [s]   ɛ[š]džɪni   'I'm singing'
           [s]   nɛ[š]yɛɬ   'I'm growing'
           [s]   ɛ[s]k'a: 'I'm gutting fish'
           [s]   ɛ[s]dan   'I'm drinking'

       b. [s]   ta[θ]tθaɬ   'I'm dying'
           [s]   ɛdɛdɛ[θ]du:θ   'I whipped myself'
           [θ]   ni[s]it'a:ts   'we got up'
           [θ]   mɛʔɛ[š]it'otš   'we are breast-feeding'
           [s]   ya[š]tɬ'ɛtš   'I splashed it'

As the forms in (115b) show, the remaining plain dental and lateral series neither trigger, block, nor undergo the rule. Since the Tahltan harmony involves more than a single feature (at least [anterior] to distinguish [s] and [š] and either [distributed] or [strident] to distinguish [s] from [θ]), the spreading must take place at the level of the Coronal articulator node.

In order to explain why the rule does not target the plain dental series [t,d,t'], Shaw underspecifies these segments, depriving them of a Place node: they are marked only for the stricture feature [−continuant] at the point where the harmony rule applies. They consequently can be neither sources of nor barriers to harmony. Finally, to explain why they themselves do not harmonize, Shaw formulates the rule in such a way that it cannot target a missing Place node, requiring the focus to be specified for coronal.

(116)   Place   Place

        ≠---------⌋

     [coron]   [coron]

This restriction is puzzling; recall that one of the diagnostics of an underspecified segment is its susceptibility to assimilation. Here the underspecified segments must be specifically excluded. More generally, Tahltan forms a virtual minimal pair with the Sanskrit *n*-retroflexion (section 9.9), where assimilation of the Coronal articulator is blocked by the plain [t,d], etc., series. In the Sanskrit phonemic inventory, [t] contrasts with [ṭ] for the [±anterior] feature that is involved in the *n*-retroflexion rule while in Tahltan it is the affricates [ts], [tš], and [tθ] that constitute the [±anterior] opposition; [t] lacks a [−anterior] counterpart in the Tahltan system and hence can be underspecified.

Feature dependency also plays a role in Shaw's analysis. It is the marked [−anterior] [š], [+distributed] [θ], and [+strident] [ts] that spread. These features are only reachable through the Coronal articulator, which consequently must be present and hence cannot be underspecified. It is the unmarked [+anterior] series [t,d,t'] that is underspecified. By parity of reasoning, the analysis must also underspecify the lateral series for Place because [dl,tl], etc., neither trigger, block, nor undergo the harmony. As Shaw observes, this analysis implies that [lateral] is not a Coronal dependent even though it is almost always executed by this articulator.

9.12   Phonetic Underspecification

Keating (1988) and Cohn (1990) argue that some segments must remain underspecified at the level of the input to phonetic implementation. This conclusion is based on a distinction between two kinds of articulatory transition.

(117)   a. | +F | −F | −F | b. | +F | 0F | −F | c. | −F | 0F | +F |

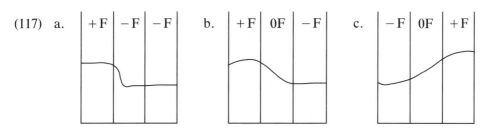

In one case two adjacent segments with opposite specifications for the feature [+F] [−F] show a more or less steady state for the corresponding articulatory gesture except at their margins, where there is a rapid transition from one state to the next (117a). This case contrasts with a hypothetical underspecified segment sandwiched between two specified ones (117b,c). Here the transition takes the form of a cline that develops more gradually over a greater portion of the segment. If the intervening segment is unspecified as [0F], then the cline can be explained as an articulatory interpolation between the adjacent [+F] [−F] or [−F] [+F] targets.

As illustration, we will look at a few examples from Cohn's study of nasality in Sundanese, French, and English. Working with a respiratory mask equipped with nasal and oral transducers, Cohn obtained measurements of nasal and oral airflow from which the action of the velum could be inferred. Recall from exercise 5.4 that Sundanese has a rule spreading nasality from a nasal consonant to following vowels. Thus, the input to the phonetic component contains both nasal and oral vowels. To illustrate the two types of transition, we can schematize the nasal airflow measurements obtained for *ŋōbah* 'change' and *ŋūliat* 'stretch' (118).

(118)

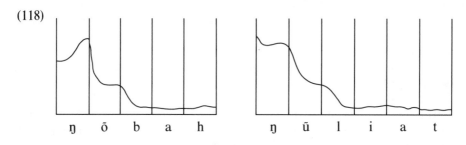

The nasal vowels show significant nasal airflow throughout. The stop [b] has a slight nasalization at its left edge followed by a sharp transition to oral. In contrast, the [l] of *ŋūliat* exhibits a more gradient decay of nasality to the following oral vowel. Cohn draws several conclusions from these data. Segments whose nasal airflow takes the form of a plateau (such as the [ō] and [b] of *ŋōbah*) reflect [+nasal] and [−nasal] phonological specifications realized as more or less steady states over the course of the entire segment; transitions are confined to the margins of these specified segments. Segments whose nasal airflow exhibits a cline (such as the [l] in *ŋūliat*) reflect a phonological [0nasal] specification. They send no instructions to the Soft Palate articulator. Their nasal airflow profile arises from an interpolation between the [+nasal] target of the preceding vowel and the [−nasal] target of the following vowel.

If this interpretation of the clines and plateaus is correct, then we can reason backward from the phonetics to infer the nature of the phonological representations that are input to the phonetics. A summary of Cohn's results for the vowels of Sundanese, French, and English illustrates this point. Sundanese vowels exhibit plateaus in essentially all environments (the single exception was a cline-like pattern for [a] before the velar nasal [ŋ]). This suggests that in the phonological input to the phonetics, vowels are fully specified as [+nasal] or [−nasal]. French vowels also contrast phonologically for nasality and so we expect the same behavior.

This makes the correct prediction for oral vowels before a nasal vowel or consonant: the [e] of *Leon de* [Leõ] has the plateau shape with the onset of nasalization
at its right margin (119a), as does the [ɔ] of *bonne tête* [bɔn tɛt].

(119) a.   Leon de   b.   dites nez deux fois

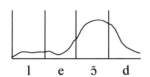

       l   e   õ   d

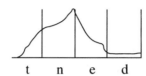

       t   n   e   d

   c.   nonne de

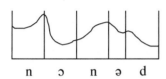

       n   ɔ   n   ə   d

We expect the same story for a phonologically oral vowel following a nasal segment. Surprisingly, the [e] in *bon héros* [bõ ero] and the [e] in *dites nez deux (fois)*
[dit ne də] show a cline-like transition throughout their duration (119b). Accordingly, Cohn postulates a phonological rule to delete [−nasal] on a vowel that
follows a [+nasal] segment. The resultant [0nasal] vowel then is interpolated
through in the phonetics. Cohn stresses that this is not autosegmental spreading
of nasality but arises from a quite different mechanism of phonetic interpolation.
Now consider what happens in a case like *nonne* [nɔn], where a phonologically
oral vowel sits between two nasal consonants. Given the rule deleting [−nasal],
a [0nasal] vowel surfaces between two [+nasal] segments. Here we find a plateau,
but one with less airflow than an underlying [+nasal] vowel (119c). It makes
sense to see this as a flatter interpolation across the [+nasal] targets.

Unlike Sundanese and French, English lacks a nasality contrast in its vowels,
which can consequently be either [0nasal] or [−nasal] as input to the phonetics.
The phonetic evidence suggests that vowels are underspecified. For the vowels
of both *den* and *Ned*, Cohn reports a cline rather than a plateau. A plateau was
found for the internasal vowels of *none* and *men;* but this is where a plateau would
be expected anyway if interpolation walks straight across from one [+nasal] target
to the next. Cohn finds an unexpected plateau on the vowel preceding a tautosyllabic nasal+voiceless stop cluster. Airflow measurements for the [ɛ] vowels
of *say s[ɛ]nt twice* and *say c[ɛ]nter twice* reveal a steady-state nasality in the
former. Furthermore, the nasal consonant is considerably reduced in this context.
Cohn sees this as phonetic evidence for the phonological rule deleting a nasal
consonant before a tautosyllabic voiceless stop (see the Introduction). The reduction must be formulated in such a way that the [+nasal] feature of the consonant persists and reattaches to the preceding vowel. This segment then enters
the phonetics as [+nasal] and hence takes the form of a plateau.

In sum, the nasal airflow measurements suggest that segments such as the
vowels of English can remain unspecified for [nasal] throughout the phonology.

Sundanese differs from French in consistently implementing its vocalic oral-nasal contrast as [−nasal] vs. [+nasal]. French represents an intermediate case; although it contrasts nasal and oral vowels like Sundanese, it systematically drops [−nasal] after [+nasal]. According to Cohn, the process also affects following voiced stops. The [d] in (119c) shows a nasal cline rather than a steady state. Voiceless stops retain their [−nasal] specification in this context. One might reinterpret these data in terms of a rule of prenasalization spreading [+nasal] to the closure phase of the following stop. This analysis sees the nasal transition on the [d] in (119c) as phonological in nature rather than the result of interpolation. The two competing analyses could be resolved by the behavior of voiced fricatives such as [z] (not studied by Cohn). Interpolation predicts a cline while prenasalization predicts a plateau (at least if we accept Steriade's bipositional representation for plosives). The restriction to voiced stops might indicate a spread of sonority along with nasality. The voicing on [d] could then reflect spontaneous voicing: a voiceless stop cannot accept [+sonorant] without giving up voicelessness.

Cohn's study thus seems to provide evidence for a three-way contrast among [+nasal], [−nasal], and [0nasal] at the point where phonology interfaces with phonetics. An alternative conclusion that a backer of privative [nasal] may wish to pursue is to say that phonetic interpretation of the lack of [nasal] as oral (a raised velum) is contextually determined. Finally, we note a parallel between the phonetics and the phonology. When abutting [+nasal] and [−nasal] segments appear in the phonetics, the former segment in general encroaches on the latter rather than vice versa. Thus, in the phonetics as well as the phonology, [+nasal] dominates [−nasal].

9.13   Rules versus Constraints

In the earliest expositions of the generative model, phonological generalizations were captured by two sorts of statements: phonological rules and morpheme structure constraints. The principal job of phonological rules was to account for alternations: systematic changes in the shapes of stems, affixes, and words as a function of the varying sounds in neighboring morphemes and words (e.g., Catalan nasal assimilation (section 5.7), Polish final devoicing (section 2.7), Tangale elision (section 3.2)). The rules thus had a certain dynamic quality relating one alternant to another (via a common underlying representation). Morpheme structure constraints accounted for more static generalizations concerning the combination of features to define the language's segment inventory and phonotactic constraints on sound sequences. Two simple examples illustrate this point. In the ubiquitous five-vowel system [i,e,a,o,u], the distribution of [round] is not free with respect to [back]. The lack of [ü] and [ɯ] might reflect a constraint against front rounded and nonlow back unrounded vowels (120a). Alternatively, the gap can be expressed by saying that the grammar does not select [round] as a distinctive feature. All lexical entries thus contain [0round] specifications, and redundancy rules fill in values for [back] in agreement with the value for [round] and otherwise assign [−round] (120b).

(120) a. $*$V   b.   V

$$\begin{bmatrix} -\text{low} \\ \alpha\text{back} \\ -\alpha\text{round} \end{bmatrix}$$ $\begin{bmatrix} -\text{low} \\ \alpha\text{back} \\ 0\text{round} \end{bmatrix} \rightarrow [\alpha\text{round}]$

$$\begin{array}{c} \text{V} \quad \rightarrow [-\text{round}] \\ [0\text{round}] \end{array}$$

In addition to such "segment structure" constraints, the set of morpheme structure constraints also included various "sequence structure" constraints. For example, in most languages, tautomorphemic nasal + consonant clusters share the
same point of articulation. Once again, this can be accounted for with a constraint
such as (121a) that bars heterorganic clusters whose first member is a nasal. But
the more popular treatment has invoked the redundancy rule format in which the
nasal is [0Place], reflecting the fact that its Place specification is predictable from
the following consonant by a rule such as (121b).

(121) a. $*$C   C   b.   [+nasal] [+cons]

$$\begin{bmatrix} +\text{nasal} \\ \alpha\text{Place} \end{bmatrix} \quad [-\alpha\text{Place}]$$

$$\begin{array}{c} \text{--------} \rceil \\ \text{Place} \end{array}$$

Underspecification theory is of course a direct continuation of this kind of attack
on the problem. An important unresolved question in generative theory is whether
underspecification or constraints are the proper approach to this issue (Mohanan
1991). The most commonly advanced argument for the underspecification-plus-
redundancy-rules position is based on the observation that morpheme structure
constraints are often extended to heteromorphemic alternations. For example, in
many five-vowel systems an umlauting process fronts back vowels by spreading
[−back] from a suffix or prefix. Recall that in Chamorro (section 1.3) [u,o,a] are
converted to [i,e,æ] – not to [ü,ö,æ]. If we adopt underspecification of [round]
and order rule (120b) after umlaut, then we automatically account for why fronted
[u] appears as [i] and not [ü]: at the point where umlaut applies all vowels are
[0round]; they only pick up their rounding specification later by (120b). But in
the analysis employing the constraint (120a), [u] is underlyingly [+round]; when
umlaut spreads [−back], the ill-formed [−back, +round] results. We would then
have to complicate the umlaut rule to delink the [+round] (as well as the original
[+back]). It is thus not immediately obvious how the constraint in (120a) will
ensure that [ü] is converted to [i] in a language such as Chamorro. Underspecification avoids this problem: the redundancy rule (120b) fills in [+round] at just
one point in the derivation.

A similar argument can be advanced for sequence structure constraints. In many
languages where tautomorphemic nasals agree in place with following consonants,
nasals assimilate across morpheme boundaries. For example, Diola Fogny (Sapir
1965) morpheme-internal NC clusters are homorganic (e.g., *bunt* 'lie', *jensu* 'un-
dershirt', *ekumbay* 'pig'). Reduplication may create a nasal + consonant sequence;
the nasal is changed to agree with the following consonant in the paradigms in
(122a).

(122) a. [ni-gam-gam] → niganɡam   'I judge'
           [ku-bɔn-bɔn]   kubɔmbɔn   'they sent'
           [na-ti:ŋ-ti:ŋ]   nati:nti:ŋ   'he cut (it) through'

       b. [+nasal]   [+cons]

           Place   Place

In this case an underlying contrast is neutralized and basic nasals radically alter their point of articulation. Once again, if we just invoke a constraint barring heterorganic clusters such as (121a), it is unclear how it can be generalized to induce the necessary feature changes across morpheme boundaries. To solve this problem, (Kiparsky (1982a) proposes that rule (121b) do double duty to both fill in zeros and change feature values across morpheme boundaries (essentially by delinking the original Place specification of the nasal, as in (122b)). The nasal assimilation process thus performs both a feature-filling and a feature-changing operation. If we grant rules this double function, the statement that nasals are homorganic with the following consonant is thus made just once in the grammar and no generalization is lost.

The first challenge to the redundancy rule (underspecification) approach to this rules-versus-constraints issue was posed by Kisseberth (1970a,b), who called attention to the fact that in a number of American Indian languages rules of vowel deletion and insertion conspire to ensure that clusters of three consonants are not created. For example, in Tonkawa a vocalic mora is deleted in word-medial position, as shown by the paradigms in (123).

(123) [picena]
       picna-noʔ   'he is cutting it'
       we-pcena-noʔ   'he is cutting them'

       [netale]
       netle-noʔ   'he is licking it'
       we-ntale-noʔ   'he is licking them'

       [na:t]
       na:t-oʔ   'he steps on it'
       we-nat-oʔ   'he steps on them'

       [c'a:px]
       c'a:px-oʔ   'he puts up a bed'
       we-c'apx-oʔ   'he puts up several beds'

       [salk]
       salk-oʔ   'he pulls sinew from meat'
       we-salk-oʔ   'he pulls sinews from meat'

Stems such as [picena] 'cut' and [netale] 'lick' lose their second vowel when suffixed and their first vowel when prefixed. Long-vowel roots such as [na:t] 'step on' and [c'a:px] 'put up a bed' shorten when prefixed; but roots of the shape CVCC such as [salk] 'pull sinews' never lose their vowel when prefixed (or suffixed). These data present a significant analytic dilemma. We might express the deletion as (124a) and the shortening as (124b).

(124) a. $V \rightarrow \emptyset / VC \underline{\quad\quad} CV$
      b. $V \rightarrow \emptyset / VC_1V \underline{\quad\quad} C_1V$

But this is unsatisfactory since both rules apply in the same medial environment and both are subject to certain additional idiosyncrasies (not discussed here), indicating that there is really just one process of medial mora deletion. Expressing it as two separate rules misses an essential descriptive generalization. Kisseberth's solution to this problem was based on the observation that Tonkawa does not allow medial CCC strings (presumably reflecting a ban on complex syllable onsets and codas plus exhaustive syllabification). If the grammar states a separate phonotactic constraint excluding *CCC, then the two branches of elision (syncope and shortening) can be collapsed into a single statement, as in (125a) (or the more contemporary (125b), where the constraint against *CCC is interpreted syllabically).

(125) a. $V \rightarrow \emptyset / X \underline{\quad\quad} Y$
          Condition: block if result violates constraint *CCC

      b. $V \rightarrow \emptyset / \sigma \underline{\quad\quad} \sigma$
          Condition: block if result is not exhaustively syllabifiable

Adopting terminology suggested by George Lakoff, Kisseberth referred to such conditions as *derivational* or *derivative* constraints. They are derivative in the sense that they reflect autonomous phonotactic constraints that must be stated independently of the elision process: it is simply a general fact that CCC strings are absent in Tonkawa (as are #CC and CC#). They constrain the derivation in the sense that a rule is blocked from applying if its output violates the condition. In this case it is clear that appeal to underspecification and a fill-in redundancy rule is of no avail. The correct analysis breaks the elision alternation into two parts: a simple rule of medial elision plus a restriction that limits the scope of the rule by reference to an independently needed phonotactic constraint. In other words, both the constraint and the rule are needed; and the mode in which the rule applies makes direct reference to the constraint.

Another celebrated example in which a constraint on syllable structure simplifies the analysis of an alternation is Itô's treatment of the Lardil final truncations discussed in section 6.9. Recall that Lardil syllables close on a single (apical) coronal consonant. The various truncations are evident in the reduplicated structures of (126a).

(126) a.   yili-yil   'oyster species'
            tipi-ti   'rock-cod species'
            kantu-kan   'red'
            muŋku-mu   'wooden axe'

      b.   V → ∅ / ____ #
            C → ∅ / C ____ #
            C → ∅ / ____ #
            [−apical]

      c.   V → ∅ / ____ #
            C′ → ∅

While earlier analyses stipulated rules of final cluster simplification followed by deletion of final nonapical ([+distributed]) coronals (126b), Itô streamlined the analysis to a simple apocope rule plus stray erasure (126c) of consonants that could not be (re)syllabified in the wake of apocope. Like Kisseberth's condition on Tonkawa elision, Lardil stray erasure is obviously defined in reference to the language's syllable structure (C′ denoting the complement of syllabified material) and so is a "derivative" condition or rule.

    These analyses have inspired the idea that certain combinations of features within the segment and certain configurations of phoneme sequences are more optimal, stable, highly valued, less marked. Morpheme concatenation (as well as perhaps the construction of redundancy-free lexical representations) creates non-optimal configurations. Phonological rules serve to advance the representation toward these more optimal configurations. A more or less equivalent expression of the same idea is that certain configurations are to be filtered out as less optimal, more costly, more marked, more complex. Morpheme combination as well as other rules may create violations of the constraint. Phonological rules serve to repair the constraint violations. In the next section we will look at a few examples where this line of thought has been pursued.

9.14   Repair Rules and Optimization

Calabrese (1988) develops an alternative to underspecification that employs filters and repair rules. Briefly, his theory is as follows. The basic claim is that filters blocking the combination of features are not arbitrary but reflect a UG preference hierarchy among phonological segments; violations of the filters that arise in the course of the derivation are repaired by a restricted set of responses. Calabrese's strongest example illustrating this general thesis involves the distribution of [ATR] with respect to the vocalic height features. Stewart (1972) noted a hierarchy in the historical merger of [ATR] contrasts in the Kwa language family such that the [ATR] contrast tends to be lost first in the low vowels, then in the high vowels, and finally in the mid vowels. Calabrese sees these developments not as sound changes reflecting the addition of a rule but rather as the reimposition of the UG hierarchy of filters in (127).

(127) a. *[−high, +ATR]
b. *[+high, −ATR]
c. *[+low, +ATR]

According to (127), the optimal five-vowel system has [i,u,ɛ,ɔ,a]. Relaxing (127a) allows [e,o]; relaxing (127b) allows [ị,ụ]; and relaxing (127c) allows [ʌ]. On this view, the Proto-Kwa ten-vowel system with [+ATR] [i,u,e,o,ʌ] and [−ATR] [ị,ụ,ɛ,ɔ,a] represents the most complex state; it can only be learned on positive evidence that the most complex segment of the system (i.e., [ʌ]) is present in the language of the environment. In the absence of such evidence, the filters exclude the relevant segment. The evolution of the various daughter languages involves simplifications of the system, reimposing the filters along the hierarchy in (127).

The filter hierarchy not only defines the underlying vocalic inventory but may monitor the output of phonological rules as well. In particular, a rule may create a segment that is excluded by the filter hierarchy. The theory allows two possible responses in this situation: take no action, and allow the illicit segment to surface (i.e., the analogue of Kiparsky's (1982a) Structure Preservation is not imposed, perhaps reflecting the rule's postlexical status). Alternatively, the ban on the illicit feature combination is still enforced, activating one of three possible UG operations: delinking, fission, or reversal.

Calabrese illustrates this aspect of the theory with an analysis of the metaphony process found in many Southern Italian dialects whereby a suffixal high vowel raises the preceding stressed stem vowel (exercise 2.7). Like Standard Italian, these dialects have an underlying seven-vowel system consisting of [i,u,e,o,ɛ,ɔ,a]. They thus have relaxed filter (127a) to allow the [e,o] mid vowels but still ban the lax high vowels [ị,ụ]. Calabrese argues that constraint (127b) is enforced in the output of metaphony, which helps us to understand the following striking asymmetry. When the underlying root vowel is [+ATR] [e,o], then the output of metaphony is uniformly [i,u] across a wide geographic area (128a). But when the root vowel is [−ATR] [ɛ,ɔ], then the product of metaphony varies considerably from one dialect to another. The three principal subtypes are tabulated in (128b) and sampled in (128c).

(128) a.

<u>sg.</u>	<u>pl.</u>	
mes-e	mís-i	'month'
króč-e	kruč-i	'cross'
<u>fem.</u>	<u>masc.</u>	
fredd-a	fridd-u	'cold'
karos-a	karus-u	'young'

b.

	[ɛ]	[ɔ]
Salentino	iɛ	uɔ (>uɛ)
Foggiano	i	u
S. Umbro	e	o

   c.   Salentino

pɛt-e sg.	piɛt-i pl.	'foot'
kɔr-e	kuɛr-i	'heart'
lɛnt-a fem.	liɛnt-u masc.	'slow'
mɔrt-a	muɛrt-u	'dead'

Foggiano

pɛt-e sg.	pit-i pl.	'foot'
grɔss-a fem.	gruss-u masc.	'big'

S. Umbro

pɛd-e sg.	ped-i pl.	'foot'
nɔstr-a fem.	nostr-u masc.	'our'

Calabrese explains the disparity as follows. Metaphony is formulated to spread [+high], delinking the [high] specification of the stem vowel.

(129)   V   V

           ⌿----------⌡

   [−high] [+high]

When rule (129) is applied to the [+ATR] mid vowels [e,o] of (128a), the resultant [+high, +ATR] is an optimal feature combination that is not excluded by the filters and so is allowed to stand. But when the root vowel is the [−ATR] [ɛ,ɔ], metaphony produces the [−ATR, +high] combination that is excluded by filter (127b). In the Salentino dialect this illicit feature combination is repaired by a *fission* process in which the incompatible features repel each other into separate segments [+high] [−ATR] to create the rising onglide diphthongs [iɛ,uɔ] (130a). The [uɔ] > [uɛ] change is a later development.

(130) a.   V   →   V   V

               | | |

          $\begin{bmatrix} -\text{ATR} \\ +\text{high} \end{bmatrix}$ [+high] [−ATR]

     b.   V   →   V

               | |

          $\begin{bmatrix} -\text{ATR} \\ +\text{high} \end{bmatrix}$ $\begin{bmatrix} +\text{ATR} \\ +\text{high} \end{bmatrix}$

     c.   V   →   V

               | |

          $\begin{bmatrix} -\text{ATR} \\ +\text{high} \end{bmatrix}$ $\begin{bmatrix} +\text{ATR} \\ -\text{high} \end{bmatrix}$

In Foggiano the illicit combination is repaired by *delinking* [−ATR] (130b), creating a [+high] vowel that becomes [+ATR] in conformity with the filter. Southern Umbro repairs the violation by *negating* each of the incompatible feature values to derive a [+ATR, −high] vowel allowed by the system (130c). Individual dialects have grammaticalized one of these three outcomes. The rather chaotic geographic distribution of the dialectal subtypes suggests that grammaticalization represented an independently developing local response at particular points rather than any broad, sweeping sound change.

If correct, this analysis has a number of theoretical implications. First, it shows that filters or constraints barring a particular structure cannot be understood to always simply suspend the application of a rule like some invisible hand staying the move of a chess piece. Rather, the rule applies and the system is left to deal with the consequences. Second, the repair is made immediately by a limited set of operations. No other language-particular rules may intervene to be triggered by the illicit [i̥,u̥] before they are repaired at a later stage of the derivation. Finally, and most significantly, the repair operations only make sense as responses to an independently defined ban on illicit segments. This is especially evident in the case of the diphthong arising from fission. If we try to explain the diphthong as simply the spread of [+high] with no delinking of the stem vowel's original [−high] (creating the analogue of a contour tone), we expect a falling, offglide diphthong [ɛi] − not the ongliding [iɛ]. In other words, these responses restore the system to a more optimal state that conforms to the constraint. Stated differently, if the segmental inventory allowed underlying [i̥,u̥], then we would not expect the range of responses in (128b) − rather, we would expect the raising of [ɛ,ɔ] → [i̥,u̥] to uniformly accompany the raising of [e,o] → [i,u].

One important issue this analysis raises is the putative universality of the segment hierarchy. For example, many Bantu languages are claimed to contrast [ATR] among the high vowels, not the mid vowels; the same situation obtains in Moore (exercise 1.8). Granted that this is the proper feature interpretation in these languages, we must modify the framework to accommodate these systems, perhaps by different ordering of the filters. If (127a) comes after (127b), then the system allows [i̥,u̥] at the expense of [ɛ,ɔ]. Another aspect of the universality issue is whether the repair mechanisms can be circumscribed in the rigid fashion Calabrese assumes. Other analysts have broadened the range, seeing a variety of rules as repair or optimization strategies. Finally, instead of encoding the relative complexity of phonological segments in a hierarchy of filters, some phonologists have built this property directly into the formal representation of a given sound. See Kaye, Lowenstamm, and Vergnaud 1985 and Anderson and Ewen 1987, among others, for developments of this hypothesis.

Phonologists have tried to bring sequential phonotactics under the constraints umbrella as well. For example, recall the Diola Fogny phonotactic whereby nasals agree with a following consonant. In many languages this reflects a more general constraint that a coda consonant agrees in place with following consonant. A number of linguists (e.g., Kaye, Lowenstamm, and Vergnaud 1990, Goldsmith 1990, Itô 1986) have characterized this phenomenon in terms of a notion of *prosodic licensing*. In the traditional generative model, once a feature is stored in the lexical representation, it will emerge to the surface unless some rule intervenes to change it. Prosodic licensing drops this assumption. Features do not automatically pass to the phonetic surface. Rather, they must go through an inspection much like passengers disembarking from an airplane. Any feature that fails this phonological customs inspection is not allowed to leave the grammar. Applying this line of reasoning to the Diola case, we might imagine that the various nodes of syllable structure are annotated with the features that they will approve. In the Diola case, the N' coda position licenses [+nasal] and [+consonantal] but not a Place feature. In contrast, the onset N" checks off both [+nasal] and [+consonantal] as well as Place. To see how this works, consider [gam + gam] → [gaŋgam].

(131) gam + gam

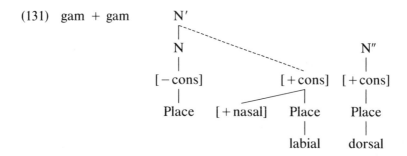

When syllabification is imposed on [gam + gam], the preconsonantal nasal is placed in coda position (131). While [+nasal] and [+consonantal] are licensed in this position, the Place features are not. If we accept Halle's (1992) idea that [+consonantal] must have an Oral Place specification, then we have two options: license the [consonantal] by negating [+consonantal] to [−consonantal], deriving the nasal glide N (and eventually perhaps a nasal vowel); alternatively, find a Place specification from the closest position that is licensed – the preceding vowel or the following consonant. If the preceding vowel is dorsal, this option might be argued to derive the velar nasal [ŋ]. Linkage to the following consonant is of course the option that Diola takes, deriving [gaŋgam], [bɔmbɔn], and [tiːntiːŋ]. The Place specification of the velar [g] in [gaŋgam] is licensed in virtue of appearing in onset position. The result is formally equivalent to a rule of nasal assimilation. But on this view, the nasal assimilation does not result directly from a rule changing one feature specification into another. Rather, it is one outcome among a (limited?) range of responses to achieve a specific and limited goal: licensing the [+consonantal] feature in the coda. If we accept this analysis, then another statement will be required to license the Place specification of word-final consonants since Diola freely contrasts nasals in this position. Such statements would be the prosodic licensing equivalent of the appendix in more traditional generative accounts of the syllable.

9.15 The Obligatory Contour Principle and Soft Universals

The Obligatory Contour Principle (OCP) was one of the first configurational constraints to arise from autosegmental phonology and has continued to be the subject of some debate. Recall that its original formulation barred underlying lexical representations from containing adjacent identical elements on an autosegmental tier. The OCP enforced the multiply linked high tone in Shona *hákáta* 'diviner's bones' (section 7.2) and the long-distance geminate in Classical Arabic *madad-na* 'we stretched' (section 8.3) crucial to explaining the phonology of these structures.

(132) hakata   CVCVC

       ⋁ | | ⋁

       H L   m   d

There have been various attempts to extend the OCP beyond underlying lexical representations. McCarthy (1986a) notes that a number of languages block syncope rules just in case they would bring together tautomorphemic identical consonants (antigemination, section 8.5). For example, Tonkawa medial syncope converts [picen-oʔ] 'he cuts' to *picnoʔ* but blocks on [hewaw-oʔ] 'he is dead', which is realized as *hewawoʔ*, not **heww-oʔ*. This phenomenon is explained if the OCP is allowed to reject the output of elision in Tonkawa because it creates a morpheme-internal sequence of identical consonants. Finally, recall from section 7.2 that Myers (1987a) proposes that the OCP merge identical high tones in Shona that straddle a morpheme boundary in order to derive the multiple linking crucial for rules applying on a later cycle.

Odden (1986, 1988) calls the scope of the OCP into question, arguing that at best it pinpoints a marked configuration that can, but need not, be repaired in a variety of ways rather than a rigid principle of phonological representation that simply blocks a rule whose output would violate it, as McCarthy seems to assume. For example, in Yir Yoront a schwa is inserted to break up stop clusters that are not homorganic: for example, [ŋat thuy] 'fish fat' is realized as *ŋatəthuy* (retroflex [ṭ] and laminal [th] count as different points of articulation). The natural analysis merges the Place nodes in homorganic clusters before the operation of epenthesis, which then blocks by geminate integrity (133a). But in other languages epenthesis applies precisely between homorganic segments and nowhere else (133b). For example, Modern Hebrew inserts [e] between stems ending in a dental stop and suffixes beginning with a dental stop: [yalad + ti] → *yiladeti* 'I gave birth'. Thus, in each case the result is avoidance of the C_iC_i configuration; but the methods to achieve this result differ. There is thus little justification to single out blockage of deletion (antigemination) as the only OCP reflex.

(133) a. $C_i + C_i$ C_i

       | | → ⋀

       X X   X X

    b. $C_i + C_i$ → $C_i\ V\ C_i$

    c. k a n ə n + i   k a n n + i   k a n + i

        | ⋀ | | | | → | ⋀ | | | → | ⋀ ⋀ |

        X X X X X X   X   X X X X X   X   X X X X X   X

Furthermore, Odden questions the generality of the antigemination phenomenon itself. There are no reported cases where the deletion of intervocalic consonants is suspended just in case it creates tautomorphemic identical vowels and indeed there are some counterexamples such as Estonian *tegema* 'to do', *teen* 'I do' from [tegem]. Also, there are counterexamples to vowel deletion such as Hindi schwa syncope, which applies in [daanəw-i] → *daanwi* 'demon' as well as in [kaanən-i] → *kaanni* 'garden'. Although Odden does not draw this conclusion, we might maintain that in these cases an OCP-motivated merger applies to the output of syncope, as in (133c). The Hindi and Estonian cases would then differ from Tonkawa in that the OCP is enforced on the output of the rule through a repair rather than by blocking the rule. Finally, Odden challenges the contention that the OCP always holds of underlying representations, calling attention to the epenthesis into geminate clusters in Yawelmani *mulil-ši?* 'deceived' (cf. *moll-onit* 'you are being duped').

We conclude that the OCP is not the rigid universal constraint on phonological representation that McCarthy (1986a) implies. But it would be equally mistaken to deny the connection among the various OCP responses sketched in (133). The OCP has the status of what Goldsmith (1990) calls a "soft" universal. It defines a marked configuration that grammars tend to avoid though they do not necessarily always succeed in doing so. Identifying such configurations, circumscribing the ways in which they are respected, and finding the proper formalism to express the phenomenon has emerged as one of the critical challenges facing contemporary phonological theory. We will close with brief discussion of a couple of attempts to confront this issue.

Yip (1988a) proposes to expand the role of the OCP considerably as the motive force behind various rules and constraints. Her proposal is cast within the framework of McCarthy (1986a), with the following key assumptions: (i) the scope of the OCP is expanded from ruling out identical root nodes to ruling out identical (Place) features as well; (ii) the OCP is a UG constraint on tautomorphemic sequences; (iii) phonemes belonging to separate morphemes are arrayed on different tiers; (iv) tier conflation may bring two identical elements together; (v) if no other rules intervene to modify the [αF] [αF] sequence, the two feature specifications are merged into one at the end of each cycle or stratum. If we agree to expand the scope of the OCP to individual feature tiers *[αF] [αF], then morpheme concatenation (and associated tier conflation) will create many sequences of identical specifications on individual Place feature tiers. The [αF] [αF] configuration elicits a variety of responses from one case to another that must be stipulated in individual grammars. But the claim is that all have the same underlying cause: avoidance of an [αF] [αF] configuration.

As illustration, let us look at a simple example from Yip's discussion of a rule of Seri (based on Marlett and Stemberger 1983) that deletes a glottal stop from the coda of the syllable just in case the onset also contains a glottal stop. Underlying [?i-?-a:?-kašni] 'my being bitten' is thus realized as *?i-?-a:-kašni*. Seri does not bar coda glottal stops in general (cf. *ko?panšX* 'run like him!') – just when the onset also contains a glottal stop. While we might express the rule as (134a), this formulation fails to distinguish the process as being any more plausible than one with [p] (or any other arbitrary consonant) as trigger (134b).

(134)   a.   [ʔ] → ∅ / [ʔ] ____   b.   [ʔ] → ∅ / [p] ____

Yip expresses the rule as (135), listing the tier along which identity is to be checked, a domain limitation (if needed), and the type of response the rule encodes – in the Seri case deletion of the second glottal stop. What is missing from the rule is the environment: this is understood to be supplied by the OCP.

(135)   <u>OCP</u>

tier:	laryngeal
domain:	syllable
structural description:	
structural change:	delete second element

We may understand this analysis as follows. The [αF] [αF] configuration of the OCP defines the core of a UG rule schema whose remaining portions must be filled in (learned) on a language-particular basis. When an [αF] [αF] sequence is created in a given language, a certain "pressure" builds up. In the absence of any other information, nothing will happen. What (135) does is to specify a particular response to release the pressure. This rule only applies to the [αF] [αF] configuration supplied by the OCP. A rule such as (134b) deleting [ʔ] after tautosyllabic [p] is thus more complex because it does not fall under the [αF] [αF] schema and hence the structural description of the rule as including [p] and [ʔ] must be stated directly. In (135) the structural description comes for free because all grammars inherit the core [αF] [αF] schema from UG. Yip assumes that if no rule crystallizes around the [αF] [αF] core, then the general merger convention proposed by Myers (1987a) collapses the two segments into one. This point seems dubious, if for no other reason than that it weakens the basic premise of the analysis; if the merger device is always available, what motivation is there for a language-particular rule?

To get a better feel for this mode of thinking, let us consider another of Yip's examples. In Cantonese Chinese there is a constraint against successive labials. Since syllable and morpheme generally coincide in Chinese, the constraint can be stated over either domain. We choose the morpheme for reasons that will become clear momentarily. The labial constraint bars the combination of labial consonants in the onset and coda (*pim, *ma:p) as well as with round nuclear vowels (*tup, *köm). The only asymmetry is that a labial onset may combine with a back rounded vowel (mou, puk, fu) but not with a front rounded vowel (*möü, *pü) – a complication we will overlook here; see Yip 1988a for discussion.

Since there is little morphology in Cantonese, it is difficult to find heteromorphemic effects of the labial constraint. One does arise in the secret language known as *La-mi*. In this speech disguise, the CVC morpheme reduplicates, the initial consonant changes to [l], and the final vowel changes to [i]: [ma] becomes [ma + ma] and then [la + mi]; [yat] becomes [yat + yat] and then [lat + yit]. According to Yip's source, when a morpheme with a coda labial reduplicates, the final one is replaced by a default coronal: [sap] and [t'im] surface as [lap + sit] and [lim + t'in] from [lap + sip] and [lim + t'im]. This suggests that the constraint against successive labials is a property of the morpheme rather than the syllable. As in the Seri case, this dissimilation is treated as a particular expansion of the OCP schema in (136).

(136)   OCP

                              tier: labial
                       domain: morpheme
        structural description:
              structural change: delete second element

Another dissimilation operates in the *La-mi* speech disguise. When the base contains an [i], the vowel of the second reduplicant surfaces as [u] instead of [i]: [kin] → [lin + kin] → [lin + kun]. This can be treated analogously as an instantiation of the OCP on Clements's V-Pl [coronal] tier, with the morpheme as the domain, and a change of the second element to [labial]. Curiously, the [i] → [u] rule is blocked when the coda itself contains a labial: [t'im] is [lim + t'in], not [lim + t'un]. Thus, here the OCP blocks a rule of dissimilation if this rule would itself create an OCP violation. Theories that see repairs as improvements of the structure see this interaction as expected; application of vocalic dissimilation to [lim + t'im] or [lim + t'in] would introduce a [labial] [labial] violation; if rules are constrained to always advance the structure to a better-formed state, vocalic dissimilation would be blocked. Alternatively, this might be a simple conflict of constraints, with the labial one winning out. In either case the OCP *[αF] [αF] configuration is the driving force behind the analysis.

A similar line of thought is pursued in Mohanan's (1992a) study of place assimilation processes. Mohanan proceeds from the observation that given a [nasal] + C cluster, a language is more likely to have nasal assimilation than not, at least syllable-internally. Similar to Yip's treatment of the OCP, Mohanan postulates the sequence [−continuant] [+consonantal] as the core of a UG rule schema. Since it is present in all grammars, the child must learn the parameters that generate the assimilatory patterns in the language of the environment. Once again, we see that the earlier generative assumption that representations emerge for free in the absence of rules is dropped. A particular phonological configuration reaches the phonetic surface only after it has passed inspection by the individual grammar's protocol for that structure.

Through study of place assimilation processes in English, Korean, Hindi, and Malayalam, Mohanan discerns certain hierarchies regarding place and sonorancy that constrain the outcome for any given combination of [−continuant] [+consonantal]. The Place hierarchy runs from weak to strong as coronal, labial, velar and is claimed to control both the target and the source of assimilation according to an intuitive notion of "strength" or dominance: the likelihood of assimilation between any given pair of segments [x] + [y] is directly proportional to the strength of the trigger and inversely related to the strength of the target. Thus, the weak coronal is most susceptible to assimilation and least likely to spread, while the strong velar is the most likely to spread and most resistant to assimilation. A similar relation ranks sonorants as weaker than obstruents, with the result that a nasal is more likely to assimilate and an oral stop is more likely to spread. These strength parameters implicate various schedules of assimilation whose validity remains to be verified: for example, if a labial assimilates, then a dental will also; if a stop assimilates, then a nasal will too.

Finally, see Archangeli and Pulleyblank 1993 and Prince and Smolensky 1993 for extensive discussion of constraints and specific proposals to integrate them into a theory of phonological rules and representations.

Suggested Readings

Archangeli, Diana, and Douglas Pulleyblank. 1989. Yoruba vowel harmony. Linguistic Inquiry 20.173–217.
Goldsmith, John. 1992. Phonology as an intelligent system. Bridges between psychology and linguistics: A Swarthmore festschrift for Lila Gleitman, ed. by D. J. Napoli and J. Kegl. Hillsdale, N.J.: Lawrence Erlbaum.
Halle, Morris. 1992. Phonological features. International encyclopedia of linguistics, vol. 3, ed. by W. Bright, 207–12. Oxford: Oxford University Press.
Kaye, Jonathan, Jean Lowenstamm, and Jean-Roger Vergnaud. 1985. The internal structure of phonological elements: A theory of charm and government. Phonology Yearbook 2.303–26.
Odden, David. 1991. Vowel geometry. Phonology 8.261–90.

Exercises

9.1 Arabic

Relying on the discussion of place features in sections 9.2 and 9.3, develop analyses for the following sound changes in various Arabic dialects.

A. In Moroccan Arabic (McCarthy 1991) labialization of consonants is restricted to the segments [k,g,q,x̣,ɣ]. Express the class of consonants that seat the labialization feature.

(1) dx^wəl   'come in'
     nɣ^wəl   'prick'
     nq̇^wəl   'copy down'
     rg^wəd   'sleep'
     nk^wər   'deny'

B. Classical Arabic [q] has changed to [ʔ] in Egyptian and most sedentary Levantine dialects and to [g] in many others such as Sudanese. State these sound changes.

C. In Lebanese Arabic (Haddad 1983) the low vowel [a] raises to [e] in certain contexts, a process known as *imaala*. One involves the feminine noun suffix

– a change found in many other Levantine dialects. Another is more characteristically Lebanese and affects the long low vowel. Examine the following examples to determine the nature of the consonants that block *imaala*. How can this be expressed formally given the feature structures introduced in section 9.2? (Transcription note: [T,D,S] are ''emphatic'' consonants.)

(2) feminine nouns

ʕuTl-e	'vacation'	furS-a	'break'
jariid-e	'newspaper'	warʔ-a	'sheet of paper'
mʕallm-e	'teacher'	laḥZ-a	'moment'
jdiid-e	'new'	ʕariiD-a	'wide'
nDiif-e	'clean'	rafiiʕ-a	'thin'

(3) template
    CaCCaaC (agentive)

rasseem	'painter'	xaTTaaT	'calligrapher'

    CaCaaCil (plural)

ʔaneebil	'bombs'	maʕaawil	'hoes'

    CaaC (past tense)

keen	'was'	Saar	'became'

    mCaaCaC-a (derived nominal)

mseeyar-a	'amusing'	mḥaawal-e	'attempt'

    CaaCiC (participle)

feeyiʔ	'awake'	Taayir	'flying'

9.2 Nisgha Reduplication

In this Tsimshian language of British Columbia (Shaw 1987, 1991b), the quality of short prefixal vowels is determined by the phonological context. Examine the following data and develop an analysis that predicts the shape of the reduplicative prefix. What aspects of feature geometry are helpful in expressing the phonological generalizations? The language has a strict ban on onsetless syllables.

(1)

labial	coronal	velar	uvular	laryngeal
p	t tˢ	k kʷ	q	ʔ
p'	t' tˢ' tɬ'	k' k'ʷ	q'	
	s ɬ	x xʷ	x̣	h
m	n l			
m'	n' l'			
	y, y'	w, w'		

(2)

wilá:x	wil-wilá:x	'to know something'
wá:x	wix-wá:x	'to paddle'
tˢám	tˢim-tˢám	'to cook'
t'á:p	t'ip-t'á:p	'to drive in'
tá:w	tuw-tá:w	'to freeze'
ɬáxʷ	ɬuxʷ-láxʷ	'to shake'
híx	hax-(h)íx	'to be fat'
ɬó:q	ɬax̣-ɬó:q	'to wake or get up early'
ɬé:x̣-kʷ	ɬax̣-ɬé:x̣-kʷ	'to have finished eating'
ʔúx	ʔax-ʔúx	'to throw'
qá:p	qap-qá:p	'to scratch'
tám'	tim-tám'	'to press'
qín'	qan-qín'	'to chew'
háw'	haw-(h)áw'	'to stop, go home'
hít'	hat-hít'	'to stick'
t'áʔ	t'ax̣-t'áʔ	'to clap'
qóʔ	qax̣-qóʔ	'to go somewhere'
t'ák	t'ix-t'ák	'to forget'
lúkʷ	luxʷ-lúkʷ	'to move'
tˢó:q	tˢax̣-tó:q	'to be embarrassed'
kikíl'	kix-kikíl'	'to look for'
t'ákʷ	t'uxʷ-t'ákʷ	'to twist'
pátˢ	pis-pátˢ	'to lift, carry'
q'útˢ	q'as-q'útˢ	'to cut'
ʔí:tˢ	ʔas-ʔí:tˢ	'to fry'
hátˢ'	has-hátˢ'	'to bite'
t'ú:tˢ'	t'is-t'ú:tˢ'	'to be black'
tˢ'átɬ'	tˢ'iɬ-tˢ'átɬ'	'to have rippled surface'
yátˢ	his-yátˢ	'to strike'
yáɬ-kʷ	hiɬ-yáɬ-kʷ	'to be smooth'
yέ:	hi-yέ:	'to walk'

9.3 Proto-Indo-European and Proto-Kachin Reconstruction

A. The following sound correspondences have been discovered among the three Indo-European languages Luvian, Sanskrit, and Greek. Reconstruct the most plausible PIE sources for each correspondence set. Characterize the individual sound changes.

(1)

PIE	Skt	Gk	Luv
———	š	k	tˢ
———	k	k	k
———	k	p	kʷ

B. PIE *gʷ has the following reflexes in various daughter languages: [g] Sanskrit, [b] Greek, [w] Luvian, [gu] Latin. Formalize the sound changes.

C. Burling (1966) reconstructs open-syllable CV and closed-syllable CVC morphemes for Proto-Kachin on the basis of correspondences such as those in (2).

(2)

	Burmese	Atsi	Maru	
CV	shú	tshú	tshàu	'fat'
	dû	dú	dāu	'dig'
	θwêi	sùi	sā	'blood'
	ù	ǔ	áu	'egg'
CVC	shóun	tshúm	tshàm	'mortar'
	bân	bàn	bīn	'flower'
	chouʔ	khyup	khyáp	'sew'
	θauʔ	šuʔ	šók	'drink'
	shaʔ	tshat	tshéʔ	'deer'

What reasons can be given for reconstructing the following cognates as open-syllable CV vs. closed-syllable CVC?

(3)

θéi	šǐ	šìt	'die'
chéi	khyí	khyìt	'leg'
myêi		myìt	'grandchild'
šèi	hǐ	ɣʔít	'in front'
chêi	khyì	khyít	'dung'
môu	màu	mùk	'sky'
ŋóu	ŋâu	ŋùk	'cry'
shôu	tsháu	tshúk	'dye'
nòu	nǎu	núk	'breast'
thôu	tháu	thúk	'stab'

9.4 Irish

As part of the well-known lenition alternation in Irish, the voiceless plain coronals [t] and [s] and their palatalized counterparts [t'] and [s'] reduce to [h] and [h'] (= [hʸ]), respectively (Ní Chiosáin 1991). How can this process be formulated? Discuss its bearing on feature geometry with respect to place and stricture features and the representation of secondary articulation.

(1)

talə	'land'	mə halə	'my land'
soləs	'light'	mə holəs	'my light'
t'o:xt	'temperature'	mə h'o:xt	'my temperature'
s'o:l	'sail'	mə h'o:l	'my sail'

9.5 Spirantization

Aspirated stops [pʰ,tʰ,kʰ] frequently turn to fricatives [f,θ,x] (e.g., Grimm's Law, Ancient Greek). Is this evidence for the proposition that [h] is properly analyzed as [+continuant]?

9.6 *Ngbaka Consonants*

Ngbaka includes the segments of (1) in its consonant inventory (Thomas 1963, Sagey 1988).

(1) p   f   t   s   k   kp
    b   v   d   z   g   gb
    mb   nd nz ŋg ŋmgb
    m   n   ñ
       l   y   w

A. The following pairs of consonants may not occur within the same (noncompound) word (in either order). Develop an analysis to explain this cooccurrence constraint.

(2) p – b   b – mb   mb – m
    t – d   d – nd   nd – n
    s – z   z – nz   nz – n
    k – g   g – ŋg   ŋg – ñ
    kp – gb   gb – ŋmgb   ŋmgb – m

    p – kp   b – kp   mb – kp   m – kp
    p – gb   b – gb   mb – gb   m – gb
    p – ŋmgb   b – ŋmgb   mb – ŋmgb   m – ŋmgb

B. However, as shown by the forms in (3), velars and labiovelars freely combine. Try to extend the analysis to these cases. Is the notion of major versus minor articulator of help?

(3) gboko   'incandescent'   kpaŋga   'large mat'
    kukpe-la   'eyelid'   gbOngO   'small basket'
    kakpe   'slave'   ŋmgboko   'he-goat'

C. Also, while pairs such as [nd] – [d] and [nz] – [z] are disallowed, [nz] – [d] and [nd] – [l], [nz] – [l] are allowed.

(4) nzidOlO   'citron'
    ndulu   'to deceive'
    nzulu   'flour'

And while [t] – [d] and [s] – [z] are disallowed, [s] – [d], [t] – [l], and [s] – [l] are permitted. Recalling the discussion of Arabic root cooccurrence constraints in section 4.3.4, try to extend your analysis to these cases.

(5) sakade   'thus'
    tolo   'strike'
    sulu   'to rain very hard'

9.7 Räto-Romansch

In the Bergüner dialect of Räto-Romansch (Kamprath 1986, 1987), the underlying and etymological glide [y] appears as the velar stop [k] in certain contexts but not others. Examine the following data and develop an analysis for the process. What bearing does it have on the status of [consonantal] as a Root feature?

(1) [krey + r] → krekr̥   'to believe'   cf. krey + a   'believes'
     [rey + r]   → rekr̥   'to laugh'   rey-ə   'laughs'
     [deyt]   → dekt   'finger'   deyt   'finger' (dialectical)
     [feyl]   → fekl̥   'thread'
     [vɛyr]   → vɛkr̥   'true'   veyr   'true' (dialectical)
     [lay]   → lay, *lak   'lake'
     [dzey]   → dzey, *dzek 'juice'

9.8 Kagoshima Japanese

In the Kagoshima dialect of Japanese word-final high vowels are dropped after a [−continuant] consonant (Haraguchi 1984, Trigo 1991). Express the subsequent development of the [−continuant] segments. N transcribes the so-called mora nasal of Japanese.

(1) obi   oʔ   'belt'
     matu   maʔ   'pine tree'
     doku   doʔ   'poison'
     kagi   kaʔ   'key'
     kami   kaN   'god'
     inu   iN   'dog'

9.9 Kammu

In the Mon-Khmer language Kammu (Svantesson 1989) the Southern and Northern dialects differ in terms of a voicing contrast on the onset consonant versus a tonal register difference in the following vowel. Characterize the difference between the two dialects and discuss the bearing of these data on the thesis of monovalent [voiced].

(1) | Southern Kammu | Northern Kammu | |
|---|---|---|
| kuŋ | kúŋ | 'village' |
| taañ | táañ | 'to weave' |
| m̥aar | máar | 'salt' |
| r̥aaŋ | ráaŋ | 'tooth' |
| | | |
| gaaŋ | kàaŋ | 'house' |
| dar | tàr | 'to run' |
| maam | màam | 'blood' |
| raaŋ | ràaŋ | 'flower' |

9.10 Polish

Recall from section 5.8.1 the rule that changes palatalized [r'] to obstruent [ž]. When this segment is preceded by a voiceless consonant, the [ž] turns to [š].

Discuss this process with respect to the theory of monovalent [voiced]. Must it be described as the spread of [−voiced]?

(1) nom.sg.   pas   mur   gr-a   kr-a
     loc.sg.   pa[ś]-e mu[ž]-e   g[ž]-e   k[š]-e
               'belt'   'wall'   'game'   'ice float'

9.11 Yucatec Maja (Straight 1976)

In Yucatec Maja consonant clusters sharing the same articulator reduce in the manner indicated in (1). Using the notions of feature geometry, try to formalize the rule. What bearing does this process have on the representation of affricates?

(1) [k + k] → [h + k]   tun kolik k'aaš → tun kolih k'aaš
                              'he's clearing brush'
     [t + č] → [h + č]   le? iŋ w ot čo → le? iŋ w oh čo
                              'that house of mine'
     [tˢ + t] → [s + t]   ?utˢ t iŋ w ič → ?us t iŋ w ič
                              'I like it'
     [č + t] → [š + t]   c'u ho?oč tik → c'u ho?oš tik
                              'he scratched it'

9.12 Sinhalese

Utilizing Steriade's aperture model for plosives, develop an analysis for the following data from Sinhalese (Feinstein 1979). Assume that the superscripted [ŋ] is the placeless nasal glide (Trigo 1988); [ⁿd] and [ᵐb] are prenasalized stops. The final schwa marks the definite; the plural form consists of the bare stem.

(1) sing.def.   pl.
     bim-ə   biᵑ   'ground'
     gam-ə   gaᵑ   'village'
     kan-ə   kaᵑ   'ear'
     liⁿd-ə   liᵑ   'well'
     aᵐb-ə   aᵑ   'mango'

In certain morphological contexts consonants are geminated. In the same contexts prenasalized stops are realized as heterosyllabic nasal-stop clusters. Develop an analysis for these cases. Compare the treatment of gemination of the prenasalized segments in Sagey's contour segment model and Steriade's aperture model. Ignore all other alternations.

(2) geminating   nongeminating
     puttu   putaa   'son'
     weddu   wedaa   'doctor'
     gonnu   gonaa   'bull'
     hombə   hoᵐbu   'chin'
     kandə   kaⁿdu   'hill'
     kondə   koⁿdu   'backbone'

9.13   Barra Gaelic Epenthesis

The Gaelic dialect of Barra Island (Outer Hebrides) is characterized by the epenthesis of a vowel within a sonorant + consonant cluster (Clements 1986, 1987).
Examine the data in (2) to identify the rules determining the quality of the epenthetic vowel. Do these data support Restricted or Radical Underspecification? C'
denotes palatalized consonants with a [−back] secondary articulation. The segment inventory is shown in (1), ignoring the phenomenon of lenition.

(1)   i   ɨ   u   p   t   t'   k   k'
      e   ʌ   o   b   d   d'   g   g'
      æ   a   ɔ   f   s   s'   x   x'
                      v   z'   ɣ
                      m   n   n'
                          r   r'
                          l   l'

(2)   mar[a]v   'dead'
      ɔr[ɔ]m   'on me'
      d'al[a]v   'picture'
      ur[u]pəl   'tail'
      dun[u]xəɣ   'Duncan'
      a.l[a]pə   'Scotland'
      tʰɔr[ɔ]mæt   'Norman'
      bɔ.r[ɔ]ɣ   'Borg'
      šal[a]k   'hunting'

      mʌr'[e]v   'the dead'
      bul'[i]k'   'bellows' gen.sg.
      dɨr'[i]çə   'darker'
      tʰʌr'[e]v   'bulls'
      lur'[i]k'n'ən   'legs'
      šær[a]v   'bitter'
      fær[a]k   'anger'
      šæn[a]xəs   'conversation'

      æm[æ]šir'   'time'
      tʰ'im[i]çal   'round about'

9.14   Russian

Teachers of Russian report that their English-speaking students have difficulty
articulating palatalized dental consonants, pronouncing *Na*[d']*a* and *Volo*[d']*a* as
either [nadya] or [naǰa], [volodya] or [voloǰa]. How might these errors be explained in Calabrese's model of filters and repair rules (section 9.14)?

9.15   English

Developing an observation made originally by Fudge (1969), and repeated by
Clements and Keyser (1983), Davis (1991) systematically surveys the range of
consonants that may substitute for C_1 and C_2 in tautomorphemic sC_1VC_2 strings
in English. The results of his computer search of a 20,000-word dictionary are

indicated in (1). How might the gaps be expressed formally? Is underspecification of use?

(1) spVC
C = labial	0	
C = alveolar	196	(spit, speed)
C = palatal	20	(speech, special)
C = velar	56	(speak, spike, spook, spaghetti)

    skVC
C = labial	58	(skip, scuba, Eskimo)
C = alveolar	151	(skit, skate, skulk, scud)
C = palatal	25	(scotch, sketch)
C = velar	1	(skuŋk ?)

    stVC
C = labial	100+	(stable, stop)
C = coronal	300+	(stone, stall, static, stadium, stash, stitch)
C = velar	100+	(stock, plastic)

9.16 *Fula Geminates*

According to Paradis (1988–89), Fula has the consonant system shown in (1).

(1)
stops	p	t	c	k
	b	d	ǰ	g
implosives	ɓ	ɗ	ʄ	
nasals	m	n	ñ	ŋ
fricatives	f	s		
liquids		l,r		
glides	w		y	h

The language contrasts simple and geminate consonants. All consonants may appear geminate except the continuants [w], [y], [f], [h], [s]: *raddo* 'hunt', *tikkere* 'anger', *ɓottude* 'to pinch', *gollaade* 'to work', *lacciri* 'couscous', *kaŋŋe* 'gold'. Certain noun stem markers trigger a gemination of the final consonant of the stem. Although no examples are cited, for purposes of this exercise you may assume the existence of hypothetical stems such as those in (2). What is cited are stems such as those in (3) ending in an underlying continuant. The consonant is changed under gemination, reflecting the absence of geminate continuants.

(2)
stem	diminutive	geminated
lam	lam-el	lamm-i
sak	sak-el	sakk-i

(3)
stem	diminutive	geminated	
kɔs		kɔcc-ɛ	'curdled milk'
lɛw	lew-el	lebb-i	'month'
ñɛw	ñew-el	ñɛbb-ɛ	'bean'
lɛf	lef-el	lepp-i	'ribbon'
wuy		guǰǰ-ɔ	'thief'

Develop an analysis for this alternation. How might the absence of geminate continuants in the phonemic inventory be expressed? Discuss the effect of this gap on the analysis of the data in (3). Does it make sense to distinguish between a constraint and a repair rule? What are the implications of the data in (4) for the analysis?

(4)	stem	diminutive	geminated	
	ñiiw		ñiib-i	'elephant'
	laaw	laaw-el	laab-i	'road'
	lɛɛs	lees-el	lɛɛc-ɛ	'bed'
	maay	maay-el	maaĵ-ɛ	'river'

9.17   Selayarese

Recall the discussion of prosodic licensing and nasal assimilation in Diola Fogny in section 9.13. The following data are from the Indonesian language Selayarese (Goldsmith 1990, based on Mithun and Basri 1986). Develop a licensing analysis of the alternations occasioned by reduplication.

(1)	pekaŋ	'hook'	pekampekaŋ	'hook-like object'
	maŋŋaŋ	'tired'	maŋŋammaŋŋaŋ	'sort of tired'
	soroŋ	'push'	soronsoroŋ	'drawer'
	dodoŋ	'sick'	dodondodoŋ	'sort of sick'
	nunruŋ	'hit'	nunrunnunruŋ	'hit lightly'
	gintaŋ	'chili'	gintaŋgintaŋ	'chili-like object'
	lamuŋ	'grow'	lamullamuŋ	'plantation'
	luŋaŋ	'pillow'	luŋalluŋaŋ	'small pillow'

9.18   Guere

Recall from section 9.11 that Guere has a root constraint that bars the combination of two nonhigh vowels in successive syllables: *[−high] [−high]. The only exceptions are geminates and identical vowels separated by a coronal. These are treated as single multiply linked phonemes and so (combined with the default coronal assumption) they can escape the constraint.

(1)	a.	nimi	'animal'	c.	bēnī	'sand'
		zIgU	'chameleon'		gwɛI	'burn'
		būi	'ashes'		meU	'tongue'
		duɗu	'chest'		gbau	'fox'
	b.	kI6o	'rat'	d.	baa	'manioc'
		glUɛ̃	'cayman'		yɛɛ	'to dry'
		kUla	'hand'		wɔɗɔ	'to wash'
		jie	'road'		beɗe	'to hang'
		6lua	'ground'			

Paradis and Prunet (1989) note that when an object pronoun is suffixed to the verb, the root vowel of the verb shortens and sometimes changes to high. The object pronouns themselves come in various types – ε, $\mathfrak{o}$, I, U – each of which reflects the noun class of the referent.

(2) UR

nɛɛ + ɛ	→ nIɛ	'stick it'
nɛɛ + ɔ	→ nIɔ	'stick it'
gblee + ɛ	→ gblIɛ	'welcome it'
gblee + ɔ	→ gblIɔ	'welcome it'
nɛɛ + U	→ nɛU	'stick it'
gblee + I	→ gbleI	'welcome them'

There is no change when the root vowel is high: *ɗu-ɛ* 'make it crush', *ɗi-ɔ* 'make it eat', *ñI-U* 'make it give', *pU-I* 'cure them'. Adopting the framework of Yip (1988a) discussed in section 9.15, how might these data be analyzed?

9.19 Berber Causative

State the rules governing the variation in the causative prefix in the following Imdlawn Berber paradigms (Elmedlaoui 1992). Ignore gemination.

verb	causative		verb	causative	
nkr	ss-nkr	'get up'	nza	zz-nza	'be sold'
uki	ss-uki	'jump'	uzzl	z-uzzl	'run'
gla	ss-gla	'moisten'	gʷraz	zz-gʷraz	'regret'
rks	ss-rks	'undress'	bruzza	z-bruzza	'crumble'
lsa	ss-lsa	'wear'	lẓa	zz-lẓa	'be soft'
kšm	šš-kšm	'enter'	bḅrḅš	š-bḅrḅš	'be gaudy'
ḥaša	š-ḥaša	'be fed up'	mmždawl	ž-mmždawl	'slip'
rša	šš-rša	'be rotten'	nžm	žž-nžm	'escape an
bbukšša	š-bukšša	'overflow'			accident'

Discuss the implications of the following data for underspecification and feature theory.

verb	causative	
rkz	ss-rkz	'dance'
ukz	ss-ukz	'recognize'
nnuqqž	š-nuqqž	not glossed
frrž	š-frrž	'be distracted'
ḥužža	š-ḥužža	'make a pilgrimage'

10   Stress

In this chapter and the next we return to the subject of prosody, examining processes that group syllables (or perhaps more accurately, syllabic nuclei) into larger metrical units. The leading idea pursued in chapter 10 is that stress (especially word stress) reflects such a grouping. Chapter 11 explores the hypothesis that processes of reduplication, truncation, and infixation also parse the string of segments into metrical constituents as a function of its syllable structure.

The discussion of stress in this chapter begins with a brief overview of the subject in generative grammar. We will then see that stress is not properly speaking a feature analogous to [nasal] or [voiced] but rather an abstract relation of prominence. Section 10.2 will introduce a graphic notation for stress (the metrical grid) that accounts for many of its special properties. In sections 10.3–10.5 we will survey the major stress patterns found in the languages of the world. Two competing models for casting these stress patterns in terms of the grid will be considered: one (developed by Halle and Vergnaud (1987) and independently by Hammond (1984)), crucially relies on metrical grouping, while the other (explored by Prince (1983), Selkirk (1984), and others) does not explicitly refer to grouping. In section 10.6 we will discuss some of the evidence that supports the grouping theory. Sections 10.7 and 10.8 will introduce the Halle-Vergnaud theory's device of conflation, which brings languages with just one stress per word into the metrical fold. In section 10.9 we will examine evidence that alternating stress is a rhythmic phenomenon. In section 10.10 we will compare the rhythmic and Halle-Vergnaud conceptions of stress with respect to several analytic and theoretical issues. Finally, in section 10.11 we will consider certain extensions and simplifications of the Halle-Vergnaud model that manipulate metrical brackets.

10.1   Background and Basic Properties

As with other aspects of phonological structure, the chief theoretical problem posed by stress is to discover a representation which permits the facts to be stated clearly so that generalizations emerge which provide the basis for an explanatory theory. The study of stress has been pursued from the beginning of generative grammar (Chomsky, Halle, and Lukoff 1956) and has always played an important part in the theory. Before we examine the contemporary conception of stress, a brief historical setting is in order. Since the work of Trager and Smith (1951), Newman (1946), and other structuralists, it was well known that English speakers can make quite subtle judgments about degrees of stress that correlate systematically with internal syntactic constituency. For example, the three-morpheme string composing *light + house + keeper* receives different interpretations depending on the stress contour: 1-3-2-4 is associated with *lighthouse keeper* (someone who keeps a lighthouse), while 2-1-3-4 is associated with *light housekeeper* (a housekeeper who is light in weight). (In this transcription 1 denotes primary stress, 2 secondary, etc.) For the structuralists, such contours were described by means of a series of four stress phonemes of decreasing strength: [ˈ], [ˆ], [ˋ], [˘]. While it is reasonable to analyze the three segments of *pin* in terms of phonemes (distinctive-feature bundles) with relatively well defined phonetic correlates, treating stress in the same fashion gave rise to a number of anomalies. For one thing, the phonetic correlates of stress proved quite elusive, so much so that even trained phoneticians could not detect the presence of [ˊ] vs. [ˋ] vs. [ˆ] without knowing the intended meaning.

In their paper Chomsky, Halle, and Lukoff showed how the distribution of the various stress levels could be predicted from a simple [±stress] distinction by remarkably precise and general rules. These rules crucially take into account the organization of the lexical items into hierarchical syntactic constituents. Such information was strictly off limits to phonemic analyses that adhered to classical structuralist tenets. The success of the Chomsky-Halle-Lukoff analysis encouraged the exploration of hypotheses that later became methodological cornerstones of generative phonology: in particular, the propositions that phonological structure can be described by general and formal rules; that the nature of these rules should be entirely a matter of empirical investigation rather than being circumscribed by a priori methodological restrictions; that the rules compute representations that may not have straightforward phonetic (material) correlates but nevertheless constitute psychologically genuine distinctions.

The rules for phrasal prominence sketched by Chomsky, Halle, and Lukoff (1956) were elaborated in Chomsky and Halle's landmark study *The Sound Pattern of English* (1968). *SPE* was the first full-scale exposition of the generative phonological model – illustrated by an in-depth description of the major phonological alternations found in English. In addition to working out the phrasal stress contours in greater detail, *SPE* demonstrated that the distribution of stressed and unstressed syllables within the word could be predicted in a large number of cases by simple and elegant rules. While the *SPE* analysis of English stress was a spectacular descriptive success, the theoretical treatment of stress in the same terms as the other distinctive features (i.e., as [±stress] analogous to [±nasal] or [±coronal]) ironically repeated the same sort of mistake made by the structuralist conception of stress as a phoneme analogous to [p]. It soon became clear that stress – especially when viewed cross-linguistically – displays a suite of properties that set it apart from other phonological features. The special status of stress remains unexplained in the *SPE* model that represents it as [±stress]. Let us enumerate some of the properties that make stress special.

First, it is well known that stress is the most phonetically elusive phonological feature. It has no invariant phonetic cues. Rather, stress is realized through the offices of other phonetic features, typical choices being the pitch contour of an intonation pattern or vowel/consonant length. Sometimes more subtle features of a given linguistic system such as (the lack of) vowel reduction or the implementation of consonantal allophones are sufficient to elicit the perception of stress.

Given the indirect relation between stress and its phonetic implementation, we might pause to ask what kinds of evidence can determine the stress properties of a given syllable. Of primary importance are the perceptions and judgments of the native speaker. For example, most English speakers discern three levels of prominence in a word such as *Alabama*. The second and fourth syllables are the weakest, while the third [bam] is judged the strongest. The initial syllable seems intermediate in character: it is not as prominent as [bam] but feels stronger than the other syllables. Of equal importance are the ways in which the syllables of the word are treated by the grammar of the language. For example, in many languages vowels reduce in unaccented positions. The patterns of reduction can be used to establish the stress contour. In *Alabama* we note that the second and fourth syllables – the ones perceived to have the weakest prominence – are reduced to schwa, while the first and third have full [æ] vowels. If we let the acute and grave accents stand for primary and secondary stress levels, then *Alabama* may be transcribed as [æ̀ləbǽmə]. Another source of evidence for stress are various adjustments a language may resort to in order to avoid a sequence of stressed syllables. A well-known rule of English transforms a word with a [...secondary...primary...] stress contour to [...primary...secondary...] when a stressed syllable follows. Thus, *ràccóon* shifts to *ráccòon* in the collocation *raccoon coat*. But the word *maroon* does not alter its stress in *maroon coat*. The contrasting behavior of *raccoon* and *maroon* is explained by the fact that these words have different stress patterns: *raccoon* has a secondary accent on the initial syllable while the initial syllable of *maroon* is unstressed. Most English speakers readily perceive this difference in prominence. This judgment is also supported by the fact that the vowel of the initial syllable is reduced in *maroon* but remains [æ] in *raccoon*. We will return to this rhythmic alternation later. Finally, in many languages intonation contours are distributed over words and phrases by reference to the strongest stress. For example, Liberman (1975) analyzes the so-called vocative chant (used to call someone out of sight) in terms of a MHM tone sequence in which the high maps to the stressed syllable and the mid tones autosegmentally associate to the surrounding syllables. The English speaker's percept that the primary word stress jumps between the first syllable in *'Isadore* and the third syllable in *Isad'ora* is dramatically highlighted by the evocations displayed in (1).

(1)   oh 'Isadore!   oh Isad'ora!

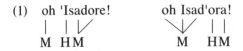

        M H M   M   H M

We have noted two respects in which stress differs from other features: the lack of uniform and precise phonetic correlates and greater-than-binary discriminations that are crucial to the operation of phonological rules. Another unusual aspect of stress is its striking long-distance effects. Most other features have local phonological determinants. For example, in many English compounds the major stress is located on the first word: *the téacher's ùnion* vs. *the tèacher's friend*. When the compounds are left-branching, the prominence of the first member keeps increasing cyclically in proportion to the depth of embedding. (We shift to a numerical notation in (2), where the magnitude of the numbers reflects degree of prominence so that 2 is stronger than 1, 3 is stronger than 2, etc.)

(2) teachers' union
　　　　2　　　1

　　　[teachers' union] president
　　　　　3　　　1　　　　2

　　　[[teachers' union] president] election
　　　　　　4　　　1　　　　2　　　　3

In the compounds of (2), the stress on *teachers'* modulates with respect to the stress values of the other elements even though the stresses of the latter can be located a considerable distance away. No other phonological property, with the possible exception of tone, exhibits such long-distance effects. An adequate theory of phonology should explain why stress has this propensity for action-at-a-distance.

　　To take another example, consider the stress pattern of Cairene Arabic (Mitchell 1960).

(3) šájara　　　　　　　　'tree' pausal form
　　　šajarátun　　　　　　nonpausal
　　　šajarátuhu　　　　　'his tree'
　　　šajaratuhúmaa　　　'their dual tree'

　　　ʔadwiyatúhu　　　　'his drugs'
　　　ʔadwiyatúhumaa　'their dual drugs'

In this dialect stress falls on one of the last three syllables of the word. But unlike many other systems with such a three-syllable window, in Cairene the assignment of stress must take into account the number and character of the syllables that precede the stressed syllable. For example, for words terminating in two light syllables, the stress varies between the second-last (penultimate) and the third-last (antepenultimate) syllable, depending on which is preceded by an even number of syllables from the beginning of the word. Thus, in four- and six-syllable words such as *šajarátun* and *šajaratuhúmaa,* the penult is stressed. But in three-syllable *šájara* and five-syllable *šajarátuhu,* the antepenult is stressed. Furthermore, the stress location at the right edge of the word can be changed by varying the weight of the syllable at the left edge: while five-syllable *šajarátuhu* has antepenultimate stress, five-syllable *ʔadwiyatúhu* has penultimate stress. In a sense to be made precise later, the prosodic shape of the entire word must be taken into account in order to determine the location of stress in Cairene Arabic.

　　Still another characteristic of stress is that in many languages a given syllable will bear stress not by virtue of its own make-up but simply due to its position in the word or phrase. For example, in Polish primary accent is regularly associated with the penultimate syllable of the word: *nauczýciel* 'teacher' nom.sg.

When a suffix is added, the accent appears to shift from the [czy] syllable to the [cie] one: *nauczyciél-a* gen.sg. In *nauczyciel-ówi* (adjectival) the stress has moved off of the stem entirely. This "shift" of stress is motivated by the relative positions of the syllables with respect to the end of the word. Once again, other phonological features such as [±nasal] or [coronal] do not behave in this way. Other common positional patterns include stress on the initial syllable of the word (e.g., Czech, Finnish, Georgian) or the final syllable (e.g., Turkish, French, Farsi).

In many languages stress involves the repetition of a basic pattern or motif. For example, the Australian language Maranungku that has figured in many generative discussions of stress is characterized by Tryon (1970b) as having primary stress on initial syllables and a secondary stress on every other syllable thereafter. The canonical prosodic shape of Maranungku words is thus CV́CV, CV́CVCV̀, CV́CVCV̀CV, CV́CVCV̀CVCV̀. Such an alternating stress pattern can be characterized as the repetition of a stressed + unstressed motif across the word. Syllables occupying an odd-numbered position are accented while those occupying an even-numbered position are unaccented. A similar phenomenon occurs on a smaller scale in English. (4) lists words with primary stress on the final or the penult.

(4)   a.   Kàlamazóo
           Mànitawáuk

      b.   Tàtamagóuchi
           Wìnnipesáukee

      c.   Àpalàchicóla
           càlifràgilístic

In (4a) the words have final stress and in (4b) penultimate stress. In both cases three syllables precede the major stressed syllable and a secondary accent appears on the initial syllable. But in (4c) four syllables precede the primary stress. Here we find two secondary accents: one on the first syllable and another on the third syllable. The pretonic string *Àpalàchicóla* displays the same strong-weak (trochaic) rhythm found in Maranungku. The syllable [la] in *Àpalàchicóla* thus bears a stress simply by virtue of its odd-numbered position in the word and not by virtue of any inherent property it possesses.

In other cases syllables bear an accent regardless of their location in the word. The most common determinant of such *inherent stress* is syllable weight: syllables with a long vowel are always stressed while the stressability of short-voweled syllables depends on location with respect to the edge of the word or to another heavy syllable. Syllables closed by a consonant pattern with long vowels in some systems and with short vowels in others. It is noteworthy that while stressability is almost invariably a function of the syllable nucleus, such properties as vowel quality are rarely taken into account (and if they are, it is to determine the degree of prominence rather than the presence or absence of stress). A language in which back vowels defined heavy syllables would be strange indeed. Again, an adequate theory will explain this fact. In addition to being determined by syllable weight, the inherent accent of a syllable may be simply an arbitrary, unpredictable property of the lexical item in which the syllable is located. Russian and Japanese have many such lexically determined accents.

Finally, in languages that allow multiple stresses per word, one is typically perceived as more prominent than the others. As our discussion of the English rhythm rule indicated, this contrast between primary and secondary accent is crucial to explaining why there is no shift of accent in *maroon coat* in contrast to *raccoon coat*. Let us look at a few more cases in which this contrast in stress levels is crucial in English. First, we note that there are large numbers of English nouns containing two stressed syllables that contrast in terms of which stress is primary (marked by the acute).

(5) húrricàne   Tènnessée
     pédigrèe   kàngaróo
     mátadòr   pàlisáde
     cántalòupe   màgazíne
     cávalcàde   chàndelíer

Second, there are alternations between the $[...\grave{V}...\acute{V}...]$ and $[...\acute{V}...\grave{V}...]$ stress contours. These take place at the phrasal level (*Tènnessée* but *Ténnessèe Ernie*) as well as in the word phonology (*Ísadòre* but *Ìsadóra*). Third, the normal method of stress enhancement at the phrasal level is for the stress of the second word of a collocation to be increased. This process is known as the nuclear stress rule (NSR). Some examples are listed in (6).

(6) red barn   John's shirt   Mary's salamander   basic mathematics
      1   2   1   2   2   3   1   2   1   3

     eat meat   be happy   judged sacrosanct   visit Alabama
      1   2   1 2   2   3   1   2   1   3

As we can see from some of these examples, when the second word has two stresses, it is uniformly the stronger one that is enhanced. In *Mary's salamander* the initial syllable of *sálamànder* has been enhanced. But in *basic mathematics* it is the second stress – the one on the penult – in *màthemátics* that has been increased. An adequate theory of phonology will explain why stress, in contrast to any other phonetic property, lends itself so easily to mirroring the syntactic constituent structure in this way and why only the highest stress in a word is subject to such enhancement under the NSR.

10.2   The Metrical Grid

Liberman's (1975) *metrical grid* is a notation that permits the special aspects of stress to be represented in a particularly perspicuous manner. For the metrical grid, stress is neither a feature nor an inherent property of syllables. Rather, stress is defined in terms of an abstract two-dimensional array that plots metrical positions for levels of prominence. Syllabic nuclei "bear" a stress by autosegmentally associating with one of these metrical positions. In this way, stress is largely autonomous from the phonemic string. In many languages the metrical grid defines three levels of prominence for the word. Following the notation of Halle and Vergnaud (1987), the grid levels are represented as lines of asterisks. Line 0 is the basic level and denotes a potentially enhanceable position. In general, every syllable in a word projects a line 0 position, though in some languages (e.g., Indonesian; Cohn 1989) schwa-like syllables may be systematically ignored. Such accentually inert syllables do not project a position on the grid and hence do not figure in any stress computations. Line 1 is sometimes called the *foot level* and line 2 the *word level*. The words *Apalachicola, Tennessee,* and *hurricane* have the metrical grids in (7).

(7)

```
2  _____*_____      _____*_____    *_____
1  *   *   *                *     *          *     *
0  * **  * **               *  *  *          *  *  *
   Apalachicola            Tennessee        hurricane
```

As in a grid, we can think of the representations in (7) as assigning every syllable a plus or minus value for each of the prominence levels. (A plus value is denoted by an asterisk and a minus value by the absence of an asterisk.) However, the metrical grids are scalar: an asterisk on any line n implies an asterisk on line $n-1$.

Now let us consider how some of the properties of stress noted earlier are naturally explained by this kind of notation. First, it is clear that the metrical grid does not treat stress as an inherent phonetic property of phonological segments analogous to features such as nasality and tone. Rather, it defines an autonomous level of representation. Second, the fact that a syllable may bear stress simply in virtue of its position in the word reflects the grid's horizontal dimension as a sequence of metrical (stressable) positions. A syllable comes to bear a stress solely in virtue of being associated with this metrical position. Third, the fact that stress encodes greater-than-binary distinctions is reflected directly in the grid's vertical dimension.

Finally, the metrical grid permits many of the long-distance features of stress to be assimilated to the more familiar, local kind of relation that we have come to expect of linguistic structure. For example, the phenomenon of stress enhancement observed in the nuclear stress rule can be accounted for very simply by assuming that each level of syntactic embedding defines a new line in the grid. Since the grid is scalar, it makes sense that the asterisk associated with the new line will attach to the most prominent element of the preceding line. Thus, to characterize the long-distance relation between the stressed syllables of *discovered* and *Mississippi* in *discovered Mississippi,* we need only stipulate that the second word in the collection is enhanced. The line 3 asterisk marking this enhancement is automatically attracted to the penult, because the penult is the only syllable in the word with a line 2 registration.

(8)

```
3  _____*____   NSR
2     *              *
1     *        *     *
0  *  *  *  *  *  *  *  *
   discovered Mississippi
```

Finally, consider how the rhythmic shift in *the Míssissìppi River* can be characterized. After the NSR enhances the stress on *River,* we have the grid in (9a).

```
(9)  a.  3 _____ * _____   RR →   b. _____ * _____
         2        *     *                        *           *
         1    *   *     *                        *    *      *
         0    *  *  *  *  * *                     *  *  *  *  * *
            Mìssissíppi River                    Míssissìppi River
```

With the grid representation, the rhythm rule (RR) can be thought of as a process that slides the line 2 asterisk leftward to the next available landing site in response to the stress clash created by the following stressed syllable in *River* (Prince 1983). In this way, the rhythmic alternation in *Míssissìppi River* also defines a local phonological relation – between positions that happen to be adjacent at a certain level in the metrical grid. For example, in (9a) the stresses associated with the [sip] and [Riv] syllables are adjacent on line 2. (No other asterisk intervenes between them.) Locality is also respected by the movement process itself: the asterisk shifts to the adjacent line 1 position. The precise definition of a stress clash is a complicated issue; see Liberman and Prince 1977, Hammond 1984, and Hayes 1984 for useful discussion.

10.3 Some Basic Parameters

In this section we will explore the basic parameters underlying the construction of metrical grids. For data we will rely heavily on the survey of the descriptive literature found in Hayes 1981. This study convinced many phonologists that the myriad stress systems of the world's languages involve variations on a small number of basic themes and hence that a parametric approach is appropriate. The chief problem is to develop a system that generates the common patterns in a simple fashion yet is robust enough to derive the more complex ones from the combinatory work of the simple ones. Considerable guesswork is involved in this enterprise. Many of the decisions that have been made in the literature are quite underdetermined by the data. Consequently, any exposition of the theory is tentative and subject to revision (sometimes radical) as new facts are discovered. One crucial issue has been whether the notion of metrical constituency needs to be recognized; another is the way in which quantity figures in stress patterns. The nature of much of the rest of the system is determined by one's position on these issues.

As noted earlier, stressed and unstressed syllables often distribute themselves in an alternating fashion. Hayes (1981) identified four basic patterns, samples of which are cited in (10).

(10) a. Maranungku (Tryon 1970b): Primary stress falls on the initial syllable, and secondary stress falls on every other syllable thereafter.

         tíralk 'saliva', mérepèt 'beard', yángarmàta 'the Pleiades', lángkaràtetì 'prawn', wélepènemànta 'kind of duck'

b. Weri (Boxwell and Boxwell 1966): Primary stress is assigned to the final syllable, and secondary stress is assigned to each preceding alternate syllable.

ŋintíp 'bee', kùlipú 'hair of arm', ulùamít 'mist', àkunètepál 'times'

c. Warao (Osborn 1966): Main stress falls on the penult, with secondary stress appearing on alternating syllables before the main stress.

yiwàranáe 'he finished it', yàpurùkitàneháse 'verily to climb', enàhoròahàkutái 'the one who caused him to eat'

d. Araucanian (Echeveria and Contreras 1965): Main stress falls on the second syllable, and secondary stress falls on alternating following syllables.

wulé 'tomorrow', țipánto 'year', elúmuyù 'give us', elúaènew 'he will give me', kimúbalùwulày 'he pretended not to know'

(11a) schematizes the stress contours each system assigns to four- and five-syllable words; (11b) distills the distribution of stressed ['V] versus unstressed [V] syllables in each type without regard to magnitude of stress.

(11)	type 1	a.	V́ V V̀ V V́ V V̀ V V̀	b.	'V V 'V V 'V V 'V V 'V
	type 2		V V̀ V V́ V̀ V V̀ V V́		V 'V V 'V 'V V 'V V 'V
	type 3		V̀ V V́ V .V V̀ V V́ V		'V V 'V V V 'V V 'V V
	type 4		V V́ V V̀ V V́ V V̀ V		V 'V V 'V V 'V V 'V V

Notice that a given stress contour appears twice in the table. For instance, the four-syllable ['V V 'V V] appears in both type 1 Maranungku and type 3 Warao. The languages differ in the stress contour they assign to five-syllable (or more generally to odd-numbered) words: in Maranungku ['V V 'V V] combines with ['V V 'V V 'V]; in Warao it combines with [V 'V V 'V V]. Similarly, five-syllable ['V V 'V V 'V] combines with ['V V 'V V] in type 1 Maranungku, but with [V 'V V 'V] in type 2 Weri. Since each contour appears twice, the occurrence of any one contour is independent from the appearance of the others. This fact suggests that the entire system results from the free combination of two more elementary factors: whether the initial assignment maps a syllable to a stressed or an unstressed position and whether the assignment starts at the left or the right edge of the word.

If stress prominence is a function of the metrical grid, then one way to build up the grids to generate the four alternating patterns of (11) is to define a mapping of syllables onto a primitive rhythmic alternation of peaks and troughs (Prince 1983). Imagine a tape of successive weak and strong positions, as depicted in (12a).

(12) a.   *   *   *
          ... * * * * * * * ...

b. [peak-first, trough-first]

c. [left-to-right, right-to-left]

The alternating stress patterns in (11b) can be generated by setting the two parameters in (12b,c). (12b) tells whether the mapping starts with a rhythmic *peak* (i.e., a position marked by a line 1 asterisk) or with a *trough* (a position lacking a line 1 asterisk). The second parameter (12c) specifies the direction of assignment. The four basic patterns arise from the parameter settings in (13).

(13)   type 1   [peak-first, L-R]
       type 2   [peak-first, R-L]
       type 3   [trough-first, R-L]
       type 4   [trough-first, L-R]

To briefly illustrate this method of grid construction, consider how the type 1 language Maranungku would be generated. According to (13), we start at the left edge of the word and map the first syllable to a rhythmic peak in the tape of (12a); remaining syllables in the word are then matched one to one with subsequent positions in the tape, as illustrated in (14a). A four-syllable word thus receives the grid in (14b).

(14)   a.   1   *   *
            0   ... * * * * * ...
                     / / / /
                    V V V V ...

       b.   1   *   *
            0   * *   * *
                 'V V 'V V

       c.   2   *
            1   * → * / # ____

       d.   2   *
            1   *   *
            0   * *   * *
                 V V V V

Enhancement of one of the line 1 asterisks introduces a distinction between primary and secondary stress. Typically, it is a marginal line 1 element that is strengthened. Maranungku and Araucanian enhance the leftmost line 1 asterisk, Weri and Warao the rightmost. The word stress rule for Maranungku is stated in (14c). It transforms (14b) into (14d).

According to the view just sketched (essentially the proposal of the influential study by Prince (1983)), stress is primarily a rhythmic phenomenon. There is no explicit notion of metrical grouping. Any given peak is equally related to the troughs on either side and any trough is equally related to its adjacent peaks. An alternative view analyzes a series of alternating stressed and unstressed syllables into binary units known as *metrical feet*. The feet differ in terms of whether the stressed position (the *head* of the foot) occurs at the left or the right edge.

(15)   metrical foot   *   *   line 1
                          (* *)   (* *)   line 0

                        left-headed   right-headed
                        (trochaic)   (iambic)

In some versions of this general approach (e.g., Halle and Vergnaud 1987, Anderson and Ewen 1987) the head is said to *govern* the adjacent unstressed position, much in the way a verb governs an adjacent direct object noun phrase. As in the first view, a {left-to-right, right-to-left} parameter specifies the direction in which syllables are grouped into metrical feet.

Consider first how a type 1 language such as Maranungku is generated in a theory employing metrical constituents. The metrical feet are left-headed and assigned from left to right. For words with an even number of syllables, the division into binary feet encompasses all the syllables in the word (16a). But when the word contains an odd number of syllables, one position is necessarily left over at the end of the parse (16b). In a type 1 language this syllable is stressed, and so it is natural to allow these leftover (orphan) syllables to form *degenerate feet* of just one syllable, assuming that the parsing is exhaustive. Since the degenerate foot is stressed, the requirement that every syllable have a head (stressed position) is still satisfied. With provision made for degenerate feet, the four- and five-syllable schemata of a type 1 language are analyzed by foot theory as in (16).

(16)   a.   1   *   *
           0   * * * *   →   (* *) (* *)
               | | | | | | | |
               V V V V   'V V 'V V

      b.   1   *   *   *
           0   * * * * *   →   (* *) (* *) (*)
               | | | | | | | | | |
               V V V V V   'V V 'V V 'V

A type 2 language arises in exactly the same way, except that the feet are assigned from right to left.

Since in a metrical constituent the head is typically signaled by greater prominence, it is natural to construe the enhancement of a line 1 asterisk as a process that organizes the asterisks of line 1 into a metrical constituent. Since the number of stressed syllables in a Maranungku word may exceed two, the resultant constituent is of *unbounded* size, taking in the entire word. The rule "organize line 1 asterisks into an unbounded left-headed constituent" transforms the grids of (16) into those in (17).

(17)   a.   2   *   b.   2   *
           1   (*   *)   1   (*   *   *)
           0   (* *) (* *)   0   (* *) (* *) (*)
               V́ V V̀ V   V́ V V̀ V V̀

To briefly summarize, the leading idea behind this alternative view is that stress reflects a grouping of the grid positions into headed constituents.

The analysis of type 3 and type 4 languages under the grouping theory is more complicated. Consider type 3. If the feet are left-headed and assigned from right to left and the parsing is exhaustive, then the leftover syllable at the beginning of the word will be assigned to a degenerate foot. We incorrectly predict that words with an odd number of syllables should begin with two successive stressed syllables. (For a type 4 language the situation is symmetric, with a stress clash predicted at the right edge.)

(18) type 3 [left-headed, R-L]

```
1                    *  *       *
0   * * * * *    →   (*)(* *) (* *)
    V V V V V         V 'V V  'V V
```

Grouping theory must invoke a rule to remove the stress clash by deleting the line 1 asterisk from the degenerate foot. Rules of this form must be allowed in any case in order to remove stress clashes arising at the phrasal level from the collocation of separate words. For example, in Icelandic (Gussmann 1985) compounding of *v'erk* 'work' and *m'aður* 'man' produces a clash that is removed by deleting the second stress in *v'erk#maður* 'good worker'; compare *v'erka#k'ona* 'female worker'. Nevertheless, the theory positing a metrical foot requires a more complex analysis of the type 3 stress pattern. An extra stress is assigned and then must be removed by another rule. The alternative "grid-only" theory, which assigns syllables directly to the alternating peaks and troughs, generates the type 3 language in one step. Other things being equal, it might appear at this point that the introduction of metrical constituency is a needless complication.

Proponents of the foot theory have argued that there are good reasons to introduce the metrical constituent in spite of the apparent complexity that arises in the analysis of a type 3 language such as Warao. First of all, it is simply untrue that languages always avoid stress clashes. An example is provided by the Algonquian language Ojibwa (Kaye 1973, Piggott 1980). Ojibwa words lacking a long vowel have stresses on even-numbered syllables counting from the left. In addition, the final syllable of every word is stressed, entailing a stress clash in words with an odd number of syllables.

(19) a.   nagámò   'he sings'
           ni-níbà   'I sleep'
           ni-bímosè   'I walk'
           ni-nágamò-mìn   'we sing'

```
     b.  1       *    *              *     *   *
         0     (* *) (* *)         (* *) (* *) (*)
               V'V   V'V            V'V   V'V  'V
```

Parsing syllables into binary right-headed feet from left to right produces the grids in (19b) for four- and five-syllable words. In this case the theory positing metrical constituents produces the surface stress patterns directly. No subsidiary rules are required to adjust the grid that arises from the initial imposition of metrical struc- ture. But since Ojibwa words contain a clash of stresses at the right edge, the "grid-only" theory that assigns syllables to the primitive rhythmic alternation of peaks and troughs cannot generate this pattern directly. Another rule must be stipulated to deliver a line 1 asterisk to the final syllable of every word. We conclude that when a larger class of languages is examined, the initial advantage that the grid-only theory seemed to enjoy disappears. (In fairness, however, it should be noted that Ojibwa appears to represent the marked situation; the avoid- ance of a stress clash at the edge of the domain appears to be the predominant pattern.)

A similar conclusion can be drawn from alternating stress patterns in which the clash posited by foot theory is resolved, not by destressing the degenerate foot, but rather through the destressing of the head of the adjacent binary (nonde- generate) foot. For example, the Australian language Garawa (Hayes 1981) is described as having an initial primary stress and secondary stress on the penult; a tertiary stress ('V) is said to lie on alternating syllables preceding the penult.

(20) a.   yámi   'eye'
          púnjala   'white'
          wátjimpàŋu   'armpit'
          náriŋinm'ukuŋj'inamìra   'at your own many'

      b.   'VV
          'VVV
          'VV'VV
          'VVV'VV
          'VV'VV'VV
          'VVV'VV'VV

In (20b) the various levels of prominence are suppressed; only the distribution of stressed versus unstressed syllables of prototypical Garawa words is displayed. When this is done, the distribution of accented and unaccented syllables in Garawa looks very similar to that in Warao: both accent the penult and alternating syllables preceding the penult. For words with an even number of syllables, stressed and unstressed positions are distributed alike. The languages differ in their stressing of words with an odd number of syllables. In Garawa the initial syllable is accented (e.g., 'V-V-V-'V-V) while in Warao the second syllable is (e.g., V-'V-V-'V-V). Under the theory that groups metrical positions into binary feet, both languages can be analyzed as being of essentially the same type [left-headed, R-L]. They differ in the way the stress clash is resolved: Garawa deletes the second line 1 asterisk, Warao the first.

(21)   *   *   *
                     (*) (* *)(* *)

       Garawa   'V V V'VV
       Warao   V 'V V'VV

Since the grid-only theory is designed to keep stresses apart, it cannot produce a sequence of stressed syllables directly. The Garawa stress pattern thus represents a complication. It can be generated with the help of two additional rules: one to accent the initial syllable of the word and a second to relieve the resultant stress clash through the deletion of the second of two adjacent asterisks. A five-syllable word thus receives the three-step derivation sketched in (22).

(22)
$$* \quad * \qquad * * \quad * \qquad * \quad *$$
$$* * * * * \rightarrow * * * * * \rightarrow * * * * * \rightarrow * * * * *$$

Thus, both approaches generate the appropriate stress patterns. They differ in their interpretation of adjacent stresses. The theory positing metrical constituents regularly generates stress clashes in the course of assigning every syllable to a metrical foot. The grid-only theory must produce clashing stresses via additional rules. Which of these two general approaches is correct continues to be a major issue in stress theory. We will return to this question in section 10.10.

Some of the strongest arguments for metrical constituency are based on the readjustments to the stress pattern that take place upon the deletion or the insertion of another syllable. Since the metrical grid, like an autosegmental tone pattern, defines a level of representation separate from the phonemes, the loss of a vowel (or syllable) will not necessarily entail the loss of the corresponding grid column; only the lowest level will be erased, since that is a projection of the syllable (nucleus). Higher grid marks may persist. In a theory with metrical constituents, it is natural that if the vowel associated to the metrical head is deleted but the stress pattern is preserved, then the stress will appear to migrate to the adjacent syllable in the foot. Consequently, we expect a correlation between the type of foot structure and the direction of accent shift. If the accented vowel in (23a) governs the vowel to the right, then, upon deletion, the accent should shift to the right (23b). But if the feet are right-headed, then the accent should shift to the left (23c). In a theory that does not impose any metrical constituency, no such correlation is predicted.

(23) a.   ... $V_1 \acute{V} V_2$ ...
 b.   ... $V_1) (\acute{V} V_2) \rightarrow V_1 \acute{V}_2$
 c.   ... $V_1 \acute{V}) (V_2 ... \rightarrow \acute{V}_1 V_2$

Several instances of the phenomenon depicted in (23) have been reported in the literature. We will review one later. If they are not simply coincidental, they constitute powerful support for the hypothesis of metrical constituency.

Even though the available evidence for metrical constituency is far from compelling (see Kenstowicz 1993 for a survey), we will adopt this hypothesis in our exposition of the theory of stress. This decision represents a guess that such an approach will prove more revealing and closer to the truth. To summarize the discussion so far, we have examined four basic alternating stress patterns. We have analyzed them in terms of two parameters: {left-to-right or right-to-left} parsing of syllables into {left-headed or right-headed} binary feet. Stress clashes may but need not be removed by an additional rule suppressing one of two adjacent grid marks.

10.4 Heavy Syllables

In the examples examined so far, syllable quantity has played no role. But in many languages the location of stress depends on a division of the syllables into light and heavy classes. Invariably, the heavy syllables attract a stress (in our terms, are assigned a more prominent grid position). To take a simple example, the Uto-Aztecan language Tübatulabal is described by Voegelin (1935) as stressing all syllables containing a long vowel, all final syllables, and alternating syllables preceding a stressed syllable.

(24) a. ipónihwín   'of his own skunk'
          witáŋhatál   'the Tejon Indians'
          wítaŋhátalá:bacú   'away from the Tejon Indians'
          yú:dú:yú:dát   'the fruit is mashing'
          haní:lá   'the house' (obj.)
          tá:háwilá:p   'in the summer'
          wašá:gáhajá   'it might flame up'
          ánaɲí:nínɨmút   'he is crying wherever he goes' (distr.)
          pɨɨtípɨtí:dinát   'he is turning it over repeatedly'

     b.   *   line 1
          * → * / ____   line 0
                 |
                 V:

The most straightforward account of this language simply postulates a rule stressing long vowels independent of their position in the string. Halle and Vergnaud (1987) postulate the rule (24b). We must now investigate how such inherently accented syllables group with adjacent syllables into metrical feet. The forms *pónihwín* and *witáŋhatál* show that Tübatulabal forms binary right-headed feet from right to left. It is thus a type 2 language. Consider the case of a long vowel in an even position counting from the right edge of the word. Two examples are cited in (25). After the application of (24b), these forms have the following grids.

(25) a. 1   *   b. 1   *
          0   * * *   0   * * * * * *
          hani:la   anaɲi:ninɨmut

Halle and Vergnaud examine two initially plausible methods to parse grids. One breaks the parse down into a two-step procedure. The first step locates the line 1 asterisks and groups them with the appropriate adjacent syllables into constituents with the long-voweled syllable as head. Since Tübatulabal feet are binary and right-headed, this initial parse derives the grids in (26a).

(26)   a.   1   *   *
           0   (* *) *   * (* *) * * *

       b.   1   * *   *   *) *   *
           0   (* *) (*)   (*) (* *) (*)(* *)
                ha ní: la   á na ɲí: ní nɨm út

In the second step the remaining unmetrified syllables are parsed from right to left to derive the grids in (26b).

An alternative procedure maintains a single right-to-left parse. But since a metrically dependent position cannot be more prominent than the head, a syllable with a line 1 asterisk may never be made sister to a head. Consequently, when such a syllable is encountered, the foot construction procedure must begin anew, assigning it to a head position. (In effect, the parsing of line 0 asterisks monitors for a line 1 asterisk.) As an example of this alternative interpretation, let us follow the parse of *ánaɲí:nínɨmút* in detail. First, the [mut] syllable is assigned as head, with [nɨ] as dependent (27a). Then the next [ni] is assigned to head (27b); but the [ɲi:] may not be assigned to a dependent position since it bears a line 1 asterisk and thus is barred from such a weak metrical position. Consequently, a degenerate monosyllabic foot is created, with [ni] as head (27b). The parsing procedure continues and [ɲi:] is assigned to a head position with the preceding [na] as its sister (27c). Finally, the initial syllable is assigned to head position and the parse terminates in (27d).

(27)

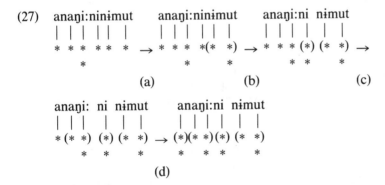

Both procedures thus succeed in assigning the correct grid structure to the representations in (25). They predict different results, however, for an initial representation such as (25b) if the parse proceeds from left to right. The two-step procedure will first organize the second and third syllables into a foot; then the initial syllable is parsed to yield a representation such as (28a). Under the one-step approach, the first and second syllables parse into a right-headed foot and then the third syllable forms a foot by itself, since it has already been supplied with a line 1 asterisk. This procedure generates the grid of (28b).

(28)   a.   *   *   b.   * *
                  (*) (* *)   (* *) (*)
                   | | | | | |
            V V V: → V V V: V V V: → V V V:

Crucial evidence for the second approach is furnished by Ojibwa. Like Tübatulabal, Ojibwa stresses all long-voweled syllables and thus has rule (24b) assigning such syllables a line 1 asterisk. The language also permits adjacent stressed
syllables to surface phonetically.

(29) bimósè: 'he walks'
      ni-bímosè:-mìn   'we walk'
      ni-níbà:-mìn   'we sleep'

We learned from (19) that Ojibwa feet are right-headed and assigned from left to
right. Words with two short syllables followed by a long one will decide between
the alternative parsing procedures. Forms such as *bimósè:* and *ni-níbà:-mìn* argue
for the second approach in which metrical organization arises exclusively from
a syllable-by-syllable transition from one edge of the word to the other.

Languages such as Tübatulabal and Ojibwa that tolerate a stress clash are significant since they permit the underlying assignment of stresses to surface directly.
A point worth bringing out here is that the theory predicts a correlation between
the type and direction of foot assignment for short-vowel words and the position
of stress clashes with respect to a long vowel. To appreciate this point, consider
Tübatulabal again. The stress contours in *pónihwín* and *witáŋhatál* suffice to establish that binary feet are right-headed and assigned from right to left. Consider
now the stress in *tá:háwilá:p*. Stressing long vowels produces the grid in (30a).

(30) a. 1 *   *   b. 1 *   *   *
          0 * * * *   0 (*) (*) (* *)

Since feet are right-headed and assigned from right to left, exhaustive parsing
groups the penult with the final syllable and places the antepenult in a foot by
itself. It follows that the bisyllabic interval between long vowels must stress the
first syllable: 'V:VV'V: → 'V:'VV'V:. This theory not only predicts the correct
form *tá:háwilá:p;* it also predicts that **tá:hawílá:p* could not in principle be the
stress assignment. The latter and obviously much stronger claim is supported by
the fact that the theory makes exactly the opposite prediction for Ojibwa. In this
language *ni-bímosè* and *ni-nágamò-mìn* establish a right-headed, left-to-right foot
structure. Since feet are imposed from left to right, we predict that an even-
syllabled interval between long vowels will have the stress clash on the right. A
form such as *ni-wì:-pimí-takkònà:n* 'I'll carry it along' confirms this prediction.

If the Tübatulabal and Ojibwa methods of filling in such short-vowel intervals
represent the general state of affairs, then we derive strong support for our general
approach to stress. After all, given a [V́: V V V́:] string, it is not obvious why a
language should systematically favor stressing one of the two intervening short
vowels. It is even less obvious that the particular decision adopted should inversely correlate with the way short-voweled words are stressed. For example,
since short syllables pair up as (V'V) in Tübatulabal, one might mistakenly expect
a short-vowel interval in [V́:-V-V-V́:] to have the stress clash on the right rather
than on the left. The correct results are obtained only if each of the various

parameters in the theory holds – in particular, that stress results from the metrical organization of all syllables in the word in a sweep from one edge to the other.

Some further support for this approach is furnished by certain Tübatulabal stems with an irregular stress. For example, the final syllable of the stem [tuguwa] 'meat' is always stressed regardless of its position in the word: *túguwá-n* 'his meat', *túguwá-yí-n* obj. The stress on the [wa] syllable is thus an idiosyncratic lexical property that must be recorded as part of the underlying representation of this lexical item. A natural way to do this is to let the [wa] project a line 1 asterisk as part of its underlying representation. The fact that the short syllable preceding the [wa] is always unaccented while a short syllable following may be accented follows from the analysis. The parallel behavior of long syllables and lexically accented syllables in Tübatulabal justifies the decision to analyze both as arising in the same way: by the assignment (either lexical or rule-governed) of a line 1 asterisk.

The discussion can be summarized by stating the following rules of grid construction (Halle and Vergnaud 1987).

(31) Tübatulabal
  a. Syllable nuclei project a line 0 asterisk.
  b. Assign a line 1 asterisk to syllables with a long vowel.
  c. Parse line 0 asterisks into binary right-headed feet from right to left and mark the heads with a line 1 asterisk.

  Ojibwa
  a. Syllable nuclei project a line 0 asterisk.
  b. Assign a line 1 asterisk to syllables with a long vowel.
  c. Parse line 0 asterisks into binary right-headed feet from left to right and mark the heads with a line 1 asterisk.

10.5 Unbounded Constituents

In this section we will extend the metrical approach to a larger class of languages. Consider first the languages that are described as having a single accent per word located on the initial or the final syllable, such as Latvian and Czech or French and Farsi. (Some may have secondary accents, but we assume that at least a subset have just a single accent per word.) In a theory that does not countenance metrical constituents such languages can be described simply by postulating a rule to assign a line 1 asterisk to the initial or final syllable. A word-level rule then singles out the only line 1 asterisk as the host for a line 2 asterisk. An initially accented word has the derivation sketched in (32).

(32)

```
                                              2  *
                        1  *                  1  *
    0  * * * *          0  * * * *            0  * * * *
       V V V V    →        V V V V     →         V V V V
```

A rather different interpretation emerges from the grouping theory. Recall that it views stress as reflecting the imposition of constituency on the metrical positions in the grid. In particular, stress marks the head of the constituent. Given this leading idea, it is natural to see initial stress as marking the head of an unbounded constituent that encompasses the remaining unstressed syllables and hence takes in the whole word. The metrical structure of a V́VVV word is thus as shown in (33).

(33) 2   *
      1   (*)
      0   (* * * *)   left-headed

If we accept this position and allow for unbounded constituents, then it is natural to require that line 0 positions be exhaustively analyzed into metrical constituents, much as we assumed that the string of phonemes is exhaustively parsed into syllables. In this way, we understand why a language such as Tübatulabal assigns stresses to light syllables even when the word has a long vowel and hence an inherent stress. While the existence of unbounded feet thus follows rather naturally from the assumption of metrical constituency, it must be recognized that to date the most impressive independent evidence confirming metrical constituency has been found in systems with binary feet. In the next section we will review three of the best cases.

10.6   Metrical Constituency

10.6.1   Dorsey's Law in Winnebago

The Siouan language Winnebago illustrates a number of issues in the metrical theory of accent. Our data come from the descriptions of Miner (1979) and of Hale and White Eagle (1980). If we restrict attention to words with just short vowels, then we find that stress appears on every odd-numbered syllable except for the first (i.e., on the third, the fifth, etc.). The one exception to this general statement is that in disyllabic words the final syllable is accented.

(34) wajé   'dress'   hipirák   'belt'
      wijúk   'cat'   hišjasú   'eye'
      hočįčínįk   'boy'   hijowíre   'fall in'
      hirawáhazrà   'the license'   hakirújikšą̀ną   'he pulls it taut'
      hokiwárokè   'swing' n.

Winnebago accent is obviously alternating. But unlike words in the previously examined patterns, the Winnebago word may begin with two unstressed syllables before a stressed one is encountered. Disyllabic words are the only exceptions to this generalization. Both peculiarities could be explained if the parsing skips the initial syllable. Then Winnebago becomes identical with a type 4 language such as Araucanian: both assign binary right-headed feet from left to right. Accordingly, we postulate a provision to exempt certain syllables from the metrical parse. Mechanically, we will assume a feature [+ *extrametrical*], which renders a syllable's line 0 asterisk invisible to the parsing procedure. Clearly, such a feature must be used sparingly. In the absence of any constraints on which syllable can be ignored, any metrical pattern could be generated and the theory loses its empirical force. Study of many languages has led to the conclusion that only material at the edges of a domain is exempt from the metrical parse. This *peripherality* condition is reminiscent of the behavior of marginal consonants in escaping syllabification and of final vowels in escaping tone spread. It is commonly assumed that the extrametricality feature is only active at the edge of a metrical domain. As soon as a syllable becomes medial (e.g., by affixation), its asterisk becomes "visible" and hence cannot be ignored by the metrical parsing rules.

Given extrametricality, we postulate the rules of (35), which generate the grids in (36). Following the notation introduced by Kager (1989), we mark extrametrical positions with angled brackets.

(35) a. Mark the line 0 asterisk of the initial syllable extrametrical.
　　 b. Group line 0 asterisks into binary right-headed constituents from left to right.
　　 c. Group line 1 asterisks into an unbounded left-headed constituent.

(36)
```
2      *              *                    *
1      *            (*  *)               (*       *)
0   〈*〉(*)      〈*〉(*  *)(*)      〈*〉(*   *) (*    *)
    wa je        ho či či nį k        hi ra wa haz ra
```

A later rule of stress clash reduction deletes the line 1 asterisk from the final syllable of *hočįčínįk*.

Hale and White Eagle (1980) and Halle and Vergnaud (1987) point to additional material from Winnebago that provides a striking argument for the postulated metrical constituents. Winnebago has a rule known as Dorsey's Law, which inserts a copy of the following vowel within a preceding voiceless obstruent-plus-sonorant cluster. This rule is stated in (37a). It is illustrated by adding the second person prefix [š-] to a stem beginning with a sonorant. Underlying [š-wažok] 'mash' is realized as *šawažók*. In some cases the vowel inserted by Dorsey's Law preserves the accent pattern (37b). But in other cases the stress shifts to the inserted vowel (37c).

(37) a. $CRV_i \rightarrow CV_iRV_i$

　　 b. [ho-š-wažá]　　　　　　$\rightarrow$　hošawažá　　　　'be sick'
　　　 [ha-ra-kí-š-rujìk-šnạ̀]　$\rightarrow$　harakíšurujìkšạnà　'pull taut' 2d
　　　 cf. ha-ki-rújik-šạ̀nạ　　　　　　　　　　　　　'pulls taut' 3d

c. mąą-ráč   'promises'
   [mąą-š-ráč] → mąą-šárač   'you promise'
   [hi-ra-kró-hò] → hirakórohò   'prepare'
    cf. [hi-kro-hó] → hikorohó   'prepares'
   [wakriprás] → wakiripáras   'flat bug'
   [hirakróhonìrà] → hirakórohònirà   'dress, get ready' 2d

For example, in *hošawažá* (UR [hošwaža]) the first accent is located on the fourth syllable of the word instead of the third; and in *harakíšurujìkšąnà* there are two unaccented syllables between the primary stress and the first secondary stress – a deviation from the otherwise strictly alternating pattern of secondary accents. Both aberrations are explained if the stress is assigned before Dorsey's Law. But in the forms of (37c) such as *hirakórohò* (UR [hirakroho]) a stress appears on the inserted vowel.

The Winnebago data thus pose two puzzles: first to find a basis for the distinction between the two groups of words and second to explain why one group preserves the underlying accent while the other does not. Hale and White Eagle (1980) had the following insight into the problem: if the representations prior to the application of Dorsey's Law are parsed into metrical feet, then for the forms in (37b) the inserted vowel falls in the gap between the feet while for the data in (37c) it disrupts the metrical foot. This point is graphically illustrated in (38).

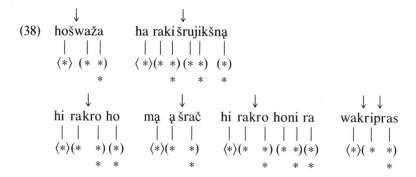

(38)

This consistent difference demonstrates that the metrical relation between a stressed and an adjacent unstressed syllable is not symmetric – a result that is expected if stresses are assigned in virtue of metrical constituents. Furthermore, the postulated right-headed iambic (VC'V) grouping helps us to understand why it is the Dorsey's Law separation of an unstressed plus stressed syllable that produces the stress shift (rather than separation of a stressed plus unstressed syllable). We assume that the vowel inserted by Dorsey's Law projects a metrical position on line 0. The new position disrupts the binary foot and hence leads to the deformation of the disturbed constituent, whose freed asterisks are then reparsed according to the parameters of (35). On this analysis, a form such as *hirakórohò* is derived as in (39).

(39)   1   * *   * *   *   *   *
      0   ⟨*⟩(* *)(*)   ⟨*⟩(* * *) (*)   (*)* * * (*)   ⟨*⟩(* *)* (*)
        hi rakro ho → hi rakoro ho → hirakoroho → hi rakoroho

In the first step Dorsey's Law injects a new metrical position within the foot. This deforms the constituent, which is then remetrified according to the parameters of the system in (35).

An underlying form such as [wakri-pras] 'cockroach' appears as *wakiripáras*. It suggests that the metrical reparsing begins with the asterisks comprising the disrupted constituent – not at the beginning of the entire string. Otherwise, we should expect stress on the third syllable instead of the fourth.

(40)   wakripr as   waki riparas   waki ripa ras

$$\langle*\rangle(*\ \ *) \quad\rightarrow\quad \langle*\rangle*(*\ *\ *) \quad\rightarrow\quad \langle*\rangle*(*\ *)(*)$$
$$*\qquad\qquad\qquad\quad *\qquad\qquad\qquad *\ \ *$$

A later rule of stress clash removal eliminates the final stress.

Another significant case is [hirakróhonìrà] → *hirakórohònirà*. It suggests that the reparsing cannot be local but affects the following stresses as well. To account for these cases, Halle and Vergnaud postulate a *Domino Condition*, which requires a deformation of the metrical constituents that follow the disrupted constituent.

(41)   hi rakro honi ra   hi rakoro honi ra   hi rako roho nira

$$\langle*\rangle(*\ \ *)(*\ *)(*) \rightarrow \langle*\rangle(*\ *\ *)(*\ *)(*) \rightarrow \langle*\rangle(*\ *)(*\ *)(**)$$
$$*\ \ \ *\ *\qquad\qquad\quad *\ \ *\ *\qquad\qquad\quad *\ \ \ *\ \ \ *$$

This condition makes sense on the view that a syllable is stressed simply in virtue of its odd/even position in the string. If its position is altered, then it becomes subject to reparsing like the constituents actually interrupted by Dorsey's Law. If this is the correct interpretation, then it constitutes another way in which stress is special in contrast to other features with more local determinants. (The Domino Condition is controversial and awaits additional support. See section 10.10 for further discussion of Dorsey's Law.)

10.6.2 *Bedouin Arabic Elision*

In this section we will see how extrametricality may combine in different ways with the parameters already developed to explain some more complex stress patterns. We will also review another argument for metrical constituency.

The Cairene dialect of Arabic has been widely discussed in the metrical literature (based on data from Mitchell 1960). The location of word stress in Cairene is summarized in three successively more inclusive statements. First, a final superheavy (CVVC, CVCC) syllable is stressed (42a). Otherwise, stress falls on a heavy (CVV, CVC) penult (42b). Finally, in all other words the stress varies between the penult and the antepenult (42c). For these, Langendoen (1968) discovered the rule that the stress falls on the penult or the antepenult, depending on which is separated from a preceding heavy syllable or the beginning of the word by an even number of light syllables.

(42) a. ḍarábt, ʔaʕmáal
      b. mustášfaa, muʕállim, muqáatil, šaabáatun
      c. kaatába, qattálat, maktábah, wálad, ráʔaa, híya, kátaba, šájarah, ʔin-
          kásara, bulahníyatun, ʔadwiyatúhu, murtabiṭátun, šajarátun, katabátaa

These data are significant in several respects. First, as noted in section 10.1, the choice between penult and antepenult in (42c) can only be resolved by scanning the entire string of preceding syllables. This implies that the stress location effectively depends on the gross syllabic profile of the entire word – a serious violation of phonological locality. However, Langendoen's rule scans the pretonic string for a very restricted type of information: the number of syllables and their weight. Furthermore, the scansion equates two light syllables with one heavy syllable. But this is exactly the kind of information computed in the analysis of alternating stress patterns.

We can capture the elusive Cairene pattern as follows (McCarthy 1979b). We assume that the mora (syllable-rimal element) is the stress-bearing unit that projects a line 0 asterisk. We then parse these elements into binary left-headed constituents from left to right – just as in the type 1 language Maranungku. The systematic exclusion of final syllables that are not superheavy is handled by extrametricality. Finally, instead of making the initial stress primary, we enhance the final one. These rules and parameter settings are stated in (43) and their operation is illustrated in (44).

(43) a. The mora is the stress-bearing unit.
      b. Final syllables that are not extraheavy are extrametrical.
      c. Group line 0 asterisks into binary left-headed feet from left to right.
      d. Enhance the rightmost stress by constructing an unbounded right-headed constituent on line 1.

(44) šajaratuhu   šaja ratu hu   šaja ratu hu   šajaratu hu
      | | | | | | | | | | | | | | | | | | | |
      * * * * ⟨*⟩   →   (* *)(* *)(*)   →   (* *)(* *)⟨*⟩   →   * *(* *)⟨*⟩
                          *   *   (*   *)   *
                                                   *

      ʔadwiyatuhu   ʔad wiya tu hu   ʔad wiya tu hu   ʔadwiyatu hu
      || | | | | || | | | | || | | | | || | | | |
      ** * * * ⟨*⟩   → (**) (* *)(*)⟨*⟩ → (**) (* *)(*) ⟨*⟩ → ** * *(*) ⟨*⟩
                          *   *   *   (*   *   *)   *
                                                      *

The first step in the derivation parses the line 0 asterisks and the second enhances the final stress. Most sources agree that Cairene has no surface secondary stresses (Welden 1980 is an exception). Thus, a rule is needed to suppress the nonprimary stresses. We follow Halle and Vergnaud and postulate a rule of conflation that deletes line 1. The result is a single stress at the right end of the word – but one whose location is crucially determined by a left-to-right parse of the entire word.

We will return to line conflation in section 10.7. At this juncture the important point is that our system captures the superficially quite different Cairene stress pattern by simply combining in new ways the various descriptive options that we have already motivated – in particular, extrametricality and stress enhancement – but at the opposite edge of the word from which the metrical parse begins. Another feature worthy of note is the decision to allow the mora to count as the stress-bearing unit.

With this combinatoric theme in mind, let us now look at two Bedouin dialects discussed by Irshied and Kenstowicz (1984). In the Bani-Hassan dialect of Jordan, stems of the shape *CaCaC* reduce to *CCaC* when followed by a vowel.

(45) sáḥab   'he pulled'   báɣal   'mule'
      saḥáb-na   'we pulled'   baɣál-na   'our mule'
      sḥáb-at   'she pulled'   bɣál-i   'my mule'

Since elision fails in such stems as *ʕasáah* 'cane', *máktab* 'office', *ʕállam-at* 'she taught', *báarak-at* 'she blessed', it appears that we must characterize the context for the rule as ____CVCV. This formulation violates phonological locality because it stipulates information beyond the syllable that is immediately adjacent to the elision site. However, if light syllables are organized into binary metrical feet from left to right, then the rule receives a simple expression: elide the short low vowel [a] from an open syllable when it occupies the initial (head) position of a disyllabic trochaic (left-headed) foot.

(46)   σ   (where σ is light)
                        |
      [a] → Ø / _____
                        |
                     (* *)   line 0
                      *   line 1

We account for the absence of elision in *CáCaC* words by assuming that final syllables are extrametrical, just as in Cairene. The form *sḥáb-at* receives the derivation in (47).

(47) saḥab-at   sḥab-at   sḥab-at
      | | | → | | → | |
      (* *)⟨*⟩   (·*)⟨*⟩   (*)⟨*⟩
      *   *   *

When the elision rule deletes the stressed vowel, the line 0 asterisk associated with [sa] loses its licenser and hence disappears. Just as the deletion of a tone-bearing unit typically leads to the shift of tone to an adjacent tone-bearing unit, so the stress in (47) is preserved. Given the hypothesis that stress indexes the head of a metrical constituent, it is natural to construe the shift of stress (the line 1 asterisk) as reflecting the conservation of metrical constituency – in the second step of (47) headship is transferred from the deleted vowel to the following one, which now becomes the leftmost element in the foot.

While this chain of reasoning may seem recondite, it has empirical consequences when the eliding stressed vowel is located in the middle of the word. Conservation of constituency predicts that the stress will shift to the left or the right as a function of whether the constituent is right- or left-headed. The Bedouin elision rule confirms this hypothesis in striking fashion.

The brief paradigms in (48) suggest that a heavy-plus-light syllable constitutes a metrical constituent in the Bani-Hassan dialect.

(48)   ʕállam   'he taught'
       ʕállam-at   'she taught'
       ʕàllam-át#uh   'she taught him'

       sáaʕad   'he helped'
       sáaʕad-at   'she helped'
       sàaʕad-át#uh   'she helped him'

       sáḥab   'he pulled'
       sḥáb-at   'she pulled'
       sḥàb-át#uh   'she pulled him'

This assumption simultaneously explains the primary stress on the [-at] suffix when it is nonfinal (not extrametrical) and the fact that the second syllable of CaCCaC stems such as [ʕallam] does not elide. As the representations in (49) show, this syllable does not satisfy rule (46).

(49)   ʕallam-at-uh   sahab-at-uh   →   shab-at-uh

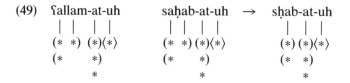

Let us now compare the Bani-Hassan paradigms of (48) with the cognate ones in (50) from the Riyadh dialect.

(50)   ʕállam   sáaʕad   sáḥab
       ʕállim-at   sáaʕad-at   sḥáb-at
       ʕallm-ít#ah   saaʕd-ít#ah   sḥáb-it#ah

The first two entries are virtually the same as those found in Bani-Hassan, save for a rule that raises the low vowel of a short open syllable when not adjacent to a guttural consonant. The two dialects diverge before the clitic object suffix. First, in CaCaC-at#V structures, Riyadh has the word stress on the root while Bani-Hassan places the accent on the suffix: compare Riyadh *sḥáb-it#ah* with Bani-Hassan *sḥàb-át#uh*. Second, in Riyadh the second vowel of CaCCaC and

CaaCaC stems elides before the [-at] suffix when the latter is in turn followed by a vowel; no such elision occurs in Bani-Hassan.

We can account for both differences if Riyadh agrees with Cairene in designating the mora as the stress-bearing unit. On this analysis, Riyadh *ʕallm-ít#ah* and *sháb-it#ah* receive the underlying metrical representations shown in (51a,b).

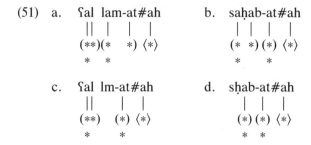

(51) a.   ʕal lam-at#ah   b.   sahab-at#ah

c.   ʕal lm-at#ah   d.   shab-at#ah

If the mora is the stress-bearing unit, then the initial heavy syllable of [ʕallam] constitutes a foot by itself. The result is that the following [la] heads a new metrical foot. When [la] joins with the following syllable in a foot, elision may now apply, leading to a shift of stress to the [at] suffix to preserve metrical constituency. The result is the representation in (51c). The segmental rule raising the low vowel of an open syllable derives *ʕallm-ít#ah*. Elision also converts (51b) into (51d).

Finally, to account for the fact that underlying [sáhab-át#ah] surfaces as *sháb-it#ah* in Riyadh, we must postulate a rule that deletes stress from a final non-branching foot. This rule is stated in (52a); it converts (52b) into (52c).

(52) a.   line 0   (*) ⟨*⟩
           line 1   * → ∅ / ____

b.   shab-at#ah   c.   shab-at#ah
     | | | | | |
     (*)(*) ⟨*⟩   (*) * ⟨*⟩
      * *   *

Rule (52a) also accounts for the retraction of stress in Riyadh *ʕállim-at* and *sáaʕad-at* vs. Cairene *ʕallám-at* and *saaʕád-at*.

To briefly summarize the discussion, the fact that the shift of stress under the Bedouin elision rule systematically correlates with left-headed feet is a surprising and significant result because the postulated metrical constituency is independently motivated by the distribution of stress. (See Al-Mozainy, Bley-Vroman, and McCarthy 1985, where the same phenomenon in a related dialect is discussed and similar conclusions are drawn.) Also, the fact that both the scope of elision and the distribution of stress covary between the two dialects suggests that whether the mora or the syllable is the stress-bearing unit is a significant parameter of difference. And more generally, since such a rich network of parameter settings is required in order to delimit the scope of elision, the evidence encourages the belief that the overall framework is on the right track.

10.6.3 *Latin Enclitic Stress*

In addition to stress shifts induced by epenthesis and elision, accentual displacements occasioned by the attachment of enclitics have proved a useful probe of
metrical structure. Steriade (1988a) develops this line of inquiry in a study of
enclitic accent in Ancient Greek and Latin. Let us briefly review her result here.

Latin stresses the antepenult unless the penult is heavy, in which case it takes
the stress: *réficit, refé:cit, reféctus*. The rules in (53) generate this paradigm,
assigning the grids in (54). (To simplify matters, only the first two lines of the
grid are shown.)

(53) a.   The syllable rime is the stress-bearing unit.
      b.   Final syllables are extrametrical.
      c.   Assign a line 1 asterisk to heavy syllables.
      d.   Group line 0 asterisks into binary left-headed constituents from right
           to left.

(54)   refe cit   re fe:cit   re fectus
        | | | | | | | | |
       (* *)⟨*⟩   (*)(*) ⟨*⟩   (*)(*) ⟨*⟩
         *   *   *   *   *

Steriade shows that enclitic stress corroborates the constituency postulated in
these representations. Latin has both monosyllabic and disyllabic clitics (55).

(55) a.   úbi   'where'   ubí#libet   'wherever'
      b.   lí:mina   'thresholds'   li:miná#que   'and thresholds'
      c.   Mú:sa   'the Muse'   Mu:sá#que   'and the Muse'

Addition of the clitic displaces the stress of the base. But there is a systematic
and intriguing difference between *ubí#libet* and *li:miná#que*. In both cases we
have a four-syllable string. But they are stressed differently. *ubí#libet* suggests
that stress assigned under enclisis can reach back to the antepenult. But when
the base is trisyllabic and the clitic monosyllabic, antepenultimate stress is
shunned in favor of penultimate stress. As Steriade observes, if we assume that
enclitic stress is assigned to a representation that already has the metrical structure
of the base word imposed, then a simple and elegant explanation emerges for the
contrasting behavior of *li:mina* and *ubi* when they host enclitics. The second
syllables in the quadrisyllabic *ubí#libet* and *li:miná#que* have a different status.
In the latter the [mi] syllable is metrified as a dependent of the stressed syllable
[li:], while in the former the [bi] syllable is unmetrified, because it is extrametrical
(56).

(56)   li:mi na   u bi
        | | | | |
       (*   *) ⟨*⟩   (*)⟨*⟩
          *   *

To explain the contrast, all we need say is that stress assignment under enclisis respects the previously established structure and is constrained to erect metrical constituents only on free, unparsed asterisks (Prince's (1985) Free Element Condition). Under this assumption, the inputs to enclitic metrification are the representations in (57a). Recall that extrametricality is subject to a peripherality condition. As soon as affixation renders an element nonperipheral, its extrametricality is lost and it becomes available for metrification. In (57a) the [na] and [bi] syllables have lost their extrametricality. The final syllables of the clitics can undergo the extrametricality rule since they are peripheral.

(57)   a.

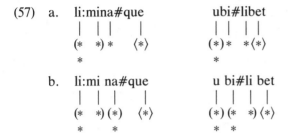

 ubí#libet (57a) contains two free positions; thus, when rule (53d) applies, a disyllabic left-headed foot is assigned (57b). But *li:miná#que* (57a) contains just a single free position and hence the enclitic stress is planted there. Enhancement of the rightmost stress then yields the correct surface forms.

The important theoretical point is that this result crucially depends on the second syllables in *ubi* and *li:mina* having a different status even though they presumably receive identical phonetic implementations as simple, unstressed syllables. They differ only in terms of the hidden (inaudible) metrical structure imputed by the rules in (53).

There is a second way in which metrical constituency is respected under enclitic stress assignment. Consider *Mu:sá#que* (55c). The rules of (53) assign the representation shown in (58a). (58b) ensues from addition of the clitic.

(58)   a.   Mu:sa   b.   Mu:sa#que   c.   Mu:sa#que

Latin metrical constituents are left-headed. (58b) contains one free asterisk preceded by a degenerate (monosyllabic) foot. A priori, there are two possible responses the theory might make in this situation. First, the boundary of the degenerate foot could expand to take in the [sa]. But if we take seriously the ideas that previously established metrical structure is inviolate and that metrical constituents are built by taking unmetrified asterisks in a right-to-left scan of the word, then we predict that the degenerate foot will not expand. Rather, the single free element will parse into a degenerate foot, as in (58c). Steriade reports that

Musá#que in fact has penultimate stress. This illustrates a second respect in which the invisible metrical structure makes its presence felt.

The Latin result raises the question of what to say about the well-known paradigms in (59).

(59) a.   comp[ə]nsation vs. cond[ɛ]nsation
      b.   órigin, oríginal, orìginálity vs. Wìnnipesáukee

As observed in section 5.3, *SPE* noted that some English dialects contrast the phonemically nearly identical four-syllable strings in (59a) in terms of whether or not the second syllable is unaccented and hence may reduce to schwa. The *SPE* analysis explains the difference in terms of the morphological bases on which the words are built: the second syllable is unstressed in *cómpensàte* (in virtue of a regular rule of English phonology) while it bears a stress in *còndénse*. In order to explain how the stress pattern of one word can determine the stress of a related but nevertheless different word, *SPE* proposed to embed the phonological derivation of the shorter word inside the derivation of the longer one. Specifically, the stress contours of *compensation* and *condensation* are computed cyclically. First, the stress of the bases *compensate* and *condense* is derived. The resultant representations then serve as the inputs [cómpensát + ion] and [cóndén + sation] for the derivations of *compensat + ion* and *condens + ation*.

Kiparsky (1979) uncovered additional evidence for the cyclic analysis of English stress. He noted a consistent difference in the behavior of trisyllabic strings of pretonic light syllables in underived words such as **Winnipesáukee** and in such morphologically complex words as **originality**. In the former class the first syllable is typically stressed and the following two unstressed: *Wìnnipesáukee*. But in the latter class a secondary stress can fall in the middle of the trisyllabic string: *orìginálity*. Clearly, this difference is a function of the existence of the related word *oríginal*. If the stress is assigned cyclically, then it is easy to see how the primary stress in *oríginal* may emerge as a secondary stress in *orìginálity*.

Kiparsky (1982a) observed that the suffixes that shift the stress in the base may also shorten its vowel. For example, *-ity* shifts the stress in *lócal, locál-ity* and shortens the vowel in *divīne, divín-ity*. To explain this correlation, we saw in section 5.5 that Kiparsky proposed that the rules of English phonology fall into two major blocks (levels or strata). Primary suffixes such as *-al, -ity* activate rules of the first level, while secondary suffixes such as *-less, -ness* activate rules of the second. If we accept this line of reasoning, then a word such as *original* is cyclically derived from the base *origin*. But by the logic of the metrical interpretation of the Latin stress rule sketched above, the latter must have the metrical structure of (60a). It then appears that the input to the derivation of *original* must be the representation shown in (60b). But if metrification is restricted to free elements, as the Latin enclitic accent suggests, then the [ri] syllable should be inaccessible.

(60) a.   ori gin   b.   ori gin al
           | | | | | | |
           (* *) ⟨*⟩   (* *) * ⟨*⟩
            *   *

Two solutions to this problem have been proposed. Inkelas (1989) suggests that underived roots may be lexically marked to skip the cyclic rules. This allows the base [origin] to bypass the first cycle. The stress assigned in [origin]*al* then operates on a metrically clean slate. An alternative tack taken by Halle and Vergnaud (1987) postulates a special Stress Erasure Convention (see section 10.8 for brief discussion) operating at the beginning of each cycle that effectively cancels the metrical structure erected on the preceding cycle. On this approach, the [ri] syllable in (60a) is now accessible to the stress rules operating on the [origin]*al* cycle. Cases like Latin enclitic stress, where the metrical structure of the base is respected and hence must be present at the point where the enclitic accent is assigned, are treated by Halle and Kenstowicz (1991) as noncyclic effects. The Latin enclitics are [−cyclic] and thus fail to activate the rules of the cyclic block – in particular, the Stress Erasure Convention. Their host must have passed through the cyclic block and thus have obtained a metrification. It is this metrical structure that is respected by the enclitic accents. Clearly, more cases of this form must be uncovered in order to strengthen the hypothesis that respecting metrical structure is a diagnostic of the noncyclic block. See Halle, Harris, and Vergnaud 1991 for further discussion.

10.7   Line Conflation

In this section we look at two Slavic languages whose stress systems are quite simple. They have certain exceptions that illuminate aspects of the theory developed to this point. In Macedonian (Lunt 1952) stress is regularly placed on the third-last (antepenultimate) syllable of the word. If a word has fewer than two syllables, then the first is stressed.

(61)   vodéničar   'miller'
       vodeníčar-ot   'the miller'
       vodeníčar-i   'millers'
       vodeničári-te   'the millers'

As developed to this point, our theory is unable to account for this simple stress system. Since there is only one stress per word, it might appear that we must invoke an unbounded foot. But an unbounded foot locates the stressed head at the initial or final syllable (the second/penult if the extrametricality option is chosen). We cannot place the head of an unbounded foot more than two syllables in from the word margin. Consequently, the foot must be binary. Winnebago showed that it is possible to place an accent three syllables in from the word margin by appeal to a binary foot plus extrametricality. If Macedonian feet are left-headed and assigned from the right word edge, we derive the grids in (62) for *vodéničar* and *vodeníčar-ot*.

(62)   a.   1   * *   b.   1   *   *
          0   (*)(* *)⟨*⟩   0   (* *)(* *)⟨*⟩
           voden i(čar)   vode niča rot

While we might invoke a rule to remove the stress clash in (62a), such a rule will not extend to (62b) because the stressed syllables are not adjacent. Nevertheless, all descriptions agree that Macedonian has just a single accent per word. The Macedonian stress system thus differs minimally from that of Winnebago. Both have binary feet plus the extrametricality option. But Winnebago has secondary stresses, while Macedonian assigns just a single phonological accent per word. Consequently, the theory must be extended to allow for a single accent per word in a system with bounded feet.

Two extensions have been proposed in the literature. First, the parse of line 0 asterisks could have the option of iterating or simply applying once. For [+iterative] Winnebago, foot construction would iterate across the word, assigning secondary accents; in [−iterative] Macedonian, it would cease after the first foot has been constructed and thus assign just a single accent. Alternatively, we might parse the entire word into metrical feet and then suppress the secondary accents. In the Halle-Vergnaud theory, this option is known as *line conflation* – a rule that collapses adjacent lines of the grid through suppression of material on the lower one. A constituent of the lower line is preserved only if its head is also the head of a constituent on the higher line. To simplify the technical discussion, we interpret conflation as the deletion of the lower line. We can in effect convert a Winnebago-like system to Macedonian by conflating lines 1 and 2 in the grid. In this way, only the rightmost line 1 asterisk persists, since it is the seat of the line 2 asterisk.

To illustrate, Halle and Vergnaud (1987) propose the rules of (63) for Macedonian.

(63) a. Syllable rimes project a line 0 asterisk.
      b. The final syllable is extrametrical.
      c. Parse line 0 asterisks into binary left-headed constituents from right to left.
      d. Group line 1 asterisks into an unbounded right-headed constituent.
      e. Conflate lines 1 and 2.

These rules complete the derivation of (62b) as in (64).

(64) 2   *
      1   (*   *)   1,2   *
      0   (**)(**)⟨*⟩   →   0   ** (**)⟨*⟩

We thus have two different proposals for extending the system. Which is correct? On conceptual grounds, the conflation solution is attractive since it assigns every syllable to a metrical constituent on the initial parse (and thus mimics syllabification). The anti-iteration proposal does not; it leaves the pretonic string in *vodeníčar-ot* unmetrified throughout the derivation. But are there any empirical consequences that differentiate the two proposals? Halle and Vergnaud point to the behavior of certain lexical items (mostly loanwords) with exceptional stress to support conflation. These items have an exceptional stress on the penult or the final syllable. According to Franks (1983), these stresses persist so long as they are found within one of the last three syllables of the word. If suffixation buries them below the antepenult, they fail to emerge and a new accent is assigned by the regular rule.

(65)   konzumátor   restorán
        konzumátor-i   restorán-i   pl.
        konzumatór-i-te   restorán-i-te   pl.def.
        'consumer'   'restaurant'

The paradigms in (65) raise two questions. First, why in a form like *restorán* is no stress assigned to the antepenult by the normal rule? Second, why is the exceptional stress on the [ma] syllable of *konzumátor* replaced by antepenultimate stress in *konzumatór-i-te?* Conflation answers both questions. As in Tübatulabal, it is natural to encode the exceptional stresses of *konzumátor* and *restorán* as line 1 accents in the lexical representations.

(66)   1   *   *
       0   *   *   * *   *   *   *
             konzumator   restoran

According to the rules in (63), each syllable of the word parses. But in virtue of rule (63e) only the rightmost line 1 stress survives to the surface. These will be the exceptional stresses of *konzumátor* and *restorán,* except in the case where the parse plants a foot to the right of these positions.

(67)   2   *   *
       1   (* *   *)   (*   *)
       0   (*)(* *)(* *)⟨*⟩   (* *)(*)   →
                kon zumat o ri te   resto ran

       1,2   *   *
       0   *   * *(* *)⟨*⟩   * *(*)
                konzumatori te   restoran

Under the [−iterative] parameter, material preceding the antepenult remains unmetrified; it thus is unexplained why the lexical stress in *konzumátor* fails to emerge when suffixation places it beyond the antepenult. An otherwise unnecessary rule is required to remove this stress. If the Macedonian suppression of lexical stresses falling outside the main stress foot represents the norm, then we have evidence for the conflation mechanism over the [±iterative] parameter. Proponents of the [±iterative] parameter have rightly pointed to the fact that very little positive evidence has so far been found that would justify the hypothetical metrification of the pretonic string that is canceled by conflation. For example, segmental rules sensitive to stress seem to fail to discriminate among the syllables composing the pretonic string. The case for conflation would be strengthened considerably if such a situation could be demonstrated empirically.

Lexical exceptions in Polish also shed light on some basic concepts of metrical phonology – in particular, line conflation and extrametricality. Recall that Polish has regular penultimate stress. In the metrical framework, there are two ways to set the parameters to obtain stress on the second-last syllable of the word. The final syllable may be extrametrical and an unbounded right-headed foot constructed. Alternatively, the word may parse into binary left-headed feet from right to left and then the conflation option suppresses the secondary accents. Certain deviations from the penultimate stress pattern argue for the latter analysis. These words (mostly of foreign origin) stress the antepenult instead of the penult.

(68)   uniwérsytet   'university' nom.sg.
       uniwersytét-a   gen.sg.
       uniwersytét-u   dat.sg.

The exceptional stress is only assigned when these items are unsuffixed. As soon as a suffix is added, the regular penultimate stress appears. If Polish feet are binary and left-headed, the exceptions can be accounted for straightforwardly by marking their final syllable extrametrical (69a). Conflation of lines 1 and 2 suppresses the secondary stresses to obtain just one surface accent.

(69)   a. 2   *   b. 2   *
           1 (*   *)   1 (*   *   *)
           0 (* *) (* *)⟨*⟩   0 (* *)(* *)(* *)
                uni wersy tet   uniwersy tet-a

Recall that exclusion of a syllable from the metrical parse by extrametricality is subject to a peripherality condition. The extrametricality feature is activated only when the syllable lies at the edge of the relevant stress domain. As soon as it becomes nonperipheral (e.g., by affixation), its lexically assigned extrametricality feature is invisible and the syllable is consequently parsed. In this way, we understand why such items as *uniwérsytet* adopt regular penultimate stress when they are suffixed (69b).

   This interpretation is available only if Polish feet are left-headed and binary. If they are unbounded, then the parameters cannot be set to generate the antepenultimate stress of *uniwérsytet*. The Polish data suggest that the metrical analysis of penultimate stress must be weighted in favor of binary (as opposed to unbounded) feet. We can obtain this result if a certain cost is associated with extrametricality. If a stress pattern can be generated without extrametricality, then the acquisition procedure will select that option first. This is a natural decision since extrametricality is a way of avoiding the basic thrust of the theory – that every syllable of the word is parsed into a metrical constituent. From this point of view, it makes sense that the only device to avoid metrification is (i) costly and (ii) restricted to peripheral positions. The fact that the number of languages with penultimate stress appears to greatly exceed the number with antepenultimate stress also is explained if extrametricality is costly. Finally, the preponderance of penultimate over antepenultimate stress may reflect the tendency for word boundaries to coincide with metrical boundaries.

10.8 Conflation: Some Extensions

Conflation allows us to account for a class of languages originally noted by Kiparsky (1973b). Like Macedonian, Eastern Cheremis has just one surface stress per word. It falls on the rightmost syllable with a nonreduced vowel. If the word contains only reduced vowels, then the initial syllable is stressed. (The data in (70) are from Hayes 1981.)

(70) šiinčáam, šlaapáažəm, kíidəštəžə, tə́ləzən

Komi is the mirror image of Eastern Cheremis: in Komi stress falls on the leftmost full vowel, otherwise on the final syllable.

Two strategies have been proposed to deal with such systems. We might permit the rules constructing line 0 constituents to inspect the internal structure of the syllable (e.g., for weight) so that only syllables of a certain type can head a constituent. For Eastern Cheremis we might imagine that the rule works from right to left, searching for a heavy syllable to seat a stress. If no such syllable is found, the search will have reached the initial syllable, which, we might imagine, receives a stress by default. Alternatively, we might postulate a rule assigning a line 1 asterisk to all syllables with nonreduced, long vowels and then group line 0 asterisks into unbounded left-headed metrical feet. For a word lacking full vowels, the resultant foot takes in the entire word. Under this analysis, forms such as *šlaapáažəm* and *tə́ləzən* receive the preliminary grids in (71a).

(71) a. 1   * *   1   *
          0   (*)(* *)   0   (* * *)

      b. 2   *   2   *
          1   (* *)   1   (*)
          0   (*)(* *)   0   (* * *)

      c. 1,2   *   1,2   *
          0   *(* *)   0   (* * * *)

To obtain the correct surface forms, the line 1 asterisks are grouped into unbounded right-headed constituents; this enhances the rightmost stress in the word (71b). Then, to account for the fact that just one stress emerges to the surface, lines 1 and 2 are conflated (71c), erasing stress on all but the rightmost full vowel.

Halle and Vergnaud (1987) argue for the second position on grounds of conceptual economy. The first analysis allows headship to be determined by examining structure internal to the syllable, while the second does not – at least not directly. The metrical parse looks only at line 0 in the grid. However, this claim of restrictedness is not as strong as it first seems, since Halle and Vergnaud permit rules to assign line 1 asterisks on the basis of syllable structure (e.g., the Eastern Cheremis rule stressing all heavy syllables). Because these syllables eventually head a constituent anyway, the ban on inspecting internal syllable structure holds only for constituents that acquire a head via the directional parsing procedure (their "constructed" constituents). It remains to be seen whether this distinction is purely theory-internal or has empirical consequences.

Stress systems minimally different from those of Eastern Cheremis and Komi have been discovered. In these too the first (or last) syllable of a certain type (typically heavy) bears the word stress. But in the absence of such syllables, stress lodges on the first (or last) syllable of the word. Khalkha Mongolian belongs to this class of "same-side" default languages. In Khalkha the first long vowel in a word is stressed (72a), otherwise the initial syllable (72b). (The data are from Hayes 1981, based on Street 1963.)

(72) a. bosgúul   'fugitive'
          bariáad   'after holding'
          xoyərdugáar   'second'
          garáasaa   'from one's own hand'

      b. áli   'which'
          xótəbərə   'leadership'

Most researchers have connected the default initial stress with the enhancement of the leftmost stressed (long) syllable. The precise implementation of this idea varies with the particular metrical theory. In the Halle and Vergnaud framework, for example, the lexically assigned asterisks of line 1 are grouped into an unbounded left-headed constituent; subsequent conflation suppresses all but the leftmost stress, just as in Eastern Cheremis.

(73) a. Group line 1 asterisks into an unbounded left-headed constituent, whose head is marked on line 2.
      b. Conflate lines 1 and 2.

To account for the default initial accent, Halle and Vergnaud propose that Khalkha differs from Eastern Cheremis in lacking a rule that metrifies line 0. As a result, the rule (73a) metrifying line 1 finds no asterisks to work with (74b).

(74) a. CVCVCVCV → b. CVCVCVCV → c. CVCVCVCV   line 0
          *   *   *   *   *   *   *   *   (*   *   *   *)
          ·   ·   ·   ·   (·   ·   ·   ·)   *   ·   ·   ·   line 1

In the absence of such raw material, a convention requires the rule to look at the immediately lower line. Since by hypothesis this line is unmetrified, the convention allows rule (73a) to push its brackets down to line 0. Since line 1 constituents are left-headed and unbounded, the word-initial syllable becomes the head, with all remaining syllables dependent (74c).

A number of Indo-European languages have stress systems that are formally identical to that of Khalkha Mongolian. For example, Russian morphemes fall into two major types: accented and unaccented. In the accented class, the location of accent is unpredictable and must be memorized as part of the lexical representation. However, when morphemes are combined, the stress contour of the resultant word is predictable by rules that essentially mirror the system proposed for Khalkha Mongolian. To see this, consider the sample inflectional paradigms for the feminine nouns in (75a).

(75) a. <u>fixed stress</u>

rýb-a	kómnat-a	koróv-a	nom.sg.
rýb-u	kómnat-u	koróv-u	acc.sg.
'fish'	'room'	'cow'	

    b. <u>mobile stress</u>

vod-á	golov-á	borod-á	nom.sg.
vód-u	gólov-u	bórod-u	acc.sg.
'water'	'head'	'beard'	

In the fixed class, stress is always bound to a particular syllable of the stem. In the mobile class, the stress alternates between the case suffix and the word-initial syllable. For feminine nouns, the nom.sg. *-a* is stressed in the mobile paradigm while the acc.sg. *-u* is stressless.

We may account for the stress of these words by the analysis proposed for Khalkha Mongolian. Fixed stress stems have lexical representations with a line 1 asterisk supplied, while mobile stems lack any lexical accent. Similarly, the nom.sg. *-a* will bear a lexical stress, while the acc.sg. *-u* is unstressed. There are four possible combinations of stem plus affix to consider. Examples appear in (76a). (76b) shows the effects of rule (73a) assigning an unbounded constituent, while (76c) shows the results of conflation and the convention interpreting empty lines. (Analysis based on Halle and Vergnaud 1987).

(76) a.

komnat-a	komnat-u	golov-a	golov-u	
* * *	* * *	* * *	* * *	line 0
* *	*	*	*	line 1

    b.

* * *	* * *	* * *	* * *	line 0
(* *)	(*)	(*)	( )	line 1
*	*	*		line 2

    c.

(* * *)	(* * *)	(* * *)	(* * *)	line 0
*	*	*	*	line 1

This analysis explains why the stem stress of the fixed class predominates over the stress of the case suffix: [kómnat + á] → *kómnata*. In a word lacking a line 1 asterisk, initial stress is imposed, just as in Khalkha: [golov + u] → *gólovu*.

10.8.1 *Dominant versus Recessive Affixes*

In systems organized like those of Khalkha and Russian, some affixes (tradition-ally termed *dominant*) suppress the stress of the base to which they are added. If these affixes are themselves stressed, the line 2 word accent shifts to them. But if they are unaccented, the result is a stem lacking any accent. By the convention for empty lines developed in the analysis of Khalkha, we predict a default initial stress.

The accent of Lithuanian nominals studied by Dudas (1972) illustrates this kind of system well. The inflection of Lithuanian nouns is organized as in Russian with fixed and mobile stems, the latter alternating in the paradigm between the initial syllable and the case suffix. However, the phonetic realization of the accent is more complex. In syllables with two moras, the accent is either falling "acute" (e.g., *káim-as* 'village') or rising "circumflex" (e.g., *vaĩk-as* 'child'). Syllables with just one mora have a simple high tone with no appreciable tonal contour; they are marked by the "grave" accent (*ùp-ė* 'river'). For purposes of discussion, we will adopt the Halle and Vergnaud (1987) analysis in which circumflex accents are lexically designated to project a line 0 asterisk from the syllable's second mora, while acute and grave accents project the first mora as the stress-bearing unit. Stress is realized phonetically as high pitch.

(77) kaim-as   vaik-as   up-ė
      | | |
      *   *   *

The partial paradigms in (78) briefly illustrate the inflectional accent. In the masculine declension, the nom.sg. *-as* and the dat.sg. *-ui* are unaccented, while the nom.pl. *-ai* and the dat.pl. *-ams* are accented. In feminine nouns, the nom.sg. *-a* and the loc.sg. *-oje* are accented, while the acc.sg. *-ą* and the dat.sg. *-ai* are unaccented.

(78)   <u>fixed</u>   <u>mobile</u>
      masculine
      mókytoj-as   pieštùk-as   ą́žuol-as   vaĩk-as
      mókytoj-ui   pieštùk-ui   ą́žuol-ui   vaĩk-ui
      mókytoj-ai   pieštùk-ai   ąžuol-aĩ   vaik-aĩ
      mókytoj-ams   pieštùk-ams   ąžuol-áms   vaik-áms
      'teacher'   'pencil'   'oak'   'child'

      feminine
      elget-a   bažnýč-ia   Lietuv-à   galv-à
      elget-oje   bažnýč-ioje   Lietuv-ojè   galv-ojè
      elget-ą   bažnýč-ią   Líetuv-ą   gálv-ą
      elget-ai   bažnýč-iai   Líetuv-ai   gálv-ai
      'beggar'   'church'   'Lithuania'   'head'

The underlying representations of *mókytoj-as, vaĩk-as, mókytoj-ai,* and *vaik-aĩ* appear in (79).

(79) mookiitooj-as   mookiitooj-ai   vaik-as   vaik-ai
      | | | | | | | | | | | |
      * * * *   * * * *   * *   * *   line 0
      *   *   *   *   line 1

As in Russian and Khalkha, rule (73a) enhances the first line 1 asterisk while conflation suppresses the remaining ones. The accentless *vaĩk-as* receives a stress on its initial syllable through the empty line convention.

With this sketch of the inflectional accent as background, let us turn to the derivational system. Derivational suffixes fall into two unequal types as far as their effect on the accent of the stem is concerned. In the present-day language there is just one suffix that behaves like a (stressed) inflectional suffix: the agentive *-inink* takes the word accent when added to an unaccented (mobile) stem, while a fixed stress stem preserves its accent intact. For example, fixed stress *áuks-as* 'gold' yields fixed stress *áuks-inink-as* 'goldsmith', while mobile *dárb-as* 'work' yields *darb-iniñk-as* 'workman'. The latter inflects as a fixed stem, as we predict if *-inink* is assigned a lexical accent on its final mora. Halle and Vergnaud (1987) report the existence of an unaccented derivational suffix from an earlier stage of the language: adjectival *-isk* yielded a fixed stress when appended to an accented stem and a mobile stress when added to an unaccented stem.

Aside from these two cases, the remaining derivational suffixes suppress the accent of the stem. The overwhelming majority of these are accented. Examples appear in (80).

(80) éln-ias   'stag'   (fixed)   eln-íen-a   'venison'   (fixed)
      vilk-as   'wolf'   (mobile)   vilk-íen-a 'wolf meat'   (fixed)
      kišk-as   'rabbit' (fixed)   kišk-ēl-is dimin.   (fixed)
      vilk-as   'wolf'   (mobile)   vilk-ēl-is dimin.   (fixed)

We might account for these cases by splitting derivation and inflection into two separate rule blocks and making line 1 constituents right-headed in the cyclic block but left-headed in the noncyclic, inflectional stratum. Assuming that conflation of lines 0 and 1 is also cyclic, this allows the accent on the derivational suffix to predominate over the stem. If more than one level of suffixation is encountered, the stress keeps migrating to the right.

(81) eln-ien   eln-ien   eln-ien
      | | | | | |
      *   *   *   *   *   *   line 0
      *   *   →   (*   *)   →   *   line 1
                         *   line 2

The problem with this approach is that there are at least two suffixes that suppress the stem stress but carry no accent themselves. The result is a grid with no line 1 asterisks. Our system correctly predicts that these constructions show the default initial accent of a mobile noun. An example of one of these unaccented dominant suffixes appears in (82).

(82) mēšk-ė 'bear'   (fixed)   mēšk-in-as 'male bear' (mobile)
      av-ìs   'sheep' (mobile)   āv-in-as   'ram'   (mobile)

But with the analysis suggested in (81), we cannot explain why a fixed stem such as *měšk-* loses its accent in nom.pl. *mešk-in-aī*. Since *-in* contributes no line 1 asterisk, it cannot head a line 1 constituent and we thus incorrectly predict stem stress.

It thus appears that we must posit a rule to delete the stress of the stem when a new derivational suffix is added. If the suffix is stressed, then it will predominate over an inflectional suffix since it becomes the leftmost line 1 asterisk. If the suffix is unaccented, then the word stress shows up on an accented desinence (case suffix); if the desinence is also unaccented, the initial default accent is assigned. It is simplest to express this process as a rule of conflation. However, the rule must be restricted to apply only in the presence of a derivational suffix. We want the accent of the derivational suffix and the lexical accent of an unsuffixed stem to survive into the inflectional rule block. The rule is stated in (83) as a rule of the cyclic stratum. The rules of line 1 metrification and conflation will be assigned to the word-level inflectional rule block.

(83)   [line 0] [   ]
     line 1 → ∅ / _____

Halle and Vergnaud (1987) see the suppression of the stem accent by the dominant suffixes as a cyclic effect and promote the stress loss to the status of a UG convention called the *Stress Erasure Convention*. Specifically, they propose that each level of affixation creates a new autosegmental plane on which the metrification process is applied. Since the suffix is new material, its lexical line 1 asterisks are visible. But the stress contours erected on the stem on line 1 and higher lines in the previous cycle exist in a different plane. The result is a family of planes – one for each level of derivation. If only the last one is submitted to the noncyclic stratum, the effect is to suppress all preceding stem accents – just like rule (83).

On this view, a word such as *kaim-iēt-is* 'villager' is derived as in (84a). In the first step the Stress Erasure Convention relegates the stress of the root [kaim] to a more remote plane. Another level of affixation pushes back the plane of the stem [kaimiēt], shifting the accent progressively to the right. In (84b) we see that the unaccented dominant suffix derives a grid that is bereft of line 1 asterisks and thus permits this derived stem to display the mobile pattern of inflection.

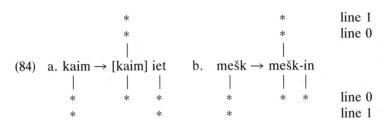

Halle and Vergnaud intend their Stress Erasure Convention to be a property of cyclic rules in general. This has some radical consequences for earlier conceptions of cyclic stress. While segmental reflexes of stress are carried over from one cycle to another, the stresses themselves no longer can be. The well-known contrast between *Wìnnipesáukee* and *orìginálity* is lost (Kiparsky 1979). In each word the main stress is preceded by a string of three light syllables. Monomorphemic stems such as *Wìnnipesaukee* characteristically have an initial secondary stress, while subsidiary stress on the second syllable in *orìginálity* reflects the main stress of the cyclic source *oríginal*. If the stress plane of one cycle is not carried forth to the next, the contrast between *orìginálity* and *Wìnnipesáukee* will be lost. Halle and Vergnaud are aware of this consequence of their proposal and offer an ad hoc remedy that we will not discuss. Suffice it to say, the construal of the dominant suffixes as a general cyclic effect is speculative and awaits supporting evidence.

10.9   Iambic versus Trochaic Rhythm

As developed to this point, the metrical parsing of the phonemic string (essentially line 0) has been determined by directionality and the location of heads. Freely combining these parameters (and a rule to eliminate stress clash) creates the typology of (85).

(85)   a.   left-headed, LR: C'VCVC'VCV, C'VCVC'VCVC'V   e.g., Maranungku
     b.   left-headed, RL: C'VCVC'VCV, CVC'VCVC'VCV   Warao
     c.   right-headed, LR: CVC'VCVC'V, C'VCVC'VCVC'VCV   Araucanian
     d.   right-headed, RL: CVC'VCVC'V, C'VCVC'VCVC'V   Weri

For quantity-sensitive metrical parsing, we posited a separate rule to assign heavy syllables a line 1 asterisk; the parsing procedure respects this structure, placing a stressed syllable in a head position. Adding quantity sensitivity thus creates four additional types of languages – one for each pattern in (85).

In an impressively documented search of the descriptive literature, Hayes (1985, 1991) discovered three surprising asymmetries in the combination of directionality, sensitivity to quantity, and the location of heads. The first two of these *Hayesian asymmetries* are stated in (86).

(86)   a.   Quantity-insensitive parses tend to be left-headed (trochaic).
     b.   Right-headed (iambic) parses do not permit a heavy syllable to occupy the dependent position.

(86a) is based on the observation that the four cells of the partition in (85) are not equally populated. While numerous examples of (85a,b) exist, (85c,d) are rarer. (86b) states that while there are left-headed trochaic systems such as Czech and Finnish in which a long-voweled (heavy) syllable can occupy the dependent position in the metrical foot ('LH), there are no right-headed iambic languages that place a long vowel in the dependent position. In other words, trochaic parsing may ignore quantity but iambic parsing may not. Abbreviating light and heavy syllables as L and H, (86b) means that systems that group a LL sequence as (L'L) cannot also group HL as (H'L).

Hayes (1991) proposes to build the asymmetries directly into the syllable-parsing procedure, yielding three disparate types. The first two are stated in (87). Following Hayes, we will refer to these as the *syllabic trochee* and *iambic parses*. As in earlier models, they freely combine with the (RL, LR) directionality parameter.

(87)   syllabic trochee parse
       Parse σ σ as (σ σ); elsewhere parse σ as (σ).
                *   *

       iambic parse
       Parse ŏ σ as (ŏ σ) and ō as (ō).
                *   *

The notation is slightly different from that of the Halle-Vergnaud model; for Hayes, the syllable is always the stress-bearing unit and hence serves as the terminal line of the grid. (For Halle and Vergnaud, the metrical parse is orthogonal to the syllabification and projected from the skeletal tier.) The iambic parse groups a light syllable with a following light or heavy as (L'L) or (L'H). But a heavy never joins with a following syllable: it may group with a preceding L or it occupies a constituent by itself. A (H'L) structure thus cannot result from either of the two parsing procedures in (87), accounting for (86b).

Functional motivation for the Hayesian asymmetries is to be found in the way in which humans perceive rhythmic groupings. An apparently well-supported generalization of experimental psychology states that quantitative distinctions induce iambic grouping while distinctions of intensity favor trochaic grouping. Bell (1977) reports experiments in which subjects listen to alternating pulses that are differentiated by an increase in intensity or duration. Hearing the former type, subjects perceive the enhanced stimulus as joined with a following nonenhanced element (88a); hearing the latter type, they group the enhanced element with the preceding weak position (88b).

(88)   a.   . . . . o . o . o . . . . → . . . . (o.)(o .)(o .) . . .   (o is louder)
       b.   . . . . - . - . - . . . . → . . . (. -)(. -)(. -) . . . .   (- is longer)

According to Hayes, this grouping principle is observed in musicians' preference rules and in verse recitation. It also underlies the response many English speakers give when asked to differentiate between iambic and trochaic verse: iambic verse is said to go *duh duuuh, duh duuuh, duh duuuh* while trochaic verse is *DUH duh, DUH duh, DUH duh*.

The departures of (86) from the theoretically expected symmetry are thus explained by assuming that alternating stress is essentially a rhythmic phenomenon. As such, an iambic grouping is naturally sensitized to quantitative distinctions and hence will not place a quantitatively prominent long vowel/heavy syllable in a rhythmically weak position. This explains why an unbalanced iamb (H'L) is avoided. On the other hand, if a system lacks a quantitative opposition, then it will tend to favor trochaic parsing. This explains why (85a,b) are more frequent than (85c,d). Czech and Warao are intermediate cases. In the former, a quantitative opposition that could support iambicity is ignored in favor of trochaic grouping; in the latter, iambic parsing is not reinforced by quantity.

Given the affinity between iambism and quantity, one expects quantitative oppositions to be encouraged in an iambic system and to be curtailed in a trochaic one. Changes of exactly this nature have been discovered. We will briefly review three cases. Perhaps the most widespread is the phenomenon of *iambic lengthening*, whereby a light syllable becomes heavy when the head of an iamb: (LL) → (LH). The increment of quantity can be realized as either vocalic lengthening or consonantal gemination. For example, in the Muskogean language Choctaw *Choctaw* (Nicklas 1975) nonfinal vowels in even-numbered light syllables counting from the left are lengthened. This process accounts for the quantitative variations in the stem of *habi:na* 'to receive a present' but *či-ha:bina* (*či-* 'you' obj.): in the former (LL)⟨L⟩ is enhanced to (LH)⟨L⟩; in the latter (LL)L⟨L⟩ is enhanced to (LH)L⟨L⟩. In some systems this process merges an underlying length contrast; in others it is the primary source for the language's long vowels or consonants. In many cases lengthened vowels are kept distinct from underlying long vowels, creating a three-way distinction (e.g., in some dialects of Muskogean).

A more spectacular example of the relation between length and iambism is furnished by the Australian language Yidin^y studied by Dixon (1977a,b) and Hayes (1982). Yidin^y has several rules that depend on whether the word contains an odd or even number of syllables. The paradigms in (89) illustrate the two major ones.

(89) root   [buNa]   [gindanu]   [gudaga]
      absolute   buNa   ginda:n   guda:ga
      ergative   buna:-ŋ   gindanu-ŋgu   gudaga-ŋgu
      genitive   buNa:-n   gindanu-ni   gudaga-ni
      comitative   buNa:-y   gindanu-yi   gudaga-yi
                    'woman'   'moon'   'dog'

One rule deletes a final postsonorant vowel from a word with an odd number of syllables; disyllabic 'woman' thus retains its final vowel in the unaffixed absolute and deletes the suffixal vowels, while trisyllabic 'moon' apocopates in the bare form but retains the suffixal vowels. Another rule lengthens the penultimate vowel, but only in words with an odd number of syllables. Once again 'woman' and 'moon' pattern inversely in the affixed and the bare forms. These rules are easy to state if the Yidin^y word parses into binary constituents from left to right. A word with an odd number of syllables terminates in a degenerate (monosyllabic) constituent. The rules are stated in (90a), using the orphan (CV) constituent as a reference point.

(90) a. V → V: / _____ (CV) #
          V → ∅ / (C _____) # (where C is [+sonorant])

      b. [buNa]   [gindanu]   [gudaga]   UR
          (buna)   (ginda)(nu)   (guda)(ga)   LR parse
          ——   (ginda:)(nu)   (guda:)(ga)   penultimate
                                                      lengthening
          ——   (ginda:n)   ———————   apocope

With these rules as background, let us now consider stress in Yidin^y. Dixon reports that when a long vowel falls in an even-numbered syllable, then the word stresses its even-numbered syllables; otherwise, the odd-numbered syllables are stressed. The paradigm for 'dog' in (91) illustrates this alternating stress pattern.

(91) absolute   gud'a:ga
      genitive   g'udag'a-ni
      reduplicated   gud'agud'a:ga

We may understand these strange stress rules by assuming that the string is parsed into binary feet from left to right and then penultimate lengthening applies to introduce a long vowel. (This is the primary source of length in the language.) The location of the stressed element within the parsed constituent is then guided by the rhythmic principle: iambic grouping if a long vowel is found in a sanctioned position (i.e., right edge of foot) and trochaic otherwise.

(92) [gudaga-ni]   [gudagudaga]   UR
      (guda)(gani)   (guda)(guda)(ga)   LR binary parse
      ──────────   (guda)(guda:)(ga)   penultimate lengthening
      ──────────   (gud'a)(gud'a:)(ga) iambic stress
      (g'uda)(g'ani)   ─────────────   trochaic stress

The Yidin^y case differs from the more common iambic lengthening of Muskogean, where the metrical parsing induces a quantity change as reinforcement; in Yidin^y quantity drives the choice between iambic and trochaic rhythm.

The final Hayesian asymmetry states that in languages that parse light syllables trochaically (producing a 'LL'LL stress contour), a left-to-right parse will stress a light syllable immediately following a heavy, despite the fact that a clash is produced. Cairene Arabic is the standard exemplar of this generalization. We saw earlier that even though Cairene deposits a single stress at the far end, metrification must cross the entire word, with conflation wiping its tracks clean. We briefly review the analysis in (93), tabulating the possible two- and three-syllable cases ending in a light.

(93) 'LL   ɣ'ada   'lunch'
      'HL   t'aani   'second'
      'LLL   k'atabu   'they wrote'
      L'HL   kat'abna   'we wrote'
      H'LL   makt'aba   'library'
      H'HL   makt'abna   'our office'

'LL and 'LLL suffice to establish trochaic parsing with final extrametricality; L'HL indicates sensitivity to quantity; and H'HL suggests enhancement of the rightmost stress and conflation of the preceding weaker ones. The surprise is a H'LL contour instead of the expected 'HLL. A traditional apology for this case is to say that the metrical parse counts moras in Cairene: binary metrification groups the two moras of a heavy syllable and hence starts a new foot on the following light syllable, correctly inducing a preconflation #(H)(L)⟨L⟩ grouping. A serious problem with this analysis is that the syllabic and metrical bracketing must coincide. Otherwise, the wrong metrification is assigned to cases such as *muqaatílatun* 'fighter' fem. and *muqaatilatúhu* 'his fighter' fem. As shown in (88), indiscriminately parsing moras without regard for the syllable breaks leads to an error: *muqaatilátuhu.

(94) muqa ati l atuhu
      | | || | | |
      (* *)(* *)(* *)(*⟩

Hayes (1987, 1991) proposes to derive this result by a third and final metrical parse, known as the *moraic trochee*. It allows trochaic rhythm to respect quantity but rigidly adheres to the syllable as the stress-bearing unit.

(95) moraic trochee parse
      Parse σ̆ σ̆ as (σ̆ σ̆) and σ̄ as (σ̄).
            *   *

This parse groups two successive light syllables or a single heavy syllable. As soon as it encounters a heavy syllable, it wraps it in brackets; metrification then begins anew, stressing the following syllable. The moraic trochee thus parses #HLL as #(H)(LL). And since the syllable is the stress-bearing unit, the initial L of a LHLLLL sequence cannot group with the following heavy. Consequently, (94) is correctly metrified as #L(H)(LL)(LL); since the moraic trochee parse (95) does not group a single light syllable (L), it requires us to drop final extrametricality for Cairene.

While the moraic trochee parse captures the behavior of initial #HL sequences in Cairene, it remains to be seen how general the third Hayesian asymmetry is. One problem is that it fails to capture the case of Bani-Hassan Arabic (section 10.6.2), where the postulated (HL) grouping explains the absence of elision in *ʕàllamátuh*. Given (HL)(L)⟨L⟩ metrification, the second syllable fails to head a (LL) constituent and thus escapes elision. A more serious problem is that there is rather convincing evidence for (HL) grouping under right-to-left trochaic parsing. For example, recall from section 10.6.3 that in Latin the *ubí#libet* vs. *li:miná#que* contrast crucially depends on the (L)⟨L⟩ vs. (HL)⟨L⟩ bracketing. If *li:mina* had the (H)L⟨L⟩ or (H)(LL) grouping required by the moraic trochee parse, we should expect the [mi] syllable to seat an enclitic accent.

Thus, while direct evidence for a (HL) trochaic foot is lacking, the circumstantial evidence supports this grouping. However, the experiments cited in (88) indicate that quantitative oppositions are not optimally compatible with trochaic rhythm. We might thus expect them to be curtailed. At least two clear cases have been discovered in which a (HL) structure shortens to (LL). They are usually interpreted as optimizing trochaic rhythm. One example is the English paradigm of (96), noticed first by Myers (1987b).

(96)   'origin   or'iginal   c'inema   cinem'atic
        p'arent   par'ental   en'igma   enigm'atic
        s'ēmen   s'ĕminal   Semīte   Sem'ĭtic
        sp'īne   sp'īnal   tōne   t'ŏnic

To briefly review the analysis, *par'ent-al* establishes *-al* as a stress-sensitive affix; the antepenultimate stress of *or'igin-al* shows it to be extrametrical. In this respect it contrasts with *-ic*, which, though also stress-sensitive, consistently shifts the accent to the preceding syllable: *cinem'at-ic, enigm'at-ic*. This contrast can be explained by treating both *-al* and *-ic* as level 1 (cyclic) affixes but differing in extrametricality. Both affixes also shorten the stressed stem vowel, regardless of whether the stress is shifted (*S'emīte, Sem'ĭt-ic*) or not (*n'āture, n'ătur-al*). But a long vowel preceding the stress is preserved: *trīumph, trī'umph-al; t'ītan, tīt'an-ic*. As Myers observes, the generalization is that shortening only takes place within a trochaic foot. We can express the trochaic shortening rule as in (97), reverting to the Halle-Vergnaud notation.

(97) $\bar{V} \rightarrow \check{V} /$ _____
                   |
              (* *)   line 0
               *   line 1

The analysis is supported by such minimal pairs as *tōne*, but *t'ŏn-ic* vs. *t'ōn-al*. In general, *-ic* shortens a preceding monosyllabic stem while *-al* does not. This striking contrast follows since *-ic* metrifies with the preceding syllable while *-al* does not: *t'ŏn-ic* thus has an underlying (HL) structure while *t'ōn-al* is (H)⟨L⟩; trochaic shortening (97) thus applies in the former but not in the latter.

On the face of it, the shortening of a stressed vowel seems strange. Stressed position is phonologically strong and typically preserves structure. Indeed, Myers analyzed the shortening as mediated by a ('V.CV) → ('VC.V) resyllabification within a trochaic foot, activating the closed-syllable shortening rule operating in *keep, kĕpt*. But in view of the equivalent (phonetic) syllabifications of the medial consonant in *t'onic* and *t'o:nal*, a resyllabification to onset must apply to undo this hypothetical change in syllabification. Proponents of the rhythmic view of stress (e.g., Prince 1990) interpret (97)'s shortening of (HL) to (LL) as restoring the balanced quantitative relation between members of a foot favored by trochaism. However, this explanation faces the problem that two other rules of English lengthen vowels when they occupy the head of a trochaic foot: one affects the first of two successive vowels, applying in *algebră, algebr'ā-ic* and *v'ary, v'ari-ous*, but *var'ī-ety*. The other lengthens nonhigh vowels in the context ____*C*iV: *'Arab, Ar'āb-ian; Sp'enser, Spens'ēr-ian*; compare *D'arwin, Darw'in-ian*. If trochaic rhythm motivates the shortening of *tōne, tŏn-ic* by (97), why do we find lengthening in a subset of the very same metrical contexts?

10.10 Outstanding Issues

In this section we will examine some of the issues that have emerged in the most recent metrical stress theory. For many of these questions two competing models exist: the Halle and Vergnaud (1987) model (and later developments in Halle 1990, Halle and Kenstowicz 1991, Halle and Idsardi 1993, Idsardi 1992) versus the model of the rhythmic theorists (Hayes 1991, Prince 1990, Kager 1991). Both accept the basic insight that stress reflects the grouping of metrical positions into headed constituents. The two models differ in their guiding intuition concerning word stress (particularly alternating stress). For Halle and Vergnaud, stress reflects the marking of headed constituents formed on the metrical grid. It is thus the grid-level instantiation of a much more general phenomenon found at many different levels of linguistic analysis in which items are concatenated. For Hayes and Prince, alternating word stress is primarily a rhythmic phenomenon governed by the iambic-trochaic disparity with respect to quantity. This disparity plays no role at higher levels of the grid, where it is unclear whether the notion of constituency is even required, as opposed to a rule that simply enhances an element at the edge of the word or phrase.

10.10.1 *Stress-Bearing Unit*

In the Halle and Vergnaud model, all stress computations are performed on the grid. The grid is projected from the skeletal tier. In the unmarked case, the head of the syllable-rime (essentially the nucleus) projects a line 0 asterisk and thus constitutes the stress-bearing unit. However, the model allows a heavy syllable the option to project two line 0 asterisks (from its first two rime slots). We informally appealed to this device to explain the different realizations of a HLLL string such as [ʕallamatah] in the two Bedouin Arabic dialects discussed in section 10.6.2: Riyadh requires a (H)(LL)⟨L⟩ parse while Bani-Hassan has (HL)(L)⟨L⟩. The latter is obtained in the normal way by having the head of the syllable nucleus project a line 0 asterisk and invoking a separate rule that assigns heavy syllables a line 1 asterisk. LR binary parsing then groups the first two syllables. The (H)(LL)⟨L⟩ grouping arises from the same left-headed parse but differs by having the heavy syllable project two line 0 asterisks – one from each rimal slot. LR binary parsing thus closes the first foot on the heavy syllable. Projecting two line 0 asterisks from a heavy syllable also generates the (H)('LL)⟨L⟩ parsing required by Cairene *makt'abatu* 'his library'. However, recall from section 10.6.2 that Cairene demands that the metrical bracketing not interrupt a syllable boundary, lest the wrong stress be assigned to *muqaat'ilatu* (98a).

(98) a. muqaat i latu → muqa ati la t u
　　　　| || | | |　　　　| | | | | |
　　　　* ** * * *　　　(* *)(* *)(*)⟨*⟩
　　　　　　　　　　　　　*　　 *　　*

　　　b. muqaatilatu → muqaatilatu → mu qaa tila tu
　　　　| || || |　　　　| || || |　　　　| || || |
　　　　* ** ** *　　　* (** ** *　　　(*)(**)(**)⟨*⟩

To handle this problem, Halle (1990) postulates a rule for Cairene that places an opening metrical bracket "(" in front of every line 0 asterisk projected from the head of a heavy syllable. This bracket must then be respected by the metrical parse (98b). The bracket has a number of consequences. Since metrical feet are binary, the parse gathers both asterisks of the heavy syllable into a foot. The foot can thus never interrupt a syllable. The parse then starts a new foot on the syllable following any heavy syllable. In this way, a heavy syllable always constitutes a foot of its own in Cairene.

For Hayes and other metrical theorists who accept the prosodic hierarchy in which moras are organized into syllables, syllables into feet, and feet into prosodic words, stress feet are necessarily composed of syllables and all metrical parsing is defined over the syllable (though the parse may look down another level to inspect the syllable's weight (mora count)). Given that the prosodic hierarchy is strictly layered, metrical footing cannot in principle interrupt the syllable. There are cases of accent assignment that target moras regardless of their syllable affiliation. For example, in the Bantu language Luganda (Hyman and Katamba 1992) certain constructions contribute a high tone, which is attracted to the second mora so long as the first mora is free.

(99)　a.　ku-lim-a　　'to cultivate'　　ku-lim-á kyàngè　　'my cultivating'
　　　　　ku-lagir-a　'to command'　　ku-lagír-à kyàngè　'my commanding'
　　　　　ku-tumul-a　'to enrage'　　ku-tumúlùl-à kyàngè　'my enraging'

　　　b.　ku-saab-a　'to smear'　　ku-sááb-à kyàngè　'my smearing'

　　　c.　ku-tamiir-a　'to get drunk'　　ku-tamîir-à kyàngè　'my getting drunk'

When the first two syllables are light, the high tone falls on the second (99a); when the first syllable is heavy, we find a rising tone, simplified to high by a general rule as in [ku-sàáb-a] → [ku-sááb-a] (99b); and finally, when the first syllable is light and the second heavy, a falling tone on the heavy syllable ensues (99c). These data might be argued to reflect an iambic parsing of the moras without regard to the syllabification. The high tone would then be realized on the head of the initial iamb, splitting the syllable in (100c).

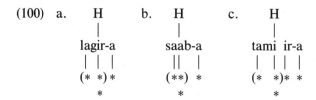

Proponents of the prosodic hierarchy could propose an alternative analysis in which the initial mora is extratonal and the high tone is then assigned to the first mora of the remaining base.

(101)   a.   H   b.   H   c.   H

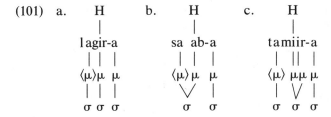

Although the syllable is split in this analysis as well, this arises from a rule defined to operate at the lower moraic level and so no violation of the prosodic hierarchy ensues. What is predicted not to occur are alternating stress patterns that split syllables.

One much-discussed case that appears to work this way is Winnebago. Recall from section 10.6 that in a string of light syllables the alternating accent starts on the third syllable, suggesting initial extrametricality and a right-headed LR parse: *hočįčínįk* is ⟨L⟩(LL)(L). However, when the first syllable contains a long vowel, stress falls on the second syllable: *taanį́žu* 'sugar' (Miner 1990). If a long vowel projects two line 0 asterisks, then initial extrametricality plus binary right-headed feet locates the stress in exactly the right positions (102a,b).

(102)   a.   ho čįčįn įk   b.   ta anįž u
             | | | | | | | |
          ⟨*⟩(* *)(*)   ⟨*⟩(* *)(*)
               * *   * *

But the metrical bracketing splits the initial syllable of *taanį́žu*. And when the first two syllables contain a long vowel, moraic parsing misaligns the metrical and syllabic structure twice: *yuukíihinaŋkì* 'if I could mix them' (Halle 1990) has the analysis shown in (103a).

(103)   a.   yu uki ihi naŋki   b.   ho kiwa roke
             | | | | | | | | | | | | | |
          ⟨*⟩(* *)(* *)(* *)   ⟨*⟩ (* *)(* *)
               *   *   *   *   *

However, the syllable division cannot be ignored entirely in Winnebago stress. The rule deleting the second of two clashing stresses must remove the second stress in (103). In order for this rule to convert [yuuk'iih'inaŋk'u] to *yuukíihinaŋkù* but to retain the accents in *hokiwároke̖*, it must be defined over the syllable. If destressing were defined solely on the grid, it would fail to distinguish the two cases since as (103a,b) show, they have equivalent grid representations.

A theory that parses iambically over syllables cannot score a direct hit in Winnebago. Initial-syllable extrametricality parses ⟨H⟩(L'L); no extrametricality delivers ('H)(L'L). Each attempt misses the second syllable target of *taanį́žu*. Recapitulating Miner's (1979) diachronic reconstruction, Hayes (1991) suggests assigning Winnebago accent in two steps. His solution drops the Halle and Vergnaud initial extrametricality and parses iambically to produce ('H)(L'L) and (L'L)(L'L). The accent is interpreted as high tone. Then a separate rule is postulated to shift the tone one syllable to the right, triggering a dissimilation of the second of two adjacent high tones.

(104)

The accent in Winnebago is apparently realized tonally (Miner 1979) and so this interpretation is possible. Furthermore, the postulated rules of tone shift and dissimilation have plausible precedents in the Bantu languages. However, just as the destressing rule of the Halle and Vergnaud analysis must look outside the postulated moraic grid structure to the syllable projection, so Hayes's tone shift cuts across the metrical bracketing imputed by the syllable-based iambic parse. In section 11.2 we will examine some cases of prosodic morphology that apparently require a moraic grouping to interrupt the syllable. While cases of this kind exist, they appear to be rare. (See Halle and Vergnaud's (1987) and Hayes's (1981) discussion of Southern Paiute for another possible example.) In the normal state of affairs, metrical bracketing and syllable bracketing coincide. Future research must decide whether deviations from the norm can be explained by some as yet unknown factor.

10.10.2 Maximal Binarity

Multiple stresses in the word typically arise from an iterative binary parse of syllables or moras. A metrical lapse of two successive unstressed positions generally reflects extrametricality at the left (Winnebago) or right (Latin) edge of the word or a rule of stress clash removal: compare *Àpalàchicóla* with *Wìnnipesáukee* (from [Wìnnipèsáukee] or [Wìnnìpesáukee], depending on the direction of assignment of secondary stresses). However, a few well-documented cases exist of systematic lapses of two successive unstressed positions. In this section we will examine two of the best-known examples and the treatments they have received.

In the Bolivian language Cayuvava (Key 1961, 1967, Levin 1988b) stress falls on the third, sixth, and ninth vowel from the right edge, with initial stress in disyllables. The data in (105) are from Hayes 1991.

(105)
'σ σ	éne	'leaf'
'σ σ σ	šákahe	'stomach'
σ 'σ σ σ	kihíβere	'I ran'
σ σ 'σ σ σ	ariúuca	'he came already'
'σ σ σ 'σ σ σ	ràibirínapu	'dampened manioc flour'
σ 'σ σ σ 'σ σ σ	maràhahaéiki	'their blankets'
σ σ 'σ σ σ 'σ σ σ	ikitàparerépeha	'the water is clean'
'σ σ σ 'σ σ σ 'σ σ σ	càadiròboβurúruce	'ninety-nine'

The paradigm in (105) appears to reflect a ('σσσ) motif. However, metrical theorists have been reluctant to admit ternary ('σσσ) or (σσ'σ) constituents directly into the theory. For one thing, the multiple 'σσσ sequences found in Cayuvava appear to be rare. More importantly, if ternary feet were admitted, then metrical parsing would violate the otherwise well-established generalization that linguistic rules do not count beyond two, in turn raising the question why counting to four or five is never found. (Counting to two can be construed as adjacency to a designated element and thus there really is no counting as such.) If this rationale is accepted, then the Cayuvava stress contour must be derived in another way.

Halle and Vergnaud (1987) suggest refining the category of bounded constituents with a [±head-terminal] classification. Since the head must be adjacent to the governed dependent in bounded constituents, the only possible ternary grouping is one in which the head is flanked by a single dependent on each side. On this analysis, Cayuvava parses into *amphibrachs* from right to left with final extrametricality (106a).

(106) a. (σ σ)(σ σ σ)⟨σ⟩   (σ σ σ)(σ σ σ)⟨σ⟩   (σ)(σ σ σ)(σ σ σ)⟨σ⟩
            *   *   *   *   *   *   *

       b. (σ σ)(σ σ σ)⟨σ⟩   (σ σ σ)(σ σ σ)⟨σ⟩   (σ)(σ σ σ)(σ σ σ)⟨σ⟩
            (*   *)   (*   *)   (*   *   *)
                     *   *   *

       c. σ σ(σ σ σ)⟨σ⟩   (σ σ σ)(σ σ σ)⟨σ⟩   σ (σ σ σ)(σ σ σ)⟨σ⟩
                (*)   (*   *)   (*   *)
                 *   *   *

The rightmost stress is then enhanced by constructing unbounded right-headed constituents on line 1. Exhaustive parsing yields binary and monosyllabic constituents at the left edge. Since these are not stressed on the surface in Cayuvava, a rule defooting nonmaximal constituents is introduced. This rule is blocked from applying to the foot that supports the main stress, allowing disyllabic *éne* to emerge. In sum, ternary amphibrachs are introduced into the Halle and Vergnaud model by refining one of the foot parameters while the rest of the system remains essentially intact.

Following Levin (1988b), Hayes (1991) objects to this analysis on the grounds that defooting normally operates under clash (Hammond's (1984) generalization) and that it is preferable to restrict the foot inventory to binary constituents. His proposal is to allow the directional parse a marked option to skip a single mora or light syllable after the construction of a foot. When combined with final extrametricality, this *weak local parsing* option generates the following representations for the three classes of Cayuvava words.

(107) (σ σ) σ (σ σ)⟨σ⟩   σ (σ σ) σ (σ σ)⟨σ⟩   σ σ (σ σ) σ (σ σ)⟨σ⟩
        *   *   *   *   *   *

In a 3-*n*+2 case such as the eight-syllable *ikitàparerépeha*, the initial stress is blocked by a ban on degenerate monosyllabic (σ) feet outside the main word stress (see below).

To briefly summarize, while one model augments the basic foot inventory in a fairly natural way, the other modifies the parsing procedure in a seemingly equally natural way. The contest between the two proposals thus will have to be resolved on empirical rather than conceptual grounds.

Another controversial example of apparent ternary footing is provided by the Chugach dialect of Alutiiq Yupik Eskimo (Leer 1985). Most Yupik dialects parse iambically from left to right with lengthening of open-syllable stressed vowels (often displacing a short versus long opposition to long versus extralong). In the Chugach dialect, sequences of light syllables allow a lapse of two unstressed syllables between each pair of stressed ones. (The transcriptions in (108) abstract away from the stressed vowel lengthening.)

(108)   pal'ayaq   'rectangular skiff'
        ak'utam'ək   'a type of food' abl.sg.
        taq'umalun'i   'apparently getting done'
        ak'utaxtun'ixtuq   'he stopped eating akutaq'
        maŋ'axsuqut'aqun'i   'if he refl. is going to hunt porpoise'

Following the analysis developed for Cayuvava, Halle (1990) assigns Chugach amphibrachs, but from left to right. Unlike in Cayuvava, nonmaximal feet are not suppressed in Chugach.

(109)   akutamək   taqumal uni   akutaxtunixtuq
        | | | | | | | | | | | | | | |
        (* * *)(*)   (* * *)(* *)   (* * *)(* * *)
           *   *   *   *   *   *

In Hayes's (1991) analysis, the feet are iambic and Chugach differs from other Yupik dialects in skipping a single mora after the construction of an iamb. On this analysis, the forms of (109) parse initially as in (110a). A later reapplication of the basic stress rule then metrifies pairs of adjacent light syllables left over from the end of the iambic parse, assigning a final stress in *ak'utam'ək* (110b). This option of "persistent footing" distinguishes Alutiiq from Cayuvava, where the lapse of two unstressed syllables is allowed to surface. Persistent footing thus works something like syllabification, ensuring that material escaping the initial parse is later metrified. The precise details of its operation have not been worked out, however.

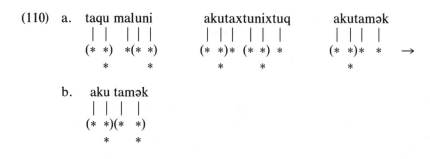

(110) a. taqu maluni   akutaxtunixtuq   akutamək
           | | | | | | | | | | | | | | |
           (* *) *(* *)   (* *)* (* *) *   (* *)* *   →
              *   *   *   *   *

       b. aku tamək
           | | | |
           (* *)(* *)
              *   *

Both analyses thus generate the ternary stress patterns with a minimal change in the basic system. Deciding between them will require finding independent evidence for metrical grouping, in particular whether or not the Chugach foot closes on the stressed vowel or takes in the following unstressed one. See Hayes 1991 and Kager 1991 for additional discussion.

10.10.3 Minimal Binarity

Alternating stress is characteristically binary. However, in many languages a lapse of two successive unstressed syllables is allowed at the end of an odd-numbered sequence. For example, in the Australian language Pintupi (data cited in Hayes 1991, from Hansen and Hansen 1969, 1978) the final syllable remains unstressed regardless of its odd or even position.

(111) páṇa   'earth'
      tʲúṭuya   'many'
      máḷawàna   'through from behind'
      púliŋkàlatʲu   'we (sat) on the hill'
      tʲámulìmpatʲùŋku   'our relation'
      tíḷiriŋulàmpatʲu   'the fire for our benefit flared up'

If metrical parsing is exhaustive, then we have two options for explaining the lack of final stress in *tʲúṭuya:* the final syllable could be extrametrical, (tʲúṭu)⟨ya⟩; or it could be parsed and then destressed by a rule eliminating degenerate nonbinary feet, (tʲuṭu)(ya) → (tʲuṭu)ya. Adapting a term from the printing trade for leftover pages in the gathering of a book, let us refer to such unmatched syllables as *orphans.* In the Halle and Vergnaud model, with its commitment to exhaustive parsing by the RL/LR iterative grouping rules, orphans are regularly parsed into degenerate constituents. When they appear unstressed on the surface, a rule eliminating degenerate constituents (typically but not always under stress clash) must be postulated. For rhythmic theorists, binary constituents pairing a stressed and an unstressed element are the norm. A monosyllabic/monomoraic constituent is rhythmically unbalanced and thus unexpected. Accordingly, some rhythmic theorists have interpreted languages such as Pintupi as reflecting a system-wide ban on degenerate feet. On this view, there is a parameter for minimal binarity that must be set. If the unmarked positive setting is chosen, then no degenerate feet are possible. In a quantity-sensitive system, the foot inventory is then limited to bimoraic (H) and (LL) plus (LH) for iambic systems and possibly (HL) for trochaic. If quantity is not relevant, then all feet are simply (σ σ). On this view, Pintupi [tʲuṭuya] thus parses directly as (tʲuṭu)ya, with an unmetrified final syllable. Hayes (1991) hypothesizes that a system will choose the marked setting licensing a stressed orphan only when it is directly under the main word stress. In this section we will briefly survey some of the characteristic behaviors displayed by orphans and how they play out in the two approaches.

The simplest way to test for degenerate constituents is to look at monosyllables. It turns out that in a significant number of cases, monosyllabic/monomoraic words are simply absent, either because such underlying representations are augmented by the addition of another mora/syllable (e.g., Lardil, Choctaw) or because they are simply missing from the lexical stock. Such is the case in Pintupi as well as in the iambic parsing Winnebago (Miner 1979) and trochaic Cairene. The absence of *subminimal words* is usually explained by appeal to the *prosodic hierarchy*. Given that phonological words are composed of metrical feet, any word must have at least one foot. The absence of monosyllabic/monomoraic words might thus reflect the absence of degenerate feet in the metrical system. In other words, the unparsed orphan of (tʲutu)*ya* and the lack of monosyllabic words are claimed to reflect the same gap in the metrical foot inventory: no (L) or (σ); see section 11.3.

Other evidence cited for minimal binarity is the tendency to reparse extra-metrical syllables to achieve binarity and hence a stress. For example, Latin displays the minimal word syndrome. Monomoraic words are absent from the nonclitic vocabulary. Allen (1973) interprets the iambic shortening that converted #L⟨H⟩# words such as *egō* 'I' and *modō* 'only' to 'ego and m'odo as an artifice to assign a word stress but still satisfy strict binarity: #L⟨H⟩# reparses as #(LL)#, with automatic shortening of the heavy syllable to maintain trochaism. #(H)⟨H⟩# *ambō* 'both' does not shorten, suggesting that (H) has no need to incorporate the final syllable since it is already a legitimate binary (bimoraic) foot. (See Mester 1993 for further discussion.)

The Peruvian language Auca represents a case where orphans are stressed. As shown by Pike (1964), stems parse trochaically from left to right while the string of suffixes parses from right to left. (112) tabulates four representative stress contours as a function of the parity of the stem and string of suffixes. In the analysis of these data by Halle and Kenstowicz (1991), the final syllable of the stem is treated as extrametrical. It groups with the suffixes in the right-to-left parse of the noncyclic (word-level) stratum. For a case such as (112b), the suffixal parse of 3#45 terminates in a stressed orphan (3)#(45), generating a clash.

(112) a. 'apæn'e#kānd'apa 'he speaks'
            123#456 → ('12)⟨3⟩#456 → ('12)3#456 → ('12)('3#4)('56)

       b. y'iwæm'ō#ŋ'āmba 'he carves'
            123#45 → ('12)⟨3⟩#45 → ('12)('3)#('45)

       c. p'ædæp'ōnō#n'āmba 'he handed it over'
            1234#56 → ('12)('3)⟨4⟩#56 → ('12)('3)('4)#('56) → ('12)('3)4#('56)

       d. 'ēŋ'a#kānd'apa 'he was born'
            12#345 → ('1)⟨2⟩#345 → ('1)2#345 → ('1)('2#3)('45)

In Hayes's (1991) analysis the stem is metrified directly, with no extrametricality; a stressed orphan is generated on stems containing an odd number of metrical positions. Although Pike does not indicate any primary versus secondary stress distinctions in his discussion or transcriptions, Hayes assembles circumstantial evidence that the final syllable of the stem carries a stronger stress than the others. If this is true, then Auca conforms to the hypothesis that stressed orphans arise only under main stress. In a case such as (112c), Halle and Kenstowicz parse the formerly extrametrical syllable of the stem as an orphan and then must invoke a rule eliminating degenerate constituents under stress clash on the left. Hayes's analysis derives this case directly: ('12)('34)#('56). However, the relative simplicity of this case is offset by a more complex treatment for words in which the stem has an even number of positions and the suffixal string an odd number. For Hayes, initial metrification generates ('12)#3('45). A rebracketing rule is then required to group the unparsed orphan 3 with the final syllable of the stem to return a ('1)('2#3)('45) representation. This reparsing is relatively unmotivated in Hayes's system since 3 falls outside the main stress and thus should, other things being equal, emerge unstressed. In sum, the two models each must postulate an extra rule in their analysis of Auca: a destressing rule in Halle and Vergnaud's system to cut back the extra stress in (112c) and a reparsing rule in Hayes's to insert an otherwise unexpected stress.

Granted that stressed orphans exist, we still might question the legitimacy of assigning a stress and then having to take it back in a case like Pintupi (tʲ'uṭu)(y'a) → (tʲ'uṭu)*ya*. Descriptively, the derivation is shorter if this extra step is not taken. More importantly, is there any positive evidence to justify the intermediate stage? If not, then strict adherence to the binary parsing option is preferable. A possible example that motivates the intermediate stage is Winnebago. Recall that this language parses iambically from left to right with initial extrametricality. Three- and five-syllable strings such as *hipirák* 'belt' and *hokiwárokè* 'swing' parse binarily as ⟨1⟩(2'3) and ⟨1⟩(2'3)(4'5). But exhaustive parsing produces a stressed orphan in even-syllabled *hočįčínịk* 'boy' ⟨1⟩(2'3)('4) that must then be eliminated (under clash). In Winnebago the main stress is at the front of the word and so a stressed orphan would not be licensed under Hayes's hypothesis. The two models thus impose quite different analyses as a function of their stand on minimal binarity and exhaustive parsing.

Recall that when Dorsey's Law epenthesis disrupts a metrical constituent in Winnebago, the string is reparsed from the spot of the foul. But when the epenthetic vowel is slipped between metrical constituents, the original stress is retained. Hale and White Eagle (1980) cite the form in (113) as an example of the latter situation.

(113)   ha rakíšrujìkšnậ   ha rakíšurujìkšậnậ
     | | | || | → | | | || | | |
   ⟨*⟩(* *)(* *) (*)   ⟨*⟩(* *)*(* *) * (*)
      *   *   *   *   *   *

The disyllabic lapse over the Dorsey's Law sequence [šuru] is not reparsed since no constituent has been disturbed. The Dorsey's Law sequence *šậnậ* has a final stress. This could only arise from an underlying stress. But in the underlying structure of this six-syllable word, [šnậ] is an orphan. We can account for this case if a stressed orphan is assigned and the rule eliminating degenerate constituents under clash is ordered after epenthesis. This example is comparable to other cases in which an epenthetic vowel allows normally hidden structure to emerge (e.g., the long vowels in Yawelmani [CVVCC] stems; section 3.4). If correct, this analysis supports the rule destressing orphans and more generally the commitment to exhaustive parsing on which it is premised. (Recall from section 10.10.1, however, Hayes's alternative analysis of Winnebago as a pitch accent system with a tone shift rule that derives all surface accents from the preceding syllable. If his analysis is correct, then the force of this example is diminished.)

Finally, let us look at two more examples illustrating different properties of degenerate constituents. In Old English (Dresher and Lahiri 1991) high vowels syncopate from an open syllable when preceded by a heavy or two lights.

(114) syncope
     gōd + u   heafud + es word + u   werud + u   færeld + u
           ↘   ↘   ↘   ↘   ↘
            ∅   ∅   ∅   ∅   ∅

     'good'   'head'   'words'   'troops'   'journey'
     nom.pl. gen.sg.
     neut.

     no syncope
     lof + u   nīten + u
     'praises'   'animals'

The equivalence of H and LL suggests that Old English parses like Cairene but with the major stress on the initial syllable. The orphan, parsed either as (L) or as a bare L, then defines the context for the syncope rule. (See Dresher and Lahiri 1991 for an alternative interpretation.)

(115) good + u   hea fud + es   word + u   werud + u   fæ reld + u
      ‖ | ‖ | ‖   ‖ | ‖ | | | ‖ |
     (**) (*)   (**)(*) (**) (**) (*) (* *) (*) (*)(**) (*)

     lof + u   nii ten + u
     | | ‖ | |
     (*   *) (**)(*   *)

In addition to defining the site of syncope, degenerate constituents are relevant for the rule of destressing in Old English. Dresher and Lahiri state that while secondary stress is retained on a heavy syllable following a heavy (*ōpèrne* 'other' acc.sg.masc.) or two lights (*ǽpelìnges* 'prince' gen.sg.), it is lost from a heavy syllable that follows a stressed light: *cýninges* 'king' gen.sg., *wésende* 'to be' pres.part. Under the bipositional representation for heavy syllables, the contrast between initial light and heavy syllables with respect to initiating stress clash removal has a natural representational difference of the kind noted by Prince (1983). The stress-bearing units are adjacent in the (L)(H) sequence but not in (H)(H), whose grid structure parallels that of a (LL)(LL) sequence.

(116) we sen de   oo þer ne
     | ‖ | ‖ ‖ |
     (*)(**)(*)   (**)(**)(*)
      *   *   *   *   *   *

This analysis claims that even though there is no phonetic manifestation of a stress curve in the bipositional heavy syllable, nevertheless the initial mora of a heavy syllable is phonologically more prominent than the second. This explains why the stress-bearing units are adjacent in the (L)(H) sequence but not in (H)(H). The second mora of the initial heavy acts as a buffer between the two stressed positions.

Kager (1992) attempts to take account of such phenomena within the rhythmic framework, with the idea that the mora may define a separate layer of prominence below the syllable level. Specifically, bimoraic heavy syllables have an inherent strong-weak prominence that is generally inaudible but may assert itself when no contradictory metrical structure is imposed at the syllable level. The falling mora prominence of a heavy syllable can also encourage certain types of clash avoidance. This explains the contrasting behavior of light and heavy syllables in two small corners of Estonian prosody. As the forms in (117a) show, Estonian freely groups light and heavy syllables in a left-to-right disyllabic trochee parse that ignores quantity (abstracting away from overlength and an optional ternary rhythm; see Prince 1980, Hayes 1991). The rule in (117b) generates the observed stress contours.

(117) a. ('LL)   ré.ti.(lì.le)   'ladder' all.sg.
           ('HL)   ép.pet.(tùs.te)lè.ki   'lessons, too' all.pl.
           ('LH)   pí.mes.(tà.vas).se   'blinding' ill.sg.
           ('HH)   vá.ra.(sèi.mat).tè.le   'earliest' all.pl.
           ('H)   pá.he.(mài)⟨t⟩   'worse' part.pl.

    b. $\sigma\sigma \rightarrow ({}'\sigma\sigma)$ left to right

However, as the forms in (118) show, a final heavy in an odd position takes a stress while a light does not. Another similar contrast between light and heavy syllables occurs in monosyllables. The Estonian minimal word consists of one heavy or two light syllables; words composed of a single light syllable are absent from the Estonian lexicon.

(118) pí.mes.tà.va.le   'blinding' ill.sg.
       pí.mes.tà.va.màit   'blinding' part.pl.

Kager explains the limited contrast between light and heavies as follows. The inherent mora prominence of the heavy syllable may be promoted to the syllable level when the syllable parse imposed by (117b) fails to assign any contradictory structure. Given strict binarity, this situation arises only with word-final orphans and monosyllables. Thus, *pi.mes.ta.va.mait* receives the analysis in (119). (119) shows the structure assigned by the syllabic (generalized) trochee. Under strict binarity, the final syllable is unparsed. The inherent moraic prominence of the final heavy syllable may be promoted to the syllable level because the syllable parse (117b) has imposed no structure at this point. But promotion of the moraic prominence of the second syllable [mes] is blocked by the weak metrical position assigned at the syllable level by (117b). Similarly, the strong position on the syllable level is passed down as a prominence to the mora level in [pi] and [ta].

(119) syllable   (*   ·) (*   ·)   ·   (*   ·) (*   ·) (*)
       mora   ·   (*·) ·   ·   (*.)   *   (*·)   *   ·   (*·)
                   [pi] [mes] [ta] [va] [mait]   →   [pi] [mes] [ta] [va] [mait]

Kager invokes the notion of clash at the moraic level to explain a curious contrast between Estonian and Finnish: Finnish systematically avoids a ('LH) trochee outside the initial two syllables of the word. As demonstrated by the paradigm in (120a), it otherwise manifests the panoply of trochaic shapes found in Estonian. The form in (120b) shows that when a LH sequence is encountered in an odd-even position, the parse skips the light syllable to place a stress on the following heavy: LLLHLLLLL → ('LL)L('HL)('LL)('LL).

(120)   a.   ('LL)   ló.pe.(tè.ta)   'finish' negative
             ('HL)   lópe.(tèt.ta).va   'to be finished'
             ('LH)   not found medially
             ('HH)   ló.pe.(tèt.tii)⟨n⟩   'one finished'
             ('H)   ló.pe.te.(tàa)⟨n⟩   'one finishes'

        b.   ká.no.ni.sòi.ma.nà.ni.kò.han   'in a state of having been
                                               canonized by me, of course'
                                               essive sg.

Kager sees Finnish as adopting the Estonian disyllabic parse of (117b) but imposing an additional requirement to avoid a clash at the mora level. As shown in (121), such a clash arises in a (LH) grouping at the syllable level when the prominence assigned to the light syllable is passed down as a prominence to the mora level.

(121)   syllable level (*   ·)   (*   ·)
        mora level   · (*·)   →   *   *·
                        [ni] [soi]   [ni] [soi]

In sum, both languages parse under strict binarity, avoiding a clash at the syllable level; Finnish imposes an additional restriction avoiding a clash at the mora level.

Kager discerns a similar minimal difference among systems that metrify by the moraic trochee. Recall that under this parse, languages such as Cairene Arabic and Cahuilla group pairs of light syllables ('LL) and single heavy syllables ('H). They avoid a clash at the mora level and so group #LH as #L('H) rather than #('L)('H). However, such parsings as #HLL → #('H)('LL) and #HHL → #('H)('H)L indicate that they readily accept a syllable clash. The forms in (122a) from the Australian language Yindjibarndi suggest that this language also groups according to the moraic trochee.

(122)   a.   'LL'H   pángkarrìi   'go' infinitive
             L'HL   purnngáarri   'cyclonic cloud'

        b.   'HH   páarnpaarn   'mulga parrot'
             'HL'L   káarrwarà   'loincloth'

    c.   LHL   palírri≈páli.ìrri   'blue-tongue lizard'
         HH   pirríi≈pírri.ì   'match'

But unlike Cairene and Cahuilla, Yindjibarndi avoids stress on two successive heavy syllables or a heavy and a light (122b), preferring 'HL'L to 'H'LL. Kager sees this language as parsing by the moraic trochee but imposing an additional avoidance of clashing syllables. HH thus groups as ('H)H rather than ('H)('H); similarly, ('H)('LL) is rejected in favor of ('H)L('L). This analysis is supported by the existence of an optional rule that breaks long high vowels into two successive light syllables (122c). The rule is apparently restricted to even-numbered syllables counting from the left. Application of the rule allows the initial syllable to be stressed but at the same time avoids a stress clash at the syllable level.

10.11   Bracket Matching and Edge Parameters

Let us close with a discussion of recent innovations in the Halle and Vergnaud framework streamlining the basic model as well as extending its empirical coverage (Idsardi 1992, Halle and Idsardi 1993). For Halle and Vergnaud (1987), metrical brackets are notational by-products of the basic act of grouping asterisks (metrical positions) into headed constituents. For Idsardi, the brackets play a more central role; the actual constituent construction is distributed through several steps and is the joint product of various rules and conventions operating at different points in the derivation.

Recall that Halle (1990) allows the grid to be annotated before constituent construction by two separate devices that guide the subsequent parse: a given syllable may be assigned a line 1 asterisk – lexically or contextually in virtue of weight – or it may trigger the insertion of a metrical bracket (Cairene, section 10.10). The iterative parse respects the preassigned brackets and makes sure that preassigned asterisks dominate a head. Idsardi proposes to dispense with the latter device in favor of the former. In his model, all asterisks above line 0 arise from marking heads and hence are the product of constituent construction. Once a bracket has been assigned, the metrical constituent is completed by a *Bracket-Matching Convention* that supplies a corresponding left or right parenthesis marking off the opposite edge of the constituent. Thus, all lines in the grid arise from projection: line 0 from projecting syllabic nuclei and syllable brackets (see below) and higher lines from projecting heads from the immediately lower line. In addition, rules of constituent construction are defined over a simple vocabulary of grid asterisks and parentheses. Unlike in the rhythmic model, they do not have the power to refer to the internal structure of the syllable.

To take a simple example, in Koya the initial syllable of the word is stressed and all noninitial long vowels carry a secondary stress. The rule for heavy syllables assigns each such syllable a left bracket on line 0 (more technically, the left syllable boundary is "projected" as a line 0 metrical bracket). Accordingly, a Koya word with the structure LLHLLLHLL receives the derivation in (123). In the first step heavy syllables are supplied with a left bracket on line 0. The Bracket-Matching

Convention then introduces a right bracket, taking in as many free positions as possible (maximization of constituents). Finally, the {right, left} headship of the resultant constituents is specified, projecting a line 1 asterisk.

(123)
```
LL H LLL HLL        LL H LLL HLL        LL H LLL H LL
|| | ||| |||   →    || | ||| |||   →    || | ||| |||
** * * * * * *      * *(* * * *(* * *    * *(* * * *)(* * *)
                                                *         *
```

Given the Bracket-Matching Convention, a constituent is ensured once one edge is laid down. A rule parsing the entire line is thus not necessarily needed. In Koya all words carry a stress on their initial syllable. Idsardi sees this fact as the product of another parameter that metrifies one edge of the word or phrase. This *Edge-Marking Parameter* is expressed as a triple of {left, right} settings that determine (i) which edge of the word is fixed, (ii) whether it is metrified with a left or a right bracket, and (iii) whether this bracket appears to the left or to the right of the first or the last asterisk of the relevant grid line. The Edge-Marking Parameter ties together several phenomena that were treated separately in earlier metrical models: extrametricality, orphans, idiosyncratic lexical stress, pre- and postaccenting morphemes.

(124) <u>Edge-Marking Parameter</u>
Place a {left,right} bracket to the {left,right} of the {left/right}most asterisk in the string.

Koya sets the Edge-Marking Parameter at {left,left,left}: a "(" is placed on the left side of the first (i.e., leftmost) line 0 asterisk in the word. The Bracket-Matching Convention then completes this constituent, taking in as many free line 0 asterisks as it can. In a word with no long vowels, the resultant constituent spans the entire word, ensuring that no other stress appears in the word – the equivalent of Halle and Vergnaud's unbounded constituents (we will see how bounded constituents are derived momentarily). The derivation of the schematic LLLL and LLHLLLHLL words is completed in (125).

(125)
```
L L L L         L L L L         L L L L
| | | |         | | | |         | | | |
* * * *    →    (* * * *    →    (* * * *)
                                     *

L L H LLL H LL              LL H LLL H LL
| | | ||| | ||             || | ||| | ||
* *(* * * *)(* * *)    →    (* *)(* * * *)(* * *)
      *        *            *     *        *
```

To summarize, metrical constituents arise from the general convention matching brackets. We have seen two sources for the initial bracketing: a rule targeting heavy syllables and the Edge-Marking Parameter metrifying the left or right edge of the word.

It is not obvious that the notion of metrical constituency is a natural one to extend to Koya. After all, in the Koya word long vowels are stressed, as is the first syllable. Why can't the stress rules assign line 1 asterisks directly in terms of these properties instead of through the intermediary of headed constituents? Two answers to this question seem plausible, one conceptual in nature, the other empirical. First, invoking constituents accords with the leading idea of metrical phonology due to Liberman (1975) that stress reflects a grouping. This idea has proved quite fruitful and so should not be abandoned. Second, metrical constituency allows the model to formally express certain other "unbounded" stress systems by simply changing the settings of basic parameters already in place.

As an example, recall Khalkha Mongolian (section 10.8), which stresses the first long vowel and otherwise the first syllable. At an abstract level, Khalkha resembles Koya save for two features. First, if the word has a long vowel, then the initial syllable is stressed in Koya but not in Khalkha. Second, Khalkha has conflation, suppressing all but the first accent. We abstract away from conflation and concentrate on the first difference. Consider the schematic 'LLLL and LL'HLLLHL words. The initial accent on 'LLLL suggests that Khalkha constituents are left-headed, just as in Koya. The problem then is to block an accent from appearing at the front end of every word with a long vowel. Khalkha stresses this syllable only when the word lacks a noninitial heavy syllable – in Idsardi's terms, when it matches a ")" bracket. A formal statement of this property has been quite problematic for earlier metrical theories: recall Halle and Vergnaud's (1987) special convention to impose the line 1 setting on line 0 if the latter lacks any constituents. Given Idsardi's distributed constituent construction, the difference can be expressed straightforwardly in terms of the Edge-Marking Parameters: Khalkha fixes the right edge of its words as R-R-R (placing a ")" bracket on the right side of the rightmost asterisk) in contrast to Koya's L-L-L setting. To see this point, let us look at the derivation of Khalkha LL'HLLLHLL and 'LLLL in (126). In the first step heavy syllables project their left bracket on line 0. Then the right edge of the word is fixed. Finally, the Bracket-Matching Convention steps in to complete the constituents. Given the {left} setting for the Head Parameter, the correct inputs to line 1 metrification are produced. Here we want to enhance the first asterisk and so set the Edge-Marking Parameter to L-L-L and the Head Parameter to {left} for line 1. Conflation yields the final result.

(126)
```
      L L H L L L H L L             L L L L
      | | | | | | | | |             | | | |
      * * * * * * * * *             * * * *

      L L H L L L H L L             L L L L
      | | | | | | | | |             | | | |
      * *( * * * *( * * *           inappl.          heavy syllables

      L L H L L L H L L             L L L L
      | | | | | | | | |             | | | |
      * *( * * * *( * * *)          * * * *)         edge: R-R-R
```

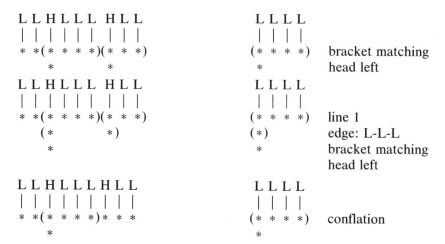

The crucial point is that Khalkha lacks the uniform bracket assignment found in Koya: the heavy syllable rule projects a left bracket "(" while the Edge-Marking Parameter inserts a right bracket ")". Constituents are completed in either case by the Bracket-Matching Convention. The difference between the two systems arises from setting a basic parameter of the model: the Edge-Marking Parameter. No special convention is required.

Several additional phenomena are expressed naturally under Idsardi's distributed constituent construction. First consider pre- and postaccenting morphemes. Recall from section 10.8 that the Russian accent system is formally equivalent to that of Khalkha Mongolian except that Russian accents are lexically contrastive instead of predictable from a vowel length contrast, as in Khalkha. The paradigms in (127a) illustrate the four possible outcomes of combining disyllabic accented and unaccented stems and monosyllabic desinences. These data motivate the lexical representations in (127b). The correct surface forms ensue from setting the Edge-Marking Parameter at R-R-R and invoking conflation to cancel all but the leftmost accent.

(127) a.

		fixed		mobile
nom.sg.	kómnat-a	koróv-a	golov-á
acc.sg.	kómnat-u	koróv-u	gólov-u
	'room'	'cow'	'head'

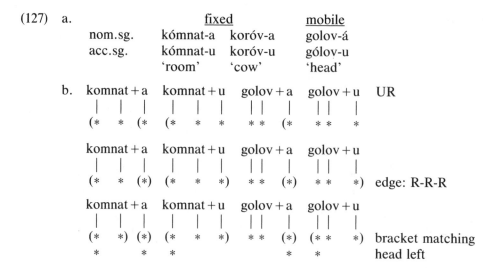

Russian in fact has an additional class of stems (128) that consistently stress the following case suffix. (Depending on declension class, the accent may be retracted in certain case forms by a subsequent rule – a detail we ignore here.) In earlier metrical models, these postaccenting stems necessitated a lexically conditioned rule to shift the accent from the stem to the ending. Under Idsardi's distributed constituent construction, they have a simpler analysis: these stems project a left bracket "(" at the right of their final syllable (128b).

(128) a.   <u>end-stressed</u>
              nom.sg.   kolbas-á
              gen.sg.   kolbas-ý
              dat.sg.   kolbas-é
              acc.sg.   kolbas-ú
              instr.sg. kolbas-ój
              loc.sg.   kolbas-é
                        'sausage'

   b.   kolbas
        | |
        * *(

   c.   kolbas + u   kolbas + u
        | | | | | |
        * *(*   →   * * (*)

When combined with an unaccented ending such as the acc.sg. *-u*, such stems force a constituent to be built on the following syllable (128c). The Edge-Marking Parameter then supplies the final closing bracket. In sum, a Russian disyllabic noun exhibits one of four different accent patterns corresponding to whether or not a "(" metrical bracketing occurs at the left or right of one of its two line 0 asterisks.

(129) komnat   korov   kolbas   golov
       | | | | | | | |
       (*   *   *(*   * *(* *

An important question that arises within this approach is whether all idiosyncratic accents can be expressed as an edge setting. We will return to this point below.

Now let us consider how distributed constituent construction accounts for alternating stress. Since the Bracket-Matching Convention automatically supplies an edge, iterative parsing need only insert a closing bracket at every second position between line 0 asterisks. Idsardi postulates the rules in (130). Going from left to right, (130a) inserts a ")" after the second of two successive free asterisks; (130b) inserts a "(" under analogous conditions going from right to left.

(130) a.   Ø →) / * * ____   (left to right)

       b.   Ø → (/ ____ * *   (right to left)

Idsardi also drops Halle and Vergnaud's (1987) assumption of exhaustive parsing. Consequently, the rules in (130) are not allowed a default option to construct degenerate constituents. To illustrate, a quantity-insensitive language such as Pintupi (section 10.10) receives the analysis in (131a). The LR iterative construction rule (130a) drops a right parenthesis between even- and odd-positioned asterisks. The Bracket-Matching Convention then closes off the constituents, and the Head Parameter emits a line 1 asterisk over the first element in the constituent. The four- and five-syllable forms *málawàna* and *púliŋkàlatju* receive the derivations indicated in (131b). In the first step a right bracket is inserted after the second of every two asterisks not interrupted by a bracket; this process proceeds across line 0 from left to right. The second step shows the effect of the Bracket-Matching Convention inserting a matching parenthesis. In the final step the left-headed constituents project an asterisk on line 1.

(131)   a.   line 0
             Heavy Syllable Parameter: inactive
             Edge-Marking Parameter: inactive
             binary parse: LR
             Head Parameter: left

             line 1
             Edge-Marking Parameter: L-L-L
             Head Parameter: left

        b.   malawana   malawana   malawana   malawana
             | | | | → | | | | → | | | | → | | | |
             * *   * *   * *) * *)   (* *)(* *)   (* *)(* *)
                                                                     *   *

             pulinkalatju   pulinkalatju   pulinkalatju   pulinkalatju
             || ||| | → || ||| | → || ||| | → || ||| |
             * * ** *   * *) * *) *   (* *) (* *) *   (* *) (* *) *
                                                                     *   *

Recall that Maranungku differs minimally from Pintupi in stressing final odd-numbered syllables: compare *yángarmàta* and *lángkaràtetì*. The Edge-Marking Parameter is pressed into service to stress these orphan syllables. Marking the far edge of the word (the opposite edge from the one where the binary parsing begins) ensures that the final asterisk will always be metrified. If it occupies an odd-numbered position, the Bracket-Matching Convention constructs a unary foot. Five-syllable *lángkaràtetì* receives the partial derivation in (132b) on the basis of the analysis in (132a).

(132)   a.   line 0
             Heavy Syllable Parameter: inactive
             Edge-Marking Parameter: R-R-R
             binary parse: LR
             Head Parameter: left

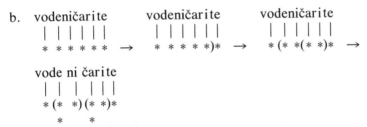

Idsardi also deploys the Edge-Marking Parameter to express extrametricality. For example, recall the Macedonian paradigm: *vodéničar, vodeníčari, vodeničárite*. By setting this option at R-L-R, a '')'' bracket is inserted to the left of the rightmost line 0 asterisk. The result is the first step in the derivation of *vodeničárite* in (133b). RL iterative footing (130b) initiates the construction of binary left-headed feet, completed as usual by bracket matching in the next step. Since the iterative parsing rules (130) are defined over successive unbracketed asterisks, they are blocked from applying to the final asterisk in (133b). The R-L-R edge marking inserting the '')'' bracket thus effectively freezes out the final asterisk from the parse. Conflation suppresses nonfinal constituents to yield *vodeničárite*.

(133) a. line 0
          Heavy Syllable Parameter: inactive
          Edge-Marking Parameter: R-L-R
          binary parse: RL
          Head Parameter: left

    b. vodeničari te   vodeničari te   vodeničari te
         | | | | | | | | | | | | | | | | | |
         * * * * * * → * * * * *)* → *(* *(* *)* →

        vode ni čari te
        | | | | | |
        (*)(* *)*
         *   *

Edge marking can also function as a lexical diacritic. For example, recall from section 10.7 the paradigm in (134) from penultimate-stressing Polish.

(134) kowálczyk   kowalczýk-a   kowalczyk-ówi
       repúblik   repúblik-a   republik-ámi
       uniwérsytet   uniwersytét-u   uniwersytet-ámi

Kowálczyk 'blacksmith' represents the normal case. It arises from imposing binary left-headed constituents with the help of (130b) and conflation. While the grammar of Polish imposes no general edge marking, certain exceptional stems (generally of foreign origin) impose their own setting for this parameter as an idiosyncratic lexical marking. *Repúblik* differs from *kowálczyk* in that its stem-final syllable is unstressable: *repúblik-a*. We may capture this fact by saying that this stem imposes a R-R-R setting on itself (135a). This bracketing has two effects. Since (130b) requires two free asterisks to work with, it ensures that the final syllable remains unmetrified (135b). It also ensures that the *-blik* syllable occupies the recessive position in the binary left-headed constituent. *Uniwérsytet* takes a R-L-R lexical setting (135c). This results in antepenultimate stress in the unaffixed form; but the regular penultimate stress is restored whenever a suffix is added (135d).

(135)   a.   republik   b.   republik-a

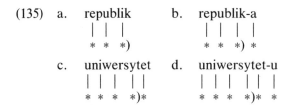

        c.   uniwersytet   d.   uniwersytet-u

The derivations in (136) illustrate these points.

(136)

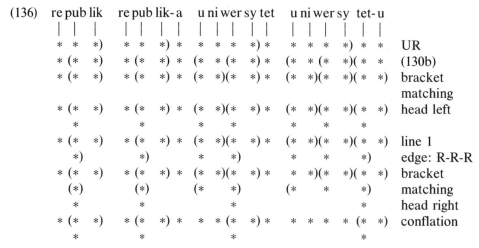

Idsardi conjectures that all lexical accent specifications can be reduced to some setting of the Edge-Marking Parameter. This implies the following analysis for the indicated Russian nouns: *márganets* 'manganese' (L-L-L), *Amérik-a* (L-R-L), and *ananás* 'pineapple' (L-L-R). What is beyond the ken of this hypothesis would be a four-syllable stem with a fixed stress on the third syllable. Russian in fact has a few words of this form (e.g., *Sevastópol, alternátor, temperáment*); but they might be analyzed with some internal morphological structure (*alterna-tor, tempera-ment*, etc.).

Let us close with a few final observations. First, in many cases the same surface distribution of stresses is compatible with more than one choice among the model's parameters. For example, returning to Koya (stress all long vowels and first syllable), the analysis in (137b) will (just like the analysis of (137a) proposed earlier) generate the appropriate stress contours, as the derivation in (137c) makes clear.

(137)   a.   line 0
             Heavy Syllable Parameter: left
             Edge-Marking Parameter: L-L-L
             Head Parameter: left

             line 1
             Edge-Marking Parameter: L-L-L
             Head Parameter: left

b. <u>line 0</u>
   Heavy Syllable Parameter: right
   Edge-Marking Parameter: R-R-L
   Head Parameter: right

   <u>line 1</u>
   Edge-Marking Parameter: L-L-L
   Head Parameter: left

c.

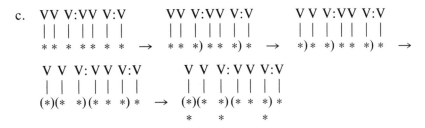

With respect to this indeterminacy problem, Halle and Idsardi (1992) suggest that, in the absence of data forcing a unique solution, the learner will prefer the analysis whose parameter settings are *homogeneous*. This forces the choice of (137a) over (137b) because in the former all settings refer to "left" while the latter mixes both "left" and "right." This seems like a natural requirement but awaits supporting evidence. Second, in later work Idsardi (1992) drops the Bracket-Matching Convention as being essentially redundant. Given that constituents are maximal, in a representation such as (138) we can infer that the left edge of the constituents will appear at the first and fourth asterisks without requiring a left-hand bracket to actually mark this position.

(138)   * * *) * * *)* *

By incorporating the iterative constituent construction rules of (130) into his model and dropping the Halle and Vergnaud (1987) requirement that these rules exhaustively parse a line, Idsardi concedes the rhythmic theorists' point that alternating stress is in essence a binary phenomenon. However, binarity is only a function of these rules and not a general representational constraint; other parameters are free to construct monopositional line 0 constituents. More generally, Idsardi maximizes the leading idea pursued in this chapter: that stress reflects projection from headed constituents.

Suggested Readings

Halle, Morris, and William Idsardi. 1993. General properties of stress and metrical structure. To appear in A handbook of phonological theory, ed. by J. Goldsmith. Oxford: Blackwell Publishers.

Halle, Morris, and Jean-Roger Vergnaud. 1987. An essay on stress. Cambridge, Mass.: MIT Press. Chapters 1, 2, 3, and 6.

Hayes, Bruce. 1991. Metrical stress theory: Principles and case studies. Chicago: University of Chicago Press.

Mester, R. Armin. 1993. The quantitative trochee in Latin. To appear in Natural Language & Linguistic Theory 11.

Prince, Alan. 1983. Relating to the grid. Linguistic Inquiry 14.19–100.

Exercises

10.1 English

Transcribe the stresses in the following English words, using numbers to mark the degrees of prominence. Compare your results with those of a good pronouncing dictionary or gazetteer that marks stress. To what extent do your judgments coincide? How many levels of prominence are distinguished by your dictionary? How is this notated?

(1) | Kalamazoo | Tennessee | engineer |
|---|---|---|
| Argentina | vegetarian | honorarium |
| volunteer | gasoline | elementary |
| onomatopeia | formaldehyde | hamamelidanthemum |

10.2 Manam

A. Manam is an Austronesian language of Papua New Guinea described by Lichtenberk (1983). Examine the data in (1) and formulate the required rules/ parameter settings to locate primary stress in the correct position.

(1) | ʔu-réba | 'you sailed' | aláŋa | 'reef' |
|---|---|---|---|
| u-píle | 'I spoke' | waríge | 'rope' |
| u-yalále | 'I went' | mótu | 'island' |
| i-panána | 'he ran' | boazíŋa | 'hole' |
| ʔi-poasagéna | 'we are tired' | moarépi | 'rice' |
| | | atabála | 'up' |

B. A lexically restricted class of suffixes, which Lichtenberk terms AP ("antepenult") suffixes, deviate from the regular pattern. Suggest an account for the AP suffixes. (The 3pl. suffix has several allomorphs including -*di*, -*i*, and -*∅*; only the first is an AP suffix. Also, the 3sg. -*i* belongs to the AP class while the 3pl. -*i* does not.)

(2) | non–AP suffixes | | AP suffixes | |
|---|---|---|---|
| táma | 'father' | táma-di | 'their father' |
| tamá-gu | 'my father' | táma-ma | 'our excl. father' |
| tamá-da | 'our incl. father' | | |
| | | | |
| u-ráraŋ-i | 'I warmed them' | u-bázi-di | 'I carried them' |
| i-ra-ʔíta | 'he talked to us incl.' | dí-te-a | 'they saw me' |
| u-taga-íʔo | 'I followed you' | i-rápuŋ-i | 'he waited for her' |
| ʔu-dóʔ-i | 'you took them' | ʔú-doʔ-i | 'you took it' |
| | | i-rápuŋ-i | 'he waited for her' |

C. The following words deviate from the stress patterns in (1) and (2). Postulate a rule to explain their behavior.

(3) malabóŋ 'flying fox'
manám 'Manam Island'

Zaranóm personal name
u-zém 'I chewed (them)'

i-ʔínt-a 'he pinched me'
u-rapún-di 'I waited for them'

Show how your analysis works by deriving the following words: *waríge, u-bázi-di, u-rapún-di, malabóŋ, ʔú-doʔ-i, ʔu-dóʔ-i*.

D. Lichtenberk notes the following generalization about the behavior of clitics (*ʔi* 'or', *be* 'and', *ʔa* focus particle) in Manam. When the word terminates in an AP suffix, stress shifts to the penult under enclisis; when the word does not terminate in an AP suffix, stress does not shift under enclisis (4). Building on the discussion of Latin enclitics in section 10.6.3, how can Lichtenberk's generalization be explained?

(4) <u>no AP suffix</u>   <u>AP suffix</u>
ʔu-dóʔ-i#ʔi 'you took them or'   ʔu-doʔ-í#ʔi 'you took it or'
i-alále#be 'he goes and'   i-pile-lá#be 'he kept talking and'
wabúbu#ʔa 'night' foc.   baga-ló#ʔa 'from the mainland' foc.
                                                     (cf. siŋába-lo 'in the bush'; -lo loc.)

10.3 Choctaw

A. Building on the analysis suggested in section 10.9, formulate rules to predict the vowel length alternations in the following paradigms from Choctaw (Nicklas 1975). Show how your analysis works by deriving *habi:na, habi:na-či,* and *či-ha:bina:-či*.

(1) či- 'you' obj., -li 'I' subj., -či causative

habi:na   pisa
či-ha:bina   či-pi:sa
habí:na-li   pisa:-li
habí:na-či   či-pi:sali
či-ha:bina:-či   či-pi:sa-či
habí:na-či:-li   pisa:-či-li
či-ha:bina:-či-li   či-pi:sa-či:li
'receive a present'   'see'

B. The data in (2) require an additional segmental rule. How must it be ordered with the rule(s) already developed? Give the derivation of *čokf-oši* and *op-o:ši*.

(2) opa   'owl'   op-o:ši   'young owl'
     čokfi   'rabbit'   čokf-oši   'young rabbit'
     yala   'grubworm'   yal-o:ba   'tadpole'
     issi   'deer'   iss-oba   'horse'

10.4 Asheninca

A. Asheninca (Payne 1990) is an Arawakan language of Peru. Examine the data
    in (1) (slightly simplified) to develop an analysis that predicts the location of
    stress. Specify all relevant parameters and rules. Long vowels are transcribed
    as geminates. *N* is a syllable-final nasal. Certain words show alternative
    stressing. Can you explain them in a natural way?

(1) háka   'here'
     nopíto   'my canoe'
     syoNkíri   'type of partridge'
     kawíniri/kawiníri   'cinnamon'
     okícoki/okicóki   'seed'
     notòNkaméNto   'my gun'
     nokòwawétaka   'I wanted (it) in vain'
     hamànaNtàkenéro   'he bought it for her'
     pamènakòweNtákero   'take care of her'

     jíñaa   'water'
     pàatikákeri   'you stepped on him'
     piñàapáake   'you saw on arrival'
     ikyàapíiNti   'he always enters'
     nomàkoryàawàitapáake   'I rested awhile'
     oNkitàitamánake   'in the morning'
     kaNtimáitacya   'however'

B. Payne singles out for special treatment a class of "extralight" syllables con-
    sisting of short [i] as nucleus and the alveolars [s] or [c] as onset ([ši] is
    transcribed as [syi], evidently indicating palatalization). These syllables are
    never stressed and can lose their vowel before a voiceless consonant by a
    late phonetic rule. Examine the data in (2) and suggest an analysis for these
    syllables. What bearing do they have on the issue of metrical constituency?

(2) óciti   'dog'
     kósyiri   'type of monkey'
     kàcitáke   'he/she hurt'
     píciciro   'type of bird'
     pìsyitáciri   'broom'
     hácikawètakána   'he almost bit me'

10.5 Creek

In Creek (Haas 1977) the accent is marked by a high tone on the final or penultimate syllable of the word. Examine the following data to predict the location of
the accent.

(1)   ifá   'dog'   hicíta   'one to see one'

ifá	'dog'	hicíta	'one to see one'
ifóci	'puppy'	ahicitá	'one to look after'
amifocí	'my puppy'	imahicíta	'one to look after for'
itiwanayipíta	'to tie each other'	isimahicitá	'one to sight at one'
cá:lo	'trout, bass'	wa:kocí	'calf'
sókca	'sack, bag'	hoktakí	'woman'
pocóswa	'axe'	iŋkosapitá	'one to implore'
famí:ca	'cantaloupe'	alpatóci	'baby alligator'
aktopá	'bridge'	yakaphoyíta	'two to walk'

10.6 Winnebago

A.   Some additional Winnebago data from Miner 1990 are listed in (1). Metrify these words according to the analysis of section 10.6. How must long vowels (transcribed as geminates) be treated?

(1)

waniǧík	'bird'	waniǧíg-ra	'the bird'
taanížu	'sugar'	taanížu-rà	'the sugar'
haakítujìk-gajà	'after I pull taut'		
hakirújik-gàjà	'after 3pl. pull taut'		

B.   In the words in (2) the underlined vowel is inserted by Dorsey's Law. Which forms are straightforwardly derived by the text analysis? Which are problematic? Discuss possible solutions for the latter. (Hint: Consider the effect of Dorsey's Law on the peripherality of extrametrical elements.)

(2)

šoróš	'deep'
šawažók	'you mash'
kerejúsep	'Black Hawk'
rukeréx	'tattoo'
hacakére	'with difficulty'
haapúruč	'common elder'
poropóro	'spherical'
hikuruní	'tangled'
wakiripáras	'flat bug'
wakiripóropòro	'spherical bug'

10.7 Bedouin Arabic

Recall the Bedouin Arabic rule of elision (46). Irshied and Kenstowicz (1984) report that their Riyadh informant can suppress this rule so that his speech more closely approximates Standard Arabic. In this case the following alternative paradigms result. How do the alternative pronunciations bear on the text analysis of section 10.6.2?

(1)

ʕállam	sáaʕad
ʕállim-at	sáaʕad-at
ʕallm-ít#ah or ʕallím-it#ah	saaʕd-ít#ah or saaʕád-it#ah

10.8   Kashmiri Stress

A.   Examine the data in (1) and specify the parameters that will position the word stress over the proper syllable.

(1)   nóyid   gánpaθya:r
      mátlab   ní:ra:zan
      dá:na: bó:la:naθ
      pé:čda:r   dé:ve:li:
      sála:m   sírinagar
      jína:b   mulá:heza
      bú:go:l   aŋgó:lika:
      phíkiri   sampaná:wun
      rə́phvarukh   ná:ra:zagi
      zitó:vuh   narpí:rasta:n
      á:yurda: maharə́:ni:
      bá:gambar   mahá:ra:zi
      masrá:wun   páharadari:
      kaḍná:wun   ardonó:ri:šor
      šá:rika: páharadari:
      bákhčanha:r

B.   What problems are presented by the data in (2)? For the latter, Bhatt (1989) suggests a restriction on the rule that projects a line 0 asterisk from coda consonants. Try to reconstruct this solution. How must the rule be ordered with respect to the other stress rules? Compare this analysis with the Domino Condition (section 10.6.1) for Winnebago suggested by Halle and Vergnaud (1987).

(2)   nuránjan
      noyídgi:
      mukáddima
      šyawánzahyum
      nandiké:šor
      bagándarladin
      yunivársiti

10.9   Indo-European

Halle (1989) has suggested that the accent rules postulated for Russian reflect the basic system of Proto-Slavic and more remotely of Proto-Indo-European. Most of the Slavic languages that have developed a predictable accent (Czech, Slovak, Early Polish) stress the initial syllable. Similarly, the majority of the Indo-European daughter languages that evolved a predictable accent have (gone through the stage of) initial stress. How might the preponderance of initial (rather than final or penultimate) stress be explained?

10.10 Russian (Leka Dialect)

In Russian stressed *o* is normally realized as open [ɔ]. The Leka dialect underwent a sound change whereby stressed *o* was raised and diphthongized to [o] or [uo]. This sound change had one systematic exception. It did not apply to the initial syllable of mobile nouns: thus, *k*[ó]*mnatu, kor*[ó]*vu* but *v*[ɔ́]*du, g*[ɔ́]*lovu*. Some scholars have interpreted this change as evidence for a special "circumflex" intonation on *g*[ɔ́]*lovu* as opposed to an "acute" accent in *k*[ó]*mnata*. In view of the discussion in section 10.8, how plausible is this speculation? Can the sound change be explained in some other way? Formulate the rule and show how it discriminates *komnata* and *vodu*.

10.11 Lithuanian Dominant and Recessive Affixes

Using the Halle and Vergnaud analysis of Lithuanian discussed in section 10.8, trace the derivation of the following forms, evaluating each affix as dominant versus recessive and accented versus unaccented. (The data are excerpted from Dudas 1972.)

(1) paūkšt-is   'bird' fixed
     paūkšt-inink-as   'bird-raiser' fixed
     paukšt-inink-ȳst-ė   'bird raising' fixed

     av-ìs   'sheep' mobile
     av-iniñk-as   'shepherd' fixed

     sēn-as   'old' mobile
     sen-ȳb-ė   'antiquity' fixed
     sen-ȳb-inink-as   'antiquarian' fixed

     sāk-o   'he says' mobile
     apý-sak-a   'story' fixed
     apy-sak-ēl-ė   'short story' fixed

     kój-a   'foot' fixed
     pa-kój-a   'footstool' fixed
     laĩk-as   'time' mobile
     pā-laik-as   'the rest, remainder' mobile

     kāp-as   'grave' mobile
     pa-kap-ē   'place near grave' mobile
     pa-kap-ȳn-ė   'area around cemetery' fixed

     kuĩn-is   'heel' mobile
     ùž-kuln-is   'back of heel' fixed
     pó-už-kuln-is   'under-part of heel' fixed

10.12 Yidinʸ Stress and Length

A. Recalling the analysis in section 10.9, supply derivations for the following Yidinʸ data, marking the appropriate stresses.

(1)   comitative + da   buNa-yi-da   gudaga-yi:-da
       comitative + ergative   buNa-yi-ŋgu   gudaga-yi:-ŋ
       genitive + ergative   buNa-nu-ŋgu   gudaga-ni:-ŋ
                                'woman'   'dog'

B.   While most long vowels in Yidinʸ derive from the penultimate lengthening
     rule, there is a small group of affixes that lengthen a preceding vowel. An
     example is the antipassive suffix, which Dixon (1978a) transcribes as [:di];
     the colon indicates a lengthening of the preceding vowel. Assume a similar
     representation with an extra skeletal position. In certain cases the length fails
     to materialize, requiring a rule Dixon calls "illicit length elimination." Ex-
     amine the data in (2) to formulate this rule. What bearing does it have on the
     issue of iambic versus trochaic rhythm? (Although the examples Dixon cites
     are compatible with a rule that simply shortens the first of two successive
     long syllables, he gives a more general formulation of the rule that refers to
     the odd/even position of the long-voweled syllable in the word.)

(2)   waw'a:-di-ŋ   'look' present
       waw'a:-di-ŋ   past
       w'uŋab'a:-di-ŋ   'hunt' past
       w'uŋab'a:-di-N'unda   dative subordinate
       g'aliŋ'a:-di-ŋ   'go' past
       barg'anda-d'i:-na   'pass by' purposive
       dund'iŋa-d'i:-Num   'play' causative subordinate

10.13   Cupan Stress Reconstruction

Cupan is a group of three closely related languages of the Takic branch of Uto-
Aztecan (Munro 1990). Disyllabic nouns with various stress patterns are cited in
(1). For each noun, reconstruct the gross CV shape and stress contour for the
protolanguage Cupan. What are the stress rules for the protolanguage? How did
the individual daughter languages evolve from Cupan? For Cahuilla singular and
plural forms (where available in the source) are shown in the third and fourth
columns, respectively. How can the V≈∅ alternation be accounted for?

(1)

	Luiseño	Cupeño	Cahuilla	
'badger'	hú:na-l	húna-l	húna-l	hún-l-am
'fish'	kiyú:-l	qəyú-l	kíyu-l	kíyu-l-am
'deer'	ṣú:ka-t	súqa-t	súka-t	súk-t-am
'oak'	wiʔá-t	wíʔa-t	wíʔa-t	
'ant'	ʔá:na-t	ʔána-t	ʔáne-t	ʔán-t-em
'blue jay'	čá:ʔi-š	čáʔi-š	čáʔi-š	čáʔ-č-em
'squirrel'	qé:ŋi-š	qíŋi-š	qíŋi-š	qíŋ-č-em
'agave'	ʔamú:-l	ʔamú-l	ʔámu-l	ʔámu-l-em
'meadowlark'	ʔisá:-l	ʔisá-l	ʔísa-l	ʔísa-l-em
'quail'	qaxá:-l	kaxá-l	qáxa-l	qáxa-l-em
'jackrabbit'	ṣuʔí-š	súʔi-š	súʔi-š	
'river'	waní-š	wáni-š	wáni-š	

	Luiseño	Cupeño	Cahuilla	
'sun'	timé-t	támi-t	támi-t	
'wildcat'	tú:ku-t	túku-t	túku-t	túk-t-em
'poison oak'	ʔiyá:-l	ʔəyá-l	ʔíya-l	ʔíya-l-em
'conifer'	tuvá-t	tə́və-t	téva-t	

10.14 Russian and Polish Edge Marking

A. Given Idsardi's (1992) distributed constituent construction discussed in section 10.11, what are the lexical representations required for the following Russian nouns?

(1) nom.sg. dám-a   stran-á   sten-á
    acc.sg. dám-u   stran-ú   stén-u
             'lady' 'country' 'wall'

B. Nouns in the mobile stress paradigm retract stress onto a proclitic preposition. Stem-stressed and end-stressed stems never exhibit this retraction. How can this asymmetry be explained?

(2) nom.sg. kómnat-a   koróv-a   kolbas-á   golov-á
    acc.sg. kómnat-u   koróv-u   kolbas-ú   gólov-u
    prep.   na kómnat-u na koróv-u na kolbas-ú ná golov-u
             'room'   'cow'   'sausage'   'head'

C. Recalling the text analysis of Polish *repúblik* and *uniwérsytet*, specify the setting of the Edge-Marking Parameter that will generate the irregular stress of *rezím, rezím-u, rezim-ámi* 'diet'.

11   Prosodic Morphology

The prototypical morphological operation is affixation to a base. In most cases affixation occurs without regard to the phonological nature of the base. For example, English's regular plural suffix -(*e*)*s* attaches to bases regardless of the number of syllables, the location of stress, or the nature of the final consonants and vowel in the base. Of course, once affixation takes place, phonological rules can be called into play. But in general, affixation occurs earlier and the phonology is left with the task of assigning to the result a phonetic representation consistent with the rules and constraints of the language.

There are, however, cases in which the affixation process itself must take account of the phonology of the base; if the requisite structure does not obtain, affixation fails to occur. For example, the comparative -*er* and the superlative -*est* of the adjectival inflection in English attach most successfully only to monosyllabic or disyllabic stressed + unstressed bases: *red-er, yellow-er, stupid-er, *beautiful-er, *American-er*. Other morphological processes refer to the phonology of the base more directly. Nicknames (*hypocoristics*) typically involve shortening the base: *Samuel → Sam; Bertram → Bert*. But which phonemes truncate and which must remain? Two other prevalent morphological operations that take account of the phonology of the base are reduplication and infixation. In *reduplication,* some portion of the base is copied. But we need to know precisely what material is copiable. *Infixation* may insert an affix or alter the phonemic make-up of the base at designated points. But how are these points located? In the earlier linear model in which phonological representations consist solely of a string of phonemes, the base has a simple, flat structure and so lacks any natural contours to which the morphological processes might refer. In this theory, morphological operations must be defined as generalized string operations or transformations (see Kenstowicz and Kisseberth 1979 for a survey). But such rules are very powerful and unconstrained, allowing for many operations that never seem to occur (e.g., "infix a nasal after the first voiced consonant in the base"). With the discovery of enriched prosodic representations, phonologists have pursued the hypothesis that such notions as "syllable" and "metrical foot" suffice to delimit the groupings over which the morphological operations of reduplication, infixation, truncation, and affixation are defined. If this *Prosodic Morphology Hypothesis* proves correct, then the operations themselves become potentially powerful additional probes of phonological representation. In this chapter we will survey this line of research, examining the major questions and the preliminary results. The discussion relies heavily on the pioneering work of McCarthy and Prince (1986, 1990, 1991).

11.1 Reduplication

Consider the reduplication paradigm in (1) from the Philippine language Ilokano that marks the progressive of the verb (McCarthy and Prince 1986).

(1)   <u>root</u>   <u>progressive</u>

      [basa]   ag-bas-basa   'read'

      [adal]   ag-ad-adal   'study'

      [da.it]   ag-da-dait   'sew'

      [takder]   ag-tak-takder   'standing'

      [trabaho]   ag-trab-trabaho   'work'

A pretheoretical characterization of the phenomenon is that some continuous substring from the initial portion of the word is copied. The copied string ranges from two to four segments in length (and could be as short as one segment, since a hypothetical root such as [a.it] should reduplicate as [ag-a-a.it]). The only common factor is the vowel: the reduplicated material thus falls under the expression $C_0V(C)$. Unfortunately, as a theoretical characterization this expression gives no insight as to why this particular 1–4 segment sequence is copied rather than, say, $V_0C(V)$, CCCC, or any other imaginable substring. Just as syntactic transformations are defined over constituents rather than arbitrary word sequences, we might expect reduplication to target such natural phonological groupings as the syllable. The Ilokano reduplication might thus be expressed as "Copy the first syllable of the base." The problem is that this rule is simply at odds with the syllabification of the language. While it works correctly for [tak.der] and [da.it], it fails in [ba.sa], [a.dal], and [tra.ba.ho], where the intervocalic consonant onsets the following vowel and thus is not a constituent of the initial syllable. In fact, Moravcsik's (1978) survey of the descriptive literature found no clear cases where a syllable is copied: that is, where *ta.pa*, *tā.pa*, and *tap.ta* reduplicate as *ta + ta.pa*, *tā + tā.pa*, and *tap + tap.ta*, respectively.

11.1.1   Segmental versus Prosodic Templates

Moravcsik's surprising generalization inspired Marantz (1982) to conclude that reduplication consists of two separate aspects: (i) copy the phonemes of the base, but (ii) how many are actually pronounced and their prosodic organization is predetermined independently of the particular base. Specifically, Marantz treats partial reduplication as mapping a copy of the base's segmental tier to a predesignated sequence of CV skeletal slots. Under this conception, partial reduplication thus reduces to a form of affixation (with which it shares certain clear parallels, especially in the types of juncture relations it contracts with the adjacent base). It is assumed that an affix lacking phonemic content activates a UG convention that copies the adjacent base's segmental tier, which then maps to as many positions in the CV template as possible, consistent with matching [+consonantal] segments with C-slots and [−consonantal] ones with V-slots. For Ilokano, the template is CCVC and the map proceeds from left to right; *trab-trabaho* receives the analysis in (2).

(2)   CCVC + CCVCVCV → CCVC + CCVCVCV → CCVC   + CCVCVCV
      | | | | | | | | | | | | | | | | | | | | | | | | |
      t r a b a h o   trabaho   t r a b a h o   t r a b a h o   t r a b a h o

Two general remarks are in order here. First, this kind of analysis is only possible in a model that distinguishes the segmental and skeletal tiers. It is unreconstructible in the earlier linear model, which required a transformational operation to describe reduplication (see Marantz 1982 for discussion). Second, reduplication is no longer a special morphological operation but can be construed as ordinary affixation. What is special is the phonological nature of affix: it lacks a specification on the segmental tier.

Marantz notes certain technical details in getting the association to work correctly. First, it must be "phoneme-driven" in the sense that segments are matched one by one to the template. Mapping in the opposite direction (from the skeletal template to the segmental tier) creates immediate problems: given the phoneme sequence [bas], mapping C_1 to [b] and C_2 to [s] prevents matching V to [a] without crossing an association line (3a).

(3)   a. C_1 C_2 V C_3 b.   C C V C   c.   C C V C
           | ⤫   ╱ | | ╱ |
           b   á   s   a   d   d a i t

Second, the mapping must restrict itself to a continuous portion of the segmental tier. It may skip positions in the template when the latter is not expanded fully: for example, in mapping [ad], we must skip the first two C-slots, and for [dait], we must skip the second C-slot (3b,c). But why can't the final C-slot match with a phoneme farther down the line, skipping the [i] and generating the impossible *[dat-da.it]? The requirement that only a continuous region of the phonemic string can be mapped blocks this unwanted outcome in (3c).

Beyond these technical issues lurks a more serious problem: characterizing the reduplication templates as skeletal slots allows many more possibilities than actually seem to occur. For example, few if any of the other fifteen possible four-position sequences that arise from interchanging V- and C-slots ever functions in the way that CCVC does in Ilokano. McCarthy and Prince (1986) had the insight that what is special about the CCVC expression in Ilokano is that it denotes the language's maximal syllable. They have developed an influential theory of prosodic morphology whose major premise is that templates are defined in terms of "authentic units of prosody." At this point we will consider their theory as it applies to the basic analysis of reduplication, examining additional aspects in later sections.

McCarthy and Prince retain Marantz's basic premise that reduplication is not syllable copying but mapping the base's segmental tier (its *melody*) to a phonemically empty affix. However, the affix is not an arbitrary sequence of skeletal slots, but rather is drawn from a restricted class of prosodic categories that includes the mora, the syllable, and the metrical foot. On this view, Ilokano reduplication can be characterized as prefixation of a [σ] to the base (4a).

(4)   σ σ ...   σ [σ σ   σ   [σ σ
      ∧ ∧   ∧ ∧   ∧ ∧
      [abcde...   →   [abcde...   →   abcde... [abcde...   →
                  (a)   (b)   (c)

      σ   σ σ   σ σ σ
      ∧   ∧ ∧   ∧ ∧ ∧
      abcde... [abcde...   →   ab[abcde
                        (d)

As in Marantz's (1982) analysis, such phonemically bare affixes trigger copying of the segmental string (4b), which then maps to the syllable similar to the way in which syllabification proceeds under template matching (4c). The major difference is that the affix is prosodically limited (e.g., in Ilokano to just one syllable), while ordinary syllabification proceeds across the segmental tier, calling as many syllables as needed to accommodate the segmental material. Finally, unlicensed material is suppressed via stray erasure (4d). Given that Ilokano syllables allow complex onsets, the [σ] template subsumes the [tr] sequence of [trabaho]. Since the template allows no consonant clustering in the rime, only one postvocalic consonant is mapped; and since just a single σ is allowed, the remaining material fails to syllabify and undergoes stray erasure.

(5)   σ   σ σ σ   σ   σ σ σ   σ   σ σ σ
                     ∧∧ ∧   ∧   ∧∧ ∧   ∧   ∧∧ ∧
      trabaho [trabaho]   →   trabaho [trabaho   →   trab [trabaho

McCarthy and Prince support the prosodic approach to reduplication over the skeletal-slot treatment of Marantz with three types of argument. First, if the reduplication template is to be characterized as a sequence of skeletal slots, then the system allows all sorts of unattested patterns of reduplication. For example, Ilokano noun plurals are also formed by reduplication (Hayes and Abad 1989). To account for *klas-kláse,* we must be able to copy up to the first four segments. If the reduplication affix is defined as a string of skeletal positions, then the simplest template would be a sequence of four skeletal slots XXXX taking in the first four segments of the base. When applied to bases such as *kaldíŋ* and *púsa,* this analysis predicts the forms in (6a). Such a reduplication paradigm not only is unattested in Ilokano but seems totally bizarre.

(6)   a.   kláse   'class'   klas-kláse
           kaldíŋ   'goat'   *kald-kaldíŋ
           púsa   'cat'   *pusa-púsa

      b.   kláse   'class'   klas-kláse
           kaldíŋ   'goat'   kal-kaldíŋ
           púsa   'cat'   pus-púsa

But if the Ilokano reduplication affix is characterized as a bimoraic heavy syllable [$\sigma_{\mu\mu}$], then exactly the right segments emerge: any number of prevocalic consonants forming a valid onset plus a single postvocalic consonant to fill the second mora.

(7)

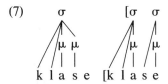

As a second reason to reject Marantz's skeletal-slot definition of the reduplication template, McCarthy and Prince argue that a prosodic characterization gives a better fix on the optional versus obligatory elements of the template. Since a heavy syllable by definition contains two moras, the language will make every effort to fill the moras. Hayes and Abad (1989) report that Ilokano *da.it* 'sew' in fact reduplicates as *ag-da:-da[ʔ]it* or *ag-dad-da[ʔ]it*, depending on the dialect. The glottal stop in *da[ʔ]it* is inserted by a hiatus-breaking rule. If this rule is ordered before reduplication, then [da?it] first reduplicates to [da?-da?it]; since glottal stop is only found in onset position in Ilokano, a deletion plus compensatory lengthening rule could explain the long vowel in [da:-da?it]. Hayes and Abad reject this analysis on the basis of monosyllables like *tra:-trák* 'trucks' and *na:-nárs* 'nurse' where, for some mysterious reason, final consonants are shielded from the phonemic melody copying. If this is indeed the case, then the lengthened vowel must arise from spreading the vowel to the second mora of the heavy syllable template rather than from compensatory lengthening due to a deleted coda consonant. The lengthening of *da:*[da?it] suggests that the second mora of the heavy syllable must be filled and requires the segmental analysis to refine the template to C_0VC. But once this move is made, it becomes unclear why the initial portion of the template can have zero positions while the postvocalic portion is obligatory. Under the prosodic view, this asymmetry makes sense: a heavy syllable is defined as bimoraic, while the number of onset consonants is prosodically irrelevant. Requiring a fixed number of onset consonants but allowing a variable number of coda consonants is impossible to express in prosodic theory. But McCarthy and Prince argue that such a template is easy to express on the segmentalist view of the template: CVC_0. However, while easy to express, CVC_0 is an unattested reduplication pattern. The conclusion is that the prosodic approach more accurately circumscribes the range of reduplication templates.

Finally, if the template is characterized prosodically, it can be expected to recapitulate the syllabic parameters of the particular language in which it is expressed. For example, the initial consonant clusters in words like *klase* and *trabaho* reflect a change in the syllabic canons of Ilokano resulting from the influx of recent loanwords. Given that the template is characterized syllabically as [$\sigma_{\mu\mu}$], we predict that Ilokano will reduplicate the cluster as soon as complex onsets are accepted by the syllable-building parameters of the system. If the template is expressed in segmental terms independent of syllable structure, then no such connection is made; a separate change would have to be made in the reduplication template to accommodate the initial consonant cluster in *klas-kláse*.

Characterizing reduplication syllabically predicts variations from one language to the next as a function of the languages' syllable-building parameters. McCarthy and Prince (1986) illustrate this point with the following paradigm from Orokaiva (Healy, Isoroembo, and Chittleborough 1969).

(8) waeke   wa-waeke   'shut'
     hirike   hi-hirike   'open'
     tiuke   ti-tiuke   'cut'
     uhuke   uh-uhuke   'blow'

Orokaiva syllables close on a consonant only when it is homorganic with a following consonant – essentially just a nasal. McCarthy and Prince suggest that this property explains why Orokaiva differs from Ilokano in not freely reduplicating a postvocalic consonant. The only systematic exception is reduplication of a postvocalic consonant when the following base is vowel-initial: *uh-uhuke*. According to McCarthy and Prince, the consonant onsets the vowel-initial base to avoid a hiatus (9a).

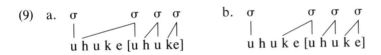

(9) a. σ   σ σ σ   b. σ   σ σ σ
     u h u k e [u h u ke]   u h u k e [u h u k e]

This analysis has two consequences. First, it seems to corroborate the assumption that the entire phonemic string of the base is copied. Although normally only the segments hosted by the syllable affix reach the surface, (9a) suggests that under the appropriate circumstances material hidden inside the copied string may emerge. Second, it strengthens the "no skipping" provision; otherwise, it is unclear why the closer [k] does not onset the initial syllable of the following base, producing *uk-uhuke (9b). (See below, however, for an alternative analysis of Orokaiva *uhuhuke*.)

In a significant number of cases, partial reduplication exceeds a single syllable. McCarthy and Prince had the important insight that these cases too can be described in natural prosodic terms as the minimal metrical foot of the language. To take a simple but striking example, consider verbal reduplication in Lardil. Like many other Australian languages, Lardil assigns trochaic, left-headed feet from left to right. A minimal word syndrome also establishes the trochee as the metrical foot. Word-final vowels delete from stems of three or more syllables. Disyllabic stems systematically fail to apocopate – a restriction that follows from the requirement that the minimal word contain a trochaic foot. Finally, underlying monomoraic stems are augmented by a suffix -*a* when they are unaffixed. The paragogic vowel is another strategy to achieve a minimal bimoraic word. (10) provides a sample of the verbal reduplication in Lardil.

(10)
base	simple	reduplicated	
[kele-th]	kele	kele-kele	'cut'
[pareli-th]	pareli	parel-pareli	'gather'
[la-th]	latha	laa-la	'spear'
[ŋaali-th]	ŋaali	ŋaal-ŋaali	'thirst'

The verbal suffix [th] (laminal) does not generally surface since it is barred from the coda by a constraint blocking the association of nonapical consonants (see discussion in section 6.8). However, when a monomoraic root such as [la] 'spear' takes the augment, the [th] emerges as onset: *latha*.

With this descriptive background, let us now consider the Lardil reduplication template. It may be succinctly characterized as a bimoraic foot. Recall from section 10.9 that Hayes's moraic trochee parse has two expansions as (LL) or (H). When possible, Lardil chooses (LL) (perhaps to allow as much phonemic material as possible to surface). However, when the root contains a single vowel, then the (H) expansion is selected, leading to the gemination of the vowel.

(11)

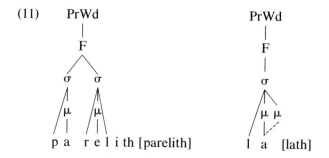

In addition to the bisyllabic foot [σσ], a reduplicating template may fix on two moras at the syllable level [σ_μμ]. Bases lacking enough phonemes to fill out the heavy syllable are then expanded. A much-discussed example is provided by the Micronesian language Mokilese (Harrison 1976).

(12)
kasɔ	kas-kasɔ	'throw'
poki	pok-poki	'beat'
wadek	wad-wadek	'read'
pɔdok	pɔd-pɔdok	'plant'
pa	paa-pa	'weave'
di.ar	dii-di.ar	'find'

Assuming a bimoraic heavy syllable template [σ_μμ], [kas-kasɔ] and [paa-pa] receive the analysis in (13). In the former, the second mora takes in the [s], and the remaining [ɔ] undergoes stray erasure. In the case of [pa], the second mora is unfilled under initial template matching. The long vowel follows from spreading the only available phoneme – the [a].

(13)

A major problem with Marantz's two-step copy and associate view of reduplication, first noticed by Levin (1983), is the fact that long vowels copy in Mokilese. If the first vowel of the root is long, then the prefix also has a long vowel.

(14) kookɔ   koo-kookɔ   'grind coconut'
      sɔɔrɔk   sɔɔ-sɔɔrɔk   'tear'
      caak   caa-caak   'bend'

Under the standardly accepted geminate representation, length is encoded not
segmentally but rather as the mapping of one segment to two skeletal slots or
moras. But if only the phonemic string is copied from the base, there is no straightforward way to correctly associate the second mora of the reduplication prefix.
kaskasɔ and *kookookɔ* have equivalent representations at the segmental level. But
in the former, the second mora of the [σμμ] prefix maps to the [s], while in the
latter, it associates with the vowel [o].

(15)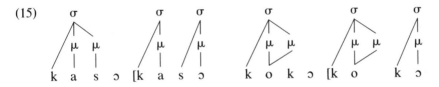

Following the term introduced by Clements (1985c), this has become known as
the *transfer problem* in the reduplication literature: information about the prosodic
structure of the base must be transferred to the reduplicating affix.

11.1.2 An Alternative Prosodic Theory

At this point we will consider a third approach to reduplication advocated by
Steriade (1988b) that is designed to surmount the transfer problem. On this view,
partial reduplication is treated as reduction from full reduplication. The entire
base morpheme is first copied, including all of its prosodic structure: [base] →
[base + base]. Transfer is no longer a problem since the two halves of the reduplication structure start out the same. The reduplicant then must be reduced in
the appropriate way (in cases of partial reduplication; full reduplication requires
no further change). Steriade does not see the construction of the reduplicated
affix as mapping to a preexistent template. Rather, the prosodic affix crystallizes
at the left or right edge of the reduplicant through an appropriate modification of
the parameters controlling the syllabic and higher-order prosodic structure in this
region of the string. Steriade thus tries to preserve McCarthy and Prince's insight

that the reduplication templates are prosodically defined. However, the method of production is different. The relevant parameters include the decision whether to form a metrical foot (as in Lardil) or not. At the syllable level, the weight parameters may be switched between monomoraic and bimoraic settings. Finally, the onset and nonmoraic codas can branch or remain nonbranching. Segmental material not falling under these parameters is then discarded by some version of stray erasure.

To illustrate this approach, let us work backward through a few examples. For Mokilese, the template emerges from setting the parameters for left edge, heavy syllable, with a complex rime (consonantal coda) permitted. The first syllable of reduplicated [kookɔ-kookɔ] satisfies these parameters directly and so no modification is required. The second syllable is not licensed by the templatic parameters and so is discarded. For [kaso-kaso] (16a), the first syllable is tuned to heavy, adding a mora on the right; this mora then maps to the following consonant; erasure of the following unlicensed syllable then yields [kas-kaso]. For [paa-pa] (16b), we must assume that the juncture between the two reduplicants inhibits consonant gemination. The mora is then filled by spreading the vowel. This default option also applies in [dii-di.ari].

(16) a.

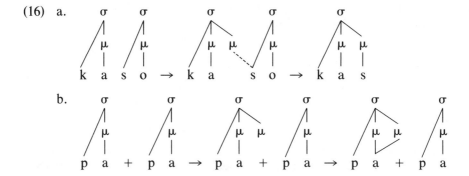

b.

To briefly summarize, where McCarthy and Prince envision one general sweep of template mapping, Steriade allows the prosodic structure to be changed "on-line." A major advantage of the latter course is a natural solution to the transfer problem. McCarthy and Prince (1988) treat the Mokilese transfer by construing the segmental tier that is copied in reduplication to include unpredictable association lines. Given that a long vowel is represented as a doubly linked geminate, the double linking is copied along with the segmental melody. Such geminates will then lock onto a bimoraic template, preempting association of a consonant to the second mora; copied material is shown in bold in (17).

(17)

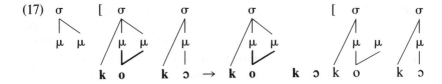

A chief difference between the two models is that in the reduction approach, the truncating syllables intervene between the reduplicant and the base at all higher prosodic levels; for McCarthy and Prince's model, no prosodic structure intervenes between the template and the following base. This difference is brought out in the two models' representations of Orokaiva [uh-uhuke], (18a) and (18b), respectively.

(18) a. σ   σ σ σ   b. σ σ   σ σ   σ σ

      u h u k e [u h u k e]   u h u k e [u h u k e]

Recall that in the McCarthy and Prince analysis, the coda bars consonants that are not homorganic with a following consonant; a consonant following the initial vowel of the reduplicant thus remains unsyllabified. But since by hypothesis no prosodic structure intervenes between the reduplicating affix and the base, the consonant [h] is free to reach across this prosodic gulf to onset the following base (18a). No such treatment is possible in (18b). We must apparently store the [h] temporarily in the coda, delete the remaining material in the reduplicant, and then resyllabify the stored consonant: [u.hu.ke + u.hu.ke] → [uh.u.ke + u.hu.ke] → [uh. + u.hu.ke] → [u.hu.hu.ke]. It remains to be seen whether this analysis is descriptively feasible.

11.1.3 *Prespecification versus Melodic Over-/Underwriting*

In many reduplication paradigms a portion of the reduplicant has a fixed melodic shape regardless of the base melody. For example, in Yoruba verb nominalizations are formed by a CV reduplicating prefix whose vowel is [i]: *lọ* 'to go', *lílọ* nominal; *dù* 'to be tasty', *dídù* nominal. In Akan the reduplicant has a fixed high vowel; only its value for round reflects the base: *seʔ, siseʔ* 'say'; *ba, biba* 'come'; *soʔ, susoʔ* 'light'; *sow, susow* 'catch'. Marantz (1982) treats the phenomenon by prespecifying the segmental template with the relevant segments or features, which then preempt the association of phonemes copied from the base to the relevant positions in the template. The Yoruba prefix thus is represented as (19a); the V-position of the template is saturated, blocking association of the copied vowel (19b). For Akan the prefixal V-slot is prespecified as [+high] (19c); only the chromatic features of [round] and [back] can seep in.

(19) a. C V   b. C V + C V   →   C V + C V

          i   i   i

      c. C V

          [+ high]

McCarthy and Prince (1986) are skeptical of the general validity of prespecification. Since their templates only contain moras as terminals, onset consonants cannot be prespecified. They observe that there are often alternative explanations for the fixed portion of the reduplicant. For example, Pulleyblank (1988) shows that [i] is the default vowel in Yoruba. If underspecification theory is accepted, then the reduplicant's [i] might arise not from prespecifying the template as in (19a) but rather from failing to copy certain material from the base. While blocking individual features from copying seems ad hoc, McCarthy and Prince argue that the theory must apparently be granted this power in any case. They observe that tonal features often fail to reduplicate, citing the Yoruba paradigm in (20) from Akinlabi 1984. (Mid tone is unmarked.)

(20)   a.   àgbà   àgbààgbà   'elder'
            òru   òròòru   'evening'
            ègbé   ègbèègbé   'side'

       b.   osù   osoosù   'month'
            ogba   ogboogba   'equal'
            alé   alaalé   'evening'

       c.   egbe   →   egbe + egbe   →   egbe + egbe
            | | | | ＼ |
            L H   L   H   L   H

            a le   →   ale + ale   →   ale + a le
            | | | | ＼ |
            MH   MH   MH

Here the tone of the reduplicant is identical with the first tone of the following base: low in (20a) and mid in (20b). This generalization follows if we stipulate that the reduplicant does not copy the base's tonal tier but instead simply assimilates an adjacent tone through regressive tone spreading (20c). If we accept the implication of this analysis that particular feature groupings may be blocked from copying, then we can extend this line of reasoning to copy just the consonants in the Yoruba *lí-lo* nominalization.

McCarthy and Prince point out that fixed segmental structure is found in total reduplication as well, where it goes under the traditional heading of "echo" words. Some examples appear in (21).

(21)   a.   English
            table   shmable
            book   shmook
            fantastic   shmantastic
            apple   shmapple
            strike   shmike

b. Kampuri

ghar-sar	'house'
gharaa-saraa	'horse'
khori-sori	'fuel'

c. Kolami

pal-gil	'tooth'
kota-gita	'bring it'
iir-giir	'water'
maasur-giisur	'men'
saa-gii	'go' cont. ger.

In these cases prespecification is of no avail. Since the echo word phenomenon is a species of full reduplication, the prosodic shape of the reduplicant cannot be determined by a template: it is a function of each individual base. But if there is no template, then there is nothing that can be prespecified. Rather, the distortions in the echo words must arise from rules defined over these constructions. McCarthy and Prince see these rules as a kind of dissimilation that modifies one of the twins in the X + X construction. Support for this view derives from the surprising generalization that echo words apparently cannot have the semblance of reduplication. For example, McCarthy and Prince's consultant for the data in (21a) reports that lexical items beginning with [shm] systematically modify the [m] to [p]: *shmaltz-shpaltz*. A similar fact is reported for Kampuri, where stems in initial [s] form echo words with [t]: *saati-taati* 'lamp'. This makes sense if the phenomenon is a type of dissimilation applying to the output of complete reduplication. It is mysterious under prespecification of the template. Why should there be a change restricted precisely to bases that match the prespecified portion of the template?

McCarthy and Prince conclude from this phenomenon and others that phonological rules must be granted the power to change phonemic content in the context of particular templates. They dub this operation *melodic overwriting*. In the next section we will see extensive melodic overwriting in their analysis of the Arabic broken plurals.

11.2 Prosodic Circumscription

For several cases of transfer, McCarthy and Prince have proposed the device of *prosodic circumscription*. The basic idea is that phonological representations can be cut into two pieces; rules of affixation and phonological change apply to one of the pieces before they are sewn back together. The fundamental hypothesis is that the same inventory of light versus heavy syllable, iambic versus trochaic foot, at the left versus right edge will suffice to identify the anatomical parts that submit to this prosodic surgery. More specifically, McCarthy and Prince propose that the base may factor into a prosodic constituent (mora, syllable, foot) plus *residue*. *Negative circumscription* operates on the residue, while *positive circumscription* isolates the prosodic constituent for phonological scrutiny. *Extrapro-*

sodicity (extrametricality, extrasyllabicity, extratonality) is the most familiar type of negative circumscription. For example, the antepenultimate stress rule factors *Ameri*⟨ca⟩ into a residue [Ameri] and extrametrical final syllable ⟨ca⟩. The metrical parse then works over the residue. Another type of circumscription, termed *prosodic delimitation*, isolates a subset of the vocabulary for morphological action. For example, in Dyirbal (Dixon 1972) the ergative suffix has two allomorphs whose distribution is determined prosodically: disyllabic stems take *-ŋgu*, while trisyllabic and longer stems take *-gu: yara-ŋgu* 'man' vs. *yamani-gu* 'rainbow'. A disyllabic structure [σσ] has a special status in Dyirbal: it constitutes the metrical foot and the *minimal word* (see below for development). The minimal word thus delimits the range of the *-ŋgu* allomorph; *-gu* is the default variant, added in the elsewhere case.

McCarthy and Prince discovered that many infixations can be understood as affixation to a positively circumscribed base. For example, in the Nicaraguan language Ulwa (Hale and Lacayo Blanco 1988), the construct state of a noun is formed by affixing *-ka*. The default option suffixes possessed noun stems with *-ka*. But a large class of nouns (many body-part and kinship terms) inject the affix into the stem. The insertion site is rigidly determined.

(22)

base	possessed	
al	al-ka	'man'
bas	bas-ka	'hair'
kii	kii-ka	'stone'
amak	amak-ka	'bee'
sana	sana-ka	'deer'
sapaa	sapaa-ka	'forehead'
suulu	suu-ka-lu	'dog'
baskarna	bas-ka-karna	'comb'
kuhbil	kuh-ka-bil	'knife'
siwanak	siwa-ka-nak	'root'
anaalaaka	anaa-ka-laaka	'chin'
karasmak	karas-ka-mak	'knee'

For example, **si-ka-wanak* and **kara-ka-smak* are impossible. Collecting all the cases, the infix appears after a single heavy syllable (*suu-ka-lu, bas-ka-karna*), after two lights (*siwa-ka-nak*), or after a light-heavy sequence (*karas-ka-mak*). This list of contexts falls exactly under the grouping delivered by an iambic parse. We may informally characterize the infixation as follows: Parse the word iambically from left to right; break off the initial iamb and suffix *-ka* to this factor; then restore the residue.

(23)

[suula]	[siwanak]	[karasmak]	
suu	siwa	karas	circumscribe iamb at left edge
suu-ka	siwa-ka	karas-ka	suffix *-ka* to circumscript
suukala	siwakanak	karaskamak	restore residue

A circumscribed foot can also serve as the base to which a reduplication template is affixed. McCarthy and Prince cite the following paradigm from the penultimate-stress language Samoan.

(24) | verb | pl. | |
|------|------|-----|
| táa | ta-taa | 'strike' |
| nófo | no-nofo | 'sit' |
| alófa | a-lo-lofa | 'love' |
| saváli | sa-va-vali | 'walk' |

In this case a (light) syllable prefixes to the bisyllabic (trochaic) stress foot. The foot also supplies the phonemic content to fill out the reduplicated affix.

(25) [savali]
vali	circumscribe trochee at right edge
σ-vali	prefix σ
va-vali	template matching
savavali	restore residue

In Samoan two operations are thus defined with respect to the circumscribed constituent: affixation of the reduplicating prefix and copy of the segmental tier.

McCarthy and Prince call on circumscription to explain a curious contrast between Lardil reduplication (discussed earlier in section 11.1) and the following paradigm from Yidin^y (Dixon 1977b).

(26) | sg. | pl. | |
|-----|-----|-----|
| mulari | mula-mulari | 'initiated man' |
| jugarba | jugar-jugarba-n | 'have an unsettled mind' |
| gindalba | gindal-gindalba | 'lizard species' |
| kalampaRa | kala-kalampaRa | 'March fly' |

Like Lardil, Yidin^y has a disyllabic stress foot; the reduplicated affix is obviously disyllabic and so the template is a foot. Unlike Lardil, however, Yidin^y carries over certain aspects of the base's syllabification to the affix. The [r] onsets the third syllable in [mu.la.ri] but closes the second syllable in [ju.gar.ba]. And in [ka.la.mpa.Ra], the homorganic nasal plus stop is a tautosyllabic onset. The onset versus coda status of these consonants is systematically reflected in their absence versus presence in the reduplicated prefix. In this respect, Yidin^y contracts minimally with Lardil, where [pa.re.li] reduplicates as *parel-pareli:* here the reduplicant copies an onset consonant, just as in Ilokano.

McCarthy and Prince propose to solve this puzzle by restricting the reduplicant's access to the phonemic melody of the base. Specifically, suppose that Yidin^y follows Samoan in recruiting the stress foot [σσ] as the base of reduplication. Then only the phonemes lying inside the foot will be visible to the copy operation and hence have a chance to appear in the affix.

(27)   [ju.gar.ba]   [mu.la.ri]
     ju.gar   mu.la   circumscribe [σσ] foot at left edge
     F-ju.gar   F-mula   prefixation of [σσ] foot template
     ju.gar-ju.gar   mula-mula   template matching
     ju.gar.ju.gar.ba   mulamulari   restore residue

In this analysis, the disyllabic metrical foot does double duty in defining both the base of affixation and the prosodic shape of the affix itself.

In the examples considered so far, circumscription has been defined over a preexisting metrical foot that independently defines the word's stress contour. One might wonder whether this is necessary or a function of the relatively small number of cases identified so far. McCarthy and Prince's (1990) analysis of the Arabic broken plural bears on this question; it is one of the most impressive applications of the prosodic morphology arsenal to a problem that seems initially quite impenetrable. Recall from 8.1 that Arabic words such as *kuutib-a* 'correspond with' (perfect passive) resolve into three intersecting morphemic tiers: a consonantal root of two to four radicals, a vocalic melody, and a skeletal template (transcribed here in CV terms).

(28)
$$[ktb] \quad \text{'write'}$$
$$CVVCVC \quad \text{measure III}$$
$$[ui] \quad \text{perfect, passive}$$

In the verbal morphology the vocalic melody is partially independent (e.g., [ui] marks the passive voice in the perfect tense); but in other cases the melody is tied to a particular morphological template (e.g., locational nouns of the pattern *ma*+CC*a*C take [a], participles of the shape CVVCVC take [ai], etc.) or to the radicals defining a given lexeme (e.g., nouns of the CVCC shape lexically contrast for the three vowels of the language: *kalb* 'dog', *rijl* 'leg', *ʔuðn* 'ear').

Although the language has affixal inflection, a good portion of the derivational morphology is nonconcatenative. Since there are no long chains of affixation, it is difficult to reconstruct the derivational history of a given word on the basis of its overt shape. Most scholars of Arabic have concluded that the morphology is root-based rather than word-based. To form a word, the root consonants are recovered and then mapped to a template. Universally, the plural of a noun is derived from the singular (rather than the inverse); this is reflected in the morphology through affixation to a singular base. Plurals of this form occur in Arabic too, where they are known as *sound plurals;* but they are a marginal phenomenon. *Broken plurals,* formed by modification of the template, pervade the system and readily apply to borrowings (e.g., *bank, bunuuk* 'bank'; *film, ʔaflaam* 'film'). McCarthy and Prince's table of broken plural patterns (based on Wright 1971) is reproduced in (29).

(29) Wright's broken plural patterns

a.	iambic	b.	trochaic	c.	monosyllabic	d.	other
5.	CiCaaC	1.	CuCaC	2.	CuCC	7.	CuC$_i$C$_i$aC
6.	CuCuuC	4.	CiCaC	@12.	CiCC + at	8.	CuC$_i$C$_i$aaC
23.	CaCaaC	#28.	CaCaC	18.	CiCC + aan		
*14.	/CaCaaC/	11.	CiCaC + at	19.	CuCC + aan		
+24.	CaCaaC + /ay/	$13.	/CaCuC/	+22.	CaCC + /ay/		
#25.	CaCiiC	3.	CuCuC	#29.	CaCC		
#26.	CuCuuC + at	9.	CaCaC + at				
#27.	CiCaaC + at	10.	CuCaC + at				
16.	CawaaCiC	20.	CuCaC + aaʔ				
17.	CaCaaʔiC	&15.	/CaCiC/ + at				
Q1.	CaCaaCiC	&21.	/CaCiC/ + aaʔ				
Q2.	CaCaaCiiC						

Sigla:

#	rare according to Wright
*	metathesizes to ʔaCCaaC
$	metathesizes to ʔaCCuC
&	metathesizes to ʔaCCiC
+	underlying /ay/ to [aa] by regular glide phonology
@	usually has CiCC + aan doublet, according to Wright

Since the patterns are so numerous and so diversified, it is not obvious that it makes any sense to say that the plural is derived from the singular the way sound plurals are. When Wright's 31 types are arranged prosodically, however, some generalizations begin to emerge. CuC$_i$C$_i$aaC (29d8) derives almost exclusively from CaaCiC participles and is best treated as gemination of the middle consonant through backward spreading to the second mora of the initial syllable. The mono-syllabic pattern is rare (only 4% in McCarthy and Prince's survey) and since most instances take a suffix, it might be argued to derive from an underlying CVCVC + VC shape through elision. The trochaic group is of some importance and even predominates in certain lexical classes; but the iambic is the truly pro-ductive pattern, ranging over the widest class of singulars and extending to loan-words. Examples appear in (30).

(30)

		sg.	pl.	
CVCC				
		nafs	nufuus	'soul'
		qidḥ	qidaaḥ	'arrow'
		ḥukm	ḥakaam*	'judgment'
CVCVC				
		ʔasad	ʔusuud	'lion'
		rajul	rijaal	'man'
		ʕinab	ʕanaab*	'grape'
CVCVVC				
		saḥaab + at	saḥaaʔib	'cloud'
		jaziir + at	jazaaʔir	'island'

CVVCVC

faakih + at	fawaakih	'fruit'
ʔaanis + at	ʔawaanis	'cheerful'

CVVCV(V)C

xaatam	xawaatim	'signet ring'
jaamuus	jawaamiis	'buffalo'

CVCCV(V)C

jundub	janaadib	'locust'
sulṭaan	salaaṭiin	'sultan'
nuwwaar	nawaawiir	'white flowers'
jilbaab	jalaabiib	'a type of garment'
zalzal + at	zalaazil	'earthquake'

[* These appear as *ʔaḥkaam* and *ʔaʕnaab* by an independently needed rule metathesizing initial C*a* strings and adding a prosthetic glottal stop.]

The only invariant that underlies these plurals is that they begin with a CVCVV shape, indicating the presence of a (LH) iamb $[\sigma_\mu \sigma_{\mu\mu}]$. However, it is not sufficient to say that they are formed by replacing the singular template with an iamb. The plural exhibits various transfer effects that depend on the prosodic structure of the singular. For example, the vowel length in the final syllable of the plural correlates with the length of the final syllable of the singular: *jundub* and *xaatam* are matched by the final short vowels of the plurals *janaadib* and *xawaatim* in the same way that the long-voweled *sulṭaan – salaaṭiin* and *jaamuus – jawaamiis* form matched sets. Also, bimoraic singulars such as *nafs* and *rajul* have disyllabic plurals while longer (trimoraic or greater) singulars form trisyllabic plurals. Finally, idiosyncratic associations of the radical consonants to the singular template are preserved in the plural. For example, in *nuwwaar – nawaawiir* from [nwr] the second radical spreads; but in *jilbaab – jalaabiib* from [jlb] the third one does. And reduplication of the biradical [zl] appears in both the singular *zalzal + at* and the plural *zalaazil*.

The prosodic structure of the final syllable thus is preserved in the plural. It is only the initial portion of the string that changes into an iamb. How can this initial portion be defined? McCarthy and Prince's answer is that the broken plurals of (31) are formed by first circumscribing the phonemes that lie within a bimoraic trochee at the left edge of the word. It is this segmental material that is mapped to the iambic template, consonantal phonemes seeking out nonmoraic, onset positions and vocalic phonemes, moraic positions. Since vowels and consonants occupy distinct tiers, the vowel melody may map to both syllables of the iamb without crossing the intervening consonant's association line. The residue is then added back and finally the vocalic melody is changed.

(31)   [nafs]   [rajil]

naf	raji	circumscribe trochee at left edge
nafaa	rajii	map to iambic template
nufuus	rijaal	restore residue and change melody

As in Yidin^y, the analysis appeals to prosodic templates at two distinct points: a bimoraic trochee isolates the phonemic raw material, which is then mapped to an iambic template. At a later stage, the vocalic melody is changed. McCarthy and Prince report that for CaCC singulars, CuCuuC is the preferred plural with [u] melody. In the other bimoraic singulars, CaCaaC predominates. The [ia] of *rijaal* is less common.

When the initial syllable of a polysyllabic singular is heavy, the residue encompasses the entire second syllable. In this case the initial bimoraic circumscript spreads to fill out the iamb, just as in *nafs – nufuus*. The quantity of the second syllable does not change because it constitutes the residue and thus is isolated from the iambicity imposed on the initial bimoraic circumscript. This accounts for the transfer effects noted earlier.

(32) [jundub]   [sulṭaan]   [zalzal]
      jun   sul   zal   circumscribe trochee of left edge
      junuu   suluu   zalaa   map to iambic template
      janaadib   salaaṭiin   zalaazil   restore residue and change melody

For the trimoraic$^+$ singulars, the plural melody [ai] predominates to the exclusion of almost all others. The [a] maps to the iamb while the [i] appears on the residue, overwriting the original vowel. McCarthy and Prince suggest that forms such as *ḥikm* sg., *ʔaḥkaam* pl. (from [ḥakaam] by metathesis) also have the [ai] plural melody; but they fail to show the [i] because their shorter bases lack a residue. This means that for the majority of broken plurals, the vowel melody is fixed at [ai].

An interesting analytic detail arises in singulars that begin with a long vowel such as *xaatam*. Here circumscription isolates a single consonant and vowel [xa]. The vowel apparently spreads to both syllables of the iamb, while the consonant refuses to budge from the onset of the initial syllable. Since Arabic syllables require an onset, a default glide [w] is inserted.

(33) [xaatam]
      xa   circumscribe trochee at left edge
      xawaa   map to iambic template
      xawaatim   restore residue and change melody

Finally, in cases such as *jaziir-at – jazaaʔir,* circumscription of the first two moras cuts through the second syllable, taking its onset and first mora. (The latter cannot be seen directly since it is covered up by melody overwriting.) The residue is thus deprived of an onset. When the two pieces are put back together, the residue receives a default glide as onset (appearing here as [ʔ] instead of [w] by an independently needed rule).

(34) [jaziir]
      jazi   circumscribe trochee at left edge
      jazii   map to iambic template
      jaziiʔir   restore residue
      jazaaʔir   change melody

To briefly summarize, while the analysis is complex, it utilizes tools that have been independently motivated: circumscribing a bimoraic sequence and mapping to an iambic template – with spreading to fill out required positions.

There is one respect in which the Arabic broken plural circumscription differs from the cases of Ulwa, Samoan, and Yidin^y. In the latter, the circumscript is identical to the metrical constituent that locates the stress (initial iambic for Ulwa, initial trochaic for Yidin^y, final trochaic for Samoan). In Arabic the broken plurals are formed at a very early stage of the derivation, before any metrical structure is assigned. It is presumably for this reason that the bimoraic parse is able to cut through a syllable. However, McCarthy and Prince see the bimoraic parse required for circumscription as still being intimately tied to the metrical structure in Arabic because there is evidence that it corresponds to the minimal word. Indeed, McCarthy and Prince hypothesize that all cases of positive prosodic circumscription will isolate the minimal word. We will return to this point after examining the evidence for this minimality.

11.3 Minimal Word Phenomenon

In many languages words of one mora or one syllable are avoided: a minimal bimoraic/disyllabic requirement is imposed. For example, while CV syllables with a lax, short vowel occur nonfinally in English, they are systematically absent at the end of a word unless the vowel is low. As a result, monomoraic CV words are absent from the lexical vocabulary (and in dialects that distinguish length in the low vowels, *Pa* and *Ma* are long). Every lexical word thus contains at least two moras. For Yidin^y, Dixon (1977b) states that all roots are built from a $CVCV(CV)^n(C)$ canon, entailing a disyllabic lower bound on major category words. Systems that impose minimal length restrictions typically allow deviations in the nonlexical vocabulary. Thus, monomoraic words are found in the English articles (*the, a*). In their discussion of the phenomenon in Arabic, McCarthy and Prince (1990) note that the major deviations from bimoraicity include monomoraic particles (*wa* 'and', *bi* 'in', *qad* past) and a handful of nouns such as *Pab* 'father', *Pax* 'brother', *dam* 'blood', *yad* 'hand' (recall that final consonants are extrasyllabic in Arabic and hence do not count for weight). The latter are restricted to kinship and body-part terms, possibly reflecting an obligatory possessive affix at an earlier stage of the language. When serving as bases for productive word formation, these items are brought up to code by the addition of a consonant. For example, compare the nisba (characteristic) adjectives in *-iy: Maṣr* 'Egypt', *Miṣr-iy* 'Egyptian' and *Pab* 'father', *Pabaw-iy* 'paternal'. Japanese (Itô 1990) has many monomoraic nouns: *su* 'vinegar', *ne* 'root', *ki* 'tree'. But when bound stems undergo productive compounding, they are lengthened: for example, the monomoraic stem for 'Tuesday' in *ka-yoobi* is lengthened in the compound *kaa-moku* 'TuTh'. Itô concludes that Japanese has a bimoraic minimality constraint that is overridden only in nonderived lexical contexts.

Minimal word requirements are often reflected in blocking the application of rules that would otherwise truncate a word below the minimum. For example, recall that apocope in Lardil freely applies to trisyllabic or longer stems but is blocked on disyllables. Apocope would push these words below the disyllabic minimum.

(35)   uninflected   inflected
       yalul   yalulu-n   'flame'
       mayar   mayara-n   'rainbow'
       karikar   karikari-n   'butter-fish'
       murkuni   murkunima-n   'nullah'
       mela   mela-n   'sea'
       ŋawa   ŋawu-n ⁊   'wife'
       wiṭe   wiṭe-n   'interior'

In Estonian (Prince 1980) trisyllabic [tænava] and HL [konna], [matsi] apocopate; but the process blocks on LL [kona] and H [koi], [maa].

(36)   base   nom.sg.
       [tænava]   tænav   'street'
       [konna]   kon:n   'frog'
       [matsi]   mat:s   'lout, bumpkin'
       [kana]   kana   *kan   'hen'
       [koi]   koi: *ko   'clothes-moth'
       [maa]   maa: *ma   'country'

Rule blockage can be understood as following from a bimoraic minimality constraint: apocope would push LL and H stems below the allowed limit. (A later morphologically restricted rule adds a mora to realize the Estonian "strong grade.")

Another reflection of minimality constraints are augmentation processes that insert a dummy mora or syllable when the base would otherwise surface with less prosodic weight than the required minimum. Such a process is evident in the Lardil paradigms in (37).

(37)   a.   kentapal   kentapal-in   'dugong'
            yaraman   yaraman-in   'horse'
            pirŋen   pirŋen-in   'woman'

       b.   yaka   yak-in   'fish'
            ṭera   ṭer-in   'thigh'
            ṛelka   ṛelk-in   'head'

In (37a) we see consonant-final stems that take the inflection *-in*. The forms in (37b) also take *-in*, suggesting that they end in a consonant. But in the unaffixed form, they appear with a final [a]. Hale (1973) analyzes these stems as underlying monosyllables. They are augmented with a final [a] in the uninflected form. The fact that augmentation applies only to monosyllables suggests that its function is to ensure that every Lardil word surfaces with at least two syllables. To take another example, in Arabic many roots lose their initial [w] when it occupies preconsonantal position: compare the perfect *wazan* 'weigh' with the imperfect *ya-zin* from [ya-wzin]. In the masdar (nominalization) *zin-at,* a semantically empty suffix -*at* is added whose only justification seems to be to ensure that the resultant stem contains two moras. Finally, in Choctaw (Lombardi and McCarthy 1991) all monosyllabic nouns have the shape CV:C. If the final consonant is extraprosodic, then the long vowel requirement on monosyllables can be understood to reflect a bimoraic requirement on noun roots. Choctaw verbs also manifest minimality, but in a slightly different fashion. As the paradigm in (38) shows, verbs fall into two groups. In the first the initial vowel is stable while in the second – all with initial [a] – the initial vowel is missing in the prefixed form.

(38) a. ani   'to fill'   iš-ani   'for you to fill'
          ona   'to arrive'   iš-ona   'for you to arrive'
          iši   'to fill'   iš-iši   'for you to fill'

      b. abi   'to kill'   iš-bi   'for you to kill'
          amo   'to gather'   iš-mo   'for you to gather'
          apa   'to eat'   iš-pa   'for you to eat'

Following Nicklas (1974, 1975), Lombardi and McCarthy suggest that the stems in (38b) have an underlying monomoraic CV shape. The bimoraic minimality requirement is satisfied through the mora provided by the prefix. In unaffixed forms such as the infinitive, the CV stems (and only these) take an [a] augment, rendering them bimoraic. Choctaw lexical categories thus differ in terms of the level when the minimality constraint is enforced: at the lexical root level for nouns; but at a later stage for verbs, allowing affixes to bring deficient roots up to the minimum.

We noted earlier that elements drawn from the nonlexical class of pronouns, prepositions, and grammatical particles frequently escape minimality restrictions. These items also often fail to receive a stress and tend to cliticize to adjacent lexical items, where they may (but need not) be taken into account by the regular stress assignment rule (see section 10.6). McCarthy and Prince (1986) have tried to tie these two properties together by expressing the minimal word requirement in terms of the prosodic hierarchy. The reasoning runs as follows. According to the *prosodic hierarchy,* the phonological word PW (McCarthy and Prince use the term *prosodic word,* abbreviated *PrWd*) is composed of metrical feet F, which in turn are composed of syllables, which in turn contain moras.

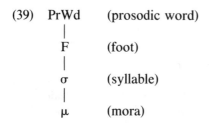

(39) PrWd   (prosodic word)
       |
       F   (foot)
       |
       σ   (syllable)
       |
       μ   (mora)

According to the syntax of (39), any PrWd must contain at least one F. If metrical feet are strictly binary (disyllabic or bimoraic), then monosyllabic/monomoraic items cannot be metrified and hence cannot stand alone as phonological words. To stand alone, a PrWd must be minimally bimoraic or disyllabic (hence the motivation for augmentation processes). A degenerate element can escape the normal stress rules and hence cliticize. Thus, clitics tend to be monosyllabic. These prosodic dwarfs reside primarily in the nonlexical region of the vocabulary. Being a closed class, they do not deploy the full distinctive capacity of the system, which is held in reserve to build up the open-ended lexical categories (nouns, verbs, adjectives).

McCarthy and Prince observe that in triggering augmentation and blocking apocope, the PrWd behaves like the other categories in the hierarchy. For example, epenthesis and gemination processes typically intervene to foster a syllable in a deficient segmental environment (section 6.6). Also, syncope is often inhibited if the output cannot be syllabified (section 9.13). Similarly, processes of iambic lengthening and trochaic shortening have been seen as optimizing the prosodic weight of a metrical foot (section 10.9).

McCarthy and Prince (1990) hypothesize that positive circumscription always isolates the system's minimal word. This yields the correct predictions for Ulwa and Yidin^y. We have seen that Dixon's root canon for Yidin^y has a disyllabic minimum and the reduplication process is built off a circumscribed disyllabic stem. Iambic-parsing Ulwa also displays a bimoraic minimality constraint over the lexical vocabulary (Green 1992). According to McCarthy and Prince, restricting positive circumscription to the minimal word ensures that the morphological operation it subserves will be defined over a substantial portion of the vocabulary. For example, circumscription of the first two moras will apply to bimoraic, trimoraic, and all longer lexical items. If circumscription were restricted to trimoraic strings, all bimoraic lexical items would escape the relevant morphological operation.

While construing minimality in terms of the prosodic hierarchy ties a number of facts together in a natural way, this proposal still faces some questions. First, as mentioned in section 10.10, it is not clear whether all systems exhibiting the minimal word syndrome can in fact be described without appealing to degenerate metrical constituents (e.g., Winnebago). Also, since the minimal word is by definition coextensive with a foot, it is difficult to assess the claim that circumscription isolates the category PrWd rather than simply the Foot. Furthermore, if the minimal element is bimoraic, it is difficult to pin down as iambic or trochaic. This is reflected in the fact that in their (1990) study of the Arabic broken plural McCarthy and Prince describe circumscription as isolating a moraic trochee, while in later work (1991) they see the bimoraic parse as isolating the (LL) and (H) species of the iamb. Relevant to this issue are systems like Auca (section 10.10) where metrical orphans and monosyllabic CV lexical words go hand in hand. In this case data from stress and word shapes converge on the conclusion that a bimoraic/disyllabic minimum is not imposed. If more cases can be discovered where stress and minimal word shapes covary in this fashion, then the claim that these various types of minimality isolate the same phenomenon will be strengthened.

Finally, there are cases in which the circumscription phenomenon does not respect the prosodic hierarchy. For example, recall that the iambic broken plural in Arabic is built on the circumscription of the first two moras of the singular. In

LH CVCVVC stems such as *jaziir-at – jazaaʔir,* circumscription splits the second syllable. If the minimal word is identified with the foot, then circumscription should fail in this case: according to the prosodic hierarchy, feet are composed of syllables and syllables of moras. Thus, a metrical foot cannot cut through a syllable; it is built on top of syllables in the prosodic architecture. In order to preserve the generalization that circumscription isolates the minimal word, McCarthy and Prince allow the broken plural circumscription to bypass the syllable and operate at the lowest level of the prosodic hierarchy: the mora. But if this is the level at which the minimal word is expressed, then we seem to lose the idea that the PrWd is reachable through the Foot level. Furthermore, it is unclear whether this is technically feasible. For McCarthy and Prince, onset consonants are not dominated by a mora but rather report directly to the syllable. Circumscription of just the moraic phonemes fails to grab the onset consonants and thus cannot transform the [r] and [j] of *rajil* into the iamb *rijaal.*

A similar issue arises in Itô's (1990) analysis of truncation in Japanese. Poser (1984) and Mester (1990) detected considerable variation in the formation of Japanese hypocoristics: for example, *Mariko* reduces as *Mari-čan* (left-to-right association), *Riko-čan* (right-to-left), and even *Mako-čan* (edge-in) or *Maa-čan.* The one constant underlying these options is mapping to a bimoraic template: **Ma-čan* is rejected. A similar process of truncation operates in the adaptation of loanwords. A sample appears in (40). Most reductions fall within the two-, three-, and four-mora range.

(40)

moras	# of cases	example	
1	2	pe(eji)	'page'
2	86	heri(koputaa)	'helicopter'
3	53	terebi(jon)	'television'
4	55	rihabiri(teešon)	'rehabilitation'
5	1	konkurii(to)	'concrete'

Poser interpreted these cases as targeting a one- or two-foot sequence. In a more systematic study of the phenomenon, Itô (1990) uncovered certain puzzling gaps in the possible patterns.

(41)   2-mora: LL, *H
        3-mora: HL, LLL, *LH
        4-mora: HH, HLL, LLH, LLLL, *LHL

First, while the two-mora case can be filled with two light syllables, a single heavy is ill formed. For example, [sutoraiki] 'strike' shortens to (LL) *suto,* but [haNgaa] 'hunger' may not shorten to (H) **haN,* and [jiiNzu] 'jeans' may not shorten to (H) **jii.* More puzzling still is the fact that reduction to (H) is found in compounds: [haNgaa-sutoraiki] 'hunger strike' appears as *haN-suto* and [jiiNzu paNtsu] 'jeans pants' truncates to *jii-paN.* A final mystery is that reduction to a light-heavy sequence is systematically avoided: [demoNsutoreešoN] 'demonstration' and [rokeešoN] 'location' reduce to (LL) *demo* and *roke,* not (LH) **demoN* and **rokee.*

Itô's analysis for these cases involves imposing two separate restrictions that the truncation operation must simultaneously satisfy. (42a) requires the truncated word to start with a bimoraic foot (a kind of prosodic "stem"); (42b) requires each word to be longer than a single syllable.

(42) a.   Min(stem) = F = [μμ]

  b.   Min(word) > σ

(42a) explains why reduction to (H) is possible in stem + stem compounds such as *jii + paN* while (42b) halts the slide into monosyllabism in cases where the word stands alone. Similarly, [maikurohoN] 'microphone' truncates to *maiku*, not **mai*. The latter fails to satisfy the disyllabic constraint on prosodic words. (H)L *maiku* fulfills both requirements: it begins with a heavy syllable that can be analyzed as a bimoraic foot; and the second syllable [ku] ensures that the disyllabic PrWd constraint is satisfied.

Itô's explanation of [demoNsutoreešoN] → *demo*, **demoN* is more subtle. **demoN* is blocked because, while it satisfies (42b), it fails to receive a proper analysis by (42a), given that the initial foot is required to be exactly two moras.

(43) a.   PrWd   b.   PrWd   c.   PrWd

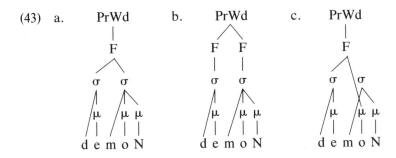

Allowing the foot to take in both syllables (43a) encompasses three moras and thus exceeds the constraint of exactly two moras called for by (42a). Distributing the two syllables over separate feet (43b) leaves the first foot too small. Finally, footing the second mora with the first instead of the third (43c) is blocked by the prosodic hierarchy, since moras can be reached only through the syllable node.

While the prosodic hierarchy helps to explain why **demoN* is ruled out, it remains unclear how *demo* is ruled in. Here the analysis into a bimoraic foot cuts across the syllable, just as in the Arabic broken plural. While we may appeal to circumscription of the first two moras, this analysis must bypass the syllable level. If such a move is permitted, then the prosodic hierarchy [PrWd > F > σ > μ] is being skipped at two points. The constraint that PrWd dominate more than one syllable skips the F level, and the circumscription of a bimoraic F skips the σ level. Such cases potentially jeopardize the claim that prosodic units are organized in a strict hierarchy. For those theories in which analysis into syllables and analysis into moras are separate projections (e.g., Halle and Vergnaud 1987), such cases are not problematic and parallel the Winnebago analysis of section 10.10 where the metrical and syllabic constituency fail to align. Another possible approach to the problem that maintains the prosodic hierarchy intact is to declare Japanese a trochaic system that is strictly binary, allowing just (LL) and (HL) constituents. To impose strict binarity on a light-heavy sequence under trochaic parsing, the second syllable must change its weight from H to L. On this view, developed by Prince (1990), the shedding of the second mora arises from imposition of a binary parse under trochaic rhythm similar to the change of *egō* to ('LL) *ego* in Latin discussed in section 10.10.

11.4   Extensions and Refinements

In more recent work McCarthy and Prince (1991) have attempted to both tighten their theory and extend its empirical coverage. In this section we will survey their major claims and results. Recall that their basic thesis is that prosodic templates are expressed as "authentic units of prosody" arrayed in the hierarchy of (44).

(44)   PrWd   (prosodic word)
         |
        F   (foot)
         |
        σ   (syllable)
         |
        μ   (mora)

The metrical feet come in several varieties depending on whether or not the language is sensitive to quantity (quantity-sensitive, QS; and quantity-insensitive, QI), and if so, then whether the rhythm is iambic or trochaic. As with stress, subminimal feet are assigned only under "duress."

(45)   <u>QI</u>   <u>QS</u>   <u>QS</u>
       genus   syllabic   trochaic   iambic

       species   (σσ)   (LL)   (LH)
                                  (H)   (H)
                                  (HL)?   (LL)

       subminimal   (σ)   (L)   (L)

       where L = σ and H =   σ
                      | /\
                      μ   μ μ

The principal claim is that the groupings that define prosodic templates and the principles deploying them in derivations will exhibit the same features and properties as those operative in the phonology of stress: for example, QI versus QS, and within the latter, iambic versus trochaic grouping. If this hypothesis proves correct, it will constitute a major discovery in the discipline. One methodological implication is that we can use prosodic morphology in addition to stress to probe metrical structure. We expect them to converge on the same structures. While much remains to be learned, the preliminary evidence for the hypothesis is impressive. Assuming that it turns out to be correct in the long run, we can ask why. A plausible answer would lie in the idea that metrical groupings are natural perceptual categories. If a morphological process is to be marked not by an affix but by imposing a shape on the string of phonemes, then it makes sense to utilize shapes to which the system is already sensitized.

Let us now turn to some of the questions that have arisen in defending the claim that templates are "authentic units of prosody" and McCarthy and Prince's answers to these questions.

11.4.1 Autotemplaticism

Some patterns that were previousely analyzed templatically can no longer be expressed as templates if the typology in (45) is correct. McCarthy and Prince reanalyze a number of these cases in such a way that the prosodic structure arises not from a morphologically or lexically induced template but simply from the ordinary syllabification resources of the language. To take a couple of simple cases, in the Ethiopian Semitic language Chaha the jussive form of the triliteral verb shows a schwa between either the first two or the second two consonants, depending on the location of the most sonorous element.

(46) yägfər   'release'   yäsərt   'cauterize'
      yäk'ßər   'plant'   yätərx   'make incision'
      yäft'əm   'block'   yägəmt'   'chew off'

In a theory where templates are segmentally specified, the jussive can, like other forms of the Chaha verb, be expressed templatically: as [yä + CCC]. The schwa is then supplied by the normal syllabically driven epenthesis process. But a vowelless template is not possible within the system of (45). Furthermore, the templates in the McCarthy and Prince typology are expressed moraically. The sonority of individual segments is not encoded and is thus inaccessible in the statement of the templates themselves. For these cases, McCarthy and Prince suggest that there simply is no template supplied by the morphology. The prosodic structure is rather projected from the string of phonemes via the independently motivated rules of syllabification operative in the language.

Another, more controversial case where such an "autotemplatic" solution is proposed is McCarthy and Prince's refinement of Archangeli's (1983, 1991) analyses of Yawelmani templates. The templatic morphology of Yawelmani operates at a certain level of abstraction and can only be glimpsed once the complex phonological alternations discussed in section 3.4.2 are undone. In Archangeli's (1991) analysis, underlying bimoraic CVVC syllables are realized as CVC via a weight-by-position rule that remaps a coda consonant to the second mora, triggering shortening of the underlying long vowel (47).

(47)

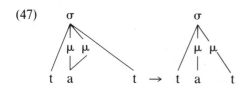

This is Archangeli's prosodic reinterpretation of closed-syllable shortening – a rule that is ordered after epenthesis, vowel lowering, and harmony. Within the verb, roots fall into three major types, each with an additional subtype reflecting another consonant. Their expression in Archangeli's (1983) segmental analysis appears in (48).

(48) | template pool | biconsonantal | | triconsonantal | |
|---|---|---|---|---|
| CVC(C) | caw- | 'shout' | hogn- | 'float' |
| CVVC(C) | c'uum- | 'devour' | cuupn- | 'consent' |
| CVCVV(C) | ninii- | 'become quiet' | yawaal- | 'follow' |

In Yawelmani some suffixes replace the underlying template of the verb root with one of their own. Both verb roots and suffixes impose the same pool of templates. For example, the continuative suffix -*Ɂaa* selects the CVVC(C) template, while the aorist -*hin* is neutral, allowing the lexical template of the root to emerge.

(49) a.
[caw + hin]	'shouted'	CVC
[c'uum + hin]	'devoured'	CVVC
[ninii + hin]	'became quiet'	CVCVV
[caaw + Ɂaa + hin]	'shout'	CVVC
[c'uum + Ɂaa + hin]	'devour'	CVVC
[niin + Ɂaa + hin]	'quieten'	CVVC

b. caw-hin
c'om-hun
ninee-hin

caw-Ɂaa-hin
c'om-Ɂaa-hin
nen-Ɂaa-hin

From the examples in (49a) we see that the neutral aorist suffix -*hin* allows each of the three template types in the lexical class to surface. We also see the change to a CVVC template induced by the -*Ɂaa* suffix on a CVC verb like 'shout' and on a CVCVV verb like 'become quiet'. These paradigms are then submitted to the regular phonological rules of the language, yielding the surface representations in (49b).

When we think about how to express these templates in prosodic terms, two problems arise. First, how do we account for the additional consonant allowed by triconsonantal roots such as [hogn], [cuupn], and [yawaal]? This is even more problematic for certain reduplicative structures where segmentalist templates such as CVCCC can be found (see below). Second, how can we represent the contrast between verbs such as [caw] and [c'uum]? If both templates are simply bimoraic, how do we ensure that second mora maps to the vowel [u] in [c'uum] but to the consonant [w] in [caw]? Archangeli's solution stipulates that consonants are not moraic at the underlying level, where the template is mapped. The weight-by-position rule (47) maps coda consonants to the second mora of the syllable, triggering vowel shortening where necessary. On this analysis, the CVCVV template of [ninii] is reinterpreted as the (LH) canonical iamb, [c'uum] is a heavy syllable (H), and [caw] is a simple (light) syllable (σ).

(50)

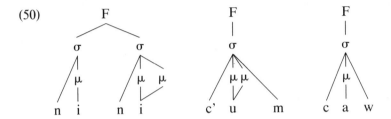

While this analysis successfully recasts the templates in the more restrictive prosodic framework, the problem from McCarthy and Prince's perspective is that a single light syllable is a valid template only in a QI language; it does not fit naturally with the (H) and (LH) iambs. If the templates truly reflect the prosody of the language, and if the latter is expressed in terms of the typology in (45), then the segmental CVC template must receive a different interpretation. McCarthy and Prince claim that the prosodic structure assigned to [caw] is not a function of the templatic morphology but simply arises from ordinary syllabification imposed on this sequence of phonemes (given that the language has obligatory onsets and no clustering in the onset or coda). This appeal to normal syllabification is the solution Archangeli (1991) suggests for the problem of the dangling consonants. For example, the reflexive suffix -iwis calls for a doubling of the root consonants. The CVVC root [laan] 'to hear' appears as *laniln-iwis* (from [lanln] by epenthesis). To account for this case, we assume that -iwis blocks the appearance of the verb's lexical template and copies the radical consonants to yield [lanln + iwis]. Syllabically driven epenthesis then derives *laniln-iwis*. The upshot of this analysis is that the prosodic templates in Yawelmani are imposed at the left edge of the verb; the rest of the verb stem plus the suffixes are assigned their prosodic structure "autotemplatically" – that is, in virtue of the normal syllabification rules of the language that produce CV, CVV, and CVC syllables.

If we accept this account, then any suffix that imposes the [σ] template in Archangeli's analysis must be reinterpreted to remove the root's lexical template but fail to assign one of its own. This suggests that template substitution breaks down into two steps: deletion of the root's original template followed by imposition of the template (if any) supplied by the suffix. More generally, while the appeal to autotemplaticism makes sense on theory-internal grounds, it remains to be seen whether this way of dividing things up has any independent justification in the morphology of Chaha and Yawelmani.

11.4.2   Foot Species and Genus

Another, more technical refinement introduced by McCarthy and Prince concerns the way in which particular species of foot templates are defined. Rather than simply listing (LL), (LH), and so on, McCarthy and Prince characterize each type in terms of two predicates: whether the number of syllables and the number of moras in the foot is maximized or minimized. A (LL) foot comes from maximizing the syllables but minimizing the moras; (LH) and (HL) maximize both syllables and moras; the bimoraic heavy syllable (H) minimizes both dimensions. These parameters are framed by the overarching condition of foot binarity. Strict binarity ensures that the foot can never exceed two syllables and if monosyllabic, never two moras. Similarly, binarity ensures that subminimal elements never define a template target. (For treatment of the light syllable affix under reduplication, see below.)

(51)   (LH)   =   max σ, max μ
       (LL)   =   max σ, min μ
       (H)   =   min σ, min μ

Given this system, the Yawelmani (LH) and (H) templates arise from calling for a minimal PrWd (one Foot), of the iambic genus, with [max σ, max μ] and [min σ, min μ] species settings, respectively.

In some prosodic morphologies, the foot species is not fixed, generating various expansions of this category. Hypocoristics often display this property. For example, the proximal vocatives in Yupik (Woodbury 1987) show monosyllabic and disyllabic variants.

(52)   full name   nickname
       Aŋukagnaq   Aŋ, Aŋuk
       Cupel:aq   Cup, Cupel
       Nupigak   Nup, Nupix/Nupik
       Qakfagalgia   Qak, Qakef/*Qakfag

We may understand this variation as follows. Recall that Yupik stress prosody is iambic and that initial closed syllables count as heavy. The monosyllabic nicknames close on a consonant, creating a heavy syllable. They thus realize the (H) expansion of the iambic foot. The disyllabic variants represent a (LL) expansion of the iambic category. *Qakfag is malformed because its (HL) structure does not match the iambic prosody. We may thus specify the Yupik vocative template as a PrWd minimally satisfied (one Foot) that belongs to the iambic genus with undefined species.

11.4.3   Strict versus Loose Expansion

Trisyllabic templates do not fit snugly in the typology of (45). An example is the Cupeño habilitative (Hill 1970, McCarthy 1984) in which the string composed of the stressed syllable plus any following unstressed ones is reparsed over a tri-syllabic span.

(53)

verb stem	habilitative	
čál	čáʔaʔal	'husk'
táw	táʔəʔəw	'see'
kəláw	kəláʔaʔaw	'gather wood'
páčik	páčiʔik	'leach acorns'
čáŋnəw	čáŋnəʔəw	'be angry'
xáləyəw	xáləyəw	'fall'

McCarthy and Prince (1991) propose to assign the habilitative template the struc-ture presumed to hold for a proparoxytone ('σσ)⟨σ⟩ under an antepenultimate stress rule such as in Latin or Macedonian. In this structure the extrametrical syllable is daughter to the prosodic word.

(54)

One consequence of this move is that the prosodic hierarchy is no longer strictly layered such that each higher-level unit is composed exclusively of elements drawn from the adjacent level in the hierarchy: (54) allows the PrWd to imme-diately dominate Foot as well as Syllable. McCarthy and Prince refer to this option as the *loose interpretation* of the notion "hierarchy" – a kind of adjunction that perhaps can be restricted to the edge of some larger domain. If we grant this move, then the template for the Cupeño habilitative can be characterized as arising from minimizing the PrWd through selection of a QI F+σ – that is, the PrWd "loosely" interpreted.

In Cupeño this template is filled through circumscription of a final foot followed by an edge-in mapping of the consonants and spreading of the vowels. Empty onsets are realized with a glottal stop. For example, *kəláʔaʔaw* receives the deri-vation sketched in (55).

(55) kə[láw] → [law] → l a w → l a ʔ a ʔ a w → kəláʔaʔaw

Loose interpretation of PrWd accommodates, at least in part, Itô's analysis of the Japanese truncation data discussed earlier.

(56)   LL   HL
      [opereešoN]   →   ope   [saikederikku]   →   saike
        'operation'   'psychedelic'

                              LL   LH   LLL
      [rokeešoN]   →   roke *rokee   [animeešoN]   →   anime
        'location'   'animation'

Recall that under Itô's analysis, the truncation template must satisfy both a bi-moraic and a disyllabic minimum. The latter explains why an initial heavy syllable such as *saikederikku* does not reduce to *sai*. Prince (1990) sees the truncation as targeting a trochaic foot; it cannot be iambic since it shuns *rokee* in favor of *roke*. On this view, *saike* receives the analysis in (57a). But the option of loose interpretation of the prosodic word allows for an alternative analysis (57b) (de-scriptively equivalent to the prosodic stem + suffix proposed by Itô).

(57)   a.   saike   b.   saike   c.   heriko

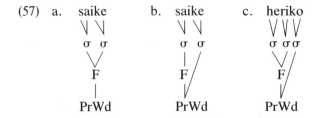

The choice between the two turns on the status of the unbalanced HL trochee. If the typology of (45) is constructed so as to exclude this foot, then (57b) is a better analysis than (57a). It is also supported by the existence of such trisyllabic truncations as *herikoputaa* → *heriko*. Like the Cupeño habilitative, such a struc-ture is beyond the ken of a simple foot and demands the loose interpretation of PrWd as F + σ (57c).

In these adjoined structures, the added syllable must be light in a QS system such as Japanese: F + L. This explains the vowel shortening in [animeešoN] → *anime* (58a). Turning to [demoNsutoreešoN] → *demo*, *demoN*, consider the possible expansions of the PrWd category in (58b,c,d).

(58)   a.   a n i m e   b.   d e m o N   c.   d e m o N   d.   d e m o N

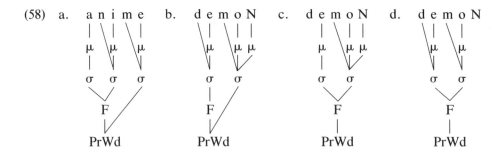

(58b) is ruled out since the foot is subminimal and the adjoined element is too heavy. (58c) is a well-formed foot, but only as an iamb. We can exclude it if we

set the QS option to trochaic – a rhythm that is independently motivated by the accent (Watanabe 1991). Only (58d) is well formed: the first two moras form a (LL) bimoraic foot that falls within the trochaic genus. In sum, the Japanese truncation can be generated by calling for a PrWd template that is minimally satisfied and loosely interpreted with the foot genus set to trochaic and the species to [max σ, min μ]. It is, however, unclear exactly how to extend this analysis to the case of four-mora truncations such as *rihabiri*(teešoN) 'rehabilitation).

11.4.4 Reduplication: Refinements

Several well-attested patterns of reduplication are not accommodated by the template typology of (45). One, misleadingly dubbed the "core syllable" template in McCarthy and Prince 1986, consists of a monomoraic light syllable with a mono-consonantal onset. An example is furnished by the perfect in Sanskrit (data from Steriade 1988b).

(59)

root	perfect		
pat	pa-pát-a	'fly, fall'	
prath	pa-práth-a*	'spread'	
kṣad	ka-kṣád-a*	'divide'	(cakṣáda)
mna:	ma-mná:-u	'note'	

Recall from section 6.5 that the root-initial clusters in (59) are core onsets in Sanskrit and thus are assigned at the initial stage of syllabification. In the prosodic morphology theory of McCarthy and Prince, templates can only be discriminated in terms of their moraic structure. Since onset material is nonmoraic by assumption, templates cannot distinguish onset positions. The fact that only a single consonant maps to the onset in (59) must consequently be explained on other grounds. McCarthy and Prince hypothesize that such onset simplification will follow from independently motivated restrictions on the syllabic structure of prefixes or affixes in the individual languages. Since it is well known that affixes often have a simpler syllabic and segmental structure in comparison to roots, this conjecture is attractive. The fact that Sanskrit has two other reduplication templates and that both also show the reduction to monoconsonantal onsets bolsters this escape from the problem raised by this reduplication type.

Another problem is posed by reduplication patterns that appear to skip word-initial syllables that begin with a vowel. The Orokaiva data discussed earlier and repeated in (60) illustrate this phenomenon.

(60)

waeke	wawaeke	'shut'
hirike	hihirike	'open'
tiuke	titiuke	'cut'
uhuke	uhuhuke	'blow'
indi	indidike	'eat'

A consonant-initial word such as *waeke* reduplicates the first syllable, but vowel-initial *uhuke* doubles the second syllable. While an analysis negatively circumscribing vowel-initial syllables could be developed, a rule singling out onsetless syllables is not particularly attractive. McCarthy and Prince (1991) suggest an alternative that more fully utilizes the descriptive resources of their theory. The proposal is that at the stage of the derivation where reduplication is defined, languages such as Orokaiva require syllables to contain a consonantal onset. Instead of supplying an onset through epenthesis, these languages are assumed to delay syllabification over vowels not preceded by a consonant. Vowel-initial words thus fail to project a syllable at their left edge. Rather, the first syllable and hence higher projections of the prosodic hierarchy are only erected when a CV sequence is reached. On these assumptions, vowel-initial *uhuke* has the structure shown in (61a).

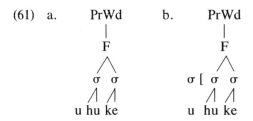

If Orokaiva reduplication is σ-prefixation to the PrWd, then from the perspective of the phonemic tier the reduplicative affix will appear infixed in such vowel-initial words as *uhuke* (61b). Admittedly, certain details in the copying and subsequent mapping of the segmental tier remain to be worked out. The viability of this solution depends on the legitimacy of the delayed prosodification of vowel-initial words – a move whose implications remain to be assessed.

Capitalizing on an observation of Steriade (1988b), McCarthy and Prince speculate that the rather heterogeneous set of descriptively attested reduplication templates can be systematized in terms of a single parameter: [±PrWd]. Steriade's observation is that a reduplication paradigm such as (62) seems to occur only in languages that do not distinguish quantity.

(62)   pa   pa-pa
       wadek   wad-wadek

If a language is quantity-sensitive in the unmarked fashion where both vowels and consonants increment weight, then *wad-wadek* results from calling for a bimoraic syllable. If templates arise from fixing the weight of a syllable, then we expect *pa:-pa* and not *pa-pa* from the $[\sigma_\mu]$ affix. The upshot is that the reduplicative template underlying the paradigm in (62) is ambiguous with respect to whether or not it realizes $[\sigma_\mu]$ or $[\sigma_{\mu\mu}]$ (in a QI language we cannot tell). However, in a QS language the heavy syllable template $[\sigma_{\mu\mu}]$ can be interpreted as a particular expansion of the PrWd, minimally satisfied.

Given this refinement (plus others discussed in this section), McCarthy and Prince reduce the full gamut of reduplication templates to three types: the heavy syllable (= PrWd), the light syllable, and the complementary syllable (see below).

To illustrate the first two, let us return to the Ilokano plural and *si* 'covered with' construction.

(63) a. pusa   pus-pusa   'cat'
           kaldiŋ   kal-kaldiŋ   'goat'

      b. buneŋ   si-bu-buneŋ   'carrying a buneng'
           pandiliŋ   si-pa-pandiliŋ 'wearing a skirt'

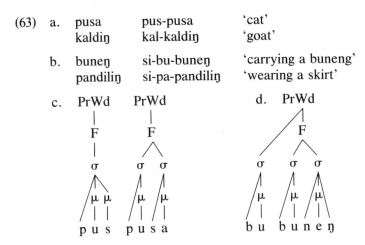

The former is said to produce structures of the form PrWd + PrWd and represents a kind of external morphology in which the PrWd is compounded with itself (63c). If this structure is accepted, it is then natural to view the light syllable template (interpreted now as [−PrWd]) as a simple affix because it is too small to stand alone as a prosodic word (63d). The putative compound versus affixational distinction implied in this analysis awaits independent confirmation. It can be tested by seeing the extent to which the postulated structures mimic simple nonreduplicative compounding versus affixation in the individual languages. We will return to this point momentarily.

    A third, less attested reduplication type appears in McCarthy and Prince's (1986) analysis of a construction in Ponapean, where the prosodic shape of the template varies as a function of the weight of the base. With monosyllabic bases, the reduplicative prefix has complementary weight, appearing as a bimoraic heavy syllable when the base has a short vowel (64a) and as a monomoraic light syllable when the base has a bimoraic heavy syllable (64b) (final consonants are extrametrical).

(64) a. pa   paa-pa   'weave'
          lal   lal-lal   'make a sound'
          pap   pam-pap   'swim'

      b. duup   du-duup   'dive'
          laud   la-laud   'big, old'
          mand ma-mand 'tame'

To account for this case, McCarthy and Prince assume that the system tries to maximize the weight of the prefixal syllable but that the result is constrained in such a way that the prefix + base must constitute a minimal word, that is, satisfy the equation [prefix + base] = MinWd. This condition is said to block lengthening of the prefix in (64b) since the resultant HH sequence cannot be subsumed under a single PrWd in a QS system. Also, on this analysis the Ponapean PrWd must be interpreted "loosely" in order to subsume both the HL sequence of (64a) and the LH of (64b). (The available materials evidently do not permit the rhythm (iambic/trochaic) to be established.) In this case, then, the minimal word template functions as an output condition constraining the overall shape of the prefix-plus-base combination.

With polysyllabic bases the weight of the prefix also varies in Ponapean.

(65)	a.	dilip	din-dilip	'mend thatch'
		rere	rer-rere	'decorticate'
		li.aan	lii-li.aan	'outgoing'
	b.	tooroor	to-tooroor	'be independent'
		waantuuke	wa-waantuuke	'count'
	c.	duupek	duu-duupek	'starved'
		peese	pee-peese	'be acquainted'

McCarthy and Prince extend the analysis developed for (64) to this paradigm as well. The next category beyond the MinWd in the prosodic hierarchy is a compound of two MinWds. Maximization of the reduplicative prefix is thus constrained so that the resultant prefix + base falls within the bounds set by the equation [prefix + base] = MinWd # MinWd. To see how this works, we start from the observation that a minimal word can contain at most one heavy syllable. The prefix can thus expand to bimoraic with the bases in (65a,c) since they contain at most a single H. For example, H-LL *din-dilip* has the analysis (H)#(LL) and thus solves for MinWd # MinWd. But the bases in (65b) start with two heavy syllables. If the prefix were to expand here as well, the [prefix + base] constituent would contain three heavy syllables and the result could not be analyzed into a compound of two minimal words. But a light syllable prefix may join with the following heavy syllable to form a PrWd ("loose"). The L-HHL sequence in *wa-waantuuke* thus solves for MinWd # MinWd.

In sum, through these clever moves the "complementary" prefix found in Ponapean reduplication can also be understood as following from choosing the [+PrWd] option; but the resultant template functions as an output condition on the [prefix + base] combination rather than on the reduplication affix itself. One implication of this analysis is that *wa-waantuuke* has a prosodic structure that is incongruous with respect to the morphological structure: a major prosodic break occurs in the middle of the root morpheme. A basic question this kind of analysis raises is whether there is independent evidence to support this type of mismatch.

To get an idea of the kind of evidence that we might expect to support such a structure, let us return to Yidin^y. Recall from section 10.9 that this language parses the word into binary feet from left to right. A final orphan (degenerate foot or unparsed syllable) triggers penultimate lengthening and suffers apocope under the appropriate segmental conditions. Finally, an iambic, right-headed stress is imposed across the word if a long vowel occupies the second position in a binary foot; trochaic, left-headed stress is assigned otherwise.

Dixon (1977b) divides the affixes of Yidin^y into a cohering and a noncohering class. The transitive verbalizing suffix [ŋa + 1] belongs to the former and the intransitive verbalizer [daga] to the latter. The past tense paradigms in (66) illustrate the phonological effects of this classification.

(66)

adjective		derived verb			
milba	'clever'	[milba + ŋa + 1 + ñu]	→	milba-ŋa-l-ñu	'made clever'
guma:ṛi	'red'	[gumaṛi + ŋa + 1 + ñu]	→	gumaṛi-ŋa:-l	'made red'
gad^{y}u:l	'dirty'	[gad^{y}ulA + ŋa + 1 + ñu]	→	gad^{y}ula-ŋa:-l	'made dirty'

The first parses as (milba)(ŋalñu) and the second as (guma)(ṛiŋal)(ñu). The latter then undergoes penultimate lengthening and apocope plus final cluster simplification.

Now consider the paradigm constructed from the same roots with a noncohering suffix.

(67)

milba	[milba + daga + ñu]	→	milba-daga:-ñ	'became clever'
guma:ṛi	[gumaṛi + daga + ñu]	→	guma:ṛi-daga:-ñ	'became red'
gad^{y}u:l	[gad^{y}ulA + daga + ñu]	→	gad^{y}u:l-daga:-ñ	'became dirty'

We note two differences. First, [daga] has a constant shape regardless of the number of syllables that precede. Second, the trisyllabic stems [gumaṛi] and [gad^{y}ulA] show penultimate lengthening (and apocope of the A morphophoneme). As Dixon demonstrates, both anomalies are explained if the morphological word is broken down into two phonological words: [milba#daga + ñu] and [gumaṛi#daga + ñu]. On this analysis, the derivations in (68) ensue.

(68)

[milba#daga + ñu]	[gumaṛi#daga + ñu]	
(milba)(daga)(ñu)	(guma)(ṛi)(daga)(ñu)	metrical parse
(milba)(daga:)(ñu)	(guma:)(ṛi)(daga:)(ñu)	penultimate length
milbadaga:ñ	guma:ṛidaga:ñ	apocope

The medial phonological word boundary is also supported by stress. For example, [waŋal#gimbal + du] 'boomerang'-'without'-ergative is realized *wáŋal#gimbá: ldu*. The penultimately lengthened vowel induces iambic stress. But this stress rhythm is not transmitted to the initial part of the string, where [wáŋal] is realized with trochaic stress. In general, each phonemic stretch separated by the # symbol is metrified independently of the others.

It turns out that the classification into cohering and noncohering affixes is phonologically based. Cohering suffixes are all monosyllabic, while noncohering ones are disyllabic. Furthermore, each type is dispersed among the inflectional and derivational classes and can thus be concatenated, ruling out a level-ordering solution in which cohering suffixes precede noncohering ones. Expressed in McCarthy and Prince's terms, [milba + ŋa + 1 + ñu] and [milba#daga + ñu] have the structure in (69).

(69)

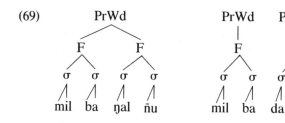

There are various options with respect to how these structures are assigned. We might stipulate that all disyllabic suffixes start with a prosodic word boundary. This solution is unsatisfactory since it fails to capture the generalization that the placement of the boundary is predictable. If the boundary is inserted by rule, then the rule must count (at least up to two). But a basic assumption of metrical phonology has been that all counting is done via the metrification process itself. Furthermore, inserting a boundary presupposes that various pieces of the prosodic structure can be referred to before the entire structure is erected – a basic premise of Idsardi's theory (section 10.11). Another analysis has been developed by Hewitt (1992), who proposes a parameter of "vertical maximization" that allows higher levels of prosodic structure to be erected before lower levels of the prosodic hierarchy have been extended across the phonemic string. Applied to Yidin^y, this means that as soon as the first two syllables of a word are parsed into a foot, the [+VMax] option allows the grammar to impose a PrWd. Further assumptions are that foot construction in Yidin^y is cyclic and noniterative, each cycle forming a separate metrical domain. Given strict binarity, a foot and, under the [+VMax] setting, a PrWd will be assigned at the left of any disyllabic cyclic domain. Thus [gumaṛi + daga + ñu] parses as {guma}ṛi on the first cycle, {guma}ṛi{daga} on the second, and {guma}ṛi{daga}ñu on the third (where braces mark PrWds). Monosyllabic suffixes will fail to initiate a foot because they are too small. [gumaṛi + ŋal + ñu] parses a foot and hence a PrWd on the root cycle {guma}ṛi. But subsequent cycles fail to generate a foot and hence a PrWd since they are initiated by monosyllabic affixes: {guma}ṛi → {guma}ṛiŋal → {guma}ṛiŋalñu. In the postcyclic phonology the parse is iterative and [−VMax] so the unmetrified syllables are grouped with the PrWd on their left.

For our purposes here, the details of how the structures of (69) are derived are less important than the fact that Yidin^y clearly establishes the point that a morphological word may contain more than one phonological word. Phonological rules sensitive to such groupings can then be used to confirm their existence and offer a potentially rich source of evidence bearing on the higher-level prosodic structures implicated by McCarthy and Prince's theory of Prosodic Morphology.

Suggested Readings

Itô, Junko. 1990. Prosodic minimality in Japanese. Chicago Linguistic Society 26. Part II: Papers from the parasession on the syllable in phonetics and phonology, ed. by K. Deaton et al., 213–39. Chicago: Chicago Linguistic Society, University of Chicago.

Lombardi, Linda, and John McCarthy. 1991. Prosodic circumscription in Choctaw morphology. Phonology 8.37–72.

Marantz, Alec. 1982. Re reduplication. Linguistic Inquiry 13.435–82.

McCarthy, John, and Alan Prince. 1990. Foot and word in prosodic morphology: The Arabic broken plural. Natural Language & Linguistic Theory 8.209–84.

Steriade, Donca. 1988. Reduplication and syllable transfer in Sanskrit and elsewhere. Phonology 5:73–155.

Exercises

11.1 Manam (Lichtenberk 1983)

Review the analysis of Manam stress in exercise 10.2. Utilizing the tools of Prosodic Morphology theory, develop an analysis for the reduplication in the following paradigm.

(1) | | | |
|---|---|---|
| salága | salagalága | 'long' |
| moíta | moitaíta | 'knife' |
| ʔarái | ʔarairái | 'ginger species' |
| láʔo | laʔoláʔo | 'go' |
| malabóŋ | malabombóŋ | 'flying fox' |
| ʔulán | ʔulanláŋ | 'desire' |

11.2 Sanskrit (Steriade 1988b)

Specify the parameters and other assumptions required to generate the following reduplication paradigm of Sanskrit. You may ignore the infixed [i].

(1) | root | intensive (full grade) | |
|---|---|---|
| krand | kan-i-krand- | 'cry out' |
| bhranç | ban-i-bhranç- | 'fall' |
| dhvans | dhan-i-dhvans- | 'sound' |
| dyaut | dau-dyaut-* | 'shine' |

11.3 Mangarayi (Merland 1982)

Develop an analysis for the following reduplication paradigm from Mangarayi.

(1) | sg. | pl. | |
|---|---|---|
| malam | malalamji | 'men' |
| yirag | yirirag | 'fathers and children' |
| gabuji | gababuji | 'old people' |
| jimgan | jimgimgan | 'knowledgeable people' |
| waŋgij | waŋgaŋgij | 'children' |
| muygji | muygjuygji | 'having a dog' |

11.4 Ilokano (Hayes and Abad 1989)

A. In Ilokano a cyclic rule converting prevocalic nonlow vowels to glides accounts for the following alternations.

(1) | | | | |
|---|---|---|---|
| babáwi | 'to regret' | babawy-én | 'regret-goal focus' |
| masáhe | 'massage' | masahy-én | 'massage-goal focus' |
| maného | 'driver' | manehw-án | 'drive-goal focus' |

With this rule as background, develop analyses for the paradigms in (2) within the McCarthy and Prince and the Steriade models of reduplication. How can the variation be explained? Is one model able to handle the data more straightforwardly? Some constructions call for heavy syllable reduplication and others such as the ʔagin- 'pretend to' call for light syllable reduplication.

(2)   heavy syllable reduplication

bwáya	'crocodile'	na-ka-bway-bwáya	'is acting like a crocodile'
		na-ka-bu:-bwáya	
lwálo	'prayer'	ʔag-lwal-lwálo	'is praying'
		ʔag-lu:-lwálo	
pyék	'chick'	pye:-pyék, pi:-pyék	'chicks'

light syllable reduplication

kwárto	'room'	si-kwa-kwárto	'be locked up in a room'
		si-ku-kwárto	
pyár	'to trust'	ʔagin-pya-pyár	'pretend to trust'
		ʔagin-pi-pyár	
pyésta	'fiesta'	ʔagin-pye-pyésta	'pretend to be celebrating'
		ʔagin-pi-pyésta	

B.   Recalling the discussion of reduplication in section 11.1, explain why the forms in the first column of (3) are acceptable, while those in the second are not.

(3)   na-ka-bway-bwáya   *na-ka-bua-bwáya
       na-ka-bu:-bwáya   *na-ka-buy-bwáya
                                                           *na-ka-bwa:-bwáya

saŋ-sáŋit	'is crying'	*sa:-sáŋit
yáman	'grateful'	
ʔag-yam-yáman	'pretend to be grateful'	*ʔag-i:-yáman

11.5   Mayo (Hagberg 1989)

In Mayo words fall into two classes as far as stress is concerned; one class has initial stress while the other stresses the second syllable. Class membership is apparently unpredictable. Suggest an analysis for the reduplication. Show how your analysis works by deriving *n'ok-nokwa*, *n'on-noka*, and *nok-n'oka*.

(1)
stem	reduplicated	
n'okwa	n'ok-nokwa	'known language'
w'attiawa	w'at-wattiawa	'put' coll.
b'uyte	b'uy-buyte	'run'
n'oka	n'on-noka	'know language'
y'uke	y'uy-yuke	'rain'
h'ima	h'ih-hima	'throw'
nok'a	nok-n'oka	'speak'
ban'a	ban-b'ana	'cry'
sim'e	sim-s'ime	'go'

11.6 Ulwa

Recall the discussion of Ulwa (section 11.2), where we find paradigms such as the following.

(1) base   construct state
     s'uula   s'uu-ka-la   'dog'
     siw'anak   siw'a-ka-nak   'root'
     an'aalaaka   an'aa-ka-laaka   'chin'

Following McCarthy and Prince, we treated this infixation of -*ka* as suffixation to a prosodically circumscribed iambic foot (= MinWd). However, we might entertain the following alternative analysis: "Insert -*ka* after the stressed syllable." Explore the theoretical consequences of such an alternative. Does it permit situations that the circumscription analysis excludes?

11.7 Koasati (Kimball 1988)

Kimball distinguishes two types of reduplication in the Muskogean language Koasati. Using the notion of circumscription, develop an analysis for each type. Discuss the analysis in terms of the McCarthy and Prince theory. Which aspects of their theory are supported by your analysis? Which (if any) are not?

(1) base   iterative
     cikáplin   cikakáplin   'to glitter'
     wacíplin   wacicíplin   'to feel a stabbing pain'
     watóhlin   watotóhlin   'to clabber'
     haytanáhkan   haytananahká:cin   'to revolve'
     hó:pan   hohó:pan   'to hurt'

     base   punctual
     taháspin   tahastó:pin   'to be light in weight'
     lapátkin   lapatló:kin   'to be narrow'
     copóksin   copokcó:sin   'to be a hill'
     tonóhkin   tonohtó:kin   'to be round'
     cofóknan   cofokcó:nan   'to be angled'

     aklátlin   akholátlin   'to be loose'
     okcáyyam   okhocáyyam   'to be alive'
     okcákkon   okhocákkon   'to be green or blue'

11.8 Axininca (Spring 1990)

In Axininca, an Arawakan language of Peru, the genitive morpheme has the allomorphs -*ni* and -*ti*. State the rule for their distribution. Is one better treated as the default, elsewhere case? Why? The language also has a general rule shortening word-final long vowels that is evident in some of the data in (1). Can this phenomenon be connected to the allomorphy rule?

(1)

noun	'my noun'	
cʰimi	no-cʰimi-ni	'water hole'
sima	no-sima-ni	'fish'
mapi	no-mapi-ni	'rock'
cʰiŋki	no-cʰiŋki-ni	'eel'
mii	no-mii-ni	'otter'
soo	no-soo-ni	'sloth'
itʰo	n-itʰo-ni	'swallow'
cʰimi	no-cʰimii-ti	'ant'
sampa	no-sampaa-ti	'balsa'
sawo	no-sawoo-ti	'cane'
maini	no-maini-ti	'bear'
airi	n-airi-ti	'bee'
cokori	no-cokori-ti	'armadillo'
tʰoŋkiri	no-tʰoŋkiri-ti	'hummingbird'
manaawawo	no-manaawawo-ti	'turtle'
cʰiriwito	no-cʰiriwito-ti	'kingfisher'

11.9 Japanese

Suggest a way to rule out the following analyses of ill-formed Japanese truncations.

(1) [demoNsutoreešoN] → *demoN   [rokeešoN] → *roke

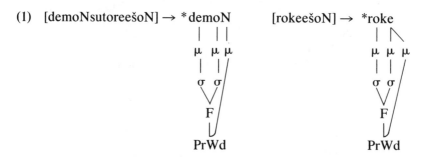

11.10 Yidinʸ (Dixon 1977b)

Extend the analysis developed in the text (section 11.4.4) to the following paradigm. Show how it works by deriving 'was going to run'.

(1)

dʸuŋga-n	'run'	dʸadʸama-n	'jump'
dʸuŋga:-ñ	'ran'	dʸadʸama-ñu	'jumped'
dʸuŋga-ŋal-ñu	'made run'	dʸadʸama-ŋa:l	'made jump'
dʸúŋga-ŋalí:-ñ	'was going to run'	dʸadʸa:ma-ŋali:-ñ	'was going to jump'

References

Abu-Salim, Issam. 1980. Epenthesis and geminate consonants in Palestinian Arabic. Studies in the Linguistic Sciences 10,2.1–11.

Akinlabi, Akinbiyi. 1984. Tonal underspecification and Yoruba tone. University of Ibadan ms.

Alfonso, P., K. Honda, T. Baer, and K. Harris. 1982. Multi-channel study of tongue EMG during vowel production. Paper presented at the 103rd Meeting of the Acoustical Society of America.

Alghazo, Mohammad. 1987. Syncope and epenthesis in Levantine Arabic: A nonlinear approach. Urbana: University of Illinois Ph.D. dissertation.

Alho, Irja. 1987. Finnish vowel harmony. Urbana: University of Illinois ms.

Allen, W. Sidney. 1973. Accent and rhythm. Cambridge: Cambridge University Press.

Al-Mozainy, Hamza. 1982. The phonology of a Bedouin Hijazi dialect. Austin: University of Texas Ph.D. dissertation.

Al-Mozainy, Hamza, Robert Bley-Vroman, and John McCarthy. 1985. Stress shift and metrical structure. Linguistic Inquiry 16.135–44.

Anderson, John, and Colin Ewen. 1987. Principles of dependency phonology. Cambridge: Cambridge University Press.

Anderson, Stephen. 1969. West Scandinavian vowel systems and the ordering of phonological rules. Cambridge, Mass.: MIT Ph.D. dissertation.

Anderson, Stephen. 1972. The Faroese vowel system. Contributions to generative phonology, ed. by M. Brame, 1–21. Austin: University of Texas Press.

Anderson, Stephen. 1974. The organization of phonology. New York: Academic Press.

Anderson, Stephen. 1976a. Nasal consonants and the internal structure of segments. Language 52.326–44.

Anderson, Stephen. 1976b. On the description of consonant gradation in Fula. Studies in African Linguistics 7.93–136.

Anderson, Stephen. 1985. Phonology in the twentieth century. Chicago: University of Chicago Press.

Archangeli, Diana. 1983. The root CV template as a property of the affix: Evidence from Yawelmani. Natural Language & Linguistic Theory 1.347–84.

Archangeli, Diana. 1984. Underspecification in Yawelmani phonology and morphology. Cambridge, Mass.: MIT Ph.D. dissertation. Published by Garland Press, New York, 1988.

Archangeli, Diana. 1988. Aspects of underspecification theory. Phonology 5.183–208.

Archangeli, Diana. 1991. Syllabification and prosodic templates. Natural Language & Linguistic Theory 9.231–83.

Archangeli, Diana, and Douglas Pulleyblank. 1993. Grounded phonology. Cambridge, Mass.: MIT Press.

Armstrong, Robert. 1968. Yala (Ikom): A terraced-level language with three tones. Journal of West African Languages 5.41–50.

Aronoff, Mark. 1976. Word formation in generative grammar. Cambridge, Mass.: MIT Press.

Avery, Peter, and Keren Rice. 1989a. Constraining underspecification. In Proceedings of NELS 19, 1–15. Amherst: GLSA, University of Massachusetts.

Avery, Peter, and Keren Rice. 1989b. On the interaction between sonorancy and voicing. Paper presented at meeting of the Canadian Linguistic Association, Laval University.

Bagemihl, Bruce. 1991. Syllable structure in Bella Coola. Linguistic Inquiry 22.589–646.

Bao, Zhiming. 1990. On the nature of tone. Cambridge, Mass.: MIT Ph.D. dissertation.

Bao, Zhiming. 1991. Tone and the geometry of laryngeal features. Madison: University of Wisconsin ms.

Barkaï, M. 1974. On duration and spirantization in Biblical Hebrew. Linguistic Inquiry 5.456–9.

Barker, M. A. R. 1964. Klamath grammar. Berkeley: University of California Press.

Bell, Alan. 1977. Accent placement and perception of prominence in rhythmic structures. Studies in stress and accent, ed. by L. Hyman, 1–14. (Southern California Occasional Papers in Linguistics 4.) Los Angeles: University of Southern California.

Bethin, Christina. 1978. Phonological rules in the nominative singular and genitive plural of the Slavic substantive declension. Urbana: University of Illinois Ph.D. dissertation.

Bhatt, Rakesh. 1989. Syllable weight and metrical structure of Kashmiri. Urbana: University of Illinois ms.

Bloomfield, Leonard. 1925. On the sound system of Central Algonquian. Language 1.130–56.

Bloomfield, Leonard. 1928. A note on sound change. Language 4.99–100.

Bloomfield, Leonard. 1930. German ç and x. Le Maître Phonétique III 20.27–8.

Bloomfield, Leonard. 1946. Algonquian. Linguistic structures of native America, ed. by H. Hojer et al., 85–129. (Viking Fund Publications in Anthropology 6.) New York: Viking Fund.

Boas, Franz. 1947. Kwakiutl grammar with a glossary of the suffixes. (Transactions of the American Philosophical Society, ns. 37,3.) Philadelphia: American Philosophical Society.

Booij, Geert, and Jerzy Rubach. 1984. Morphological and prosodic domains in lexical phonology. Phonology Yearbook 1.1–27.

Booij, Geert, and Jerzy Rubach. 1987. Postcyclic versus postlexical rules in lexical phonology. Linguistic Inquiry 18.1–44.

Borowsky, Toni. 1985. Empty and unspecified segments. Proceedings of the West Coast Conference on Formal Linguistics 4, 46–57. Stanford, Calif.: Stanford Linguistics Association, Stanford University.

Borowsky, Toni. 1986. Topics in the lexical phonology of English. Amherst: University of Massachusetts Ph.D. dissertation. Published by Garland Press, New York, 1990.

Borowsky, Toni. 1989. Structure preservation and the syllable coda in English. Natural Language & Linguistic Theory 7.145–66.

Borowsky, Toni. 1992. On the word-level. To appear in Studies in lexical phonology, ed. by S. Hargus and E. Kaisse. San Diego, Calif.: Academic Press.

Boxwell, H., and M. Boxwell. 1966. Weri phonemes. Papers in New Guinea Linguistics no. 5, ed. by S. Wurm, 77–93. Canberra: Australian National University.

Brame, Michael. 1970. Arabic phonology: Implications for phonological theory and historical Semitic. Cambridge, Mass.: MIT Ph.D. dissertation.

Bright, William. 1957. The Karok language. (University of California Publications in Linguistics 13.) Berkeley: University of California Press.

Bright, William. 1972. The enunciative vowel. International Journal of Dravidian Linguistics 1,1.26–55.

Bromberger, Sylvain, and Morris Halle. 1989. Why phonology is different. Linguistic Inquiry 20.51–70.

Broselow, Ellen. 1982. On predicting the interaction of stress and epenthesis. Glossa 16.115–32.

Broselow, Ellen, and Alice Niyondagara. 1989. Morphological structure and Kirundi palatalization: Implications for feature geometry. To appear in Studies in interlacustrine Bantu phonology, ed. by F. Katamba. Cologne: Afrikanistische Arbeitspapier.

Browman, Catherine, and Louis Goldstein. 1989. Articulatory gestures as phonological units. Phonology 6.201–51.

Buck, Carl D. 1933. Comparative grammar of Greek and Latin. Chicago: University of Chicago Press.

Burling, Robbins. 1966. The addition of final stops in the history of Maru. Language 42.581–6.

Burzio, Luigi. 1988. English stress. Certamen phonologicum. Papers from the 1987 Cortona Phonology Meeting, ed. by P. M. Bertinetto and M. Loporcaro, 63–76. Turin: Rosenberg & Sellier.

Calabrese, Andrea. 1984. Metaphony in Salentino. Rivista di Grammatica Generativa 9–10.1–140.

Calabrese, Andrea. 1988. Towards a theory of phonological alphabets. Cambridge, Mass.: MIT Ph.D. dissertation.

Calabrese, Andrea. 1992. On palatalization processes: An inquiry about the nature of a sound change. Cambridge, Mass.: Harvard University ms.

Carreira, Maria. 1988. The representation of diphthongs in Spanish. Studies in the Linguistic Sciences 18,1.1–24.

Cassimjee, Farida. 1983. An autosegmental analysis of Venda nominal tonology. Studies in the Linguistic Sciences 13,1.43–72.

Cassimjee, Farida. 1987. An autosegmental analysis of Venda tonology. Urbana: University of Illinois Ph.D. dissertation. Published by Garland Press, New York, 1990.

Chambers, J. 1973. Canadian raising. Canadian Journal of Linguistics 18.113–35.

Chang, Kun, and Betty Shefts Chang. 1968. Vowel harmony in spoken Lhasa Tibetan. Project on Linguistic Analysis. Reports, second series, no. 7, 1–81. Berkeley: Phonology Laboratory, Department of Linguistics, University of California.

Chao, Yuan-ren. 1930. A system of tone letters. Le Maître Phonétique 45.24–47.

Charette, Monik. 1991. Conditions on phonological government. Cambridge: Cambridge University Press.

Chen, Matthew. 1985. Tianjin tone sandhi: Erratic rule application. San Diego: University of California ms.

Chen, Matthew. 1987. The syntax of Xiamen tone sandhi. Phonology Yearbook 4.109–49.

Chen, Matthew. 1991. An overview of tone sandhi phenomena across Chinese dialects. Languages and dialects of China, ed. by W. Wang, 113–58. Journal of Chinese Linguistics, monograph series no. 3.

Cheng, Chin-Chuan, and Charles Kisseberth. 1979. Ikorovere Makua tonology (part 1). Studies in the Linguistic Sciences 9,1.31–63.

Cheng, Chin-Chuan, and Charles Kisseberth. 1980. Ikorovere Makua tonology (part 2). Studies in the Linguistic Sciences 10,1.15–44.

Cheng, Chin-Chuan, and Charles Kisseberth. 1981. Ikorovere Makua tonology (part 3). Studies in the Linguistic Sciences 11,1.181–202.

Cheng, Lisa. 1989. Feature geometry of vowels and co-occurrence restrictions in Cantonese. Cambridge, Mass.: MIT ms.

Chiba, T., and J. Kajiyama. 1941. The vowel: Its nature and structure. Tokyo: Tokyo Kaiseikan Publishing Company.

Chierchia, Gennaro. 1986. Length, syllabification and the phonological cycle in Italian. Journal of Italian Linguistics 8.5–34.

Chomsky, Noam. 1973. Conditions on transformations. A festschrift for Morris Halle, ed. by S. Anderson and P. Kiparsky, 232–86. New York: Holt, Rinehart and Winston.

Chomsky, Noam. 1986. Knowledge of language: Its nature, origin, and use. New York: Praeger.

Chomsky, Noam, and Morris Halle. 1968. The sound pattern of English. New York: Harper & Row.

Chomsky, Noam, Morris Halle, and Fred Lukoff. 1956. On accent and juncture in English. For Roman Jakobson, ed. by Morris Halle et al., 65–80. The Hague: Mouton.

Christdas, Prathima. 1988. The phonology and morphology of Tamil. Ithaca, N.Y.: Cornell University Ph.D. dissertation.

Clark, John, and Colin Yallop. 1990. An introduction to phonetics and phonology. Oxford: Blackwell Publishers.

Clements, George N. 1978. Tone and syntax in Ewe. Elements of stress, tone, and intonation, ed. by D. J. Napoli, 21–99. Washington, D.C.: Georgetown University Press.

Clements, George N. 1979. The description of terraced-level tone languages. Language 55.536–58.

Clements, George N. 1980. Vowel harmony in nonlinear generative phonology. Bloomington: Indiana University Linguistics Club.

Clements, George N. 1985a. The geometry of phonological features. Phonology Yearbook 2.225–52.

Clements, George N. 1985b. Akan vowel harmony: A nonlinear analysis. African linguistics: Essays in memory of M. W. K. Semikenke, ed. by D. Goyvaerts, 55–98. Amsterdam: Benjamins.

Clements, George N. 1985c. The problem of transfer in nonlinear phonology. Working papers in linguistics 5, 38–73. Ithaca, N.Y.: Cornell University.

Clements, George N. 1986. Syllabification and epenthesis in the Barra dialect of Gaelic. The phonological representation of suprasegmentals, ed. by K. Bogers et al., 317–36. Dordrecht: Foris.

Clements, George N. 1987. Phonological feature representation and the description of intrusive stops. Papers from the Twenty-third Meeting, Chicago Linguistic Society, vol. 2, 29–50. Chicago: Chicago Linguistic Society, University of Chicago.

Clements, George N. 1990. The role of the sonority cycle in core syllabification. Papers in laboratory phonology 1: Between the grammar and physics of speech, ed. by J. Kingston and M. Beckman, 283–333. Cambridge: Cambridge University Press.

Clements, George N. 1991a. Place of articulation in consonants and vowels: A unified theory. Working papers of the Cornell Phonetics Laboratory 5, 77–123. Ithaca, N.Y.: Cornell University.

Clements, George N. 1991b. Vowel height assimilation in Bantu languages. Working papers of the Cornell Phonetics Laboratory 5, 37–76. Ithaca, N.Y.: Cornell University.

Clements, George N., and Kevin Ford. 1979. Kikuyu tone shift and its synchronic consequences. Linguistic Inquiry 10.179–210.

Clements, George N., and Samuel Jay Keyser. 1983. CV phonology: A generative theory of the syllable. Cambridge, Mass.: MIT Press.

Clements, George N., and Engin Sezer. 1982. Vowel and consonant disharmony in Turkish. The structure of phonological representations (part II), ed. by H. van der Hulst and N. Smith, 213–55. Dordrecht: Foris.

Clivio, Gianrenzo. 1971. Vocalic prothesis, schwa-deletion and morphophonemics in Piedmontese. Zeitschrift für Romanische Philologie 87.334–44.

Cohn, Abigail. 1989. Stress in Indonesian and bracketing paradoxes. Natural Language & Linguistic Theory 7.167–216.

Cohn, Abigail. 1990. Phonetic and phonological rules of nasalization. (Working Papers in Phonetics 76.) Los Angeles: University of California.

Cook, Eung-Do. 1987. An autosegmental analysis of Chilcotin flattening. Papers from the Twenty-third Regional Meeting, Chicago Linguistic Society, vol. 2, 51–65. Chicago: Chicago Linguistic Society, University of Chicago.

Coupez, A. 1969. Une leçon de linguistique. Africa-Tervuren 15.33–7. Musée Royal de l'Afrique Centrale.

Cowan, William. 1972. Workbook in historical linguistics. New York: Holt, Rinehart and Winston.

Davis, Stuart. 1991. Coronals and the phonotactics of nonadjacent consonants in English. In Paradis and Prunet 1991, 49–60.

Delattre, Pierre. 1971. Pharyngeal features in the consonants of Arabic, German, Spanish, French, and American English. Phonetica 23.129–55.

Delattre, Pierre, Alvin Liberman, and Franklin Cooper. 1955. Acoustic loci and transitional cues for consonants. Journal of the Acoustical Society of America 27.769–73.

Dell, François, and Mohamed Elmedlaoui. 1985. Syllabic consonants and syllabification in Imdlawn Tashlhiyt Berber. Journal of African Languages and Linguistics 7.105–30.

Dell, François, and Oufae Tangi. 1991a. Syllabification and empty nuclei in Ath-Sidhar Rifian Berber. Paris: Centre National de la Recherche Scientifique ms.

Dell, François, and Oufae Tangi. 1991b. Partially syllabified representations: Evidence from Ath-Sidhar Rifian Berber. Paris: Centre National de la Recherche Scientifique ms.

Demers, Richard, and Ann Farmer. 1991. A linguistics workbook. Cambridge, Mass.: MIT Press.

de Rijk, Rudolf. 1970. Vowel interactions in Bizcayan Basque. Fontes Linguae Vasconum 2,5.149–67.

Dixon, Robert. 1972. The Djirbal language of North Queensland. Cambridge: Cambridge University Press.

Dixon, Robert. 1977a. A grammar of Yidiny. Cambridge: Cambridge University Press.

Dixon, Robert. 1977b. Some phonological rules in Yidiny. Linguistic Inquiry 8.1–34.

Dixon, Robert. 1988. A grammar of Boumaa Fijian. Chicago: University of Chicago Press.

Doke, Clement. 1931. A comparative study of Shona phonetics. Johannesburg: University of Witwatersrand Press.

Downing, Laura. 1988. Local and metrical tone shift in Zulu and Xhosa. Paper presented at the annual meeting of the Linguistic Society of America, New Orleans, December 1988.

Dresher, Elan, and Aditi Lahiri. 1991. The Germanic foot: Metrical coherence in Old English. Linguistic Inquiry 22.251–86.

Duanmu, San. 1990. A formal study of syllable, tone, stress, and domain in Chinese languages. Cambridge, Mass.: MIT Ph.D. dissertation.

Dudas, Karen. 1972. The accentuation of Lithuanian derived nominals. Studies in the Linguistic Sciences 2,2.103–36.

Durand, Jacques. 1987. On the phonological status of glides: The evidence from Malay. Explorations in dependency phonology, ed. by J. Anderson and J. Durand, 79–108. Dordrecht: Foris.

Durand, Jacques. 1990. Generative and nonlinear phonology. London: Longmans.

Echeveria, Max, and Heles Contreras. 1965. Araucanian phonemics. International Journal of American Linguistics 31.132–5.

Eimas, P., E. Siqueland, P. Jusczyk, and J. Vigorito. 1971. Speech perception in infants. Science 171.303–6.

Elmedlaoui, Mohamed. 1992. Aspects des representations phonologiques dans certains langues chamito-semitiques. Thèse de Doctorat d'Etat. Rabat: Université Mohammed V.

Ewen, Colin. 1982. The internal structure of complex segments. The structure of phonological representations (part II), ed. by H. van der Hulst and N. Smith, 27–68. Dordrecht: Foris.

Fabb, Nigel. 1988. English suffixation is constrained only by selectional restrictions. Natural Language & Linguistic Theory 6.527–39.

Feinstein, Mark. 1979. Prenasalization and syllable structure. Linguistic Inquiry 10.243–78.

Franks, Steven. 1983. Stress in Polish and Macedonian. Ithaca, N.Y.: Cornell University ms.

Fudge, Eric. 1969. Syllables. Journal of Linguistics 5.253–87.

Geary, James. 1941. Proto-Algonquian *çk: Further examples. Language 17.304–10.

Ghazeli, Salem. 1977. Back consonants and backing coarticulation in Arabic. Austin: University of Texas Ph.D. dissertation.

Gleason, Henry. 1961. An introduction to descriptive linguistics. New York: Holt, Rinehart and Winston.

Goddard, Ives. 1974. An outline of the historical phonology of Arapaho and Atsina. International Journal of American Linguistics 40.102–16.

Goddard, Ives. 1979. Comparative Algonquian. The languages of North America, ed. by L. Campbell and M. Mithun, 70–132. Austin: University of Texas Press.

Goldsmith, John. 1976 Autosegmental phonology. Cambridge, Mass.: MIT Ph.D. dissertation. Distributed by Indiana University Linguistics Club. Published by Garland Press, New York, 1979.

Goldsmith, John. 1990. Autosegmental and metrical phonology. Oxford: Blackwell Publishers.

Goldsmith, John. 1993. Harmonic phonology. To appear in the last phonological rule: Reflections on constraints and derivations, ed. by J. Goldsmith. Chicago: University of Chicago Press.

Goldsmith, John, and Gary Larson. 1990. Local modeling and syllabification. Papers from the Twenty-sixth Meeting, Chicago Linguistic Society, vol. 2, 129–41. Chicago: Chicago Linguistic Society, University of Chicago.

Golston, Chris. 1990. Enclitic accent in Ancient Greek. Los Angeles: University of California ms.

Goodman, M. 1967. Prosodic features of Bravanese, a Swahili dialect. Journal of African Languages 6.278–84.

Gorecka, Alicja. 1989. Phonology of articulation. Cambridge, Mass.: MIT Ph.D. dissertation.

Gorecka, Alicja. 1992. The matter of two high front rounded vowels and the feature theory. Paper presented at West Coast Conference on Formal Linguistics 9.

Green, Thomas. 1992. Notes on the morphophonology of Ulwa. Cambridge, Mass.: MIT ms.

Greenberg, Joseph. 1948. The tonal system of proto-Bantu. Word 4.196–208.

Greenberg, Joseph. 1950. The patterning of root morphemes in Semitic. Word 6.162–81.

Greenberg, Joseph. 1978. Universals of language. Vol. 2: Phonology. Stanford, Calif.: Stanford University Press.

Guerssel, Mohamed. 1977. Constraints on phonological rules. Linguistic Analysis 3.267–305.

Guerssel, Mohamed. 1978. A condition on assimilation rules. Linguistic Analysis 4.225–54.

Guerssel, Mohamed. 1986. Glides in Berber and syllabicity. Linguistic Inquiry 17.1–12.

Gussmann, Edmund. 1985. The morphology of a phonological rule: Icelandic vowel length. Phono-morphology, ed. E. Gussmann, 75–94. Lublin: Redakcja Wydawnictw Katolickiego Uniwersytetu Lubelskiego.

Gussmann, Edmund. 1992. Resyllabification and delinking: The case of Polish voicing. Linguistic Inquiry 23.29–56.

Haas, Mary. 1941. The classification of the Muskogean languages. Language, culture, and personality, ed. L. Spier et al., 41–56. Menasha, Wis.: Sapir Memorial Fund.

Haas, Mary. 1945. Dialects of the Muskogee language. International Journal of American Linguistics 11.69–74.

Haas, Mary. 1947. Development of Proto-Muskogean *kw. International Journal of American Linguistics 13.135–7.

Haas, Mary. 1977. Tonal accent in Creek. Studies in stress and accent, ed. by L. Hyman, 195–208. (Southern California Occasional Papers in Linguistics.) Los Angeles: University of Southern California.

Haddad, Ghassan. 1983. Problems and issues in the phonology of Lebanese Arabic. Urbana: University of Illinois Ph.D. dissertation.

Haddad, Ghassan. 1984. Epenthesis and sonority in Lebanese Arabic. Studies in the Linguistic Sciences 14,1.57–88.

Hagberg, Larry. 1989. Mayo reduplication. Tucson: University of Arizona ms.

Hale, Kenneth. 1973. Deep-surface canonical disparities in relation to analysis and change: An Australian example. Current Trends in Linguistics 11.401–58.

Hale, Kenneth, and A. Lacayo Blanco. 1988. Vocabulario preliminar del ULWA (sumu meridional). Cambridge, Mass.: Center for Cognitive Science, MIT.

Hale, Kenneth, and Josie White Eagle. 1980. A preliminary metrical account for Winnebago accent. International Journal of American Linguistics 46.117–32.

Halle, Morris. 1962. Phonology in generative grammar. Word 18.54–72.

Halle, Morris. 1978. Formal versus functional considerations in phonology. Bloomington: Indiana University Linguistics Club.

Halle, Morris. 1983. On distinctive features and their articulatory implementation. Natural Language & Linguistic Theory 1.91–105.

Halle, Morris. 1989. On stress placement and metrical structure. Papers from the Twenty-fifth Regional Meeting, Chicago Linguistic Society, 157–73. Chicago: Chicago Linguistic Society, University of Chicago.

Halle, Morris. 1990. Respecting metrical structure. Natural Language & Linguistic Theory 8.149–76.

Halle, Morris. 1992. Phonological features. International encyclopedia of linguistics, vol. 3, ed. by W. Bright, 207–12. Oxford: Oxford University Press.

Halle, Morris, James Harris, and Jean-Roger Vergnaud. 1991. The Stress Erasure Convention and cliticization in Spanish. Linguistic Inquiry 22.339–63.

Halle, Morris, and William Idsardi. 1993. General properties of stress and metrical structure. To appear in A handbook of phonological theory, ed. by J. Goldsmith. Oxford: Blackwell Publishers.

Halle, Morris, and Michael Kenstowicz. 1991. The Free Element Condition and cyclic versus noncyclic stress. Linguistic Inquiry 22.457–501.

Halle, Morris, and Kenneth Stevens. 1969. On the feature 'advanced tongue root'. Quarterly Progress Report 94, 209–15. Cambridge, Mass.: Research Laboratory of Electronics, MIT.

Halle, Morris, and Kenneth Stevens. 1971. A note on laryngeal features. Quarterly Progress Report 101, 198–212. Cambridge, Mass.: Research Laboratory of Electronics, MIT.

Halle, Morris, and Kenneth Stevens. 1991. Knowledge of language and the sounds of speech. Music, language, speech and brain, ed. by J. Sundberg et al., 1–19. London: Macmillan.

Halle, Morris, and Jean-Roger Vergnaud. 1980. Three dimensional phonology. Journal of Linguistic Research 1.83–105.

Halle, Morris, and Jean-Roger Vergnaud. 1987. An essay on stress. Cambridge, Mass.: MIT Press.

Hamid, Abdel Halim. 1984. The phonology of Sudanese Arabic. Urbana: University of Illinois Ph.D. dissertation.

Hammond, Michael. 1984. Constraining metrical theory: A modular theory of rhythm and destressing. Los Angeles: University of California Ph.D. dissertation. Distributed by Indiana University Linguistics Club. Published by Garland Press, New York, 1988.

Hansen, K., and L. Hansen. 1969. Pintupi phonology. Oceanic Linguistics 8.153–70.

Hansen, K., and L. Hansen. 1978. The core of Pintupi grammar. Alice Springs, North Territory, Australia: Institute for Aboriginal Development.

Haraguchi, Shosuke. 1984. Some tonal and segmental effects of vowel height in Japanese. Language sound structure, ed. by M. Aronoff and R. Oehrle, 145–56. Cambridge, Mass.: MIT Press.

Harms, Robert. 1968. Introduction to phonological theory. Englewood Cliffs, N.J.: Prentice-Hall.

Harris, James. 1983. Syllable structure and stress in Spanish: A nonlinear analysis. Cambridge, Mass.: MIT Press.

Harris, James. 1985a. Autosegmental phonology and liquid assimilation in Havana Spanish. Papers from the 13th Linguistic Symposium on Romance Languages, ed. by L. King and C. Maley, 127–48. Amsterdam: Benjamins.

Harris, James. 1985b. Spanish diphthongization and stress: A paradox resolved. Phonology Yearbook 2.31–45.

Harris, John. 1989. Towards a lexical analysis of sound change in progress. Journal of Linguistics. 35–56.

Harris, John. 1990. Segmental complexity and phonological government. Phonology 7.255–300.

Harris, John, and Jonathan Kaye. 1990. A tale of two cities: London glottalling and New York City tapping. The Linguistic Review 7.251–74.

Harrison, Sheldon. 1976. Mokilese reference grammar. Honolulu: University of Hawaii Press.

Hayes, Bruce. 1981. A metrical theory of stress rules. Cambridge, Mass.: MIT Ph.D. dissertation. Revised version distributed by Indiana University Linguistics Club. Published by Garland Press, New York, 1985.

Hayes, Bruce. 1982. Metrical structure as the organizing principle of Yidin^y phonology. The structure of phonological representations (part I), ed. by H. van der Hulst and N. Smith, 97–110. Dordrecht: Foris.

Hayes, Bruce. 1984. The phonology of rhythm in English. Linguistic Inquiry 15.33–74.

Hayes, Bruce. 1985. Iambic and trochaic rhythm in stress rules. Proceedings of the 13th Meeting of the Berkeley Linguistics Society, 429–46. Berkeley: Berkeley Linguistics Society, University of California.

Hayes, Bruce. 1986a. Inalterability in CV phonology. Language 62.321–51.

Hayes, Bruce. 1986b. Assimilation as spreading in Toba Batak. Linguistic Inquiry 17.467–99.

Hayes, Bruce. 1987. A revised parametric metrical theory. Proceedings of NELS 17, vol. 1, 274–89. Amherst: GLSA, University of Massachusetts.

Hayes, Bruce. 1989. Compensatory lengthening in moraic phonology. Linguistic Inquiry 20.253–306.

Hayes, Bruce. 1990. Precompiled phrasal phonology. In Inkelas and Zec 1990, 85–108.

Hayes, Bruce. 1991. Metrical stress theory: Principles and case studies. Los Angeles: University of California ms.

Hayes, Bruce, and May Abad. 1989. Reduplication and syllabification in Ilokano. Lingua 77.331–74.

Healy, Alan, Ambrose Isoroembo, and Martin Chittleborough. 1969. Preliminary notes on Orokaeva grammar. Papers in New Guinea Linguistics 9.33–64.

Herzallah, Rukayyah. 1990. Aspects of Palestinian Arabic phonology: A nonlinear approach. Ithaca, N.Y.: Cornell University Ph.D. dissertation. Working Papers of the Cornell Phonetics Laboratory, no. 4.

Hewitt, Mark. 1992. Vertical maximization and metrical theory. Waltham, Mass.: Brandeis University Ph.D. dissertation.

Hewitt, Mark, and Alan Prince. 1989. OCP, locality, and linking: The N. Karanga verb. Proceedings of the West Coast Conference on Formal Linguistics 8, 176–91. Stanford, Calif.: Stanford Linguistics Association, Stanford University.

Hill, Jane. 1970. A peeking rule in Cupeño. Linguistic Inquiry 1.534–9.

Hockett, Charles. 1948. Implications of Bloomfield's Algonquian studies. Language 24.117–31.

Hockett, Charles. 1955. A manual of phonology. International Journal of American Linguistics. Memoir 11.

Hoffman, Carl. 1963. A grammar of the Margi language. London: Oxford University Press.

Hombert, Jean-Marie. 1986. Word games: Some implications for analysis of tone and other phonological constructs. Experimental phonology, ed. by J. Ohala and J. Jaeger, 175–86. Orlando, Fla.: Academic Press.

Hooper, Joan. 1978. Constraints on schwa-deletion in American English. Recent developments in historical phonology, ed. by J. Fisiak, 183–207. The Hague: Mouton.

Hou, J.-Y. 1980. Pinyao fangyan de liandu biandiao. [Tone sandhi in the Pinyao dialect]. Fangyan 1980 1.1–14.

Hualde, José. 1987. On Basque affricates. Proceedings of the West Coast Conference on Formal Linguistics 6, 77–89. Stanford, Calif.: Stanford Linguistics Association, Stanford University.

Hualde, José. 1991. Basque phonology. London: Routledge.

Huang, C.-T. James. 1985. The autosegmental and metrical nature of tone terracing. African linguistics: Essays in memory of M. W. K. Semikenke, ed. by D. Goyvaerts, 209–38. Amsterdam: Benjamins.

Hulst, Harry van der. 1989. Atoms of segmental structure: Components, gestures, and dependency. Phonology 6.253–84.

Hume, Elizabeth. 1990. Front vowels, palatal consonants, and the rule of umlaut in Korean. Proceedings of NELS 20, 230–43. Amherst: GLSA, University of Massachusetts.

Hume, Elizabeth. 1992. Front vowels, coronal consonants and their interaction in nonlinear phonology. Ithaca, N.Y.: Cornell University Ph.D. dissertation.

Hutchinson, Sandra. 1974. Spanish vowel sandhi. Papers from the Parasession on Natural Phonology, ed. by A. Bruck et al., 184–92. Chicago: Chicago Linguistic Society, University of Chicago.

Hyman, Larry. 1981. Tonal accent in Somali. Studies in African Linguistics 12.169–203.

Hyman, Larry. 1985. A theory of phonological weight. Dordrecht: Foris.

Hyman, Larry. 1988. Underspecification and vowel height transfer in Esimbi. Phonology 5.255–73.

Hyman, Larry, and Francis Katamba. 1992. A new approach to tone in Luganda. Berkeley: University of California ms.

Idsardi, William. 1992. The computation of prosody. Cambridge, Mass.: MIT Ph.D. dissertation.

Inkelas, Sharon. 1989. Prosodic constituency in the lexicon. Stanford, Calif.: Stanford University Ph.D. dissertation. Published by Garland Press, New York, 1990.

Inkelas, Sharon, and Draga Zec, eds. 1990. The phonology-syntax connection. Chicago: University of Chicago Press.

IPA. 1949. Principles of the International Phonetic Association. London: Department of Phonetics, University College.

Irshied, Omar. 1984. The phonology of Bani-Hassan Arabic. Urbana: University of Illinois Ph.D. dissertation.

Irshied, Omar, and Michael Kenstowicz. 1984. Some phonological rules of Bani-Hassan Arabic. Studies in the Linguistic Sciences 14,1.109–48.

Itô, Junko. 1986. Syllable theory in prosodic phonology. Amherst: University of Massachusetts Ph.D. dissertation. Published by Garland Press, New York, 1988.

Itô, Junko. 1989. A prosodic theory of epenthesis. Natural Language & Linguistic Theory 7.217–59.

Itô, Junko. 1990. Prosodic minimality in Japanese. Chicago Linguistic Society 26. Part II: Papers from the parasession on the syllable in phonetics and phonology, ed. by K. Deaton et al., 213–39. Chicago: Chicago Linguistic Society, University of Chicago.

Itô, Junko, and R. Armin Mester. 1986. The phonology of voicing in Japanese. Linguistic Inquiry 17.49–73.

Iverson, Gregory. 1987. On glottal width features. Lingua 60.331–9.

Iverson, Gregory. 1989. On the category supralaryngeal. Phonology 6.285–304.

Jakobson, Roman. 1941. Kindersprache, Aphasie und allgemeine Lautgesetze. Selected writings, vol. 1, 328–401. The Hague: Mouton, 1971.

Jakobson, Roman, Gunnar Fant, and Morris Halle. 1951. Preliminaries to speech analysis. Cambridge, Mass.: MIT Press.

James, Deborah. 1981. An autosegmental analysis of Siane. Norman, Okla.: Summer Institute of Linguistics ms.

Jeffers, Robert, and Ilse Lehiste. 1979. Principles and methods for historical linguistics. Cambridge, Mass.: MIT Press.

Joos, Martin. 1942. A phonological dilemma in Canadian English. Language 18.141–4.

Joos, Martin, ed. 1957. Readings in linguistics I. Chicago: University of Chicago Press.

Ka, Omar. 1988. Wolof phonology and morphology: A nonlinear approach. Urbana: University of Illinois Ph.D. dissertation.

Ka, Omar. 1989. Wolof syllable structure: Evidence from a secret code. Eastern States Conference on Linguistics 5, 261–74. Columbus: Department of Linguistics, Ohio State University.

Kager, René. 1989. A metrical theory of stressing and destressing in English and Dutch. Dordrecht: Foris.

Kager, René. 1991. Alternatives to the iambic-trochaic law. To appear in Natural Language & Linguistic Theory.

Kager, René. 1992. Shapes of the generalized trochee. To appear in Proceedings of the West Coast Conference on Formal Linguistics 11.

Kahn, Daniel. 1976. Syllable-based generalizations in English phonology. Cambridge, Mass.: MIT Ph.D. dissertation. Distributed by Indiana University Linguistics Club.

Kaisse, Ellen. 1985. Connected speech: The interaction of syntax and phonology. Orlando, Fla.: Academic Press.

Kaisse, Ellen. 1987. Rhythm and the cycle. Papers from the Twenty-third Regional Meeting, Chicago Linguistic Society, vol. 2, 199–209. Chicago: Chicago Linguistic Society, University of Chicago.

Kaisse, Ellen. 1992. Can [consonantal] spread? Language 68.313–32.

Kaisse, Ellen, and Arnold Zwicky, eds. 1987. Syntactic conditions on phonological rules. (Phonology Yearbook 4.) Cambridge: Cambridge University Press.

Kamprath, Christine. 1986. The syllabification of consonantal glides: Postpeak distinctions. Proceedings of NELS 16, 217–29. Amherst: GLSA, University of Massachusetts.

Kamprath, Christine. 1987. Suprasegmental structures in a Räto-Romansh dialect: A case study in metrical and lexical phonology. Austin: University of Texas Ph.D. dissertation.

Kaye, Jonathan. 1973. Odawa stress and related phenomena. Odawa language project: Second report, ed. by G. Piggott and J. Kaye. Toronto: Centre for Linguistic Studies, University of Toronto.

Kaye, Jonathan. 1990a. Government in phonology: The case of Moroccan Arabic. The Linguistic Review 6.131–59.

Kaye, Jonathan. 1990b. "Coda" licensing. Phonology 7.301–30.

Kaye, Jonathan. 1990c. What ever happened to dialect B? Grammar in progress: GLOW essays for Henk van Riemsdijk, ed. by J. Mascaró and M. Nespor, 259–63. Dordrecht: Foris.

Kaye, Jonathan. 1992. Do you believe in magic? The story of s + C sequences. London: School of Oriental and African Studies ms.

Kaye, Jonathan, and Jean Lowenstamm. 1984. De la syllabicité. Forme sonore du langage, ed. by F. Dell et al., 123–59. Paris: Hermann.

Kaye, Jonathan, Jean Lowenstamm, and Jean-Roger Vergnaud. 1985. The internal structure of phonological elements: A theory of charm and government. Phonology Yearbook 2.303–26.

Kaye, Jonathan, Jean Lowenstamm, and Jean-Roger Vergnaud. 1990. Constituent structure and government in phonology. Phonology 7.193–231.

Kaye, Jonathan, and Jean-Roger Vergnaud. 1990. Phonology, morphology and the lexicon. Paper presented at GLOW 13, Cambridge.

Keating, Patricia. 1988. Underspecification in phonetics. Phonology 5.275–92.

Kenstowicz, Michael. 1970. On the notation of vowel length in Lithuanian. Papers in Linguistics 3.73–113.

Kenstowicz, Michael. 1979. Chukchee vowel harmony and epenthesis. The elements: Parasession on linguistic units and levels, 402–12. Chicago: Chicago Linguistic Society, University of Chicago.

Kenstowicz, Michael. 1982. Gemination and spirantization in Tigrinya. Studies in the Linguistic Sciences 12,1.103–22.

Kenstowicz, Michael. 1986a. The phonology of Chukchee consonants. Studies in the Linguistic Sciences 16,1.79–96.

Kenstowicz, Michael. 1986b. Notes on syllable structure in three Arabic dialects. Revue québécoise de linguistique 16.101–28.

Kenstowicz, Michael. 1992. American structuralist phonology. International encyclopedia of linguistics, vol. 3, ed. by W. Bright, 215–17. Oxford: Oxford University Press.

Kenstowicz, Michael. 1993. Evidence for metrical constituency. The view from Building 20: Essays in linguistics in honor of Sylvain Bromberger, ed. by K. Hale and S. J. Keyser. Cambridge, Mass.: MIT Press.

Kenstowicz, Michael, and Charles Kisseberth. 1977. Topics in phonological theory. New York: Academic Press.

Kenstowicz, Michael, and Charles Kisseberth. 1979. Generative phonology: Description and theory. New York: Academic Press.

Kenstowicz, Michael, Emmanuel Nikiema, and Meterwa Ourso. 1988. Tonal polarity in two Gur languages. Studies in the Linguistic Sciences 18,1.77–104.

Kenstowicz, Michael, and Charles Pyle. 1973. On the phonological integrity of geminate clusters. Issues in phonological theory, ed. by M. Kenstowicz and C. Kisseberth, 27–43. The Hague: Mouton.

Kenstowicz, Michael, and Jerzy Rubach. 1987. The phonology of syllabic nuclei in Slovak. Language 63.463–97.

Key, Harold. 1961. Phonotactics of Cayuvava. International Journal of American Linguistics 27.143–50.

Key, Harold. 1967. Morphology of Cayuvava. The Hague: Mouton.

Keyser, Samuel J., and Paul Kiparsky. 1984. Syllable structure in Finnish phonology. Language sound structure, ed. by M. Aronoff and R. Oehrle, 2–31. Cambridge, Mass.: MIT Press.

Kidda, Mairo. 1982. Hausa adjectives: A three-dimensional analysis. Urbana: University of Illinois ms.

Kidda, Mairo. 1985. Tangale phonology: A descriptive analysis. Urbana: University of Illinois Ph.D. dissertation.

Kim, Chin-Wu. 1965. On the autonomy of the tensity feature in stop classification. Word 21.339–59.

Kim, Chin-Wu. 1972. Two phonological notes: A-sharp and B-flat. Contributions to generative phonology, ed. by M. Brame, 155–70. Austin: University of Texas Press.

Kimball, Geoffrey. 1988. Koasati reduplication. In honor of Mary Haas, ed. by W. Shipley, 431–42. Berlin: Mouton.

Kiparsky, Paul. 1968a. Linguistic universals and language change. Universals in linguistic theory, ed. by E. Bach and R. Harms, 191–212. New York: Holt, Rinehart and Winston. Reprinted in Kiparsky 1982b, 13–44.

Kiparsky, Paul. 1968b. How abstract is phonology? Distributed by Indiana University Linguistics Club. Reprinted in Kiparsky 1982b, 119–64.

Kiparsky, Paul. 1971. Historical linguistics. A survey of linguistic science, ed. by W. Dingwall, 576–649. College Park: Linguistics Program, University of Maryland. Reprinted in Kiparsky 1982b, 57–80.

Kiparsky, Paul. 1973a. Abstractness, opacity, and global rules. Bloomington: Indiana University Linguistics Club. Also in Three dimensions of linguistic theory, ed. by O. Fujimura, 57–86. Tokyo: TEC.

Kiparsky, Paul. 1973b. "Elsewhere" in phonology. A festschrift for Morris Halle, ed. by S. Anderson & P. Kiparsky, 93–106. New York: Holt, Rinehart and Winston.

Kiparsky, Paul. 1979. Metrical structure assignment is cyclic. Linguistic Inquiry 10.421–42.

Kiparsky, Paul. 1981. Remarks on the metrical structure of the syllable. Phonologica 1980, ed. by W. Dressler et al., Innsbruck.

Kiparsky, Paul. 1982a. Lexical phonology and morphology. Linguistics in the morning calm, ed. by I. S. Yang, 3–91. Seoul: Hanshin. Abridged version published as "From cyclic to lexical phonology" in The structure of phonological representations (part I), ed. by H. van der Hulst and N. Smith, 131–75. Dordrecht: Foris.

Kiparsky, Paul. 1982b. Explanation in phonology. Dordrecht: Foris.

Kiparsky, Paul. 1984. On the lexical phonology of Icelandic. Nordic phonology III, ed. by C. Elert et al., 135–64. Stockholm: Almqvist & Wiksell.

Kiparsky, Paul. 1985. Some consequences of lexical phonology. Phonology Yearbook 2.83–138.

Kiparsky, Paul. 1992. Blocking in non-derived environments. To appear in Studies in lexical phonology, ed. by S. Hargus and E. Kaisse. San Diego, Calif: Academic Press.

Kisseberth, Charles. 1969. Theoretical implications of Yawelmani phonology. Urbana: University of Illinois Ph.D. dissertation.

Kisseberth, Charles. 1970a. On the functional unity of phonological rules. Linguistic Inquiry 1.291–306.

Kisseberth, Charles. 1970b. Vowel elision in Tonkawa and derivational constraints. Studies presented to Robert B. Lees by his students, ed. by J. Sadock and A. Vanek, 109–38. Edmonton: Linguistic Research, Inc.

Kisseberth, Charles. 1973a. Is rule ordering necessary in phonology? Issues in linguistics: Papers in honor of Henry and Renée Kahane, ed. by B. Kachru, 418–41. Urbana: University of Illinois Press.

Kisseberth, Charles. 1973b. On the alternation of vowel length in Klamath: A global rule. Issues in phonological theory, ed. by M. Kenstowicz and C. Kisseberth, 9–26. The Hague: Mouton.

Kisseberth, Charles. 1986. Lectures on phonological phrasing. Urbana: University of Illinois.

Kisseberth, Charles, and Mohammad Abasheikh. 1974. Vowel length in Chi Mwi:ni: A case study of the role of grammar in phonology. Papers from the parasession on natural phonology, ed. by A. Bruck et al., 193–209. Chicago: Chicago Linguistic Society, University of Chicago.

Krause, Scott. 1979. Topics in Chukchee phonology and morphology. Urbana: University of Illinois Ph.D. dissertation.

Kruger, John. 1962. A grammar of Yakut. Bloomington: Indiana University Press.

Kuhl, P., and A. Meltzoff. 1982. The bimodal perception of speech in infancy. Science 218.1134–8.

Kumbaraci, T. 1966. Consonantally conditioned alternation of vocalic morphophonemes in Turkish. Anthropological Linguistics 8.11–24.

Kuroda, S.-Y. 1967. Yawelmani phonology. Cambridge, Mass.: MIT Press.

Ladefoged, Peter. 1962. Elements of acoustic phonetics. Chicago: University of Chicago Press.

Ladefoged, Peter. 1975. A course in phonetics. New York: Harcourt Brace Jovanovich.

Ladefoged, Peter. 1982. A course in phonetics. 2d ed. New York: Harcourt Brace Jovanovich.

Ladefoged, Peter. 1993. A course in phonetics. 3d ed. New York: Harcourt Brace Jovanovich.

Ladefoged, Peter, and Ian Maddieson. 1988. Phonological features for place of articulation. Language, speech, and mind: Studies in honour of Victoria A. Fromkin, ed. by L. Hyman and C. Li, 49–61. London: Routlege.

Lahiri, Aditi, and William Marslen-Wilson. 1991. The mental representation of lexical form: A phonological approach to the recognition lexicon. Cognition 38.245–94.

Langendoen, D. Terence. 1968. The London school of linguistics: A study of the linguistic theories of B. Malinowski and J. R. Firth. Cambridge, Mass.: MIT Press.

Lass, Roger. 1976. English phonology and phonological theory. London: Cambridge University Press.

Leben, William. 1973. Suprasegmental phonology. Cambridge, Mass.: MIT Ph.D. dissertation.

Leben, William. 1980. A metrical analysis of length. Linguistic Inquiry 10.497–509.

Leer, Jeff. 1985. Evolution of prosody in the Yupik languages. Yupik Eskimo prosodic systems: Descriptive and comparative studies, ed. by M. Krauss, 135–57. Fairbanks: Alaska Native Language Center.

Levin, Juliette. 1983. Reduplication and prosodic structure. Cambridge, Mass.: MIT ms.

Levin, Juliette. 1985. A metrical theory of syllabicity. Cambridge, Mass.: MIT Ph.D. dissertation.

Levin, Juliette. 1988a. A place for lateral in the feature geometry. Austin: University of Texas ms.

Levin, Juliette. 1988b. Generating ternary feet. Texas Linguistic Forum 29, 97–113. Austin: Department of Linguistics, University of Texas.

Liberman, Alvin. 1970. The grammars of speech and language. Cognitive Psychology 1.301–23.

Liberman, Alvin, Franklin Cooper, F. Shankweiler, and Michael Studdert-Kennedy. 1967. Perception of the speech code. Psychological Review 74.431–61.

Liberman, Alvin, and Ignatius Mattingly. 1985. The motor theory of speech perception revised. Cognition 21.1–36.

Liberman, Mark. 1975. The intonational system of English. Cambridge, Mass.: MIT Ph.D. dissertation. Distributed by Indiana University Linguistics Club.

Liberman, Mark, and Alan Prince. 1977. On stress and linguistic rhythm. Linguistic Inquiry 8.249–336.

Lichtenberk, F. 1983. A grammar of Manam. Honolulu: University of Hawaii Press.

Lieberman, Philip. 1984. The biology and evolution of language. Cambridge, Mass.: Harvard University Press.

Lieberman, Philip, and Sheila Blumstein. 1988. Speech physiology, speech perception, and acoustic phonetics. New York: Cambridge University Press.

Lightner, Theodore. 1965. On the description of vowel and consonant harmony. Word 21.224–50.

Lightner, Theodore. 1972. Problems in the theory of phonology: Russian phonology and Turkish phonology. Edmonton: Linguistic Research, Inc.

Lombardi, Linda. 1990. The nonlinear organization of the affricate. Natural Language & Linguistic Theory 8.375–426.

Lombardi, Linda. 1991. Laryngeal features and laryngeal neutralization. Amherst: University of Massachusetts Ph.D. dissertation.

Lombardi, Linda, and John McCarthy. 1991. Prosodic circumscription in Choctaw morphology. Phonology 8.37–72.

Loporcaro, Michele. 1988. Grammatica storica del dialetto di Altamura. Pisa: Giradini.

Lowenstamm, Jean, and Jonathan Kaye. 1986. Compensatory lengthening in Tiberian Hebrew. Studies in compensatory lengthening, ed. by L. Wetzels and E. Sezer, 97–132. Dordrecht: Foris.

Lowenstamm, Jean, and Jean-François Prunet. 1986. Le Tigrinya et le principe du contour obligatoire. Revue québécoise de linguistique 16,1.181–208.

Lü, Shu-Xiang. 1980. Danyang fangyan de shengdiao xitong. [The tonal system of the Danyang dialect.] Fangyan 2.85–122.

Lunt, Horace. 1952. A grammar of the Macedonian literary language. Skopje.

Ma Newman, Roxana. 1971. Downstep in Ga'anda. Journal of African Languages 10.15–27.

Maddieson, Ian. 1984. Patterns of sounds. Cambridge: Cambridge University Press.

Maddieson, Ian. 1987. The Margi vowel system and labiocoronals. Studies in African Linguistics 18.327–56.

Makkai, Valeri Becker, ed. 1972. Phonological theory: Evolution and current practice. New York: Holt, Rinehart and Winston.

Malécot, A. 1960. Vowel nasality as a distinctive feature in American English. Language 36.222–9.

Mandelbaum, David, ed. 1949. Selected writings of Edward Sapir in language, culture, and personality. Berkeley: University of California Press.

Marantz, Alec. 1982. Re reduplication. Linguistic Inquiry 13.435–82.

Marlett, Stephen, and Joseph Stemberger. 1983. Empty consonants in Seri. Linguistic Inquiry 14.617–39.

Marshad, Hassan. 1982. Kiamu phonology. Urbana: University of Illinois ms.

Mascaró, Joan. 1976. Catalan phonology and the phonological cycle. Cambridge, Mass.: MIT Ph.D. dissertation. Distributed by Indiana University Linguistics Club.

Mascaró, Joan. 1987. A reduction and spreading theory of voicing and other sound effects. Universitat Autònoma de Barcelona ms.

Mattingly, Ignatius, and Alvin Liberman. 1990. Speech and other auditory modules. Sign and sense, ed. by G. Edelman et al., 501–20. New York: Wiley.

McCarthy, John. 1979a. Formal problems in Semitic phonology and morphology. Cambridge, Mass.: MIT Ph.D. dissertation. Distributed by Indiana University Linguistics Club. Published by Garland Press, New York, 1985.

McCarthy, John. 1979b. On stress and syllabification. Linguistic Inquiry 10.443–65.

McCarthy, John. 1981. A prosodic theory of nonconcatenative morphology. Linguistic Inquiry 12.373–418.

McCarthy, John. 1983. Consonantal morphology in the Chaha verb. Proceedings of the West Coast Conference on Formal Linguistics 2, 176–88. Stanford, Calif.: Stanford Linguistics Association, Stanford University.

McCarthy, John. 1984. Prosodic organization in morphology. Language sound structure, ed. by M. Aronoff and R. Oehrle, 299–317. Cambridge, Mass.: MIT Press.

McCarthy, John. 1986a. OCP effects: Gemination and antigemination. Linguistic Inquiry 17.207–63.

McCarthy, John. 1986b. Lexical phonology and nonconcatenative morphology in the history of Chaha. Revue québécoise de linguistique 16.209–28.

McCarthy, John. 1988. Feature geometry and dependency: A review. Phonetica 43:84–108.

McCarthy, John. 1989. Linear order in phonological representations. Linguistic Inquiry 20.71–99.

McCarthy, John. 1991. The phonetics and phonology of Semitic pharyngeals. To appear in Papers in laboratory phonology III: Phonological structure and phonetic form, ed. by P. Keating. London: Cambridge University Press.

McCarthy, John, and Alan Prince. 1986. Prosodic morphology. Waltham, Mass.: Brandeis University ms.

McCarthy, John, and Alan Prince. 1988. Quantitative transfer in reduplicative and templatic morphology. Linguistics in the morning calm 2, 3–35. Seoul: Hanshin.

McCarthy, John, and Alan Prince. 1990. Foot and word in prosodic morphology: The Arabic broken plural. Natural Language & Linguistic Theory 8.209–84.

McCarthy, John, and Alan Prince. 1991. Lectures on prosodic morphology. Linguistic Society of America Summer Institute, University of California, Santa Cruz.

McCarthy, John, and Alison Taub. 1992. Review of Paradis and Prunet 1991. Phonology 9.363–70.

Meeussen, Albert. 1959. Essai de grammaire rundi. Tervuren: Musée royal du Congo Belge.

Mehler, Jacques, J. Dommergues, Uli Frauenfelder, and Juan Segui. 1981. The syllable's role in speech segmentation. Journal of Verbal Learning and Verbal Behavior 20.298–305.

Meillet, Antoine. 1926–1936. Les langues du monde. Paris.

Meredith, Scott. 1990. Issues in the phonology of prominence. Cambridge, Mass.: MIT Ph.D. dissertation.

Merlan, F. 1982. Mangarayi. Lingua Descriptive Series 4.1–242.

Mester, R. Armin. 1990. Patterns of truncation. Linguistic Inquiry 21.478–85.

Mester, R. Armin. 1993. The quantitative trochee in Latin. To appear in Natural Language & Linguistic Theory 11.

Mester, R. Armin, and Junko Itô. 1989. Feature predictability and underspecification: Palatal prosody in Japanese mimetics. Language 65.258–93.

Michailovsky, Boyd. 1975. On some Tibeto-Burman sound changes. Proceedings of the First Annual Meeting of the Berkeley Linguistics Society. Berkeley: Berkeley Linguistics Society, University of California.

Miller, George. 1956. The perception of speech. For Roman Jakobson, ed. by M. Halle et al., 353–60. The Hague: Mouton.

Miller, George, and Patricia Gildea. 1987. How children learn words. Scientific American 257,6.94–9.

Miner, Kenneth. 1979. Dorsey's law in Winnebago-Chiwere and Winnebago accent. International Journal of American Linguistics 45.25–33.

Miner, Kenneth. 1990. Winnebago accent: The rest of the data. Lawrence: University of Kansas ms.

Minifie, F., T. Hixon, and F. Williams. 1973. Normal aspects of speech, hearing and language. Englewood Cliffs, N.J.: Prentice-Hall.

Mitchell, T. F. 1960. Prominence and syllabification in Arabic. Bulletin of the School of Oriental and African Studies 23.369–89.

Mithun, Marianne, and Hasan Basri. 1986. The phonology of Selayarese. Oceanic Linguistics 25.210–54.

Mohanan, K. P. 1982. Lexical phonology. Cambridge, Mass.: MIT Ph.D. dissertation. Distributed by Indiana University Linguistics Club. Published by Reidel, Dordrecht, 1986.

Mohanan, K. P. 1991. On the bases of radical underspecification. Natural Language & Linguistic Theory 9.285–325.

Mohanan, K. P. 1992a. Feature network and naturalness. To appear in The last phonological rule, ed. by J. Goldsmith. Chicago: University of Chicago Press.

Mohanan, K. P. 1992b. Describing the phonology of non-native varieties of language. National University of Singapore ms.

Moltmann, Friederike. 1990. Syllabification and lexical phonology in German. Cambridge, Mass.: MIT ms.

Montreuil, Jean-Pierre. 1988. On assimilation through schwa. Austin: University of Texas ms.

Moravcsik, E. 1978. Reduplicative constructions. Universals of human language, vol. 3, ed. by J. Greenberg, 297–334. Stanford, Calif.: Stanford University Press.

Munro, Pamela. 1990. Stress and vowel length in Cupan absolute nouns. International Journal of American Linguistics 56.217–50.

Murray, Robert, and Theo Vennemann. 1983. Sound change and syllable structure in Germanic phonology. Language 59.514–28.

Myers, Scott. 1987a. Tone and the structure of words in Shona. Amherst: University of Massachusetts Ph.D. dissertation. Published by Garland Press, New York, 1990.

Myers, Scott. 1987b. Vowel shortening in English. Natural Language & Linguistic Theory 5.485–518.

Nespor, Marina, and Irene Vogel. 1986. Prosodic phonology. Dordrecht: Foris.

Newman, Paul. 1974. The Kanakuru language. (West African Language Monographs 9.) Leeds: Institute of Modern English Language Studies.

Newman, Paul. 1986a. Tone and affixation in Hausa. Studies in African Linguistics 17.249–67.

Newman, Paul. 1986b. Contour tones as phonemic primes in Grebo. The phonological representation of suprasegmentals, ed. by K. Bogers et al., 175–94. Dordrecht: Foris.

Newman, Paul. 1986c. Reduplicated nouns in Hausa. Journal of African Languages & Linguistics 8.115–32.

Newman, Stanley. 1944. Yokuts language of California. (Viking Fund Publications in Anthropology 2.) New York: Viking Fund.

Ní Chiosáin, Máire. 1991. Topics in the phonology of Irish. Amherst: University of Massachusetts Ph.D. dissertation.

Nicklas, Thurston. 1974. The elements of Choctaw. Ann Arbor: University of Michigan Ph.D. dissertation.

Nicklas, Thurston. 1975. Choctaw morphophonemics. Studies in Southeastern Indian languages, ed. by J. Crawford, 237–50. Athens: University of Georgia Press.

Nikiema, Emmanuel. 1989. Vocalic epenthesis reanalyzed: The case of Tangale. Current approaches to African linguistics, vol. 7, ed. by J. Hutchison and V. Manfredi, 41–51. Dordrecht: Foris.

Noyer, Rolf. 1991. Verner's law and underspecification theory. Cambridge, Mass.: MIT ms.

Odden, David. 1989. Associative tone in Shona. Journal of Linguistic Research 1,2.37–51.

Odden, David. 1984. Stem tone assignment in Shona. Autosegmental studies in Bantu tone, ed. by G. N. Clements and J. Goldsmith, 255–80. Dordrecht: Foris.

Odden, David. 1986. On the role of the Obligatory Contour Principle in phonological theory. Language 62.353–83.

Odden, David. 1987. Kimatuumbi phrasal phonology. Phonology Yearbook 4:13–26.

Odden, David. 1988. Anti Antigemination and the OCP. Linguistic Inquiry 19.451–75.

Odden, David. 1989. Kimatuumbi phonology and morphology. Columbus: Ohio State University ms.

Odden, David. 1990. Syntax, lexical rules and postlexical rules in Kimatuumbi. In Inkelas and Zec 1990, 259–78.

Odden, David. 1991. Vowel geometry. Phonology 8.261–90.

Ohala, John. 1986. Consumer's guide to evidence in phonology. Phonology Yearbook 3.3–26.

Orešnik, Janez. 1972. On the epenthesis rule in modern Icelandic. Arkiv för Nordisk Filologi 87.1–32.

Osborn, H. 1966. Warao I: Phonology and morphophonemics. International Journal of American Linguistics 32.108–23.

Ourso, Meterwa. 1989. Lama phonology and morphology. Urbana: University of Illinois Ph.D. dissertation.

Padgett, Jaye. 1991. Stricture in feature geometry. Amherst: University of Massachusetts Ph.D. dissertation.

Paradis, Carole. 1986. Lexical phonology and morphology: The nominal classes in Fula. Montreal: University of Montreal Ph.D. dissertation. Published by Garland Press, New York, 1992.

Paradis, Carole. 1988a. Glide alternation in Pulaar and the theory of dominance. Current approaches to African linguistics, vol. 4, ed. by D. Odden, 327–39. Dordrecht: Foris.

Paradis, Carole. 1988–89. On constraints and repair strategies. The Linguistic Review 6.71–97.

Paradis, Carole, and Jean-François Prunet. 1989. On coronal transparency. Phonology 6.317–48.

Paradis, Carole, and Jean-François Prunet, eds. 1991. The special status of coronals: Internal and external evidence. (Phonology and Phonetics 2.) San Diego, Calif.: Academic Press.

Payne, Judith. 1990. Asheninca stress patterns. Amazonian linguistics, ed. by D. Payne, 185–212. Austin: University of Texas Press.

Perkell, Joseph. 1980. Phonetic features and the physiology of speech production. Language production 1: Speech and talk, ed. by B. Butterworth, 337–72. New York: Academic Press.

Pesetsky, David. 1979. Russian morphology and lexical theory. Cambridge, Mass.: MIT ms.

Pesetsky, David. 1985. Morphology and logical form. Linguistic Inquiry 16.193–246.

Peterson, G., and H. Barney. 1952. Control methods used in a study of vowels. Journal of the Acoustical Society of America 24.174–84.

Piggott, Glyne. 1980. Aspects of Odawa morphophonemics. New York: Garland.

Piggott, Glyne. 1992. Variability in feature dependency: The case of nasality. Natural Language & Linguistic Theory 10.33–78.

Pike, Kenneth. 1964. Stress trains in Auca. In honour of Daniel Jones, ed. by D. Abercrombie et al., 425–31. London: Longmans. Reprinted in Selected writings, ed. by R. Brend, 186–91. Mouton: The Hague.

Poser, William. 1982. Phonological representations and action at a distance. The structure of phonological representations (part II), ed. by H. van der Hulst and N. Smith, 121–58. Dordrecht: Foris.

Poser, William. 1984. Hypocoristic formation in Japanese. Proceedings of the West Coast Conference on Formal Linguistics 3,218–29. Stanford, Calif.: Stanford Linguistics Association, Stanford University.

Prince, Alan. 1980. A metrical theory for Estonian quantity. Linguistic Inquiry 11.511–62.

Prince, Alan. 1983. Relating to the grid. Linguistic Inquiry 14.19–100.

Prince, Alan. 1984. Phonology with tiers. Language sound structure, ed. by M. Aronoff and R. Oehrle, 234–44. Cambridge, Mass.: MIT Press.

Prince, Alan. 1985. Improving tree theory. Proceedings of the Eleventh Annual Meeting of the Berkeley Linguistics Society, 471–90. Berkeley: Berkeley Linguistics Society, University of California.

Prince, Alan. 1990. Quantitative consequences of rhythmic organization. Papers from the Twenty-sixth Regional Meeting, Chicago Linguistic Society, vol. 2, 355–98. Chicago: Chicago Linguistic Society, University of Chicago.

Prince, Alan, and Paul Smolensky. 1993. Optimality theory. Rutgers University ms.

Pryor, David, and John Clifton. 1987. Nasalization in Kire. Studies in Melanesian orthographies, ed. by J. Clifton, 31–44. Data Papers on Papua New Guinea Languages 33.

Pulleyblank, Douglas. 1986. Tone in lexical phonology. Dordrecht: Reidel.

Pulleyblank, Douglas. 1988. Vocalic underspecification in Yoruba. Linguistic Inquiry 19.233–70.

Pulleyblank, Edwin. 1989. The role of coronal in articulator based features. Papers from the Twenty-fifth Regional Meeting, Chicago Linguistic Society, vol. 1, 379–93. Chicago: Chicago Linguistic Society, University of Chicago.

Pullum, Geoffrey, and William Ladusaw. 1986. Phonetic symbol guide. Chicago: University of Chicago Press.

Quackenbush, Hiroko. 1970. Studies in the phonology of some Truckic dialects. Ann Arbor: University of Michigan Ph.D. dissertation.

Rialland, Annie. 1991. L'allongement compensatoire: Nature et modèles. To appear in

Architecture des représentations phonologiques, ed. by B. Laks and A. Rialland. Presse du CNRS.

Rialland, Annie, and Mamadou Badjimé. 1989. Réanalyse des tons du Bambara: Des tons du nom à l'organization générale du système. Studies in African Linguistics 20.1–28.

Ringen, Catherine. 1975. Vowel harmony: Theoretical implications. Bloomington: Indiana University Ph.D. dissertation. Published by Garland Press, New York, 1988.

Robins, R. H. 1953. The phonology of nasalized verbal forms in Sundanese. Bulletin of the School of Oriental and African Studies 15.138–45.

Robins, R. H. 1957. Vowel nasality in Sundanese: A phonological and grammatical study. Studies in linguistic analysis, 87–103. Oxford: Blackwell Publishers.

Rubach, Jerzy. 1984. Cyclic and lexical phonology. The structure of Polish. Dordrecht: Foris.

Rubach, Jerzy. 1990. Final devoicing and cyclic syllabification in German. Linguistic Inquiry 21.79–94.

Rubach, Jerzy. 1992a. Affricates as strident stops in Polish. Iowa City: University of Iowa ms. To appear in Linguistic Inquiry.

Rubach, Jerzy. 1992b. Skeletal versus moraic representations in Slovak. To appear in Natural Language & Linguistic Theory.

Rubach, Jerzy, and Geert Booij. 1990. Syllable structure assignment in Polish. Phonology 7.121–58.

Sagey, Elizabeth. 1986. The representation of features and relations in nonlinear phonology. Cambridge, Mass.: MIT Ph.D. dissertation. Published by Garland Press, New York, 1990.

Sagey, Elizabeth. 1988. Degree of closure in complex segments. Features, segmental structure and harmony processes (part I), ed. by H. van der Hulst and N. Smith, 169–208. Dordrecht: Foris.

Saint, Rachel, and Kenneth Pike. 1962. Auca phonemics. Studies in Ecuadorian Indian languages, ed. by B. Elson, 2–30. Norman, Okla.: Summer Institute of Linguistics.

Sampson, Geoffrey. 1973. Duration in Hebrew consonants. Linguistic Inquiry 4.101–4.

Sapir, Edward. 1925. Sound patterns in language. Language 1.37–51. Reprinted in Mandelbaum 1949, 33–45, Joos 1957, 19–25, and Makkai 1972, 13–21.

Sapir, Edward. 1931. The concept of phonetic law as tested in primitive languages by Leonard Bloomfield. Methods in social science: A case book, ed. by S. Rice, 297–306. Chicago: University of Chicago Press. Reprinted in Mandelbaum 1949, 73–82.

Sapir, Edward. 1933. The psychological reality of phonemes. In Mandelbaum 1949, 46–60, and Makkai 1972, 22–31.

Sapir, Edward, and Morris Swadesh. 1939. Nootka texts. Baltimore, Md.: Linguistic Society of America.

Sapir, J. David. 1965. A grammar of Diola Fogny. (West African Language Monographs 3.) London: Cambridge University Press.

Schane, Sanford. 1984. The fundamentals of particle phonology. Phonology Yearbook 1.129–55.

Schein, Barry. 1981. Spirantization in Tigrinya. Theoretical issues in the grammars of Semitic languages, ed. by H. Borer and J. Aoun, 32–42. (MIT Working Papers in Linguistics 3.) Cambridge, Mass.: Department of Linguistics and Philosophy, MIT.

Schein, Barry, and Donca Steriade. 1986. On geminates. Linguistic Inquiry 17.691–744.

Schneiderman, C. 1984. Basic anatomy and physiology in speech and hearing. London: Croom Helm.

Seiler, Hansjakob. 1977. Cahuilla grammar. Banning, Calif.: Malki Museum Press.

Selkirk, Elisabeth. 1982a. The syntax of words. Cambridge, Mass.: MIT Press.

Selkirk, Elisabeth. 1982b. The syllable. The structure of phonological representations (part II), ed. by H. van der Hulst and N. Smith, 337–83. Dordrecht: Foris.

Selkirk, Elisabeth. 1984. Phonology and syntax. Cambridge, Mass.: MIT Press.

Selkirk, Elisabeth. 1986. On derived domains in sentence phonology. Phonology Yearbook 3.371–405.

Selkirk, Elisabeth. 1988. Dependency, place, and the notion "tier." Amherst: University of Massachusetts ms.

Selkirk, Elisabeth. 1991. On the inalterability of geminates. Certamen phonologicum II: Papers from the Second Cortona Phonology Meeting, ed. by P. M. Bertinetto et al. Turin: Rosenberg & Sellier.

Sezer, Engin. 1986. An autosegmental analysis of compensatory lengthening in Turkish. Studies in compensatory lengthening, ed. by L. Wetzels and E. Sezer, 227–50. Dordrecht: Foris.

Shaw, Patricia. 1987. Nonconservation of melodic structure in reduplication. Papers from the Twenty-third Regional Meeting, Chicago Linguistic Society, vol. 2, 291–306. Chicago: Chicago Linguistic Society, University of Chicago.

Shaw, Patricia. 1991a. Consonant harmony systems: The special status of coronal harmony. In Paradis and Prunet 1991, 125–57.

Shaw, Patricia. 1991b. The laryngeal/postlaryngeal connection. Paper presented at Conference on Phonological Feature Organization, University of California, Santa Cruz.

Siebert, Frank. 1941. Certain proto-Algonquian consonant clusters. Language 17.298–303.

Siegel, Dorothy. 1978. The adjacency condition and the theory of morphology. Proceedings of NELS 8, 189–97. Amherst: GLSA, University of Massachusetts.

Sohn, Hyang-Sook. 1987. Underspecification in Korean phonology. Urbana: University of Illinois Ph.D. dissertation.

Sonesson, B. 1968. The functional anatomy of the speech organs. Manuel of phonetics, ed. by B. Malmberg. Amsterdam: North Holland.

Spaandonck, Marcel van. 1971. L'analyse morphotonologique dans les langages bantoues. Paris: Société des études linguistiques et anthropologiques de France, vol. 23–24.

Spring, Cari. 1990. Implications of Axininca Campa for prosodic morphology and reduplication. Tucson: University of Arizona Ph.D. dissertation.

Stallcup, K. 1980. A brief account of nominal prefixes and vowel harmony in Esimbi. L'expansion bantoue, vol. 2, ed. by L. Bouquiaux, 435–41. Paris: Société des études linguistiques et anthropologiques de France.

Steriade, Donca. 1982. Greek prosodies and the nature of syllabification. Cambridge, Mass.: MIT Ph.D. dissertation. Published by Garland Press, New York, 1990.

Steriade, Donca. 1986. A note on coronal. Cambridge, Mass.: MIT ms.

Steriade, Donca. 1987a. Locality conditions and feature geometry. Proceedings of NELS 17,595–618. Amherst: GLSA, University of Massachusetts.

Steriade, Donca. 1987b. Redundant values. Papers from the Twenty-third Regional Meeting, Chicago Linguistic Society, vol. 2, 339–62. Chicago: Chicago Linguistic Society, University of Chicago.

Steriade, Donca. 1988a. Greek accent: A case for preserving structure. Linguistic Inquiry 19.271–314.

Steriade, Donca. 1988b. Reduplication and syllable transfer in Sanskrit and elsewhere. Phonology 5.73–155.

Steriade, Donca. 1989. Affricates and stops. Paper presented at the Features Conference, MIT, Cambridge, Mass.

Steriade, Donca. 1990. Moras and other slots. Formal Linguistics Society of Midamerica 1,254–80. Madison: Department of Linguistics, University of Wisconsin.

Steriade, Donca. 1991a. Aperture positions and syllable structure. Paper presented at Conference, The Organization of Phonology: Features and Domains. University of Illinois, Urbana.

Steriade, Donca. 1991b. Closure, release, and nasal contours. Los Angeles: University of California ms.

Stevens, Kenneth. 1972. The quantal nature of speech: Evidence from articulatory-acoustic data. Human communication: A unified view, ed. by E. David and P. Denes, 51–66. New York: McGraw-Hill.

Stevens, Kenneth. 1989. On the quantal nature of speech. Journal of Phonetics 17,1–2.3– 46.

Stevens, Kenneth, and Samuel Jay Keyser. 1989. Primary features and their enhancement in consonants. Language 65.81–106.

Stevick, E. 1965. Shona basic course. Washington, D.C.: Foreign Service Institute.

Stewart, John. 1967. Tongue root position in Akan vowel harmony. Phonetica 16.185–204.

Stewart, John. 1972. Niger-Congo, Kwa. Linguistics in subsaharan Africa, ed. by T. Sebeok, 179–213. (Current Trends in Linguistics 7.) The Hague: Mouton.

Straight, H. 1976. The acquisition of Maya phonology: Variation in Yucatec child language. New York: Garland.

Street, J. C. 1963. Khalkha structure. Bloomington: Indiana University Press.

Summerfield, Quentin. 1991. Visual perception of phonetic gestures. Modality and the motor theory of speech perception, ed. by I. Mattingly and M. Studdert-Kennedy, 117– 38. Hillsdale, N.J.: Lawrence Erlbaum.

Svantesson, Jan-Olof. 1989. Tonogenetic mechanisms in Northern Mon-Khmer. Phonetica 46.60–79.

Thomas, J. M. C. 1963. Le parler Ngbaka de Bokanga. The Hague: Mouton.

Thráinsson, H. 1978. On the phonology of Icelandic aspiration. Nordic Journal of Linguistics 1.3–54.

Topping, Donald. 1968. Chamorro vowel harmony. Oceanic Linguistics 7.67–79.

Trager, George, and Henry L. Smith. 1951. An outline of English structure. (Studies in Linguistics; Occasional Papers 3.) Norman, Okla.: Battenburg Press.

Traill, Anthony. 1985. Phonetic and phonological studies of !Xoo Bushman. Hamburg: H. Buske.

Trigo, Rosario L. 1988. On the phonological behavior and derivation of nasal glides. Cambridge, Mass.: MIT Ph.D. dissertation.

Trigo, Rosario L. 1991. The inherent structure of nasal segments. Boston: Boston University ms.

Tryon, D. T. 1970a. Conversational Tahitian. Berkeley: University of California Press.

Tryon, D. T. 1970b. An introduction to Maranungku. (Pacific Linguistics Monographs, Series B, no. 14.) Canberra: Australian National University.

Tucker, A. N., and P. E. Hackett. 1959. Le groupe linguistique zande. (Annales du Musée Royal du Congo Belge, Sciences de l'homme, linguistique, 22.) Tervuren.

Tyndall, John. 1896. Sound. New York: Appleton.

Välimaa-Blum, Riitaa. 1986. Finnish vowel harmony as a prescriptive and descriptive rule: An autosegmental account. Eastern States Conference on Linguistics 2,511–22. Columbus: Department of Linguistics, Ohio State University.

Vanelli, Laura. 1979. L'allungamento delle vocali in Friulano. Ce fastu? 55.66–76.

Vanelli, Laura. 1986. La fonologia dei prestiti in friulano. Raetia antiqua et moderna, ed. by G. Holtus and K. Ringer, 355–76. Tübingen: Max Niemeyer Verlag.

Voegelin, C. 1935. Tübatulabal grammar. Berkeley: University of California Press.

Walsh, D. S., and Bruce Biggs. 1966. Proto-Polynesian word list I. Auckland: Linguistics Society of New Zealand.

Wang, P. 1983. Patterns of tone sandhi in Suzhou bisyllables. Fangyan 4.286–96.

Wang, William. 1967. The phonological features of tone. International Journal of American Linguistics 33.93–105.

Watanabe, Akira. 1991. Accent assignment in Japanese and the phonological status of stems and affixes. Cambridge, Mass.: MIT ms.

Wehr, Hans. 1976. Arabic-English dictionary. (The Hans Wehr dictionary of modern written Arabic, ed. by J. M. Cowan.) Ithaca, N.Y.: Spoken Language Services.

Welden, Ann. 1980. Stress in Cairo Arabic. Studies in the Linguistic Sciences 10,2.99–120.

Wells, John. 1982. Accents of English. Cambridge: Cambridge University Press.

Welmers, William. 1962. The phonology of Kpelle. Journal of African Languages 1.69–93.

Welmers, William. 1973. African language structures. Berkeley: University of California Press.

Werker, Janet. 1989. Becoming a native listener. American Scientist 77,1.54–9.

Wilkinson, Karina. 1988. Prosodic structure and Lardil phonology. Linguistic Inquiry 19.325–34.

Wiltshire, Caroline. 1992. Syllabification and rule application in harmonic phonology. Chicago: University of Chicago Ph.D. dissertation.

Wong-opasi, Uthaiwan. 1986. Lexical phonology and the Spanish lexicon. Urbana: University of Illinois Ph.D. dissertation. Distributed by Indiana University Linguistics Club.

Woo, Nancy. 1969. Prosody and phonology. Cambridge, Mass.: MIT Ph.D. dissertation.

Wood, S. 1982. X-ray and model study of vowel articulation. (Working Paper 23.) Lund: Department of Linguistics, Lund University.

Woodbury, Anthony. 1987. Meaningful phonological processes: A consideration of Central Alaskan Yupik Eskimo prosody. Language 63.685–740.

Wright, W. 1971. A grammar of the Arabic language. Cambridge: Cambridge University Press.

Yip, Moira. 1980. The tonal phonology of Chinese. Cambridge, Mass.: MIT Ph.D. dissertation. Distributed by Indiana University Linguistics Club. Published by Garland Press, New York, 1990.

Yip, Moira. 1988a. The Obligatory Contour Principle and phonological rules: A loss of identity. Linguistic Inquiry 19.65–100.

Yip, Moira. 1988b. Template morphology and the direction of association. Natural Language & Linguistic Theory 6.551–77.

Yip, Moira. 1989. Contour tones. Phonology 6.149–74.

Yip, Moira. 1991. Coronals, consonant clusters, and the coda condition. In Paradis and Prunet 1991, 61–78.

Younes, R. 1983. The representation of geminate consonants. Austin: University of Texas ms.

Zec, Draga. 1988. Sonority constraints on prosodic structure. Stanford, Calif.: Stanford University Ph.D. dissertation.

Zemlin, W. 1968. Speech and hearing science. Englewood Cliffs, N.J.: Prentice-Hall.

Abbreviations

A	amplitude of wave, aperture node	SPE	Sound Pattern of English (Chomsky and Halle 1968)
ATB	across-the-board application of rule	SSP	Sonority Sequencing Principle
ATR	advanced tongue root feature	SV	spontaneous voicing node
C	consonant	T	period of vibration
C_0	zero or more consonants	TBU	tone bearing unit
CL	compensatory lengthening	TSL	trisyllabic laxing
cps	cycles per second	UAC	Universal Association Convention
f	frequency of wave, feminine gender	UG	Universal Grammar
f_0	fundamental frequency	V	vowel
F	metrical foot	V	unassociated vowel
H	high tone, heavy syllable	vf	vocal folds
Hz	Hertz	WBP	weight by position rule
IE	Indoeuropean	WFR	word formation rule
IJAL	International Journal of American Linguistics	X	skeletal slot
IPA	International Phonetics Association	α	variable feature coefficient (plus or minus)
L	low tone, light syllable	λ	wave length
LI	Linguistic Inquiry	μ	mora
LR	left to right	σ	syllable
m	masculine gender	τ	tone
MSC	morpheme structure constraint	á	high tone, primary stress
n	neuter gender	à	low tone, secondary stress
N	nucleus of syllable	ǎ	rising tone
N′	rime of syllable	â	falling tone
N″	syllable	a:, ā, aa	long vowel
NLLT	Natural Language & Linguistic Theory	ă	short vowel
NSR	nuclear stress rule	ã	nasal vowel
OCP	Obligatory Contour Principle	#	word boundary
PIE	Proto Indoeuropean	+	morpheme boundary
pl	plural	−	morpheme boundary
PrWd	prosodic word	*	ungrammatical form, reconstructed form, metrical grid slot, major articulator
QI	quantity insensitive		
QS	quantity sensitive	(,)	metrical bracket
RL	right to left	[,]	stem boundary
RTR	retracted tongue root feature	⟨a⟩	extraprosodic (extrametrical, extrasyllabic, extratonal) element
SC	structural change of rule		
SCC	Strict Cycle Condition	a≈b	a alternates with b
SD	structural description of rule	→	"becomes" in synchronic rule
SDP	Sonority Dispersion Principle	>	"becomes" in diachronic rule
sg	singular	/xyz/	underlying representation
SP	soft palate	[xyz]	intermediate, phonetic representation

Language Index

Subject Index

Abad, M. 625, 659
ablaut 33
absolute neutralization 111, 112, 227
accommodation 484
adjacency 335, 346, 368
advanced tongue root [ATR] 14, 476, 528
affricate consonant 31–2, 499–506
Alghazo, M. 399
Allen, S.
  Greek syllable weight 439
  Latin iambic shortening 600
  Latin stress 292
allomorphy 105
allophone 66
Almozainy, H.
  speech disguise 409
alternations 19
  analysis 91, 103
  multiple 103–4
  in paradigm 89
alveolar 27
alveopalatal 27
amplitude of wave 168
anaptyxis 399
[anterior] 28
antigemination 418, 533
aperture 477, 503
apical consonant 30
apocope 105
appendix of syllable 260
[approximant] 34, 255
Archangeli, D.
  default vowel 402
  radical underspecification 507
  Yawelmani templates 647–8
Armstrong, R. 368
Aronoff, M.
  latinate vocabulary 211
  level ordering 234
  morpheme 210
Articulator Model 452–5
articulators 14, 139–45, 164
  adjacency 165
  feedback 145

larynx 14, 139
tongue root 14
aspiration 39
assimilation 21, 150–8
association lines 316, 327
autosegmental phonology
  adjacency 164, 335, 368
  assimilation 151, 153, 155, 420
  association
    delinking 159
    directional 323
    edge-in 369, 372
    lines 316
    multiple linking 407, 410
    parameters 374
    path 371
    Universal Association Convention (UAC) 317
  line crossing ban 317, 354
  locality 343
  melody 428
  Obligatory Contour Principle (OCP) 323
  tier 153, 164, 315, 395
  tier conflation 419
  tone
    default 319
    extratonality 332
    floating 321, 366
    latent 364
    melody 313
    polarity 313
    stabilty 321
    tone bearing unit 316
  underspecification 162
  vowel harmony 346
    disharmonic root 350
    floating autosegment 355
    neutral vowel 357
    opaque vowel 351
autotemplatic syllabification 647

Bagemihl, B. 289–91
Bao, Z.
  contour tone 378, 381